AN INDEX
TO BOOK REVIEWS
IN THE HUMANITIES

VOLUME 24

1983

PHILLIP THOMSON

WILLIAMSTON, MICHIGAN

This volume of the INDEX contains data collected up to 31 December 1983.

This is an index to book reviews in humanities periodicals. Beginning with volume 12 of this Index (dated 1971), the former policy of selectively indexing reviews of books in certain subject categories only was dropped in favor of a policy of indexing all reviews in the periodicals indexed, with the one exception of children's books — the reviews of which will not be indexed.

The form of the entries used is as follows:

> Author. Title.
> Reviewer. Identifying Legend.

The author's name used is the name that appears on the title-page of the book being reviewed, as well as we are able to determine, even though this name is known to be a pseudonym. The title only is shown; subtitles are included only where they are necessary to identify a book in a series. The identifying legend consists of the periodical, each of which has a code number, and the date and page number of the periodical where the review is to be found. PMLA abbreviations are also shown (when a periodical has such an abbreviation, but such abbreviations are limited to four letters) immediately following the code number of the periodical. To learn the name of the periodical in which the review appears, it is necessary to refer the code number to the numerically-arranged list of periodicals beginning on page iii. This list also shows the volume and number of the periodical issues indexed.

Reviews are indexed as they appear and no attempt is made to hold the title until all the reviews are published. For this reason it is necessary to refer to previous and subsequent volumes of this Index to be sure that the complete roster of reviews of any title is seen. As an aid to the user, an asterisk (*) has been added immediately following any title that was also indexed in Volume 23 (1982) of this Index.

Authors with hyphenated surnames are indexed under the name before the hyphen, and the name following the hyphen is not cross-indexed. Authors with more than one surname, but where the names are not hyphenated, are indexed under the first of the names and the last name is cross-indexed. When alphabetizing surnames containing umlauts, the umlauts are ignored. Editors are always shown in the author-title entry, and they are cross indexed (except where the editor's surname is the same as that of the author). Translators are shown only when they are necessary to identify the book being reviewed (as in the classics), and they are not cross-indexed unless the book being reviewed has no author or editor. Certain reference works and anonymous works that are known primarily by their title are indexed under

that title and their editors are cross-indexed.

A list of abbreviations used is shown on page ii.

ABBREVIATIONS

```
Anon.........Anonymous
Apr..........April
Aug..........August
Bk...........Book
Comp(s)......Compiler(s)
Cont.........Continued
Dec..........December
Ed(s)........Editor(s) [or] Edition(s)
Fasc.........Fascicule
Feb..........February
Jan..........January
Jul..........July
Jun..........June
Mar..........March
No...........Number
Nov..........November
Oct..........October
Prev.........Previous volume of this Index
Pt...........Part
Rev..........Revised
Sep..........September
Ser..........Series
Supp.........Supplement
Trans........Translator(s)
Vol..........Volume
* (asterisk)....This title was also shown
                in the volume of this Index
                immediately preceding this
                one
```

The periodicals in which the reviews appear are identified in this Index by a number. To supplement this number, and to promote ready identification, PMLA abbreviations are also given following this number. Every attempt will be made to index those issues shown here as "missing" in a later volume of this Index.

The following is a list of the periodicals indexed in volume 24:

2(AfrA) - African Arts. Los Angeles.
    Nov81 thru Aug82 (vol 15 complete)
9(AlaR) - Alabama Review. University.
    Jan82 thru Oct82 (vol 35 complete)
14 - American Archivist. Chicago.
    Winter82 thru Fall82 (vol 45 complete)
16 - American Art Journal. New York.
    Winter82 thru Autumn82 (vol 14 complete)
18 - American Film. Washington.
    Oct81 thru Sep83 (vols 7 and 8 complete)
24 - American Journal of Philology. Baltimore.
    Spring82 thru Winter82 (vol 103 complete)
26(ALR) - American Literary Realism, 1870-1910. Arlington.
    Spring82 and Autumn82 (vol 15 complete)
27(AL) - American Literature. Durham.
    Mar82 thru Dec82 (vol 54 complete)
29 - The American Poetry Review. Philadelphia.
    Jan-Feb83 thru Nov-Dec83 (vol 12 complete)
31(ASch) - American Scholar. Washington.
    Winter81/82 thru Autumn82 (vol 51 complete)
35(AS) - American Speech. University.
    Spring82 thru Winter82 (vol 57 complete)
37 - The Américas. Washington.
    Jan-Feb82 thru Nov-Dec82 (vol 34 complete)
38 - Anglia. Tübingen.
    Band 100 complete
39 - Apollo. London.
    Jan82 thru Dec82 (vols 115 and 116 complete)
42(AR) - Antioch Review. Yellow Springs.
    Winter82 thru Fall82 (vol 40 complete)
43 - Architectura. Munich.
    Band 12 complete
45 - Architectural Record. New York.
    Nov81 and Jan82 thru Dec82 (vol 169 no 15, vol 170 complete)
46 - Architectural Review. London.
    Jan82 thru Dec82 (vols 171 and 172 complete)
48 - Archivo Español de Arte. Madrid.
    Jan-Mar80 and Apr-Jun80, Jan-Mar82 thru Oct-Dec82 (vol 53 no 209 and 210, vol 55 complete) [Jul-Sep 80 and Oct-Dec80 still missing]
49 - Ariel. Calgary.
    Jan82 thru Oct82 (vol 13 complete)

50(ArQ) - Arizona Quarterly. Tucson.
    Spring82 thru Winter82 (vol 38 complete)
52 - Arcadia. Berlin.
    Band 16 complete
53(AGP) - Archiv für Geschichte der Philosophie. Berlin.
    Band 64 complete
54 - Art Bulletin. New York.
    Mar82 thru Dec82 (vol 64 complete)
55 - Art News. New York.
    Jan82 thru Dec82 (vol 81 complete)
57 - Artibus Asiae. Ascona.
    Vol 43 complete
59 - Art History. Henley-on-Thames.
    Mar82 thru Dec82 (vol 5 complete)
60 - Arts of Asia. Hong Kong.
    Jan-Feb82 thru Nov-Dec82 (vol 12 complete)
61 - Atlantic Monthly. Boston.
    Jan83 thru Dec83 (vols 251 and 252 complete)
62 - Artforum. New York.
    Sep82 thru Summer83 (vol 21 complete)
63 - Australasian Journal of Philosophy. Canberra.
    Mar82 thru Dec82 (vol 60 complete)
64(Arv) - ARV: Scandinavian Yearbook of Folklore. Uppsala.
    Vol 36
67 - AUMLA [Journal of the Australasian Universities Language and Literature Assn.] Hobart.
    May82 and Nov82 (no 57 and 58)
69 - Africa. Manchester.
    Vols 51 and 52 complete
71(ALS) - Australian Literary Studies. St. Lucia.
    May82 and Oct82 (vol 10 no 3 and 4)
72 - Archiv für das Studium der neueren Sprachen und Literaturen. Braunschweig.
    Band 218 complete
73 - Art Magazine. Toronto.
    Sep/Oct81 thru Summer83 (vols 13 and 14 complete)
77 - Biography. Honolulu.
    Winter82 thru Fall82 (vol 5 complete)
78(BC) - Book Collector. London.
    Spring82 thru Winter82 (vol 31 complete)
83 - The British Journal for Eighteenth-Century Studies. Oxford.
    Spring82 and Autumn82 (vol 5 complete)
84 - The British Journal for the Philosophy of Science. Aberdeen.
    Mar82 thru Dec82 (vol 33 complete)
85(SBHC) - Studies in Browning and His Circle. Waco.
    Spring82 and Fall82 (vol 10 complete)
86(BHS) - Bulletin of Hispanic Studies. Liverpool.
    Jan82 thru Oct82 (vol 59 complete)
88 - Blake, An Illustrated Quarterly. Albuquerque.
    Summer82 thru Spring83 (vol 16 complete)

iii

89(BJA) - The British Journal of Aesthetics. London.
Winter82 thru Autumn82 (vol 22
complete)
90 - Burlington Magazine. London.
Jan82 thru Dec82 (vol 124 complete)
95(CLAJ) - CLA Journal. Atlanta.
Sep81 thru Jun83 (vols 25 and 26
complete)
97(CQ) - The Cambridge Quarterly.
Vol 11 complete
98 - Critique. Paris.
Jan82 thru Dec82 (vol 38 complete)
99 - Canadian Forum. Toronto.
Apr82 thru Mar83 (vol 62 complete)
102(CanL) - Canadian Literature. Vancouver.
Winter81 thru Autumn82 (no 91
thru no 94)
104(CASS) - Canadian-American Slavic
Studies/Revue canadienne-américaine
d'études slaves. Tempe.
Spring82 thru Fall-Winter82 (vol
16 complete)
105 - Canadian Poetry. London, Ontario.
Spring/Summer82 and Fall/Winter82
(no 10 and 11)
106 - The Canadian Review of American
Studies. Winnipeg.
Spring82 thru Winter82 (vol 13
complete)
107(CRCL) - Canadian Review of Comparative Literature/Revue Canadienne de
Littérature Comparée. South Edmonton.
Sep81 thru Dec82 (vol 8 no 3 and
4, vol 9 complete)
108 - Canadian Theatre Review. Downsview.
Winter82 thru Fall82 (no 33 thru
36)
113 - Centrum. Minneapolis.
Spring82 (vol 2 no 1)
114(ChiR) - Chicago Review.
Summer81 thru Summer83 (vol 33
complete)
121(CJ) - Classical Journal. Greenville.
Oct/Nov82 thru Apr/May83 (vol 78
complete)
122 - Classical Philology. Chicago.
Jan82 thru Oct82 (vol 77 complete)
123 - Classical Review. London.
Vol 32 complete
124 - Classical World. Pittsburgh.
Sep/Oct82 thru Jul/Aug83 (vol 76
complete)
125 - Clio. Ft. Wayne.
Fall81 thru Summer82 (vol 11 complete)
127 - Art Journal. New York.
Spring82 thru Winter82 (vol 42
complete)
128(CE) - College English. Champaign.
Jan82 thru Dec82 (vol 44 complete)
130 - Comparative Drama. Kalamazoo.
Spring82 thru Winter82/83 (vol 16
complete)
131(CL) - Comparative Literature. Eugene.
Winter82 thru Fall82 (vol 34 complete)
133 - Colloquia Germanica. Lexington.
Band 15 complete

134(CP) - Concerning Poetry. Bellingham.
Spring82 and Fall182 (vol 15 complete)
135 - Connoisseur. New York.
Jan82 thru Sep82 and Nov82 (vols
209 and 210 complete, vol 211 no
847 and 849) [issues dated Oct82
and Dec82 missing]
136 - Conradiana. Lubbock.
Vol 14 complete
137 - CV/II: Contemporary Verse Two.
Winnipeg.
Winter82 thru Aug82 (vol 6 complete)
139 - American Craft. New York.
Feb/Mar82 thru Oct/Nov82 (vol 42
no 1-5)
140(CR) - The Critical Review. Melbourne.
No 24 [no reviews indexed]
141 - Criticism. Detroit.
Winter82 thru Fall82 (vol 24 complete)
142 - Philosophy and Social Criticism.
Dordrecht.
Spring81 thru Winter81 (vol 8 complete)
145(Crit) - Critique. Washington.
Vol 24 no 1 and 2
148 - Critical Quarterly. Manchester.
Spring82 thru Winter82 (vol 24
complete)
149(CLS) - Comparative Literature Studies.
Champaign.
Spring82 thru Winter82 (vol 19
complete)
150(DR) - Dalhousie Review. Halifax.
Spring82 thru Winter82/83 (vol 62
complete)
151 - Dance Magazine. New York.
Jan82 thru Jun82 (vol 56 no 1-6)
152(UDQ) - The Denver Quarterly.
Spring81 thru Winter83 (vols 16
and 17 complete)
153 - Diacritics. Baltimore.
Spring82 thru Winter82 (vol 12
complete)
154 - Dialogue. Ottawa.
Mar82 thru Dec82 (vol 21 complete)
155 - The Dickensian. London.
Spring82 thru Autumn82 (vol 78
complete)
157 - Drama/The Quarterly Theatre Review.
London.
Spring82 thru Winter82 (no 143-
146)
161(DUJ) - Durham University Journal.
Dec81 and Jun82 (vol 74 complete)
165(EAL) - Early American Literature.
Amherst.
Winter82/83 and Spring83 (vol 17
no 3 and vol 18 no 1)
167 - Erkenntnis. Dordrecht.
Jan82 thru Nov82 (vols 17 and 18
complete)
168(ECW) - Essays on Canadian Writing.
Downsview.
Spring82 and Winter-Spring82/83
(no 23 and 24/25)
172(Edda) - Edda. Oslo.
1982/1 thru 1982/6 (vol 82 complete)

173(ECS) - Eighteenth-Century Studies.
Northfield.
Fall81 thru Summer83 (vols 15 and
16 complete)
174(Éire) - Éire-Ireland. St. Paul.
Spring82 thru Winter82 (vol 17
complete)
175 - English. London.
Spring82 thru Autumn82 (vol 31
complete)
177(ELT) - English Literature in Transition. Tempe.
Vol 25 complete
178 - English Studies in Canada. Edmonton.
Mar82 thru Dec82 (vol 8 complete)
179(ES) - English Studies. Lisse.
Feb82 thru Dec82 (vol 63 complete)
180(ESA) - English Studies in Africa.
Johannesburg.
Mar81 and Sep81 (vol 24 complete)
[no reviews indexed]
181 - Epoch. Ithaca.
Fall80 thru Spring-Summer83 (vols
30, 31 and 32 complete)
183(ESQ) - ESQ: A Journal of the American
Renaissance. Pullman.
Vol 28 complete
184(EIC) - Essays in Criticism. Oxford.
Jan82 thru Oct82 (vol 32 complete)
185 - Ethics. Chicago.
Oct82 thru Jul83 (vol 93 complete)
186(ETC.) - ETC. San Francisco.
Spring82 thru Winter82 (vol 39
complete)
187 - Ethnomusicology. Ann Arbor.
Jan83 thru Sep83 (vol 27 complete)
188(ECr) - L'Esprit Créateur. Baton
Rouge.
Spring82 thru Winter82 (vol 22
complete)
189(EA) - Etudes Anglaises. Paris.
Jan-Mar82 thru Oct-Dec82 (vol 35
complete)
191(ELN) - English Language Notes. Boul-
der.
Sep81 thru Mar/Jun83 (vols 19 and
20 complete)
192(EP) - Les Études Philosophiques. Paris.
Jan-Mar81 thru Oct-Dec82
193(ELit) - Études Littéraires. Montreal.
Apr82 thru Dec82 (vol 15 complete)
196 - Fabula. Berlin.
Band 23 complete
198 - The Fiddlehead. Fredericton.
Jan82 thru Oct82 (no 131-134)
199 - Field. Oberlin.
Fall82 and Spring83 (no 27 and 28)
200 - Films in Review. New York.
Jan82 thru Dec82 (vol 33 complete)
203 - Folklore. London.
Vol 93 complete
207(FR) - French Review. Champaign.
Oct82 thru May83 (vol 56 complete)
208(FS) - French Studies. London.
Jan82 thru Oct82 (vol 36 complete)
209(FM) - Le Français Moderne. Paris.
Jan82 thru Oct82 (vol 50 complete)
210(FrF) - French Forum. Lexington.
Jan82 thru Sep82 (vol 7 complete)
214 - Gambit. London.
Vol 10 no 38

215(GL) - General Linguistics. University Park.
Spring82 thru Winter82 (vol 22
complete)
219(GaR) - Georgia Review. Athens.
Spring82 thru Winter82 (vol 36 complete)
220(GL&L) - German Life and Letters.
Oxford.
Oct82/Jan83 thru Jul83 (vol 36
complete)
221(GQ) - German Quarterly. Cherry Hill.
Jan82 thru Nov82 (vol 55 complete)
222(GR) - Germanic Review. Washington.
Winter82 thru Fall82 (vol 57 complete)
224(GRM) - Germanisch-Romanische Monats-
schrift. Heidelberg.
Band 32 complete
227(GCFI) - Giornale Critico della Filosofia Italiana. Firenze.
Jan-Apr82 thru Sep-Dec82 (vol 2
fasc 1-3)
228(GSLI) - Giornale storico della letteratura italiana. Torino.
Vol 159 complete
231 - Harper's Magazine. New York.
Jan83 thru Dec83 (vols 266 and
267 complete)
234 - The Hemingway Review. Ada.
Fall82 and Spring83 (vol 2 complete)
236 - The Hiram Poetry Review. Hiram.
Spring-Summer82 and Fall-Winter82
(no 32 and 33)
238 - Hispania. University.
Mar82 thru Dec82 (vol 65 complete)
240(HR) - Hispanic Review. Philadelphia.
Winter82 thru Autumn82 (vol 50
complete)
241 - Hispanófila. Chapel Hill.
Jan82 thru Sep82 (no 74-76)
244(HJAS) - Harvard Journal of Asiatic
Studies. Cambridge.
Jun82 and Dec82 (vol 42 complete)
249(HudR) - Hudson Review. New York.
Spring82 thru Winter82/83 (vol 35
complete)
250(HLQ) - The Huntington Library Quarterly. San Marino.
Winter82 thru Autumn82 (vol 45
complete)
255(HAB) - Humanities Association Review/
La Revue de l'Association des Humani-
tés. Kingston.
Winter/Spring80 (vol 31 no 1/2)
[no reviews indexed]
256 - Humanities in Society. Los Angeles.
Winter and Spring82 (vol 5 no 1/2)
[no reviews indexed]
257(IRAL) - IRAL: International Review of
Applied Linguistics in Language Teaching. Heidelberg.
Feb82 thru Nov82 (vol 20 complete)
258 - International Philosophical Quarterly. New York and Heverlee-Leuven.
Mar82 thru Dec82 (vol 22 complete)
259(IIJ) - Indo-Iranian Journal. Dordrecht.
Jan80 thru Oct80 and Jan82 thru
Oct82 (vols 22 and 24 complete)

260(IF) - Indogermanische Forschungen.
Berlin.
Band 86
262 - Inquiry. Oslo.
Mar82 thru Dec82 (vol 25 complete)
263(RIB) - Revista Interamericana de Bib-
liografía/Inter-American Review of
Bibliography. Washington.
Vol 32 complete
268(IFR) - The International Fiction Review. Fredericton.
Winter83 and Summer83 (vol 10
complete)
269(IJAL) - International Journal of American Linguistics. Chicago.
Jan82 thru Oct82 (vol 48 complete)
271 - The Iowa Review. Iowa City.
Winter82 and Spring82 (vol 13
no 1 and 2)
273(IC) - Islamic Culture. Hyderabad.
Jan82 thru Oct82 (vol 56 complete)
276 - Italica. New York.
Spring82 thru Winter82 (vol 59
complete)
283 - Jabberwocky - the Journal of the
Lewis Carroll Society. Burton-on-
Trent.
Winter81/82 and Spring82 (vol 11
no 1 and 2) [Summer81 and Autumn81
missing]
284 - The Henry James Review. Baton Rouge.
Fall82 thru Spring83 (vol 4 complete)
285(JapQ) - Japan Quarterly. Tokyo.
Jan-Mar82 thru Oct-Dec82 (vol 29
complete)
287 - Jewish Frontier. New York.
Jan82 thru Dec82 (vol 49 complete)
289 - The Journal of Aesthetic Education.
Urbana.
Spring82 thru Winter82 (vol 16
complete)
290(JAAC) - Journal of Aesthetics and Art
Criticism. Greenvale.
Fall82 thru Summer83 (vol 41 complete)
292(JAF) - Journal of American Folklore.
Washington.
Jan-Mar82 thru Oct-Dec82 (vol 95
complete)
293(JASt) - Journal of Asian Studies. Ann
Arbor.
Nov81 thru Aug82 (vol 41 complete)
294 - Journal of Arabic Literature. Leiden.
Vol 13
295(JML) - Journal of Modern Literature.
Philadelphia.
Vol 9 no 1 thru Dec82 (vol 9 complete)
296(JCF) - Journal of Canadian Fiction.
Guelph.
No 33
297(JL) - Journal of Linguistics. Cambridge.
Mar82 and Sep82 (vol 18 complete)
298 - Journal of Canadian Studies/Revue
d'études canadiennes. Peterborough.
Spring82 thru Winter82/83 (vol
17 complete)
299 - Journal of Beckett Studies. London.
Spring82 (no 7)

301(JEGP) - Journal of English and Germanic Philology. Champaign.
Jan82 thru Oct82 (vol 81 complete)
303(JoHS) - Journal of Hellenic Studies.
London.
Vol 102
304(JHP) - Journal of Hispanic Philology.
Tallahassee.
Spring82 thru Winter83 (vol 6 no 3,
vol 7 no 1 and 2)
305(JIL) - The Journal of Irish Literature. Newark.
Jan-May82 and Sep82 (vol 11 complete)
307 - Journal of Literary Semantics. Heidelberg.
Apr82 (vol 11 no 1)
308 - Journal of Music Theory. New Haven.
Spring82 and Fall82 (vol 26 complete)
311(JP) - Journal of Philosophy. New York.
Jan82 thru Dec82 (vol 79 complete)
313 - Journal of Roman Studies. London.
Vol 72
314 - Journal of South Asian Literature.
East Lansing.
Winter-Spring82 and Summer-Fall82
(vol 17 complete)
316 - Journal of Symbolic Logic. Providence.
Mar82 thru Dec82 (vol 47 complete)
317 - Journal of the American Musicological Society. Richmond.
Spring82 thru Fall82 (vol 35 complete)
318(JAOS) - Journal of the American Oriental Society. New Haven.
Jan-Mar81 thru Oct-Dec81 (vol 101
complete)
319 - Journal of the History of Philosophy. San Diego.
Jan82 thru Oct83 (vols 20 and
21 complete)
320(CJL) - Canadian Journal of Linguistics. Toronto.
Spring82 and Fall82 (vol 27 complete)
321 - The Journal of Value Inquiry. The
Hague.
Vol 16 complete
322(JHI) - Journal of the History of Ideas.
Philadelphia.
Jan-Mar82 thru Oct-Dec82 (vol 43
complete)
323 - The Journal of the British Society
for Phenomenology. Manchester.
Jan82 thru Oct82 (vol 13 complete)
324 - Journal of the Royal Society of
Arts. London.
Dec82 thru Nov83 (vol 131 complete)
325 - Journal of the Society of Archivists.
London.
Apr82 and Oct82 (vol 7 no 1 and 2)
329(JJQ) - James Joyce Quarterly. Tulsa.
Fall81 thru Summer83 (vols 19 and
20 complete)
339(KSMB) - The Keats-Shelley Memorial
Assn. Bulletin. Heslington.
No 31-33
340(KSJ) - Keats-Shelley Journal. New
York.
Vol 31

341 - Konsthistorisk Tidskrift. Stockholm.
    Vol 51 no 1-3 [Vol 50 no 4 is missing]
342 - Kant-Studien. Berlin.
    Band 73 complete
344 - The Kenyon Review. Gambier.
    Winter83 thru Fall83 (vol 5 complete)
345(KRQ) - Kentucky Romance Quarterly. Lexington.
    Vol 29 complete
349 - Language and Style. Flushing.
    Winter82 thru Fall82 (vol 15 complete) [no reviews indexed]
350 - Language. Baltimore.
    Mar83 thru Dec83 (vol 59 complete)
351(LL) - Language Learning. Ann Arbor.
    Jun82 and Dec82 (vol 32 complete)
353 - Linguistics. The Hague.
    Vol 19 complete
354 - The Library. London.
    Mar82 thru Dec82 (vol 4 complete)
355(LSoc) - Language in Society. Cambridge.
    Apr82 thru Dec82 (vol 11 complete)
356(LR) - Les Lettres Romanes. Louvain.
    Feb82 thru Nov83 (vol 36 complete)
360(LP) - Lingua Posnaniensis. Poznań.
    Vols 24 and 25
361 - Lingua. Amsterdam.
    Jan82 thru Nov/Dec82 (vols 56-58 complete)
362 - The Listener. London.
    6Jan83 thru 30Jun83, 7 Jul83 thru 10Nov83 and 8Dec83 thru 22/29Dec 83 (vol 109 complete, vol 110 no 2816-2834 and 2836-2838) [vol 110 no 2835 is missing]
363(LitR) - The Literary Review. Madison.
    Winter82 and Fall82 thru Summer83 (vol 25 no 2, vol 26 complete)
364 - London Magazine. London.
    Apr/May82 thru Mar83 (vol 22 complete)
365 - Literary Research Newsletter. Brockport.
    Fall82 thru Spring83 (vol 7 no 4, vol 8 no 1 and 2)
366 - Literature and History. London.
    Spring82 and Autumn82 (vol 8 complete)
367(L&P) - Literature and Psychology. Teaneck.
    Vol 30 complete
377 - Manuscripta. St. Louis.
    Nov81 thru Nov82 (vol 25 no 3, vol 26 complete)
381 - Meanjin Quarterly. Parkville.
    Jul81 thru Dec82 (vol 40 no 2-4, vol 41 complete)
382(MAE) - Medium Aevum. Oxford.
    1982/1 and 1982/2 (vol 51 complete)
385(MQR) - Michigan Quarterly Review. Ann Arbor.
    Winter83 thru Fall83 (vol 22 complete)
390 - Midstream. New York.
    Jan82 thru Dec82 (vol 28 complete)
391 - Milton Quarterly. Athens.
    Mar82 thru Dec82 (vol 16 complete)

392 - The Mississippi Quarterly. Mississippi State.
    Winter81/82 thru Fall82 (vol 35 complete)
393(Mind) - Mind. Oxford.
    Jan82 thru Oct82 (vol 91 complete)
394 - Mnemosyne. Leiden.
    Vol 35 complete
395(MFS) - Modern Fiction Studies. West Lafayette.
    Spring81 thru Winter82/83 (vols 27 and 28 complete)
396(ModA) - Modern Age. Bryn Mawr.
    Winter82 thru Summer/Fall82 (vol 26 complete)
397(MD) - Modern Drama. Toronto.
    Mar82 thru Dec82 (vol 25 complete)
399(MLJ) - Modern Language Journal. Madison.
    Spring82 thru Winter82 (vol 66 complete)
400(MLN) - MLN [Modern Language Notes]. Baltimore.
    Jan82 thru Dec82 (vol 97 complete)
401(MLQ) - Modern Language Quarterly. Seattle.
    Mar82 thru Sep82 (vol 43 no 1-3)
402(MLR) - Modern Language Review. London.
    Jan82 thru Oct82 (vol 77 complete)
405(MP) - Modern Philology. Chicago.
    Aug82 thru May83 (vol 80 complete)
406 - Monatshefte. Madison.
    Spring82 thru Winter82 (vol 74 complete)
407(MN) - Monumenta Nipponica. Tokyo.
    Spring82 thru Winter82 (vol 37 complete)
408 - Mosaic. Winnipeg.
    Winter82 thru Dec82 (vol 15 complete)
410(M&L) - Music & Letters. London.
    Jan81 thru Jul/Oct82 (vols 62 and 63 complete)
412 - Music Review. Cambridge.
    Feb81 thru Aug-Nov81 (vol 42 complete)
414(MusQ) - Musical Quarterly. New York.
    Jan82 thru Oct82 (vol 68 complete)
415 - Musical Times. London.
    Jan82 thru Dec82 (vol 123 complete)
418(MR) - Massachusetts Review. Amherst.
    Spring82 thru Winter82 (vol 23 complete)
424 - Names. Saranac Lake.
    Mar82 thru Dec82 (vol 30 complete)
432(NEQ) - New England Quarterly. Boston.
    Mar82 thru Dec82 (vol 55 complete)
433 - Neophilologus. Groningen.
    Jan82 thru Oct82 (vol 66 complete) [no reviews indexed]
434 - New England Review and Bread Loaf Quarterly. Lyme.
    Autumn-Winter82 thru Summer83 (vol 5 complete)
435 - New Orleans Review. New Orleans.
    Spring/Summer82 thru Winter82 (vol 9 complete)
436(NewL) - New Letters. Kansas City.
    Fall82 thru Spring/Summer83 (vol 49 complete)

437 - New Universities Quarterly. Oxford.
Winter81/82 thru Autumn82 (vol 36 complete)
439(NM) - Neuphilologische Mitteilungen. Helsinki.
1982/1 thru 1982/4 (vol 83 complete)
441 - New York Times Book Review.
2Jan83 thru 25Dec83 (vol 88 complete)
442(NY) - New Yorker. New York.
3Jan83 thru 26Dec83 (vol 58 no 46-52, vol 59 no 1-45) [vol 59 begins with the 21Feb83 issue]
445(NCF) - Nineteenth-Century Fiction. Berkeley.
Jun82 thru Mar83 (vol 37 complete)
446(NCFS) - Nineteenth-Century French Studies. Fredonia.
Fall-Winter82/83 and Spring-Summer83 (vol 11 complete)
447(N&Q) - Notes & Queries. London.
Feb81 thru Dec81 (vol 28 complete)
448 - Northwest Review. Eugene.
Vol 20 complete
449 - Noûs. Bloomington.
Mar82 thru Nov82 (vol 16 complete)
450(NRF) - La Nouvelle Revue Francaise. Paris.
Jan82 thru Dec82 (vols 59 and 60 complete)
451 - 19th Century Music. Berkeley.
Summer82 thru Spring83 (vol 6 complete)
453(NYRB) - The New York Review of Books.
20Jan83 thru 22Dec83 (vol 29 no 21/22, vol 30 no 1-20)
454 - Novel. Providence.
Fall82 thru Spring83 (vol 16 complete)
459 - Obsidian. Detroit.
Spring81 and Summer/Winter81 (vol 7 complete)
460(OhR) - The Ohio Review. Athens.
No 30 and 31 [no reviews indexed]
461 - The Ontario Review. Princeton.
Spring-Summer82 and Fall-Winter 82/83 (no 16 and 17)
463 - Oriental Art. Richmond.
Spring82 thru Winter82/83 (vol 28 complete)
468 - Paideuma. Orono.
Spring82 thru Winter82 (vol 11 complete)
469 - Parabola. New York.
Vol 8 complete
471 - Pantheon. München.
Jan/Feb/Mar82 thru Oct/Nov/Dec82 (vol 40 complete)
472 - Parnassus: Poetry in Review. New York.
Fall/Winter82 and Spring/Summer83 (vol 10 no 2 and vol 11 no 1)
473(PR) - Partisan Review. Boston.
1/1982 thru 4/1982 (vol 49 complete)
474(PIL) - Papers in Linguistics. Edmonton.
Vol 14 complete
475 - Papers on French Seventeenth Century Literature. Tübingen.
No 16, pt 1 and 2, vol 9 no 17

477(PLL) - Papers on Language and Literature. Edwardsville.
Winter82 thru Autumn82 (vol 18 complete)
478 - Philosophy and Literature. Baltimore.
Oct82 (vol 6 no 1 and 2)
479(PhQ) - Philosophical Quarterly. Oxford.
Jan82 thru Oct82 (vol 32 complete)
480(P&R) - Philosophy & Rhetoric. University Park.
Winter82 thru Fall82 (vol 15 complete)
481(PQ) - Philological Quarterly. Iowa City.
Winter81 thru Fall82 (vols 60 and 61 complete)
482(PhR) - Philosophical Review. Ithaca.
Jan82 thru Oct82 (vol 91 complete)
483 - Philosophy. Cambridge.
Jan82 thru Oct82 (vol 57 complete) [Oct81 issue missing]
484(PPR) - Philosophy and Phenomenological Research. Providence.
Sep82 thru Jun83 (vol 43 complete)
485(PE&W) - Philosophy East & West. Honolulu.
Jan82 thru Oct82 (vol 32 complete)
486 - Philosophy of Science. East Lansing.
Mar82 thru Dec82 (vol 49 complete)
487 - Phoenix. Toronto.
Spring82 thru Winter82 (vol 36 complete)
488 - Philosophy of the Social Sciences. Waterloo.
Mar82 thru Dec82 (vol 12 complete)
489(PJGG) - Philosophisches Jahrbuch. Freiburg.
Band 89 complete
490 - Poetica. Amsterdam.
Band 13 complete
491 - Poetry. Chicago.
Apr82 thru Mar83 (vols 140 and 141 complete)
492 - Poetics. Amsterdam.
Mar82 thru Dec82 (vol 11 complete)
493 - Poetry Review. London.
Dec81 thru Jan83 (vol 71 no 4, vol 72 complete)
494 - Poetics Today. Cambridge.
Winter82 and Spring82 (vol 3 no 1 and 2)
495(PoeS) - Poe Studies. Pullman.
Jun82 and Dec82 (vol 15 complete)
497(PolR) - Polish Review. New York.
Vol 27 complete
498 - Popular Music and Society. Bowling Green.
Vol 8 complete
500 - Post Script. Jacksonville.
Winter83 and Spring/Summer83 (vol 2 no 2 and 3)
502(PrS) - Prairie Schooner. Lincoln.
Spring82 thru Winter82/83 (vol 56 complete)
503 - The Private Library. Pinner.
Spring82 thru Winter82 (vol 5 complete)
504 - Praxis. Los Angeles.
No 5 and 6
505 - Progressive Architecture. New York.
Jan82 thru Dec82 (vol 63 complete)

506(PSt) - Prose Studies. London.
  May82 thru Dec82 (vol 5 complete)
517(PBSA) - Papers of the Bibliographical
Society of America. New York.
  Vol 76 complete
518 - Philosophical Books. Oxford.
  Jan82 thru Oct82 (vol 23 complete)
519(PhS) - Philosophical Studies. Dordrecht.
  Jan82 thru Nov82 (vols 41 and 42
  complete)
520 - Phronesis. Assen.
  Vols 26 and 27 complete
526 - Quarry. Kingston.
  Winter82 thru Autumn82 (vol 31
  complete)
529(QQ) - Queen's Quarterly. Kingston.
  Spring82 thru Winter82 (vol 89
  complete)
535(RHL) - Revue d'Histoire Littéraire
de la France. Paris.
  Jan-Feb82 thru Sep-Dec82 (vol 82
  complete)
539 - Renaissance and Reformation/Renais-
sance et Réforme. Mississauga.
  Feb83 thru Aug83 (vol 7 no 1-3)
540(RIPh) - Revue Internationale de Philosophie. Wetteren.
  Vol 36 complete
541(RES) - Review of English Studies.
London.
  Feb82 thru Nov82 (vol 33 complete)
542 - Revue Philosophique de la France et
de l'Étranger. Paris.
  Jan-Mar82 thru Oct-Dec82 (vol 172
  complete)
543 - Review of Metaphysics. Washington.
  Sep81 thru Jun82 (vol 35 complete)
545(RPh) - Romance Philology. Berkeley.
  Aug81 thru May82 (vol 35 complete)
546(RR) - Romanic Review. New York.
  Jan82 thru Nov82 (vol 73 complete)
547(RF) - Romanische Forschungen. Frankfurt am Main.
  Band 93 and 94 complete
549(RLC) - Revue de Littérature Comparée.
Paris.
  Jan-Mar82 thru Oct-Dec82 (vol 56
  complete)
550(RusR) - Russian Review. Stanford.
  Jan82 thru Oct82 (vol 41 complete)
551(RenQ) - Renaissance Quarterly. New
York.
  Spring81 thru Winter82 (vols 34
  and 35 complete)
552(REH) - Revista de estudios hispánicos. University.
  Jan82 thru Oct82 (vol 16 complete)
553(RLiR) - Revue de Linguistique Romane.
Strasbourg.
  Jan-Jun81 thru Jul-Dec82 (vols 45
  and 46 complete)
554 - Romania. Paris.
  Vol 102 complete
555 - Revue de Philologie. Paris.
  Vols 55 and 56 complete
556 - Russell. Hamilton.
  Summer81 thru Winter82/83 (new
  series, vols 1 and 2 complete)
557(RSH) - Revue des Sciences Humaines.
Lille.
  1982/1 thru 1982/4 (no 185-188)
  [no reviews indexed]

558(RLJ) - Russian Language Journal. East
Lansing.
  Winter-Spring82 and Fall82 (vol
  36 complete)
559 - Russian Linguistics. Dordrecht.
  Nov81 thru Jun82 (vol 6 complete)
560 - Salmagundi. Saratoga Springs.
  Spring82 thru Fall82/Winter83
  (no 56 thru 58/59)
561(SFS) - Science-Fiction Studies. Mon-
tréal.
  Mar82 thru Nov82 (vol 9 complete)
563(SS) - Scandinavian Studies. Lawrence.
  Winter82 thru Autumn82 (vol 54
  complete)
564 - Seminar. Toronto.
  Feb81 thru Nov82 (vols 17 and
  18 complete)
565 - Stand. Newcastle upon Tyne.
  Vol 23 complete
566 - The Scriblerian. Philadelphia.
  Autumn82 and Spring83 (vol 15 complete)
567 - Semiotica. The Hague.
  Vols 37 thru 41 complete
568(SCN) - Seventeenth-Century News.
University Park.
  Spring-Summer82 thru Winter82 (vol
  40 complete)
569(SR) - Sewanee Review. Sewanee.
  Winter82 thru Fall82 (vol 90 complete)
570(SQ) - Shakespeare Quarterly. Washington.
  Spring82 thru Winter82 (vol 33
  complete)
571(ScLJ) - Scottish Literary Journal.
Aberdeen.
  May82 thru Winter82 (vol 9 complete, plus supp 16 and 17)
572 - Shaw: The Annual of Bernard Shaw
Studies. University Park.
  Vol 3
573(SSF) - Studies in Short Fiction. New-
berry.
  Winter82 thru Fall82 (vol 19 complete)
574(SEEJ) - Slavic and East European
Journal. Tucson.
  Spring82 thru Winter82 (vol 26
  complete)
575(SEER) - Slavonic and East European
Review. London.
  Jan82 thru Oct82 (vol 60 complete)
576 - Journal of the Society of Architectural Historians. Philadelphia.
  Mar82 thru Dec82 (vol 41 complete)
577(SHR) - Southern Humanities Review.
Auburn.
  Winter82 thru Fall82 (vol 16 complete)
578 - Southern Literary Journal. Chapel
Hill.
  Spring83 and Fall83 (vol 15 no 2
  and vol 16 no 1)
579(SAQ) - South Atlantic Quarterly. Durham.
  Winter82 thru Autumn82 (vol 81 complete)
580(SCR) - The South Carolina Review.
Clemson.
  Fall82 and Spring83 (vol 15 complete)

581 - Southerly. Sydney.
        Mar82 thru Dec82 (vol 42 complete)
582(SFQ) - Southern Folklore Quarterly.
    Gainesville.
        Vol 43 complete
583 - Southern Speech Communication Jour-
    nal. Tampa.
        Fall82 thru Summer83 (vol 48 com-
        plete)
584(SWR) - Southwest Review. Dallas.
        Winter82 thru Autumn82 (vol 67
        complete)
585(SoQ) - The Southern Quarterly. Hat-
    tiesburg.
        Fall81 thru Summer82 (vol 20 com-
        plete)
587(SAF) - Studies in American Fiction.
    Boston.
        Spring82 and Autumn82 (vol 10
        complete)
588(SSL) - Studies in Scottish Literature.
    Columbia.
        Vol 17
589 - Speculum. Cambridge.
        Jan82 thru Oct82 (vol 57 complete)
590 - Studies in the Humanities. Indiana,
    Pennsylvania.
        Jun83 (vol 10 no 1)
591(SIR) - Studies in Romanticism. Bos-
    ton.
        Spring82 thru Winter82 (vol 21
        complete)
592 - Studio International. London.
        1/1978, 2/1978 and 1/1980 thru vol
        195 no 997 (vols 194 and 195 com-
        plete)
593 - Symposium. Washington.
        Spring82, Fall82 and Winter82/83
        (vol 36 no 1, 3 and 4) [Summer82
        issue missing]
594 - Studies in the Novel. Denton.
        Spring82 thru Winter82 (vol 14
        complete)
595(ScS) - Scottish Studies. Edinburgh.
        Vol 25
596(SL) - Studia Linguistica. Lund.
        Vol 36 complete
597(SN) - Studia Neophilologica. Stock-
    holm.
        Vol 54 complete
598(SoR) - The Southern Review. Baton
    Rouge.
        Winter83 thru Autumn83 (vol 19
        complete)
599 - Style. De Kalb.
        Winter82 thru Fall82 (vol 16 com-
        plete)
600 - Simiolus. Utrecht.
        Vol 12 no 4
602 - Sprachkunst. Vienna.
        Vol 13 complete
603 - Studies in Language. Amsterdam.
        Vol 6 complete
604 - Spenser Newsletter. Albany.
        Winter82 thru Fall82 (vol 13 com-
        plete)
605(SC) - Stendhal Club. Grenoble.
        15Oct82 thru 15Jul83 (vol 25 com-
        plete)
606 - Synthese. Dordrecht.
        Jan82 thru Dec82 (vols 50-53 com-
        plete)

607 - Tempo. London.
        Mar82 thru Dec82 (no 140-143)
608 - TESOL Quarterly. Washington.
        Mar83 thru Dec83 (vol 17 complete)
609 - Theater. New Haven.
        Winter82 thru Summer/Fall83 (vol
        14 complete)
611(TN) - Theatre Notebook. London.
        Vol 36 complete
612(ThS) - Theatre Survey. Albany.
        May82 and Nov82 (vol 23 complete)
613 - Thought. Bronx.
        Mar82 thru Dec82 (vol 57 complete)
        [no reviews indexed]
614 - The Textile Booklist. Lopez Island.
        Winter83 thru Fall83 (vol 8 com-
        plete)
617(TLS) - Time Literary Supplement. Lon-
    don.
        7Jan83 thru 30Dec83 (no 4162-
        4213)
619 - Transactions of the Charles S.
    Peirce Society.
        Winter82 thru Fall82 (vol 18 com-
        plete)
627(UTQ) - University of Toronto Quarterly.
        Fall81 thru Summer82 (vol 51 com-
        plete) [in Summer issue, only the
        "Humanities" section is indexed]
628(UWR) - University of Windsor Review.
    Windsor.
        Fall-Winter82 and Spring-Summer83
        (vol 17 complete)
636(VP) - Victorian Poetry. Morgantown.
        Spring82 thru Autumn/Winter82 (vol
        20 complete)
637(VS) - Victorian Studies. Bloomington.
        Autumn81 thru Summer82 (vol 25
        complete)
639(VQR) - Virginia Quarterly Review.
    Charlottesville.
        Winter82 thru Autumn82 (vol 58
        complete)
646(WWR) - Walt Whitman Review. Detroit.
        Mar82 and Jun-Sep-Dec82 (vol 28
        complete)
648(WCR) - West Coast Review. Burnaby.
        Summer81 thru Apr83 (vols 16 and
        17 complete)
649(WAL) - Western American Literature.
    Logan.
        Spring82 thru Winter83 (vol 17
        complete)
650(WF) - Western Folklore. Los Angeles.
        Jan82 thru Oct82 (vol 41 complete)
651(WHR) - Western Humanities Review.
    Salt Lake City.
        Spring82 thru Winter82 (vol 36 com-
        plete)
656(WMQ) - William and Mary Quarterly.
    Williamsburg.
        Jan82 thru Oct82 (vol 39 complete)
658 - Winterthur Portfolio. Chicago.
        Spring82 thru Winter82 (vol 17
        complete)
659(ConL) - Contemporary Literature. Madi-
    son.
        Spring83 thru Winter83 (vol 24
        complete)
660(Word) - Word. New York.
        Apr81 thru Dec82 (vols 32 and 33
        complete)

661(WC) - The Wordsworth Circle. Philadelphia.
>Winter82 thru Autumn82 (vol 13
complete)
675(YER) - Yeats Eliot Review. Edmonton.
>Jun82 (vol 7 no 1/2)
676(YR) - Yale Review. New Haven.
>Autumn82 thru Summer83 (vol 72
complete)
677(YES) - The Yearbook of English Studies.
London.
>Vol 12
678(YCGL) - Yearbook of Comparative and
General Literature. Bloomington.
>No 30
679 - Zeitschrift für allgemeine Wissenschaftstheorie. Wiesbaden.
>Band 13 complete
680(ZDP) - Zeitschrift für deutsche Philologie. Berlin.
>Band 101 complete
682(ZPSK) - Zeitschrift für Phonetik,
Sprachwissenschaft und Kommunikations-
forschung. Berlin.
>Band 34 and 35 complete
683 - Zeitschrift für Kunstgeschichte.
München.
>Band 45 complete
684(ZDA) - Zeitschrift für deutsches
Altertum und deutsche Literatur [An-
zeiger section]. Wiesbaden.
>Band 111 complete
685(ZDL) - Zeitschrift für Dialektologie
und Linguistik. Wiesbaden.
>2/1981 and 3/1981, 1/1982 thru
3/1982 (vol 48 no 2 and 3, vol 49
complete)
686(ZGL) - Zeitschrift für germanistische
Linguistik. Berlin.
>Band 8 thru 11 complete [no
reviews indexed]
687 - Zeitschrift für Philosophische Forschung. Meisenheim/Glan.
>Jan-Mar81 thru Oct-Dec82 (Band 35
and 36 complete)
688(ZSP) - Zeitschrift für slavische
Philologie. Heidelberg.
>Band 43 Heft 1

Each year we are unable (for one reason
or another) to index the reviews appearing
in all of the periodicals scanned. The
following is a list of the periodicals
whose reviews were not included in this
volume of the Index. Every attempt will
be made to index these reviews in the next
volume of the Index:

44 - Architectural History. London.
70(AN&Q) - American Notes & Queries.
Owingsville.
110 - Carolina Quarterly. Chapel Hill.
112 - Celtica. Dublin.
116 - Chinese Literature: Essays, Articles,
Reviews. Madison.
204(FdL) - Forum der Letteren. Muider-
berg.
261 - Indian Linguistics. Poona.
272(IUR) - Irish University Review. Dublin.
277(ITL) - ITL, a Review of Applied Linguistics. Leuven.
279 - International Journal of Slavic
Linguistics and Poetics. Columbus.
300 - Journal of English Linguistics.
Bellingham.
302 - Journal of Oriental Studies. Hong
Kong.
398(MPS) - Modern Poetry Studies. Buffalo.
462(OL) - Orbis Litterarum. Copenhagen.
476 - Performing Arts Review. Washington.
513 - Perspectives of New Music. Annandale-
on-Hudson.
537 - Revue de Musicologie. Paris.
562(Scan) - Scandinavica. Norwich.
586(SoRA) - Southern Review. Adelaide.
610 - Theatre Research International.
London.
615(TJ) - Theatre Journal. Washington.
654(WB) - Weimarer Beiträge. Berlin.

Ackroyd, P. The Last Testament of Oscar
Wilde.
A. Hislop, 617(TLS):15Apr83-375
J. Mellors, 362:5May83-27
Ackroyd, P. Ezra Pound and his World.*
J. Saunders, 565:Vol23No1-73
295(JML):Dec82-515
"Acta Universitatis Carolinae, Philologica
1, 1975."
G. Weise, 682(ZPSK):Band34Heft3-388
"Actas del Simposio Internacional de
Estudios Hispánicos."
D-H. Pageaux, 549(RLC):Apr-Jun82-231
"Actes du Colloque du Bicentenaire de
l'Indépendance Américaine, Brest 1976."
J. Gury, 549(RLC):Jan-Mar82-111
"Actes du premier congrès d'histoire et de
la civilisation du Maghreb."
R. Bidwell, 69:Vol51No3-800
Acton, E. Alexander Herzen and the Role
of the Intellectual Revolutionary.*
M. Confino, 550(RusR):Jan82-74
"Acts and Letters of the Apostles." (R.
Lattimore, trans)
M. Goulder, 617(TLS):28Oct83-1199
Adair, G. Vietnam on Film.
J. Beaver, 200:Feb82-124
J. Rosenbaum, 18:Apr82-71
639(VQR):Summer82-100
Adam, H. and H. Giliomee. Ethnic Power
Mobilised.
B. Munslow, 69:Vol52No4-91
Adam, R. I'm Not Complaining.
P. Craig, 617(TLS):18Nov83-1294
Adam, W. Vitruvius Scoticus.* (J. Simp-
son, ed)
R. Ormond, 90:Mar82-168
Adams, A. Rich Rewards.
J.L. Halio, 598(SoR):Winter83-203
Adams, B. London Illustrated 1604-1851.
D. Piper, 617(TLS):25Nov83-1330
Adams, D. Life, the Universe and Every-
thing.*
G. Jonas, 441:23Jan83-24
Adams, D.W. - see Jefferson, T.
Adams, E. and D. Redstone. Bow Porcelain.
T. Hughes, 324:Jan83-108
G. Wills, 39:Aug82-122
Adams, G. Games of the Strong.
G. Manning, 381:Dec82-486
Adams, G. The Hottest Night of the Cen-
tury.
E. Webby, 381:Jul81-200
Adams, H. The Letters of Henry Adams.
(J.C. Levenson and others, eds)
W.S. McFeely, 441:6Mar83-9
Adams, I. S: Portrait of a Spy.
J.L. Granatstein, 529(QQ):Autumn82-529
Adams, I.H. and G. Fortune - see Lindsay,
A.
Adams, J.C. - see Roberts, C.G.D.
Adams, J.G. Without Precedent.
R. Sherrill, 441:5Jun83-11
Adams, J.Q. Diary of John Quincy Adams.*
(Vols 1 and 2) (D.G. Allen and others,
eds)
R.H. Ferrell, 432(NEQ):Dec82-606
Adams, M., ed. Ethnologische Zeitschrift
Zurich I/1980.
R.M. Fulton, 2(AfrA):Nov81-81
Adams, R.M. Decadent Societies.
F. Kermode, 441:3Jul83-7
N. Stone, 617(TLS):25Jul83-758

Adams, R.M. - see Jonson, B.
Adams, S. The Homosexual as Hero in Con-
temporary Fiction.
J. Stokes, 402(MLR):Apr82-437
Adams, T.R. The American Controversy.*
M. Kallich, 173(ECS):Winter82/83-221
Adams, T.R. American Independence.*
M. Kallich, 173(ECS):Winter82/83-220
Adams, W.H. Monticello.
P. Goldberger, 441:11Dec83-13
C. Tomkins, 442(NY):19Dec83-127
Adams, W.P. The First American Constitu-
tions.*
A.N., 185:Jul83-835
Adams, W.Y. Nubia.
H. Goedicke, 318(JAOS):Apr-Jun81-251
Adamson, D. Balzac: "Illusions perdues."*
B.G. Hourcade, 446(NCFS):Spring-Summer
83-368
Adamson, J. "Othello" as Tragedy.*
C. Kahn, 551(RenQ):Summer82-336
Adaqi, Y. and U. Sharvit. A Treasury of
Jewish Yemenite Chants.
S. Staub, 187:Sep83-553
Adburgham, A. Silver Fork Society.
D.A. Low, 617(TLS):8Jul83-721
Adcock, F. Selected Poems. The Virgin
and the Nightingale.
A. Motion, 617(TLS):2Sep83-922
Addison, J. The Freeholder.* (J. Leheny,
ed)
F.P. Lock, 677(YES):Vol 12-279
P. Rogers, 541(RES):Aug82-330
Addison, J. and R. Steele. Selections
from "The Tatler" and "The Spectator"
of Steele and Addison. (A. Ross, ed)
566:Spring83-134
Addiss, S. and C-T. Li, eds. Catalogue of
the Oriental Collection.
U. Roberts, 60:Mar-Apr82-137
"Lady Addle Remembers." (M. Dunn, ed)
A. Huth, 362:22and29Dec83-37
Ades, D. Dalí.
R.S. Short, 617(TLS):25Mar83-309
Adey, L. C.S. Lewis's "Great War" with
Owen Barfield.
J.K. Johnstone, 178:Jun82-243
Adhyatman, S. - see under Sumarah Adhyat-
man
Adilman, M.E. Piece Work.*
P. Monk, 529(QQ):Summer82-419
J.A. Wainwright, 102(CanL):Winter81-
148
Adkins, G. A Difficult Peace.
L. Mackinnon, 617(TLS):8Apr83-356
Adler, H., ed. Literarische Geheimber-
ichte.
H. Steinecke, 221(GQ):May82-475
Adler, J.S. War in Melville's Imagina-
tion.*
W. Harris, 49:Apr82-83
R. Lehan, 445(NCF):Jun82-127
I. Melada, 594:Summer82-220
Adler, M.J. A Pragmatic Logic for Com-
mands.*
D.H., 355(LSoc):Dec82-493
Adler, R. Pitch Dark.
M. Spark, 441:18Dec83-1
Adler, R. Women of the Shtetl.
N. Wachtel, 390:Mar82-55
Adler, W. American Sextet.
N. Callendar, 441:20Mar83-27

Adler, W. Jan Wildens.
    K. Renger, 471:Jan/Feb/Mar82-74
Adloff, J.G., ed. Sartre: Index du Corpus
philosophique. (Vol 1)
    T.R. Flynn, 319:Jul83-418
Adorno, T. In Search of Wagner.*
    R. Hollingrake, 410(M&L):Jul/Oct81-436
    R.L.J., 412:Aug-Nov81-288
    J. Kerman, 453(NYRB):22Dec83-27
    H. McQueen, 381:Apr82-84
Adorno, T.W. Prisms.*
    C. Koelb, 395(MFS):Winter82/83-694
Adrados, F.R., ed. Diccionario griego-
español. (Vol 1)
    C. Brixhe, 555:Vol56fasc1-112
    M.L. West, 303(JoHS):Vol 102-256
    N.G. Wilson, 123:Vol32No2-210
Adrados, F.R. El mundo de la lírica
griega antigua.
    J. Péron, 555:Vol56fasc2-315
Aelfric. Aelfric's Catholic Homilies: The
Second Series, Text.* (M. Godden, ed)
    T.D. Hill, 301(JEGP):Jul82-404
    J.C. Pope, 541(RES):Feb82-66
Aepinus, F. Aepinus's Essay on the Theory
of Electricity and Magnetism. (R.W.
Home, ed)
    D. Knight, 161(DUJ):Jun82-287
Aers, D. Chaucer, Langland, and the Crea-
tive Imagination.*
    J.D. Burnley, 541(RES):Aug82-309
Aers, D., J. Cook and D. Punter. Romanti-
cism and Ideology.
    T. Eagleton, 366:Autumn82-255
Aers, D., B. Hodge and G. Kress. Litera-
ture, Language and Society in England,
1580-1680.
    L.C. Knights, 551(RenQ):Winter82-651
Aeschylus. The Oresteia. (T. Harrison,
trans)
    D. Devlin, 157:Summer82-52
Aeschylus. The Suppliants. (H.F. Johan-
sen and E.W. Whittle, eds)
    J. Diggle, 123:Vol32No2-127
    R.W., 555:Vol56fasc2-327
"Aeschylus: 'Prometheus Bound.'" (M.
Griffith, ed)
    J.H.C. Leach, 617(TLS):15Jul83-756
Afanas'ev, I.N. Istorizm protiv eklek-
tiki.
    G.M. Enteen, 550(RusR):Apr82-215
Agassi, J. Science and Society.
    R.H., 185:Jan83-418
Agawa, H. The Reluctant Admiral.*
    G.R. Nunn, 77:Fall82-370
Agee, J. Twelve Years.*
    J. Stern, 364:Aug/Sep82-134
Agel, J. and E. Boe. Deliverance in Shang-
hai.
    J.J. Osborne, Jr., 441:23Oct83-26
Ager, D.E., F.E. Knowles and J. Smith, eds.
Advances in Computer-Aided Literary and
Linguistic Research.
    M. Johnson, 350:Jun83-466
    E. Mater, 682(ZPSK):Band34Heft3-389
Agesthialingom, S. and K.K. Gowda, eds.
Dravidian Case System.
    D.W. McAlpin, 318(JAOS):Oct-Dec81-492
Agler-Beck, G. Der von Kürenberg.*
    H. Homann, 406:Spring82-94

Agüera, H.C. and M.M. Díaz. Lecturas
básicas: A Cultural Reader. (2nd ed)
    M.S. Arrington, 399(MLJ):Spring82-97
    R. Romeu, 238:Sep82-477
Aguilera-Malta, D. Seven Serpents and
Seven Moons.
    T. Lochhaas, 114(ChiR):Winter83-130
Aguinaga, C.B., J. Rodríguez Puértolas and
I.M. Zavala - see under Blanco Aguinaga,
C., J. Rodríguez Puértolas and I.M.
Zavala
Aguirre, J.M. - see Manrique, J.
Agulhon, M., ed. Histoire de la France
urbaine. (Vol 4)
    E. Weber, 617(TLS):7Oct83-1077
Agulhon, M. Marianne into Battle.*
    639(VQR):Winter82-22
Agulhon, M. - see Renouvier, C.
Agulló, M. and others. Madrid hasta 1875.
    D. Angulo Íñiguez, 48:Apr-Jun80-214
Ahmed, A.S. Pukhtun Economy and Society.
    C. Lindholm, 293(JASt):Nov81-163
Ahmed, E., ed. Bangladesh Politics.
    M. Franda, 293(JASt):Aug82-857
Ahmed, M. Bangladesh.
    M. Franda, 293(JASt):Aug82-857
Ahuja, G.B. - see under Bravo Ahuja, G.
Aichinger, P. Earle Birney.
    G. Coggins, 178:Dec82-520
    J.H. Ferres, 102(CanL):Spring82-108
Aichinger, P. - see de Lorimier, C.
Aidala, T. and C. Bruce. The Great Houses
of San Francisco.
    D.J. Hibbard, 658:Spring82-90
Aiken, C. Selected Letters of Conrad
Aiken. (J. Killorin, ed)
    H. Bak, 179(ES):Feb82-80
Aikens, C.M. and T. Higuchi. Prehistory
of Japan.
    C. Keally, 407(MN):Autumn82-405
Aili, H. The Prose Rhythm of Sallust and
Livy.*
    P. Flobert, 555:Vol56fasc2-346
Ainsworth, M.W. and others. Art and Auto-
radiography.
    C. Brown, 90:Dec82-772
Aitchison, J. Language Change.
    P. Baldi, 350:Jun83-411
Aithal, K.P., ed. Āśvalāyanagṛhyasūtrab-
hāṣya.
    H.W. Bodewitz, 259(IIJ):Oct82-305
Aitken, A.J. and T. McArthur, eds. Lan-
guages of Scotland.*
    A. Ward, 447(N&Q):Jun81-258
Aitken, R. Taking the Path of Zen.
    T. Lippe, 469:Vol8No1-118
Aitmatov, C. The Day Lasts More Than A
Hundred Years.
    M. Seton-Watson, 617(TLS):4Nov83-1215
Aiyar, K.N. - see "Thirty Minor Upanishads,
including the Yoga Upanishads"
Ajame, P. 300 heros et personnages du
roman français d'Atala à Zazie.
    C. Coustou, 450(NRF):Feb82-128
Ajdukiewicz, K. The Scientific World-
Perspective and Other Essays, 1931-1963.
(J. Giedymin, ed)
    C. Lejewski, 316:Jun82-457
Akatsuka Kiyoshi. Chūgoku kodai no shūkyō
to bunka — In ōchō no saishi.
    D.N. Keightley, 244(HJAS):Jun82-267

3

Akehurst, A.J. To Raise Myself a Little.
  (T. Dyer, ed)
    639(VQR):Autumn82-117
Akenson, D.H. A Protestant in Purgatory.
  S. Cronin, 174(Érie):Summer82-153
Akerman, J. Black Around the Eyes.
  M. Fee, 102(CanL):Summer82-138
  A.T. Seaman, 198:Apr82-97
Akers, G.A. Phonological Variation in the
  Jamaican Continuum.
    R.A. Hall, Jr., 350:Jun83-452
Akhtar, M.S. - see Herāwī, M.Q.
Akimoto, T. - see Kamata, K.
Akira, F. - see Fujiwara Akira
Aksakov, S. Years of Childhood.
  G.S., 617(TLS):20May83-527
Aksyonov, V. The Island of Crimea.
  I. Gold, 441:11Dec83-11
Aksyonov, V. and others, eds. Metropol.
  H. Muchnic, 441:27Feb83-1
"Akten zur deutschen auswärtigen Politik,
  1918-1945." (Ser B, Vol 14)
    F.L. Carsten, 575(SEER):Jul82-474
"Akten zur deutschen auswärtigen Politik,
  1918-1945." (Ser B, Vol 15)
    F.L. Carsten, 575(SEER):Jan82-139
"Aktuální otázky jazykové kultury v
  socialistické společnosti."
    M. Renský, 355(LSoc):Dec82-439
    W. Schmidt, 682(ZPSK):Band34Heft3-354
Akurgal, E., ed. The Art and Architecture
  of Turkey.*
    H. Crane, 576:May82-163
Akutin, J.M. - see Vel'tman, A.F.
Al, B.P.F. La notion de grammaticalité
  en grammaire générative-transformation-
  nelle.*
    J. Sumpf, 209(FM):Jan82-88
Alan of Lille. The Plaint of Nature.*
  (J.J. Sheridan, ed and trans)
    P.G. Walsh, 487:Autumn82-293
Alas, L. Su único hijo. (C. Richmond, ed)
    G. Sobejano, 240(HR):Autumn82-496
Alatis, J.E., H.B. Altman and P.M. Alatis,
  eds. The Second Language Classroom.
    D.L. Lange, 399(MLJ):Autumn82-317
Alatri, P. Gabriele D'Annunzio.
    S. Vinall, 617(TLS):14Oct83-1132
Alba, M.S. - see under Sito Alba, M.
Albert of Metz. Alpertus van Metz:
  "Gebeurtenissen van deze tijd & Een frag-
  ment over bisschop Diederik I van Metz."
    B.M. Kaczynski, 589:Apr82-342
Albert, M. Un Pari pour L'Europe.
    A. Forbes, 362:22Sep83-22
Albert, M.H. Operation Lila.
    P. Andrews, 441:22May83-42
Albert, M.L. and others. Clinical Aspects
  of Dysphasia.
    M.W. Salus, 350:Dec83-941
Albert, P.J., ed. The American Federation
  of Labor Records: The Samuel Gompers Era.
  (Pts 1 and 2)
    M. Nash, 14:Winter82-64
Albert, S. Bellum iustum.
    J.W. Rich, 313:Vol72-181
    J-C. Richard, 555:Vol55fasc2-385
Albert, S.R., ed. Knitting for Babies.
    C.J. Mouton, 614:Winter83-18
Alberti, O. Un Jasmin ivre.
    R. Turrini, 450(NRF):Dec82-95

Alberti, R. The Lost Grove. (G. Berns,
  ed and trans)
    A. Ruiz Salvador, 150(DR):Summer82-328
Albisetti, J.C. Secondary School Reform
  in Imperial Germany.
    G.G. Field, 617(TLS):2Sep83-942
Albjerg, A. Ludvig Holbergs poetiske mask-
  erade.
    J.A. Parente, Jr., 563(SS):Summer82-
    261
Alborg, J.L. Historia de la literatura
  española. (Vol 4)
    J.M. López de Abiada, 547(RF):Band93
    Heft1/2-298
Albrecht, E. Weltanschauung — Methodol-
  ogie — Sprache.
    M. Uesseler, 682(ZPSK):Band34Heft2-222
Albrecht, M. Kants Antinomie der praktis-
  chen Vernunft.*
    V. Gerhardt, 687:Oct-Dec82-655
Albright, D. Representation and the
  Imagination.
    E. Brater, 651(WHR):Spring82-91
Albright, H. Wheat Fields. Portmanteaux.
    B. Meyer, 102(CanL):Spring82-88
Albury, W.R. - see de Condillac, E.B.
Alcalá, A. - see Servet, M.
Alcázar, R. El cuento social boliviano.
    E. Echevarría, 268(IFR):Winter83-71
Alcover, M. Poullain de la Barre.
    S. Romanowski, 475:Vo'9No17-729
Aldan, D. The Art and Craft of Poetry.
    639(VQR):Spring82-56
Aldcroft, D. and M. Freeman, eds. Trans-
  port in the Industrial Revolution.
    T.C. Barker, 617(TLS):16Dec83-1410
Alden, D. Marcel Proust's Grasset Proofs.*
    L.B. Price, 207(FR):Oct82-159
Alden, D.W. and R.A. Brooks, eds. A Criti-
  cal Bibliography of French Literature.*
  (Vol 6)
    J. Cruickshank, 402(MLR):Jan82-215
    S.E. Gray, 149(CLS):Spring82-76
    D. Leuwers, 535(RHL):Jul-Aug82-678
Alden, J., with D.C. Landis, eds. Euro-
  pean Americana.* (Vol 1)
    D.B. Quinn, 551(RenQ):Winter81-570
Alden, J. and D.C. Landis, eds. European
  Americana. (Vol 2)
    D. McKitterick, 617(TLS):10Jun83-612
Alderman, G. The Jewish Community in Brit-
  ish Politics.
    W.J. Fishman, 617(TLS):17Jun83-634
Alderman, H. Nietzsche's Gift.*
    J. Tietz, 648(WCR):Spring82-37
Alderman, S.D. and K. Wertenberger. Hand-
  woven, Tailormade.
    P. Bach, 614:Fall83-20
Alderson, B. - see Darton, F.J.H.
Aldhelm. The Prose Works.* (M. Lapidge
  and M. Herren, trans)
    G.H. Brown, 589:Apr82-340
    V.E. Watts, 161(DUJ):Jun82-297
Aldington, R. and L. Durrell. Literary
  Lifelines. (I.S. MacNiven and H.T.
  Moore, eds)
    H.H. Watts, 395(MFS):Summer82-281
    42(AR):Winter82-116
    639(VQR):Winter82-17
Aldiss, B. This World and Nearer Ones.
    42(AR):Winter82-117
Aldiss, B.W. Helliconia Summer.
    C. Greenland, 617(TLS):2Dec83-1358

Aldridge, J.W. The American Novel and the Way We Live Now.
R.J. Margolis, 441:19Jun83-16
Aldridge, M.V. English Quantifiers.
M. Celce-Murcia, 350:Jun83-440
Alegría, F. The Chilean Spring.
J.F. Donahue, 37:Mar-Apr82-58
Alegría, F., ed. Chilean Writers in Exile.
C. Wright, 676(YR):Winter83-xiii
Aleichem, S. Marienbad.*
M. Haltrecht, 617(TLS):11Feb83-131
Alemán, M. Guzmán de Alfarache. (B. Brancaforte, ed)
C.B. Johnson, 240(HR):Winter82-100
Ales Bello, A., ed. The Great Chain of Being and Italian Phenomenology.
P. Simpson, 323:May82-202
Alexander of Aphrodisias. The "De Anima" of Alexander of Aphrodisias. (A.P. Fotinis, ed and trans)
A. Preus, 319:Oct82-427
Alexander, B. British Volunteers for Liberty.
B. Knox, 617(TLS):29Jul83-800
Alexander, C. The Early Writings of Charlotte Brontë.
A. Leighton, 617(TLS):4Nov83-1213
Alexander, C. The Linz Café.
P. Buchanan, 46:Nov82-81
Alexander, C. - see Brontë, C.
Alexander, C.C. Here the Country Lies.*
D.W. Bjork, 579(SAQ):Summer82-347
Alexander, E. The Resonance of Dust.*
M. Shapiro, 301(JEGP):Oct82-609
T. Ziolkowski, 569(SR):Fall82-592
Alexander, G.M. The Prelude to the Truman Doctrine.
D. Hunt, 617(TLS):11Feb83-138
Alexander, J. Voices and Echoes.
V. Glendinning, 617(TLS):9Sep83-971
Alexander, J.H. "Marmion."
J. Rubenstein, 571(ScLJ):Winter82-82
Alexander, J.T. Bubonic Plague in Early Modern Russia.*
I. de Madariaga, 575(SEER):Jan82-115
Alexander, K.C. Rural Organizations in South India.
A.A. Yang, 293(JASt):May82-608
Alexander, L. The Doll Dressmaker's Guide to Patternmaking.
P. Bach, 614:Spring83-18
Alexander, M. Geoffrey Chaucer: Prologue to the "Canterbury Tales."
R.T. Davies, 447(N&Q):Jun81-256
Alexander, M. Old English Riddles from the Exeter Book.
D. Gifford, 203:Vol93No2-237
Alexander, M. The Poetic Achievement of Ezra Pound.*
G. Dekker, 402(MLR):Oct82-947
C. Froula, 405(MP):Aug82-103
W. Harmon, 569(SR):Spring82-279
Alexander, M., H. Hecker and M. Lammich - see Stökl, G.
Alexander, P. Roy Campbell.*
R.G. Freebairn, 364:Jun82-87
Alexander, S. Very Much a Lady.
A. Bernays, 441:27Mar83-13
Alexander, W. William Dean Howells.
K. Vanderbilt, 26(ALR):Autumn82-274
Alföldi, M.R. Antike Numismatik. (Vols 1 and 2)
P. Kinns, 303(JoHS):Vol 102-292

Alfonso XI. Libro de la montería. (D.P. Seniff, ed)
J.E. Keller, 304(JHP):Winter83-144
Alford, N. The Rhymer's Club.*
S. Bassett, 637(VS):Summer82-497
Algeo, J. - see Pyles, T.
Algren, N. The Devil's Stocking.
P-L. Adams, 61:Oct83-122
J.W. Aldridge, 441:9Oct83-9
Ali, M.M. and M.S. Unpublished Letters of the Ali Brothers. (S. Muhammad, ed)
R. Kemal, 273(IC):Jan82-78
Princess Alice, Duchess of Gloucester. Memoirs. (J.S. McEwen, ed)
I. Colegate, 617(TLS):29Apr83-428
J. Vaizey, 362:5May83-25
Alighieri, D. - see under Dante Alighieri
Alinder, J. - see "Wright Morris: Photographs and Words"
Alitto, G.S. The Last Confucian.
C. Furth, 244(HJAS):Jun82-327
Alkire, L.G., Jr. New Periodical Title Abbreviations. (Vol 1) (3rd ed)
K.B. Harder, 424:Jun82-123
Alkon, P.K. Defoe and Fictional Time.*
A. Varney, 447(N&Q):Feb81-78
Allaby, M. and J. Lovelock. The Great Extinction.
P-L. Adams, 61:Apr83-133
W.H. McCrea, 617(TLS):29Jul83-796
Allain, M.F. The Other Man.
A. Hislop, 617(TLS):1Jul83-710
P. Kemp, 362:12May83-24
Allan, D.G.C. and R.E. Schofield. Stephen Hales.*
J.L. Abbott, 173(ECS):Spring83-352
G.L. Turner, 447(N&Q):Dec81-551
Allan, J.W. Persian Metal Technology 700-1300 A.D.
P. Meyers, 318(JAOS):Apr-Jun81-222
Allan, S. Arrow in the Dark.
M. Laski, 362:19May83-24
Allard, J-L. L'éducation à la liberté ou la philosophie de l'éducation de Jacques Maritain.
R. Prévost, 192(EP):Apr-Jun81-242
Allard, L. Mademoiselle Hortense ou l'école du septième rang.*
P. Collet, 102(CanL):Summer82-122
Allard, Y. Ecrits sur l'avenir.
M.A., 561(SFS):Mar82-102
Allason, R. The Branch.
T. Parker, 617(TLS):10Jun83-610
Allbeury, T. The Other Side of Silence.*
639(VQR):Spring82-54
Allbeury, T. Shadow of Shadows.*
N. Callendar, 441:2Jan83-26
Allchin, F.R. and D.K. Chakrabarti, eds. A Source Book of Indian Archaeology. (Vol 1)
H.S. Converse, 318(JAOS):Jul-Sep81-385
Alldritt, K. Eliot's "Four Quartets."
A.C. Bolgan, 178:Jun82-215
Allemand, A. L'Oeuvre romanesque de Nathalie Sarraute.*
S. Jüttner, 547(RF):Band93Heft1/2-287
L.S. Roudiez, 546(RR):Jan82-128
M. Tison-Braun, 535(RHL):Sep-Dec82-982
Allen, B. and L. Montell. From Memory to History.
F.A. de Caro, 650(WF):Apr82-148

5

Allen, C., ed. Tales from the South China Seas.
  A. Ross, 617(TLS):29Jul83-811
Allen, C.B. The New Lottie Moon Story.
  R. Armour, 9(AlaR):Jan82-63
Allen, D.G. In English Ways.
  P. Greven, 656(WMQ):Apr82-365
Allen, D.G. and others - see Adams, J.Q.
Allen, E. A Shored Up House.
  D. Barbour, 648(WCR):Summer81-83
  B. Pell, 102(CanL):Spring82-128
Allen, E.D. and others. ¿Habla español?
  (rev)
  L.E. Haughton, 399(MLJ):Spring82-96
Allen, G.F. Railways.
  S. Bailey, 617(TLS):25Feb83-196
Allen, G.W. Waldo Emerson.*
  R. Giuffrida, 619:Fall82-383
  W.H. Pritchard, 249(HudR):Winter82/83-619
  R.D. Richardson, 152(UDQ):Spring82-121
  P. Wild, 50(ArQ):Summer82-190
Allen, H. and J. Wilbur. The Worlds of the Early Greek Philosophers. The Worlds of Plato and Aristotle. (2nd ed)
  W. Watson, 321:Vol 16No3-241
Allen, H.W. Poindexter of Washington.
  J. Benjamin, 583:Summer83-399
Allen, J. Theatre in Europe.
  R. Findlater, 157:Winter82-45
Allen, J.B. and T.A. Moritz. A Distinction of Stories.
  T.H. Bestul, 589:Oct82-850
  E. Brown, Jr., 301(JEGP):Oct82-554
  K.J. Harty, 573(SSF):Winter82-81
  R.M. Jordan, 150(DR):Spring82-164
  T.A. Stroud, 405(MP):Nov82-177
Allen, J.S. Popular French Romanticism.*
  T. Gretton, 208(FS):Apr82-223
  J.S. Patty, 345(KRQ):Vol29No2-215
Allen, M. The Birth Symbol in Traditional Women's Art from Eurasia and the Western Pacific.
  R.L. Shep, 614:Spring83-16
Allen, M.J.B. - see Ficino, M.
Allen, M.J.B. and D.G. Calder, eds and trans. Sources and Analogues of Old English Poetry.
  G.H. Brown, 38:Band100Heft3/4-493
Allen, M.J.P. and K. Muir - see Shakespeare, W.
Allen, M.V. The Achievement of Margaret Fuller.*
  V. Strong-Boag, 106:Spring82-97
Allen, N.J. Sketch of Thulung Grammar.
  J.A. Matisoff, 318(JAOS):Oct-Dec81-435
Allen, R. The Hawryliw Process.
  D. Barbour, 102(CanL):Winter81-162
Allen, R., S. Luxton and M. Teicher. Late Romantics.*
  T. Goldie, 102(CanL):Summer82-149
  B. Whiteman, 529(QQ):Spring82-223
Allen, R.E. Socrates and Legal Obligation.
  J. Cropsey, 185:Apr83-623
  O.D.D., 543:Jun82-847
  D.S. Hutchinson, 123:Vol132No1-98
  P. Woodruff, 319:Jan83-93
Allen, R.R. - see "The Eighteenth Century: A Current Bibliography"
Allen, W. As I Walked Down New Grub Street.*
  M. Maddocks, 569(SR):Fall82-569
  H.H. Watts, 395(MFS):Winter82/83-646

Allen, W. Four Films of Woody Allen.*
  T. Wiener, 18:Mar83-74
Allen, W. The Short Story in English.*
  M-C. Birmann, 189(EA):Oct-Dec82-431
  J. Lothe, 172(Edda):1982/2-116
  W. Peden, 395(MFS):Winter81/82-767
  W. Sullivan, 579(SAQ):Winter82-117
  42(AR):Winter82-117
  295(JML):Dec82-377
Allerton, D.J. Essentials of Grammatical Theory.*
  P. Mühlhäusler, 541(RES):Nov82-449
Allerton, D.J., E. Carney and D. Holdcroft, eds. Function and Context in Linguistic Analysis.
  G. Öhlschläger, 72:Band218Heft1-150
Alley, R., comp. Catalogue of the Tate Gallery's Collection of Modern Art other than Works by British Artists.
  R. Pickvance, 39:Apr82-295
Alley, R. Graham Sutherland.
  D. Sutton, 39:Aug82-72
Alleyne, M.C. Comparative Afro-American.*
  J.R. Rickford, 350:Sep83-670
  B.M.H. Strang, 677(YES):Vol 12-264
Allin, T.R. Vocabulario resígaro.
  H.E. Manelis Klein, 269(IJAL):Oct82-484
Allison, F., ed-in-chief. Music in Colonial Massachusetts, 1630-1820. (Vol 1)
  D. McKay, 414(MusQ):Jul82-428
Allman, E.J. Player-King and Adversary.*
  G.K. Hunter, 569(SR):Spring82-273
  T.F. Van Laan, 551(RenQ):Spring82-121
Allman, J. Walking Four Ways in the Wind.
  C. Berger, 491:Apr82-35
Allnutt, G. Spitting the Pips Out.
  L. Sail, 565:Vol23No4-74
Allon, Y. Communicating Vessels.
  N. Rotenstreich, 390:Apr82-46
Allott, K. - see Arnold, M.
Allott, M. - see Arnold, M.
Allshouse, R.H. - see Prokudin-Gorskii, S.M.
Allyson, J., with F.S. Leighton. June Allyson.
  M. Buckley, 200:Aug-Sep82-444
Almeder, R. The Philosophy of Charles S. Peirce.
  C.J.D., 543:Jun82-849
  C.F. Delaney, 619:Spring82-195
  C. Hookway, 479(PhQ):Jan82-87
  M. Thompson, 185:Oct82-187
  R. Tursman, 319:Jan83-118
Almeida, A. and J. da Silva. Sprachvergleich Portugiesisch-Deutsch.
  H. Schulz, 682(ZPSK):Band34Heft2-257
Almeida, E.R. - see under Rodriguez Almeida, E.
de Almeida, H. Byron and Joyce Through Homer.*
  K.E. Marre, 395(MFS):Summer82-266
de Almeida, J. Introdução ao estudo das perífrases verbais de infinitivo.
  A. Brakel, 552(REH):Jan82-159
Almon, B. Gary Snyder.
  G.F. Day, 649(WAL):Summer82-173
Aloni, A. Le Muse di Archiloco.
  D.E. Gerber, 487(Autumn82-283
Alonso, L.R. El Supremísimo.
  O. Rossardi, 37:May-Jun82-64
Alonso, S. - see Gracián, B.

6

Alpers, A. The Life of Katherine Mans-
field.*
D. Davies, 184(EIC):Apr82-194
D.W. Kleine, 396(ModA):Winter82-106
Alpers, H.J., W. Fuchs and R.M. Hahn, eds.
Reclams Science Fiction Führer.
M.W. Heiderich, 268(IFR):Summer83-141
Alpers, P. The Singer of the "Eclogues."*
K.S. Datta, 551(RenQ):Summer82-322
R.F. Thomas, 122:Oct82-370
Alpers, S. The Art of Describing.
E.H. Gombrich, 453(NYRB):10Nov83-13
J. Nash, 617(TLS):4Nov83-1211
J. Russell, 441:4Dec83-13
Alquié, F. Le rationalisme de Spinoza.
G. Courtois, 192(EP):Oct-Dec82-461
Alquié, F. - see Kant, I.
Alsop, J. The Rare Art Traditions.*
M. Kemp, 617(TLS):25Mar83-294
J. Walker, 39:Oct82-275
Alston, A.J. Saṃkara on The Absolute.
J.W. de Jong, 259(IIJ):Jan82-60
Alt, A.T. - see Storm, T. and E. Esmarch
Altenberg, B. The Genitive v. the "of"-
Construction.
J.M. Anderson, 596(SL):Vol36No2-168
Alter, I. The Good Man's Dilemma.
S. Cohen, 577(SHR):Spring82-178
J.A. Ward, 395(MFS):Summer82-315
Alter, P. Wissenschaft, Staat, Mäzene.
P. Kennedy, 617(TLS):20May83-518
Alter, R. The Art of Biblical Narrative.*
E. Kreizman, 400(MLN):Dec82-1243
H.J. Levine, 219(GaR):Winter82-900
E. Robertson, 175:Autumn82-274
L. Stern, 290(JAAC):Spring83-340
Althaus, H.P., H. Henne and H.E. Wiegand,
eds. Lexikon der Germanistischen Lin-
guistik.* (2nd ed)
W.S. Bennett, 301(JEGP):Oct82-528
S. Grosse, 685(ZDL):1/1982-67
L. Lipka, 38:Band100Heft1/2-135
Althusser, L. Elements of Self-Criticism.
M. Poster, 504:No5-113
Althusser, L. For Marx. Lenin and Philos-
ophy. Essays in Self-Criticism.
J.H. Kavanagh, 153:Spring82-25
Althusser, L. and E. Balibar. Reading
Capital.
J.H. Kavanagh, 153:Spring82-25
Altick, R.D. The Art of Literary Research.
(3rd ed rev by J.J. Fenstermaker)
W. Kupersmith, 365:Spring83-75
Altick, R.D. The Shows of London.
P. van der Merwe, 611(TN):Vol36No2-89
Altick, R.D. - see Browning, R.
Altieri, C. Act and Quality.*
P.A. Bové, 659(ConL):Fall83-379
P. Hernadi, 290(JAAC):Winter82-227
J. Reichert, 113:Spring82-82
R. Shusterman, 89(BJA):Summer82-280
Altman, J.B. The Tudor Play of Mind.*
M. Trousdale, 570(SQ):Autumn82-414
Altman, J.G. Epistolarity.
B. Duyfhuizen, 454:Fall82-91
G.S. Rousseau, 617(TLS):7Jan83-20
Altman, R., ed. Genre: The Musical.
M. Wood, 18:Dec81-77
Altmann, G., ed. Glottometrika 1.
L. Hoffmann, 682(ZPSK):Band34Heft5-647
Alton, J. and B. Jeffery. Bele Buche e
bele parleure.
C.A. Robson, 410(M&L):Jul/Oct81-417

Alvar Ezquerra, M. Concordancias e
indices léxicos de la "Vida de San
Ildefonso."
R. Pellen, 553(RLiR):Jun-Dec82-440
Alvarado Tenorio, H. La poesía española
contemporánea.
W.D. Barnette, 238:May82-309
Alvarez, A. The Biggest Game in Town.
P-L. Adams, 61:Jun83-105
M. Richler, 441:8May83-7
R. Sale, 453(NYRB):2Jun83-35
Alvarez, A. Life After Marriage.*
N. Berry, 364:Dec82/Jan83-130
639(VQR):Summer82-90
Álvarez de Miranda, P., ed. Tratado sobre
la Monarquía Columbina.
S. Cro, 304(JHP):Fall182-78
Alver, B. Guten i gadden.
O. Holzapfel, 196:Band23Heft1/2-115
Alvis, J. and T.G. West, eds. Shakespeare
as a Political Thinker.
C. Hill, 570(SQ):Winter82-529
J.V. Schall, 396(ModA):Summer/Fall182-
411
Amabile, G. The Presence of Fire.
J. Peirce, 99:Oct82-27
Amacher, R.E. and V. Lange, eds. New Per-
spectives in German Literary Criticism.*
S. Deetz and L.L. Nelson, 290(JAAC):
Summer83-468
J.M. Ellis, 678(YCGL):No30-87
J.F. Hyde, Jr., 406:Fall82-336
"Amadís de Gaula." (J. di Algaba, trans;
Z. Malachi, ed)
B. Sholod, 304(JHP):Spring82-242
Amalrik, A. Notes of a Revolutionary.*
L. Schapiro, 453(NYRB):20Jan83-3
C. Wheeler, 362:6Jan83-23
Amalrik, A. Raspoutine.
I. Vinogradoff, 617(TLS):14Jan83-31
Amann, R. and J. Cooper, eds. Industrial
Innovation in the Soviet Union.
A. Brown, 617(TLS):1Apr83-333
Ambrière-Fargeaud, M. - see de Balzac, H.
Ambrose, S.E. Eisenhower. (Vol 1)
D. Middleton, 362:18Sep83-9
Amburger, E. Ingermanland.*
J. Cracraft, 550(RusR):Apr82-200
T.U. Raun, 104(CASS):Summer82-250
Ameln, K., M. Jenny and W. Lipphardt, eds.
Das deutsche Kirchenlied. (Vol 1, Pt 1)
J. Janota, 684(ZDA):Band111Heft4-171
"American Coverlets of the 19th Century
from the Helen Louise Allen Textile Col-
lection.
R.L. Shep, 614:Winter83-13
"American Folk Portraits."
M.S. Young, 39:Sep82-201
"The American Heritage Dictionary." (2nd
College ed)
K, Kalfus, 441:16Jan83-14
"American Literary Scholarship 1975." (J.
Woodress, ed) "American Literary Schol-
arship 1977." (J. Woodress, ed) "Amer-
ican Literary Scholarship 1978." (J.A.
Robbins, ed)
E. Gallafent, 677(YES):Vol 12-364
"American Literary Scholarship, 1976."
(J.A. Robbins, ed)
E. Gallafent, 677(YES):Vol 12-364
A. Hook, 447(N&Q):Aug81-375
Améry, J. At the Mind's Limits.
E. Alexander, 390:Dec82-57

Ames, R.T.   The Art of Rulership.
   M. Loewe, 617(TLS):9Dec83-1383
Ames, W.L.   Police and Community in Japan.
   R.J. Smith, 293(JASt):Feb82-353
Ames-Lewis, F.   Drawing in Early Renais-
   sance Italy.*
   G. Baker, 135:Feb82-88
de Amescua, M. - see under Mira de Amescua
Amichai, Y.   Great Tranquillity.
   R. Pinsky, 441:13Nov83-27
Amiel, H-F.   Journal intime.
   J-L. Chrétien, 98:Mar82-251
Amigues, M.   Le chrétien devant le refus
   de la mort.
   M. Adam, 542:Oct-Dec82-665
Amirthanayagam, G., ed.   Writers in East-
   West Encounter.
   G. Salgãdo, 617(TLS):14Jan83-43
Amis, K.   Collected Short Stories.
   P. Craig, 617(TLS):18Nov83-1294
Amis, M.   Other People.*
   G.W. Jarecke, 577(SHR):Spring82-157
   P. Lewis, 565:Vol23No1-51
Ammons, A.R.   A Coast of Trees.*
   L.L. Martz, 676(YR):Autumn82-63
Ammons, A.R.   Lake Effect Country.
   A. Corn, 441:4Sep83-8
Ammons, A.R.   The Snow Poems.
   M. McFee, 114(ChiR):Summer81-32
Ammons, A.R.   Worldly Hopes.*
   H. Vendler, 491:Oct82-26
Ammons, E., ed.   Critical Essays on Har-
   riet Beecher Stowe.*
   C. Perotin, 189(EA):Jul-Sep82-361
Ammons, E.   Edith Wharton's Argument with
   America.*
   L. Waldeland, 395(MFS):Winter81/82-725
Amor, A.C.   Mrs. Oscar Wilde.
   J. Stokes, 617(TLS):24Jun83-650
Amorós, A. - see Pérez de Ayala, R.
Amorosi, R.   A Generous Wall.
   M. Lammon, 436(NewL):Winter82/83-109
Amory, M. - see Waugh, E.
Amos, A.C.   Linguistic Means of Determin-
   ing the Dates of Old English Literary
   Texts.
   M. Rissanen, 589:Jan82-112
Amossy, R.   Les Jeux de l'allusion littér-
   aire dans "Un Beau Ténébreux" de Julien
   Gracq.*
   O. de Mourgues, 208(FS):Oct82-496
   L.K. Penrod, 207(FR):May83-954
   S.R. Suleiman, 210(FrF):Jan82-91
Amossy, P.   Parcours symboliques chez
   Julien Gracq.
   A. Cismaru, 395(MFS):Winter82/83-711
Amossy, R. and E. Rosen.   Les Discours du
   cliché.
   W. Woodhull, 207(FR):Feb83-524
Amprimoz, A.L.   Other Realities.*
   P. Monk, 102(CanL):Winter81-171
Amy, R. and P. Gros.   La Maison Carrée de
   Nîmes.
   D.E.E. and F.S. Kleiner, 576:Mar82-56
Anacleti, A.O., ed.   Jipemoyo.   (Vol 2)
   M. Etherton, 69:Vol51No4-863
Ananaba, W.   The Trade Union Movement in
   Africa.
   M. Peil, 69:Vol51No1-531
Ananthanarayana, H.S.   Four Lectures on
   Pa:ṇini's Aṣṭa:dhya:yi:.*
   G. Cardona, 259(IIJ):Oct82-301

Anawalt, P.R.   Indian Clothing before
   Cortés.
   L. Milazzo, 584(SWR):Winter82-v
   N.P. Troike, 263(RIB):Vol32No2-207
Anaxagoras.   The Fragments of Anaxagoras.
   (D. Sider, ed)
   M. Schofield, 123:Vol32No2-189
Anaya, R.A.   Tortuga.
   A. Miguélez, 152(UDQ):Fall81-120
Ancelet, D.   Cuisine of France.
   W. and C. Cowen, 639(VQR):Spring82-65
And, M.   A Pictorial History of Turkish
   Dancing.
   T. Buckland, 203:Vol193No2-240
Andelson, R.V., ed.   Critics of Henry
   George.
   J.L. Green, 577(SHR):Fall182-380
Andersen, F.G. and others, eds.   Medieval
   Iconography and Narrative.
   G.S. Tate, 563(SS):Spring82-164
Andersen, H.C.   Tales and Stories by Hans
   Christian Andersen.*   (P. Conroy and S.
   Rossel, eds and trans)
   S. Pickering, 569(SR):Spring82-300
Anderson, A., Jr. - see Smith, D.
Anderson, A.B. and J.S. Frideres.   Ethnic-
   ity in Canada.
   R.T. Bowles, 298:Spring82-131
Anderson, B.   Internal Migration during
   Modernization in Late Nineteenth-Century
   Russia.
   A. Helgeson, 550(RusR):Apr82-217
Anderson, C., J. Gordon and N.W. Towner.
   Beiderwand?
   P. Bach, 614:Spring83-15
Anderson, D.K.   Charles T. Griffes.
   A.F.L.T., 412:Feb81-61
Anderson, E.   The Technique of Soft Toy-
   making.
   M. Cowan, 614:Summer83-22
Anderson, E.W.   Animals as Navigators.
   J.L. Cloudsley-Thompson, 617(TLS):
      22Jul83-786
Anderson, F. and others - see Twain, M.
Anderson, F.W. and E. Cesar.   Incredible
   Rogers Pass.
   529(QQ):Autumn82-687
Anderson, F.W., H. Rowed and D. Stewart.
   Majestic Jasper.
   529(QQ):Autumn82-687
Anderson, G.L.   Asian Literature in
   English.
   354:Jun82-205
Anderson, J.   Education and Inquiry.
   P.J. Crittenden, 63:Sep82-299
Anderson, J., ed.   Language Form and Lin-
   guistic Variation.
   R.K.S. Macaulay, 350:Sep83-686
Anderson, J.   The Milky Way.
   W. Logan, 617(TLS):10Jun83-614
Anderson, J.   The One and Only.*
   R. Philp, 151:Jan82-92
Anderson, J.   Selected Poems.
   P. Lopate, 441:2Oct83-15
Anderson, J., with J. Boyd.   Fiasco.
   J. Fallows, 441:27Nov83-7
Anderson, J.M.   The Truth of Freedom.
   H.W. Johnstone, Jr., 480(P&R):Fall182-
      281
Anderson, J.R.L.   Death in the City.
   N. Callendar, 441:10Apr83-32

Anstruther, I. Oscar Browning.
P.N. Furbank, 617(TLS):25Nov83-1303
D. Newsome, 362:27Oct83-33
Anthony, G. Gwen Pharis Ringwood.
J. Hoffman, 108:Summer82-150
W.N., 102(CanL):Summer82-163
Antoine, G. Liberté, Égalité, Fraternité
ou les fluctuations d'une devise.
M. Piron, 209(FM):Jan82-82
Anton, J.P., ed. Science and the Sciences
in Plato.
I. Bulmer-Thomas, 123:Vol32No2-196
D.F., 185:Oct82-210
D.J. Zeyl, 124:Sep/Oct82-53
Antonaci, A. Ricerche sull'aristotelismo
del Rinascimento: Marcantonio Zimara.*
(Vol 2)
J-R. Armogathe, 192(EP):Oct-Dec81-469
Antonov-Ovseyenko, A. The Time of Stalin.*
S. Hook, 31(ASch):Spring82-291
639(VQR):Winter82-21
Antunes, A.L. South of Nowhere.
A. Cheuse, 441:24Jul83-10
J.M., 231:Aug83-76
N. Shakespeare, 617(TLS):16Dec83-1413
"Anuarul de Folclor I."
H. Stein, 196:Band23Heft3/4-304
Anz, T. and M. Stark, eds. Expression-
ismus.
W. Paulsen, 222(GR):Fall82-166
H. Steinecke, 680(ZDP):Band101Heft4-
603
Anzieu, D. Le Corps de l'oeuvre.
P. Fédida, 450(NRF):Feb82-144
Anzilotti, R., ed. Robert Lowell.*
R. Pooley, 677(YES):Vol 12-329
Aoki, H. Nez Percé Texts.
G.F. Meier, 682(ZPSK):Band35Heft5-594
Aoki, M.Y. and M.B. Dardess, eds. As the
Japanese See It.
J. Abrams, 407(MN):Summer82-261
L.L. Johnson, 293(JASt):Aug82-835
Aono, H. and S. Birukawa, eds. Nihon
Chishi.
J.D. Eyre, 293(JASt):Nov81-130
Apel, K-O. Die Erklären.*
J.B., 543:Jun82-851
E.M. Lange, 687:Oct-Dec82-642
Apel, K-O. Die Idee der Sprache in der
Tradition des Humanismus von Dante bis
Vico.
J. Poulain, 98:Feb82-130
Apel, K-O. Charles S. Peirce.
V.G. Potter, 619:Fall82-376
H.S. Thayer, 319:Jul83-412
Apollinaire, G. Calligrammes.* (A.H.
Greet, trans)
M. Davies, 402(MLR):Jul82-730
Apollonius of Rhodes. Apollonios de
Rhodes, "Argonautiques." (Vol 2) (F.
Vian, ed; E. Delage, trans)
M. Campbell, 123:Vol32No1-14
P. Chuvin, 555:Vol156fasc2-331
Apollonius of Rhodes. Apollonios de
Rhodes, "Argonautiques." (Vol 3) (F.
Vian and É. Delage, eds)
M. Campbell, 123:Vol32No2-137
Apostle, H.G. - see Aristotle
Apostolidès, J-M. Le Roi-machine.
J. Barchilon, 207(FR):Dec82-362
P. France, 402(MLR):Oct82-956
H. Phillips, 208(FS):Oct82-472

Appel, D.H., ed. An Album for Americans.
B. Dobell, 441:4Dec83-62
Appelfeld, A. The Age of Wonders.*
B.T. Birmelin, 363(LitR):Spring83-460
D. Flower, 249(HudR):Summer82-274
M. Levene, 99:Jun/Jul82-27
Appelfeld, A. Badenheim 1939.*
W. Phillips, 473(PR):1/1982-139
T. Ziolkowski, 569(SR):Fall82-592
Appelfeld, A. Tzili.
R.M. Adams, 453(NYRB):16Jun83-34
J.C. Oates, 441:27Feb83-9
442(NY):25Apr83-152
Appia, A. Staging Wagnerian Drama.
J. Kerman, 453(NYRB):22Dec83-27
Applbaum, R.L. and K.W.E. Anatol. Effec-
tive Oral Communication for Business and
the Professions.
S.H. Brown, 583:Spring83-308
Apple, M., ed. Southwest Fiction.*
D. Johnson, 649(WAL):Spring82-72
Apple, M.W., ed. Cultural and Economic
Reproduction in Education.
J.M.G., 185:Apr83-637
Applewhite, J. Following Gravity.*
R. Tillinghast, 569(SR):Spring82-291
Applewhite, P.B. Molecular Gods.
J.M. Bristow, 529(QQ):Winter82-919
"Appraisal of the Records of the Federal
Bureau of Investigation."
F.G. Ham, 14:Fall82-475
Apresjan, J.D. Tipy informacci dlja pov-
erxnostno-semantičeskogo komponenta
modeli "smysl-tekst."
F.E. Knowles, 575(SEER):Jan82-94
Apter, T.E. Thomas Mann.*
S. Mandel, 395(MFS):Summer81-406
Apter, T.E. Virginia Woolf.*
F.W. Bradbrook, 447(N&Q):Aug81-364
Apthorp, M.J. The Manuscript Evidence for
Interpolation in Homer.
S. West, 123:Vol32No1-1
Åqvist, L. and F. Guenthner. Tense Logic.
M. Boudot, 192(EP):Jul-Sep81-329
Arac, J. Commissioned Spirits.*
R. Bennett, 541(RES):Feb82-101
Aragon, L. and J. Cocteau. Conversations
on the Dresden Gallery.
R. Cardinal, 617(TLS):8Apr83-361
Arant, P.M. Russian for Reading.
J.J. Rinkus, 399(MLJ):Winter82-433
Araya, G., H. Haverkate and K. van Leuven,
eds. Los clíticos en el español actual.
T.R. Arrington, 238:Sep82-476
J.N. Green, 402(MLR):Jul82-742
F.H. Nuessel, Jr., 361:Sep/Oct82-192
Arbasino, A. Matinée.
K. Bosley, 617(TLS):14Oct83-1136
Arbatov, G.A. and W. Oltmans. The Soviet
Viewpoint.
M.D. Shulman, 441:10Jul83-11
Arbuthnot, J. The History of John Bull.
(A.W. Bower and R.A. Erickson, eds)
P. Dixon, 447(N&Q):Aug81-340
Arbuzov, A. Selected Plays.
J. Curtis, 617(TLS):17Jun83-639
Arce, J. La poesía del siglo ilustrado.
R.P. Sebold, 240(HR):Summer82-297
Archambault, G. The Umbrella Pines.
J.J. O'Connor, 102(CanL):Winter81-128
Archard, D. Marxism and Existentialism.
D. Lamb, 323:Jan82-92

Archbold, A. The Traditional Arts and
Crafts of Warren County, Kentucky.
C. Camp, 650(WF):Oct82-313
Archer, M. India and British Portraiture,
1770-1825.
J.E. van Lohuizen-de Leeuw, 57:Vol43
No1/2-165
Archibald, D. Yeats.
D. Donoghue, 441:5Jun83-7
"An Architectural and Historical Inventory
of Raleigh, North Carolina."
D.J. Hibbard, 658:Spring82-90
"Architecture of Russia from Old to Mod-
ern." (Vol 1)
M. Winokur, 574(SEEJ):Spring82-111
"Archives de philosophie du droit." (Vol
26)
J-L. Gardies, 542:Jan-Mar82-76
Ardagh, J. France in the 1980s.*
J.K. Davison, 441:10Apr83-16
J. Mellors, 364:Nov82-101
Ardao, A. Estudios latinoamericanos de
historia de las ideas.
Z. Kouřím, 542:Oct-Dec82-655
Ardao, A. Génesis de la idea y el nombre
de América Latina.*
J.C. Torchia Estrada, 263(RIB):Vol132
No1-47
Arden, H. Fools' Plays.*
B.C. Bowen, 551(RenQ):Autumn81-436
Ardley, G. The Common Sense Philosophy of
James Oswald.
M.J. Cormack, 571(ScLJ):Spring82-7
M. Kuehn, 518:Oct82-209
Arellano, J. La existencia cosificada.
A. Reix, 542:Oct-Dec82-656
Arellano, J.E. and J. Jirón Terán. Con-
tribuciones al estudio de Rubén Darío e
investigaciones en torno a Rubén Darío.
I.M. Zuleta, 263(RIB):Vol32No3/4-367
Arenas, R. Termina el Desfile.
O. Rossardi, 37:Jan-Feb82-63
Arendt, H. Lectures on Kant's Political
Philosophy. (R. Beiner, ed)
W.H. Walsh, 617(TLS):3Jun83-566
442(NY):21Feb83-134
Arendt, H. La vie de l'esprit.* (Vol 1)
M. Adam, 542:Oct-Dec82-656
Arendt, J.D., D.L. Lange and P.J. Myers,
eds. Foreign Language Learning, Today
and Tomorrow.*
G.L. Ervin, 399(MLJ):Winter82-416
Arens, B. Katzengold.
M. Hofmann, 617(TLS):4Mar83-223
Arens, W. The Man-Eating Myth.
J.R. Rayfield, 488:Mar82-106
Argue, V. and R. Ullmann. Sur une ligne
aérienne.
L. Vines, 399(MLJ):Summer82-215
Argueta, M. One Day of Life.
A. Josephs, 441:20ct83-15
Argyle, G. German Elements in the Fiction
of George Eliot, Gissing, and Meredith.*
J. McMaster, 178:Sep82-372
Arhin, K. West African Traders in Ghana
in the Nineteenth and Twentieth Centur-
ies.
J. Middleton, 69:Vol51No4-884
Arias, J. "Guzmán de Alfarache."*
H. Klüppelholz, 356(LR):Aug82-267
Arias, R. The Spanish Sacramental Plays.
W.F. Hunter, 402(MLR):Oct82-976
C. Stern, 238:Mar82-140

Ariès, P. The Hour of Our Death.*
G. Strauss, 589:Jul82-583
Arieti, S. The Parnas.
C. Leviant, 390:Feb82-62
Ariosto, L. Orlando furioso. (E. Bigi,
ed)
O. Ragusa, 276:Winter82-354
Ariosto, L. Der rasende Roland (Orlando
furioso). (J.D. Gries, trans; S. Evers-
mann, ed)
W. Hirdt, 52:Band16Heft2-193
Aris, M. Bhutan.
E. Gellner, 293(JASt):May82-609
J.W. de Jong, 259(IIJ):Oct82-318
Aristides. Aristides Quintilianus on
Music. (T.J. Mathiesen, ed)
E.K. Borthwick, 617(TLS):11Nov83-1250
Aristides. P. Aelius Aristides, The
Complete Works. (Vol 2) (C.A. Behr, ed
and trans)
I. Avotins, 124:Sep/Oct82-56
A.R.R. Sheppard, 123:Vol132No2-144
Aristides. P. Aelii Aristidis, Opera quae
exstant omnia. (Vol 1, fasc 1-4) (F.W.
Lenz and C.A. Behr, eds)
A.H.M. Kessels, 394:Vol35fasc3/4-383
Aristotle. Aristote, "Anthropologie."
(J-C. Fraisse, ed and trans)
A. Reix, 192(EP):Apr-Jun81-245
Aristotle. Aristote, "La poétique."* (R.
Dupont-Roc and J. Lallot, eds and trans)
M. Bal, 494:Winter82-171
Aristotle. Aristotele: "La Poetica."
(D. Pesce, trans)
P. Somville, 542:Apr-Jun82-449
Aristotle. Aristotele's Metaphysik. (Bks
1-14) (H. Seidl, ed)
J-F. Courtine, 192(EP):Jul-Sep82-373
Aristotle. Aristotle's Categories and
Propositions (De Interpretatione).
(H.G. Apostle, ed and trans)
G.K. Plochmann, 319:Apr83-243
Aristotle. Aristotle's "De Motu Animal-
ium."* (M.C. Nussbaum, ed and trans)
D.M. Balme, 319:Jan82-92
A.G., 543:Mar82-619
J. Scarborough, 121(CJ):Oct/Nov82-74
Aristotle. Aristotle's Eudemian Ethics.*
(Bks 1, 2 and 8) (M. Woods, trans)
R.J. Sullivan, 319:Oct83-557
Aristotle. Aristotle's "Posterior Analy-
tics." (H.G. Apostle, ed and trans)
R. Smith, 319:Jul83-395
Aristotle. Poetics. (J. Hutton, ed and
trans)
A.P., 617(TLS):26Aug83-915
Aristotle. The Politics. (T.A. Sinclair,
trans; rev by T.J. Saunders)
R.W., 555:Vol56fasc1-136
Arkes, H. The Philosopher in the City.
J.L.G., 185:Jan83-435
Arkoun, M. Lectures du Coran.
B. Lewis, 453(NYRB):30Jun83-35
"Arktouros, Hellenic Studies presented to
Bernard M.W. Knox."
R. Aélion, 555:Vol56fasc2-336
Arlacchi, P. Mafia, Peasants and Great
Estates.
J. Davis, 617(TLS):30Dec83-1465
Arlen, M.J. The Camera Age.* Thirty Sec-
onds.*
P. Brantlinger, 128(CE):Sep82-475

11

Arlott, J. Fred.
    A.J.H., 617(TLS):20May83-527
Arlott, J. Jack Hobbs.
    A.J.H., 617(TLS):22Apr83-415
Arlt, W., ed. Basler Jahrbuch für histor-
ische Musikpraxis. (Vol 1)
    J. Stevens, 410(M&L):Jul/Oct82-311
de Armas, F.A. The Invisible Mistress.
    J.A. Silveira y Montes de Oca, 241:
    May82-96
de Arams, F.A., D.M. Gitlitz and J.A. Mad-
rigal, eds. Critical Perspectives on
Calderón de la Barca.
    D.J. Hill, 304(JHP):Spring82-250
Armistead, S.G. and J.H. Silverman. Tres
calas en el Romancero sefardí (Rodas,
Jerusalén, Estados Unidos).*
    J.G. Cummins, 402(MLR):Apr82-474
    P. Díaz-Mas, 240(HR):Summer82-357
Armour, L. The Idea of Canada and the
Crisis of Community.
    S. Burns, 150(DR):Summer82-315
Armour, L. and E. Trott. The Faces of
Reason.
    S. Burns, 150(DR):Summer82-315
    J.T. Stevenson, 99:Jun/Jul82-31
    G. Woodcock, 102(CanL):Autumn82-164
Arms, G. and C.K. Lohmann - see Howells,
W.D.
Armstrong, B. Sable Island.
    529(QQ):Summer82-460
Armstrong, C.A.J. England, France and
Burgundy in the Fifteenth Century.
    M. Jones, 617(TLS):11Nov83-1252
Armstrong, D.M. The Nature of Mind and
Other Essays.*
    B.F. Scarlett, 63:Jun82-182
    R.B. Schultz, 185:Jul83-805
Armstrong, D.M. A Theory of Universals.
    M. Woods, 483:Jul82-408
Armstrong, D.M. Universals and Scientific
Realism.
    R. Grossmann, 449:Mar82-133
Armstrong, J.A. Nations before National-
ism.
    E. Kedourie, 617(TLS):19Aug83-873
Armstrong, L. Renaissance Miniature Paint-
ers and Classical Imagery.*
    N. Barker, 78(BC):Winter82-523
Armstrong, M.W. Rolle und Charakter.
    D.H. Green, 402(MLR):Jan82-226
Armstrong, R.P. The Powers of Presence.
    H. Osborne, 289:Fall82-122
    J.M. Vlach, 2(AfrA):Aug82-82
Armstrong, R.W. The Chases of Cimarron.
    L. Milazzo, 584(SWR):Winter82-v
Arnason, D. Marsh Burning.
    D. Barbour, 648(WCR):Summer81-83
    B. Whiteman, 102(CanL):Winter81-172
Arnason, H.H. and others. Robert Mother-
well. (rev)
    R. Cohen, 55:Nov82-44
Árnason, K. Quantity in Historical Phonol-
ogy.*
    J.E. Cathey, 301(JEGP):Apr82-305
    W.G. Moulton, 297(JL):Sep82-492
Arnaud, N. and H. Bordillon - see Jarry, A.
Arnaut Daniel. The Poetry of Arnaut
Daniel. (J.J. Wilhelm, ed and trans)
    J.C. Hirsh, 468:Spring82-177
    N.B. Smith, 207(FR):Oct82-145

Arndt, K.J.R. The Annotated and Enlarged
Edition of Ernst Steiger's Precentennial
Bibliography "The Periodical Literature
of the United States."
    P. Herminghouse, 406:Spring82-85
Arndt, P.H. Der Erzähler bei Hartmann von
Aue.
    D.H. Green, 402(MLR):Apr82-484
Arndt, W. - see Busch, W.
Arnell, P. and T. Bickford, eds. A Tower
for Louisville.
    A.L. Huxtable, 453(NYRB):8Dec83-29
Arnhart, L. Aristotle on Political Reason-
ing.
    C.H.W., 185:Apr83-641
Arnheim, R. The Power of the Center.
    F.D. Martin, 290(JAAC):Summer83-448
    D. Rosand, 55:Nov82-46
von Arnim, E. Fraulein Schmidt and Mr.
Anstruther. Vera.
    P. Craig, 617(TLS):29Jul83-820
Arnold, A., ed. Georg Kaiser.
    R.H. Lawson, 221(GQ):May82-449
Arnold, A. and J. Schmitt, eds. Reclams
Kriminalromanführer.
    D. Gutzen, 52:Band16Heft1-102
Arnold, B. Running to Paradise.
    M.K. Benet, 617(TLS):22Apr83-400
Arnold, D. Giovanni Gabrieli and the
Music of the Venetian High Renaissance.*
    E. Rosand, 551(RenQ):Summer81-245
    J. Steele, 410(M&L):Jan81-80
Arnold, D., general ed. The New Oxford
Companion to Music.
    C. Wintle, 617(TLS):30Dec83-1451
Arnold, E. In America.
    B. Dobell, 441:4Dec83-62
Arnold, G. Held Fast for England.
    R. Kiely, 637(VS):Autumn81-87
Arnold, H.L., ed. Büchner I/II.
    H-G. Werner, 406:Fall82-364
Arnold, K. Kind und Gesellschaft in Mit-
telalter und Renaissance.
    D. Herlihy, 551(RenQ):Winter82-592
    R.B. Lyman, Jr., 589:Apr82-349
Arnold, M. The Complete Poems. (K.
Allott, ed; 2nd ed rev by M. Allott)
    R.J. Dingley, 447(N&Q):Aug81-353
    S. Lavabre, 189(EA):Oct-Dec82-476
Arnold, M.I. Zimbabwean Stone Sculpture.
    D. Brokensha, 2(AfrA):Aug82-23
Arnold, R. and K. Hansen. Englische
Phonetik.
    A. Wollmann, 38:Band100Heft3/4-463
Arnold, W. China Gate.
    J.J. Osborne, Jr., 441:30Oct83-33
Arnold, W. Eine norddeutsche Fürstenbib-
liothek des Frühen 18. Jahrhunderts.
    D.L. Paisey, 78(BC):Spring82-117
Arnott, W.G. - see "Menander"
Arntzen, E. and R. Rainwater. Guide to
the Literature of Art History.
    G. Baker, 135:Jan82-13
    H. Honour, 59:Sep82-370
Aron, R. In Defense of Decadent Europe.
    R.A. Cooper, 390:Dec82-56
Aron, R. Mémoires.
    A. Forbes, 362:22Sep83-22
    D. Johnson, 617(TLS):9Dec83-1378
Aron, R., with J-L. Missika and D. Walton.
The Committed Observer.
    D. Johnson, 617(TLS):9Dec83-1378

Aspin, C. The Woollen Industry.
  R. Hoffman, 614:Winter83-22
Aspital, A.W., comp. Catalogue of the
Pepys Library at Magdalene College,
Cambridge. (Vol 3, Pt 1)
  D. McKitterick, 78(BC):Spring82-109
Aspiz, H. Walt Whitman and the Body
Beautiful.*
  R. Asselineau, 189(EA):Oct-Dec82-489
  L. Cederstrom, 106:Winter82-349
  D. Middlebrook, 301(JEGP):Jan82-152
Asquith, H.H. H.H. Asquith: Letters to
Venetia Stanley.* (M. and E. Brock,
eds)
  N. Bliven, 442(NY):15Aug83-88
  G. Hodgson, 441:3Apr83-3
Asquith, S. Children and Justice.
  T. Campbell, 617(TLS):10Jun83-610
Asselineau, R. The Transcendentalist Con-
stant in American Literature.*
  L. Buell, 587(SAF):Spring82-117
  L. Cederstrom, 106:Winter82-349
  S. Paul, 301(JEGP):Jan82-151
Assouline, P. Monsieur Dassault.
  D. Johnson, 617(TLS):18Nov83-1282
Aston, T.H. and others, eds. Social Rela-
tions and Ideas.
  J.A. Tuck, 617(TLS):12Aug83-865
"At the Edge of Asia."
  R.L. Shep, 614:Spring83-15
Atanagi, D. Rime d'encomio e morte. (G.
De Santi, ed)
  E. Favretti, 228(GSLI):Vol 159fasc507-
439
Atherton, S.S. Alan Sillitoe.*
  K. MacKinnon, 268(IFR):Summer83-146
  B. Stovel, 178:Sep82-388
Atiyah, P.S. Promises, Morals and Law.
  A.D. Woozley, 518:Jul82-170
Atiyah, P.S. The Rise and Fall of Freedom
of Contract.
  R. McGowen, 637(VS):Spring82-386
Atkins, B.T. and others - see "Collins/
Robert French-English, English-French
Dictionary"
Atkins, G.D. The Faith of John Dryden.*
  J.M. Aden, 579(SAQ):Spring82-242
  J.V. Guerinot, 568(SCN):Fall82-46
  P. Harth, 173(ECS):Winter81/82-210
  C.H. Hinnant, 191(ELN):Sep82-51
  A. Poyet, 189(EA):Jul-Sep82-329
Atkins, J. J.B. Priestley.
  A.E. Kalson, 395(MFS):Summer82-286
  295(JML):Dec82-518
Atkins, L.R. The Valley and the Hills.
  J. Fuller, 9(AlaR):Apr82-142
Atkinson, B. Sean O'Casey. (R.G. Lowery,
ed)
  J.S. Bratton, 617(TLS):14Jan83-38
Atkinson, J.E. A Commentary on Q. Curtius
Rufus' "Historiae Alexandri Magni" books
3 and 4.
  S. Hornblower, 303(JoHS):Vol 102-272
"Atlas Linguarum Europae."* (Introduction,
First questionnaire, and Second question-
naire) (A. Weijnen and others, eds)
  J. Göschel, 685(ZDL):2/1981-228
Attar, S. The Intruder in Modern Drama.
  L.P. Gabbard, 397(MD):Jun82-326
Attebery, B. The Fantasy Tradition in
American Literature.*
  N. Khouri, 106:Winter82-407
  D.M. Miller, 395(MFS):Summer82-321

Attenborough, R. In Search of Gandhi.
  F. Watson, 362:20Jan83-27
Attfield, R. God and the Secular.*
  J.E. Force, 319:Jul82-315
"Atti del convegno internazionale di studi
danteschi."*
  A.S. Bernardo, 551(RenQ):Summer81-218
Attman, A. The Bullion Flow between
Europe and the East 1000-1750.
  R.W. Unger, 104(CASS):Fall-Winter82-
533
Attman, A. and others, eds. Ekonomiche-
skie sviazi mezhdu Rossiei i Shvetsiei v
XVII v. Ekonomiska förbindelser mellan
Sverige och Russland under 1600-talet.
  W. Kirchner, 550(RusR):Jan82-68
Attridge, D. The Rhythms of English
Poetry.
  T. Disch, 617(TLS):28Oct83-1194
Attwood, W. Making It through Middle Age.
  639(VQR):Autumn82-136
Atwood, M. Bodily Harm.*
  M. Dixon, 198:Apr82-87
  M. Dyment, 526:Spring82-73
  D. Flower, 249(HudR):Summer82-274
  L. Howe, 363(LitR):Fall82-177
  J. Mellors, 364:Jun82-61
  M.L. Moore, 181:Winter-Spring83-169
  G. Woodcock, 461:Spring-Summer82-106
  G. Woodcock, 529(QQ):Winter82-744
Atwood, M. Dancing Girls and Other
Stories.*
  A. Duchêne, 617(TLS):7Jan83-23
  J. Mellors, 362:6Jan83-24
  M.L. Moore, 181:Winter-Spring83-169
Atwood, M. Second Words.
  W.J. Keith, 99:Feb83-26
Atwood, M. True Stories.
  F. Adcock, 617(TLS):18Mar83-278
  D. Barbour, 648(WCR):Oct82-37
  D. Davis, 362:5May83-24
  A. Mandel, 198:Jan82-63
  M.L. Rosenthal, 441:13Mar83-6
  B. Whiteman, 298:Summer82-150
Atwood, M. Two-Headed Poems and Others.*
  D. Gioia, 491:May82-102
  R. Tillinghast, 569(SR):Spring82-291
Atwood, M. and J. Barkhouse. Anna's Pet.
  M. Whitaker, 102(CanL):Spring82-95
Atwood, R. The Hessians.
  W.B. Willcox, 656(WMQ):Apr82-377
Atwood, W.G. The Lioness and the Little
One.*
  L.J. Austin, 208(FS):Jan82-80
  B.T. Lupack, 497(PolR):Vol127No1/2-141
Aubenque, P., ed. Concepts et catégories
dans la pensée antique.
  P. Pellegrin, 542:Apr-Jun82-450
Aubenque, P., ed. Etudes sur la "Méta-
physique" d'Aristote.*
  B. Dumoulin, 192(EP):Jan-Mar81-77
Aubert, J. and M. Jolas, eds. Joyce and
Paris 1902 ... 1920-1940 ... 1975.
  R.A. Day, 189(EA):Jan-Mar82-101
  V. Mahon, 402(MLR):Jan82-188
Aubreton, R., with F. Buffière, eds and
trans. Anthologie grecque. (Pt 2, Vol
13)
  C. Dobias-Lalou, 555:Vol56fasc2-320
Auburn, M.S. - see Dryden, J.
Auchincloss, L. Narcissa and Other Fables.
  F. Taliaferro, 441:3Apr83-6

14

Aron, T. L'Objet du texte et le texte objet.*
B. Beugnot, 535(RHL):May-Jun82-498
Aronowitz, S. The Crisis in Historical Materialism.
A.L., 185:Jan83-431
Aronowitz, S. Working Class Hero.
S.M. Lipset, 441:11Dec83-3
Aronson, A. Music and the Novel.*
J. Batchelor, 410(M&L):Apr81-218
Aronson, H.B. Love and Sympathy in Theravāda Buddhism.
C. Hallisey, 293(JASt):Aug82-859
Aronson, R. Jean-Paul Sartre.*
A. Demaitre, 577(SHR):Summer82-284
Aronson, S.M.L. Hype.
J. Lieberson, 453(NYRB):16Jun83-30
Aronson, T. Royal Family.
J. Grigg, 617(TLS):18Nov83-1293
Arrabal, F. Théâtre XIII.
J. Spinale, 207(FR):May83-971
Arrillaga Torrens, R. Kant y el idealismo Transcendental.
R. Rovira, 342:Band73Heft2-241
Arseguel, G. Les Bleus du procédé.
F. Coulange, 450(NRF):Feb82-137
Arsenault, G. Complaintes acadiennes de l'Ile-du-Prince-Edouard.
G. Thomas, 102(CanL):Spring82-130
"Art to Wear."
R.L. Shep, 614:Summer83-16
"Arte Italiana 1960-82."
W. Zanuszczak, 592:Vol 195No997-82
Arthur, E. Beyond the Mountain.
A. Hoffman, 441:20Nov83-14
Arthur, P. With Brendan Behan.
F. McCluskey, 305(JIL):Sep82-110
Artibise, A.F.J. and G. Stelter. Canada's Urban Past.
H. Tuck, 150(DR):Winter82/83-721
Artinian, R.W. and A., comps. Maupassant Criticism.
E.D. Sullivan, 446(NCFS):Spring-Summer 83-396
Artisien, P.F.R. Friends or Foes?
D.A. Dyker, 575(SEER):Apr82-317
Asals, F. Flannery O'Connor.
B.L. Clark, 454:Spring83-265
W. McBrien, 617(TLS):21Jan83-56
W.J. Stuckey, 395(MFS):Autumn82-508
Asals, H.A.R. Equivocal Predication.*
D. Benet, 391:Mar82-23
A. Rudrum, 627(UTQ):Summer82-417
Ascher, C. Simone de Beauvoir.*
M.B. Pringle, 395(MFS):Winter82/83-714
S. Reynolds, 402(MLR):Oct82-967
Ascherson, N. The Polish August.*
A.J. Matejko, 497(PolR):Vol27No3/4-196
Asfour, J. Land of Flowers and Guns.
R. Geiger, 198:Oct82-120
Ash, B. Who's Who in H.G. Wells.
J-T. Vernier, 189(EA):Oct-Dec82-476
Ash, J. The Goodbyes.*
H. Lomas, 364:Dec82/Jan83-100
Ash, M. The Strange Death of Scottish History.
J. Anderson, 588(SSL):Vol 17-294
A. Hook, 571(ScLJ):Winter82-89
Ashbee, A., ed. Lists of Payments to the King's Musick in the Reign of Charles II (1660-1685).
P. Holman, 415:May82-334

Ashbery, J. As We Know.*
R. Pybus, 565:Vol123No3-61
Ashbery, J. Shadow Train.*
T. Dooley, 493:Jun82-64
D. Revell, 134(CP):Spring82-92
V. Shetley, 491:Jul82-236
Ashbery, J. and K. Moffett. Fairfield Porter.
K. Flint, 617(TLS):7Oct83-1072
Ashbrook, J. In the Footsteps of the Opium Eater.
L. Sail, 565:Vol123No4-73
Ashbrook, W. Donizetti and His Operas.*
P. Gossett, 453(NYRB):31Mar83-30
Ashby, C. and S.D. May. Trouping Through Texas.
D.B. Wilmeth, 612(ThS):Nov82-250
Ashby, W.J. Clitic Inflection in French.
K. Connors, 545(RPh):Nov81-434
Asher, F.M. The Art of Eastern India, 300-800.
J.L., 90:Mar82-200
J. Williams, 293(JASt):Aug82-861
Ashhurst, A.W. La literatura hispano-americana en la crítica española.*
F. Dauster, 240(HR):Summer82-374
Ashley, M. England in the Seventeenth Century. (new ed)
D.L. Russell, 568(SCN):Fall82-48
Ashley, M. The People of England.*
442(NY):12Sep83-156
Ashton, D. American Art Since 1945.*
D. Saatchi, 90:Sep82-567
M. Sawin, 127:Winter82-351
Ashton, D. and D.B. Hare. Rosa Bonheur.*
J.H., 90:May82-328
B. Scott, 39:Apr82-294
Ashton, R. The German Idea.*
F. Bolton, 189(EA):Jan-Mar82-89
R.J. Dingley, 447(N&Q):Jun81-272
J. Forster, 72:Band218Heft1-153
W. Stafford, 366:Autumn82-261
Ashworth, E.J. Language and Logic in the Post-Medieval Period.
G.F. Meier, 682(ZPSK):Band35Heft6-727
Asimov, I. Exploring the Earth and the Cosmos.
W.H. McCrea, 617(TLS):10Jun83-594
Asimov, I. The Roving Mind.
J.R. Durant, 617(TLS):23Sep83-1008
Asimov, I., C.G. Waugh and M. Greenberg, eds. Isaac Asimov Presents the Best Science Fiction of the 19th Century.
C. Greenland, 617(TLS):5Aug83-843
Asin Palacios, M. Saint John of the Cross and Islam.
S. Vahiduddin, 273(IC):Apr82-168
Aslet, C. The Last Country Houses.*
N. Annan, 453(NYRB):3Mar83-16
Asmundsson, D.R. Georg Brandes.
G.S. Argetsinger, 563(SS):Summer82-266
Assor Rosa, A., ed. Letteratura italiana (Vol 1)
P. Shaw, 617(TLS):7Oct83-1083
Aspaturian, V., J. Valenta and D. Burke, eds. Eurocommunism between East and West.
H. Hanak, 575(SEER):Jan82-148
Aspetsberger, F. Literarisches Leben im Austrofaschismus.*
F. Kadrnoska, 602:Vol 13No2-352
A. Obermayer, 564:Feb81-89

Aspin, C. The Woollen Industry.
R. Hoffman, 614:Winter83-22
Aspital, A.W., comp. Catalogue of the
Pepys Library at Magdalene College,
Cambridge. (Vol 3, Pt 1)
D. McKitterick, 78(BC):Spring82-109
Aspiz, H. Walt Whitman and the Body
Beautiful.*
R. Asselineau, 189(EA):Oct-Dec82-489
L. Cederstrom, 106:Winter82-349
D. Middlebrook, 301(JEGP):Jan82-152
Asquith, H.H. H.H. Asquith: Letters to
Venetia Stanley.* (M. and E. Brock,
eds)
N. Bliven, 442(NY):15Aug83-88
G. Hodgson, 441:3Apr83-3
Asquith, S. Children and Justice.
T. Campbell, 617(TLS):10Jun83-610
Asselineau, R. The Transcendentalist Con-
stant in American Literature.*
L. Buell, 587(SAF):Spring82-117
L. Cederstrom, 106:Winter82-349
S. Paul, 301(JEGP):Jan82-151
Assouline, P. Monsieur Dassault.
D. Johnson, 617(TLS):18Nov83-1282
Aston, T.H. and others, eds. Social Rela-
tions and Ideas.
J.A. Tuck, 617(TLS):12Aug83-865
"At the Edge of Asia."
R.L. Shep, 614:Spring83-15
Atanagi, D. Rime d'encomio e morte. (G.
De Santi, ed)
E. Favretti, 228(GSLI):Vol 159fasc507-
439
Atherton, S.S. Alan Sillitoe.*
K. MacKinnon, 268(IFR):Summer83-146
B. Stovel, 178:Sep82-388
Atiyah, P.S. Promises, Morals and Law.
A.D. Woozley, 518:Jul82-170
Atiyah, P.S. The Rise and Fall of Freedom
of Contract.
R. McGowen, 637(VS):Spring82-386
Atkins, B.T. and others - see "Collins/
Robert French-English, English-French
Dictionary"
Atkins, G.D. The Faith of John Dryden.*
J.M. Aden, 579(SAQ):Spring82-242
J.V. Guerinot, 568(SCN):Fall82-46
P. Harth, 173(ECS):Winter81/82-210
C.H. Hinnant, 191(ELN):Sep82-51
A. Poyet, 189(EA):Jul-Sep82-329
Atkins, J. J.B. Priestley.
A.E. Kalson, 395(MFS):Summer82-286
295(JML):Dec82-518
Atkins, L.R. The Valley and the Hills.
J. Fuller, 9(AlaR):Apr82-142
Atkinson, B. Sean O'Casey. (R.G. Lowery,
ed)
J.S. Bratton, 617(TLS):14Jan83-38
Atkinson, J.E. A Commentary on Q. Curtius
Rufus' "Historiae Alexandri Magni" books
3 and 4.
S. Hornblower, 303(JoHS):Vol 102-272
"Atlas Linguarum Europae."* (Introduction,
First questionnaire, and Second question-
naire) (A. Weijnen and others, eds)
J. Göschel, 685(ZDL):2/1981-228
Attar, S. The Intruder in Modern Drama.
L.P. Gabbard, 397(MD):Jun82-326
Attebery, B. The Fantasy Tradition in
American Literature.*
N. Khouri, 106:Winter82-407
D.M. Miller, 395(MFS):Summer82-321

Attenborough, R. In Search of Gandhi.
F. Watson, 362:20Jan83-27
Attfield, R. God and the Secular.*
J.E. Force, 319:Jul82-315
"Atti del convegno internazionale di studi
danteschi."*
A.S. Bernardo, 551(RenQ):Summer81-218
Attman, A. The Bullion Flow between
Europe and the East 1000-1750.
R.W. Unger, 104(CASS):Fall-Winter82-
533
Attman, A. and others, eds. Ekonomiche-
skie sviazi mezhdu Rossiei i Shvetsiei v
XVII v. Ekonomiska förbindelser mellan
Sverige och Russland under 1600-talet.
W. Kirchner, 550(RusR):Jan82-68
Attridge, D. The Rhythms of English
Poetry.
T. Disch, 617(TLS):28Oct83-1194
Attwood, W. Making It through Middle Age.
639(VQR):Autumn82-136
Atwood, M. Bodily Harm.*
M. Dixon, 198:Apr82-87
M. Dyment, 526:Spring82-73
D. Flower, 249(HudR):Summer82-274
L. Howe, 363(LitR):Fall82-177
J. Mellors, 364:Jun82-61
M.L. Moore, 181:Winter-Spring83-169
G. Woodcock, 461:Spring-Summer82-106
G. Woodcock, 529(QQ):Winter82-744
Atwood, M. Dancing Girls and Other
Stories.*
A. Duchêne, 617(TLS):7Jan83-23
J. Mellors, 362:6Jan83-24
M.L. Moore, 181:Winter-Spring83-169
Atwood, M. Second Words.
W.J. Keith, 99:Feb83-26
Atwood, M. True Stories.
F. Adcock, 617(TLS):18Mar83-278
D. Barbour, 648(WCR):Oct82-37
D. Davis, 362:5May83-24
A. Mandel, 198:Jan82-63
M.L. Rosenthal, 441:13Mar83-6
B. Whiteman, 298:Summer82-150
Atwood, M. Two-Headed Poems and Others.*
D. Gioia, 491:May82-102
R. Tillinghast, 569(SR):Spring82-291
Atwood, M. and J. Barkhouse. Anna's Pet.
M. Whitaker, 102(CanL):Spring82-95
Atwood, R. The Hessians.
W.B. Willcox, 656(WMQ):Apr82-377
Atwood, W.G. The Lioness and the Little
One.*
L.J. Austin, 208(FS):Jan82-80
B.T. Lupack, 497(PolR):Vol127No1/2-141
Aubenque, P., ed. Concepts et catégories
dans la pensée antique.
P. Pellegrin, 542:Apr-Jun82-450
Aubenque, P., ed. Etudes sur la "Méta-
physique" d'Aristote.*
B. Dumoulin, 192(EP):Jan-Mar81-77
Aubert, J. and M. Jolas, eds. Joyce and
Paris 1902 ... 1920-1940 ... 1975.
R.A. Day, 189(EA):Jan-Mar82-101
V. Mahon, 402(MLR):Jan82-188
Aubreton, R., with F. Buffière, eds and
trans. Anthologie grecque. (Pt 2, Vol
13)
C. Dobias-Lalou, 555:Vol156fasc2-320
Auburn, M.S. - see Dryden, J.
Auchincloss, L. Narcissa and Other Fables.
F. Taliaferro, 441:3Apr83-6

de Ayala, P.L. - see under López de Ayala, P.

de Ayala, R.P. - see under Pérez de Ayala, R.

Ayandele, E.A. Nigerian Historical Studies.
  C. Fyfe, 69:Vol51No3-797

Aycock, W.M., ed. The Teller and the Tale.
  T.A. Gullason, 573(SSF):Fall82-391

Aycock, W.M. and S.P. Cravens, eds. Calderón de la Barca at the Tercentenary.
  M.D. McGaha, 304(JHP):Winter83-159

Aycock, W.M. and T.M. Klein, eds. Classical Mythology in Twentieth-Century Thought and Literature.
  M. Mueller, 678(YCGL):No30-100

Ayer, A.J. Hume.
  C. Battersby, 402(MLR):Apr82-412

Ayer, A.J. Philosophy in the Twentieth Century.*
  M. Platts, 617(TLS):11Mar83-246

Ayers, J. Far Eastern Ceramics in the Victoria and Albert Museum.*
  U. Roberts, 60:Jul-Aug82-138

Ayers, R.W. - see Milton, J.

Aymard, M., ed. Dutch Capitalism and World Capitalism/Capitalisme hollandais et Capitalisme mondial.
  A. Carter, 617(TLS):8Apr83-362

Ayres, J. English Naive Painting, 1750-1900.
  R.L. Patten, 637(VS):Winter82-243

Ayres, P.J. - see Munday, A.

Ayres, R.L. Banking on the Poor.
  C. Marcy, 441:21Aug83-11

Ayrton, E. English Provincial Cooking.
  W. and C. Cowen, 639(VQR):Autumn82-138

Azar, I. Discurso retórico y mundo pastoral en la Égloga segunda de Garcilaso.
  P. Waley, 304(JHP):Fall82-67

Azarpay, G., with others. Sogdian Painting.*
  B. Gray, 39:Mar82-208
  W. Watson, 89(BJA):Autumn82-367

Azevedo, M.M. A Contrastive Phonology of Portuguese and English.
  T.R. Arrington, 350:Mar83-232
  A. Brakel, 660(Word):Aug81-153
  H.M. Fraser, 399(MLJ):Summer82-222
  W.W. Megenney, 263(RIB):Vol32No3/4-367

Aziz, M. - see James, H.

Azzario, E. La prosa autobiográfica de Mariano Picón Salas.
  J. Febles, 238:Dec82-667

Baader, H., ed. Voltaire.
  S. Jüttner, 547(RF):Band93Heft1/2-268
  U. van Runset, 535(RHL):Jan-Feb82-115

Baader, R., ed. Molière.*
  G. Conesa, 535(RHL):Sep-Dec82-893
  W. Henning, 547(RF):Band93Heft3/4-447

Baader, R. and D. Fricke, eds. Die französische Autorin vom Mittelalter bis zur Gegenwart.*
  P. Cantraine, 547(RF):Band93Heft3/4-436

Baader, U. Kinderspiele und Spiellider.
  J.R. Dow, 292(JAF):Apr-Jun82-243

Baark, E. and J. Sigurdson. Indo-China Comparative Research Technology and Science for Development.
  P. Suttmeier, 293(JASt):Feb82-301

Babb, J., with P.E. Taylor. Border Healing Woman.
  A.N. Goldblatt, 584(SWR):Winter82-102

Babington, K.G. The Kremlin Cat and the Bomb.
  J. Mellors, 362:10Mar83-27

Babington Smith, C. Iulia de Beausobre.
  K. Fitz Lyon, 617(TLS):12Aug83-864
  C. Lock, 362:30Jun83-26

Babiniotis, G. Theōrētikē glōssologia.
  A. Kakouriotis, 361:Mar/Apr82-360

Babson, M. Death Beside the Sea.*
  N. Callendar, 441:1May82-27

Babson, M. Death Warmed Up.*
  N. Callendar, 441:6Feb83-20

Babson, M. A Fool for Murder.
  T.J. Binyon, 617(TLS):19Aug83-890

Babula, W. Shakespeare in Production, 1935-1978.
  C.H. Shattuck, 570(SQ):Summer82-243

Babyonyshev, A., ed. On Sakharov.
  L.R. Graham, 441:23Jan83-7

Bacarisse, S., ed. Contemporary Latin American Fiction.*
  D. Kadir, 395(MFS):Summer81-423

Bach, H. Handbuch der Luthersprache. (Vol 1)
  H. Wolf, 685(ZDL):2/1981-260

Bach, K. and R.M. Harnish. Linguistic Communication and Speech Acts.*
  G.M. Green, 350:Sep83-627
  W. Ingber, 482(PhR):Jan82-134

Bacharach, S.B. and E.J. Lawler. Bargaining.
  S.P., 185:Oct82-204

Bachem, M. Heimito von Doderer.
  E.C. Hesson, 268(IFR):Winter83-73
  R. Ruppel, 221(GQ):May82-450

Bacher, J. Die deutsche Sprachinsel Lusern.
  H. Tyroller, 685(ZDL):2/1981-255

Bachrach, A.G.H. and R.G. Collmer - see Huygens, L.

Baciu, S., ed. Antología de la poesía surrealista latinoamericana.
  C. Mathieu-Higginbotham, 263(RIB):Vol32No1-55

Back, M. Die sassanidischen Staatsinschriften.*
  M.J. Dresden, 318(JAOS):Oct-Dec81-465

Backès, J-L. Racine.
  R.W. Tobin, 207(FR):Oct82-151

Backhouse, J. The Lindisfarne Gospels.
  C. Tyerman, 59:Jun82-255
  639(VQR):Spring82-63

Bäckman, S. Tradition Transformed.*
  D. Hibberd, 447(N&Q):Aug81-359

Bacon, E.E. Central Asians under Russian Rule.
  I. Kreindler, 550(RusR):Oct82-512

Bacon, N. The Papers of Nathaniel Bacon of Stiffkey. (Vol 1) (A.H. Smith, G.M. Baker and R.W. Kenny, eds)
  J.M.W. Bean, 551(RenQ):Winter82-637

Bacon, R. Roger Bacon's Philosophy of Nature. (D.C. Lindberg, ed)
  J. North, 617(TLS):21Oct83-1163

Bacou, R.. Piranesi, Etchings and Drawings.
  R. Middleton, 576:Dec82-333

Badawi, A. and others. Milenerio de Avicena.
  A. Reix, 542:Jul-Sep82-530

Badawi, M.M. Background to Shakespeare.
  L. Scragg, 148:Summer82-84
Badawy, A. Coptic Art and Archaeology.
  P. van Moorsel, 318(JAOS):Oct-Dec81-
  460
Badcock, C.R. Madness and Modernity.
  R. Littlewood, 617(TLS):18Nov83-1266
Badia, L.V. Akademik A.M. Pankratova-
  istorik rabochego klassa SSSR.
  C. Wynn, 550(RusR):Apr82-216
Badian, E. - see Syme, R.
Badiou, A. Théorie du sujet.
  G.L., 185:Jul83-830
Badt, K. Paolo Veronese.
  G. Schweikhart, 471:Apr/May/Jun82-165
Baehr, C. Nothing to Lose.
  J. Neville, 617(TLS):8Jul83-725
Baender, P. - see Twain, M.
Baer, J.T. Arthur Schopenhauer and die
  russische Literatur des späten 19. und
  frühen 20. Jahrhunderts.
  S. McLaughlin, 574(SEEJ):Winter82-474
Baesjou, R., ed. An Asante Embassy on the
  Gold Coast.
  K. Arhin, 69:Vol51No4-886
Bagdikian, B.H. The Media Monopoly.
  A. Hacker, 441:26Jun83-11
Bagley, D. Windfall.*
  N. Callendar, 441:16Jan83-26
Bagley, M. The Plutonium Factor.
  T.J. Binyon, 617(TLS):21Jan83-66
Baguley, D. Bibliographie de la critique
  sur Émile Zola, 1971-1980.
  L. Kamm, 446(NCFS):Fall-Winter82/83-
  194
Bahmueller, C.F. The National Charity
  Company.
  C.S., 185:Jan83-429
Bahr, E. Nelly Sachs.
  G. Stern, 221(GQ):Nov82-614
Baier, S. An Economic History of Central
  Niger.
  G. Nicolas, 69:Vol52No1-93
Baile, D. Gershom Scholem.
  R.H. Popkin, 319:Apr82-213
Bailey, A. Along the Edge of the Forest.
  W. Goodman, 441:10Jul83-12
Bailey, A. America, Lost and Found.
  S. Brown, 569(SR):Spring82-250
Bailey, A. Walt Disney's World of Fantasy.
  N. Roddick, 617(TLS):25Feb83-178
Bailey, A. Miramichi Lightning.
  J. Peirce, 99:Jun/Jul82-41
Bailey, D. Bailey NW1.
  J. Naughton, 362:6Jan83-22
Bailey, D.R.S. - see under Shackleton
  Bailey, D.R.
Bailey, F.G. The Tactical Uses of Passion.
  L. Hudson, 617(TLS):11Nov83-1235
Bailey, C.W.S. Privacy and the Mental.
  B.F. Scarlett, 63:Jun82-186
Bailey, H.W., comp. Dictionary of Khotan
  Saka.*
  M.J. Dresden, 318(JAOS):Oct-Dec81-466
Bailey, J. Norman Mailer.*
  P. Murphy, 541(RES):May82-234
Bailey, J. The Moon Baby.
  S. Gunew, 381:Jun82-277
Bailey, L. Lee Bailey's Country Weekends.
  M. Burros, 441:11Dec83-36
Bailey, M.J. Those Glorious Glamour Years.
  M. Whitehead, 200:May82-316

Bailey, P. An English Madam.*
  G. Ewart, 364:Nov82-71
Bailey, R.N. Viking Age Sculpture in
  Northern England.
  H. Chickering, 589:Jul82-586
Bailey, T. and others. The Lord's Taver-
  ners Fifty Greatest.
  A. Ross, 617(TLS):16Sep83-987
Bain, G.S., ed. Industrial Relations in
  Britain.
  C. Crouch, 617(TLS):25Nov83-1328
Bain, I. Thomas Bewick.
  78(BC):Spring82-7
Bain, I., ed. The Watercolours and Draw-
  ings of Thomas Bewick and his Workshop
  Apprentices.*
  A. Bell, 90:Dec82-774
  J. Glynne, 59:Sep82-353
  G. Reynolds, 39:May82-415
  78(BC):Spring82-7
Bainbridge, B. A Weekend with Claude.*
  (rev)
  P. Craig, 617(TLS):29Jul83-820
Baines, B. Fashion Revivals from the
  Elizabethan Age to the Present Day.
  B. Scott, 39:Sep82-198
Bair, D. Samuel Beckett.*
  D.L. Eder, 367(L&P):Vol30No2-83
Baird, J.D. and C. Ryskamp - see Cowper, W.
Bakan, D. And They Took Themselves Wives.
  A.N., 185:Oct82-195
Baker, A. Ship or Sheep? (2nd ed)
  L.E. Henrichsen, 399(MLJ):Autumn82-356
Baker, A.J. Anderson's Social Philosophy.
  J.L. Mackie, 63:Jun82-175
Baker, C. Baby Doll.
  M. Haskell, 441:30Oct83-9
Baker, C. - see Hemingway, E.
Baker, D. Laws of the Land.
  G. Holthaus, 649(WAL):Winter83-378
Baker, D. Space Shuttle.
  529(QQ):Autumn82-691
Baker, D. - see Latini, B.
Baker, G.P. and P.M.S. Hacker. Wittgen-
  stein.*
  J. Burnheim, 63:Sep82-282
  D.R. Lachterman, 480(P&R):Summer82-212
  R. Nowak, 489(PJGG):Band89Heft1-187
  C. Radford, 393(Mind):Jul82-441
Baker, H.A., Jr. The Journey Back.*
  R.K. Barksdale, 191(ELN):Dec81-167
Baker, J. Time and Mind in Wordsworth's
  Poetry.*
  G. Durrant, 178:Dec82-509
  J.A.W. Heffernan, 591(SIR):Summer82-
  253
Baker, K.L., R.J. Dalton and K. Hilde-
  brandt. Germany Transformed.
  H. Speier, 221(GQ):May82-477
Baker, L. Miranda.
  A.M. Dershowitz, 441:26Jun83-10
  442(NY).18Jul83-98
Baker, L. The Percys of Mississippi.
  R. Coles, 441:18Dec83-11
Baker, L.F. and others. Collage.
  B. Ebling, 207(FR):Oct82-194
  R.J. Melpignano, 399(MLJ):Summer82-209
Baker, M. The Folklore of the Sea.
  M.N. Schatz, 292(JAF):Jul-Sep82-362
Baker, M. Nam.
  P. Beidler, 577(SHR):Spring82-181
Baker, P.R. Richard Morris Hunt.*
  M.E. Shapiro, 54:Mar82-159

17

de Balzac, H. La Comédie humaine. (Vols 8 and 9) (P-G. Castex, ed)
M. Ménard, 535(RHL):Mar-Apr82-295
de Balzac, H. La Comédie humaine. (Vol 11) (P-G. Castex, ed)
R. Quinsat, 535(RHL):Mar-Apr82-299
de Balzac, H. La Comédie humaine. (Vol 12) (P-G. Castex, ed)
D. Bellos, 535(RHL):Sep-Dec82-926
de Balzac, H. Louis Lambert, Les Proscrits, Jésus-Christ en Flandre. (S.S. de Sacy, ed) Ursule Mirouët. (M. Ambrière-Fargeaud, ed)
J. Mileham, 207(FR):Feb83-486
de Balzac, H. Mémoires de deux jeunes mariées. (A. Michel, ed)
C. Smethurst, 208(FS):Jan82-79
Bambara, T.C. The Salt Eaters.*
N. Harris, 459:Spring81-101
W.M. Shipley, 95(CLAJ):Sep82-125
Bambeck, M. Studien zu Dantes "Paradiso."
J.P. Williams, 589:Oct82-962
Bamber, L. Comic Women, Tragic Men.
F. Kermode, 453(NYRB):28Apr83-30
Bamborschke, U. and others. Die Erzählung über Petr Ordynskij.
R.D. Bosley, 575(SEER):Oct82-623
Bambrough, R. Moral Scepticism and Moral Knowledge.*
F.R.B., 543:Mar82-589
Bamford, J. The Puzzle Palace.*
W. Laqueur, 617(TLS):11Feb83-137
T. Powers, 453(NYRB):3Feb83-12
Banac, I., J.G. Ackerman and R. Szporluk, eds. Nation and Ideology.
G. Augustinos, 104(CASS):Fall-Winter82-572
Bancquart, M-C. Maupassant conteur fantastique.
P.J. Whyte, 208(FS):Jan82-86
Bancquart, M-C. - see de Maupassant, G.
Bancroft, M. Autobiography of a Spy.
B. Shulgasser, 441:21Aug83-16
442(NY):29Aug83-93
Bańczerowski, J. Systems of Semantics and Syntax.
J. Pogonowski, 360(LP):Vol25-121
Bandy, M. Mind Forg'd Manacles.
W.H. Galperin, 577(SHR):Fall82-360
W. Keach, 661(WC):Summer82-142
J. Wittreich, 405(MP):May83-428
Banerji, S.C. Tantra in Bengal.
L. Sternbach, 318(JAOS):Oct-Dec81-488
Banham, P.R. Scenes in America Deserta.
D. Quammen, 441:20Feb83-9
C. Vita-Finzi, 617(TLS):18Feb83-150
Banham, R. Design by Choice.* (P. Sparke, ed)
A. Betsky, 505:Aug82-102
Bankowski, Z. and G. Mungham, eds. Essays in Law and Society.
C.S., 185:Oct82-204
Banks, H. The Rise and Fall of Freddie Laker.
M. Goldring, 617(TLS):7Jan83-10
Banks, P.N. A Selective Bibliography on the Conservation of Research Library Materials.
J. Segal, 325:Apr82-48
"The Bannatyne Manuscript: National Library of Scotland Advocates' MS 1. 1. 6."
N. Jacobs, 382(MAE):1982/2-243
M. Seymour, 354:Dec82-428

Banner, L.W. American Beauty.
P-L. Adams, 61:Mar83-117
C.N. Degler, 441:17Apr83-12
A. Lurie, 453(NYRB):2Jun83-20
Bannerman, D.A. and W.M. The Birds of the Balearics.
B. Urquhart, 617(TLS):22Jul83-786
Bannert, R. Mittelbairische Phonologie auf akustischer und perzeptiver Basis.
G.F. Meier, 682(ZPSK):Band34Heft6-750
Bannikov, N., comp. Three Centuries of Russian Poetry.
P.R. Hart, 399(MLJ):Winter82-435
Bannister, R.C. Social Darwinism.
W.A. Waiser, 106:Winter82-341
Bantel, L. The Alice M. Kaplan Collection.
E. Young, 39:Apr82-293
Banton, M. Racial and Ethnic Competition.
K. Kirkwood, 617(TLS):28Oct83-1190
Banu, G. Bertolt Brecht.
J. Guérin, 450(NRF):Jul-Aug82-206
Banville, J. Kepler.
R. McCormmach, 441:29May83-10
442(NY):9May83-134
Bar-Zohar, M. and E. Haber. The Quest for the Red Prince.
J.M. Markham, 441:10Jul83-3
Baradi, E.R. The Philippines.
C.R. Bryant, 293(JASt):May82-636
Baratin, M. and F. Desbordes, eds. Signification et référence dans l'antiquité et au moyen âge.
P. Swiggers, 350:Jun83-434
Barbaria, F.A. Modern "Asiatic" Despotism Masquerading in Communist Workers' Ideology.
W. Ratliff, 550(RusR):Jul82-348
Barbarino, J.L. The Evolution of the Latin /b/-/u/ Merger.
P.A. Gaeng, 276:Summer82-109
G. Price, 208(FS):Jan82-117
Barber, G. - see Contat, N.
Barber, R. The Reign of Chivalry.
T. Ehlert, 680(ZDP):Band101Heft1-124
Barbéris, P. "Le Colonel Chabert" de Balzac.
O.N. Heathcote, 208(FS):Oct82-482
Barbey, B. Portrait of Poland.
D. Gillard, 362:20Jan83-26
Barbier, J-P. and others. Exotische Kunst.
M. Adams, 2(AfrA):Feb82-17
Barbieri, F. and F. Fiorese - see Dragonzino, G.
Barbour, D. Worlds Out of Words.
G. Wolfe, 561(SFS):Mar82-98
Barbour, D. and S. Scobie. The Pirates of Pen's Chance.
B. Henderson, 99:Apr82-34
Barbour, R. Greek Literary Hands (A.D. 400-1600).
D. des Places, 555:Vol36Fasc1-114
"Barbour's Bruce." (Vol 2) (M.P. McDiarmid and J.A.C. Stevenson, eds)
K. Bitterling, 38:Band100Heft3/4-504
de la Barca, P.C. - see under Calderón de la Barca, P.
Barchilon, J. and P. Flinders. Charles Perrault.
M. Franko, 546(RR):Nov82-521
Barclay, B. Summer of the Hungry Pup.
B. Pirie, 102(CanL):Autumn82-139

Bardach, J., B. Leśnodorski and M. Pietrzak. Historia panstwa i prawa polskiego.
 P.J. Best, 497(PolR):Vol27No3/4-239
Bardelli, R. Centro Africa.
 R. Gray, 69:Vol151No3-798
Bardon, J. Belfast.
 S. Gribbon, 617(TLS):11Mar83-251
Bareau, M. - see García, C.
Bareham, T., ed. Anthony Trollope.*
 S. Monod, 189(EA):Apr-Jun82-222
 R. Tracy, 637(VS):Autumn81-99
Barentsen, A.A., B.M. Groen and R. Sprenger - see "Studies in Slavic and General Linguistics"
Barfield, O. Orpheus. (J.C. Ulreich, Jr., ed)
 R.J. Reilly, 469:Vol8No2-100
Barfoot, C.C. The Thread of Connection.
 L.R. Leavis, 179(ES):Apr82-189
Barfoot, J. Abra.*
 C. McLay, 296(JCF):No33-134
Bargen, W. Fields of Thenar.
 M. Lammon, 436(NewL):Winter82/83-107
Barguillet, F. Le Roman au XVIIIe siècle.
 E. Showalter, Jr., 207(FR):Apr83-770
Baricelli, J-P. - see Chekhov, A.
Barickman, R.,* S. MacDonald and M. Stark. Corrupt Relations.
 A. Sanders, 617(TLS):25Mar83-288
Barish, J. The Antitheatrical Prejudice.*
 J.I. Cope, 141:Winter82-73
 E. Fischer, 397(MD):Sep82-435
 T.M. Greene, 551(RenQ):Winter82-669
 T. Helton, 568(SCN):Winter82-72
 G. Weales, 651(WHR):Spring82-85
 B. Wilshire, 290(JAAC):Fall82-101
Barke, J. - see Burns, R.
Barker, A.W. Letters to an Australian Publisher.
 J. Neville, 617(TLS):7Oct83-1100
Barker, F. and R. Hyde. London As It Might Have Been.*
 J.S. Curl, 324:Feb83-156
Barker, G. Anno Domini.
 A. Thwaite, 617(TLS):29Jul83-813
Barker, H. No End of Blame.
 D. Devlin, 157:Summer82-52
Barker, J. Soviet Historians in Crisis, 1928-1932.
 R. Szporluk, 550(RusR):Oct82-492
Barker, P. Union Street.
 I. Gold, 441:2Oct83-9
 J.S., 231:Nov83-76
Barker, R. Innings of a Lifetime.
 T.D. Smith, 617(TLS):28Jan83-91
Barker, S. A Fire in the Rain.
 M. Hofmann, 617(TLS):8Apr83-356
Barker, T. The Transport Contractors of Rye: John Jempson & Son.
 S. Alderson, 324:Mar83-227
Barksdale, E.C. Daggers of the Mind.*
 N. Pervukhina-Kamyshnikova, 395(MFS):Summer81-416
Barley, N. The Innocent Anthropologist.
 A. Barnard, 617(TLS):5Aug83-824
Barlow, G. Gumbo.*
 639(VQR):Winter82-26
Barlow, J.D. German Expressionist Film.
 J. Hoberman, 18:Jan-Feb83-62
Barmash, I. Always Live Better Than Your Clients.
 G.A. De Candido, 441:18Dec83-14

Barnard, J. Walter Reuther and the Rise of the Auto Workers.
 442(NY):9May83-134
Barnard, R. The Case of the Missing Brontë.
 N. Callendar, 441:13Nov83-33
Barnard, R. Death and the Princess.*
 N. Callendar, 441:6Feb83-20
Barnard, R. A Little Local Murder.
 N. Callendar, 441:8May83-27
Barnard, R. The Missing Brontë.
 T.J. Binyon, 617(TLS):18Feb83-149
 M. Laski, 362:19May83-24
Barnes, D. Creatures in an Alphabet.
 A. Field, 441:9Jan83-9
Barnes, D. Selected Works of Djuna Barnes.
 D. Seed, 189(EA):Apr-Jun82-234
Barnes, D. Smoke and Other Early Stories. (D. Messerli, ed)
 V. Cunningham, 617(TLS):21Jan83-50
 A. Field, 441:9Jan83-9
 E. Hardwick, 617(TLS):7Oct83-1071
 442(NY):3Jan83-70
Barnes, J. Sartre and Flaubert.*
 C. Howells, 208(FS):Oct82-495
 L.M. Porter, 395(MFS):Summer82-332
 L.A. Slade, Jr., 95(CLAJ):Sep81-109
Barnes, J. The American Book of the Dead.*
 M.D. Lammon, 436(NewL):Fall82-116
Barnes, J. Aristotle.
 S. Waterlow, 617(TLS):11Mar83-247
Barnes, J. Before She Met Me.*
 J. Mellors, 364:Apr/May82-133
Barnes, J. The Presocratic Philosophers.*
 J. Bernhardt, 319:Jul82-301
Barnes, J. The Rise of the Cinema in Great Britain. (Vol 2)
 S. Mills, 617(TLS):18Nov83-1276
Barnes, J. This Crazy Land.
 M. Lammon, 436(NewL):Winter82/83-111
Barnes, J. - see "Joseph Furphy"
Barnes, J., M. Schofield and R. Sorabji. Articles on Aristotle, 4.
 D.A. Rees, 123:Vol32No1-99
Barnes, L. Bitter Finish.
 N. Callendar, 441:20Mar83-27
Barnes, P. and others. Best Radio Plays of 1981.
 R. Belben, 157:Winter82-44
Barnes, T.D. Constantine and Eusebius.
 H.A. Drake, 24:Winter82-462
Barnet, R.J. The Alliance.
 D. Yergin, 441:18Dec83-6
 442(NY):19Dec83-142
Barnett, A. Iron Britannia.
 G. Wheatcroft, 617(TLS):13May83-490
Barnett, L.D. Bret Harte.*
 R. Asselineau, 189(EA):Jan-Mar82-113
Barnett, L.K. Swift's Poetic Worlds.*
 A.B. England, 566:Spring83-124
 B.S. Hammond, 83:Autumn82-242
Barnett, R.B. North India Between Empires.
 M.N. Pearson, 293(JASt):May82-611
Barney, G.O., P.H. Freeman and C.A. Ulinski. Global 2000.
 J.D. Todd, 529(QQ):Winter82-866
Barney, S.A. Allegories of History, Allegories of Love.*
 R.T. Davies, 402(MLR):Jan82-139
 W. Rothwell, 208(FS):Jan82-112
Barney, S.A., ed. Chaucer's "Troilus."
 D. Staines, 589:Apr82-351

Barnhardt, D. Bird Bubble and Stream.
P. Monk, 529(QQ):Summer82-419
Barnhart, C.L. and others, eds. The
Second Barnhart Dictionary of New Eng-
lish.*
G. Cannon, 350:Jun83-442
G. Cannon, 660(Word):Dec82-265
J.K. Chambers, 320(CJL):Spring82-65
J.R. Gaskin, 569(SR):Winter82-143
H. Käsmann, 38:Band100Heft1/2-162
Barnickel, K-D. Farbe, Helligkeit und
Glanz im Mittelenglischen.
D. Nehls, 260(IF):Band86-367
Barnouw, E. The Sponsor.
D. Millar, 161(DUJ):Jun82-279
Barnstone, A. and W., eds. A Book of
Women Poets from Antiquity to Now.
A. Oktenberg, 436(NewL):Winter82/83-
112
Barnstone, W. - see Borges, J.L.
Barnum, P.H., ed. Dives and Pauper. (Vol
1, Pt 2)
K. Bitterling, 38:Band100Heft3/4-508
Barnum, P.T. Selected Letters of P.T.
Barnum. (A.H. Saxon, ed)
C.B. Mills, 617(TLS):29Apr83-423
B. Shulgasser, 441:5Jun83-16
Barnum, P.T. Struggles and Triumphs. (C.
Bode, ed)
M. Mudrick, 249(HudR):Winter82/83-581
Barnwell, H.T. The Tragic Drama of Cor-
neille and Racine.
J.H. Mason, 617(TLS):21Jan83-68
Barolsky, P. Infinite Jest.
B. Dodge, 627(UTQ):Fall81-125
Baron, C. - see Neville, G.H.
Baron, F., E.S. Dick and W.R. Maurer, eds.
Rilke.
J. Ryan, 564:May82-151
Baron, N.S. Speech, Writing, and Sign.*
W. Walker, 350:Mar83-219
Baron, S.H. Muscovite Russia.*
C.J. Halperin, 104(CASS):Spring82-155
Barr, J.G. Rowdy Tales from Early Ala-
bama.* (G.W. Hubbs, ed)
G.H. Gates, 9(AlaR):Jan82-47
Barraclough, G. From Agadir to Armageddon.
J. Keegan, 453(NYRB):18Aug83-50
Z. Steiner, 617(TLS):22Apr83-406
Barral, M. L'Imparfait du subjonctif.
R. Martin, 553(RLiR):Jul-Dec82-473
C. Wimmer, 209(FM):Jul82-268
Barratt, A. Yurii Olesha's "Envy."
R. Russell, 402(MLR):Oct82-1004
Barratt, K. Logic and Design.
D.F. Anstis, 324:Feb83-159
Barrell, J. The Dark Side of the Land-
scape.*
A.M. Duckworth, 191(ELN):Mar/Jun83-52
K. Garlick, 447(N&Q):Dec81-559
Barrell, J. English Literature in History
1730-80.
J.P. Kenyon, 617(TLS):29Apr83-437
Barrère, J-B. Claudel.
M. Wood, 546(RR):Mar82-268
Barrett, C. Boundweave.
P. Bach, 614:Spring83-16
Barrett, C. and E. Smith. Double Two-Tie
Unit Weaves.
P. Bach, 614:Summer83-18

Barrett, L.I. Gambling With History.
J. Fallows, 453(NYRB):27Oct83-68
N. Lemann, 441:26Jun83-7
442(NY):25Jul83-88
Barrett, W. The Truants.*
J.B. Gilbert, 385(MQR):Winter83-151
M. Maddocks, 569(SR):Fall82-569
S. Pinsker, 219(GaR):Fall82-655
J.P. Sisk, 31(ASch):Autumn82-579
Barricelli, J-P., ed. Chekhov's Great
Plays.
J.M. Curtis, 397(MD):Sep82-438
A.R. Durkin, 550(RusR):Jul82-353
Barrientos, A. and V.G. de la Concha. El
arte literario de santa Teresa.
M. Tietz, 72:Band218Heft1-212
Barrington, M. David's Daughter Tamar.
M.G. McCulloch, 617(TLS):21Jan83-69
Barrocchi, P. - see del Riccio, A.
Barroero, L. and others. Pittura del Sei-
cento e del Settecento.
F. Russell, 39:May82-411
Barron, N., ed. Anatomy of Wonder.
R.M.P., 561(SFS):Fall82-353
Barron, W.R.J. "Trawthe" and Treason.*
C.D. Benson, 589:Apr82-353
Barrow, C.W. Montage in James Joyce's
"Ulysses."
B. Benstock, 395(MFS):Summer81-310
L.V. Harrod, 174(Éire):Fall82-153
R.D. Newman, 577(SHR):Winter82-80
Barrow, G.L. The Round Towers of Ireland.
P. Harbison, 174(Éire):Fall82-148
Barrow, G.W.S. The Anglo-Norman Era in
Scottish History.
R. Nicholson, 589:Oct82-855
J. Wormald, 382(MAE):1982/1-121
Barrow, J.D. and J. Silk. The Left Hand
of Creation.
T. Ferris, 441:20Nov83-12
Barrow, K. Flora.*
B.A. Young, 157:Summer82-50
Barrows, S. Distorting Mirrors.
J.H. Matthews, 446(NCFS):Fall-Winter
82/83-176
Barry, D.D. and C. Barner-Barry. Contempo-
rary Soviet Politics.* (2nd ed)
M. McCauley, 575(SEER):Oct82-638
Barry, J. Infamous Woman.
C. Colter, 436(NewL):Fall82-108
Barry, M.V., ed. Aspects of English Dia-
lects in Ireland. (Vol 1)
L. Todd, 38:Band100Heft3/4-480
Barry, W.J. Perzeption und Produktion im
sub-phonemischen Bereich.
G.F. Meier, 682(ZPSK):Band35Heft3-368
Barson, J. La Grammaire à l'oeuvre.*
(3rd ed)
J. Ludwig, 399(MLJ):Summer82-208
Barszczewski, S. Związek Narodowy Polski
w Stanach Zjednoczonych Ameryki Połnoc-
nej.
D.E. Pienkos, 497(PolR):Vol27No1/2-180
Bartenieff, I., with D. Lewis. Body Move-
ment.
J.L. Hanna, 187:Jan83-124
Barth, F. Features of Person and Society
in Swat.
K.E.S., 185:Oct82-196
Barth, F. Process and Form in Social
Life. (Vol 1)
P.R.S., 185:Jan83-422

Batchelor, J.C. The Birth of the People's
Republic of Antarctica.
T.R. Edwards, 441:29May83-1
442(NY):9May83-134
Bately, J., ed. The Old English Orosius.
C. von Nolcken, 405(MP):Nov82-175
Bateman, F. and T. Weiss. A Deplorable
Scarcity.
F.N. Boney, 9(AlaR):Jan82-62
639(VQR):Spring82-43
Bateman, W.G. Bateman Blend Weaves. (V.I.
Harvey, ed)
P. Bach, 614:Winter83-13
Bater, J.H. The Soviet City.*
G. Hodge, 529(QQ):Winter82-870
R.N. North, 104(CASS):Summer82-277
Bates, D. Normandy before 1066.
R.H.C. Davis, 617(TLS):21Jan83-62
Bates, R.H. Markets and States in Tropi-
cal Africa.*
R.H., 185:Oct82-196
Bateson, W. Problems of Genetics.
R.M. Burian, 486:Mar82-147
Bathe, W. A Brief Introduction to the
True Art of Music. (C. Hill, ed)
A.E. Walters, 308:Fall82-349
Baticle, J. and C. Marinas, with others.
La Galerie Espagnole de Louis-Philippe
au Louvre, 1838-1848.
J. Brown, 90:Apr82-250
Batiffol, H. Problèmes de base de philos-
ophie du droit.
S. Goyard-Fabre, 192(EP):Oct-Dec82-476
J. Parain-Vial, 540(RIPh):Vol36fasc3-
376
Bator, R., ed. Signposts to Criticism of
Children's Literature.
G. Avery, 617(TLS):22Jul83-775
Bätschmann, O. Dialektik der Malerei von
Nicolas Poussin.
B. Growe, 471:Oct/Nov/Dec82-353
Batson, C.D. and W.L. Ventis. The Reli-
gious Experience.
J.W. Bowker, 617(TLS):13May83-494
Batten, C.L., Jr. Pleasurable Instruction.
J.A. Downie, 506(PSt):May82-171
J. Mezciems, 677(YES):Vol 12-276
Battersby, J.L. Rational Praise and Natu-
ral Lamentation.*
H. Weinbrot, 173(ECS):Winter81/82-238
Battilana, C. Reflexiones sobre "Hijo de
hombre" de Augusto Roa Bastos.
M.I. Lichtblau, 552(REH):Jan82-157
Battiscombe, G. Christina Rossetti.
639(VQR):Spring82-52
Battisti, E. Filippo Brunelleschi.*
A. Blunt, 46:Oct82-108
C. Elam, 59:Dec82-489
T.G. Smith, 505:Nov82-152
Battle, L. War Brides.
639(VQR):Summer82-97
Baude, M. P.H. Azaïs, témoin de son temps
d'apres son journal inédit (1811-1844).
F. Bassan, 207(FR):Apr83-773
J-R. Derré, 535(RHL):Sep-Dec82-921
Baude, M. and M-M. Münch, eds. Romantisme
et religion.*
V. Kapp, 547(RF):Band93Heft3/4-463
Baudelaire, C. Les Fleurs du Mal.* (R.
Howard, trans)
W. Fowlie, 569(SR):Fall82-lxxxii
P.N. Furbank, 362:3Feb83-24
[continued]

[continuing]
A. de Jonge, 617(TLS):21Jan83-68
R. Sieburth, 676(YR):Winter83-263
Baudisch, A. and others. Decidability and
Generalized Quantifiers.
J. Cowles, 316:Dec82-907
Bauen, M. Sprachgemischter Mundartaus-
druck in Rimella (Valsesia, Piemont).
H-E. Keller, 545(RPh):Aug81-269
Bauer, C. Graded French Reader: Deuxième
Etape. (2nd ed)
B.E. Gesner, 207(FR):Mar83-647
Bauer, H. and B. Rupprecht. Corpus der
Barocken Deckenmalerei in Deutschland.
P. Cannon-Brookes, 90:Jun82-368
Bauer, L. and others. American English
Pronunciation. American English Pronun-
ciation Supplement: Comparison with
Danish.
N. Davidsen-Nielsen, 179(ES):Jun82-260
Bauer, W., ed. Studia Sino-Mongolica.
R.I. Meserve, 293(JASt):Nov81-93
Bauer, Y. American Jewry and the Holo-
caust.
E. Matz, 390:Jan82-56
Bauer, Y. The Jewish Emergence from Power-
lessness.
N. Frankel, 390:Jan82-53
Bauer-Lechner, N. Recollections of Gustav
Mahler.* (P.R. Franklin, ed)
J.B., 412:Feb81-60
M. Kennedy, 410(M&L):Apr81-208
Bauerle, R., ed. The James Joyce Songbook.
M. Hodgart, 617(TLS):14Jan83-38
Baum, E. Katalog des Österreichischen
Barockmuseums im Unteren Belvedere
in Wien.
A. Laing, 90:Mar82-170
C. Maué, 471:Jan/Feb/Mar82-74
Baum, G. Catholics and Canadian Socialism.
J. Dutka, 529(QQ):Spring82-187
Baum, J.M. The Theoretical Compositions
of the Major English Romantic Poets.
J.W. Ehrstine, 130:Spring82-82
Baumann, B. Dino Buzzati.
U. Schulz-Buschhaus, 547(RF):Band93
Heft1/2-290
Baumann, C.C. Wilhelm Müller.
B. Turchin, 222(GR):Winter82-46
Baumann, W. Die Zukunftsperspektiven des
Fürsten V.F. Odoevskij.
A. McMillin, 575(SEER):Jan82-102
Baumert, M. Englische Frage-Antwort-
Strukturen.
A.R.T., 189(EA):Jan-Mar82-115
Baumgartner, A.J. Untersuchungen zur
Anthologie des Codex Salmasianus.
E.J. Kenney, 123:Vol32No2-278
Baumgartner, E., ed and trans. Merlin le
Prophète ou le livre du Graal.
P. Noble, 208(FS):Oct82-457
Baumgartner, E. Le "Tristan en prose."
M-C. Struyf, 356(LR):Feb82-78
Baumgartner, W. Triumph des Irrealismus.*
H.S. Naess, 406:Spring82-86
S.H. Rossel, 301(JEGP):Jan82-98
J. Sjåvik, 563(SS):Spring82-178
H. Uecker, 52:Band16Heft3-291
Baur, J.I.H. The Inlander.
A. Berman, 55:Nov82-43
Baur, U. Dorfgeschichte.
N.A. Kaiser, 406:Spring82-106

23

Baur, U. and E. Castex, eds. Robert Musil Untersuchungen.
   L.L. Titche, 221(GQ):Mar82-268
Bauschinger, S. Else Lasker-Schüler.*
   G.J. Carr, 402(MLR):Oct82-999
   W.E. Riedel, 564:Nov81-326
Bautier, R-H. and M. Gilles, with A-M. Bautier, eds and trans. Chronique de Saint-Pierre-le-Vif de Sens, dite de Clarius (Chronicon Sancti Petri Vivi Senonensis).
   G.M. Spiegel, 589:Jan82-114
Bawden, N. The Ice House.
   A. Duchêne, 617(TLS):22Jul83-791
   J. Mellors, 362:18Aug83-23
Bax, A. Dermot O'Byrne. (L. Foreman, ed)
   P. Dickinson, 410(M&L):Apr81-203
Bax, D. Heironymous Bosch.
   C. Brown, 39:Mar82-210
Baxandall, M. The Limewood Sculptors of Renaissance Germany.*
   R. Marks, 90:Jul82-451
"Glen Baxter: His Life." (Vol 1)
   P.N. Furbank, 362:15Sep83-23
Baxter, J. Shakespeare's Poetic Styles.
   T. Hawkes, 551(RenQ):Spring82-124
   G.K. Hunter, 569(SR):Spring82-273
   G.T. Wright, 570(SQ):Spring82-111
Baxter, J.K. Collected Poems.* (J.E. Weir, ed)
   T. Eagleton, 565:Vol23No2-62
Baxter, S.B., ed. England's Rise To Greatness, 1660-1763.
   G. Holmes, 617(TLS):4Nov83-1228
Bayer, H. Gralsburg und Minnegrotte.*
   H. Brall and U. Küsters, 684(ZDA): Band111Heft3-120
Bayles, M.D. Morality and Population Policy.*
   P.A. McAuliffe, 518:Jul82-177
Bayles, M.D. Professional Ethics.
   R.E.G., 185:Oct82-213
Bayley, E.R. Joe McCarthy and the Press.
   P. Bixler, 42(AR):Summer82-365
Bayley, J. Shakespeare and Tragedy.*
   G.K. Hunter, 569(SR):Spring82-273
   R. Jacobs, 175:Spring82-55
   H. Levin, 551(RenQ):Autumn82-514
Bayley, P. French Pulpit Oratory, 1598-1650.*
   C.M. Probes, 475:No16Pt2-416
Bayley, S. The Albert Memorial.
   A.J.G.H., 617(TLS):24Jun83-683
Baylis, J. and G. Segal, eds. Soviet Strategy.
   S.S. Kaplan, 550(RusR):Jul82-343
Baylon, C. and P. Fabre. La Sémantique.
   R. Martin, 553(RLiR):Jan-Jun81-234
Bayly, C.A. Rulers, Townsmen and Bazaars.
   H. Tinker, 617(TLS):1Jul83-708
Baym, N. Woman's Fiction.*
   L. Buell, 183(ESQ):Vol28No1-63
Bayne, S.P. Tears and Weeping.
   J. Moravcevich, 475:Vol9No17-731
Baynes-Cope, A.D. Caring for Books and Documents.
   D.G. Vaisey, 325:Oct82-125
"Barbara Baynton." (S. Krimmer and A. Lawson, eds)
   K. Stewart, 71(ALS):Oct82-541
Bayo, G. Au sommet de la nuit.
   D. Pobel, 450(NRF):Feb82-120

Bayor, R.H. Neighbors in Conflict.
   W. Maslow, 390:Apr82-63
Beach, D., ed. Aspects of Schenkerian Theory.
   C. Wintle, 617(TLS):1Jul83-697
Beach, M.C. The Grand Mogul, Imperial Painting in India 1600-1660.
   M.W. Meister, 318(JAOS):Oct-Dec81-476
Beadle, R., ed. The York Plays.
   P. Neuss, 617(TLS):11Nov83-1257
Beal, P., comp. Index of English Literary Manuscripts. (Vol 1)
   H. Kelliher, 354:Dec82-435
   P. Lefranc, 189(EA):Jan-Mar82-76
Bealer, G. Quality and Concept.
   G. Hunter, 617(TLS):14Jan83-40
Bean, C.E.W. Gallipoli Correspondent. (K. Fewster, ed)
   E. de Mauny, 617(TLS):7Oct83-1098
Bean, P. Punishment.*
   S.L. Mendus, 518:Oct82-252
Bean, S.S. Symbolic and Pragmatic Semantics.
   R.W. Casson, 355(LSoc):Dec82-442
Beard, G. Craftsmen and Interior Decoration in England, 1660-1820.*
   P. Thornton, 90:Mar82-167
Beard, G. Stucco and Decorative Plasterwork in Europe.
   A. Laing, 617(TLS):12Aug83-863
Beard, J. Beard on Pasta.
   M. Burros, 441:11Dec83-12
Beard, J. The New James Beard.
   W. and C. Cowen, 639(VQR):Spring82-66
Beard, R. The Indo-European Lexicon.
   M. Aronoff, 350:Jun83-439
Beare, G. Index to the "Strand Magazine," 1891-1950.
   J. Sutherland, 617(TLS):9Dec83-1379
Beasley, W.G. The Modern History of Japan. (3rd ed)
   T.J. Pempel, 293(JASt):Aug82-837
"Cecil Beaton War Photographs 1939-1945."
   V. Powell, 39:Mar82-209
Beaton, R. Folk Poetry of Modern Greece.*
   G. Morgan, 203:Vol193No2-231
Beatson, P. "The Eye in the Mandala."
   J.F. Burrows, 677(YES):Vol 12-360
Beattie, A. The Burning House.*
   P. Iyer, 364:Mar83-87
   J. Mellors, 362:9Jun83-26
Beattie, S. Annie's Story.
   J. Motion, 617(TLS):12Aug83-866
Beattie, S. The New Sculpture.
   G. Grigson, 362:8Dec83-33
Beauchamp, T.L. Philosophical Ethics.
   E.R., 185:Jan83-414
Beauchamp, T.L. and others, eds. Ethical Issues in Social Science Research.
   I.S., 185:Jul83-841
Beauchamp, T.L. and J.E. Childress. Principles of Biomedical Ethics.
   W.E.M., 543:Mar82-590
Beauchamp, T.L. and A. Rosenberg. Hume and the Problem of Causation.*
   A.G.N. Flew, 518:Jul82-135
   R.J. Fogelin, 319:Jul83-429
   J.L. Mackie, 518:Jul82-129
   R.H.P., 543:Jun82-853
Beauchemin, Y. Le Matou.*
   M. Genuist, 102(CanL):Spring82-111

Beaudin-Beaupré, A. L'Aventure de Blanche
Morti.
M. Cagnon, 207(FR):Dec82-332
Beaugrand, H. Jeanne la fileuse.
J. Warwick, 102(CanL):Summer82-137
de Beaugrande, R. Factors in a Theory of
Poetic Translating.*
Z. Szabó, 353:Vol 19No3/4-373
de Beaugrande, R. Text, Discourse, and
Process.*
J.R. Hobbs, 355(LSoc):Aug82-291
de Beaugrande, R-A. and W.U. Dressler.
Einführung in die Textlinguistik.
T.F. Shannon, 350:Jun83-462
Beaujeu, J. - see Cicero
Beaujour, M. Miroirs d'encre.*
E.S. Burt, 153:Winter82-17
A.J. McKenna, 207(FR):Dec82-311
C. Miething, 547(RF):Band94Heft2/3-292
S.F.R., 131(CL):Summer82-272
Beaulieu, A. - see Mersenne, P.M.
Beaulieu, V-L. Una.*
E-M. Kroller, 102(CanL):Winter81-127
Beauman, N. A Very Great Profession.
L. Taylor, 617(TLS):29Jul83-799
de Beaumarchais, P.A.C. Correspondance.
(Vol 4) (B.N. Morton and D.C. Spinelli,
eds)
J-P. de Beaumarchais, 535(RHL):Jan-
Feb82-125
Beaumont, B. Thanks to Rugby.
J. Barnes, 617(TLS):28Jan83-91
Beaumont, F. and J. Fletcher. The Drama-
tic Works in the Beaumont and Fletcher
Canon.* (Vol 4) (F. Bowers, ed)
G.K. Hunter, 402(MLR):Jul82-700
Beaurline, L.A. Jonson and Elizabethan
Comedy.*
M. Charney, 551(RenQ):Spring81-151
E. Platz-Waury, 38:Band100Heft3/4-522
de Beauvais, P. and others. Bestiaires du
Moyen Age. (G. Bianciotto, trans)
D.A. Fein, 207(FR):Oct82-144
de Beauvoir, S. La Cérémonie des Adieux.
P. Bourgeade, 450(NRF):Feb82-127
M. Naudin, 207(FR):Dec82-334
de Beauvoir, S. When Things of the Spirit
Come First.*
442(NY):10Jan83-98
Bebek, B. The Third City.
J. Loudon, 469:Vol18No3-99
Bec, P. La Lyrique française au moyen âge
(xiie-xiiie siècles).
L.T.T., 382(MAE):1982/1-124
Béchade, H.D. Les Romans comiques de
Charles Sorel.
J. Alter, 207(FR):May83-941
Bechert, H., ed. Buddhism in Ceylon and
Studies on Religious Syncretism in Bud-
dhist Countries.
T.W. de Jong, 259(IIJ):OcL00-311
Bechert, H., ed. Die Sprache der ältesten
buddhistischen Überlieferung/The Lan-
guage of the Earliest Buddhist Tradition.
J.W. de Jong, 259(IIJ):Jul82-215
Bechert, H. and V. Moeller - see von Glase-
napp, H.
Bechmann, R. Les Racines des Cathédrales.
R. Elvin, 46:Apr82-81
Bechtel, F. Kleine onomastische Studien.
C. Brixhe, 555:Vol56fasc1-113
P.M. Fraser, 123:Vol32No1-104

Beck, H. Folklore and the Sea.
R. Rufty, 582(SFQ):Vol43No3/4-338
Beck, J., ed. Le Concile de Basle (1434).*
C.C. Willard, 551(RenQ):Autumn81-434
Beck, J. Early Renaissance Painting.
C. Eisler, 55:Feb82-27
Beck, J. Italian Renaissance Painting.
M. Larsen, 324:Sep83-630
F. Russell, 39:May82-411
Beck, J.C. To Windward of the Land.*
V. Newall, 203:Vol193No2-240
V. Newall, 650(WF):Apr82-161
Beck, K. - see "Das Stefan Zweig Buch"
Beck, L.W. Essays on Kant and Hume.
H. Hoppe, 53(AGP):Band64Heft3-331
Becker, A.L. and A.A. Yengoyan, eds. The
Imagination of Reality.
S. Errington, 293(JASt):Nov81-190
Becker, G.J. D.H. Lawrence.*
L. Hamalian, 363(LitR):Spring83-451
M. Magalaner, 395(MFS):Summer81-307
H.T. Moore, 402(MLR):Apr82-433
Becker, H.S. Art Worlds.
V. Kavolis, 290(JAAC):Winter82-226
Becker, J. Aller Welt Freund.
M. Butler, 617(TLS):7Oct83-1094
Becker, J. Traditional Music in Modern
Java.
H. Susilo, 293(JASt):Feb82-410
A. Toth, 187:Jan83-137
Becker, K-P. and others, eds. Stottern.
H-J. Bastian, 682(ZPSK):Band34Heft3-
382
Becker, M.B. Medieval Italy.*
M. Danesi, 399(MLJ):Autumn82-343
Becker, R.A. Revolution, Reform, and the
Politics of American Taxation, 1763-
1783.*
H.J. Henderson, 656(WMQ):Apr82-381
Becker, R.P. A War of Fools.
F.L. Borchardt, 221(GQ):Nov82-593
Becker, W. and W.K. Essler, eds. Konzepte
der Dialektik.
R.P. Horstmann, 687:Jul-Dec81-648
Becker-Grüll, S. Vokabeln der Not.
J. Ryan, 221(GQ):Mar82-270
Beckerman, W. and S. Clark. Poverty and
Social Security in Britain since 1961.
D. Donnison, 617(TLS):25Feb83-195
Beckett, D. Brunel's Britain.
J. Ranlett, 637(VS):Winter82-254
Beckett, J.C. The Anglo-Irish Tradition.
William Butler Yeats.
P-Y. Petillon, 98:Jun-Jul82-537
Beckett, L., ed. Richard Wagner:
"Parsifal."*
D.R. Murray, 410(M&L):Jul/Oct82-296
Beckett, O. J.F. Herring & Sons.*
T. Crombie, 39:Jun82-511
Beckett, S. Company.* (French title:
Compagnie.)
P. Fenves, 114(ChiR):Summer81-104
P.D. Henry, 219(GaR):Summer82-429
R. Kostelanetz, 473(PR):1/1982-156
J. Pilling, 299:Spring82-127
Beckett, S. Worstward Ho.
H. Kenner, 441:18Dec83-9
Beckman, B.J. Underlying Word Order.*
G. Mallinson, 361:Mar/Apr82-364
Beckman, G. Hittite Birth Rituals.
C. Carter, 318(JAOS):Oct-Dec81-456

Becksmann, R. Die mittelalterlichen Glas-
malereien in Baden und in der Pfalz,
ohne Freiburg-i-B.
  M.H. Caviness, 589:Oct82-857
Beckson, K. - see Wratislaw, T.
Beckwith, C. and M. van Offelen. Nomads
of Niger.
  P-L. Adams, 61:Dec83-117
  P. Zweig, 441:4Dec83-15
Beckwith, C.A. and D. Knox. Delta Force.
  M. Kempton, 453(NYRB):22Dec83-26
Bedarida, R. L'Irlande.
  R. Fréchet, 189(EA):Oct-Dec82-480
Bedau, H.A. The Death Penalty in America.
(3rd ed)
  J.D., 185:Apr83-642
Bédé, J-A. and W. Edgerton, eds. Columbia
Dictionary of Modern European Litera-
ture.* (2nd ed)
  P. Garavaso and others, 400(MLN):Dec82-
  1186
Bedell, M. The Alcotts.*
  V. Bassil, 191(ELN):Sep82-77
  D. Maginnes, 9(AlaR):Jan82-60
Bedell, S. Up the Tube.
  S. Weaver, 18:Dec81-80
Bédouelle, G. Le "Quincuplex Psalterium"
de Lefèvre d'Étaples.* [shown in prev
under Lefèvre d'Étaples, J.]
  K.M. Hall, 208(FS):Apr82-194
Beecher, D. - see de Turnèbe, O.
Beeching, J. The Galleys at Lepanto.*
  442(NY):22Aug83-93
Beehler, R. Moral Life.*
  J.T.K., 543:Jun82-855
Beer, B.L. Rebellion and Riot.
  J.A. Guy, 617(TLS):25Feb83-199
Beer, P. The Lie of the Land.
  D. Davis, 362:28Jul83-23
  T. Dooley, 617(TLS):27May83-549
Beesly, P. Room 40.
  W. Laqueur, 617(TLS):11Feb83-137
van Beethoven, L. Violin Sonata in G
major, op. 30, no. 3. String Quartet
Opus 59 No. 1. String Quartet Opus 59
No. 2. [facsimiles]
  R. Kramer, 451:Summer82-76
Beetz, K.H. Algernon Charles Swinburne: A
Bibliography of Secondary Works, 1861-
1980.
  T.L. Meyers, 365:Spring83-84
Beevor, A. The Faustian Pact.
  K. Jeffery, 617(TLS):22Apr83-400
Beevor, A. The Spanish Civil War.
  D. Mitchell, 617(TLS):4Feb83-117
Beg, M.A.J. - see under Jabbar Beg, M.A.
Begiebing, R.J. Acts of Regeneration.
  H. Parker, 587(SAF):Spring82-121
  S. Pinsker, 395(MFS):Winter81/82-740
Behal, M. and others. Heinrich Heine.
  R.C. Figge, 301(JEGP):Apr82-294
Behan, B. After the Wake. (P. Fallon,
ed)
  P. Craig, 617(TLS):22Apr83-412
Behlmer, R. America's Favorite Movies.
  J. Beaver, 200:Oct82-507
  P. Craig, 18:Nov82-81
Behr, C.A. - see under Aristides
Behr, H-J. Herzog Ernst.
  J.L. Flood, 680(ZDP):Band101Heft1-131

Behr, H-J. Politische Realität und litera-
rische Selbstdarstellung.
  H. Herkommer, 52:Band16Heft1-81
  E. Könsgen, 680(ZDP):Band101Heft3-452
Behr, S.R. L'art de bien danser oder.
  W. Dimter, 684(ZDA):Band111Heft2-
  77
Behrens, S.A. Directory of Foreign Lan-
guages Service Organizations.
  L.A. Strasheim, 399(MLJ):Winter82-411
Behschnitt, W.D. Nationalismus bei Serben
und Kroaten 1830-1914.
  S.Z. Pech, 104(CASS):Summer82-306
Beichman, A. and M.S. Bernstam. Andropov.
  J.M. Burns, 441:6Nov83-13
Beidler, P.D. American Literature and the
Experience of Vietnam.
  W. Alexander, 385(MQR):Fall83-664
Beier, R. Englische Fachsprache.
  G.B., 189(EA):Apr-Jun82-238
Beier, U. Yoruba Beaded Crowns.
  J.B. Donne, 617(TLS):27May83-552
Beiersdorff, H-G. Das Angebot zur franzö-
sischen Literatur in den Lehrveranstalt-
ungsankündigungen der bundesrepublikan-
ischen Universitäten 1948-1973.
  C. Wentzlaff-Eggebert, 547(RF):Band94
  Heft2/3-313
Beierwaltes, W. Marsilio Ficinos Theorie
des Schönen im Kontext des Platonismus.
  A. Sheppard, 123:Vol32No1-119
Beile, W. and A. Sprechintentionen
Modelle 4.
  D.C. Hausman, 399(MLJ):Winter82-425
Beiner, R. - see Arendt, H.
Beinhauer, W. Stilistisch-phraseolog-
isches Wörterbuch spanisch-deutsch.
  H. Müller, 72:Band218Heft1-201
Beit-Arié, M. and C. Sirat. Manuscrits
médiévaux en caractères hébraïques por-
tant des indications de date jusqu'a
1540. (Pt 2)
  S.D. Goitein, 589:Jan82-116
Beitl, K. Volksglaube.
  E. Ettlinger, 203:Vol93No2-233
Beitl, R. and K. Wörterbuch der deutschen
Volkskunde. (3rd ed)
  E. Ettlinger, 203:Vol93No2-233
Bekaert, G., ed. A la recherche de
Viollet-le-Duc.
  A.L. van Zanten, 576:May82-160
Bekerman, G. Marx and Engels.
  J. Gray, 617(TLS):30Dec83-1459
Belamich, A. - see Lorca, F.G.
Belasco, W.J. Americans on the Road.
  F.T. Kihlstedt, 658:Summer/Autumn82-
  169
Belay, M. La mort dans le théâtre de
Gabriel Marcel.
  A. Reix, 542:Jan-Mar82-60
Belford, K. Sign Language.
  P. Mitcham, 102(CanL):Spring82-92
Belgrader, M. Das Märchen von dem Machan-
delboom (KHM 47).
  W.F.H. Nicolaisen, 292(JAF):Apr-Jun82-
  240
  H-J. Uther, 196:Band23Heft3/4-306
Bélil, M. see Greenwich.
  L. Rochette, 102(CanL):Autumn82-158
Belkin, K.L. Corpus Rubenianum Ludwig
Burchard.* (Pt 24)
  J.S. Held, 90:Apr82-245
  S.M. Newton, 39:May82-418

Bence-Jones, M. Burke's Guide to Country Houses. (Vol 1)
D. Watkin, 39:Aug82-128
Bence-Jones, M. The Viceroys of India.
K. Ballhatchet, 617(TLS):18Mar83-274
Lord Holderness, 324:Apr83-291
Benchley, P. The Girl of the Sea of Cortez.*
R.M. Mandojana, 37:Nov-Dec82-60
Bender, T.K. and J.W. Parins. A Concordance to Conrad's "The Nigger of the Narcissus."
E.D. Bevan, 136:Vol 14No1-73
Benderly, B.L. Dancing Without Music.*
W.L. Coleman, 35(AS):Fall82-213
Bendersky, J.W. Carl Schmitt.
G.A. Craig, 617(TLS):12Aug83-851
Benditt, T.M. Rights.
H.A.B., 185:Apr83-627
Benecke, G. Maximilian I (1459-1519).
H. Cohn, 617(TLS):2Sep83-942
Benedetti, J. Stanislavski.
M. Kahan, 617(TLS):2Sep83-926
di Benedetto, V. L'ideologia del potere e la tragedia greca.*
A.M. van Erp Taalman Kip, 394:Vol135 fasc3/4-369
Benedict, K.M., ed. A Select Bibliography on Business Archives and Records Management.
E. Hedlin, 14:Spring82-197
Benedict, M. and B. Men, Women and Money in Seychelles.
D. Wilson, 617(TLS):23Sep83-1027
Benedict, S., ed. The Literary Guide to the United States.
M.G. Porter, 649(WAL):Nov82-288
Benedikt, M. The Badminton at Breat Barrington; or, Gustave Mahler and the Chattanooga Choo-Choo.
R. Tillinghast, 569(SR):Spring82-291 639(VQR):Winter82-27
Benediktsson, J., ed. "Catilina" and "Jugurtha" by Sallust and "Pharsalia" by Lucan in Old Norse.
E.J. Crook, 589:Jan82-184
Benediktsson, T.E. George Sterling.*
R. Asselineau, 189(EA):Jul-Sep82-362
Benet, J. A Meditation.*
L.H. Chambers, 152(UDQ):Fall82-86
Bengtson, H. Die Flavier.*
A.N. Sherwin-White, 123:Vol32No1-67
Benigni, J. Wortschatz und Lautgebung der Innsbrucker Stadtmundart im Wandel dreier Generationen.
B.F. Steinbruckner, 685(ZDL):2/1981-253
Benito, F. and J. Berchez. Presencia del Renaixement a Valencia.
A.E. Pérez Sánchez, 48:Oct-Dec82-393
Benjamin, R. and K. Ori. Tradition and Change in Postindustrial Japan.
T.J. Pempel, 293(JASt):Aug82-837
Benjamin, W. Das Passagen-Werk. (R. Tiedemann, ed)
M. Rosen, 617(TLS):4Feb83-109
Benkovitz, M.J. Aubrey Beardsley.*
L. Dowling, 637(VS):Winter82-239
Benmayor, R., ed. Romances judeo-españoles de Oriente.
M. da Costa Fontes, 240(HR):Winter82-91

Benn, S., with others. Political Participation.
R.F. Khan, 63:Mar82-99
Bennet, G. Beyond Endurance.
J.F. Watkins, 617(TLS):12Aug83-860
Bennett, A. Arnold Bennett: Sketches for Autobiography.* (J. Hepburn, ed)
D.E. Nord, 506(PSt):Sep82-265
E.E. Stevens, 177(ELT):Vol25No3-187
Bennett, B. Horatio Alger, Jr.
P.B. Eppard, 517(PBSA):Vol76No3-364
Bennett, B., ed. Cross Currents.
M. Duwell, 71(ALS):Oct82-541
Bennett, B. Modern Drama and German Classicism.*
G. Gillespie, 149(CLS):Winter82-475
V.W. Hill, 406:Summer82-202
L. Löb, 402(MLR):Jan82-232
Bennett, B.T. - see Shelley, M.W.
Bennett, C.E. Florida's "French" Revolution, 1793-1795.
R.R. Rea, 9(AlaR):Oct82-280
Bennett, J.A.W. Chaucer at Oxford and at Cambridge.
K. Reichl, 38:Band100Heft3/4-498
Bennett, J.A.W. Essays on Gibbon.
C.J. Rawson, 677(YES):Vol 12-285
Bennett, J.A.W. The Humane Medievalist. (P. Boitani, ed) Poetry of the Passion.
S. Medcalf, 617(TLS):1Apr83-317
Bennett, M.J. Community, Class and Careerism.
G. Holmes, 617(TLS):1Jul83-704
Bennett, P. Talking with Texas Writers.*
D.C. Grover, 649(WAL):Spring82-81
Bennett, R. Images of Summer.
J. Saunders, 565:Vol123No3-73
Bennett, R. River.
G. Catalano, 381:Oct81-349
D. Haskell, 581:Sep82-348
Bennett, R.J. and R.J. Chorley. Environmental Systems.
R.H. Wills, 488:Jun82-235
Bennett, T. Formalism and Marxism.*
J.R. Bennett, 599:Winter82-98
J.W. Davidson, 477(PLL):Winter82-428
B. Foley, 405(MP):May83-443
J.H. Kavanagh, 153:Spring82-25
Benoist, J. Les Carnets d'un guérisseur réunionnais.
A.M. Gardella, 69:Vol152No2-120
Benoist, J-P. Les Fonctions de l'ordre des mots en russe moderne, romans et nouvelles de Gorki.
K.L. Nalibow, 574(SEEJ):Fall82-375
Bénouis, M.K. Le Français économique et commercial.
J.T. Chamberlain, 207(FR):Dec82-347
Benrekassa, G. Le Concentrique et l'excentrique.
B. Baczko, 535(RHL):Sep-Dec82-909
P. Stewart, 400(MLN):May82-1008
Bensko, J. Green Soldiers.*
R. Pybus, 565:Vol123No3-61
Benson, C.D. The History of Troy in Middle English Literature.*
C. Gauvin, 189(EA):Oct-Dec82-452
E. Wilson, 447(N&Q):Dec81-528
Benson, J. British Coalminers in the Nineteenth Century.
R. Price, 637(VS):Autumn81-111
Benson, J. The Penny Capitalist.
P. Joyce, 617(TLS):11Nov83-1258

Benson, L.D., ed. King Arthur's Death.
K.H. Göller, 38:Band100Heft1/2-193
Benson, L.D. and J. Leyerle, eds. Chivalric Literature.
E.M. Orsten, 627(UTQ):Summer82-409
Benson, R.G. Medieval Body Language.
W. Habicht, 38:Band100Heft3/4-500
H.S. Houghton, 382(MAE):1982/2-261
A.A. MacDonald, 179(ES):Oct82-474
Benstock, B. James Joyce: the Undiscover'd Country.
A. Topia, 98:Jun-Jul82-499
Benstock, B., ed. The Seventh of Joyce.
R. Brown, 617(TLS):29Apr83-440
Benstock, S. and B. Who's He When He's at Home.*
M.P. Gillespie, 594:Spring82-116
M. Power, 395(MFS):Summer81-316
Bensusan-Butt, J. On Naturalness in Art.
J.B. Smith, 39:Aug82-126
Bent, M. Dunstaple.
D. Stevens, 415:May82-334
Bentham, J. Constitutional Code. (Vol 1)
(F. Rosen and J.H. Burns, eds)
D.D. Raphael, 617(TLS):2Sep83-941
Bentham, J. Deontology, together with A Table of the Springs of Action and the Article on Utilitarianism. (A. Goldworth, ed)
D.D. Raphael, 617(TLS):2Sep83-941
Bentley, E. The Brecht Commentaries.
J. Fuegi, 397(MD):Dec82-577
A.P.H., 148:Spring82-94
Bentley, E.C. and others. The First Clerihews.
I. Shenker, 442(NY):25Apr83-148
Bentley, G.E., Jr. Blake Books.
J.E. Grant, 481(PQ):Summer82-277
Bentley, G.E., Jr. - see Blake, W.
Bentley, J. The Importance of Being Constance.
J. Stokes, 617(TLS):24Jun83-650
Bentley, M. and J. Stevenson, eds. High and Low Politics in Modern Britain.
J.A. Turner, 617(TLS):16Dec83-1409
Bentley, U. The Natural Order.*
D. Durrant, 364:Nov82-87
442(NY):14Feb83-114
Benvenga, N. Kingdom on the Rhine.
J. Kerman, 453(NYRB):22Dec83-27
Benveniste, E. Etudes sogdiennes.
M.J. Dresden, 318(JAOS):Oct-Dec81-464
Beny, R., with P. Gunn. The Churches of Rome.*
J. Lees-Milne, 39:Sep82-196
T.G. Smith, 505:Nov82-152
"Beowulf." (M. Swanton, ed and trans)
D.M.E. Gillam, 179(ES):Jun82-278
S.B. Greenfield, 38:Band100Heft1/2-168
"Beowulf, l'épopée fondamentale de la littérature anglaise."* (J. Queval, ed and trans)
J-C. Masson, 450(NRF):Jan82-141
Beradt, M. Der deutsche Richter. Die Verfolgten.
R.C. Holub, 406:Spring82-72
Berberova, N. Zheleznaia zhenshchina.
N. Kolchevska, 550(RusR):Oct82-521
de Berceo, G. Signos que aparecerán antes del Juicio Final, Duelo de la Virgen, Martirio de San Lorenzo.* (A.M. Ramoneda, ed)
T. Montgomery, 240(HR):Spring82-226
P. Such, 402(MLR):Oct82-974

Berchet, J-C. - see Gautier, T.
Berchez, J. and V. Corell. Catálogo de los Diseños de Arquitectura de la Real Academia de B.B.A.A. de San Carlos de Valencia 1768-1846.
A. Bustamante García, 48:Jan-Mar82-120
Bercovitch, S. The American Jeremiad.*
F. Shuffelton, 173(ECS):Winter81/82-232
Bercuson, D.J. and P.A. Buckner, eds. Eastern and Western Perspectives.
R. Ommer, 99:Apr82-31
Berenson, E.M. Understanding Persons.*
R. Cigman, 89(BJA):Autumn82-380
M.R. Haight, 518:Apr82-124
Berenson, M. Mary Berenson: A Self-Portrait from her Letters and Diaries.
(B. Strachey and J. Samuels, eds)
V. Glendinning, 617(TLS):3Jun83-561
Beres, L.R. Apocalypse.
A. Denman, 42(AR):Summer82-363
Beresford-Howe, C. The Marriage Bed.
A.S. Brennan, 198:Jul82-82
Berg, S., ed. In Praise of What Persists.
M. Bayles, 441:7Aug83-15
Berg, S. With Akhmatova at the Black Gates.*
R. Pybus, 565:Vol23No3-61
Berg, S.B. The Book of Esther.
A. Berlin, 318(JAOS):Oct-Dec81-443
Berg, W. Uneigentliches Sprechen.
W. Oesterreicher, 353:Vol 19No9/10-1026
J. Villwock, 224(GRM):Band32Heft2-243
Berg, W.J., G. Moskos and M. Grimaud. Saint/Oedipus.
A. Israel-Pelletier, 446(NCFS):Spring-Summer83-372
A. Thorlby, 617(TLS):14Jan83-39
van Bergen, E. and S. Barbour - see Lamb, C. and M.A.
Berger, B. and P.L. The War Over the Family.
R. Coles, 441:15May83-7
Berger, B.M. The Survival of a Counter-culture.
42(AR):Winter82-118
Berger, E. and R. Lullies. Antike Kunst-werke aus der Sammlung Ludwig. (Vol 1)
D. Williams, 303(JoHS):Vol 102-287
Berger, J. Another Way of Telling.
J. Naughton, 362:6Jan83-22
Berger, J. Success and Failure of Picasso.
N. Wadley, 592:Vol 195No993/994-103
Berger, K. Theories of Chromatic and Enharmonic Music in Late 16th Century Italy.*
A.F. Carver, 410(M&L):Jan/Apr82-132
M. Lindley, 551(RenQ):Autumn81-432
Berger, M.L. The Devil Wagon in God's Country.
F.T. Kihlstedt, 658:Summer/Autumn82-169
Berger, P. and H. Kellner. Sociology Reinterpreted.
D.N.L., 185:Jul83-828
Berger, T. The Feud.
A. Tyler, 441:8May83-1
442(NY):23May83-120
Berger, T. Reinhart's Women.*
G.W. Jarecke, 577(SHR):Spring82-160

Berger, T.R.   Fragile Freedoms.*
    A.A. Borovoy, 99:Apr82-28
    G.W., 102(CanL):Spring82-162
Bergeron, L.   Dictionnaire de la langue
    québécoise.*
    B. Dunn-Lardeau, 553(RLiR):Jan-Jun82-
    204
    E. Seutin, 320(CJL):Fall82-191
Bergeron, L.   Dictionnaire de la langue
    québécoise: Supplément 1981.
    T.R. Wooldridge, 627(UTQ):Summer82-485
Berghahn, K.L. and B. Pinkerneil.   Am
    Beispiel Wilhelm Meister.
    D.F. Mahoney, 222(GR):Winter82-45
Berghahn, V.R.   Militarism.
    G. Best, 617(TLS):18Mar83-261
Berghaus, F-G.   Die Verwandtschaftsverhält-
    nisse der altenglischen Interlinearver-
    sionen des Psalters und der Cantica.
    T.F. Hoad, 447(N&Q):Oct81-436
    E.G. Stanley, 541(RES):Feb82-113
van den Berghe, P.L., ed.   The Liberal
    Dilemma in South Africa.
    B. Munslow, 69:Vol152No4-91
Bergin, T.G.   Boccaccio.*
    D.J. Donno, 551(RenQ):Winter82-602
    L.V.R., 568(SCN):Fall82-57
Berglund, G.   Der Kampf um den Leser im
    Dritten Reich.
    W.D. Elfe, 221(GQ):Mar82-276
Bergman, H.E. and S.E. Szmuk.   A Catalogue
    of Comedias sueltas in the New York
    Public Library.
    M.V. Boyer, 304(JHP):Spring82-256
    K. and R. Reichenberger, 547(RF):Band
    94Heft4-505
Bergman, J.   Vera Zasulich.
    J. Keep, 617(TLS):14Oct83-1114
Bergman, R.P.   The Salerno Ivories, Ars
    Sacra from Medieval Amalfi.
    P. Williamson, 90:May82-299
Bergmann, E.L.   Art Inscribed.
    A. Terry, 131(CL):Fall82-371
Bergmann, M., J. Moor and J. Nelson.   The
    Logic Book.
    C.S. Hill, 316:Dec82-915
Bergmann, R., W. König and H. Stopp.   Bib-
    liographie zur Namenforschung.
    R. Bauer, 72:Band218Heft2-402
Bergmann, R. and P. Pauly.   Einführung in
    die Sprachwissenschaft.
    K.E. Sommerfeldt, 682(ZPSK):Band34
    Heft5-648
Bergquist, G.N.   The Pen and the Sword.
    A. Klein, 38:Band100Heft3/4-546
Bergson, A. and H.S. Levine, eds.   The
    Soviet Economy.
    A. Nove, 617(TLS):5Aug83-836
Bergsten, S.   Gamle Kant.
    L. Aagaard-Mogensen, 342:Band73Heft1-
    95
Berke, B.   Tragic Thought and the Grammar
    of Tragic Myth.
    C.A. Troutman, 350:Dec83-943
Berke, R.   Bounds Out of Bounds.*
    L. Bartlett, 649(WAL):Spring82-84
    G. Burns, 584(SWR):Summer82-354
    C. Falck, 493:Sep82-70
    T. Mallon, 134(CP):Spring82-88
Berkowitz, F.P.   Popular Titles and Sub-
    titles of Musical Compositions.   (2nd ed)
    A.F.L.T., 412:Feb81-61

Berkowitz, R. and M. Callen, with R. Dwor-
    kin.   How to Have Sex in an Epidemic.
    J. Lieberson, 453(NYRB):18Aug83-17
Berl, E.   Présence des morts.
    J. Aeply, 450(NRF):Jul-Aug82-166
Berland, A.   Culture and Conduct in the
    Novels of Henry James.*
    J.P. Dyson, 627(UTQ):Summer82-432
    R. Hewitt, 395(MFS):Winter81/82-719
    A. Gribben, 27(AL):Mar82-127
    R.B. Yeazell, 445(NCF):Mar83-611
Berlász, J.   Az Országos Széchényi könyv-
    tár története 1802-1867.
    354:Dec82-470
Berlin, A.   Enmerkar and Ensuḫkešdanna.
    W. Heimpel, 318(JAOS):Jul-Sep81-404
Berlin, I., with J.P. Reidy and L.S. Row-
    land, eds.   Freedom.   (Ser 2)
    C.V. Woodward, 441:13Feb83-9
Berlin, E.A.   Ragtime.
    P. Dickinson, 410(M&L):Apr81-215
    M. Harrison, 415:Apr82-263
Berlin, I., ed.   Freedom.   (Ser 2)
    442(NY):21Mar83-132
Berlin, I.   Personal Impressions.*   (H.
    Hardy, ed)
    E. Wasiolek, 114(ChiR):Summer81-99
Berlin, I.   Vico and Herder.
    E. Namer, 192(EP):Apr-Jun81-238
Berlin, I. and R. Hoffman, eds.   Slavery
    and Freedom in the Age of the American
    Revolution.
    J. White, 617(TLS):30Sep83-1066
Berling, J.A.   The Syncretic Religion of
    Lin Chao-en.
    D.L. Overmyer, 293(JASt):Nov81-95
Berman, A.   Forestville Tales.
    E. Walter, 608:Mar83-132
    J. Zukowski/Faust, 608:Mar83-131
Berman, M.   All That Is Solid Melts Into
    Air.*
    H. McQueen, 381:Dec82-493
Berman, M.   The Reenchantment of the World.
    M. Jacob, 322(JHI):Apr-Jun82-331
Berman, M.   Take Note.
    L. Hamp-Lyons, 608:Mar83-109
Berman, N.D.   Playful Fictions and Fic-
    tional Players.
    D. Johnson, 577(SHR):Fall82-382
    W.J. Palmer, 395(MFS):Winter81/82-743
Bermant, C.   The House of Women.
    B. Morton, 617(TLS):8Apr83-360
    442(NY):12Sep83-154
Bermejo, E.   La pintura de los primitivos
    flamencos en España.
    D. Angulo Íñiguez, 48:Apr-Jun80-213
Bernard, S. and A. Guyaux - see Rimbaud, A.
Bernardini, J.   Singapore: A Novel of the
    Bronx.
    D. Evanier, 441:30Oct83-15
Bernardo, A.S., ed.   Francesco Petrarca,
    Citizen of the World.
    J.L. Smarr, 551(RenQ):Summer82-261
    S. Sturm-Maddox, 589:Oct82-859
Bernardus Silvestris.   The Commentary on
    the First Six Books of Virgil's "Aeneid."
    (E.G. Schreiber and T.E. Maresca, eds
    and trans)
    C.S.F. Burnett, 447(N&Q):Aug81-329
Bernardus Silvestris.   Cosmographia.   (P.
    Dronke, ed)
    K. Brownlee, 545(RPh):Nov81-403

30

Bernays, A. The Address Book.
　　A. Roiphe, 441:13Nov83-12
　　442(NY):7Nov83-182
Bernd, C.A. German Poetic Realism.
　　L.A. Lensing, 221(GQ):May82-426
Berner, C. and others, eds. Sowjetunion
　　1980-81.
　　M. McCauley, 575(SEER):Apr82-317
Bernhard, M. Wortkonkordanz zu Anicius
　　Manlius Severinus Boethius "De institu-
　　tione musica."
　　S. Lusignan, 589:Oct82-862
Bernhard, T. Beton.
　　D. McLintock, 617(TLS):4Mar83-223
Bernhard, T. L'Imitateur.
　　B. Bayen, 450(NRF):Apr82-143
Bernhard, T. Wittgensteins Neffe.
　　G. Steiner, 617(TLS):22Jul83-788
Bernhardt-Kabisch, E. Robert Southey.
　　J. Raimond, 189(EA):Apr-Jun82-218
Bernikow, L. Abel.
　　W. Laqueur, 617(TLS):11Feb83-137
Bernini, D., ed. Raphael Vrbinas.
　　J. Pope-Hennessy, 453(NYRB):22Dec83-44
Berns, G. - see Alberti, R.
Berns, J.J. - see Schottelius, J.G.
Bernshtam, M.S., ed. Nezavisimoe rabochee
　　dvizhenie v 1918 godu.
　　P. Avrich, 550(RusR):Apr82-208
Bernstein, C.L. Precarious Enchantment.*
　　W.F. Wright, 637(VS):Winter82-248
Bernstein, J. Hans Bethe.
　　D. Layzer, 473(PR):2/1982-305
Bernstein, J.A. Shaftesbury, Rousseau,
　　and Kant.
　　R.W., 185:Apr83-640
Bernstein, L.F. and J. Haar - see Gero, I.
Bernstein, M.A. The Tale of the Tribe.*
　　J. Barbarese, 295(JML):Dec82-515
　　C. Froula, 405(MP):Aug82-103
　　W. Harmon, 569(SR):Spring82-279
　　L. Kramer, 301(JEGP):Apr82-279
　　L. Surette, 408:Jun82-57
Bernstein, R. From the Center of the
　　Earth.*
　　D.S.G. Goodman, 617(TLS):24Jun83-675
Bernstein, S.J. The Strands Entwined.
　　I.R. Hark, 130:Winter82/83-376
　　C. Werner, 397(MD):Jun82-322
Bernstein, W. and R. Cawker. Building
　　with Words.
　　A. Penney, 150(DR):Summer82-336
Le Chevalier de Berquin. Brefve admoni-
　　tion de la maniere de prier. (É-V.
　　Telle, ed)
　　P. Aquilon, 535(RHL):Mar-Apr82-286
Berreman, G.D. Caste and Other Inequities.
　　P. Kolenda, 293(JASt):Aug82-863
Berriault, G. The Infinite Passion of
　　Expectation.
　　D. Milton, 441.9Jan83-0
Berridge, A. - see Thomas, E.
Berrin, K., ed. Art of the Huichol
　　Indians.
　　J. Christian, 292(JAF):Apr-Jun82-215
Berry, A. The Super-Intelligent Machine.
　　S. Sutherland, 617(TLS):13May83-492
Berry, C.R. The Reform in Oaxaca, 1856-
　　76.
　　R.N. Sinkin, 263(RIB):Vol32No1-56
Berry, F. Langston Hughes.
　　B. Beckham, 441:11Sep83-14
　　442(NY):18Jul83-99

Berry, H., ed. The First Public Play-
　　house.*
　　J. Reibetanz, 551(RenQ):Autumn81-448
Berry, R. Changing Styles in Shake-
　　speare.*
　　A. Leggatt, 627(UTQ):Summer82-414
　　N. Pennell, 108:Spring82-208
Berry, W. The Gift of Good Land.*
　　R. Pevear, 249(HudR):Summer82-341
　　639(VQR):Summer82-100
Berry, W. Recollected Essays, 1965-1980.
　　M. Coiner, 42(AR):Spring82-244
　　C. Hudson, 219(GaR):Spring82-220
　　R. Pevear, 249(HudR):Summer82-341
　　H.P. Simonson, 649(WAL):Nov82-263
Berry, W. Standing by Words. A Place on
　　Earth. (rev)
　　N. Perrin, 441:18Dec83-8
Berry, W. The Wheel.
　　M. Kinzie, 29:Jan/Feb83-28
　　N. Perrin, 441:18Dec83-8
Bersani, J., M. Raimond and J. Yves-Tadié,
　　eds. Etudes proustiennes, IV.
　　V. Minogue, 617(TLS):27May83-548
Bersani, L. The Death of Stéphane Mal-
　　larmé.*
　　C.M. Crow, 208(FS):Jul82-352
　　U. Franklin, 446(NCFS):Fall-Winter
　　82/83-170
　　J.P. Houston, 207(FR):Mar83-638
　　R. Howard, 676(YR):Autumn82-108
Berschin, W. Griechisch-lateinisches Mit-
　　telalter.
　　H-J. Zimmermann, 72:Band218Heft2-372
Berst, C.A., ed. Shaw and Religion.
　　J.P. Wearing, 177(ELT):Vol25No4-249
Bertaud, M. La Jalousie dans la littéra-
　　ture au temps de Louis XIII.
　　R. Danner, 546(RR):Nov82-518
　　G. Gerhardi, 547(RF):Band94Heft2/3-321
　　M-O. Sweetser, 475:Vol9No17-733
Bertaux, É. L'art dans l'Italie méridion-
　　ale. (Vols 4-6) (A. Prandi, ed)
　　R.P. Bergman, 54:Mar82-141
　　D. Glass, 589:Jan82-163
Bertelli, C. and T.V. Salamon, eds. Gra-
　　fica grafica II. (Pt 2)
　　R. Middleton, 576:Dec82-333
Bertelli, S. and P. Innocenti. Bibliogra-
　　fia machiavelliana.*
　　H.K. Moss, 402(MLR):Apr82-470
Berthel, W., ed. Über Stanislaw Lem.
　　H. Stephan, 574(SEEJ):Winter82-503
Berthier, P. - see Gautier, T.
Berthoff, W. A Literature Without Quali-
　　ties.*
　　G. Wickes, 395(MFS):Summer81-358
Berthoud, A. Aristote et l'argent.
　　P. Pellegrin, 542:Oct-Dec82-631
Berthoud, J. Joseph Conrad: The Major
　　Phase.*
　　J. McLauchlan, 136:Vol 14No2-141
Berthoud, R. Graham Sutherland.*
　　A. Ross, 364:Jul82-6
　　D. Sutton, 39:Aug82-72
Bertier, J. and others - see Plotinus
Bertin, C. Marie Bonaparte.*
　　P. Roazen, 617(TLS):6May83-451
　　A. Storr, 441:6Feb83-8
Bertram, P. White Spaces in Shakespeare.
　　J.P. Hammersmith, 577(SHR):Fall82-356

Bertrand, A. Gaspard de la Nuit.* (M. Milner, ed)
  J-L. Steinmetz, 535(RHL):Sep-Dec82-924
Bertrand, J. Dictionnaire pratique des faux frères.
  G. Price, 208(FS):Jan82-120
Bertrand de Muñoz, M. La Guerra civil española en la novela.
  H.R. Southworth, 617(TLS):4Nov83-1231
Bertuccelli Papi, M. Studi sulla diatesi passiva in testi italiani antichi.
  R.A. Hall, Jr., 350:Jun83-444
  M. Ulleland, 597(SN):Vol54No1-203
Berwanger, E.H. The West and Reconstruction.
  W. Nugent, 579(SAQ):Autumn82-474
Besemeres, J.F. Socialist Population Politics.*
  J. Krase, 497(PolR):Vol27No1/2-157
Bessai, D., ed. Prairie Performance.
  A. Filewood, 108:Spring82-200
Bessai, D. and D. Jackel, eds. Figures in a Ground.*
  E.J. Hinz, 178:Jun82-227
Besserman, L.L. The Legend of Job in the Middle Ages.*
  J.B. Allen, 301(JEGP):Jul82-405
Bessette, G. Le Cycle. La Garden-Party de Christophine.
  M.J. Edwards, 102(CanL):Winter81-117
Best, A. and H. Wolfschütz, eds. Modern Austrian Writing.
  A. Obermayer, 564:Nov81-331
  J. Strelka, 680(ZDP):Band101Heft2-314
  B. Wichmann, 395(MFS):Summer81-408
  W.E. Yates, 402(MLR):Apr82-503
Best, G. Honour Among Men and Nations.
  M.R.D. Foot, 617(TLS):8Jul83-718
Best, H. Debrett's Texas Peerage.
  N. Lemann, 441:11Dec83-34
Best, M. Ramón Pérez de Ayala.
  J.J. Macklin, 86(BHS):Oct82-345
"Best Radio Plays of 1981: The Giles Cooper Award Winners."
  F.A. Hume, 214:Vol 10No38-135
Besterman, T. - see de Voltaire, F.M.A.
Bethea, D.M. Khodasevich.
  R.P. Hughes, 441:27Nov83-9
Betjeman, J. Uncollected Poems.*
  R. Brain, 617(TLS):11Feb83-142
  A. Hollinghurst, 493:Jan83-57
Bettagno, A. Disegni di Giambattista Piranesi.
  R. Middleton, 576:Dec82-333
Bettagno, A., ed. Piranesi, incisioni-rami-legature architetture.
  R. Middleton, 576:Dec82-333
Bettelheim, B. Freud and Man's Soul.
  P-L. Adams, 61:Feb83-105
  F. Kermode, 441:6Feb83-9
  S.S. Prawer, 617(TLS):29Jul83-812
Bettoni, C. Italian in North Queensland.
  A. Pauwels, 67:Nov82-226
Betts, D. Heading West.*
  D. Flower, 249(HudR):Summer82-274
  J.L. Halio, 598(SoR):Winter83-203
Betts, G.R. Writers in Residence.*
  J.J. Murphy, 649(WAL):Spring82-64
Betty, L.S. Vādirāja's Refutation of Śaṅkara's Non-Dualism.
  S. Elkman, 318(JAOS):Jul-Sep81-384
"Between Continents/Between Seas."
  B. Braun, 55:Apr82-27

Betz, P.F. - see Wordsworth, W.
Beugnot, B. Jean-Louis Guez de Balzac. (Supp 2)
  R. Lathuillère, 535(RHL):May-Jun82-461
Beutin, W. and others. Deutsche Literaturgeschichte. [shown in prev under Buetin, W. and others]
  J. Hermand, 406:Fall81-338
Beutler, G. Adivinanzas Españolas de la Tradición Popular Actual de Mexico, Principalmente de las Regiones de Puebla-Tlaxcala.
  W.J. Pepicello, 292(JAF):Jul-Sep82-364
Bevan, J. - see Walton, I.
Beveridge, C.E. and C.C. McLaughlin, with D. Schuyler - see Olmsted, F.L.
Beverley, J. - see de Góngora, L.
Beverley, J.R. Aspects of Góngora's "Soledades."*
  T.E. Lewis, 494:Spring82-183
Bevis, R.W. The Laughing Tradition.*
  J.B. Kern, 173(ECS):Spring83-324
  A. Leggatt, 178:Dec82-501
  S.M. Tave, 612(ThS):May82-126
  C. Worth, 67:May82-77
Bew, P. Land and the National Question in Ireland 1858-82. C.S. Parnell.
  G. Eley, 385(MQR):Winter83-107
Bew, P., P. Gibbon and H. Patterson. The State in Northern Ireland 1921-72.
  G. Eley, 385(MQR):Winter83-107
Beyeler, E. and R. Hohl. Picasso.
  L. Cooke, 59:Sep82-338
Beyer, E. and R. Matzen. Atlas linguistique et ethnographique de l'Alsace. (Vol 1)
  P. Wiesinger, 685(ZDL):2/1982-234
Beyer, J. The Art and Technique of Making Medallion Quilts.
  R.L. Shep, 614:Summer83-15
Beyerlin, W., ed. Near Eastern Religious Texts Relating to the Old Testament.
  S.D. Sperling, 318(JAOS):Oct-Dec81-448
Beyrie, J. Galdós et son mythe.
  W.T. Pattison, 240(HR):Autumn82-494
Beyssade, J-M. La philosophie première de Descartes.
  J-L. Marion, 192(EP):Jan-Mar81-87
Bezzel, I. Erasmusdrucke des 16. Jahrhunderts in bayerischen Bibliotheken.*
  C.H. Miller, 551(RenQ):Winter82-615
Bezzerides, A.I. William Faulkner.
  J.G. Watson, 395(MFS):Summer81-365
"The Bhagavad Gītā."* (W. Sargeant, trans) "The Bhagavadgītā."* (K.W. Bolle, trans)
  L. Sternbach, 318(JAOS):Oct-Dec81-479
Bharati, S. Poems of Subramania Bharati.
  N. Cutler, 293(JASt):Feb82-393
Bhargava, A. The Poetry of W.B. Yeats.
  B. Dolan, 305(JIL):Sep82-114
"Bhartṛharis Vākyapadīya." (W. Rau, ed)
  G. Cardona, 259(IIJ):Jan80-53
Bhaskar, R. The Possibility of Naturalism.*
  G.N. Cantor, 479(PhQ):Jul82-280
  D. Papineau, 84:Dec82-444
Bhat, D.N.S. The Sixth Sense.
  R.A. Fox, 350:Dec83-938
Bhatnagar, S.C. A Neurolinguistic Analysis of Paragrammatism.
  P.G. Patel, 350:Jun83-460

Bhatt, B. The Canonical Nikṣepa.
  J.W. de Jong, 259(IIJ):Jan80-77
Bhattacharjee, J.M. Catalogus Catalogorum
  of Bengali Manuscripts. (Vol 1)
    A.N. Sarkar, 293(JASt):May82-612
    A.N. Sarkar, 318(JAOS):Oct-Dec81-500
Bhattacharyya, B. An Introduction to Bud-
  dhist Esoterism.
    M. Tatz, 293(JASt):May82-614
Biagini, H.E. Cómo fue la generación del
  80.
    A. Blasi, 238:Dec82-662
Bialer, S., ed. The Domestic Context of
  Soviet Foreign Policy.
    W.C. Clemens, Jr., 550(RusR):Jan82-90
Bianca, C. and others, eds. Scrittura,
  biblioteche e stampa a Roma nel Quattro-
  cento.
    J. Monfasani, 551(RenQ):Summer82-265
Biancardi, E. - see de Somaize, A.B.
Bianchi, U., ed. La "doppia creazione"
  dell'uomo negli Alessandrini, nei
  Cappadoci e nella gnosi.
    É. Des Places, 555:Vol55fasc1-168
Bianciotti, H. L'Amour n'est pas aimé.
    F. de Martinoir, 450(NRF):Dec82-109
Bianconi, S. Lingua matrigna.
    H.W. Haller, 350:Dec83-917
Biard, J.D. Lexique pour l'explication de
  texte.*
    M. Cranston, 207(FR):Mar83-625
Biasutti, F. La dottrina della scienza in
  Spinoza.
    R. Sasso, 192(EP):Oct-Dec81-470
Bichakjian, B.H., ed. From Linguistics
  to Literature.
    M.W. Epro, 350:Sep83-689
Bickerton, D. Roots of Language.*
    P. Muysken, 350:Dec83-884
Bickley, R.B., Jr. Joel Chandler Harris.
    S.I. Bellman, 573(SSF):Winter82-84
Bickman, M. The Unsounded Centre.*
    L. Cederstrom, 106:Winter82-349
Bicknell, P. Beauty, Horror and Immensity.
    G. Reynolds, 39:May82-415
Bidart, F. The Sacrifice.
    L. Simpson, 441:27Nov83-13
Bideau, D. Sur les pas de Stendhal.
    V.D.L., 605(SC):15Jul83-553
Bieber, M. The History of the Greek and
  Roman Theater. (2nd ed)
    W.S. Rodner, 130:Fall82-288
Bieck, D.S. The Art of Spinning in the
  Grease.
    R.L. Shep, 614:Spring83-14
Biedermann, J. Grammatiktheorie und gram-
  matische Deskription in Russland in der
  2. Hälfte des 18. und zu Anfang des 19.
  Jahrhunderts.
    S. Kempgen, 559:Jun82-386
Biehl, W. - see Euripides
Bielenberg, C. The Past is Myself.
    V.R., 617(TLS):18Mar83-275
Bielski, N. Oranges for the Son of Alex-
  ander Levy.
    J. Pilling, 617(TLS):7Jan83-23
Bien, H., with G. Sokoll, eds. Nordisk
  Litteraturhistorieskriving.
    K. Gulbrandsen, 172(Edda):1982/5-307
Bienek, H. Erde und Feuer.
    J.J. White, 617(TLS):4Mar83-223

Bierbrier, M.L. The Tomb-Builders of the
  Pharaohs.
    K. Kitchen, 617(TLS):4Feb83-118
Biere, B.U. Kommunikation unter Kindern.
    K. Meng, 682(ZPSK):Band34Heft3-362
Bieri, P., R-P. Horstmann and L. Krüger,
  eds. Transcendental Arguments and
  Science.
    R. Aschenberg, 687:Apr-Jun81-313
    P.F. Strawson, 311(JP):Jan82-45
Biers, W.R. The Archaeology of Greece.*
    C.E. Vafopoulou-Richardson, 123:Vol132-
      No1-108
Bierstedt, R. American Sociological The-
  ory.
    J.S., 185:Oct82-202
Biet, C., J-P. Brighelli and J-L. Rispail.
  XVIe-XVIIe Siècles. XVIIe-XVIIIe
  Siècles.
    R. Danner, 207(FR):May83-964
Biet, C., J-P. Brighelli and J-L. Rispail.
  Manuel du XIXe siècle.*
    R. Danner, 207(FR):Apr83-810
Biggs, J.R. Lettercraft.
    W. Gardner, 324:Jun83-417
Bigi, E. - see Ariosto, L.
Bigler, N. Mundartwandel im mittleren
  Aargau.
    G.A. Plangg, 685(ZDL):3/1982-395
Bigras, J. Le Choc des oeuvres d'art.
    F. Sparshott, 627(UTQ):Summer82-490
Bigsby, C.W.E., ed. Contemporary English
  Drama.
    J. Schlueter, 397(MD):Jun82-314
Bihari, A., comp and trans. A Catalogue
  of Hungarian Folk Belief Legends.
    B. af Klintberg, 64(Arv):Vol36-211
Bilan, R.P. The Literary Criticism of F.R.
  Leavis.*
    R.G. Cox, 447(N&Q):Aug81-369
    A.D. Nuttall, 541(RES):Feb82-110
"Bildwörterbuch Deutsch und Vietnamesisch."
  (Pts 1 and 2)
    G.F. Meier, 682(ZPSK):Band35Heft3-336
Bilik, D.S. Immigrant-Survivors.*
    L. Field, 395(MFS):Summer82-340
    L.I. Yudkin, 148:Spring82-92
    T. Ziolkowski, 569(SR):Fall82-592
Billcliffe, R. Mackintosh Textile Designs.
    R.L. Shep, 614:Spring83-21
    M. Straub, 324:May83-355
Billerbeck, M. Der Kyniker Demetrius.*
    A.A. Long, 303(JoHS):Vol 102-260
Billeskov Jansen, F.J. Holberg og hans
  tid.
    J.A. Parente, Jr., 563(SS):Summer82-
      261
Billington, J.H. Fire in the Minds of
  Men.*
    J.A. Leith, 529(QQ):Summer82-439
Billington, R. Occasion of Sin.*
    A. McCarthy, 441:1May83-11
Billington, R.A. Land of Savagery, Land
  of Promise.*
    D. Kirby, 639(VQR):Spring82-333
    R.W. Paul, 649(WAL):Summer82-158
Billington, R.A. and A. Camarillo. The
  American Southwest.
    B. Lawson-Peebles, 541(RES):Nov82-490
    C. Pérotin, 189(EA):Jan-Mar82-114
Binchy, M. Dublin 4.
    P. Craig, 617(TLS):1Apr83-324

Blanchard, M-E. Saint-Just & Cie.
T. Conley, 188(ECr):Spring82-93
N. Hampson, 208(FS):Apr82-210
Blanchot, J-J. and C. Graf, eds. Actes du
2è Colloque de Langue et Littérature
Ecossaises (Moyen Age et Renaissance).
W. Scheps, 588(SSL):Vol 17-284
Blanco, J.J.R. - see under Rivera Blanco,
J.J.
Blanco Aguinaga, C., J. Rodríguez Puer-
tolas and I.M. Zavala. Historia social
de la literatura española (en lengua
castellana).*
J.M. López de Abiada, 547(RF):Band93
Heft1/2-293
Bland, A. The Royal Ballet.
M.J. Warner, 529(QQ):Winter82-874
Bland, L.I. and S.R. Ritenour - see Mar-
shall, G.C.
Blandford, L. America on Five Valium a
Day.
N. Kenyon, 362:28Jul83-22
J. Stokes, 617(TLS):3Jun83-576
Blank, R.H. The Political Implications of
Human Genetic Technology.
T.R.M., 185:Oct82-214
Blansitt, E.L., Jr. and R.V. Teschner, eds.
Festschrift for Jacob Ornstein.
B.S. Hartford, 399(MLJ):Winter82-447
Blanzat, J. Le Faussaire.
F. de Martinoir, 450(NRF):Apr82-124
Blasberg, R.W., with C.L. Bohdan. Fulper
Art Pottery.
R.I. Weidner, 658:Summer/Autumn82-162
Blaser, R. - see Bowering, G.
Blasi, A.J. Segregationist Violence and
Civil Rights Movements in Tuscaloosa.
W.D. Barnard, 9(Ala):Jan82-48
Blasier, C. The Giant's Rival.
W.S. Smith, 441:25Dec83-10
Blassingame, J.W. and others - see Doug-
lass, F.
Blatty, W.P. Legion.
J.J. Osborn, Jr., 441:3Jul83-9
Blau, E. Ruskinian Gothic.*
D. Johnson, 453(NYRB):31Mar83-13
Blau, J. The Renaissance of Modern Hebrew
and Modern Standard Arabic.
A. Fox, 350:Mar83-233
Blau, R.M. The Body Impolitic.
R. Mason, 447(N&Q):Oct81-445
Blauberg, I.V., V.N. Sadovsky and E.G.
Yudin. Systems Theory.
G. Morgan, 154:Jun82-336
Blavier, A. Les Fous littéraires.
W.D. Redfern, 617(TLS):13May83-496
Blayney, P.W.M. The Texts of "King Lear"
and their Origins. (Vol 1)
R. Proudfoot, 617(TLS):9Dec83-1381
Blázquez, J.M. Historia de España Antiqua.
(Vol 1)
J. Elayi, 318(JAOS):Oct-Dec81-455
Blech, U. Germanistische Glossenstudien
zu Handschriften aus französischen Bib-
liotheken.
R. Bergmann, 680(ZDP):Band101Heft3-442
Blecher, M.J. and G. White. Micropolitics
in Contemporary China.
G. Young, 293(JASt):Nov81-97
Bledsoe, C.H. Women and Marriage in
Kpelle Society.
J. Gay, 69:Vol51No4-881

Bleecker, S.E. The Politics of Architec-
ture.*
C.H. Krinsky, 576:May82-168
Bleicher, J. Contemporary Hermeneutics.*
C. Griswold, 290(JAAC):Fall82-106
Bleiler, E.F., ed. A Treasury of Victor-
ian Detective Stories.
B.F. Fisher 4th, 191(ELN):Dec81-158
Bleser, C., ed. The Hammonds of Red-
cliffe.*
L.H. MacKethan, 578:Fall83-113
Blessing, R. A Closed Book.*
D. Hopes, 236:Fall-Winter82[No33]-27
L.L. Lee, 649(WAL):Summer82-169
Blessington, F.C. "Paradise Lost" and the
Classical Epic.*
A. Burnett, 402(MLR):Jan82-161
M. Evans, 541(RES):Aug82-318
M.B. Raizis, 399(MLJ):Spring82-75
Blet, P. and others, eds. Actes et docu-
ments du Saint Siège relatifs à la
seconde guerre mondiale. (Vol 11)
J.S. Conway, 617(TLS):14Jan83-33
Blewett, D. Defoe's Art of Fiction.*
T. Lohman, 152(UDQ):Summer81-123
J. McLaverty, 447(N&Q):Dec81-548
M.E. Novak, 402(MLR):Jan82-168
J. Richetti, 173(ECS):Fall82-108
Blickle, P. The Revolution of 1525.
639(VQR):Summer82-85
Blishen, E. A Cackhanded War. Uncommon
Entrance.
A.J.G.H., 617(TLS):29Jul83-819
Blishen, E. Donkey Work.
D.J. Enright, 362:8Sep83-21
Bliss, A. Spoken English in Ireland, 1600-
1740.*
A. Ward, 541(RES):May82-192
Bliss, A. - see Tolkien, J.R.R.
Bliss, L. The World's Perspective.
L. Mackinnon, 617(TLS):29Jul83-817
Blissett, W. The Long Conversation.*
A. Causey, 90:Sep82-566
V. Powell, 39:Apr82-296
T.R. Whitaker, 627(UTQ):Summer82-436
Blitz, M. Heidegger's "Being and Time"
and the Possibility of Political Philoso-
phy.*
L.G., 185:Jan83-431
Bloch, D. Faroese Flowers.
H. Brønner, 563(SS):Winter82-80
Bloch, E. Experimentum Mundi. (G. Raulet,
ed and trans)
J.B. Ayoub, 154:Jun82-333
Bloch, K.F. Die Atomistik bei Hegel und
die Atomtheorie der Physik.
P. Rohs, 53(AGP):Band64Heft3-340
Bloch, M. Marxism and Anthropology.
A. Wooldridge, 617(TLS):25Mar83-302
Bloch, M. Les Rois thaumaturges.
P. Burke, 617(TLS):8Jul83-723
Bloch, S. and P. Chodoff, eds. Psychiat-
ric Ethics.
J.D., 185:Apr83-646
Block, A.F. The Early French Parody Noël.
D. Fallows, 617(TLS):23Dec83-1428
Block, A.F. and C. Neuls-Bates, eds.
Women in American Music.
A.F.L.T., 412:Feb81-61
Block, I., ed. Perspectives on the Philos-
ophy of Wittgenstein.*
J. Burnheim, 63:Sep82-282

Block, L. The Burglar Who Painted Like
  Mondrian.
    N. Callendar, 441:20Nov83-41
Block, N., ed. Readings in Philosophy of
  Psychology. (Vol 1)
    K.V. Wilkes, 84:Jun82-227
Block, W. and E. Olsen, eds. Rent Control.
    L.B. Smith, 529(QQ):Spring82-194
Blocker, H.G. The Metaphysics of Absurd-
  ity.
    E.F. Kaelin, 289:Summer82-118
    P.S. Nichols, 395(MFS):Winter81/82-659
Blocker, H.G. and E.H. Smith, eds. John
  Rawls' Theory of Social Justice.*
    D.D. Raphael, 479(PhQ):Apr82-190
Blodgett, E.D. Configuration.
    E. Thompson, 628(UWR):Spring-Summer83-
  83
Blofeld, J. The Wheel of Life.
    S. Lombardo, 318(JAOS):Oct-Dec81-433
Blok, A. Selected Poems.*
    D. McDuff, 565:Vol23No1-58
Blokker, R., with R. Dearling. The Music
  of Dmitri Shostakovich: the Symphonies.
    E. Roseberry, 410(M&L):Jan81-65
Blom, F.J.M. Christoph and Andreas Arnold
  and England.
    L. Forster, 179(ES):Jun82-287
Blom, J.P. and others, eds. Norwegian
  Folk Music. (Vol 7)
    P. Hopkins, 187:May83-370
Blomqvist, J. The Date and Origin of the
  Greek Version of Hanno's Periplus.
    J. Desanges, 555:Vol155fasc1-162
Bloodworth, B.E. and A.C. Morris. Places
  in the Sun.
    P.A. Bulger, 292(JAF):Jul-Sep82-363
Bloom, C. Limelight and After.*
    D. Hughes, 157:Autumn82-45
Bloom, E.A. and L.D., eds. Addison and
  Steele: The Critical Heritage.*
    R.H. Dammers, 173(ECS):Fall82-112
    P. Rogers, 541(RES):Aug82-330
    A. Varney, 506(PSt):Dec82-337
Bloom, E.A. and L.D. Satire's Persuasive
  Voice.*
    G. Ahrends, 38:Band100Heft1/2-207
    F.M. Keener, 402(MLR):Jan82-149
    P. Rogers, 447(N&Q):Feb81-81
Bloom, H. Agon.*
    H. Bloom, 676(YR):Autumn82-116
    W. Freedman, 134(CP):Fall82-89
    D. O'Hara, 141:Summer82-297
    639(VQR):Summer82-79
Bloom, H. The Breaking of the Vessels.*
    H. Bloom, 676(YR):Autumn82-116
    D. O'Hara, 290(JAAC):Fall82-99
Bloom, H. Poetry and Repression.
    R. Machin, 89(BJA):Autumn82-377
Bloom, H. and others. Deconstruction and
  Criticism.*
    P. Hamilton, 541(RES):Nov82-504
    C. Norris, 447(N&Q):Aug81-376
Bloor, D. Knowledge and Social Imagery.
    A. Flew, 262:Sep82-365
Blostein, D.A. - see Marston, J.
Blotner, J. - see Faulkner, W.
Blount, P.G. George Sand and the Victor-
  ian World.*
    R. Miles, 402(MLR):Jan82-181
Blount, R. One Fell Soup.
    J. Stokes, 617(TLS):3Jun83-576

Bludau, B. Frankreich im Werk Nietzsches.*
    A. Flécheux, 192(EP):Oct-Dec82-479
Blüher, K-A. and J. Schmidt-Radefeldt, eds.
  Poétique et Communication: Paul Valéry.*
    C. Miething, 72:Band218Heft1-222
Blum, L.A. Friendship, Altruism, and
  Morality.
    J. Campbell, 63:Jun82-194
    R.F. Chadwick, 518:Jul82-175
    R.A. Duff, 479(PhQ):Apr82-181
    N.C. Gillespie, 185:Apr83-596
    C.W. Gowans, 258:Mar82-101
Blume, B. Existenz und Dichtung.
    N. Ritter, 406:Winter82-499
Blume, H-D. Menanders Samia.
    J.T.M.F. Pieters, 394:Vol35fasc1/2-174
Blumenberg, H. Die Lesbarkeit der Welt.
    G. Müller, 680(ZDP):Band101Heft4-622
Blumenkranz, B., ed. Art et archéologie
  des Juifs en France médiévale.
    C.F. Barnes, Jr., 589:Oct82-852
Blumenthal, P. La syntaxe du message.
    H. Bonnard, 209(FM):Apr82-155
    G. Kleiber, 553(RLiR):Jan-Jun82-174
Blumhardt, D. and B. Blake. Craft New
  Zealand.
    M.W. Phillips, 139:Feb/Mar82-43
Blumin, S. The Short Season of Sharon
  Springs.
    42(AR):Winter82-120
Blumstein, P. and P. Schwartz. American
  Couples.
    C. Tavris, 441:23Oct83-7
Blumstock, R., ed. Békévar.
    R.B. Klymasz, 292(JAF):Jul-Sep82-368
    M. Laba, 650(WF):Jul82-238
Blundell, J. Menander and the Monologue.
    S.M. Goldberg, 121(CJ):Dec82/Jan83-173
    E.G. Turner, 123:Vol32No1-94
Blussé, L. and F. Gaastra, eds. Companies
  and Trade.
    C.R. Boxer, 617(TLS):29Apr83-435
Bly, P.A. Galdós's Novel of the Histor-
  ical Imagination.
    A.F. Lambert, 617(TLS):5Aug83-838
Bly, R. The Man in the Black Coat Turns.*
    C. Molesworth, 649(WAL):Nov82-282
Bly, R., ed. News of the Universe.*
    L. Bartlett, 649(WAL):Spring82-66
Bly, R. - see Machado, A.
Bly, R. - see Rilke, R.M.
Blythe, R. Characters and Their Land-
  scapes.
    P. Fussell, 61:Sep83-120
Blythe, R. From the Headlands.*
    P. Dickinson, 364:Mar83-105
Boardman, J. Greek Sculpture: The Archaic
  Period.*
    R. Higgins, 39:May82-413
Boase, P.H., ed. The Rhetoric of Protest
  and Reform 1878-1898.^
    M.P. Kelley, 599:Winter82-74
Bobango, G.J. Religion and Politics.
    S.D. Spector, 104(CASS):Fall-Winter82-
  610
Bobbio, N. and M. Bovero. Società e Stato
  nella filosofia politica moderna.
    F. Volpi, 489(PJGG):Band89Heft2-439
Bobunova, A.N. and V.K. Morozov. Russian
  for Businessmen.
    V.G. Brougher, 574(SEEJ):Spring82-132
    J.S. Elliott, 399(MLJ):Autumn82-345

Boccazzi, F.V. Pittoni.
  D.C. Miller, 54:Dec82-672
Bocheński, J.M. Qu'est-ce que l'autorité?
  (P. Secrétan, ed and trans)
  A. Reix, 542:Jan-Mar82-77
Bochmann, K., ed. Die Analyse politischer
  Texte.
  J. Erfurt, 682(ZPSK):Band35Heft6-731
Bochmann, K. Der Politisch-Sozial Wort-
  schatz des Rumänischen von 1821 bis 1850.
  A. Beyrer, 682(ZPSK):Band35Heft3-337
  H. Misterski, 360(LP):Vol25-148
Bochmann, K., ed. Soziolinguistische
  Aspekte der rumänischen Sprache.
  A. Beyrer, 682(ZPSK):Band35Heft5-571
Bock, S. Literatur, Gesellschaft, Nation.
  B. Einhorn, 221(GQ):May82-460
  H.T. Tewarson, 222(GR):Spring82-82
Bockris, V. A Report from the Bunker,
  with William Burroughs.
  H. Williams, 364:Feb83-107
Bodard, L. Anne Marie.
  M. Naudin, 207(FR):Dec82-332
Bode, C. - see Barnum, P.T.
Bodel, J. Le "Jeu de saint Nicolas" de
  Jehan Bodel. (3rd ed) (A. Henry, ed and
  trans)
  D. Evans, 208(FS):Jan82-51
  G. Roques, 553(RLiR):Jul-Dec82-501
  E.R. Sienaert, 356(LR):Aug82-265
  N.B. Smith, 589:Jan82-184
Boden, M. Artificial Intelligence and
  Natural Man.
  P. Danielson, 488:Mar82-105
Boden, M.A. Minds and Mechanisms.*
  W.H.P., 185:Jan83-417
Bodi, L. Tauwetter in Wien.
  F. Rau, 224(GRM):Band32Heft1-107
"Bodleian Library MS Fairfax 16."*
  M. Seymour, 354:Dec82-428
Bodson, L. Iera Zōia.
  G.J.D. Aalders H. Wzn., 394:Vol35fasc
  1/2-193
Boehm, R. Vom Gesichtspunkt der Phänomen-
  ologie. (Vol 2)
  S.L., 227(GCFI):May-Aug82-249
Boehne, P.J. J.V. Foix.*
  D. Keown, 86(BHS):Apr82-161
Boelen, B.J. Personal Maturity.
  C.O.S., 543:Sep81-113
Boelhower, W.Q. - see Goldmann, L.
den Boer, W., ed. Les études classiques
  aux XIXe et XXe siècles.
  E.J. Kenney, 123:Vol132No1-86
den Boer, W. Private Morality in Greece
  and Rome.*
  K.J. Dover, 303(JoHS):Vol 102-260
Boerens, T. Of Daydreams and Memories.
  M. Cowan, 614:Fall83-22
Bogarde, D. A Gentle Occupation.
  J.L. Halio, 598(SoR):Winter83-203
Bogarde, D. An Orderly Man.
  C. Brown, 617(TLS):29Apr83-429
  V. Glendinning, 362:14Apr83-25
  B. Shulgasser, 441:9Oct83-16
  442(NY):7Nov83-184
Bogdan, R.J., ed. Keith Lehrer: Profiles.
  P.D. Klein, 484(PPR):Mar83-409
Bogdan, R.J., ed. Patrick Suppes.
  J.D. Quesada, 167:Jan82-113
  F. Suppe, 482(PhR):Jul82-484
Bogdanor, V., ed. Liberal Party Politics.
  S. Koss, 617(TLS):3Jun83-564

Boghardt, C., M. Boghardt and R. Schmidt.
  Die zeitgenössischen Drucke von Klop-
  stocks Werken.
  J.L. Flood, 354:Dec82-450
  J.E. Walsh, 517(PBSA):Vol76No3-353
Boghardt, M. Analytische Druckforschung.
  G. Lohse, 684(ZDA):Band111Heft1-37
Boglioni, P., ed. La culture populaire au
  moyen âge.*
  F.L. Cheyette, 589:Jan82-185
Bohm, D. Wholeness and the Implicate
  Order.*
  R.H., 543:Sep81-114
  D.L. Schindler, 258:Dec82-315
Böhme, R. Der Sänger der Vorzeit.
  É. Des Places, 555:Vol156fasc2-312
Bohn, V., ed. Literaturwissenschaft.
  J.H. Petersen, 52:Band16Heft3-302
Bohrer, K.H. Die Ästhetik des Schreckens.
  M.T. Jones, 221(GQ):May82-442
Boime, A. Thomas Couture and the Eclectic
  Vision.*
  E. Mai, 471:Jan/Feb/Mar82-76
de Boisdeffre, P. Le Roman français
  depuis 1900.*
  R. Tarica, 207(FR):May83-951
Boismenu, G., L. Mailhot and J. Rouillard.
  Le Québec en textes 1940-1980.
  M. Lebel, 102(CanL):Summer82-135
Boissel, J. Gobineau (1816-1882).*
  M.D. Biddiss, 208(FS):Jul82-341
  M. Donaldson-Evans, 207(FR):Apr83-774
Boisvert, C. Tranches de néant.
  H.R. Runte, 102(CanL):Autumn82-144
Boisvert, L., M. Juneau and C. Poirier -
  see "Travaux de linguistique québécoise"
Boitani, P. - see Bennett, J.A.W.
Boixo, J.C.G. - see under González Boixo,
  J.C.
Bojko-Blochyn, J. Gegen den Strom.
  H. Rösel, 688(ZSP):Band43Heft1-227
Bok, S. Secrets.
  I. Hacking, 453(NYRB):31Mar83-7
  R. Sennett, 441:20Feb83-3
  442(NY):4Apr83-134
Bokser, B.Z. The Jewish Mystical Tradi-
  tion.
  B.W. Holtz, 390:Oct82-58
Boland, E. Introducing Eavan Boland.*
  L. Goldstein, 385(MQR):Winter83-160
  J. Parini, 569(SR):Fall82-623
  V. Young, 249(HudR):Spring82-139
Bold, A. MacDiarmid.
  N. Corcoran, 617(TLS):26Aug83-909
Bold, A. Modern Scottish Literature.
  I. Campbell, 617(TLS):26Aug83-909
Bold, A. Mounts of Venus.
  P-G. Boucé, 189(EA):Oct-Dec82-437
Bold, A. The Sensual Scot.
  G. Ewart, 617(TLS):22Apr83-397
Bold, A., ed. Smollett.
  M. Doody, 617(TLS):3Jun83-560
Boldt, P. Junge Pferde! Junge Pferde!
  W. Paulsen, 133:Band15Heft1/2-175
Boldy, S. The Novels of Julio Cortázar.*
  R.K. Britton, 402(MLR):Jan82-221
Bolger, D. Finglas Lilies.
  T.F. Merrill, 305(JIL):Sep82-3
"Lord Bolingbroke: Contributions to the
  'Craftsman.'" (S. Varey, ed)
  W.A. Speck, 617(TLS):21Jan83-64
Bolinger, D. Language — the Loaded Weapon.
  N. Fairclough, 355(LSoc):Apr82-110

Böll, H. Fürsorgliche Belagerung.
  D. Myers, 268(IFR):Winter83-65
Böll, H. Irish Journal. (French title:
  Journal irlandais.)
  J-P. Lefebvre, 98:Jun-Jul82-576
  W.T. Touwen, 617(TLS):19Aug83-892
Böll, H. The Safety Net.*
  B. Andrews, 364:Apr/May82-129
  D. Flower, 249(HudR):Summer82-274
  P. Lewis, 565:Vol23No3-68
Boll, M.M. The Petrogard Armed Workers
  Movement in the February Revolution
  (February-July 1917).
  R.A. Wade, 550(RusR):Jan82-78
Bollack, J. and A. Laks, eds. Cahiers de
  Philologie. (Vol 1)
  J.M. Rist, 122:Oct82-377
Bolle, K.W. - see "The Bhagavadgītā"
Bollée, W.B. Studien zum Sūyagaḍa.
  J.W. de Jong, 259(IIJ):Jan80-75
Boller, P.F., Jr. Presidential Anecdotes.
  R. Morgan, 584(SWR):Winter82-97
Bollino, F. Teoria e sistema delle belle
  arti.
  A. Becq, 535(RHL):May-Jun82-478
  R.G. Saisselin, 173(ECS):Fall81-113
Bollvåg, M.A. Kjaerlighetsbegrepet i
  Sigurd Hoels forfatterskap.
  J. de Mylius, 172(Edda):1982/1-62
Bolotin, D. Plato's Dialogue on Friend-
  ship.*
  L. Brown, 447(N&Q):Jun81-280
  D.B. Robinson, 123:Vol32No1-42
Bolt, S. A Preface to James Joyce.
  M.P. Gillespie, 395(MFS):Winter82/83-
  625
Bolton, D. An Approach to Wittgenstein's
  Philosophy.*
  T.E. Burke, 393(Mind):Oct82-614
  R. Fogelin, 482(PhR):Jan82-119
Bolton, W.F. Alcuin and "Beowulf."*
  J.S. Wittig, 38:Band100Heft1/2-172
Bombal, M.L. New Islands.*
  F. Partridge, 617(TLS):9Dec83-1372
Bömer, F. P. Ovidius Naso, "Metamorpho-
  sen:" Kommentar Buch IV-V, VI-VII.
  P.H. Schrijvers, 394:Vol35fasc3/4-410
Bömer, F. P. Ovidius Naso, "Metamor-
  phosen:" Kommentar Buch X-XI.
  E.J. Kenney, 123:Vol32No2-165
Bonaccorso, G. L'Oriente nella narrativa
  di Gustave Flaubert. (Pt 1, Vols 1 and
  2)
  A. Fairlie, 208(FS):Apr82-214
Bonali-Fiquet, F. - see de Chandieu, A.
Bonanno, J., with S. Lalli. A Man of
  Honour.
  R. Fox, 617(TLS):23Sep83-1012
Bonaventura da Brescia. Rules of Plain
  Music (Breviloquium Musicale). (A.
  Seay, trans)
  A.E. Walters, 308:Fall82-349
Saint Bonaventure. Disputed Questions on
  the Mystery of the Trinity.* (Z. Hayes,
  ed and trans)
  A.B.W., 543:Sep81-117
Bonavia, D. The Chinese.
  E.W., 617(TLS):11Feb83-143
Bond, D. The Temptation of Despair.
  A. Mitcham, 268(IFR):Winter83-60
Bond, E.J. Reason and Value.
  S. Blackburn, 617(TLS):27May83-535
Bond, G.W. - see Euripides

Bondanella, P. Italian Cinema.
  V. de Grazia, 18:Jul-Aug83-54
Bondanella, P. and J.C., eds. The Macmil-
  lan Dictionary of Italian Literature.
  M. Mann, 447(N&Q):Feb81-89
Bondarko, L.V. Zvukovoj stroj sovremen-
  nogo russkogo jazyka.
  F.E. Vejsalov, 682(ZPSK):Band34Heft2-
  224
Bondeson, W.B. and others, eds. New Know-
  ledge in the Biomedical Sciences.
  P.S., 185:Jul83-836
Bondzio, W., ed. Einführung in die Grund-
  fragen der Sprachwissenschaft.
  H. Schmidt, 682(ZPSK):Band35Heft6-732
Bones, J., Jr. Texas West of the Pecos.
  L. Milazzo, 584(SWR):Winter82-v
Bonet, L. - see de Pereda, J.M.
Bonet Correa, A. and others. Bibliografía
  de arquitectura, ingeniería y urbanismo
  en España (1498-1880).
  J.B. Bury, 46:Jul82-75
Bonfatti, E. La "Civil Conversazione" in
  Germania.
  R. Zeller, 52:Band16Heft2-204
Bonfield, L. Marriage Settlements, 1601-
  1740.
  P. Clark, 617(TLS):25Nov83-1302
Bongie, L.L. - see de Condillac, E.B.
Bonitzer, P. Le Champ aveugle.
  J. Prieur, 450(NRF):Nov82-138
Bonnefis, P. Comme Maupassant.
  P.W. Lasowski, 450(NRF):Jun82-98
Bonnefis, P., ed. Jules Laforgue.
  C.W. Thompson, 402(MLR):Apr82-458
Bonnefis, P. and P. Reboul, eds. Des mots
  et des couleurs.
  J-M. Bailbé, 535(RHL):Jan-Feb82-139
Bonnefoy, Y. Entretiens sur la poésie.
  G. Gasarian, 98:May82-375
  M. Treharne, 208(FS):Jul82-360
Bonnefoy, Y. L'Improbable. Poèmes. Le
  nuage rouge. Rue Traversière.
  G. Gasarian, 98:May82-375
Bonnell, P. and F. Sedwick. Conversation
  in French. (3rd ed)
  P. Stevens, 399(MLJ):Autumn82-330
Bonner, S.E. and D. Kellner, eds. Passion
  and Rebellion.
  I.B. Whyte, 617(TLS):9Dec83-1386
Bonner, T., Jr., comp. William Faulkner.
  J.G. Watson, 395(MFS):Summer81-365
Bonnet, H. and B. Brun - see Proust, M.
Bonnevie, P. and P. Amiel, general eds.
  Dictionnaire Hachette juniors.
  B.A. Byers, 207(FR):May83-963
Bonney, R. The King's Debts.*
  639(VQR):Autumn82-128
Bonney, W.W. Thorns and Arabesques.*
  R.K. Anderson, 395(MFS):Summer81-333
  J. Pinsker, 136:Vol 14No2-151
Bonta, J.P. Architecture and its Inter-
  pretation.*
  W. Widdowson, 658:Summer/Autumn82-173
Bony, J. The English Decorated Style.
  P. Draper, 54:Jun82-330
Bonython, E. King Cole.
  T. Russell-Cobb, 324:Apr83-292
Booij, G.E., J.B. Kerstens and H.J. Ver-
  kuyl. Lexicon van de taalwetenschap.
  K.C. Rothacker, 350:Jun83-436

"Bookman's Price Index." (Vol 21) (D.F. McGrath, ed)
   C.W. Mann, 568(SCN):Spring-Summer82-23
Boolos, G. The Unprovability of Consistency.*
   R.M.M., 543:Mar82-592
van den Boom, R. Die Bedienten und das Herr-Diener-Verhältnis in der deutschen Komödie der Aufklärung (1742-1767).
   A.J. Camigliano, 406:Fall82-354
Boon, J.A. Other Tribes, Other Scribes.
   D. Sperber, 617(TLS):4Nov83-1224
Boorstin, D.J. The Discoverers.
   E.E. Morison, 441:27Nov83-1
Booth, M.R. Prefaces to English Nineteenth-Century Theatre.
   J.S. Moy, 130:Winter82/83-380
   G. Rowell, 611(TN):Vol36No2-95
Booth, M.R. Victorian Spectacular Theatre 1850-1910.
   A. McKinnon, 214:Vol 10No38-124
   H.F. Salerno, 177(ELT):Vol25No1-52
   J.W. Stedman, 637(VS):Spring82-380
   H.W., 636(VP):Spring82-92
Booth, M.W. The Experience of Song.
   C.S. Brown, 131(CL):Summer82-269
Booth, P. Before Sleep.*
   D. Gioia, 491:May82-102
   R. Jackson, 502(PrS):Spring82-91
Booth, W.C. Critical Understanding.*
   E. Rooney, 400(MLN):Dec82-1232
Booth, W.C. The Rhetoric of Fiction.
   R.B., 617(TLS):29Jul83-819
de Booy, J.T. - see Diderot, D.
Bora, G. I disegni lombardi e genovesi del Cinquecento.
   N.W. Neilson, 90:Jul82-453
Borchmeyer, D. Dienst und Herrschaft.
   M. Brändle, 67:May82-91
   M. Holona, 133:Band15Heft1/2-178
   J. Schmidt, 221(GQ):Mar82-269
Borchmeyer, D. - see Wagner, R.
Bord, J. and C. Earth Rites.
   V. Newall, 617(TLS):7Jan83-11
Bord, L-J. Généalogie commentée des rois de France.
   M.G. Hydak, 207(FR):Oct82-193
Bordillon, H. - see Jarry, A.
Borel, P. Opera Polemica.* (B. Pompili, ed) Critica degli Spettacoli.
   R. Lloyd, 208(FS):Jul82-339
Borgatti, J. Levels of Reality.
   S.P. Blier, 2(AfrA):Aug82-80
Borges, J.L. Borges at Eighty. (W. Barnstone, ed)
   639(VQR):Autumn82-116
Borges, J.L. An Introduction to American Literature.
   R.A. Rand, 135:Nov82-162
Borges, J.L. and A. Bioy-Casares. Six Problems for Don Isidro Parodi.
   M. Boccia, 502(PrS):Spring82-88
Borghese, A. The Great Year-Round Turkey Cookbook.
   W. and C. Cowen, 639(VQR):Spring82-66
Borghouts, J.F. Ancient Egyptian Magical Texts.
   V.L. Davis, 318(JAOS):Oct-Dec81-437
Borie, J. Mythologies de l'hérédité au XIXe siècle.
   M. Lukacher, 400(MLN):May82-1018

Boring, P.Z. Víctor Ruiz Iriarte.*
   D. Gagen, 86(BHS):Apr82-159
   R. Lima, 397(MD):Jun82-328
   G. Martínez Lacalle, 402(MLR):Oct82-979
Bork, H.D., A. Greive and D. Woll, eds. Romanica Europaea et Americana.
   G. Ernst, 547(RF):Band93Heft3/4-407
Borkenau, F. End and Beginning. (R. Lowenthal, ed)
   V. Nemoianu, 400(MLN):Dec82-1235
Borkowski, M., M. Murch and V. Walker. Martial Violence.
   H. Rubinstein, 617(TLS):20May83-506
Bormanshinov, A. Lama Arkad Chubanov, his Predecessors and Successors.
   H. Ermolaev, 575(SEER):Jan82-155
Born, A. South Devon.
   P. Beer, 617(TLS):28Oct83-1192
Born, N. The Deception.
   D.J. Enright, 362:14Jul83-24
   E. Pawel, 441:27Feb83-8
   T. Sutcliffe, 617(TLS):20May83-526
Bornert, R. La réforme protestante du culte à Strasbourg au XVIe siècle (1523-1598).
   M.U. Chrisman, 551(RenQ):Summer82-282
Bornkamm, H. Martin Luther in der Mitte seines Lebens.
   J.R. Stephenson, 161(DUJ):Jun82-282
Bornstein, M., Z. Gitelman and W. Zimmerman, eds. East-West Relations and the Future of Eastern Europe.
   J.C. Campbell, 550(RusR):Oct82-514
   C.D. Jones, 104(CASS):Fall-Winter82-597
Borodine, L. Récit d'une époque étrange.
   J. Blot, 450(NRF):Nov82-135
Boronkai, I. - see Vitéz de Zredna, I.
Borque, J.M.D. - see under Díez Borque, J.M
Borroff, M. Language and the Poet.*
   R. Pooley, 677(YES):Vol 12-329
Borsa, G. Clavis typographorum librariorumque Italiae 1465-1600.
   J.E. Walsh, 517(PBSA):Vol76No2-227
Borsody, S. The Tragedy of Central Europe.
   R.C. Monticone, 497(PolR):Vol27No3/4-210
   D. Stafford, 104(CASS):Summer82-265
Borson, R. Rain.
   A. Todkill, 526:Summer82-120
Borsook, E. The Mural Painters of Tuscany. (2nd ed)
   H. Belting, 683:Band45Heft4-423
   J. Gardner, 90:Feb82-104
Borsook, E. and J. Offerhaus. Francesco Sassetti and Ghirlandaio et S. Trinita, Florence.
   H. Belting, 683:Band45Heft4-423
Borst, R.R. Henry David Thoreau.
   G. Palmer, 78(BC):Winter82-515
   27(AL):Oct82-481
Borthwick, J.S. The Case of the Hook-Billed Kites.
   N. Callendar, 441:9Jan83-41
Børtnes, J. Episke problemer.
   E. Kraggerud, 172(Edda):1982/3-181
Borys, J. The Sovietization of Ukraine, 1917-1923.
   D.E. Davis, 104(CASS):Summer82-286
Borzello, F. The Artist's Model.
   R. Hewison, 617(TLS):21Jan83-67

du Bos, C. Robert et Elizabeth Browning ou la plénitude de l'amour humain.
  A. Hayter, 617(TLS):13May83-478
Bosanquet, N. After the New Right.
  G. Sampson, 617(TLS):2Dec83-1340
Boscán de Lombardi, L. Aproximaciones críticas a la narrativa de Ernesto Sábato.
  J.E. Ciruti, 552(REH):Jan82-120
Bosch, G., J. Carswell and G. Petherbridge. Islamic Bindings and Bookmaking.
  O. Watson, 463:Winter82/83-383
de Boschère, J. Fragments du Journal d'un rebelle solitaire. (Vol 2) (Y-A. Favre, ed)
  J. Onimus, 535(RHL):Sep-Dec82-976
Bose, M. The Lost Hero.*
  A. Dickins, 364:Oct82-94
Bosmajian, H. Metaphors of Evil.*
  O.F. Best, 406:Fall82-348
  T.C. Hanlin, 295(JML):Dec82-343
  S. Mews, 221(GQ):Jan82-126
  T. Ziolkowski, 569(SR):Fall82-592
Bosque, I. Sobre la negación.
  F.H. Nuessel, Jr., 353:Vol 19No3/4-365
Bosquet, A. Speech is Plurality.
  G.D. Martin, 208(FS):Oct82-497
Bosse, M. The Warlord.
  J.G. Zorn, 441:5Jun83-15
Bosshard, H.H. Mundartnamen von Bäumen und Sträuchern in der deutschsprachigen Schweiz und im Fürstentum Liechtenstein.
  K. Kehr, 685(ZDL):3/1982-394
Bosshard, H.H. Natur-Prinzipien und Dichtung.
  D.F. Mahoney, 133:Band15Heft1/2-168
Bossong, G. Probleme der Übersetzung wissenschaftlicher Werke aus dem Arabischen in das Altspanische zur Zeit Alfons des Weisen.
  J.M., 554:Vol 102No4-569
Bostock, D. Logic and Arithmetic.* (Vols 1 and 2)
  M.D. Resnik, 316:Sep82-708
Boström, I. La morfosintassi dei pronomi personali soggetti della terza persona in italiano e in fiorentino.
  L. Wolf, 685(ZDL):3/1981-398
Boswell, J. Boswell: The Applause of the Jury 1782-1785.* (I.S. Lustig and F.A. Pottle, eds)
  O.W. Ferguson, 579(SAQ):Autumn82-467
Boswell, J. Walt Whitman and the Critics.
  W. White, 365:Fall82-163
Bosworth, A.B. A Historical Commentary on Arrian's History of Alexander.* (Vol 1)
  S.I. Oost, 122:Apr82-167
Botha, R.P. The Conduct of Linguistic Inquiry.
  A.R. Tellier, 189(EA):Jul-Sep82-322
Botha, R.P. On the Galilean Style of Linguistic Inquiry.
  J. Klausenburger, 350:Jun83-434
Botha, T. Generalizations About Synthetic Compounding in Afrikaans.
  M. Peet, 350:Jun83-445
Bothwell, R. and J.L. Granatstein, eds. The Gouzenko Transcripts.
  F. Park, 99:Mar83-30
Bots, H. and P. Leroy - see Rivet, A. and C. Sarrau
Botsch, B.E. We Shall Not Overcome.*
  W. Flynt, 577(SHR):Summer82-272

Bottigheimer, K.S. Ireland and the Irish.
  R. Foster, 617(TLS):20May83-512
Bottomley, G. After the Odyssey.
  R. Clogg, 617(TLS):12Aug83-861
Bottomore, T., with others, eds. A Dictionary of Marxist Thought.
  J. Gray, 617(TLS):30Dec83-1459
  R. Williams, 441:27Nov83-14
Bottomore, T. and others. Marxism and Alternatives.
  L.A. Barth, 104(CASS):Fall-Winter82-606
Bottomore, T.B., ed. Karl Marx.*
  E. Kamenka, 63:Mar82-81
Bottoms, D. Shooting Rats at the Bibb County Dump.*
  C. Berger, 491:Apr82-35
Bottorff, W.K. Thomas Jefferson.
  J.A.L. Lemay, 677(YES):Vol 12-286
Bouamrane, C. Le Problème de la liberté humaine dans la pensée musulmane (solution mu'tazilite).
  R.M. Frank, 318(JAOS):Apr-Jun81-222
Bouboulidis, P. and G. Bibliographia Neoellēnikēs Philologias tōn Etōn 1977-1978.
  J.E. Rexine, 399(MLJ):Autumn82-329
Boucé, P-G., ed. Sexuality in Eighteenth-Century Britain.
  K. Walker, 617(TLS):25Feb83-174
Bouchard, C. La Mort après la mort.
  E. Dansereau, 102(CanL):Spring82-84
Bouchard, P. and S. Beauchamp-Achim. Le Français, langue des commerces et des services publics.
  R. Le Page, 207(FR):Oct82-199
Bouchard, R., ed. Culture populaire et littératures au Québec.
  L. Brind'Amour, 188(ECr):Summer82-73
  S. Litton, 399(MLJ):Winter82-422
  C. May, 208(FS):Oct82-506
Boudaille, G. Expressionists.
  J.B. Smith, 39:Nov82-348
Boudon, P. and P. Deshayes. Viollet-le-Duc/Le Dictionnaire d'architecture, Relevés et observations.
  A.L. van Zanten, 576:May82-160
Boudon, R. The Logic of Social Action.
  D.S., 185:Jan83-423
Bouffartigue, J. and A-M. Delrieu. Trésors des racines grecques. Trésors des racines latines.
  P-L. Rey, 450(NRF):May82-111
Bouffartigue, J. and M. Patillon - see Porphyry
Bouillier, V. Naître Renonçant.
  R. Burghart, 293(JASt):Nov81-167
Boulanger, D. Connaissez-vous Maronne?
  F. de Martinoir, 450(NRF):Feb82-132
Boulanger, J-C. Bibliographie linguistique de la néologie 1960-1980. (Vol 1)
  J-Y. Dugas, 553(RLiR):Jul-Dec82-468
Boulger, J.D. The Calvinist Temper in English Poetry.
  M.I. Lowance, Jr., 661(WC):Summer82-157
  C.F. Main, 551(RenQ):Spring82-138
Boulton, J.T. - see Lawrence, D.H.
Bounemeur, A. Les bandits de l'Atlas.
  F. Ghilès, 617(TLS):6May83-464
Bouraoui, H. and S. Field. Tales of Heritage.
  L. Welch, 198:Oct82-99

Bourcier, G. An Introduction to the History of the English Language.
S.M. Embleton, 320(CJL):Fall82-183
Bourdeaux, M. Risen Indeed.
R.T.B., 617(TLS):20May83-527
Bourdieu, P. Algeria 1960.
G. Stanton, 69:Vol52No2-121
Bourdieu, P. Ce que parler veut dire.
R. Harris, 617(TLS):20May83-524
Bourdieu, P. La distinction.*
P. Somville, 542:Jan-Mar82-77
Bourel, D. - see Mendelssohn, M.
Bourg, J., P. Dupont and P. Geneste - see de Quevedo, F.
Bourgeade, P. Les Serpents.
F. Ghilès, 617(TLS):6May83-464
Bourgeault, C. - see Smoldon, W.L.
Bourgeois, J-L. Spectacular Vernacular.
P-L. Adams, 61:Nov83-148
Bourgeois, R. L'Ironie romantique.
S. Bisarello, 356(LR):Nov82-360
Bourget, J-L. Le cinéma américain 1895-1980.
C. MacCabe, 617(TLS):18Nov83-1277
le Bour'his, J.M. - see under Morris le Bour'his, J.
Bourke, J.G. Les Rites scatologiques. (D-G. Laporte, ed)
A. Reix, 542:Jan-Mar82-79
Bourmeyster, A., ed. Le 14 Decembre 1825.
G. Barratt, 104(CASS):Summer82-259
Bourquin, G. "Piers Plowman."
D. Pearsall, 402(MLR):Oct82-915
Bourricaud, F. The Sociology of Talcott Parsons.
K.S., 185:Jul83-832
de Bouscal, D.G. - see under Guérin de Bouscal, D.
de Bouscal, G.G. - see under Guérin de Bouscal, G.
Bousquet, F. and others. La croyance.
A. Reix, 542:Oct-Dec82-657
Bousquet, J. Recherches sur le séjour des peintres français à Rome au XVIIème siècle.
P. Conisbee, 59:Sep82-363
90:Nov82-730
Bouvet, F. Bonnard, the Complete Graphic Work.
R. Hobbs, 59:Dec82-511
Bouvier, J-C. and C. Martel. Anthologie des expressions en Provence.
P. Rézeau, 553(RLiR):Jun-Dec82-453
Bouvier, N. Le Poisson-scorpion.
J. Aeply, 450(NRF):May82-116
Bouzek, J. and others. Kyme 2.
J.M. Cook, 303(JoHS):Vol 102-283
Bowden, J. Edward Schillebeeckx.
P. Hebblethwaite, 617(TLS):7Oct83-1103
Bowden, M.W. Washington Irving.
R. Willett, 402(MLR):Oct82-930
Bowder, D., ed. Who Was Who in the Greek World: 776 B.C. - 30 B.C.* Who Was Who in the Roman World: 753 B.C. - A.D. 476.*
D.J.R. Bruckner, 441:16Jan83-11
Bowdler, G.A. and P. Cotter. Voter Participation in Central America, 1954-1981.
V.C. Peloso, 263(RIB):Vol32No3/4-368
Bowen, E. The Collected Stories of Elizabeth Bowen.*
R. Buffington, 569(SR):Spring82-264

Bowen, J. Squeak.
J. Mellors, 362:15Dec83-30
Bowen, R. - see Spencer, B.
Bowen, R.W. Rebellion and Democracy in Meiji Japan.*
G. Akita, 293(JASt):May82-590
Bowen, Z. - see "Irish Renaissance Annual II"
Bower, A.W. and R.A. Erickson - see Arbuthnot, J.
Bower, T.G.R. Le développement psychologique de la première enfance.
L. Millet, 192(EP):Oct-Dec81-472
Bowering, G. Burning Water.*
A.S. Brennan, 198:Jan82-85
Bowering, G. Particular Accidents.* (R. Blaser, ed)
S. Thorne, 526:Winter82-91
Bowering, G. A Way with Words.
R. Mathews, 99:Nov82-31
Bowering, G. West Window.
J. Peirce, 99:Oct82-27
Bowering, M. Giving Back Diamonds.
B. Whiteman, 99:Mar83-30
Bowering, M. Sleeping with Lambs.
D. Barbour, 648(WCR):Jun82-33
Bowers, E. Witnesses.*
J. Finlay, 598(SoR):Winter83-181
D. Gioia, 249(HudR):Autumn82-483
Bowers, F. - see Beaumont, F. and J. Fletcher
Bowers, F. - see Nabokov, V.
Bowers, J.Z. When the Twain Meet.
S.O. Long, 407(MN):Spring82-134
W.E. Steslicke, 293(JASt):Aug82-839
Bowers, N. Theodore Roethke.
N. Corcoran, 617(TLS):8Jul83-716
Bowersock, G.W. Julian the Apostate.
P.W. van der Horst, 394:Vol135fasc1/2-207
Bowie, M. Proust, Jealousy, Knowledge.*
G. Craig, 402(MLR):Oct82-963
Bowie, M. - see Fairlie, A.
Bowie, N. Business Ethics.
M.S.M., 185:Jan83-441
Bowle, J. John Evelyn and His World.
M. Jacob, 322(JHI):Apr-Jun82-331
Bowle, J. - see Evelyn, J.
Bowler, P.J. The Eclipse of Darwinism.
F.B. Churchill, 617(TLS):9Dec83-1366
Bowles, E.A. Musikleben im 15. Jahrhundert.
H.M. Brown, 410(M&L):Jan81-71
Bowles, P. Midnight Mass.
J. Ridland, 472:Spring/Summer83-191
H. Weber, 573(SSF):Fall82-389
Bowles, P. Next to Nothing.
J. Ridland, 472:Spring/Summer83-191
Bowles, S., D.M. Gordon and T.E. Weisskopf. Beyond the Waste Land.
J.K. Galbraith, 453(NYRB):2Jun83-3
P. Passell, 441:31Jul83-7
Bowling, A. and A. Cartwright. Life After a Death.
N. Roberts, 617(TLS):18Mar83-270
Bowman, F.P. Le Discours sur l'Éloquence sacrée à l'époque romantique.*
P.J. Bayley, 208(FS):Jan82-76
Bowman, J. De Valera and the Ulster Question 1917-1973.
D.W. Harkness, 617(TLS):11Feb83-127

42

Bowman, S. and others, eds. Studies in
Honor of Gerald E. Wade.
   M-A. Börger-Reese, 240(HR):Autumn82-
   481
Bowne, B.P. Representative Essays of
Borden Parker Bowne. (W.E. Steinkraus,
ed)
   J. Howie, 319:Jan83-117
   E.K., 543:Dec81-412
Bowring, R. - see "Murasaki Shikibu: Her
Diary and Poetic Memoirs"
Bowron, E.P. - see Clark, A.M.
Bowsky, W.M. A Medieval Italian Commune.*
   R.A. Goldthwaite, 377:Nov82-187
   D. Wootton, 150(DR):Winter82/83-713
Box, M. Rebel Advocate.
   D. Pannick, 362:19May83-19
   A. Paterson, 617(TLS):27May83-534
Boxer, C.R. João de Barros.
   M.N. Pearson, 293(JASt):May82-614
Boxer, C.R., ed. A Descriptive List of
the State Papers Portugal, 1661-1780 in
the Public Record Office, London. (Vols
1 and 2)
   R. Ollard, 617(TLS):8Apr83-362
Boxer, C.R. Jan Compagnie in War and
Peace 1602-1799.
   R. Rocher, 318(JAOS):Oct-Dec81-470
Boxer, C.R. Portuguese India in the Mid-
Seventeenth Century.
   M.N. Pearson, 293(JASt):May82-614
Boyazoglu, J. and L. de Neuville. Les
Faïences de Delft.
   G. Wills, 39:Apr82-297
Boyce, D.G. Nationalism in Ireland.
   G. Eley, 385(MQR):Winter83-107
Boyce, M. A Word-List of Manichaean
Middle Persian and Parthian. (3rd Ser,
Vol 2)
   J.P. Asmussen, 259(IIJ):Apr80-170
Boyd, M. William Mathias.
   T. Bray, 410(M&L):Jul/Oct81-416
Boyd, M. Grace Williams.*
   A. Whittall, 410(M&L):Jan/Apr82-112
Boyd, W. A Good Man in Africa.*
   J. Wolcott, 231:Mar83-61
Boyd, W. An Ice-Cream War.*
   R. Boscombe, 364:Nov82-91
   M. Gorra, 441:27Feb83-8
   R. Towers, 453(NYRB):2Jun83-42
   J. Wolcott, 231:Mar83-62
   442(NY):25Apr83-154
Boyd Whyte, I. Bruno Taut and the Archi-
tecture of Activism.
   R. Banham, 617(TLS):7Jan83-19
Boyde, P. Dante Philomythes and Philoso-
pher.
   J.A. Scott, 402(MLR):Jul82-737
Boyer, J. Political Radicalism in Late
Imperial Vienna.
   D. Barnouw, 221(GQ):May82-463
Boyer, L.B. Childhood and Folklore.*
   G.A. Fine, 650(WF):Jan82-69
Boyers, R. R.P. Blackmur, Poet-Critic.*
   W.E. Cain, 639(VQR):Spring82-360
Boylan, C. Holy Pictures.
   A. McCarthy, 441:20Nov83-9
   J. Mellors, 362:10Mar83-27
   L. Taylor, 617(TLS):11Mar83-248
Boylan, C. A Nail on the Head.
   P. Craig, 617(TLS):15Jul83-745
Boyle, A.J., ed. Ancient Pastoral.
   K.W. Gransden, 313:Vol72-206

Boyle, C. House of Cards.
   T. Dooley, 617(TLS):7Jan83-17
   H. Lomas, 364:Dec82/Jan83-100
Boyle, K. Fifty Stories.*
   W. Boyd, 364:Jun82-96
Boyle, M.O. Christening Pagan Mysteries.
   F.L. Borchardt, 221(GQ):Nov82-594
   L.V.R., 568(SCN):Spring-Summer82-34
   J.K. Sowards, 551(RenQ):Autumn82-479
Boyle, R. Selected Philosophical Papers
of Robert Boyle.* (M.A. Stewart, ed)
   D. Knight, 161(DUJ):Jun82-323
   A. Stroup, 568(SCN):Winter82-80
Boyle, R.H. and R.A. Acid Rain.
   T. Chaffin, 441:24Jul83-17
Boyle, R.J. John Twachtman.
   A. Davis, 106:Spring82-109
Boyle, T.C. Water Music.*
   C. Hope, 364:Jul82-80
   G. Kearns, 249(HudR):Autumn82-499
Bozzolo, C. and E. Ornato. Pour une his-
toire du livre manuscrit au moyen âge.*
   P. Saenger, 589:Jul82-590
van Brabant, J.M. Socialist Economic
Integration.
   K. Botos, 575(SEER):Jan82-144
Brabazon, J. Dorothy L. Sayers.
   C.G. Heilbrun, 31(ASch):Autumn82-552
Brabec, B. Creative Cash.
   R.L. Shep, 614:Winter83-14
Bracher, K.D. Zeit der Ideologien.
   J. Joll, 617(TLS):25Mar83-300
Bracken, P. The Command and Control of
Nuclear Forces.
   M. Bundy, 441:9Oct83-1
Brackenbury, A. Dreams of Power.*
   M. O'Neill, 493:Apr82-59
   J. Saunders, 565:Vol23No3-73
Brackert, H., ed. Und wenn sie nicht
gestorben sind...
   H. Lixfeld, 196:Band23Heft1/2-117
Brackman, A.C. The Luck of Nineveh.
   J. Leopold, 637(VS):Spring82-389
Bradbrook, M.C. The Collected Papers of
Muriel Bradbrook.* (Vol 1)
   F. Kermode, 453(NYRB):28Apr83-30
Bradbrook, M.C. Themes and Conventions of
Elizabethan Tragedy. (2nd ed)
   J.A. Bryant, Jr., 569(SR):Spring82-
   xxviii
Bradbrook, M.C. John Webster.*
   J.A. Bryant, Jr., 569(SR):Spring82-
   xxviii
   F. Lagarde, 189(EA):Oct-Dec82-462
   D.B.J. Randall, 579(SAQ):Spring82-244
Bradbury, M. Rates of Exchange.
   R. Billington, 441:20Nov83-15
   D.J. Enright, 362:21Apr83-24
   B. Morrison, 617(TLS):8Apr83-345
   F. Taliaferro, 231:Nov83-74
Bradbury, M. and D. Palmer, eds. The
Contemporary English Novel.*
   L. Bonnerot, 189(EA):Jan-Mar82-102
Bradbury, M. and D. Palmer, with I. Flet-
cher, eds. Decadence and the 1890s.
   J. Baird, 541(RES):May82-225
Bradbury, M. and H. Temperley, eds. Intro-
duction to American Studies.*
   J. Rivière, 189(EA):Jul-Sep82-356
Bradbury, N. Henry James: The Later
Novels.*
   B. Richards, 447(N&Q):Dec81-567
                                 [continued]

43

Bradbury, N. Henry James: The Later
Novels. [continuing]
   J.C. Rowe, 445(NCF):Jun82-113
   J.A. Ward, 284:Winter83-146
Bradby, D., L. James and B. Sharratt, eds.
Performance and Politics in Popular
Drama.*
   D. Jarrett, 447(N&Q):Oct81-461
Bradby, D. and J. McCormick. People's
Theatre.
   A. Munton, 299:Spring82-153
Brademann, K. Die Bezeichnungen für den
Begriff des "Erinnerns" im Alt- und
Mittelfranzösischen.
   R. Martin, 553(RLiR):Jan-Jun81-254
Braden, G. The Classics and English
Renaissance Poetry.*
   E. Häublein, 38:Band100Heft1/2-200
Braden, W.W., ed. Oratory in the New
South.
   T. Bonner, Jr., 392:Fall82-457
Bradford, B.T. Voice of the Heart.
   M. Watkins, 441:24Apr83-16
Bradford, D.E. The Concept of Existence.
   M.S.G., 543:Mar82-592
Bradford, S. Disraeli.
   V. Bogdanor, 617(TLS):28Jan83-81
   P. Stansky, 441:10Jul83-1
   442(NY):16May83-133
Bradley, A., ed. Contemporary Irish
Poetry.*
   J. Parini, 569(SR):Fall82-623
   T. Parkinson, 219(GaR):Fall82-662
Bradley, A. and T. Smith, eds. Australian
Art and Architecture.
   T. Crombie, 39:Sep82-199
   J. Stringer, 127:Spring82-79
Bradley, B.L. Zu Rilkes "Malte Laurids
Brigge."*
   J. Ryan, 221(GQ):Mar82-270
Bradley, D. Proto-Loloish.*
   J.K. Wheatley, 293(JASt):Feb82-411
Bradley, I. - see Gilbert, W.S. and A.S.
Sullivan
Bradley, L. Inkle Weaving.
   P. Bach, 614:Fall83-21
Bradley, M.Z. The Mists of Avalon.
   M. Quilligan, 441:30Jan83-11
Bradley, O.N. and C. Blair. A General's
Life.
   C. Barnett, 617(TLS):14Oct83-1116
   G.A. Craig, 453(NYRB):30Jun83-17
   D. Middleton, 441:20Feb83-4
Bradley, R. and N. Swartz. Possible
Worlds.*
   H.A. Lewis, 479(PhQ):Oct82-382
   D.E. Over, 518:Jan82-39
Bradley, S. - see Whitman, W.
Bradley, S.A.J. Anglo-Saxon Poetry.
   M. Godden, 617(TLS):8Jul83-736
Bradshaw, B. The Irish Constitutional
Revolution of the Sixteenth Century.
   J.M.W. Bean, 551(RenQ):Winter81-605
Bradsher, H.S. Afghanistan and the Soviet
Union.
   E. Mortimer, 453(NYRB):22Dec83-3
   M. Yapp, 617(TLS):4Nov83-1212
Bradstreet, A. The Complete Works of Anne
Bradstreet. (J.R. McElrath, Jr. and A.P.
Robb, eds)
   J.B. Buchanan, 165(EAL):Spring83-111
[continued]

[continuing]
   K.Z. Derounian, 568(SCN):Spring-
   Summer82-24
   E.S. Fussell, 27(AL):Mar82-123
Brady, J. The Craft of the Screenwriter.
   R. Hooley, 18:Mar82-77
Brady, J. Holy Wars.
   S. Ellin, 441:3Jul83-8
Brady, T.A., Jr. Ruling Class, Regime and
Reformation at Strassbourg, 1520-1555.
   D. Bitton, 551(RenQ):Spring81-109
Brady, V. A Crucible of Prophets.
   K. Gelder, 71(ALS):Oct82-531
Braegger, C. Das Visuelle und das Plas-
tische.*
   P. Stenberg, 564:Feb82-77
Braekman, W.L. The Treatise on Angling
on The Boke of St. Albans (1496).
   C.C. Morse, 589:Oct82-863
Braet, H. Deux lais féeriques bretons du
XIIIe siècle.
   S. Kay, 208(FS):Jan82-46
Bragg, M. Kingdom Come.*
   M. Thery, 189(EA):Jan-Mar82-101
Bragg, M. Land of the Lakes.
   N. Nicholson, 617(TLS):1Jul83-692
Bragg, M. Love and Glory.
   P. Kemp, 617(TLS):9Sep83-950
   K.C. O'Brien, 362:15Sep83-23
Braham, R.L. The Politics of Genocide.*
   J.S. Conway, 104(CASS):Summer82-300
   D. Stone, 287:Apr82-28
Brain, R. Art and Society in Africa.
   J. Maquet, 2(AfrA):Nov81-24
   F. Willett, 59:Jun82-227
Braithwaite, E., ed. Savacou 14/15.
   S. Brown, 493:Dec81-65
Bräkling-Gersuny, G. Orpheus, der Logos-
Träger.
   A. Hillach, 224(GRM):Band32Heft4-470
Bramble, F. Fools.
   J.K.L. Walker, 617(TLS):11Feb83-131
   442(NY):14Mar83-158
Brame, M.K. Base Generated Syntax.
Essays toward Realistic Syntax.
   G. Gazdar, 297(JL):Sep82-464
Brams, S.J. Biblical Games.*
   R. Polzin, 529(QQ):Spring82-227
Brancaforte, B. Guzmán de Alfarache.*
   J.A. Jones, 86(BHS):Apr82-152
Brancaforte, B. - see Alemán, M.
Brancaforte, B. and C.L. La primera tra-
ducción italiana del "Lazarillo de Tor-
mes" por Giulio Strozzi.*
   J-P. Leroy, 549(RLC):Jan-Mar82-107
Brancaforte, B., E. Mulvihill and R. Sán-
chez, eds. Homenaje a Antonio Sánchez
Barbudo.
   K. Schwartz, 238:May82-305
Branch, E.M. and R.H. Hirst, with H.E.
Smith - see Twain, M.
Brand, M., ed. The Nature of Causation.
   F. Jackson, 316:Jun82-470
Brand, M. Wild Freedom.
   J.D. Nesbitt, 649(WAL):Summer82-185
Brandauer, F.P. Tung Yüeh.
   R.M. Somers, 293(JASt):May82-572
Brandes, S. Metaphors of Masculinity, Sex
and Status in Andalusian Folklore.
   J.P. Leary, 650(WF):Jan82-67
Brandl, H. Persönlichkeitsidealismus und
Willenskult.
   H. Uecker, 52:Band16Heft3-291

Brandt, B., ed. Russistik in der DDR.
　P. Bruhn, 688(ZSP):Band43Heft1-217
Brandt, G.W., ed. British Television
　Drama.*
　P. Hollindale, 437:Spring82-200
　M. Lyons, 214:Vol 10No38-142
　E. Northey, 565:Vol23No2-36
Brandt, R., ed. John Locke: Symposium Wol-
　fenbüttel 1979.
　A. Morvan, 189(EA):Jul-Sep82-330
Brandt, R.B. A Theory of the Good and the
　Right.
　N. Daniels, 185:Jul83-772
　G. Harman, 519(PhS):Jul82-119
　D.L.S., 543:Dec81-367
　N.L. Sturgeon, 482(PhR):Jul82-389
　J-C. Wolf, 687:Apr-Jun81-307
Branford, J. A Dictionary of South Afri-
　can English.*
　J. Honey, 179(ES):Apr82-184
Brann, N.L. The Abbot Trithemius (1462-
　1516.)
　L.V.R., 568(SCN):Fall82-59
Brannen, J. and J. Collard. Marriages in
　Trouble.
　H. Rubinstein, 617(TLS):4Feb83-113
Brant, S. and E. Cullman. Small Folk.
　S. Pickering, 569(SR):Spring82-300
Branyan, L., N. French and J. Sandon.
　Worcester Blue and White Porcelain, 1751-
　1790.
　G. Wills, 39:Apr82-297
Brasch, C. Indirections.
　T. James, 364:Aug/Sep82-114
Brasch, J.D. and J. Sigman. Hemingway's
　Library.
　E.S. Fussell, 27(AL):Dec82-623
　S. Wertheim, 234:Fall82-81
Brasch, W.M. Black English and the Mass
　Media.
　D. Noonan-Wagner, 351(LL):Jun82-223
Braselmann, P.M.E. Konnotation, Verstehen,
　Stil.
　R. Martin, 553(RLiR):Jul-Dec82-424
Brassaï. The Artists of My Life.*
　J. Naughton, 362:6Jan83-22
Braswell, L.N. Western Manuscripts from
　Classical Antiquity to the Renaissance.
　R.P. Oliver, 121(CJ):Apr/May83-367
Bratchell, D.F. The Impact of Darwinism.
　R.O., 617(TLS):22Jul83-786
Brathwaite, E.K. Sun Poem.
　F. Adcock, 617(TLS):18Feb83-160
　S. Brown, 493:Jan83-59
　C. Hope, 364:Dec82/Jan83-106
Bratton, J.S. The Impact of Victorian
　Children's Fiction.
　G.E. Sadler, 445(NCF):Sep82-240
Braude, S.E. ESP and Psychokinesis.
　R.N. Giere, 482(PhR):Apr82-288
Braudel, F. Civilisation and Capitalism
　15th-18th Century. (Vol 2: The Wheels
　of Commerce.)
　N. Bliven, 442(NY):18Jul83-94
　J. Israel, 617(TLS):21Jan83-63
　P. Johnson, 362:10Feb83-23
　J. Spence, 441:10Jul83-1
Braun, E. and S. Macdonald. Revolution in
　Miniature.
　442(NY):25Apr83-156
Braun, T. - see Rosenthal-Schneider, I.

Braune, W. Gotische Grammatik. (19th ed)
　(E.A. Ebbinghaus, ed)
　A. Liberman, 215(GL):Summer82-121
Braunfels, W. Die Kunst im Heiligen
　Römischen Reich Deutscher Nation.*
　(Vol 1)
　H. Glaser, 471:Jan/Feb/Mar82-77
Braunfels, W. Die Kunst im Heiligen Römis-
　chen Reich Deutscher Nation.* (Vol 2)
　H. Glaser, 471:Oct/Nov/Dec82-354
Braunfels, W. Die Kunst im Heiligen Röm-
　ischen Reich Deutscher Nation. (Vol 3)
　H. Boockmann, 683:Band45Heft2-208
　H. Glaser, 471:Oct/Nov/Dec82-354
Braunthal, J. History of the Interna-
　tional, 1943-1968. (Vol 3)
　H. Gruber, 550(RusR):Apr82-211
Brautigan, R. So The Wind Won't Blow It
　All Away.*
　D. Montrose, 617(TLS):22Apr83-399
Bravo Ahuja, G. La Enseñanza del Español
　a los Indígenas Mexicanos.
　J.H. Hill, 269(IJAL):Apr82-238
de Bray, R.G.A. Guide to the Slavonic Lan-
　guages.* (Vol 1: Guide to the South
　Slavonic Languages.) (3rd ed)
　O. Frink, 399(MLJ):Spring82-106
　P. Herrity, 575(SEER):Jan82-91
　K.E. Naylor, 574(SEEJ):Spring82-126
　G. Schaarschmidt, 104(CASS):Spring82-
　113
de Bray, R.G.A. Guide to the Slavonic Lan-
　guages.* (Vol 2: Guide to the West
　Slavonic Languages.) (3rd ed)
　O. Frink, 399(MLJ):Spring82-106
　G. Schaarschmidt, 104(CASS):Spring82-
　113
　G. Stone, 575(SEER):Jan82-93
　C.E. Townsend, 574(SEEJ):Spring82-122
de Bray, R.G.A. Guide to the Slavonic Lan-
　guages.* (Vol 3: Guide to the East
　Slavonic Languages.) (3rd ed)
　O. Frink, 399(MLJ):Spring82-106
　G. Schaarschmidt, 104(CASS):Spring82-
　113
Brazeau, P. Parts of a World.
　R. Ellmann, 453(NYRB):24Nov83-16
　W. Pritchard, 441:20Nov83-3
Brazier, M. and S. Davies. Viva Macau!
　U. Roberts, 60:Jan-Feb82-139
Bream, F. The Vicar Done It.
　T.J. Binyon, 617(TLS):8Jul83-732
Breasted, M. I Shouldn't Be Telling You
　This.
　C. Schine, 441:19Jun83-12
Brecht, B. Briefe.* (G. Glaeser, ed)
　R. Speirs, 220(GL&L):Jul83-374
Brecht, B. Gedichte aus dem Nachlass.
　(H. Ramthun, ed)
　P. Brady, 617(TLS):27May83-550
Brecht, B. Poems 1913-1956.* (J. Willett
　and R. Manheim, with E. Fried, eds)
　T. Eagleton, 565:Vol23No2-42
Brecht, B. Short Stories, 1921-46. (J.
　Willett and R. Manheim, eds)
　442(NY):29Aug83-92
Brecht, M. and R.F. Paulus - see Hahn, P.M.
Bredsdorff, T. Tristans børn.
　T. Moi, 172(Edda):1982/4-257
Brée, G. Twentieth-Century French Litera-
　ture, 1920-1970.
　R. Buss, 617(TLS):16Dec83-1408
　J. Sturrock, 441:31Jul83-10

Breen, J.L. Listen for the Click.
 N. Callendar, 441:28Aug83-21
Breen, R. Made for TV.
 N. Callendar, 441:13Mar83-21
Breen, T.H. Puritans and Adventurers.*
 J.E. Crowley, 656(WMQ):Jul82-534
 J.K. Nelson, 579(SAQ):Winter82-116
Bréhier, E. Histoire de la Philosophie.
 J. Bernhardt, 542:Oct-Dec82-658
Breitenbürger, G. Metaphora.
 J. Villwock, 224(GRM):Band32Heft2-244
Breitman, E. Art and the Stage.
 S. Elchen, 108:Winter82-113
Brekle, H.E. - see Mertian, I.
Bremmer, J. The Early Greek Concept of
 the Soul.
 M. Schofield, 617(TLS):26Aug83-896
Brenan, G. Thoughts in a Dry Season.*
 R. Mason, 447(N&Q):Jun81-287
Brendle, O.J. The Visible Idea.
 R.R.R. Smith, 313:Vol72-198
Brendon, P. The Life and Death of the
 Press Barons.*
 R. Foster, 617(TLS):18Feb83-163
Brenkert, G.G. Marx's Ethics of Freedom.
 J. Gray, 617(TLS):30Dec83-1459
Brenman-Gibson, M. Clifford Odets.*
 J.E. Mack, 676(YR):Winter83-305
 C.C. Nash, 50(ArQ):Autumn82-268
 295(JML):Dec82-508
Brennan, C. Prose-Verse-Poster-Algebraic-
 Symbolico-Riddle Musicopoematographo-
 scope.
 L.J. Austin, 208(FS):Jul82-354
Brennan, J. The Original Thai Cookbook.
 W. and C. Cowen, 639(VQR):Spring82-68
Brennan, P. Zarkeen.
 M. Harry, 150(DR):Winter82/83-704
Brennecke, D. Strindberg und Ernst Brause-
 wetter.
 H. Uecker, 52:Band16Heft3-291
Brenner, J. Histoire de la littérature
 française de 1940 à nos jours.
 G. Cesbron, 356(LR):May82-178
Brentano, C. and S. Mereau. Lebe der
 Liebe und liebe das Leben. (D. von Gers-
 dorff, ed)
 K. Feilchenfeldt, 680(ZDP):Band101-
 Heft4-596
Brentano, F. The Theory of Categories.*
 J. Howarth, 323:Oct82-307
Brereton, G.F. and J.M. Ferrier - see
 "Le Menagier de Paris"
Bresc-Bautier, G. Artistes, Patriciens et
 Confréries.
 H. Belting, 683:Band45Heft4-423
da Brescia, B. - see under Bonaventura da
 Brescia
Breslauer, G.W. Khrushchev and Brezhnev
 as Leaders.
 A. Brown, 617(TLS):1Apr83-333
Bresler, F. The Mystery of Georges
 Simenon.
 D. Pryce-Jones, 617(TLS):1Apr83-316
 J. Symons, 441:30Oct83-12
Breslin, T.A. China, American Catholicism,
 and the Missionary.
 S.W. Barnett, 293(JASt):Feb82-311
Bretensky, D.F., E.A. Hovanec and A.N.
 Skomra, comps. Patch/Work Voices.
 R. Conrad, 650(WF):Jan82-71

Brett, P., ed. Benjamin Britten: "Peter
 Grimes."
 P. Driver, 617(TLS):15Jul83-751
Brett, R.L., ed. Andrew Marvell.*
 P. Burdon, 447(N&Q):Feb81-75
 P. Cullen, 551(RenQ):Winter81-629
Brett, S. Murder in the Title.
 T.J. Binyon, 617(TLS):8Jul83-732
 N. Callendar, 441:13Nov83-34
 442(NY):12Sep83-158
Brettell, R. and C. Lloyd. A Catalogue of
 Drawings by Camille Pissarro in the
 Ashmolean Museum, Oxford.
 R. Thomson, 90:Mar82-163
Brettschneider, W. Die Parabel vom verlor-
 enen Sohn.
 N. Oellers, 52:Band16Heft2-187
Brettschneider, W. Zorn und Trauer.
 A. Stephan, 406:Fall82-347
Bretz, G. Die mundartliche Frachsprache
 der Spinnerei und Weberei in Heltau, Sie-
 benbürgen, in ihren räumlichen, zeit-
 lichen und sachlichen Bezügen.
 K. Manherz, 685(ZDL):2/1982-251
Bretz, M.L. La evolución novelística de
 Pío Baroja.*
 P. Smith, 240(HR):Winter82-107
Breu, W. Semantische Untersuchungen zum
 Verbalaspekt im Russischen.
 F.E. Knowles, 575(SEER):Jan82-95
Breuer, D. Oberdeutsche Literatur 1565-
 1650.
 M.R. Sperberg-McQueen, 406:Summer82-
 198
Breuer, H. Vorgeschichte des Fortschritts.
 H. Zander, 490:Band13Heft3/4-360
Breunig, L.C. and others. Forme et fond.*
 (2nd ed)
 D.C. Spinelli, 399(MLJ):Summer82-213
Brewer, A.M., ed. Dictionaries, Encyclope-
 dias, and other Word-Related Books.
 (Vol 1) (3rd ed)
 K.B. Harder, 424:Jun82-123
Brewer, D. Symbolic Stories.*
 C. Gauvin, 189(EA):Oct-Dec82-439
 R.W. Hanning, 589:Oct82-864
 C. Lindahl, 292(JAF):Oct-Dec82-469
 B. White, 203:Vol93No2-241
Brewer, K. Collected Poems of Mongrel.
 S. Hamill, 649(WAL):Winter83-367
Bricke, J. Hume's Philosophy of Mind.*
 E. Craig, 53(AGP):Band64Heft3-329
 A. Flew, 393(Mind):Jan82-128
 C. Thompson, 518:Jul82-159
Briçonnet, G. and Marguerite d'Angoulême.
 Correspondance (1521-1524).* (Vol 2)
 (C. Martineau and M. Veissière, with H.
 Heller, eds)
 K.M. Hall, 208(FS):Apr82-195
 P.E. Hughes, 551(RenQ):Spring81-107
Bridenbaugh, C. Early Americans.
 E.G. Evans, 656(WMQ):Jul82-536
Bridges, D.S. Constructive Functional
 Analysis.
 F. Richman, 316:Sep82-703
Bridgman, R. Dark Thoreau.
 P.F. Gura, 432(NEQ):Sep82-448
 M. Meyer, 27(AL):Dec82-612
Bridson, G.D.R., V.C. Phillips and A.P.
 Harvey, comps. Natural History Manu-
 script Resources in the British Isles.
 S. Raphael, 325:Oct82-128

46

Broeckx, J.L. Contemporary Views on Musical Style and Aesthetics.
G.D.P., 412:Aug-Nov81-293

Brogan, T.V.F. English Versification, 1570-1980.
J.W. Page, 88:Fall82-125
G.T. Wright, 113:Spring82-73

Broide, E. Chekhov — myslitel'-khudoz-hnik.*
R. Lindheim, 104(CASS):Spring82-134

Brokensha, D.W., D.M. Warren and O. Werner, eds. Indigenous Knowledge Systems and Development.
M. Etherton, 69:Vol51No4-863

Brome, V. Ernest Jones.
M. Jones, 362:17Feb83-21
P. Roazen, 617(TLS):6May83-451

Bronk, W. Life Supports.
S.F. Morse, 491:Nov82-105
639(VQR):Spring82-59

Bronsen, D., ed. Jews and Germans from 1860 to 1933.
R. Kauf, 406:Spring82-87

Brontë, A. The Poems of Anne Brontë.* (E. Chitham, ed)
J.R. Watson, 677(YES):Vol 12-326

Brontë, C. Ashworth. (M.J. Monahan, ed)
R. Barnard, 179(ES):Apr82-178

Brontë, C. Shirley.* (H. Rosengarten and M. Smith, eds)
D. Hewitt, 447(N&Q):Aug81-348

Brontë, C. Something about Arthur. (C. Alexander, ed and trans)
R.D. Haynes, 67:Nov82-203

Brook, G.L. Books and Book-collecting.
517(PBSA):Vol76No4-508

Brook, G.L. and R.F. Leslie - see Layamon

Brook, S., ed. The Oxford Book of Dreams.
R. Dinnage, 617(TLS):7Oct83-1085
S. Spender, 362:13Oct83-26
B.F. Williamson, 441:18Dec83-14
442(NY):26Dec83-72

Brook-Shepherd, G. November 1918.*
639(VQR):Summer82-85

Brooke, C.N.L. and R.A.B. Mynors - see Map, W.

Brooke, J. The Image of a Drawn Sword.
V. Cunningham, 617(TLS):4Feb83-97
J. Mellors, 364:Mar83-106

Brooke, N. Horrid Laughter in Jacobean Tragedy.*
C. Asp, 568(SCN):Spring-Summer82-6

Brooke-Rose, C. A Rhetoric of the Unreal.
G.K. Wolfe, 561(SFS):Nov82-330

Brooker, B. Sounds Assembling. (B. Sproxton, ed)
S. Grace, 102(CanL):Spring82-110

Brooker, P. A Student's Guide to the Selected Poems of Ezra Pound.
W. Harmon, 569(SR):Spring82-279

Brookner, A. Jacques-Louis David.*
P. Conrad, 31(ASch):Spring82-282
T. Crow, 59:Mar82-109

Brookner, A. Look at Me.
M. Cantwell, 441:22May83-14
A. Duchêne, 627(TLS):25Mar83-289
J. Mellors, 362:14Apr83-32
A. Roston, 231:Jul83-75

Brooks, C. William Faulkner.*
D. Meindl, 38:Band100Heft1/2-236
J. Newman, 161(DUJ):Jun82-319

Brooks, C. William Faulkner: First Encounters.
B.F. Williamson, 441:13Nov83-19

Brooks, H.A., ed. Writings on Wright.
D. Hoffman, 576:Oct82-245
J.V. Turano, 16:Winter82-78

Brooks, H.F. - see Shakespeare, W.

Brooks, L. Lulu in Hollywood.*
W.K. Everson, 200:Aug-Sep82-441
G. Kaufman, 362:6Oct83-23
A. Ross, 364:Oct82-4
W. Rothman, 18:Oct82-66

Brooks, P. Speaking for Nature.*
C. Beyers, 649(WAL):Spring82-88

Brooks, P.N., ed. Seven-Headed Luther.
H.A. Oberman, 617(TLS):18Nov83-1286

Brophy, B. The Prince and the Wild Geese.
G. Annan, 617(TLS):10Jun83-596
D.J. Enright, 362:24Feb83-24

Brotherston, G. The Emergence of the Latin American Novel.
R.A. Young, 107(CRCL):Dec81-565

Broudy, H. Soundings.
D. Barbour, 648(WCR):Jun82-33

Broughton, G. and others. Teaching English as a Foreign Language.*
H. Bennemann, 682(ZPSK):Band34Heft3-383

Broughton, P.R., ed. The Art of Walker Percy.*
J.W. Tuttleton, 677(YES):Vol 12-362

Broun, H. Odditorium.
S. Isaacs, 441:27Mar83-14

Broun, H.H. Whose Little Boy Are You?
P-L. Adams, 61:Jul83-108
B. Shulgasser, 441:5Jun83-16
442(NY):13Jun83-131

Brower, K. A Song for Satawal.
C. McGregor, 441:8May83-14

Brown, A. By Green Mountain.*
A. Todkill, 526:Summer82-123

Brown, A. Sketches from Life.
L. Rogers, 102(CanL):Summer82-156

Brown, A. and others - see "The Cambridge Encyclopedia of Russia and the Soviet Union"

Brown, A. and F.N. Cheney - see Tate, A.

Brown, A. and M. Kaser, eds. Soviet Policy for the 1980s.
K. Dawisha, 617(TLS):30Sep83-1062

Brown, A.C. - see under Cave Brown, A.

Brown, A.C. and C.B. MacDonald - see under Cave Brown, A. and C.B. MacDonald

Brown, C. Days Without Weather.
D. Bradley, 441:17Apr83-26

Brown, C. Carel Fabritius.*
U. Hoff, 39:Jun82-510
W. Liedtke, 90:May82-303
R. Ruurs, 600:Vol 12No4-263

Brown, C. Van Dyck.
M. Jordan, 441:17Apr83-9
O. Millard, 617(TLS):25Mar83-308

Brown, C. and L. Cunliffe. The Book of Royal Lists.*
J.K. Davison, 441:8May83-22

Brown, C.C. - see Townshend, A.

Brown, D. Killdeer Mountain.
J. Coleman, 441:5Jun83-15

Brown, D. Walter Scott and the Historical Imagination.*
J.H. Raleigh, 677(YES):Vol 12-289

Brown, D. Tchaikovsky. (Vol 1)
H.Z., 412:Aug-Nov81-290

Brown, D. Tchaikovsky.* (Vol 2: The Crisis Years, 1874-1878.)
　H. Cole, 362:5May83-26
　442(NY):25Apr83-154
Brown, D.A. Raphael and America.
　D.H. Wright, 453(NYRB):2Jun83-6
Brown, E.K. and J.E. Miller. Syntax.*
　P. Baldi, 215(GL):Winter82-267
　G.S. Nathan, 350:Jun83-438
Brown, F. Theater and Revolution.*
　V. Brown, 31(ASch):Summer82-423
Brown, G., K.L. Currie and J. Kenworthy. Questions of Intonation.*
　A. Crompton, 297(JL):Sep82-419
Brown, G.M. - see under Mackay Brown, G.
Brown, H. Thinking About National Security.
　R. Halloran, 441:7Aug83-11
　S. Hoffmann, 453(NYRB):29Sep83-48
Brown, J. and J.H. Elliott. A Palace for a King.* (Spanish title: Un Palacio para el Rey.)
　P. Ilie, 238:Mar82-141
　D. Linstrum, 324:Jan83-106
　V. Tovar Martín, 48:Jul-Sep82-319
　M.C. Volk, 54:Mar82-155
Brown, J.E. The Spiritual Legacy of the American Indian.
　W. Least Heat Moon, 441:8May83-14
　C. Vecsey, 469:Vol8No2-108
Brown, J.L. Valery Larbaud.
　P. McCarthy, 207(FR):May83-950
　P. Mahillon, 450(NRF):Mar82-120
Brown, J.M. Dickens.*
　G.H. Ford, 445(NCF):Sep82-214
　N. Russell, 155:Autumn82-169
Brown, J.R. Discovering Shakespeare.*
　S. Barnet, 551(RenQ):Winter82-660
Brown, J.R. Shakespeare and his Theatre.
　S. Wells, 157:Autumn82-45
Brown, J.R., ed. Shakespeare: "Much Ado About Nothing" and "As You Like It:" A Casebook.
　K. Muir, 677(YES):Vol 12-258
Brown, J.S.H. Strangers in Blood.
　R. Cook, 656(WMQ):Jan82-240
Brown, L. A Catalogue of British Historical Medals 1760-1960.* (Vol 1)
　G. Wills, 39:Nov82-349
Brown, L. English Dramatic Form, 1660-1760.*
　J. Hamard, 189(EA):Oct-Dec82-466
　C. Hill, 366:Spring82-126
　J.B. Kern, 173(ECS):Spring83-324
　J.S. Malek, 141:Spring82-183
　J. Milhous, 301(JEGP):Oct82-567
　566:Autumn82-54
Brown, M. The Shape of German Romanticism.*
　J. Fetzer, 406:Fall82-356
　J. Neubauer, 173(ECS):Spring83-356
Brown, M.E. Double Lyric.*
　F. Chappell, 579(SAQ):Summer82-348
Brown, M.J.E. The New Grove Schubert.
　A. Blackwood, 617(TLS):9Sep83-954
Brown, P. Country and Eastern.
　G. Catalano, 381:Oct81-349
Brown, P. Indian Painting Under the Mughals A.D. 1550 to A.D. 1750.
　M.W. Meister, 318(JAOS):Oct-Dec81-475
Brown, P. and S. Gaines. The Love You Make.
　J. Stokes, 617(TLS):2Dec83-1356

Brown, P.G. and H. Shue, eds. Boundaries.
　B.B., 185:Oct82-220
Brown, R.M. The Ceramics of South-East Asia.
　L. Craighill, 318(JAOS):Jul-Sep81-395
Brown, R.M. Sudden Death.
　E. Jakab, 441:19Jun83-12
Brown, S. The Facts of Power.
　442(NY):3Oct83-129
Brown, S.A. The Collected Poems of Sterling A. Brown.* (M.S. Harper, ed)
　E. Hirsch, 459:Spring81-93
Brown, T. Amusements Serious and Comical.
　566:Autumn82-55
Brown, T. The Fate of the Dead.*
　P. Horden, 447(N&Q):Feb81-70
Brown, T. Life as a Party.
　I. Moncreiffe, 362:27Oct83-35
Brown, T.H. Thèmes et Discussions.
　J. Spinale, 207(FR):Feb83-526
Brown, V.P. and L. Owens. Toting the Lead Row.
　M. McPherson, 9(AlaR):Apr82-147
Brown, W., Jr. - see Genet, E.C.C.
Brown, W.E. A History of Eighteenth Century Russian Literature.
　K.A. Papmehl, 104(CASS):Spring82-124
Brown, W.E. A History of Seventeenth Century Russian Literature.*
　J.V. Haney, 104(CASS):Spring82-123
Brown, W.N. India and Indology. (R. Rocher, ed)
　M.B. Emeneau, 318(JAOS):Apr-Jun81-236
　J.W. de Jong, 259(IIJ):Apr80-153
　F. Staal, 293(JASt):Feb82-269
Browne, E.M., with H. Browne. Two in One.
　A. Emmet, 611(TN):Vol36No3-135
Browne, G.L. Baltimore in the Nation, 1789-1861.*
　P.F. Lachance, 106:Spring82-53
Browne, G.M., ed. Michigan Coptic Texts.*
　O. Wintermute, 318(JAOS):Oct-Dec81-458
Browne, P.C. The Land of Look Behind.
　N. Besner, 102(CanL):Winter81-131
Browne, R.B. The Alabama Folk Lyric.
　B. Feintuch, 650(WF):Jul82-232
Brownell, B.A. and D.R. Goldfield, eds. The City in Southern History.
　P.F. Lachance, 106:Spring82-53
Browning, E.B. The Letters of Elizabeth Barrett Browning to Mary Russell Mitford 1836-1854. (M.B. Raymond and M.R. Sullivan, eds)
　B. Hardy, 617(TLS):1Jul83-688
Browning, E.B. A Variorum Edition of Elizabeth Barrett Browning's "Sonnets from the Portuguese." (M.W. Dow, ed)
　D. Karlin, 541(RES):Aug82-351
Browning, R. The Poems.* (J. Pettigrew, with T.J. Collins, eds)
　P. Davison, 354:Sep82-347
　M. Hicks, 148:Winter82-89
　W. Scammell, 364:Feb83-98
　529(QQ):Autumn82-690
Browning, R. Political and Constitutional Ideas of the Court Whigs.
　L. Colley, 617(TLS):21Jan83-64
Browning, R. The Ring and the Book. (R.D. Altick, ed)
　M. Hicks, 148:Winter82-89

49

Browning, R. and F. Furnivall. Browning's
Trumpeter.* (W.S. Peterson, ed)
 P. Drew, 541(RES):May82-218
 I. Jack, 447(N&Q):Dec81-564
Brownlee, M.S. The Poetics of Literary
Theory.
 F.L. Yudin, 304(JHP):Spring82-247
Brownlow, K. Napoleon: Abel Gance's
Classic Film.
 D. Coward, 617(TLS):9Sep83-957
 G. Kaufman, 362:6Oct83-23
 B. Shulgasser, 441:13Nov83-20
Brownstein, O.L. and D.M. Daubert. Ana-
lytical Sourcebook of Concepts in Dra-
matic Theory.
 M. Carlson, 612(ThS):May82-113
Brownstein, R. and N. Easton. Reagan's
Ruling Class.
 J. Fallows, 453(NYRB):27Oct83-68
Brownstein, R.M. Becoming a Heroine.*
 A. Barton, 453(NYRB):21Jul83-30
Bruandet, P. Painting on Silk.
 P. Bach, 614:Winter83-20
Bruccoli, M.J. James Gould Cozzens.
 J.W. Aldridge, 441:3Jul83-4
Bruccoli, M.J. Some Sort of Epic Gran-
deur.*
 J.A. Glusman, 639(VQR):Summer82-537
 M. Mudrick, 249(HudR):Summer82-290
 L.W. Wagner, 27(AL):May82-304
 R.P. Weeks, 395(MFS):Summer82-295
 295(JML):Dec82-446
Bruccoli, M.J. - see Sayre, J. and M.
Faulkner
Bruccoli, M.J. and R. Layman - see "Fitz-
gerald/Hemingway Annual, 1979"
Bruce-Novoa, J.D. Chicano Authors.
 D. Schmidt, 152(UDQ):Fal181-118
 C. Tatum, 238:Dec82-668
"Bruckmanns Lexikon der Münchner Kunst Mün-
chner Maler im 19. Jahrhundert." (Vols
1 and 2) (H. Ludwig and others, comps)
 E. Ruhmer, 471:Oct/Nov/Dec82-354
Brückner, H. Zum Beweisverfahren Śaṃkaras.
 J.W. de Jong, 259(IIJ):Apr82-158
Bruckner, M.T. Narrative Invention in the
Twelfth-Century French Romance.*
 G.M. Cropp, 67:Nov82-202
 E. Finazzi Agrò, 547(RF):Band94Heft1-
 106
"Bruckner-Jahrbuch 1980." (F. Grasberger,
ed)
 P. Banks, 410(M&L):Jul/Oct81-398
Bruderer, H.E. Handbuch der maschinellen
und maschinengestüzten Sprachübersetzung.
 G.F. Meier, 682(ZPSK):Band35Heft5-574
Bruegmann, R. Benicia.
 R. Winter, 576:Oct82-249
Brugière, B. L'univers imaginaire de
Robert Browning.*
 P. Drew, 541(RES):May82-218
Bruhn, P. and H. Glade. Heinrich Böll in
der Sowjetunion (1952-1979).
 W. Busch, 688(ZSP):Band43Heft1-223
 M. Kuxdorf, 221(GQ):Mar82-284
Bruhns, H. Caesar und die römische Ober-
schicht in den Jahren 49-44 v. Chr.*
 E.J. Jonkers, 394:Vol35fasc1/2-199
Bruman, H.J. and C.W. Meighan. Early
California.
 J. Béranger, 189(EA):Jul-Sep82-357

Brumbaugh, R.S. The Philosophers of
Greece.
 A. Reix, 542:Apr-Jun82-457
Brumberg, A., ed. Poland.
 M. Bayles, 441:24Jul83-16
 T. Garton Ash, 617(TLS):4Nov83-1229
 M. Malia, 453(NYRB):29Sep83-18
Brumberg, J.J. Mission for Life.
 L.N. Allen, 9(AlaR):Jan82-70
Brumble, H.D., 3d. An Annotated Bibliogra-
phy of American Indian and Eskimo Autobi-
ographies.
 C.A. Milner 2d, 649(WAL):Spring82-90
Brumfield, W.C. Gold in Azure.
 J.H. Billington, 617(TLS):9Dec83-1369
 P. Goldberger, 441:11Dec83-37
Brumm, U. Geschichte und Wildnis in der
amerikanischen Literatur.
 H. Friedl, 72:Band218Heft1-184
Brummack, J. Satirische Dichtung.
 B. Hannemann, 406:Summer82-206
Brummack, J. - see Heine, H.
Brun, J. Les masques du désir.
 G. Hottois, 540(RIPh):Vol36fasc3-378
 A. Reix, 542:Oct-Dec82-659
Brun, V., ed and trans. Sug, the Trick-
ster Who Fooled the Monk.
 D.K. Swearer, 318(JAOS):Oct-Dec81-496
Bruneau, J. - see Flaubert, G.
Bruneau, T.C. The Church in Brazil.
 D.A. Chalmers, 263(RIB):Vol132No3/4-369
Brunel, G., ed. Piranèse et les français.
 R. Middleton, 576:Dec82-333
Brunel, G. and P. Arizzoli, eds. Piranèse
et les français 1740-1790.
 R. Middleton, 576:Dec82-333
"Filippo Brunelleschi."
 C. Elam, 59:Dec82-489
Brunet, E. Le Vocabulaire de Jean Girau-
doux.
 A.G. Raymond, 399(MLJ):Spring82-85
Brunet, E. Le vocabulaire français de
1789 à nos jours, d'après les données du
Trésor de la Langue Française.
 A. Schneider, 553(RLiR):Jul-Dec82-461
Brunkhorst, M. Tradition und Transforma-
tion.*
 T. Gelzer, 490:Band13Heft1/2-163
 W. Riehle, 602:Vol 13No1-202
 W. Zacharasiewicz, 52:Band16Heft2-205
 F. Zaic, 72:Band218Heft2-439
Brunner, H., U. Müller and F.V. Spechtler
- see Walther von der Vogelweide
Brunner, J. The Crucible of Time.
 G. Jonas, 441:6Nov83-38
Brunner, K. Oppositionelle Gruppen im
Karolingerreich.
 T.F.X. Noble, 589:Apr82-358
Brunngraber, R. Karl und das 20. Jahr-
hundert.
 R.C. Holub, 406:Spring82-72
Bruns, A. Übersetzung als Rezeption.
 S.H. Rossel, 406:Summer82-209
 H. Uecker, 52:Band16Heft3-291
Brunsdale, M.M. The German Effect on D.H.
Lawrence and His Works 1885-1912.
 R. Gray, 402(MLR):Oct82-996
Brunvand, J.H. The Vanishing Hitchhiker.*
 G.A. Fine, 650(WF):Apr82-156
Bruschi, A. Bramante.*
 M. Licht, 576:May82-159

Bruschi, A. and others. Scritti rinascimentali di architettura.
R.J. Betts, 576:Mar82-61
Brush, S.G. The Kind of Motion We Call Heat.
P. Clark, 84:Jun82-165
Brushwood, J.S. Genteel Barbarism.
F.W. Murray, 263(RIB):Vol132No3/4-370
Bruss, E.W. Beautiful Theories.
T. Eagleton, 617(TLS):27May83-546
Bruss, P. Victims.
D.J. Cahill, 659(ConL):Fall83-395
S. Fogel, 395(MFS):Summer82-306
Brutus, É.J. Vindiciae contra tyrannos.*
(A. Jouanna and others, eds)
F.M. Higman, 208(FS):Jan82-59
de Bruyn, L. Woman and the Devil in Sixteenth-Century Literature.*
P. Rackin, 551(RenQ):Winter81-609
Bruzina, R. and B. Wilshire, eds. Crosscurrents in Phenomenology.
A. Reix, 542:Jan-Mar82-60
Bryan, C.D.B. Beautiful Women; Ugly Scenes.
A. Adams, 441:28Aug83-10
J. Atlas, 61:Aug83-96
J. Wolcott, 231:Aug83-62
Bryan, S. Salt Air.
A. Williamson, 441:13Nov83-26
Bryant, W.C. The Letters of William Cullen Bryant. (Vol 3) (W.C. Bryant 2d and T.G. Voss, eds)
D.A. Ringe, 27(AL):Oct82-446
Bryce, J.C. - see Smith, A.
Bryer, J.R. - see O'Neill, E.
Brym, R.J. and R.J. Sacouman, eds. Underdevelopment and Social Movements in Atlantic Canada.
J. Fingard, 150(DR):Summer82-341
Bryson, J. Whoring Around.
J. Mellors, 364:Feb83-112
Bryson, N. Vision and Painting.
R. Arnheim, 617(TLS):7Oct83-1080
Bryson, N. Word and Image.
M. Hobson, 208(FS):Oct82-474
B. Scott, 39:Jul82-66
R. Wollheim, 617(TLS):13May83-477
Bryusov, V. The Diary of Valery Bryusov (1893-1905) with Reminiscences by V.F. Khodasevich and Marina Tsetaeva.* (J.D. Grossman, ed and trans)
J. Graffy, 575(SEER):Jul82-451
A. Pyman, 402(MLR):Apr82-506
Brzezina, M. Języki mniejszości narodowych w tekstach literackich i folklorystycznych. (Vol 1)
N.G. Jacobs, 497(PolR):Vol27No3/4-234
Brzezinski, Z. Power and Principle.
S. Hoffmann, 453(NYRB):29Sep83-48
F. Lewis, 441:17Apr83-3
442(NY):18Apr83-152
Buah, F.K. A History of Ghana.
R. Rathbone, 69:Vol52No2-123
Buber, M. Judaïsme.
A. Reix, 542:Oct-Dec82-660
"Buch und Sammler."
E. Mass, 547(RF):Band93Heft3/4-456
Buchan, J. Castle Gay.
P. Craig, 617(TLS):19Aug83-890
Buchan, J. Sick Heart River.
G.W., 102(CanL):Autumn82-167
Buchan, W. John Buchan.*
K. Hillier, 364:Aug/Sep82-127

Buchan, W. - see Masefield, J.
Buchanan, A.E. Marx and Justice.
A.L., 185:Apr83-639
Buchanan, J.M. What Should Economists Do?
E.J.G., 185:Jan83-427
Bucher, M. and others, eds. Manifeste und Dokumente zur deutschen Literatur — Realismus und Grundzeit.
H. Steinecke, 680(ZDP):Band101Heft4-603
Buchholz, H.G. and J. Wiesner. Kriegswesen.
J.M. Hemelrijk, 394:Vol35fasc1/2-158
Buchholz, P. Vorzeitkunde.*
H.R.E. Davidson, 203:Vol193No1-121
P. Schach, 589:Oct82-868
Buchloh, P.G. and J.P. Becker, eds. Der Detektiverzählung auf der Spur.
B. Schulte-Middelich, 38:Band100 Heft1/2-257
Büchner, G. Woyzeck. (G. Schmid, ed)
R. Grimm, 406:Fall82-360
H. Wetzel, 564:Sep82-222
Büchner, K. Römische Dichtung.
J. Soubiran, 555:Vol56fasc1-158
Buck, A. Forschungen zur romanischen Barockliteratur.
W. Floeck, 535(RHL):Sep-Dec82-875
W. Theile, 547(RF):Band93Heft1/2-238
Buck, G. The History of King Richard the Third (1619).* (A.N. Kincaid, ed)
D.M. Loades, 161(DUJ):Jun82-281
Buck, H. At the Window.
A. Stevenson, 617(TLS):15Jul83-757
Buck, K., E.G. Fichtner and K.M. Helmers, eds. Teaching Business and Technical German.
A. Galt, 399(MLJ):Autumn82-336
Buck, M. Politics, Finance and the Church in the Reign of Edward II.
E. Miller, 617(TLS):1Jul83-704
Buck, P. American Science and Modern China 1876-1936.
N. Sivin, 293(JASt):Nov81-98
Buck, R.J. A History of Boeotia.*
B. Jordan, 122:Apr82-155
Buck-Morss, S. The Origin of Negative Dialectics.
L.J. Ray, 488:Sep82-340
Buckland, P. A History of Northern Ireland.
S. Cronin, 174(Éire):Summer82-147
Buckle, R. The Most Upsetting Woman.
V. Powell, 39:Apr82-296
Buckler, J. The Theban Hegemony, 371-362 B.C.
J.T. Roberts, 24:Spring82-107
A. Schachter, 487:Autumn82-289
Buckler, W.E. On the Poetry of Matthew Arnold.
M. Allott, 617(TLS):6May83-468
Buckler, W.E. The Victorian Imagination.*
S. Lavabre, 189(EA):Jul-Sep82-341
I. Milligan, 506(PSt):Dec82-344
P. Zietlow, 637(VS):Winter82-242
Buckley, C. Steaming to Bamboola.*
J. Hanley, 364:Dec82/Jan83-140
Buckley, R. Occupation Diplomacy.
C. Thorne, 617(TLS):11Feb83-138
Buckley, W.F., Jr. Overdrive.
P-L. Adams, 61:Sep83-124
J.G. Dunne, 453(NYRB):13Oct83-20

[continued]

Buckley, W.F., Jr. Overdrive. [continuing]
  N. Ephron, 441:7Aug83-7
  R. Koenig, 231:Oct83-72
Bucknall, B.J. Ursula K. Le Guin.
  M.A., 561(SFS):Jul82-223
Budbill, D. Pulp Cutters' Nativity.
  D. Hall, 271:Winter82-170
Budd, J., comp. Eight Scandinavian Novel-
  ists.
  A. Jørgensen, 172(Edda):1982/6-375
Budd, L.J., E.H. Cady and C.L. Anderson,
  eds. Toward a New American Literary His-
  tory.
  K. Carabine, 447(N&Q):Oct81-463
Buddecke, W. and H. Fuhrmann. Das deutsch-
  sprachige Drama seit 1945.
  H.A. Pausch, 564:May82-153
Budden, J. The Operas of Verdi.* (Vol 3)
  W. Dean, 410(M&L):Jan/Apr82-91
  J.A. Hepokoski, 317:Fall82-577
Buel, R., Jr. Dear Liberty.
  J.R. Daniell, 432(NEQ):Mar82-128
  L.R. Gerlach, 656(WMQ):Apr82-375
Buetin, W. and others - see under Beutin,
  W. and others
Bufalino, G. L'amaro miele.
  K. Bosley, 617(TLS):14Oct83-1136
Büff, R. Ruelle und Realität.
  C. Schlumbohm, 547(RF):Band94Heft1-113
Buford, B. - see "Granta 7"
Buford, B. - see "Granta 8: Dirty Realism"
Buican, D. L'éternel retour de Lyssenko.
  A. Tétry, 192(EP):Jan-Mar81-88
"The Buildings of Biloxi: An Architectural
  Survey."
  D.J. Hibbard, 658:Spring82-90
Buisson, L. Der Bildstein Ardre VIII auf
  Gotland.
  G.W. Weber, 589:Apr82-359
van Buitenen, J.A.B. - see "The Mahābhā-
  rata"
Bukdahl, E.M. Diderot, critique d'art.*
  (Vol 1)
  J. Chouillet, 535(RHL):Jan-Feb82-118
  P. Conisbee, 90:Jul82-455
  G. May, 54:Jun82-342
  R. Wrigley, 59:Sep82-358
Bukovsky, V. To Build a Castle.
  A. Yanov, 550(RusR):Jan82-82
Bulciolu, M.T. L'École saint-simonienne
  et la femme.*
  F. Daenens, 356(LR):May82-169
Bulhof, I.N. Wilhelm Dilthey.
  T. Plantinga, 319:Apr83-257
Bull, G. Venice.
  J.G. Links, 39:Jul82-67
Bull, G. - see Vasari, G.
Bullard, M.M. Filippo Strozzi and the
  Medici.
  P. Partner, 551(RenQ):Spring82-86
Buller, E. Indigenous Performing and
  Ceremonial Arts in Canada.
  A. Wagner, 108:Spring82-211
"Bulletin de l'Institut de Phonétique de
  Grenoble." (Vols 4-6)
  G.F. Meier, 682(ZPSK):Band34Heft3-363
Bullion, J.L. A Great and Necessary
  Measure.
  P.D.G. Thomas, 617(TLS):27May83-551
Bullitt, O.H. Phoenicia and Carthage.
  L. Vann, 121(CJ):Dec82/Jan83-163

Bullock, A. Ernest Bevin: Foreign Secre-
  tary, 1945-1951.
  J. Grigg, 362:10Nov83-26
  K.O. Morgan, 617(TLS):11Nov83-1243
Bullock, A. and R.B. Woodings, eds. The
  Fontana Biographical Companion to Modern
  Thought.
  S. Collini, 617(TLS):9Dec83-1367
  E. Griffiths, 362:3Nov83-26
Bullock, C. and D. Peck, comps. Guide to
  Marxist Literary Criticism.
  A. Wald, 42(AR):Spring82-241
Bulmahn, H. Adolf Glassbrenner.
  C.V. Miller, 406:Spring82-106
Bülow, E. and P. Schmitter, eds. Inte-
  grale Linguistik.*
  G.F. Meier, 682(ZPSK):Band35Heft3-344
Bultmann, R. Primitive Christianity in
  its Contemporary Setting.
  M.T., 617(TLS):21Oct83-1171
Bulychev, K. Gusliar Wonders.
  P-L. Adams, 61:Jul83-109
  442(NY):18Jul83-96
Bumke, J. Mäzene im Mittelalter.*
  D.H. Green, 402(MLR):Apr82-479
  C.S. Jaeger, 221(GQ):Jan82-111
  W. Störmer, 72:Band218Heft1-156
Bump, J. Gerard Manley Hopkins.
  M.D. Moore, 150(DR):Winter82/83-709
Bumsted, J.M. The People's Clearance 1770-
  1825.
  W.R. Brock, 617(TLS):3Jun83-569
Bunce, V. Do New Leaders Make a Differ-
  ence?
  G.W. Breslauer, 550(RusR):Oct82-502
Bunge, M. The Mind-Body Problem.*
  G. Berger, 167:May82-399
Bunge, M. Scientific Materialism.
  D.M. Armstrong, 63:Dec82-373
Bunge, M. Treatise on Basic Philosophy.
  (Vol 4)
  J.E., 543:Mar82-595
Bungert, H., ed. Die amerikanische Lit-
  eratur der Gegenwart.*
  M. Schulze, 72:Band218Heft2-448
Bünker, J.R. Schwänke, Sagen und Märchen
  in heanzischer Mundart. (K. Haiding, ed)
  E. Moser-Rath, 196:Band23Heft3/4-308
Bunnens, G. L'expansion phénicienne en
  Méditerranée.
  J. Raison, 555:Vol55fasc2-328
Buñuel, L., with J-C. Carrière. My Last
  Sigh. (French title: Mon Dernier Sou-
  pir.)
  J. Kirkup, 364:Nov82-64
  P. Schjeldahl, 441:13Nov83-10
  M. Wood, 453(NYRB):10Nov83-6
Bunyan, J. John Bunyan: The Poems. (G.
  Midgley, ed)
  E.B., 189(EA):Apr-Jun82-238
  P. Hammond, 541(RES):Nov82-470
  N.H. Keeble, 447(N&Q):Aug81-339
Bunyan, J. The Holy War.* (R. Sharrock
  and J.F. Forrest, eds)
  E. Bourcier, 189(EA):Jul-Sep82-328
  R. Edgecombe, 506(PSt):Sep82-254
  N.H. Keeble, 447(N&Q):Dec81-541
Bunyan, J. The Miscellaneous Works of
  John Bunyan. (Vol 1) (T.L. Underwood,
  ed)
  E. Bourcier, 189(EA):Apr-Jun82-213
  N.H. Keeble, 447(N&Q):Jun81-264

Bunyan, J. A Treatise of the Fear of God;
The Greatness of the Soul; A Holy Life.
(R.L. Greaves, ed)
J.B.H. Alblas, 179(ES):Dec82-576
Burawoy, M. and T. Skocpol. Marxist
Inquiries.
J. Gray, 617(TLS):30Dec83-1459
Burbank, J. and P. Steiner - see Mukařov-
ský, J.
Burch, J. Lubyanka.
P. Van Rjndt, 441:25Sep83-21
Burch, N. To the Distant Observer.
M. Le Fanu, 97(CQ):Vol 11No3-417
Burchfield, R.W. - see "A Supplement to
the Oxford English Dictionary"
Burck, E., ed. Das römische Epos.
J. Perret, 555:Vol56fasc1-159
Burd, V.A. - see La Touche, R.
Burden, R. John Fowles, John Hawkes,
Claude Simon.
P. Stevick, 395(MFS):Winter81/82-748
Bureau, C. Syntaxe fonctionnelle du fran-
çais.
J-M. Léard, 320(CJL):Spring82-85
G. Price, 208(FS):Apr82-241
Burford, E.J., ed. Bawdy Verse.
C. Hawtree, 364:Mar83-112
C. James, 453(NYRB):13Oct83-16
Burg, B.R. Sodomy and the Perception of
Evil.
C. Hill, 453(NYRB):12May83-42
G. Scammell, 617(TLS):1Jul83-694
Burger, H., A. Buhofer and A. Sialm. Hand-
buch der Phraseologie.
E. Haggblade, 350:Dec83-922
Burger, R. Plato's "Phaedrus."*
C. Gill, 478:Oct82-217
Burgess, A. Earthly Powers.*
C. Hawtree, 364:Apr/May82-138
Burgess, A. The End of the World News.*
J. Mellors, 364:Nov82-74
M. Wood, 441:6Mar83-3
442(NY):11Apr83-134
Burgess, A. This Man and Music.*
P-L. Adams, 61:Oct83-123
R. Craft, 453(NYRB):22Dec83-50
K. Walker, 364:Oct82-111
Burgis, N. - see Dickens, C.
Burk, D. A Brush with the West.
R. Thacker, 649(WAL):Nov82-280
Burkard, M. Ruby for Grief.
D. St. John, 42(AR):Spring82-226
Burke, P. Helden, Schurken und Narren.
(R. Schenda, ed)
E. Moser-Rath, 196:Band23Heft3/4-310
Burke, P. Montaigne.
I.W.F. Maclean, 208(FS):Jul82-321
Burkert, W. Griechische Religion der
archaischen und klassischen Epoche.
G. Nagy, 122:Jan82-70
Burkert, W. Structure and History in
Greek Mythology and Ritual.*
W.O. Hendricks, 567:Vol39No1/2-131
C. Leach, 447(N&Q):Jun81-259
G. Nagy, 122:Apr82-159
Burkhard, M., ed. Gestaltet und gestalt-
end.
M.K. Flavell, 402(MLR):Apr82-491
Burkhard, M. Conrad Ferdinand Meyer.
D.W.P. Lewis, 221(GQ):Jan82-123

Burkhard, M. and G. Labroisse, eds. Zur
Literatur der deutschsprachigen Schweiz.*
D. Bell, 402(MLR):Apr82-497
H. Böschenstein, 564:Sep81-246
Burkhardt, F., F. Bowers and I.K.
Skrupskelis - see James, W.
Burkhardt, F.H. and I.K. Skrupskelis - see
James, W.
Burkhardt, H. Logik und Semiotik in der
Philosophie von Lebniz.
W. Redmond, 319:Oct83-571
Burkholz, H. and C. Irving. The Sleeping
Spy.
S. Ellin, 441:13Feb83-14
Burki, S.J. Pakistan Under Bhutto 1971-
1977.
C. Baxter, 293(JASt):May82-615
K.B. Sayeed, 529(QQ):Autumn82-678
Burks, A.W. Chance, Cause, Reason.
I. Levi, 449:Nov82-619
Burley, W.J. Wycliffe and the Beales.
T.J. Binyon, 617(TLS):23Dec83-1437
Burley, W.J. Wycliffe's Wild Goose Chase.*
442(NY):14Feb83-120
Burn, A.R. and M. The Living Past of
Greece.
C.E. Vafopoulou-Richardson, 123:Vol32-
No1-107
Burne-Jones, E. The Little Holland House
Album. (J. Christian, ed)
R. Mander, 39:Aug82-125
L.O., 90:Mar82-200
Burne-Jones, E. Pre-Raphaelite Drawings.
G. Reynolds, 39:Aug82-122
Burne-Jones, E.C. Burne-Jones Talking,
His Conversations 1895-1898.* (M. Lago,
ed)
Q. Bell, 90:Dec82-776
A. Phillips, 364:Aug/Sep82-123
Burnett, A. Milton's Style.
R. Flannagan, 391:Oct82-74
Burnett, D. Guido Molinari.
C.A. Phillips, 529(QQ):Winter82-854
Burnett, J. Hélène Bébé.
M.K. Benet, 617(TLS):8Apr83-360
Burnett, T.A.J. The Rise and Fall of a
Regency Dandy.*
P.W. Graham, 579(SAQ):Autumn82-455
Burnett, V. Towers at the Edge of a World.
M.J. Evans, 102(CanL):Spring82-86
Burnett, V., S. MacKinnon and W.K. Thomas,
eds. Four-Square Garden.
J. Carson, 526:Autumn82-75
Burnham, D. The Rise of the Computer
State.
R. Asahina, 441:21Aug83-8
L.D. Burnard, 617(TLS):25Nov83-1328
Burnier, M-A. Le Testament de Sartre.
A. Whitmarsh, 617(TLS):13May83-483
Burnley, J.D. Chaucer's Language and the
Philosophers' Tradition.*
D.M.E. Gillam, 179(ES):Aug82-360
P. Hardman, 541(RES):Feb82-71
P. Mack, 402(MLR):Apr82-404
G. Schmitz, 38:Band100Heft1/2-183
Burns, A. Nature and Culture in D.H.
Lawrence.*
D.R. Schwarz, 395(MFS):Winter81/82-682
Burns, A. and C. Sugnet, eds. The Imagina-
tion on Trial.*
D.W. Madden, 594:Winter82-388
Burns, D.D. Feeling Good.
G.R. Lowe, 529(QQ):Spring82-161

Burns, G. Boccherini's Minuet.
  B. Sileski, 584(SWR):Winter82-111
Burns, H., with L. Fairbairn and B.
  Boucher. Andrea Palladio 1508-1580.
  W. Cross, 43:Band12Heft1-84
Burns, J. New Zealand Novels and Novel-
  ists 1861-1979.
  S.F.D. Hughes, 395(MFS):Winter82/83-
  738
Burns, R. The Avenging Angel.
  N. Callendar, 441:24Apr83-21
  442(NY):16May83-136
Burns, R. Kantoj Poemoj kaj Satiroj.
  M. Boulton, 447(N&Q):Feb81-85
Burns, R. Learning to Talk.
  J. Saunders, 565:Vol23No3-73
Burns, R. Poems and Songs of Robert Burns.
  (J. Barke, ed)
  J.C., 617(TLS):29Jul83-819
Burns, R. Tree.
  T. Eagleton, 565:Vol23No2-62
Burns, R. and G. Gömöri, eds. Homage to
  Mandelstam.
  D. McDuff, 565:Vol23No1-59
Burns, R.M. The Great Debate on Miracles.
  J.M. Hill, 566:Spring83-142
Burnshaw, S. The Refusers.*
  N. Fruman, 390:Aug/Sep82-58
Burnyeat, M. and others. Notes on Book
  Zeta of Aristotle's "Metaphysics."
  R.M. Dancy, 482(PhR):Jan82-112
  J.D.G. Evans, 518:Jan82-15
Burnyeat, M.F. Conflicting Appearances.
  R.H., 543:Mar82-596
Buroker, J.V. Space and Incongruence.
  D.J. Martin, 319:Oct83-575
  G. Nerlich, 63:Dec82-369
  R.B.P., 543:Jun82-856
Burow, J. Corpus Vasorum Antiquorum.
  (Deutschland, Vol 47)
  B.A. Sparkes, 303(JoHS):Vol 102-285
Burros, M. Keep it Simple.
  W. and C. Cowen, 639(VQR):Spring82-67
Burroughs, W.S. Cities of the Red Night.*
  (French title: Les Cités de la nuit
  écarlate.)
  W.D. Blackmon, 152(UDQ):Summer81-122
  C. Jordis, 450(NRF):Apr82-140
  R. Kostelanetz, 473(PR):1/1982-156
Burrow, J.A. Medieval Writers and Their
  Work.*
  J.J.A., 148:Autumn82-92
Burrow, J.W. A Liberal Descent.*
  639(VQR):Autumn82-128
Burrow, T. The Problem of Shwa in San-
  skrit.*
  R. Rocher, 318(JAOS):Apr-Jun81-244
Burrowes, J. Benny Lynch.
  V. Scannell, 617(TLS):14Jan83-32
Bursen, H.A. Dismantling the Memory
  Machine.*
  P. Danielson, 488:Mar82-104
  J.L., 543:Jun82-859
Burstow, C.A. The Songs of Bathsheba.
  R.J. Merrett, 529(QQ):Winter82-893
Burstyn, J.N. Victorian Education and the
  Ideal of Womanhood.
  B. Caine, 637(VS):Autumn81-107
Burt, J.R. From Phonology to Philology.*
  J.W. Brown, 238:Mar82-150
Burton, A. Embrace of the Butcher.
  N. Callendar, 441:16Jan83-26

Burton, D. Dialogue and Discourse.
  N.E. Enkvist, 603:Vol6No1-107
  J.S. Ryan, 67:Nov82-222
Burton, F. and P. Carlen. Official Dis-
  course.
  R. Fowler, 599:Winter82-67
Burton, I.J. Out of Season.
  P. Lewis, 565:Vol23No1-51
Burton, J.E. The Yorkshire Nunneries in
  the Twelfth and Thirteenth Centuries.
  M. Harvey, 161(DUJ):Jun82-281
Burton, R.D. The Context of Baudelaire's
  "Le Cygne."
  R. Chambers, 446(NCFS):Spring-Summer83-
  376
  R.A. York, 402(MLR):Apr82-455
Burton, R.W.B. The Chorus in Sophocles'
  Tragedies.
  J. Diggle, 123:Vol132No1-12
  P.G. Mason, 303(JoHS):Vol 102-248
Burton, S.H. and C.J.H. Chacksfield. Afri-
  can Poetry in English.
  G. Moore, 447(N&Q):Oct81-471
  M.V. Mzamane, 402(MLR):Jul82-713
Busby, K. Gauvain in Old French Litera-
  ture.*
  C. Roussel, 356(LR):Feb82-76
Busch, F. Take This Man.*
  W.H. Pritchard, 249(HudR):Spring82-159
Busch, W. The Genius of Wilhelm Busch.*
  (W. Arndt, ed and trans)
  G.W. Oldham, 42(AR):Summer82-362
  C.G. Thayer, 219(GaR):Fall82-688
  639(VQR):Summer82-98
Buschhausen, H. Der Verduner Altar.
  F. Deuchler, 589:Oct82-963
Buschmann, E. Untersuchungen zum Begriff
  der Materie bei Avicenna.
  W. Kluxen, 687:Apr-Jun82-299
Bush, D. and J.E. Shaw, eds. A Variorum
  Commentary on the Poems of John Milton.
  (Vol 1) (rev by A.B. Giamatti)
  C. Schaar, 179(ES):Feb82-75
Bushaway, B. By Rite.
  V. Newall, 617(TLS):23Sep83-1027
Bushell, P. London's Secret History.
  E.S. Turner, 617(TLS):5Aug83-826
Bushell, S.W. Oriental Ceramic Art.
  M. Medley, 39:Aug82-123
Bushkova, N.N. and others, eds. The
  United States and Russia: The Beginning
  of Relations, 1765-1815/Rossiia i SShA:
  Stanovlenie otnoshenii 1765-1815.
  J.A. White, 104(CASS):Summer82-255
Bushman, C.L. "A Good Poor Man's Wife."
  L.L. Stevenson, 432(NEQ):Jun82-306
Bushnell, H. Maria Malibran.
  W. Dean, 410(M&L):Apr81-206
Bushrui, S.B. and B. Benstock, eds. James
  Joyce; an International Perspective.
  W. Herman, 329(JJQ):Summer83-463
Busi, F. The Transformations of Godot.*
  H.P. Abbott, 299:Spring82-144
  A.B. Moorjani, 577(SHR):Winter82-77
  L. Powlick, 130:Winter82/83-388
Busnel, R.G. and A. Classe. Whistled Lan-
  guages.*
  G.F. Meier, 682(ZPSK):Band34Heft4-483
Bustin, F.L. Paroles au choix.*
  J.W. Cross, 399(MLJ):Spring82-84
Butcher, J.G. The British in Malaya 1880-
  1941.
  W.R. Roff, 293(JASt):Nov81-193

Butchvarov, P. Being qua Being.*
  D.E. Bradford, 321:Vol 16No3-239
  J.F. Rosenberg, 449:Mar82-143
Buteux, P. The Politics of Nuclear Consul-
tation in NATO 1965-1980.
  L. Martin, 617(TLS):11Nov83-1240
Butler, C. After the Wake.*
  D.G. Campbell, 127:Summer82-175
  B. Stoltzfus, 395(MFS):Winter81/82-651
  L. Thiesmeyer, 184(EIC):Oct82-374
Butler, D. Governing Without a Majority.
  N. Gash, 617(TLS):3Jun83-565
Butler, D. Lusitania.
  P-L. Adams, 61:Feb83-105
Butler, F. and others - see "Children's
Literature"
Butler, J. Churchill's Secret Agent.
  M.R.D. Foot, 617(TLS):19Aug83-874
Butler, M. Peacock Displayed.*
  F.W. Bradbrook, 677(YES):Vol 12-295
  P.H. Butter, 339(KSMB):No33-91
  D. Gallon, 541(RES):Aug82-343
Butler, M. Romantics, Rebels, and Reac-
tionaries.*
  T. Boorman, 175:Summer82-150
  R. Lehan, 445(NCF):Sep82-248
  V. Nemoianu, 400(MLN):Dec82-1245
  M. Scrivener, 141:Summer82-286
  C. Woodring, 88:Spring83-232
Butler, N. Theatre in Colchester.
  S. Rosenfeld, 611(TN):Vol36No3-129
Butler, R. Balzac and the French Revolu-
tion.
  N. Hampson, 617(TLS):4Nov83-1225
Butler, R. Choiseul. (Vol 1)
  J.S. Bromley, 83:Spring82-139
Butler, R., ed. Vanishing Canada.
  F. Rasky, 73:Summer83-53
Butler, R. Western Sculpture, Definitions
of Man.
  P. Cannon-Brookes, 39:Aug82-125
Butler, R.O. Sun Dogs.
  D. Quammen, 441:9Jan83-12
Butler, T., ed and trans. Monumenta Serbo-
croatica.*
  W.W. Derbyshire, 104(CASS):Spring82-
  147
Butlin, M. The Paintings and Drawings of
William Blake.*
  R.N. Essick, 88:Summer82-22
  P. Quennell, 39:Apr82-295
  I. Tayler, 127:Spring82-66
  W. Vaughan, 59:Mar82-106
  J. Ziff, 54:Dec82-673
Butlin, M. Turner: Later Works.
  E. Joll, 39:Jul82-65
Butlin, R. The Exquisite Instrument.
  M. Hofmann, 617(TLS):8Apr83-356
Butlin, R. The Tilting Room.
  G. Mangan, 617(TLS):30Dec83-1462
Butor, M Letters from the Antipodes.
  A.S. Newman, 67:Nov82-211
Butor, M. Vanité.
  J. Pfeiffer, 450(NRF):Oct82-118
Butt, J. Oxford History of English Litera-
ture.* (Vol 8: The Mid-Eighteenth Cen-
tury.) (ed and completed by G. Carnall)
  D. Daiches, 571(ScLJ):Winter82-63
  566:Autumn82-55
Butt, W. Mobilmachung des Elfenbeinturms.
  H. Uecker, 52:Band16Heft3-292
Butter, P.H. - see Blake, W.

Butterfield, F. China.*
  D. Wilson, 617(TLS):8Apr83-348
Butters, G. Francis Ponge.
  B. Beugnot, 535(RHL):May-Jun82-496
  E. Ruhe, 547(RF):Band93Heft1/2-284
  F.R. Smith, 208(FS):Jan82-95
Butterworth, C.E. - see Rousseau, J-J.
Butterworth, K. and J.E. Kibler, Jr.,
comps. William Gilmore Simms.
  M.A. Wimsatt, 365:Winter83-23
Butterworth, M. The Man Who Broke the
Bank at Monte Carlo.
  N. Callendar, 441:18Sep83-45
Büttner, F. Peter Cornelius — Fresken und
Freskenprojekte. (Vol 1)
  E. Mai, 471:Oct/Nov/Dec/82-356
Buttrey, T.V. Documentary Evidence for
the Chronology of the Flavian Titulature.
  I.A. Carradice, 313:Vol72-189
  B.M. Levick, 123:Vol132No1-106
Buttrey, T.V. and M.T.M. Moevs. Cosa: the
Coins and Italo-Megarian Ware at Cosa.
  R. Reece, 123:Vol132No2-294
Butts, R.E. and J.C. Pitt, eds. New Per-
spectives on Galileo.*
  M.E. Finocchiaro, 488:Mar82-99
  W. Leszl, 687:Jan-Mar82-123
Buvalelli, R. Le poesie.* (E. Melli, ed)
  F.M. Chambers, 545(RPh):Feb82-552
Buxton, C. and A. Price. Survival: South
Atlantic.
  N. Shakespeare, 617(TLS):28Oct83-1192
Buxton, J., ed. The Birds of Wiltshire.
  R. O'Hanlon, 617(TLS):15Apr83-381
Buxton, J. The Grecian Taste.*
  J.R. Watson, 339(KSMB):No31-68
Buxton, R.G.A. Persuasion in Greek Trag-
edy.
  R. Parker, 617(TLS):11Mar83-242
Buzzati, D. Nous sommes au regret de ...
  L. Séjor, 98:Nov82-943
Buzzati, D. Restless Nights.
  J. Cary, 469:Vol18No4-120
Byatt, I.C.R. The British Electrical
Industry 1875-1914.
  M. Turner, 637(VS):Autumn81-89
Bynner, W. The Chinese Translations.
  V. Young, 472:Spring/Summer83-168
Bynner, W. Selected Letters of Witter
Bynner. (J. Kraft, ed)
  42(AR):Winter82-117
Bynum, C.W. Jesus as Mother.
  B. Ward, 617(TLS):1Apr83-318
Bynum, D.E. The Daemon in the Wood.*
  R.B. Klymasz, 107(CRCL):Dec81-534
Bynum, D.E., ed. Serbo-Croatian Heroic
Songs.* (Vols 6 and 14)
  J. Kolsti, 292(JAF):Apr-Jun82-247
Bynum, D.E. - see Međedović, A.
Byrd, M, Finders Weepers.
  N. Callendar, 441:30Oct83-31
Byrne, J.H. Mrs. Byrne's Dictionary of
Unusual, Obscure, and Preposterous Words.
  B. Cottle, 541(RES):Nov82-445
Byrne, K.D. and R.C. Snyder. Chrysalis.
  L. Waldeland, 395(MFS):Winter81/82-725
Byrne, M.S., ed. The Elizabethan Zoo.
  B.E. Brandt, 152(UDQ):Winter82-118
Byrne, M.S., ed. The Lisle Letters.*
  S. Foister, 90:Jun82-367
  M. Levine, 551(RenQ):Autumn82-491
  R.J. Schoeck, 191(ELN):Sep82-27
[continued]

Cain, R. Whole Lotta Shakin' Goin' On.
  B.L. Cooper, 498:Vol8No1-65
Cain, T.H. Praise in "The Faerie Queene."
  O.B. Hardison, Jr., 551(RenQ):Spring81-139
  D.A. Richardson, 125:Spring82-316
Cairns, F. Tibullus.*
  R.J. Ball, 121(CJ):Apr/May83-362
  H.F. Guite, 487:Winter82-378
  J.K. Newman, 122:Oct82-374
Cairns, H.S. and C.E. Psycholinguistics.
  H. Wode, 38:Band100Heft1/2-138
Cairns, R. and G. Turner. Glenn Turner's
  Century of Centuries.
  A.L. Le Quesne, 617(TLS):16Sep83-987
Calabi, D., ed. Architettura domestica in
  Gran Bretagna 1890-1939.
  A. Saint, 617(TLS):14Oct83-1122
Calasso, R. La rovina di Kasch.
  M. d'Amico, 617(TLS):14Oct83-1132
Calcraft, R.P. The Sonnets of Luis de
  Góngora.
  E. Bergmann, 304(JHP):Fall82-74
  J.F.G. Gornall, 402(MLR):Jul82-748
Caldarini, E. - see du Bellay, J.
Calder, J., ed. Robert Louis Stevenson: A
  Critical Celebration.
  R. Brebach, 395(MFS):Winter81/82-698
  R. Kiely, 637(VS):Autumn81-87
Calder, J. Robert Louis Stevenson: A Life
  Study.*
  R. Kiely, 637(VS):Autumn81-87
  S. Pickering, 569(SR):Fall82-xciv
Calder, J., ed. Stevenson and Victorian
  Scotland.
  I. Campbell, 571(ScLJ):Winter82-92
Calder, N. Nuclear Nightmares.
  G. Ignatieff, 529(QQ):Summer82-352
Caldera, R-T. Le jugement par inclination
  chez Saint Thomas D'Aquin.
  J.O., 543:Dec81-369
Calderon, E. Erma.
  V.A. Smith, 569(SR):Spring82-xxxvii
Calderón, E.C. - see under Caballero Cal-
  derón, E.
Calderón, E.C. - see under Correa Calderón,
  E.
Calderón de la Barca, P. Celos aun del
  aire matan. (M.D. Stroud, ed and trans)
  K.C. Gregg, 238:Sep82-463
Calderón de la Barca, P. Four Comedies by
  Pedro Calderón de la Barca.* (K. Muir,
  trans; A.L. Mackenzie, ed)
  W.R. Blue, 238:Mar82-144
  G. Edwards, 86(BHS):Jan82-74
  A. Limoges-Miller, 568(SCN):Fall82-38
  J. Lyons, 214:Vol 10No38-140
  C.G. Peale, 399(MLJ):Autumn82-349
Calderón de la Barca, P. La vida es sueño.
  (E. Rull, ed)
  K. and R. Reichenberger, 72:Band218
  Heft2-475
Calderwood, J.L. Metadrama in Shake-
  speare's Henriad.*
  J. Hasler, 179(ES):Jun82-282
Caldicott, C.E.J. - see Guérin de Bouscal,
  D.
Caldini, R.M. - see under Montanari Cal-
  dini, R.
Caldwell, D. American-Soviet Relations
  from 1947 to the Nixon-Kissinger Grand
  Design.
  R.R. Pope, 550(RusR):Oct82-513

Caldwell, E. Stories of Life/North and
  South. (E.C. Lathem, ed)
  S.J. Cook, 578:Fall83-126
Caldwell, J. George R. Stewart.
  A.R. Huseboe, 649(WAL):Summer82-176
Čale, F., ed. Petrarca i petrarkizam u
  slavenskim zemljama/Petrarca e il pet-
  rarchismo nei paesi slavi.
  F. Mouret, 549(RLC):Jan-Mar82-99
Calero, G.P. - see under Pérez Calero, G.
Calhoun, C. The Question of Class Strug-
  gle.
  D. Thompson, 617(TLS):18Feb83-162
Calhoun, J.C. The Papers of John C. Cal-
  houn. (Vol 8) (C.N. Wilson, ed)
  A.V. Huff, Jr., 579(SAQ):Winter82-127
Calhoun, T.O. Henry Vaughan.*
  F. Fogle, 551(RenQ):Summer82-343
  K. Lynch, 568(SCN):Winter82-69
  T-L. Pebworth, 191(ELN):Mar/Jun83-63
Calì, M. Da Michelangelo all'Escorial.
  A.W.A. Boschloo, 90:Aug82-509
Calisher, H. Mysteries of Motion.
  J.C. Oates, 441:6Nov83-7
Calisher, H., with S. Ravenel, eds. The
  Best American Short Stories 1981.*
  D. Grumbach, 219(GaR):Fall82-668
Calkins, R.G. Illuminated Books of the
  Middle Ages.
  R. McKitterick, 617(TLS):30Dec83-1468
Callado, A. Sempreviva.
  M. Silverman, 399(MLJ):Spring82-108
Callaghan, J. Boycott.
  T.D. Smith, 617(TLS):28Jan83-91
Callaghan, M.R. Mothers.
  J.L. Halio, 598(SoR):Winter83-203
Callahan, W.J. La Santa y Real Hermandad
  del Refugio y Piedad de Madrid 1618-
  1832.
  P. Deacon, 86(BHS):Jan82-74
Callahan, W.J. and D. Higgs, eds. Church
  and Society in Catholic Europe of the
  Eighteenth Century.
  S. Gilley, 83:Autumn82-253
Callan, E. Auden.
  P-L. Adams, 61:Apr83-132
Callan, E. Crystal Dalmation.
  D. Haskell, 581:Sep82-348
Callenbach, E. Ecotopia Emerging.
  T.J. Lyon, 649(WAL):Spring82-71
Callinicos, A. The Revolutionary Ideas of
  Karl Marx. Marxism and Philosophy.
  J. Gray, 617(TLS):30Dec83-1459
Callinicos, A. Southern Africa after
  Zimbabwe.
  B. Munslow, 69:Vol52No4-91
Callmer, C. Königin Christina, ihre Bib-
  liothekare und ihre Handschriften.
  R. Düchting, 72:Band218Heft2-374
Callot, F. La philosophie de la science
  et de la nature.*
  A. Reix, 192(EP):Oct-Dec82-487
Calloway, S. English Prints for the Col-
  lector.*
  D. Robinson, 39:Sep82-200
Calvert, P. The Concept of Class.
  P.N. Furbank, 362:13Jan83-20
  G. Sampson, 617(TLS):4Mar83-218
Calvert, P. The Falklands Crisis.
  G. Wheatcroft, 617(TLS):13May83-490
Calvet, L-J. Chanson et Société.
  C. Pinet, 207(FR):Mar83-658

Calvet de Magalhaes, T. Signe ou symbole.
  C. Morier, 567:Vol39No3/4-343
Calvin, W.H. The Throwing Madonna.
  P-L. Adams, 61:Aug83-100
  M. Pines, 441:21Aug83-8
Calvino, I. Adam, One Afternoon.
  J. Astor, 362:17Mar83-24
  T. Sutcliffe, 617(TLS):2Sep83-921
Calvino, I. If on a winter's night a tra-
  veler.*
  G.W. Jarecke, 577(SHR):Spring82-155
Calvino, I. Marcovaldo.
  T. Sutcliffe, 617(TLS):2Sep83-921
Cambon, G. Ugo Foscolo.
  M. Ambrose, 161(DUJ):Dec81-144
  J.H. Whitfield, 591(SIR):Summer82-260
"The Cambridge Encyclopedia of Africa."
  S.L. Kasfir, 2(AfrA):Aug82-84
"The Cambridge Encyclopedia of Russia and
  the Soviet Union."* (A. Brown and
  others, general eds)
  M. McCauley, 575(SEER):Oct82-612
"Cambridge University Library MS Ff. II.
  38."
  M. Mills, 382(MAE):1982/2-246
  M. Seymour, 354:Dec82-428
"Cambridge University Library MS Gg. IV.
  27."
  M. Seymour, 354:Dec82-434
Cameron, A. Earth Witch.
  B. Serafin, 648(WCR):Apr83-45
Cameron, A. and J. Jones. The L.L. Bean
  Game and Fish Cookbook.
  M. Burros, 441:11Dec83-12
Cameron, E. Hugh MacLennan.*
  H. Dahlie, 49:Jul82-92
  R. Hyman, 627(UTQ):Summer82-452
Cameron, I.A. Crime and Repression in the
  Auvergne and the Guyenne 1720-1790.
  N. Hampson, 208(FS):Oct82-476
Cameron, J. Prisons and Punishment in
  Scotland from the Middle Ages to the
  Present.
  M. Ignatieff, 617(TLS):23Sep83-1030
Cameron, K. Agrippa d'Aubigné.
  I.D. McFarlane, 208(FS):Jan82-56
Cameron, K., ed. Montaigne and His Age.
  E. Armstrong, 208(FS):Jul82-322
  P. Burke, 402(MLR):Jul82-720
  F. Gray, 551(RenQ):Summer82-306
Cameron, K. - see Meigret, L.
Cameron, S. The Corporeal Self.
  E. Carton, 594:Winter82-391
  E.A. Dryden, 445(NCF):Sep82-223
Camp, J. Draw.
  90:Dec82-794
de la Campa, R.V. José Triana.
  A. Kapcia, 86(BHS):Jan82-86
Campagna, A.F. and P. Grundlehner.
  Pointes de Vue.*
  M.R. Kaufman, 399(MLJ):Autunn82-331
Campagnoli, R. Forme, Maniere, Manierismi.
  M. Simonin, 535(RHL):Jul-Aug82-648
Campan, R. L'animal et son univers.
  J-M. Gabaude, 542:Jan-Mar82-88
Campanella, A.P. - see Garibaldi, G.
Campanella, T. La Città del Sole: Dialogo
  Poetico/The City of the Sun: A Poetical
  Dialogue. (D.J. Donno, ed and trans)
  P.M.S. Dawson, 148:Autumn82-72
Campbell, B.F. Ancient Wisdom Revived.
  W. Halbfass, 318(JAOS):Oct-Dec81-473

Campbell, D. Blether.
  R. Watson, 588(SSL):Vol 17-218
Campbell, D. War Plan UK.
  M. Carver, 617(TLS):4Feb83-98
Campbell, D.A. The Golden Lyre.
  R. Stoneman, 617(TLS):10Jun83-599
Campbell, E.D.C., Jr. The Celluloid South.
  J.R. Millichap, 392:Fall82-439
Campbell, G. - see Milton, J.
Campbell, H.H. James Thomson.
  A.J. Sambrook, 677(YES):Vol 12-281
Campbell, I. The Kailyard.
  I. Murray, 571(ScLJ):Winter82-93
Campbell, I.R. "Kudrun."*
  C. Love, 406:Spring82-95
Campbell, J. Grammatical Man.*
  P.N. Johnson-Laird, 617(TLS):4Nov83-
  1205
Campbell, J. Historical Atlas of World
  Mythology. (Vol 1)
  W. O'Flaherty, 441:18Dec83-3
Campbell, J. Roy Jenkins.
  A. Howard, 362:26May83-20
Campbell, J. F.E. Smith.
  S. Koss, 617(TLS):23Dec83-1419
Campbell, J. and J. Doyle, eds. The Prac-
  tical Vision.
  H. Kreisel, 107(CRCL):Dec81-540
Campbell, J.L., ed and trans. Hebridean
  Folksongs.* (Vol 3)
  P. Cooke, 410(M&L):Jan/Apr82-116
Campbell, L. Van der Weyden.*
  E. Dhanens, 90:Jun82-367
Campbell, R. Dark Companions.
  G. Locklin, 573(SSF):Fall83-398
Campbell, R. Self-Love and Self-Respect.*
  T.E. Hill, Jr., 482(PhR):Jul82-470
  J. Narveson, 154:Sep82-531
  A.W. Price, 518:Oct82-250
Campbell, R.W. Fat Tuesday.
  R. Freedman, 441:6Mar83-10
Campbell, R.W. Soviet Energy Technologies.
  J.P. Stern, 104(CASS):Summer82-278
Campbell, S.C. Only Begotten Sonnets.*
  K. Muir, 570(SQ):Spring82-116
Campbell, S.C. - see Shakespeare, W.
Campbell, S.L. The Second Empire Revis-
  ited.
  M. Siegel, 125:Winter82-211
Campbell, W., A. Lampman and D.C. Scott.
  At the Mermaid Inn.
  T. Goldie, 178:Jun82-240
Campbell, W.D. The Glad River.
  639(VQR):Autumn82-129
Campe, J.H. Robinson der Jüngere, zur
  angenehmen und nützlichen Unterhaltung
  für Kinder.
  E.G. von Bernstorff, 133:Band15Heft4-
  369
Campeau, L. Établissement à Québec (1616-
  1634).
  J. Axtell, 656(WMQ):Oct82-696
Campion, E.J. - see Quinault, P.
Campo, M. Cristiano Wolff e il razional-
  ismo precritico.
  J. Ecole, 192(EP):Jul-Sep81-343
Campos, J. - see Machado, M.
Campos, M.R. - see under Rodríguez Campos,
  M.
Camus, R. Journal d'un voyage en France.
  E. Marty, 98:May82-452
Cañada Castillo, P. and others - see
  Rodríguez Moñino, A.R.

Cardonia, M., ed. Tina Modotti: Photo-
graphs.
  B.L., 55:Nov82-59
Cardoza, A.L. Agrarian Elites and Italian
Fascism.
  T. Abse, 617(TLS):3Jun83-580
Carduner, S. and M.P. Hagiwara. D'Accord.*
  L. Kikuchi, 207(FR):Dec82-351
Cardus, N. The Roses Matches 1919-1939.*
  A.L. Le Quesne, 617(TLS):20May83-522
Cardwell, G. - see Twain, M.
Cardwell, R.A. - see de Espronceda, J.
Carême, M. Petites Légendes.
  M-J. Renaudie, 207(FR):Dec82-333
Carey, G. Katharine Hepburn.
  A. Mars-Jones, 617(TLS):18Nov83-1291
Carey, G. Judy Holliday.
  M. Buckley, 200:Oct82-505
  J. Stokes, 617(TLS):1Apr83-319
Carey, G.O., ed. Faulkner.
  J.G. Watson, 395(MFS):Summer81-365
Carey, J. John Donne.*
  R.B., 617(TLS):22Apr83-415
  G.M. Crump, 191(ELN):Sep82-34
  M.J.M. Ezell, 184(EIC):Jan82-69
  D. Karlin, 175:Summer82-142
  N.R. McMillan, 577(SHR):Fall82-358
  R. Messenger, 568(SCN):Spring-Summer82-
  10
  J. Stachniewski, 148:Winter82-84
  G.W. Williams, 579(SAQ):Autumn82-471
Carey, J., ed. English Renaissance Stud-
ies Presented to Dame Helen Gardner in
Honour of Her Seventieth Birthday.*
  M. Grivelet, 189(EA):Jan-Mar82-78
  R. Harrier, 551(RenQ):Summer81-277
  C.F. Williamson, 541(RES):Nov82-458
Carey, P. Bliss.*
  P. Pierce, 381:Dec81-522
Cargile, J. Paradoxes.*
  J.A. Benardete, 154:Jun82-342
Cargill, J. The Second Athenian League.*
  S. Hornblower, 123:Vol132No2-235
  S.M. Sherwin-White, 303(JoHS):Vol 102-
  269
Carlile, H. Running Lights.
  K. Cherry, 134(CP):Spring82-100
  D. Hall, 271:Winter82-166
  M. Lammon, 436(NewL):Winter82/83-104
Carlisle, J. The Sense of an Audience.
  G.H. Ford, 445(NCF):Sep82-214
Carlo, A.M. - see under Millares Carlo, A.
Carlson, H.G. Strindberg and the Poetry
of Myth.
  R. Brustein, 453(NYRB):20Jan83-29
  P. Engel, 441:20Feb83-9
Carlson, I., ed. The Pastoral Care.* (Pt
2) (completed by L-G. Hallander, with M.
Löfvenberg and A. Rynell)
  J. Bately, 382(MAE):1982/1-108
Carlson, J. George C. Wallace and the
Politics of Powerlessness.
  V.V. Hamilton, 9(AlaR):Jan82-50
Carlson, L.H. Martin Marprelate, Gentle-
man.
  W.T. MacCaffrey, 551(RenQ):Summer82-
  312
Carlson, M. The Italian Stage from
Goldoni to D'Annunzio.
  S.V. Longman, 612(ThS):May82-128
Carlson, P. Roughneck.
  R.J. Margolis, 441:4Sep83-10

Carlsson, J. The Limits to Structural
Change.
  D. Rimmer, 69:Vol152No2-122
Carlton, C. Charles I.
  R. Lockyer, 617(TLS):8Jul83-720
Carlton, D. Anthony Eden.*
  639(VQR):Spring82-52
Carlut, C., ed. Essais sur Flaubert.*
  A. Lacy, 546(RR):Mar82-265
Carlyle, T. and J.W. The Collected Let-
ters of Thomas and Jane Welsh Carlyle.
(Vols 1-7) (C.R. Sanders, J. Butt and
K.J. Fielding, eds)
  G.B. Tennyson, 506(PSt):Sep82-239
Carlyle, T. and J.W. The Collected Let-
ters of Thomas and Jane Welsh Carlyle.*
(Vols 8 and 9) (C.R. Sanders and K.J.
Fielding, eds)
  C. Moore, 588(SSL):Vol 17-254
  G.B. Tennyson, 506(PSt):Sep82-239
Carlyle, T. and J. Ruskin. The Correspon-
dence of Thomas Carlyle and John Ruskin.*
(G.A. Cate, ed)
  D. Johnson, 453(NYRB):31Mar83-13
Carmack, R.M. The Quiché Mayas of Utat-
lán.
  E.P. Bensen, 37:Sep-Oct82-61
Carman, B. Letters of Bliss Carman. (H.P.
Gundy, ed)
  D.M.R. Bentley, 105:Spring/Summer82-
  112
Carman, B. and J. McPherson - see McPher-
son, J.
Carmean, E.A., Jr. Picasso The Saltim-
banques.
  L. Cooke, 59:Sep82-338
Carmely, K.P. Das Identitätsproblem jüdi-
scher Autoren im deutschen Sprachraum.
  G. Brude-Firnau, 564:May82-150
Carmi, T., ed and trans. The Penguin Book
of Hebrew Verse.*
  A. Alcalay, 472:Spring/Summer83-85
  W. Bargad, 399(MLJ):Winter82-427
Carmichael, J. The Death of Jesus.
  N. Fruman, 390:May82-55
Carnall, G. - see Butt, J.
Carnell, P., comp. Ballads in the Charles
Harding Firth Collection of the Univer-
sity of Sheffield.
  A.C. Percival, 203:Vol193No2-230
Carnesale, A. and others. Living With
Nuclear Weapons.
  J. Fallows, 441:26Jun83-3
Carney, T.M., ed. Communist Party Power
in Kampuchea (Cambodia).
  M. Ebihara, 293(JASt):Nov81-63
Caro, A. The Scruffy Scoundrels. (M.
Ciavolella and D. Beecher, eds and trans)
  D. Radcliff-Umstead, 539:Feb83-63
Caro, R. Días geniales o lúdicros. (J-P.
Etienvre, ed)
  H. Iventosch, 552(REH):Jan82-146
Caro, R.A. The Years of Lyndon Johnson:
The Path to Power.*
  M. Kempton, 453(NYRB):17Feb83-25
  P. Whitehead, 362:16Jun83-24
  G.K. Wilson, 617(TLS):25Mar83-287
Caron, L. Le Canard de bois.
  A.B. Chartier, 207(FR):Feb83-504
Caron, L. The Draft Dodger.
  H.R. Runte, 102(CanL):Winter81-124
Carpenter, C.A. Modern British Drama.
  E.H. Mikhail, 397(MD):Sep82-440

60

Carpenter, D.B. - see Emerson, E.T.
Carpenter, H. W.H. Auden.*
   H. Carruth, 249(HudR):Summer82-334
   A. Levitin, 31(ASch):Autumn82-572
   J. Matthias, 598(SoR):Winter83-184
   T. Paulin, 569(SR):Winter82-73
   J. Replogle, 577(SHR):Fall82-373
   42(AR):Summer82-369
   295(JML):Dec82-402
Carpenter, K.E., ed. Books and Society in
History.
   G. Barber, 617(TLS):24Jun83-679
Carpentier, A. La Novela Latinoamericana
en Visperas de un Nuevo Siglo y Otros
Ensayos.
   O. Rossardi, 37:May-Jun82-64
Carpio, L.D. - see under de Vega Carpio, L.
Carpio, O.G. - see under Gete Carpio, O.
Carr, E.H. The Twilight of Comintern,
1930-35.
   A. Dallin, 441:29May83-8
   L. Labedz, 617(TLS):10Jun83-605
   W. Pfaff, 442(NY):21Nov83-214
Carr, F. Ivan the Terrible.
   D. Atkinson, 550(RusR):Apr82-199
Carr, R.A. Pierre Boaistuau's "Histoires
Tragiques."*
   C. Clark, 208(FS):Jan82-58
Carr, S. and R. Fox-Hunting.
   B. Gutteridge, 364:Feb83-119
Carrasco, D. Quetzalcoatl and the Irony
of Empire.
   G. Brotherston, 617(TLS):7Oct83-1090
le Carré, J. The Little Drummer Girl.
   T.J. Binyon, 617(TLS):25Mar83-289
   W.F. Buckley, Jr., 441:13Mar83-1
   M. Laski, 362:21Apr83-27
   J. Wolcott, 453(NYRB):14Apr83-19
   442(NY):4Apr83-132
Carré, O., ed. L'Islam et l'état dans le
monde d'aujourd'hui.
   B. Lewis, 453(NYRB):30Jun83-35
Carrell, S.L. Le Soliloque de la passion
féminine ou le dialogue illusoire.
   B. Bray, 475:Vol9No17-746
Carrera, A. Nívia.
   J. Kirkup, 617(TLS):4Feb83-117
Carrère d'Encausse, H. Confiscated Power.
   L. Schapiro, 453(NYRB):20Jan83-3
Carrier, R. Les Fleurs vivent-elles ail-
leurs que sur la terre? La Céleste
Bicyclette.
   E. Dansereau, 102(CanL):Autumn82-143
Carrier, R. The Hockey Sweater and Other
Stories.
   N. Besner, 102(CanL):Winter81-131
Carrington, G.W. Foreigners in Formosa,
1841-1874.
   J.E. Wills, Jr., 318(JAOS):Oct-Dec81-
426
Carrión, A.M., with others - see under
Morales Carrión, A., with others
Carrive, P. Bernard Mandeville.
   J-L. Dumas, 192(EP):Jan-Mar82-111
Carroll, J. The Cultural Theory of Mat-
thew Arnold.
   C. Baldick, 617(TLS):16Sep83-976
Carroll, J.M. Toward a Structural Psychol-
ogy of Cinema.*
   T. Docherty, 89(BJA):Spring82-187
Carroll, L. Lewis Carroll and the Kit-
chins. (M.N. Cohen, ed)
   R. Dupree, 191(ELN):Dec82-119

Carroll, L. The Letters of Lewis Carroll.*
(M.N. Cohen, with R.L. Green, eds)
   R. Dupree, 191(ELN):Dec82-119
Carroll, L. The Pennyroyal Alice. (S.H.
Goodacre, ed) The Hunting of the Snark.
(J. Tanis and J. Dooley, eds)
   J.C. Oates, 191(ELN):Dec82-109
Carroll, L.L. Language and Dialect in
Ruzante and Goldoni.
   R.A. Hall, Jr., 350:Jun83-445
"Lewis Carroll, Photographer of Children."
   R. Dupree, 191(ELN):Dec82-119
Carroll, P.N. The Other Samuel Johnson.*
   B. Tucker, 173(ECS):Fall81-111
Carruth, H. The Sleeping Beauty.
   R.W. Flint, 472:Spring/Summer83-17
   H. Leibowitz, 441:21Aug83-12
Carruth, H. Working Papers.* (J. Weiss-
man, ed)
   J.D. Bloom, 27(AL):Dec82-625
   R.W. Flint, 472:Spring/Summer83-17
Carson, C. The New Estate.
   J. Parini, 569(SR):Fall82-623
Carson, N. Arthur Miller.*
   A.P. Hinchliffe, 148:Autumn82-83
Carson, N., ed. New Canadian Drama 1.
   R. Plant, 102(CanL):Spring82-103
   T. Stephenson, 108:Spring82-201
Carson, P. James van Artevelde.
   B. Lyon, 589:Oct82-870
Carson, R.A.G. Principal Coins of the
Romans.* (Vol 3)
   D. Nash, 123:Vol32No2-301
Carstairs, G.M. Death of a Witch.
   D. Pocock, 617(TLS):21Oct83-1153
Carsten, F.L. War against War.*
   D.P.L., 185:Jul83-840
Carswell, C. The Savage Pilgrimage.
   J. Meckier, 579(SAQ):Autumn82-462
   639(VQR):Summer82-81
Carswell, J. The Exile.
   A.S. Byatt, 617(TLS):2Dec83-1338
Carter, A. The Passion of New Eve.
   P. Craig, 617(TLS):21Jan83-69
Carter, E.C. 2d and others - see Latrobe,
B.H.
Carter, G.M. Which Way is South Africa
Going?*
   B. Munslow, 69:Vol152No4-91
Carter, G.M. and P. O'Meara, eds. South-
ern Africa.
   B. Munslow, 69:Vol152No4-91
Carter, H. The Tomb of Tutenkhamen.
   M.F., 617(TLS):29Jul83-819
Carter, J. Keeping Faith.*
   R.J. Barnet, 442(NY):17Jan83-107
Carter, J. Work, for the Night is Coming.*
   S.C. Behrendt, 502(PrS):Summer82-90
   D. Gioia, 491:May82-102
   R. Pybus, 565:Vol23No3-61
Carter, J.R., ed. Religiousness in Sri
Lanka.
   H.L. Seneviratne, 293(JASt):Feb82-379
Carter, M.G., ed. Arab Linguistics.
   A.S. Kaye, 350:Sep83-698
Carter, R.B. Descartes' Medical Philoso-
phy.
   J. Cottingham, 617(TLS):11Nov83-1239
Carton, D. and A. Caprio. En Français.*
(2nd ed)
   H. Wilkes, 399(MLJ):Summer82-211

Cátedra, P. - see de Córdoba, A.

Catley, R. and B. McFarlane. Australian
Capitalism in Boom and Depression.
K. Tsokhas, 381:Dec82-499

Catlow, L., ed and trans. Pervigilium
Veneris.
J. Chomarat, 555:Vol156fasc2-301

Cato, M.P. Marcus Porcius Cato, "Vom
Landbau." (O. Schönberger, ed)
P-P. Corsetti, 555:Vol156fasc1-152

"Catullus." (G.P. Goold, ed and trans)
R. Wells, 617(TLS):14Oct83-1120

"Catullus."* (D.F.S. Thomson, ed)
R.T. van der Paardt, 394:Vol135fasc3/4-
404

Caudill, H. The Mountain, the Miner, and
the Lord.
R. Manley, 292(JAF):Oct-Dec82-479

Caufield, C. The Emperor of the United
States of America and Other Magnificent
British Eccentrics.
639(VQR):Autumn82-136

Caute, D. The K-Factor.
R. Owen, 617(TLS):3Jun83-562

Caute, D. Under the Skin.
C. Style, 362:24Feb83-27
G. Wheatcroft, 617(TLS):11Mar83-234

Cavaillès, J. Méthode axiomatique et
formalisme.
A. Reix, 542:Jul-Sep82-542

Cavalieri, L.F. The Double-Edged Helix.*
639(VQR):Winter82-14

Cavaliero, G. Elegy For St. Anne's.
L. Mackinnon, 617(TLS):8Apr83-356

Cavaliero, G. A Reading of E.M. Forster.*
K. Watson, 447(N&Q):Oct81-451

Cavaliero, G. Charles Williams.
S. Medcalf, 617(TLS):21Oct83-1150

Cavarero, A. Dialettica e politica in
Platone.
J. Moreau, 192(EP):Apr-Jun81-236

Cave, M. Computers and Economic Planning.*
D.A. Dyker, 575(SEER):Jan82-147

Cave, M. and P. Hare. Alternative
Approaches to Economic Planning.
D.A. Dyker, 575(SEER):Jul82-469

Cave, O. Cut-Work Embroidery.
P. Bach, 614:Spring83-18

Cave, R.A. A Study of the Novels of
George Moore.*
H. Robinson, 677(YES):Vol 12-334

Cave Brown, A. The Last Hero.
E.J. Epstein, 441:16Jan83-1
T. Powers, 453(NYRB):12May83-29
442(NY):14Feb83-117

Cave Brown, A. and C.B. MacDonald. On a
Field of Red.*
N. Weyl, 390:Nov82-57

Cavell, S. The Claim of Reason.*
T.D. Eisele, 396(ModA):Spring82-199
A.D. Nuttall, 541(RES):Aug82-368
A. Palmer, 393(Mind):Apr82-292

Cavell, S. Pursuits of Happiness.*
N. Carroll, 290(JAAC):Fall82-103
A. La Valley, 18:Jan/Feb82-66
D. Turner, 141:Summer82-300

Caven, B. The Punic Wars.
J.W. Rich, 313:Vol72-182

Cavendish, G. Metrical Visions. (A.S.G.
Edwards, ed)
A.G. Petti, 405(MP):Feb83-302

Caviró, B.M. - see under Martínez Caviró,
B.

Caws, I. Boy with a Kite.
L. Sail, 565:Vol23No4-73

Caws, M.A. The Eye in the Text.
E. Higdon, 290(JAAC):Winter82-221
J.C. O'Neal, 546(RR):Mar82-269
J.B. Smith, 39:Aug82-126
M. Tison-Braun, 188(ECr):Summer82-72
639(VQR):Spring82-57

Caws, M.A. La Main de Pierre Reverdy.*
F.R. Smith, 208(FS):Jul82-357

Caws, M.A., ed. Le Siècle éclaté, 2.
A-M. Christin, 535(RHL):Jul-Aug82-675

Caws, P. Sartre.*
T. Baldwin, 393(Mind):Apr82-288
T.R.F., 543:Sep81-118
P. Trotignon, 542:Jan-Mar82-61

Caws, P., ed. Two Centuries of Philosophy
in America.
S. Harrison, 619:Summer82-273

Cayrol, J. Il était une fois Jean Cayrol.*
F. de Martinoir, 450(NRF):Jul-Aug82-
168
M. Naudin, 207(FR):Feb83-505

Cazelles, B. La Faiblesse chez Gautier de
Coinci.*
W. Rothwell, 208(FS):Jan82-49

Cazeneuve, J. La raison d'être.
M. Adam, 542:Oct-Dec82-661

Cazotte, J. Le Diable amoureux, suivi de
la prophétie de Cazotte rapportée par La
Harpe, de ses Révélations, d'extraits de
sa correspondance, ainsi que d'Ollivier
et de l'Histoire de Maugraby. (G.
Décote, ed)
C. Todd, 208(FS):Oct82-476

Cèbe, J-P. - see Varro

"Cebes' Tablet."
F. Rädle, 52:Band16Heft2-188
W. Schleiner, 551(RenQ):Spring81-121

Cecchi, G.M. The Horned Owl. (K. Eisenbichler, ed and trans)
D. Radcliff-Umstead, 539:Feb83-63

Cecil, D. A Portrait of Charles Lamb.
J. Gross, 453(NYRB):16Jun83-11
D.A.N. Jones, 362:7Jul83-26
G. Lindop, 617(TLS):10Jun83-588

Cecil, D. A Portrait of Jane Austen.*
J.M.B., 179(ES):Apr82-144

Cedeño, R.A.N. - see under Núñez Cedeño,
R.A.

Céline, L-F. Romans I. (H. Godard, ed)
B. Vercier, 535(RHL):Sep-Dec82-968

Cell, J.W. The Highest Stage of White
Supremacy.
K. Ingham, 617(TLS):16Sep83-982

Cella, C.R. Mary Johnston.
C. Allen, 26(ALR):Spring82-136
G.C. Longest, 392:Spring82-133

Cellard, J. and A. Rey. Dictionnaire du
français non-conventionnel.
P. Rézeau, 209(FM):Oct82-365
G. Roques, 553(RLiR):Jan-Jun81-258

Cellard, J. and M. Sommant. 500 mots
nouveaux définis et expliqués.*
F.H., 209(FM):Oct82-384

Cellucci, C. Teoria della dimostrazione.
F. Previale, 316:Mar82-220

Cendrars, B. Gold.
P.L. Bowles, 617(TLS):4Feb83-116

"Census-Catalogue of Manuscript Sources of
Polyphonic Music, 1400-1550." (Vol 1)
F. Tirro, 551(RenQ):Autumn81-431

"Centennale des artistes français: Le
Salon 1881-1981."
  N. Green, 59:Mar82-128
Centi, B.L.W. Relining Coats and Jackets.
  P. Bach, 614:Spring83-23
Cercignani, F. Shakespeare's Works and
Elizabethan Pronunciation.*
  W.N. Francis, 350:Dec83-915
Cervantes, L.D. Emplumada.
  M. Hall, 152(UDQ):Winter82-110
de Cervantes Saavedra, M. Don Quijote de
la Mancha. (B. Pallares, ed)
  M.I. and M.A. Arenas, 238:Mar82-143
de Cervantes Saavedra, M. Don Quixote.
  (J. Ormsby, trans; J.R. Jones and K.
Douglas, eds)
  T.A. Lathrop, 304(JHP):Winter83-152
Cervigni, D.S. The "Vita" of Benvenuto
Cellini.*
  A. Mazzocco, 276:Winter82-350
Cervoni, J., K. Schlyter and A. Vassant -
see Moignet, G.
Cetron, M. and T. O'Toole. Encounters
with the Future.
  639(VQR):Autumn82-137
Chabot, C.B. Freud on Schreber.
  N. Lukacher, 400(MLN):Dec82-1239
Chabot, D. Eldorado on Ice.* (French
title: L'Eldorado des glaces.)
  E. Dansereau, 526:Spring82-86
  D. Duffy, 529(QQ):Winter82-761
  M. Fee, 102(CanL):Summer82-138
Chace, W.M. Lionel Trilling.*
  S. Schwartz, 185:Oct82-189
Chacon, L. and others. Bilingual Business
Grammar/Gramática Comercial Bilingüe.
  D.E. Rivas, 399(MLJ):Autumn82-351
Chadwick, J. The Unofficial Commonwealth.
  H.S. Ferns, 617(TLS):7Jan83-16
  J.K. Thompson, 324:Mar83-225
Chadwick, O. Hensley Henson.
  M. Ramsey, 617(TLS):19Aug83-878
Chadwick, O. Newman.
  I. Ker, 617(TLS):1Apr83-331
  A. Ryan, 362:17Mar83-22
Chadwick, O. The Popes and European Revo-
lution.
  S. Gilley, 83:Autumn82-255
Chafe, W.L., ed. American Indian Lan-
guages and American Linguistics.
  P. Swiggers, 353:Vol 19No5/6-543
Chailley, J. La musique grecque antique.*
  A. Bélis, 555:Vol56fasc2-316
Chaillou, M. Domestique chez Montaigne.
  T. Cave, 617(TLS):3Jun83-579
Chakravarti, A. The Sdok Kak Thom Inscrip-
tion. (Pt 1)
  L. Sternbach, 318(JAOS):Oct-Dec81-482
Chalfant, E. Both Sides of the Ocean.
  R. Walters, 441:9Jan83-16
Chaliand, G. Report from Afghanistan.
  E. Mortimer, 453(NYRB):22Dec83-3
Chalidze, V., comp. SSSR: Vnutrennie prot-
ivorechiia.
  J. Bushnell, 550(RusR):Oct82-506
Chalier, C. Figures du féminin.
  H. Valavanidis-Wybrands, 450(NRF):
Jul-Aug82-187
"The Challenge of Peace: God's Promise
and Our Response."
  M. Bundy, 453(NYRB):16Jun83-3

Chalmurzaev, T.C. Status urdu v sovre-
mennoj Indii i tendencii ego razvitija.
  M. Gatzlaff, 682(ZPSK):Band35Heft2-218
Chamanga, M.A. and N-J. Gueunier. Le dic-
tionnaire Comorien-Français et Français-
Comorien du R.P. Sacleux.
  S. Brauner, 682(ZPSK):Band34Heft6-753
Chamberlain, J. A Life with the Printed
Word.
  W. Goodman, 441:23Jan83-10
Chamberlain, M.E. Lord Aberdeen.
  K. Bourne, 617(TLS):9Dec83-1380
Chamberlin, R. Loot!
  T. Phillips, 617(TLS):11Nov83-1245
Chambers, J.K., ed. The Languages of
Canada.
  A. Kramer-Dahl, 102(CanL):Winter81-136
Chambers, J.K. and P. Trudgill. Dialec-
tology.*
  G.M. Awbery, 297(JL):Sep82-431
  M.I. Miller, 35(AS):Winter82-291
  J.S. Ryan, 67:Nov82-224
"Chambers Twentieth Century Dictionary."
(new ed) (E.M. Kirkpatrick, ed in chief)
  J. Acworth, 617(TLS):19Aug83-888
Chamot, M. Turner: Early Works.
  E. Joll, 39:Jul82-65
Champion, L.S. "King Lear."
  A. Wertheim, 365:Spring83-87
Champion, L.S. Perspective in Shake-
speare's English Histories.*
  R.A. Rebholz, 551(RenQ):Winter81-618
  J. Wilders, 570(SQ):Winter82-540
Champlin, E. Fronto and Antonine Rome.*
  A.K. Bowman, 487:Autumn82-278
  R. Mellor, 24:Winter82-459
Chan, M. Music in the Theatre of Ben Jon-
son.*
  M. Emslie, 611(TN):Vol36No3-127
  E.B. Jorgens, 551(RenQ):Summer82-339
  P. Walls, 410(M&L):Jul/Oct81-380
Chand, M. The Bonsai Tree.
  N. Irving, 617(TLS):6May83-465
  442(NY):5Sep83-112
Chandernagor, F. L'Allée du Roi.
  N. Aronson, 475:Vol19No17-751
de Chandieu, A. Octonaires sur la vanité
et inconstance du monde.* (F. Bonali-
Fiquet, ed)
  M-C. Wrage, 207(FR):Dec82-315
Chandler, D., with B. Kiernan and M.H. Lim.
The Early Phases of Liberation in North-
west Cambodia.
  M. Ebihara, 293(JASt):Nov81-63
Chandler, K. Kett's Rebellion and Other
Poems.
  D. Davis, 617(TLS):8Apr83-356
Chandler, R. Selected Letters of Raymond
Chandler.* (F. MacShane, ed)
  27(AL):Mar82-151
Chandra, P. The Ṭūṭī-Nāma of the Cleve-
land Museum of Art and the Origins of
Mughal Painting.
  M.W. Meister, 318(JAOS):Oct-Dec81-476
Chanfón, C., ed. El libro de Villard de
Honnecourt.
  D. Angulo Íñiguez, 48:Jan-Mar80-133
Chanfón, C. - see García, S.
Chang, C-G. Der Held im europäischen und
koreanischen Märchen.
  D. Eikemeier, 196:Band23Heft3/4-311
Chang, K-C. Shang Civilization.
  D.N. Keightley, 293(JASt):May82-549

Chang, K.S. The Evolution of Chinese
"Tz'u" Poetry from Late T'ang to
Northern Sung.*
  A.C. Yu, 293(JASt):Feb82-315
Chang-Rodríguez, R. and D.A. Yates, eds.
Homage to Irving A. Leonard.
  W.P. Scott, 552(REH):Jan82-154
Changeux, J-P. L'Homme neuronal.
  D. Bodanis, 617(TLS):4Nov83-1206
"La Chanson de Roland."* (P. Jonin, ed
and trans)
  F. Goldin, 589:Oct82-968
  D.D.R. Owen, 208(FS):Apr82-183
de Chantelou, P.F. Journal du voyage du
Cavalier Bernin en France.
  A. Blunt, 90:Dec82-770
Chanteur, J. Platon, le désir et la cité.
  M. Lassègue, 192(EP):Jan-Mar82-112
Chantraine, G. Erasme et Luther.
  A.M. O'Donnell, 551(RenQ):Winter82-620
Chantraine, P. and others. Dictionnaire
étymologique de la langue grecque.*
(Vol 4, Pt 2)
  C.J. Ruijgh, 361:Sep/Oct82-202
Chao, P. Chinese Kinship.
  J.L. Watson, 617(TLS):24Jun83-652
"Chapeau Bas."
  L.E. Doucette, 627(UTQ):Summer82-481
  I. Joubert, 298:Fall82-149
Chapman, A. Drama and Power in a Hunting
Society.
  P. Henley, 617(TLS):18Mar83-277
Chapman, G., B. Jonson and J. Marston.
Eastward Ho.* (R.W. Van Fossen, ed)
  T.W. Craik, 161(DUJ):Jun82-303
  G.K. Hunter, 677(YES):Vol 12-247
Chappell, F. Earthsleep.*
  R. Tillinghast, 569(SR):Spring82-291
  E. Tucker, 114(ChiR):Summer81-85
Chappell, F. Midquest.
  639(VQR):Autumn82-134
Chappell, W., ed. Edward Burra.
  A. Powell, 39:Aug82-120
  A. Ross, 364:Apr/May82-5
Chapple, G. and H.H. Schulte, eds. The
Turn of the Century.
  E. Timms, 617(TLS):15Apr83-383
Chapple, J.A.V. - see Gaskell, E.
Chapple, R.L. Soviet Satire of the Twen-
ties.*
  N. Pervukhina-Kamyshnikova, 395(MFS):
Summer81-416
  H. Stephan, 104(CASS):Spring82-138
Char, L.H. Indonesia.
  C.R. Bryant, 293(JASt):May82-636
Char, R. Oeuvres complètes.
  D. Gascoyne, 617(TLS):14Oct83-1137
Charak, S.S. History and Culture of Hima-
layan States. (Vol 2)
  R.J. Young, 318(JAOS):Oct-Dec81-498
Charet, M. Le Thé au Harem d'Archi Ahmed.
  J. Kirkup, 617(TLS):6May83-464
Charette, G. Vanishing Spaces.
  G.W., 102(CanL):Winter81-184
Charlebois, G. Aléola.
  M. Fraser, 102(CanL):Winter81-139
Charleston, R.J. Masterpieces of Glass.*
  U.G. Dietz, 658:Spring82-83
Charleston, R.J., W. Evans and A. Polak,
eds. The Glass Circle 3.
  G. Wills, 39:Jun82-512
Charlot, M. and others. Britain Revisited.
  J. Leruez, 189(EA):Jul-Sep82-353

Charlton, M. The Price of Victory.
  S. Jacobson, 362:13Oct83-27
Charmasson, T. Recherches sur une tech-
nique divinatoire.
  D. Pingree, 589:Oct82-964
Charney, M. Comedy High and Low.*
  F. Bloch, 447(N&Q):Jun81-283
Charney, M. Sexual Fiction.
  S. Fogel, 395(MFS):Summer82-306
  M.B. Goodman, 594:Summer82-216
  L. Hamalian, 295(JML):Dec82-330
Charny, I.W. How Can We Commit the Un-
thinkable?
  D.P.L., 185:Jul83-839
Charpentier, C. Le Thème de la claustra-
tion dans "The Unicorn" d'Iris Murdoch.
  J. Lorch, 402(MLR):Jul82-712
Charpentier, F. Pour une lecture de la
tragédie humaniste: Jodelle, Garnier,
Montchrestien.
  C-G. Dubois, 535(RHL):Mar-Apr82-289
Charpentier, M-A. Pestis Mediolanensis
(The Plague of Milan). (H.W. Hitchcock,
ed)
  G. Dixon, 161(DUJ):Jun82-322
de Charrière, I. Romans.
  L. Herlin, 450(NRF):Oct82-115
de Charrière, I./B. de Zuylen. Oeuvres
complètes. (Vol 1) (S. and P. Dubois,
eds)
  M.B. Lacy, 173(ECS):Fall82-96
"Le Charroi de Nîmes, chanson de geste
anonyme du XIIe siècle." (F. Gégou,
trans)
  J.L. Grigsby, 545(RPh):Feb82-532
Charron, D. - see Rotrou, J.
Charrue, J-M. Plotin, lecteur de Platon.
  M. Lassègue, 192(EP):Jan-Mar81-111
Charteris, L. The Fantastic Saint. (M.H.
Greenberg and C.G. Waugh, eds)
  T.J. Binyon, 617(TLS):13May83-498
  T.J. Binyon, 617(TLS):8Jul83-732
Charters, S. Mr. Jabi and Mr. Smythe.
  C. Hope, 617(TLS):3Jun83-582
  E. Milton, 441:10Apr83-14
Charvet, J. A Critique of Freedom and
Equality.*
  D. Johnston, 185:Jul83-806
Charyn, J. Pinocchio's Nose.
  S. Maloff, 441:17Jul83-11
Chase, C., ed. The Dating of "Beowulf."
  R.D. Fulk, 481(PQ):Summer82-341
de Chase, C.S.S. Correlación entre al-
gunos procedimientos estilísticos y la
temática en la ficción extensa de Alejo
Carpentier hasta "El siglo de las luces."
  A. Bernal, 238:May82-314
Chase, G. The Distress of Harvest.
  E. Thompson, 102(CanL):Summer82-133
Chase, J. During the Reign of the Queen
of Persia.
  M. Atwood, 441:12Jun83-9
Chase, J. Exterior Decoration.
  R. Banham, 617(TLS):25Mar83-306
Chase, M. Elie Halévy.
  R. Jann, 637(VS):Spring82-381
  F.M.L. Thompson, 366:Spring82-119
Chastain, K. Toward a Philosophy of
Second-Language Learning and Teaching.*
  D.W. Birckbichler, 399(MLJ):Summer82-
196
  D.J. Curland, 238:May82-319

Chastel, A. The Sack of Rome, 1527.
P. Partner, 453(NYRB):31Mar83-20
442(NY):16May83-134
Chateau, D., A. Gardies and F. Jost, eds.
Cinémas de la modernité.
A. Thiher, 207(FR):Dec82-358
de Chateaubriand, F.R. Correspondance
Générale.* (Vol 1 ed by B. d'Andlau;
Vol 2 ed by P. Riberette)
B. Bray, 549(RLC):Oct-Dec82-519
de Chateaubriand, F.R. Correspondance
générale.* (Vol 3) (P. Riberette, ed)
F. Bassan, 446(NCFS):Spring-Summer83-
397
A. Clerval, 450(NRF):Jun82-96
Châtelet, A. Early Dutch Painting.
90:Apr82-264
Châtelet, F. and E. Pisier-Kouchner. Les
conceptions politiques du XXe siècle.
A. Reix, 542:Jan-Mar82-80
Chatillon, J. and others. Le Pouvoir.
A. Reix, 192(EP):Jan-Mar81-113
Chatman, S. Story and Discourse.*
U. Margolin, 107(CRCL):Mar82-76
Chatman, S., U. Eco and J-M. Klinkenberg,
eds. A Semiotic Landscape.
S. Schmidt-Wulffen and M. Faust,
260(IF):Band86-329
Chatterjee, L. Housing in Indonesia.
T. McGee, 293(JASt):Feb82-412
Chatterji, S.K. Select Writings. (Vol
1) (A.K. Kanjilal, ed) Select Papers.
(Vol 2) (A.K. Kanjilal and others, eds)
M.C. Shapiro, 293(JASt):May82-617
Chattopadhyaya, D.P. Individuals and
Worlds.
J.N. Mohanty, 449:Mar82-150
Chatwin, B. On the Black Hill.*
P-L. Adams, 61:Mar83-116
L. Jones, 364:Dec82/Jan83-136
V.S. Pritchett, 453(NYRB):20Jan83-6
F. Taliaferro, 231:Jan83-74
R. Towers, 441:2Jan83-1
J. Updike, 442(NY):21Mar83-126
Chaubey, B.B., ed. Bhāṣikasūtra of Mahar-
ṣi Kātyāyana with the Commentaries of
Mahāsvāmin and Anantabhaṭṭa.
L. Sternbach, 318(JAOS):Oct-Dec81-483
Chaucer, G. The Canterbury Tales. (P.G.
Ruggiers, ed)
W.C. McAvoy, 377:Nov81-183
D. Pearsall, 179(ES):Dec82-568
Chaucer, G. La Rakontoj de Canterbury,
Prologo.
M. Boulton, 447(N&Q):Jun81-277
Chaucer, G. "Troilus and Criseyde:" A
Facsimile of Corpus Christi College Cam-
bridge MS 61.
M.C. Seymour, 354:Jun82-190
Chaudhry, G.A. Studies in Dickens.
M. Reynolds, 155:Spring82-53
Chaudhuri, K.N. and C.J. Dewey, eds.
Economy and Society.
N.B. Dirks, 293(JASt):Nov81-168
Chaudhuri, S. Index Indo-Asiaticus.
L. Sternbach, 318(JAOS):Oct-Dec81-489
Chaumont, M. Orthographe avec ou sans
dictée.
N. Gueunier, 209(FM):Apr82-172
Chaunu, P. Histoire et décadence.
Y. Kempf, 450(NRF):Jun82-129
Chaurette, N. Fêtes d'automne.
S.R. Schulman, 207(FR):Apr83-785

Chaurette, N. Rêve d'une nuit d'hôpital.
J.M. Weiss, 102(CanL):Spring82-143
Chaze, E. Goodbye Goliath.
N. Callendar, 441:24Apr83-21
442(NY):6Jun83-146
Checinski, M. Poland.
M. Bernhard, 287:Nov82-17
A. Brumberg, 453(NYRB):2Jun83-37
Checkland, O. Philanthropy in Victorian
Scotland.
M.J. Moore, 637(VS):Winter82-257
Checkland, S. British Public Policy 1776-
1939.
H. Perkin, 617(TLS):10Jun83-589
Cheetham, N. Keepers of the Keys.
P. Hebblethwaite, 617(TLS):18Feb83-166
Cheetham, N. Mediaeval Greece.
P. Charanis, 589:Jul82-679
Cheever, J. Oh What a Paradise It Seems!*
D. Flower, 249(HudR):Summer82-274
639(VQR):Summer82-97
Cheever, S. The Cage.*
B. Morton, 617(TLS):11Feb83-130
Chefdor, M. Blaise Cendrars.*
H. Nitzberg, 207(FR):Dec82-327
Chekhov, A. Chekhov: The Early Stories,
1883-1888.* (P. Miles and H. Pitcher,
eds and trans)
H. Moss, 453(NYRB):8Dec83-3
442(NY):15Aug83-90
Chekhov, A. Chekov's Great Plays. (J-P.
Baricelli, ed)
M. Ehre, 574(SEEJ):Fall82-359
Chellas, B.F. Modal Logic.*
S.J. Kuhn, 154:Sep82-545
Chen, C-Y. Hsün Yüeh (A.D. 143-209).
C. Hansen, 318(JAOS):Jul-Sep81-388
Ch'en, C-Y. Hsün Yüeh and the Mind of
Late Han China.
B.B. Blakeley, 485(PE&W):Jan82-112
W.A. Rickett, 293(JASt):Nov81-100
Chen, J. The Chinese of America.
S.F. Chung, 293(JASt):Feb82-304
Chen Jo-hsi. The Execution of Mayor Yin
and Other Stories from the Great Prole-
tarian Cultural Revolution.
A. Chan, 318(JAOS):Oct-Dec81-429
Chen, L. and L. Wu, eds. Chinese Knotting.
R.L. Shep, 614:Spring83-16
Chenel, L. and L. Siegfried. Chèvre!
M. Burros, 441:11Dec83-36
Cheney, M.G. Roger, Bishop of Worcester,
1164-1179.
R.B. Patterson, 589:Oct82-872
Chenkin, K. Okhotnik vverkh nogami.
W. Laqueur, 617(TLS):11Feb83-137
Cherchi, P. Andrea Cappellano, i trova-
tori e altri temi romanzi.
F.M. Chambers, 545(RPh):Nov81-438
Cherfas, J. Man-Made Life.
A. Mackay, 617(TLS):15Apr83-381
G.S. Stent, 441:23Oct83-28
Cherlin, G. Model Theoretic Algebra.
U. Felgner, 316:Mar82-222
Chern, K.C. Dilemma in China.
N.B. Tucker, 293(JASt):Nov81-102
Chernaik, W.L. The Poet's Time.
L. Mackinnon, 617(TLS):16Sep83-992
Chernin, K. In My Mother's House.
D. McWhorter, 441:21Aug83-14
Chernyshevsky, N.G. What Is To Be Done?
K. Fitz Lyon, 617(TLS):20May83-525

Church, R., ed. The Dynamics of Victorian Business.
  M. Turner, 637(VS):Autumn81-89
Churchill, K. Italy and English Literature 1764-1930.
  D. Paroissien, 637(VS):Spring82-96
  T. Webb, 339(KSMB):No33-81
Churchland, P.M. Scientific Realism and the Plasticity of Mind.*
  M.E. Levin, 449:Sep82-461
  A. Morton, 482(PhR):Apr82-299
Chusid, M. - see Verdi, G.
Chuvin, P. - see Nonnus
Ciardi, J. A Browser's Dictionary and Native's Guide to the Unknown American Language.*
  J.R. Gaskin, 569(SR):Winter82-143
Ciardi, J. For Instance.
  D. Gioia, 491:May82-102
Ciavolella, M. and D. Beecher - see Caro, A.
Cibber, C. The Plays of Colley Cibber. [intro by R.L. Hayley]
  566:Spring83-137
Cicero. Cicéron, Correspondance. (Vol 7) (J. Beaujeu, ed and trans)
  E. Rawson, 123:Vol32No1-97
  H. Zehnacker, 555:Vol56fasc1-153
Cicero. Epistulae ad Familiares.* (D.R. Shackleton Bailey, ed)
  J.H. Brouwers, 394:Vol35fasc3/4-402
Cieszkowski, A. Prolegomena zur Historiosophie.
  L.S.S., 543:Jun82-860
Cifelli, E.M. David Humphreys.
  J.D. Wallace, 165(EAL):Winter82/83-254
Ciment, M. Kubrick. Schatzberg, de la photo au cinéma.
  D. Robinson, 617(TLS):23Sep83-1015
Cioranescu, A. Ion Barbu. (E. Tappe, ed and trans)
  D. Deletant, 402(MLR):Oct82-1007
  V. Nemoianu, 617(TLS):11Mar83-250
Ciplijauskaité, B. - see de Góngora, L.
Cipolla, W.R. A Catalog of the Works of Arthur Foote (1853-1937).
  A.F.L.T., 412:Feb81-61
Cipriani, G. Il mito etrusco nel rinascimento fiorentino.
  A. Hus, 555:Vol56fasc2-373
  B. Mitchell, 276:Winter82-345
  D.J. Wilcox, 551(RenQ):Summer82-257
Cirre, J.F. and M.M. España y los españoles. (2nd ed)
  V.R. Foster, 238:May82-323
  C.T. Hartl, 399(MLJ):Spring82-98
Ciruelo, P. Reprovación de las supersticiones y hechicerías. (A.V. Ebersole, ed)
  M. Embeita, 552(REH):Jan82-139
Cisneros, A. Helicopters in the Kingdom of Peru.
  D. McDuff, 565:Vol23No1-59
Čistova, K.V. and T.A. Bernštam, eds. Russkij narodnyj svadebnyj obrjad.
  J.L. Conrad, 292(JAF):Jul-Sep82-357
Citino, D. The Appassionata Poems.
  J. Ditsky, 628(UWR):Spring-Summer83-82
Citron, S. and M-C. Junod, eds. Registres de la Compagnie des Pasteurs de Genève. (Vol 6)
  J. Raitt, 551(RenQ):Spring82-101

Ciucci, G. and others. The American City: From the Civil War to the New Deal.*
  T. Walton, 576:Dec82-351
Claes, F. Bibliographisches Verzeichnis der deutschen Vokabulare und Wörterbucher gedruckt bis 1600.
  W.J. Jones, 685(ZDL):3/1981-359
Claiborne, R. Our Marvelous Native Tongue.
  P-L. Adams, 61:May83-104
  M. Bayles, 441:18Sep83-28
  442(NY):6Jun83-144
Clair, A. Pseudonymie et paradoxe.
  M. Carignan, 154:Mar82-137
Clampitt, A. The Kingfisher.
  R. Howard, 472:Spring/Summer83-271
  W. Logan, 617(TLS):10Jun83-614
  R. Tillinghast, 441:7Aug83-12
  H. Vendler, 453(NYRB):3Mar83-19
Clanchy, M.T. England and Its Rulers 1066-1272.
  W.L. Warren, 617(TLS):30Sep83-1040
Clanchy, M.T. From Memory to Written Record.*
  W. Rothwell, 208(FS):Apr82-190
Clancy, L. Xavier Herbert.
  J.J. Healy, 71(ALS):Oct82-535
Clancy, L. Christina Stead's "The Man Who Loved Children" and "For Love Alone."
  J. Croft, 71(ALS):May82-400
Clapperton, C.M., ed. Scotland.
  C. Harvie, 617(TLS):26Aug83-908
Clardy, J.V. and B.S. The Superfluous Man in Russian Letters.*
  M. Raskin, 395(MFS):Summer81-412
Clare, G. Last Waltz in Vienna.*
  639(VQR):Autumn82-118
Clare, J. John Clare: The Journal, Essays, The Journey from Essex. (A. Tibble, ed)
  J.A. Kearney, 506(PSt):Dec82-340
Clare, J. John Clare's Autobiographical Writings. (E. Robinson, ed)
  A. Motion, 617(TLS):25Nov83-1306
Clare, J. John Clare's Birds. (E. Robinson and R. Fitter, eds)
  R. O'Hanlon, 617(TLS):21Jan83-70
Clare, J. The Midsummer Cushion. (A. Tibble and R.K.R. Thornton, eds)
  P.M. Ball, 677(YES):Vol 12-300
Clark, A. Christopher Brennan.*
  L.J. Austin, 208(FS):Jul82-354
  T. Sturm, 71(ALS):May82-402
Clark, A. Lewis Carroll.
  R. Dupree, 191(ELN):Dec82-119
Clark, A. Psychological Models and Neural Mechanisms.*
  P.S. Churchland, 311(JP):Feb82-98
  K.V. Wilkes, 84:Jun82-230
Clark, A. Working Life of Women in the Seventeenth Century.
  A. Goreau, 617(TLS):7Jan83-20
Clark, A.M. Studies in Roman Eighteenth-Century Painting.* (E.P. Bowron, ed)
  T.J. McCormick, 39:Jun82-509
Clark, C.E.F., Jr. - see "The Nathaniel Hawthorne Journal 1977"
Clark, D.R. "That Black Day."
  S.B., 675(YER):Jun82-146
  B. Dolan, 305(JIL):Sep82-114
Clark, F. Hats.
  R.L. Shep, 614:Summer83-16
Clark, G. The Identity of Man.
  D.A. Roe, 617(TLS):17Jun83-621

Clark, I. Christ Revealed.
E.R. Cunnar, 391:Dec82-103
Clark, J.G. La Rochelle and the Atlantic
Economy during the Eighteenth Century.
D. Geggus, 617(TLS):28Jan83-89
Clark, K. Piero della Francesca.
R. Cocke, 59:Dec82-508
F. Russell, 39:May82-411
Clark, K. Moments of Vision.
D. Thomas, 324:Feb83-155
Clark, K. The Soviet Novel.*
R.L. Chapple, 104(CASS):Fall-Winter82-528
H. McLean, 550(RusR):Jan82-108
S.J. Rabinowitz, 574(SEEJ):Spring82-109
M. Raskin, 395(MFS):Winter82/83-709
Clark, K. What is a Masterpiece?
P. Joannides, 97(CQ):Vol 11No3-390
Clark, L.D. The Fifth Wind.
L. Davis, 649(WAL):Nov82-297
Clark, L.D. The Minoan Distance.*
L. Hamalian, 363(LitR):Spring83-451
M. Magalaner, 395(MFS):Summer81-307
Clark, M. The Place of Syllogistic in
Logical Theory.
P.M. Simons, 479(PhQ):Apr82-175
P. Thom, 518:Apr82-73
Clark, R. Bertrand Russell and His World.*
H. Ruja, 556:Winter81/82-171
Clark, R.J. Catabasis.*
P. Chuvin, 555:Vol155fasc2-365
H.W. Stubbs, 203:Vol193No2-234
Clark, R.P., ed. Best Newspaper Writing
1979. Best Newspaper Writing 1980.
Best Newspaper Writing 1981.
E.A. Nickerson, 599:Fall82-458
Clark, R.W. Benjamin Franklin.
P. Maier, 441:6Feb83-23
A. Sheps, 617(TLS):16Sep83-984
E.S. Turner, 362:28Apr83-25
Clark, S. Social Origins of the Irish
Land War.*
P. Bew, 161(DUJ):Jun82-295
Clark, W. and J. Page. Energy, Vulnerabil-
ity, and War.
639(VQR):Spring82-50
Clark, W.B., ed. Critical Essays on Rob-
ert Penn Warren.
A. Shepherd, 392:Winter81/82-53
Clarke, A. Selected Poems. (T. Kinsella,
ed)
J. Parini, 569(SR):Fall82-623
Clarke, A.C. 2010: Odyssey Two.*
C. Greenland, 617(TLS):21Jan83-69
G. Jonas, 441:23Jan83-24
Clarke, A.F.N. Contact.
R. West, 617(TLS):6May83-455
Clarke, G. Letter from a Far Country.
D. Davis, 362:5May83-24
M. Kinzie, 29:Nov/Dec83-40
A. Stevenson, 617(TLS):15Jul83-757
Clarke, H. Homer's Readers.
M.W. Edwards, 121(CJ):Apr/May83-369
Clarke, J.W. American Assassins.*
P.J. Parish, 617(TLS)28Jan83-80
Clarke, M. The Tempting Prospect.*
L. Ormond, 90:May82-308
G. Reynolds, 39:May82-415
Clarke, M. and C. Crisp. The Ballet-
Goer's Guide.
R. Philp, 151:Jun82-85

Clarke, M. and N. Penny, eds. The Arro-
gant Connoisseur.
R. Jenkyns, 339(KSMB):No33-75
Clarke, P. and J.S. Gregory, eds. Western
Reports on the Taiping.
R. Harris, 617(TLS):24Jun83-675
Clarke, S. The Foundations of Structural-
ism.*
D. Wood, 208(FS):Apr82-239
Clarke, S. Marx, Marginalism and Modern
Sociology.
K. Minogue, 617(TLS):13May83-482
Clarkson, S. The Soviet Theory of Develop-
ment.
P. Desai, 550(RusR):Jan82-96
Claudel, C.A. Fools and Rascals.*
E.C. Lynskey, 585(SoQ):Spring82-94
Claudian. Claudius Claudianus: Cl.
Claudiani "De bello Gothico." (Vol 1)
(G. Garuti, ed and trans)
M. McCormick, 24:Summer82-226
M. Reydellet, 555:Vol56fasc1-168
Claudon, F. Hofmannsthal et la France.
H-G. Ruprecht, 107(CRCL):Jun82-301
Claudon, F. L'idée et l'influence de la
musique chez quelques romantiques fran-
çais et notamment Stendhal.
J-M. Bailbé, 535(RHL):Jan-Feb82-133
Claus, D.B. Toward the Soul.
D.F., 185:Oct82-210
S.D. Sullivan, 487:Autumn82-272
Clausen, A. Austin, Texas Austin, Texas.
D. Lehman, 181:Spring-Summer83-277
Clausen, C. The Place of Poetry.*
W. Harmon, 491:Jan83-237
A. Krystal, 31(ASch):Autumn82-583
J. Olney, 569(SR):Summer82-456
295(JML):Dec82-388
Clavaud, R. Le Ménexène de Platon et la
rhétorique de son temps.
Y. Lafrance, 154:Mar82-156
Clavell, L. El nombre propio de Dios
según Santo Tomás de Aquino.
A. Reix, 542:Jul-Sep82-535
Clay, G. Close-Up.
T.J. Schlereth, 658:Winter82-289
Clay, H. The Papers of Henry Clay. (Vol
6) (M.W.M. Hargreaves and J.F. Hopkins,
eds)
639(VQR):Autumn82-120
Clayton, B.D. Life After Doomsday.
G. Ignatieff, 529(QQ):Summer82-352
Clayton, J.D. and G. Schaarschmidt, eds.
Poetica Slavica.
P. Austin, 104(CASS):Fall-Winter82-518
Clayton, P.A. The Rediscovery of Ancient
Egypt.
J.M. Crook, 617(TLS):18Feb83-150
Clayton, T., ed. Cavalier Poets.*
K. Bartenschlager, 38:Band100Heft3/4-526
Cleaves, F.W., ed and trans. The Secret
History of the Mongols. (Vol 1)
C.R. Bawden, 617(TLS):24Jun83-669
Clebsch, W.A. - see Donne, J.
Clecak, P. America's Quest for the Ideal
Self.
J.M., 231:Jul83-75
R.J. Margolis, 441:17Apr83-18
Clegg, J. Ruskin and Venice.
D. Howard, 90:Dec82-775
D. Johnson, 453(NYRB):31Mar83-13

Clemeau, C. The Adriadne Clue.
T.J. Binyon, 617(TLS):18Feb83-149
Clement of Alexandria. Clément d'Alexan-
drie, "Les Stromates;" "Stromate V." (A.
le Boulluec, ed; P. Voulet, trans)
É. des Places, 555:Vol56fasc1-138
Clément, C. Vies et légendes de Jacques
Lacan.
J. Forrester, 208(FS):Jan82-96
H. Rapaport, 435:Spring/Summer82-89
Clements, P. and J. Grindle, eds. The
Poetry of Thomas Hardy.*
M. Bird, 175:Autumn82-262
K. Brady, 637(VS):Spring82-390
H.L. Weatherby, 569(SR):Spring82-313
Clemoes, P., ed. Anglo-Saxon England.
(Vol 8)
A. Crépin, 189(EA):Jan-Mar82-74
Clemoes, P., ed. Anglo-Saxon England.
(Vol 9)
J.J. Campbell, 377:Jul82-114
B.E. Yorke, 366:Autumn82-257
Clendenning, P. and R. Bartlett. Eigh-
teenth-Century Russia.
J.M. Hartley, 575(SEER):Apr82-311
Clerc, C., ed. Approaches to "Gravity's
Rainbow."
C. Baldick, 617(TLS):3Jun83-576
de Clercq-Fobe, D. Epingles votives du
Luristan (Iran).
O.W. Muscarella, 318(JAOS):Apr-Jun81-
228
Clifford, J. Person and Myth.
P. Gathercole, 617(TLS):11Feb83-136
Clifford, W. An Ache In The Ear.
D. Barbour, 648(WCR):Oct82-37
Clifton, T. and C. Leroy. God Cried.
M. Yapp, 617(TLS):26Aug83-911
Cline, C.T. The Attorney Conspiracy.
N. Callendar, 441:10Apr83-32
Clinton, C. The Plantation Mistress.
P-L. Adams, 61:Feb83-105
Clinton, D. and M. Liquorice - see Taylor,
R.
Clipman, W. Dog Light.
V. Young, 249(HudR):Spring82-139
Clissold, S. Djilas.
R.K. Kindersley, 617(TLS):30Dec83-1461
Clogg, M.J. and R., comps. Greece.
S. Wichert, 575(SEER):Apr82-300
Clogg, R., ed. Balkan Society in the Age
of Greek Independence.
P. Auty, 575(SEER):Jul82-461
S. Fischer-Galati, 104(CASS):Fall-
Winter82-574
Clopper, L.M., ed. Records of Early En-
glish Drama: Chester.*
A. Hudson, 541(RES):Aug82-313
V.B. Richmond, 551(RenQ):Spring81-129
Clothier, C. Death Mask.*
D. Graham, 565:Vol23No2-74
Cloudsley, A. Women of Omdurman.
J. Murray, 69:Vol51No4-879
Clough, C.H. The Duchy of Urbino in the
Renaissance.
L. Tenenbaum, 276:Winter82-346
Cloulas, I. Catherine de Médicis.
N. Cazauran, 535(RHL):Jul-Aug82-649
Clover, C.J. The Medieval Saga.
H. O'Donoghue, 617(TLS):25Feb83-197
Clubb, L.G. - see Della Porta, G.
Clubbe, J. - see Froude, J.A.

Clucas, H. Gods and Mortals.*
M. O'Neill, 493:Sep82-56
Cluck, N.A., ed. Literature and Music.
K. Price, 290(JAAC):Winter82-236
Clurman, H. Ibsen.
D. Jarrett, 447(N&Q):Aug81-356
Cluysenaar, A. and S. Hewat. Double Helix.
A. Stevenson, 617(TLS):15Jul83-757
Clyne, M., ed. Australia Talks.
B. Rigsby, 355(LSoc):Apr82-126
Coakley, J. and L. Harris. The City of
Capital.
J.H.C. Leach, 617(TLS):9Dec83-1368
Coale, A.J., B.A. Anderson and E. Härm.
Human Fertility in Russia since the
Nineteenth Century.*
T.S. Fedor, 550(RusR):Jan82-85
Coates, C. Claret.
J. Robinson, 617(TLS):6May83-452
Coates, C.A. John Cowper Powys in Search
of a Landscape.
P. Redgrove, 617(TLS):27May83-536
Cobb, M.G. - see Debussy, C.
Cobb, R. French and Germans, Germans and
French.
J. Grigg, 362:28Jul83-23
S. Hoffmann, 441:18Dec83-6
R.O. Paxton, 453(NYRB):16Jun83-9
E. Weber, 617(TLS):12Aug83-850
Cobb, R. Promenades.*
I. Collins, 366:Spring82-118
Cobb, R. Still Life.
N. Annan, 362:27Oct83-30
M. Neve, 617(TLS):21Oct83-1149
Coble, P.M., Jr. The Shanghai Capitalists
and the Nationalist Government, 1927-
1937.
S. Cochran, 293(JASt):Feb82-319
Cobley, J., ed. Sydney Cove 1793-1795.
N. McLachlan, 617(TLS):7Oct83-1097
Coburn, D. and others, eds. Health and
Canadian Society.
M.G. Taylor, 529(QQ):Autumn82-671
Coburn, K. Experience into Thought.*
J.D. Gutteridge, 447(N&Q):Aug81-348
M.E. Holstein, 627(UTQ):Summer82-424
G. Little, 541(RES):Nov82-482
Cochin, A. L'Esprit du jacobinisme.
P. Higonnet, 617(TLS):14Oct83-1141
Cochran, C.E. Character, Community and
Politics.
P.S., 185:Jul83-827
Cochran, S. Big Business in China.
P. West, 293(JASt):Nov81-105
Cochran, S., and A.C.K. Hsieh, with J.
Cochran, eds and trans. One Day in
China: May 21, 1936.
J.B. Grieder, 441:19Jun83-8
H.R. Isaacs, 453(NYRB):10Nov83-48
W.J.F. Jenner, 617(TLS):14Oct83-1133
Cochrane, E. Historians and Historiogra-
phy in the Italian Renaissance.*
P. Zagorin, 551(RenQ):Winter82-590
Cochrane, I. The Slipstream.
J. Melmoth, 617(TLS):19Aug83-875
Cockburn, A. The Threat.
W.E. Colby, 441:26Jun83-3
D. Holloway, 453(NYRB):2Jun83-22
T. Powers, 61:May83-93
Cockfield, J.H., ed. Dollars and Diplo-
macy.*
J. Keep, 575(SEER):Apr82-315

Cocking, J.M. Proust.*
D. May, 362:18Aug83-19
A.R. Pugh, 268(IFR):Summer83-145
Cocks, R. Diary Kept by the Head of the
English Factory in Japan.
M. Cooper, 407(MN):Summer82-265
Cockshaw, P., M-C. Garand and P. Jodogne,
eds. Miscellanea codicologica F. Masai
dicata MCMLXXIX.
M. McCormick, 24:Summer82-227
Codignola, L., ed. Canadiana.
R.A. Cavell, 107(CRCL):Dec81-572
Codoñer Merino, C. - see Seneca
Cody, L. Bad Company.*
N. Callendar, 441:10Apr83-32
Coe, B. and M. Haworth-Booth. A Guide to
Early Photographic Processes.
C. Ford, 617(TLS):24Jun83-668
Coetzee, J.M. Dusklands.
R. Owen, 617(TLS):14Jan83-30
Coetzee, J.M. Life and Times of Michael K.
D.J. Enright, 617(TLS):30Sep83-1037
J. Mellors, 362:13Oct83-31
C. Ozick, 441:11Dec83-1
Coetzee, J.M. Waiting for the Barbarians.*
P. Lewis, 565:Vol23No2-44
L. Whiteson, 99:Oct82-26
Coffey, T.M. Hap.
J. Keegan, 61:Jan83-96
Coffin, D., ed. The Italian Garden.
W.H. Adams, 127:Fall82-255
Coffin, D.R. The Villa in the Life of
Renaissance Rome.*
G.L. Hersey, 551(RenQ):Summer81-249
Coffin, F.M. The Ways of a Judge.
H.T. Silsby 2d, 432(NEQ):Jun82-313
Coffin, T.P., with R.D. Renwick. The
British Traditional Ballad in North
America. (rev)
E.B. Lyle, 203:Vol93No2-229
Cogswell, F. A Long Apprenticeship.
D. Barbour, 648(WCR):Summer81-80
P. Morley, 102(CanL):Winter81-109
Cohen, A. Music in the French Royal
Academy of Sciences.
P. Gouk, 410(M&L):Jul/Oct82-314
Cohen, A.A. An Admirable Woman.
E. Shorris, 441:20Nov83-9
Cohen, A.B. Poor Pearl, Poor Girl!
J.S. Bratton, 203:Vol93No2-239
Cohen, G.A. Karl Marx's Theory of His-
tory.*
D.F. Calhoun, 125:Fall81-94
J. Cohen, 311(JP):May82-253
E. Kamenka, 63:Mar82-81
J.S.M., 543:Dec81-374
J. Nida-Rümelin, 167:Nov82-421
Cohen, G.A., ed. U.S. College-Sponsored
Programs Abroad. Vacation Study Abroad.
R. Neff, 399(MLJ):Summer82-196
Cohen, H., ed. The Public Enemy.
J. Basinger, 18:Jul-Aug82-72
Cohen, H. Werke. (Vol 7, Pt 2: Ethik des
reinen Willens.) (H. Holzhey, ed)
J.M. Krois, 319:Jul83-417
Cohen, H. - see Thew, H.
Cohen, H.R. Biblical Hapax Legomena in
the Light of Akkadian and Ugaritic.
P.T. Daniels, 318(JAOS):Oct-Dec81-440
Cohen, I.B. The Newtonian Revolution.
A.R. Hall, 84:Sep82-305
Cohen, J. Le haut langage.*
J-M. Klinkenberg, 209(FM):Apr82-144

Cohen, J.A., R.R. Edwards and F-M.C. Chen,
eds. Essays on China's Legal Tradition.
B.C. Terrell, 293(JASt):Feb82-320
Cohen, J.L. Class and Civil Society.
J. Gray, 617(TLS):30Dec83-1459
Cohen, J.R. Charles Dickens and his
Original Illustrators.*
M. Baumgarten, 651(WHR):Autumn82-279
C. Fox, 90:Dec82-778
N.K. Hill, 191(ELN):Sep81-73
S. Monod, 402(MLR):Jul82-708
Cohen, K. Film and Fiction.*
J.G. Saunders, 541(RES):Aug82-367
Cohen, L.H. The Revolutionary Histories.
D.F. Hawke, 125:Spring82-296
A.H. Shaffer, 656(WMQ):Apr82-383
Cohen, M. Flowers of Darkness.*
J. Kertzer, 198:Jan82-81
Cohen, M. The Sweet Second Summer of
Kitty Malone.*
F. Mansbridge, 296(JCF):No33-121
Cohen, M., T. Nagel and T. Scanlon, eds.
Marx, Justice and History.
A.P. Simonds, 185:Jul83-792
Cohen, M.J. Palestine.
D. Stone, 287:Jun/Jul82-29
Cohen, M.N. Lewis Carroll and Alice, 1832-
1982.
P. Heath, 191(ELN):Dec82-126
Cohen, M.N. - see Carroll, L.
Cohen, M.N., with R.L. Green - see Carroll,
L.
Cohen, M.R. Jewish Self-Government in
Medieval Egypt.
S. Bowman, 589:Jul82-593
Cohen, N. Long Steel Rail.
B.L. Pearson, 187:May83-376
Cohen, R.D. and R.A. Mohl. The Paradox of
Progressive Education.
J. Abbott, 106:Spring82-87
Cohen, S. The Truth About the Neutron
Bomb.
T. Powers, 441:1May83-9
Cohen, S.A. English Zionists and British
Jews.
W.J. Fishman, 617(TLS):4Mar83-204
Cohen, T. and P. Guyer, eds. Essays in
Kant's Aesthetics.
J. Kulenkampff, 290(JAAC):Spring83-337
Cohen, U. and K-H. Osterloh. Zimmer frei.
A. Galt, 399(MLJ):Autumn82-337
Cohen, W.B. Français et Africains.
H. Cronel, 450(NRF):Sep82-145
Cohen-Solal, A., with H. Nizan. Paul
Nizan, communiste impossible.
W.D. Redfern, 402(MLR):Apr82-462
Cohn, A.M. and K.K. Collins. The Cumu-
lated Dickens Checklist, 1970-1979.
T. Wortham, 445(NCF):Mar83-619
Cohn, D. La Transparence intérieure.
P. Dulac, 450(NRF):Mar82-130
Cohn, D. Transparent Minds.*
M.G. Rose, 107(CRCL):Dec81-536
H.H. Weinberg, 446(NCFS):Spring-Summer
83-358
W. Zacharasiewicz, 52:Band16Heft1-73
Cohn, J. Improbable Fiction.*
V. Strong-Boag, 106:Spring82-97
Cohn, R. Just Play.*
A.P. Hinchliffe, 148:Spring82-87
Cohn, R. New American Dramatists 1960-
1980.*
A.P. Hinchliffe, 148:Autumn82-83

Cohn, R.G. Toward the Poems of Mallarmé.
J. Newton, 546(RR):May82-393
Cohn, S.K., Jr. The Laboring Classes in Renaissance Florence.*
R.A. Goldthwaite, 551(RenQ):Autumn82-472
L. Martines, 589:Jul82-595
Coianiz, A. and V. Allouche. Grammaire du français langue étrangère.
P. Trescases, 207(FR):May83-965
Coirault, Y. L'Horloge et le Miroir.
P. Hourcade, 535(RHL):Mar-Apr82-292
Coke, V.D. Avant-Garde Photography in Germany, 1919-1939.
J. Willett, 453(NYRB):17Feb83-31
Colace, P.R. - see Choerilus of Samos
Colaiaco, J.A. James Fitzjames Stephen and the Crisis of Victorian Thought.
S. Collini, 617(TLS):16Sep83-975
Colbert, E.H. Dinosaurs.
M. Levine, 441:11Dec82-35
Colby, B.N. and L.M. The Daykeeper.
D. Hendrix, 37:Sep-Oct82-62
Colby, D. As the Curtain Rises.
J. Schlueter, 397(MD):Jun82-314
Colby, R.A. Thackeray's Canvass of Humanity.*
S.M. Adamson, 447(N&Q):Jul81-271
C. MacKay, 594:Summer82-218
G.C. Sorensen, 301(JEGP):Apr82-274
J. Sutherland, 677(YES):Vol 12-314
Coldham, J.D. Lord Harris.
P.H. Sutcliffe, 617(TLS):24Jun83-657
Coldham, P.W. English Estates of American Colonists. Lord Mayor's Court of London Depositions Relating to Americans 1641-1736.
B.R. Masters, 325:Apr82-40
Cole, B. Masaccio and the Art of Early Renaissance Florence.*
F. Ames-Lewis, 90:May82-300
M. Boskovits, 551(RenQ):Autumn81-415
Cole, B. The Renaissance Artist at Work.
F. Ames-Lewis, 617(TLS):2Dec83-1337
Cole, B. Sienese Painting.*
F. Ames-Lewis, 90:May82-300
Cole, D. Rough Road to Rome.
R. Trevelyan, 362:2Jun83-26
Cole, D. The Work of Sir Gilbert Scott.*
S. Muthesius, 637(VS):Summer82-508
Cole, H.C. The "All's Well" Story from Boccaccio to Shakespeare.*
J.J. O'Connor, 551(RenQ):Autumn82-517
Cole, H.M. Mbari.
W. Muensterberger, 90:Dec82-779
Cole, L. Hollywood Red.
V.S. Navasky, 18:Mar82-72
Cole, W.S. Roosevelt and the Isolationists, 1932-45.
A. Schlesinger, Jr., 453(NYRB):24Nov83-36
Coleman, D.G. The Chaste Muse.*
D. Maskell, 541(RES):Nov82-465
Coleman, D.G. The Gallo-Roman Muse.*
D. Ménager, 535(RHL):Mar-Apr82-287
Coleman, E.J. - see Shih T'ao
Coleman, J. Medieval Readers and Writers 1350-1400.
F.C. Robinson, 569(SR):Fall82-608
639(VQR):Autumn82-116
Coleman, K. Colonial Georgia.*
F. Shuffelton, 173(ECS):Summer83-415

Coleman, P. The Heart of James McAuley.
L. Hergenhan, 71(ALS):May82-413
Coleman, V. Miles Franklin in America.
D. Kirby, 71(ALS):Oct82-548
Coleman, W. Mad Dog Black Lady.
Y. Komunyakaa, 459:Summer/Winter81-229
Coleridge, S.T. The Collected Works of Samuel Taylor Coleridge. (Vol 7: Biographia Literaria, or Biographical Sketches of My Literary Life and Opinions.) (J. Engell and W.J. Bate, eds)
R. Ashton, 617(TLS):26Aug83-913
J. Curtis, 648(WCR):Apr83-53
Coleridge, S.T. The Collected Works of Samuel Taylor Coleridge.* (Vol 12: Marginalia, I.) (G. Whalley, ed)
J.R. Barth, 611(WC):Summer82-106
D. Degrois, 189(EA):Oct-Dec82-474
E. Shaffer, 591(SIR):Fall82-531
Coleridge, S.T. The Collected Works of Samuel Taylor Coleridge. (Vol 13: Logic.) (J.R.D. Jackson, ed)
D. Emmet, 627(UTQ):Summer82-422
R. Modiano, 661(WC):Summer82-108
Coles, D. The Prinzhorn Collection.
A. Morton, 526:Autumn82-72
J. Peirce, 99:Oct82-27
Coles, R. Flannery O'Connor's South.*
R. Gray, 447(N&Q):Oct81-466
P.G. Hogan, Jr., 573(SSF):Fall82-395
D. McGifford, 106:Winter82-389
W.J. Stuckey, 395(MFS):Autumn82-508
Colette. The Collected Stories of Colette. (R. Phelps, ed)
V.S. Pritchett, 442(NY):19Dec83-137
P. Rose, 441:25Dec83-3
Colette. Letters from Colette.* (R. Phelps, ed and trans)
H. Harris, 364:Jun82-97
Colette, J. - see Schulz, W.
Colin, R-P. Schopenhauer en France.*
Y. Chevrel, 549(RLC):Oct-Dec82-523
J. Lefranc, 192(EP):Jan-Mar82-116
R. Pouilliart, 356(LR):Feb82-83
Collaer, P. Musique traditionnelle sicilienne.
B. Lortat-Jacob, 187:Sep83-551
Collard, E. The Cut and Construction of Women's Dress in the 1930's.
R.L. Shep, 614:Summer83-18
Collard, P. Ramón J. Sender en los años 1930-1936.
C.L. King, 238:May82-309
M.C. Peñuelas, 240(HR):Summer82-368
A.M. Trippett, 86(BHS):Apr82-159
Collcutt, M. Five Mountains.*
C. Bielefeldt, 293(JASt):Aug82-841
"College and University Archives: Selected Readings."*
M. Cook, 325:Apr82-47
Colles, H.C. and J. Cruft. The Royal College of Music.
R. Crichton, 617(TLS):1Jul83-697
Colley, I. Dos Passos and the Fiction of Despair.*
H. Claridge, 447(N&Q):Aug81-365
Colli, G. Dopo Nietzsche.
R.P.H., 543:Sep81-119
Colli, G. Naissance de la philosophie.
J-M. le Sidaner, 450(NRF):May82-128
Colli, G. La Ragione errabonda. (E. Colli, ed)
L. Pompa, 617(TLS):6May83-463

Colli, G. La Sapienza greca.* (Vol 3)
    D. Pralon, 555:Vol56fasc1-129
Collie, M. The Alien Art.*
    P. Keating, 447(N&Q):Feb81-90
Collier, D., ed. The New Authoritarianism
in Latin America.
    F. Lambert, 86(BHS):Oct82-349
Collier, J.L. Louis Armstrong.
    M. Lydon, 441:30Oct83-12
Collier, R. The Road to Pearl Harbor:
1941.
    639(VQR):Spring82-44
Collinet, J-P. - see Perrault, C.
Collins, B. and I. Mees. The Sounds of
English and Dutch.
    W.S. Allan and P. Nieuwenhuis, 361:
    Sep/Oct82-189
Collins, D. Sartre as Biographer.*
    A. Demaitre, 577(SHR):Summer82-284
    S.B. John, 402(MLR):Apr82-464
Collins, J. Hollywood Wives.
    J. Bass, 441:11Sep83-18
Collins, L. and D. Lapierre. The Fifth
Horseman.
    A. Denman, 42(AR):Summer82-363
Collins, M. The Baby Blue Rip-Off.
    N. Callendar, 441:20Mar83-27
Collins, M. Freak.
    N. Callendar, 441:20Mar83-27
Collins, M.A. No Cure for Death.
    N. Callendar, 441:30Oct83-31
Collins, P., ed. ·Dickens: Interviews and
Recollections.
    A. Easson, 155:Autumn82-166
    A.D. Hutter, 445(NCF):Jun82-105
Collins, P., ed. Thackeray: Interviews
and Recollections.
    J. Keates, 617(TLS):5Aug83-826
Collins, R. Sociology since Midcentury.
    K.E.S., 185:Jan83-433
Collins, W. The Haunted Hotel.
    A.J.G.H., 617(TLS):28Jan83-79
Collins, W. Rambles Beyond Railways.
    A.P., 617(TLS):18Mar83-279
Collins, W. The Works of William Col-
lins.* (R. Wendorf and C. Ryskamp, eds)
    F. Felsenstein, 83:Autumn82-239
    M. New, 173(ECS):Spring82-359
"Collins/Robert French-English, English-
French Dictionary."* (B.T. Atkins and
others, eds)
    R.E. Asher, 402(MLR):Apr82-441
Collinson, P. Archbishop Grindal, 1519-
1583.
    D. Loades, 551(RenQ):Spring82-107
Collinson, P. The Religion of Protestants.
    C. Hill, 617(TLS):18Mar83-257
Collison, R.L., ed. World Bibliographical
Series. (Vol 2: Uganda.)
    D. McMaster, 69:Vol152No1-102
Collodi, C. Le Avventure di Pinocchio.
(O.C. Pollidori, ed) Le avventure di
Pinocchio. (F. Tempesti, ed)
    A. Kurzweil, 617(TLS):25Nov83-1320
Colloms, B. Victorian Visionaries.
    A. Phillips, 364:Aug/Sep82-123
Collymore, P. The Architecture of Ralph
Erskine.
    E. Denby, 324:Oct83-701
Colodny, R.G. - see Nalimov, V.V.
Colombo, J.R., ed. Friendly Aliens.
    J. Doyle, 102(CanL):Summer82-160

Colombo, J.R., ed. Windigo.
    M. Abley, 617(TLS):13May83-480
Colombo, J.R. and others, comps. CDN SF &
F.
    D. Barbour, 107(CRCL):Mar82-122
Colombo, J.R. and M. Richardson, eds. Not
To Be Taken At Night.
    C. Fagan, 99:Apr82-35
    L. Rogers, 102(CanL):Autumn82-165
Colón, G. and A-J. Soberanas - see de
Nebrija, E.A.
Colquhoun, A. Essays in Architectural
Criticism.
    J.P. Bonta, 290(JAAC):Spring83-352
    R. Maxwell, 46:Oct82-108
    W.H. Schallenberg, 576:Oct82-257
Colquhoun, K. Kiss of Life.
    T. Fitton, 617(TLS):14Oct83-1110
Coltheart, M., K. Patterson and J.C. Mar-
shall, eds. Deep Dyslexia.*
    E. Zurif and F. Pastouriaux, 353:
    Vol 19No11/12-1193
Colvin, C., ed. Maria Edgeworth in France
and Switzerland.
    R. Fréchet, 189(EA):Jan-Mar82-89
    J. Lough, 208(FS):Apr82-209
    G. O'Brien, 677(YES):Vol 12-288
    F.B. Pinion, 541(RES):Feb82-90
Colvin, H. Unbuilt Oxford.
    M. Girouard, 362:8Dec83-32
    D. Watkin, 617(TLS):4Nov83-1221
Colvin, H. and J. Newman - see North, R.
Colvin, H.M., general ed. The History of
the King's Works. (Vol 4, Pt 2)
    M. Girouard, 617(TLS):25Mar83-292
    D. Linstrum, 324:Apr83-290
Colwin, L. Family Happiness.*
    V. Rothschild, 617(TLS):6May83-465
Colwin, L. The Lone Pilgrim.
    N.Y. Hoffman, 573(SSF):Summer82-293
Comaroff, J.L. and S. Roberts. Rules and
Processes.*
    D.D.L., 185:Jan83-427
Combalia Dexeus, V., ed. Estudios sobre
Picasso.
    T. Crombie, 39:May82-417
Combet, L. Cervantès ou les incertitudes
du désir.*
    R. El Saffar, 400(MLN):Mar82-422
Comeau, R.F., F. Bustin and N.S. Lamoureux.
Ensemble. (2nd ed)
    W. Wrage, 207(FR):Apr83-812
"Comecon Foreign Trade Data, 1980."
    A.H. Smith, 575(SEER):Apr82-307
Comotti, G. Storia della musica. (Vol 1,
Pt 1)
    E.K. Borthwick, 303(JoHS):Vol 102-263
Compagnon, A. Nous, Michel de Montaigne.
    A.M. Hardee, 546(RR):Nov82-515
    M. McGowan, 208(FS):Jul82-322
    G. Nakam, 535(RHL):Jan-Feb82-99
    S.F.R., 131(CL):Winter82-70
Compagnon, A. La Seconde Main.*
    S.F.R., 131(CL):Winter82-70
Compañy, F.D. - see under Domínguez Com-
pañy, F.
"Comparative Criticism."* (Vol 1) (E.
Shaffer, ed)
    J.D. Johansen, 678(YCGL):No30-88
    E. Mendelson, 402(MLR):Jan82-132
    C. Rodiek, 52:Band16Heft3-311
Compton, M.D. Ricardo Palma.
    J.W. Brown, 263(RIB):Vol32No3/4-371

Compton-Burnett, I. Elders and Betters.
More Women than Men.
P. Craig, 617(TLS):18Nov83-1294
Comrie, B. Aspect.
A.F. Majewicz, 360(LP):Vol24-128
Comrie, B. Language Universals and Lin-
guistic Typology.
S. De Lancey, 350:Jun83-406
Comrie, B. The Languages of the Soviet
Union.
C.E. Gribble, 399(MLJ):Summer82-219
I. Kreindler, 550(RusR):Jul82-358
J.I. Press, 575(SEER):Apr82-275
Comrie, B., ed. Studies in the Languages
of the USSR.
S.M. Embleton, 350:Sep83-697
Comrie, B. and G. Stone. The Russian Lan-
guage since the Revolution.*
D. Milivojević, 558(RLJ):Winter-
Spring82-275
Comyns, B. Our Spoons Came From Wool-
worths.
P. Craig, 617(TLS):29Jul83-820
Conacher, D.J. Aeschylus' "Prometheus
Bound."*
C.H. Herington, 487:Spring82-77
P.G. Mason, 123:Vol32No1-6
Conche, M. Lucrèce et l'expérience.
A. Reix, 542:Apr-Jun82-458
Conde, J.F. - see under Fernández Conde, J.
Condé, M. Une Saison à Rihata.
C. Zimra, 207(FR):Oct82-165
de Condillac, E.B. La Langue des calculs.
(A-M. Chouillet, ed)
M. Hobson, 208(FS):Jan82-72
de Condillac, E.B. La Logique. (W.R.
Albury, ed and trans)
J.W. Yolton, 518:Jul82-158
de Condillac, E.B. Les Monades.* (L.L.
Bongie, ed)
S. Auroux, 535(RHL):Sep-Dec82-907
W.H. Barber, 402(MLR):Jan82-210
J. Pappas, 207(FR):Feb83-485
Condominas, G. L'Espace Social à propos
de l'Asie du Sud-Est.
L.M. Hanks, 293(JASt):Aug82-879
Condon, R. A Trembling Upon Rome.
J.J. Osborn, Jr., 441:4Sep83-4
Condorelli, S. - see Gargilius
Condous, J., J. Howlett and J. Skull, eds.
Arts in Cultural Diversity.
J. Lovano-Kerr, 289:Summer82-124
Cone, C.B. Hounds in the Morning.
639(VQR):Summer82-99
Coney, M. Cat Karina.
J. Clute, 617(TLS):5Aug83-843
Congdon, L. The Young Lukács.
M. Jay, 617(TLS):7Oct83-1092
Conger, S.M. and J.R. Welsch, eds. Narra-
tive Strategies.
M. Deutelbaum, 395(MFS):Summer82-367
F. McConnell, 678(YCGL):No30-97
"Congrès de Psychiatrie et de Neurologie
de Langue française."
A. Reix, 542:Jan-Mar82-90
Congreve, W. The Comedies of William Con-
greve. (A.G. Henderson, ed)
I. Donaldson, 617(TLS):28Oct83-1183
Conibear, F. and J.L. Blundell. The Wise
One. (abridged)
M. Whitaker, 102(CanL):Summer82-142

Conisbee, P. Painting in Eighteenth-
Century France.*
J. Ingamells, 90:Jul82-454
Conlon, J.J. Walter Pater and the French
Tradition.
J. Uglow, 617(TLS):3Jun83-578
Conlon, P.M. Ouvrages français relatifs
à Jean-Jacques Rousseau, 1751-1799.
P. Robinson, 83:Autumn82-266
Conn, D. Ticket Stubs for the Bullgang.
D. Barbour, 648(WCR):Summer81-82
Conn, R. Native American Art in the
Denver Art Museum.
F.J. Dockstader, 292(JAF):Apr-Jun82-
210
Connell, E.S. Mrs. Bridge. Mr. Bridge.
B. Landon, 271:Winter82-148
D. Montrose, 617(TLS):29Jul83-805
W.H. Pritchard, 249(HudR):Spring82-159
Connell, E.S., Jr. Saint Augustine's
Pigeon.* (G. Blaisdell, ed)
B. Landon, 271:Winter82-148
639(VQR):Spring82-55
Connell, R.W. and T.H. Irving. Class
Structure in Australian History.
T. Rowse, 381:Jul81-259
Conners, B.F. Dancehall.
N. Callendar, 441:28Aug83-21
Conniff, R., ed. The Devil's Book of
Verse.
P-L. Adams, 61:May83-105
Connolly, C. The Unquiet Grave. The Rock
Pool.
M. Mudrick, 231:Jan83-57
"Cyril Connolly: Journal and Memoir." (D.
Pryce-Jones, ed)
A. Forbes, 362:14Jul83-23
J. Symons, 617(TLS):8Jul83-721
Connolly, R. Stardust Memories.
C. Brown, 617(TLS):2Dec83-1356
Connor, N. and others. Talitha Cumi.
M. Hofmann, 617(TLS):18Nov83-1272
Connor, T. New and Selected Poems.
N. Corcoran, 617(TLS):27May83-549
D. Gioia, 249(HudR):Winter82/83-640
Connors, J.J. Borromini and the Roman Ora-
tory.*
A. Blunt, 90:Apr82-247
A. Braham, 46:Mar82-60
Conolly, L.W. and J.P. Wearing. English
Drama and Theatre, 1800-1900.
J. Woodfield, 178:Mar82-122
Conot, R.E. Justice at Nuremberg.
J.K. Davison, 441:10Jul83-16
K. Kyle, 362:15Dec83-27
Conrad, J. The Collected Letters of
Joseph Conrad. (Vol 1) (F.R. Karl
and L. Davies, eds)
M. Mudrick, 231:Jan83-60
F.W. Said, 441:11Dec83 7
Conrad, J. Joseph Conrad.*
J. Halperin, 395(MFS):Summer82-260
R.G. Hampson, 136:Vol 14No2-148
Conrad, P. Imagining America.*
M.G. Perloff, 402(MLR):Apr82-425
A. Rodway, 447(N&Q):Aug81-375
R.G. Walker, 395(MFS):Summer81-347
Conrad, P. Television.*
N. Berry, 364:Aug/Sep82-140
Conrad, R.C. Heinrich Böll.
W.G. Cunliffe, 564:Nov82-307
M. Jurgensen, 133:Band15Heft1/2-184
L.W. Tusken, 395(MFS):Winter82/83-700

Conrady, K.O., ed. Deutsche Literatur zur
Zeit der Klassik.
　H.M.K. Riley, 406:Summer82-203
Conrath, K. Die Volkssprache der unteren
Saar und der Obermosel.
　W. Kleiber, 685(ZDL):3/1981-383
Conron, J.P. Socorro.
　J.C. Henry, 576:Oct82-248
Conroy, J.F. A l'aventure!
　P. Siegel, 207(FR):Apr83-813
Conroy, P. and S. Rossel - see Andersen,
H.C.
"The Conservation and Development Pro-
gramme for the UK."
　D. Poore, 324:Oct83-699
"Conservation and Restoration for Small
Museums."
　J. de Boer, 614:Fall83-18
Constable, F. and S. Simon. The England
of Eric Ravilious.*
　A. Ross, 364:Dec82/Jan83-132
Constable, J. Constable with his Friends
in 1806.* (G. Reynolds, ed)
　J. Egerton, 90:Dec82-773
Constant, B. Recueil d'articles 1820-
1824.* (E. Harpaz, ed)
　B. Fink, 207(FR):Mar83-634
Constantine, D. Watching for Dolphins.
　M. Hofmann, 617(TLS):18Nov83-1272
Constantine, K.C. Always a Body to Trade.
　N. Callendar, 441:21Aug83-23
Contat, M. and M. Rybalka, with others -
see Sartre, J-P.
Contat, N. Anecdotes typographiques.* (G.
Barber, ed)
　D.J. Shaw, 447(N&Q):Dec81-554
"Contemporary Swedish Poetry."* (J. Mat-
thias and G. Printz-Påhlson, trans)
　J. Lutz, 563(SS):Autumn82-326
Contoski, V. Names.
　D. Low, 436(NewL):Fall82-106
Contosta, D.R. Henry Adams and the Ameri-
can Experiment.
　S.J. Whitfield, 639(VQR):Winter82-143
Contreras, R.L. - see under Ruiz Contreras,
L.
Conway, H. Ernest Race.
　R.W. Grant, 324:Jun83-415
Conze, E. The Prajñāpāramitā Literature.*
(2nd ed)
　D.S. Ruegg, 318(JAOS):Oct-Dec81-471
Conze, E. A Short History of Buddhism.*
　D.W. Mitchell, 485(PE&W):Jan82-109
Cook, A. French Tragedy.*
　R.L. Frautschi, 568(SCN):Fall82-39
Cook, A.H. and H. Hayashi. Working Women
in Japan.
　S.J. Pharr, 293(JASt):Feb82-354
Cook, A.J. The Privileged Playgoers of
Shakespeare's London, 1576-1642.*
　A.C. Dessen, 130:Winter82/83-372
　K. Muir, 570(SQ):Autumn82-411
　M.T. Rozett, 612(ThS):May82-117
　639(VQR):Spring82-57
Cook, A.S. Myth and Language.*
　J. Bolland, 366:Spring82-112
Cook, B. Brecht in Exile.
　P. Engel, 441:20Feb83-14
　442(NY):21Mar83-132
Cook, C. Joyce Cary.
　E. Christian, 594:Fall82-301
　H.H. Watts, 395(MFS):Summer82-281
　295(JML):Dec82-421

Cook, D.A. A History of Narrative Film.*
　P. Valenti, 500:Spring/Summer83-65
Cook, F.H. Hua-yen Buddhism.
　W.W. Lai, 318(JAOS):Apr-Jun81-234
Cook, F.J. The Great Energy Scam.
　P. Engel, 441:27Mar83-16
　442(NY):14Feb83-118
Cook, J. Shakespeare's Players.
　S. Wells, 617(TLS):2Sep83-935
Cook, J.M. The Persian Empire.
　P.R.S. Moorey, 617(TLS):25Feb83-198
Cook, M. Archives and the Computer.
　M.G. Underwood, 325:Oct82-127
Cook, P. Massey at the Brink.
　P. Marchak, 99:Aug82-38
Cook, P. - see Doepler, C.E.
Cook, R. Godplayer.
　J. Coleman, 441:24Jul83-11
Cook, R.F. "Chanson d'Antioche," chanson
de geste.
　G.R. Mermier, 207(FR):May83-937
　L.A.M. Sumberg, 589:Apr82-363
Cook, R.I. Sir Samuel Garth.*
　E. Duthie, 447(N&Q):Dec81-546
　A. Pailler, 189(EA):Oct-Dec82-469
　P. Roberts, 677(YES):Vol 12-273
Cook, R.M. Clazomenian Sarcophagi.
　D.C. Kurtz, 123:Vol32No2-248
Cooke, A. Masterpieces.*
　P. Ackroyd, 157:Autumn82-47
Cooke, D. I Saw the World End.*
　J. Kerman, 453(NYRB):22Dec83-27
Cooke, D. Vindications.
　R. Swanston, 607:Dec82-39
Cooke, J.E. Georges Bernanos.
　T. Field, 208(FS):Oct82-491
Cooke, M.G. Acts of Inclusion.*
　E.B. Murray, 541(RES):Feb82-92
　S.M. Tave, 402(MLR):Jan82-174
Cooke, T.D. The Old French and Chaucerian
Fabliaux.*
　R. O'Gorman, 481(PQ):Fall81-538
Cooley, D., ed. Draft.
　A. Brooks, 102(CanL):Autumn82-138
Cooley, D. Leaving.*
　D. Barbour, 648(WCR):Summer81-83
Cooley, D. - see Suknaski, A.
Cooley, J.K. Libyan Sandstorm.
　M. Yapp, 617(TLS):15Apr83-368
Cooley, J.R. Savages and Naturals.
　R. Phillips, 114(ChiR):Summer83-71
Cooley, M. Architect or Bee?
　R.E. Pahl, 437:Winter81/82-107
Coolhaas, W.P. A Critical Survey of Stud-
ies on Dutch Colonial History. (2nd ed
rev by G.J. Schutte)
　W.H. Frederick, 293(JASt):Nov81-195
Coolidge, A.C., Jr. Beyond the Fatal
Flaw.*
　R. Aélion, 555:Vol56fasc2-324
　P.G. Mason, 123:Vol32No2-280
Coombs, V.M. A Semantic Syntax of Grammat-
ical Negation in Older Germanic Dialects.
　C.M. Barrack, 685(ZDL):2/1982-247
Coomer, J. The Decatur Road.
　442(NY):26Dec83-71
Cooper, A.A. (Lord Shaftesbury). Complete
Works, Selected Letters, and Posthumous
Writings in English with Parallel German
Translation. (Pt 1, Vol 1) (G. Hemme-
rich and W. Benda, eds and trans)
　J.A. Dussinger, 149(CLS):Winter82-472
　S. Grean, 319:Oct82-434

76

Cooper, B. Merleau-Ponty and Marxism.
S.M. Corbett, 529(QQ):Summer82-347
Cooper, D. and D. A Durable Fire. (A.
Cooper, ed)
V. Glendinning, 617(TLS):7Oct83-1079
J. Vaizey, 362:20Oct83-25
Cooper, D.E. Illusions of Equality.*
J. White, 393(Mind):Apr82-302
Cooper, E. A History of World Pottery.
G. Wills, 39:Apr82-297
Cooper, G. and C. Wortham - see "Everyman"
Cooper, H.S.F., Jr. Imaging Saturn.
L.S. Robinson, 441:6Nov83-16
Cooper, J.F. The American Democrat.
M.D. Clark, 396(ModA):Summer/Fall182-
424
Cooper, J.M., Jr. The Warrior and the
Priest.
D.M. Kennedy, 441:20Nov83-7
Cooper, J.S. The Return of Ninurta to
Nippur.
W.W. Hallo, 318(JAOS):Apr-Jun81-253
Cooper, L., ed. La gran conquista de
ultramar.
C. González, 304(JHP):Winter83-149
J.E. Keller, 238:Mar82-138
Cooper, N. The Diversity of Moral Think-
ing.*
N.J.H. Dent, 518:Jan82-52
J. Harrison, 479(PhQ):Oct82-374
Cooper, R.M., ed. Essays on Richard Cra-
shaw.
J.H. Ottenhoff, 568(SCN):Spring-
Summer82-14
Cooper, W. Scenes from Later Life.
J. Mellors, 362:22Sep83-25
J. Melmoth, 617(TLS):9Sep83-950
Cooper, W. Scenes from Provincial Life
[and] Scenes from Metropolitan Life.*
W. Boyd, 441:9Oct83-9
Cooper, W.A. In Praise of America.
A.S. Roe, 54:Dec82-675
R.H. Saunders, 658:Spring82-84
Cooper, W.E. and J.M. Sorensen. Fundamen-
tal Frequency in Sentence Production.*
I. Lehiste, 215(GL):Summer82-123
Cooperman, S. Greco's Last Book. (F.
Candelaria, ed)
D. Watmough, 102(CanL):Winter81-146
Coote, S., ed. The Penguin Book of Homo-
sexual Verse.
A. Hollinghurst, 617(TLS):22Apr83-397
Cope, J.I. Joyce's Cities.*
R.M. Kain, 395(MFS):Winter81/82-671
K. Lawrence, 141:Summer82-294
L. Orr, 329(JJQ):Fall82-141
Cope, J.I. and G. Green, eds. Novel vs.
Fiction.
W. Bache, 395(MFS):Winter82/83-732
Cope, W. Across the City.
I. McMillan, 493:Jun82-71
Cope, W. and others. Poetry Introduction
5.*
M. O'Neill, 493:Jun82-68
Copeland, J.G., R. Kite and L. Sandstedt.
Intermediate Spanish. (2nd ed)
G. Guntermann, 399(MLJ):Spring82-100
Copeland, R. Spode's Willow Pattern and
Other Designs after the Chinese.
G.L. Miller, 658:Winter82-272

Copenhaver, B.P. Symphorien Champier and
the Reception of the Occultist Tradition
in Renaissance France.
B. Hansen, 551(RenQ):Spring82-104
Copleston, F.C. On the History of Philos-
ophy, and Other Essays.*
M.J. Inwood, 393(Mind):Jul82-455
Copleston, F.C. Philosophies and Cultures.
M. Sprung, 529(QQ):Winter82-906
Copley, I.A. The Music of Peter Warlock.*
D. Wulstan, 410(M&L):Apr81-205
Coppel, A. The Burning Mountain.
R. Freedman, 441:6Mar83-10
Copperud, R.H. American Usage and Style.*
J.R. Gaskin, 569(SR):Winter82-143
Corbeil, J-C. L'aménagement linguistique
du Québec.
J-C. Boulanger, 209(FM):Apr82-175
Corcoran, N. The Song of Deeds.
G. Jones, 617(TLS):8Apr83-349
Cordes, A. The Descent of the Doves.*
P.S. Nichols, 395(MFS):Winter81/82-659
Cordner, M. - see Etherege, G.
de Córdoba, A. Commemoración breve de los
reyes de Portugal. (P. Cátedra, ed) Un
sermón castellano del siglo XV. (R.E.
Surtz, ed)
E.M. Gerli, 304(JHP):Winter83-150
Cordwell, J., ed. The Visual Arts.
J. Picton, 59:Jun82-219
Cordwell, J.M. and R.A. Schwarz, eds. The
Fabrics of Culture.
J.B. Eicher, 2(AfrA):Nov81-17
J. Picton, 59:Jun82-219
Corey, S. The Last Magician.
639(VQR):Spring82-60
Corinth, T., ed. Lovis Corinth: Eine Doku-
mentation.*
A. Mochon, 54:Sep82-520
Corkin, J. Twelve Canadians.
W.N., 102(CanL):Spring82-162
Cormeau, C., ed. Deutsche Literatur im
Mittelalter.
D.H. Green, 402(MLR):Jan82-223
W. Schröder, 684(ZDA):Band111Heft1-28
Cormier, R. and J.L. Pallister. Waiting
for Death.*
D.H. Hesla, 299:Spring82-139
Corn, A. A Call in the Midst of the Crowd.
G.E. Murray, 472:Spring/Summer83-277
Corn, A. The Various Light.*
G.E. Murray, 472:Spring/Summer83-277
R. Tillinghast, 569(SR):Spring82-291
Corneille, P. La Galerie du Palais ou
l'Amie Rivale. (M.R. Margitić, ed)
W. Leiner, 475:No16Pt2-369
H.B. McDermott, 207(FR):Mar83-631
Corneille, P. Oeuvres complètes.* (Vol 1)
(G. Couton, ed)
R. Zuber, 535(RHL):May-Jun82-461
Cornelia, M. The Function of the Masque
in Jacobean Tragedy and Tragicomedy.
D.L. Russell, 568(SCN):Spring-Summer82-
7
Cornman, J.W. Skepticism, Justification
and Explanation.
L. Bon Jour, 482(PhR):Oct82-612
R. Feldman, 484(PPR):Sep82-111
D. Odegard, 518:Jan82-34
A. O'Hear, 393(Mind):Apr82-295
Corns, T.N. The Development of Milton's
Prose Style.
R. Flannagan, 391:Oct82-75

Cornu, M. Existence et séparation.
  J. Brun, 192(EP):Jan-Mar82-117
Cornwall, J., ed. The County Community
  under Henry VIII.
  C. Rawcliffe, 325:Oct82-119
Cornwell, R. God's Banker.
  R. Fox, 362:1Sep83-22
  C. Moorehead, 617(TLS):23Sep83-1012
Corominas, J. Breve Diccionario Etimol-
  ógico de la Lengua Castellana. (3rd ed)
  M. Perl, 682(ZPSK):Band35Heft3-338
Corominas, J.M. Castiglione y "La Arau-
  cana."
  R. Chang-Rodríguez, 238:Mar82-148
Coromines, J., with J. Gulsoy and M. Cal-
  mer. Diccionari etimològic i complemen-
  tari de la llengua catalana. (Vol 1)
  R.A. Hall, Jr., 350:Mar83-194
del Corral, L.D. - see under Díez del Cor-
  ral, L.
Correa, A.B. and others - see under Bonet
Correa, A. and others
Correa, G., ed. Antología de la poesía
  española (1900-1980).
  D.P. Hill, 238:May82-308
Correa Calderón, E. - see de Larra, M.J.
Corrigan, T. Coleridge, Language, and
  Criticism.
  I. McGilchrist, 617(TLS):27May83-555
Corrington, J.W. The Southern Reporter.*
  J. Bathanti, 573(SSF):Winter82-99
Corsi, P. and P. Weindling, eds. Informa-
  tion Sources in the History of Science
  and Medicine.
  R. Porter, 617(TLS):21Oct83-1165
Corsinovi, G. Pirandello e l'Espression-
  ismo.
  F. De Nicola, 228(GSLI):Vol 159fasc505-
  139
Corson, R. Stage Makeup. (6th ed)
  N. Welsh, 108:Winter82-113
Cortázar, J. Nous l'aimons tant, Glenda,
  et autres récits.
  F. de Martinoir, 450(NRF):Nov82-130
Cortázar, J. Queremos Tanto a Glenda.
  O. Rossardi, 37:May-Jun82-64
Cortázar, J. We Love Glenda So Much.
  P. Zweig, 441:27Mar83-1
Cortazzi, H. Isles of Gold.
  E. Seidensticker, 441:11Dec83-14
Cortazzi, H. - see Fraser, M.C.
Cortelazzo, M. I dialetti e la dialettol-
  ogia in Italia (fino al 1800).
  E. Radtke, 72:Band218Heft2-466
Cortelazzo, M. and P. Zolli. Dizionario
  etimologico della lingua italiana. (Vol
  2)
  H. Meier, 547(RF):Band94Heft4-457
Cortesii, P. De hominibus doctis. (G.
  Ferraù, ed)
  M. Pozzi, 228(GSLI):Vol 159fasc505-136
Corti, M. Dante a un nuovo crocevia.*
  M. Marti, 228(GSLI):Vol 159fasc506-299
Corwin, J.H. Easy to Make Appliqué Quilts
  for Children.
  M. Cowan, 614:Winter83-16
Coser, L.A., C. Kadushin and W.W. Powell.
  Books.
  W.B. Goodman, 676(YR):Autumn82-112
Cosgrove, R.A. The Rule of Law.*
  T.J. Toohey, 637(VS):Autumn81-94

Ćosić, D. Reach to Eternity. South to
  Destiny.
  C. Hawkesworth, 617(TLS):27May83-538
Cossé, L. Les Chambres du Sud.
  P. Olivier, 450(NRF):Jan82-120
Cosslett, T. The "Scientific Movement"
  and Victorian Literature.
  P. Kemp, 617(TLS):25Mar83-288
Costa, F. and others. La Civilisation
  britannique.
  J. Leruez, 189(EA):Jul-Sep82-352
Costa, G. La antichità germaniche nella
  cultura italiana da Machiavelli a Vico.*
  B.L.O. Richter, 276:Summer82-113
de Costa, R. The Poetry of Pablo Neruda.
  O. Hahn, 240(HR):Winter82-111
Costa, R.H. Edmund Wilson.*
  J.V. Hagopian, 395(MFS):Winter81/82-
  732
  D.R. Noble, 577(SHR):Summer82-277
Costas Rodríguez, J. Aspectos del vocabu-
  lario de Q. Curtius Rufus.
  L.D. Stephens, 350:Sep83-659
Costello, B. Marianne Moore.*
  B.F. Engel, 27(AL):Mar82-140
  V.M. Kouidis, 577(SHR):Spring82-177
  T. Martin, 295(JML):Dec82-501
Costich, J.F. The Poetry of Change.*
  M. Sheringham, 402(MLR):Jan82-217
Coston, H. Lectures Françaises.
  M.G. Hydak, 207(FR):Oct82-193
"Costume through the Ages."
  R.L. Shep, 614:Winter83-14
Cotnam, J., A. Oliver and C.D.E. Tolton,
  eds. Perspectives contemporaines.*
  D.H. Walker, 208(FS):Oct82-488
Cott, J. Pipers at the Gates of Dawn.
  R. Lipsey, 469:Vol18No3-94
  C. Ozick, 441:1May83-7
  441(NY):4Jul83-91
Cotter, M.G. Vietnam.
  C.R. Bryant, 293(JASt):May82-636
Cotterell, A. The First Emperor of China.
  M. Medley, 39:Jul82-65
Cottez, H. Dictionnaire des structures du
  vocabulaire savant.
  M. Tournier, 209(FM):Oct82-371
Cotton, J. The Totleigh Riddles. Day
  Book.
  I. McMillan, 493:Jun82-71
Cotton, N. Women Playwrights in England
  c. 1363-1750.
  T. Helton, 568(SCN):Fall82-46
  J.B. Kern, 173(ECS):Spring83-324
Cottrell, A.P. Goethe's View of Evil and
  the Search for a New Image of Man in our
  Time.
  M. Swales, 617(TLS):1Apr83-339
Cottrell, R.D. Sexuality/Textuality.
  C. Clark, 208(FS):Oct82-463
  F. Gray, 551(RenQ):Summer82-306
Coulmas, F., ed. Conversational Routine.
  P. Brown, 350:Mar83-215
Couloubaritsis, L. L'avènement de la
  science physique.
  P. Louis, 555:Vol56fasc1-135
  P. Pellegrin, 542:Apr-Jun82-458
Couloumbis, T.A. and J.O. Iatrides, eds.
  Greek American Relations.
  R. Clogg, 617(TLS):12Aug83-861
Coulter, J. The Social Construction of
  Mind.*
  S.J.O., 543:Jun82-861

Counter, S.A. and D.L. Evans. I Sought My Brother.
    J. Povey, 2(AfrA):Feb82-79
Countryman, E. A People in Revolution.
    R. Middlekauf, 165(EAL):Spring83-102
    J.R. Pole, 617(TLS):18Feb83-153
    G.S. Wood, 453(NYRB):3Feb83-16
Coupe, W.A. The Continental Renaissance.
    W. Cherry, 241:Sep82-65
Couper-Kuhlen, E. The Prepositional Passive in English.*
    R. Hudson, 297(JL):Mar82-210
Courbin, P. Delos. (fasc 33)
    R.A. Tomlinson, 303(JoHS):Vol 102-280
Cournot, A-A. Oeuvres complètes. (Vol 5)
    (C. Salomon-Bayet, ed)
    A. Reix, 192(EP):Oct-Dec81-475
Coursen, H.R., Jr. Christian Ritual and the World of Shakespeare's Tragedies.
    J.L. Styan, 125:Winter82-189
Coursodon, J-P. and P. Sauvage. American Directors.
    P. Biskind, 441:15May83-14
Court, F.E., ed. Walter Pater.
    D.E. Van Tassel, 395(MFS):Summer81-337
Courtauld, G. An Axe, A Spade and Ten Acres.
    R. Blythe, 617(TLS):16Sep83-998
    A. Huth, 362:15Dec83-26
Courtney, C.P. A Bibliography of Editions of the Writings of Benjamin Constant to 1833.
    A. Zielonka, 446(NCFS):Spring-Summer83-394
Courtney, C.P. A Preliminary Bibliography of Isabelle de Charrière (Belle de Zuylen).*
    D. Wood, 402(MLR):Apr82-453
Courtney, E. A Commentary on the Satires of Juvenal.*
    G.B. Townend, 313:Vol72-208
Courtney, R. The Dramatic Curriculum.
    J. Doolittle, 108:Spring82-198
Courtney, W.F. Young Charles Lamb 1775-1802.*
    J. Gross, 453(NYRB):16Jun83-11
Couser, G.T. American Autobiography.*
    E. Waterston, 106:Fall82-193
Cousin, J. - see Quintilian
Cousins, N. Anatomy of an Illness as Perceived by the Patient.
    P.P. Morgan, 529(QQ):Summer82-411
Coutinho, E.D. The Process of Revitalization of the Language and Narrative Structure in the Fiction of João Guimarães Rosa and Julio Cortázar.
    P.W. Borgeson, Jr., 552(REH):Oct82-473
    B.J. Chamberlain, 238:Dec82-669
Couton, G. - see Corneille, P.
Couturat, L. and L. Leau. Histoire de la langue universelle.
    G.F. Meier, 682(ZPSK):Band34Heft6-753
Couturier, F. Monde et être chez Heidegger.
    M. Haar, 192(EP):Apr-Jun81-235
Cowan, I.B. and D. Shaw, eds. The Renaissance and Reformation in Scotland.
    E. Playfair, 617(TLS):26Aug83-910
Cowan, P. Mobiles.
    E. Webby, 381:Jul81-200
Cowan, P. An Orphan in History.*
    J-A. Mort, 287:Nov82-18

Cowan, R.C. Hauptmann-Kommentar zum dramatischen Werk.
    P. Skrine, 402(MLR):Jan82-241
Cowan, W., ed. Papers of the Thirteenth Algonquian Conference.
    I. Goddard, 350:Sep83-702
Coward, B. The Stanleys, Lords Stanley and Earls of Derby 1358-1672.
    M. James, 617(TLS):9Sep83-966
Coward, H.G. Sphoṭa Theory of Language.
    G.W. Houston, 485(PE&W):Apr82-226
Coward, N. The Collected Stories of Noël Coward. (British title: The Collected Short Stories.)
    A. Hollinghurst, 617(TLS):25Mar83-289
    J. McCourt, 441:18Dec83-9
    442(NY):26Dec83-71
Coward, N. Pomp and Circumstance.
    A. Hollinghurst, 617(TLS):25Mar83-289
Coward, R. and J. Ellis. Language and Materialism.
    M.M. Bryant, 660(Word):Apr81-63
    J.H. Kavanagh, 504:No5-118
Cowart, D. Thomas Pynchon.*
    K. Tölölyan, 454:Winter83-165
Cowart, D. and T.L. Wymer, eds. Twentieth-Century American Science Fiction Writers.
    354:Jun82-206
Cowart, G. The Origins of Modern Musical Criticism.
    A. Cohen, 410(M&L):Jan/Apr82-121
Cowen, R.C. Hauptmann-Kommentar zum Dramatischen Werk.*
    S. Hoefert, 406:Summer82-209
    G. Oberembt, 680(ZDP):Band101Heft4-611
Cowie, P. Ingmar Bergman.*
    R. Combs, 617(TLS):10Jun83-611
    J. Simon, 18:Mar83-71
Cowper, W. The Letters and Prose Writings of William Cowper.* (Vol 1) (J. King and C. Ryskamp, eds)
    J. Barrell, 541(RES):Nov82-476
    N. Dalrymple-Champneys, 447(N&Q):Feb81-82
    P. Danchin, 179(ES):Apr82-177
    P. Rogers, 617(TLS):8Apr83-343
    P.M. Spacks, 301(JEGP):Apr82-264
Cowper, W. The Letters and Prose Writings of William Cowper.* (Vol 2) (J. King and C. Ryskamp, eds)
    P. Craddock, 405(MP):Feb83-308
    P. Rogers, 617(TLS):8Apr83-343
    639(VQR):Winter82-16
Cowper, W. The Letters and Prose Writings of William Cowper. (Vol 3) (J. King and C. Ryskamp, eds)
    P. Rogers, 617(TLS):8Apr83-343
Cowper, W. The Poems of William Cowper.* (Vol 1) (J.D. Baird and C. Ryskamp, eds)
    P. Craddock, 405(MP):Feb83-308
    P.M. Spacks, 301(JEGP):Apr82-264
Cox, G. See It Happen.
    P. Whitehead, 362:21Jul83-26
Cox, G.S.A. Folk Music in a Newfoundland Outport.*
    D. Kodish, 292(JAF):Apr-Jun82-237
Cox, J. Take a Cold Tub, Sir!
    P. Keating, 617(TLS):25Feb83-181
Cox, L. Lincoln and Black Freedom.
    P. Maslowski, 579(SAQ):Autumn82-464

Cruz, M. and R. A Chicano Christmas Story.
V. Allen, 399(MLJ):Autumn82-353
Cruz, V.H. By Lingual Wholes.
R. Elman, 441:18Sep83-36
Cruz Hernandez, M. El pensamiento de
Ramon Llull.
A. Llinarès, 192(EP):Jul-Sep81-348
Cruz Valdovinos, J.M. and J.M. García
López. Platería religiosa en Ubeda y
Baeza.
A. López-Yarto, 48:Jan-Mar80-126
Crystal, D. Directions in Applied Lin-
guistics.
F. Gomes de Matos, 351(LL):Dec82-439
Crystal, D. A First Dictionary of Linguis-
tics and Phonetics.*
G. Bourcier, 189(EA):Oct-Dec82-447
E.G. Fichtner, 660(Word):Apr81-67
N.V. Smith, 297(JL):Sep82-461
Crystal, D. Introduction to Language Path-
ology.
W. Weidner, 583:Summer83-398
Csampai, A., ed. Wolfgang Amadeus Mozart:
Don Giovanni.
J. Rushton, 410(M&L):Jul/Oct81-393
Csenki, S. and J. Vekerdi, eds. Ilona
Tausendschön.
I. Köhler-Zülch, 196:Band23Heft1/2-120
Csonka, F. - see Schesaeus, C.
Cude, W. A Due Sense of Differences.*
R. Lecker, 395(MFS):Winter81/82-745
J. Moss, 178:Dec82-529
M.A. Peterman, 627(UTQ):Summer82-439
M.L. Ross, 102(CanL):Spring82-78
Cudjoe, S.R. Resistance and Caribbean
Literature.
E. Baugh, 529(QQ):Winter82-897
de Cuenca, L.A. Floresta española de
varia caballería.
B. Mujica, 552(REH):Oct82-475
Cuénin, M. Roman et société sous Louis
XIV: Mme. de Villedieu.*
E. Woodrough, 402(MLR):Jul82-723
Cuénin, M. - see Madame de Lafayette
de la Cueva, J. Los Inventores de las
Cosas. (B. Weiss and L.C. Pérez, eds)
S. Hernandez-Araico, 238:Dec82-655
Cuevas, J.L. Cartas para una Exposición.
B. Novoa, 37:Sep-Oct82-63
Cugusi, P. Epistolographi Latini minores.
(Vol 2)
J. André, 555:Vol55fasc1-174
Čukovskaja, L. Zapiski ob Anne Axmatovoj.
(Vol 2)
A.L. Crone, 558(RLJ):Winter-Spring82-
297
S. Ketchian, 574(SEEJ):Spring82-102
Culhane, J. Walt Disney's "Fantasia."
J. Maslin, 441:4Dec83-73
Cullen, P. and T.P. Roche, Jr. - see
"Spenser Studies"
Culler, J. Barthes.
A. Jefferson, 617(TLS):15Jul83-761
Culler, J. On Deconstruction.
C. Craig, 617(TLS):27May83-546
J.R. Searle, 453(NYRB):27Oct83-74
Culler, J. The Pursuit of Signs.*
S. Briosi, 603:Vol6No3-435
W.E. Cain, 580(SCR):Fall82-118
J.W. Davidson, 477(PLL):Winter82-428
M. Green, 363(LitR):Fall82-139
R. Magliola, 395(MFS):Winter81/82-759
[continued]

[continuing]
V. Milicic, 134(CP):Fall82-101
J. Phelan, 405(MP):Nov82-222
C. Rigolot, 207(FR):Apr83-759
N. Smith, 493:Sep82-72
Cullingford, E. Yeats, Ireland and Fas-
cism.*
R.W. Dasenbrock, 400(MLN):Dec82-1262
B. John, 627(UTQ):Spring82-303
Cullup, M. Reading Geographies.
D. Davis, 617(TLS):8Apr83-356
Culot, P., with A. Rey. Jean-Claude
Bozerian.
A. Hobson, 90:Oct82-636
Culver, C.M. and B. Gert. Philosophy in
Medicine.
P.S., 185:Jul83-836
Culver, M. A Garden of Cucumbers.
M. Lammon, 436(NewL):Winter82/83-105
Cumings, B. The Origins of the Korean
War.*
Kamata Mitsuto, 285(JapQ):Apr-Jun82-
248
J. Merrill, 293(JASt):Aug82-853
Cumming, R.D. Starting Point.*
M. Adam, 542:Oct-Dec82-678
Cumming, V. Gloves.
R.L. Shep, 614:Summer83-16
Cummings, W.K. Education and Equality in
Japan.*
V.N. Kobayashi, 293(JASt):Nov81-132
Cummins, J.G. El habla de Coria y sus
cercanías.
E. Keas, 545(RPh):May82-652
Cummins, J.G. - see de Mena, J.
Cummins, P.W. Commercial French.
J.T. Chamberlain, 207(FR):Apr83-814
Cunningham, E. - see Poe, S.
Cunningham, E.V. The Case of the Kid-
napped Angel.
T.J. Binyon, 617(TLS):5Aug83-843
N. Callendar, 441:2Jan83-26
Cunningham, S. Language and the Phenomen-
ological Reductions of Edmund Husserl.
H-U. Hoche, 53(AGP):Band64Heft3-343
Cunninghame Graham, R.B. Selected Writ-
ings of Cunninghame Graham.* (C. Watts,
ed)
J. Walker, 136:Vol 14No3-237
Cunninghame Graham, R.B. The South Ameri-
can Sketches of R.B. Cunninghame Graham.*
(J. Walker, ed)
S.A. Stoudemire, 241:Sep82-68
Cuomo, G. Family Honor.
J.J. Osborn, Jr., 441:13Nov83-18
Čurčić, S. Gračanica.*
P. Hetherington, 90:Jan82-46
Curcio, L.L. and others. Nouveau Visage
du monde français. (2nd ed)
R. Danner, 207(FR):Oct82-195
"Curial and Guelfa." (P. Waley, trans)
A. Terry, 617(TLS):25Feb83-197
Curl, J.S. The Egyptian Revival.
P.A. Clayton, 324:Jul83-487
J.M. Crook, 617(TLS):18Feb83-150
D. Watkin, 46:Nov82-80
Curl, J.S. The Life and Work of Henry
Roberts 1803-1876.
A. Saint, 617(TLS):18Nov83-1265
Curley, E.M. Descartes against the Skep-
tics.*
J.M. Beyssade, 53(AGP):Band64Heft3-323
[continued]

Daley, R. The Dangerous Edge.
S. Ellin, 441:25Sep83-19
442(NY):3Oct83-128
Lord Dalhousie. The Dalhousie Journals.
(Vol 2) (M. Whitelaw, ed)
G.W., 102(CanL):Summer82-173
Dallapiccola, A.L., with S.Z-A. Lallemant,
eds. The Stūpa.
J.W. de Jong, 259(IIJ):Oct82-316
Dallas, G. The Imperfect Peasant Economy.
P.K. O'Brien, 617(TLS):1Jul83-706
Dallek, R. The American Style of Foreign
Policy.
G. Smith, 441:27Mar83-9
Dallmayr, F.R. Twilight of Subjectivity.
A.R., 185:Jul83-827
Dally, A. Inventing Motherhood.
P. Robinson, 441:24Jul83-8
442(NY):25Jul83-87
Dalmonte, R., ed. Il gesto della forma.
D. Osmond-Smith, 410(M&L):Jan/Apr82-
101
d'Alpuget, B. Monkeys in the Dark.
P. Pierce, 381:Dec81-522
d'Alpuget, B. Turtle Beach.
J. Klein, 441:23Oct83-12
P. Pierce, 381:Dec81-522
Dalton, R. Unconscious Structure in "The
Idiot."*
G.S. Morson, 494:Spring82-157
Daly, H.E., ed. Economics, Ecology,
Ethics.
M. Bradfield, 529(QQ):Autumn82-585
Daly, P.J. This Day's Importance.
T.F. Merrill, 305(JIL):Sep82-3
Daly, P.M., ed. The European Emblem.*
G.A. Davies, 86(BHS):Jan82-71
A.M. Gibbs, 541(RES):May82-197
B.G. Lyons, 551(RenQ):Summer81-273
R.E. Schade, 221(GQ):May82-413
Daly, P.M. Literature in the Light of the
Emblem.*
A.M. Gibbs, 541(RES):May82-197
B.G. Lyons, 551(RenQ):Summer81-273
Dalyell, T. One Man's Falklands ...
C. Wain, 362:3Mar83-20
G. Wheatcroft, 617(TLS):13May83-490
Dam-Mikkelsen, B. and T. Lundbaek, eds.
Ethnographic Objects in the Royal Danish
Kunstkammer 1650-1800.
W.B.R. Neave-Hill, 463:Spring82-89
d'Amboise, C. Leap Year.
D. Harris, 441:2Jan83-4
d'Amico, F. - see Baldini, G.
D'Amico, J.F. Renaissance Humanism in
Papal Rome.
C. Cairns, 617(TLS):30Dec83-1465
D'Amico, M. Dieci secoli di teatro
inglese 970-1980.
K. Elam, 617(TLS):8Apr83-359
Damrosch, L., Jr. Symbol and Truth in
Blake's Myth.*
H. Adams, 405(MP):Feb83-316
J. Blondel, 189(EA):Jul-Sep82-332
M. Eaves, 301(JEGP):Jul82-438
R.F. Gleckner, 591(SIR):Winter82-666
Damsteegt, T. Epigraphical Hybrid San-
skrit.*
J.W. de Jong, 259(IIJ):Oct80-313
Dana, R. In a Fugitive Season.*
J. Saunders, 565:Vol23No1-73

Dance, F.E.X., ed. Human Communication
Theory.
J.T. Wood, 583:Summer83-403
Danchin, P., ed. The Prologues and Epi-
logues of the Restoration 1660-1700.
(Pt 1)
R.D. Hume, 612(ThS):May82-120
F. Schunck, 38:Band100Heft1/2-209
Danckert, L. Directory of European Porce-
lain.
G. Wills, 39:Apr82-297
Dancourt, F.C. Le Chevalier à la mode
(1687). (R.H. Crawshaw, ed)
A. Blanc, 535(RHL):Jan-Feb82-109
B. Russell, 402(MLR):Apr82-452
d'Andlau, B. - see de Chateaubriand, F.R.
Daneš, F. and D. Viehweger, eds. Probleme
der Textgrammatik.
E. Wittmers, 682(ZPSK):Band34Heft6-766
Danforth, L.M. The Death Rituals of Rural
Greece.
M. Alexiou, 617(TLS):6May83-450
Daniel, A. - see under Arnaut Daniel
Daniel, S. - see Philo of Alexander
Daniel, W.C. Black Journals of the United
States.
S.B. Garren, 95(CLAJ):Jun82-476
Daniell, D. "Coriolanus" in Europe.*
G.K. Hunter, 569(SR):Spring82-273
Daniels, S. The Salt Doll.
A. Rollings, 114(ChiR):Summer81-112
Danielson, D. Milton's Good God.
G. Campbell, 391:Oct82-76
Danielson, H. Ādideśa: The Essence of Su-
preme Truth (Paramārthasāra).
S. Elkman, 293(JASt):Nov81-171
J.W. de Jong, 259(IIJ):Oct82-310
Danielsson, B. - see Twiti, W.
Danly, R.L. In the Shade of Spring Leaves.
F. Bach, 651(WHR):Winter82-362
W.E. Naff, 407(MN):Summer82-257
Danly, R.L. - see Higuchi Ichiyo
Dannenbaum, J. Fast and Fresh.
W. and C. Cowen, 639(VQR):Spring82-67
Danninger, E. Sieben politische Gedichte
der HS. B.L. Harley 2253.
S. Wenzel, 38:Band100Heft1/2-177
Dansereau, L-M. La Trousse.
J. Moss, 102(CanL):Spring82-122
Danset-Léger, J. L'enfant et les images
de la littérature enfantine.
L. Millet, 192(EP):Jan-Mar82-118
Dante Alighieri. Dante, The Divine Comedy.
(C.H. Sisson, trans)
J.F. Cotter, 249(HudR):Summer82-306
M. Davie, 402(MLR):Oct82-971
Dante Alighieri. Dante's Inferno. (M.
Musa, trans) Dante's Purgatorio. (M.
Musa, trans) Purgatorio. (A. Mandel-
baum, trans)
J.F. Cotter, 249(HudR):Summer82-306
Dante Alighieri. Inferno.* (A. Mandel-
baum, trans)
J.F. Cotter, 249(HudR):Summer82-306
M. Davie, 402(MLR):Oct82-971
J.M. Ferrante, 551(RenQ):Autumn82-452
Danto, A.C. Sartre.
A.G. Pleydell-Pearce, 323:Jan82-90
Danto, A.C. The Transfiguration of the
Commonplace.*
M. Devereaux, 127:Winter82-347
F. Schier, 617(TLS):4Feb83-111

Daoust, Y. Roger Planchon.
  C. Campos, 208(FS):Jul82-362
  R.C. Lamont, 397(MD):Sep82-446
  M. Sadler, 402(MLR):Oct82-968
  J.R. Taylor, 157:Spring82-59
Darby, E. and N. Smith. The Cult of the
  Prince Consort.
  R. Foster, 617(TLS):2Dec83-1344
  E.S. Turner, 362:15Dec83-23
Darby, H.C. The Changing Fenland.
  L.R. Poos, 617(TLS):21Oct83-1166
Darby, T. The Feast.
  B. Cooper, 150(DR):Winter82/83-707
D'Arcy, M. and J. Arden. Vandaleur's
  Folly.
  R.J. Steen, 214:Vol 10No38-139
Dardis, T. Harold Lloyd.
  J. Davison, 441:18Sep83-26
  A. Reilly, 18:Jun83-69
  442(NY):5Sep83-112
Darkers, C. The Blue Plaque Guide to
  London.
  639(VQR):Summer82-100
Darlaston, P., ed. Presents.
  M. Cowan, 614:Spring83-22
Darling, M.E., ed. A.J.M. Smith.
  W.J. Keith, 627(UTQ):Summer82-455
  I.S. MacLaren, 105:Fall/Winter82-141
Darling, M.L. The Punjab Peasant in Pros-
  perity and Debt.
  D. Gilmartin, 293(JASt):Nov81-171
Darling, S.S. Chicago Ceramics and Glass.
  C. Robertson, 658:Summer/Autumn82-160
Darlington, B. - see Wordsworth, W. and M.
Darnton, R. The Business of Enlighten-
  ment.*
  R. Shackleton, 517(PBSA):Vol76No1-89
Darras, J. Joseph Conrad and the West.
  C.R. La Bossière, 268(IFR):Winter83-75
Darroch, L. Bright Land.
  F. Rasky, 73:Summer83-52
  W.N., 102(CanL):Summer82-174
Darroch, L.A., ed. Between Fire and Love.
  E.M. Aldrich, Jr., 238:Dec82-667
Darton, F.J.H. Children's Books in En-
  gland.* (3rd ed rev by B. Alderson)
  J.G. Schiller, 78(BC):Winter82-516
Daruwalla, K.N. Sword and Abyss.
  A. Hashmi, 314:Summer-Fall82-243
Daruwalla, K.N., ed. Two Decades of
  Indian Poetry (1960-1980).
  F.E. Krishna, 436(NewL):Winter82/83-
  120
Darvi, A. Pretty Babies.
  M. Haskell, 441:30Oct83-9
Darwin, C. Voyage d'un naturaliste autour
  du monde. (Vols 1 and 2)
  J. Aeply, 450(NRF):Dec82-97
Darwin, E. The Letters of Erasmus Darwin.*
  (D. King-Hele, ed)
  D.M. Hassler, 661(WC):Summer82-137
Dary, D. Cowboy Culture.*
  J.R. Nicholl, 649(WAL):Winter83-373
  639(VQR):Spring82-63
Das, G.K. and J. Beer, eds. E.M. Forster.*
  E. Heine, 677(YES):Vol 12-339
  K. Watson, 447(N&Q):Oct81-452
Das, R.P. - see Neisser, W.
Dascotte, R. Etude dialectologique, ethno-
  graphique et folklorique sur l'élevage
  dans le Centre.
  L. de Cock, 553(RLiR):Jul-Dec81-505

Dasher, T.E. William Faulkner's Charac-
  ters.
  D. Minter, 578:Fall83-123
Dathorne, O.R. Dark Ancestor.*
  C.E. Mushel, 114(ChiR):Vol33No2-156
Dauben, J.W. Georg Cantor, His Mathemat-
  ics and Philosophy of the Infinite.
  A. Oberschelp, 316:Jun82-456
  M.E. Tiles, 518:Jan82-21
Daubert, H. and others - see "Lexicon der
  Kinder — und Jugendliteratur"
Dauenhauer, B.P. Silence.
  C. Chalier, 192(EP):Oct-Dec82-488
  M.E. Zimmerman, 258:Sep82-219
Daugherty, S.B. The Literary Criticism of
  Henry James.* [incorrectly shown in
  prev under James, H.]
  A.W. Bellringer, 506(PSt):May82-175
  C.L. Eichelberger, 27(AL):Mar82-145
  R. Hewitt, 395(MFS):Winter81/82-719
  R.A. Hocks, 183(ESQ):Vol128No4-261
  J.E. Miller, Jr., 284:Winter83-151
  R.B. Yeazell, 445(NCF):Mar83-611
Dault, G.M. - see "Barker Fairley Por-
  traits"
Daumal, R. René Daumal ou le retour à soi.
  A. Reix, 542:Jan-Mar82-62
Dauphin, J-P., ed. L-F. Céline 4.
  L. Davis, 208(FS):Oct82-492
Dauses, A. Das Imperfekt in den romanis-
  chen Sprachen.
  J. Klausenburger, 350:Jun83-444
Dauzat, A., G. Deslandes and C. Rostaing.
  Dictionnaire étymologique des noms de
  rivières et de montagnes en France.
  J. Bourguignon, 553(RLiR):Jan-Jun81-
  265
Dave, J.H. - see "Manu-smriti with Nine
  Commentaries"
Davenport, G. Eclogues.*
  F. Goellner-Cortwright, 114(ChiR):
  Vol33No2-150
  P. La Salle, 573(SSF):Summer82-291
  639(VQR):Spring82-55
Davenport, G. The Geography of the Imagin-
  ation.*
  S.E. Lauzen, 560:Summer82-181
  295(JML):Dec82-370
  639(VQR):Winter82-9
Davenport, M. The Unpretentious Pose.
  L. Milazzo, 584(SWR):Spring82-v
Davern, J. and others. Architecture 1970-
  1980.
  P. Blake, 576:Mar82-80
Davey, F. Louis Dudek and Raymond
  Souster.*
  R. Gibbs, 198:Jul82-105
  R. Hatch, 102(CanL):Summer82-157
  W.J. Keith, 627(UTQ):Summer82-457
  F.W. Watt, 99:Apr82-32
Davey, P. Arts and Crafts Architecture.*
  C. Ashwin, 592:Vol 195No995-93
  A. Crawford, 637(VS):Summer82-501
  J.D. Kornwolf, 576:Mar82-77
  P. Skipwith, 90:May82-309
Daviau, D.G. - see Schnitzler, A.
Daviault, A. Comoedia Togata: Fragments.
  H.D. Jocelyn, 123:Vol132No2-154
David, C., ed. Franz Kafka.*
  C. Koelb, 680(ZDP):Band101Heft4-614
  H.J. Meyer-Wendt, 221(GQ):May82-436
  J. Strelka, 133:Band15Heft1/2-177
  J.J. White, 402(MLR):Apr82-500

David, D. Fictions of Resolution in Three
Victorian Novels.*
W.L. Reed, 637(VS):Winter82-256
David, M. and F.G. Ham, and others. Archi-
val Preservation of Machine-Readable
Records.
V.I. Walch, 14:Fall82-480
David-Neel, A. and L. Yongden. The Power
of Nothingness.
A. van Buren, 469:Vol8No1-112
Davidian, H.H. The Rhododendron Species.
(Vol 1)
A. Paterson, 617(TLS):22Jul83-786
Davidsen, E. Henrik Ibsen og Det konge-
lige Teater.*
C. Waal, 563(SS):Spring82-176
Davidsen-Nielsen, N. English Phonetics.
B.S. Andrésen, 179(ES):Jun82-255
Davidsen-Nielsen, N. Neutralization and
Archiphoneme.*
A. Zettersten, 179(ES):Aug82-369
Davidson, A. North Atlantic Seafood.
W. and C. Cowen, 639(VQR):Spring82-67
Davidson, A.A. Early American Modernist
Painting, 1910-1935.*
A. Berman, 55:May82-29
M. Sawin, 127:Winter82-351
M. Yorke, 324:Mar83-228
Davidson, A.E. and C.N., eds. The Art of
Margaret Atwood.
I. Ferris, 627(UTQ):Summer82-466
W.J. Keith, 168(ECW):Spring82-88
Davidson, A.K. The Art of Zen Gardens.
E. Seidensticker, 441:11Dec83-14
Davidson, C., ed. A Middle English Trea-
tise on the Playing of Miracles.
T. Coletti, 130:Summer82-184
Davidson, C.N., ed. Critical Essays on
Ambrose Bierce.
J.R. Brazil, 26(ALR):Autumn82-282
Davidson, D. Essays on Actions and
Events.*
T. Burge, 185:Apr83-608
A.C.D., 543:Sep81-122
J. Heal, 483:Jan82-133
J-L. Petit, 192(EP):Oct-Dec82-488
Davidson, H.E. - see Saxo Grammaticus
Davidson, J.P. David Teniers the Younger.*
B. Wind, 568(SCN):Winter82-78
Davidson, M.B. The American Wing.
M.S. Young, 39:Feb82-133
Davidson, M.B. The Bantam Illustrated
Guide to Early American Furniture.*
M.S. Young, 39:Feb82-133
Davidson, M.B. The Drawing of America.
B. Dobell, 441:4Dec83-12
Davidson, R. Tracks.
S. Brown, 569(SR):Spring82-250
Davie, D. Collected Poems 1971-1983.
E. Griffiths, 362:1Sep83-22
Davie, D. These the Companions.*
P. Dickinson, 364:Nov82-76
Davie, D. and R. Stevenson. English Hym-
nology in the Eighteenth Century.
J. Michon, 189(EA):Oct-Dec82-470
Davies, A. An Annotated Critical Bibliog-
raphy of Modernism.
E. Mendelson, 617(TLS):26Aug83-901
Davies, C. Latin Writers of the Renais-
sance.*
J.W. Binns, 123:Vol32No1-120

Davies, H. and M-H. Holy Days and Holi-
days.
R.A. Fletcher, 617(TLS):2Dec83-1354
Davies, J. - see Esenin, S.
Davies, J.A. John Forster.
G. Lindop, 617(TLS):14Oct83-1111
Davies, N. The Aztecs.
P.T. Bradley, 86(BHS):Oct82-348
Davies, N. God's Playground.
M. Malia, 453(NYRB):29Sep83-18
Davies, P. God and the New Physics.
T. Ferris, 441:20Nov83-12
B. Pippard, 617(TLS):29Jul83-795
Davies, P. and J. and A. Huxley. Wild
Orchids of Britain and Europe.
W.T. Stearn, 617(TLS):20May83-522
Davies, R. The Enthusiasms of Robertson
Davies.* (J.S. Grant, ed)
J. Hoffman, 108:Summer82-148
Davies, R. High Spirits.
442(NY):19Dec83-140
Davies, R. The Rebel Angels.*
J. Harris, 296(JCF):No33-112
W.J. Keith, 298:Spring82-135
J. Mills, 198:Oct82-117
G. Woodcock, 529(QQ):Winter82-744
Davies, R. The Well-Tempered Critic.*
(J.S. Grant, ed)
W. Cude, 627(UTQ):Summer82-456
J. Hoffman, 108:Summer82-148
W.J. Keith, 298:Spring82-135
Davies, R., A.R. George and G. Rupp, eds.
A History of the Methodist Church in
Great Britain. (Vol 3)
D. Martin, 617(TLS):1Apr83-329
Davies, R.W. The Industrialization of
Soviet Russia.*
J.R. Millar, 550(RusR):Jan82-60
Davies, S. Emily Brontë.
A. Leighton, 617(TLS):4Nov83-1213
Davies, T. Merlyn the Magician and the
Pacific Coast Highway.
A. Sutherland, 362:3Feb83-26
Davies, W. Wales in the Early Middle Ages.
C. Thomas, 617(TLS):18Feb83-165
Davies, W. - see Hopkins, G.M.
Davies, W.D. The Territorial Dimension of
Judaism.
H. Maccoby, 617(TLS):1Jul83-702
I. Youdovin, 287:Dec82-26
Davis, A. Frontier of Our Dreams.
N. Luckyj, 529(QQ):Autumn82-630
Davis, A.J. Rural Residences, etc.
G.B. Tatum, 576:Dec82-357
Davis, A.P. From the Dark Tower.
E. Guereschi, 395(MFS):Winter82/83-682
Davis, B.H. and R.K. O'Cain, eds. First
Person Singular.*
C.M. Rulon, 35(AS):Fall82-221
Davis, C. Waiting For It.
R.A. Schroth, 436(NewL):Fall82-95
Davis, C.B. The Animal Motif in African
Art.
P.J. Imperato, 2(AfrA):Nov81-84
Davis, C.T. Black Is the Color of the
Cosmos. (H.L. Gates, Jr., ed)
I. Reed, 676(YR):Summer83-619
Davis, D. Seeing the World.*
M. Kinzie, 29:Jul/Aug83-33
Davis, D. Stars!
J. Maslin, 441:4Dec83-72
Davis, D. Theatre for Young People.
J. Doolittle, 108:Spring82-198

Davis, D. Wisdom and Wilderness.
  D. Davie, 617(TLS):5Aug83-840
  D. Middleton, 598(SoR):Autumn83-919
Davis, D.H. Fire Falcon.
  T.J. Binyon, 617(TLS):30Dec83-1462
Davis, F. A Fearful Innocence.*
  639(VQR):Summer82-86
Davis, F. Living Alive!
  G.R. Lowe, 529(QQ):Spring82-161
Davis, H. and P. Walton, eds. Language,
  Image, Media.
  M. Warnock, 617(TLS):8Jul83-722
Davis, H.C. and others, eds. Essays in
  Honour of John Humphreys Whitfield Pre-
  sented to Him on His Retirement from the
  Serena Chair of Italian at the Univer-
  sity of Birmingham.
  C. Kleinhenz, 545(RPh):May82-677
Davis, H.L. Robert Desnos.
  A. Duhamel-Ketchum, 207(FR):Feb83-492
  A.M. Russo, 188(ECr):Summer82-69
Davis, J.B. La Quête de Paul Gadenne.
  J.O. Lowrie, 207(FR):Feb83-493
Davis, J.C. Utopia and the Ideal Society.*
  N.P. Eurich, 551(RenQ):Winter82-642
  L.T. Sargent, 322(JHI):Oct-Dec82-681
Davis, J.E. Chrysalis.
  E. Manwaring, 649(WAL):Spring82-82
Davis, J.F. Heresy and Reformation in the
  South-East of England 1520-1559.
  D.M. Loades, 617(TLS):21Oct82-1169
Davis, J.T. Dramatic Pairings in the
  Elegies of Propertius and Ovid.
  J.H. Brouwers, 394:Vol35fasc3/4-415
Davis, K.F. Désiré Charnay.
  L. Milazzo, 584(SWR):Winter82-v
Davis, L.H. Theory of Action.*
  M.M., 543:Jun82-864
Davis, M., ed. Zionism in Transition.
  M.I. Urofsky, 390:Jan82-59
Davis, M.C. Hebrew Bible Manuscripts in
  the Cambridge Genizah Collections.
  (Vol 1)
  E.J. Revell, 318(JAOS):Apr-Jun81-260
Davis, M.C. Hebrew Bible Manuscripts in
  the Cambridge Genizah Collections. (Vol
  2)
  E.J. Revell, 318(JAOS):Oct-Dec81-444
Davis, N., ed. Non-Cycle Plays and The
  Winchester Dialogues.*
  D. Bevington, 402(MLR):Jul82-692
Davis, N. and others, comps. A Chaucer
  Glossary.*
  S.A. Barney, 402(MLR):Oct82-920
Davis, N.Z. The Return of Martin Guerre.
  D. Isaac, 441:20ct83-13
  E. Le Roy Ladurie, 453(NYRB):22Dec83-
  12
Davis, P. Hometown.*
  639(VQR):Summer82-91
Davis, R. The English Rothschilds.
  R. Foster, 617(TLS):14Oct83-1108
Davis, R.C., ed. The Fictional Father.*
  S.S. Curry, 295(JML):Dec82-332
  S.S. Curry, 546(RR):Mar82-273
  S.G. Kellman, 395(MFS):Summer82-349
  P. McCallum, 49:Jan82-73
  N. Schor, 454:Fall82-88
Davis, R.M. A Catalogue of the Evelyn
  Waugh Collection at the Humanities
  Research Center, the University of
  Texas at Austin.
  P. Miles, 354:Dec82-460

Davis, R.M. Evelyn Waugh, Writer.*
  A.A. De Vitis, 651(WHR):Winter82-369
  M. Stannard, 184(EIC):Oct82-384
  R.J. Voorhees, 395(MFS):Summer82-285
Davis, S. and P. Simon. Reggae Interna-
  tional.
  D. Rimmer, 362:19May83-22
Davis, S.T.W. Intellectual Change and
  Political Development in Early Modern
  Japan.*
  R.W. Bowen, 293(JASt):Nov81-133
Davis, T.M. Faulkner's "Negro."
  L. Mackinnon, 617(TLS):3Jun83-568
Davis, T.M. and V.L. - see Taylor, E.
Davis, W. The Rich.*
  442(NY):20Jun83-102
Davis, W.C., ed. The Image of War, 1861-
  1865. (Vol 1)
  M.P. Musick, 14:Spring82-202
  H.H. Shapley, 50(ArQ):Spring82-90
  639(VQR):Summer82-82
Davis, W.C., ed. The Image of War, 1861-
  1865.* (Vol 2)
  H.H. Shapley, 50(ArQ):Spring82-90
Davis, W.V. One Way to Reconstruct the
  Scene.
  C. Berger, 491:Apr82-35
  J. Saunders, 565:Vol23No1-73
  D.R. Solheim, 152(UDQ):Summer81-124
Davison, P. Barn Fever and Other Poems.
  D. Davis, 362:5May83-24
  S. Sandy, 491:Aug82-293
Davy, K. Richard Foreman and the Onto-
  logical-Hysteric Theatre.
  T.J. Taylor, 612(ThS):Nov82-252
Daw, S. The Music of Johann Sebastian
  Bach: the Choral Works.*
  R. Jones, 410(M&L):Jul/Oct82-348
Dawe, C.W. and E.A. Dornan. One to One.
  M. Schneider, 608:Sep83-484
Dawe, R.D. - see Sophocles
Dawe, R.D. and J. Diggle - see Page, D.L.
Dawidowicz, L.S. The Holocaust and the
  Historians.*
  S. Friedlander, 473(PR):3/1982-464
  T. Ziolkowski, 569(SR):Fall82-592
Dawisha, K. and P. Hanson, eds. Soviet-
  East European Dilemmas.
  J.F. Triska, 550(RusR):Apr82-231
Dawson, A.C. and L.M. Dicho y hecho.
  L. Soto-Ruiz, 238:Mar82-154
Dawson, C. and J. Pfordresher, eds. Mat-
  thew Arnold, Prose Writings: The Criti-
  cal Heritage.
  R.J. Dingley, 447(N&Q):Aug81-353
  S. Monod, 402(MLR):Oct82-936
Dawson, J.G. 3d. Army Generals and Recon-
  struction.
  639(VQR):Autumn82-128
Dawson, L.H. - see Walker, J.
Dawson, P.M.S. The Unacknowledged Legis-
  lator.*
  J. Buxton, 541(RES):Nov82-488
  D.H. Reiman, 340(KSJ):Vol31-214
  B. Ruddick, 366:Spring82-129
Day, A.G., ed. Modern Australian Prose,
  1901-1975.*
  L. Hergenhan, 71(ALS):May82-407
  S.F.D. Hughes, 395(MFS):Spring81-173
Day, D. By Little and by Little. (R.
  Ellsberg, ed)
  J.K. Davison, 441:7Aug83-15

Day, R.R., ed. Issues in English Creoles.
  G. Escure, 355(LSoc):Dec82-473
  L. Todd, 38:Band100Heft1/2-141
"The Day After Midnight."
  M. Howard, 231:Feb83-66
Daydí-Tolson, S. and others. Vicente
  Aleixandre.
  R. Ruiz, 238:Sep82-465
Daymond, D. - see de la Roche, M.
Dazzi, M. and E. Merkel. Catalogo della
  Pinacoteca della Fondazione Scientifica
  Querini Stampalia.
  G. Robertson, 90:Dec82-764
Deacon, M. Philip Doddridge of Northamp-
  ton, 1702-51.
  M.P., 189(EA):Jan-Mar82-116
Dean, D. The Thirties.
  J.M. Richards, 617(TLS):1Jul83-690
Dean, J.F. Tom Stoppard.*
  M. Lammon, 436(NewL):Winter82/83-104
Dean, J.W. 3d. Lost Honor.
  N. Horrock, 441:9Jan83-10
Dean, S.F.X. Such Pretty Toys.
  T.J. Binyon, 617(TLS):3Jun83-582
  T.J. Binyon, 617(TLS):8Jul83-732
  M. Laski, 362:19May83-24
Dean, W. The New Grove Handel.
  A. Blackwood, 617(TLS):9Sep83-954
De Andrea, W.L. Killed With a Passion.
  N. Callendar, 441:22May83-49
Deane, B. Alun Hoddinott.
  T. Bray, 410(M&L):Jul/Oct81-416
Deane, J.F. High Sacrifice.
  L.M. Harrod, 174(Éire):Fall82-145
Dearden, J.S. Turner's Isle of Wight
  Sketchbook.
  E. Joll, 39:Feb82-136
De Arment, R.K. Knights of the Green
  Cloth.
  584(SWR):Summer82-v
Dearnley, M. Margiad Evans.
  K.O. Morgan, 617(TLS):8Apr83-349
Deathridge, J. and C. Dahlhaus. The New
  Grove Wagner.
  J. Kerman, 453(NYRB):22Dec83-27
Debevec, A., comp. United States Docu-
  ments in the Propaganda Fide Archives.
  (Vol 8) (M. Kiemen and A. Wyse, eds)
  S. Gilley, 161(DUJ):Dec81-126
Debray-Genette, R., ed. Flaubert à
  l'Oeuvre.*
  A. Fairlie, 208(FS):Apr82-214
Debrie, J. and R. Moeurs épulaires pic-
  ardes.
  L. de Cock, 553(RLiR):Jul-Dec81-506
Debru, C. Analyse et Représentation.
  H.W. Arndt, 342:Band73Heft4-476
Debus, F. and J. Hartwig, eds. Fest-
  schrift für Gerhard Cordes zum 65.
  Geburtstag. (Vols 1 and 2)
  H. Niebaum, 685(ZDL):2/1981-238
Debussy, C. The Poetic Debussy. (M.G.
  Cobb, ed)
  R.L. Smith, 617(TLS):18Mar83-265
Decalo, S. Historical Dictionary of Niger.
  A.H.M. Kirk-Greene, 69:Vol51No3-798
Décaudin, M., ed. Les Poètes fantaisistes.
  J. Réda, 450(NRF):Apr82-120
Décaudin, M. - see Verlaine, P.
De Coster, C. Pedro Antonio de Alarcón.*
  P.L. Ullman, 593:Spring82-92
Décote, G. - see Cazotte, J.

Decoufle, A-C. Traité élémentaire de pré-
  vision et de prospection.
  J. Donzelot, 98:Feb82-97
  R. Prévost, 192(EP):Apr-Jun82-243
"La Découverte de la France au XVIIe
  siècle."
  P. Hourcade, 475:No16Pt2-370
  M-O. Sweetser, 535(RHL):May-Jun82-459
Dedijer, V. Novi prilozi za biografiju
  Josipa Broza Tita.*
  S. Clissold, 575(SEER):Oct82-632
Deduck, P.A. Realism, Reality, and the
  Fictional Theory of Alain Robbe-Grillet
  and Anais Nin.
  M. Simonton, 268(IFR):Summer83-151
Deeney, J.J., ed. Chinese-Western Compara-
  tive Literature.
  A.E. Kunst, 678(YCGL):No30-90
Defaux, G. Molière, ou les métamorphoses
  du comique.*
  B. Beugnot, 210(FrF):Jan82-76
  L. Gossman, 402(MLR):Apr82-447
  M. Gutwirth, 535(RHL):May-Jun82-471
  W. Matzat, 547(RF):Band94Heft2/3-324
Defoe, D. Roxana, The Fortunate Mistress.
  566:Autumn82-56
Defoe, D. The Versatile Defoe.* (L.A.
  Curtis, ed)
  D. Blewett, 173(ECS):Summer82-477
De Francis, J. Beginning Chinese Reader.
  (2nd ed)
  T. Light, 318(JAOS):Oct-Dec81-430
Deftereos, A.N. Bread at Birth and Death.
  [in Greek]
  G. Morgan, 203:Vol193No1-121
Degen, R., W.W. Müller and W. Röllig. New
  Ephemeris für Semitische Epigraphik.
  (Vol 3)
  S. Segert, 318(JAOS):Oct-Dec81-451
Degenhart, B. and A. Schmitt. Corpus der
  italienischen Zeichnungen, 1300-1450.
  (Pt 2)
  E. Borsook, 551(RenQ):Spring82-74
Degering, K. Defoes Gesellschaftskonzep-
  tion.
  M.E. Novak, 402(MLR):Jan82-168
Dégh, L., ed. Indiana Folklore.
  R. Wehse, 196:Band23Heft3/4-312
De Giorgi, R. Scienza del diritto e legit-
  timazione.
  F. Volpi, 489(PJGG):Band89Heft2-441
De Giovanni, B. La teoria politica delle
  classi nel "Capitale."
  F. Volpi, 489(PJGG):Band89Heft2-439
Degl'Innocenti Pierini, R. Studi su
  Accio.* [shown in prev under Pierini,
  R.D.]
  P. Flobert, 555:Vol55fasc2-377
Degrada, F., ed. Vivaldi Veneziano Euro-
  peo.
  E. Cross, 415:Jan82-31
Deguise, A. Trois Femmes.
  M.B. Lacy, 207(FR):Mar83-633
Deguy, M. Donnant Donnant.*
  M. Bishop, 207(FR):Dec82-335
Deidda, A. Infelix Austria.
  I. Solbrig, 133:Band15Heft3-274
Deighton, L. Berlin Game.
  T.J. Binyon, 617(TLS):21Oct83-1170
Dekeyser, X. and others. Foundations of
  English Grammar.
  A. Juul, 179(ES):Dec82-559

Dekeyser, X. and P.D.S. Sheldon. An Introduction to the Articulation of RP Phonemes.
A. Wollmann, 38:Band100Heft3/4-466
Dekker, G. Coleridge and the Literature of Sensibility.
J.R.D. Jackson, 173(ECS):Fall81-97
Dekker, T. The Shoemaker's Holiday.*
(R.L. Smallwood and S. Wells, eds)
T.W. Craik, 161(DUJ):Jun82-303
G.K. Hunter, 677(YES):Vol 12-247
De Kovic, G. "En directo" desde España.
J.A. Castañeda, 399(MLJ):Summer82-232
Dêl, R. Tū'điển Việt - Gia Rai.
A.F. Majewicz, 360(LP):Vol24-166
Delacampagne, C. and R. Magiori, eds. Philosopher, les interrogations contemporaines, matériaux pour un enseignement.*
J. Lefranc, 192(EP):Oct-Dec82-490
Delacroix, E. Journal 1822-63.
J. Russell, 617(TLS):15Jul83-744
Delage, R. Iconographie musicale: Chabrier.
R. Orledge, 410(M&L):Jul/Oct82-328
Delamater, J. Dance in the Hollywood Musical.
J.P. Telotte, 500:Winter83-62
Delaney, F. James Joyce's Odyssey.
M.P. Gillespie, 395(MFS):Winter82/83-625
R.M. Kain, 329(JJQ):Summer82-466
De-la-Noy, M. Elgar.
M. Trend, 617(TLS):15Jul83-751
Delany, P. D.H. Lawrence's Nightmare.*
B. Whiteman, 556:Summer82-78
Delany, S.R. Neveryona.
G. Jonas, 441:31Jul83-13
Delarue, C. La Chute de l'ange.
L. Kovacs, 450(NRF):Jun82-126
Delbaere, J., ed. Bird, Hawk, Bogie.
S.F.D. Hughes, 395(MFS):Spring81-173
Delbanco, A. William Ellery Channing.*
J. Myerson, 432(NEQ):Dec82-618
Delbanco, N. About My Table.
E. Milton, 441:18Sep83-14
Delblanc, S. Speranza.
J.B., 231:Nov83-75
D. Evanier, 441:30Oct83-15
Delblanc, S. Treklöver.
R. Wright, 563(SS):Winter82-95
Delclos, J-C. Le Témoignage de Georges Chastellain, historiographe de Philippe le Bon et de Charles le Téméraire.*
D. Hoeges, 547(RF):Band93Heft3/4-443
R. Vaughan, 382(MAE):1982/2-259
Delebecque, E. Construction de l'Odyssée.
P.V. Jones, 123:Vol32No1-82
Deleuze, G. Francis Bacon, logique de la sensation.*
J. Clair, 450(NRF):Mar82-151
P. Vauday, 98:Nov82-956
Deleuze, G. Nietzsche and Philosophy.
R. Rorty, 617(TLS):17Jun83-619
Deleuze, G. Spinoza: Philosophie Pratique.
T. Cordellier, 450(NRF):Jan82-129
Delevoy, R.L. Journal du Symbolisme.
G. Roque, 107(CRCL):Dec81-552
Delevoy, R.L. Der Symbolismus in Wort und Bild.
M. Gsteiger, 52:Band16Heft2-222
Delgado, J.J. - see under Jiménez Delgado, J.

de Delgaty, A.H.V. and A. Ruíz Sánchez. Diccionario Tzotzil de San Andrés con Variaciones Dialectales.
C.G. Craig and N.C. England, 269(IJAL):Apr82-226
Delibes, M. The Hedge.
T. Talbot, 441:11Dec83-11
De Lillo, D. The Names.*
M.K. Benet, 617(TLS):9Dec83-1373
442(NY):4Apr83-132
Delius, H. Self-Awareness.
J.F.M. Hunter, 518:Jul82-191
Dell, F. Generative Phonology and French Phonology.*
B.K. Barnes, 399(MLJ):Summer82-204
B. Rochet, 320(CJL):Spring82-93
D.C. Walker, 297(JL):Mar82-206
Della Porta, G. Gli duoi fratelli rivali/The Two Rival Brothers. (L.G. Clubb, ed and trans)
N. Dersofi, 276:Winter82-348
Della Valle, D. and A. Carriat - see Guérin de Bouscal, G.
Della Volpe, G. Critique of Taste.
R.E.I., 543:Sep81-123
Dellheim, C. The Face of the Past.
D. Watkin, 617(TLS):29Apr83-427
Del Litto, V., ed. Le Journal intime et ses formes littéraires.
F.P. Bowman, 535(RHL):May-Jun82-499
Del Litto, V. - see Stendhal
Delmaire, B. Le compte général de receveur d'Artois pour 1303-1304.
B. Lyon, 589:Apr82-448
Del Mar, N. Anatomy of the Orchestra.*
P.P. Nash, 607:Sep82-51
L. Salter, 415:May82-332
Del Mar, N. Orchestral Variations.
S. Sadie, 415:Aug82-548
Deloffre, F. - see de Voltaire, F.M.A.
Deloffre, F. and J. van den Heuvel - see de Voltaire, F.M.A.
Delort, R. Le commerce des fourrures en Occident à la fin du moyen âge.
R.C. Hoffmann, 589:Apr82-365
Deluca, A.R. Great Power Rivalry at the Turkish Straits.
M.S. Anderson, 575(SEER):Apr82-299
De Luca, V.A. Thomas De Quincey.
M.E. Holstein, 627(UTQ):Summer82-427
J.R. Nabholtz, 191(ELN):Sep82-68
Demaray, J.G. Milton's Theatrical Epic.*
E.R. Cunnar, 191(ELN):Mar82-280
A. Low, 551(RenQ):Summer81-294
Demélier, J. Les Nouvelles Lettres de mon Moulin.
V. Beauvois, 450(NRF):Oct82-122
Demerson, G., ed. Poétiques de la Métamorphose de Pétrarque à John Donne.
M. McGowan, 402(MLR):Oct82-949
L. Nelson, Jr., 551(RenQ):Winter82-646
U. Schulz-Buschhaus, 547(RF):Band94Heft2/3-297
Demeter, R.S. and P.S. Obrazcy fol'klora Cygan-Këldërarej.
F.B.J. Kuiper, 259(IIJ):Oct82-328
D'Emilio, J. Sexual Politics, Sexual Communities.
R.J. Margolis, 441:22May83-18
Deming, S. Not Tonight.
P. Nightingale, 102(CanL):Autumn82-155

Demos, J.P. Entertaining Satan.*
    C.F. Karlsen, 676(YR):Summer83-612
    D. Levin, 165(EAL):Spring83-95
    A. Macfarlane, 617(TLS):13May83-493
Demougeot, E. La formation de l'Europe et
les invasions barbares. (Vol 2)
    M. Reydellet, 555:Vol55fasc1-186
Dempsey, H.A. and J.R. Harper. History
In Their Blood.
    K. Kritzwiser, 73:Dec82/Jan/Feb83-58
Dempster, B. Fables for Isolated Men.
    R.D. MacKenzie, 628(UWR):Spring-
      Summer83-86
d'Encausse, H.C. - see under Carrère
d'Encausse, H.
Dendle, B.J. Galdós: the Mature Thought.*
    R. Ricard, 356(LR):May82-171
    S.E. Schyfter, 593:Fall82-273
    D.F. Urey, 400(MLN):Mar82-432
Denecke, L. Jacob Grimm und sein Bruder
Wilhelm.
    I. Regener and W. Neumann, 682(ZPSK):
      Band35Heft2-239
De Neef, A.L. Spenser and the Motives of
Metaphor.
    H.R. Woudhuysen, 617(TLS):12Aug83-867
Denès, F. Catalogue raisonné des objets
en bois provenant de Dunhuang et con-
servés au musée Guimet.
    M.M. Rhie, 318(JAOS):Oct-Dec81-434
Denham, R.D. Northrop Frye and Critical
Method.
    T. Rajan, 627(UTQ):Fall81-93
Deniaux, E. Recherches sur les amphores
antiques de Basse-Normandie.
    R. Reece, 123:Vol32No2-296
Denieul-Cormier, A. Wise and Foolish
Kings.
    639(VQR):Spring82-46
Denis, E. La Lokapaññatti et les idées
cosmologiques du bouddhisme ancien.*
    J.W. de Jong, 259(IIJ):Jan80-70
Denisova, M.A. Lingvo-Stranovedčeskij
Slovar'.
    D. Milivojević, 558(RLJ):Winter-
      Spring82-282
Denkler, H., ed. Romane und Erzählungen
des bürgerlichen Realismus.
    G.W. Field, 564:Nov81-321
    F. Martini, 680(ZDP):Band101Heft2-262
Denktash, R.R. The Cyprus Triangle.
    C. Hitchens, 453(NYRB):20Jan83-31
Dennett, D.C. Brainstorms.*
    J. Haugeland, 449:Nov82-613
Denoon, D. Settler Capitalism.
    C. Ehrlich, 617(TLS):7Oct83-1097
Dens, J-P. L'Honnête Homme et la critique
du goût.
    S.R. Baker, 207(FR):Apr83-768
Dent, P. Distant Lamps.
    L. Sail, 565:Vol23No4-73
Denux, R. La terrible course de Chateau-
briand.
    M. Schaettel, 356(LR):May82-167
Denyer, N. Time, Action and Necessity.*
    T.M.R., 185:Jan83-416
    P. Simpson, 63:Dec82-374
Depestre, R. Alléluia pour une femme-
jardin.
    C. Zimra, 207(FR):Mar83-662

Deprun, J. La philosophie de l'inquiétude
en France au XVIIIe siècle.*
    R. Grimsley, 208(FS):Jul82-334
    M. Phillips, 192(EP):Apr-Jun81-239
De Rijk, L.M. Die mittelalterlichen Trak-
tate De modo opponendi et respondendi.
    I. Angelelli, 319:Apr83-249
    V. Muñoz Delgado, 53(AGP):Band64Heft2-
      198
Dernberger, R.F., ed. China's Development
Experience in Comparative Perspective.
    V.D. Lippit, 293(JASt):Aug82-817
De Rocher, F. and G. Options.*
    T.M. Scanlan, 399(MLJ):Summer82-207
Derolez, A. The Library of Raphael de Mar-
catellis.*
    P.E. Webber, 377:Mar82-61
De Rosalia, A. Iscrizioni latine arcaiche.
(2nd ed)
    P. Flobert, 555:Vol56fasc2-339
De Rose, P.L. Jane Austen and Samuel
Johnson.
    D. McCracken, 405(MP):Nov82-196
Deroux, C., ed. Studies in Latin Litera-
ture and Roman History. (Vol 1)
    P. Jal, 555:Vol55fasc2-382
Deroux, C., ed. Studies in Latin Litera-
ture and Roman History. (Vol 2)
    D. Porte, 555:Vol55fasc2-382
Derré, J.R. - see Ballanche, P.S.
Derrett, J.D.M. Essays in Classical and
Modern Hindu Law. (Vol 4)
    L. Rocher, 318(JAOS):Oct-Dec81-463
Derrida, J. Dissemination. (B. Johnson,
ed and trans)
    483:Jan82-146
Derrida, J. Margins of Philosophy.
    A.C. Danto, 617(TLS):30Sep83-1035
Derrida, J. Of Grammatology.
    S. Rosen, 480(P&R):Winter82-66
Derrida, J. Positions.* (A. Bass, ed and
trans)
    P. McCallum, 49:Jan82-73
Derrida, J. Writing and Difference.
    P. Hamilton, 541(RES):Nov82-504
Derry, T.K. A History of Scandinavia.
    R. McKnight, 563(SS):Winter82-81
Derry, T.K. - see Greve, T.
Dershowitz, A.M. The Best Defense.*
    J. Riemer, 287:Nov82-22
Dervillez-Bastuji, J. Structures des rela-
tions spatiales dans quelques langues
naturelles.
    G. Kleiber, 553(RLiR):Jul-Dec82-419
Desai, A. Clear Light of Day.*
    S. Daniels, 114(ChiR):Summer81-107
    A. Hashmi, 268(IFR):Winter83-56
De Salvo, L.A. Virginia Woolf's First
Voyage.*
    A.L. McLaughlin, 395(MFS):Summer81-320
Desanges, J. - see Pliny
De Santi, G. - see Atanagi, D.
Desbarats, P. Canada Lost/Canada Found.*
    G.W., 102(CanL):Spring82-163
Desbordes, F. Argonautica.
    J-P. Cèbe, 555:Vol55fasc1-181
Descartes, R. Le Monde. (M. Mahoney, ed
and trans)
    D.M. Clarke, 518:Apr82-82
Deschamps, N., R. Héroux and N. Villeneuve.
Le Mythe de Maria Chapdelaine.*
    L. Rochette, 102(CanL):Spring82-94

Deschaux, R., ed. Les oeuvres de Pierre Chastellain et de Vaillant.
   G. Roques, 553(RLiR):Jul-Dec82-504
Deschoux, M. Comprendre Platon.
   W.J. Verdenius, 394:Vol35fasc3/4-373
Deschoux, M. Platon ou le Jeu philosophique.
   P. Pellegrin, 542:Apr-Jun82-460
Descombes, V. Le même et l'autre.
   P. Lewis, 153:Spring82-2
Descombes, V. Modern French Philosophy.
   G.H. Bauer, 207(FR):Feb83-473
   M. Quirk, 258:Jun82-211
   R. Young, 400(MLN):May82-975
Desfosses, H., ed. Soviet Population Policy.
   A. Helgeson, 550(RusR):Apr82-224
Desgraves, L. Elie Vinet humaniste de Bordeaux (1509-1587).
   I.D. McFarlane, 208(FS):Jan82-55
Deshpande, M.M. Evolution of Syntactic Theory in Sanskrit Grammar.*
   W.P. Lehmann, 660(Word):Dec81-245
   R. Rocher, 318(JAOS):Jul-Sep81-383
   T. Venkatacharya, 259(IIJ):Apr82-132
Desné, R. - see Meslier, J.
Desnoes, E., ed. Los dispositivos en la flor.
   S. Menton, 238:Sep82-470
Des Périers, B. Nouvelles Récréations et joyeux devis I-XC.* (K. Kasprzyk, ed)
   P. Chilton, 402(MLR):Jan82-201
Despeux, C. - see Mazu
Dessaix, R. and M. Ulman - see Svirski, G.
Dessaux-Berthonneau, A-M., ed. Théories linguistiques et traditions grammaticales.
   J. Chaurand, 209(FM):Jul82-272
Desvignes, L., ed. Travaux comparatistes.
   P. Chavy, 107(CRCL):Dec81-538
Desvignes, L. - see Mareschal, A.
d'Étaples, J.L. - see under Lefèvre d'Étaples, J.
Detienne, M. Dionysios Slain.
   J.W. Dye, 125:Fall81-109
   S. Loveday, 447(N&Q):Jun81-260
Detienne, M. Dionysos mis à mort.
   J.H. Croon, 394:Vol35fasc1/2-194
Detienne, M. L'Invention de la mythologie.
   J-P. Guinle, 450(NRF):May82-129
Detienne, M. and J-P. Vernant. Cunning Intelligence in Greek Culture and Society.
   N.D. Smith, 125:Fall81-107
Deuchler, F. and J. Wirth. Reclams Kunstführer Frankreich II.
   V. Beyer, 471:Jul/Aug/Sep82-264
Deutsch, E. On Truth.*
   J.N. Mohanty, 485(PEGW):Jan82-123
   E.P., 543:Mar82-600
"Deutschkanadisches Jahrbuch/German-Canadian Yearbook." (Vols 1-5) (H. Fröschle, ed)
   J. Eichhoff, 406:Summer82-185
Deva, B.C. The Music of India.
   E.O. Henry, 187:Sep83-557
Devahuti, ed. Problems of Indian Historiography.
   M.N. Pearson, 318(JAOS):Jul-Sep81-381
Devaulx, N. Le Pressoir mystique.
   F. de Martinoir, 450(NRF):Sep82-128
Devereux, G. Femme et mythe.
   M. Lefkowitz, 617(TLS):6May83-450

Devereux, W. Adult Education in Inner London, 1870-1980.
   J.S. Hurt, 324:Apr83-294
Devine, L. Nile.
   D. Cole, 441:6Mar83-28
Devine, P.E. The Ethics of Homicide.*
   B. Paskins, 483:Apr82-272
Devine, T.M. and D. Dickson, eds. Ireland and Scotland 1600-1850.
   F.M.L. Thompson, 617(TLS):26Aug83-910
De Vitis, A.A. and A.E. Kalson. J.B. Priestley.
   P. Brigg, 397(MD):Jun82-319
   P. Wolfe, 395(MFS):Summer81-351
De Vivo, A. Tacito e Claudio.
   M. Griffin, 313:Vol72-188
Devlamminck, B. and G. Jucquois. Compléments aux dictionnaires étymologiques du gotique. (Vol 1)
   E. Seebold, 260(IF):Band86-362
Devlin, A.J. Eudora Welty's Chronicle.
   F.C. Watkins, 578:Fall83-131
Devlin, D. A Speaking Part.*
   J.W. Lambert, 157:Winter82-45
Devlin, D.D. Wordsworth and the Poetry of Epitaphs.
   J.A.W. Heffernan, 591(SIR):Summer82-253
   K. Horowitz, 184(EIC):Jan82-74
Devlin, P. All of Us There.
   A. Duchêne, 617(TLS):7Oct83-1079
De Voogd, P.J. Henry Fielding and William Hogarth.
   P. Crowther, 89(BJA):Winter82-88
   D. Profumo, 566:Autumn82-49
De Vos, M. L'egittomania in pitture e mosaici romano-campani della prima età imperiale.
   H. Whitehouse, 313:Vol72-199
De Voto, M. - see Piston, W.
De Vries, P. Sauce for the Goose.*
   D. Flower, 249(HudR):Summer82-274
De Vries, P. Slouching Towards Kalamazoo.
   P-L. Adams, 61:Aug83-100
   W. Balliett, 442(NY):29Aug83-90
   E. Korn, 617(TLS):26Aug83-898
   T. Meehan, 441:14Aug83-7
Dewar, D. Saint of Auschwitz.
   P. Hebblethwaite, 617(TLS):22Apr83-394
Dewar, M. - see Smith, T.
Dewdney, C. Alter Sublime.*
   D. Barbour, 648(WCR):Oct82-37
Dewdney, S. Christopher Breton.
   E. Overend, 296(JCF):No33-118
De Witt, H.A. Chuck Berry.
   B.L. Cooper, 498:Vol18No2-129
Dexeus, V.C. - see under Combalia Dexeus, V.
Dezső, L. and W. Nemser, eds. Studies in English and Hungarian Contrastive Linguistics.
   J. Haiman, 350:Jun83-446
Dhanens, E. Hubert and Jan van Eyck.
   L. Campbell, 90:Feb82-106
"Dharmakośa, Rājanītikāṇḍa." (Vol 4, Pts 5 and 6) (L. Joshi, ed)
   L. Sternbach, 318(JAOS):Oct-Dec81-482
Dhôtel, A. Je ne suis pas d'ici.
   C. Dis, 450(NRF):Jun82-112
d'Hulst, R.A. Jacob Jordaens.
   D. Freedberg, 617(TLS):12Aug83-863

Didion, J. Salvador.
　　P-L. Adams, 61:Apr83-132
　　W. Hoge, 441:13Mar83-3
　　D. Leppard, 362:28Apr83-23
　　R. Stone, 231:Dec83-70
　　L. Whitehead, 617(TLS):24Jun83-663
　　442(NY):18Apr83-150
Didsbury, P. The Butchers of Hull.
　　H. Lomas, 364:Feb83-73
　　S. Regan, 493:Sep82-64
　　W. Scammell, 617(TLS):7Jan83-17
"1616 — Anuario de la Sociedad Española de
　　Literatura General y Comparada." (Vol 1)
　　C. Rodiek, 52:Band16Heft3-311
Diederich, B. Somoza.
　　639(VQR):Spring82-50
Diederichs, U. - see Frobenius, L.
Diefendorf, B.B. Paris City Councillors
　　in the Sixteenth Century.
　　R. Bonney, 617(TLS):1Jul83-706
de Diéguez, M. L'Idole monothéiste.
　　T. Cordellier, 450(NRF):Feb82-141
　　A. Reix, 542:Oct-Dec82-664
Diehl, J.F. Dickinson and the Romantic
　　Imagination.*
　　C.N. Davidson, 27(AL):Oct82-451
　　W. Martin, 661(WC):Summer82-135
　　C. Miller, 405(MP):Feb83-326
Diehl, W. Chameleon.*
　　639(VQR):Summer82-96
Dieter, W. Hunter's Orange.
　　442(NY):8Aug83-93
Diethart, J.M. Prosopographia Arsinoitica
　　I, s. vi-viii (Pros. Ars. I).
　　P.M. Fraser, 123:Vol132No2-260
Dietz, K. Senatus contra principem.
　　J.H.W.G. Liebeschuetz, 123:Vol132No1-
　　106
Dietz, S. Asine: Results of the Excava-
　　tions East of the Acropolis 1970-74.
　　(fasc 2)
　　O.T.P.K. Dickinson, 303(JoHS):Vol 102-
　　278
Díez Borque, J.M., ed. Historia de la
　　literatura española. (Vol 2)
　　M. Wilson, 86(BHS):Oct82-337
Díez Borque, J.M., ed. Historia de las
　　literaturas hispánicas no castellanas.
　　F. Pierce, 86(BHS):Jan82-77
Díez Borque, J.M. Lope de Vega.
　　N.L. D'Antuono, 552(REH):Jan82-130
Díez del Corral, L. Velázquez, la Monar-
　　quía e Italia.
　　D. Angulo Íñiguez, 48:Apr-Jun80-209
Diffey, N.R. Jakob Michael Reinhold Lenz
　　and Jean-Jacques Rousseau.
　　M. Hadley, 564:Sep82-213
　　E. McInnes, 680(ZDP):Band101Heft4-593
Digance, R. Run Out In The Country,
　　G. Ewart, 617(TLS):12Aug83-867
Digby, K.H. Lawyer in the Wilderness.
　　R. Pringle, 293(JASt):May82-629
Diggory, T. Yeats and American Poetry.
　　D. Donoghue, 441:5Jun83-7
Di Girolamo, C. A Critical Theory of Lit-
　　erature.
　　R.A. Hall, Jr., 350:Jun83-465
van Dijk, H. Het Roelantslied.
　　C. Gellinek, 589:Jan82-199
van Dijk, J., ed and trans. Lugal Ud Me-
　　Lám-bi Gál.
　　A. Millard, 617(TLS):4Nov83-1208

van Dijk, T.A. Text and Context.
　　Z. Szabó, 353:Vol 19No1/2-190
Dil, A.S. - see Emeneau, M.B.
Dil, A.S. - see Frake, C.O.
Dil, A.S. - see Friedrich, P.
Dillard, A. Teaching a Stone to Talk.*
　　442(NY):14Feb83-118
Dillard, J.L. Lexicon of Black English.
　　J.A. Hirshberg, 35(AS):Spring82-52
Dillard, J.L., ed. Perspectives on Ameri-
　　can English.
　　H. Pilch, 38:Band100Heft3/4-482
Dillard, J.L. - see Marckwardt, A.H.
Dillard, R.H.W. The First Man on the Sun.
　　J. Clute, 617(TLS):25Nov83-1329
Dillard, R.H.W. The Greeting.
　　L.L. Lee, 134(CP):Spring82-98
　　639(VQR):Summer82-94
Dille, G.F., ed. La comedia llamada Sera-
　　fina.
　　R.J. Nelson, 552(REH):Jan82-141
Diller, H-J. Metrik und Verslehre.*
　　G. Graustein, 682(ZPSK):Band34Heft3-
　　390
Diller, H-J. and J. Kornelius. Linguis-
　　tische Probleme der Übersetzung.*
　　P. Robberecht, 179(ES):Apr82-185
Diller, K.C., ed. Individual Differences
　　and Universals in Language Learning
　　Aptitude.
　　U. Reichenbach, 221(GQ):Nov82-587
　　M-A. Reiss, 399(MLJ):Summer82-194
Dilligan, R.J., J.W. Parins and T.K. Ben-
　　der. A Concordance to Ezra Pound's
　　"Cantos."
　　468:Fall82-356
Dillon, G.L. Constructing Texts.*
　　J. Hagge, 113:Spring82-61
Dillon, J. Shakespeare and the Solitary
　　Man.
　　R.C. Jones, 130:Winter82/83-384
Dillon, M. A Little Original Sin.
　　639(VQR):Winter82-16
Dilman, I. Morality and the Inner Life.*
　　A.W.H. Adkins, 185:Jan83-406
Dilman, I. Studies in Language and Reason.
　　J.D., 185:Oct82-195
　　O. Hanfling, 518:Oct82-230
Dilthey, W. Selected Writings.* (H.P.
　　Rickman, ed) Descriptive Psychology and
　　Historical Understanding.*
　　T.E. Huff, 488:Mar82-81
　　T.E. Huff, 488:Jun82-205
Dimic, M.V. and E. Kushner, general eds.
　　Actes du VIIe Congrès de l'Association
　　Internationale de Littérature Comparée/
　　Proceedings of the VIIth Congress of
　　the International Comparative Literature
　　Association.*
　　U. Weisstein, 107(CRCL)·Jun82-223
Dimić, M.V. and E. Kushner, eds. Compara-
　　tive Literature Today. (Vol 2)
　　H. Pausch, 678(YCGL):No30-103
Dimitrescu, F. Dicţionar de cuvinte
　　recente.
　　A. Lombard, 553(RLiR):Jul-Dec82-433
Dimitrov, T.D., ed. World Bibliography of
　　International Documentation.
　　T.L. Welch, 263(RIB):Vol132No1-59

Dimnik, M. Mikhail, Prince of Chernigov
and Grand Prince of Kiev, 1224-1246.
   A.M. Kleimola, 104(CASS):Fall-Winter82-
   535
   T.S. Noonan, 550(RusR):Apr82-197
Dimter, M. Textklassenkonzepte heutiger
Alttagssprache.
   B.J. Koekkoek, 221(GQ):Mar82-235
el-Din el-Shazali Ibrahim, S. Beyond
Underdevelopment.
   C. Jedrej, 69:Vol52No2-118
Dinesen, I. Letters from Africa 1914-
1931.* (F. Lasson, ed)
   M.J. Blackwell, 563(SS):Autumn82-319
   M.F., 617(TLS):18Mar83-279
   R. Langbaum, 219(GaR):Spring82-213
   M.B. Pringle, 395(MFS):Winter82/83-714
   G.B. Saul, 50(ArQ):Winter82-377
Dingwall, R. and P. Lewis, eds. The
Sociology of the Professions.
   L. Taylor, 617(TLS):24Jun83-659
Dini, B. Una pratica di mercatura in for-
mazione (1394-1395).
   L.B. Robbert, 589:Oct82-965
Dinnerstein, D. The Mermaid and the Mino-
taur.
   B. Johnson, 153:Summer82-2
   C. Kahn, 153:Summer82-32
Dinsmoor, W.B., Jr. The Propylaia to the
Athenian Akropolis.* (Vol 1)
   W.R. Biers, 124:Jan/Feb83-186
   C.W.J. Eliot, 487:Summer82-184
   R.A. Tomlinson, 303(JoHS):Vol 102-280
Dinzelbacher, P. Vision und Visionslitera-
tur im Mittelalter.
   F. Wagner, 196:Band23Heft3/4-313
Dion, M. État, Église et luttes popu-
laires.
   W.R. Ward, 161(DUJ):Jun82-290
Di Pierro, J.C. Structures in Beckett's
"Watt."
   M.W. Blades, 207(FR):Mar83-643
   S. Smith, 188(ECr):Summer82-70
Di Pietro, R.J., ed. Linguistics and the
Professions.
   R.B. Kaplan, 350:Sep83-711
Dippie, B.W. Remington and Russell.
   L. Milazzo, 584(SWR):Autumn82-vi
Dipple, E. Iris Murdoch.*
   P. O'Donnell, 50(ArQ):Winter82-378
   J. Pickering, 395(MFS):Winter82/83-643
Dirlmeier, C. and K. Sprigade. Quellen
zur Geschichte der Alamannen. (Vols 3
and 4)
   B.S. Bachrach, 589:Jan82-187
Disch, T.M. ABCDEFG HIJKLM NPOQRST UVWXYZ.
   D. Lehman, 181:Spring-Summer83-277
"Il Disegno Interrotto."
   S.B. Butters, 59:Dec82-480
Diskin, L. Theodore Sturgeon.
   D.M. Hassler, 561(SFS):Nov82-336
Disraeli, B. Benjamin Disraeli: Letters.*
   (Vols 1 and 2) (J.A.W. Gunn and others,
   eds)
   P. Burroughs, 150(DR):Autumn82-517
Disraeli, B. and S. A Year at Hartlebury,
or The Election.
   M. Foot, 362:7Jul83-24
   J. Keates, 617(TLS):14Oct83-1115
Ditsky, J. Friend and Lover.
   E. Jones, 150(DR):Spring82-168
   R. Phillips, 461:Spring-Summer82-98

Ditsky, J. The Onstage Christ.
   J. Schlueter, 397(MD):Sep82-437
Dittmann, J., ed. Arbeiten zur Konversa-
tionsanalyse.*
   R. Kanth, 685(ZDL):1/1982-114
Dix, C. D.H. Lawrence and Women.*
   K.M. Hewitt, 541(RES):Aug82-360
   R. Mason, 447(N&Q):Oct81-453
Dixon, R.J. Essential Idioms in English.
   (rev)
   H.K. Fragiadakis, 608:Dec83-676
Dixon, R.M.W. The Languages of Australia.*
   S. Feld, 355(LSoc):Apr82-133
   J. Heath, 297(JL):Mar82-190
Dixon, V. - see de Vega Carpio, L.
Dixson, R.J. Modern American English.
   (Vols 1-5)
   D.L.F. Nilsen, 399(MLJ):Summer82-224
Djordjevic, D. and S. Fischer-Galati. The
Balkan Revolutionary Tradition.*
   D.J. Farsolas, 104(CASS):Fall-Winter82-
   570
   K.S. Pavlowitch, 575(SEER):Jan82-109
Djurić, V., ed. Sava Nemjanić — Sveti
Sava.
   M. Heppell, 402(MLR):Apr82-509
Dmytryshyn, B. and E.A.P. Crownhart-
Vaughan - see Golovin, P.N.
Doane, A.N., ed. Genesis A.* (new ed)
   J. Roberts, 447(N&Q):Apr81-177
   E.G. Stanley, 72:Band218Heft1-162
Dobbs, K. Pride and Fall.
   G. Woodcock, 529(QQ):Winter82-744
Dobkin, M.H. - see Thomas, M.C.
Döblin, A. A People Betrayed.
   E. Pawel, 441:17Apr83-11
Dobson, E.J. and F.L. Harrison. Medieval
English Songs.*
   H. Cooper, 541(RES):Feb82-69
Dobyns, S. Dancer With One Leg.
   N. Callendar, 441:13Nov83-33
   442(NY):6Jun83-142
Dobyns, S. Heat Death.
   R. Jackson, 502(PrS):Spring82-91
Doca, G. Analyse psycholinguistique des
erreurs faites lors de l'apprentissage
d'une langue étrangère.
   S.H. Elgin, 350:Jun83-427
Doctorow, E.L. Loon Lake.*
   J.L. Halio, 598(SoR):Winter83-203
Dodd, P., ed. Walter Pater.
   J.J. Conlon, 177(ELT):Vol25No3-186
   P. Lewis, 89(BJA):Autumn82-375
Dodd, W. The Names You Gave It.
   R. Pybus, 565:Vol23No3-61
Dodds-Parker, D. Setting Europe Ablaze.
   M.R.D. Foot, 617(TLS):19Aug83-874
Doderer, G. Orgelmusik und Orgelbau im
Portugal des 17. Jahrhunderts.
   J. Dalton, 410(M&L):Jan81-75
Dodge, G.H. Benjamin Constant's Philos-
ophy of Liberalism.*
   É. Harpaz, 535(RHL):Jan-Feb82-127
Dodwell, C.R. Anglo-Saxon Art.
   J. Graham-Campbell, 617(TLS):4Feb83-
   118
Doepler, C.E. A Memoir of Bayreuth 1876
related by Carl Emil Doepler. (P. Cook,
ed and trans)
   R.L.J., 412:Aug-Nov81-288
Doern, R. Wednesdays Are Cabinet Days.
   N. Wiseman, 99:Apr82-33

Dogbé, Y-E. Morne soliloque.
C.V. Michael, 207(FR):Apr83-786
Doggett, F. and R. Buttel, eds. Wallace Stevens.*
L. Surette, 106:Spring82-135
Dohalská-Zichová, M. Analyse spectrographique des voyelles françaises basée sur l'examen de la chaîne parlée.
J. Klare, 682(ZPSK):Band34Heft2-259
Doisneau, R. Three Seconds from Eternity.
J. Guimond, 219(GaR):Winter82-894
Dolan, T.P. - see Dunning, T.P.
Dolet, É. Préfaces francaises.* (C. Longeon, ed)
J.R. Henderson, 551(RenQ):Summer81-238
F. Higman, 208(FS):Apr82-195
Dolezelová-Velingerová, M., ed. The Chinese Novel at the Turn of the Century.
B-H. Lu, 395(MFS):Summer81-399
C.D.K. Yee, 293(JASt):May82-574
Dollarhide, L. and A.J. Abadie, eds. Eudora Welty.
W.J. Stuckey, 395(MFS):Autumn82-507
Domanski, D. War in an Empty House.
E. Jones, 150(DR):Spring82-168
Dombrowski, D.A. Plato's Philosophy of History.
S.U., 543:Sep81-125
Domingo, P. My First Forty Years.
P.G. Davis, 441:20ct83-12
Domínguez Compañy, F. Estudios Sobre las Instituciones Locales Hispanoamericanas.
J.M. Ribas, 37:May-Jun82-60
H.J. Tanzi, 263(RIB):Vol32No1-59
Dominguin, L.M. and G. Boudaille. Pablo Picasso Toros and Toreros.
L. Cooke, 59:Sep82-338
Dominic, R.B. A Flaw in the System.
T.J. Binyon, 617(TLS):25Nov83-1301
T.J. Binyon, 617(TLS):23Dec83-1437
Dominicis, M.C. and J.A. Cussen. Casos y cosas.*
E.D. Myers, 238:Mar82-152
Donadio, S. Nietzsche, Henry James, and the Artistic Will.*
R.A. Hocks, 183(ESQ):Vol28No4-261
D.H. Ohi, 152(UDQ):Spring81-113
Donahue, T.J. The Theater of Fernando Arrabal.*
P. Macnaughton, 214:Vol 10No38-126
Donaldson, F. P.G. Wodehouse.*
C. Hawtree, 364:Oct82-109
Donaldson, G. All the Queen's Men.
J. Wormald, 617(TLS):28Oct83-1198
Donaldson, G., ed. Four Centuries.
J. Campbell, 617(TLS):23Sep83-1030
Donaldson, I. The Rapes of Lucretia.*
A. Barton, 453(NYRB):21Jul83-30
Donaldson, R.H., ed. The Soviet Union in the Third World.
C.E. Ziegler, 550(RusR):Jan82-94
Donaldson, S.R. White Gold Wielder.
S. Frank, 441:14Aug83-13
Donaldson, T. Corporations and Morality.
M.S.M., 185:Jan83-441
Donaldson, W. and D. Young, eds. Grampian Hairst.
C. Lamont, 571(ScLJ):Spring82-25
Donaldson-Evans, L.K. Love's Fatal Glance.
D.G. Coleman, 210(FrF):Sep82-269
G. Joseph, 207(FR):Dec82-314
J.C. Nash, 551(RenQ):Autumn82-510
di Donato, R. - see Gernet, L.

Doncaster, S. Some Notes on Bewick's Trade Blocks.*
78(BC):Spring82-7
Donghi, T.H. - see under Halperín Donghi, T.
Donia, R.J. Islam under the Double Eagle.
T. Stoianovich, 104(CASS):Fall-Winter 82-576
Donington, R. Baroque Music.
N. Zaslaw, 415:Dec82-842
Donington, R. The Rise of Opera.*
D. Arnold, 415:Apr82-259
F.W. Sternfeld, 410(M&L):Jul/Oct82-325
Donini, P.L. and G.F. Gianotti. Modelli filosofici e letterari.
J-M. André, 555:Vol56fasc1-161
Donker, M. and G.M. Muldrow. A Dictionary of Literary-Rhetorical Conventions of the English Renaissance.
W.F.M., 604:Fall82-49
C. Spivack, 365:Spring83-73
Donkin, E. - see Brisebarre, J.
Donleavy, J.P. Leila.
J. Moynahan, 441:30Oct83-11
D. Profumo, 617(TLS):28Oct83-1185
Donne, J. The Epithalamions, Anniversaries and Epicedes.* (W. Milgate, ed)
G. Pursglove, 161(DUJ):Jun82-308
Donne, J. Paradoxes and Problems.* (H. Peters, ed)
J.M. Mueller, 551(RenQ):Autumn81-458
G. Pursglove, 161(DUJ):Jun82-308
Donne, J. Poèmes de John Donne. (J. Fuzier and Y. Denis, trans)
J.V. Guerinot, 568(SCN):Spring-Summer82-13
Donne, J. Suicide. (W.A. Clebsch, ed)
G.S., 617(TLS):21Oct83-1171
Donnell, D. Dangerous Crossings.*
D. Barbour, 648(WCR):Summer81-81
B. Meyer, 137:Winter82-82
P. Monk, 529(QQ):Summer82-419
K. Norris, 137:Aug82-34
Donnelly, H.M., with R.N. Billings. Sara and Gerald.
A. Latham, 441:13Feb83-12
Donnelly, M. Glasgow Stained Glass.
L. Ormond, 39:Aug82-123
Donner, F. Shabono.*
P. Henley, 617(TLS):14Jan83-41
Donnison, D. The Politics of Poverty.
S. Jackson, 437:Autumn82-392
Donno, D.J. - see Campanella, T.
Donno, F. Opere. (G. Rizzo, ed)
D. Conrieri, 228(GSLI):Vol 159fasc507-449
Donovan, R.J. Tumultuous Years.*
H. Brogan, 617(TLS):26Aug83-902
Donzelli, G.B. Studio sull'"Elettra" di Euripide.
D. Bain, 123:Vol32No2-272
Donzelot, J. The Policies of Families.
D. Levine, 529(QQ):Autumn82-618
Doody, T. Confession and Community in the Novel.
J.M. Mellard, 395(MFS):Summer81-391
Dooley, D.J. Moral Vision in the Canadian Novel.*
F. Zichy, 298:Summer82-143
Doolittle, I.G. The City of London and its Livery Companies.
F. Sheppard, 617(TLS):10Jun83-589

Dop, J.A. Eliza's Knights.
 H.H. Rowen, 551(RenQ):Spring82-109
Doppagne, A. Les régionalismes du fran-
 çais. Belgicismes de bon aloi.
 M. Piron, 209(FM):Jan82-84
Doppler, B. Katholische Literatur und
 Literaturpolitik: Enrica von Handel-
 Mazzetti.
 L.E. Kurth-Voigt, 301(JEGP):Oct82-538
Dopsch, H., ed. Geschichte Salzburgs.
 (Vol 1, Pt 1)
 J.B. Freed, 589:Oct82-878
Dor, G. Du Sang bleu dans les veines.
 C.F. Coates, 207(FR):Mar83-663
Doret, M.R. Topologie. Antipalinodie.
 B.C. Freeman, 207(FR):May83-973
Dörfer, I. Arms Deal.
 L. Freedman, 617(TLS):26Aug83-900
Dorfman, A. The Empire's Old Clothes.
 A. Hacker, 441:8May83-15
Dorfman, A. Widows.
 A. Cheuse, 441:24Jul83-10
 N. Rankin, 617(TLS):9Dec83-1372
Dorge, C. Le Roitelet.*
 S.P. Knutson, 102(CanL):Winter81-151
Dorian, N.C. Language Death.*
 J.D. McClure, 571(ScLJ):Spring82-1
d'Ormesson, J. Mon dernier rêve sera pour
 vous.*
 M. Mohrt, 450(NRF):Dec82-91
Dorn, E. Yellow Lola, Formerly Titled
 Japanese Neon.*
 K. Shevelow, 114(ChiR):Summer81-101
Dornberg, J. The Putsch That Failed.
 J.D. Noakes, 617(TLS):17Jun83-640
Dorson, R.M. Land of the Millrats.
 T.C. Humphrey, 650(WF):Apr82-150
 42(AR):Fall82-487
Doty, M.A. Tell Me Who I Am.
 V.A. Kramer, 392:Spring82-127
 J.A. Ward, 395(MFS):Summer82-315
Doucette, L. Skill and Status.
 J.D.A. Widdowson, 203:Vol93No1-125
Dougan, C. and others. The Vietnam Experi-
 ence. (Vols 1-6)
 R. Rosenblatt, 441:11Sep83-13
Dougherty, D.M. and E.B. Barnes, eds. Le
 "Galien" de Cheltenham.
 N.J. Lacy, 207(FR):Apr83-764
Doughty, M. Merchant Shipping and War.
 P. Nailor, 617(TLS):18Mar83-260
Doughty, O. Perturbed Spirit.
 T. McFarland, 676(YR):Autumn82-95
Douglas, C. A Cure For Living.
 C. Hawtree, 617(TLS):6May83-465
Douglas, E. A Lifetime Burning.*
 P.R. Broughton, 617(TLS):22Jul83-791
Douglas, M. and A. Wildavsky. Risk and
 Culture.*
 D. Martin, 617(TLS):18Mar83-270
Douglas, R.A. - see "John Prince, 1796-
 1870"
Douglass, D. and J. Krieger. A Miner's
 Life.
 P. Willmott, 617(TLS):27May83-540
Douglass, F. The Frederick Douglass
 Papers.* (Ser, 1 Vol 1) (J.W. Blassin-
 game and others, eds)
 R. Felgar, 392:Fall82-427
Doumas, C., ed. Thera and the Aegean
 World.* (Vol 1)
 W.R. Biers, 124:Sep/Oct82-54

Doumas, C., ed. Thera and the Aegean
 World. (Vol 2)
 W.R. Biers, 124:Sep/Oct82-54
 E. Schofield, 123:Vol32No2-246
Dover, K. The Greeks.
 E.E. Best, Jr., 219(GaR):Summer82-457
Dover, K. - see Plato
Dovlatov, S. The Compromise.
 P-L. Adams, 61:Nov83-147
 T.G., 231:Sep83-76
 F. Williams, 617(TLS):16Dec83-1413
Dow, M.W. - see Browning, E.B.
Dowell, C. White on Black on White.
 D. Evanier, 441:13Nov83-14
Dowell, R.W., with J.L.W. West and N.M.
 Westlake - see Dreiser, T.
Dowling, W.C. The Boswellian Hero.*
 P. Alkon, 301(JEGP):Jul82-434
Dowling, W.C. Language and Logos in Bos-
 well's "Life of Johnson."
 J.A. Buttigieg, 77:Summer82-267
 J.A. Dussinger, 405(MP):Nov82-191
 R.J. Merrett, 150(DR):Winter82/83-700
Downes, D.A. Ruskin's Landscapes of
 Beatitude.*
 J. Batchelor, 447(N&Q):Oct81-446
Downes, L.S. Palavras Amigas da Onça.
 N.T. Baden, 238:Mar82-152
Downie, F. Plainsong.*
 J. Saunders, 565:Vol23No3-73
Downie, J.A. Robert Harley and the Press.*
 F. Doherty, 541(RES):May82-207
 M.C. Jacob, 173(ECS):Summer82-467
Downie, M.A. The King's Loon.
 M.J. Evans, 102(CanL):Spring82-86
Downie, M.A. and J. Honor Bound.
 M. Whitaker, 102(CanL):Spring82-95
Downie, M.A. and G. Rawlyk. A Proper
 Acadian.
 M. Whitaker, 102(CanL):Summer82-142
Downie, R.S. and E. Telfer. Caring and
 Curing.
 J.C.M., 185:Oct82-215
 D. Watson, 479(PhQ):Apr82-186
Downs, B. Sacred Places.*
 H. Kalman, 529(QQ):Summer82-404
Downs, R.B. Books that Changed the World.
 (2nd ed)
 42(AR):Summer82-372
Downs, R.B. and E.C. British and Irish
 Library Resources.
 354:Dec82-466
Dowty, D.R. Word Meaning and Montague
 Grammar.*
 J.N. Pankhurst, 361:Sep/Oct82-181
 T. Parsons, 482(PhR):Apr82-290
Doyle, A.C. Essays on Photography.* (J.M.
 Gibson and R.L. Green, eds)
 A. Ross, 364:Feb83-3
Doyle, D.N. and O.D. Edwards, eds. Ameri-
 ca and Ireland, 1776-1976.
 F.M. Carroll, 174(Éire):Fall82-154
Doyle, J. Annie Howells and Achille
 Fréchette.
 C. Thomas, 178:Mar82-103
Doyle, J., ed. Yankees in Canada.
 R. Labrie, 102(CanL):Spring82-120
 E. Waterston, 627(UTQ):Summer82-444
Doyle, R.L. Victor Hugo's Drama.
 R.B. Grant, 207(FR):Apr83-776
 P. Ward, 446(NCFS):Fall-Winter82/83-
 192

Doyle, W. The Old European Order, 1660-1800.
  J. Black, 161(DUJ):Dec81-121
Doyon-Ferland, M. Jeux, rythmes et divertissements traditionnels.
  G. Thomas, 102(CanL):Spring82-130
Drabble, M. The Middle Ground.*
  J.L. Halio, 598(SoR):Winter83-203
Drabble, M. A Writer's Britain.
  D. Davie, 569(SR):Winter82-79
Dragonzino, G. Nobilità di Vicenza. (F. Barbieri and F. Fiorese, eds)
  M. Pozzi, 228(GSLI):Vol 159fasc508-601
Draï, R. La Politique de l'Inconscient.
  A. Jacob, 542:Jan-Mar82-81
Drakakis, J., ed. British Radio Drama.
  P. Hollindale, 437:Spring82-200
  M. Lyons, 214:Vol 10No38-142
  E. Northey, 565:Vol23No2-36
Drake, S. Cause, Experiment and Science.
  M.A. Finocchiaro, 551(RenQ):Winter82-610
Drake, S. Galileo at Work.*
  M.S. Mahoney, 551(RenQ):Spring81-102
Dralle, L. Slaven am Havel und Spree.
  M. Todd, 575(SEER):Jul82-456
Draper, T. Present History.
  R.J. Margolis, 441:22May83-16
  C.C. O'Brien, 453(NYRB):29Sep83-10
Dray, W. Perspectives on History.*
  D. Braybrooke, 154:Dec82-782
  G.H. Martin, 366:Spring82-116
  W.H. Walsh, 125:Spring82-293
Dreben, B. and W.D. Goldfarb. The Decision Problem.
  P.B. Andrews, 316:Jun82-452
Dreher, D. From the Neck Up.
  H. Barglebaugh, 614:Winter83-17
Dreiser, T. An Amateur Laborer. (R.W. Dowell, with J.L.W. West and N.M. Westlake, eds)
  E.L. Doctorow, 441:4Dec83-9
Dreiser, T. The American Diaries 1902-1926.* (T.P. Riggio, J.L.W. West 3d and N.M. Westlake, eds)
  K.S. Lynn, 31(ASch):Autumn82-568
  27(AL):Oct82-480
Dreiser, T. Sister Carrie.* (J.L.W. West 3d and others, eds)
  S.C. Brennan, 594:Summer82-211
  R. Hansen, 385(MQR):Fall83-661
  L.E. Hussman, 42(AR):Winter82-114
Drescher, H.W., with R. Ahrend and K-H. Stoll, eds. Lexikon der englischen Literatur.
  D. Mehl, 52:Band16Heft2-178
Dressler, W.U. and J. Hufgard. Études Phonologiques sur le Breton Sud-Bigouden.
  M. Rockel, 682(ZPSK):Band33Heft3-369
Dretske, F.I. Knowledge and the Flow of Information.*
  B. Loewer, 486:Jun82-297
  J. Moor, 518:Oct82-235
  D. Odegard, 154:Dec82-778
  J.S., 185:Oct82-202
Drew, E. Politics and Money.
  D.H. Wrong, 441:11Sep83-12
Drew, E. Portrait of an Election.*
  639(VQR):Winter82-10
Drew, P. The Meaning of Freedom.*
  R. Lehan, 445(NCF):Sep82-247
Drewitz, I., ed. Märkische Sagen.
  E.H. Rehermann, 196:Band23Heft3/4-314

Drewnowski, J., ed. Crisis in the East European Economy.
  P. Hanson, 617(TLS):16Sep83-977
Drexler, A. Transformations in Modern Architecture.
  P. Blake, 576:Mar82-80
Dreyer, E.L. Early Ming China.
  D. Rimmington, 617(TLS):24Jun83-672
Dreyfus, F-G. De Gaulle et le Gaullisme.
  H. Peyre, 207(FR):Apr83-801
Dreyfus, H.L. and P. Rabinow. Michel Foucault.
  C. Gordon, 617(TLS):15Jul83-761
Dreyfus, J. A History of the Nonesuch Press.*
  78(BC):Summer82-143
Drieu la Rochelle, P. Fragments de Mémoires 1940-1941.
  D. Johnson, 617(TLS):1Apr83-316
Drijvers, H.J.W. Cults and Beliefs at Edessa.
  J.H. Marks, 318(JAOS):Oct-Dec81-441
Driver, C. The British at Table 1940-1980.
  K. Amis, 617(TLS):15Jul83-747
  H. Wackett, 362:11Aug83-20
Driver, C.E. - see Moore, M.
Drobnic, K., S. Abrams and M. Morray. Reading and Writing the English of Science and Technology.
  M.R. Miller, 399(MLJ):Autumn82-357
Drochner, K-H., ed. Deutsche Fragen.
  P.F. Dvorak, 399(MLJ):Summer82-215
Droguet, H. Le Contre-dit.
  L. Ray, 450(NRF):Sep82-118
Dronke, P. - see Bernardus Silvestris
Dronke, U. and others, eds. Speculum Norroenum.
  R. Simek, 602:Vol 13No2-338
Drower, J. Good Clean Fun.
  P. Smith, 617(TLS):15Apr83-382
Druet, P-P. Pour vivre sa mort.
  M. Adam, 542:Oct-Dec82-665
Drummond, H.J.H., comp. A Short Title Catalogue of Books Printed on the Continent of Europe, 1501-1600, in Aberdeen University Library.
  R.J. Roberts, 447(N&Q):Aug81-342
Drummond, J.D. Opera in Perspective.
  W. Dean, 415:Apr82-259
  F.W. Sternfeld, 410(M&L):Jul/Oct81-374
Drummond, P. The German Concerto.*
  C.M. Carroll, 173(ECS):Fall82-101
  S. Davis, 415:Apr82-261
  A. Hutchings, 410(M&L):Apr81-198
Drury, A. Decision.
  E. Hunter, 441:30Oct83-14
Druskin, M. Igor Stravinsky.
  G. Abraham, 617(TLS):17Jun83-635
Dryden, J. Marriage à la Mode. (M.S. Auburn, ed)
  J.D. Canfield, 566:Autumn82-57
  J.V. Guerinot, 568(SCN):Winter82-74
Dryden, J. The Works of John Dryden. (Vol 2 ed by H.T. Swedenberg, Jr. and V.A. Dearing; Vol 3 ed by E. Miner and V.A. Dearing, with others; Vol 10 ed by M.E. Novak and G.R. Guffey)
  B. Olinder, 38:Band100Heft1/2-211
Dryden, J. The Works of John Dryden.* (Vol 15 ed by E. Miner and G.R. Guffey; Vol 19 ed by A. Roper and V.A. Dearing)
  P. Hammond, 541(RES):Aug82-325

97

Dryden, J. The Works of John Dryden. (Vol 17) (S.H. Monk, A.E.W. Maurer and V.A. Dearing, with others, eds)
P. Hammond, 541(RES):Aug82-325
B. Olinder, 38:Band100Heft1/2-211
Dryden, K. The Game.
442(NY):19Dec83-142
Drysdale, V.L., ed. The Gift of the Sacred Pipe.
C. Vecsey, 469:Vol8No2-108
Drzemczewski, A.Z. European Human Rights Convention in Domestic Law.
D. Pannick, 617(TLS):12Aug83-849
Duane, P.A. Gentlemen Emigrants.
G.W., 102(CanL):Autumn82-184
Duarte, C.F. Historia de la Alfombra en Venezuela. Historia de la Escultura en Venezuela: Época colonial.
D. Angulo Íñiguez, 48:Jan-Mar80-127
Du Bartas, S. La Sepmaine.* (Y. Bellenger, ed)
T.C. Cave, 208(FS):Jul82-324
M. Hugues, 549(RLC):Jul-Sep82-387
J. Pineaux, 535(RHL):Sep-Dec82-872
J. Sproxton, 402(MLR):Jul82-719
D. Stone, Jr., 207(FR):Feb83-479
Dubé, L. La Mariakèche.
E. Hamblet, 207(FR):May83-973
Dube, W-D. Expressionist and Expressionism.
J. Russell, 441:4Dec83-65
Dublin, T., ed. Farm to Factory.
639(VQR):Spring82-52
Dubois, C. - see Schelling, F.W.J.
Dubois, D. and H. Prade. Fuzzy Sets and Systems.
I. Grattan-Guinness, 316:Sep82-702
Du Bois, E.C. Feminism and Suffrage.
A.C. Fellman, 106:Spring82-61
Dubois, J. Versailles.
442(NY):26Dec83-74
Dubois, J. and others. Dictionnaire du français contemporain illustré.
F. Helgorsky, 209(FM):Oct82-380
Dubois, R-D. Panique à Longueil.
J.M. Weiss, 102(CanL):Spring82-143
Dubois, S. and P. - see de Charrière, I./B. Zuylen
Dubos, R. The Wooing of the Earth.
E.L. Jackson, 658:Summer/Autumn82-178
Dubuc, J-G. Nos Valeurs en ébullition.
M. Lebel, 102(CanL):Spring82-100
Dubus, A. The Times Are Never So Bad.
J.C. Oates, 441:26Jun83-12
442(NY):13Jun83-130
Duby, G. The Age of the Cathedrals.
M.T. Davis, 576:May82-156
C.T. Wood, 589:Jul82-599
Duby, G. Le Chevalier, la femme et le prêtre.*
N. Aronson, 207(FR)Mar83-657
Ducatillon, J. Polémiques dans la Collection Hippocratique.*
E. Hussey, 123:Vol32No1-16
Ducháček, O. L'évolution de l'articulation linguistique du domaine esthétique du latin au français contemporain.*
H. Geckeler, 72:Band218Heft2-453
H-M. Militz, 682(ZPSK):Band34Heft5-628
Ducharme, R. HA ha!
S. Smith, 207(FR):May83-974
Duchêne, R. - see Madame de Sévigné

Duchet, C. and J. Neefs, eds. Balzac.
D.G. Clinton, 446(NCFS):Spring-Summer 83-365
Duchet, J-L. La Phonologie.
F. Carton, 209(FM):Apr82-174
Duck, S. Friends, For Life.
L. Hudson, 617(TLS):8Jul83-717
d'Uckermann, R.P. Ernest Hébert 1817-1908.
V.D.L., 605(SC):15Jul83-552
Duckworth, D. The Influence of Biblical Terminology and Thought on Wolfram's "Parzival."
A. Closs, 680(ZDP):Band101Heft1-140
D.H. Green, 402(MLR):Jan82-227
Ducout, F. A petit feu.
D.C. Cooper, 207(FR):Oct82-167
Ducrot, O. and others. Les Mots du Discours.*
F. Récanati, 192(EP):Oct-Dec82-490
Ducrot, O. and T. Todorov. Encyclopaedic Dictionary of the Sciences of Language.*
N. Rojas, 399(MLJ):Summer82-203
N.V. Smith, 297(JL):Sep82-461
Dudden, F.E. Serving Women.
T. Chaffin, 441:24Apr83-14
Dudek, L. Continuation 1.
M. Darling, 102(CanL):Autumn82-114
Dudek, L. and the Véhicule Poets. A Real Good Goosin'.
M. Darling, 102(CanL):Autumn82-114
Dudin, M. Nightingales.
T.J. Lewis, 399(MLJ):Winter82-433
Dudley Edwards, R. An Atlas of Irish History. (2nd ed)
G. Eley, 385(MQR):Winter83-107
Dudman, J., ed. International Music Guide 1982.
A. Jacobs, 415:May82-337
Due, B. Antiphon.
C.W. MacLeod, 123:Vol32No1-95
Duff, D. George and Elizabeth.
J. Grigg, 617(TLS):2Sep83-924
Duffy, C. Russia's Military Way to the West.*
P. Dukes, 83:Autumn82-280
Duffy, D. Gardens, Covenants, Exiles.
C.T. Bissell, 150(DR):Summer82-322
R. Mathews, 99:May82-34
C.R. Steele, 49:Oct82-132
Duffy, E. Rousseau in England.*
R. Trousson, 149(CLS):Fall82-396
Duffy, J. The Songs and Motets of Alfonso Ferrabosco, the Younger (1575-1628).
M. Chan, 410(M&L):Jan/Apr82-130
Duffy, M. Londoners.
G. Strawson, 617(TLS):7Oct83-1095
Duffy, M. That's How it Was.
P. Craig, 617(TLS):1Jul83-711
Duffy, M.J. Guide to the Parochial Archives of the Episcopal Church in Boston.
V.N. Bellamy, 14:Fall82-482
Dufour-Kowalska, G. Michel Henry, un philosophe de la vie et de la praxis.
W.L.M., 543:Dec81-382
Dufrenne, M. Esthétique et philosophie. (Vol 3)
H. Osborne, 89(BJA):Summer82-279
Dufwa, J. Winds from the East.
D. Waterhouse, 407(MN):Winter82-550
Dugast, D. La Statistique lexicale.*
A. Raphael, 353:Vol 19No1/2-180

Dugast, D. Vocabulaire et Discours.
   A. Raphael, 353:Vol 19No1/2-179
   A.G. Raymond, 399(MLJ):Spring82-85
Duggan, A. Thomas Becket.
   R.M. Fraher, 589:Apr82-449
Dugger, R. The Life and Times of Lyndon
Johnson.
   M. Beloff, 617(TLS):7Jan83-18
Dugger, R. The Politician.*
   639(VQR):Autumn82-118
Duhamel, L. Les Soviétiques et les Voies
de la Révolution en Europe Occidentale
de Lénine à Brejnev.
   R.E. Kanet, 104(CASS):Fall-Winter82-
   580
Duignan, P. and A. Rabushka, eds. The
United States in the 1980s.*
   W.W. Kulski, 497(PolR):Vol27No3/4-202
Duisit, L. Satire, parodie, calembour.*
   S. Golopentia-Eretescu, 400(MLN):May82-
   1024
Dujarric, G. Précis chronologique d'his-
toire de France des origines à nos jours.
   (new ed) (Y.D. Papin, ed)
   A. Sokalski, 207(FR):Apr83-798
Duke, D.C. Distant Obligations.
   T. Chaffin, 441:19Jun83-17
Dukore, B.F. Money and Politics in Ibsen,
Shaw, and Brecht.*
   G. Weales, 397(MD):Dec82-578
Dukore, B.F. Harold Pinter.*
   A.P. Hinchliffe, 148:Autumn82-83
Dukore, B.F. The Theatre of Peter Barnes.
   I. Todd, 397(MD):Jun82-316
Dukore, B.F. - see Shaw, G.B.
Dukore, M.M. A Novel Called Heritage.
   J.L. Halio, 598(SoR):Winter83-203
Dulles, A. A Church To Believe In.
   D. Tracy, 441:3Apr83-10
Duman, D. The English and Colonial Bars
in the Nineteenth Century.
   Z. Cowen, 617(TLS):1Apr83-320
Duman, D. The Judicial Bench in England
1727-1875.
   Z. Cowen, 617(TLS):1Apr83-320
Dumas, M-C. Robert Desnos ou l'explora-
tion des limites.
   M. Bonnet, 535(RHL):Sep-Dec82-961
Dumestra, G., ed and trans. La geste de
Ségou, raconté par des griots bambara.
   G. Innes, 69:Vol51No1-535
Dumitriu, A. History of Logic.* (Vols 1-
4)
   J. Bacon, 258:Mar82-106
   A. Perreiah and D. Howard, 319:Jan82-
   101
Dumitriu, P. Comment ne pas l'aimer.
   J. Bastaire, 450(NRF):Jan82-135
Dumitriu, P. To the Unknown God.*
   (French title: Au Dieu inconnu.)
   R.T.B., 617(TLS):11Feb83-143
Dummett, M. Frege: Philosophy of Lan-
guage.* (2nd ed)
   R. Buhr, 350:Mar83-236
   S. Shanker, 154:Sep82-565
Dummett, M. The Interpretation of Frege's
Philosophy.*
   S. Shanker, 154:Sep82-565
Dummett, M. Principles of Intuitionism.
   H.T. Hodes, 482(PhR):Apr82-253
Dumont, F. L'anthropologie en l'absence
de l'homme.
   J-P. Audet, 154:Jun82-317

Dumont, L. Affinity as a Value.
   E. Leach, 617(TLS):21Oct83-1153
Dumouchel, P. and J-P. Dupuy. L'enfer des
choses.
   C. Chalier, 192(EP):Oct-Dec81-477
Dun, S. Memoirs of the Four-Foot Colonel.
   M.M. Gyi, 293(JASt):Feb82-430
Dunae, P.A. Gentlemen Emigrants.
   M. Abley, 617(TLS):3Jun83-569
   J. Parr, 150(DR):Winter82/83-693
Dunant, G. and L. Kahil. Corpus Vasorum
Antiquorum. (Suisse, fasc 3)
   B.A. Sparkes, 303(JoHS):Vol 102-285
Dunaway, D.K. How Can I Keep From Singing.
   G. Bluestein, 187:Jan83-127
   R.S. Denisoff, 498:Vol8No2-129
Dunaway, J.M. Jacques Maritain.
   G. Cesbron, 356(LR):Nov82-364
   J.C. McLaren, 207(FR):Mar83-641
Dunbar, A.P.D. Against the Grain.*
   R. Coles, 639(VQR):Summer82-501
Dunbar, P. William Blake's Illustrations
to the Poetry of Milton.*
   J-J. Mayoux, 189(EA):Apr-Jun82-216
   W. Vaughan, 59:Mar82-106
Dunbar, W. The Poems of William Dunbar.
   (J. Kinsley, ed)
   F.H. Ridley, 551(RenQ):Spring81-132
Duncan, D. Ben Jonson and the Lucianic
Tradition.*
   W.D. Kay, 402(MLR):Jan82-158
Duncan, D.J. The River Why.
   D. Profumo, 617(TLS):27May83-553
   D. Quammen, 441:24Apr83-12
Duncan, R. Working with Britten.
   N. Goodwin, 415:Jun82-417
   D. Matthews, 607:Dec82-34
   J. Matthias, 598(SoR):Winter83-184
Duncan, S.J. Sara Jeannette Duncan,
Selected Journalism. (T.E. Tausky, ed)
   C. Gerson, 102(CanL):Spring82-113
Duncan, W.R., ed. Soviet Policy in the
Third World.
   E.K. Valkenier, 550(RusR):Jul82-344
Duncanson, D. Changing Qualities of
Chinese Life.
   R. Harris, 617(TLS):8Apr83-348
Duncombe, J. The Feminiad.
   T. Atkins, 566:Spring83-143
Dundes, A., ed. Cinderella.
   T.A. Shippey, 617(TLS):22Jul83-781
Dundes, A. Interpreting Folklore.*
   C. Nash, 402(MLR):Jul82-689
   J. Simpson, 203:Vol93No1-127
Dunjwa-Blajberg, J. Sprache und Politik
in Südafrika.
   S. Brauner, 682(ZPSK):Band35Heft5-570
Dunlop, R. Donovan.
   T. Powers, 453(NYRB):12May83-29
Dunmore, M. The Apple Fall.
   M. Hofmann, 617(TLS):18Nov83-1272
Dunn, D. Europa's Lover.
   T. Dooley, 617(TLS):19Aug83-886
Dunn, D., ed. A Rumoured City.
   H. Lomas, 364:Feb83-73
   M. O'Neill, 493:Jan83-48
   W. Scammell, 617(TLS):7Jan83-17
Dunn, D. St. Kilda's Parliament.*
   M. O'Neill, 493:Apr82-59
Dunn, G. The Fellowship of Song.
   A.C. Percival, 203:Vol93No2-230

Dunn, J. Political Obligation in its Historical Context.*
D.R. Knowles, 518:Jan82-58
Dunn, J. Timor.
P. Burnett, 617(TLS):16Dec83-1391
Dunn, J. and C. Kendrick. Siblings.
J. Bruner, 453(NYRB):27Oct83-84
Dunn, L.A. Controlling the Bomb.*
639(VQR):Autumn82-123
Dunn, M. - see "Lady Addle Remembers"
Dunn, M.M. and R.S. - see Penn, W.
Dunn, N. Steaming.
D. Devlin, 157:Summer82-52
Dunn, S. Nerval et le roman historique.
R. Chambers, 446(NCFS):Fall-Winter 82/83-162
R.T. Denommé, 207(FR):May83-947
Dunn, S. Work and Love.
R.B. Shaw, 491:Dec82-170
639(VQR):Autumn82-135
Dunn, S.P. The Fall and Rise of the Asiatic Mode of Production.
E. Gellner, 617(TLS):14Jan83-27
Dünnhaupt, G. Bibliographisches Handbuch der Barockliteratur. (Pts 1 and 2)
G. Hoffmeister, 597(SN):Vol154No2-329
J.R. Paas, 221(GQ):May82-409
D. Paisey, 354:Dec82-446
L.S. Thompson, 133:Band15Heft3-266
Dünnhaupt, G. Bibliographisches Handbuch der Barockliteratur. (Pt 3)
G. Hoffmeister, 597(SN):Vol154No2-329
D. Paisey, 354:Dec82-446
L.S. Thompson, 133:Band15Heft3-266
Dunning, A. Count Unico Wilhelm van Wassenaer (1692-1766).
S. Sadie, 415:Jan82-32
Dunning, T.P. "Piers Plowman:" An Interpretation of the A Text. (2nd ed) (T.P. Dolan, ed)
J.A. Alford, 589:Apr82-367
S.S. Hussey, 447(N&Q):Dec81-527
Dunphy, J. First Wine.
442(NY):14Mar83-157
Dunsby, J. Structural Ambiguity in Brahms.
M. Musgrave, 410(M&L):Jan/Apr82-118
R. Pascall, 415:Apr82-262
Dupin, J. The Growing Dark.
D. McDuff, 565:Vol23No1-59
Duplat, A. - see de la Vigne, A.
Dupont-Roc, R. and J. Lallot - see Aristotle
Dupree, L. Afghanistan.
P. Stuchen, 529(QQ):Winter82-850
Durán, G. and M. Vivir hoy. (2nd ed)
M.E. Beeson, 238:Mar82-153
Durán, M. - see Marqués de Santillana
Durán, M. and M. Safir. Earth Tones.
J. von Stackelberg, 547(RF):Band94 Heft1-142
Durand, J. Les formes de la communication.
L. Millet, 192(EP):Oct-Dec82-492
F. Woerly, 542:Jan-Mar82-89
Durand, J.R. and C. Lévêque. Flore et faune aquatiques de L'Afrique: Sahelo-Soudanienne.
J.L. Cloudsley-Thompson, 69:Vol152No1-88
Durand, L. The Angkor Massacre.
J. Sullivan, 441:10Apr83-29
Durand, R., ed. La relation théâtrale.
K. Elam, 397(MD):Sep82-448

Durant, A. Ezra Pound.*
W. Harmon, 569(SR):Spring82-279
Durante, I.S. - see under Soldevila Durante, I.
Duranton, H., ed. Journal de la Cour et de Paris depuis le 28 novembre 1732 jusques au 30 novembre 1733.
P. Jansen, 535(RHL):Sep-Dec82-906
Duranton, H. - see Hotman, F.
Duras, M. L'Homme atlantique.
F. de Mèredieu, 450(NRF):Sep82-157
Duras, M. La maladie de la mort.
G. Craig, 617(TLS):15Jul83-760
Durbach, E., ed. Ibsen and the Theatre.*
C.L. Anderson, 579(SAQ):Spring82-238
Durcan, P. Jesus, Break his Fall.
T.F. Merrill, 305(JIL):Sep82-3
Durcan, P. The Selected Paul Durcan. (E. Longley, ed)
D. Profumo, 617(TLS):19Aug83-886
d'Urfé, H. L'Astrée. (M. Gaume, ed)
L.K. Horowitz, 207(FR):May83-943
Durham, F. and R.D. Purrington. Frame of the Universe.
J. North, 617(TLS):25Nov83-1331
Durkin, A.R. Sergei Aksakov and Russian Pastoral.
V.L. Smith, 617(TLS):20May83-525
Duro, A., comp. Concordanze e Indici di frequenza dei Principj di una scienza nuova — 1725 di Giambattista Vico.
D.P. Verene, 319:Jul83-408
Durrell, L. Collected Poems, 1931-1974.* (J.A. Brigham, ed)
W.H., 148:Summer82-93
J.D. McClatchy, 491:Jun82-170
Durrell, L. Sebastian, or Ruling Passions.
V. Cunningham, 617(TLS):28Oct83-1184
Dürrenmatt, F. Werkausgabe in dreissig Bänden.
G.P. Knapp, 406:Summer82-179
Dury, I., ed. Hard Lines.
G. Ewart, 617(TLS):25Feb83-182
P. Kemp, 362:3Feb83-27
Durzak, M. Das Amerika-Bild in der deutschen Gegenwartsliteratur.
K-H. Schoeps, 406:Spring82-89
Durzak, M. Die deutsche Kurzgeschichte der Gegenwart.
H. Kreuzer, 133:Band15Heft1/2-186
Dusinberre, W. Henry Adams.*
R. Mane, 125:Spring82-313
S.J. Whitfield, 639(VQR):Winter82-143
Duso, G., ed. La politica oltre lo Stato.
F. Volpi, 489(PJGG):Band89Heft2-440
Dussel, E. A History of the Church in Latin America. (A. Neely, ed and trans)
D. Tracy, 441:3Apr83-10
Dussère, C.T. The Image of the Primitive Giant in the Works of Gerhart Hauptmann.
R.C. Cowen, 680(ZDP):Band101Heft2-309
Dutton, D., ed. The Forger's Art.
P-L. Adams, 61:Aug83-101
B. Shulgasser, 441:13Nov83-20
R. Wollheim, 617(TLS):30Dec83-1449
Dutton, P. Right Hemisphere, Left Ear.
L. Lemire-Tostevin, 102(CanL):Spring82-141
Duval, E.M. Poesis and Poetic Tradition in the Early Works of Saint-Amant.
R.T. Corum, Jr., 207(FR):Feb83-481
J. Marmier, 475:No16Pt2-376
C. Rolfe, 402(MLR):Jul82-721

Eck, W. Die staatliche Organisation
Italiens in der hohen Kaiserzeit.*
   A.N. Sherwin-White, 313:Vol72-191
Eckard, R.D. and M.A. Kearny. Teaching
Conversation Skills in ESL.
   B. Powell, 399(MLJ):Winter82-448
Ecker, D.W. and S.S. Madeja. Pioneers in
Perception.
   J. Fisher, 289:Spring82-110
Ecker, G. Einblattdrucke von den Anfängen
bis 1555.
   W.A. Coupe, 402(MLR):Jul82-756
Eckert, T.E. and L.R. Stark, eds. Histori-
cal Records of Washington State.
   R.L. Schaadt, 14:Spring82-199
Eckholm, E. Down to Earth.
   T. Cantell, 324:Jun83-415
Eckman, F.R. and A.J. Hastings, eds.
Studies in First and Second Language
Acquisition.
   M. Paradis, 320(CJL):Spring82-90
Eckstein, A., ed. Quantitative Measures
of China's Economic Output.
   J.C.H. Fei, 293(JASt):Nov81-107
Eco, U. The Name of the Rose. (Italian
title: Il nome della rosa.)
   P-L. Adams, 61:Jul83-108
   R. Ellmann, 453(NYRB):21Jul83-11
   F. Ferrucci, 441:5Jun83-1
   R. Fox, 362:60ct83-25
   C.D. Lobner, 329(JJQ):Summer82-468
   J.S., 231:Aug83-75
   J. Updike, 442(NY):14Nov83-188
   J. van de Wetering, 469:Vol8No4-98
Eco, U. The Role of the Reader.*
   R.E.I., 543:Sep81-126
"Economic Consequences of the New Rice
Technology."
   D.O. Dapice, 293(JASt):Feb82-305
"Economic Reforms in Eastern Europe and
Prospects for the 1980s."
   B. Mieczkowski, 497(PolR):Vol27No1/2-
   155
"Die Edda." (F. Genzmer, with K. Schier,
trans)
   K. Düwel, 196:Band23Heft3/4-315
Eddy, P. and others. War in the Falklands.
(British title: The Falklands War.)
   N. Bliven, 442(NY):12Sep83-148
   G. Smith, 441:9Jan83-10
   C. Wain, 362:3Mar83-20
   G. Wheatcroft, 617(TLS):13May83-490
Ede, M. Arts and Society in England under
William and Mary.
   566:Autumn82-57
Edel, A. Science, Ideology, and Value.*
(Vols 1 and 2)
   D.M. Emmet, 518:Jul82-187
Edel, L. Bloomsbury.*
   B. Ruddick, 148:Spring82-86
Edel, L. Stuff of Sleep and Dreams.*
   A. Phillips, 364:Oct82-96
Edel, L. - see James, H.
Edel, L. - see Wilson, E.
Edelen, G. - see Hooker, R.
Edelhart, M., with J. Lindenmann. Inter-
feron.
   R. Hasselback, 529(QQ):Winter82-884
Edelman, B. L'homme des foules.
   M. Adam, 542:Oct-Dec82-669
Edelstein, M. Overseas Investment in the
Age of High Imperialism.
   S. Pollard, 617(TLS):25Feb83-196

Eden, E. Up The Country.
   A.P., 617(TLS):21Oct83-1171
Eder, W. Servitus publica.
   A. Lintott, 123:Vol32No2-290
   J-C. Richard, 555:Vol56fasc2-364
Edgren, J.S., comp. Catalogue of the Nor-
denskiöld Collection of Japanese Books
in the Royal Library.
   P.F. Kornicki, 244(HJAS):Jun82-334
Edmond, L. - see Fairburn, A.R.D.
Edmond, M. Hilliard and Oliver.
   G. Reynolds, 617(TLS):26Aug83-897
Edmonds, M. Lytton Strachey.
   G. Merle, 189(EA):Oct-Dec82-479
   517(PBSA):Vol76No4-502
Edmunds, L. The Silver Bullet.
   C.D. Ryals, 579(SAQ):Winter82-123
Edmunds, L. The Sphinx in the Oedipus
Legend.
   C. Callanan, 196:Band23Heft3/4-316
Edwardes, M. Back from the Brink.
   R. Hattersley, 362:21Apr83-24
   R.J. Overy, 617(TLS):6May83-452
Edwards, A. The Road to Tara.
   D. McWhorter, 441:28Aug83-13
   J. O'Faolain, 617(TLS):22Jul83-771
Edwards, A. Sonya.*
   D. Kirby, 150(DR):Winter82/83-719
Edwards, A.B. A Thousand Miles Up the
Nile.
   A.J.G.H., 617(TLS):11Feb83-143
Edwards, A.D. Language in Culture and
Class.*
   M.M. Bryant, 660(Word):Aug81-167
Edwards, A.S.G. - see Cavendish, G.
Edwards, C. The Lion's Mouth.
   M. Harry, 150(DR):Winter82/83-704
Edwards, G. The Prison and the Labyrinth.
   A.A. Parker, 86(BHS):Oct82-340
Edwards, G.B. The Book of Ebenezer Le
Page.*
   J.L. Halio, 598(SoR):Winter83-203
Edwards, J. Christian Córdoba.
   P. Linehan, 617(TLS):29Apr83-435
Edwards, J. Superweapon.
   L. Freedman, 617(TLS):26Aug83-900
Edwards, J. The Works of Jonathan Edwards.
(Vol 6: Scientific and Philosophical
Writings.) (W. Anderson, ed)
   M. Vetö, 192(EP):Oct-Dec81-479
Edwards, P. Heidegger on Death.
   J. Llewelyn, 479(PhQ):Oct82-388
Edwards, P. Peggy Salté.
   D. Cole, 441:11Dec83-16
   B. Morton, 617(TLS):25Nov83-1329
Edwards, P. Threshold of a Nation.*
   D. Donoghue, 551(RenQ):Summer81-279
   A.H. Elliott, 447(N&Q):Dec81-573
   M. Hattaway, 541(RES):May82-240
   H. Lindenberger, 677(YES):Vol 12-243
Edwards, P., I-S. Ewbank and G.K. Hunter,
eds. Shakespeare's Styles.*
   J. Drakakis, 447(N&Q):Dec81-535
   D. Hamer, 541(RES):Nov82-466
   P. Hyland, 67:Nov82-198
Edwards, P.G. Prime Ministers and Diplo-
mats.
   J. Cable, 617(TLS):2Dec83-1355
Edwards, R.B. Kadmos the Phoenician.*
   J.T. Hooker, 303(JoHS):Vol 102-276
Edwards, R.B. Pleasures and Pains.*
   W.P. Alston, 482(PhR):Jan82-143

Edwards, R.D. - see under Dudley Edwards, R.

Edwards, T.R.N. Three Russian Writers and the Irrational.
H. Ermolaev, 550(RusR):Oct82-531

Effe, B. Dichtung und Lehre.*
P.H. Schrijvers, 394:Vol35fasc3/4-400

van Effenterre, H. Le palais de Mallia et la cité minoenne.
S. Hood, 303(JoHS):Vol 102-277

Egan, D. and M. Hartnett. Choice. (2nd ed)
S. Fauchereau, 98:Jun-Jul82-628

Egan, D.R. and M.A. Leo Tolstoy.*
A.V. Knowles, 447(N&Q):Oct81-477

Egan, J. Elena.
639(VQR):Winter82-19

Egan, J. The Inward Teacher.*
J. Stephens, 568(SCN):Spring-Summer82-9

Egbert, D.D. The Beaux-Arts Tradition in French Architecture. (D. Van Zanten, ed)
R.D. Middleton, 54:Jun82-340
B. Scott, 39:Feb82-136

Egerton, G. Keynotes and Discords.
P. Craig, 617(TLS):1Jul83-711

Egerton, J. British Sporting and Animal Paintings 1665-1867 [together with]
Egerton, J. and D. Snelgrove. British Sporting and Animal Drawings 1500-1850.*
L. Lambourne, 90:Mar82-167

Egerton, J. Generations.
A. Tyler, 441:6Nov83-3

Eggebrecht, H.H., ed. Handwörterbuch der musikalischen Terminologie. (Pt 7)
J. Caldwell, 410(M&L):Apr81-211

Eggermont, P.H.L. Alexander's Campaigns in Sind and Baluchistan and The Siege of The Brahmin Town of Harmatelia.
L. Rocher, 318(JAOS):Oct-Dec81-464

Eggleston, W. Literary Friends.*
S. Neuman, 102(CanL):Spring82-125

Egleton, C. A Conflict of Interests.
N. Callendar, 441:20Nov83-41

Egleton, C. The Russian Enigma.
T.J. Binyon, 617(TLS):8Jul83-732

Egremont, M. Balfour.
D. Beales, 637(VS):Summer82-511

Egremont, M. The Ladies' Man.
A. Hislop, 617(TLS):11Feb83-130

Eguchi, P.K. Fulfulde Tales of North Cameroon.
A.H.M. Kirk-Greene, 69:Vol51No4-891

von Ehingen, G. Reisen nach der Ritterschaft. (G. Ehrmann, ed)
M. Wis, 439(NM):1982/4-471

Ehrenpreis, I. Acts of Implication.*
R.J. Merrett, 150(DR):Winter82/83-700
D.L. Patey, 191(ELN):Sep82 56

Ehrenreich, B. The Hearts of Men.
C. Hitchens, 617(TLS):12Aug83-858
C. Tavris, 441:5Jun83-12

Ehresmann, J.M. The Pocket Dictionary of Art Terms. (rev by J. Hall)
D. Thompson, 592:Vol 195No993/994-102

Ehrismann, O. Der mittelhochdeutsche Reinhart Fuchs, Abbildungen und Materialien zur handschriflichen Überlieferung.
T.W. Best, 221(GQ):Mar82-244

Ehrlich, E. and others - see "Oxford American Dictionary"

Ehrlich, E. and G. Carruth. The Oxford Illustrated Literary Guide to the United States.
J. Russell, 617(TLS):10Jun83-608

Ehrlich, P. and A. Extinction.
A. Mackay, 617(TLS):15Apr83-381

Ehrman, J. The Younger Pitt. (Vol 2)
L. Colley, 617(TLS):24Jun83-649
J. Grigg, 362:23Jun83-24

Ehrmann, G. - see von Ehingen, G.

Eich, G. Valuable Nail.
S. Bauschinger, 221(GQ):Nov82-617

Eicher, J.B. Nigerian Handcrafted Textiles.*
R.L. Shep, 614:Winter83-20

Eichhoff, J. Wortatlas der deutschen Umgangssprachen. (Vols 1 and 2)
I. Reiffenstein, 685(ZDL):2/1981-234

Eichhorn, D.M. Evangelizing the American Jew.
J.D. Sarna, 390:Feb82-63

Eichinger, L.M. Syntaktische Transposition und semantische Derivation.
W.P. Ahrens, 350:Dec83-909

Eichmann, A. Eichmann Interrogated. (J. von Lang, with C. Sibyll, eds)
W. Laqueur, 441:10Jul83-13

Eidlin, F.H. The Logic of "Normalization."
K. Dawisha, 104(CASS):Fall-Winter82-592

Eigeldinger, M. and M. Milner, eds. Balzac.
M. Naudin, 207(FR):Oct82-156

Eigen, M. and R. Winkler. Laws of the Game.
R. Gregory, 617(TLS):26Aug83-914

"Eight Dynasties of Chinese Painting."
60:Jul-Aug82-137

"The Eighteenth Century: A Current Bibliography." (Vols 3 and 4) (R.R. Allen, ed)
J. Freehafer, 566:Autumn82-58

Eikhenbaum, B. Tolstoi in the Sixties.*
Tolstoi in the Seventies.*
S. Karlinsky, 617(TLS):18Feb83-161

Eimer, H. rNam thar rgyas pa.
D.S. Ruegg, 259(IIJ):Jan82-74

Eimer, H. Skizzen des Erlösungsweges in buddhistischen Begriffsreihen.
J. May, 259(IIJ):Jul80-249

Einarsson, M. Everyman's Heritage.
C.H. Carpenter, 582(SFQ):Vol43No3/4-333

Einstein, C. Werke.
L. Meffre, 98:Feb82-176

Eis, G. Kleine Schriften zur Altdeutschen Weltlichen Dichtung.*
N.F. Palmer, 447(N&Q):Jun81-281

Eisele, C. Studies in the Scientific and Mathematical Philosophy of Charles S. Peirce. (R.M. Martin, ed)
R.S. Robin, 619:Fall82-367

Eisele, C. - see Peirce, C.S.

Eisele, U. Der Dichter und sein Detektiv.
P. Brewster, 406:Spring82-107

Eisenbach, A. Wielka Emigracja wobec kwestii żydowskiej 1832-1849.
G.J. Lerski, 497(PolR):Vol27No3/4-229

Eisenberg, D. Romances of Chivalry in the Spanish Golden Age.
F. Pierce, 304(JHP):Fall82-65

Eisenberg, P., ed. Maschinelle Sprachanalyse.
G.F. Meier, 682(ZPSK):Band34Heft6-754

Eisenberg, P., ed. Semantik und künst-
liche Intelligenz.
  G.F. Meier, 682(ZPSK):Band35Heft3-363
Eisenbichler, K. - see Cecchi, G.M.
Eisenhower, D.D. The Eisenhower Diaries.
(R.H. Ferrell, ed)
  H. Brogan, 617(TLS):3Jun83-574
Eisenman, P. House X.
  A.L. Huxtable, 453(NYRB):8Dec83-29
Eisenman, R.H. Islamic Law in Palestine
and Israel.
  D.F. Forte, 318(JAOS):Oct-Dec81-462
Eisenstein, E.L. The Printing Press as
an Agent of Change.*
  N. Barker, 617(TLS):24Jun83-679
  P. Laslett, 551(RenQ):Spring81-82
  R.J. Schoeck, 191(ELN):Sep82-109
Eisenstein, S.M. Immoral Memories.
  P. Schjeldahl, 441:13Nov83-10
  442(NY):28Nov83-190
Eisler, B. Class Act.
  B. Ehrenreich, 441:18Dec83-10
Eitel, W. Balzac in Deutschland.*
  G.R. Kaiser, 224(GRM):Band32Heft3-370
  V. Neuhaus, 52:Band16Heft2-220
Eiteljorg, H. Treasures of the American
West.
  584(SWR):Summer82-v
Eitner, L.E.A. Géricault.
  F. Haskell, 617(TLS):15Jul83-743
Eitner, W.H. Walt Whitman's Western Jaunt.
  J.R. Nicholl, 649(WAL):Spring82-70
Ek, K-G. The Development of OE āe (i-muta-
ted ā) before Nasals and OE āe in South-
Eastern Middle English.
  C.M. Barrack, 685(ZDL):3/1982-374
Ekberg, C.J. The Failure of Louis XIV's
Dutch War.
  R. Mettam, 161(DUJ):Dec81-122
Ekirch, A.R. "Poor Carolina."
  R. Middlekauf, 165(EAL):Spring83-102
  J.J. Nadelhaft, 656(WMQ):Oct82-707
Eklof, P.C. Set Theoretic Methods in
Homological Algebra and Abelian Groups.
  M. Huber, 316:Sep82-701
Ekman, B. The End of a Legend.*
  W.J. Stuckey, 395(MFS):Autumn82-507
Elam, K. The Semiotics of Theatre and
Drama.*
  J. Féral, 397(MD):Mar82-182
  A. Helbo, 567:Vol139No1/2-125
El'baum, G. Analiz iudejskix glav Mastera
i Margarity M. Bulgakova.
  E.C. Haber, 574(SEEJ):Winter82-489
Elder, C. Appropriating Hegel.
  D.D., 543:Jun82-866
Elder, N. This Thing of Darkness.
  639(VQR):Winter82-28
Eldredge, N. and I. Tattersall. The Myths
of Human Evolution.
  J.R. Durant, 617(TLS):18Feb83-152
  R.C. Lewontin, 453(NYRB):16Jun83-21
Eleen, L. The Illustration of the Pauline
Epistles in French and English Bibles of
the Twelfth and Thirteenth Centuries.
  C.R. Dodwell, 617(TLS):8Apr83-363
Elegant, R. Mandarin.
  J.J. Osborne, Jr., 441:23Oct83-24
Elert, C-C., ed. Internordisk språkfor-
ståelse.*
  N. Hasselmo, 355(LSoc):Dec82-458
Elfriede, N., ed. Geschichtsdrama.
  E. Huge, 221(GQ):Jan82-106

Eliach, Y., ed. Hasidic Tales of the
Holocaust.*
  G. Josipovici, 617(TLS):14Oct83-1113
Eliade, M. Autobiography.* (Vol 1)
  529(QQ):Autumn82-689
Eliade, M. A History of Religious Ideas.*
(Vol 1)
  H. McDonald, 396(ModA):Spring82-201
Elias, A.C., Jr. Swift at Moor Park.*
  D. Nokes, 566:Spring83-127
Elias, N. The Court Society.
  R. Mettam, 617(TLS):5Aug83-842
Eliot, G. George Eliot: A Writer's Note-
book, 1854-1879 and Uncollected Writings.
(J. Wiesenfarth, ed)
  W. Baker, 354:Mar82-80
  K. McSweeney, 637(VS):Autumn81-109
Eliot, G. The George Eliot Letters.*
(Vols 8 and 9) (G.S. Haight, ed)
  R. Ashton, 541(RES):May82-222
  J. Beaty, 402(MLR):Jan82-184
Eliot, G. George Eliot's "Middlemarch"
Notebooks.* (J.C. Pratt and V.A. Neu-
feldt, eds)
  I. Adam, 178:Mar82-91
  R. Ashton, 541(RES):May82-222
  F.B., 189(EA):Jan-Mar82-116
  W. Baker, 354:Mar82-80
  J. Beaty, 301(JEGP):Oct82-583
Eliot, G. Middlemarch. (A. Loisy, trans)
  A. Jumeau, 189(EA):Jul-Sep82-341
Eliot, G. The Mill on the Floss.* (G.S.
Haight, ed)
  F. Bolton, 189(EA):Jan-Mar82-91
Elison, G. and B.L. Smith, eds. Warlords,
Artists, and Commoners.
  R.L. Backus, 407(MN):Spring82-130
Princess Elizabeth of Toro. African
Princess.
  D. Hunt, 362:10Nov83-27
Elkann, A. Stella Oceanis.
  I. Quigly, 617(TLS):6May83-464
Elkins, A.J. The Dark Place.
  N. Callendar, 441:30Oct83-31
Elkins, A.J. Fellowship of Fear.
  N. Callendar, 441:6Feb83-20
Ellen, R.F. and D. Reason, eds. Classifi-
cations in Their Social Context.
  S. Feld, 355(LSoc):Dec82-493
Ellenberger, B. The Latin Element in the
Vocabulary of the Earlier Makars Henry-
son and Dunbar.*
  J.D. McClure, 571(ScLJ):Spring82-4
Eller, J. Rage of Heaven.
  N. Callendar, 441:6Mar83-31
Ellin, S. The Dark Fantastic.
  P. van Rjndt, 441:11Sep83-16
Elliot, A. Talking Back.*
  A. Hollinghurst, 617(TLS):30Sep83-1061
Elliot, A.J. Child Language.
  S. Foster, 350:Jun83-458
Elliot, L. Little Flower.
  T. Chaffin, 441:10Jul83-17
Elliott, E. Revolutionary Writers.*
  R.A. Bosco, 432(NEQ):Dec82-622
Elliott, J. Magic.
  L. Duguid, 617(TLS):9Sep83-950
Elliott, J.E. Russian for Trade Negotia-
tions with the USSR.
  V.G. Brougher, 574(SEEJ):Winter82-499
Elliott, M. Partners in Revolution.
  R.B. McDowell, 617(TLS):11Feb83-127

Elliott, S.B. Some Data and Other Stories
of Southern Life.
  B. Hooper, 573(SSF):Spring82-181
Ellis, A.T. The Birds of the Air.*
  639(VQR):Winter82-20
Ellis, A.T. The Other Side of the Fire.
  J. Mellors, 362:15Dec83-30
  P. Raine, 617(TLS):18Nov83-1269
Ellis, A.T. - see Keene, M.
Ellis, B.D. Rational Belief Systems.*
  J.E. Tiles, 518:Jan82-38
Ellis, J.M. Heinrich von Kleist.
  M. Totten, 406:Fall82-358
Ellis, J.M. One Fairy Story Too Many.
  P-L. Adams, 61:Dec83-116
Ellis-Fermor, U. Shakespeare's Drama. (K.
Muir, ed)
  G.K. Hunter, 569(SR):Spring82-273
  K. Smidt, 179(ES):Dec82-576
  J. Voisine, 549(RLC):Jul-Sep82-391
Ellison, G.R. More Tales from Slim Elli-
son.
  L. Milazzo, 584(SWR):Spring82-v
Ellmann, R. The Identity of Yeats.
  R.B., 617(TLS):21Oct83-1171
Ellmann, R. - see Joyce, J.
Ellsberg, R. - see Day, D.
Ellsworth, L.E. Charles Lowder and the
Ritualist Movement.
  P. Butler, 617(TLS):7Jan83-22
Elrod, J.W. Kierkegaard and Christendom.*
  J.S. Boozer, 319:Oct83-578
Elsen, A.E. In Rodin's Studio.
  J. Tancock, 90:Jan82-45
Elshtain, J.B. Public Man, Private Woman.*
  J.L.H., 185:Jan83-425
Elsom, J., ed. Post-War British Theatre
Criticism.*
  S. Rusinko, 397(MD):Jun82-317
  R.J. Steen, 214:Vol 10No38-130
Elson, V. Where in the Sun to Stand.
  D. Hopes, 236:Fall-Winter82[No33]-27
Elster, J. Explaining Technical Change.
  N. Rescher, 617(TLS):26Aug83-914
Elster, J. Sour Grapes.
  A. Ryan, 617(TLS):14Oct83-1112
Elton, G.R. Studies in Tudor and Stuart
Politics and Government. (Vol 3)
  C. Haigh, 617(TLS):15Apr83-371
Elton, W.R. Shakespeare's World.
  J. van Dorsten, 570(SQ):Winter82-532
  C. Spivack, 365:Fall82-161
Elvers, R. and E. Vögel, eds. Festschrift
Hans Schneider zum 60. Geburtstag.
  A.H. King, 410(M&L):Jul/Oct82-292
Elwert, W.T. Die romanischen Sprachen und
Literaturen.*
  C. Blaylock, 240(HR):Autumn82-479
Ely, J.H. Democracy and Distrust.
  C. Arnold and H.S. Fairley, 185:Apr83-
  615
Elytis, O. Selected Poems. (E. Keeley
and P. Sherrard, eds)
  P. Merchant, 493:Jun82-75
  639(VQR):Autumn82-134
Emeljanov, V., ed. Chekhov: The Critical
Heritage.
  J. Curtis, 130:Summer82-192
  G. McVay, 575(SEER):Apr82-314
  L. Smith, 402(MLR):Jul82-765
  J. Uglow, 617(TLS):2Sep83-928

Emeneau, M.B. Language and Linguistic
Area.* (A.S. Dil, ed)
  H.M. Hoenigswald, 318(JAOS):Apr-Jun81-
  238
  K.R. Norman, 361:Jan82-93
Emerson, E.T. The Life of Lidian Jackson
Emerson.* (D.B. Carpenter, ed)
  J.H. McElroy, 50(ArQ):Winter82-380
  P.A. Palmieri, 432(NEQ):Jun82-303
Emerson, R.W. Emerson in His Journals.*
  (J. Porte, ed)
  R. Lipsey, 469:Vol8No1-114
  A.E. Stone, 27(AL):Dec82-607
Emerson, S. Listeners.
  L. Taylor, 617(TLS):6May83-465
Emery, J. Summer Ends Now.
  E. Webby, 381:Jul81-200
Emery, J.S. Stage Costume Technique.
  A. Curtis, 108:Winter82-112
Emery, M. Furniture by Architects.
  P. Goldberger, 441:11Dec83-37
Emiliani, A. Le Collezioni d'Arte della
Cassa di Risparmio in Bologna.
  J.T. Spike, 90:Feb82-108
Eminescu, M. Opere. (Vol 9)
  D. Deletant, 575(SEER):Apr82-281
Emlyn-Jones, C.J. The Ionians and Hellen-
ism.*
  C. Tuplin, 303(JoHS):Vol 102-265
Emmanuel, P. L'Autre.
  D. O'Connell, 207(FR):Oct82-169
Emmel, H. Geschichte des deutschen Romans.
  (Vols 2 and 3)
  G.C. Avery, 406:Summer82-192
Emmerson, R.K. Antichrist in the Middle
Ages.
  R.E. Lerner, 589:Jul82-601
Emmison, F.G., ed. Elizabethan Life.*
  I. Gray, 325:Oct82-121
Emond, P. Plein la vue.
  H. Le Mansec, 207(FR):Apr83-787
Empaytaz de Croome, D. Albor.*
  J.G. Cummins, 402(MLR):Apr82-473
Empedocles. The Extant Fragments.* (M.R.
Wright, ed)
  J. Barnes, 123:Vol32No2-191
"Employment and Earnings."
  A. Hacker, 453(NYRB):30Jun83-27
Enayat, H. Modern Islamic Political
Thought.*
  B. Lewis, 453(NYRB):30Jun83-35
"The Encyclopedia of American Cities."
  529(QQ):Summer82-458
Ende, M. The Neverending Story.
  D. Quammen, 441:6Nov83-14
Enders, H.W. and J. Pinborg - see Radul-
phus Brito
Endler, D. and H. Walter. Wörterbuch
Bulgarisch-Deutsch.
  G. Brandt, 682(ZPSK):Band35Heft2 236
Endo, S. The Samurai.*
  B. Powell, 362:4Aug83-20
Endo, S. Wonderful Fool.
  A. Cheuse, 441:13Nov83-13
Endres, C. Joannes Secundus.*
  J.W. Binns, 551(RenQ):Autumn82-499
"Energy in Transition 1985-2010."
  C.K. Rush, 529(QQ):Spring82-197
Engberg, R. and D. Wesling - see Muir, J.
Engberg, S. Pastorale.
  R. Banks, 441:20Feb83-6

Engberg-Pedersen, T. Aristotle's Theory of Moral Insight.
A.W. Price, 617(TLS):2Dec83-1336
Engel, A.J. From Clergyman to Don.
D.A.N. Jones, 362:17Mar83-22
E. Norman, 617(TLS):18Feb83-151
Engel, B.A. Mothers and Daughters.
A. Kelly, 617(TLS):30Dec83-1454
Engel, L. Words With Music.
J. Bridges, 498:Vol8No3/4-139
Engel, M. Fish.
W.H. Pritchard, 249(HudR):Spring82-159
Engel, M. The Glassy Sea.
C. Ross, 296(JCF):No33-138
Engel, M. Lunatic Villas.*
M. Gadpaille, 102(CanL):Autumn82-127
B. Godard, 198:Apr82-90
B. Greenwood, 526:Winter82-96
Engel, M. and J.A. Kraulis. The Islands of Canada.
529(QQ):Summer82-459
Engelbrecht, L.C. and J-M.F. Henry C. Trost, Architect of the Southwest.
W.B. Robinson, 576:Dec82-351
Engelhardt, K. and V. Roloff. Daten der französischen Literatur.*
M. Cranston, 207(FR):Oct82-142
Engell, J. The Creative Imagination.*
R. Beum, 569(SR):Spring82-xxxix
G. Chapman, 152(UDQ):Spring81-106
R. Cohen, 141:Spring82-174
D. Degrois, 189(EA):Oct-Dec82-473
L.R. Furst, 301(JEGP):Apr82-268
Z. Leader, 175:Autumn82-252
T. McFarland, 340(KSJ):Vol31-198
A. Page, 661(WC):Summer82-150
R. Quintana, 402(MLR):Jul82-688
F.W. Shilstone, 577(SHR):Fall82-362
L.J. Swingle, 401(MLQ):Mar82-89
H. Trowbridge, 405(MP):Nov82-185
Engell, J. and W.J. Bate - see Coleridge, S.T.
Engels, J. Vivaldi in Early Fall.*
E. Grosholz, 249(HudR):Summer82-319
J.D. McClatchy, 491:Sep82-346
Engen, R. Kate Greenaway.*
V. Powell, 39:Feb82-132
Enggass, C. and R. - see Malvasia, C.C.
England, A.B. Energy and Order in the Poetry of Swift.*
P. Brückmann, 627(UTQ):Summer82-419
P. Thorpe, 577(SHR):Winter82-68
D.M. Vieth, 173(ECS):Winter82/83-198
Englander, D. Landlord and Tenant in Urban Britain 1838-1918.
F.M.L. Thompson, 617(TLS):22Jul83-785
Englebretsen, G. Three Logicians. Logical Negation.
P. Thom, 63:Dec82-381
Engstrand, I.H.W. Spanish Scientists in the New World: The Eighteenth-Century Expeditions.
J. Dowling, 83:Autumn82-278
E.J. Goodman, 37:Nov-Dec82-62
E.J. Goodman, 263(RIB):Vol32No1-62
Engström-Persson, G. Zum Konjunktiv im Deutschen um 1800.
A. Lötscher, 685(ZDL):3/1982-387
Enlart, J. Adam ou la géométrie incarnée.
M. Adam, 542:Oct-Dec82-669
Ennis, J. At The Frontier.
G. Szirtes, 617(TLS):15Jul83-757

Ennius. Quinto Ennio.* (P. Magno, ed and trans)
P. Flobert, 555:Vol56fasc2-340
Enright, D.J. Collected Poems.*
M. Imlah, 493:Apr82-55
P. Swinden, 148:Autumn82-85
M. Wood, 617(TLS):9Sep83-951
Enright, D.J. A Mania for Sentences.
R. Davies, 362:25Aug83-22
M. Wood, 617(TLS):9Sep83-951
Enright, D.J., ed. The Oxford Book of Contemporary Verse, 1945-80.
R.B., 189(EA):Jan-Mar82-117
M. Thorpe, 179(ES):Feb82-82
Enright, D.J., ed. The Oxford Book of Death.
R. Blythe, 362:21Apr83-25
A. Burgess, 617(TLS):6May83-449
D.O., 231:Aug83-75
W.H. Pritchard, 441:19Jun83-3
P. Zaleski, 469:Vol8No4-108
442(NY):6Jun83-143
Enslin, T. Ranger. (Vols 1 and 2)
B. Ahearn, 472:Spring/Summer83-178
Entenza de Solare, B.E., ed. Poesías varias (Ms. 1132 de la Biblioteca Nacional de Madrid).
D.C. Clarke, 545(RPh):May82-689
Enyedi, G. and J. Mészaros, eds. Development of Settlement Systems.*
L.A. Kosiński, 104(CASS):Summer82-314
Enzensberger, H.M. Critical Essays. (R. Grimm and B. Armstrong, eds)
K. Acker, 62:Jan83-71
Enzensberger, H.M. The Sinking of the Titanic.*
D. Dunn, 493:Apr82-53
D. McDuff, 565:Vol23No1-58
Eörsi, I. - see Lukács, G.
Ephron, N. Heartburn.
G. Glueck, 441:24Apr83-3
J. Neville, 617(TLS):16Sep83-1001
M.L. Moore, 181:Spring-Summer83-283
J. Wolcott, 231:Aug83-64
Epstein, C.F. Women in Law.
R.M. Kanter, 676(YR):Winter83-x
Epstein, E.J. The Diamond Invention.
R. West, 617(TLS):7Jan83-10
Epstein, E.L., ed. A Starchamber Quiry.
M.P. Gillespie, 329(JJQ):Spring83-361
M.T. Reynolds, 395(MFS):Winter82/83-629
S. Whittaker, 594:Winter82-394
Epstein, J. Ambition.
S. Brown, 569(SR):Spring82-250
Epstein, J., ed. Masters.
S.I. Bellman, 50(ArQ):Summer82-188
A.J. Bingham, 577(SHR):Spring82-179
S. Pickering, 569(SR):Summer82-474
Erasmus. Cinq Banquets. (J. Chomarat and D. Ménager, eds and trans)
F. Bierlaire, 535(RHL):Sep-Dec82-862
Erasmus. Collected Works of Erasmus.* (Vols 23 and 24) (C.R. Thompson, ed)
G.K. Hunter, 402(MLR):Apr82-397
Erasmus. Opera Omnia. (Vol 4, Pt 3) (C.H. Miller, ed)
W.D. Key, 551(RenQ):Autumn81-395
Erasmus. The Praise of Folly.* (C.H. Miller, ed and trans)
D.F. Bratchell, 447(N&Q):Aug81-331
M-M. Martinet, 189(EA):Apr-Jun82-204
J.D. Tracy, 551(RenQ):Spring82-90

Erbse, H. Scholia Graeca in Homeri Iliadem. (Vol 5)
  M. van der Valk, 394:Vol35fasc3/4-350
Erdmann, P. Inversion im heutigen Englisch.
  P.A. Jorgensen, 35(AS):Fall82-218
  W. Zydatiss, 257(IRAL):May82-161
Erdmann, P. There Sentences in English.
  P.W. Kunsmann, 257(IRAL):Feb82-75
Erens, P. Sexual Stratagems.
  J. Nelson, 529(QQ):Summer82-451
Erfurth, S. Harry Martinsons barndoms-värld.
  K. Petherick, 563(SS):Spring82-181
Erhart, A. and R. Večerka. Úvod do etymologie.
  K. Müller, 682(ZPSK):Band35Heft5-597
Erhart, K.P., J. Frel and S. Nodelman. Roman Portraits.
  S. Wood, 54:Jun82-327
Erickson, C. The First Elizabeth.
  M. Quilligan, 441:3Apr83-9
  442(NY):11Apr83-136
Erickson, J.D. Nommo.*
  E. Müller-Bochat, 547(RF):Band94Heft1-135
  C. Wake, 208(FS):Jul82-371
Erickson, J.D. and I. Pagès, eds. Proust et le texte producteur.*
  W.A. Strauss, 399(MLJ):Spring82-92
Erickson, J.R. The Modern Cowboy.
  R.D. Keller, 649(WAL):Nov82-294
Erickson, K.V., ed. Plato.
  T.M. Lentz, 480(P&R):Summer82-215
Erickson, K.V. Plato: True and Sophistic Rhetoric.
  J-P. Levet, 555:Vol55fasc2-338
Ericson, E.E., Jr. Solzhenitsyn.*
  C.R. Goldfarb, 579(SAQ):Winter82-121
  M. Raskin, 395(MFS):Summer81-412
Erikson, E.H. The Life Cycle Completed.
  P. Sedgwick, 617(TLS):9Sep83-968
Eriksson, B. L'emploi des modes dans la subordonnée relative en français moderne.*
  H. Berschin, 547(RF):Band93Heft1/2-206
  G. Price, 208(FS):Apr82-243
Erkkila, B. Walt Whitman Among the French.*
  R. Asselineau, 189(EA):Oct-Dec82-490
  M.A. Caws, 131(CL):Winter82-85
  L. Cederstrom, 106:Winter82-349
  D. Middlebrook, 301(JEGP):Jan82-152
  R.J. Scholnick, 149(CLS):Winter82-487
Erler, A. and E. Kaufmann, with R. Schmidt-Wiegand, eds. Handwörterbuch zur deutschen Rechtsgeschichte. (Vols 1-3)
  R. Gmür, 684(ZDA):Band111Heft3-107
Erlich, V. Russian Formalism. (3rd ed)
  F.C.M. Kitch, 575(SEER):Apr02 315
Erlmann, V. Die Macht des Wortes.
  K.A. Gourlay, 69:Vol51No4-890
Ermolaev, H. Mikhail Sholokhov and His Art.*
  D. Kiziria, 550(RusR):Oct82-533
  V.D. Mihailovich, 268(IFR):Winter83-67
  295(JML):Dec82-533
Ernst, T. and E. Smith, eds. Lingua Pranca.
  I. Andrews, 257(IRAL):Feb82-82
Erofeev, B. Moscow Circles.*
  R. Blount, Jr., 441:20Mar83-9
  J. Updike, 442(NY):21Feb83-126

Erskine-Hill, H. The Augustan Idea in English Literature.
  C. Rawson, 617(TLS):12Aug83-847
Erskine-Hill, H. and G. Storey, eds. Revolutionary Prose of the English Civil War.
  S. Wintle, 617(TLS):16Sep83-992
Eruvbetine, A.E. Intellectualized Emotions and the Art of James Joyce.
  M. Power, 395(MFS):Summer81-316
Ervin, S.J., Jr. Humor of a Country Lawyer.
  R. Reed, 441:25Dec83-8
Erzgräber, W., ed. Europäisches Spätmittelalter.
  F.B. Parkes-Perret, 481(PQ):Summer81-422
  K. Rossenbeck, 597(SN):Vol54No1-179
Erzgräber, W., ed. Hamlet-Interpretationen.
  M. Pfister, 72:Band218Heft2-432
Esberey, J.E. Knight of the Holy Spirit.*
  D. Swainson, 529(QQ):Autumn82-611
Escarpit, D. La Littérature d'enfance et de jeunesse.
  R. Robert, 535(RHL):Sep-Dec82-992
von Eschenbach, W. - see under Wolfram von Eschenbach
Escobar, A., J. Matos Mar and G. Alberti. Perú, país bilingüe?
  G.F. Meier, 682(ZPSK):Band34Heft2-226
Escudé, C. Gran Bretaña, Estados Unidos y la declinación argentina, 1942-1949.
  D. Rock, 617(TLS):23Dec83-1435
Esenin, S. A Biography in Memoirs, Letters, and Documents. (J. Davies, ed and trans)
  L. Visson, 574(SEEJ):Winter82-490
Esher, L. A Broken Wave.*
  R. Sheppard, 46:Jan82-77
Eskola, A. and J. Salminen. Puhe on Suomesta.
  R.G. Selleck, 563(SS):Summer82-275
Esland, G. and G. Salaman, eds. The Politics of Work and Occupations.
  G. Hunnius, 99:May82-35
Esposito, J. Evolutionary Metaphysics.
  S.B.R., 543:Jun82-867
Esposito, R. La politica e la storia.
  F. Volpi, 489(PJGG):Band89Heft2-437
de Espronceda, J. El estudiante de Salamanca and Other Poems. (R.A. Cardwell, ed)
  H-J. Lope, 547(RF):Band94Heft1-138
  D.L. Shaw, 402(MLR):Apr82-478
  M.A. Wellington, 238:Dec82-657
Espy, W.R. The Garden of Eloquence.
  P-L. Adams, 61:Oct83-122
Esquirol, E. Des passions considérées comme causes, symptômes et moyens curatifs de l'aliénation mentale.
  A. Reix, 542:Jan-Mar82-90
Esser, J. Intonationszeichen im Englischen.*
  G.F. Meier, 682(ZPSK):Band35Heft4-481
Esser, J.B. Faces of Fiesta.
  C.F. Klein, 2(AfrA):Aug82-89
Essick, R.N. William Blake, Printmaker.*
  D. Irwin, 161(DUJ):Dec81-112
  D.M. Read, 661(WC):Summer82-139
Essler, W.K. Wissenschaftstheorie IV.
  N. Froese, 167:Jan82-123

Esslin, M. Mediations.*
  A. Schwarz, 397(MD):Sep82-441
Estermann, A. Die deutschen Literatur-
  Zeitschriften 1815-1850.* (Vol 10)
  H. Steinecke, 221(GQ):Jan82-131
Estess, T.L. Elie Wiesel.
  L. Field, 395(MFS):Summer82-340
Estienne, H. Deux Dialogues du nouveau
  langage francois ...* (P-M. Smith, ed)
  C.E. Campbell, 207(FR):Apr83-766
Estleman, L.D. The Glass Highway.
  N. Callendar, 441:23Oct83-38
de Estrada, D. Octavas rimas a la insigne
  victoria conseguida por el Marqués de
  Santa Cruz. (H.M. Ettinghausen, ed)
  B.W. Ife, 402(MLR):Jan82-220
  D.G. Walters, 86(BHS):Oct82-339
Estrada, F.L. and others - see under López
  Estrada, F. and others
Estrin, M.W. Lillian Hellman.
  B.F. Dick, 397(MD):Dec82-587
Etcheverry, J. El Evasionista/The Escape
  Artist.
  M.T. Lane, 198:Jul82-100
Etherege, G. The Plays of Sir George
  Etherege. (M. Cordner, ed)
  I. Donaldson, 617(TLS):28Oct83-1183
Etherton, M. The Development of African
  Drama.
  D. Walder, 617(TLS):14Jan83-43
"Ethnic Recordings in America."
  M. Slobin, 187:Sep83-542
Étiemble. Quelques essais de littérature
  universelle.*
  M.F. Meurice, 450(NRF):Sep82-122
Etiemble, R. Mes Contrepoisons.
  P. Nagy, 549(RLC):Oct-Dec82-527
Etienne, R. and D. Knoepfler. Hyettos de
  Béotie et la chronologie des archontes
  fédéraux entre 250 et 171 avant J.-C.
  S.C. Bakhuizen, 394:Vol35fasc3/4-435
Etienvre, J-P. - see Caro, R.
Etter, D. Cornfields.
  M. Lammon, 436(NewL):Winter82/83-110
Ettinger, S. Form und Funktion in der
  Wortbildung.* (2nd ed)
  G.F. Meier, 682(ZPSK):Band34Heft4-487
Ettinghausen, H.M. - see de Estrada, D.
Ettore, E.M. Lesbians, Women, and Society.
  A. Karlen, 560:Fal182/Winter83-300
"Les études classiques aux XIXe et XXe
  siècles."
  R.W., 555:Vol56fasc1-143
"Études rabelaisiennes." (Vol 15)
  F. Charpentier, 535(RHL):May-Jun82-453
"Études seiziémistes offertes à Monsieur
  le Professeur V.-L. Saulnier par plusi-
  eurs de ses anciens doctorants."
  I.D. McFarlane, 208(FS):Oct82-466
  M. Quainton, 402(MLR):Jan82-200
"Eubulus: The Fragments." (R.L. Hunter,
  ed)
  J.H.C. Leach, 617(TLS):22Apr83-398
Euler, W. Indoiranisch-griechische Geme-
  insamkeiten der Nominalbildung und deren
  indogermanische Grundlagen.
  J-L. Perpillou, 555:Vol56fasc1-115
Euripides. Euripide, "Ion." (W. Biehl,
  ed)
  G. Ronnet, 555:Vol55fasc1-157
Euripides. Heracles. (G.W. Bond, ed)
  R.W., 555:Vol56fasc2-328

Euripides. Tragedie di Euripide. (Vol 1)
  (O. Musso, ed and trans)
  J. Diggle, 123:Vol32No1-91
Eustathius. Eustathii Archiepiscopi
  Thessalonicensis Commentarii ad Homeri
  "Iliadem" Pertinentes. (Vol 3) (M. van
  der Valk, ed)
  F.M. Combellack, 122:Apr82-184
  N.G. Wilson, 123:Vol32No1-119
Eutropius. Eutropii Breuiarium ab Vrbe
  condita. (C. Santini, ed)
  J. Hellegouarc'h, 555:Vol56fasc1-169
Evanier, D. The One-Star Jew.
  I. Gold, 441:14Aug83-12
Evans, B. Shakespeare's Tragic Practice.*
  R.A. Foakes, 677(YES):Vol 12-255
  M.M. Mahood, 570(SQ):Spring82-107
  J. Rees, 447(N&Q):Aug81-335
  S. Snyder, 551(RenQ):Spring81-146
  G. Taylor, 541(RES):Feb82-76
Evans, B.H. Daylight in Architecture.
  S. Matthews, 505:Apr82-204
Evans, C. Landscapes of the Night. (ed
  and completed by P. Evans)
  R. Dinnage, 617(TLS):7Oct83-1085
Evans, D. Mather Brown.
  P. Greenham, 617(TLS):5Aug83-831
Evans, E. Eudora Welty.
  K. Cushman, 573(SSF):Winter82-100
  W.J. Stuckey, 395(MFS):Autumn82-507
  639(VQR):Winter82-8
Evans, G. The Varieties of Reference.
  (J. McDowell, ed)
  C. Taylor, 617(TLS):11Mar83-230
Evans, G. and J. McDowell, eds. Truth and
  Meaning.*
  M. Bell, 606:Jul82-135
Evans, G.R. Augustine on Evil.
  C. Kirwan, 617(TLS):22Jul83-784
Evans, G.R. Old Arts and New Theology.*
  S.C. Ferruolo, 589:Apr82-370
Evans, H. Good Times, Bad Times.
  O.R. McGregor, 617(TLS):16Dec83-1395
  D. Trelford, 362:27Oct83-34
Evans, J., ed. London Tales.
  D. Montrose, 617(TLS):25Nov83-1301
Evans, J.L. The Kievan Russian Principal-
  ity, 860-1240.
  T.S. Noonan, 550(RusR):Oct82-472
Evans, J.M. Guide to the Amerikansky
  Russky Viestnik. (Vol 1)
  R.H. Burger, 575(SEER):Apr82-313
Evans, J.S.T. The Psychology of Deductive
  Reasoning.
  O.J.F., 185:Apr83-629
Evans, M. Lucien Goldmann.*
  T. Eagleton, 208(FS):Jul82-363
Evans, M. Nightstar: 1973-78.
  D. Dorsey, 95(CLAJ):Sep81-107
Evans, M.K. The Truth about Supply-Side
  Economics.
  R. Lekachman, 61:Jul83-96
Evans, P. The Englishman's Daughter.
  442(NY):23May83-120
Evans, P. The Music of Benjamin Britten.*
  J. Bach, 414(MusQ):Jan82-138
Evans, R.J., ed. The German Working Class,
  1888-1933.
  639(VQR):Summer82-85
Evans, T.S. Formen der Ironie in Conrad
  Ferdinand Meyers Novellen.*
  G. Reinhardt, 222(GR):Summer82-124

Faulconer, A.M. The Season.
  N. Shack, 617(TLS):21Oct83-1157
Faulkes, A., ed. Two Versions of Snorra
  Edda from the 17th Century.
  J. Harris, 589:Oct82-966
Faulkner, P. Against the Age.
  A. Bacon, 506(PSt):Dec82-345
Faulkner, P. Robert Bage.*
  P.J. Weston, 161(DUJ):Jun82-311
Faulkner, P. Angus Wilson.*
  J.L. Halio, 402(MLR):Apr82-436
  H.H. Watts, 395(MFS):Winter81/82-702
Faulkner, R.K. Richard Hooker and the
  Politics of a Christian England.
  G.R. Elton, 551(RenQ):Winter82-640
Faulkner, W. Helen.
  D.P. Ragan, 392:Summer82-337
Faulkner, W. Lettres choisies. (J. Blot-
  ner, ed) (D. Coupaye and M. Gresset,
  trans)
  S. Koster, 98:May82-466
Faulkner, W. Sanctuary. (N. Polk, ed)
  529(QQ):Summer82-457
"Faulkner Studies." (Vol 1) (B. Gutten-
  berg, ed)
  S.M. Ross, 395(MFS):Winter81/82-729
Fauré, G. Gabriel Fauré: Correspondance.
  (J-M. Nectoux, ed)
  R. Orledge, 410(M&L):Jul/Oct81-354
Faurot, J.L., ed. Chinese Fiction from
  Taiwan.
  N.K. Mao, 293(JASt):May82-575
Faust, B. Women, Sex and Pornography.
  H. Garner, 381:Jul81-147
Faust, D. James Henry Hammond and the
  Old South.
  E.D. Genovese, 453(NYRB):31Mar83-23
Faust, D.G., ed. The Ideology of Slavery.
  639(VQR):Summer82-85
Faust, W. Russlands goldener Boden.
  M. von Hagen, 550(RusR):Jan82-76
  D.S.M. Williams, 575(SEER):Jan82-120
Favier, J., ed. Les Archives Nationales.
  G. Westfall, 14:Spring82-201
Favier, J. François Villon.
  P.S. Lewis, 617(TLS):15Apr83-372
"Favorite Knitting and Crochet Patterns."
  M. Cowan, 614:Spring83-19
Favre, Y-A. - see de Boschère, J.
Favret Saada, J. and J. Contreras. Corps
  pour corps, enquête sur la sorcellerie
  dans le Bocage.
  H. Cronel, 450(NRF):Oct82-132
Fawcett, B. Aggressive Transport.
  B. Serafin, 648(WCR):Apr83-45
Fawcett, B. Tristram's Book.
  E. Thompson, 102(CanL):Summer82-133
Fawcett, E. and T. Thomas. America, Ameri-
  cans.
  A. Quinton, 617(TLS):28Jan83-80
"Faxue Cidian."
  W.C. Jones, 293(JASt):Feb82-323
"Jean-Pierre Faye." (M. Partouche, ed)
  M. Bishop, 207(FR):Oct82-175
Fayolle, R. La Critique.
  S. Sarkany, 106(CRCL):Jun82-241
Fazzini Giovannucci, E. Die alemannischen
  im westlichen Norditalien.
  P. Zürrer, 685(ZDL):3/1981-393
Feagin, C. Variation and Change in Ala-
  bama English.*
  B.H. Davis, 355(LSoc):Apr82-139
  H. Ulherr, 38:Band100Heft3/4-484

Feather, J. The English Provincial Book
  Trade before 1850.
  D. Pearson, 83:Autumn82-263
  F. Strong, 325:Oct82-123
Feaver, V. Close Relatives.*
  J. Saunders, 565:Vol23No3-73
February, V.A. Mind Your Colour.
  M.V. Mzamane, 402(MLR):Jul82-714
Febvre, L. The Problem of Unbelief in the
  Sixteenth Century.
  P. Burke, 617(TLS):8Jul83-723
  D.P. Walker, 453(NYRB):31Mar83-36
Fedeli, P. Sesto Properzio.* [shown in
  prev under Propertius]
  L. Richardson, Jr., 121(CJ):Feb/Mar83-
  260
Feder, L. Madness in Literature.*
  J. Berman, 191(ELN):Dec81-169
  S.M. Gilbert, 301(JEGP):Apr82-244
  A. Morvan, 189(EA):Apr-Jun82-195
  B.A. Rosenberg, 149(CLS):Winter82-486
"Federal Records Management."
  M. Brichford, 14:Fall82-477
Federici Vescovini, G. Astrologia e
  scienza.
  E. Rosen, 551(RenQ):Spring81-100
Federman, R. The Twofold Vibration.*
  D. Lehman, 676(YR):Spring83-xii
Fedorowicz, J.K., ed and trans. A Repub-
  lic of Nobles.*
  M. Malia, 453(NYRB):29Sep83-18
Feduchi, L. A History of World Furniture.
  G. Wills, 39:Apr82-297
Fee, J. The Sweater Workshop.
  C. Mouton, 614:Fall83-24
Feeley, M.F. Court Reform on Trial.
  G. Hughes, 453(NYRB):10Nov83-28
Feenberg, A. Lukács, Marx and the Sources
  of Critical Theory.*
  W.L. Adamson, 319:Apr83-264
Feer, L. Avadâna-çataka.
  259(IIJ):Jan82-81
Feher, F., A. Heller and G. Markus. Dicta-
  torship over Needs.
  A. Nove, 617(TLS):23Sep83-1014
Feher, M.I. Jean-Paul Sartre.
  É. Martonyi, 535(RHL):Sep-Dec82-970
von der Fehr, D. Myte og roman.
  J. de Mylius, 172(Edda):1982/6-376
Fehrenbacher, D.E. The South and Three
  Sectional Crises.
  W. Flynt, 577(SHR):Summer82-271
Feibleman, J.K. Assumptions of Grand
  Logics.
  R.M.M., 543:Mar82-601
Feiffer, J. Jules Feiffer's America. (S.
  Heller, ed)
  R. Davies, 362:10Feb83-27
Feigenbaum, E.A. and P. McCorduck. The
  Fifth Generation.
  J. Weizenbaum, 453(NYRB):27Oct83-58
Feinberg, J. Rights, Justice and the
  Bounds of Liberty.*
  A.G.N. Flew, 518:Jan82-55
  D. Vandeveer, 484(PPR):Sep82-120
Feinberg, R.E. The Intemperate Zone.
  C. Marcy, 441:21Aug83-11
Feirstein, F. Manhattan Carnival.*
  D. Gioia, 249(HudR):Winter82/83-640
Feist, L. An Introduction to Popular
  Music Publishing in America.
  J. Bridges, 498:Vol8No1-61

Fekete, É. and É. Karádi, eds. Georg Lukács.*
    E. Keller, 67:Nov82-218
Fekete, É. and É. Karádi - see Lukács, G.
Feld, R. Only Shorter.
    G. Kearns, 249(HudR):Autumn82-499
Feldbaek, O. Denmark and the Armed Neutrality 1800-1801.
    R.K. Debo, 104(CASS):Summer82-257
Felde, A.Z. - see under Zum Felde, A.
Felder, E. Germanische Personennamen auf merowingischen Münzen.
    H. Beck, 680(ZDP):Band101Heft1-129
Feldman, A. and E. O'Doherty. The Northern Fiddler.*
    L.E. McCullough, 292(JAF):Apr-Jun82-249
Feldman, R. The Ambition of Ghosts.
    M. Hindus, 390:Mar82-50
Feldstein, M. Inflation, Tax Rules, and Capital Formation.
    L.C. Thurow, 453(NYRB):22Dec83-47
Felix, D. Marx as Politician.
    J. Gray, 617(TLS):30Dec83-1459
Fell, J.P. Heidegger and Sartre.*
    J. Butler, 482(PhR):Oct82-641
Fellini, F. Moraldo in the City [and] A Journey with Anita. (J.C. Stubbs, ed and trans)
    M. Wood, 617(TLS):18Nov83-1275
Fellman, A.C. and M. Making Sense of Self.
    L.G. Zatlin, 651(WHR):Winter82-372
Fellows, J. Ruskin's Maze.*
    Q. Bell, 90:Sep82-560
    D. Johnson, 453(NYRB):31Mar83-13
    639(VQR):Spring82-57
Fellows, O. and D.G. Carr - see "Diderot Studies"
Felman, S. Le scandale du corps parlant.*
    L. Tyler, 580(SCR):Spring83-117
Felperin, H. Shakespearean Representation.
    D. Mehl, 570(SQ):Spring82-106
Felsenstein, F. - see Smollett, T.
Felstiner, J. Translating Neruda.
    D. Schier, 569(SR):Spring82-323
Felten, H. Französische Literatur der Julimonarchie.
    D. Bellos, 208(FS):Jan82-79
Fenger, H. Kierkegaard.
    B. Dewey, 563(SS):Spring82-173
Fenlon, I., ed. Early Music History. (Vol 1)
    R. Woodley, 410(M&L):Jul/Oct82-341
Fenlon, I. Music and Patronage in Sixteenth Century Mantua.* (Vol 1)
    D. Arnold, 410(M&L):Jul/Oct82-303
    J. Chater, 415:Jan82-31
    J.A. Owens, 317:Summer82-334
Fenlon, I. Music and Patronage in Sixteenth-Century Mantua. (Vol 2)
    D. Stevens, 617(TLS):4Mar83-206
Fenlon, I., ed. Music in Medieval and Early Modern Europe.
    R. Strohm, 410(M&L):Jan/Apr82-133
Fennell, J.L.I., A.E. Pennington and I.P. Foote - see "Oxford Slavonic Papers"
Fennell, T.B. and H. Gelsen. A Grammar of Modern Latvian.
    W.R. Schmalstieg, 215(GL):Summer82-139
Fenner, B. Friedrich Hebbel zwischen Hegel und Freud.
    D.J. Parent, 221(GQ):May82-432

Fennis, J. La "Stolonomie" 1547-1550 et son vocabulaire maritime marseillais.*
    H. and R. Kahane, 545(RPh):Nov81-348
Fensk, H. Schweizerische und österreichische Besonderheiten in deutschen Wörterbuchern.
    G. Lipold and H. Tatzreiter, 685(ZDL):1/1982-78
Fenstad, J.E. General Recursion Theory.
    D. Cenzer, 316:Sep82-696
Fenstermaker, J.J. - see Altick, R.D.
Fenton, J. The Memory of War.*
    G. Ewart, 364:Oct82-67
    C. Rumens, 493:Jan83-51
Fenton, J. You Were Marvellous.
    A. Wesker, 362:25Aug83-21
Ferber, R. Zenons Paradoxien der Bewegung und die Struktur von Raum und Zeit.
    M. Schofield, 123:Vol32No2-188
Ferenczy, E. From the Patrician State to the Patricio-Plebeian State.
    A. Drummond, 313:Vol72-176
Ferge, Z. A Society in the Making.
    R. Blumstock, 104(CASS):Summer82-302
Fergus, J. Jane Austen and the Didactic Novel.
    D. Monaghan, 268(IFR):Summer83-139
    N. Spoliar, 617(TLS):19Aug83-884
Ferguson, A.B. Clio Unbound.*
    M-M. Martinet, 189(EA):Apr-Jun82-205
    R.J. Schoeck, 551(RenQ):Winter81-611
    A.J. Slavin, 125:Fall81-84
    J.M. Steadman, 301(JEGP):Jan82-104
Ferguson, J. Callimachus.
    M. Campbell, 123:Vol33No1-94
Ferguson, R.H. Laforgue y Lugones.
    D. Harris, 402(MLR):Oct82-977
Ferguson, T. and J. Rogers, eds. The Hidden Election.*
    639(VQR):Spring82-48
Fergusson, D.A., A.I. MacDhomhnuill and J.F. Gillespie, eds. From the Farthest Hebrides (Bho Na H-Innse Gall An Iomallaiche).
    J. Porter, 187:Jan83-128
Ferling, J.E. A Wilderness of Miseries.
    I.D. Gruber, 656(WMQ):Jul82-546
Ferlinghetti, L. Endless Life.
    L. Bartlett, 50(ArQ):Autumn82-275
    J. Trimbur, 649(WAL):Spring82-79
Ferlinghetti, L. and N.J. Peters. Literary San Francisco.
    A. Frietzsche, 649(WAL):Nov82-264
Fernández, A.L. - see under Labandeira Fernández, A.
Fernández, C. Paracuellos del Jarama.
    P. Preston, 617(TLS):13May83-483
Fernandez, D. Dans la main de l'ange.
    A. Lavers, 617(TLS):7Jan83-23
Fernandez, D. - see de Maupassant, G.
Fernandez, D.G. The Iloilo Zarzuela: 1903-1930.
    D.L. Szanton, 293(JASt):Nov81-196
Fernández-Armesto, F. Sadat and his Statecraft.
    P.J. Vatikiotis, 617(TLS):26Aug83-911
Fernández Conde, J., ed. La Iglesia en la España de los siglos VIII-XIV.
    P. Linehan, 617(TLS):4Feb83-117
Fernández de Avellaneda, A. Don Quixote de La Mancha. (Pt 2) (A.W. Server and J.E. Keller, eds and trans)
    S.H. Ackerman, 238:Sep82-462

Fernández de Heredia, J. Aragonese Version of the "Libro de Marco Polo." (J.J. Nitti, ed)
  S. Baldwin, 589:Oct82-881
Fernández de la Vega, O. and J.E. Hernández-Miyares. Ortografía activa.
  M. Iglesias, 399(MLJ):Spring82-101
Fernández de Lizardi, J.J. El Periquillo Sarniento. (L. Sáinz de Medrano, ed)
  J. Roy, 552(REH):Jan82-129
Fernandez-Galiano, E. Léxico de los Himnos de Calimaco.* (Vol 4) [entry in prev was of Vols 1-4]
  R.W., 555:Vol55fasc2-345
Fernández González, E. La escultura románica en la zona de Villaviciosa (Asturias).
  I. Mateo Gómez, 48:Apr-Jun82-220
Fernández Moreno, C., J. Ortega and I.A. Schulman, eds. Latin America in Its Literature.*
  D. Kadir, 395(MFS):Winter81/82-769
Fernández-Morera, D. The Lyre and the Oaten Flute.
  A.J. Cascardi, 304(JHP):Spring82-245
Fernández-Puertas, A. La Fachada del Palacio de Comares. (Vol 1)
  D. Angulo Íñiguez, 48:Jan-Mar82-114
Fernández Retamar, R. Para una teoría de la literatura hispanoamericana y otras aproximaciones.
  R.A. Young, 107(CRCL):Dec81-565
Ferneyhough, F. Steam Up!
  D. Luckhurst, 324:Sep83-634
Ferns, C.S. Aldous Huxley: Novelist.*
  J. Meckier, 395(MFS):Winter81/82-693
Ferns, J. A.J.M. Smith.
  J.H. Ferres, 102(CanL):Spring82-108
  P. Stevens, 105:Fall/Winter82-136
Ferrard, J. Orgues du Brabant Wallon.
  P. Williams, 410(M&L):Jul/Oct82-310
Ferrars, E.X. Death of a Minor Character.
  442(NY):29Aug83-94
Ferrars, E.X. Skeleton in Search of a Closet.* (British title: Skeleton in Search of a Cupboard.)
  442(NY):24Jan83-109
Ferraté, J. - see March, A.
Ferrater Mora, J. De la materia a la razón.*
  A. Reix, 192(EP):Oct-Dec81-483
Ferraù, G. - see Cortesii, P.
Ferreira, M.J. Doubt and Religious Commitment.
  P.J. Sherry, 518:Oct82-212
Ferrell, R.H. - see Eisenhower, D.D.
Ferrell, R.H. - see Hagerty, J.C.
Ferrell, R.H. - see Truman, H.S.
Ferreres, R. - see March, A.
Ferrier-Caverivière, N. L'image de Louis XIV dans la littérature française de 1660 à 1715.
  P. Ronzeaud, 475:Vol9No17-760
Ferris, P. Richard Burton.*
  M. Norgate, 157:Spring82-58
Ferris, P. A Distant Country.
  H. Davies, 617(TLS):22Jul83-791
Ferro, M. Comment on raconte l'Histoire aux enfants à travers le monde entier.
  C. Zimra, 207(FR):Dec82-365
Ferron, J. L'Amélanchier.
  V. Raoul, 102(CanL):Winter81-155

Ferrucci, F. The Poetics of Disguise.
  A. Paolucci, 551(RenQ):Summer81-223
Fessard, G. Chrétiens marxistes et théologie de la libération. Eglise de France, prends garde de perdre la foi.
  E.L.F., 543:Sep81-128
Fessard, G. La philosophie historique de Raymond Aron.
  A. Reix, 542:Jan-Mar82-62
Festa-McCormick, D. Honoré de Balzac.*
  C. Smethurst, 208(FS):Jul82-339
Festugière, A.J. - see Hippocrates
Fet, A. I Have Come to Greet You.
  J. Grayson, 617(TLS):28Jan83-86
Fetler, J. Impossible Appetites.
  C. Colter, 436(NewL):Fall82-108
Fetter, F.W. The Economist in Parliament: 1780-1868.
  S. Hollander, 637(VS):Summer82-505
Feuchtwanger, E.J. and P. Nailor, eds. The Soviet Union and the Third World.
  C.W. Lawson, 575(SEER):Oct82-636
  E.K. Valkenier, 550(RusR):Oct82-515
Feuerstein, G. - see Patañjali
Feuerwerker, Y-T.M. Ding Ling's Fiction.
  W.J.F. Jenner, 617(TLS):24Jun83-676
Feustle, J.A. Poesía y mística.
  J.G. Johnson, 552(REH):Jan82-152
Fewster, K. - see Bean, C.E.W.
Feyerabend, P. Science in a Free Society.*
  R.H.S., 543:Dec81-383
Feyerabend, P. Der Wissenschaftstheoretische Realismus und die Autorität der Wissenschaften.
  E. Zahar, 84:Dec82-397
Fiacc, P. The Selected Padraic Fiacc.
  L.M. Harrod, 174(Éire):Fall82-145
Fiacre, K-J. Historische Lautlehre des Dialektes von Bévercé (Kanton Malmédy, Belgien).
  G. Roques, 553(RLiR):Jan-Jun81-265
Fichte, J.G. Gesamtausgabe der Bayerischen Akademie der Wissenschaften. (Vol 2, Pt 5 and Vol 4, Pts 1 and 2) (R. Lauth, H. Jacob and H. Gliwitzky, eds)
  J. Widmann, 489(PJGG):Band89Heft1-204
Fichte, J.G. Machiavel et autres écrits philosophiques et politiques de 1806-1807.
  S.L., 227(GCFI):May-Aug82-244
Fichte, J.O. Chaucer's "Art Poetical."*
  D. Mehl, 38:Band100Heft1/2-181
Fichter, A. Poets Historical.
  S. Wintle, 617(TLS):12Aug83-867
Ficino, M. Marsilio Ficino and the Phaedran Charioteer. (M.J.B. Allen, ed and trans)
  L.V.R., 568(SCN):Fall82-58
  P. Vicari and J. Warden, 604:Spring-Summer82-29
  D.P. Walker, 551(RenQ):Autumn82-455
Ficino, M. Marsilio Ficino: The Book of Life. (C. Boer, trans)
  M.J.B. Allen, 551(RenQ):Spring82-69
Fick, B.W. El libro de viajes en la España medieval.
  P.A. Bly, 552(REH):Jan82-145
Fickelson, M. La Vie intérieure.*
  C. Coustou, 450(NRF):Jul-Aug82-173
Fiddian, R. Ignacio Aldecoa.*
  J. Ferrán, 593:Spring82-94
Fiedler, J. and J. Mele. Isaac Asimov.
  M. Tritt, 561(SFS):Nov82-334

Fiedler, L. What Was Literature?*
    A. Kazin, 61:Jan83-92
Fiedler, L.A. The Inadvertent Epic.
    G. Wickes, 395(MFS):Summer81-358
Fiedler, L.A. Olaf Stapledon.
    B. Aldiss, 617(TLS):23Sep83-1007
Fiedler, L.A. and H.A. Baker, Jr., eds.
    English Literature.*
    W.E. Cain, 580(SCR):Fall82-118
Fieguth, M. Vancouver Island and the Gulf
    Islands.
    529(QQ):Summer82-459
Fieguth, R. - see Norwid, C.
Field, A. Djuna.
    P. Rose, 441:26Jun83-9
    J.S., 231:Jul83-76
    442(NY):20Jun83-102
Field, A. The Formidable Miss Barnes.
    E. Hardwick, 617(TLS):7Oct83-1071
Field, A. Vladimir Nabokov.
    J. Aeply, 450(NRF):Oct82-128
Field, F.V. From Right to Left.
    R. Sherrill, 441:16Oct83-3
Field, G.G. Evangelist of Race.
    V.A. Rudowski, 580(SCR):Spring83-130
Field, H.H. Science Without Numbers.*
    F.J. Clendinnen, 606:May82-283
    M. Lockwood, 479(PhQ):Jul82-281
    D. Malament, 311(JP):Sep82-523
    M.E. Tiles, 518:Apr82-90
Field, J. Place-Names of Greater London.*
    K. Ames, 292(JAF):Oct-Dec82-490
Field, L. Bendor.
    E.S. Turner, 617(TLS):2Sep83-924
Field, L. - see Wolfe, T.
Fielding, H. - see under Richardson, S.
Fields, K. The Odysseus Manuscripts.
    T. Diggory, 560:Summer82-159
    W.S. Di Piero, 598(SoR):Spring83-456
Fiennes, C. The Journeys of Celia Fiennes.
    A.J.G.H., 617(TLS):22Apr83-415
Fiering, N. Jonathan Edwards's Moral
    Thought and Its British Context.
    N.S. Grabo, 27(AL):Dec82-608
    P.F. Gura, 639(VQR):Summer82-526
    C.A. Holbrook, 656(WMQ):Oct82-689
    D. Weber, 432(NEQ):Jun82-285
Fiering, N. Moral Philosophy at Seven-
    teenth-Century Harvard.
    J.L. Blau, 619:Spring82-191
    P.F. Gura, 639(VQR):Summer82-526
    A. MacIntyre, 656(WMQ):Oct82-687
    V.C. Punzo, 377:Jul82-117
    J. Schwartz, 568(SCN):Spring-Summer82-
    25
    D. Weber, 432(NEQ):Jun82-285
Fierstein, F. Manhattan Carnival.
    F. Turner, 461:Spring-Summer82-93
Fifield, W. In Search of Genius.
    G.A. De Candido, 441:13Feb83-16
Figes, E. Light.
    J.C. Oates, 441:16Oct83-11
    K.C. O'Brien, 362:10Nov83-30
    L. Taylor, 617(TLS):26Aug83-898
    442(NY):7Nov83-182
Figes, E. Sex and Subterfuge.
    K. Sutherland, 148:Autumn82-90
Figes, E. Waking.*
    P. Craig, 617(TLS):18Nov83-1294
Filion, P. Juré craché.
    J.J. Herlan, 207(FR):Mar83-664
Filippova, B.A. - see Leont'ev, K.

Fill, A. Wortdurchsichtigkeit im Eng-
    lischen.*
    H. Sauer, 38:Band100Heft3/4-467
Filler, L. - see Hardy, I.
Fillion, J. Il est bien court, le temps
    des cerises.
    P. Collet, 102(CanL):Summer82-122
    M. Gaulin, 207(FR):Dec82-336
Filliozat, P., ed and trans. Le Mahāb-
    hāṣya de Patañjali, avec le Pradīpa de
    Kaiyaṭa et l'Uddyota de Nāgeśa.*
    R. Rocher, 318(JAOS):Oct-Dec81-468
"Film Review Annual, 1981." (J.S. Ozer,
    ed)
    M. Vaughan, 18:Mar83-73
Finch, P. God, Guts, and Guns.
    J.B., 231:May83-92
Finch, R. The Primal Place.
    A. Wilkinson, 441:31Jul83-8
Finch, R. Variations and Theme.
    S. Gingell-Beckmann, 168(ECW):Spring82-
    157
    M. Thorpe, 102(CanL):Winter81-144
Finder, J. Red Carpet.
    J.K. Galbraith, 441:17Jul83-7
"The Findern Manuscript (C.U.L. MS Ff. 1.
    6)."
    M. Seymour, 354:Dec82-428
Findlater, R., ed. At the Royal Court.
    D.R., 214:Vol 10No38-144
Findlay, J.N. Kant and the Transcendental
    Object.*
    D.P.L., 185:Oct82-208
    R. Meerbote, 319:Oct82-439
    C.M.S., 543:Mar82-602
    W.H. Walsh, 483:Jul82-415
Findley, C.V. Bureaucratic Reform in the
    Ottoman Empire.
    D.M. Lang, 161(DUJ):Dec81-125
Findley, T. Famous Last Words.*
    A.S. Brennan, 198:Jul82-82
    K. Garebian, 526:Summer82-93
    J.F. Hulcoop, 102(CanL):Autumn82-117
    G. Woodcock, 529(QQ):Winter82-744
    42(AR):Fall82-489
Fine, E.S. Legacy of Night.
    T. Ziolkowski, 569(SR):Fall82-592
Finegan, E. Attitudes Toward English
    Usage.
    W.W. Douglas, 128(CE):Jan82-72
Finegold, L. Linguadex: Key-Word Index to
    Spoken Russian.*
    R. Hagglund, 574(SEEJ):Summer82-257
Fingard, J. Jack in Port.
    D.F. Chard, 150(DR):Winter82/83-716
Fingleton, D. Kiri Te Kanawa.
    L. Schwarzbaum, 441:29May83-12
Fink, S.R. Aspects of a Pedagogical
    Grammar.
    R. Emons, 38:Band100Heft3/4-451
Finkel, D. What Manner of Beast.*
    R.B. Shaw, 491:Dec82-170
    639(VQR):Autumn82-133
Finkelman, P. An Imperfect Union.*
    J.V. Matthews, 106:Winter82-333
Finkelstein, B., ed. Regulated Children/
    Liberated Children.
    J. Abbott, 106:Spring82-87
Finlay, R. Politics in Renaissance Venice.
    P.F. Grendler, 551(RenQ):Winter81-596
Finlayson, C.P. Clement Litill and His
    Library.
    T.H. Howard-Hill, 588(SSL):Vol 17-287

Finley, G. Landscapes of Memory.*
  K. Kroeber, 571(ScLJ):Spring82-13
Finley, G. Turner and George the Fourth
in Edinburgh, 1822.
  E. Joll, 39:Jul82-65
Finley, G.E. George Heriot.
  D.W. Rozniatowski, 529(QQ):Summer82-405
Finley, M.I. Economy and Society in Ancient Greece.* (B.D. Shaw and R.P. Saller, eds)
  J. Briscoe, 123:Vol32No2-287
  T.E.J. Wiedemann, 437:Summer82-298
Finley, M.I., ed. The Legacy of Greece.*
  R.W., 555:Vol56fasc1-143
Finley, M.I. Mythe, mémoire, histoire.
  P. Pellegrin, 542:Jul-Sep82-529
Finley, M.I. Politics in the Ancient World.
  O. Murray, 617(TLS):26Aug83-895
  A. Ryan, 362:28Jul83-24
Finn, T. Three Men (not) in a Boat.
  C. Hawtree, 617(TLS):27May83-553
Finney, J. Forgotten News.
  P-L. Adams, 61:May83-104
Finnigan, J. This Series Has Been Discontinued.*
  E. Thompson, 102(CanL):Summer82-133
  B. Whiteman, 198:Apr82-112
Finnis, J.M. Natural Law and Natural Rights.*
  T.R., 543:Mar82-604
  D.A.J. Richards, 185:Oct82-169
Finocchiaro, M.A. Galileo and the Art of Reasoning.
  F.D. Anderson, 480(P&R):Spring82-136
  C. Perelman, 480(P&R):Spring82-134
  J.M.Q., 543:Dec81-385
  W.A. Wallace, 319:Jul82-307
Fioravanti, M. Giuristi e Costituzione Politica nell'Ottocento Tedesco.
  R. Brandt, 489(PJGG):Band89Heft2-441
Fiore, P.A. Milton and Augustine.
  M.A. Mikolajczak, 568(SCN):Fall82-63
Fiorenza, E.S. In Memory of Her.
  P. Trible, 441:1May83-28
Fiorina, M.P. Retrospective Voting in American National Elections.
  E.M.U., 185:Oct82-205
"Fire Insurance Maps in the Library of Congress."
  J.E. Fraser, 14:Winter82-62
"Firebird I."
  L. Jones, 364:Jun82-102
Firestone, O.J. The Other A.Y. Jackson.
  R. Stacey, 627(UTQ):Summer82-492
First, R. and A. Scott. Olive Schreiner.*
  M. McQuade, 114(ChiR):Winter83-134
Fischer, F. Politics, Values, and Public Policy.
  C.W. Anderson, 185:Apr83-625
Fischer, H. Citoyens sculpteurs.
  F. Treuttel, 46:Feb82-75
Fischer, H. Erzählgut der Gegenwart.*
  O. Reichmann, 685(ZDL):1/1982-95
Fischer, H. L'Histoire de l'art est terminée.
  B. Scott, 39:Aug82-126
  F. Treuttel, 46:Feb82-75
Fischer, J.I. On Swift's Poetry.*
  W. Kinsley, 173(ECS):Summer82-442
Fischer, K-D. Pelagonii Ars Veterinaria.
  J.N. Adams, 123:Vol32No2-180

Fischer, L., ed. Zeitgenosse Büchner.
  D.G. Richards, 221(GQ):May82-425
Fischer, N., L. Pastouras and N. Georgopoulos, eds. Continuity and Change in Marxism.
  J. Gray, 617(TLS):30Dec83-1459
Fischer, T. Seleukiden und Makkabäer.
  A. Momigliano, 122:Jul82-262
Fischer, V. and L. Salamo, with M.J. Jones - see Twain, M.
Fischer, W. Die andere Tradition.
  R. Elvin, 46:Dec82-72
Fischer-Galati, S., ed. Eastern Europe in the 1980s.*
  H. Hanak, 575(SEER):Jul82-476
Fish, L.M. The Folklore of the Coal Miners of the Northeast of England.
  R.S. McCarl, 650(WF):Apr82-153
Fish, S. Is There a Text in This Class?*
  P. Barry, 175:Spring82-79
  R.P. Bilan, 627(UTQ):Fall81-102
  J.M. Ellis, 478:Oct82-207
  C. Gallagher, 153:Winter82-40
  D.H. Hirsch, 569(SR):Winter82-119
  S. Raval, 50(ArQ):Summer82-186
  S. Rendall, 153:Winter82-49
  A. Rosmarin, 152(UDQ):Spring81-100
  J.J. Sosnoski, 395(MFS):Winter81/82-753
  M. Steig, 128(CE):Feb82-182
  R. Young, 506(PSt):Dec82-353
  A.C. Yu, 405(MP):Aug82-113
Fish, S. The Living Temple.*
  A.J. Smith, 677(YES):Vol 12-266
Fishbane, M. Text and Texture.*
  J.C. Exum, 318(JAOS):Oct-Dec81-447
Fishburn, A. Batsford Book of Home Furnishings.
  R.H. Hoffman, 614:Spring83-15
Fishburn, E. The Portrayal of Immigration in Nineteenth Century Argentine Fiction (1845-1902).
  R. González Echevarría, 263(RIB):Vol32No3/4-373
Fisher, B. Joyce Cary.*
  E. Christian, 594:Fall82-301
  B. Murray, 395(MFS):Summer81-330
Fisher, H. UHFO.
  V. Trueblood, 271:Spring82-132
Fisher, J., ed. Thorburn's Birds. (rev by J. Parslow)
  R. O'Hanlon, 617(TLS):6May83-466
Fisher, L.H. A Literary Gazeteer of England.
  D. Davie, 569(SR):Winter82-79
Fisher, M.F.K. As They Were.*
  42(AR):Fall82-488
Fisher, M.F.K. Sister Age.
  F. Taliaferro, 441:29May83-10
Fisher, R. and H. Johnston, eds. Captain James Cook and His Times.*
  W.M. Fowler, Jr., 173(ECS):Summer82-482
  C. Harris, 656(WMQ):Jul82-554
Fisher, R.H. The Voyage of Semen Dezhnev in 1648.
  J.B. Gibson, 104(CASS):Fall-Winter82-541
  B. Haney, 550(RusR):Oct82-476
Fisher, W.A. The Soviet Marriage Market.
  D.E. Powell, 550(RusR):Oct82-506

Fleischmann, F., ed. American Novelists
Revisited.
   B.L. Clark, 454:Spring83-265
Fleisher, D. and D.M. Freedman. Death of
an American.
   M. Kramer, 441:11Dec83-9
Fleishman, A. Figures of Autobiography.
   A.O.J. Cockshut, 617(TLS):5Aug83-841
Fleishman, L. Boris Pasternak v dvadt-
satye gody.
   J.D. Clayton, 104(CASS):Fall-Winter82-
   529
   V. Erlich, 550(RusR):Jul82-355
   D.L. Plank, 574(SEEJ):Summer82-246
Fleisser, M. Avant-garde.
   R. Micha, 98:Apr82-369
Fleming, C.A. George Edward Lodge, Unpub-
lished Bird Paintings.
   R. O'Hanlon, 617(TLS):16Dec83-1414
Fleming, G. Hitler und die Endlösung.
   G.A. Craig, 453(NYRB):21Jul83-4
   H. Trevor-Roper, 617(TLS):28Jan83-75
Fleming, G.H. The Unforgettable Season.
   639(VQR):Winter82-27
Fleming, P. One's Company.
   K.M., 617(TLS):22Apr83-415
Fleming, R. and E., eds. Sinclair Lewis.
   R.S., 189(EA):Oct-Dec82-496
Fleming, R.E. Charles F. Lummis.
   A.R. Huseboe, 649(WAL):Summer82-176
Flemming, D.N. and R.G. Mowry. Sobre
héroes y rumbos.
   E. Spinelli, 399(MLJ):Winter82-443
Flemming, L.A. Another Lonely Voice.*
   R.K. Barz, 259(IIJ):Oct82-325
Fletcher, A. Selected Political Writings
and Speeches. (D. Daiches, ed)
   J.A. Downie, 677(YES):Jul82-272
   A.H. MacLaine, 541(RES):Feb82-73
Fletcher, C. The Man from the Cave.
   S. Brown, 569(SR):Spring82-250
Fletcher, H.G., ed. A Miscellany for Bib-
liophiles.
   J. Porter, 503:Autumn82-161
Fletcher, I., ed. Decadence and the
1890's.
   S. Bassett, 637(VS):Summer82-497
Fletcher, I. and J. Lucas - see Fraser,
G.S.
Fletcher, J. Humanhood.
   P. Carrive, 192(EP):Oct-Dec81-481
Fletcher, J. Novel and Reader.
   R. Moss, 402(MLR):Jan82-142
Fletcher, M.D. - see Carver, A.J.
Fletcher, P. Roll Over Rock.
   D. Young, 607:Jun82-35
Fletcher, P. and M. Garman, eds. Language
Acquisition.*
   D. Keller-Cohen, 355(LSoc):Dec82-453
Fletcher, W.C. Soviet Believers
   D.V. Pospielovsky, 550(RusR):Oct82-508
Fleuret, C. Rousseau et Montaigne.
   J-L. Lecercle, 535(RHL):Jan-Feb82-124
Flew, A. The Politics of Procrustes.*
   D. Browne, 63:Dec82-392
   G. Graham, 479(PhQ):Apr82-187
   P. Widulski, 258:Jun82-209
Flew, A. A Rational Animal and Other Phil-
osophical Essays on the Nature of Man.
   S. Richmond, 488:Dec82-448
Flexner, S.B. Listening to America.
   W. Cole, 441:16Jan83-14

Fliegelman, J. Prodigals and Pilgrims.*
   J.J. Ellis, 165(EAL):Winter82/83-249
   G.S. Wood, 453(NYRB):3Feb83-16
Flint, R. Resuming Green.
   D. Bromwich, 441:9Oct83-12
Flippo, C. Your Cheatin' Heart.*
   J.W. Lee, 577(SHR):Spring82-182
   M.K. Smith, 498:Vol8No1-62
Floeck, W. Die Literaturästhetik des
französischen Barock.*
   W. Leiner, 475:Vol9No17-765
   U. Schulz-Buschhaus, 72:Band218Heft2-
   469
Flood, C.B. Lee: The Last Years.
   J.M. Cox, 676(YR):Spring83-420
   R.N. Current, 9(AlaR):Jul82-233
Flood, J. Archaeology of the Dreamtime.
   B.A.L. Cranstone, 617(TLS):7Oct83-1098
Flood, J.A. Barristers' Clerks.
   M. Cain, 617(TLS):25Nov83-1304
Flook, M. Reckless Wedding.
   A. Williamson, 441:1May83-15
Flora, J.M. Hemingway's Nick Adams.
   S. Pinsker, 395(MFS):Winter82/83-673
Flore, J. Comptes amoureux. (G-A.
Pérouse and others, eds)
   P. Chilton, 402(MLR):Jul82-718
"Florence and Venice." (Vol 1)
   A. Molho, 551(RenQ):Spring82-72
Flores, E. Le scoperte di Poggio e il
testo di Lucrezio.
   E.J. Kenney, 313:Vol72-220
Flórez, L. Apuntes de español.
   S.N. Dworkin, 545(RPh):Nov81-431
Flory, W.S. Ezra Pound and "The Cantos."*
   S.J. Adams, 106:Fall82-245
   M. Alexander, 179(ES):Dec82-567
   C. Froula, 405(MP):Aug82-103
   T. Grieve, 648(WCR):Jun82-52
   W. Harmon, 577(SHR):Winter82-83
   P. Makin, 402(MLR):Apr82-431
   L. Surette, 408:Jun82-60
Floud, J. and W. Young. Dangerousness and
Criminal Justice.
   R.B.C., 185:Oct82-213
Flower, J.E., ed. France Today. (4th ed)
   N. Aronson, 399(MLJ):Autumn82-333
   S. Smith, 207(FR):Dec82-359
Flower, R. The Palace.
   D. Gillard, 362:20Jan83-26
Floyd, V., ed. Eugene O'Neill.
   G. Anthony, 106:Fall82-231
Floyd, V. - see O'Neill, E.
Fluchère, H. - see Shakespeare, W.
Flukinger, R., L. Schaaf and S. Meacham.
Paul Martin.
   B. Jay, 637(VS):Summer82-515
Flutre, L-F. Du Moyen Picard au picard
moderne.
   N.L. Corbett, 545(RPh):Nov81-432
   J. Kramer, 547(RF):Band93Heft3/4-424
Flynn, C.H. Samuel Richardson.
   G.S. Rousseau, 617(TLS):7Jan83-20
Flynn, D. Murder Isn't Enough.
   N. Callendar, 441:13Nov83-34
Flynt, J.W. Dixie's Forgotten People.*
   W.B. McCarthy, 292(JAF):Apr-Jun82-230
Flynt, J.W. and D.S. Southern Poor Whites.
   M.A. McLaurin, 9(AlaR):Oct82-283
Fo, D. and F. Rame. Female Parts.*
   R. Shade, 214:Vol 10No38-137

Fodor, J. The Modularity of Mind.
    M. Piattelli-Palmarini, 617(TLS):
    2Dec83-1357
Fodor, J.A. Representations.*
    J. Heil, 518:Oct82-229
    J.S., 185:Jan83-417
Fog, D. Grieg-Katalog.
    J.H., 412:Feb81-67
    P.W. Jones, 410(M&L):Jul/Oct82-310
Fogel, D.M. Henry James and the Structure
    of the Romantic Imagination.*
    R.A. Hocks, 183(ESQ):Vol28No4-261
    R. Lehan, 445(NCF):Jun82-127
    J. Rambeau, 395(MFS):Winter82/83-662
    R.B. Yeazell, 445(NCF):Mar83-611
    295(JML):Dec82-470
Fok Tou-hui. An-hui "San-shih wei-shih
    shih."
    J.W. de Jong, 259(IIJ):Oct82-324
Foladare, J. Boswell's Paoli.*
    J.C. Beasley, 402(MLR):Jul82-701
    W.C. Dowling, 173(ECS):Fall81-115
Folejewski, Z. Futurism and its Place in
    the Development of Modern Poetry.*
    U. Weisstein, 149(CLS):Winter82-479
Foley, J.A. Theoretical Morphology of the
    French Verb.*
    J. Durand, 297(JL):Sep82-474
Foley, J.M., ed. Oral Traditional Litera-
    ture.
    W. Parks, 104(CASS):Fall-Winter82-517
    Z.D. Zimmerman, 574(SEEJ):Fall82-363
Foley, M. The Go Situation.*
    I. McMillan, 493:Jun82-71
Fölkel, F. and C.L. Cergoly. Trieste
    Provincia Imperiale.
    N. Stone, 617(TLS):12Aug83-862
Folkenflik, R., ed. The English Hero,
    1660-1800.
    R. Halsband, 617(TLS):4Mar83-217
Follain, J. Transparence of the World.
    (W.S. Merwin, ed and trans) D'Après
    Tout. A World Rich in Anniversaries.
    Canisy.
    D. Young, 199:Spring83-60
Follett, K. On Wings of Eagles.
    H. Goodman, 441:23Oct83-20
Folmar, J.K. - see Williams, J.M.
Folsom, J.K., ed. The Western.
    M. Gilliland, 106:Spring82-75
Fónagy, I. La Métaphore en phonétique.*
    L. Guierre, 189(EA):Jul-Sep82-324
Fónagy, I. and P.R. Léon, eds. L'accent
    en français contemporain.*
    A. Marchal, 320(CJL):Spring82-89
Fondane, B. Le faux traité d'esthétique.*
    C. Thieck, 98:Nov82-975
Fondane, B. Rencontres avec Léon Chestov.
    T. Cordellier, 450(NRF):Dec82-99
Foner, P.S. and R.L. Lewis, eds. The
    Black Worker from 1900 to 1919.
    E.F. Haas, 9(AlaR):Jan82-71
Fong, W., ed. The Great Bronze Age of
    China.*
    M. Medley, 39:Sep82-197
Fontaine, J. Études sur la poésie latine
    tardive d'Ausone à Prudence.
    R. Braun, 555:Vol56fasc2-354
Fontaine, J. L'art préroman hispanique.
    (Vol 2)
    O.K. Werckmeister, 589:Jul82-604

Fontaine, J. Naissance de la poésie dans
    l'Occident chrétien.
    P. Flobert, 555:Vol56fasc2-355
Fontana, B.L. Of Earth and Little Rain.
    E.H. Spicer, 50(ArQ):Autumn82-264
Fontana, V. and P. Morachiello, eds. Vit-
    ruvio e Raffaello.
    J.J. Rasch, 43:Band12Heft2-184
Fontanella de Weinberg, M.B. La asimila-
    ción lingüística de los immigrantes.
    Dinámica social de un cambio lingüís-
    tico.
    F.L. Tarallo, 355(LSoc):Dec82-446
Fontenay, C.L. Estes Kefauver.
    M.R. Winchell, 585(SoQ):Spring82-95
de Fontenay, É. Diderot ou le matérial-
    isme enchanté.*
    P. Saint-Amand, 400(MLN):May82-1002
    S. Tomaselli, 83:Autumn82-273
Fontenrose, J. The Delphic Oracle.*
    M. Herzfeld, 567:Vol38No1/2-169
    N. Robertson, 487:Winter82-358
Fontenrose, J. Steinbeck's Unhappy Valley.
    S.E. Marovitz, 649(WAL):Summer82-167
Foot, D. Harold Gimblett.
    A.L. Le Quesne, 617(TLS):4Mar83-207
Foot, P. Red Shelley.*
    P. Story, 340(KSJ):Vol31-218
Foot, P. Virtues and Vices and Other
    Essays in Moral Philosophy.
    S.B. Cunningham, 154:Mar82-133
Foraboschi, D. Papiri della Università
    degli Studi di Milano VII.
    E.G. Turner, 123:Vol132No2-298
Forbes, J. Stalin's Holidays.*
    G. Catalano, 381:Oct81-349
Forcadel, É. Oeuvres poétiques.* (F.
    Joukovsky, ed)
    I.D. McFarlane, 208(FS):Apr82-196
Forché, C. The Country Between Us.*
    J.F. Cotter, 249(HudR):Autumn82-471
    S. Doubiago, 29:Jan/Feb83-35
    W. Logan, 617(TLS):10Jun83-614
    G.E. Murray, 385(MQR):Fall83-643
    P. Stitt, 219(GaR):Winter82-911
    C. Wright, 271:Winter82-130
    639(VQR):Autumn82-133
Forché, C. El Salvador. (H. Mattison, S.
    Meiselas and F. Rubenstein, eds)
    A. Grundberg, 441:4Dec83-76
    R. Stone, 231:Dec83-71
Forcione, A.K. Cervantes and the Humanist
    Vision.
    A.J. Close, 617(TLS):24Jun83-662
Ford, B., ed. Medieval Literature.
    J.J.A., 148:Autumn82-92
Ford, C. The Womb Rattles Its Pod.
    G. Chase, 526:Autumn82-80
Ford, C. and B. Harrison. A Hundred Years
    Ago.
    442(NY):23May83-123
Ford, D. The Unquiet Man.
    K. Brownlow, 617(TLS):25Feb83-178
Ford, E. Missed Connections.
    J.B., 231:Mar83-76
    F. Prose, 441:24Apr83-12
Ford, F.M. The English Novel.
    A. Mars-Jones, 617(TLS):30Sep83-1058
Ford, F.M. The Rash Act.*
    A. Fothergill, 617(TLS):30Sep83-1059
Ford, J. The Broken Heart.* (T.J.B.
    Spencer, ed)
    M.L. Kessel, 568(SCN):Winter82-74

Ford, P.J. George Buchanan.
  J.B. Trapp, 617(TLS):15Jul83-755
Ford, T.W. A.B. Guthrie, Jr.
  J. Allred, 651(WHR):Spring82-88
  J.D. Nesbitt, 649(WAL):Winter83-365
"Foreign Versions of English Names and
  Foreign Equivalents of United States
  Military and Civilian Titles."*
  J.A., 35(AS):Fall82-223
Foreman, L. Bax.
  D. Puffett, 617(TLS):29Jul83-810
Foreman, L. Arthur Bliss.
  P.W. Jones, 410(M&L):Jan/Apr82-125
Foreman, L., ed. The Percy Grainger Com-
  panion.*
  T.H.W.A., 412:Aug-Nov81-291
  A. Pople, 410(M&L):Jul/Oct82-322
Foreman, L. - see Bax, A.
Forest, A. Essai sur les formes du lien
  spirituel.
  M. Adam, 542:Oct-Dec82-670
Forest, J. Thomas Merton.
  M.W. Higgins, 106:Spring82-127
Forestier, G. Le Théâtre dans le théâtre
  sur la scène française du XVIIe siècle.
  H.T. Barnwell, 402(MLR):Oct82-953
  W.O. Goode, 207(FR):May83-942
Forestier, L., ed. Arthur Rimbaud, 4.
  A. Guyaux, 535(RHL):Sep-Dec82-939
Forge, A. Balinese Traditional Paintings.*
  J.S. Lansing, 293(JASt):May82-630
Forge, S. Victorian Splendour.
  S. Dillon-Gibbons, 324:Feb83-160
Forkner, B., ed. Modern Irish Short
  Stories.*
  P. Craig, 617(TLS):18Nov83-1294
  J.A. Glusman, 152(UDQ):Summer81-116
  J. Kilroy, 569(SR):Winter82-89
Forkner, B. and P. Samway, eds. Stories
  of the Modern South.
  L. Jones, 364:Jul82-91
Fornaro, P. Flavio Giuseppe, Tacito e
  L'Impero.
  M.D. Goodman, 123:Vol32No1-105
Forni, L. The Dove and the Bear.
  P. Nichols, 617(TLS):29Jul83-803
Forrest, K. The Paintings of Frederick
  Nicholas Loveroff.
  D. Farr, 529(QQ):Winter82-856
Forrest-Thomson, V. Poetic Artifice.
  B. McHale, 494:Winter82-141
  M. McKie, 175:Summer82-162
Forrester, D.B. Caste and Christianity.
  P.G. Hiebert, 293(JASt):Aug82-865
Forrester, M. Moral Language.
  N.F., 185:Apr83-627
Forrester, T., ed. The Microelectronic
  Revolution.
  C.A.T. Salama, 529(QQ):Spring82-231
Forrester, V. Van Gogh ou l'enterrement
  dans les blés.
  D. Gascoyne, 617(TLS):9Dec83-1386
Forsgren, K-Å. Wortdefinition und Feld-
  struktur.
  U. Schröter, 682(ZPSK):Band34Heft2-228
Forsgren, M. La place de l'adjectif
  épithète en français contemporain.
  K.E.M. George, 208(FS):Jan82-118
Forssman, B. - see Sommer, F.
Forssman, B. - see Wackernagel, J.

Forssman, E. Karl Friedrich Schinkel:
  Bauwerke und Baugedanken.
  R. Elvin, 46:Jan82-78
  H. Kauffmann, 683:Band45Heft4-431
Forster, E.M. Arctic Summer and Other Fic-
  tion.* (E. Heine and O. Stallybrass,
  eds)
  E. Hanquart, 189(EA):Apr-Jun82-165
Forster, E.M. A Passage to India.* The
  Manuscripts of "A Passage to India."*
  (O. Stallybrass, ed of both)
  M. Bowen, 405(MP):Aug82-61
Forster, E.M. Selected Letters of E.M.
  Forster. (Vol 1) (M. Lago and P.N.
  Furbank, eds)
  A. Hollinghurst, 617(TLS):18Nov83-1267
  S. Spender, 362:3Nov83-25
Forster, M.H. Historia de la poesía his-
  panoamericana.
  M. Agosin, 263(RIB):Vol32No2-209
Forster, P.G. The Esperanto Movement.
  F. Nuessel, 350:Sep83-706
Forster, R. Merchants, Landlords, Magis-
  trates.
  H.C. Payne, 173(ECS):Summer83-459
Forsyth, K. "Ariadne Auf Naxos" by Hugo
  von Hofmannsthal and Richard Strauss.
  R. Anderson, 415:Sep82-617
  M. Tanner, 617(TLS):11Mar83-243
Forsyth, P.Y. Atlantis.*
  J.V. Luce, 487:Summer82-174
Fortassier, R. - see Huysmans, J-K.
Fortescue, W. Alphonse de Lamartine.
  N. Hampson, 617(TLS):20May83-503
Forti, F. Lo stile della meditazione.
  A. Cottignoli, 228(GSLI):Vol 159
  fasc508-618
Fortier, A. Le Texte et la Scène.*
  L.E. Doucette, 627(UTQ):Summer82-481
  E.F. Nardocchio, 108:Spring82-209
Fortier, P.A. Structures et communication
  dans "La Jalousie" d'Alain Robbe-Grillet.
  B. Stoltzfus, 207(FR):Mar83-646
Fortin, E.L. Dissidence et philosophie au
  moyen âge.*
  J.M. Ferrante, 551(RenQ):Winter82-595
Fortis, P-N. Lamennais et 1848.
  J-R. Derré, 535(RHL):Jul-Aug82-670
Fortune, N. - see Westrup, J.A.
Fosburgh, L. Old Money.
  C. See, 441:2Oct83-14
Foss, C. Ephesus after Antiquity.
  S. Hill, 303(JoHS):Vol 102-296
Fossat, J-L. Dictionaire occitan-français
  de l'agriculture.
  J-P. Chambon, 553(RLiR):Jun-Dec82-452
Fossey, D. Gorillas in the Mist.
  K. Bouton, 441:4Sep83-2
Foster, D. Moonlite.
  P. Pierce, 381:Dec81-522
Foster, D.W. Mexican Literature.
  D. Parle, 263(RIB):Vol32No2-210
Foster, D.W. Studies in the Contemporary
  Spanish-American Short Story.*
  J. Gledson, 86(BHS):Oct82-350
  G. Guinness, 395(MFS):Summer81-419
Foster, D.W. and R. Reis, comps. A Dic-
  tionary of Contemporary Brazilian
  Authors.
  A.E. Severino, 263(RIB):Vol32No3/4-374
Foster, F.S. Witnessing Slavery.*
  L. Buell, 183(ESQ):Vol28No1-63

Fragnito, G. Memoria individuale e cos-
truzione biografica.
  A. Santosuosso, 551(RenQ):Autumn81-410
Fraisse, J-C. L'oeuvre de Spinoza.*
  J. Rouveyrol, 192(EP):Jan-Mar81-91
Fraisse, J-C. - see Aristotle
Fraisse, S., ed. Charles Péguy, I.
  A. Roche, 535(RHL):Sep-Dec82-950
Frake, C.O. Language and Cultural Descrip-
tion. (A.S. Dil, comp)
  A.A. Yengoyan, 293(JASt):Nov81-198
Frame, D.M. and M.B. McKinley, eds. Colum-
bia Montaigne Conference Papers.
  C. Clark, 208(FS):Oct82-463
Frame, J. To the Is-Land.*
  A. Chisholm, 617(TLS):8Jul83-737
  442(NY):24Jan83-108
Frampton, K. Modern Architecture.*
  A.L. Huxtable, 453(NYRB):22Dec83-55
  S. Polyzoides, 45:Jan82-47
Francard, M. Le parler de Tenneville.
  Y-C. Morin, 553(RLiR):Jul-Dec82-485
France, P. Poets of Modern Russia.
  D. McDuff, 617(TLS):1Jul83-703
France, P. - see Williams, D.
"La France et la question juive 1940-1944."
  J. Paulhan, 207(FR):Dec82-363
Franciosi, G. Clan gentilizio e strutture
monogamiche.
  J-C. Richard, 555:Vol56fasc1-173
Francis, C. and F. Gontier - see Proust, M.
Francis, D. Banker.*
  P-L. Adams, 61:May83-105
  E. Hunter, 441:27Mar83-15
  M. Laski, 362:20Jan83-23
  A. Ross, 364:Feb83-6
  442(NY):11Apr83-138
Francis, D. The Danger.
  T.J. Binyon, 617(TLS):11Nov83-1255
Francis, R.G. The Utah Photographs of
George Edward Anderson.
  R.C. Poulsen, 292(JAF):Jan-Mar82-100
Francisco, R.A., B.A. Laird and R.D. Laird,
eds. Agricultural Policies in the USSR
and Eastern Europe.
  A.W. Wright, 550(RusR):Apr82-226
Franck, D. Chair et corps.
  P. Guenancia, 98:Dec82-1039
Franck, F., ed. The Buddha Eye.
  R.A.F. Thurman, 469:Vol8No1-120
Franck, F. The Supreme Koan.
  J.C. Rochelle, 469:Vol8No2-116
Franck, T.M., ed. The Tethered Presidency.
  639(VQR):Winter82-14
Francke, L.B. Growing Up Divorced.
  D. Goldstine, 441:24Jul83-9
Francoeur, L. Neons in the Night.
  D. O'Rourke, 102(CanL):Autumn82-149
François, F., ed. Linguistique.
  H.P. Hagiwara, 399(MLJ):Spring82-71
François, J. Les Amantes.
  M. Le Clézio, 207(FR):Feb83-507
François, J. Les Bonheurs.
  N. Shaw, 207(FR):Mar83-665
François, J. Joue-nous "España."
  N. Shaw, 207(FR):Feb83-508
Francovich, G. Ensayos Pascalianos.
  P. Rivas, 535(RHL):Sep-Dec82-881
Franey, P. More 60-Minute Gourmet.
  W. and C. Cowen, 639(VQR):Autumn82-140
Frank, E.E. Literary Architecture.*
  J. Bump, 131(CL):Winter82-88
  B. Richards, 184(EIC):Jul82-283

Frank, J. Cromwell's Press Agent.
  L. Miller, 391:Mar82-23
Frank, J-M. Le Christ est du matin.
  P. Jaccottet, 450(NRF):Mar82-114
Franke, R. London und Prag.
  F.L. Carsten, 575(SEER):Jan82-136
Franke, R.O. Kleine Schriften. (O. von
Hinüber, ed)
  J.W. de Jong, 259(IIJ):Jan80-73
  L. Sternbach, 318(JAOS):Oct-Dec81-486
Frankel, J. Prophecy and Politics.*
  S. Beller, 575(SEER):Jul82-462
  N.M. Naimark, 550(RusR):Jul82-326
  S.J. Zipperstein, 287:Aug/Sep82-21
Frankena, W.K. Thinking About Morality.
  S.L. Darwall, 482(PhR):Jul82-454
Franklin, B. The Autobiography of Benja-
min Franklin.* (J.A.L. Lemay and P.M.
Zall, eds)
  P. Davison, 354:Jun82-200
Franklin, B. 5th and D. Schneider. Anaïs
Nin.
  E.J. Hinz, 106:Winter82-373
  M. Leaf, 447(N&Q):Oct81-467
  L. Waldeland, 395(MFS):Winter81/82-725
Franklin, C. Fond of Printing.
  D. Chambers, 503:Winter82-211
Franklin, H.B. Robert A. Heinlein.
  N. Khouri, 106:Winter82-407
  S. Stone-Blackburn, 529(QQ):Spring82-
  201
Franklin, J.L., Jr. Pompeii.
  B. Levick, 123:Vol132No1-69
Franklin, M. On Dearborn Street.
  D. Kirby, 71(ALS):May82-409
Franklin, P.R. - see Bauer-Lechner, N.
Franklin, R.W. - see Dickinson, E.
Franklin, U. The Rhetoric of Valéry's
Prose "Aubades."*
  N. Celeyrette-Pietri, 535(RHL):Mar-
  Apr82-311
Franklin, V.P. The Education of Black
Philadelphia.
  J. Abbott, 106:Spring82-87
Franks, C.S. Beyond The Well of Loneli-
ness.
  M. Baker, 617(TLS):1Jul83-710
Franks, F. Polywater.
  J.D. McCowan, 529(QQ):Winter82-913
Franolić, B. Les mots d'emprunt Français
en Croate.
  A. de Vincenz, 260(IF):Band86-359
Franolić, B. A Short History of Literary
Croatian.*
  G. Thomas, 402(MLR):Apr82-510
Frantzen, A.J. The Literature of Penance
in Anglo-Saxon England.
  P. Godman, 617(TLS):29Apr83-442
Franz, N. Groteske Strukturen in der
Prosa Zamjatins.
  J.T. Baer, 574(SEEJ):Spring82-101
  C.J. Barnes, 575(SEER):Apr82-284
Fraser, D. Alanbrooke.*
  639(VQR):Summer82-86
Fraser, D. And We Shall Shock Them.
  M. Carver, 617(TLS):10Jun83-590
Fraser, D. August 1988.
  C. Greenland, 617(TLS):2Sep83-940
Fraser, D. - see Watt, C.
Fraser, G.M. Mr. American.
  R. Schmudde, 649(WAL):Summer82-190
Fraser, G.M. The Pyrates.
  D. Profumo, 617(TLS):2Dec83-1345

Fraser, G.S. Poems of G.S. Fraser. (I.
Fletcher and J. Lucas, eds)
  B. Bergonzi, 148:Spring82-19
  L. Sail, 565:Vol23No4-73
Fraser, G.S. A Stranger and Afraid.
  A. Crook, 362:22Sep83-23
  J.A. Smith, 617(TLS):5Aug83-839
Fraser, J. America and the Pattern of
Chivalry.
  R. Lehan, 617(TLS):15Jul83-750
Fraser, J.T. The Genesis and Evolution of
Time.
  D. Finkelstein, 469:Vol8No3-102
Fraser, M.C. A Diplomat's Wife in Japan.*
(H. Cortazzi, ed)
  C. Blacker, 617(TLS):23Sep83-1029
  M. Cooper, 407(MN):Winter82-548
Fraser, R. A Mingled Yarn.*
  J.B. Gilbert, 385(MQR):Winter83-151
  M.K. Spears, 249(HudR):Autumn82-453
  R.E. Spiller, 27(AL):Oct82-462
  295(JML):Dec82-412
Frassanito, W.A. Grant and Lee.
  442(NY):5Sep83-114
Frassica, P. and A. Carrara. Per modo di
dire.*
  F.A. Bassanese, 276:Autumn82-193
Frassinetti, P. and L. Di Salvo, eds and
trans. Satire.
  J. André, 555:Vol55fasc2-375
Frayling, C. Spaghetti Westerns.*
  E. Brater, 651(WHR):Winter82-376
Frayn, J.M. Subsistence Farming in Roman
Italy.
  G. Barker, 313:Vol72-192
Frazer, D. Reptiles and Amphibians in
Britain.
  P. Morris, 617(TLS):22Jul83-786
Fréchet, A. John Galsworthy.
  J. Batchelor, 617(TLS):20May83-513
  W.W. Robson, 189(EA):Jan-Mar82-93
Frede, H.J., ed. Vetus Latina. (fasc 25)
  M-J. Rondeau, 555:Vol56fasc2-360
Fredericks, C. The Future of Eternity.
  T.A. Shippey, 617(TLS):13May83-479
Frederickson, G.M. White Supremacy.
  R.F. Durden, 579(SAQ):Winter82-113
  T.D. Moodie, 529(QQ):Winter82-794
Fredouille, J-C. - see Tertullian
Fredrickson, H. Baudelaire: Héros et Fils.
  E. Hartman, 546(RR):Jan82-121
Freed, A.F. The Semantics of English
Aspectual Complementation.*
  E. Jelinek, 606:Oct82-143
Freed, L. T.S. Eliot.*
  A.D. Moody, 402(MLR):Jan82-192
  A.D. Nuttall, 541(RES):Feb82-110
  T. Pinkney, 366:Autumn82-248
Freedberg, S.J. Circa 1600.
  F. Haskell, 453(NYRB):12May83-25
Freedeman, C.E. Joint-Stock Enterprise in
France, 1807-1867.
  R.C. Michie, 161(DUJ):Jun82-289
Freedman, L. The Evolution of Nuclear
Strategy.*
  M. Bundy, 453(NYRB):17Mar83-3
  M. Howard, 231:Feb83-66
Freedman, R., ed. Virginia Woolf.*
  V.S. Middleton, 594:Fall82-289
Freeling, N. The Back of the North Wind.
  T.J. Binyon, 617(TLS):19Aug83-890
  M. Laski, 362:11Aug83-24

Freeman, D. Flytrap.
  A. Messenger, 102(CanL):Spring82-101
Freeman, D. Margaret Mead and Samoa.
  J. Clifford, 617(TLS):13May83-475
  G.E. Marcus, 441:27Mar83-3
Freeman, G. An Easter Egg Hunt.
  639(VQR):Spring82-54
Freeman, J.A. Milton and the Martial
Muse.*
  J.S. Lawry, 191(ELN):Mar82-279
  J. Wittreich, 551(RenQ):Spring82-133
Freeman, M. Edmund Burke and the Critique
of Political Radicalism.*
  J. Cannon, 83:Spring82-143
  P. Gottfried, 173(ECS):Winter82/83-214
  D.J., 185:Jan83-429
Freeman, M. - see Walker, J.
Freeman, M.A. The Poetics of "Translatio
Studii" and "Conjointure."*
  M. Offord, 208(FS):Jan82-45
Freeman, M.E.W. Selected Stories of Mary
E. Wilkins Freeman. (M. Pryse, ed)
  442(NY):25Jul83-86
Freer, C. The Poetics of Jacobean Drama.*
  R. Levin, 401(MLQ):Sep82-293
Frege, G. Philosophical and Mathematical
Correspondence.* (B. McGuinness, ed; H.
Kaal, trans)
  G. Currie, 84:Mar82-65
  A. Reix, 542:Jan-Mar82-64
Frege, G. Posthumous Writings.* (H.
Hermes, F. Kambartel and F. Kaulbach,
eds)
  E-H.W. Kluge, 482(PhR):Jan82-115
  J. Mosconi, 542:Jan-Mar82-110
Frege, G. Wissenschaftlicher Briefwechsel.
(G. Gabriel and others, eds)
  C. Parsons, 606:Aug82-325
Frei, N. Theodor Fontane.*
  A. Obermayer, 564:Nov81-323
  M. Walter-Schneider, 680(ZDP):Band101-
  Heft2-304
  I.H. Washington, 301(JEGP):Jan82-94
Frei-Lüthy, C. Der Einfluss der griechis-
chen Personennamen auf die Wortbildung.
  J-L. Perpillou, 555:Vol55fasc2-325
von Freiberg, D. Abhandlung über den
Intellekt und den Erkenntnisinhalt. (B.
Mojsisch, ed)
  J-F. Courtine, 192(EP):Jul-Sep82-373
von Freiberg, D. Opera omnia. (Vols 1
and 2)
  J-F. Courtine, 192(EP):Oct-Dec81-476
Freiberg, M., ed. Journals of the House
of Representatives of Massachusetts,
1772-1773 and 1773-1774. (Vols 49 and
50)
  J.A. Schutz, 432(NEQ):Dec82-614
Freiberg, S.K. Nightmare Tales.
  R. Lecker, 102(CanL):Autumn82-141
Freidus, A.J. Sumatran Contributions to
the Development of Indonesian Literature,
1920-1942.
  J.M. Echols, 318(JAOS):Oct-Dec81-494
Freitus, J. The Natural World Cookbook.
  T. Whittaker, 529(QQ):Winter82-872
Fremerey, M. Studenten und Politik in
Indoesien.
  M.F.S. Heidhues, 293(JASt):Nov81-199
French, D. Jitters.
  M. Fraser, 102(CanL):Winter81-139

122

French, M. Shakespeare's Division of
Experience.*
   G.K. Hunter, 569(SR):Spring82-273
   L. Scragg, 148:Winter82-83
French, P., ed. The Third Dimension.
   R. Davies, 617(TLS):23Dec83-1439
French, P. and M. MacLure, eds. Adult-
Child Conversation.
   C.M. Scotton, 350:Jun83-459
French, P.A. The Scope of Morality.*
   S. Conly, 482(PhR):Jul82-457
   F. Feldman, 449:Sep82-486
   D.P.L., 185:Jan83-414
French, P.A., T.E. Uehling, Jr. and H.K.
Wettstein, eds. Contemporary Perspec-
tives in the Philosophy of Language.*
   A. Akhtar, 320(CJL):Fall82-170
French, S.G., ed. Philosophers Look at
Canadian Confederation.*
   J. King-Farlow, 154:Jun82-374
French, W., ed. The South and Film.
   J.R. Millichap, 392:Fall82-439
Frere, S. Verulamium Excavations. (Vol 2)
   M. Harrison, 617(TLS):23Sep83-1028
Frere, S.S. and J.K.S. St. Joseph. Roman
Britain From the Air.
   K. Branigan, 617(TLS):23Sep83-1028
Frerichs, L.C.J. Italiaanse Tekeningen II.
   D. Scrase, 90:Jul82-454
Freson, R. The Taste of France.
   M. Burros, 441:11Dec83-12
Fretwell, M.E. This So Remote Frontier.
   R.G. Mitchell, 9(AlaR):Apr82-146
Freudenberg, R. Der alemannisch-bairische
Grenzbereich in Diachronie und Syn-
chronie.
   W. Kleiber, 685(ZDL):3/1981-381
Freudenstein, R., ed. Language Learning.
   G. Weise, 682(ZPSK):Band34Heft3-367
Frey, G. Theorie des Bewusstseins.
   R. Margreiter, 484(PPR):Sep82-127
   R. Margreiter, 489(PJGG):Band89Heft1-
   217
Frey, J.A. The Aesthetics of the "Rougon-
Macquart."*
   R. Lethbridge, 208(FS):Jul82-350
Frey, R.G. Interests and Rights.*
   S.R.L. Clark, 393(Mind):Jul82-459
Freyer, G. W.B. Yeats and the Anti-
Democratic Tradition.*
   B. Dolan, 305(JIL):Sep82-114
Fricke, H. Die Sprache der Literatur-
wissenschaft.*
   G. Michel, 682(ZPSK):Band34Heft2-230
Friday, N. My Mother/My Self.
   B. Johnson, 153:Summer82-2
Fridolin. E Baseldytsch-Sammlig. (4th
ed)
   A. Lötscher, 685(ZDL):1/1982-91
Friebertshäuser, H., ed. Dialektlexiko-
graphie.
   E. Künebacher, 685(ZDL):2/1981-245
Fried, C. Contract as Promise.*
   R.N. Bronaugh, 518:Jul82-171
Fried, E. One Hundred Poems Without a
Country.*
   A. Otten, 42(AR):Fall82-483
Fried, J.L. and others, eds. Guatemala in
Rebellion.
   J. Davison, 441:2Oct83-18
Fried, L. and T. Janericco, eds. Cooking
by Degrees.
   W. and C. Cowen, 639(VQR):Spring82-66

Fried, M. Absorption and Theatricality.*
   P. Conisbee, 90:Jul82-455
   P. Conrad, 31(ASch):Spring82-282
   L. Gossman, 210(FrF):Sep82-271
   R. Wrigley, 59:Sep82-358
Friedberg, M. A Decade of Euphoria.
   B. Scherr, 558(RLJ):Winter-Spring82-
   310
Friedemann, J. Le Rire dans l'univers
tragique d'Elie Wiesel.
   R.C. Lamont, 207(FR):May83-958
de Friedemann, N.S. and J. Arocha. Here-
deros del jaguar y la anaconda.
   B.J. Meggers, 263(RIB):Vol32No3/4-374
Frieden, N.M. Russian Physicians in an
Era of Reform and Revolution, 1856-1905.
   G.M. Hamburg, 104(CASS):Fall-Winter82-
   551
   R. Wortman, 550(RusR):Oct82-481
Friedenreich, K. Christopher Marlowe.
   R.Y. Turner, 551(RenQ):Spring81-137
   J. Weil, 677(YES):Vol 12-261
Friedman, A. - see Wycherley, W.
Friedman, B.H. The Polygamist.
   W.H. Pritchard, 249(HudR):Spring82-159
Friedman, E.G. Joyce Carol Oates.*
   Z. Mistri, 395(MFS):Summer81-377
Friedman, G. The Political Philosophy of
the Frankfurt School.
   J. Schmidt, 185:Jan83-397
Friedman, J.B. The Monstrous Races in
Medieval Art and Thought.
   D.C. Baker, 191(ELN):Sep82-23
   L.W. Patterson, 141:Winter82-70
   P. Riesenberg, 589:Oct82-882
   S. Wenzel, 301(JEGP):Oct82-551
Friedman, J.M. Dancer and Other Aesthetic
Objects.
   G. McFee, 89(BJA):Spring82-180
   D. Snyder, 289:Winter82-103
Friedman, L.J. Gregarious Saints.
   D. Macleod, 617(TLS):8Jul83-730
Friedman, M. Bright Promises, Dismal Per-
formance.
   R. Lekachman, 61:Jul83-96
Friedman, M. Martin Buber's Life and Work:
The Early Years 1878-1923.
   P. Vermes, 617(TLS):7Jan83-22
Friedman, M. Martin Buber's Life and Work:
The Middle Years 1923-45.
   P.L. Berger, 441:31Jul83-3
Friedman, M., ed. De Stijl, 1917-1931.
   A.L. Huxtable, 453(NYRB):8Dec83-29
Friedman, M. Foundations of Space-Time
Theories.
   H.R. Pagels, 441:21Aug83-9
Friedman, M. Hurricane Season.
   N. Callendar, 441:27Nov83-28
Friedman, M., with others. Hockney Paints
the Stage.
   J. Russell, 441:4Dec83-65
Friedman, P. Roads to Extinction. (A.J.
Friedman, ed)
   L. Field, 395(MFS):Summer82-340
   J.L. Lichten, 497(PolR):Vol27No3/4-216
Friedman, P.G. Interpersonal Communica-
tion.
   H.L. Goodall, Jr., 583:Fall82-94
Friedman, S.S. The Incident at Massena.
   J.D. Sarna, 390:Feb82-63

123

Friedman, S.S. Psyche Reborn.
S.M. Gilbert, 659(ConL):Winter83-496
I. Gregson, 184(EIC):Oct82-381
A. Morris, 481(PQ):Summer82-363
E. Prioleau, 27(AL):Oct82-456
Friedmann, H. A Bestiary for Saint Jerome.
E. Cropper, 551(RenQ):Autumn82-463
Friedrich, P. Language, Context, and the
Imagination.* (A.S. Dil, comp)
J.J. Chew, 320(CJL):Spring82-67
Friedrich, P. The Meaning of Aphrodite.
N. Loraux, 303(JoHS):Vol 102-261
Friedrichs, C.R. Urban Society in an Age
of War.
R. Hatton, 161(DUJ):Dec81-119
Friedrichs, E., comp. Die deutschsprachi-
gen Schriftstellerinnen des 18. und 19.
Jahrhunderts.
M. Lichterfeld, 221(GQ):Nov82-624
Friel, B. The Diviner.
F. Tuohy, 617(TLS):3Jun83-582
Friel, B. Translations.*
S. Fauchereau, 98:Jun-Jul82-628
Frier, B.W. Landlords and Tenants in
Imperial Rome.
W.M. Gordon, 123:Vol32No1-103
J. Humphrey, 487:Winter82-370
Frier, B.W. Libri annales pontificum maxi-
morum.*
J-C. Richard, 555:Vol55fasc2-383
G.V. Sumner, 487:Summer82-189
Friese, W., ed. Strindberg und die
deutschsprachigen Länder.*
B. Lide, 301(JEGP):Apr82-308
H. Uecker, 52:Band16Heft3-291
Friesen, P. The Shunning.
R. Phillips, 461:Spring-Summer82-98
Friess, H.L. Felix Adler and Ethical Cul-
ture.* (F. Weingartner, ed)
H.B. Radest, 619:Summer82-269
Frisbie, C.J., ed. Southwestern Indian
Ritual Drama.
P.V. Kroskrity, 187:May83-373
Frisby, D. Sociological Impressionism.
C. Pletsch, 676(YR):Winter83-viii
Frisby, J.P. Seeing.
529(QQ):Summer82-455
Frisch, M. Bluebeard.* (German title:
Blaubart.)
R.M. Adams, 453(NYRB):29Sep83-14
R. Gilman, 441:10Jul83-9
Frisé, A. Plädoyer für Robert Musil.
H. Reiss, 402(MLR):Jan82-246
Frith, S. Sound Effects.*
C. Keil, 187:Sep83-547
Frith, U., ed. Cognitive Processes in
Spelling.
B.J. Koekkoek, 399(MLJ):Summer82-193
Fritzen, B. and H.F. Taylor, eds. Fried-
rich Dürrenmatt.
D.G. Daviau, 221(GQ):Nov82-619
Fritzsch, H. Quarks.
442(NY):20Jun83-103
Frobenius, L. Schwarze Sonne Afrika. (U.
Diederichs, ed)
E. Dammann, 196:Band23Heft1/2-123
Fröberg, I. Une "histoire secrète" à
matière nordique.
V. Fournier, 597(SN):Vol54No2-346
Froissart, J. "Dits" et "Débats." (A.
Fourrier, ed)
N. Wilkins, 208(FS):Apr82-186

Frolic, B.M. Mao's People.* (French
title: Le Peuple de Mao.)
H. Cronel, 450(NRF):Dec82-104
"From Talbot to Stieglitz."
A. Ross, 364:Jun82-99
Fromkin, V.A., ed. Errors in Linguistic
Performance.*
C.A. Fowler, 353:Vol 19No7/8-819
F. Nolan, 297(JL):Sep82-483
Fromkin, V.A., ed. Tone.
G.N. Clements, 361:Feb82-192
Frontain, R-J. and J. Wojcik, eds. The
David Myth in Western Literature.
A. Avni, 107(CRCL):Jun82-259
A.J. Gedalof, 173(ECS):Spring82-356
Fröschle, H. - see "Deutschkanadisches
Jahrbuch/German-Canadian Yearbook"
Frost, D.L. - see Middleton, T.
Frost, L.A. Custer Legends.
J.V. Holleran, 649(WAL):Nov82-299
"Robert Frost and Sidney Cox."* (W.R.
Evans, ed)
M.V. Allen, 27(AL):Mar82-120
W. Tefs, 106:Fall82-223
Frost, S.B. McGill University. (Vol 1)
P. Axelrod, 529(QQ):Spring82-137
Froude, J.A. Froude's Life of Carlyle.*
(ed and abridged by J. Clubbe)
P. Morgan, 179(ES):Jun82-284
P. Scott, 588(SSL):Vol 17-272
Frude, N. The Intimate Machine.
S. Sutherland, 617(TLS):13May83-492
Frühwald, W. and W. Schieder, eds. Leben
im Exil.
J. Strelka, 221(GQ):Nov82-610
Fry, D.K. Norse Sagas Translated into
English.
M. Ciklamini, 563(SS):Spring82-165
Fry, E.C. Book of Knots and Ropework.
P. Bach, 614:Winter83-13
Fry, P.H. The Poet's Calling in the
English Ode.*
D.R. Anderson, 173(ECS):Winter82/83-
179
A.H. Fairbanks, 191(ELN):Dec81-145
V. Madsen, 134(CP):Spring82-84
Fry, P.S. and F.S. - see under Somerset
Fry, P. and F.
Fry, T. and others, eds. RB 1980: The
Rule of St. Benedict.
C.W. Bynum, 589:Jul82-607
Fryde, E.B. Studies in Medieval Trade and
Finance.
M. Prestwich, 617(TLS):12Aug83-865
Frye, N. Creation and Recreation.*
D. Jeffrey, 102(CanL):Winter81-111
J.M. Mellard, 395(MFS):Summer81-391
D. Tolomeo, 178:Jun82-245
Frye, N. Divisions on a Ground. (J. Polk,
ed)
R. Brown, 99:Dec82/Jan83-39
R. Woodman, 105:Spring/Summer82-124
Frye, N. The Great Code.*
P.H. Fry, 676(YR):Summer83-605
H.J. Levine, 219(GaR):Winter82-900
E. Mandel, 99:Sep82-30
E. Robertson, 175:Autumn82-274
R.D.S., 604:Fall82-51
F. Sparshott, 478:Oct82-180
L. Stern, 290(JAAC):Spring83-340
T. Willard, 50(ArQ):Autumn82-280
R. Woodman, 105:Spring/Summer82-124

Frye, R.M. Milton's Imagery and the
Visual Arts.*
J.B. Trapp, 402(MLR):Jan82-162
Frye, R.M. Shakespeare.
L. Scragg, 148:Autumn82-75
Fryer, B. and others, eds. Law, State and
Society.
D.R., 185:Oct82-203
Fryer, H. Magnificent Yellowhead Highway.
529(QQ):Autumn82-687
Fu, C.W-H. and W-T. Chan. Guide to Chi-
nese Philosophy.*
F. Rieman, 485(PE&W):Jul82-353
Fu, S.C.Y. and others. Traces of the
Brush.*
M. Medley, 39:Sep82-197
Fuchs, C. La paraphrase.
G. Kleiber, 553(RLiR):Jul-Dec82-426
Fuchs, C. and A-M. Léonard. Vers une thé-
orie des aspects.
B. Comrie, 353:Vol 19No3/4-383
Fuchs, H.J. Entfremdung und Narzissmus.
J-R. Armogathe, 535(RHL):Mar-Apr82-332
Fuchs, V. Of Ice and Men.
P. Beck, 617(TLS):18Mar83-260
Fuchs, V.R. How We Live.
A. Hacker, 453(NYRB):30Jun83-27
P. Passell, 441:1May83-12
Fuchs, W. Die Bilderalben für die Süd-
reisen des Kaisers Kienlung im 18. Jahr-
hundert.
D.L. Rosenzweig, 318(JAOS):Oct-Dec81-
427
Fuchser, L.W. Neville Chamberlain and
Appeasement.
J.P. Fox, 617(TLS):30Sep83-1064
Fuentes, C. Distant Relations.*
D. Tipton, 364:Oct82-105
639(VQR):Autumn82-131
Fuentes, C. Une certaine parenté.
M.F. Meurice, 450(NRF):May82-141
Fuglesang, S.H. Some Aspects of the Ring-
erike Style.
H. Chickering, 589:Jul82-609
Fuhrer, H.R. Spionage gegen die Schweiz.
W. Laqueur, 617(TLS):11Feb83-137
Fuhrmann, J.T. Tsar Alexis.
D.H. Kaiser, 104(CASS):Fall-Winter82-
539
P. Longworth, 575(SEER):Jan82-112
D.B. Miller, 550(RusR):Jan82-68
Fujimura, O., ed. Three Dimensions of Lin-
guistic Theory.
G.F. Meier, 682(ZPSK):Band34Heft2-253
Fujiwara Akira. Nihongo wa doko kara kita
ka.
R.A. Miller, 350:Mar83-207
Fukutake, T. The Japanese Social Struc-
ture.
J.A.A. Stockwin, 617(TLS):25Nov83-1324
Fukutake Tadashi. Rural Society in Japan.*
K. Brown, 293(JASt):Feb82-356
Fuller, D. Passage.
442(NY):4Jul83-92
Fuller, J. The Beautiful Inventions.
D. Nokes, 617(TLS):13May83-480
Fuller, J. Convergence.
T.J. Binyon, 617(TLS):22Apr83-400
N. Callendar, 441:2Jan83-26
M. Laski, 362:9Jun83-24
Fuller, J. Flying to Nowhere.
J. Mellors, 362:5May83-27
D. Nokes, 617(TLS):13May83-480

Fuller, J. Waiting for the Music.*
C. Hope, 364:Dec82/Jan83-106
S. Regan, 493:Sep82-64
Fuller, J. - see Gay, J.
Fuller, J.G. Are the Kids All Right?
R.S. Denisoff, 498:Vol8No3/4-137
Fuller, L.L. The Principles of Social
Order. (K.I. Winston, ed)
T.D. Eisele, 396(ModA):Summer/Fall82-
440
Fuller, M. The Letters of Margaret Fuller.
(R.N. Hudspeth, ed)
J.R. Mellow, 441:19Jun83-1
442(NY):18Jul83-98
Fuller, P. Robert Natkin.
R. Cohen, 55:Nov82-44
Fuller, R. Vamp Till Ready.*
J. Mellors, 364:Oct82-98
Fuller, R.B. Critical Path.
P.B. Checkland, 617(TLS):28Oct83-1196
Fuller, R.B. Grunch of Giants.
P. Engel, 441:17Jul83-16
Fullerton, A. The Torch Bearers.
M. Trend, 617(TLS):23Dec83-1437
Fullinwider, R.K. The Reverse Discrimina-
tion Controversy.*
M.D. Bayles, 311(JP):Aug82-455
Fulton, R. Fields of Focus.
M. Hofmann, 617(TLS):8Apr83-356
Fulton, R. Selected Poems 1963-1978.
R. Watson, 588(SSL):Vol 17-218
Fulton, R. - see Garioch, R.
Fumaroli, M. L'Age de l'éloquence.*
L. Brind'Amour, 188(ECr):Summer82-64
P. France, 402(MLR):Jan82-203
O. Ranum, 400(MLN):May82-1040
P. Zoberman, 546(RR):Jan82-110
Fumaroli, M., ed. Le Statut de la littéra-
ture.
H. Peyre, 207(FR):May83-935
"Fund og Forskning XXIV."
B.G. Fletcher Holt, 78(BC):Autumn82-
380
Furber, D. and A. Callahan. Erotic Love
in Literature.
N.J. Lacy, 446(NCFS):Spring-Summer83-
357
von Fürer-Haimendorf, C. Highlanders of
Arunachal Pradesh.
N.J. Allen, 617(TLS):11Feb83-136
von Fürer-Haimendorf, C. Tribes of India.
F.G. Bailey, 617(TLS):8Jul83-735
Furet, F. L'Atelier de l'histoire.
P. Higonnet, 617(TLS):14Oct83-1141
Furet, F. Penser la Révolution française.
F. George, 98:May82-394
Furetière, A. Le Roman bourgeois. (J.
Prévot, ed)
W. Leiner, 475:Vol19No17-792
A. Niderst, 535(RHL):Sep-Dec82-889
Furlong, M. Cousins.
L. Duguid, 617(TLS):17Jun83-642
Furlong, M. Merton.*
M.W. Higgins, 106:Spring82-127
P. O'Connor, 42(AR):Winter82-114
42(AR):Summer82-369
Furman, L. Watch Time Fly.
W. Lesser, 441:9Oct83-15
Furness, R. Wagner and Literature.*
R. Hollinrake, 410(M&L):Jul/Oct82-330
"Joseph Furphy." (J. Barnes, ed)
K. Stewart, 71(ALS):Oct82-541

125

Furst, L.R. The Contours of European
Romanticism.*
  R.A. Foakes, 541(RES):Nov82-477
  G. Gillespie, 345(KRQ):Vol29No2-216
  R. Hauptman, 395(MFS):Winter81/82-762
  J.E. Jordan, 149(CLS):Spring82-81
  R. Littlejohns, 402(MLR):Jan82-156
Furst, L.R., comp. European Romanticism.*
  R.A. Foakes, 541(RES):Nov82-477
Furst, P.T. and J.L. North American
Indian Art.*
  R.L. Shep, 614:Spring83-21
Furth, D.L. The Visionary Betrayed.
  R. Hewitt, 395(MFS):Winter81/82-719
Fuss, A. Paul Claudel.
  A. Espiau de La Maëstre, 535(RHL):
  May-Jun82-495
Fussell, P. Abroad.*
  B. Allen, 569(SR):Spring82-xlv
  T. Brooks, 184(EIC):Jul82-297
  R.G. Walker, 395(MFS):Summer81-347
  42(AR):Winter82-115
Fussell, P. The Boy Scout Handbook and
Other Observations.*
  G.C., 569(SR):Fall82-cx
  Z. Leader, 617(TLS):11Feb83-129
Fussell, P. Class.
  A. Lurie, 441:13Nov83-7
  W. Sheed, 61:Oct83-104
Fussell, P. - see Sassoon, S.
Futrell, A.W. and C.R. Wordell - see
Maurer, D.W.
Futuyma, D.J. Science on Trial.
  R.C. Lewontin, 453(NYRB):16Jun83-21
Fyle, C.N. and E.D. Jones, eds. A Krio-
English Dictionary.
  P. Baker, 69:Vol51No3-803
  D.K. Nylander, 603:Vol6No3-441
Fyler, J.M. Chaucer and Ovid.*
  R.T. Davies, 402(MLR):Apr82-403
  G. Schmitz, 38:Band100Heft1/2-186
Fyvel, T.R. George Orwell.*
  P. Martin, 364:Dec82/Jan83-142
  V.S. Pritchett, 442(NY):7Mar83-130

Gaan, M. Little Sister.
  442(NY):21Mar83-130
Gabaude, J-M., ed. La pédagogie contem-
poraine.
  E. Diet, 542:Jan-Mar82-37
Gabba, E. and M. Pasquinucci. Strutture
agrarie e allevamento transumante nell'-
Italia romana (III-I sec. A.C.).
  G. Barker, 313:Vol72-192
Gabba, E. and G. Vallet, eds. La Sicilia
Antica.*
  J. de Romilly, 555:Vol56fasc1-120
Gabel, G.U. and G.R. La littérature fran-
çaise.
  O. Klapp, 547(RF):Band94Heft4-481
Gabka, K., ed. Die russische Sprache der
Gegenwart.
  G. Schaarschmidt, 574(SEEJ):Winter82-
  496
Gabriel, G. Prose and Passion.
  S.J. Gaies, 399(MLJ):Autumn82-358
Gabriel, G. and others - see Frege, G.
Gabrielsen, V. Remuneration of State
Officials in Fourth-Century B.C. Athens.
  D.M. Lewis, 303(JoHS):Vol 102-269

Gabszewicz, A. and G. Freeman. Bow Porce-
lain.
  T. Hughes, 324:Jan83-108
Gache, L-H. A Frenchman, A Chaplain, A
Rebel.
  O.H. Lipscomb, 9(AlaR):Jul82-230
Gadamer, H-G. Dialogue and Dialectic.*
  (P.C. Smith, ed and trans)
  J.P. Conway, 258:Mar82-104
Gadda, C.E. Il tempo e le opere.
  U. Varnai, 617(TLS):24Jun83-680
Gadenne, P. Siloé. Le vent noir.
  R. Buss, 617(TLS):15Jul83-760
Gaeng, P.A. A Study of Nominal Inflection
in Latin Inscriptions.*
  K. Hunnius, 547(RF):Band93Heft3/4-418
Gagarin, M. Drakon and Early Athenian
Homicide Law.
  D.M. MacDowell, 123:Vol32No2-208
Gage, J. - see von Goethe, J.W.
Gage, J.T. In the Arresting Eye.*
  W. Harmon, 569(SR):Spring82-279
  C. Norris, 89(BJA):Spring82-184
  R. Overstreet, 583:Spring83-307
Gage, N. Eleni.
  T. Morgan, 441:1May83-1
  C.M. Woodhouse, 453(NYRB):18Aug83-25
Gagne, C. and T. Caras. Soundpieces.
  M. Hayes, 607:Sep82-50
Gagnon, J. Les Vaches sont de braves
types et trois autres pièces.*
  J. Moss, 102(CanL):Spring82-122
Gagnon, M. Au coeur de la lettre.
  K. Gould, 207(FR):May83-975
Gaide, F. - see Avianus
Gaines, E.J. A Gathering of Old Men.
  R. Price, 441:30Oct83-15
  442(NY):24Oct83-163
Gair, R. The Children of Paul's.
  J. Hankey, 617(TLS):22Apr83-393
Gaite, C.M. - see under Martín Gaite, C.
Gaitskell, H. The Diary of Hugh Gaitskell,
1945-1956. (P.M. Williams, ed)
  K.O. Morgan, 617(TLS):11Nov83-1243
  J. Vaizey, 362:29Sep83-26
Gal, A. Brandeis of Boston.
  S.Z. Abramov, 390:Feb82-54
  S.E. Kennedy, 432(NEQ):Mar82-140
Galante, M. La datazione dei documenti
del "Codex Diplomaticus Cavensis."
  A. Várvaro, 545(RPh):May82-647
Galassi, J. - see Montale, E.
Galassi, P. Before Photography.
  G. Perez, 249(HudR):Summer82-266
Galavaris, G. The Illustrations of the
Prefaces in Byzantine Gospels.
  L. Nees, 589:Apr82-373
Galay, J-L. Philosophie et invention tex-
tuelle.
  J-C. Margolin, 192(EP):Jul-Sep81-345
Galbis, I.R.M. De Mío Cid a Alfonso Reyes.
  T. Guerra de Gloss, 238:Dec82-655
Galbraith, J.K. The Anatomy of Power.
  L. Coser, 441:9Oct83-1
  G. Wills, 61:Nov83-145
Galbraith, J.K. The Voice of the Poor.
  L. Silk, 441:10Apr83-9
  442(NY):4Apr83-133
Gale, B.G. Evolution Without Evidence.
  E.C. Lewontin, 453(NYRB):16Jun83-21
  D. Snow, 617(TLS):4Mar83-216
Gale, R.L. Charles Marion Russell.
  G.F. Day, 649(WAL):Summer82-173

Galeano, E. Les Veines ouvertes de
l'Amérique latine.
F. Trémolières, 450(NRF):Jan82-139
Galey, A. 1,50 fr. la ligne.
A.T. Harrison, 207(FR):Apr83-806
Galindo, L.O. - see under Ortega Galindo,
L.
Galinsky, H. Das amerikanische Englisch.
J-P. Schultze, 682(ZPSK):Band34Heft6-
758
Gall, S. Behind Russian Lines.
E. Mortimer, 453(NYRB):22Dec83-3
M. Yapp, 617(TLS):4Nov83-1212
Gall, S. Don't Worry about the Money Now.
R. Boston, 617(TLS):8Jul83-737
Gallacher, D.B. Les chartes de la
Salvetat-Mondragon.
Å. Grafström, 554:Vol 102No2-260
Gallacher, T. Apprentice.
D. Dunn, 617(TLS):8Jul83-732
Gallagher, E. and S. Worrall. Christians
in Ulster 1968-1980.
D. Hetherington, 617(TLS):1Apr83-332
Gallagher, E.J., J.A. Mistichelli and J.A.
Van Eerde. Jules Verne.*
A. Martin, 402(MLR):Apr82-457
F. Raymond, 535(RHL):Sep-Dec82-943
Gallagher, J. The Decline, Revival and
Fall of the British Empire. (A. Seal,
ed)
V.G. Kiernan, 617(TLS):7Jan83-16
Gallant, C. Blake and the Assimilation of
Chaos.
S.D. Cox, 173(ECS):Winter81/82-205
J.E. Swearingen, 125:Winter82-208
Gallardo, F.V. - see under Vivas Gallardo,
F.
Gallas, H. Das Textbegehren des "Michael
Kohlhaas."
J. Jacobs, 680(ZDP):Band101Heft2-301
Gallati, E. Frédéric Soret und Goethe.
H. Eichner, 406:Fall82-327
R. Gould, 564:Feb82-76
H. Reiss, 133:Band15Heft3-269
Gallay, P., with M. Jourjon - see Saint
Gregory of Nazianzus
Galle, R. Tragödie und Aufklärung.
A. Adler, 72:Band218Heft2-391
Gállego, J. El pintor de artesano a
artista.
F. Marías, 48:Jan-Mar80-131
Gallet, M. Claude-Nicolas Ledoux 1736-
1806.
J-M. Pérouse de Montclos, 576:Oct82-
261
Gallistl, B. Teiresias in den Bakchen des
Euripides.
J. Diggle, 123:Vol32No1-92
Gallo, B. Linguaggio come Pornotopia in
Dylan Thomas.
A.R. Tellier, 189(EA):Apr-Jun82-224
Gallo, P.L. and F. Sedwick. French for
Careers.*
D.E. Rivas, 399(MLJ):Spring82-83
Gallop, J. The Daughter's Seduction.
M. Homans, 676(YR):Spring83-445
S. Relyea, 454:Winter83-187
Gallop, J. Feminism and Psychoanalysis.
J. Mitchell, 617(TLS):14Jan83-39
Gallop, J. Intersections.
P. Collier, 402(MLR):Oct82-967
M.B. Holland, 208(FS):Jul82-360
Gallup, D. - see O'Neill, E.

Galluzzi, P. Momento.
W.A. Wallace, 551(RenQ):Autumn81-400
Galston, W.A. Justice and the Human Good.
R.K. Fullinwider, 185:Oct82-157
E.F. Kingdom, 518:Jul82-179
Galt, J. The Provost.
J.K.L. Walker, 617(TLS):4Mar83-205
Galvin, J. Imaginary Timber.*
T. Swiss, 584(SWR):Summer82-345
Gambarara, D. and P. Ramat, eds. Dieci
anni di linguistica italiana (1965-1975).
G.F. Meier, 682(ZPSK):Band34Heft5-641
Gamberini, L. Plutarco "Della musica."
A. Bélis, 555:Vol56fasc2-332
Gammond, P. and P. Horricks, eds. Music
on Record 2.
M. Harrison, 415:Aug82-549
Gandy, D.R. Marx and History.
D.F. Calhoun, 125:Fall81-94
Gann, L.H. and P. Duignan. Why South
Africa will Survive.
B. Munslow, 69:Vol152No4-91
Gannon, P. and P. Czerniewska. Using Lin-
guistics.
A. Roca, 399(MLJ):Winter82-444
Gans, H. and others, eds. On the Making
of Americans.
J.S. Drew, 658:Winter82-284
Gans, H.J. Deciding What's News.
P. Brantlinger, 128(CE):Sep82-475
Gansberg, A.L. Little Caesar.
J. Marsh, 617(TLS):18Nov83-1291
Ganz, A. Realms of the Self.
E. Brater, 130:Summer82-180
T.R. Whitaker, 397(MD):Dec82-569
Ganzel, D. Fortune and Men's Eyes.
R.A. Foakes, 250(HLQ):Autumn82-317
A. Freeman, 617(TLS):22Apr83-391
Garapon, R. - see Scarron, P.
Garasa, D.L. Paseos literarios por Buenos
Aires.
M. Camurati, 263(RIB):Vol32No2-211
Garavini, F. La casa dei giochi.*
G. Malquori Fondi, 475:Vol9No17-772
Garber, F. The Autonomy of the Self from
Richardson to Huysmans.
P.L. Thorslev, Jr., 401(MLQ):Sep82-302
639(VQR):Summer82-81
Garber, F. Thoreau's Redemptive Imagina-
tion.*
M.L. Ross, 107(CRCL):Dec81-544
García, C. La Oposición y conjunción de
los dos grandes Luminares de la Tierra o
la antipatía de Franceses y Españoles.*
(M. Bareau, ed)
D-H. Pageaux, 107(CRCL):Jun82-270
García, E.E. - see Tirso de Molina
García, M. Desert Immigrants.
L. Hall, 584(SWR):Summer82-349
García, O. Compendio de arquitectura y
simetría de los templos. (C. Chanfón,
ed)
D. Angulo Íñiguez, 48:Jan-Mar80-133
García Castañeda, S. Don Telesforo de
Trueba y Cosío (1799-1835).*
I. Bergquist, 173(ECS):Winter82/83-194
R.P. Sebold, 345(KRQ):Vol29No3-323
García Márquez, G. Chronicle of a Death
Foretold.* (Spanish title: Crónica de
una Muerte Anunciada.)
P-L. Adams, 61:May83-103
R.M. Adams, 453(NYRB):14Apr83-3
[continued]

García Márquez, G. Chronicle of a Death
Foretold. [continuing]
J.R.B., 148:Winter82-93
J. Fowles, 219(GaR):Winter82-721
L. Michaels, 441:27Mar83-1
N.M. Scott, 37:Jan-Feb82-60
D. Tipton, 364:Oct82-105
García y García, A., ed. Constitutiones
Concilii Quarti Lateranensis una cum
Commentariis Glossatorum.
P.R. Hyams, 382(MAE):1982/2-266
Gardam, J. The Pangs of Love and Other
Stories.
A. Duchêne, 617(TLS):11Feb83-131
J. Mellors, 362:9Jun83-26
Garde, P. Grammaire Russe. (Vol 1)
P. Mayo, 104(CASS):Spring82-120
Gardies, J-L. Essai sur la logique des
modalités.*
A. Reix, 192(EP):Apr-Jun82-235
Gardiner, J.R. Going On Like This.
E. Milton, 441:14Aug83-12
Gardiner, M. Code Name "Mary."
R. Dinnage, 617(TLS):19Aug83-874
H.R., 231:Jul83-76
442(NY):23May83-123
Gardner, H. Art, Mind, and Brain.
E. Rothstein, 441:6Feb83-13
Gardner, H. Artful Scribbles.*
K.M. Lansing, 289:Summer82-120
Gardner, H. Frames of Mind.
J. Bruner, 453(NYRB):27Oct83-84
G.A. Miller, 441:25Dec83-5
B. Singer, 231:Dec83-76
Gardner, H. In Defense of the Imagina-
tion.*
H.M. Solomon, 577(SHR):Fall82-377
639(VQR):Autumn82-115
Gardner, I. New and Selected Poems.
C. Hebald, 436(NewL):Fall82-118
Gardner, J. The Art of Living.
M. Kreyling, 573(SSF):Winter82-77
A. Mars-Jones, 617(TLS):29Jul83-805
Gardner, J. Icebreaker.
T.J. Binyon, 617(TLS):22Jul83-769
M. Laski, 362:11Aug83-24
M. Watkins, 441:24Apr83-16
Gardner, J. On Becoming a Novelist.
P. Engel, 441:10Jul83-17
von Gardner, J. Orthodox Worship and
Hymnography.
D. Hiley, 415:Apr82-262
Gardner, J. The Quiet Dogs.
M. Laski, 362:20Jan83-23
Gardner, J.A. Legal Imperialism.
D.J. Padilla, 263(RIB):Vol32No1-63
Gardner, M. Order and Surprise.
A. Quinton, 617(TLS):2Dec83-1335
442(NY):14Nov83-208
Gardner, M. Science Fiction Puzzle Tales.
P.F.S., 617(TLS):26Aug83-915
Gardner, M. The Whys of a Philosophical
Scrivener.
G. Groth, 453(NYRB):8Dec83-41
A. Quinton, 617(TLS):2Dec83-1335
Gardner, W. Alphabet at Work.
B. Wolpe, 324:Nov83-780
Garfinkel, A. Forms of Explanation.
M. Hollis, 311(JP):May82-283
D-H. Ruben, 84:Dec82-438
S.W., 185:Oct82-194

Garfitt, J.S.T. The Work and Thought of
Jean Grenier (1898-1971).
J. Cruickshank, 617(TLS):2Sep83-920
Gargano, J.W., ed. Critical Essays on
John William De Forest.
A.E. Rowe, 26(ALR):Spring82-139
Gargett, G. Voltaire and Protestantism.*
J.A. Perkins, 207(FR):Dec82-320
Gargilius. Gargilii Martialis quae extant.
(Vol 1) (S. Condorelli, ed)
P. Flobert, 555:Vol55fasc1-179
Garibaldi, G. Manlio. (A.P. Campanella,
ed)
M. Clark, 617(TLS):14Oct83-1132
Gariépy, R. Voice Storm.
P. Monk, 102(CanL):Winter81-171
Garioch, R. Complete Poetical Works. (R.
Fulton, ed)
N. McCaig, 617(TLS):18Nov83-1272
Garland, H. The Berlin Novels of Theodor
Fontane.*
F. Betz, 301(JEGP):Jan82-95
R.L. Jamison, 221(GQ):Mar82-263
G.B. Pickard, 395(MFS):Summer82-326
A.R. Robinson, 402(MLR):Jan82-239
Garland, M.M. Cambridge Before Darwin.
A. Engel, 637(VS):Autumn81-104
de Garlandia, J. Concerning Measured
Music (De Mensurabili Musica).* (S.H.
Birnbaum, trans)
R. Erickson, 308:Spring82-169
Garlington, A.S., Jr. Sources for the
Study of Nineteenth Century Opera in the
Syracuse University Libraries.
S. Maguire, 410(M&L):Jul/Oct81-414
Garmey, J. Great British Cooking.
W. and C. Cowen, 639(VQR):Autumn82-139
Garner, A. Conversationally Speaking.
M. Hickson 3d, 583:Fall82-92
Garner, P., ed. Phaidon Encyclopaedia of
Decorative Arts 1890-1940.
G. Wills, 39:Apr82-297
Garner, W. Think Big, Think Dirty.
T.J. Binyon, 617(TLS):5Aug83-843
M. Laski, 362:11Aug83-24
Garnett, W. The Extraordinary Landscape.
P-L. Adams, 61:Jan83-103
C. Vita-Finzi, 617(TLS):18Feb83-150
Garnon, G. La nouvelle Justine.
F. Champarnaud, 98:Oct82-871
Garnsey, P., ed. Non-Slave Labour in the
Greco-Roman World.
T.E.J. Wiedemann, 123:Vol32No1-73
Garnsey, P., K. Hopkins and C.R. Whittaker,
eds. Trade in the Ancient Economy.
J. D'Arms, 617(TLS):29Jul83-802
Garon, P. Blues and the Poetic Spirit.
J.T. Titon, 187:Jan83-130
Garoutte, S., ed. Uncoverings 1981.
P. Bach, 614:Winter83-22
Garrard, J. Leadership and Power in Vic-
torian Industrial Towns 1830-80.
P.J. Waller, 617(TLS):8Apr83-351
Garrard, T.F. Akan Weights and the Gold
Trade.*
F. Willett, 59:Jun82-227
Garrett, G. The Succession.
M. Quilligan, 441:25Dec83-6
Garrett, J. The Triumphs of Providence.
639(VQR):Summer82-84

Garrett, P.K. The Victorian Multiplot
Novel.*
    R. Mason, 447(N&Q):Jun81-269
    A. Welsh, 301(JEGP):Jan82-129
Garrick, D. David Garrick: Selected
Verse. (J.D. Hainsworth, ed)
    J. Newman, 83:Autumn82-245
Garrick, D. The Plays of David Garrick.
(Vols 1 and 2) (H.W. Pedicord and F.L.
Bergmann, eds)
    P. Davison, 354:Sep82-343
    L. Hughes, 405(MP):May83-398
Garrick, D. The Plays of David Garrick.*
(Vols 3 and 4) (H.W. Pedicord and F.L.
Bergmann, eds)
    P. Davison, 354:Sep82-343
    L. Hughes, 405(MP):May83-398
    R. Savage, 617(TLS):2Sep83-936
Garrick, D. The Plays of David Garrick.
(Vols 5-7) (H.W. Pedicord and F.L. Berg-
mann, eds)
    R. Savage, 617(TLS):2Sep83-936
Garrow, D.J. The FBI and Martin Luther
King, Jr.
    L.W. Dunbar, 639(VQR):Autumn82-702
    J.M. Thornton 3d, 9(AlaR):Oct82-278
Garson, H.S. Truman Capote.
    F. Baldanza, 395(MFS):Summer81-370
    S. Fogel, 106:Fall82-267
Garuti, G. - see Claudian
Garvin, H.R. and M.D. Payne, eds. Shake-
speare: Contemporary Critical Approaches.
    C.W. Cary, 130:Fall82-272
Gary, R. King Solomon.
    P. Keegan, 617(TLS):29Jul83-804
    J. Weightman, 441:10Jul83-9
Gascoigne, B. Quest for the Golden Hare.
    P.J. Kavanagh, 617(TLS):8Jul83-722
    E.S. Turner, 362:23Jun83-27
Gascoigne, G. George Gascoigne: The Green
Knight, Selected Poetry and Prose. (R.
Pooley, ed)
    C. Nicholl, 617(TLS):19Aug83-884
Gascón Vera, E. Don Pedro, Condestable de
Portugal.
    A. Mutton, 402(MLR):Jul82-744
Gash, J. The Sleepers of Erin.
    N. Callendar, 441:8May83-27
    M. Laski, 362:19May83-24
Gasiorowska, X. The Image of Peter the
Great in Russian Fiction.*
    T.I. Whittaker, 574(SEEJ):Spring82-92
Gaskell, E. Elizabeth Gaskell: A Portrait
in Letters. (J.A.V. Chapple, ed)
    B. Shulgasser, 441:13Nov83-19
Gaskell, P. Trinity College Library: The
First 150 Years.*
    D.G. Davis, Jr., 517(PBSA):Vol76No2-
230
Gaspar, J. Égée [suivi de] Judée.*
    Y-A. Favre, 450(NRF):Jul-Aug82-163
Gašparíková, V. Povesti o zbojníkoch zo
slovenských a pol'ských Tatier.
    J. Jech, 196:Band23Heft1/2-126
Gasparini, G. and L. Margolies. Inca
Architecture.*
    F.J. Prestamo, 37:Mar-Apr82-56
Gasparini, L. Breaking and Entering.
    B. Whiteman, 102(CanL):Winter81-172
Gassendi, P. Institutio Logica. (H.
Jones, ed and trans)
    A. Back, 319:Oct82-432
    E.D. James, 208(FS):Oct82-469

Gasset, J.O. - see under Ortega y Gasset,
J.
Gatenby, G. Growing Still.*
    R.J. Merrett, 529(QQ):Winter82-893
    E. Thompson, 102(CanL):Summer82-133
    E. Trethewey, 198:Oct82-111
Gates, E.M. End of the Affair.*
    639(VQR):Summer82-84
Gates, H.L., Jr. - see Davis, C.T.
Gates, H.L., Jr. - see "Our Nig"
"Gathering What the Great Nature Pro-
vided."*
    W.N., 102(CanL):Spring82-160
Gatti Perer, M.L. Umanesimo a Milano.
    I. Hyman, 551(RenQ):Autumn81-425
Gaudiani, C. Teaching Writing in the FL
Curriculum.
    A. Malinowski, 207(FR):Mar83-649
Gaudiani, C.L. The Cabaret Poetry of Thé-
ophile de Viau.
    G. Saba, 475:No16Pt2-379
Gaudon, J. - see Gautier, T.
Gauger, H-M., W. Oesterreicher and R. Win-
disch. Einführung in die romanische
Sprachwissenschaft.
    I. Söhrman, 597(SN):Vol54No2-337
Gauger, J-D. Beiträge zur jüdischen Apolo-
getik.
    A. Momigliano, 122:Jul82-258
Gaukroger, S., ed. Descartes: Philosophy,
Mathematics and Physics.
    D.M. Clarke, 518:Apr82-82
    J.R. Milton, 208(FS):Apr82-198
Gaulin, A. Entre la neige et le feu.*
    M.J. Edwards, 102(CanL):Summer82-161
Gaume, M. - see de Belleforest, F.
Gaume, M. - see d'Urfé, H.
Gauna, M. - see Tahureau, J.
Gaur, G., comp. Catalogue of Panjabi
Printed Books added to the India Office
Library 1902-1964.
    I.D. Serebryakov, 259(IIJ):Apr80-166
de Gaury, G. Traces of Travel.
    S. Runciman, 617(TLS):2Sep83-924
de Gaury, G. and H.V.F. Winstone, eds.
The Road to Kabul.*
    V. Young, 249(HudR):Winter82/83-660
Gaus, G.F. The Modern Liberal Theory of
Man.
    M. Freeden, 617(TLS):23Sep83-1014
Gautier, T. "La Morte amoureuse," "Avatar"
et autres récits fantastiques. (J. Gau-
don, ed)
    A.B. Smith, 207(FR):Mar83-637
    J. Van Eerde, 446(NCFS):Fall-Winter
82/83-158
Gautier, T. Voyage en Espagne suivi de
España. (P. Berthier, ed) Voyage en
Espagne. (J-C. Berchet, ed)
    K H. Darsch, 207(FR):Mar83-636
    A-M. Christin, 535(RHL):Sep-Dec82-930
"Gautier de Dargies Poesie." (A.M. Rau-
gei, ed)
    G. Roques, 553(RLiR):Jul-Dec82-499
Gavel, J. Colour.
    S.Y. Edgerton, Jr., 551(RenQ):Autumn81-
421
    J. Harris, 289:Spring82-115
Gay, J. John Gay: Dramatic Works. (J.
Fuller, ed)
    P. Rogers, 617(TLS):2Sep83-925
Gay, M. Plaque Tournante.
    M.G. Rose, 207(FR):May83-980

Gentikow, B. Skandinavien als präkapital-
istische Idylle.* Skandinavische und
deutsche Literatur.
  H. Uecker, 52:Band16Heft3-291
Gentili, B. Theatrical Performances in
the Ancient World.
  R.M. Pinkerton, 313:Vol72-202
Genzmer, F., with K. Schier - see "Die
Edda"
Geoghegan, C. Louis Aragon.
  W. Babilas, 72:Band218Heft1-231
  S. Ravis-Françon, 535(RHL):Mar-Apr82-
  326
Georgacas, D.G. Ichthyological Terms for
the Sturgeon and Etymology of the Inter-
national Terms "Botargo," "Caviar" and
"Congeners."*
  J. André, 555:Vol55fasc1-173
George, D.H. Blake and Freud.*
  Z. Leader, 591(SIR):Winter82-683
  M. Steig, 648(WCR):Oct82-46
  T.A. Vogler, 88:Fall82-121
  B. Wilkie, 301(JEGP):Jan82-115
George, E. - see Radnóti, M.
George, F.H. Philosophical Foundations
of Cybernetics.
  Y. Wilks, 84:Sep82-335
George, K. Murder at Tomorrow.
  N. Callendar, 441:16Jan83-26
George, M. Australia and the Indonesian
Revolution.
  A. Kahin, 293(JASt):May82-633
George, M.C.H. Mary Bonner.
  584(SWR):Summer82-v
George, W.R.P. Lloyd George: Backbencher.
  K.O. Morgan, 617(TLS):16Dec83-1409
Georges, R.A. and M.O. Jones. People
Studying People.
  N.V. Rosenberg, 650(WF):Jan82-73
Georgiades, T. Music and Language.
  W. Mellers, 617(TLS):17Jun83-624
Georgiev, V.I. Introduction to the His-
tory of the Indo-European Languages.
  J.A.C. Greppin, 617(TLS):1Jul83-709
  L.D. Stephens, 350:Dec83-912
Geraghty, T. Who Dares Wins. This is the
SAS.
  C. Wain, 362:18Aug83-21
Gerald of Wales. The Jewel of the Church.
(J.J. Hagen, trans)
  D. Luscombe, 382(MAE):1982/1-129
von Geramb, V. Kinder-und Hausmärchen aus
der Steiermark. (5th ed, rev by K. Haid-
ing)
  E. Moser-Rath, 196:Band23Heft3/4-308
Gérard, J. L'exclamation en français.*
  J-H. Boisset, 215(GL):Spring82-59
Gérard, J. La ponctuation trochaïque dans
l'hexamètre latin d'Ennius à Juvenal.
  E.J. Kenney, 123:Vol32No2-218
Gerber, J.C., P. Baender and T. Firkins -
see Twain, M.
Gerber, L.A. Married to their Careers.
  B. Hepburn, 617(TLS):28Oct83-1196
Gerbner, G., C.J. Ross and E. Zigler, eds.
Child Abuse.
  B.J. McConville, 529(QQ):Spring82-189
Gerdts, W.H. American Impressionism.
  A. Davis, 106:Spring82-109
Gerdts, W.H. and T.E. Stebbins, Jr. "A
Man of Genius."*
  A. Davis, 106:Spring82-109

Geretsegger, H. and M. Peintner. Otto
Wagner 1841-1918.
  R.H. Bletter, 576:May82-161
Gerhart, M. The Question of Belief in
Literary Criticism.
  M. Murray, 478:Oct82-214
Gérin, W. Anne Thackeray Ritchie.*
  C. MacKay, 637(VS):Summer82-514
Gerlach, I. Der schwierige Fortschritt.
  B. Einhorn, 221(GQ):May82-462
"'The Germ:' The Literary Magazine of the
Pre-Raphaelites."
  C.R.P. Tyzack, 506(PSt):Sep82-260
Germain, D. La Vengeance de l'original.
  H.R. Runte, 102(CanL):Autumn82-144
Germain, E.B., ed. English and American
Surrealist Poetry.
  D. Hillery, 161(DUJ):Dec81-153
Germann, G. Einführung in die Geschichte
der Architekturtheorie.
  H. Lorenz, 683:Band45Heft3-297
Gerndt, S. Idealisierte Natur.
  P.D. Sweet, 221(GQ):Mar82-234
Gernet, J. A History of Chinese Civilisa-
tion.* Chine et Christianisme.
  D. Rimmington, 617(TLS):24Jun83-672
Gernet, L. Les Grecs sans miracle. (R.
di Donato, ed)
  R. Buxton, 617(TLS):7Oct83-1084
Gero, J. Il primo libro de' madrigali
italiani et canzino francese a due voci.
(L.F. Bernstein and J. Haar, eds)
  M. Picker, 551(RenQ):Summer82-299
Gerould, D. Witkacy.
  B.L. Knapp, 295(JML):Dec82-554
  T. Venclova, 395(MFS):Winter82/73-717
Gerould, D. and J. Kosicka - see Witkie-
wicz, S.I.
von Gersdorff, D. - see Brentano, C. and
S. Mereau
Gersh, S. From Iamblichus to Eriugena.*
  L.G. Westerink, 394:Vol35fasc1/2-183
Gershuny, J. After Industrial Society?
  A.L. Stinchcombe, 185:Oct82-114
Gerstenkorn, A. Das "Modal-" System im
heutigen Deutsch.
  A. Krivonosov, 682(ZPSK):Band35Heft5-
  575
Gervers, V. The Influence of Ottoman Turk-
ish Textiles and Costume in Eastern
Europe.
  R.L. Shep, 614:Spring83-20
"Gesamtverzeichnis österreichischer Dis-
sertationen XIII."
  S.M. Patsch, 602:Vol 13No1-209
Gessinger, J. Sprache und Bürgertum.
  J. Schildt, 682(ZPSK):Band35Heft5-579
Gete Carpio, O. - see Secundus, J.
Gethmann, C.F. Protologik.
  W. Breidert, 687:Apr-Jun82-293
Gettel, R.E. Twice Burned.
  N. Callendar, 441:17Apr83-21
Gettleman, M.E. and others, eds. El
Salvador.*
  J. Shevin, 287:Jun/Jul82-28
Getz, L.M. Flannery O'Connor.
  J. Schlueter, 573(SSF):Winter82-92
  W.J. Stuckey, 395(MFS):Autumn82-507
Geuss, R. The Idea of a Critical Theory.*
  A. Rapaczynski, 185:Jul83-811
Geyer, F.R. and D. Schweitzer, eds. Alien-
ation.
  S.K., 185:Apr83-635

Gier, N.F. Wittgenstein and Phenomenology.
J. Burnheim, 63:Sep82-282
Giese, H. Franz von Matsch.
N. Powell, 39:Nov82-347
Giesen, W. Zur Geschichte des buddhis-
tischen Ritualgesangs in Japan.
E.J. Markham, 410(M&L):Jan81-79
Giffhorn, J. Studien am "Survey of
English Dialects."
D. Jost, 589:Oct82-883
G. Kristensson, 179(ES):Aug82-371
Gifford, D. Joyce Annotated.
R.B., 617(TLS):29Jul83-819
M.P. Gillespie, 395(MFS):Winter82/83-
625
Gifford, H. Tolstoy.*
S. Karlinsky, 617(TLS):18Feb83-161
Gifford, P. and W.M.R. Louis, eds. The
Transfer of Power in Africa.
C. Ehrlich, 617(TLS):27May83-552
Gifford, T. and N. Roberts. Ted Hughes.
M. Waterhouse, 148:Spring82-87
Gilbar, S. The Book Book.
639(VQR):Spring82-61
Gilbert, A.J. Literary Language from
Chaucer to Johnson.*
S. Logan, 447(N&Q):Dec81-575
Gilbert, B. Westering Man.
W.S. McFeely, 441:14Aug83-10
442(NY):10Oct83-167
Gilbert, C. Nerval's Double.*
S. Noakes, 591(SIR):Spring82-114
Gilbert, E.L. - see Kipling, R.
Gilbert, F. The Pope, His Banker, and
Venice.
M.M. Bullard, 551(RenQ):Winter81-593
Gilbert, G.G. - see Schuchardt, H.
Gilbert, H. The Riding Mistress.
K.C. O'Brien, 362:14Jul83-28
J. Pilling, 617(TLS):17Jun83-642
Gilbert, J.G. Edmund Waller.*
T.G.S. Cain, 447(N&Q):Aug81-337
Gilbert, M. Auschwitz and the Allies.
S. Friedlander, 473(PR):3/1982-464
E. Matz, 390:Apr82-59
Gilbert, M. The Black Seraphim.
T.J. Binyon, 617(TLS):2Dec83-1358
Gilbert, M. Winston S. Churchill. (Vol 6:
Finest Hour 1939-1941.)
P. Johnson, 362:30Jun83-25
S. Koss, 617(TLS):1Jul83-689
G. Smith, 441:25Dec83-1
N. Stone, 453(NYRB):10Nov83-43
Gilbert, M. The Final Throw.
T.J. Binyon, 617(TLS):15Apr83-374
M. Laski, 362:19May83-24
Gilbert, M. Smallbone Deceased.
R. Lekachman, 135:Jul82-122
Gilbert, P. Dictionnaire des mots contem-
porains.
G. Marié, 209(FM):Oct82-354
Gilbert, S.M. and S. Gubar. The Madwoman
in the Attic.*
J. Blondel, 189(EA):Oct-Dec82-433
P. Boumelha, 541(RES):Aug82-345
J. Dusinberre, 447(N&Q):Aug81-351
Gilbert, W.S. The Lost Stories of W.S.
Gilbert.* (P. Haining, ed)
R. Robbins, 617(TLS):4Feb83-112
Gilbert, W.S. and A. Sullivan. La Piratoj
de Penzanco, au Sklavo de la Devo.
M. Boulton, 447(N&Q):Feb81-85

Gilbert, W.S. and A.S. Sullivan. The Anno-
tated Gilbert and Sullivan. (I. Bradley,
ed)
A.J.G.H., 617(TLS):11Feb83-143
Gilchrist, E. The Annunciation.
F. Taliaferro, 231:Jun83-76
Gilchrist, E. In the Land of Dreamy
Dreams.*
D. Grumbach, 219(GaR):Fall82-668
J. Mellors, 362:6Jan83-24
Gildea, J., ed. L'Hystore Job. (Vol 1)
R.F. Cook, 545(RPh):Feb82-565
Giliomee, H. The Parting of the Ways.
K. Ingham, 617(TLS):4Feb83-98
Gilkey, L. Reaping the Whirlwind.
L. Dupré, 322(JHI):Jul-Sep82-509
Gill, A. The Early Mallarmé.* (Vol 1)
F. Lestringant, 535(RHL):Mar-Apr82-310
Gill, B. McGarr and the P.M. of Belgrave
Square.
N. Callendar, 441:18Dec83-29
442(NY):26Dec83-74
Gill, D., ed. The Book of the Piano.
G. Poole, 415:Mar82-187
Gill, J.H. Wittgenstein and Metaphor.
W.L. Blizek, 290(JAAC):Fall82-111
Gill, L. Novena to St. Jude Thaddeus.
R. Sward, 137:Winter82-80
Gill, O. and B. Jackson. Adoption and
Race.
M. Banton, 617(TLS):1Jul83-705
Gille, K.F., ed. Karl August Varnhagen
von Ense.
T.H. Pickett, 221(GQ):Nov82-596
Gillespie, R. Soldiers of Perón.
T. Halperin-Donghi, 617(TLS):6May83-
454
Gillessen, H. Pierre Emmanuel: Jacob.
F.R. Smith, 208(FS):Apr82-234
Gilliatt, P. Mortal Matters.
J. Mellors, 362:15Dec83-30
J. Neville, 617(TLS):16Dec83-1412
442(NY):7Nov83-182
Gilligan, C. In a Different Voice.*
P.S., 185:Jul83-822
Gillis, D. Collaboration with the Per-
sians.
É. Will, 555:Vol55fasc2-333
Gillispie, C.C. The Montgolfier Brothers
and the Invention of Aviation, 1783-1784.
J. Bernstein, 442(NY):25Jul83-84
J.H. Plumb, 453(NYRB):10Nov83-24
G.C. Ward, 441:24Jul83-6
Gillispie, C.C. - see "Dictionary of
Scientific Biography"
Gillon, A. Joseph Conrad.
J.V. Knapp, 395(MFS):Winter82/83-621
Gillon, W. Collecting African Art.*
J. Picton, 59:Jun82-219
Gilman, S. Caldós and the Art of the Euro-
pean Novel: 1867-1887.*
E. Sánchez, 395(MFS):Summer82-335
Gilman, S.L., ed. Begegnungen mit Nietz-
sche.
R.F. Krummel, 133:Band15Heft3-277
Gilman, S.L. Wahnsinn, Text und Kontext.
W. Nehring, 221(GQ):Nov82-628
Gilmore, M. Letters of Mary Gilmore.*
(W.H. Wilde and T.I. Moore, eds) The
Passionate Heart and Other Poems.
D. Modjeska, 381:Jun82-228

Gilmour, D. Lebanon.
  P. Mansfield, 362:11Aug83-21
  M. Yapp, 617(TLS):26Aug83-911
Gilmour, I. Britain Can Work.
  S.H. Beer, 617(TLS):3Jun83-563
  J. Critchley, 362:3Mar83-21
Gilmour, R. The Idea of the Gentleman in
  the Victorian Novel.
  J. Halperin, 395(MFS):Summer82-259
  A.J.S., 148:Autumn82-93
Gilot, M. and J. Sgard, eds. Le Vocabu-
  laire du sentiment dans l'oeuvre de J-J.
  Rousseau.
  J.C. O'Neal, 207(FR):May83-945
Gilsenan, M. Recognizing Islam.*
  S. Bakhash, 441:8May83-9
  C.J. Heywood, 617(TLS):22Apr83-405
Gilson, E. L'athéisme difficile.
  M.D.J., 543:Dec81-387
Gimson, A.C. An Introduction to the Pro-
  nunciation of English. (3rd ed)
  G. Graustein, 682(ZPSK):Band35Heft3-
  340
"Alberto Ginastera: A Catalogue of his Pub-
  lished Works."
  A.F.L.T., 412:Feb81-61
Ginger, J. The Notable Man.
  P.J. de Gategno, 173(ECS):Fall81-106
Ginori Lisci, L. Cabrei in Toscana rac-
  colte di mappe, prospetti e vedute sec.
  XVI-sec. XIX.
  S.B. Butters, 59:Dec82-480
Ginsburg, J. Tradition and Theme in the
  "Annals" of Tacitus.
  M. Griffin, 313:Vol72-215
Ginsburgs, G. and R.M. Slusser, eds. A
  Calendar of Soviet Treaties, 1958-1973.
  J.F. Triska, 550(RusR):Apr82-234
Ginzburg, C. The Cheese and the Worms.*
  F. Chiappelli, 551(RenQ):Autumn81-397
Ginzburg, C. Erkundigungen über Piero.
  H. Belting, 683:Band45Heft4-423
Ginzburg, C. Indagini su Piero.*
  R. Cocke, 59:Dec82-508
Ginzburg, N. La famiglia Manzoni.
  F. Donini, 617(TLS):24Jun83-680
Giochalâs, T.P. Tò ellēno-albanikòn lexi-
  kòn tū Márku Mpotsarē.
  J. Irmscher, 682(ZPSK):Band35Heft5-
  581
Giochi, F.M. and A. Mordenti. Annali
  della tipografia in Ancona, 1512-1799.
  354:Jun82-208
Giono, J. Cahiers Giono II. (H. Godard,
  ed)
  M.I. Madden, 207(FR):May83-976
Giono, J. Coeurs, passions, caractères.*
  M.I. Madden, 207(FR):May83-976
  F. de Martinoir, 450(NRF):Oct82-120
"Giono aujourd'hui."
  R. Ricatte, 193(ELit):Dec82-461
Giovannangeli, D. Ecriture et répétition
  (Approche de Derrida).
  P. Somville, 542:Jan-Mar82-64
Giovanni di Conversino da Ravenna. Drag-
  malogia de eligibili vite genere. (H.L.
  Eaker, ed and trans)
  G. Holmes, 551(RenQ):Spring82-67
  R.G. Witt, 589:Jul82-611
Giovannini, A. and G. Gottlieb. Thukydi-
  des und die Anfänge der athenischen
  Arche.
  H.D. Westlake, 123:Vol32No1-60

Giovannucci, E.F. - see under Fazzini
  Giovannucci, E.
Gipper, H. Sprachwissenschaftliche Grund-
  begriffe und Forschungsrichtungen.
  A.W. Stanforth, 685(ZDL):1/1982-71
Gippert, J. Zur Syntax der infinitivis-
  chen Bildungen in den indogermanischen
  Sprachen.
  H-E. Seidel, 260(IF):Band86-336
Gippius, V.V. Gogol. (R.A. Maguire, ed
  and trans)
  G. Cox, 574(SEEJ):Spring82-97
Girard, G., R. Ouellet and C. Rigault.
  L'Univers du théâtre.
  D. Knowles, 208(FS):Jan82-113
Girardot, N.J. and M.L. Ricketts, eds.
  Imagination and Meaning.
  639(VQR):Autumn82-116
Giraud, Y., ed. La vie théâtrale dans les
  provinces du Midi.
  P. Ronzeaud, 535(RHL):Mar-Apr82-290
Giraud, Y. - see Scarron, P.
Giraud, Y. - see Sorel, C.
Gireev, D. Mikhail Bulgakov na beregakh
  Tereka.
  E.C. Haber, 550(RusR):Oct82-532
dei Girolami, R. - see under Remigio dei
  Girolami
Girouard, M. The Return to Camelot.*
  529(QQ):Summer82-453
Girouard, M. Robert Smythson and the
  Elizabethan Country House.
  J. Buxton, 617(TLS):23Dec83-1427
  P. Goldberger, 441:11Dec83-13
  P. Johnson, 362:29Sep83-21
Giroux, R. The Book Known as Q.*
  F. Kermode, 453(NYRB):28Apr83-30
  639(VQR):Autumn82-117
Gissing, G. Denzil Quarrier.* (J. Hal-
  perin, ed)
  P. Coustillas, 189(EA):Jan-Mar82-92
Gitlin, T. Inside Prime Time.
  R. Sklar, 441:20ct83-12
Gitlin, T. The Whole World Is Watching.
  P. Brantlinger, 128(CE):Sep82-475
Gitlitz, D.M. La estructura lírica de la
  comedia de Lope de Vega.
  I.P. Rothberg, 238:May82-306
Gittinger, M. Master Dyers to the World.
  R.L. Shep, 614:Winter83-19
Giudici, E. Louise Labé: Essai.*
  Y. Bellenger, 535(RHL):Sep-Dec82-870
  M-R. Logan, 551(RenQ):Winter82-649
Giudici, E. - see Labé, L.
Giusti-Lanham, H. and A. Dodi. The
  Cuisine of Venice. [shown in prev under
  Guisti-Lanham]
  W. and C. Cowen, 639(VQR):Spring81-71
Giustiniani, V.R. Neulateinische Dich-
  tung in Italien 1850-1950.*
  J. IJsewijn, 52:Band16Heft1-108
  R. Kassel, 547(RF):Band94Heft4-512
Givner, J. Katherine Anne Porter.*
  I. Ehrenpreis, 453(NYRB):20Jan83-13
  J. Symons, 617(TLS):10Jun83-593
Givón, T., ed. Syntax and Semantics.*
  (Vol 12)
  P.A. Shaw, 399(MLJ):Summer82-199
Glaeser, E., ed. Fazit.
  R.C. Holub, 406:Spring82-72
Glaeser, G. - see Brecht, B.
Glanz, D. How the West Was Drawn.
  J.V. Turano, 16:Autumn82-86

Glare, P.G.W. - see "Oxford Latin Dictionary"
von Glasenapp, H. Ausgewählte Kleine
Schriften. (H. Bechert and V. Moeller,
eds)
    L. Sternbach, 318(JAOS):Jul-Sep81-378
von Glasenapp, H. Von Buddha zu Gandhi.
    J.W. de Jong, 259(IIJ):Jan82-65
Glaser, H., ed. The German Mind of the
19th Century.
    D.L. Hoffmeister, 399(MLJ):Winter82-
    425
Glaser, H. Literatur des 20. Jahrhunderts
in Motiven. (Vol 2)
    K. Binneberg, 52:Band16Heft1-109
Glass, F.W. The Fertilizing Seed.
    J. Kerman, 453(NYRB):22Dec83-27
Glasse, H. The Art of Cookery Made Plain
and Easy.
    C. Driver, 617(TLS):23Dec83-1442
Glassie, H. All Silver and No Brass.
    P. Craig, 617(TLS):23Dec83-1428
Glassman, E. and M.F. Symmes. Cliché-
verre.
    K.F. Beall, 127:Summer82-179
    R.L. Patten, 637(VS):Winter82-243
Glassner, B. Essential Interactionism.
    S. Woolpert, 185:Oct82-186
Glatigny, M. and J. Guilhaumou, eds.
Peuple et Pouvoir.
    J-P. Seguin, 209(FM):Apr82-185
Glattauer, W. Strukturelle Lautgeographie
der Mundarten im südlichen Niederöster-
reich und in den angrenzenden Gebieten
des Burgenlandes und der Steiermark.
    L. Zehetner, 685(ZDL):2/1981-250
Glatzer, N.N. - see Kafka, F.
Glaze, A. I Am the Jefferson County Court-
house.
    J.D. McClatchy, 491:Sep82-346
Glaze, A.J. Art and Death in a Senufo Vil-
lage.
    P.L. Ravenhill, 2(AfrA):May82-26
Glazer, N. Ethnic Dilemmas 1964-1982.
    M. Walzer, 441:2Oct83-7
Gleason, A. Young Russia.*
    E.W., 617(TLS):23Sep83-1031
Gleason, W.J. Moral Idealists, Bureauc-
racy and Catherine the Great.
    W.R. Augustine, 104(CASS):Fall-Winter
    82-544
Glees, A. Exile Politics during the
Second World War.
    K.O. Morgan, 617(TLS):15Jul83-748
Glen, D. Realities/Poems.*
    R. Watson, 588(SSL):Vol 17-218
Glen, H. Vision and Disenchantment.
    C. Baldick, 617(TLS):19Aug83-884
Glendinning, N. and N. Harrison - see de
Cadalso, J.
Glendinning, V. Edith Sitwell.*
    M. Goldstein, 569(SR):Winter82-xiii
Glendinning, V. Vita.
    R. Blythe, 362:8Dec83-29
    M. Holroyd, 617(TLS):30Sep83-1038
    S. Hynes, 441:23Oct83-1
Glenn, K.M. Azorín (José Martínez Ruiz).
    S.K. Ugalde, 238:Sep82-464
Gless, D.J. "Measure for Measure," the
Law, and the Convent.*
    M. Rose, 551(RenQ):Spring81-145

Glick, T.F. Islamic and Christian Spain
in the Early Middle Ages.
    A.J. Forey, 161(DUJ):Dec81-118
    A. Mackay, 86(BHS):Apr82-148
Glidden, H.H. The Storyteller as Humanist.
    F. Rigolot, 207(FR):May83-938
Glissant, É. Le Discours antillais.
    J. Silenieks, 207(FR):Apr83-806
Glob, P.V. The Bog People.
    J-M. Rabaté, 98:Jun-Jun82-512
"The Global 2000 Report to the President."
    T.C. Holyoke, 42(AR):Summer82-364
Glofcheskie, J.M. Folk Music of Canada's
Oldest Polish Community.*
    R.B. Klymasz, 292(JAF):Oct-Dec82-491
Glorieux, G., ed. Belgica typographica,
1541-1600. (Vol 2)
    R. Hirsch, 551(RenQ):Winter81-567
"Glossaire des patois de la Suisse
romande." (fasc 70 and 71)
    P. Swiggers, 353:Vol 19No9/10-1035
"Glossarium Artis — Wörterbuch der Kunst."
(Vols 6 and 7)
    W. Müller-Wiener, 43:Band12Heft1-83
Glover, A. Next.
    R. Maud, 648(WCR):Oct82-58
Glover, D.E. C.S. Lewis.
    H.H. Watts, 395(MFS):Summer82-281
Gloversmith, F., ed. Class, Culture and
Social Change.*
    M.E. Rose, 366:Autumn82-261
Glowacki, J. Give Us This Day.
    L. Jones, 617(TLS):3Jun83-582
Gloy, K. Die Kantische Theorie der
Naturwissenschaft.*
    R. Stuhlmann-Laeisz, 53(AGP):Band64-
    Heft1-100
Glück, L. Descending Figure.*
    A.W. Fisher, 502(PrS):Fall82-93
    R. Jackson, 502(PrS):Spring82-91
    R. Tillinghast, 569(SR):Spring82-291
Glucker, J. Antiochus and the Late Acad-
emy.*
    D. Sedley, 520:Vol26No1-67
    J.C.M. van Winden, 394:Vol135fasc3/4-
    379
Glymour, C. Theory and Evidence.*
    P. Horwich, 311(JP):Dec82-775
    M.A. Kaplan, 185:Apr83-613
    I. Levi, 482(PhR):Jan82-124
    R.S. Woolhouse, 518:Apr82-96
    J. Worrall, 167:Jul82-105
Glynn, P. Skin to Skin.*
    A. Lurie, 453(NYRB):2Jun83-20
"Glyph 3." "Glyph 4." "Glyph 5." (S.
Weber and H. Sussman, eds of all)
    T. Hawkes, 447(N&Q):Feb81-94
"Glyph 6." (S. Weber and H. Sussman, eds)
    P. Bleton, 107(CRCL):Jun82-245
Gnoli, R., ed. The Gilgit Manuscript of
the Śayanāsanavastu and the Adhikaraṇa-
vastu.
    J. May, 259(IIJ):Jul80-249
Gnoli, R., with T. Venkatacharya, eds.
The Gilgit Manuscript of the Saṅghabheda-
vastu.
    J. May, 259(IIJ):Jul80-249
Gnolli, U. Pittori miniatori nell 'Umbria.
    C.B. Strehlke, 39:May82-417
Gobes, S. and others. Not Just Another
Quilt.
    M. Cowan, 614:Fall83-22

Gochet, P. Outline of a Nominalist Theory of Propositions.*
 I.G. McFetridge, 518:Jan82-41
Gochet, P. Quine en Perspective.*
 S. Rosen, 480(P&R):Spring82-144
Gockel, H. Max Frisch: "Gantenbein."*
 (2nd ed)
 R. Kieser, 222(GR):Winter82-37
Godard, H. - see Céline, L-F.
Godard, H. - see Giono, J.
Goddard, C. Jazz Away from Home.
 M. Harrison, 415:Jan82-33
Godden, M. - see Aelfric
Godfrey, J. 1204, the Unholy Crusade.
 J.W. Barker, 377:Nov81-179
 G.W. Day, 589:Jan82-189
Godfrey, L.R., ed. Scientists Confront Creationism.
 M. Bayles, 441:15May83-16
 R. Dawkins, 617(TLS):4Nov83-1206
Godley, W. and F. Cripps. Macroeconomics.
 P. Seabright, 617(TLS):16Sep83-977
 J. Vaizey, 362:9Jun83-22
Godwin, G. Mr. Bedford and the Muses.
 J. Gies, 441:18Sep83-14
Godwin, J. Mystery Religions in the Ancient World.*
 R.M. Ogilvie, 123:Vol32No1-102
Goebbels, J. The Goebbels Diaries 1939-1941. (F. Taylor, ed)
 H. James, 617(TLS):18Mar83-275
 442(NY):11Apr83-137
Goeppert, S., ed. Perspektiven psycho-analytischer Literaturkritik.
 A. Lange-Kirchheim, 224(GRM):Band32 Heft1-104
Goethals, G.T. The TV Ritual.
 P. Brantlinger, 128(CE):Sep82-475
von Goethe, J.W. The Eternal Feminine. (F. Ungar, ed)
 W.H. Clark, 399(MLJ):Summer82-217
von Goethe, J.W. Goethe on Art.* (J. Gage, ed and trans)
 M.L. Baeumer, 221(GQ):Mar82-250
 E.H. Gombrich, 59:Jun82-237
von Goethe, J.W. Goethe, Selected Poems. (C. Middleton, ed and trans)
 M. Perloff, 29:Sep/Oct83-10
von Goethe, J.W. Traité des couleurs. (H. Bideau, trans)
 E. Escoubas, 98:Mar82-231
Goetz, H-W. Die Geschichtstheologie des Orosius.
 J.M. Alonso-Núñez, 313:Vol72-219
Goetzmann, W.H. and J.C. Porter. The West as Romantic Horizon.
 584(SWR):Summer82-v
 639(VQR):Autumn82-136
Goff, T.W. Marx and Mead.*
 D.N. Levine, 185:Oct82-184
 J. Walton, 319:Apr83-258
Goffart, W. Barbarians and Romans.
 J.A.S. Evans, 529(QQ):Autumn82-478
 E. James, 589:Oct82-885
 N. Wagner, 684(ZDA):Band111Heft2-57
Goffman, E. Forms of Talk.*
 M. Botwinick, 186(ETC.):Winter82-394
 S.U. Philips, 350:Jun83-429
 K.S., 185:Jul83-826
Goguel, C.M. and F. Viatte. Roman Drawings of the Sixteenth Century from the Musée du Louvre, Paris.
 A.S. Harris, 551(RenQ):Summer81-251

Gohin, Y. - see Hugo, V.
Gohorry, J. Understudies.
 I. McMillan, 493:Jun82-71
Goines, D.L. A Constructed Roman Alphabet.
 D.J.R.B., 441:30Jan83-14
Golbert de Goodbar, P. Epu Peñiwen ("Los Dos Hermanos").
 H.E. Manelis Klein, 269(IJAL):Oct82-484
Gold, A. Before Romantic Words.
 D. Barbour, 648(WCR):Oct82-37
Gold, B.K., ed. Literary and Artistic Patronage in Ancient Rome.*
 T. Russell-Cobb, 324:Jul83-488
Gold, G.L. The Role of France, Quebec and Belgium in the Revival of French in Louisiana Schools.
 C.R. Pons, 207(FR):Oct82-202
Goldbarth, A. Original Light.
 P. Lopate, 441:2Oct83-15
Goldbarth, A. Who Gathered and Whispered Behind Me.
 J. Addiego, 448:Vol20No1-136
Goldberg, H. Israel Salanter.
 A.J., 185:Apr83-640
Goldberg, J. Endlesse Worke.
 D.C., 604:Spring-Summer82-34
 K. Gross, 676(YR):Autumn82-x
 M. McCanles, 141:Summer82-282
 E. Sacks, 400(MLN):Dec82-1298
Goldberg, R., ed. Tonos a lo divino y a lo humano.
 E.T. Howe, 304(JHP):Spring82-254
Goldberg, S.M. The Making of Menander's Comedy.*
 E. Fantham, 487:Spring82-87
 J. Tatum, 24:Fall82-154
Goldberger, P. The Skyscraper.*
 D. Gebhard, 576:Dec82-353
 P. Missac, 98:Oct82-880
 M.L. Wang, 505:Mar82-141
Goldblatt, R.I. Topoi.
 J.L. Bell, 84:Mar82-95
 P.J. Scott, 316:Jun82-445
Goldemberg, I. The Fragmented Life of Don Jacobo Lerner. (Spanish title: La Vida a Plazos de Don Jacobo Lerner.)
 P.K. Speck, 37:May-Jun82-63
Goldemberg, I. Hombre De Paso/Just Passing Through.
 Z. Shanken, 287:Aug/Sep82-26
Golden, M. Migrations of the Heart.
 G.D. Kendrick, 95(CLAJ):Mar83-362
 D. McWhorter, 441:1May83-16
 442(NY):21Feb83-134
Golden, R.M. The Godly Rebellion.
 D. Parker, 617(TLS):9Sep83-965
Goldensohn, L. The Tether.
 M. Kinzie, 29:Jul/Aug83-33
Golding, W. Parade sauvage.
 C. Jordis, 450(NRF):Feb82-154
Golding, W. Rites of Passage.*
 J.L. Halio, 598(SoR):Winter83-203
Goldman, A.H. Elvis.
 J.T., 585(SoQ):Summer82-118
Goldman, A.H. Justice and Reverse Discrimination.*
 M.D. Bayles, 311(JP):Aug82-455
 B.R. Gross, 393(Mind):Oct82-632
 C.P., 189(EA):Oct-Dec82-497
Goldman, M. China's Intellectuals.*
 L. Dittmer, 293(JASt):Aug82-810

Goldman, M.I. The Enigma of Soviet Petro-
leum.
E.A. Hewett, 550(RusR):Jan82-89
Goldman, M.I. U.S.S.R. in Crisis.
P. Hanson, 617(TLS):16Sep83-977
E.A. Hewett, 441:10Jul83-11
L.C. Thurow, 61:Feb83-102
Goldman, P. and T. Fuller, with others.
Charlie Company.
T. Buckley, 441:1May83-12
Goldman, S.M. Contemporary Mexican Paint-
ing in a Time of Change.
J. Stringer, 127:Spring82-79
Goldman, W. Adventures in the Screen
Trade.
J. Maslin, 441:20Mar83-14
442(NY):18Apr83-151
Goldmann, L. Method in the Sociology of
Literature. (W.Q. Boelhower, ed and
trans)
R. Best, 89(BJA):Spring82-183
Goldschläger, A. Simone Weil et Spinoza.
J.B. Ayoub, 154:Dec82-774
Goldschmidt, H., ed. Zu Beethoven.*
B. Cooper, 410(M&L):Jul/Oct81-406
Goldsmith, U.K., with T. Schneider and S.S.
Coleman, eds. Rainer Maria Rilke: A
Verse Concordance to His Complete Lyri-
cal Poetry.*
T.J. Casey, 402(MLR):Jan82-245
S. Hoefert, 564:Feb81-88
Goldstein, D.I. Dostoyevsky and the Jews.
M. Banerjee, 395(MFS):Winter81/82-663
M.V. Jones, 575(SEER):Jul82-449
H.K. Schefski, 550(RusR):Apr82-236
Goldstein, I. Jewish Justice and Concilia-
tion.
J.M. Rosenberg, 390:Oct82-60
Goldstein, J.K. The Modern American Vice
Presidency.*
639(VQR):Autumn82-124
Goldstein, M. Library Research in Spanish,
French and German Literature.
N.C. Ekstein, 207(FR):Feb83-527
Goldstein, R. The Mind-Body Problem.
C. Seebohm, 441:25Sep83-14
F. Taliaferro, 231:Dec83-74
Goldthwaite, R.A. The Building of Renais-
sance Florence.*
A. Molho, 589:Oct82-886
P. Partner, 576:Mar82-60
N. Rubinstein, 551(RenQ):Summer82-274
Goldworth, A. - see Bentham, J.
Golemba, H.L. Frank R. Stockton.
R.L. Buckland, 573(SSF):Winter82-90
Golffing, F. Collected Poems.
J.D. McClatchy, 491:Jun82-170
J. Ridland, 472:Spring/Summer83-191
Göller, K.H., ed. The Alliterative Morte
Arthure.
J.L. Boren, 481(PQ):Fall82-491
Gollin, R.K. Nathaniel Hawthorne and the
Truth of Dreams.*
E. Wright, 677(YES):Vol 12-311
Golovin, P.N. The End of Russian America.*
(B. Dmytryshyn and E.A.P. Crownhart-
Vaughan, eds and trans)
G. Barratt, 575(SEER):Jan82-122
Gom, L. Land of the Peace.*
M.T. Lane, 198:Jan82-71
S. Shreve, 648(WCR):Jun82-45
C. Wiseman, 102(CanL):Summer82-140

Gombrich, E.H. Art and Illusion.* (Span-
ish title: Arte e ilusión.)
D. Angulo Íñiguez, 48:Apr-Jun80-212
Gombrich, E.H. Ideals and Idols.
P. Burke, 90:Feb82-107
P. Joannides, 97(CQ):Vol 11No3-390
D.D. Todd, 154:Jun82-381
Gombrich, E.H. The Sense of Order.*
Y. Michaud, 98:Jan82-22
Gómez, L.O. and H. Woodward, Jr., eds.
Barabudur.
P. Mitter, 576:Oct82-258
Gómez de Castro, Á. Sonetti. (I. Pepe
Sarno, ed)
F. Pierce, 86(BHS):Oct82-339
Gómez Ramos, R. Las empresas artísticas
de Alfonso X el Sabio.
I. Mateo Gómez, 48:Apr-Jun80-211
Gomme, A.H., ed. D.H. Lawrence.*
B. Caplan, 219(GaR):Spring82-194
Gomme, A.W., A. Andrewes and K.J. Dover.
A Historical Commentary on Thucydides.*
(Vol 5, Bk 8)
M.F. McGregor, 487:Summer82-167
Gonda, J. Hymns of the Ṛgveda Not
Employed in the Solemn Ritual.
H.W. Bodewitz, 259(IIJ):Apr80-149
Gonda, J. The Mantras of the Agnyupasthāna
and the Sautrāmaṇī.
K. Mylius, 259(IIJ):Jan82-53
Gonda, J. The Medium in the Ṛgveda.
R. Rocher, 318(JAOS):Oct-Dec81-467
Gonda, J. The Praügaśastra.
K. Mylius, 259(IIJ):Oct82-307
Gonda, J. Triads in the Veda.
T.Y. Elizarenkova, 259(IIJ):Jan80-47
Gonda, J. Vedic Ritual.
F. Staal, 293(JASt):Feb82-269
Gonda, J. - see te Nijenhuis, E.
Gondos, V., Jr. J. Franklin Jameson and
the Birth of the National Archives, 1906-
1926.
H.T. Pinkett, 14:Spring82-193
de Góngora, L. Letrillas. (R. Jammes,
ed)
J.F.G. Gornall, 402(MLR):Jul82-748
de Góngora, L. Soledades. (J. Beverley,
ed)
D. Fernández-Morera, 240(HR):Winter82-
103
de Góngora, L. Sonetos. (B. Ciplijaus-
kaité, ed)
W. Pabst, 547(RF):Band94Heft2/3-369
"Göngu-Hrolfs Saga."* (H. Pálsson and P.
Edwards, trans)
S.A. Mitchell, 563(SS):Summer82-258
K.H. Ober, 301(JEGP):Jul82-400
Gonin, È. Le Point de vue d'Ellénore.
N. King, 208(FS):Oct82-477
P-L. Rey, 450(NRF):Jun82-104
Gonzales, L. El Vago.
P-L. Adams, 61:Jun83-104
D. Cole, 441:30Oct83-33
Gonzalez, A. Collected Poems.
S. Brown, 493:Dec81-65
González, A.L. Ser y participación.
A. Reix, 542:Jul-Sep82-535
González, E.F. - see under Fernández
González, E.
González, J.J.M. - see under Martín Gon-
zález, J.J.

González Boixo, J.C. Claves narrativas de
Juan Rulfo.
P.R. Beardsell, 86(BHS):Apr82-163
González-del-Valle, L. and A. Correspon-
dencia comercial. (2nd ed)
M. Iglesias, 399(MLJ):Summer82-226
González-del-Valle, L.T. El teatro de
Federico García Lorca y otros ensayos
sobre literatura española e hispano-
americana.*
M.T. Halsey, 552(REH):Oct82-469
González Jiménez, M. and A. González
Gómez. El Libro del Repartimiento de
Jerez de la Frontera.
D.W. Lomax, 86(BHS):Oct82-330
T.F. Ruiz, 589:Jul82-682
González Ollé, F. - see de Horozco, S.
González Reboredo, V. Nueva visión de la
novela "Doña Bárbara."
D.L. Shaw, 86(BHS):Jan82-85
Goodacre, S.H. - see Carroll, L.
Goodall, B. The Homilies of St. John
Chrysostom on the Letters of St. Paul
to Titus and Philemon.
J.N. Birdsall, 303(JoHS):Vol 102-297
É. Des Places, 555:Vol55fasc1-167
de Goodbar, P.G. - see under Golbert de
Goodbar, P.
Goodell, G. Independent Feature Film
Production.
M. Block, 18:Apr83-62
Goodenough, S. The Country Parson.
G. Irvine, 617(TLS):1Apr83-318
Gooders, J. Birds that Came Back.
R. O'Hanlon, 617(TLS):16Nov83-998
Goodfield, J. An Imagined World.*
D.W. Noble, 106:Winter82-321
Goodin, R.E. Manipulatory Politics.*
S. Bok, 185:Oct82-177
W.L.M., 543:Dec81-389
Goodman, J., with I. Moncreiffe of that
Ilk. Debrett's Royal Scotland.
C. Bingham, 617(TLS):23Sep83-1030
Goodman, M.B. Contemporary Literary Cen-
sorship.
T.J. Main, 114(ChiR):Winter83-81
R.E. Ziegfeld, 395(MFS):Summer82-322
Goodman, N. The Structure of Appearance.
(3rd ed)
R. Farrell, 63:Jun82-170
Goodman, N. Ways of Worldmaking.
R. Farrell, 63:Jun82-170
R. Howell, 482(PhR):Apr82-262
J.F. Rosenberg, 449:May82-307
Goodrich, L. Thomas Eakins.
A. Berman, 55:Nov82-43
J. Wilmerding, 441:2Jan83-5
Goodway, D. London Chartism 1838-1848.
F.M.L. Thompson, 617(TLS):21Jan83-65
Goodwin, B. Social Science and Utopia.
L.T. Sargent, 322(JHI):Oct-Dec82-681
Goodwin, B. and K. Taylor. The Politics
of Utopia.
J. Lively, 617(TLS):4Mar83-218
Goodwin, E.C. The Magistracy Rediscovered.
B.C. Daniels, 656(WMQ):Oct82-700
Goodwin, G.L. The Ontological Argument of
Charles Hartshorne.
T.R.V., 543:Jun82-870
Goodwin, J. - see Hall, P.
Goodwin, K. Understanding African Poetry.
M.M. Carlin, 617(TLS):16Sep83-996

Goodwin, R.A. Troika.
K. Parthé, 399(MLJ):Summer82-218
D. Phillips, 574(SEEJ):Spring82-134
Goody, J. The Development of the Family
and Marriage in Europe.
G. Duby, 617(TLS):14Oct83-1107
Goodyear, F.H., Jr. Contemporary American
Realism since 1960.
G. Baker, 135:Jan82-13
M.S. Young, 39:Jun82-511
Goodyear, F.R.D. - see Tacitus
Goold, G.P. - see "Catullus"
Goorney, H. The Theatre Workshop Story.
D.R., 214:Vol 10No38-144
Goossens, J. Deutsche Dialektologie.
M. Philipp, 685(ZDL):3/1981-379
Goossens, J., ed. Westfälisches Wörter-
buch. (Vol 1, Pts 2-4)
U. Scheuermann, 685(ZDL):1/1982-79
Goossens, J. and T. Sodman, eds. Reynaert
Reynard Reynke.
T.W. Best, 221(GQ):Mar82-245
Gopal, S. - see "Jawaharlal Nehru"
Gordimer, N. July's People.*
J.L. Halio, 598(SoR):Winter83-203
Gordis, R. The Book of Job.
Y. Gitay, 318(JAOS):Apr-Jun81-248
Gordon, A. An American Dreamer.*
C.E. Eisinger, 395(MFS):Summer81-372
H. Parker, 587(SAF):Spring82-121
Gordon, B. Defects of the Heart.
P. van Rjndt, 441:3Jul83-9
Gordon, B. The Final Steps.
R.L. Shep, 614:Spring83-20
Gordon, B. Shaker Textile Arts.*
E.J. Gehret, 292(JAF):Jul-Sep82-354
Gordon, C. The Collected Stories of Caro-
line Gordon.*
W. Buchanon, 573(SSF):Winter82-80
R. Buffington, 569(SR):Spring82-264
639(VQR):Winter82-19
Gordon, C. - see Foucault, M.
Gordon, C. - see "Erskine May's Parliamen-
tary Practice"
Gordon, D.C. The French Language and
National Identity.
G. Sankoff, 355(LSoc):Apr82-135
Gordon, D.C. The Republic of Lebanon.
M. Yapp, 617(TLS):26Aug83-911
Gordon, G. - see Shakespeare, W.
Gordon, J. James Joyce's Metamorphoses.*
K.E. Marre, 395(MFS):Summer82-266
Gordon, L. Robert Coover.
J.A. Varsava, 268(IFR):Summer83-136
Gordon, M. Head of the Harbour.
C. Klein, 99:Mar83-342
Gordon, M. The Kanner Aliyah.
A.T. Seaman, 198:Apr82-97
Gordon, R. and A. Forge. Monet.
C. Tomkins, 442(NY):19Dec83-125
Gorecki, J. Capital Punishment.
D. Pannick, 617(TLS):23Dec83-1426
Gorer, G. Africa Dances.
A.J.G.H., 617(TLS):18Mar83-279
Gori, F. and C. Questa, eds. La Fortuna
di Tacito dal sec. XV ad oggi.*
J. Hellegouarc'h, 555:Vol56fasc1-164
Gorilovics, T. La Légende de Victor Hugo
de Paul Lafargue.
J. Flower, 208(FS):Apr82-212
Görlach, M. Einführung ins Frühneu-
englische.*
D. Nehls, 257(IRAL):May82-168

Gornick, V. Women in Science.
  M.W. Rossiter, 441:2Oct83-11
Górnowicz, H. Toponimia Powiśla Gdań-
  skiego.
  Z. Zagórski, 360(LP):Vol25-150
Gorny, J. The British Labour Movement and
  Zionism 1917-1948.
  W.J. Fishman, 617(TLS):13May83-497
Görög, V. and others. Histoires d'enfants
  terribles (Afrique noire).
  E. Dammann, 196:Band23Heft1/2-128
  L. Todd, 203:Vol93No1-124
Gorsky, S.R. Virginia Woolf.
  R.D. Newman, 577(SHR):Winter82-82
Görtzen, R. Jürgen Habermas.
  J.B. Thompson, 617(TLS):8Apr83-357
Gorz, A. Farewell to the Working Class.
  M. Poole, 362:26May83-20
Gose, E.B., Jr. The Transformation
  Process in Joyce's "Ulysses."*
  B. Benstock, 395(MFS):Summer81-310
  S. Feshbach, 329(JJQ):Winter83-240
  P. Herring, 659(ConL):Fall83-387
  R.D. Newman, 577(SHR):Fall82-369
Gosling, J.C.B. and C.C.W. Taylor. The
  Greeks on Pleasure.
  T. Irwin, 617(TLS):16Sep83-1003
Gosling, P. The Woman in Red.
  T.J. Binyon, 617(TLS):30Sep83-1037
Gosse, I. A Frolilege.
  B.N. Lee, 503:Winter82-210
Gossen, C.T. - see von Wartburg, W.
Gossip, C.J. An Introduction to French
  Classical Tragedy.
  H.R. Allentuch, 612(ThS):May82-119
  P.V. Conroy, Jr., 130:Winter82/83-378
  R. McBride, 402(MLR):Jul82-722
  P.J. Yarrow, 208(FS):Apr82-202
  E.M. Zimmermann, 207(FR):Mar83-630
Gossman, L. The Empire Unpossess'd.
  M. Baridon, 189(EA):Oct-Dec82-471
  D. La Capra, 131(CL):Winter82-78
Gothot-Mersch, C. - see Flaubert, G.
Gothot-Mersch, C. and others. Lire Sime-
  non, Réalité/Fiction/Écriture.
  B. Vercier, 535(RHL):Sep-Dec82-967
Gotlieb, S. A Woman of Consequence.
  E. Jakab, 441:19Jun83-12
Gotoff, H.C. Cicero's Elegant Style.*
  C. Moussy, 555:Vol55fasc2-378
  E. Rawson, 447(N&Q):Feb81-88
Götte, C. Das Menschen- und Herrscherbild
  des "rex maior" im "Ruodlieb."
  F.P. Knapp, 684(ZDA):Band111Heft4-159
Göttert, K-H. and W. Herrlitz. Linguis-
  tische Propädeutik.
  G. Starke, 682(ZPSK):Band34Heft2-232
Gottfried von Strassburg. Tristan. (R.
  Krohn, ed and trans)
  C.S. Jaeger, 589:Jul82-613
Gottfried, R.K. The Art of Joyce's Syntax
  in "Ulysses."
  S. Ehrlich, 320(CJL):Spring82-75
  M.P. Gillespie, 594:Spring82-116
  V. Mahon, 402(MLR):Jan82-188
  R.D. Newman, 577(SHR):Winter82-80
  M. Power, 395(MFS):Summer81-316
  M.T. Reynolds, 329(JJQ):Winter83-235
Gottfried, R.S. The Black Death.
  P-L. Adams, 61:Aug83-100
  J. Davison, 441:28Aug83-13
  W.H. McNeill, 453(NYRB):21Jul83-28

Gottlieb, D. Ontological Economy.*
  M. Jubien, 311(JP):Dec82-781
  C. Parsons, 84:Dec82-409
  M.E. Tiles, 518:Apr82-90
  T.S. Weston, 316:Jun82-473
Gottlieb, E. Lost Angels of a Ruined
  Paradise.
  A. McWhir, 627(UTQ):Summer82-420
Gottschalk, H.B. Heraclides of Pontus.
  J.D.G. Evans, 303(JoHS):Vol 102-250
  A.A. Long, 123:Vol132No2-200
Goudzwaard, B. Capitalism and Progress.
  A.L. Stinchcombe, 185:Oct82-114
Gough, B.M. Distant Dominion.*
  C. Harris, 656(WMQ):Jul82-554
Gould, A. Astral Sea.
  G. Catalano, 381:Oct81-349
Gould, C. Bernini in France.*
  A. Blunt, 90:Dec82-770
  B. Scott, 39:Sep82-198
Gould, C.C. Marx's Social Ontology.*
  D. Lamb, 323:Oct82-304
  C. Melakopides, 529(QQ):Spring82-148
Gould, E. Mythic Intentions in Modern Lit-
  erature.
  W. Sypher, 569(SR):Fall82-575
  J.B. Vickery, 395(MFS):Summer82-352
Gould, S.J. Hen's Teeth and Horse's Toes.
  S. Rose, 441:8May83-3
  442(NY):9May83-135
Gould, T. Inside Outsider.
  G. Ewart, 617(TLS):16Sep83-979
  S. Moorsom, 362:15Sep83-22
Goulding, M. The Fishes and the Forest.
  Man and Fisheries on an Amazon Frontier.
  S.H. Weitzman, 37:Jul-Aug82-61
Goulson, C.F. A Source Book of Royal Com-
  missions and Other Major Governmental In-
  quiries in Canadian Education 1787-1978.
  W. Downes, 298:Winter82/83-133
Gourlay, E. Songs and Dances.
  B. Whiteman, 198:Apr82-112
de Gourmont, R. Sixtine [suivi de] Let-
  tres à Sixtine. Histoires Magiques et
  autres récits.
  P. Fawcett, 617(TLS):7Oct83-1076
Gourou, P. Terres de Bonne Espérance.
  J. Gottmann, 617(TLS):14Jan83-41
Goux, J-P. La Fable des jours.
  J. Pfeiffer, 450(NRF):Jan82-122
Govier, K. Going Through the Motions.
  D. Myers, 441:17Apr83-26
Gow, B. Madagascar and the Protestant
  Impact.
  M. Bloch, 69:Vol51No1-540
Gower, J. Confessio Amantis. (M. Ito,
  trans)
  S. Ando, 382(MAE):1982/2-263
Gowing, L. Lucian Freud.
  C. Lampert, 617(TLS):7Jan83-8
Goyard-Fabre, S. Kant et le problème du
  droit.
  J-L. Dumas, 192(EP):Apr-Jun81-233
Goyard-Fabre, S. - see Abbé de Saint-
  Pierre
Goyen, W. Arcadio.
  P-L. Adams, 61:Nov83-148
  R. Gibbons, 441:6Nov83-14
Goyen, W. La Maison d'haleine.
  C. Jordis, 450(NRF):Dec82-106
Goyet, T. and J-P. Collinet, eds. Jour-
  nées Bossuet.*
  C.M. Probes, 475:No16Pt2-419

Goytisolo, J. Makbara.
  C. Dis, 450(NRF):Jul-Aug82-204
Gozzano, G. Tutte le poesie. (A. Rocca, ed)
  M. Mari, 228(GLSI):Vol 159fasc505-141
Grab, W. Ein Mann, der Marx Ideen gab. Wilhelm Schulz.
  A. Ruiz, 224(GRM):Band32Heft1-111
Grabar, O. and others. City in the Desert.
  A.M. Watson, 589:Jan82-128
Grabar, O. and S. Blair. Epic Images and Contemporary History.*
  J.W. Clinton, 589:Oct82-891
Grabes, H. The Mutable Glass.
  A. Fowler, 617(TLS):19Aug83-872
Grabo, N.S. The Coincidental Art of Charles Brockden Brown.*
  E. Emerson, 27(AL):Oct82-445
  W.L. Hedges, 445(NCF):Sep82-220
  E.J. Sundquist, 580(SCR):Spring83-132
Grabowicz, G.G. The Poet as Mythmaker.
  A. McMillin, 617(TLS):20May83-525
Grabowicz, G.G. Toward a History of Ukrainian Literature.
  O.S. Ilnytzkyj, 550(RusR):Oct82-523
Grace, G.W. An Essay on Language.
  C. Abdul-Ghani, 350:Sep83-684
Grace, S. Violent Duality.*
  I. Ferris, 627(UTQ):Summer82-466
  W.J. Keith, 168(ECW):Spring82-88
Gracián, B. El criticón. (S. Alonso, ed)
  M.Z. Hafter, 240(HR):Autumn82-493
Gracq, J. En lisant, en écrivant.*
  R. Amossy, 400(MLN):May82-1037
Gracy, D.B. 2d. An Introduction to Archives and Manuscripts.
  E. Oetting, 14:Summer82-330
Gradidge, R. Dream Houses: The Edwardian Ideal.*
  J. Lubbock, 46:Mar82-61
  P. Skipwith, 90:May82-309
Gradman, B. Metamorphosis in Keats.*
  C.L. Bernstein, 661(WC):Summer82-154
  L. Waldoff, 340(KSJ):Vol31-220
Gradon, P. - see "Dan Michel's 'Ayenbite of Inwyt'"
Grady, J. Catch the Wind.
  C.L. Rawlins, 649(WAL):Spring82-91
Graf, R. Der Konjunktiv in gesprochener Sprache.*
  A. Lötscher, 685(ZDL):3/1982-388
Graff, G. Literature Against Itself.*
  J.W. Davidson, 477(PLL):Winter82-428
  C. Gallagher, 153:Winter82-40
  R.A. Lanham, 599:Winter82-65
  R.D. Stock, 396(ModA):Winter82-102
Grafton, A. Joseph Scaliger. (Vol 1)
  E.J. Kenney, 617(TLS):19Aug83-871
Grafton, C.B. Decorative Alphabets for Needleworkers, Craftsmen and Artists.
  M. Cowan, 614:Winter83-15
Graham, H.F. - see Skrynnikov, R.G.
Graham, J. Erosion.
  M. Kinzie, 29:Nov/Dec83-40
  W. Logan, 617(TLS):10Jun83-614
  H. Vendler, 441:17Jul83-10
Graham, J. Hybrids of Plants and of Ghosts.*
  C. Berger, 491:Apr82-35
  W. Logan, 472:Spring/Summer83-211
  T. Swiss, 584(SWR):Summer82-345
Graham, J. In the Company of Others.
  A. Chisholm, 617(TLS):20May83-506

Graham, K. J.L. Austin.
  A.K., 543:Jun82-872
Graham, L.R. Between Science and Values.*
  K.E.S., 185:Jan83-418
Graham, M. The Notebooks of Martha Graham.
  P.J. Rosenwald, 135:Sep82-168
Graham, R. and F. Gibson - see Neatby, H.
Graham, R.B.C. - see under Cunninghame Graham, R.B.
Graham, W.S. Collected Poems 1942-1977.
  R. Watson, 588(SSL):Vol 17-218
Graham, W.T., Jr. "The Lament for the South."
  D.R. Knechtges, 244(HJAS):Dec82-668
"Grammatičeskaja leksikologija russkogo jazyka."
  A. Bartoszewicz, 360(LP):Vol125-176
Grammaticus, S. - see under Saxo Grammaticus
Gran, P. Islamic Roots of Capitalism.
  P. Cachia, 318(JAOS):Oct-Dec81-462
Granatstein, J.L. The Ottawa Men.
  A. Andrew, 150(DR):Autumn82-511
  R. Whitaker, 99:Nov82-30
Grandstaff, P.J. Interregional Migration in the USSR.
  P.E. Lydolph, 550(RusR):Apr82-218
Grandy, R.E. Advanced Logic for Applications.
  N. Tennant, 316:Sep82-714
Granger, B. American Essay Serials from Franklin to Irving.*
  W.L. Hedges, 173(ECS):Summer82-454
Granger, B. The Shattered Eye.
  E. Hunter, 441:9Jan83-13
Grannes, A. Loan Compounds in Bulgarian Reflecting the Turkish Indefinite "Izafet"-Construction.
  C. Kramer, 574(SEEJ):Spring82-137
  G.A.M.W. Moudrova, 575(SEER):Jan82-97
Granoff, P.E. Philosophy and Argument in Late Vedānta.*
  L.T. O'Neil, 485(PE&W):Jul82-342
Gransden, A. Historical Writing in England, II.
  R.B. Dobson, 617(TLS):18Mar83-276
Grant, E. Much Ado about Nothing.
  D.C. Lindberg, 551(RenQ):Autumn82-448
  C.B. Schmitt, 319:Apr83-278
Grant, I.F. Along a Highland Road.
  E.R. Cregeen, 595(ScS):Vol125-81
Grant, J., ed. La Passiun de Seint Edmund.
  M. Boulton, 545(RPh):Feb82-566
  A.D. Wilshere, 402(MLR):Jan82-197
Grant, J.E., E.J. Rose and M.J. Tolley - see Blake, W.
Grant, J.S. - see Davies, R.
Grant, M. Dawn of the Middle Ages.
  639(VQR):Summer82-84
Grant, M. From Alexander to Cleopatra.
  J.K. Davison, 441:8May83-18
  A.A. Long, 617(TLS):1Apr83-338
Grant, P. Images and Ideas in Literature of the English Renaissance.*
  E.H. Hageman, 551(RenQ):Summer81-271
Grant, P. Six Modern Authors and Problems of Belief.*
  N. Jacobs, 541(RES):Aug82-362
  B. Reynolds, 402(MLR):Oct82-940
  K. Watson, 447(N&Q):Oct81-473
"Granta 7." (B. Buford, ed)
  P. Kemp, 617(TLS):15Apr83-374

"Granta 8: Dirty Realism." (B. Buford, ed)
L. Sage, 617(TLS):12Aug83-866

Granvik, R. Vallpojken till regeringsborgen.
R.G. Selleck, 563(SS):Summer82-275

Grape, A., G. Kallstenius and O. Thorell - see Sturluson, S.

Grape-Albers, H. Spätantike Bilder aus der Welt des Arztes.
L.E. Voigts, 589:Oct82-893

Grasberger, F., ed. Anton Bruckner in Wien.
P. Banks, 410(M&L):Jul/Oct81-397

Grasberger, F. - see "Bruckner-Jahrbuch 1980"

Grass, G. Headbirths, or The Germans are Dying Out.*
B. Andrews, 364:Apr/May82-129
P. Lewis, 565:Vol23No3-68

Grass, G. The Meeting at Telgte.*
P. Lewis, 565:Vol23No2-44

Grass, R. and W.R. Risley, eds. Waiting for Pegasus.*
M.R. Coke, 402(MLR):Jul82-750

Grassi, E. Rhetoric as Philosophy.*
R.D., 543:Sep81-131
C. Perelman, 319:Apr83-256
D. Robey, 506(PSt):May82-165

Grattan, V.L. Mary Coulter.
J.C. Henry, 576:Mar82-77

Grätzer, G. Universal Algebra. (2nd ed)
H. Werner, 316:Jun82-450

Graumann, G. "La Guerre de Troie" aura lieu.*
R. Laubreaux, 535(RHL):Mar-Apr82-315

Graus, F. Die Nationenbildung der Westslaven im Mittelalter.
K. Górski, 575(SEER):Apr82-288
H. Kaminsky, 589:Oct82-895

Graves, M.A.R. The House of Lords in the Parliaments of Edward VI and Mary I.*
S.E. Lehmberg, 551(RenQ):Autumn82-495

Graves, R. In Broken Images: Selected Letters of Robert Graves, 1914-1946. (P. O'Prey, ed)
I. Hamilton, 453(NYRB):18Aug83-38
M. Imlah, 493:Sep82-67

Graves, R. Wife to Mr. Milton.
J. Egan, 568(SCN):Fall82-44

Graves, R.P. The Brothers Powys.
C. Lock, 362:5May83-23
P. Redgrove, 617(TLS):27May83-536

Graves, R.P. A.E. Housman.*
R.G. Thomas, 541(RES):Feb82-107
H.W., 636(VP):Spring82-90
N. White, 447(N&Q):Aug81-358

Gray, A. Unlikely Stories, Mostly.
A. Mars-Jones, 617(TLS):18Mar83-258
J. Mellors, 362:9Jun83-26

Gray, B. The World History of Rashid al-Din.
D. James, 463:Winter82/83-382

Gray, D. Robert Henryson.*
J. Kerling, 179(ES):Apr82-163
F.H. Ridley, 589:Jul82-626

Gray, E. The Great Uranium Cartel.
M.L. Cross, 150(DR):Summer82-346

Gray, E.A. By Candlelight.
M. Pelling, 617(TLS):30Dec83-1450

Gray, H. On-Loom Cardweaving.
P. Bach, 614:Summer83-20

Gray, I. Antiquaries of Gloucestershire and Bristol.
B. Smith, 325:Oct82-122

Gray, J. Mill on Liberty: A Defence.
R. Lindley, 617(TLS):3Jun83-566

Gray, J.M. Thro' the Vision of the Night.*
E.W. Slinn, 67:Nov82-201
M. Woodfield, 72:Band218Heft2-443

Gray, N. The Painted Inscriptions of David Jones.
D. Farr, 39:Aug82-121

Gray, R., ed. Robert Penn Warren.
A. Shepherd, 392:Winter81/82-53

Gray, S. Beyond the Veil.
J.K. Davison, 441:10Apr83-18

Gray, T. Thomas Gray: Selected Poems. (J. Heath-Stubbs, ed)
M. O'Neill, 83:Spring82-160

Gray, V.B. "Invisible Men's" Literary Heritage.*
H. Beaver, 677(YES):Vol 12-320

Grayson, C., ed. The World of Dante.*
J.C. Barnes, 382(MAE):1982/2-266

Grayson, C., ed. The World of Egypt.
R.H. Lansing, 276:Spring82-59

Grayson, R. I Brake for Delmore Schwartz.
I. Gold, 441:14Aug83-12

de Grazia, E. and R.K. Newman. Banned Films.
G. Cowan, 441:6Feb83-16
T. Wiener, 18:Jun83-68

Grazia Profeti, M. Per una bibliografia di J. Pérez de Montalbán.
K. and R. Reichenberger, 547(RF): Band93Heft3/4-484

Greaves, R.L. - see Bunyan, J.

Greaves, R.L. and R. Zaller, eds. Biographical Dictionary of British Radicals in the Seventeenth Century. (Vol 2)
C. Hill, 617(TLS):21Oct83-1169

Greber, J.M. Abraham und David Roentgen: Möbel für Europa.*
C. Witt-Dörring, 471:Apr/May/Jun82-166

Greeley, A.M. Ascent Into Hell.
W. Schott, 441:3Jul83-8

Green, A. Flaubert and the Historical Novel.*
S. Haig, 207(FR):Mar83-637
A.W. Raitt, 208(FS):Jul82-343

Green, A. The Tragic Effect.*
E. Slater, 447(N&Q):Feb81-92

Green, C.L. Edward Albee.*
F.E. Eddleman, 397(MD):Dec82-585

Green, D. Great Cobbett.
J. Stevenson, 617(TLS):9Dec83-1380

Green, D.H. The Art of Recognition in Wolfram's "Parzival."
A. Groos, 617(TLS):29Apr83-442

Green, D.H. Irony in the Medieval Romance.*
M.W. Bloomfield, 589:Apr82-377
D. Mehl, 677(YES):Vol 12-232
B.N. Sargent-Baur, 545(RPh):May82-671
J. Stevens, 131(CL):Winter82-65
S.C. Van D'Elden, 406:Winter82-476

Green, D.H. and L.P. Johnson. Approaches to Wolfram von Eschenbach.
N.F. Palmer, 382(MAE):1982/1-131

Green, E. and M. Moss. A Business of National Importance.
P.N. Davies, 617(TLS):6May83-452

Green, G. Literary Criticism and the Structures of History.
    G. Steiner, 617(TLS):25Mar83-304
Green, J. Come From Away.
    D. Duffy, 529(QQ):Winter82-761
    A.T. Seaman, 198:Apr82-97
Green, J. Newspeak: A Dictionary of Jargon.
    R. Boston, 617(TLS):23Dec83-1441
Green, J. The Small Theatre Handbook.
    T. Small, 130:Fall82-277
Green, J. and J. Maritain. Une grande amitié. (J-P. Pirion, ed)
    A. Reix, 542:Jan-Mar82-65
Green, J.A. - see Schwob, M.
Green, J.R. Corpus Vasorum Antiquorum.* (New Zealand, fasc 1)
    B.A. Sparkes, 303(JoHS):Vol 102-285
Green, L.C. How Melanchthon Helped Luther Discover the Gospel.
    C.G. Nauert, Jr., 551(RenQ):Spring82-95
Green, M. Dreams of Adventure, Deeds of Empire.*
    J. Batchelor, 541(RES):Aug82-335
Green, M. Tolstoy and Gandhi, Men of Peace.
    M. Mudrick, 231:Jul83-60
    M. Muggeridge, 441:28Aug83-9
Green, M.J.M. Louis Guilloux.*
    M. Rieuneau, 535(RHL):Sep-Dec82-974
Green, R. Ford Madox Ford.*
    V. Cheng, 401(MLQ):Jun82-187
    J. Halperin, 395(MFS):Winter82/83-617
    S. Weintraub, 598(SoR):Winter83-233
Green, R., ed. The Train.*
    442(NY):3Jan83-72
Green, R. and others. Herrad of Hohenbourg, "Hortus Deliciarum."*
    E. Kitzinger, 54:Mar82-142
Green, R.F. Poets and Princepleasers.*
    R.M. Jordan, 529(QQ):Spring82-205
    D. Pearsall, 447(N&Q):Jun81-254
Green, R.L. and D. Crutch - see Williams, S.H. and F.W. Madan
Green, T. The New World of Gold.
    R. West, 617(TLS):7Jan83-10
Greenbaum, S., G. Leech and J. Svartvik, eds. Studies in English Linguistics for Randolph Quirk.*
    F.G.A.M. Aarts, 179(ES):Apr82-181
    J. Algeo, 660(Word):Dec81-249
    T. Thrane, 603:Vol6No2-253
Greenberg, J.B. Santiago's Sword.
    N.R. Crumrine, 263(RIB):Vol32No2-212
Greenberg, M.H. and C.G. Waugh - see Charteris, L.
Greenberg, R. The Drawings of Alfred Pellan.
    D.W. Rozniatowski, 529(QQ):Summer82-405
Greenberg, S.B. Race and State in Capitalist Development.
    T.D. Moodie, 529(QQ):Winter82-794
Greenberg, V.D. Literature and Sensibilities in the Weimar Era.
    C. Bedwell, 395(MFS):Winter82/83-698
Greenbie, B.B. Spaces.
    D. Bowen, 324:Jan83-105
Greenblatt, S., ed. The Power of Forms in the English Renaissance.
    G. Bradshaw, 617(TLS):30Sep83-1065

Greenblatt, S. Renaissance Self-Fashioning.*
    P. Edwards, 551(RenQ):Summer82-317
    T.M. Greene, 131(CL):Spring82-184
    A.K. Hieatt, 301(JEGP):Jul82-408
    J.N. King, 405(MP):Nov82-183
    F.P., 604:Winter82-1
Greenblatt, S.J., ed. Allegory and Representation.
    P. Piehler, 604:Fall82-56
Greene, G. J'Accuse.*
    R. Schieder, 99:Dec82/Jan83-41
Greene, G. Monsieur Quixote.*
    D. Coles, 99:Sep82-32
    J. Mellors, 364:Nov82-74
Greene, G. Ways of Escape.*
    M. Allott, 506(PSt):Dec82-350
    A.E. de Arboleda, 37:Mar-Apr82-57
    R.G. Walker, 396(ModA):Spring82-218
    P. Wolfe, 395(MFS):Winter81/82-706
    P. Wolfe, 502(PrS):Summer82-94
Greene, M.T. Geology in the Nineteenth Century.
    H. Torrens, 617(TLS):26Aug83-903
Greene, R.W. Six French Poets of Our Time.*
    M. Collot, 535(RHL):Sep-Dec82-965
Greene, S. Lost and Found.*
    J.L. Halio, 598(SoR):Winter83-203
Greene, T.M. The Light in Troy.
    T. Cave, 617(TLS):4Mar83-211
Greenfield, R. Temple.
    A. Cheuse, 441:13Feb83-1
    442(NY):7Feb83-121
Greenfield, S.B. and F.C. Robinson. A Bibliography of Publications on Old English Literature to the End of 1972.
    C.T. Berkhout, 589:Oct82-897
    D.K. Fry, 191(ELN):Sep82-11
    H. Gneuss, 38:Band100Heft3/4-487
Greenfield, S.M., ed. La generación de 1898 ante España.
    A.A. Borrás, 238:Dec82-658
Greengarten, I.M. Thomas Hill Green and the Development of Liberal-Democratic Thought.
    G.F.G., 185:Oct82-206
    H.D. Lewis, 319:Jul83-411
Greenhalgh, P. Pompey.* (Vol 1)
    J. Briscoe, 313:Vol72-184
Greenhalgh, P. Pompey.* (Vol 2)
    J. Briscoe, 313:Vol72-184
    B.R. Katz, 24:Fall82-350
Greenland, C. The Entropy Exhibition.
    G. Feeley, 617(TLS):23Sep83-1008
Greenleaf, S. Fatal Obsession.
    N. Callendar, 441:21Aug83-23
Greenleaf, W.H. The British Political Tradition.
    N. Annan, 453(NYRB):27Oct83-89
    J. Harris, 617(TLS):11Nov83-1241
Greenstein, F.I., ed. The Reagan Presidency.
    J. Fallows, 453(NYRB):27Oct83-68
    S.M. Halpern, 441:18Dec83-14
Greenway, D.E. - see Le Neve, J.
Greet, A.H. Apollinaire et le livre de peintre.*
    A-M. Christin, 535(RHL):Jul-Aug83-674
Greger, D. Movable Islands.*
    C. Berger, 491:Apr82-35
Gregersen, E.A. Language in Africa.
    K. Legère, 682(ZPSK):Band35Heft3-342

Gregg, E. Queen Anne.*
  H.T. Dickinson, 161(DUJ):Dec81-113
  M.C. Jacob, 173(ECS):Summer82-467
Gregg, L. Too Bright to See.*
  A.W. Fisher, 114(ChiR):Vol33No2-158
  D. Hall, 271:Winter82-165
  639(VQR):Winter82-24
Gregg, L.W. and E.R. Steinberg, eds. Cog-
  nitive Processes in Writing.
  W.E. Cooper, 353:Vol 19No9/10-1019
Crégoire, R. Homéliaires liturgiques
  médiévaux.
  R.W. Pfaff, 589:Oct82-899
Gregor, A. A Longing in the Land. Embodi-
  ment and other Poems.
  D. Lehman, 441:30Oct83-34
Gregor, I., ed. Reading the Victorian
  Novel.*
  N. Bradbury, 541(RES):Aug82-347
  W.L. Reed, 637(VS):Winter82-256
  J.W. Tuttleton, 677(YES):Vol 12-306
Gregor-Dellin, M. Richard Wagner.
  J. Kerman, 453(NYRB):22Dec83-27
  M. Tanner, 617(TLS):17Jun83-620
Gregor-Dellin, M. and D. Mack - see Wagner,
  C.
Saint Gregory of Nazianzus. Grégoire de
  Nazianze, "Discours" 24-26. (J. Mossay,
  with G. Lafontaine, eds and trans)
  É. des Places, 555:Vol56fasc2-334
Saint Gregory of Nazianzus. Grégoire de
  Nazianze, "Discours" 27-31. (P. Gallay,
  with M. Jourjon, eds and trans)
  É. Des Places, 555:Vol55fasc1-166
Gregory, F. Scientific Materialism in
  Nineteenth Century Germany.
  K. Bayertz, 53(AGP):Band64Heft3-341
Gregory, H., ed. Controversies About Stut-
  tering Therapy.
  R. Hand, 583:Winter83-202
Gregory, K., ed. The Second Cuckoo.
  B. Shulgasser, 441:18Sep83-23
Gregory, R.L. Mind in Science.*
  K.V. Wilkes, 483:Jul82-412
Greiff, C.M. John Notman, Architect 1810-
  1865.*
  K.N. Morgan, 576:May82-166
"Greifswalder Germanistische Forschungen."
  K-D. Ludwig, 682(ZPSK):Band34Heft3-392
Greiner, D.J., ed. American Poets Since
  World War II.
  M.H. Fleming, 365:Spring83-89
  L. Ziff, 402(MLR):Apr82-435
Greiner, D.J. The Other John Updike.
  V.D. Balitas, 27(AL):Mar82-144
  W.T.S., 395(MFS):Winter81/82-742
Grelsson, S. Les Adverbes en "-ment."
  J.T. Chamberlain, 207(FR):May83-959
  C. Wimmer, 553(RLiR):Jul-Dec82-475
Grene, N. Shakespeare, Jonson, Molière.
  J. Arnold, 568(SCN):Spring-Summer82-1
  J.A. Barish, 551(RenQ):Autumn82-521
  O.C. Brockett, 130:Spring82-94
  W. Green, 570(SQ):Winter82-536
Grenet, J. Chine et christianisme.
  G. Sartoris, 450(NRF):Jul-Aug82-191
Grenier, R. The Marrakesh One-Two.
  G. Stade, 441:17Apr83-15
Gresset, M. Faulkner ou la fascination.
  A. Bleikasten, 395(MFS):Winter82/83-
  675

Greve, T. Haakon VII of Norway.* (T.K.
  Derry, ed and trans)
  M.R.D. Foot, 617(TLS):17Jun83-626
Grévin, J. La Trésorière. (E. Lapeyre,
  ed)
  M. Lazard, 535(RHL):Sep-Dec82-867
  D. Stone, Jr., 207(FR):Oct82-147
Grey, H. Tales From the Mohaves.
  A.O. Wiget, 292(JAF):Oct-Dec82-477
von Greyerz, K. The Late City Reformation
  in Germany.
  S. Ozment, 551(RenQ):Autumn81-402
Gribbin, J. and J. Cherfas. The Monkey
  Puzzle.*
  R.C. Lewontin, 453(NYRB):16Jun83-21
Gridley, R.E. The Brownings and France.
  A. Hayter, 617(TLS):13May83-478
Grierson, P. Byzantine Coins.
  J.P.C. Kent, 617(TLS):1Apr83-338
Grieve, C.M. Annals of the Five Senses.
  N. Corcoran, 617(TLS):26Aug83-909
Griffin, D.H. Alexander Pope.*
  J. McLaverty, 447(N&Q):Feb81-79
Griffin, J. Homer on Life and Death.*
  J.S. Clay, 24:Spring82-102
  M. Lynn-George, 303(JoHS):Vol 102-239
Griffin, J., comp. Snobs.
  C. Hawtree, 364:Jun82-101
Griffin, S. Women and Nature.
  N.O. Keohane, 185:Oct82-102
Griffin-Collart, E. La philosophie écos-
  saise du sens commun.
  M. Kuehn, 319:Jan83-105
Griffith, M. - see "Aeschylus: 'Prometheus
  Bound'"
Griffiths, A.P., ed. Of Liberty.
  J. Waldron, 617(TLS):16Sep83-976
Griffiths, J. The Book of English Inter-
  national Rugby 1871-1982.
  J. Barnes, 617(TLS):28Jan83-91
Griffiths, J.C. Afghanistan.
  A.S. Ahmed, 293(JASt):Nov81-73
Griffiths, P. Cage.
  P. Dickinson, 415:May82-333
  P. Rapoport, 607:Mar82-36
  A. Whittall, 410(M&L):Jul/Oct82-305
Griffiths, P. Peter Maxwell Davies.*
  M. Hayes, 607:Jun82-30
Griffiths, P. Modern Music.
  M. Hayes, 607:Mar82-35
Griffiths, P., ed. Igor Stravinsky: "The
  Rake's Progress."
  P. Porter, 617(TLS):28Jan83-88
Griffiths, P. The String Quartet.
  S. Johnson, 617(TLS):30Dec83-1451
Griffiths, R. S.O. Davies.
  K.O. Morgan, 617(TLS):14Oct83-1130
Griffiths, S. Anglesey Material.
  D. Graham, 565:Vol123No2-74
Grigg, D. The Dynamics of Agricultural
  Change
  G.E. Mingay, 617(TLS):18Feb83-162
Grigorenko, P.G. Memoirs.
  J.B. Dunlop, 617(TLS):22Jul83-772
  L. Schapiro, 453(NYRB):13Oct83-9
  R.C. Tucker, 441:2Jan83-8
  442(NY):24Jan83-107
Grigson, G. Blessings, Kicks and Curses.*
  G. Lindop, 617(TLS):11Feb83-141
  W. Scammell, 364:Mar83-114
Grigson, G. Collected Poems 1963-1980.*
  G. Lindop, 617(TLS):11Feb83-141

Grossvogel, D.I. Mystery and its Fictions.*
    R.J. Dingley, 447(N&Q):Aug81-380
Grosu, A. Approaches to Island Phenomena.
    W. Wilkins, 350:Dec83-902
Grosz, G. A Small Yes and a Big No.*
    A. Ross, 364:Nov82-3
Grothusen, K-D. and others, eds. Südost-europa-Handbuch. (Vol 3)
    R. Clogg, 617(TLS):12Aug83-861
Grottanelli, V.L., ed. Una societa' Guineana: gli Nzema. (Vol 1)
    M.C. Roncoli, 69:Vol52No2-121
Grotzer, P. - see Raymond, M. and G. Poulet
Groupe μ. A General Rhetoric.*
    C.C. Arnold, 480(P&R):Spring82-139
    R. Fowler, 141:Summer82-273
    M-R. Logan, 477(PLL):Winter82-459
Grout, D.J. Alessandro Scarlatti: An Introduction to His Operas.
    C.M.B., 412:Feb81-56
Grover, R.S. Ernest Chausson.
    R. Nichols, 415:Feb82-112
    R.L. Smith, 410(M&L):Jan81-67
Grow, M. The Good Neighbor Policy and Authoritarianism in Paraguay.
    H.F. Peterson, 263(RIB):Vol32No1-65
Grubb, D. Beneath the Visiting Moon.
    V. Powell, 617(TLS):22Apr83-396
Grubb, D.M. A Practical Writing System and Short Dictionary of Kwakw'ala (Kwakiutl).
    P.J. Wilson, 269(IJAL):Apr82-232
Grübel, R.G. Russischer Konstruktivismus.
    J.E. Bowlt, 550(RusR):Oct82-534
Grudzińska-Gross, I. and J.T. Gross, eds. War through Children's Eyes.
    N.M. Naimark, 550(RusR):Jul82-337
Gruen, J. The World's Great Ballets.
    R. Philp, 151:Jan82-91
Grundstein, N. The Managerial Kant.
    T.D., 185:Jul83-842
Grundy, J. Hardy and the Sister Arts.*
    J. Halperin, 395(MFS):Winter82/83-617
Gruner, C.R. Understanding Laughter.
    E. Oring, 650(WF):Jan82-62
Grünert, H. Sprache und Politik.
    K.H. Schmidt, 685(ZDL):3/1981-405
Grunmann-Gaudet, M. and R.F. Jones, eds. The Nature of Medieval Narrative.
    S. Kay, 402(MLR):Apr82-442
    I. Short, 208(FS):Jan82-53
    F.P. Sweetser, 207(FR):Dec82-313
de Grunne, B. Terres Cuites Anciennes de L'ouest Africain.*
    N. Barley, 90:May82-312
de Grunne, B. and G.N. Preston. Ancient Treasures in Terra Cotta of Mali and Ghana.
    P.C. Coronel, 2(AfrA)·Aug82 80
Crusa, J. Prière pour une ville.
    L. Kovacs, 450(NRF):Feb82-156
Grushkin, P., C. Bassett and J. Grushkin. Grateful Dead.
    J. Maslin, 441:4Dec83-73
Gruslin, A. Le Théâtre et l'état au Québec.
    L.E. Doucette, 627(UTQ):Summer82-481
Gruys, J.A. The Early Printed Editions (1518-1664) of Aeschylus.
    J. Diggle, 123:Vol132No2-303

Gruys, J.A. and C. de Wolf. Typographi & Bibliopolae Neerlandici usque ad annum MDCC: Thesaurus.
    A.E.C. Simoni, 78(BC):Autumn82-383
Gruzenburg, O.O. Yesterday. (D.C. Rawson, ed)
    N.M. Naimark, 550(RusR):Apr82-206
    M. Stanislawski, 104(CASS):Fall-Winter 82-552
Grylls, D. Guardians and Angels.*
    G.A. Starr, 402(MLR):Apr82-415
Grymonprez, P., ed. "Here men may se the vertues off herbes."
    H. Hargreaves, 589:Jul82-684
Gschwind-Holtzer, G. Analyse sociolinguistique de la communication et didactique.
    P. Hagiwara, 207(FR):Feb83-523
Gsell, O. Gegensatzrelationen im Wortschatz romanischer Sprachen.
    R. Martin, 553(RLiR):Jan-Jun81-236
Guadalupi, G. and A. Manguel. Guide de nulle part et d'ailleurs. (P. Reumaux, ed and trans)
    G. Lascault, 450(NRF):Jun82-107
Guarducci, M. La cosiddetta Fibula Prenestina.
    A.E. Gordon, 121(CJ):Oct/Nov82-64
Guariglia, O.N. Quellenkritische und logische Untersuchungen zur Gegensatzlehre des Aristoteles.
    J.O., 543:Dec81-390
Guarino, A. La Rivoluzione della Plebe.
    A. Drummond, 313:Vol72-177
Guboglo, M.N. Razvitie dvujazyija v Moldavskoj SSR.
    H. Jachnow, 559:Nov81-162
Gude, M.L. "Le Page disgracié."*
    F. Assaf, 475:No16Pt2-443
    J. Prévot, 535(RHL):Jul-Aug82-651
Guenther, R.J. - see Orlova, A.
Guéraud, O. and P. Nautin - see Origen
Guéret, M., A. Robinet and P. Tombeur. Spinoza, "Ethica."*
    J-L. Marion, 192(EP):Jul-Sep81-347
Guérin, M. L'Oeuvre Gravé de Gauguin.
    R. Pickvance, 39:Feb82-136
Guérin, M. La politique de Stendhal.
    V. Brombert, 617(TLS):27May83-547
    A. Clerval, 450(NRF):Sep82-134
    V.D.L., 605(SC):15Oct82-87
Guérin, R. L'Apprenti.
    G. Quinsat, 450(NRF):May82-112
Guérin de Bouscal, D. Dom Quixote de la Manche. (D. Della Valle and A. Carriat, eds)
    C.E.J. Caldicott, 535(RHL):Sep-Dec82-882
    J-P. Leroy, 549(RLC):Jul-Sep82-395
Guérin de Bouscal, D. Le Gouvernement de Sanche Pansa. (C.E.J. Caldicott, ed)
    G. Forestier, 475:No16Pt2-383
Guerlac, H. Newton on the Continent.*
    639(VQR):Summer82-99
Guerlac, R. - see Hutton, J.
Guerlac, R. - see Vives, J.L.
Guerra-Cunningham, L. La narrativa de María Luisa Bombal.
    M. Agosin, 263(RIB):Vol32No1-66
    V.M. Valenzuela, 238:Dec82-663
Guerrini, R. Studi su Valerio Massimo.
    J.B. Trapp, 123:Vol132No2-279

Guertler, J. and A. Newburger, eds. The Records of Baltimore's Private Organizations.
K.A. Jacob, 14:Winter82-61

Guez Ricord, C.G. Le Dernier Anneau.
G. Macé, 450(NRF):Feb82-122

Guggenheim-Grünberg, F., ed. Schweizer Dialekt in Text und Ton. (Section 1, Heft 4)
H. Tatzreiter, 685(ZDL):3/1981-391

"Guía artística de Sevilla y su provincia."
I. Mateo Gómez, 48:Jan-Mar82-121

Guibal, F. ...et combien de dieux nouveaux: Heidegger.
M. Haar, 192(EP):Jul-Sep81-356
E. Joós, 154:Dec82-761

Guibal, F. ...et combien de dieux nouveaux: Lévinas.
E. Joós, 154:Dec82-761
A.L., 543:Sep81-132

"Guides to Sources for British History based on the National Register of Archives." (Vols 1-3)
D.G. Vaisey, 617(TLS):8Apr83-363

Guidi, G. Il governo della città-repubblica di Firenze del primo Quattrocento.
L. Martines, 551(RenQ):Winter82-604

Guidi, J., M-F. Piéjus and A-C. Fiorato. Images de la femme dans la littérature italienne de la Renaissance.
P.H. Labalme, 551(RenQ):Summer82-258

Guidieri, R. La route des morts.
L-V. Thomas, 542:Jan-Mar82-82

Guild, N. Chain Reaction.
442(NY):22Aug83-96

Guiliano, E., ed. Lewis Carroll: A Celebration.*
K. Blake, 191(ELN):Dec82-131

Guiliano, E. Lewis Carroll: An Annotated International Bibliography, 1960-77.*
P. Heath, 191(ELN):Dec82-126

Guillaud, J. and M., ed. Turner en France.
C. Powell, 59:Jun82-254

Guillaume de Lorris and Jean de Meun. Der Rosenroman. (Vols 1-3) (K.A. Ott, ed and trans)
C. Strosetzki, 547(RF):Band93Heft1/2-241

Guillaumin, E. The Life of a Simple Man. (E. Weber, ed; rev trans by M. Crosland)
D. Coward, 617(TLS):20May83-526

Guillemin-Flescher, J. Syntaxe comparée du français et de l'anglais.
D.A. Kibbee, 207(FR):Apr83-808

Guillermus de Podio. Ars Musicorum — Libri VI et VIII. (A. Seay, ed)
A.E. Walters, 308:Fall82-349

Guiomar, M. Trois paysages du "Rivage des Syrtes."
P-L. Rey, 450(NRF):Nov82-122

Guiral, P. and G. Thuillier. La Vie quotidienne des professeurs de 1870 à 1940.
E. Weber, 617(TLS):4Mar83-219

Guiraud, P. Le langage du corps.
G. Kirouac, 567:Vol40No1/2-167

Guisti-Lanham, H. and A. Dodi - see under Giusti-Lanham, H. and A. Dodi

Guitard, A. Les Corps communicants.
M. Genuist, 102(CanL):Spring82-111

Guiton, J., ed. The Ideas of Le Corbusier on Architecture and Urban Planning.
R. Wesley, 576:Oct82-253

Gulick, S.L. A Chesterfield Bibliography to 1800.* (2nd ed)
C. Price, 402(MLR):Oct82-926

Gullans, C. Many Houses.*
J. Finlay, 598(SoR):Winter83-181
D. Gioia, 249(HudR):Autumn82-483

Gulsoy, J. and J.M. Sola-Solé, eds. Catalan Studies/Estudis sobre el català.
C.T. Mason, 545(RPh):Aug81-296

Gumb, R.D. Evolving Theories.
W.H. Hanson, 316:Jun82-454

Gumbrecht, H.U. Funktionen parlamentarischer Rhetorik in der Französischen Revolution.
J-R. Armogathe, 535(RHL):Mar-Apr82-294

Gumperz, J.J. Discourse Strategies.
R. Harris, 617(TLS):14Jan83-37

Gunda, B. Ethnographica Carpatho-Balcanica.
W.F.H. Nicolaisen, 203:Vol193No1-122

Gundolf, F. Beiträge zur Literatur- und Geistesgeschichte. (V.A. Schmitz and F. Martini, eds)
J. Strelka, 133:Band15Heft3-259

Gundy, H.P. - see Carman, B.

Gunn, D.W. Tennessee Williams.*
F.E. Eddleman, 397(MD):Dec82-585

Gunn, G., ed. New World Metaphysics.
G. Smith, 569(SR):Winter82-v

Gunn, J.A.W. and others - see Disraeli, B.

Gunn, J.S. and B. Levy. A Word History of Bushranging.
J.S. Ryan, 67:Nov82-220

Gunn, T. Games of Chance.
D. Gioia, 249(HudR):Autumn82-471

Gunn, T. The Occasions of Poetry.*
N. Rhodes, 493:Jan83-52
H. Williams, 364:Mar83-94

Gunn, T. The Passages of Joy.*
M. Kinzie, 29:Jan/Feb83-28
N. Rhodes, 493:Jan83-52
H. Williams, 364:Mar83-94

Gunnars, K. One-Eyed Moon Maps.*
G. Johnston, 102(CanL):Spring82-73

Gunnars, K. Settlement Poems I.* Settlement Poems II.
D. Barbour, 648(WCR):Summer81-83
G. Johnston, 102(CanL):Spring82-73

"Gunnlaugs saga ormstungu." (E. Mundal, ed)
J.E. Knirk, 563(SS):Spring82-167

Gunny, A. Voltaire and English Literature.*
A. Vartanian, 546(RR):Jan82-119

Guntharp, M.G. Learning the Fiddler's Ways.
B. Owen, 292(JAF):Jul-Sep82-355
A.C. Percival, 203:Vol193No2-231

Günther, U. and L. Petazzoni - see Verdi, G.

Günzler, C. Bildung und Erziehung im Denken Goethes.
H. Eichner, 406:Fall82-327

Guppy, S. Ghost Catcher.
D. Barbour, 648(WCR):Oct82-37

Gupta, A. The Logic of Common Nouns.
J.D. McCawley, 311(JP):Sep82-512
R.R. Rockingham Gill, 518:Oct82-241

Gupta, B.S. The Afghan Syndrome.
O. Pick, 617(TLS):8Jul83-719

Gupta, S.B. Monetary Planning for India.
V.V. Bhatt, 293(JASt):Feb82-383

Haakonssen, K. The Science of a Legis-
lator.*
    K. Campbell, 63:Dec82-389
    K.E. Smith, 83:Autumn82-261
Haaland, G., ed. Problems of Savannah
Development.
    M.E. Adams, 69:Vol51No4-897
Haarberg, R. and J. Nature and Language.
    C. Baranger, 189(EA):Apr-Jun82-194
Haarder, A. Det episke liv.
    M. Lantz, 64(Arv):Vol36-209
Haarmann, H. Grundzüge der Sprachtypol-
ogie.*
    G.F. Meier, 682(ZPSK):Band35Heft4-
    482
Haarmann, H. and A.L.V., eds. Sprachen
und Staaten: Festschrift Heinz Kloss.*
    K. Kehr, 685(ZDL):2/1981-247
Haarscher, G. L'Ontologie de Marx.
    A.L., 185:Oct82-209
Haas, A.M. and H. Stirnimann, eds. Das
"einig ein."
    G.J. Lewis, 564:Nov81-319
Haas, C. L'Esprit français.
    M. Naudin, 207(FR):Oct82-170
Haas, W. Sprachwandel und Sprachgeo-
graphie.
    C.E. Reed, 301(JEGP):Jan82-73
Haas, W. - see under Linke, K.
Haase, W. - see Aveling, J.C.H., D.M.
Loades and H.R. McAdoo
Habegger, A. Gender, Fantasy and Realism
in American Literature.
    T.A. Shippey, 617(TLS):13May83-479
Haber, B. - see "The Women's Annual"
Haber, C. Beyond Sixty-Five.
    J. Davison, 441:19Jun83-16
Haberly, D.T. Three Sad Races.
    J.G. Merquior, 617(TLS):7Oct83-1090
Haberman, J. Maimonides and Aquinas.*
    K.P. Bland, 318(JAOS):Oct-Dec81-453
Habermas, J. Theorie des kommunikativen
Handelns.
    J.B. Thompson, 617(TLS):8Apr83-357
Haberstroh, C.J., Jr. Melville and Male
Identity.
    J.S. Adler, 395(MFS):Winter81/82-715
    R. Lehan, 445(NCF):Jun82-126
Habicht, C. Untersuchungen zur politis-
chen Geschichte Athens im 3. Jahrhundert
v. Chr.*
    M.J. Osborne, 303(JoHS):Vol 102-273
    É. Will, 555:Vol55fasc2-346
Hackelsberger, C. Das k.k. österreich-
ische Festungsviereck in Lombardo-
Venetien.*
    K. Lankheit, 43:Band12Heft1-87
Hacker, A., ed. U/S.
    C. Jencks, 441:10Apr83-7
Hacker, P. Kleine Schriften.* (L. Schmit-
hausen, ed)
    J.W. de Jong, 259(IIJ):Jan80-78
Hacker, P.M.S. and G.P. Baker. Wittgen-
stein.
    D. Bell, 479(PhQ):Oct82-363
Hackett, C.A. Rimbaud.
    M. Davies, 208(FS):Apr82-222
    J.P. Houston, 207(FR):Feb83-488
    D.W.P. Hackett, 446(NCFS):Fall-Winter
    82/83-168
Hackett, J. The Profession of Arms.
    J. Terraine, 617(TLS):18Nov83-1284

Hackett, S.C. Oriental Philosophy.*
    W.E.S., 543:Mar82-605
Hadas, P.W. Beside Herself.
    R.B. Shaw, 441:4Sep83-8
Haddad, G. L'Enfant illégitime.
    J. le Hardi, 450(NRF):Mar82-135
Hadden, J.K. and C.E. Swann. Prime Time
Preachers.
    639(VQR):Summer82-90
Haddon, C. The Limits of Sex.
    J. Ryle, 617(TLS):18Mar83-262
Hadjinicolaou, N. Art History and Class
Struggle.
    A. Wallach, 504:No6-177
Hadlich, R.L. Gramática transformativa
del español.
    S. Pieczara, 360(LP):Vol124-147
Hadot, P. Exercices spirituels et philos-
ophie antique.
    R. Brague, 192(EP):Oct-Dec82-492
Haeck, P. La Parole verte.
    P.G. Lewis, 207(FR):May83-977
Haese, R. Rebels and Precursors.
    U. Hoff, 39:Aug82-129
Haeusler, M. Das Ende der Geschichte in
der mittelalterlichen Weltchronistik.
    R.E. Lerner, 589:Jul82-616
Haffenden, J. John Berryman.*
    R. Labrie, 106:Winter82-397
Haffenden, J. The Life of John Berryman.*
    W. Harmon, 344:Summer83-112
    N. Miller, 42(AR):Fall82-485
    M. Perloff, 29:May/Jun83-32
Haffenden, J. Poets in Conversation.
    S. Fauchereau, 98:Jun-Jul82-628
Hagen, J.S. Tennyson and His Publishers.*
    B. Southam, 677(YES):Vol 12-313
Hagen, W.W. Germans, Poles, and Jews.
    R.J. Bazillion, 104(CASS):Summer82-291
Hageneder, O., W. Maleczek and A.A. Strnad,
eds. Die Register Innocenz' III. (Vol
2)
    L.E. Boyle, 589:Oct82-966
Hager, P.E. and D. Taylor. The Novels of
World War I.
    M. Taylor, 365:Winter83-35
Hagerty, J.C. The Dairy of James C.
Hagerty. (R.H. Ferrell, ed)
    R. Sherrill, 441:18Sep83-9
Haggard, M., with P. Russell. Sing Me
Back Home.
    R.S. Denisoff, 498:Vol8No3/4-136
Haggard, W. The Heirloom.
    T.J. Binyon, 617(TLS):13May83-498
    T.J. Binyon, 617(TLS):27May83-553
    M. Laski, 362:19May83-24
Haggie, P. Britannia at Bay.
    639(VQR):Winter82-22
Hagiwara, M.P. and F. de Rocher. Thème et
variations.* (2nd ed)
    R. Danner, 399(MLJ):Spring82-81
Hagstrum, J.H. Sex and Sensibility.*
    R.F. Brissenden, 566:Autumn82-48
    D. Brooks-Davies, 402(MLR):Jan82-150
    P. Brückmann, 627(UTQ):Spring82-298
    A. Morvan, 189(EA):Oct-Dec82-436
    J.C. Robinson, 191(ELN):Sep82-63
    P.M. Spacks, 173(ECS):Winter82/83-175
Hahn, H. Empiricism, Logic, and Mathemat-
ics.* (B. McGuinness, ed)
    D.A. Gillies, 84:Jun82-217
    R. Haller, 53(AGP):Band64Heft2-212

Hahn, H.G. Henry Fielding.*
P. Rogers, 447(N&Q):Feb81-80
D.L. Vander Meulen, 173(ECS):Summer83-439
Hahn, L. and M. Muirragui. Historical Dictionary of Libya.
D.B.C. O'Brien, 69:Vol52No4-97
Hahn, P.M. Die Kornwestheimer Tagebücher, 1772-1777. (M. Brecht and R.F. Paulus, eds)
W. Grossmann, 173(ECS):Winter81/82-215
Hahn, S. The Roots of Southern Populism.
R.J. Margolis, 441:23Oct83-16
Hahn, U. and M. Töteberg. Günter Wallraff.
B.L. Bradley, 221(GQ):Mar82-279
Hahn, W.G. Postwar Soviet Politics.
L.K.D. Kristof, 550(RusR):Oct82-500
639(VQR):Summer82-84
Hahnemann, S. Organon of Medicine.
R. Cooter, 617(TLS):9Sep83-955
Hai, T.S. and H. Sendut, eds. Public and Private Housing in Malaysia.
T. McGee, 293(JASt):Feb82-412
Haiding, K. - see Bünker, J.R.
Haiding, K. - see von Geramb, V.
Haig-Brown, R. The Master and his Fish.
G.W., 102(CanL):Winter81-173
Haig-Brown, R. Writings and Reflections. (V. Haig-Brown, ed)
442(NY):14Mar83-159
Haight, G.S. - see Eliot, G.
Haight, M.R. A Study of Self-Deception.*
T.S. Champlin, 483:Jan82-144
D.W. Hamlyn, 479(PhQ):Apr82-184
A. Paskow, 518:Apr82-121
Haile, H.G. Invitation to Goethe's "Faust."
H. Reiss, 133:Band15Heft1/2-164
Haile, H.G. Luther.*
H. Blum, 301(JEGP):Jan82-79
D.W. Lotz, 222(GR):Fall82-163
Hailey, E.F. Life Sentences.*
T. Warr, 617(TLS):21Jan83-69
Lord Hailsham. Hamlyn Revisited.
D. Pannick, 362:9Jun83-25
Haines, J. News from the Glacier.*
A. Turner, 199:Spring83-69
Haining, P. - see Gilbert, W.S.
Hainsworth, J.D. - see Garrick, D.
Hair, D.S. Domestic and Heroic in Tennyson's Poetry.*
R. Pattison, 637(VS):Summer82-510
Haitsma Mulier, E.O.G. The Myth of Venice and Dutch Republican Thought in the Seventeenth Century.
H.H. Rowen, 551(RenQ):Winter81-598
Hakes, D.T. The Development of Metalinguistic Abilities in Children.
K. Aronsson, 596(SL):Vol36No1-106
K. Meng, 682(ZPSK):Band35Heft3-343
Hakuar, V. Equality, Liberty and Perfectionism.*
O. O'Neill, 393(Mind):Oct82-625
Hakutani, Y. Young Dreiser.*
R. Asselineau, 189(EA):Jul-Sep82-363
Halabi, R. The West Bank Story.*
J.J. Goldberg, 287:Jun/Jul82-24
Halász, K. Structures narratives chez Chrétien de Troyes.
M.T. Bruckner, 589:Oct82-900
Halberstam, D. The Breaks of the Game.*
639(VQR):Spring82-61

Halbherr, F. and others. Haghia Triada nel periodo palaziale.
P. Warren, 303(JoHS):Vol 102-276
Hale, J.R., ed. A Concise Encyclopaedia of the Italian Renaissance.*
G. Baker, 135:Feb82-89
M.J. Kraus, 42(AR):Fall82-484
Hale, W.G. - see "Eric Hosking's Waders"
Halewood, W.H. Six Subjects of Reformation Art.
M. Warner, 617(TLS):25Mar83-310
Halimi, A. Le délation sous l'occupation.
E. Weber, 617(TLS):12Aug83-850
Halio, J.L. - see "Dictionary of Literary Biography"
Halka, C.S. Melquíades, Alchemy and Narrative Theory.
M.A. Aaron, 238:Dec82-664
Halkett, A. and A. Fanshawe. The Memoirs of Anne, Lady Halkett and Ann, Lady Fanshawe.* (J. Loftis, ed)
P. Cheney, 568(SCN):Spring-Summer82-18
A. Smallwood, 447(N&Q):Feb81-77
Hall, A. The Peking Target.
N. Callendar, 441:13Mar83-21
Hall, B. The Proms, and the Men Who Made Them.
N. Goodwin, 415:Feb82-111
Hall, D., ed. The Oxford Book of American Literary Anecdotes.
O.W. Ferguson, 579(SAQ):Summer82-358
W.H., 148:Spring82-93
D. Kirby, 364:Apr/May82-141
K.M. Roemer, 26(ALR):Spring82-141
Hall, D.E. Musical Acoustics.
D.A. Damschroder, 308:Fall82-370
Hall, D.G.E. A History of South-East Asia. (4th ed)
C.M. Wilson, 293(JASt):Aug82-882
Hall, D.J. Clifford Sifton. (Vol 1)
G.W., 102(CanL):Spring82-161
Hall, E.S., Jr., M.B. Blackman and V. Rickard. Northwest Coast Indian Graphics.
K. Ecclin, 99:Jun/Jul82-24
Hall, E.T. The Dance of Life.
D. Finkelstein, 469:Vol8No3-102
Hall, H.W. - see "Science Fiction Book Review Index, 1974-1979"
Hall, J. The Transforming Image.*
T.L. Bond, 577(SHR):Winter82-72
C. Castan, 67:Nov82-196
P.M.S. Dawson, 340(KSJ):Vol31-216
W. Keach, 184(EIC):Jan82-82
Hall, J. - see Ehresmann, J.M.
Hall, J.B. Her Name.
J.F. Cotter, 249(HudR):Autumn82-471
Hall, J.B. The Short Hall.
D. Grumbach, 219(GaR):Fall82-668
C. Halstead, 648(WCR):;Jun82-47
Hall, J.W. and T. Takeshi, eds. Japan in the Muromachi Age.
W.E. Naff, 318(JAOS):Jul-Sep81-394
Hall, K.M. - see Jodelle, É.
Hall, K.R. Trade and Statecraft in the Age of the Cōlas.
G.W. Spencer, 293(JASt):Aug82-867
Hall, M.B. Renovation and Counter-Reformation.*
C. Hope, 90:Aug82-513
Hall, N.J. Trollope and His Illustrators.*
A. Pollard, 366:Spring82-130
Hall, N.J., ed. The Trollope Critics.*
G. Butte, 637(VS):Summer82-502

Hall, O. The Children of the Sun.
D. Cole, 441:23Oct83-24
Hall, P. Peter Hall's Diaries. (J. Goodwin, ed)
M. Kustow, 617(TLS):2Sep83-939
S. Trotter, 362:20Sep83-24
Hall, P. Homes.
D. Barbour, 648(WCR):Summer81-81
Hall, R., ed. The Collins Book of Australian Poetry.
H. Lomas, 617(TLS):7Oct83-1100
C. Pollnitz, 581:Dec82-476
Hall, R. Fifty Years of Hume Scholarship.
J.W. Oliver, 588(SSL):Vol 17-296
Hall, R. Just Relations.
B. De Mott, 441:13Mar83-7
J. Neville, 617(TLS):24Jun83-682
F. Taliaferro, 231:Mar83-74
442(NY):18Apr83-149
Hall, R. The Most Beautiful World.
D. Haskell, 581:Sep82-348
J. Tranter, 381:Sep82-399
Hall, R.A., Jr. The Kensington Rune-Stone Is Genuine.
E. Wahlgren, 350:Mar83-231
Hall, R.A., Jr., F.A. Hall and S.Z. Garau. 2001 Italian and English Idioms/2001 Locuzioni Italiane e Inglesi.
S.E. Lindenau, 399(MLJ):Summer82-223
Hall, R.W. Plato.
N.J.H. Dent, 518:Jul82-149
R.G.M., 185:Jan83-428
Hall, T.H. Dorothy L. Sayers.
E.S. Lauterbach, 395(MFS):Summer81-356
Hall, W.E. Shadowy Heroes.
R.M. Kain, 395(MFS):Winter81/82-671
Hallam, A. Great Geological Controversies.
R. Porter, 617(TLS):26Aug83-903
Hallam, A.H. The Letters of Arthur Henry Hallam.* (J. Kolb, ed)
D.G. Riede, 636(VP):Summer82-205
Hallander, L-G., with M. Löfvenberg and A. Rynell - see Carlson, I.
Halle, M., J. Bresnan and G.A. Miller, eds. Linguistic Theory and Psychological Reality.*
J.S., 185:Jan83-419
Haller, R. Studien zur österreichischen Philosophie.
E. Paczkowska-Lagowska, 323:May82-195
Hallett, C.A. and E.S. The Revenger's Madness.*
L.S. Champion, 301(JEGP):Apr82-252
C. Hill, 366:Autumn82-258
J. Limon, 577(SHR):Summer82-257
Halliburton, D. Poetic Thinking.
G. Desjardins, 617(TLS):14Jan83-40
639(VQR):Summer82-81
Halliday, F. Ambler.
N. Callendar, 441:5Jun83-37
Halliday, F.E. Shakespeare and his World.*
M.M. Reese, 570(SQ):Spring82-124
Halliday, M. - see Grossman, A.
Hallier, J-E. Fin de siècle.
M-N. Little, 207(FR):Oct82-171
Halligan, T.A., ed. The Booke of Gostlye Grace of Mechtild of Hackeborn.*
C. von Nolcken, 447(N&Q):Apr81-181
M. Rigby, 541(RES):May82-194
Halliwell, L. Halliwell's Hundred.
P. Craig, 18:Apr83-61

Hallmann, J.C. Sämtliche Werke. (Vol 2) (G. Spellerberg, ed)
P. Skrine, 402(MLR):Apr82-488
Hallowell, C. People of the Bayou.
M.C. Brown, 585(SoQ):Spring82-92
Halls, W.D. The Youth of Vichy France.*
P.J. Kingston, 208(FS):Apr82-234
Hallyn, F., ed. Onze études sur la mise en abyme.
A. Goulet, 535(RHL):Sep-Dec82-987
S. Sykes, 208(FS):Jan82-112
Halperin, J. Gissing.*
J.S. Collis, 362:13Jan83-22
Halperin, J., ed. Trollope Centenary Essays
J. Keates, 617(TLS):20May83-513
Halperin, J. - see Gissing, G.
Halperin, J.U. Félix Fénéon and the Language of Art Criticism.
P. Berthier, 535(RHL):Sep-Dec82-945
Halperín Donghi, T. Guerra y finanza en los orígenes del estado argentino (1790-1850).
D. Rock, 617(TLS):23Dec83-1435
Halpern, D. Seasonal Rights.
R. Tillinghast, 441:1May83-15
Halpern, J. Critical Fictions.
R. Goldthorpe, 208(FS):Jan82-98
Halpin, M. and M.M. Ames, eds. Manlike Monsters on Trial.
J. Alm, 650(WF):Oct82-312
Halpin, M.M. Totem Poles.
K. Ecclin, 99:Jun/Jul82-28
Halporn, J.W., M. Ostwald and T.G. Rosenmeyer. The Meters of Greek and Latin Poetry. (rev)
T. Fleming, 121(CJ):Oct/Nov82-71
Halsband, R. "The Rape of the Lock" and its Illustrations 1714-1896.*
M.R. Brownell, 173(ECS):Fall82-90
P. Brückmann, 627(UTQ):Spring82-298
Halsey, M.T. - see Rodríguez Méndez, J.M.
Halttunen, K. Confidence Men and Painted Women.
J. Hopkins, 617(TLS):29Apr83-423
van Ham, L. and R. van Dijk. Africa: Art and Culture from the Upper Volta.
C.D. Roy, 2(AfrA):Aug82-17
Hamada, Y. Kanto Rinrigaku no Seiritsu.
Kogaku Arifuku, 342:Band73Heft3-364
Hamalian, L., ed. Ladies on the Loose.*
V. Young, 249(HudR):Winter82/83-660
Hamberg, P.G. Vasatiden och den karolinska tiden.
I. Sjöström, 341:Vol51No1-37
Hambrick-Stowe, C. The Practice of Piety.
P.F. Gura, 165(EAL):Winter82/83-253
Hamburger, K. Wahrheit und ästhetische Wahrheit.*
B.W. Seiler, 490:Band13Heft1/2-149
Hamburger, M. Literarische Erfahrungen. (H. Hartung, ed)
H. Hatfield, 221(GQ):May82-394
Hamburger, R. All the Lonely People.
R.J. Margolis, 441:4Sep83-10
Hamelin, J. and J. Provencher. Breve Histoire du Québec.
G.R. Montbertrand, 207(FR):Apr83-802
Hamill, S. At Home in the World.
M. Halperin, 448:Vol20No1-157
Hamilton, A.C. - see Spenser, E.

Hamilton, B. The Latin Church in the
Crusader States.
  J.A. Brundage, 589:Jan82-131
Hamilton, C.D. Sparta's Bitter Victories.*
  J.T. Roberts, 24:Spring82-109
Hamilton, I. Koestler.*
  J. Mellors, 364:Aug/Sep82-120
Hamilton, I. Robert Lowell.*
  P-L. Adams, 61:Feb83-105
  W. Harmon, 344:Summer83-112
  A. Kazin, 617(TLS):6May83-447
  M. Perloff, 29:May/Jun83-32
  N. Shrimpton, 362:12May83-22
Hamilton, J. Sagacity.
  D. Duffy, 529(QQ):Winter82-761
  D. Reynolds, 150(DR):Autumn82-520
Hamilton, J.F. Rousseau's Theory of Liter-
ature.*
  R. Grimsley, 208(FS):Jan82-70
Hamilton, K.G., ed. Studies in the Recent
Australian Novel.
  S.F.D. Hughes, 395(MFS):Spring81-173
Hamilton, M. The Tin-lined Trunk.
  M. Whitaker, 102(CanL):Summer82-142
Hamilton, N. Monty.
  P. Johnson, 362:27Oct83-26
  E.N. Luttwak, 617(TLS):18Nov83-1284
  639(VQR):Spring82-51
Hamilton, O. The Divine Country.*
  F. Tuohy, 364:Aug/Sep82-133
Hamilton, P. The Slaves of Solitude.
  L.D., 617(TLS):8Apr83-360
Hamilton, R. Collected Words.*
  M. Hartney, 592:Vol 195No997-83
  A. Ross, 364:Nov82-6
Hamilton, R.F. Who Voted for Hitler?*
  I. Deak, 453(NYRB):3Mar83-13
  639(VQR):Autumn82-128
Hamilton, W.S. Introduction to Russian
Phonology and Word Structure.*
  J.E. Augerot, 104(CASS):Spring82-119
Hamlyn, D.W. Perception, Learning and the
Self.
  P. Snowdon, 617(TLS):18Nov83-1283
Hamlyn, D.W. Schopenhauer.*
  D.L.L., 543:Sep81-134
  F.C. White, 63:Sep82-289
Hamm, C. Music in the New World.
  P. Dickinson, 617(TLS):28Oct83-1191
Hamm, M. Coffee Houses of Europe.
  442(NY):9May83-135
Hammacher, A.M. and R. Van Gogh.
  C. Zemel, 617(TLS):8Jul83-731
Hammar, R.A. Singing — An Extension of
Speech.
  H.B.R., 412:Aug-Nov81-294
Hammer, C. Victor Hammer.
  N. Barker, 78(BC):Winter82-513
  D. Chambers, 503:Winter82 211
Hammer, R.D., ed. Critical Perspectives
on V.S. Naipaul.
  R. Mane, 189(EA):Apr-Jun82-229
Hammer, S. Passionate Attachments.
  G.A. De Candido, 441:13Feb83-18
Hammer-Schenk, H. Synagogen in Deutsch-
land.
  C.H. Krinsky, 576:Oct82-249
Hammerstein, R. Tanz und Musik des Todes.
  T. Seebass, 317:Summer82-329
Hammond, C.M., Jr. The Image Decade.
  P. Brantlinger, 128(CE):Sep82-475
Hammond, G. The Game.*
  N. Callendar, 441:6Mar83-31

Hammond, G. The Making of the English
Bible.
  P.N. Brooks, 617(TLS):15Jul83-762
Hammond, G. The Reader and Shakespeare's
Young Man Sonnets.*
  J. Pequigney, 551(RenQ):Spring82-119
Hammond, J., with I. Townsend. John Ham-
mond on Record.
  R. Middleton, 410(M&L):Jul/Oct82-324
Hammond, J.R. A George Orwell Companion.
  J. Thompson, 617(TLS):29Apr83-440
Hammond, J.R. An Edgar Allan Poe Compan-
ion.
  R.P. Benton, 495(PoeS):Jun82-26
  B.F. Fisher 4th, 27(AL):Mar82-124
Hammond, J.R., ed. H.G. Wells.
  J.R. Reed, 395(MFS):Winter81/82-695
  J-P. Vernier, 189(EA):Jul-Sep82-350
Hammond, J.R. An H.G. Wells Companion.*
  P. Parrinder, 447(N&Q):Oct81-449
  J-P. Vernier, 189(EA):Jul-Sep82-349
Hammond, N. Venture Into Greece.
  D. Hunt, 617(TLS):15Jul83-748
Hammond, N.G.L. Alexander the Great.
  S. Hornblower, 123:Vol132No1-65
Hammond, N.G.L., ed. Atlas of the Greek
and Roman World in Antiquity.*
  H.J.K. Usher, 123:Vol132No2-222
Hammond, T.T. Red Flag over Afghanistan.
  E. Mortimer, 453(NYRB):22Dec83-3
Hammond, T.T., ed. Witnesses to the
Origins of the Cold War.
  639(VQR):Autumn82-126
Hamon, H. and P. Rotman. Les intello-
crates.*
  M. Pierssens, 98:May82-423
  H.B. Sutton, 207(FR):Mar83-651
Hamon, P. Le Personnel du roman.
  C. Smethurst, 617(TLS):25Nov83-1327
Hamovitch, M.B., ed. The "Hound and Horn"
Letters.*
  L.D. Rubin, Jr., 344:Summer83-121
Hampe, R. and E. Simon. The Birth of
Greek Art.*
  R. Higgins, 39:May82-413
  A.M. Snodgrass, 54:Sep82-495
Hampl, P. A Romantic Education.
  E. Alarcón, 152(UDQ):Spring82-123
Hampshire, G., ed. The Bodleian Library
Account Book 1613-1646.
  J.C.T. Oates, 617(TLS):2Dec83-1359
Hampshire, S. Morality and Conflict.
  M. Warnock, 362:15Dec83-25
Hampson, N. Will and Circumstance.
  C. Lucas, 617(TLS):23Sep83-1022
Hampsten, E. Read This Only to Yourself.
  27(AL):Oct82-471
  639(VQR):Autumn82-118
Hampton, C. A Cornered Freedom.
  L. Sail, 565:Vol123No4-74
Hampton, C. Socialism in a Crippled World.
  R. Poole, 437:Summer82-287
Hampton, S. Costumes.
  J. Maiden, 381:Sep82-401
Hampton, S.B. A Divided Heart. (A.F.
Hampton, ed)
  A.F. Scott, 579(SAQ):Summer82-357
Hana, C. Sun Yat-sen's Parteiorgan "Chien-
she" (1919-1920).
  A.J. Gregor, 293(JASt):Aug82-811
Hanan, P. The Chinese Vernacular Story.*
  A. Lévy, 244(HJAS):Dec82-679

Hand, W.D., A. Casetta and S.B. Thiederman, eds. Popular Beliefs and Superstitions.
N. Philip, 203:Vol93No2-242
Handelsman, M.H. El modernismo en las revistas literarias del Ecuador: 1895-1930.
O. Olivera, 238:Sep82-471
Handelsman, M.H., W.H. Heflin, Jr. and R.E. Hernández. La cultura hispana.
F.H. Nuessel, Jr., 399(MLJ):Autumn82-352
M. Prado, 238:May82-317
Handler, A. Blood Libel at Tiszaeszlár.
G.B. Cohen, 104(CASS):Summer82-298
Handlin, O. The Distortion of America.
A. Denman, 42(AR):Summer82-366
639(VQR):Winter82-12
Hanen, M.P., M.J. Osler and R.G. Weyant. Science, Pseudo-Science and Society.
R.P. Thompson, 529(QQ):Winter82-915
Hanf, T., H. Weiland and G. Vierdag. South Africa.*
H. Wolpe, 69:Vol52No4-94
Hanfling, O., ed. Essential Readings in Logical Positivism.*
J. Largeault, 542:Jan-Mar82-103
Hanfling, O. Logical Positivism.*
J. Largeault, 542:Jan-Mar82-103
Hani, J. - see Plutarch
Hanisch, G.S. Love Elegies of the Renaissance.*
S.M. Carrington, 207(FR):Oct82-148
T. Cave, 535(RHL):Jul-Aug82-647
K.F. Wiley, 551(RenQ):Autumn81-438
Hankey, J. - see Shakespeare, W.
Hankin, C.A. - see Murry, J.M.
Hankins, J.E. Backgrounds of Shakespeare's Thought.*
T. Hawkes, 570(SQ):Spring82-110
E. Jones, 677(YES):Vol 12-252
Hanley, A. Hart Crane's Holy Vision.
27(AL):Oct82-473
Hanley, G. Noble Descents.
W. Boyd, 364:Dec82/Jan83-134
Hanley, J. Against the Stream.*
B. Allen, 569(SR):Summer82-493
Hanna, P.R. and J.S. Frank Lloyd Wright's Hanna House.
D. Hoffman, 576:Oct82-245
Hannaford, R.G. Samuel Richardson.
S.W.R. Smith, 566:Autumn82-47
Hannah, B. Ray.
C. Platt, 152(UDQ):Summer81-120
Hannah, B. The Tennis Handsome.
I. Gold, 441:1May83-11
Hannan, J. For the Coming Surface.
B. Meyer, 102(CanL):Spring82-88
Hannay, M.P. C.S. Lewis.
H.H. Watts, 395(MFS):Winter82/83-646
Hannerz, U. Exploring the City.
G. Barth, 658:Winter82-287
Hanning, B.R. Of Poetry and Music's Power.
A. Newcomb, 551(RenQ):Winter81-590
Hanrahan, J.D. Government by Contract.
R.J. Margolis, 441:10Jul83-16
Hanscombe, G.E. The Art of Life.
A. Marlow, 364:Nov82-102
T. Warr, 617(TLS):25Feb83-176
Hansen, A.S. Hamsun og Publikum.
D. Buttry, 563(SS):Summer82-271
Hansen, B. Mexican Cookery.*
W. and C. Cowen, 639(VQR):Spring82-69

Hansen, F.E. The Grammar of Gregorian Tonality.
D. Hiley, 415:May82-335
Hansén, I. Les adverbes prédicatifs français en -ment.
J. Brill, 350:Sep83-692
R. Martin, 553(RLiR):Jul-Dec82-477
Hansen, J. Backtrack.
N. Callendar, 441:16Jan83-26
442(NY):7Feb83-123
Hansen, M. Ezra Pounds frühe Poetik und Kulturkritik zwischen Aufklärung und Avantgarde.
M. Pfister, 490:Band13Heft1/2-166
Hansen, W. and H. Kreft. Fachwerk im Weserraum.
J. Cramer, 43:Band12Heft2-185
Hansen, W.F., ed. Saxo Grammaticus and the Life of Hamlet.
H.R.E. Davidson, 617(TLS):27May83-537
Hanson, C. and A. Gurr. Katherine Mansfield.
C. Sprague, 395(MFS):Summer82-275
Hanson, P. Trade and Technology in Soviet-Western Relations.
P. Marer, 104(CASS):Fall-Winter82-589
A.H. Smith, 575(SEER):Apr82-306
Hanson, W.S. and G.S. Maxwell. Rome's North West Frontier.
V. Maxfield, 617(TLS):28Oct83-1197
Hansson, C. and K. Liden. Moscow Women.
S. Jacoby, 441:7Aug83-14
"Hanyu chengyu cidian."
A.J. Majewicz, 360(LP):Vol124-172
Hao, W. - see under Wang Hao
Happé, P., ed. Four Morality Plays.
A.C. Cawley, 447(N&Q):Apr81-181
Harada, H. - see Lull, R.
Haran, M. Temples and Temple-Service in Ancient Israel.
J. Milgrom, 318(JAOS):Apr-Jun81-261
Harari, J.V., ed. Textual Strategies.*
R. Lewis, 153:Spring82-2
R. Magliola, 395(MFS):Winter81/82-759
C. Rubino, 400(MLN):Dec82-1213
Haraszti, É.H. The Invaders.
J. Joll, 617(TLS):30Sep83-1064
Harbert, E.N., ed. Critical Essays on Henry Adams.
J.M. Cox, 432(NEQ):Dec82-619
R.F. Sommer, 577(SHR):Spring82-170
Harbsmeier, C. Aspects of Classical Chinese Syntax.
S. De Lancey, 350:Dec83-934
Harcourt, J. and J. Metcalf, eds. 77 Best Canadian Stories.
D. Stephens, 296(JCF):No33-130
Härd, J.E. Studien zur Struktur mehrgliedriger deutscher Nebensatzprädikate.
W.P. Ahrens, 350:Sep83-695
Hardeman, N.P. Shucks, Shocks, and Hominy Blocks.
639(VQR):Winter82-22
Harden, D.B., with V.A. Tatton-Brown. Catalogue of Greek and Roman Glass in the British Museum. (Vol 1)
R. Higgins, 39:Sep82-199
Harden, E.F. The Emergence of Thackeray's Serial Fiction.*
N. Pickwoad, 541(RES):Aug82-355
G.C. Sorensen, 301(JEGP):Apr82-274

Harder, H-B. and H. Rothe, eds. Goethe
und die Welt der Slawen.
T.E. Little, 575(SEER):Oct82-637
V. Terras, 301(JEGP):Jul82-387
Hardie, R. The Burma-Siam Railway.
H. Toye, 617(TLS):2Dec83-1355
Hardie, W.F.R. Aristotle's Ethical Theory.
(2nd ed)
J.L. Ackrill, 123:Vol32No1-99
Hardin, R.F., ed. Survivals of Pastoral.*
P. Lindenbaum, 678(YCGL):No30-93
O.F. Sigworth, 402(MLR):Apr82-402
Harding, J. Maurice Chevalier.
G. O'Connor, 617(TLS):21Jan83-71
Harding, L., ed. The Altered I.
S. Gunew, 381:Jun82-277
Harding, L. Displaced Person.
S. Gunew, 381:Jun82-277
Harding, L., ed. Rooms of Paradise.
S. Gunew, 381:Jun82-277
Harding, N. Lenin's Political Thought.
(Vol 2)
J. Keep, 575(SEER):Apr82-295
R.H.W. Theen, 550(RusR):Oct82-497
Harding, W. and M. Meyer. The New Thoreau
Handbook.*
M. Granger, 189(EA):Apr-Jun82-230
L. Lane, Jr., 106:Fall82-199
Hardison, O.B., Jr. Entering the Maze.
A.N. Jeffares, 651(WHR):Autumn82-285
M. Williams, 639(VQR):Summer82-514
Hardwick, E. Bartleby in Manhattan and
Other Essays.
D. Donoghue, 441:12Jun83-7
D.A.N. Jones, 362:29Sep83-23
D. Lodge, 617(TLS):11Nov83-1237
Hardwick, E. A View of My Own.
V. Trueblood, 271:Spring82-132
Hardwick, M. and M. Alfred Deller.
E. Forbes, 415:Jul82-481
Hardy, E. The Countryman's Ear and other
Essays on Thomas Hardy.
P. Dickinson, 364:Jul82-92
Hardy, H. - see Berlin, I.
Hardy, I. An Ohio School Mistress. (L.
Filler, ed)
42(AR):Fall82-487
Hardy, J. Values in Social Policy.
T.M.R., 185:Oct82-214
Hardy, J.P. Samuel Johnson.
R. Folkenflik, 677(YES):Vol 12-283
Hardy, P. The Film Encyclopedia. (Vol 1)
C. Frayling, 617(TLS):18Nov83-1264
Hardy, T. The Collected Letters of Thomas
Hardy.* (Vol 2) (R.L. Purdy and M. Mill-
gate, eds)
J.L. Bradley, 402(MLR):Jul82-709
R. Brebach, 395(MFS):Winter81/82-698
Hardy, T. Thomas Hardy's Chosen Poems.
(F.S. Puk, ed)
T.R. Watson, 677(TLS):Vol 12-326
Hardy, T. Selected Poems of Thomas Hardy.
(J. Reeves and R. Gittings, eds)
H.L. Weatherby, 569(SR):Spring82-313
Hardy, T. The Woodlanders. (D. Kramer,
ed)
S. Gatrell, 445(NCF):Jun82-122
A.L. Manford, 517(PBSA):Vol76No4-491
R.C. Schweik, 177(ELT):Vol125No3-179
Hardyment, C. Dream Babies.
R. Dinnage, 617(TLS):4Feb83-113
Hare, A. George Frederick Cooke.*
A. Woods, 612(ThS):Nov82-245

Hare, G.E. Alphonse Daudet.*
B.C. Swift, 208(FS):Jul82-347
Hare, R.M. Moral Thinking.*
N. Fotion, 185:Jul83-800
B. Mayo, 518:Jul82-173
Hare, R.M. Plato.
S. Waterlow, 617(TLS):11Mar83-247
Hare, W. Open-Mindedness and Education.*
A.S. Carson, 154:Jun82-394
Harel, D. First-Order Dynamic Logic.
J. Tiuryn, 316:Jun82-453
Harenberg, E.J., with F. Ketner and M.
Dillo, eds. Oorkondenboek van Gelre en
Zutphen tot 1326, 28 aug 1214-9 juni
1322.
T. Evergates, 589:Oct82-902
Hareven, T.K. and M.A. Vinovskis, eds.
Family and Population in Nineteenth-
Century America.
A.C. Fellman, 106:Spring82-61
Harger-Grinling, V. and T. Goldie, eds.
Violence in the Canadian Novel Since
1960.
B-Z. Shek, 627(UTQ):Summer82-471
Hargreaves, A.G. The Colonial Experience
in French Fiction.
J. Flower, 402(MLR):Oct82-961
M.G. Lerner, 208(FS):Oct82-487
L.M. Porter, 395(MFS):Summer82-332
Hargreaves, M.W.M. and J.F. Hopkins - see
Clay, H.
Hargreaves-Mawdsley, W.N. Eighteenth-
Century Spain, 1700-1788.
W.J. Callahan, 173(ECS):Fall82-82
Harington, J. A Supplie or Addicion to
the Catalogue of Bishops to the Yeare
1608. (R.H. Miller, ed)
P. Collinson, 354:Jun82-198
Harjan, G. Leonid Leonov.*
B.T. Urbanic, 574(SEEJ):Summer82-247
Harlan, L.R. Booker T. Washington. (Vol
2)
P.J. Parish, 617(TLS):9Dec83-1371
C.V. Woodward, 441:22May83-13
Harlan, R.D. Chapter Nine.
D. Chambers, 503:Winter82-211
Harland, R. Testimony.
D. Haskell, 581:Sep82-348
Harland, R. and K. Spike. Fast Fashion
Jeans for Family Fun.
P. Bach, 614:Winter83-16
Harlass, G. and H. Vater. Zur aktuellen
deutschen Wortschatz.
E. Beneš, 685(ZDL):2/1981-266
Harlech, P. Practical Guide to Cooking,
Entertaining and Household Management.
W. and C. Cowen, 639(VQR):Spring82-65
Harlfinger, D., ed. Griechische Kodi-
kologie und Textüberlieferung.
P. Hoffmann, 555:Vol133Fasc2-362
Harman, B.L. Costly Monuments.
A.D. Nuttall, 617(TLS):22Jul83-787
Harman, C. - see Warner, S.T.
Harmatta, J., ed. Prolegomena to the
Sources on the History of Pre-Islamic
Central Asia. Studies in the Sources
on the History of Pre-Islamic Central
Asia.
J.W. de Jong, 259(IIJ):Jul82-219

Harmer, L.C. Uncertainties in French Grammar.* (P. Rickard and T.G.S. Combe, eds)
  C. Sanders, 402(MLR):Jan82-193
  B. Tranel, 545(RPh):May82-665
Harms, W. and H. Reinitzer, eds. Natura loquax.
  U-K. Ketelsen, 133:Band15Heft4-354
Harms, W., with M. Schilling and A. Wang, eds. Deutsche illustrierte Flugblätter des 16. and 17. Jahrhunderts. (Vol 2)
  W.A. Coupe, 402(MLR):Oct82-991
  R. Schenda, 196:Band23Heft3/4-318
Harning, K.E. The Analytic Genitive in the Modern Arabic Dialects.
  A.S. Kaye, 350:Sep83-699
Harou, L. Chroniques souterraines.
  M.J. Green, 207(FR):Dec82-337
Haroutunian, J. Covered Things.
  M. Cowan, 614:Winter83-14
Harpaz, E. - see Constant, B.
Harper, F. and D.E. Presley. Okefinokee Album.
  M.C. Brown, 585(SoQ):Spring82-92
Harper, G.M. W.B. Yeats and W.T. Horton.*
  B. Dolan, 305(JIL):Sep82-114
Harper, G.M. and W.K. Hood - see Yeats, W.B.
Harper, K. Suffixes of the Eskimo Dialects of Cumberland Peninsula and North Baffin Island.
  M.D. Fortescue, 269(IJAL):Jan82-91
Harper, M.S. - see Brown, S.A.
Harper, W.L., R. Stalnaker and G. Pearce, eds. Ifs, Conditionals, Belief, Decision, Chance and Time.
  J. van Benthem, 603:Vol6No1-125
Harrauer, H. and S.M.E. van Lith. Corpus Papyrorum Raineri. (Vol 6)
  E. Boswinkel, 394:Vol35fasc3/4-397
Harré, R. Social Being.*
  J.D. Moon, 185:Apr83-611
Harrell, B. Anatolian Knitting Designs.
  R.L. Shep, 614:Fall83-15
Harries, K. The Bavarian Rococo Church.
  J. Rykwert, 453(NYRB):24Nov83-42
Harries-Jenkins, G., ed. Armed Forces and the Welfare Societies.
  J. Gooch, 617(TLS):20May83-507
Harrigan, S. Aransas.*
  K. Fontenot, 436(NewL):Fall82-121
Harrington, L. Syllables of Recorded Time.
  D. Duffy, 627(UTQ):Summer82-448
Harrington, M. Decade of Decision.*
  639(VQR):Winter82-12
Harrington, M. The Politics at God's Funeral.
  P.L. Berger, 441:9Oct83-7
Harrington, M. and B. Adelman. The Next America.
  J.V. Mallow, 287:Nov82-19
Harris, A. Night's Black Agents.
  S. Hannaford, 568(SCN):Spring-Summer82-21
  K. Robinson, 447(N&Q):Aug81-336
Harris, D.A. Inspirations Unbidden.
  R. Moss, 617(TLS):28Oct83-1194
Harris, E. Velázquez.
  M. Jaffé, 617(TLS):28Oct83-1195
Harris, E.P. - see "Lessing Yearbook"
Harris, E.T. Handel and the Pastoral Tradition.*
  D.R.B. Kimbell, 410(M&L):Jan/Apr82-102

Harris, F.J. Encounters with Darkness.
  M. Tilby, 617(TLS):25Nov83-1327
Harris, H., ed. John Creasey's Crime Collection 1983.
  T.J. Binyon, 617(TLS):2Dec83-1358
Harris, J. The Artist and the Country House.*
  A. Crookshank, 90:May82-308
Harris, J. The Palladians.
  T. Connor, 90:Jun82-369
  I. Gow, 324:Jan83-106
  J. Lees-Milne, 39:Jun82-511
Harris, J. William Talman.
  J.M. Richards, 617(TLS):7Jan83-19
Harris, J. Violence and Responsibility.*
  A. Collier, 393(Mind):Jan82-151
Harris, J. and B. McKinnon, eds. Pulp Mill.
  D. Stephens, 296(JCF):No33-130
Harris, J.G. - see Mandelstam, O.
Harris, J.S., ed. TV Guide: The First 25 Years.
  A.H. Marill, 200:Oct82-509
Harris, K. Attlee.*
  G. Hodgson, 441:28Aug83-8
  P. Vansittart, 364:Dec82/Jan83-121
Harris, L.L., ed. Nineteenth-Century Literature Criticism. (Vol 2)
  T. Wortham, 445(NCF):Mar83-620
Harris, M. America Now.*
  M. Kammen, 42(AR):Fall82-479
Harris, M. Saul Bellow: Drumlin Woodchuck.*
  P. Balbert, 594:Spring82-95
  C.E. Eisinger, 395(MFS):Summer81-372
  S. Fogel, 106:Fall82-267
Harris, M. Cultural Materialism.
  A. Sandstrom, 125:Spring82-315
Harris, M. The Evolution of French Syntax.
  W.J. Ashby, 350:Jun83-414
  J. Klausenburger, 297(JL):Mar82-176
Harris, M. Screenplay.*
  L. Jones, 617(TLS):22Apr83-400
Harris, M.C. and R.G. Wright. Index to Birthplaces of United Kingdom Authors.
  D. Eagle, 447(N&Q):Aug81-341
Harris, N. Humbug.
  M. Mudrick, 249(HudR):Winter82/83-581
Harris, P. Political China Observed.
  R. Vohra, 293(JASt):Nov81-109
Harris, R., ed. Approaches to Language.
  T. Moore, 617(TLS):1Jul83-709
Harris, R. Gotcha!
  C. Wain, 362:3Mar83-20
  G. Wheatcroft, 617(TLS):13May83-490
Harris, R. The Language-Maker.*
  J.D., 185:Jan83-420
Harris, R. and J. Paxton. A Higher Form of Killing.
  639(VQR):Summer82-91
Harris, R.H. Modern Drama in America and England, 1950-1970.
  P. Davison, 354:Dec82-463
  A. Wertheim, 365:Winter83-38
Harris, T. From Mammies to Militants.
  Y.B. Kemp, 95(CLAJ):Dec82-262
  F.R. Schumer, 441:6Mar83-18
Harris, W. Morocco That Was.
  A.H.M.K-G., 617(TLS):23Dec83-1443
Harris, W.V. British Short Fiction in the Nineteenth Century.*
  N. Bradbury, 541(RES):Aug82-347

Harris, W.V. The Omnipresent Debate.
 K. Beckson, 651(WHR):Winter82-366
Harris, W.V. War and Imperialism in Repub-
lican Rome 327-70 B.C.
 S.I. Oost, 122:Jan82-81
Harrison, A.T., ed. The Graham Indian
Mutiny Papers.
 T.R. Metcalf, 293(JASt):Feb82-385
Harrison, B. An Introduction to the Phi-
losophy of Language.*
 D. Papineau, 393(Mind):Oct82-610
Harrison, B. Peaceable Kingdom.
 P. Clarke, 617(TLS):18Feb83-163
Harrison, C. English Art and Modernism
1900-1939.*
 D. Farr, 39:May82-415
 N. Wadley, 592:Vol 195No995-92
Harrison, D., ed. Crossing Frontiers.
 A. Collins, 178:Mar82-108
Harrison, D. The Limits of Liberalism.
 L. Marsden, 99:Mar83-26
 J. Stolzman, 150(DR):Summer82-344
Harrison, G.A. The Enthusiast.
 P-L. Adams, 61:Dec83-116
 J. Atlas, 441:6Nov83-11
Harrison, J. A Good Day To Die.
 G.E. Selander, 649(WAL):Nov82-276
Harrison, J. Hume's Theory of Justice.*
 E.P. Brandon, 479(PhQ):Oct82-384
 D.F. Norton, 319:Jul83-433
Harrison, J. Selected and New Poems.*
 W. Harmon, 472:Spring/Summer83-129
Harrison, M.J. The Ice Monkey.
 C. Greenland, 617(TLS):8Jul83-725
Harrison, R.P. The Cartoon.
 P. Fresnault-Deruelle, 567:Vol139No3/4-
367
Harrison, S.S. In Afghanistan's Shadow.
 A.S. Ahmed, 293(JASt):Aug82-869
Harrison, T. Continuous.*
 C.B. Cox, 148:Winter82-3
 M. O'Neill, 493:Apr82-59
Harrison, T. A Kumquat for John Keats.*
 U.S. Martial.*
 M. O'Neill, 493:Apr82-59
Harrison, T. The Last Horizon.
 F. Rasky, 73:Summer83-53
Harrison, W. and S. le Fleming. Russian-
English and English-Russian Dictionary.
 W.V. Tuman, 399(MLJ):Autumn82-346
Harrison-Matthews, L. Mammals in the
British Isles.
 P. Morris, 617(TLS):18Feb83-152
Harrod, D. Making Sense of the Economy.
 F. Cairncross, 617(TLS):2Sep83-923
Harrod, H.L. The Human Center.
 D.E.M., 185:Oct82-194
Harsanyi, J.C. Rational Behavior and Bar-
gaining Equilibrium in Games and Social
Situations.
 A.C. Michalos, 488:Dec82-444
Hart, D. The Colonel.
 C. Hawtree, 617(TLS):17Jun83-642
Hart, F.R. The Scottish Novel: From Smol-
lett to Spark.
 R.A. Day, 173(ECS):Fall81-99
Hart, G.L. 3d. Poets of the Tamil Anthol-
ogies.*
 R. Ramamurti, 318(JAOS):Oct-Dec81-501
Hart, H.L.A. Essays on Bentham.
 W. Twining, 617(TLS):11Feb83-124

Hart, K. The Lines of the Hand.*
 G. Catalano, 381:Oct81-349
 D. Haskell, 581:Sep82-348
Hart-Davis, R. - see Lyttelton, G. and R.
Hart-Davis
Hart-Davis, R. - see Sassoon, S.
Harter, H.A. Gertrudis Gómez de Avellan-
eda.
 R.M. Cabrera, 238:Sep82-470
Hartford, R., ed. Bayreuth: The Early
Years.*
 639(VQR):Winter82-27
Hartig, M. Sozialer Wandel und Sprachwan-
del.
 T.F. Shannon, 350:Jun83-454
Hartigan, K. The Poets and the Cities.*
 S. Bertman, 487:Summer82-194
Hartland, M. Down Among the Dead Men.
 T.J. Binyon, 617(TLS):30Sep83-1037
 M. Laski, 362:11Aug83-24
Hartley, B. and J. Wacher, eds. Rome and
her Northern Provinces.
 K. Branigan, 617(TLS):23Sep83-1028
Hartley, K. NATO Arms Co-operation.
 M. Carver, 617(TLS):29Jul83-803
Hartley, N. Shadowplay.
 T.J. Binyon, 617(TLS):21Jan83-66
Hartley, T.E., ed. Proceedings of the
Parliaments of Elizabeth I. (Vol 1)
 J.H. Hexter, 617(TLS):21Jan83-51
Härtling, P. Das Windrad.
 W. Larrett, 617(TLS):14Oct83-1142
Hartman, C.O. Free Verse.*
 J. Duemer, 134(CP):Fall82-108
Hartman, G.H. Criticism in the Wilder-
ness.*
 J.W. Davidson, 477(PLL):Winter82-428
 R.B. Hauck, 395(MFS):Summer81-388
 S. Lawall, 131(CL):Spring82-177
 H. Lindenberger, 401(MLQ):Jun82-194
 P. McCallum, 49:Jan82-73
 A.D. Nuttall, 402(MLR):Apr82-439
Hartman, G.H., ed. Psychoanalysis and the
Question of the Text.*
 A. Jefferson, 447(N&Q):Jun81-284
Hartman, G.H. Saving the Text.*
 G.P. Bennington, 208(FS):Jul82-365
 R.A. Cohen, 478:Oct82-223
 D.H. Hirsch, 569(SR):Winter82-119
 W.J. Kennedy, 221(GQ):May82-387
 H. Lindenberger, 401(MLQ):Jun82-194
 R. Moynihan, 141:Summer82-277
 W.J. Ong, 480(P&R):Fall82-274
 T. Rajan, 579(SAQ):Autumn82-465
 S. Raval, 50(ArQ):Autumn82-263
 S.S., 148:Summer82-92
Hartman, L.F. and A.A. Di Lella. The Book
of Daniel.
 S.A. Kaufman, 318(JAOS):Apr-Jun81-250
Hartmann, D., H. Linke and O. Ludwig, eds.
Sprache in Gegenwart und Geschichte.
 G. Lipold, 685(ZDL):3/1982-368
 J. Schildt, 682(ZPSK):Band34Heft5-642
Hartmann, J.B. Antike Motive bei Thorvald-
sen.*
 L.O. Larsson, 341:Vol51No1-40
Hartmann, N. and H. Heimsoeth. Nicolai
Hartmann und Heinz Heimsoeth im Brief-
wechsel. (F. Hartmann and R. Heimsoeth,
eds)
 B. Liebrucks, 342:Band73Heft1-82

Hartmann, R. Richard Strauss: The Staging of his Operas and Ballets.
  R. Anderson, 415:Sep82-617
  M. Tanner, 617(TLS):11Mar83-243
Hartmann, R.R.K. Contrastive Textology.
  M. Celce-Murcia, 350:Jun83-432
  M.C. Jacobs, 399(MLJ):Autumn82-325
Hartmann, S. Altersdichtung und Selbstdarstellung bei Oswald von Wolkenstein.
  F.V. Spechtler, 602:Vol 13No2-333
Hartog, F. Le Miroir d'Hérodote.*
  H. Cronel, 450(NRF):Jan82-137
Hartung, G., ed. Beiträge zur Lessing-Konferenz 1979.
  A. Scott-Prelorentzos, 221(GQ):Mar82-249
Hartung, H. - see Hamburger, M.
Hartwig, G.W. and K.D. Patterson, eds. Disease in African History.
  P. Richards, 69:Vol51No1-528
Harvard, S. An Italic Copybook.
  N. Barker, 78(BC):Winter82-513
Harvey, A. A Full Circle.
  J. Saunders, 565:Vol23No3-73
Harvey, A. A Journey in Ladakh.
  M. Amis, 61:Jul83-100
  J.H. Crook, 617(TLS):19Aug83-889
  R. Towers, 441:7Aug83-7
  E.S. Turner, 362:26May83-22
  442(NY):22Aug83-94
Harvey, A.D. English Literature and the Great War with France.
  J. Raimond, 189(EA):Oct-Dec82-472
Harvey, G. The Art of Anthony Trollope.*
  R. Tracy, 637(VS):Autumn81-99
Harvey, J. Provence.
  I. McMillan, 493:Jun82-71
Harvey, R.A. A Commentary on Persius.
  J.R. Jenkinson, 123:Vol32No2-167
  T.G. Palaima, 124:Jan/Feb83-185
Harvey, S. and others, eds. Reappraisals of Rousseau.*
  M. Delon, 535(RHL):Jul-Aug82-662
  P. France, 402(MLR):Apr82-452
Harvey, V.I. - see Bateman, W.G.
Harweg, R. Pronomina und Textkonstitution. (2nd ed)
  P. Suchsland, 682(ZPSK):Band35Heft3-370
Harwood, G. The Lion's Bride.*
  B. Beaver, 381:Sep82-403
Hasegawa, T. The February Revolution: Petrograd, 1917.*
  J. Bushnell, 550(RusR):Oct82-489
  639(VQR):Winter82-23
Haskell, B. Marsden Hartley.
  M.S. Young, 39:Nov82-348
Haskell, F. and N. Penny. Taste and the Antique.*
  P.P. Bober, 551(RenQ):Autumn82-460
  M.H. Bogart, 219(GaR):Spring82-208
  F. Felsenstein, 83:Autumn82-287
  H.D. Lutteman, 341:Vol51No1-39
  P. Mauriès, 98:Apr82-312
  J. Montagu, 59:Mar82-117
  H. Plommer, 123:Vol32No2-264
  M. Pointon, 89(BJA):Spring82-176
Haskins, D. Reclamation.
  L. Ricou, 102(CanL):Spring82-90
Hasler, P.W., ed. The History of Parliament: The House of Commons 1558-1603.
  J.H. Hexter, 617(TLS):21Jan83-51

Hasluck, N. The Hat on the Letter O.
  E. Webby, 381:Jul81-200
Hassall, A.J. Henry Fielding's "Tom Jones."*
  J.C. Beasley, 677(YES):Vol 12-281
  B.S. Hammond, 83:Autumn82-242
  J. Hay, 566:Autumn82-2
Hassan, I. The Right Promethean Fire.*
  C. Caramello, 114(ChiR):Winter83-78
  J. Martin, 27(AL):Dec82-604
  E. Webb, 648(WCR):Jun82-58
Hassan, S.Q. Les instruments de musique en Iraq.
  H.H. Touma, 187:Jan83-132
Hassel, R.C., Jr. Faith and Folly in Shakespeare's Romantic Comedies.
  F.D. Hoeniger, 551(RenQ):Summer81-283
Hassel, R.C., Jr. Renaissance Drama and the English Church Year.*
  R. Fraser, 301(JEGP):Jan82-106
  R.M. Frye, 570(SQ):Autumn82-410
Hassett, C.W. The Elusive Self in the Poetry of Robert Browning.
  A. Hayter, 617(TLS):13May83-478
Hastings, D. and T. Eckert, eds. Historical Records of Washington State.
  R.L. Schaadt, 14:Spring82-199
Hastings, M. Carnival War/Midnite at the Starlite.
  D. Devlin, 157:Summer82-52
Hastings, M. The Shotgun.
  H.L. Blackmore, 39:Jul82-67
Hastings, M. and S. Jenkins. The Battle for the Falklands.
  C. Wain, 362:3Mar83-20
  G. Wheatcroft, 617(TLS):13May83-490
Hasubek, P., ed. Die Fabel.
  T. Elm, 680(ZDP):Band101Heft4-630
Hatch, E. Culture and Morality.
  P. Winch, 617(TLS):18Mar83-277
Hathaway, L. Der Mundartwandel in Imst in Tirol zwischen 1897 und 1973.
  E. Bauer, 685(ZDL):3/1982-401
Hatley, G. and L. Portnoy. Horse Camping.
  529(QQ):Autumn82-687
Hattersley, R. Politics Apart.*
  A. Brownjohn, 617(TLS):7Jan83-4
Hattersley, R. Press Gang.
  G. Kaufman, 362:30Jun83-24
Hattersley, R. A Yorkshire Boyhood.
  G. Kaufman, 362:30Jun83-24
  K.O. Morgan, 617(TLS):29Jul83-800
Hatto, A.T. Essays on Medieval German and Other Poetry.
  I. Glier, 221(GQ):Mar82-243
  N.F. Palmer, 447(N&Q):Jun81-258
  A. Wolf, 406:Summer82-193
Hatto, A.T., ed. Traditions of Heroic and Epic Poetry. (Vol 1)
  R. Finnegan, 575(SEER):Apr82-278
  W.B. Stanford, 677(YES):Vol 12-226
Hatzopoulos, M.B. and L.D. Loukopoulos, eds. Philip of Macedon.
  C. Tuplin, 123:Vol32No2-239
Haubrichs, W., ed. Erzählforschung.* (Vols 1-3)
  H. Mayer, 564:Feb81-83
Haudry, J. L'emploi des cas en Védique.
  T.J. Elizarenkova, 259(IIJ):Jan82-43
Haudry, J. L'indo-européen.
  P. Flobert, 555:Vol55fasc1-171

Haug, C.J. Leisure and Urbanism in Nineteenth-Century Nice.
E. Weber, 617(TLS):28Jan83-87
Haug, W., ed. Formen und Funktionen der Allegorie.
D.H. Green, 402(MLR):Oct82-980
Haugeland, J., ed. Mind Design.
J.D., 185:Oct82-201
Haugen, E. Scandinavian Language Structures.
J.T. Jensen, 350:Dec83-928
Haugen, J. Diktersfinxen.
Å.H. Lervik, 172(Edda):1982/4-251
Haumann, H. Kapitalismus im zaristischen Staat, 1906-1917.
T.C. Owen, 104(CASS):Fall-Winter82-548
Haupt, G.E. - see More, T.
Hauser, T. Agatha's Friends.
N. Callendar, 441:10Apr83-32
Häusle, H. Einfache und frühe Formen des griechischen Epigramms.
P.A. Hansen, 123:Vol32No1-34
Hausman, D.M. Capital, Profits and Prices.
J. McMillan, 486:Dec82-651
Hausman, J.J., with J. Wright, eds. Arts and the Schools.*
K. Marantz, 289:Winter82-118
Hausmann, F.J. Louis Meigret humaniste et linguiste.*
C. Demaizière, 535(RHL):Sep-Dec82-865
Hausmann, F.J. - see Meigret, L.
Hausmann, F.J. - see Söll, L.
Häussler, R. Das historische Epos der Griechen und Römer bis Vergil. Das historische Epos von Lucan bis Silius und seine Theorie.
J. Perret, 555:Vol55fasc2-375
Havard, W.C. and W. Sullivan, eds. A Band of Prophets.
639(VQR):Autumn82-115
Havelka, J. Reflections and Preoccupations.
D. O'Rourke, 102(CanL):Autumn82-149
Havelock, E.A. The Greek Concept of Justice.*
H. Lloyd-Jones, 303(JoHS):Vol 102-258
M.M. Mackenzie, 319:Apr82-197
Havelock, E.A. The Literate Revolution in Greece and Its Cultural Consequences.
J.E. Rexine, 124:Mar/Apr83-251
Havens, T.R.H. Artist and Patron in Postwar Japan.
L. Allen, 617(TLS):4Feb83-114
Haverkate, H. Impositive Sentences in Spanish.*
A. Bell, 353:Vol 19No1/2-182
Hawes, L. Presences of Nature.
R. Lister, 324:Aug83-571
G. Reynolds, 617(TLS):29Apr83-438
Hawkes, E. and P. Manso. The Shadow of the Moth.
P-L. Adams, 61:Mar83-116
N. Callendar, 441:22May83-49
J.R., 231:Feb83-76
Hawkes, J. Virginie.*
C. Berryman, 114(ChiR):Summer83-74
P. Kemp, 617(TLS):28Jan83-79
Hawkins, J.A. Definiteness and Indefiniteness.*
H. Vater, 603:Vol6No2-261

Hawthorne, N. The Haunting Tales of Nathaniel Hawthorne. (M. Hayes, ed)
E. Wright, 677(YES):Vol 12-309
"The Nathaniel Hawthorne Journal 1977." (C.E.F. Clark, Jr., ed)
B. Lawson-Peebles, 541(RES):Nov82-490
E. Wright, 677(YES):Vol 12-309
Hayami, Y. and others. Anatomy of a Peasant Economy.
M. Takaki, 293(JASt):Nov81-201
Hayashi, T. Steinbeck and Hemingway.
K.Z. Derounian, 234:Fall82-85
Hayashi, T. The Theory of English Lexicography 1530-1791.
D.M.E. Gillam, 179(ES):Apr82-165
H. Käsmann, 38:Band100Heft1/2-160
Hayashima, K. and others, eds. Tibetan Tripiṭaka, Sde dge edition, Bstan ḥgyur: Dbu ma.
J.W. de Jong, 259(IIJ):Jul80-260
Hayden, D. The Grand Domestic Revolution.
E.L. Birch, 576:Mar82-75
N.F. Cott, 453(NYRB):17Mar83-36
S. Francis, 46:Sep82-94
J. Gordon, 658:Winter82-283
Hayden, J.O. Polestar of the Ancients.
D. Bartine, 301(JEGP):Jan82-102
D. Hopkins, 402(MLR):Jul82-690
B.R. Rees, 123:Vol32No1-101
S. Trombley, 541(RES):Nov82-502
Hayden, J.O. - see Wordsworth, W.
Hayden, R. American Journal.
G.E. Murray, 385(MQR):Fall83-643
J.S. Wright, 219(GaR):Winter82-904
639(VQR):Autumn82-134
Hayek, F.A. Law, Legislation and Liberty.* (Vols 1 and 2)
J.E.J. Altham, 483:Apr82-274
Hayek, F.A. Law, Legislation and Liberty.* (Vol 3)
J.E.J. Altham, 483:Apr82-274
T.R. Machan, 488:Sep82-332
Hayes, E.M. The Fine Gossoon.
J.M. Davies, 305(JIL):Sep82-116
Hayes, J. The Art of Graham Sutherland.*
A. Causey, 39:Feb82-137
F. Spalding, 90:Jan82-46
Hayes, J. The Landscape Paintings of Thomas Gainsborough.
R. Paulson, 617(TLS):25Mar83-283
Hayes, J.W. Ancient Lamps in the Royal Ontario Museum 1.
J.J. Dobbins, 487:Winter82-376
Hayes, J.W. Supplement to Late Roman Pottery.
R. Reece, 123:Vol32No1-111
Hayes, M. - see Hawthorne, N.
Hayes, T.W. Winstanley the Digger.*
P. Horden, 447(N&Q):Dec81-544
F.L. Huntley, 551(RenQ):Spring82-136
J.R. Knott, Jr., 539:Feb83-73
Hayes, Z. - see Saint Bonaventure
Hayley, B. Carleton's Traits and Stories and the 19th Century: Anglo-Irish Tradition.
P. Craig, 617(TLS):16Dec83-1415
Hayman, J. - see Ruskin, J.
Hayman, R. Artaud and After.*
P.S. Thompson, 207(FR):May83-955
Hayman, R. Brecht.
T. Garton Ash, 617(TLS):9Dec83-1363
P. Gay, 441:27Nov83-14

157

Hayman, R. Kafka.*
    C.S. Brown, 569(SR):Fall82-583
    C. Koelb, 395(MFS):Winter82/83-694
Hayman, R. Nietzsche.
    A. Nehamas, 319:Jan82-98
    J. Tietz, 648(WCR):Spring82-37
Haymon, S.T. Ritual Murder.*
    N. Callendar, 441:13Feb83-31
    M. Laski, 362:20Jan83-23
Haynal, A., M. Molnar and G. de Puymège.
Fanaticism.
    M.F., 231:Feb83-75
Haynes, D. Greek Art and the Idea of
Freedom.*
    J.F. Healy, 39:Jan82-67
Haynes, R.D. H.G. Wells.
    P. Faulkner, 447(N&Q):Oct81-450
    J. Huntington, 395(MFS):Summer81-327
    M.A. Sperber, 637(VS):Spring82-384
    J-P. Vernier, 677(YES):Vol 12-331
Hayton, D. and C. Jones, eds. A Register
of Parliamentary Lists 1660-1761.
    H.S. Cobb, 325:Apr82-41
Hayward, H. and P. Kirkham. William and
John Linnell.*
    H-O. Boström, 341:Vol51No2-88
    G. Wills, 39:Feb82-131
Hayward, M. Writers in Russia: 1917-1978.
(P. Blake, ed)
    J. Bayley, 453(NYRB):22Dec83-22
    D. Fanger, 617(TLS):11Nov83-1251
    H. Robinson, 441:9Oct83-13
    442(NY):3Oct83-130
Haywood, D. Crazy Quilting with a Differ-
ence.
    M. Cowan, 614:Winter83-14
Hazel, R. Who Touches This.
    T. Houghton, 152(UDQ):Spring81-122
Hazeldine, P. Raptures of the Deep.
    S. Pickles, 617(TLS):28Oct83-1185
Hazlehurst, F.H. Gardens of Illusion.*
    G. Walton, 54:Sep82-517
Hazlewood, A. The Economy of Kenya: The
Kenyatta Era.
    A. O'Connor, 69:Vol51No1-543
Hazlitt, W. The Letters of William Haz-
litt. (H.M. Sikes, with W.H. Bonner and
G. Lahey, eds)
    J.H. Alexander, 402(MLR):Jan82-176
    E.D. Mackerness, 447(N&Q):Dec81-560
Head, E. and P. Calistro. Edith Head's
Hollywood.
    M. Haskell, 441:30Oct83-9
Headley, J.M. The Emperor and his Chancel-
lor.
    I.A.A. Thompson, 617(TLS):8Jul83-739
Headrick, D.R. The Tools of Empire.
    P.W. Fay, 293(JASt):Aug82-807
Heal, F. Of Prelates and Princes.
    A.J. Slavin, 551(RenQ):Summer81-260
Heald, T. Networks.
    T. Brown, 617(TLS):21Oct83-1168
Healey, A.D., ed. The Old English Vision
of St. Paul.* [shown in prev under
Healy]
    J.E. Cross, 447(N&Q):Feb81-62
    A. Hudson, 677(YES):Vol 12-227
Healey, A.D. and R.L. Venezky, comps. A
Microfiche Concordance to Old English.
    F.C. Robinson, 589:Jan82-133

Healey, R., ed. Reduction, Time and Real-
ity.
    C. Nerlich, 479(PhQ):Jul82-272
    T.E. Wilkerson, 483:Jul82-410
Healy, D. Banished Misfortune.*
    J. Mellors, 364:Feb83-112
Healy, J.J. Literature and the Aborigine
in Australia, 1770-1975.
    S.F.D. Hughes, 395(MFS):Spring81-173
Heaney, S. Field Work.*
    J. Parini, 569(SR):Fall82-623
    T. Parkinson, 219(GaR):Fall82-662
    J-M. Rabaté, 98:Jun-Jul82-512
Heaney, S. The Makings of a Music.
    R.F., 189(EA):Apr-Jun82-239
Heaney, S. North.
    J-M. Rabaté, 98:Jun-Jul82-512
Heaney, S. Poems, 1965-1975.*
    T. Parkinson, 219(GaR):Fall82-662
    J-M. Rabaté, 98:Jun-Jul82-512
    S. Regan, 627(UTQ):Spring82-306
Heaney, S. Preoccupations.*
    S. Fauchereau, 98:Jun-Jul82-628
    J-M. Rabaté, 98:Jun-Jul82-512
    S. Regan, 627(UTQ):Spring82-306
Heard, N.C. House of Slammers.
    M. Watkins, 441:11Dec83-16
Heard-Bey, F. From Trucial States to
United Arab Emirates.
    M. Yapp, 617(TLS):6May83-454
Hearn, M.F. Romanesque Sculpture.
    E. Fernie, 59:Mar82-130
    P. Williamson, 90:Dec82-765
Heartz, D. and B. Wade, eds. Interna-
tional Musicological Society: Report of
the Twelfth Congress, Berkeley 1977.
    D. Leech-Wilkinson, 410(M&L):Jul/Oct82-
    338
Heath, C., D. Kerr and A. Szumigalski, eds.
The Best of Grain.
    N. Zacharin, 137:Aug82-50
Heath, J. Linguistic Diffusion in Arnhem
Land.*
    A. Rumsey, 297(JL):Mar82-173
Heath, J. The Picturesque Prison.
    C. Hawtree, 364:Aug/Sep82-136
    M. Magalaner, 395(MFS):Winter82/83-649
    J.A. Quinn, 628(UWR):Fall-Winter82-127
Heath, J., ed. Profiles in Canadian Lit-
erature. (Vols 1 and 2)
    S. Kane, 627(UTQ):Summer82-440
Heath, S. The Sexual Fix.
    J. Ryle, 617(TLS):18Mar83-262
Heath, T. Interstices of Night.*
    D. Barbour, 648(WCR):Summer81-83
Heath-Agnew, E. A History of Hereford
Cattle and their Breeders.
    J. Urquhart, 617(TLS):21Oct83-1166
Heath-Stubbs, J. Naming the Beasts.*
    H. Lomas, 364:Jul82-66
Heath-Stubbs, J. - see Gray, T.
Heatter, M. Maida Heatter's Book of Great
Chocolate Desserts.
    W. and C. Cowen, 639(VQR):Spring82-65
Hebblethwaite, P. The New Inquisition?
    C. Davis, 529(QQ):Spring82-225
Hebden, M. Pel and the Bombers.
    M. Laski, 362:19May83-24
Hebdige, D. Subcultures.
    P. Delany, 529(QQ):Spring82-182
Hebel, F. Spielraum und Festlegung.
    K.F. Geiger, 196:Band23Heft1/2-129

Heintel, P. and L. Nagl, eds. Zur Kant-Forschung der Gegenwart.
  T. Macho, 489(PJGG):Band89Heft2-432
Heinz, T.A. Frank Lloyd Wright.
  D. Hoffman, 576:Oct82-245
Heinze, R-I. The Role of the Sangha in Modern Thailand.
  D.K. Swearer, 293(JASt):Aug82-883
Heinzig, D. Sowjetische Militärberater bei der Kuomintang, 1923-1927.
  H. Hanak, 575(SEER):Apr82-298
Heinzle, J. Mittelhochdeutsche Dietrich-epik.*
  W. Schröder, 680(ZDP):Band101Heft3-466
Heiskanen, P. - see Tuominen, A.
Heisserer, A.J. Alexander the Great and the Greeks.
  P.M. Fraser, 123:Vol32No2-241
  S. Hornblower, 303(JoHS):Vol 102-271
  S.I. Oost, 122:Apr82-169
  M.B. Walbank, 487:Summer82-186
Heissig, W., ed. Die Geheime Geschichte der Mongolen.
  M. Adamović, 196:Band23Heft3/4-321
Heissig, W. The Religions of Mongolia.*
  W. Schlepp, 293(JASt):Nov81-110
Heitz, C. L'architecture religieuse caro-lingienne.
  C.B. McClendon, 576:Mar82-58
Hélal, G. La philosophie comme panphys-ique.*
  M. Boudot, 192(EP):Oct-Dec81-483
  L.S.F., 543:Mar82-607
Helbig, G., ed. Beiträge zu Problemen der Satzglieder.
  G. Starke, 682(ZPSK):Band34Heft3-358
Helbig, L.F. - see Lessing, G.E.
Helbo, A., ed. Le Champ sémiologique.*
  M-L. Ryan, 494:Winter82-191
Held, D. Introduction to Critical Theory.
  A. Rapaczynski, 185:Jul83-811
Held, J., ed. The Modernization of Agri-culture.
  F. Dovring, 104(CASS):Summer82-297
Held, J.S. The Oil Sketches of Peter Paul Rubens.*
  S. Alpers, 551(RenQ):Spring82-113
  M. Jaffé, 39:Jan82-61
  J.R. Martin, 90:May82-301
Held, K. Heraklit, Parmenides und der Anfang von Philosophie und Wissenschaft.
  W. Pohle, 319:Apr83-247
Heleniak, K.M. William Mulready.*
  A. Rorimer, 54:Sep82-518
Hélias, P.J. L'Herbe d'Or.
  D. Brautman, 207(FR):May83-979
Hell, V. L'idée de culture.
  A. Reix, 542:Oct-Dec82-672
Helleman-Elgersma, W. Soul-Sisters.*
  M.J. Atkinson, 123:Vol32No1-23
  D. O'Brien, 192(EP):Jul-Sep82-351
Heller, A. Renaissance Man.*
  W.C. Watterson, 125:Spring82-299
Heller, A. A Theory of History.
  A. Morton, 617(TLS):11Mar83-247
Heller, G. Un Allemand à Paris, 1940-1944.*
  A. Dulière, 356(LR):Feb82-86
Heller, M. Knowledge.*
  J. Saunders, 565:Vol23No1-73
Heller, M.A. A Palestinian State.
  D. Pryce-Jones, 441:8May83-9
Heller, S. - see Feiffer, J.

Hellerstein, E.O., L. Park-Hume and K.M. Offen, eds. Victorian Women.*
  D.S. Gardner, 14:Winter82-57
Hellgardt, E. Die exegetischen Quellen von Otfrids Evangelienbuch.
  A.C. Schwarz, 406:Winter82-481
Hellie, R. Slavery in Russia, 1450-1725.
  I. de Madariaga, 617(TLS):19Aug83-885
Hellinga, L. Caxton in Focus.
  G.D. Painter, 617(TLS):4Feb83-119
Hellman, J. Emmanuel Mounier and the New Catholic Left, 1930-1950.*
  G. Baum, 99:Apr82-30
  E. Morot-Sir, 207(FR):Apr83-799
  C. Taylor, 319:Jul83-414
Hellman, P. The Auschwitz Album.*
  M.W. Kiel, 287:Aug/Sep82-24
  T. Ziolkowski, 569(SR):Fall82-592
Hellmann, J. Fables of Fact.*
  P.D. Beidler, 579(SAQ):Autumn82-470
  S. Brown, 569(SR):Spring82-250
  M. Cross, 599:Fall82-462
  J. Hollowell, 395(MFS):Summer82-312
Hellmann, M., K. Zernack and G. Schramm, eds. Handbuch der Geschichte Russlands. (Vol 1, fasc 7-9)
  D.H. Kaiser, 589:Jul82-685
Hellwig, D. Adikia in Platons "Politeia."
  J. Annas, 123:Vol32No1-41
  P. Louis, 555:Vol56fasc1-135
Hellyer, J. Song of the Humpback Whales.
  D. Haskell, 581:Sep82-348
Helm, A. The English Mummers' Play.
  M. Preston, 191(ELN):Sep82-21
Helm, M., ed. Conversations with Bull-whackers, Muleskinners, Pioneers, Pros-pectors, '49ers, Indian Fighters, Trap-pers, Ex-Barkeepers, Authors, Preachers, Poets and Near Poets, and All Sorts and Conditions of Men.
  L.L. Willis, 649(WAL):Summer82-192
Helm, M. - see Lockley, F.
Helmer, H. The 40-Second Omelet Guaran-teed.
  W. and C. Cowen, 639(VQR):Autumn82-141
Helmreich, E.C. The German Churches under Hitler.
  J. Patrick, 396(ModA):Winter82-84
Helprin, M. Winter's Tale.
  A. Bold, 617(TLS):25Nov83-1329
  B. De Mott, 441:4Sep83-1
  J. Rubins, 453(NYRB):24Nov83-40
  R. Towers, 61:Sep83-122
Helsinger, E.K. Ruskin and the Art of the Beholder.*
  D. Johnson, 453(NYRB):31Mar83-13
Helterman, J. Symbolic Action in the Plays of the Wakefield Master.
  B.D. Palmer, 130:Summer82-182
Helterman, J. and R. Layman, eds. Ameri-can Novelists Since World War II.
  L. Ziff, 402(MLR):Apr82-435
Helvétius. Correspondance générale d'Hel-vétius. (Vol 1) (A. Dainard and others, eds)
  J.F. Jones, Jr., 546(RR):Nov82-522
Helweg, A.W. Sikhs in England.
  R. Russell, 293(JASt):Nov81-172
Helwig, D., ed. The Human Elements. (2nd Ser)
  L. McMullen, 102(CanL):Autumn82-151
Helwig, D. It Is Always Summer.
  M. Penman, 99:Jun/Jul82-38

Helwig, D. The King's Evil.*
  D. Duffy, 529(QQ):Winter82-761
  B. Gillespie, 526:Summer82-98
  J. Kertzer, 198:Jan82-81
Hemingway, E. Selected Letters, 1917-
1961.* (C. Baker, ed)
  J.R. Bryer, 573(SSF):Summer82-283
  P. Lukacs, 560:Summer82-172
  M.S. Reynolds, 27(AL):Mar82-119
  L.D. Rubin, Jr., 569(SR):Winter82-167
  G. Wickes, 395(MFS):Summer82-292
Hemingway, M. Emilia Pardo Bazán.
  G.M. Scanlon, 617(TLS):5Aug83-838
Heminway, J. No Man's Land.
  H. Goodman, 441:30Oct83-16
Hemme, A. Das lateinische Sprachmaterial
im Wortschatz der deutschen, französis-
chen und englischen Sprache.
  H-O. Kröner, 224(GRM):Band32Heft3-364
Hemmerich, G. Christoph Martin Wielands
"Geschichte des Agathon."
  J. Jacobs, 52:Band16Heft2-209
Hemmerich, G. and W. Benda - see Cooper,
A.A.
Hemmings, F.W.J. Baudelaire the Damned.*
  P.N. Furbank, 362:3Feb83-24
  A. de Jonge, 617(TLS):21Jan83-68
Hempel, R. The Golden Age of Japan.
  E. Seidensticker, 441:11Dec83-33
Henckmann, W., ed. Ästhetik.
  J. Kulenkampff, 687:Jan-Mar81-162
Henderson, A.A.R. - see Ovid
Henderson, A.G. - see Congreve, W.
Henderson, J., ed. Aristophanes.
  R.A. Hornsby, 130:Fall82-281
  639(VQR):Winter82-9
Henderson, J. The Maculate Muse.
  W.J. Verdenius, 394:Vol35fasc1/2-165
Henderson, L.D. The Fourth Dimension and
Non-Euclidean Geometry in Modern Art.
  P.L. Jones, 617(TLS):30Dec83-1449
Henderson, L.K. and S. Koploy. The Sub-
lime Heritage of Martha Mood. (Vol 2)
  P. Bach, 614:Summer83-22
Henderson, N. The Birth of NATO.
  M. Carver, 617(TLS):21Jan83-57
Hendrick, G. - see Hosmer, H.
Hendricks, K. and M. Tadashi Nakayama.
  E. Seidensticker, 441:11Dec83-33
Hendrickson, J. and A. Labarca. The Spice
of Life.
  K.M. Sayers, 608:Mar83-127
Hendrickson, P. Seminary.
  E. Kennedy, 441:10Apr83-12
  H.R., 231:Mar83-75
Hendry, J.F. The Sacred Threshold.
  I. Parry, 617(TLS):23Dec83-1434
Hendry, J.F. A World Alien.
  C. Milton, 571(ScLJ):Spring82-19
Heng, L. and J. Shapiro - see under Liang
Hong and J. Chapiro
den Hengst, D. The Prefaces in the "His-
toria Augusta."
  H.W. Benario, 121(CJ):Apr/May83-363
Henighan, T. Natural Space in Literature.
  N. Page, 150(DR):Winter82/83-711
Henke, J.T. Courtesans and Cuckolds.
  G. Williams, 677(YES):Vol 12-244
Henkel, A. and A. Schöne, eds. Emblemata.
(supp)
  W. Harms, 684(ZDA):Band111Heft1-39
Henkels, R.M., Jr. Robert Pinget.*
  J. Waelti-Walters, 208(FS):Jul82-361

Henkin, L., ed. The International Bill of
Rights.
  S.P., 185:Apr83-643
Henkle, R.B. Comedy and Culture, England
1820-1900.*
  J. Halperin, 395(MFS):Summer81-341
  J. Lucas, 366:Spring82-132
Henn, B. Mundartinterferenzen.
  I. Guentherodt, 685(ZDL):2/1982-257
Henne, H., ed. Praxis der Lexikographie.
  R.R.K. Hartmann, 257(IRAL):May82-169
Henne, H. and others, eds. Interdisziplin-
äres deutsches Wörterbuch in der Diskus-
sion.
  E. Bauer, 685(ZDL):3/1981-365
  D. Herberg, 682(ZPSK):Band35Heft2-221
Henne, H. and H. Rehbock. Einführung in
die Gesprächsanalyse.*
  O. Müller, 355(LSoc):Dec82-449
Hennequin, J. Henri IV dans ses oraisons
funèbres ou la naissance d'une légende.*
  C.M. Probes, 475:No16Pt2-412
Hennig, D., ed. Jacob und Wilhelm Grimm
über ihre Entlassung.
  E. Moser-Rath, 196:Band23Heft1/2-130
Hennig, J. Literatur und Existenz.
  A.P. Cottrell, 221(GQ):Nov82-578
Henningsen, B. Politik eller Kaos?
  R. Kejzlar, 172(Edda):1982/1-57
Henningsen, G. The Witches' Advocate.
  J. Simpson, 203:Vol93No2-232
Henrici, G. Die Binarismus-Problematik in
der neueren Linguistik.
  G.F. Meier, 682(ZPSK):Band35Heft5-582
Henry of Ghent. Henrici de Gandavo: Opera
Omnia I. (R. Macken, ed)
  J.F.W., 543:Sep81-136
Henry of Ghent. Henrici de Gandavo: Opera
Omnia V. (R. Macken, ed)
  J.F.W., 543:Sep81-137
Henry, A. Marcel Proust.
  F.C. St. Aubyn, 207(FR):May83-952
Henry, A. - see Bodel, J.
Henry, E.P. Chinese Amusement.*
  G.A. Hayden, 244(HJAS):Dec82-660
Henryson, R. The Poems of Robert Henryson.
  (D. Fox, ed)
  P. Morère, 189(EA):Jul-Sep82-325
  F. Riddy, 571(ScLJ):Winter82-59
  F.H. Ridley, 589:Jul82-626
  C. Weinberg, 148:Summer82-84
Hensellek, W. Sprachstudien an Augustins
"De Vera Religione."
  M. Winterbottom, 123:Vol32No1-98
Henshall, K.G. - see Katai, T.
Henslee, H. Pretty Redwing.
  S. Isaacs, 441:27Mar83-14
Henson, N., comp. Index of the Probate
Records of the Bangor Consistory Court.
(Vol 1)
  G.H. Williams, 325:Apr82-39
Henson, R. Transports and Disgraces.
  J.C. Voelker, 573(SSF):Winter82-91
Hentoff, N. Blues for Charlie Darwin.*
  T.J. Binyon, 617(TLS):30Sep83-1037
Hentschel, C. - see Powys, J.C.
Heny, F., ed. Binding and Filtering.
  D.J. Napoli, 350:Jun83-360
Henze, P.B. The Plot to Kill the Pope.
  P. Hebblethwaite, 617(TLS):16Dec83-
1406

Hepburn, A.C. The Conflict of Nationality in Modern Ireland.
R. Frēchet, 189(EA):Jul-Sep82-353
Hepburn, J., ed. Arnold Bennett: The Critical Heritage.
J. Halperin, 395(MFS):Winter82/83-617
E.E. Stevens, 177(ELT):Vol25No3-187
Hepburn, J. - see Bennett, A.
Hepp, N. and J. Hennequin, eds. Les valeurs chez les mémorialistes français du XVIIe siècle avant la Fronde.*
V. Kapp, 547(RF):Band93Heft1/2-260
Hepp, N. and G. Livet, eds. Héroïsme et création littéraire sous les règnes d'Henri IV et de Louis XIII.
V. Kapp, 547(RF):Band93Heft1/2-258
Heppenstall, R. Tales from the Newgate Calendar.
C. Rawson, 83:Autumn82-281
566:Autumn82-59
Herald, J. Renaissance Dress in Italy 1400-1500.
F. Russell, 39:May82-411
Herāwi, M.Q. The Majma' al-Shu'arā-i Jahāngīr Shāhi. (M.S. Akhtar, ed)
N. Ahmed, 273(IC):Jul82-243
Herbert, F. The White Plague.*
R. Kaveney, 617(TLS):11Mar83-249
Herbert, I., with C. Baxter and R.E. Finley - see "Who's Who in the Theatre"
Herbert, R.T. Paradox and Identity in Theology.*
M.J. McGhee, 479(PhQ):Jan82-90
K. Ward, 483:Oct82-565
Herbert, T.W., Jr. Marquesan Encounters.*
J.S. Adler, 395(MFS):Winter81/82-715
Herbst, T., D. Heath and H-M. Dederding. Grimm's Grandchildren.
E.G. Fichtner, 660(Word):Aug81-171
Herdeg, K. The Decorated Diagram.
A.L. Huxtable, 453(NYRB):22Dec83-55
de Heredia, J.F. - see under Fernández de Heredia, J.
de Heredia, J-M. Les Trophées.* (W.N. Ince, ed)
E.J. Kearns, 161(DUJ):Dec81-147
D. Leuwers, 450(NRF):Jul-Aug82-158
Hering, D. and F. Fehl. Giselle & Albrecht.
R. Philp, 151:Jan82-93
Heringer, H.J., B. Strecker and R. Wimmer. "Syntax."
K-E. Sommerfeldt, 682(ZPSK):Band35 Heft5-584
"The Heritage of Australia."
M. Girouard, 381:Dec81-461
van Herk, A. The Tent Peg.
B. Godard, 198:Apr82-90
C. Kerr, 102(CanL):Spring82-149
Herlin, H. Solo Run.
P. van Rjndt, 441:24Jul83-11
Herlyn, H. Heinrich Böll und Herbert Marcuse.
G.P. Knapp, 406:Summer82-227
Herman, A.L. An Introduction to Indian Thought.
P. Mundschenk, 485(PE&W):Jan82-120
Herman, D.J. The Philosophy of Henri Bergson.
P.A.Y.G., 543:Mar82-609

Hermary-Vieille, C. Le Grand Vizir de la nuit.
A. Clerval, 450(NRF):Feb82-135
P.L. Horn, 207(FR):Mar83-666
Hermerén, L. On Modality in English.*
E. Edgren, 597(SN):Vol154No2-324
Hermes, H., F. Kambartel and F. Kaulbach - see Frege, G.
Hermlin, S. Evening Light.
J. Agee, 441:18Sep83-7
Hernadi, P., ed. The Horizon of Literature.
F.S. Schwarzbach, 617(TLS):1Jul83-707
Hernadi, P., ed. What Is Criticism?*
W.E. Cain, 580(SCR):Fall82-118
A. Louch, 478:Oct82-190
M. Swales, 221(GQ):Nov82-568
42(AR):Spring82-245
Hernandez, M.C. - see under Cruz Hernandez, M.
Herndon, M. and N. McLeod. Music as Culture. (rev)
D.P. McAllester, 187:Jan83-123
Herondas. The Mimes of Herondas. (G. Davenport, trans)
M. Stephens, 609:Spring83-82
Herren, P. Beharren und Verwandeln.
W.D. Elfe, 133:Band15Heft3-283
Herrera, H. Frida.
L.R. Lippard, 441:24Apr83-10
442(NY):21Mar83-131
Herrero, J. and F. Sánchez de Lozada. Gramática quechua.
L. Hart-González, 269(IJAL):Oct82-477
Herrero, J. and F. Sánchez de Lozada. Método práctico para la enseñanza y aprendizaje de la lengua quechua.
L. Hart-González, 269(IJAL):Oct82-480
Herrmann, C. Les Voleuses de langue.
E. Copeland, 659(ConL):Summer83-276
von Herrmann, F-W. Heideggers Philosophie der Kunst.*
R. Brague, 192(EP):Oct-Dec82-494
Herrmann, H-V. Die Kessel der orientalisierenden Zeit. (Vol 2)
P. Cartledge, 303(JoHS):Vol 102-289
Herrmann-Winter, R. Studien zur gesprochenen Sprache im Norden der DDR.
G. Lerchner, 682(ZPSK):Band34Heft5-648
Hers, F. and S. Ristelhueber. Intérieurs.
P. Roussin, 98:Mar82-268
Hersey, G.L. Architecture, Poetry and Number in the Royal Palace at Caserta.
A. Braham, 617(TLS):14Oct83-1122
Hersh, S.M. The Price of Power. (British title: Kissinger: The Price of Power.)
H. Brogan, 362:27Oct83-29
S. Hoffmann, 441:3Jul83-1
A. Watson, 617(TLS):28Oct83-1176
G. Wills, 231:Sep83-70
Hershcher, U.D. Jewish Agricultural Utopias in America, 1880-1910.
A.L. Kagedan, 287:Apr82-27
Hershinow, S.J. Bernard Malamud.*
S. Fogel, 106:Fall82-267
Hertel, H. and S.M. Kristensen, eds. The Activist Critic.*
E. Bredsdorff, 402(MLR):Jan82-248
H-J. Müllenbrock, 189(EA):Oct-Dec82-440
S.H. Rossel, 563(SS):Spring82-179
K. Sørensen, 179(ES):Feb82-86

Hertsgaard, M. Nuclear Inc.
  D. Yergin, 441:31Ju183-7
Herttrich, E. - see Kobylańska, K.
Heruka, T.N. The Life of Marpa the Trans-
lator.
  D.S. Lopez, Jr., 469:Vol8No4-122
Hervey, S. Semiotic Perspectives.
  T. Hawkes, 617(TLS):25Mar83-304
Herz, J.S. and R.K. Martin, eds. E.M.
Forster.*
  A.M. Wyatt-Brown, 395(MFS):Winter82/83-
  641
Herzinger, K.A. D.H. Lawrence in His
Time.
  J.E. Michaels, 268(IFR):Winter83-61
Herzog, W. Fitzcarraldo.
  J. Hurley, 200:Dec82-636
von Hesberg, H. Konsolengeisa des Hellen-
ismus und der frühen Kaiserzeit.
  R.A. Tomlinson, 123:Vol32No2-293
Heseltine, H., ed. The Penguin Book of
Modern Australian Verse.
  G. Catalano, 381:Oct81-349
Heslep, R.D. The Mental in Education.
  T.M.R., 185:Apr83-646
Hess, K. Martha Washington's Booke of
Cookery.
  W. and C. Cowen, 639(VQR):Autumn82-139
Hess, L. - see Kabir
Hess, S. Ramón Menéndez Pidal.
  M.E. Lacarra, 304(JHP):Fal182-55
Hesse, E.W. and H.H. Orjuela. Spanish
Review. (5th ed)
  L.S. Glaze, 399(MLJ):Winter82-443
Hesse, G. Staatsaufgaben.
  G. Kirsch, 687:Oct-Dec82-646
Hesse, H. Le Poète chinois.
  J-L. Gautier, 450(NRF):Oct82-136
Hesse, K. Baining Dances.
  D. Niles, 187:Jan83-141
Hesse, M. Revolutions and Reconstructions
in the Philosophy of Science.*
  K.E. Jones, 84:Sep82-331
Hester, M.T. Kinde Pitty and Brave Scorn.
  L. Mackinnon, 617(TLS):24Jun83-681
Hetherington, M.S. The Beginnings of Old
English Lexicography.
  B. Cottle, 541(RES):Nov82-446
  M. Görlach, 133:Band15Heft3-257
Hetzer, A. Lehrbuch der vereinheitlichten
albanischen Schriftsprache.
  G-D. Nehring, 682(ZPSK):Band34Heft5-
  631
Heunemann, A., ed. Der Schlangenkönig.
  H. Mode, 196:Band23Heft3/4-323
de Heusch, L. Rois nés d'un coeur de
vache.
  B. Burn-Schmidt, 450(NRF):Jun82-133
Hewison, R. Footlights!
  R. Davies, 617(TLS):2Sep83-938
Hewison, R. In Anger.*
  J. Gindin, 396(ModA):Spring82-206
  J. Hunter, 249(HudR):Summer82-348
Hewison, R., ed. New Approaches to Rus-
kin.*
  D. Johnson, 453(NYRB):31Mar83-13
  N. Lightman, 175:Autumn82-257
Hewitt, D. - see Scott, W.
Hewitt, J. Loose Ends.
  E. Longley, 617(TLS):21Oct83-1162
Hewitt, J.R. André Malraux.
  J. Dale, 208(FS):Oct82-493

Hewson, J. Beothuk Vocabularies.
  W. Cowan, 320(CJL):Fal182-174
Hey, G. Die slavischen Siedlungen im
Königreich Sachsen mit Erklärung ihrer
Namen.
  G. Schaarschmidt, 104(CASS):Fall-
  Winter82-515
Heyd, D. Musil-Lektüre.
  J. Strutz, 602:Vol 13No1-197
Heyde, H. Trompeten Posaunen Tuben.
  N. O'Loughlin, 415:Apr82-261
Heymann, C.D. American Aristocracy.*
  P.C. Wermuth, 432(NEQ):Mar82-156
Heynen, J. A Suitable Church.
  G. Bennett, 649(WAL):Winter83-355
  D. Hall, 271:Winter82-162
Heyworth, P.L., ed. Medieval Studies for
J.A.W. Bennett Aetatis Suae LXX.
  A.V.C. Schmidt, 382(MAE):1982/2-234
Hibbard, C.M. Charles I and the Popish
Plot.
  R. Lockyer, 617(TLS):27May83-551
Hibbard, G.R. The Making of Shakespeare's
Dramatic Poetry.
  A. Leggatt, 627(UTQ):Summer82-412
  G.T. Wright, 570(SQ):Spring82-111
Hibbard, H. Caravaggio.
  F. Haskell, 453(NYRB):12May83-25
Hibbert, C. Africa Explored.*
  E. Claridge, 364:Dec82/Jan83-75
Hickerson, T. Archives and Manuscripts.
  B.G. Thompson, 14:Spring82-194
Hickman, L. Modern Theories of Higher
Level Predicates.*
  R.A.F., 543:Jun82-873
  J-L. Gardies, 542:Jan-Mar82-104
Hickok, L. One Third of a Nation. (R.
Lowitt and M. Beasley, eds)
  639(VQR):Winter82-23
Hicks, J. In the Singer's Temple.*
  S. Fogel, 395(MFS):Summer82-306
  J. Klinkowitz, 587(SAF):Spring82-118
  T. Samet, 27(AL):May82-306
Hicks, J.V. Winter Your Sleep.
  B.K. Filson, 526:Winter82-77
  C. Wiseman, 102(CanL):Summer82-140
Hiddleston, J.A. Essai sur Laforgue et
les "Derniers Vers" suivi de Laforgue
et Baudelaire.*
  F.S. Heck, 546(RR):Jan82-122
  P.G. Lewis, 207(FR):Oct82-157
  R.L. Mitchell, 210(FrF):Sep82-276
  C.W. Thompson, 402(MLR):Jul82-728
Hieatt, A.K. and M. Lorch - see Valla, L.
Hiebert, P. For the Birds.
  L.K. MacKendrick, 102(CanL):Winter81-
  164
Hiesinger, K.B. and G.H. Marcus, eds.
Design since 1945.
  P. Goldberger, 441:11Dec83-37
Higginbotham, J. Fast Train Russia.
  442(NY):16May83-135
Higginbotham, V. Luis Buñuel.
  A. Sarris, 18:Apr83-59
Higgins, A. Bornholm Night-Ferry.
  J. Mellors, 362:18Aug83-23
  L. Taylor, 617(TLS):24Jun83-660
Higgins, J. and others. Government and
Urban Poverty.
  C. Madge, 617(TLS):15Ju183-759
Higgins, R. Greek and Roman Jewellery.
(2nd ed)
  C.A. Picón, 123:Vol32No1-76

Higgins, R. Minoan and Mycenaean Art.
(rev)
  S. Hood, 123:Vol32No1-109
Higgs, R.J. Laurel and Thorn.
  F. Chappell, 219(GaR):Fall82-693
  W.J. Palmer, 395(MFS):Summer82-317
  E. Segal, 617(TLS):10Jun83-609
High-Wasikhongo, F. Traditional African
Art.
  L. Aronson, 2(AfrA):Aug82-88
Higham, C. and R. Moseley. Merle.
  A. Mars-Jones, 617(TLS):18Nov83-1291
Highfield, A. and A. Valdman, eds. His-
toricity and Variation in Creole Studies.
  C. Corne, 350:Mar83-176
Highfill, P.H., Jr., K.A. Burnim and E.A.
Langhans. A Biographical Dictionary of
Actors, Actresses, Musicians, Dancers,
Managers and other Stage Personnel in
London 1660-1800. (Vols 7 and 8)
  J. Keates, 617(TLS):18Mar83-265
Highsmith, P. People Who Knock on the
Door.
  H. Eley, 617(TLS):4Feb83-104
  J. Mellors, 362:17Feb83-24
Highwater, J. The Primal Mind.
  B. Cox, 529(QQ):Winter82-892
  K. Kroeber, 649(WAL):Summer82-166
Highwater, J. The Sweet Grass Lives On.
  J. Povey, 2(AfrA):Feb82-82
Higuchi Ichiyo. In the Shade of Spring
Leaves. (R.L. Danly, ed and trans)
  Cheng Lok Chua, 573(SSF):Fall82-397
Hijmans, B.L., Jr. and others. Apuleius
Madaurensis, "Metamorphoses."* (Bk 4,
Pts 1-27)
  J.A. Willis, 394:Vol35fasc1/2-184
Hijuelos, O. Our House in the Last World.
  E. Milton, 441:15May83-12
Saint Hilaire de Poitiers. La Trinité (De
Fide). (L. Brésard, trans)
  G. Sartoris, 450(NRF):May82-118
Hilbert, G.S. Sammlungsgut in Sicherheit.
(Pt 1, Vol 1)
  B. Heimberg, 471:Jan/Feb/Mar82-79
Hildebidle, J. The Old Chore.
  T. Kooser, 502(PrS):Winter82/83-84
Hildebrand, J. and C. Theuerkauff. Die
Brandenburgisch-Preussische Kunstkammer.
  J. Hayward, 90:Aug82-508
Hildebrand, K. and K.F. Werner, eds.
Deutschland und Frankreich 1936-1939.
  R. Morgan, 617(TLS):4Nov83-1230
Hildesheimer, W. Marbot.
  P-L. Adams, 61:Oct83-123
  G. Schiff, 453(NYRB):12May83-43
  J. Simon, 441:9Oct83-11
  M. Tanner, 617(TLS):7Oct83-1074
  442(NY):7Nov83-182
Hildesheimer, W. Mozart.*
  H. Cole, 362:5May83-26
  R. Craft, 61:Apr83-130
  M. Tanner, 617(TLS):7Oct83-1074
Hiley, J. Theatre at Work.*
  D. Devlin, 157:Spring82-58
  D.R., 214:Vol 10No38-144
Hilfer, A.C. The Ethics of Intensity in
American Fiction.*
  E.A. Dryden, 141:Winter82-90
  W. French, 395(MFS):Winter82/83-656
  J.W. Tuttleton, 27(AL):Mar82-146

Hilfstein, E. Starowolski's Biographies
of Copernicus.
  P.W. Knoll, 497(PolR):Vol27No3/4-220
Hilfstein, E., P. Czartoryski and F.D.
Grande, eds. Science and History.
  E. Grant, 551(RenQ):Summer81-213
Hilgartner, S., R.C. Bell and R. O'Connor.
Nukespeak.
  J. Woodcock, 441:16Jan83-18
Hill, A. The Plays of Aaron Hill. (C.
Winton, ed)
  566:Spring83-138
Hill, A.A. Constituent and Pattern in
Poetry.
  H. Penzl, 685(ZDL):1/1982-108
Hill, A.G. - see Wordsworth, W. and D.
Hill, C. Some Intellectual Consequences
of the English Revolution.
  I. Roots, 366:Spring82-125
Hill, C., ed. Winstanley.
  S. Wintle, 617(TLS):16Sep83-992
Hill, C. - see Bathe, W.
Hill, C., B. Reay and W. Lamont. The
World of the Muggletonians.
  H. Trevor-Roper, 362:14Apr83-26
  S. Wintle, 617(TLS):16Sep83-992
Hill, C.R. Change in South Africa.
  L. Mair, 617(TLS):28Oct83-1190
Hill, D. The Second Trap.
  S. Ruddell, 99:Nov82-33
Hill, D.G. The Freedom-Seekers.
  R.W. Winks, 529(QQ):Autumn82-640
Hill, D.L. - see Pater, W.
Hill, D.R., ed and trans. The Book of
Ingenious Devices (Kitāb al-Ḥiyal).
  G. Saliba, 318(JAOS):Apr-Jun81-226
Hill, E.E., comp. Guide to Records in the
National Archives of the United States
Relating to American Indians.
  R.N. Ellis, 14:Fall82-483
Hill, E.E. The Preparation of Inventories.
  A.J. Breton, 14:Fall82-484
Hill, G. The Mystery of the Charity of
Charles Péguy.
  E. Griffiths, 362:4Aug83-22
Hill, J. Rita Hayworth.
  A. Mars-Jones, 617(TLS):18Nov83-1291
Hill, J. The Letters and Papers of Sir
John Hill (1714-1775). (G.S. Rousseau,
ed)
  A.T. McKenzie, 566:Spring83-142
Hill, L.E. - see von Weizsäcker, E.
Hill, M.A. Charlotte Perkins Gilman.*
  V. Strong-Boag, 106:Spring82-97
Hill, N.K. A Reformer's Art.
  M. Reynolds, 155:Autumn82-170
Hill, P. A Place of Ravens.
  J.A.S. Miller, 571(ScLJ):Spring82-22
Hill, R. Blue Rise.
  W. Balliett, 442(NY):28Feb83-116
  J. Moynahan, 441:10Apr83-14
  L. Taylor, 617(TLS):9Dec83-1373
Hill, R. Traitor's Blood.
  T.J. Binyon, 617(TLS):23Dec83-1437
  M. Laski, 362:11Aug83-24
Hill, R. A Very Good Hater.
  442(NY):24Jan83-108
Hill, R.J. Soviet Politics, Political
Science and Reform.*
  D.E. Powell, 104(CASS):Summer82-273

Hill, R.J. and P. Frank. The Soviet Communist Party.
B. Harasymiw, 104(CASS):Fall-Winter82-581
R.J. Osborn, 550(RusR):Jul82-341
Hill, S., ed. Ghost Stories.
P. Craig, 617(TLS):14Oct83-1110
Hill, S., ed. People.
E.S. Turner, 362:22Sep83-24
Hill, S. The Woman in Black.
P. Craig, 617(TLS):14Oct83-1110
Hill, S.S., Jr. The South and the North in American Religion.
F. Hobson, 392:Winter81/82-73
Hill, V.W. Bertolt Brecht and Post-War French Drama.
J.G. Miller, 406:Summer82-225
Hill, W.S. - see Hooker, R.
Hillaby, J. Journey Home.
A. Nicolson, 617(TLS):28Oct83-1192
Hillard, A.E. and C.G. Botting. Elementary Greek Exercises.
J.E. Rexine, 399(MLJ):Autumn82-328
Hillary, R. The Last Enemy.
R.J. Margolis, 441:22May83-16
Hillebrand, B., ed. Gottfried Benn.
R. Rumold, 406:Fall82-371
Hillebrandt, A. Vedic Mythology. (Vol 1)
F. Staal, 293(JASt):Feb82-269
Hiller, H.H. Society and Change.
L. Marsden, 99:Mar83-26
Hillerman, T. The Dark Wind.*
T.J. Binyon, 617(TLS):13May83-498
T.J. Binyon, 617(TLS):27May83-553
F. Hoxie, 42(AR):Summer82-362
M. Laski, 362:19May83-24
Hillery, D. Music and Poetry in France from Baudelaire to Mallarmé.
A. Laster, 535(RHL):Sep-Dec82-941
D. Scott, 208(FS):Apr82-225
Hilles, R. Look The Lovely Animal Speaks. The Surprise Element.
D. Barbour, 648(WCR):Jun82-33
Hillgarth, J.N. - see "Pere II of Catalonia (Pedro IV of Aragon): Chronicle"
Hilliard, N. The Arte of Limning. (R.K.R. Thornton and T.G.S. Cain, eds)
G. Reynolds, 39:Feb82-135
Hills, P. David Jones.
D. Farr, 39:Aug82-121
Hills, P. Alice Neel.
J. Russell, 441:4Dec83-65
Hills, R.I. The General Strike in York, 1926.
R. Storey, 325:Apr82-43
Hillway, T. Herman Melville.
H. Beaver, 677(YES):Vol 12-320
Hilmar, R. Katalog der Musikhandschriften, Schriften und Studien Alban Bergs im Fond Alban Berg und der weiteren handschriftlichen Quellen im Besitz der Österreichischen Nationalbibliothek.
D. Jarman, 410(M&L):Jul/Oct82-285
Hilpinen, R., ed. Rationality in Science.
M.A. Kaplan, 185:Oct82-191
Hilscher, E. Der Morgenstern oder die vier Verwandlungen eines Mannes, Walther von der Vogelweide genannt.
T. Ehlert, 680(ZDP):Band101Heft3-460
Hilton, J. Georg Büchner.*
A.P. Hinchliffe, 148:Autumn82-83
Hilton, J.B. The Asking Price.
T.J. Binyon, 617(TLS):2Dec83-1358

Hilton, J.B. Mr. Fred.
M. Laski, 362:19May83-24
Hilton, T. and R. Penrose. Picasso's Picassos.
L. Cooke, 59:Sep82-338
Hilts, P.J. Scientific Temperaments.
P. Engel, 441:2Jan83-11
Hinchcliffe, A.P., ed. Drama Criticism: Developments Since Ibsen.
D. Jarrett, 447(N&Q):Aug81-356
Hincmar of Rheims. Hinkmar von Reims: "De ordine palatii." (T. Gross and R. Schieffer, eds)
K.F. Morrison, 589:Apr82-450
Hinde, R.A. Ethology.*
S.R.L. Clark, 617(TLS):24Jun83-658
Hinde, T. A Field Guide to the English Country Parson.
G. Irvine, 617(TLS):2Dec83-1353
Hinde, T. Stately Gardens of Britain.
R.I. Ross, 617(TLS):16Sep83-998
Hinderer, W., ed. Goethes Dramen.
H. Eichner, 406:Fall82-327
G. Marahrens, 564:Sep82-217
Hinderer, W., ed. Kleists Dramen.
J. Müller, 680(ZDP):Band101Heft2-295
Hinderer, W. - see von Kleist, H.
Hinderling, R. and V. Weibel, eds. Fimfchustim.
T.L. Keller, 685(ZDL):3/1982-370
Hinderschiedt, I. Zur Heliandmetrik.*
G. Wieland, 564:Sep81-250
R. Zanni, 406:Fall82-351
Hindmarsh, L. A Notebook for Kenyan Dyers.
R.L. Shep, 614:Summer83-20
Hindus, M.S. Prison and Plantation.
J.V. Matthews, 106:Winter82-333
Hine, D. Selected Poems.
D. Barbour, 648(WCR):Jun82-33
D. Tacium, 137:Aug82-57
639(VQR):Spring82-59
Hine, R.V. Community on the American Frontier.
H.R. Lamar, 651(WHR):Spring82-80
Hines, B. Unfinished Business.
J. Melmoth, 617(TLS):21Oct83-1157
Hines, D.M., ed. Tales of the Okanogans.
N.R. Grobman, 582(SFQ):Vol43No3/4-347
Hines, J. Great Singers on Great Singing.
A. Alexander, 617(TLS):6May83-470
Hines, S. Alberta.
529(QQ):Autumn82-687
Hines, S. Atlantic Canada.
F. Rasky, 73:Summer83-53
529(QQ):Summer82-460
Hingley, R. Nightingale Fever.*
G. Clifford, 493:Jun82-77
Hingley, R. Pasternak.
J. Bayley, 441:30Oct83-7
A. Livingstone, 617(TLS):26Aug83-912
Hingley, R. The Russian Mind.
A.D.P. Briggs, 447(N&Q):Jun81-278
Hinnells, J.R., ed. Mithraic Studies.
J.W. de Jong, 259(IIJ):Jan80-80
Hinrichsen, I. Der Romancier als Übersetzer.*
W. Riedel, 107(CRCL):Dec81-576
Hinson, M. The Piano in Chamber Ensemble.
A.F.L.T., 412:Feb81-61
Hintikka, J., I. Niiniluoto and E. Saarinen, eds. Essays on Mathematical and Philosophical Logic.*
S.M. Embleton, 660(Word):Dec81-238

Hinton, H.C., ed. The People's Republic of China, 1949-1979.
M. Blecher, 293(JASt):May82-577
Hinton, J. Labour and Socialism.
B. Pimlott, 617(TLS):9Dec83-1382
Hinton, W. Shenfan.
P-L. Adams, 61:Jun83-104
R. Bernstein, 441:3Jul83-6
von Hinüber, O. - see Franke, R.O.
Hinxman, M. The Corpse Now Arriving.
T.J. Binyon, 617(TLS):8Jul83-732
Hinz, E.J. and J.J. Teunissen - see Miller, H.
Hinz, R., ed. Kathe Kollwitz: Graphics, Posters, Drawings (1981).
D. Thompson, 592:Vol 195No993/994-86
Hipp, M-T. - see Mme de Villedieu
von Hippel, T.G. Theodor Gottlieb von Hippel "On Improving the Status of Women." (T.F. Sellner, ed and trans)
K. Goodman, 406:Fall82-352
Hippocrates. Hippocrate, "L'Ancienne Médecine." (A.J. Festugière, ed and trans)
R.W., 555:Vol55fasc1-159
Hiriart, R. Un poeta en el tiempo: Ildefonso-Manuel Gil.
E. Irizarry, 240(HR):Autumn82-499
Hirsch, E. For the Sleepwalkers.
J.D. McClatchy, 491:Sep82-347
A. Shapiro, 472:Spring/Summer83-286
P. Stitt, 219(GaR):Summer82-438
Hirsch, E.D., Jr. The Philosophy of Composition.
M. Kleine and J. Liebman-Kleine, 113:Spring82-45
Hirsch, H. Sophie von Hatzfeldt in Selbstzeugnissen, Zeit- und Bilddokumenten.
J.L. Sammons, 221(GQ):Nov82-600
Hirsch, H.N. The Enigma of Felix Frankfurter.
T.D. Eisele, 396(ModA):Winter82-77
Hirsch, M. Beyond the Single Vision.
D. Rice, 207(FR):May83-956
M. Schmeling, 547(RF):Band94Heft2/3-311
Hirsch, P. - see Privat, E. and R. Rolland
Hirschbach, F.D. and others, eds. Germany in the Twenties.
C. Hill, 221(GQ):Nov82-606
Hirschen, J., ed. Art in the Ancient World.
R. Higgins, 39:May82-413
Hirschman, A.O. Shifting Involvements.*
M. Banton, 617(TLS):28Jan83-90
Hirschmann, G. Kulturkampf im historischen Roman der Gründerzeit 1859-1878.
B. Zimmermann, 133:Band15Heft4-378
Hirsh, J.E. The Structure of Shakespearean Scenes.*
S. Snyder, 401(MLQ):Jun82-174
Hirsh, S.L. Ferdinand Hodler.
J.B., 55:Nov82-50
G. Eisler, 617(TLS):8Apr83-361
Hirst, M. Sebastiano del Piombo.*
C. Gould, 39:Feb82-133
C. Hope, 90:Oct82-637
T. Puttfarken, 59:Dec82-497
Hirst, P. On Law and Ideology.
R. Wess, 504:No6-181
Hirst, P.Q. Durkheim, Bernard and Epistemology.
T.O.B., 543:Sep81-139

Hirszowicz, M. The Bureaucratic Leviathan.*
A.J. Matejko, 104(CASS):Summer82-312
Hiskes, R.P. Community without Coercion.
W.J.S., 185:Apr83-631
"Histoire et christianisme chez Jacques Maritain."
F. Sauvageot, 192(EP):Apr-Jun82-239
"Histoire et langage dans 'L'Éducation sentimentale' de Flaubert."
E.F. Gray, 446(NCFS):Fall-Winter82/83-163
A. de Toro, 547(RF):Band94Heft4-500
Hitchcock, B. Richard Malcolm Johnston.*
S.I. Bellman, 573(SSF):Spring82-183
Hitchcock, H-R. German Renaissance Architecture.*
B. Bergdoll, 45:Apr82-49
B. Boucher, 39:Oct82-278
J. Summerson, 46:Jun82-81
Hitchcock, H.W. - see Charpentier, M-A.
Hitching, F. The Neck of the Giraffe.*
639(VQR):Autumn82-137
Hitchman, S. The World as Theatre in the Works of Franz Grillparzer.
R. Nicholls, 564:May81-179
Hitt, H.C. Old Chinese Snuff Bottles.
U. Roberts, 60:Jan-Feb82-136
Hitzler, E. Sel — Untersuchungen zur Geschichte des isländischen Sennwesens seit der Landnahmezeit.
J.M. Jochens, 563(SS):Winter82-83
Hix, J. The Glass House.
J. Maass, 576:Dec82-348
Hjort, A. Savanna Town.
A. O'Connor, 69:Vol51No4-899
Hoagland, E. The Tugman's Passage.*
G.C., 569(SR):Fall82-cix
Hoare, K. The Art of Tatting.
R.L. Shep, 614:Fall83-16
Hoban, R. Kleinzeit.
P-L. Adams, 61:Dec83-115
N. Perrin, 441:27Nov83-12
Hoban, R. The Lion of the Boaz-Jachin and Jachin-Boaz.
N. Perrin, 441:27Nov83-12
Hoban, R. Pilgermann.
J. Conarroe, 441:29May83-1
D. Durrant, 364:Mar83-109
Z. Leader, 617(TLS):18Mar83-259
J. Mellors, 362:10Mar83-27
J.S., 231:Apr83-75
442(NY):8Aug83-92
Hoban, R. Riddley Walker.
42(AR):Summer82-374
Hobart, M.E. Science and Religion in the Thought of Nicolas Malebranche.
R.A. Watson, 319:Oct83-570
Hobbes, T. Computatio sive Logica. (A.P. Martinich, ed and trans)
J.W. Yolton, 518:Jul82-158
Hobbes, T. Computatio sive Logica: De Corpore, Part I. (I.C. Hungerland and G.R. Vick, eds)
J.B., 543:Jun82-874
J. Kaminsky, 319:Jul83-402
Hobbie, M., comp. Museums, Sites, and Collections of Germanic Culture in North America.
F.C. Luebke, 292(JAF):Oct-Dec82-489

Hobbs, A.H. and J. Adzigian. A Complete
Guide to Egypt and the Achaeological
Sites.
  E.L. Bleiberg, 529(QQ):Winter82-878
Hobbs, R.C. and G. Levin. Abstract Expres-
sionism: The Formative Years.
  D. Saatchi, 90:Sep82-567
Hoberman, J. and J. Rosenbaum. Midnight
Movies.
  E. Mordden, 441:10Apr83-11
Hobhouse, H. Prince Albert.
  E.S. Turner, 362:15Dec83-23
Hobhouse, J. Dancing in the Dark.
  J. Astor, 362:16Jun83-28
  M. Furness, 617(TLS):17Jun83-622
  442(NY):13Jun83-130
Hobhouse, J. Nellie Without Hugo.*
  J. Mellors, 364:Apr/May82-133
Hobhouse, P. - see "Gertrude Jekyll on
Gardening"
Hobsbaum, P. Essentials of Literary Criti-
cism.
  B.M. Tonkin, 617(TLS):23Sep83-1024
Hobsbaum, P. Tradition and Experiment in
English Poetry.*
  R.B. Shaw, 677(YES):Vol 12-230
Hobsbawm, E. and T. Ranger, eds. The
Invention of Tradition.
  N. Bliven, 442(NY):10Oct83-162
  H. Seton-Watson, 617(TLS):18Nov83-1270
Hobsbawm, E.J., ed. The History of Marx-
ism. (Vol 1)
  A.G. Meyer, 550(RusR):Oct82-496
  A. Wald, 385(MQR):Winter83-158
  639(VQR):Summer82-82
Hobson, L.Z. Laura Z.
  N. Johnson, 441:23Oct83-15
Hobson, M. The Object of Art.
  D. Carrier, 290(JAAC):Summer83-455
  M. Podro, 617(TLS):26Aug83-897
Hoccleve, T. Selections from Hoccleve.
  (M.C. Seymour, ed)
  D. Pearsall, 38:Band100Heft3/4-506
Hochberg, B. Fibre Facts.
  P. Bach, 614:Winter83-16
Hochberg, B. Reprints of Bette Hochberg's
Textile Articles.
  P. Bach, 614:Winter83-21
Hochberg, H. Thought, Fact, and Refer-
ence.*
  C.F.K., 543:Jun82-877
Hochman, B. The Test of Character.
  S.R. Letwin, 617(TLS):30Dec83-1447
Hochman, S., ed. From Quasimodo to Scar-
lett O'Hara.
  P. Aufderheide, 18:May83-75
Hochschild, A.R. The Managed Heart.
  G. Sheehy, 441:23Oct83-7
Hochschild, J. What's Fair?
  J.R.C., 185:Apr83-636
Hochstein, R. Table 47.
  E. Jakab, 441:300ct83-33
"David Hockney Photographs."
  A. Ross, 364:Dec82/Jan83-132
  S. Schwartz, 453(NYRB):14Apr83-7
Hocquet, J-C. Le sel et la fortune de
Venise.
  S. Chojnacki, 589:Apr82-379
Hodard, P. Sartre entre Marx et Freud.
  P. Trotignon, 542:Jan-Mar82-66
Hodder, I. Symbols in Action.
  P.J. Ucko, 617(TLS):7Jan83-21

Hodder, I., G. Isaac and N. Hammond, eds.
Pattern of the Past.
  P.J. Ucko, 617(TLS):7Jan83-21
Hoddinott, R.F. The Thracians.
  R. Higgins, 39:May82-413
Hodge, A. Nigeria's Traditional Crafts.
  J.B. Donne, 617(TLS):27May83-552
Hodges, A. Alan Turing.
  D.R. Hofstadter, 441:13Nov83-1
Hodges, D.C. The Bureaucratization of
Socialism.
  R.J. Burkhardt, 154:Sep82-588
Hodgins, J. The Barclay Family Theatre.
  M. Abley, 102(CanL):Summer82-120
  A. Mandel, 198:Oct82-89
Hodgins, J. The Resurrection of Joseph
Bourne.*
  L.R. Ricou, 296(JCF):No33-127
Hodgkins, G. Providence and Art.
  R. Anderson, 415:Dec82-843
Hodgkinson, A.W. and R.E. Sheratsky. Hum-
phrey Jennings.
  A. Marwick, 617(TLS):10Jun83-611
Hodgson, J. The God of the Xhosa.
  E. Gillies, 617(TLS):21Oct83-1153
Hodgson, J.A. Wordsworth's Philosophical
Poetry, 1797-1814.*
  J.H. Averill, 301(JEGP):Jan82-119
  D. McCracken, 405(MP):May83-430
Hoeges, D. Literatur und Evolution.*
  D. Shepheard, 208(FS):Jan82-91
  J. Thomas, 547(RF):Band93Heft1/2-271
Hoekstra, A. Epic Verse before Homer.
  P. Monteil, 555:Vol56fasc2-313
Hoekstra, T., H. van der Hulst and M.
Moortgat, eds. Lexical Grammar.
  M.A. Covington, 350:Jun83-402
Hoenigswald, H.M., ed. The European Back-
ground of American Linguistics.*
  P. Swiggers, 353:Vol 19No5/6-543
Hoenigswald, H.M. Studies in Formal His-
torical Linguistics.
  G.F. Meier, 682(ZPSK):Band34Heft5-632
Hoeveler, J.D., Jr. James McCosh and the
Scottish Intellectual Tradition.
  P.F. Boller, Jr., 396(ModA):Summer/
  Fall82-421
  J.E. Hamilton, 619:Fall82-370
  J.C. Stewart-Robertson, 319:Jul83-409
Hoevels, F.E. Märchen und Magie in den
"Metamorphosen" des Apuleius von
Madaura.*
  R.T. van der Paardt, 394:Vol35fasc3/4-
  417
von Hofe, H., ed. Die Mittelstufe. (4th
ed)
  R. Ambacher, 399(MLJ):Spring82-102
Hoffman, D. Brotherly Love.*
  R. Asselineau, 189(EA):Oct-Dec82-493
  J.D. McClatchy, 491:Sep82-347
  D.F. Stanford, 656(WMQ):Jul82-542
  P. Stitt, 219(GaR):Summer82-438
Hoffman, M.A. Egypt Before the Pharaohs.*
  F.A. Hassan, 318(JAOS):Oct-Dec81-459
Hoffman, R. Almost Family.
  A. Gottlieb, 441:13Feb83-26
  442(NY):11Apr83-134
Hoffman, R. and P.J. Albert, eds. Diplo-
macy and Revolution.
  M.R. Zahniser, 656(WMQ):Oct82-721
Hoffman, R.L. More than a Trial.
  F. Busi, 207(FR):Oct82-191

Hoffmann, A. Das Gartenstadion in der Villa Hadriana.
  A. Frazer, 576:Mar82-57
  N. Purcell, 123:Vol32No2-249
Hoffmann, F., ed. Dialektologie heute/ Pour une dialectologie moderne.
  J. Kramer, 547(RF):Band94Heft1-89
Hoffmann, F. The Literature of Rock, 1954-1978.
  B.L. Cooper, 498:Vol18No1-60
Hoffmann, F. Sprachen in Luxemburg.
  J. Kramer, 547(RF):Band93Heft1/2-177
Hoffmann, F. Zwischenland.
  M. Clyne, 67:May82-95
Hoffmann, F. and J. Berlinger. Die neue Deutsche Mundartdichtung.*
  K. Kehr, 685(ZDL):1/1982-108
Hoffmann, G., ed. Peregrinuslevelek 1711-1750.
  G. Gömöri, 575(SEER):Oct82-626
Hoffmann, K. Aufsätze zur Indoiranistik. (J. Narten, ed)
  K. Mylius, 682(ZPSK):Band34Heft1-120
Hoffmann, P. La femme dans la pensée des lumières.*
  J. Schlobach, 547(RF):Band93Heft1/2-263
Hoffmann, R. António Vieiras Rochuspredigt aus dem Restaurationskriegsjahr 1642.
  D. Briesemeister, 547(RF):Band94Heft4-511
Hoffmann, S. Duties Beyond Borders.*
  C.R. Beitz, 185:Jul83-814
Hoffmann, V., ed. Ausgewählte Briefe des "Simplicissimus" Dichters Dr. Owlglass.
  H.G. Nerjes, 221(GQ):Nov82-608
Hoffmann, W. Das Siegfriedbild in der Forschung.
  H.M. Heinrichs, 133:Band15Heft1/2-153
  W. McConnell, 406:Winter82-480
Hoffmann, Y. The Idea of Self East and West.
  A. Adams, 485(PE&W):Apr82-228
Hoffmeister, G. Deutsche und europäische Romantik.*
  G. Gillespie, 597(SN):Vol54No2-332
  R. von Tiedemann, 52:Band16Heft1-90
Hoffmeister, G. España y Alemania.
  N.R. Orringer, 238:Mar82-137
Hoffmeister, G. Goethezeit.
  H. Eichner, 406:Fal182-327
Hoffmeister, W. Sprachwechsel in Ost-Lothringen.
  J. Eichhoff, 685(ZDL):3/1982-407
Hofinger, M. Études sur le vocabulaire du grec archaïque.
  G.P. Edwards, 123:Vol32No2-213
Höfler, M. Dictionnaire des anglicismes.
  G. Roques, 553(RLiR):Jul-Dec82-464
Höfler, M., H. Vernay and L. Wolf, eds. Festschrift Kurt Baldinger zum 60. Geburtstag, 17. November 1979.
  G. Ineichen, 260(IF):Band86-284
  C. Thomasset, 553(RLiR):Jan-Jun81-222
Höfler, O. Über somatische, psychische und kulturelle Homologie.*
  P. Buccholz, 203:Vol93No1-124
Hofman, P. Rome.
  P. Filo della Torre, 617(TLS):20May83-505

Hofmann, E. Les "Principes de politique" de Benjamin Constant. (Vol 1)
  P. Deguise, 535(RHL):Sep-Dec82-918
  M. Winkler, 547(RF):Band94Heft1-122
Hofmann, E. Les "Principes de politique" de Benjamin Constant. (Vol 2)
  P. Deguise, 535(RHL):Sep-Dec82-918
Hofmann, E., with others. Bibliographie analytique des écrits sur Benjamin Constant, 1796-1980.
  É. Harpaz, 535(RHL):Jan-Feb82-132
Hofmann, G. Der Turm.
  C. Russ, 617(TLS):4Mar83-223
Hofmann, N. Redundanz und Äquivalenz in der literarischen Übersetzung, dargestellt an fünf deutschen Übersetzungen des Hamlet.
  W. von Koppenfels, 38:Band100Heft1/2-166
Hofmekler, O. Hofmekler's People.
  S.H., 441:27Mar83-13
Hofstadter, D.R. Gödel, Escher, Bach.*
  U.J. Hansen, 529(QQ):Summer82-410
Hoftijzer, J. and G. van der Kooij, eds. Aramaic Texts from Deir 'Alla.
  B.A. Levine, 318(JAOS):Apr-Jun81-195
Höftmann, H. Wörterbuch Swahili-Deutsch.
  S. Brauner, 682(ZPSK):Band34Heft1-122
Hogan, M. The Broken Face of Summer.
  S. Hamill, 649(WAL):Winter83-366
Hogan, R. The Macmillan Dictionary of Irish Literature.
  A.E. McGuinness, 677(YES):Vol 12-241
Hogan, R.S., L. Sawin and L.L. Merrill, eds. A Concordance to the Poetry of George Meredith.
  R.F. Giles, 365:Winter83-24
Hogarth, P. Arthur Boyd Houghton.
  T. Russell-Cobb, 324:Sep83-634
Hoge, J.O. - see "Lady Tennyson's Journal"
Höger, A. Frank Wedekind.*
  V. Hertling, 221(GQ):Mar82-275
Hogg, J. Highland Tours. (W.F. Laughlan, ed)
  D. Gifford, 571(ScLJ):Winter82-84
Hogg, J. James Hogg: Selected Stories and Sketches. (D.S. Mack, ed)
  P. Rogers, 617(TLS):27May83-555
Hoggart, R. An English Temper.*
  G. Mortimer, 364:Jul82-93
  639(VQR):Autumn82-124
Hoghughi, M. The Delinquent.
  D.J. West, 617(TLS):5Aug83-830
Hogwood, C. and R. Luckett, eds. Music in Eighteenth-Century England.
  J. Keates, 617(TLS):18Mar83-265
Hohendahl, P.U. The Institution of Criticism.
  J. Hermand, 221(GQ):Nov82-572
  M. Rapisarda, 395(MFS):Winter82/83-725
  639(VQR):Autumn82-116
Höhler, G. Niemandes Sohn.
  B. Maché, 406:Summer82-217
  J. Ryan, 221(GQ):Mar82-270
Holcombe, A.M. and M.Y. Ashcroft, eds. John Sell Cotman in the Cholmeley Archive.
  D. Robinson, 39:Sep82-200
Holcombe, B. - see Fagg, W.
Holdcroft, D. Words and Deeds.*
  W.P. Alston, 449:Nov82-623
  B. Loar, 482(PhR):Apr82-303

Hösle, J. Grundzüge der italienischen
Literatur des 19. und 20. Jahrhunderts.
W. Hirdt, 547(RF):Band93Heft3/4-481
Hosmer, C.B., Jr. Preservation Comes of
Age.
E.A. Connally, 576:Oct82-263
W. French, 585(SoQ):Spring82-88
R.W. Longstreth, 658:Winter82-292
Hosmer, H. Remembrances of Concord and
the Thoreaus.* (G. Hendrick, ed)
R.H. Du Pree, 577(SHR):Spring82-166
Hospers, J. Understanding the Arts.
F. Sparshott, 290(JAAC):Spring83-335
Hotman, F. Antitribonian ou discours d'un
grand et renommé Jurisconsulte de nostre
temps, sur l'estude des loix, fait par
l'advis de feu Monsieur de l'Hospital
Chancelier de France en l'an 1567. (H.
Duranton, ed)
F.M. Higman, 208(FS):Jan82-59
Hotson, L. Shakespeare by Hilliard.
P. Bertram, 570(SQ):Spring82-121
Hottois, G. L'inflation du langage dans
la philosophie contemporaine.
A. Reix, 192(EP):Oct-Dec81-486
Hottois, G. Pour une métaphilosophie du
langage.
M. Adam, 542:Oct-Dec82-672
Hotzenköcherle, R. and R. Brunner, eds.
Schweizer Dialekte in Text und Ton.
(Section 1, Heft 5)
H. Tatzreiter, 685(ZDL):3/1981-391
Houde, C.F. Not Just Another Pretty Dress.
R.L. Shep, 614:Summer83-20
Hough, R. Edwina.
A. Chisholm, 617(TLS):18Nov83-1293
Hough, R. The Great War at Sea 1914-1918.
B. Ranft, 617(TLS):30Dec83-1466
"The Houghton 'Shahnameh.'"* (M.B. Dick-
son and S.C. Welch, eds)
B. Gray, 39:Jul82-83
Houlgate, L.D. The Child and the State.*
H. La Follette, 482(PhR):Oct82-651
Hourantier, M-J. Le Chant de la colline,
Rituel de Réjouissance, suivi de A
l'aube de la conscience, Rituel de Mort.
H.A. Waters, 207(FR):Mar83-676
House, E.R. Evaluating with Validity.
M.J. Parsons, 289:Summer82-115
Household, G. Rogue Justice.
P. Andrews, 441:22May83-42
H.R., 231:Feb83-76
442(NY):21Feb83-132
Household, G.A., ed. To Catch a Sunbeam.
R.L. Patten, 637(VS):Winter82-243
Houseman, J. Final Dress.
J. Lardner, 441:11Sep83-11
Houston, D. Jazz Baby.
M. Haskell, 441:30Oct83-9
Houston, J., ed. Lucie Rie.
W. MacKenzie, 139:Apr/May82-88
Houston, J.P. French Symbolism and the
Modernist Movement.*
S. Lawall, 210(FrF):Jan82-88
Houston, J.P. The Traditions of French
Prose Style.
J. Brody, 210(FrF):Sep82-284
R.T. Denommé, 446(NCFS):Fall-Winter
82/83-181
W. Fowlie, 569(SR):Spring82-xxiv
E. Showalter, Jr., 207(FR):Mar83-625
Houston, L. At the Mercy.*
L. Sail, 565:Vol23No4-73

Houston, P. Argument of Idea.
D. Hall, 271:Winter82-159
Hovanec, E.A. Henry James and Germany.*
J.K. Fugate, 406:Spring82-83
Hovenkamp, H. Science and Religion in
America, 1800-1860.*
W.A. Waiser, 106:Winter82-341
Hoving, T. King of the Confessors.*
D. Sutton, 39:Mar82-142
639(VQR):Winter82-28
Howard, D. The Architectural History of
Venice.*
S. Connell, 90:Aug82-512
Howard, D.R. Writers and Pilgrims.*
E. Reiss, 579(SAQ):Winter82-126
D.W. Rowe, 589:Jan82-135
Howard, E.J. Getting It Right.*
E. Ottenberg, 441:6Mar83-28
Howard, H. War Toys.
E. Jakab, 441:22May83-43
442(NY):16May83-136
Howard, M. The Causes of Wars and Other
Essays.
K. Robbins, 617(TLS):29Apr83-426
Howard, M. Clausewitz.
K. Robbins, 617(TLS):29Apr83-426
A. Ryan, 362:17Mar83-22
Howard, M. The Franco-Prussian War.
J. Hartman, 446(NCFS):Fall-Winter82/83-
196
Howard, P., ed. C.W. von Gluck: "Orfeo."*
F.W. Sternfeld, 410(M&L):Jul/Oct82-295
Howard, P. A Word In Your Ear.
E.S. Turner, 362:25Aug83-23
Howard, P. Words Fail Me.*
J.R. Gaskin, 569(SR):Winter82-143
Howard, R. In Search of My Father.
P. Cotes, 157:Summer82-51
Howard, R. Poisons in Public.
G.W. Brandie, 529(QQ):Winter82-882
Howard, T.T. The Novels of Charles Wil-
liams.
S. Medcalf, 617(TLS):21Oct83-1150
Howard-Hill, T.H. British Bibliography
and Textual Criticism. (Vols 4-6)
P. Davison, 354:Jun82-185
Howarth, S. The Knights Templar.*
639(VQR):Autumn82-129
Howarth, W. The Book of Concord.*
P.F. Gura, 432(NEQ):Sep82-448
Howarth, W.D., ed. Comic Drama.*
C. Price, 447(N&Q):Apr81-191
Howe, C. Acquiring Language in a Conversa-
tional Context.
B. McKinney, 351(LL):Jun82-219
Howe, E. The Black Game.
D. Hunt, 617(TLS):20May83-519
Howe, I. A Margin of Hope.*
R. Brustein, 453(NYRB):3Feb83-5
H. Maccoby, 362:26May83-23
J. Symons, 617(TLS):4Mar83-203
M. Syrkin, 287:Dec82-24
Howe, I., ed. "1984" Revisited.
A. Schlesinger, Jr., 441:25Sep83-1
Howell, C. Though Silence.*
639(VQR):Summer82-93
Howell, D. British Workers and the
Independent Labour Party 1888-1906.
J. Saville, 617(TLS):9Dec83-1382
Howell, J.M. John Gardner.
J.S. Crane, 517(PBSA):Vol76No4-496
R.A. Morace, 594:Spring82-119

Howell, P. A Commentary on Book One of the Epigrams of Martial.
J.G. Griffith, 123:Vol32No2-170
Howells, C. Sartre's Theory of Literature.*
S.B. John, 402(MLR):Apr82-464
Howells, C.A. Love, Mystery and Misery.*
R. Kiely, 301(JEGP):Jul82-437
Howells, W.D. Novels, 1875-1886.
G. Vidal, 453(NYRB):27Oct83-45
Howells, W.D. Selected Letters.* (Vol 2, G. Arms and C.K. Lohmann, eds) (Vol 3; R.C. Leitz 3d, with R.H. Ballinger and C.K. Lohmann, eds)
G. Monteiro, 26(ALR):Spring82-130
A. Trachtenberg, 445(NCF):Sep82-229
Howells, W.D. Selected Letters. (Vol 4) (T. Wortham, with C.K. Lohmann and D. Nordloh, eds)
G. Fortenberry, 26(ALR):Spring82-125
J. Katz, 579(SAQ):Summer82-357
A. Trachtenberg, 445(NCF):Sep82-229
Howes, M. Lying in Bed.
B. Whiteman, 198:Apr82-112
Howland, B. Things to Come and Go.
J. Kaplan, 441:20Mar83-13
Howlett, D. The Critical Way in Religion.
G. Colwell, 154:Sep82-584
Hoyle, F. The Intelligent Universe.
J. Durant, 617(TLS):9Dec83-1366
Hoyt, E.P. Pacific Destiny.
639(VQR):Summer82-85
Hoyt, R. The Siskiyou Two-Step.
N. Callendar, 441:13Nov83-33
Hsieh, J-C.C. Structure and History of a Chinese Community in Taiwan.
H.J. Lamley, 293(JASt):Aug82-812
Hsieh, S-Y. The Life and Thought of Li Kou (1009-1059).*
H.C. Tillman, 293(JASt):Nov81-111
Hsü, I.C.Y. The Rise of Modern China. (3rd ed)
J. Cotton, 617(TLS):24Jun83-654
Hsu, K-Y. and T. Wang, eds. Literature in the People's Republic of China.*
M. McCaskey, 399(MLJ):Spring82-114
Hsun, L. - see under Lu Hsun
Huang, P. Autocracy at Work.
K.C. Smith, 318(JAOS):Jul-Sep81-390
Huang, P.C.C., ed. The Development of Underdevelopment in China.
W.E. Willmott, 293(JASt):Nov81-113
Huang, R. 1587, A Year of No Significance.
J.B. Parsons, 293(JASt):Feb82-327
Hubala, E. Johann Michael Rottmayr.
W.J. Hofmann, 471:Jul/Aug/Sep82-265
Hubbard, W. Complicity and Conviction.*
R. Arnheim, 289:Spring82-107
Hubbeling, H.G. Spinoza.
R. Sasso, 192(EP):Jan-Mar81-102
Hubbs, G.W. - see Barr, J.G.
Hubbs, V.C., ed. Hessian Journals.
K.J.R. Arndt, 564:Sep82-215
Huber, L.W. Creole Collage.
M.F., 189(EA):Jul-Sep82-372
Huber, O. Zur Logik multidimensionaler Präferenzen in der Entscheidungstheorie.
E. Morscher, 687:Jan-Mar82-130
Huber, T.M. The Revolutionary Origins of Modern Japan.
Minamoto Ryōen, 285(JapQ):Jan-Mar82-115

Hubin, A.J. Crime Fiction, 1749-1980. (rev)
N. Callendar, 441:11Dec83-38
Hübscher, A. Schopenhauer-Bibliographie.
M. Hielscher, 489(PJGG):Band89Heft2-435
Hübscher, A. - see Schopenhauer, A.
Huchel, P. The Garden of Theophrastus and Other Poems.
D.J. Enright, 617(TLS):14Oct83-1136
Huchon, M. Rabelais grammairien.
R.M. Berrong, 400(MLN):May82-1010
G. Defaux, 551(RenQ):Autumn82-504
F.J. Hausmann, 547(RF):Band94Heft4-470
F. Rigolot, 546(RR):May82-386
G. de Rocher, 207(FR):Feb83-476
"Huck Embroidery."
P. Bach, 614:Fall83-21
Hucke, K-H. Utopie und Ideologie in der expressionistischen Lyrik.*
A. Arnold, 564:Nov81-325
H.F. Pfanner, 406:Fall82-368
Hudson, G., ed. Linguistics and the University Education.
R.K.S. Macaulay, 350:Sep83-710
Hudson, K. A Social History of Archaeology.
J. Leopold, 637(VS):Spring82-389
Hudson, L. Bodies of Knowledge.
R. Hewison, 617(TLS):21Jan83-67
Hudson, R.A. Sociolinguistics.*
A.S. Kroch, 350:Mar83-211
Hudson, W.H. Vertes demeures.
C. Jordis, 450(NRF):Jul-Aug82-197
Hudson, W.S. The Cambridge Connection and the Elizabethan Settlement of 1559.
P. Lefranc, 189(EA):Jul-Sep82-327
S.E. Lehmberg, 551(RenQ):Spring81-115
Hudspeth, R.N. - see Fuller, M.
Hue, J-L. Le Chat dans tous ses états.
J. Kirkup, 617(TLS):8Apr83-350
Hue de Rotelande. Ipomedon. (A.J. Holden, ed)
J.H. Marshall, 402(MLR):Jan82-196
Huebel, H.R. Jack Kerouac.*
G.F. Day, 649(WAL):Summer82-173
Huet, M-H. Rehearsing the Revolution.
J.H. Mason, 617(TLS):2Sep83-926
Hügel, H-O. Untersuchungsrichter — Diebsfänger — Detektive.*
U. Schulz-Buschhaus, 52:Band16Heft1-98
Huggins, N.I. Slave and Citizen.
R. Felgar, 392:Fall82-427
Hughes, A. Henry Irving, Shakespearean.*
R. Berry, 108:Summer82-150
R. Jackson, 637(VS):Spring82-388
J. McDonald, 610:Autumn81-223 [this citation inadvertently not shown in prev]
J.S. Bogere, 611(TN):Vol36No2-87
Hughes, A. Medieval Manuscripts for Mass and Office.
R.M. Haines, 150(DR):Autumn82-518
Hughes, D. Dryden's Heroic Plays.*
C.H. Hinnant, 173(ECS):Summer83-461
Hughes, D. The Imperial German dinner service.
D. Montrose, 617(TLS):16Sep83-1002
Hughes, E.J. Marcel Proust.
D. May, 362:18Aug83-19
Hughes, G. Where I Used to Play on the Green.*
442(NY):6Jun83-142

Hughes, G.T. Romantic German Literature.*
   M. Brown, 149(CLS):Spring82-89
   J. Neubauer, 173(ECS):Spring83-356
Hughes, H.S. Prisoners of Hope.
   B. Knox, 453(NYRB):18Aug83-6
Hughes, J. and B. Mercer. Dearest Beatie/
My Darling Jack.
   G. Battiscombe, 617(TLS):18Feb83-154
Hughes, J. and W.S. Ramson. Poetry of the
Stewart Court.
   D. Fox, 617(TLS):30Sep83-1065
Hughes, K., ed and trans. Franz Kafka.
   J.L. Hibberd, 268(IFR):Summer83-148
   C. Koelb, 395(MFS):Winter82/83-694
   S. Pinsker, 573(SSF):Summer82-287
Hughes, K. and D. Ifans - see Kilvert, F.
Hughes, M.G. The Calling.
   J. Tobin, 573(SSF):Winter82-97
   639(VQR):Winter82-19
Hughes, P. Eighteenth-Century France and
the East.
   B. Scott, 39:Apr82-294
Hughes, S. Glyndebourne.
   A. Jacobs, 415:Jan82-32
Hughes, T. River.
   P. Redgrove, 617(TLS):11Nov83-1238
Hughes, T. Under the North Star.*
   J. Saunders, 565:Vol23No3-73
   A.K. Weatherhead, 448:Vol20No1-154
Hughes, T. - see Plath, S.
Hughes, T. and F. McCullough - see Plath,
S.
Hughes, T.P. Networks of Power.
   P.V. Danckwerts, 617(TLS):28Oct83-1179
Hughes, W. The Maniac in the Cellar.*
   S. Hudson, 577(SHR):Winter82-76
   S. Mitchell, 637(VS):Autumn81-81
Hugo, R. Death and the Good Life.
   M.S. Allen, 649(WAL):Winter83-363
Hugo, R. The Hitler Diaries.*
   P. Andrews, 441:22May83-42
Hugo, V. Les Travailleurs de la mer.* (Y.
Gohin, ed)
   W.J.S. Kirton, 208(FS):Oct82-482
Huguet, L. L'oeuvre d'Alfred Döblin ou la
dialectique de l'exode, 1878-1918.*
   W. Stauffacher, 406:Summer82-221
Huidobro, M.M. - see under Montes Huidobro,
M.
Huish, I. Horváth.*
   H. Knust, 301(JEGP):Jan82-96
Hulanicki, B. From A to Biba.
   M. Furness, 617(TLS):21Oct83-1168
   A. Huth, 362:29Sep83-22
Hules, V.T. and M. Grimaud. Le Français
Littéraire Fondamental.
   N.E. Klayman, 399(MLJ):Winter82-417
Hulin, J-P. and P. Coustillas, eds. Vic-
torian Writers and the City.
   T.J. Winnifrith, 677(YES):Vol 12-305
Hulin, M. Hegel et l'Orient.
   D. Janicaud, 192(EP):Oct-Dec81-487
Hulin, M. Sāṃkhya Literature.
   W. Halbfass, 318(JAOS):Oct-Dec81-474
Hull, R.E. Nathaniel Hawthorne.*
   J.L. Idol, Jr., 580(SCR):Fall82-128
   T. Martin, 27(AL):Oct82-448
Hulme, G. The Lionel Touch.
   M. Fraser, 102(CanL):Winter81-139
Hulse, C. Metamorphic Verse.*
   D.C., 604:Fall82-57
Hulse, M. Knowing and Forgetting.*
   J. Saunders, 565:Vol23No3-73

Hultkrantz, Å. The Religions of the Amer-
ican Indians.
   T.A. Green, 292(JAF):Apr-Jun82-217
Humbach, H. and P.O. Skjaervø. The Sassan-
ian Inscription of Paikuli. (Pt 1)
   M.J. Dresden, 318(JAOS):Oct-Dec81-465
Humbert, C. Islamic Ornamental Design.
   U. Roberts, 60:Jan-Feb82-138
Hume, I.N. Martin's Hundred.*
   D.B. Quinn, 617(TLS):7Jan83-9
Hume, L.J. Bentham and Bureaucracy.*
   C.S., 185:Apr83-639
Hume, R.D., ed. The London Theatre World,
1660-1800.*
   G.L. Anderson, 130:Fall82-270
   L. Bertelsen, 173(ECS):Fall82-98
   J. Hamard, 189(EA):Oct-Dec82-467
   A. Kaufman, 301(JEGP):Oct82-570
Hume, R.D. The Rakish Stage.
   E. Burns, 617(TLS):11Nov83-1257
Hume, S. Signs Against an Empty Sky.
   K. Norris, 137:Aug82-34
   L. Ricou, 102(CanL):Spring82-90
Humes, W.M. and H.M. Paterson, eds. Scot-
tish Culture and Scottish Education 1800-
1980.
   C. Harvie, 617(TLS):18Mar83-272
Humesky, A. Modern Ukrainian.
   V. Babenko-Woodbury, 399(MLJ):Winter82-
   437
   G.A. Perfecky, 574(SEEJ):Spring82-134
Humfrey, B. John Dyer.
   D.W. Lindsay, 677(YES):Vol 12-280
Hummer, T.R. The Angelic Orders.
   D. Baker, 434:Spring83-422
Humphrey, C. - see Vainshtein, S.
Humphrey, N. Consciousness Regained.
   M. Ridley, 617(TLS):23Sep83-1009
   M. Warnock, 362:29Sep83-25
Humphreys, S. The Family, Women and Death.
   M. Alexiou, 617(TLS):15Jul83-756
Humphreys, S.C. and H. King, eds. Mortal-
ity and Immortality.
   D. Ridgway, 617(TLS):7Jan83-21
Humphries, B. A Nice Night's Entertain-
ment.
   J. Davidson, 381:Oct81-400
Hung-Tao, Y. - see under Yuan Hung-Tao
Hunger, H. Antiker und byzantinischer
Roman.
   J.R. Morgan, 123:Vol32No1-118
Hunger, H. Die hochsprachliche profane
Literatur der Byzantiner.* (Vols 1 and
2)
   J. Bompaire, 555:Vol56fasc1-140
Hungerland, I.C. and G.R. Vick - see
Hobbes, T.
Hunt, A. The Language of Television.*
   J. Corner, 437:Winter81/82-109
   D.R., 214:Vol 10No38-133
Hunt, C. "Lycidas" and the Italian
Critics.*
   L. Lerner, 131(CL):Winter82-74
   P. Palmer, 402(MLR):Jan82-160
Hunt, D., ed. Footprints in Cyprus.
   D. Gillard, 362:20Jan83-26
   C.M. Woodhouse, 617(TLS):25Feb83-198
Hunt, G. John Updike and the Three Great
Secret Things.
   W.T.S., 395(MFS):Summer81-374
Hunt, H. The Abbey.*
   N. Grene, 677(YES):Vol 12-351
   H. Kosok, 72:Band218Heft1-190

Hunt, J.D. The Wider Sea.*
   Q. Bell, 90:Sep82-560
   D. Johnson, 453(NYRB):31Mar83-11
   M. Lutyens, 39:Sep82-196
   A. Phillips, 364:Jul82-82
   W.R., 148:Winter82-94
Hunt, J.D. and F.M. Holland, eds. The Rus-
kin Polygon.*
   D. Johnson, 453(NYRB):31Mar83-13
   N. Lightman, 175:Autumn82-257
   M. Lutyens, 39:Sep82-196
   M. Warner, 90:Sep82-561
   G. Wills, 400(MLN):Dec82-1248
Hunt, M.H. The Making of a Special Rela-
tionship.
   J.K. Fairbank, 617(TLS):24Jun83-652
Hunt, T. Kerouac's Crooked Road.
   C.L. Crow, 649(WAL):Winter83-371
   W. French, 587(SAF):Spring82-115
   J.Z. Guzlowski, 395(MFS):Winter81/82-
736
Hunt, W. Oceans and Corridors of Orpheus.
   T. Diggory, 560:Summer82-159
   W.S. Di Piero, 598(SoR):Spring83-456
Hunt, W. The Puritan Moment.
   A. Fletcher, 617(TLS):8Jul83-720
   442(NY):14Mar83-159
Hunter, E. Far From the Sea.
   R. Freedman, 441:16Jan83-12
   H.R., 231:Jan83-76
Hunter, G.K. and C.J. Rawson - see "The
Yearbook of English Studies"
Hunter, I. Malcolm Muggeridge.
   K. Zaretzke, 396(ModA):Winter82-94
Hunter, J. Edwardian Fiction.*
   T.K. Bender, 141:Fall82-392
   J. Halperin, 395(MFS):Winter82/83-617
Hunter, L. G.K. Chesterton.*
   F. McCombie, 447(N&Q):Aug81-360
Hunter, M. Science and Society in Restora-
tion England.
   J.M. Hill, 566:Autumn82-59
   M. Jacob, 322(JHI):Apr-Jun82-331
Hunter, R.G. Shakespeare and the Myster-
ies of God's Judgments.
   E. Jones, 677(YES):Vol 12-253
Hunter, R.L. - see "Eubulus"
Huntingford, G.W.B., ed and trans. The
Periplus of the Erythraean Sea.*
   R. Pankhurst, 69:Vol51No1-540
Huntington, S.P. American Politics.
   639(VQR):Winter82-10
Huntley, F.L. Essays in Persuasion on
Seventeenth-Century English Literature.
   G. Hemphill, 569(SR):Winter82-x
Huntley, F.L. Bishop Joseph Hall and
Protestant Meditation in Seventeenth-
Century England.
   L.L. Martz, 191(ELN):Mar82-287
Huntley, F.L. Bishop Joseph Hall, 1574
1656.*
   A. Assmann, 72:Band218Heft2-436
   B. Vickers, 551(RenQ):Summer81-285
Huot, H. Enseignement du français et lin-
guistique.
   S.S. Magnan, 207(FR):Apr83-807
le Huray, P. and J. Day, eds. Music and
Aesthetics in the Eighteenth and Early
Nineteenth Centuries.
   H. Serwer, 410(M&L):Jul/Oct82-316
   E.R. Sisman, 317:Fall82-565
Hurd, M. Vincent Novello — and Company.
   A. Jacobs, 415:May82-334

Hurd, M. The Orchestra.*
   J.B., 412:May81-152
Hurlebusch, K. and K.L. Schneider - see
Stadler, E.
Hurst, C., comp. Catalogue of the Wren
Library of Lincoln Cathedral: Books
Printed before 1801.
   D. Shaw, 617(TLS):19Aug83-891
Hurtado, O. Political Power in Ecuador.
   W.P. Carty, 37:Jul-Aug82-60
Hurwitz, E.S. Prince Andrej Bogoljubskij.
   C.J. Halpern, 550(RusR):Jul82-323
Husserl, E. Aufsätze und Rezensionen
(1890-1910).* (B. Rang, ed)
   J. Colette, 192(EP):Jul-Sep81-349
   R.S.S., 543:Sep81-140
Husserl, E. Phantasie, Bildbewusstsein,
Erinnerung.* (E. Marbach, ed)
   J. Colette, 192(EP):Jul-Sep81-351
   R.S.S., 543:Sep81-143
Husserl, E. Phenomenology and the Founda-
tions of the Sciences.
   M. Kroy, 63:Dec82-383
Hussey, S.S. Chaucer.
   J.J.A., 148:Spring82-93
Huston, J.D. Shakespeare's Comedies of
Play.
   A.K. Nardo, 579(SAQ):Autumn82-476
   639(VQR):Summer82-81
Hutcheon, L. Narcissistic Narrative.
   G. Good, 627(UTQ):Summer82-404
   M.A. Massé, 678(YCGL):No30-96
   G. Prince, 210(FrF):Jan82-92
   C. Snider, 395(MFS):Winter81/82-765
Hutchings, B. The Poetry of William Cow-
per.
   P. Rogers, 617(TLS):8Apr83-343
Hutchins, F.G. Young Krishna.*
   D.J. Ehnbom, 293(JASt):May82-619
Hutchinson, R.C. The Unforgotten Prisoner.
   V. Cunningham, 617(TLS):23Sep83-1010
Hutson, J.H. John Adams and the Diplomacy
of the American Revolution.*
   D.R. Hickey, 396(ModA):Winter82-82
   639(VQR):Winter82-22
Hutton, J. Accidental Crimes.
   T.J. Binyon, 617(TLS):11Mar83-248
Hutton, J. Essays on Renaissance Poetry.
(R. Guerlac, ed)
   G. Hemphill, 569(SR):Winter82-x
   M.L. Lord, 551(RenQ):Summer82-325
Hutton, J. - see Aristotle
Huxley, A. Moksha. (M. Horowitz and C.
Palmer, eds)
   G.S., 617(TLS):22Apr83-415
Huygens, L. The English Journal, 1651-
1652. (A.G.H. Bachrach and R.G. Collmer,
eds and trans)
   K.H.D. Haley, 617(TLS):4Mar83-222
Huylus-Armanet, V. Des structures syntax-
iques de l'espagnol à l'analyse relation-
nelle des textes.
   R. Pellen, 553(RLiR):Jan-Jun82-170
Huysmans, J-K. A rebours. (R. Fortassier,
ed)
   J. Hytier, 546(RR):May82-394
   W. Theile, 547(RF):Band94Heft2/3-349
Huyssen, A. Drama des Sturm und Drang.
   A. von Bormann, 224(GRM):Band32Heft4-
482
   M.O. Kistler, 301(JEGP):Jan82-86
   A. Scott-Prelorentzos, 564:Feb81-87
   L. Sharpe, 402(MLR):Oct82-994

Hwang Chun-ming. The Drowning of an Old
Cat and Other Stories.
  P.G. Pickowicz, 293(JASt):Feb82-329
Hyams, J. Murder at the Academy Awards.
  N. Callendar, 441:8May83-27
Hyams, P.R. King, Lords and Peasants in
Medieval England.
  R.H. Helmholz, 589:Jul82-621
Hyde, C. The Icarus Seal.
  T.J. Binyon, 617(TLS):8Jul83-732
  T.J. Binyon, 617(TLS):13May83-498
Hyde, G.M. D.H. Lawrence and the Art of
Translation.
  J. Meyers, 395(MFS):Winter82/83-638
Hyde, H.M. The Atom Bomb Spies.*
  J.L. Granatstein, 529(QQ):Autumn82-529
Hyde, H.M. The Londonderrys.
  R. Fréchet, 189(EA):Apr-Jun82-226
  A.J. Heesom, 161(DUJ):Dec81-114
Hyde, L. The Gift.
  M. Bayles, 441:15May83-16
  C.J. Corkery, 434:Spring83-417
Hyde, M. - see Shaw, G.B. and A. Douglas
Hyland, P. Poems of Z.
  L. Mackinnon, 617(TLS):8Apr83-356
Hyman, L.M. and J. Voorhoeve, eds.
L'expansion bantoue.
  B.G. Blount, 350:Sep83-700
"Hymns Ancient and Modern: The New Stan-
dard Edition."
  G. Priestland, 362:23Jun83-25
"Hymns for Today's Church."
  F. Spiegl, 362:6Jan83-21
Hyslop, L.B. Baudelaire.*
  R.T. Cargo, 345(KRQ):Vol129No1-109
  F.S. Heck, 210(FrF):Jan82-82
  E.J. Kearns, 161(DUJ):Dec81-146
  R.A. York, 402(MLR):Apr82-455
Hyvrard, J. Le Corps défunt de la comédie.
  P. Olivier, 450(NRF):Jun82-105

de Ibarbourou, J. Antología de poemas y
prosas. (A.S. Visca and J.C. Da Rosa,
eds)
  G. Figueira, 263(RIB):Vol132No1-67
Ibargüengoitia, J. The Dead Girls.
  J. Astor, 362:17Mar83-24
  N. Rankin, 617(TLS):18Mar83-259
"Iberiul-k'avk'asiuri enatmecnierebis
c'elic'deuli, III."
  G.F. Meier, 682(ZPSK):Band34Heft5-633
"Iberiul-k'avk'asiuri enatmecnierebis
c'elic'deuli IV."
  G.F. Meier, 682(ZPSK):Band35Heft4-484
Iberville, P.L. Iberville's Gulf Journals.
(R.G. McWilliams, ed and trans)
  R.R. Rea, 9(AlaR):Apr82-145
Ibrahim, S.E. - see under el-Din el-
Shazali Ibrahim, S.
Ibsen, H. Peer Gynt.* (2nd ed) (R.
Fjelde, trans)
  M. Wells, 130:Fall82-295
Ichiyo, H. - see under Higuchi Ichiyo
Ide, R.S. Possessed with Greatness.*
  A.R. Braunmiller, 570(SQ):Winter82-538
  W. Rosen, 551(RenQ):Summer82-338
Idiens, D. and K.G. Ponting, eds. Tex-
tiles of Africa.*
  J.B. Eicher, 2(AfrA):Nov81-17
  M.V. Gilbert, 69:Vol51No4-888
  F. Willett, 59:Jun82-227

Idzerda, S.J. and others - see Marquis de
Lafayette
Iggers, G.G. and H.T. Parker, eds. Inter-
national Handbook of Historical Studies.
  K. Shipps, 125:Winter82-206
Iglesias, M. and W. Meiden. Spanish for
Oral and Written Review. (2nd ed)
  M.E. Beeson, 399(MLJ):Winter82-441
Iglesias Rouco, L.S. Urbanismo y Arquitec-
tura de Valladolid. Burgos en el siglo
XIX.
  A. Bustamante García, 48:Jan-Mar80-126
Ignatow, D. Open Between Us. (R.J. Mills,
Jr., ed)
  K. Taylor, 436(NewL):Fall82-97
Ignatow, D. Whisper to the Earth.*
  639(VQR):Summer82-93
Ihara, S. - see under Saikaku Ihara
Ihle, S.N. Malory's Grail Quest.
  C. La Farge, 617(TLS):8Jul83-736
Ihnken, T., ed. Die Inschriften von
Magnesia am Sipylos.*
  P.M. Fraser, 123:Vol132No2-300
  A.G. Woodhead, 303(JoHS):Vol 102-294
Iijima, S., Seiji Imahori and Kanesaburo
Gushima - see under Soichi Iijima, Seiji
Imahori and Kanesaburo Gushima
Ikonné, C. From Du Bois to Van Vechten.
  E. Guereschi, 395(MFS):Winter82/83-682
Ikvai, N., ed. Börzsöny néprajza.
  G.F. Cushing, 575(SEER):Apr82-292
Iles, N. The Pagan Carols Restored.
(Vol 1)
  L. Sail, 565:Vol23No4-74
Ileto, R.C. "Pasyon" and Revolution.
  B.J. Kerkvliet, 293(JASt):Feb82-414
Ilie, P. Literature and Inner Exile.
  D. Kadir, 395(MFS):Winter81/82-669
  J.W. Kronik, 400(MLN):Mar82-437
  M.C. Peñuelas, 238:May82-310
Iliescu, M. and others. Vocabularul mini-
mal al limbii romāne.
  P. Tekavčic, 553(RLiR):Jan-Jun82-182
Illič-Svityč, V.M. Opyt sravnenija nostra-
tičeskich jazykov.
  R. Eckert, 682(ZPSK):Band34Heft4-487
Illich, I. Gender.
  A.R. Hochschild, 441:30Jan83-7
  P. Robinson, 231:Mar83-71
  K. Thomas, 453(NYRB):12May83-6
Illich-Svitych, V.M. Nominal Accentuation
in Baltic and Slavic.*
  D.F. Robinson, 574(SEEJ):Summer82-258
Illick, J.E. Colonial Pennsylvania.*
  F. Shuffelton, 173(ECS):Summer83-415
"Imagen Romántica de España."
  E. Trevelyan, 90:Apr82-251
Imai, R. and H.S. Rowen. Nuclear Energy
and Nuclear Proliferation.
  P.F. Langer, 293(JASt):Nov81-135
Imbert, E.A. - see under Anderson Imbert,
E.
Imbert, P. Sémiotique et description bal-
zacienne.*
  P-L. Vaillancourt, 107(CRCL):Jun82-294
Imbs, P. - see "Trésor de la langue fran-
çaise"
Imerslund, K. Den estetisk-filosofiske
skole i norsk litteraturforskning — mål
og metode.
  T. Schiff, 563(SS):Summer82-268
Imhof, R. Harold Pinters Dramentechnik.
  R. Halbritter, 38:Band100Heft1/2-228

Imlah, M. The Zoologist's Bath and Other
  Adventures.*
    M. O'Neill, 493:Jan83-48
Immerman, R.H. The CIA in Guatemala.*
    S.C. Ropp, 263(RIB):Vol32No2-213
Inamdar, F.A. Image and Symbol in Joseph
  Conrad's Novels.
    J.J. Soldo, 136:Vol 14No1-63
Ince, W.N. Heredia.*
    E.J. Kearns, 161(DUJ):Dec81-147
Ince, W.N. - see de Heredia, J-M.
Inchbald, P. Short Break in Venice.
    T.J. Binyon, 617(TLS):23Dec83-1437
Inchbald, P. Sweet Short Grass.*
    N. Callendar, 441:27Feb83-45
"Index to Reviews of Bibliographical Publi-
  cations." (Vol 3) (L.T. Oggel, with R.
  Hewitt, eds)
    D. Traister, 517(PBSA):Vol76No4-504
"Index to Reviews of Bibliographical Publi-
  cations." (Vol 4) (L.T. Oggel and R.
  Hewitt, with G.M. Sadlek, eds)
    517(PBSA):Vol76No4-504
"Index to the Letters and Papers of Edward
  White Benson, Archbishop of Canterbury
  1883-1896, in Lambeth Palace Library."
    M. Bond, 325:Apr82-43
"Indianisme et bouddhisme."
    J.W. de Jong, 259(IIJ):Oct82-311
Indich, W.M. Consciousness in Advaita
  Vedānta.
    A. Adams, 485(PE&W):Oct82-468
    F. Staal, 293(JASt):Feb82-269
Ineichen, G. - see Renzi, L.
Inés de la Cruz, J. Selección. (L.
  Ortega Galindo, ed)
    C.S. Crantford, 552(REH):Oct82-472
Infeld, L. Quest.
    A.B. Stewart, 42(AR):Winter82-113
Ingalls, R. Binstead's Safari.
    A. Mars-Jones, 617(TLS):13May83-481
Ingalls, R. Mrs. Caliban.*
    442(NY):25Jul83-87
Ingamells, J. The English Episcopal Por-
  trait 1559-1835.
    D. Piper, 39:Jul82-66
Ingham, R. and L. Covey. The Costume
  Designer's Handbook.
    R.L. Shep, 614:Summer83-17
Ingle, S. Socialist Thought in Imagina-
  tive Literature.*
    J. Lucas, 677(YES):Vol 12-348
    J.R. Reed, 395(MFS):Winter81/82-695
    L.T. Sargent, 322(JHI):Oct-Dec82-681
    A. Wald, 125:Fall81-104
Inglis, F. The Promise of Happiness.
    M.K. Loges, 152(UDQ):Summer82-133
Ingram, R.W. John Marston.*
    G.K. Hunter, 677(YES):Vol 12-263
Ingram, W.G. and T. Redpath - see Shake-
  speare, W.
Ingrams, R. and J. Piper. Piper's Places.
    L. Ellmann, 617(TLS):21Oct83-1148
Ingwersen, N., ed. Seventeen Danish Poets.
    F. Hugus, 563(SS):Autumn82-321
Íñiguez, D.A. - see under Angulo Íñiguez,
  D.
Inkster, I. and J. Morrell, eds. Metropo-
  lis and Province.
    D.M. Knight, 617(TLS):20May83-518
Inkster, T. Blue Angel.
    L. Welch, 198:Oct82-99

Inman, B.A. Walter Pater's Reading.
    E.R. Hall, 148:Winter82-82
    D.L. Hill, 517(PBSA):Vol76No4-488
Innes, C. Holy Theatre.*
    M. Esslin, 157:Spring82-57
    B.L. Knapp, 397(MD):Jun82-312
    B. Lecker, 108:Summer82-146
    A. McKinnon, 214:Vol 10No38-128
Innes, C.D. Modern German Drama.*
    W.G. Cunliffe, 406:Fall82-339
    J. Fuegi, 397(MD):Jun82-311
Innes, C.L. and B. Lindfords, eds. Criti-
  cal Perspectives on Chinua Achebe.
    R. Mane, 189(EA):Apr-Jun82-229
Innes, M. Appleby and Honeybath.
    T.J. Binyon, 617(TLS):3Jun83-582
    T.J. Binyon, 617(TLS):8Jul83-732
Innes, M. Sheiks and Adders.*
    N. Callendar, 441:13Feb83-31
Innis, R.E. Karl Bühler.*
    T.F. Shannon, 350:Dec83-942
Inoue, Y. Chronicle of My Mother.
    E. Milton, 441:26Jun83-13
    442(NY):18Jul83-97
Inoura, Y. and T. Kawatake. The Tradi-
  tional Theater of Japan.
    F.T. Motofuji, 407(MN):Winter82-551
Insdorf, A. Indelible Shadows.
    D. Isaac, 441:2Oct83-13
"Inventaire des particularités lexicales
  du français en Afrique Noire (C-F)."
    J. Pohl, 553(RLiR):Jan-Jun82-206
Ionesco, M-F. and P. Vernois, eds. Iones-
  co, situation et perspectives.
    J. Jomaron, 535(RHL):Sep-Dec82-981
Ions, E. Against Behaviouralism.
    R.F. Kitchener, 488:Dec82-445
Ioppolo, A.M. Aristone di Chio e lo
  stoicismo antico.
    J.G.F. Powell, 123:Vol32No1-101
Iranzo, C. Antonio García Gutiérrez.*
    M.A. Rees, 402(MLR):Jan82-221
Iranzo, C. Juan Eugenio Hartzenbusch.
    M. López, 552(REH):Jan82-138
Ireland, D. City of Women.
    P. Pierce, 381:Dec81-522
Irick-Nauer, T. The First Price Guide to
  Antique and Vintage Clothes.
    R.L. Shep, 614:Fall83-19
Irigaray, L. Speculum. Amante marine.
    E.L. Berg, 153:Summer82-11
"Irish Renaissance Annual II." (Z. Bowen,
  ed)
    K.E. Marre, 395(MFS):Summer82-266
Iriye, A. Power and Culture.
    S. Pelz, 293(JASt):Feb82-359
Irizarry, E. Rafael Dieste.*
    L. Hickey, 402(MLR):Jan82-222
Irmscher, H.D. and E. Adler, comps. Der
  handschriftliche Nachlass Johann Gott-
  fried Herders.
    H.B. Nisbet, 301(JEGP):Apr82-287
Irmscher, J., ed. Antikerezeption, deut-
  sche Klassik und sozialistische Gegen-
  wart.
    R.C. Holub, 406:Spring82-93
Irvin, H.D. Women in Kentucky.
    A.C. Fellman, 106:Spring82-61
Irving, C. Tom Mix and Pancho Villa.*
    639(VQR):Autumn82-131
Irving, D. The Secret Diaries of Hitler's
  Doctor.
    G.A. Craig, 453(NYRB):21Jul83-4

Irving, J. The Hotel New Hampshire.*
  J.T. Hospital, 529(QQ):Autumn82-651
  W.H. Pritchard, 249(HudR):Spring82-159
Irving, R.G. Indian Summer.*
  M. Lutyens, 39:May82-416
Irving, T.B. Kalila e Dimna.
  J.E. Keller, 86(BHS):Oct82-330
Irving, W. Journals and Notebooks.* (Vol
  2) (W.A. Reichart and L. Schlissel, eds)
  Miscellaneous Writings, 1803-1859.*
  (Vols 1 and 2) (W.R. Kime, ed)
  R. Willett, 402(MLR):Oct82-930
Irwin, D. John Flaxman 1755-1826.*
  T.J. McCormick, 173(ECS):Summer83-468
Irwin, J.T. American Hieroglyphics.*
  H. Beaver, 402(MLR):Jul82-703
  B. Cowan, 598(SoR):Autumn83-913
  D.B. Stauffer, 301(JEGP):Jul82-463
  A.E. Stone, 131(CL):Winter82-86
Irwin, T. - see Plato
Isaac, R. The Transformation of Virginia
  1740-1790.
  J. Greene, 617(TLS):25Feb83-177
  E.S. Morgan, 453(NYRB):20Jan83-38
Isaac, R.J. Party and Politics in Israel.*
  J. Sinai, 287:Mar82-29
Isaacs, A.R. Without Honor.
  D. Pike, 441:16Oct83-9
Isaacs, E. An Introduction to the Poetry
  of Yvor Winters.
  R. Labrie, 106:Winter82-397
Isaacs, N.D. and R.A. Zimbardo, eds.
  Tolkien.
  D.M. Miller, 395(MFS):Winter81/82-708
Isaev, M.I. and others, eds. Problemy
  interlingvistiki.
  D. Blanke, 682(ZPSK):Band34Heft2-234
Isaksson, H. Lars Gyllensten.
  B. Lide, 563(SS):Winter82-99
Isenberg, M.T. War on Film.
  J. Beaver, 200:Feb82-124
Iser, W. Spenser's Arcadia.
  D.C., 604:Fall82-58
Iserloh, E. - see Eck, J.
Isern, T.D. Custom Combining on the Great
  Plains.
  L. Milazzo, 584(SWR):Spring82-v
Isherwood, C. Rencontre au bord du fleuve.
  Mon Gourou et son disciple.
  C. Jordis, 450(NRF):Oct82-135
Ishiguro, K. A Pale View of Hills.*
  B. Powell, 362:4Aug83-20
Ishumi, A.G.M. Kiziba.
  J. Beattie, 69:Vol51No4-894
Saint Isidore of Seville. Isidorus His-
  palensis, "Etymologiae XVII": Isidore de
  Séville, "Étymologies," livre XVII. (J.
  André, ed and trans)
  I. Opelt, 555:Vol56fasc2-361
Iskander, F. Sandro of Chegem.
  S. Jacoby, 441:15May83-9
  M. Scammell, 617(TLS):4Nov83-1215
Islam, J.N. The Ultimate Fate of the
  Universe.
  W.H. McCrea, 617(TLS):7Oct83-1091
Islam, S. Chronicles of the Raj.*
  E. Hanquart, 189(EA):Jan-Mar82-98
Ismailova, A.M. Oriental Miniatures of
  Abu Raihon Beruni Institute of Orientol-
  ogy of the USSR Academy of Sciences.
  B.W. Robinson, 463:Spring82-89

Isnardi Parente, M. Studi sull' Accademia
  Platonica antica.
  H. Krämer, 53(AGP):Band64Heft1-76
Issa. Everything Under Heaven. (C.
  Edwards, trans)
  B.M. Wilson, 485(PE&W):Apr82-216
Issorel, J., ed. Papel de Aleluyas.
  R. Andioc, 240(HR):Summer82-367
"Istorija romantizma v russkoj literature:
  Romantizm v russkoj literature 20-30X
  godov XIXv, 1825-1840."
  L.G. Leighton, 574(SEEJ):Summer82-239
"Istorija romantizma v russkoj literature:
  Vozniknovenie i utverždenie romantizma v
  russkoj literature 1790-1825."
  L.G. Leighton, 574(SEEJ):Summer82-239
Italiani, G. La tradizione esegetica nel
  commento ai Re de Claudio di Torino.
  E.A. Matter, 589:Oct82-967
Italicus, T.C.S. - see under Silius
  Italicus, T.C.
Itoh, T. Traditional Japanese Houses.
  E. Seidensticker, 441:11Dec83-14
Itzin, C. Stages in the Revolution.*
  C. Barker, 611(TN):Vol36No2-93
  G.K. Hunter, 612(ThS):May82-135
Ivask, I., ed. Odysseus Elytis.
  P. Bien, 651(WHR):Winter82-345
  E. Piliouni-Bousouloupoulos, 577(SHR):
  Fall82-378
"Ívens Saga." (F.W. Blaisdell, ed)
  T.D. Hill, 301(JEGP):Oct82-527
  P. Skårup, 563(SS):Winter82-73
Iversen, G., ed. Tropes de l'Agnus Dei.
  J. Caldwell, 410(M&L):Jan/Apr82-146
  R. Steiner, 589:Oct82-905
Ives, E.D. Joe Scott.*
  P. Smith, 203:Vol193No1-123
Ives, E.D. The Tape-Recorded Interview.*
  N.V. Rosenberg, 650(WF):Jan82-73
Ives, E.W. The Common Lawyers of Pre-
  Reformation England.
  G.R. Elton, 617(TLS):1Jul83-694
Izutsu, T. Toward a Philosophy of Zen
  Buddhism.
  M. Ury, 318(JAOS):Apr-Jun81-234
Izutsu, T. and T. The Theory of Beauty in
  the Classical Aesthetics of Japan.
  N. McAdoo, 89(BJA):Autumn82-363
Izzo, H.J., ed. Italic and Romance.*
  S.N. Dworkin, 320(CJL):Fall82-180

Jabbar Beg, M.A. Fine Arts in Islamic Civ-
  ilization.
  M. Kalimullah, 273(IC):Oct82-317
Jabès, E. The Book of Questions.
  M. Palmer, 441:21Aug83-13
Jablinski, M. Theodor W. Adorno.
  M.T. Jones, 221(GQ):Mar82-226
Jaccottet, P. Beauregard. La Promenade
  sous les arbres.
  M. Bishop, 207(FR):Feb83-510
Jack, D. Rogues, Rebels and Geniuses.
  G. Bilson, 529(QQ):Winter82-862
Jack, R.D.S. and A. Noble, eds. The Art
  of Robert Burns.
  W.R., 148:Winter82-93
Jackel, S. A Flannel Shirt and Liberty.
  J. Parr, 150(DR):Winter82/83-693
Jackendoff, R. X̄ Syntax.
  F. Stuurman, 297(JL):Sep82-409

Jackman, B. The Marsh Lions.
  M. Levine, 441:11Dec83-15
Jackman, J.C. and C.M. Borden, eds. The
  Muses Flee Hitler.
  S. Kauffmann, 441:10Jul83-12
Jackowska, N. Earthwalks.
  F. Adcock, 617(TLS):18Mar83-278
Jackowska, N. The Knot Garden.
  I. McMillan, 493:Jun82-71
Jackson, A.M. Illustration and the Novels
  of Thomas Hardy.*
  S.C., 148:Autumn82-94
  M. Millgate, 445(NCF):Jun82-119
  D.E. Van Tassel, 395(MFS):Summer82-255
  H.L. Weatherby, 569(SR):Spring82-313
Jackson, D. Thomas Jefferson and the
  Stony Mountains.
  J.P. Ronda, 656(WMQ):Apr82-390
  B.W. Sheehan, 639(VQR):Spring82-345
Jackson, J.C. and M. Rudner, eds. Issues
  in Malaysian Development.
  K. Mulliner, 293(JAS):Feb82-416
Jackson, J.R.D. Poetry of the Romantic
  Period.*
  J. Blondel, 189(EA):Jul-Sep82-334
  M.G. Cooke, 340(KSJ):Vol31-206
  E.D. Mackerness, 447(N&Q):Oct81-438
  E.B. Murray, 541(RES):May82-209
Jackson, J.R.D. - see Coleridge, S.T.
Jackson, K.D. and L.W. Pye, eds. Politi-
  cal Power and Communications in Indo-
  nesia.
  J. Mangan, 318(JAOS):Oct-Dec81-436
Jackson, L. Progress of Stories.
  G. Kearns, 249(HudR):Autumn82-499
Jackson, L. (Riding). The Poems of Laura
  Riding.*
  T.D. Young, 569(SR):Summer82-lxvi
Jackson, R. Fantasy.*
  S.S. Prawer, 402(MLR):Jan82-154
Jackson, R.L. The Afro-Spanish American
  Author.*
  L. King, 86(BHS):Oct82-349
Jackson, R.L. The Art of Dostoevsky.*
  A.R. Durkin, 104(CASS):Fall-Winter82-
  520
  D. Fanger, 550(RusR):Oct82-526
  G.D. Fitzgerald, 268(IFR):Winter83-62
  G.R. Jahn, 395(MFS):Winter82/83-703
  V.D. Mihailovich, 573(SSF):Summer82-
  288
  G. Woodcock, 569(SR):Fall82-589
  639(VQR):Summer82-79
Jackson, R.L. Black Writers in Latin
  America.*
  G. Guinness, 395(MFS):Summer81-419
Jackson, W. The Probable and the Marvel-
  ous.*
  L. Tannenbaum, 173(ECS):Summer82-463
Jackson, W.T.H. The Hero and the King.
  639(VQR):Summer82-81
Jackson, W.T.H., ed. The Interpretation
  of Medieval Lyric Poetry.
  R.T. Davies, 447(N&Q):Jun81-257
  P.F. Dembowski, 589:Apr82-383
  G.D. Economou, 222(GR):Winter82-38
  S. Westphal-Wihl, 221(GQ):Jan82-108
Jacob, E. Dancing.
  E. Zimmer, 151:Apr82-89
Jacob, F. Le jeu des possibles.
  F. George, 98:Oct82-855
  G. Sartoris, 450(NRF):Apr82-128

Jacob, J.R. Henry Stubbe.
  B. Worden, 617(TLS):5Aug83-837
Jacob, P. L'empirisme logique.
  E.R. Eames, 319:Jan83-125
Jacobs, A. and M. Barton - see "British
  Music Yearbook 1982"
Jacobs, D. ...But We Need the Eggs.
  T. Wiener, 18:Mar83-74
Jacobs, D.N. Borodin.*
  J.D. Hartgrove, 550(RusR):Oct82-494
Jacobs, R.A. and P.S. Rosenbaum. Readings
  in English Transformational Grammar.
  P.C. Bjarkman, 399(MLJ):Summer82-201
Jacobsen, J. The Chinese Insomniacs.*
  S.M. Gilbert, 472:Spring/Summer83-147
  X.J. Kennedy, 491:Mar83-349
Jacobson, D. The Confessions of Josef
  Baisz.
  P. Lewis, 565:Vol23No2-44
Jacobson, D. The Story of the Stories.*
  J.M. Cameron, 453(NYRB):29Sep83-45
Jacobson, H. Coming from Behind.
  J. Astor, 362:16Jun83-28
  J.K.L. Walker, 617(TLS):8Apr83-345
Jacobus, M., ed. Women Writing, and Writ-
  ing About Women.*
  K.M. Hewitt, 447(N&Q):Jun81-274
  J. Marcus, 395(MFS):Winter82/83-735
  J. Simons, 541(RES):Aug82-365
Jacoby, S. Wild Justice.
  S. Toulmin, 441:23Oct83-14
Jacques, F. Dialogiques.
  M. Longeart-Roth, 154:Jun82-397
Jaegar, P. - see Heidegger, M.
Jaeger, D. Settlement Patterns and Rural
  Development.
  J.R. Rogge, 69:Vol52No2-117
Jaeggi, U. Grundrisse.
  P. Labanyi, 617(TLS):7Oct83-1094
Jaffé, A. C.G. Jung.
  S.S. Curry, 77:Summer82-271
Jaffe, E.D. Letters to Yitz.
  J. Riemer, 390:Apr82-62
Jaffee, A.W. Adult Education.*
  J.L. Halio, 598(SoR):Winter83-203
Jaffrey, M. Vegetarian Cooking.
  W. and C. Cowen, 639(VQR):Autumn82-141
Jafri, S.H.M. The Origins and Early Devel-
  opment of Shia Islam.
  S. Kazim, 273(IC):Jul82-241
Jagchid, S. and P. Hyer. Mongolia's Cul-
  ture and Society.
  D. Rosenberg, 244(HJAS):Jun82-348
Jäger, B. "Durch reimen gute lere geben."*
  A. Schnyder, 680(ZDP):Band101Heft1-134
Jäger, K-H. Untersuchungen zur Klassifika-
  tion gesprochener deutscher Standard-
  sprache.
  K-E. Sommerfeldt, 682(ZPSK):Band34
  Heft2 260
Jägerskiöld, S. Suomen marsalkka: Gustaf
  Mannerheim, 1941-1944.
  M. Rintala, 550(RusR):Jan82-80
Jaggar, A.M. and P.R. Struhl, eds.
  Feminist Frameworks.
  M. Fox, 154:Mar82-141
Jagger, P.J. Clouded Witness.
  P. Butler, 617(TLS):27May83-554
Jagu, A. - see Musionus Rufus
Jahan, R. Bangladesh Politics.
  M. Franda, 293(JASt):Aug82-857

179

Jahn, M. Night Rituals.
  N. Callendar, 441:9Jan83-41
  442(NY):21Feb83-135
"Jahrbuch der Oswald-von-Wolkenstein-
  Gesellschaft." (Vol 1) (H-D. Mück and U.
  Müller, eds)
  S.L. Wailes, 406:Winter82-492
"Jahrbuch Deutsch als Fremdsprache 7." (A.
  Wierlacher, ed)
  C.E. Putnam, 399(MLJ):Winter82-413
Jain, D., with N. Singh and M. Chand.
  Women's Quest for Power.
  R.B. Dixon, 293(JASt):Nov81-173
Jain, J. The Vasudevahiṇḍi.
  L. Sternbach, 318(JAOS):Oct-Dec81-485
Jaini, P.S., ed and trans. Amṛtacandra-
  sūri's Laghutattvasphoṭa.
  W. Halbfass, 318(JAOS):Oct-Dec81-473
Jaini, P.S. Sāratamā.
  D.S. Ruegg, 259(IIJ):Apr82-156
Jaki, S.L. The Road of Science and the
  Ways to God.
  M. Birnbaum, 396(ModA):Winter82-80
Jakobson, M. Paasikivi Tukholmassa.
  M. Rintala, 563(SS):Autumn82-328
Jakobson, R. The Framework of Language.
  A. Liberman, 353:Vol 19No9/10-1028
Jakobson, R. Selected Writings.* (Vol 5)
  (S. Rudy and M. Taylor, eds)
  T. Eekman, 104(CASS):Summer82-247
  S. Senderovich, 567:Vol40No3/4-347
Jakobson, R. and L.R. Waugh, with M.
  Taylor. The Sound Shape of Language.*
  D. Brenneis, 292(JAF):Jan-Mar82-93
  R. Coates, 307:Apr82-63
  A. Liberman, 353:Vol 19No5/6-531
Jakubec, D. Sylvain Pitt ou les Avatars
  de la Liberté.
  D.F. Bradshaw, 208(FS):Apr82-226
Jalland, P. The Liberals and Ireland.
  G. Eley, 385(MQR):Winter83-107
"The Jamaican National Bibliography, 1964-
  1974."
  L.S. Thompson, 263(RIB):Vol32No1-67
Jamalzadeh, S.M.A. Isfahan is Half the
  World.
  T. Modarressi, 441:14Aug83-10
James, A. The Death and Letters of Alice
  James.* (R.B. Yeazell, ed)
  N. Baym, 301(JEGP):Jan82-144
  R. Hewitt, 395(MFS):Winter81/82-719
  J. Rivkin, 114(ChiR):Summer81-49
James, B. Manuel de Falla and the Spanish
  Musical Renaissance.*
  R. Orledge, 410(M&L):Jul/Oct81-420
James, C. Brilliant Creatures.
  J. Mellors, 362:21Jul83-27
  L. Taylor, 617(TLS):22Jul83-769
James, C. Contrastive Analysis.
  R. Coulon, 257(IRAL):Aug82-241
James, C. Poem of the Year.
  A. Huth, 362:22and29Dec83-38
James, C. Unreliable Memoirs.
  S. Brown, 569(SR):Spring82-250
  P. Shaw, 31(ASch):Spring82-299
James, D. George Büchner's "Dantons Tod."
  T.J. Reed, 617(TLS):22Jul83-788
James, H. The Europeans: A Facsimile of
  the Manuscript.
  R. Hewitt, 395(MFS):Winter81/82-719
James, H. Henry James: Letters.* (Vol 3)
  (L. Edel, ed)
  M. Bell, 473(PR):4/1982-613

James, H. The Literary Criticism of Henry
  James - see Daugherty, S.B.
James, H. The Tales of Henry James.*
  (Vols 1 and 2) (M. Aziz, ed)
  T. Colson, 178:Mar82-87
  D. Mehl, 72:Band218Heft1-179
James, I.M. Sewing Specialties.
  P. Bach, 614:Fall83-23
James, K., R.R. Jordan and A.J. Matthews.
  Collins Listening Comprehension and Note-
  Taking Course.
  L. Hamp-Lyons, 608:Mar83-109
James, M.R. A Descriptive Catalogue of
  the Latin Manuscripts in the John Ry-
  lands University Library. (F. Taylor,
  ed)
  N. Barker, 78(BC):Winter82-523
James, M.R. - see Map, W.
James, P.D. The Skull Beneath The Skin.*
  M. Laski, 362:20Jan83-23
James, R.R. - see under Rhodes James, R.
James, S. The Death of Innocence.
  T.C. Holyoke, 42(AR):Summer82-366
James, S.V. Colonial Rhode Island.*
  F. Shuffelton, 173(ECS):Summer83-415
James, W. Essays in Philosophy.* (F.H.
  Burkhardt and I.K. Skrupskelis, eds)
  P. Carrive, 192(EP):Apr-Jun82-236
James, W. "Kwanim Pa."
  J. Middleton, 69:Vol51No4-896
James, W. The Principles of Psychology.
  (F. Burkhardt, F. Bowers and I.K.
  Skrupskelis, eds)
  F. Tanikawa, 319:Apr83-270
Jameson, F. Fables of Aggression.*
  J. Mitchell, 599:Winter82-87
  W.G. Regier, 152(UDQ):Winter82-99
  M. Sprinker, 153:Fall82-57
  M. Wilding, 402(MLR):Oct82-944
Jameson, F. The Political Unconscious.*
  J. Arac, 395(MFS):Winter82/83-723
  G. Bennington, 153:Fall82-23
  M. Clark, 494:Winter82-159
  M. Danahy, 446(NCFS):Fall-Winter82/83-
  197
  J.W. Davidson, 477(PLL):Winter82-428
  J.D. Erickson, 207(FR):Mar83-626
  J.A. Flieger, 153:Fall82-47
  A. Gelber, 400(MLN):Dec82-1228
  W.G. Regier, 152(UDQ):Winter82-99
  G. Shapiro, 478:Oct82-206
  M. Sprinker, 153:Fall82-57
  J. Weinsheimer, 136:Vol 14No2-131
  639(VQR):Winter82-9
Jamie, K. Black Spiders.
  V. Feaver, 617(TLS):18Feb83-160
Jamme, F.A. L'Ombre des biens à venir.
  D. Leuwers, 450(NRF):May82-106
Jammes, A. and E.P. Janis. The Art of
  French Calotype.
  A. Grundberg, 441:15May83-15
Jammes, R. - see de Góngora, L.
Janata, A. Schmuck in Afghanistan.
  P.A. Andrews, 39:Nov82-346
Janericco, T. The Book of Great Hors
  d'Oeuvres.
  W. and C. Cowen, 639(VQR):Spring82-65
Janert, K.L. - see Lommel, H.
Janes, P. Light and Dark.
  R.J. Merrett, 529(QQ):Winter82-893
Janeway, E. Cross Sections.
  D. Bair, 441:23Jan83-10

Jankélévitch, V. Le Paradoxe de la morale.
  T. Cordellier, 450(NRF):May82-121
Janko, R. Homer, Hesiod and the Hymns.
  S. West, 617(TLS):11Mar83-242
Jannach, H. German for Reading Knowledge.
  (3rd ed)
  J. Jahn, 399(MLJ):Autumn82-338
Janney, F. Alejo Carpentier and His Early
  Works.
  G. Pontiero, 86(BHS):Oct82-351
Jannini, P.A. Un Altro Corbière.
  M. Tilby, 208(FS):Jan82-89
Jannuzi, F.T. and J.T. Peach. The Agrar-
  ian Structure of Bangladesh.
  D.W. Attwood, 293(JASt):Nov81-175
Janos, A.C. The Politics of Backwardness
  in Hungary 1825-1945.
  A. Sked, 617(TLS):11Mar83-250
Janota, J., ed. Eine Wissenschaft etab-
  liert sich 1810-1870.*
  U. Meves, 680(ZDP):Band101Heft1-150
Janov, A. Prisoners of Pain.
  G.R. Lowe, 529(QQ):Spring82-161
Janovy, J., Jr. Back in Keith County.
  C. Rawlins, 649(WAL):Summer82-182
Janowitz, P. Visiting Rites.
  I. Salusinszky, 617(TLS):9Dec83-1384
  H. Seidman, 441:20Feb83-6
Jansen, F. The Earliest Portuguese Lyrics.
  A-M. Quint, 549(RLC):Jan-Mar82-96
Jansen, F.J.B. - see under Billeskov Jan-
  sen, F.J.
Jansen, M. The Battle of Beirut.
  M. Howard, 617(TLS):15Apr83-367
Jansen, M.B. Japan and Its World.*
  K.B. Pyle, 293(JASt):May82-593
Jansen, W. Das Groteske in der deutschen
  Literatur der Spätaufklärung.
  W. Beck, 602:Vol 13No2-344
  A.R. Schmitt, 221(GQ):Jan82-117
Janson, T. Mechanisms of Language Change
  in Latin.*
  P. Flobert, 555:Vol56fasc1-144
  A. Maniet, 487:Summer82-188
  W. Zonneveld, 361:Sep/Oct82-197
Janssen, T.A.J.M. Hebben-konstrukties en
  indirekt-objektskonstrukties.
  H. Hipp, 682(ZPSK):Band34Heft2-261
Jansson, V., B. Nordberg and M. Thelander,
  eds. Ord och struktur.
  J.E. Cathey, 563(SS):Winter82-78
Janton, P. Einführung in die Esperantol-
  ogie.
  F. Häusler, 682(ZPSK):Band35Heft5-586
Jantzen, J. Parmenides zum Verhältnis von
  Sprache und Wirklichkeit.
  W.J. Verdenius, 394:Vol135fasc1/2-162
Janz, C.P. Friedrich Nietzsche Biographie.
  (Vol 1)
  A. Flécheux, 192(EP):Oct-Dec82-481
"Japonisme in Art."
  D. Johnson, 90:Sep82-561
Jaques, E. The Form of Time. Free Enter-
  prise, Fair Employment.
  S. Sutherland, 617(TLS):8Apr83-350
Jarausch, K.H. Students, Society, and
  Politics in Imperial Germany.
  D. Blackbourn, 617(TLS):10Jun83-604
Jardine, L. Still Harping on Daughters.
  I-S. Ewbank, 617(TLS):2Sep83-934
  F. Kermode, 453(NYRB):28Apr83-30

Jarman, A.O.H. and G.R. Hughes, eds. A
  Guide to Welsh Literature. (Vol 2)
  P.K. Ford, 589:Jan82-137
Jarman, D. Kurt Weill.
  P. Engel, 441:20Feb83-15
  P. O'Connor, 617(TLS):12Aug83-852
Jarman, M. The Rote Walker.
  J.F. Cotter, 249(HudR):Autumn82-471
Jarrell, R. The Complete Poems.
  R. Pybus, 565:Vol23No3-60
Jarrell, R. Kipling, Auden & Co.*
  H.L. Weatherby, 396(ModA):Winter82-100
Jarry, A. Gestes et opinions du Docteur
  Faustroll, pataphysicien [suivi de]
  L'Amour absolu. (N. Arnaud and H.
  Bordillon, eds) Leda. (H. Bordillon,
  ed)
  H. Béhar, 535(RHL):Sep-Dec82-947
Jarvis, G.A. and others. Connaître et se
  connaître.* (2nd ed)
  A.S. Caprio, 399(MLJ):Autumn82-334
Jarvis, G.A. and others. Vivent les dif-
  férences.* (2nd ed)
  R.E. Hiedemann, 399(MLJ):Winter82-421
Jasinski, B. - see Madame de Staël
Jasinski, R. A travers le XVIIème siècle.
  J. Morel, 475:Vol9No17-779
Jason, H. and D. Segal, eds. Patterns in
  Oral Literature.
  K. Dierks, 38:Band100Heft3/4-548
Jaspers, K. Raison et existence.
  C. Roels, 192(EP):Apr-Jun82-242
Jassem, W. and D. Gembiak. Subiektywne
  prawdopodobieństwo wyrazów polskich.
  H. Zgółkowa, 360(LP):Vol25-178
Jastrow, R. The Enchanted Loom.*
  T.C. Holyoke, 42(AR):Spring82-241
Jauss, H.R. Aesthetic Experience and Lit-
  erary Hermeneutics.* (German title:
  Aesthetische Erfahrung und literarische
  Hermeneutik.)
  J.S. Hans, 344:Summer83-117
Jauss, H.R. Alterität und Modernität der
  mittelalterlichen Literatur.*
  F. Goldin, 107(CRCL):Mar82-115
Jauss, H.R. Die nicht mehr schönen Künste.
  G. Kortian, 98:Jan82-72
Jauss, H.R. Toward an Aesthetic of Recep-
  tion.
  D.B. Polan, 290(JAAC):Spring83-354
  M. Sprinker, 400(MLN):Dec82-1205
Jauss, H.R. and E. Köhler, eds. Grundriss
  der Romanischen Literaturen des Mittel-
  alters. (Vol 2)
  W. Rothwell, 208(FS):Oct82-460
Jauss, H.R. and E. Köhler, eds. Grundriss
  der Romanischen Literaturen des Mittel-
  alters. (Vol 4, Pt 1)
  W. Rothwell, 208(FS):Jul82-317
Jay, E., ed. The Evangelical and Oxford
  Movements.
  B. Martin, 617(TLS):13May83-494
Jay, E. The Religion of the Heart.*
  J. Dusinberre, 447(N&Q):Jun81-270
Jayne, S. Library Catalogues of the
  English Renaissance.
  C. Davies, 617(TLS):8Jul83-738
Jazayery, M.A., E.P. Polomé and W. Winter,
  eds. Linguistic and Literary Studies in
  Honor of Archibald A. Hill.* (Vol 3)
  S. Johnson, 353:Vol 19No9/10-1025
Jeal, T. Carnforth's Creation.
  A. Mars-Jones, 617(TLS):2Sep83-940

Jeancolas, J-P. Le Cinéma des Français:
la Ve République 1958-1978.
　　J. Paulhan, 207(FR):Oct82-184
Jeancolas, J-P. 15 ans d'années trente.
　　D. Coward, 617(TLS):18Nov83-1274
Jeanneret, M. La Lettre perdue.*
　　N. Rinsler, 208(FS):Jan82-82
Jeanson, F. Sartre and the Problem of
Morality.*
　　C. Howells, 323:Jan82-85
　　D. Leland, 185:Oct82-151
　　P.S. Nichols, 395(MFS):Winter81/82-659
Jefferies, R. The Life of the Fields.
　　M.F., 617(TLS):18Mar83-279
Jeffers, H.P. Murder Most Irregular.
　　N. Callendar, 441:6Nov83-53
Jeffers, R. "What Odd Expedients" and
Other Poems.* (R.I. Scott, ed)
　　639(VQR):Winter82-26
Jeffers, R.J. and I. Lehiste. Principles
and Methods for Historical Linguistics.*
　　P. Swiggers, 355(LSoc):Aug82-321
Jeffers, T.L. Samuel Butler Revalued.
　　H-P. Breuer, 395(MFS):Summer82-263
　　J. Hunter, 249(HudR):Summer82-348
Jefferson, A. The Nouveau Roman and the
Poetics of Fiction.*
　　B. Morrissette, 131(CL):Winter82-93
　　J. Sturrock, 402(MLR):Jan82-218
Jefferson, G. Edward Garnett.*
　　F. Tuohy, 364:Jun82-80
Jefferson, T. Jefferson's Extracts from
the Gospels. (D.W. Adams, ed)
　　G. Wills, 453(NYRB):24Nov83-48
Jeffrey, F. Jeffrey's Criticism. (P.F.
Morgan, ed)
　　J. Campbell, 617(TLS):18Mar83-271
Jeffrey, I. Photography.
　　P. Galassi, 62:Feb83-2
Jeffrey, J.R. Frontier Women.
　　M.J. Rohrbough, 658:Summer/Autumn82-
　　147
Jeffrey, R. Formal Logic.
　　A. Kerr-Lawson, 154:Dec82-769
Jeffrey, R., ed. People, Princes and
Parmount Power.*
　　R. Rocher, 318(JAOS):Oct-Dec81-471
Jeffrey, R.C., ed. Studies in Inductive
Logic and Probability. (Vol 2)
　　S. Spielman, 486:Jun82-293
Jeffries, A. Among the Living.
　　G. Catalano, 381:Oct81-349
Jehasse, L. Salamine de Chypre.* (Vol 8)
　　J-J. Maffre, 555:Vol56fasc2-307
Jehenson, M.Y. The Golden World of the
Pastoral.
　　L.K. Horowitz, 207(FR):May83-943
Jehmlich, R. Science Fiction.*
　　P. Nusser, 564:Nov81-330
Jekutsch, U. Das Lehrgedicht in der rus-
sischen Literatur des 18. Jahrhunderts.
　　L. Hecht, 574(SEEJ):Winter82-472
Jekyll, G. and E. Mawley. Roses for
English Gardens. (rev by G.S. Thomas)
　　A.P., 617(TLS):21Oct83-1171
"Gertrude Jekyll on Gardening." (P. Hob-
house, ed)
　　A. Paterson, 617(TLS):1Jul83-692
Jelinek, E. Die Klavierspielerin.
　　J. Neves, 617(TLS):7Oct83-1094
Jencks, C. Skyscrapers, Skyprickers, Sky-
cities.
　　D. Gebhard, 576:Dec82-353

Jencks, C., with W. Chaitkin. Architec-
ture Today.*
　　A.L. Huxtable, 453(NYRB):8Dec83-29 and
　　22Dec83-55
Jencks, C. and W. Chaitkin. Current Archi-
tecture.
　　M. Girouard, 362:3Feb83-23
　　A. Saint, 617(TLS):29Apr83-427
Jencks, C.A. The Language of Post-Modern
Architecture. (rev)
　　P. Missac, 98:Oct82-879
Jenkins, D. Baja Oklahoma.
　　639(VQR):Winter82-19
Jenkins, E. The Shadow and the Light.
　　M. Mason, 617(TLS):28Jan83-81
Jenkins, E. The Tortoise and The Hare.
　　M. Furness, 617(TLS):13May83-499
Jenkins, H. - see Shakespeare, W.
Jenkins, I. Social Order and the Limits
of Law.*
　　R.V. Andelson, 396(ModA):Summer/Fall182-
　　436
　　L.H. Carter, 185:Jan83-392
　　J.P.D., 543:Jun82-878
Jenkins, J.H. Printer in Three Republics.
　　L. Milazzo, 584(SWR):Winter82-v
Jenkins, J.J. Understanding Locke.
　　D. Smith, 617(TLS):11Nov83-1239
Jenkins, L. Faulkner and Black-White Rela-
tions.
　　J.V. Hagopian, 27(AL):Mar82-135
　　S.M. Ross, 395(MFS):Winter81/82-729
　　H.M. Ruppersburg, 392:Summer82-342
Jenkins, M.F.O. Artful Eloquence.*
　　T. Thomson, 402(MLR):Apr82-446
　　R. Vallet, 535(RHL):Sep-Dec82-863
Jenkins, P. The Making of a Ruling Class.
　　L. Colley, 617(TLS):22Jul83-785
Jenkins, R. The Cone-Gatherers.
　　J.A.S. Miller, 571(ScLJ):Spring82-22
Jenkins, S. and J. Ditchburn. Images of
Hampstead.
　　D. Bindman, 617(TLS):25Feb83-194
Jenkinson, J.R. - see Persius
Jenkyns, R. The Victorians and Ancient
Greece.*
　　F. Bolton, 189(EA):Jul-Sep82-339
　　R. Lunt, 541(RES):Nov82-492
　　L. Ormond, 90:Aug82-517
　　W.B. Stanford, 402(MLR):Apr82-422
　　M.R. Stopper, 520:Vol126No3-267
Jenner, P.N., ed. Mon-Khmer Studies.*
(Vol 6)
　　G.F. Meier, 682(ZPSK):Band34Heft1-127
Jennings, E. Celebrations and Elegies.*
　　D. Davis, 362:5May83-24
　　M. O'Neill, 493:Sep82-56
Jennings, L.B. and G. Schulz-Behrend, eds.
Vistas and Vectors.
　　C. Dussère, 133:Band15Heft3-261
Jennings, M. The Hardman County Sequence.*
　　W.S. Penn, 577(SHR):Summer82-281
Jenny, M., ed. Das deutsche Kirchenlied.
(Vol 1, Pt 2)
　　J. Janota, 684(ZDA):Band111Heft4-171
Jensen, B. Sigurd Hoel om seg selv.
　　J. de Mylius, 172(Edda):1982/1-64
Jensen, E. and R. Colonial Architecture
in South Australia.*
　　D.L. Johnson, 576:Mar82-65

Johnson, D. The Shadow Knows.
E. Hower, 181:Winter-Spring83-173
Johnson, D.L. and G.P. Landow. Fantastic
Illustration and Design in Britain, 1850-
1930.*
R.L. Patten, 637(VS):Winter82-243
Johnson, E.W. Teaching School.
P. Rothman, 42(AR):Spring82-240
Johnson, F. Election Year.
A. Huth, 362:22and29Dec83-38
Johnson, F. - see "Rockwell Kent: An
Anthology of his Works"
Johnson, G.B. and G.G. Research in Serv-
ice to Society.
R.F. Durden, 639(VQR):Winter82-171
Johnson, J. Maroni de Chypre.*
Y. Calvet, 555:Vol56fasc2-311
Johnson, J. Minor Characters.
J. Atlas, 61:Feb83-100
J. Campbell, 617(TLS):3Jun83-576
H. Chasin, 441:16Jan83-9
442(NY):2May83-131
Johnson, L. The Paintings of Eugène
Delacroix.*
N. Bryson, 208(FS):Apr82-211
P. Joannides, 59:Sep82-348
M. Pointon, 89(BJA):Autumn82-370
J. Russell, 617(TLS):15Jul83-744
Johnson, L.A. Mary Hallock Foote.*
M.F., 189(EA):Jul-Sep82-371
Johnson, M., ed. Philosophical Perspec-
tives on Metaphor.
R. Greene, 400(MLN):Dec82-1222
M.R., 185:Apr83-630
J. Stern, 290(JAAC):Winter82-231
Johnson, M.M. Idea to Image.
K. Andrews, 39:Oct82-279
Johnson, M.M., with J. Forbes and K.
Delaney. Historic Colonial French Dress.
P. Bach, 614:Spring83-20
Johnson, M.M. and N.F. Kallaus. Records
Management. (3rd ed)
T.G. Buter, 14:Fall82-479
Johnson, O.A. Skepticism and Cognitivism.*
R.H. Feldman, 449:Mar82-166
R. McLaughlin, 63:Jun82-177
Johnson, P. Modern Times. (British title:
A History of the Modern World from 1917
to the 1980s.)
N. Annan, 453(NYRB):27Oct83-89
H. Brogan, 362:26May83-19
R. Nisbet, 441:26Jun83-1
S. Spender, 61:Aug83-98
H. Thomas, 617(TLS):8Jul83-718
Johnson, R. Carmen Laforet.
C. Galerstein, 238:Sep82-466
M.E.W. Jones, 86(BHS):Apr82-161
Johnson, R.R. Adjustment to Empire.*
F.J. Bremer, 656(WMQ):Jul82-523
D.C. Wilson, 432(NEQ):Sep82-459
Johnson, S. Oskar Maria Graf.
G. Helmes, 133:Band15Heft1/2-183
Johnson, S. Late Roman Fortifications.
J.J. Wilkes, 617(TLS):19Aug83-877
Johnson, S. The Plays of Samuel Johnson
of Cheshire. (V.C. Rudolph, ed)
566:Autumn82-59
Johnson, T. Swerving Straight.
639(VQR):Winter82-26
Johnson, T.O. Synge: The Medieval and the
Grotesque.
J. Elsom, 617(TLS):25Mar83-295

Johnson, U. Jahrestage 4.
G.P. Butler, 617(TLS):14Oct83-1142
Johnson, U.E. American Prints and Print-
makers.
K.F. Beall, 127:Summer82-179
Johnson, W. Poetry and Speculation of the
Ṛg Veda.
F. Staal, 293(JASt):Feb82-269
G. Turchetto, 485(PE&W):Jul82-356
Johnson, W.L. Ray Bradbury.
N. Khouri, 106:Winter82-407
Johnson, W.R. The Idea of Lyric.
C. Martindale, 617(TLS):17Jun83-628
Johnston, A. Of Earth and Darkness.
J. Huntington, 395(MFS):Summer81-327
Johnston, A.F. and M. Rogerson, eds.
Records of Early English Drama: York.*
S. Lindenbaum, 405(MP):Aug82-80
Johnston, B. Chatterboxes.
P. Black, 362:11Aug83-23
Johnston, B. To the Third Empire.*
E. Sprinchorn, 301(JEGP):Jul82-401
Johnston, C. Choiseul and Talleyrand.
J. Grayson, 617(TLS):28Jan83-86
Johnston, C. Talk About the Last Poet.*
D. McDuff, 565:Vol23No1-58
Johnston, C.M. McMaster University.
(Vols 1 and 2)
P. Axelrod, 529(QQ):Spring82-137
Johnston, E.H. and A. Kunst, eds. The
Dialectical Method of Nāgārjuna (Vigra-
havyāvartinī). (K. Bhattacharya, trans)
P. Granoff, 293(JASt):Feb82-378
Johnston, G. Taking a Grip.
D. Barbour, 648(WCR):Jun82-33
Johnston, J. Mother Bound.
H. Chasin, 441:10Apr83-12
Johnston, M. The Collected Short Stories
of Mary Johnston. (A. and H.C. Wood-
bridge, eds)
639(VQR):Autumn82-132
Johnston, P.A. Vergil's Agricultural
Golden Age.*
K.W. Gransden, 313:Vol72-207
M.C.J. Putnam, 122:Apr82-171
Johnston, S. and C. Phillipson, eds.
Older Learners.
D.R. Harris, 324:Nov83-778
Johnston, S. and A. Tennant, eds. The
Picnic Papers.
C. Blackwood, 617(TLS):3Jun83-581
Johnstone, K. IMPRO.
A. Stockwell, 108:Spring82-210
Johnstone, P.T. Topos Theory.
R. Seely, 316:Jun82-448
Johnstone, R. The Will to Believe.*
P. Martin, 364:Aug/Sep82-137
L.M. Schwerdt, 395(MFS):Winter82/83-
651
Johnstone, W. Points in Time.
J. Burr, 39:Sep82-198
Jokinen, U. Les Relatifs en moyen fran-
çais.
P. Ménard, 545(RPh):May82-662
Jolley, E. The Travelling Entertainer.
E. Webby, 381:Jul81-200
Jolly, R. The Red and Green Life Machine.
G. Wheatcroft, 617(TLS):13May83-490
Jomaron, J. Georges Pitoëff metteur en
scène.
J-J. Roubine, 535(RHL):Mar-Apr82-313

184

Jones-Davies, M., ed. La Magie et ses langages.
  G. Bullough, 189(EA):Oct-Dec82-456
Jones-Davies, M-T. Ben Jonson.
  G. Bullough, 189(EA):Oct-Dec82-461
Jones-Davies, M.T., ed. Monstres et prodiges au temps de la Renaissance.
  M. Hugues, 549(RLC):Jul-Sep82-383
Jones-Davies, M.T. Victimes et rebelles.
  G. Bullough, 189(EA):Oct-Dec82-456
  V.F. Stern, 551(RenQ):Winter81-621
de Jonge, J.W., ed. Nāgārjuna: Mūlamadhyamakakārikāḥ.
  D.S. Ruegg, 259(IIJ):Jul80-247
de Jonge, A. The Life and Times of Grigorii Rasputin.*
  I. Vinogradoff, 617(TLS):14Jan83-31
de Jonge, C. De Irenische Ecclesiologie van Franciscus Junius (1545-1602).
  K. Taylor, 551(RenQ):Winter81-579
de Jong, P. Philological and Historical Commentary on Ammianus Marcellinus.* (Bks 17 and 18)
  G.J.M. Bartelink, 394:Vol35fasc1/2-181
Jongen, R., ed. La Métaphore.
  M. Evans, 307:Apr82-68
Jongen, R. Phonologie der Moresneter Mundart. Rheinische Akzentuierung und sonstige prosodische Erscheinungen.
  D. Stellmacher, 685(ZDL):3/1981-384
Jonin, P. - see "La Chanson de Roland"
Jönsjö, J. Studies on Middle English Nicknames.* (Vol 1)
  C. Clark, 179(ES):Apr82-168
  B. Cottle, 541(RES):Feb82-68
Jonson, B. Ben Jonson's Plays and Masques.* (R.M. Adams, ed)
  J. Creaser, 402(MLR):Jul82-699
Jonsson, H. The Laryngeal Theory.
  F.O. Lindeman, 260(IF):Band86-325
Joost, U. and A. Schöne - see Lichtenberg, G.C.
Joppich-Hagemann, U. and U. Korth. Untersuchungen zu Wortfamilien der Romania Germanica.
  M. Pfister, 72:Band218Heft1-197
Jordan, B. Servants of the Gods.
  A.L. Boegehold, 122:Jul82-263
  N.J. Richardson, 303(JoHS):Vol 102-268
Jordan, D.P. The King's Trial.
  A.J. Bingham, 399(MLJ):Spring82-91
  H. Cohen, 207(FR):Dec82-364
  A. Williams, 173(ECS):Spring82-346
Jordan, J. Civil Wars.
  E. Hower, 181:Spring-Summer83-281
Jordan, J. Passion.
  M.J. Boyd, 459:Summer/Winter81-226
Jordan, M.V. De ta Soeur, Sara Riel.*
  S.P. Knutson, 102(CanL):Winter81-151
Jordan, N. The Dream of a Beast.
  P. Keegan, 617(TLS):11Nov83-1255
  J. Mellors, 362:13Oct83-31
Jordan, T. Cowgirls.
  L. Milazzo, 584(SWR):Autumn82-vi
Jordan, W.C. Louis IX and the Challenge of the Crusade.*
  A.J. Forey, 161(DUJ):Jun82-280
Jordan, W.K. The Fizz Inside.
  A. Morvan, 189(EA):Oct-Dec82-440
Jordan-Horstmann, M. Sadani.
  R.K. Barz, 259(IIJ):Apr82-139
Jordens, A-M. The Stenhouse Circle.*
  B. Kiernan, 541(RES):Nov82-494

Jorg, C.J.A. Porcelain and the Dutch China Trade.
  C.R. Boxer, 617(TLS):28Jan83-89
Jorgens, E.B. The Well-Tun'd Word.
  C.S. Brown, 219(GaR):Summer82-449
  R.F., 391:May82-51
Jørgensen, J.C. Den sande kunst.
  M. Brøndsted, 52:Band16Heft3-326
  V. Greene-Gantzberg, 563(SS):Winter82-89
Jørgensen, P. Die dithmarsische Mundart von Klaus Groths "Quickborn."
  B.J. Koekkoek, 221(GQ):Nov82-582
Jørgensen, P.A., ed. Vort modersmål er ...
  C. Henriksen, 563(SS):Winter82-76
Jose, F.S. My Brother, My Executioner.
  B.J. Kerkvliet, 293(JASt):Feb82-417
Jose, N. The Possession of Amber.
  E. Webby, 381:Jul81-200
Joseph, B. A Shakespeare Workbook.
  W.J. Meserve, 130:Fal182-279
Joseph, G.M. Revolution from Without.
  J.M. Hart, 263(RIB):Vol132No3/4-375
Joseph, J. Beyond Descartes.
  T. Dooley, 617(TLS):27May83-549
Josephson, D.S. John Taverner.
  M. Smith, 607:Mar82-38
Josephus. Flavius Josèphe, "Guerre des Juifs." (Vol 2, Bks 2 and 3) (A. Pelletier, ed and trans)
  R.W., 555:Vol55fasc2-351
Josephy, A.M., Jr. Now That the Buffalo's Gone.
  W. Least Heat Moon, 441:8May83-14
  D.P. McAllester, 469:Vol8No3-106
Joshi, A.K., B.L. Webber and I.A. Sag, eds. Elements of Discourse Understanding.
  B. MacWhinney, 350:Mar83-214
Joshi, L. - see "Dharmakośa, Rājanītikāṇḍa"
Joshi, S.D. - see Kiparsky, P.
Joshi, S.D. and J.A.F. Roodbergen - see "Patañjali's Vyākaraṇa-Mahābhāṣya, Anabhihitāhnika (P.2.3.1-2.3.17)"
Joshi, S.D. and J.A.F. Roodbergen - see "Patañjali's Vyākaraṇa-Mahābhāṣya, Vibhaktyāhnika (P. 2.3.18 - 2.3.45)"
Josipovici, G. Writing and the Body.
  D. Donoghue, 617(TLS):7Jan83-6
Jöst, E., ed. Die Historien des Neithart Fuchs.
  F.V. Spechtler, 602:Vol 13No2-333
Josten, D. Sprachvorbild und Sprachnorm im Urteil des 16. und 17. Jahrhunderts.
  J. Schildt, 682(ZPSK):Band34Heft5-635
Jouanna, A. and others - see Brutus, É.J.
Jouary, J-P. Comprendre les illusions.
  M. Adam, 542:Oct-Dec82-673
Joubert, J. The Notebooks of Joseph Joubert. (P. Auster, ed and trans)
  P. Zaleski, 469:Vol8No4-108
Joubert, L. Treatise on Laughter. (G.D. de Rocher, ed and trans)
  J.L. Pallister, 568(SCN):Spring-Summer82-22
Joukovsky, F. - see Forcadel, É.
"Journées Bossuet: La Prédication au XVIIe siècle."
  J. Hennequin, 535(RHL):May-Jun82-473
"The Journey to the West."* (Vols 1, 2 and 4) (A.C. Yu, ed and trans)
  P. Jordan-Smith, 469:Vol8No3-122
  D. Lattimore, 441:6Mar83-7

186

"The Journey to the West." (Vol 3) (A.C. Yu, ed and trans)
  R.E. Hegel, 293(JASt):Nov81-129
  P. Jordan-Smith, 469:Vol8No3-122
  D. Lattimore, 441:6Mar83-7
Joyce, D. Stone Wear [together with] Tihanya, E. A Sequence of the Blood.
  R.D. MacKenzie, 628(UWR):Spring-Summer83-86
Joyce, J. Finnegans Wake. (L. Schenoni, trans)
  C. del Greco Lobner, 329(JJQ):Winter83-246
Joyce, J. Le gesta di Stephen. (C. Linati, G. Melchiori and G. Monicelli, trans; G. Melchiori, ed)
  C. del Greco Lobner, 329(JJQ):Spring82-356
Joyce, J. The James Joyce Archive. (M. Groden and others, eds)
  P.F. Herring, 329(JJQ):Fall81-85
Joyce, J. Lettres III. (R. Ellmann, ed; M. Tadié, trans)
  G. Quinsat, 450(NRF):Jan82-144
Joyce, P. Work, Society and Politics.
  M. Charlot, 189(EA):Apr-Jun82-223
  S. Meacham, 637(VS):Autumn81-82
Judd, A. A Breed of Heroes.
  W. Scammell, 364:Jun82-95
Judd, D. and P. Slinn. The Evolution of the Modern Commonwealth, 1902-80.
  H.S. Ferns, 617(TLS):7Jan83-16
Judge, A. and F.G. Healey. A Reference Grammar of Modern French.
  P. Rickard, 617(TLS):30Dec83-1467
Judge, R. The Jack in the Green.
  L. Haring, 292(JAF):Apr-Jun82-218
Judson, J. North of Athens.
  M. Lammon, 436(NewL):Winter82/83-110
Judy, S. and S.J. An Introduction to the Teaching of Writing.
  E. McKee, 399(MLJ):Spring82-70
Juhl, M. and B.H. Jørgensen. Dianas Haevn.
  W. Mishler, 563(SS):Summer82-273
Juhl, P.D. Interpretation.*
  R.P. Bilan, 627(UTQ):Fall81-102
  A. Ellis, 89(BJA):Spring82-181
  D.H. Hirsch, 569(SR):Winter82-119
  C. Norris, 402(MLR):Jan82-130
  S.H. Olsen, 262:Jun82-263
  C.J. Radford, 518:Apr82-118
  M. Warner, 478:Oct82-172
Juin, H. Victor Hugo, 1802-1843.* (Vol 1)
  F. Bassan, 446(NCFS):Fall-Winter82/83-189
Juin, H. - see de Maupassant, G.
Julia, D. Les Trois Couleurs du Tableau Noir, la Révolution.
  H. Cronel, 450(NRF):Feb82-149
Julian. Giuliano Imperatore, "Misopogon."* (G. Prato and D. Micalella, eds and trans)
  J. Bouffartigue, 555:Vol55fasc2-353
Juliano, A. Treasures of China.
  E. Capon, 463:Autumn82-284
Junankar, N.S. Gautama: The Nyāya Philosophy.*
  L. Davis, 318(JAOS):Apr-Jun81-245
Jung, H. Die Pastorale.
  F.W. Sternfeld, 410(M&L):Jul/Oct81-364
Jung, M.L. Reflections on the English Progressive.
  J. Pauchard, 189(EA):Jul-Sep82-317

Jungandreas, W. Zur Geschichte des Moselromanischen.
  C. Schmitt, 553(RLiR):Jul-Dec82-478
Junghare, I.Y. Topics in Pāli Historical Phonology.*
  G. Cardona, 660(Word):Dec82-272
  M.C. Shapiro, 293(JASt):May82-619
Jungraithmayr, H., ed. Struktur und Wandel afrikanischer Sprachen.
  S. Brauner, 682(ZPSK):Band34Heft6-760
Junius Brutus, É. - see under Brutus, É.J.
Junji, K. - see under Kinoshita Junji
Junnarkar, P.B. An Introduction to Pāṇini.* (Bk 1)
  R. Rocher, 318(JAOS):Oct-Dec81-468
  R.N. Sharma, 259(IIJ):Jan80-56
Junor, P. Margaret Thatcher.
  J. Wells, 617(TLS):2Dec83-1340
Junquera, J.J., P. Thornton and T. Talbot Rice. Il mobile.
  M. Paz Aguiló, 48:Jul-Sep82-321
Junwen, L. - see under Liu Junwen
Jürgens-Lochthove, K. Heinrich Wittenwilers "Ring" im Kontext hochhöfischer Epik.
  D.H. Green, 402(MLR):Apr82-484
Jurgensen, M. Ingeborg Bachmann.
  A. Obermayer, 564:Sep82-230
Jurgensen, M. Thomas Bernhard.
  A. Obermayer, 564:Nov82-304
Jurgensen, M. Erzählformen des fiktionalen Ich.
  W. Koepke, 301(JEGP):Jul82-394
  J.W. Rohlfs, 402(MLR):Jan82-247
Jurgensen, M. Das fiktionale Ich.*
  D. Barnouw, 221(GQ):Jan82-134
  F. Voit, 406:Winter82-502
  R. Whitinger, 564:Nov82-305
Jurgensen, M., ed. Handke.*
  H.P. Braendlin, 406:Fall82-373
Justus, J.H. The Achievement of Robert Penn Warren.
  C. Bohner, 395(MFS):Winter82/83-680
  J.A. Grimshaw, Jr., 578:Spring83-112
  F.C. Watkins, 401(MLQ):Jun82-193
  T.D. Young, 392:Winter81/82-41
  295(JML):Dec82-547
Juvenal. Sixteen Satires Upon the Ancient Harlot. (S. Robinson, trans)
  C. Martindale, 617(TLS):14Oct83-1120
Juxon, J. Lewis and Lewis.
  E.S. Turner, 362:7Jul83-27

Kaarsted, T. Georg Brandes.
  G.S. Argetsinger, 563(SS):Summer82-266
Kabell, A. Metrische Studien I.
  A. Quak, 684(ZDA):Band111Heft3-113
Kabir. The Bījak of Kabir. (L. Hess, ed and trans)
  J.S. Hawley, 469:Vol8No3-95
Kabutogi Shōkō. Stein Pelliot shūshū Tonkō Hokkekyo mokuroku. Tonkō mokuroku taishō teihon Hokkekyō hakkan Kasuga-ban Tōshōdaijizō.
  J.W. de Jong, 259(IIJ):Oct80-316
Kádár, L. Our Changing Planet, the Earth. (Vol 1)
  G. Lachenaud, 555:Vol56fasc1-133
Kádár, Z. Survivals of Greek Zoological Illuminations in Byzantine Manuscripts.*
  W.K. Kraak, 394:Vol35fasc3/4-395

Kadaré, I. Le Pont aux trois arches.
    L. Kovacs, 450(NRF):Jul-Aug82-202
Kadish, A. The Oxford Economists in the
Late Nineteenth Century.
    D. Winch, 617(TLS):25Feb83-196
Kaelin, E.F. The Unhappy Consciousness.
    E. Sellin, 290(JAAC):Spring83-350
Kaës, R. L'idéologie.
    L. Millet, 192(EP):Oct-Dec82-499
Kaes, R. and others. Crise, rupture et
dépassement.
    L. Millet, 192(EP):Jul-Sep82-361
Kafka, F. The Complete Novels. The Com-
plete Short Stories. (N.N. Glatzer, ed)
Stories 1904-1924. (J.A. Underwood,
trans) Letters to Milena.
    S.S. Prawer, 617(TLS):14Oct83-1127
Kafka, F. Letters to Ottla and the Fam-
ily.* (N.N. Glatzer, ed)
    C. Koelb, 395(MFS):Winter82/83-694
Kafka, F. Das Schloss. (M. Pasley, ed)
Der Verschollene. (J. Schillemeit, ed)
    R. Robertson, 617(TLS):14Oct83-1129
Kafker, F.A., ed. Notable Encyclopedias
of the Seventeenth and Eighteenth Cen-
turies.
    J. Lough, 83:Spring82-158
Kagan, D. The Peace of Nicias and the
Sicilian Expedition.*
    R. Sealey, 24:Fall82-338
Kahn, C. Man's Estate.
    A. Kirsch, 570(SQ):Summer82-252
Kahn, C.H., ed and trans. The Art and
Thought of Heraclitus.*
    J. Barnes, 393(Mind):Jan82-121
    J. Bernhardt, 319:Oct82-425
Kahn, H. The Coming Boom.*
    J. Vaizey, 362:10Feb83-25
Kahn, J. Imperial San Francisco.
    H.L. Horowitz, 658:Summer/Autumn82-156
Kahneman, D., P. Slovic and A. Tversky,
eds. Judgment under Uncertainty.
    A. Margalit, 617(TLS):26Aug83-914
Kahsnitz, R. Der Werdener Psalter in
Berlin Ms. theol. lat. fol. 358.
    W. Cahn, 54:Jun82-328
    R. Deshman, 589:Jan82-140
Kaimio, J. The Romans and the Greek Lan-
guage.*
    P. Flobert, 555:Vol56fasc1-146
    M.D. MacLeod, 123:Vol32No2-216
Kainz, H.P. The Unbinding of Prometheus.
    W.L.M., 543:Dec81-392
Kaiser, D.H. The Growth of the Law in
Medieval Russia.
    D.B. Miller, 589:Apr82-386
    D.C. Waugh, 104(CASS):Spring82-153
Kaiser, E. Strukturen der Frage im Franzö-
sischen.
    A. Greive, 72:Band218Heft2-462
    R. Martin, 553(RLiR):Jul-Dec82-471
Kaiser, E., ed. Gesellschaftliche Sin-
nangebote mittelalterlicher Literatur.
    J.A. Davidson, 221(GQ):Mar82-238
    S.L. Wailes, 589:Jul82-623
Kaiser, G. Georg Kaiser: Briefe. (G.M.
Valk, ed)
    W. Paulsen, 301(JEGP):Apr82-296
Kaiser, G.R. Einführung in die Ver-
gleichende Literaturwissenschaft.*
    W.W. Holdheim, 221(GQ):Mar82-221
    U. Schulz-Buschhaus, 52:Band16Heft3-305
    U. Weisstein, 133:Band15Heft1/2-137

Kajanto, I. Classical and Christian.
    J.G. Bernstein, 551(RenQ):Autumn81-413
Kajencki, F.C. Star on Many a Battlefield.
    J.S. Pula, 497(PolR):Vol27No1/2-174
Kajino, K. La création chez Stendhal et
chez Prosper Mérimée.
    V.D.L., 605(SC):15Oct82-86
Kakar, S. Shamans, Mystics and Doctors.
    R. Dinnage, 453(NYRB):17Feb83-15
Kalbouss, G. Russian Culture. (2nd ed)
    T.E. Little, 402(MLR):Oct82-1003
    L. Visson, 574(SEEJ):Summer82-252
Kalcher, J. Perspektiven des Lebens in
der Dramatik um 1900.
    A. Arnold, 221(GQ):May82-434
Kalectaca, M. Lessons in Hopi. (R.W.
Langacker, ed)
    D.L. Shaul, 269(IJAL):Jan82-105
Kalinowski, G. L'impossible métaphysique.
    M. Adam, 542:Oct-Dec82-674
Kalish, S.S. Oriental Rugs in Needlepoint.
    P. Bach, 614:Spring83-22
Kalland, A. Shingū.
    E. Norbeck, 407(MN):Spring82-136
Kallir, J. The Folk Art Tradition.
    J.V. Turano, 16:Autumn82-88
Kallir, J. Gustav Klimt and Egon Schiele.
    N. Powell, 39:Apr82-294
Kallmann, H., G. Potvin and K. Winters,
eds. Encyclopedia of Music in Canada.
    T. Hathaway, 529(QQ):Autumn82-514
    J. Lawrence, 99:Aug82-37
    C. Morey, 627(UTQ):Summer82-501
    W.N., 102(CanL):Summer82-172
Kalmár, I. Case and Context in Inuktitut
(Eskimo).
    M.D. Fortescue, 269(IJAL):Jan82-91
Kalnins, M. - see Lawrence, D.H.
Kaluza, H. The Use of Articles in Contem-
porary English.
    J.P., 189(EA):Jul-Sep82-370
Kalverkämper, H. Orientierung zur Textlin-
guistik.
    B.J. Koekkoek, 221(GQ):Mar82-235
    P. Wodak, 133:Band15Heft1/2-135
Kamachi, N., J.K. Fairbank and C. Ichiko.
Japanese Studies of Modern China Since
1953.
    P. Berton, 318(JAOS):Oct-Dec81-431
Kamata, S. Japan in the Passing Lane. (T.
Akimoto, ed and trans)
    S. Lohr, 441:6Mar83-12
    K. Thurley, 617(TLS):1Jul83-695
Kamen, H. Spain in the Later Seventeenth
Century, 1665-1700.
    J. Fisher, 86(BHS):Oct82-343
Kamen, R.H. British and Irish Architec-
tural History.
    H. Colvin, 46:Mar82-61
    J.S. Curl, 324:Apr83-294
Kamenka, E., R. Brown and A.E-S. Tay, eds.
Law and Society.
    R.F. Khan, 63:Mar82-100
Kamenka, E. and A.E-S. Tay, eds. Human
Rights.
    R.F. Khan, 63:Mar82-100
Kamenka, E. and A.E-S. Tay, eds. Justice.*
    A. Ryan, 393(Mind):Apr82-308
Kamerbeek, J.C. The Plays of Socrates.*
(Vol 6: The Philoctetes.)
    A.L. Brown, 303(JoHS):Vol 102-246
Kaminskaya, D. Final Judgment.
    L. Schapiro, 617(TLS):11Nov83-1251

Karlinger, F. and E. Laserer, eds. Baskische Märchen.
  H-J. Uther, 196:Band23Heft3/4-332
Karlinsky, S. - see Nabokov, V. and E. Wilson
Karlinsky, S. - see Zlobin, V.
Karlsson, K.E. Syntax and Affixation.
  R. de Gorog, 660(Word):Dec81-258
Karmiloff-Smith, A. A Functional Approach to Child Language.
  R. Fink, 320(CJL):Spring82-77
Karnein, A., ed. Salman und Morolf.*
  W. Schröder, 684(ZDA):Band111Heft2-60
Karnezē, I.É. Omērika.
  P. Monteil, 555:Vol56fasc1-122
Karnow, S. Vietnam.
  D. Pike, 441:16Oct83-9
Karow, O. and I. Hilgers-Hesse. Indonesisch-Deutsches Wörterbuch/Kamus Bahasa Indonesia-Djerman. (2nd ed)
  J.M. Echols, 318(JAOS):Oct-Dec81-495
Karp, I. and C.S. Bird, eds. Explorations in African Systems of Thought.
  J. Middleton, 69:Vol52No4-101
Karpiński, J. Count-Down.*
  M. Malia, 453(NYRB):29Sep83-18
Karpinski, M. La Soif du Domaine.
  C. Dis, 450(NRF):Oct82-125
Karrer, W. and E. Kreutzer. Daten der englischen und amerikanischen Literatur von 1700 bis 1890.
  W. Bies, 52:Band16Heft3-317
Kars, H. Le Portrait chez Marivaux.
  C. Bonfils, 535(RHL):Sep-Dec82-904
  G.E. Rodmell, 402(MLR):Jul82-725
Karsh, Y. Karsh: A Fifty-Year Retrospective.
  J. Maslin, 441:4Dec83-12
Karstedt, P. Ideologie.
  J-M. Gabaude and E. Harmat, 542:Jan-Mar82-67
Karstien, H. Infixe im Indogermanischen.
  E. Neu, 260(IF):Band86-335
Kartiganer, D.M. The Fragile Thread.*
  J. Griffin, 106:Fall82-253
Kartomi, M.J., ed. Five Essays on the Indonesian Arts.
  D.L. Harwood, 187:Jan83-133
Kartun, D. Beaver to Fox.
  T.J. Binyon, 617(TLS):23Sep83-1011
"Kartvelur enata st'rukt'uris sak'itxebi."
  G.F. Meier, 682(ZPSK):Band34Heft1-123
Kasatkina, L.L., E.V. Nemčenko and T.J. Stroganovoj, eds. Russkie govory.
  V. Živov, 559:Nov81-151
Kaschnitz, M.L. Selected Later Poems of Marie Luise Kaschnitz.*
  K. Weissenberger, 133:Band15Heft3-285
Kasell, W. Marcel Proust and the Strategy of Reading.*
  H. Nitzberg, 207(FR):Feb83-490
  J.E. Rivers, 210(FrF):Jan82-86
Käsermann, M-L. Spracherwerb und Interaktion.
  K. Meng, 682(ZPSK):Band35Heft5-588
Kashner, R. Bed Rest.
  W.H. Pritchard, 249(HudR):Spring82-159
Käsler, D., ed. Klassiker des soziologischen Denkens. (Vol 2)
  B. Schlöder, 53(AGP):Band64Heft2-214
Kasparek, J.L. Molière's "Tartuffe" and the Traditions of Roman Satire.*
  R. Guichemerre, 535(RHL):May-Jun82-470

Kasprzyk, K. - see Des Périers, B.
Kassay, J. The Book of Shaker Furniture.*
  P.H. Hammell, 658:Summer/Autumn82-151
"The John Philip Kassebaum Collection." (Vol 1)
  G. Wills, 39:Apr82-297
Kassler, J. Gay Men's Health.
  J. Lieberson, 453(NYRB):18Aug83-17
Kassler, J.C. The Science of Music in Britain, 1714-1830.*
  P. le Huray, 410(M&L):Jan/Apr82-128
Kästner, H. Harfe und Schwert.
  G.P. Knapp, 221(GQ):Nov82-588
Kasulis, T.P. Zen Action/Zen Person.
  C. Davis, 529(QQ):Winter82-921
  S. Heine, 485(PE&W):Jul82-343
Katai, T. The Quilt and Other Stories by Tayama Katai.* (K.G. Henshall, ed and trans)
  Cheng Lok Chua, 573(SSF):Spring82-179
  R.L. Danly, 293(JASt):May82-594
  P.I. Lyons, 407(MN):Autumn82-403
Katerinov, K. and M.C. Borioski Katerinov. Lingua e Vita d'Italia.
  L. Farna, 399(MLJ):Winter82-429
Katkov, N. Blood and Orchids.
  P. van Rjndt, 441:11Sep83-16
Katona, A.B. Mihály Vitéz Csokonai.*
  G. Gömöri, 402(MLR):Jan82-253
Katsimanis, K.S. Étude sur le rapport entre le Beau et le Bien chez Platon.
  P. Louis, 555:Vol56fasc1-134
Katsouris, A.G. Tragic Patterns in Menander.
  S.M. Goldberg, 121(CJ):Dec82/Jan83-173
Kattan, N. Le Sable de l'ile.
  C.F. Coates, 207(FR):Oct82-172
Katz, B. Herbert Marcuse and the Art of Liberation.
  J.J., 185:Jul83-832
Katz, D.S. Philo-Semitism and the Readmission of the Jews to England 1603-1655.*
  R.H. Popkin, 319:Oct83-568
Katz, J. Artists in Exile.
  B. Shulgasser, 441:5Jun83-18
Katz, J. From Prejudice to Destruction.*
  S.P., 185:Jan83-440
Katz, J.J. Language and Other Abstract Objects.*
  K. Allan, 350:Sep83-678
Katz, N., ed. Buddhist and Western Philosophy.
  A. Reix, 542:Oct-Dec82-675
Katz, R. Boiling Energy.
  A. Barnard, 617(TLS):25Mar83-302
  E.N. Wilmsen, 469:Vol8No1-124
Katz, S. The Hollow Peace.
  P.E. Goldman, 390:May82-61
Katzenstein, M.F. Ethnicity and Equality.
  W.K. Andersen, 293(JASt):Feb82-385
Kauffman, C.J. Faith and Fraternalism.
  L.J. Daly, 377:Nov82-188
Kauffmann, C.M. Catalogue of Paintings in the Wellington Museum.
  E. Waterhouse, 90:Dec82-763
Kauffmann, J. Aspects d'André Maurois biographe.
  J. Kolbert, 207(FR):Dec82-329
Kaufman, D. and M. Horn. A Liberation Album.
  L. McIntyre, 298:Winter82/83-130

190

Kaufmann, W. Discovering the Mind.*
(Vols 1-3)
  B-A. Scharfstein, 319:Apr83-244
Kaufmann, Y. History of the Religion of
Israel. (Vol 4)
  J.M. Miller, 318(JAOS):Oct-Dec81-446
Kaulbach, F. Das Prinzip Handlung in der
Philosophie Kants.
  K. Konhardt, 687:Jan-Mar81-150
Kaussen, W. Spaltungen.
  H.F. Pfanner, 221(GQ):Nov82-613
Kautsky, J.H. The Politics of Aristocra-
tic Empires.
  E. Kedourie, 617(TLS):9Dec83-1383
Kavanagh, J.R. and R.L. Venezky, eds.
Orthography, Reading, and Dyslexia.
  P.G. Patel, 350:Sep83-636
Kavanagh, P., ed. The Members of the
Orchestra.
  D. Haskell, 581:Sep82-348
Kavanagh, P.J. Selected Poems.*
  M. O'Neill, 493:Sep82-56
Kavanagh, P.J. - see Gurney, I.
Kawin, B.F. The Mind of the Novel.
  I. Salusinszky, 617(TLS):1Jul83-707
Kawoya, V.F.K. Yiga Kiswahili — Jifunze
Luganda.
  K. Legère, 682(ZPSK):Band34Heft1-124
Kay, B., ed. Odyssey.
  D. Buchan, 571(ScLJ):Winter82-97
Kay, G. and J. Mott. Political Order and
the Law of Labour.
  C. Crouch, 617(TLS):25Nov83-1328
Kay, R. Dante's Swift and Strong.*
  L. Baldassaro, 276:Spring82-55
Kaye, K. The Mental and Social Life of
Babies.
  J. Bruner, 453(NYRB):27Oct83-84
Kaye, M.M. Death in Zanzibar.
  T.J. Binyon, 617(TLS):19Aug83-890
Kaye, M.M. Trade Wind.
  639(VQR):Winter82-19
Kaye-Smith, S. Joanna Godden. Susan
Spray.
  P. Craig, 617(TLS):29Jul83-820
Kazan, E. The Anatolian.*
  S.S. Prawer, 617(TLS):12Aug83-854
Kazantzakis, N. The Suffering God.*
  J. Graham, 152(UDQ):Spring81-119
Kea, R.A. Settlements, Trade, and Poli-
ties in the Seventeenth-Century Gold
Coast.
  J.D. Fage, 617(TLS):15Apr83-386
Kean, B.W. All the Empty Palaces.
  J. Milner, 617(TLS):21Oct83-1148
  H. Robinson, 441:28Aug83-12
Keane, D. Tape Music Composition.
  R.D. Morris, 308:Fall82-331
Keane, M. Time After Time.
  J. Grant, 617(TLS):30Sep83-1059
Keane, P.J. A Wild Civility.
  P. Hobsbaum, 677(YES):Vol 12-346
Kearney, P. A History of Erotic Litera-
ture.
  A. Ross, 364:Feb83-3
Kearney, P.J., comp. The Private Case.
  S. Matusak, 517(PBSA):Vol76No2-234
Kearney, R. and J.S. O'Leary, eds. Heideg-
ger et la question de Dieu.
  192(EP):Jul-Sep81-353
Kearns, E.J. Ideas in Seventeenth-Century
France.*
  F. Assaf, 475:No16Pt2-386

Kearns, G. Guide to Ezra Pound's "Se-
lected Cantos."*
  W. Harmon, 569(SR):Spring82-279
  L. Surette, 408:Jun82-60
Kearns, K.C. Georgian Dublin.
  M. Craig, 617(TLS):12Aug83-848
  S. Gardiner, 362:11Aug83-22
Kearon, T.P. and M.A. di Lorenzo-Kearon.
Medical Spanish.
  J. Shreve, 399(MLJ):Summer82-228
Keat, R.N. The Politics of Social Theory.
  J. Daly, 518:Oct82-254
  J.M.G., 185:Jan83-430
Keates, J. Allegro Postillions.
  T.D. White, 617(TLS):9Dec83-1372
Keaton, D. and M. Heiferman. Still Life.
  A. Grundberg, 441:4Dec83-14
Keats, J. The Poems of John Keats. (J.
Stillinger, ed)
  J. Barnard, 591(SIR):Fall82-541
Keaveney, A. Sulla.
  R. Seager, 617(TLS):18Nov83-1285
Keay, D. Royal Pursuit.
  J. Grigg, 617(TLS):18Nov83-1293
Keay, J. Eccentric Travellers.*
  A. Sutherland, 362:3Feb83-26
Keay, J. India Discovered.
  M. Archer, 39:Mar82-212
Keble Martin, W. The New Concise British
Flora. (D.H. Kent, ed)
  R. O'Hanlon, 617(TLS):25Feb83-192
Kebric, R.B. In the Shadow of Macedon:
Duris of Samos.*
  R.W., 555:Vol55fasc2-345
Keddie, N. and others, eds. Modern Iran.
  A.H.H. Abidi, 273(IC):Jan82-77
Kedourie, E. Islam in the Modern World
and Other Studies.*
  N. Rejwan, 390:Oct82-51
Keeble, B. - see Raine, K.
Keeble, J. Yellowfish.*
  C. Kizer, 448:Vol20No1-149
Keefer, S.L. The Old English Metrical
Psalter.*
  J. Hill, 72:Band218Heft2-420
Keegan, J. and J. Darracott. The Nature
of War.
  639(VQR):Winter82-27
Keeler, M.F., ed. Sir Francis Drake's
West Indian Voyage, 1585-86.*
  D.B. Quinn, 551(RenQ):Winter82-639
Keeler, M.F., M.J. Cole and W.B. Bidwell,
eds. Proceedings in Parliament 1628.
(Vols 5 and 6)
  G.R. Elton, 617(TLS):16Sep83-991
Keeley, E. and P. Sherrard - see Elytis, O.
Keene, D. Yokomitsu Riichi, Modernist.*
  N.M. Lippit, 293(JASt):Nov81-137
Keene, M. Mrs. Donald. (A.T. Ellis, ed)
  A. Duchêne, 617(TLS):?Dec83 1343
Keener, F.M. The Chain of Becoming.
  J.H. Mason, 617(TLS):5Aug83-841
Kehoe, A. North American Indians.
  H. Adams, 529(QQ):Winter82-889
Keightley, D.N. The Origins of Chinese
Civilization.
  W. Watson, 617(TLS):24Jun83-669
Keil, C. Tiv Song.*
  P. Richards, 69:Vol152No1-97
Keillor, G. Happy to Be Here.*
  639(VQR):Summer82-96
Keisler, H.J. - see Robinson, A.

Keith, W.J. Epic Fiction.*
  B.N.S. Gooch, 102(CanL):Autumn82-131
  J. Kertzer, 627(UTQ):Summer82-464
Keith, W.J. The Poetry of Nature.*
  P.J. Casagrande, 301(JEGP):Jan82-122
  A. McWhir, 49:Apr82-92
  L. Metzger, 191(ELN):Dec81-148
  W.J.B. Owen, 178:Dec82-507
Keith, W.J., ed. A Voice in the Land.
  J. Kertzer, 627(UTQ):Summer82-464
  K.P. Stich, 102(CanL):Autumn82-146
Keith, W.J. and B.Z. Shek, eds. The Arts
in Canada: The Last Fifty Years.*
  R. Mane, 189(EA):Jul-Sep82-354
Keitner, W. Ralph Gustafson.
  J. Ferns, 677(YES):Vol 12-359
Kekes, J. The Nature of Philosophy.*
  M. Adam, 542:Oct-Dec82-676
  N.C., 543:Jun82-879
  D.J. Shaw, 518:Jan82-28
Keller, A. Scandalous Lady.
  639(VQR):Winter82-17
Keller, E.F. A Feeling for the Organism.
  M.W. Rossiter, 441:2Oct83-11
Keller, G. Stories. (F.G. Ryder, ed)
  J. Agee, 441:13Feb83-27
Keller, H. and M. Cosman. Stravinsky:
Seen and Heard.*
  G. Abraham, 617(TLS):17Jun83-635
  M. Hayes, 607:Jun82-34
Keller, J.E. Pious Brief Narrative in
Medieval Castilian and Galician Verse
from Berceo to Alfonso X.
  R. Di Franco, 552(REH):Jan82-133
Keller, K. The Only Kangaroo Among the
Beauty.*
  A. Gibson, 175:Spring82-68
  G. Monteiro, 651(WHR):Autumn82-282
  A.M. Woodlief, 577(SHR):Spring82-168
Keller, O. Döblins Montageroman als Epos
der Moderne.
  O.F. Best, 301(JEGP):Apr82-300
  W. Koepke, 221(GQ):May82-441
Keller, W.B. A Catalogue of the Cary Col-
lection of Playing Cards in the Yale
University Library.
  V. Wayland, 517(PBSA):Vol76No1-93
Kellerman, M. The Forgotten Third Skill.
  J.K. Swaffar, 399(MLJ):Autumn82-318
Kelley, C.F. Meister Eckhart on Divine
Knowledge.
  A.W.J. Harper, 154:Mar82-147
Kelley, D.R. The Beginning of Ideology.
  S. Ozment, 551(RenQ):Autumn82-502
  M. Prestwich, 617(TLS):14Jan83-42
Kelley, D.R. - see de Seyssel, C.
Kelley, J.B. Arabia, The Gulf and the
West.
  R. Saidel, 390:Jan82-61
Kellner, S. "Le Docteur Pascal" de Zola.*
  L.M. Porter, 395(MFS):Summer82-332
Kelly, A. Mikhail Bakunin.
  L. Schapiro, 617(TLS):13May83-495
Kelly, A. The Descent of Darwin.
  R. Rinard, 221(GQ):Jan82-133
Kelly, A.A. Mary Lavin.*
  S. Neuman, 395(MFS):Summer81-323
Kelly, D. Medieval Imagination.*
  J.B. Allen, 125:Winter82-213
Kelly, F.K. Court of Reason.
  A.P. Cappon, 436(NewL):Winter82/83-116
Kelly, L. The Kemble Era.*
  R. Berry, 108:Summer82-150

Kelly, L.G. The True Interpreter.*
  L.V. Fainberg, 545(RPh):Nov81-420
  C.R. Taber, 355(LSoc):Aug82-314
Kelly, M. Pioneer of the Catholic Revival.
  R. Griffiths, 208(FS):Apr82-231
Kelly, M.T. The More Loving One.*
  R.M. Brown, 198:Apr82-103
Kelman, J. Not Not While the Giro and
Other Stories.
  G. Mangan, 617(TLS):30Dec83-1462
Kelman, S. Regulating America, Regulating
Sweden.
  G. Majone and T.R. Marmor, 185:Jul83-
    816
Kelman, S. What Price Incentives?
  R.E.G., 185:Oct82-220
Kemal, Y. They Burn the Thistles.
  C. Hawtree, 364:Nov82-98
Kemball, R. - see Tsvetaeva, M.
Kemp, A. The Unknown Battle.
  639(VQR):Winter82-24
Kemp, C. Angewandte Emblematik in süddeut-
schen Barockkirchen.
  C-P. Warncke, 683:Band45Heft3-302
Kemp, J.A. - see Lepsius, R.
Kemp, J.C. Robert Frost and New England.*
  W. Tefs, 106:Fall82-223
Kemp, M. Leonardo da Vinci.*
  C.H. Clough, 324:Mar83-226
Kemp, P. H.G. Wells and the Culminating
Ape.*
  R. O'Hanlon, 617(TLS):4Feb83-112
van Kempen-van Dijk, P.M.A. Monnica.
  C.W. Wolfskeel, 394:Vol35fasc1/2-190
Kempowski, W. Days of Greatness.*
  L. Jones, 364:Apr/May82-143
Kempter, G. Ganymed.
  A.H. van Buren, 589:Jul82-624
Kempton, R. French Literature.*
  F. Bassan, 446(NCFS):Spring-Summer83-
    393
  O. Klapp, 547(RF):Band93Heft3/4-435
Kendrick, W.M. The Novel-Machine.*
  A. Pollard, 366:Spring82-130
  R. Tracy, 637(VS):Autumn81-99
Kendris, C. French Now! Le Français act-
uel!
  G. Crouse, 399(MLJ):Summer82-210
Keneally, T. Outback.
  A. Ross, 617(TLS):16Dec83-1393
Keneally, T. Schindler's List.* (British
title: Schindler's Ark.)
  J. Gross, 453(NYRB):17Feb83-3
  M. Hulse, 364:Feb83-103
Kenedi, J. Do It Yourself.*
  P. Sherwood, 575(SEER):Jul82-475
Kenen, I.L. Israel's Defense Line.
  M.I. Urofsky, 390:Aug/Sep82-63
Kengen, J.H.L., ed. Memoriale Credencium.*
  A. Hudson, 447(N&Q):Apr81-183
  S.J. Ogilvie-Thomson, 541(RES):Nov82-
    457
Kenkel, K. Medea-Dramen.*
  B. Bittrich, 52:Band16Heft2-181
  M. Mueller, 107(CRCL):Jun82-262
Kenna, R. and A. Mooney. People's Palaces.
  A. Smith, 617(TLS):15Jul83-747
Kennan, G.F. The Decline of Bismarck's
European Order.*
  R.J. Crampton, 161(DUJ):Dec81-123
Kennan, G.F. The Nuclear Delusion.*
  M. Howard, 231:Feb83-68

Kiernan, K.S. "Beowulf" and the "Beowulf" Manuscript.
R.D. Fulk, 481(PQ):Summer82-341
Kihlman, C. Sweet Prince.
D.J. Enright, 617(TLS):29Jul83-804
Kilby, C.S. and M.L. Mead - see Lewis, W.H.
Kiley, D. The Peter Pan Syndrome.
H. Goodman, 441:30Oct83-16
Kilian, M. Northern Exposure.
D. Flower, 441:10Apr83-30
Kilian, M. and A. Sawislak. Who Runs Washington?
639(VQR):Autumn82-124
Lord Killanin. My Olympic Years.
C. Booker, 617(TLS):8Jul83-737
Killorin, J. - see Aiken, C.
Kilminster, R. Praxis and Method.
M.A. Finocchiaro, 488:Dec82-456
Kilvert, F. The Diary of Francis Kilvert, April-June 1870. (K. Hughes and D. Ifans, eds)
A.L. Le Quesne, 617(TLS):21Jan83-70
Kim, C-W. and H. Stahlke, eds. Papers in African Linguistics.
S. Brauner, 682(ZPSK):Band34Heft1-138
Kim, H-K., ed. Studies on Korea.
E.W. Wagner, 293(JASt):Aug82-846
Kim, I. New Urban Immigrants.
G.A. De Vos, 293(JASt):Aug82-849
Kim, Y.C. Japanese Journalists and Their World.
J.H. Bailey, 293(JASt):May82-596
Kim, Y.C. Oriental Thought.
M. Yahuda, 293(JASt):Nov81-89
Kimball, P. The File.
P-L. Adams, 61:Dec83-116
T. Powers, 441:11Dec83-9
Kimball, R. - see Porter, C.
Kimbell, D.R.B. Verdi in the Age of Italian Romanticism.*
W. Dean, 410(M&L):Jul/Oct82-281
Kime, W.R. - see Irving, W.
Kincaid, A.N. - see Buck, G.
Kindem, G., ed. The American Movie Industry.
P. French, 617(TLS):29Apr83-429
Kinder, P.J. and S. McCracken. Connaissance du droit anglais.
A. Cocatre-Zilgien, 189(EA):Oct-Dec82-441
Kindrick, R.L. Robert Henryson.
P. Bawcutt, 677(YES):Vol 12-238
F.H. Ridley, 589:Jul82-626
Kindstrand, J.F. Anacharsis.
J.G.F. Powell, 123:Vol32No2-202
Kindstrand, J.F. - see Porphyrogenitus: 'Praefatio in Homerum'"
King, A. The Writings of Camara Laye.
P.R. Bernard, 207(FR):May83-936
King, A.H. Printed Music in the British Museum.
P.W. Jones, 410(M&L):Apr81-200
King, B., ed. West Indian Literature.*
R.M., 189(EA):Apr-Jun82-239
King, F. Act of Darkness.
A. Desai, 441:25Dec83-7
J. Mellors, 362:13Oct83-31
A. Motion, 617(TLS):23Sep83-1011
442(NY):26Dec83-71
King, F. - see Ackerley, J.R.
King, J. and C. Ryskamp - see Cowper, W.
King, J.C. - see Notker der Deutsche
King, J.M. - see Tsvetaeva, M.

King, J.N. English Reformation Literature.
S. Wintle, 617(TLS):4Mar83-211
King, K. Ten Modern American Playwrights.
A. Wertheim, 365:Winter83-21
King, L.D. and M. Suñer. Para a Frente!
B.J. Chamberlain, 399(MLJ):Autumn82-344
F.P. Ellison, 238:Dec82-671
King, L.L. The Whorehouse Papers.*
R. Stuart, 108:Fall82-128
King, L.S. The Philosophy of Medicine: The Early Eighteenth Century.
H.T. Engelhardt, Jr., 486:Mar82-149
J.P. Wright, 154:Mar82-153
King, P.R. Nine Contemporary Poets.
C. Wiseman, 49:Jan82-93
King, R. - see Thornton, R.
King, R.H. A Southern Renaissance.*
C. Mulvey, 366:Autumn82-268
King, R.R. A History of the Romanian Communist Party.
G. Schöpflin, 575(SEER):Oct82-634
King, S. Christine.
P. van Rjndt, 441:3Apr83-12
King, S. Pet Sematary.
A. Gottlieb, 441:6Nov83-15
King, T. Caretakers.
J.B., 231:Oct83-75
J. Bass, 441:23Oct83-27
King, U. Towards a New Mysticism.
J.Y. Fenton, 485(PE&W):Oct82-466
King, W.L. Theravāda Meditation.
H. Coward, 485(PE&W):Oct82-463
J.C. Holt, 293(JASt):Feb82-420
King-Hamilton, A. And Nothing But the Truth.
D. Pannick, 362:17Mar83-21
A.W.B. Simpson, 617(TLS):27May83-534
King-Hele, D. - see Darwin, E.
"Henry Kingsley." (J.S.D. Mellick, ed)
K. Stewart, 71(ALS):Oct82-541
Kingsley, M. Travels in West Africa.
E. Claridge, 364:Dec82/Jan83-75
Kington, M. Nature Made Ridiculously Simple.
A. Huth, 362:22and29Dec83-37
Kinkade, M.D., K.L. Hale and O. Werner, eds. Linguistics and Anthropology.
E.P. Hamp, 269(IJAL):Jul82-327 and 344
M.B. Kendall, 269(IJAL):Jul82-334
H. Landar, 269(IJAL):Jul82-335
N.B. McNeill, 269(IJAL):Jul82-339
M. Silverstein, 269(IJAL):Jul82-342
K.V. Teeter, 269(IJAL):Jul82-332
Kinmonth, E.H. The Self-Made Man in Meiji Japanese Thought.
A.M. Craig, 407(MN):Winter82-538
Matsubara Haruo, 285(JapQ):Jul-Sep82-373
Kinnard, D. The Secretary of Defense.
J.H. Napier 3d, 9(AlaR):Oct82-284
639(VQR):Spring82-48
Kinnell, G. There Are Things I Tell To No One.
D. Gioia, 249(HudR):Autumn82-483
Kinney, A.F., ed. Critical Essays on William Faulkner: The Compson Family.
K.J. Phillips, 268(IFR):Summer83-157
Kinoshita Junji. Between God and Man.*
B. de Bary, 293(JASt):Feb82-361
Kinross Smith, G. Australia's Writers.
B. Andrews, 71(ALS):May82-405

195

Kinsella, T. Peppercanister Poems, 1972–
1978.*
  J. Parini, 569(SR):Fall82-623
  T. Parkinson, 219(GaR):Fall82-662
Kinsella, T. Poems, 1956-1973.*
  J. Parini, 569(SR):Fall82-623
  T. Parkinson, 219(GaR):Fall82-662
Kinsella, T. - see Clarke, A.
Kinsella, W.P. Born Indian.
  A. Blott, 198:Jul82-91
  I.B. McLatchie, 102(CanL):Summer82-145
Kinsella, W.P. Shoeless Joe.* (Canadian
  title: Shoeless Joe Jackson Comes to
  Iowa.)
  J. Wasserman, 102(CanL):Winter81-106
Kinsley, D.R. The Divine Player.
  N. Hein, 293(JASt):Nov81-178
Kinsley, J. - see Dunbar, W.
Kinsley, W. Contexts Two.*
  C. Fabricant, 402(MLR):Jan82-172
Kintgen, E.R. The Perception of Poetry.
  K. Arthur, 617(TLS):28Oct83-1194
Kinzer, B.L. The Ballot Question in Nine-
  teenth-Century English Politics.
  B. Harrison, 617(TLS):19Aug83-876
Kinzie, M. The Threshold of the Year.
  E. Grosholz, 434:Summer83-634
Kiparsky, P. Pāṇini as a Variationist.
  (S.D. Joshi, ed)
  H. Scharfe, 260(IF):Band86-351
Kipling, R. American Notes.* (A.M. Gib-
  son, ed)
  177(ELT):Vol25No4-254
Kipling, R. "O Beloved Kids." (E.L.
  Gilbert, ed)
  C. Raine, 617(TLS):4Nov83-1203
Kippenhahn, R. 100 Billion Suns.
  H.R. Pagels, 441:21Aug83-9
Kippur, S.A. Jules Michelet.*
  T. Moreau, 535(RHL):Sep-Dec82-931
  42(AR):Winter82-121
Kirby, D. America's Hive of Honey, or
  Foreign Influences on American Fiction
  through Henry James.*
  R. Asselineau, 189(EA):Jul-Sep82-364
Kirby, D. Grace King.*
  T. Bonner, Jr., 392:Fall82-457
Kirchert, K. Der Windberger Psalter.*
  A.L. Lloyd, 301(JEGP):Oct82-535
  N.F. Palmer, 402(MLR):Jan82-231
  P.W. Tax, 589:Jan82-143
Kirchhoff, F. William Morris.
  G.M. La Regina, 677(YES):Vol 12-322
Kirk, G.S. The Nature of Greek Myths.
  J. Peradotto, 124:Sep/Oct82-57
Kirk, I. Anton Chekhov.
  W.G. Jones, 402(MLR):Jul82-764
Kirk, M. and A. Strathern. Man as Art.*
  J. Povey, 2(AfrA):Feb82-81
Kirk-Greene, C.W.E. French False Friends.
  B.G. Hirsch, 399(MLJ):Winter82-420
  F. Lagarde, 189(EA):Oct-Dec82-446
Kirkby, J., ed. The American Model.
  D. Anderson, 381:Dec82-479
  M. Duwell, 71(ALS):Oct82-541
Kirkham, M. Jane Austen: Feminism and
  Fiction.
  A. Leighton, 617(TLS):15Apr83-384
Kirkness, A. and others, eds. Deutsches
  Fremdwörterbuch. (Vols 3 and 4)
  H.H. Munske, 685(ZDL):3/1981-357
Kirkpatrick, E.M. - see "Chambers Twenti-
  eth Century Dictionary"

Kirkpatrick, R. Dante's "Paradiso" and
  the Limitations of Modern Criticism.
  T. Barolini, 545(RPh):Nov81-409
  A.A. Iannucci, 276:Spring82-62
Kirkpatrick, R. Domenico Scarlatti.
  A. Suied, 450(NRF):Dec82-124
Kirmānī, A. Heart's Witness.
  S. Vahiduddin, 485(PE&W):Apr82-221
Kirp, D.L. Just Schools.
  C.N.S., 185:Jul83-837
Kirsch, A. Shakespeare and the Experience
  of Love.*
  639(VQR):Summer82-79
Kirsch, G.B. Jeremy Belknap.
  L.L. Tucker, 432(NEQ):Sep82-474
Kirschke, J.J. Henry James and Impression-
  ism.
  M. Deakin, 395(MFS):Summer82-290
  R.A. Hocks, 183(ESQ):Vol128No4-261
  R. Lehan, 445(NCF):Jun82-128
  J.C. Wolf, 26(ALR):Spring82-134
  295(JML):Dec82-471
Kiš, D. Sablier.
  L. Kovacs, 450(NRF):Dec82-115
Kishtainy, K. The Prostitute in Progres-
  sive Literature.
  J. Mellors, 364:Mar83-117
Kiss, L. Földrajzi Nezek Etimológiai Szó-
  tara.
  J. Kölzow, 682(ZPSK):Band35Heft5-597
Kissinger, H. For the Record.
  D.E. Mayo, 432(NEQ):Mar82-147
Kisslinger, E. and M. Rost. Listening
  Focus.
  L. Hamp-Lyons, 608:Mar83-109
Kitagawa, H. and B.T. Tsuchida - see "The
  Tale of the Heike"
Kitchen, K.A. Pharaoh Triumphant.
  J. Baines, 617(TLS):21Oct83-1152
Kitcher, P. Abusing Science.*
  R.C. Lewontin, 453(NYRB):16Jun83-21
  A. Mackay, 617(TLS):15Apr83-381
Kitching, C.J., ed. London and Middlesex
  Chantry Certificate 1548.
  L.S. Snell, 325:Apr82-38
Kitson, L. The Falklands War.
  A. Ross, 364:Feb83-7
Kitson, M. Claude Lorrain: Liber Veritas.
  M. Chiarini, 54:Mar82-157
Kivy, P. The Corded Shell.*
  J. Hospers, 289:Winter82-105
  R.A. Sharpe, 89(BJA):Winter82-81
  R. Taruskin, 414(MusQ):Apr82-287
  J.O. Urmson, 410(M&L):Jan/Apr82-111
  P. Wilson, 308:Spring82-166
Kiyoshi, A. - see under Akatsuka Kiyoshi
Kizer, C. - see Peterson, R.
Klafkowski, P., ed and trans. The Secret
  Deliverance of the Sixth Dalai Lama as
  Narrated by Dharmatāla.
  J.W. de Jong, 259(IIJ):Jul82-223
Klappenbach, R. Studien zur modernen
  deutschen Lexikographie.* (W. Abraham,
  with J.F. Brand, eds)
  H. Moser, 680(ZDP):Band101Heft1-148
Klaus, H.G., ed. The Socialist Novel in
  Britain.
  R. Lehan, 445(NCF):Sep82-249
Klauser, T. and others - see "Reallexikon
  für Antike und Christentum"
Kleiber, G. Problèmes de référence.
  R. Martin, 553(RLiR):Jul-Dec82-416

Kleiber, W., K. Kunze and H. Löffler. Historischer Südwestdeutscher Sprachatlas.
   J. Goossens, 684(ZDA):Band111Heft2-51
   W.G. Moulton, 133:Band15Heft3-255
Klein, A. Antirazionalismo di Kierkegaard.
   J. Colette, 192(EP):Jan-Mar81-91
Klein, A. Figurenkonzeption und Erzählform in den Kurzgeschichten Sherwood Andersons.
   K. Lubbers, 38:Band100Heft1/2-234
Klein, A.M. Beyond Sambation. (M.W. Steinberg and U. Caplan, eds)
   M. Finkelstein, 99:Nov82-33
Klein, D.A. Peter Shaffer.
   F. Doherty, 447(N&Q):Oct81-460
Klein, E., K.J. Mattheier and H. Mickartz. Rheinisch.*
   I. Guentherodt, 685(ZDL):3/1982-403
Klein, G. and M.J. Reban, eds. The Politics of Ethnicity in Eastern Europe.
   P. Shoup, 104(CASS):Fall-Winter82-609
Klein, H., ed. The First World War in Fiction.
   F. Mielke, 549(RLC):Apr-Jun82-226
Klein, H.G. Tempus, Aspekt, Aktionsart.
   J. Klare, 682(ZPSK):Band34Heft4-490
Klein, H.M. - see Shakespeare, W.
Klein, H.M. - see "Westward for Smelts"
Klein, K.K. and L.E. Schmitt, eds. Siebenbürgisch-Deutscher Sprachatlas. (Vol 1)
   E. Seidelmann, 685(ZDL):2/1982-222
Klein, L.R. The Economics of Supply and Demand.
   F. Cairncross, 617(TLS):9Dec83-1368
Klein, L.S., ed. Encyclopedia of World Literature in the 20th Century. (Vol 1) (2nd ed)
   T.A. Sackett, 399(MLJ):Winter82-451
Klein, M. Foreigners.*
   E. Labor, 395(MFS):Winter82/83-665
   J.F. Light, 27(AL):May82-308
   J.E. Miller, Jr., 651(WHR):Autumn82-283
   B.A. Stonehill, 405(MP):May83-436
   J. Yow, 219(GaR):Summer82-461
   639(VQR):Winter82-7
Klein, P.D. Certainty.
   D. Odegard, 518:Oct82-193
Klein, R., ed. Marc Aurel.
   A. Chastagnol, 555:Vol56fasc1-175
Klein, W. and N. Dittmar. Developing Grammars.*
   S. Gal, 660(Word):Dec81-254
   F. Hundsnurscher, 685(ZDL):2/1981-261
   P. Suchsland, 682(ZPSK):Band35Heft2-223
Klein, W. and W.J.M. Levelt, eds. Crossing the Boundaries in Linguistics.
   M. Barnes, 660(Word):Dec82-253
   A. Zwicky, 350:Mar83-225
"William Klein, Photographs."*
   J. Guimond, 219(GaR):Winter82-894
Kleinbaum, A.W. The War Against the Amazons.
   G.A. De Candido, 441:20Mar83-20
Kleinberg, E.M. Infinitary Combinatorics and the Axiom of Determinateness.
   H. Becker, 316:Sep82-698
Kleinschmidt, E., ed. Das Windschiff aus Schlaraffenland.
   J. Janota, 684(ZDA):Band111Heft4-166
Kleinzahler, A. A Calendar of Airs.
   D. Barbour, 648(WCR):Oct82-37

von Kleist, H. An Abyss Deep Enough.* (P.B. Miller, ed and trans)
   J. Agee, 441:24Jul83-3
   R. Leiter, 31(ASch):Autumn82-561
   S. Schwartz, 453(NYRB):20Jan83-40
von Kleist, H. Heinrich von Kleist: Plays. (W. Hinderer, ed)
   J. Agee, 441:24Jul83-3
   S. Schwartz, 453(NYRB):20Jan83-40
von Kleist, H. Prince Friedrich von Homburg.
   J.T. Brewer, 399(MLJ):Autumn82-342
Klemke, E.D., ed. The Meaning of Life.
   T.M.R., 185:Oct82-193
Klemm, C. Kataloge des Kunstmuseum Düsseldorf: Gaspard Dughet und die ideale Landschaft, Handzeichnungen.
   A. Blunt, 90:May82-306
Klenk, U. Formale Sprachen mit Anwendungen auf die Beschreibung natürlicher Sprachen.
   G. Kleiber, 553(RLiR):Jul-Dec81-481
Klenke, M.A. Chrétien de Troyes and "Le Conte del Graal."
   T. Hunt, 208(FS):Oct82-456
   N.J. Lacy, 207(FR):Feb83-475
Klepac, R.L. Mr. Mathews at Home.
   J. Ellis, 611(TN):Vol36No1-40
Klieneberger, H.R. The Novel in England and Germany.
   J.K. Brown, 678(YCGL):No30-83
   J.V. Knapp, 395(MFS):Winter82/83-621
Klier, J. and I. Hacker-Klier. Die Gitarre.
   B. Robinson, 415:Nov82-764
Klijn, A.F.J. Seth in Jewish, Christian, and Gnostic Literature.
   E.H. Pagels, 318(JAOS):Jul-Sep81-415
Klimowicz, T. Dmitrij Mamin-Sibiriak i problemy naturalizmu w literaturze rosyjskiej.
   K. Blanck, 688(ZSP):Band43Heft1-200
"Klimt, Schiele, Kokoschka: Drawings and Watercolours." (notes by C.M. Nebehay)
   N. Powell, 39:Feb82-132
Klinger, H. Konstantin Nikolaevič Bestužev-Rjumins Stellung in der russischen Historiographie und seine gesellschaftliche Tätigkeit; Ein Beitrag zur russischen Geistesgeschichte des 19. Jahrhunderts.*
   R.P. Bartlett, 575(SEER):Jan82-121
Klinghoffer, A.J. The Angolan War.*
   B. Ipatov, 550(RusR):Jan82-98
Klingmann, U. Religion und Religiosität in der Lyrik von Nelly Sachs.
   E. Petuchowski, 221(GQ):May82-459
Klinkenberg, J-M., D. Racelle-Latin and G. Connolly, eds. Langages et collectivités: le cas du Quebec.
   C. Callahan, 207(FR):Dec82-354
Klinkenberg, R.H. Die "Reisebilder" Heinrich Heines.
   L.D. Wells, 221(GQ):Nov82-598
Klinkenborg, V., H. Cahoon and C. Ryskamp, eds. British Literary Manuscripts.*
   D. Chambers, 503:Winter82-208
Klinkowitz, J. The American 1960's.*
   S. Fogel, 106:Fall82-267
   G. Wickes, 395(MFS):Summer81-358
Klinkowitz, J. Literary Disruptions.* (2nd ed)
   M. Terrier, 189(EA):Oct-Dec82-491

Knutson, L. Synthetic Dyes for Natural Fibers.
P. Bach, 614:Winter83-22
Kobilarov-Götze, G. Die deutschen Lehnwörter in der ungarischen Gemeinsprache.
T. Kesztyüs, 685(ZDL):1/1982-99
Kobylańska, K. Frédéric Chopin.* (E. Herttrich, ed)
H. Ferguson, 410(M&L):Jan81-87
Koch, H-A. and U., eds. Internationale Germanistische Bibliographie 1980.
R.F. Krummel, 221(GQ):Nov82-579
K. Nyholm, 439(NM):1982/2-217
H. Penzl, 350:Mar83-228
J. Strelka, 133:Band15Heft4-345
Koch, K. The Burning Mystery of Anna in 1951.
D. Spurr, 29:Mar/Apr83-42
Koch, W.E. Folklore from Kansas.
J.A. Chinn, 292(JAF):Oct-Dec82-480
G. Logsdon, 650(WF):Jan82-66
Kochetov, V. The Zhurbins.
T.J. Lewis, 399(MLJ):Autumn82-347
Kochman, T. Black and White Styles in Conflict.
D. Schiffrin, 350:Jun83-456
Kocks, D. Jean Baptiste Carpeaux.
K. Türr, 471:Apr/May/Jun82-167
Kodjak, A., M.J. Connolly and K. Pomorska, eds. The Structural Analysis of Narrative Texts.*
D.B. Johnson, 104(CASS):Spring82-116
Kodjak, A., K. Pomorska and K. Taranovsky, eds. Alexander Puškin: Symposium II.*
L.G. Leighton, 104(CASS):Spring82-126
T.E. Little, 575(SEER):Oct82-615
S. Sandler, 550(RusR):Jan82-102
Koehler, L. N.F. Fedorov.*
M. Hagemeister, 688(ZSP):Band43Heft1-203
Koehler, L. A Search for Power.*
J.J. Waters, 656(WMQ):Jan82-238
Koenker, D. Moscow Workers and the 1917 Revolution.
A. Wildman, 550(RusR):Jul82-332
Koerner, E.F.K. Western Histories of Linguistic Thought.*
J. Dietze, 682(ZPSK):Band34Heft2-262
Koertge, R. Life on the Edge of the Continent.
W. Harmon, 472:Spring/Summer83-129
Koestenbaum, P. oh I can't she says.
R. Hass, 448:Vol20No1-53
Kofas, J.V. International and Domestic Politics in Greece during the Crimean War.
J.S. Curtiss, 104(CASS):Summer82-261
Kofman, S. Aberrations.
C. Chalier, 192(EP):Apr-Jun81-229
Kofman, S. L'Enigme de la femme.
D.L. Deig, 155.Summer82-11
C. Chalier, 192(EP):Oct-Dec82-502
A. Reix, 542:Jan-Mar82-91
Koh, H.C. Korean Family and Kinship Studies Guide.
C.N. Goldberg, 293(JASt):Feb82-372
Kohl, N. Oscar Wilde.
R. Eichler, 189(EA):Oct-Dec82-477
Kohler, G. Geschmacksurteil und ästhetische Erfahrung.
D.D., 543:Jun82-880
T. Mestmäcker-Poll, 687:Apr-Jun82-306
W. Steinbeck, 342:Band73Heft2-250

Kohlmaier, G. and B. von Sartory. Das Glashaus.
J. Hix, 46:Jan82-77
J. Maass, 576:Dec82-348
Kohrt, M. Koordinationsreduktion und Verbstellung in einer generativen Grammatik des Deutschen.
G. Kolde, 260(IF):Band86-378
Kohrt, M. and J. Lenerz, eds. Sprache: Formen und Strukturen.
T.F. Shannon, 350:Jun83-436
Kojève, A. Esquisse d'une phénoménologie du droit.
J-P. Guinle, 450(NRF):Jul-Aug82-184
Kokott, H. Reynke de Vos.
T.W. Best, 221(GQ):May82-404
Kolakowski, L. Main Currents of Marxism.*
J. Satterwhite, 142:Spring81-117
Kolakowski, L. Religion: If there is no God ... *
B. Godlee, 617(TLS):4Mar83-221
D.S., 185:Jul83-825
Kolar, W.W. and A.H. Várdy, eds. The Folk Arts of Hungary.
E. Whittaker, 104(CASS):Fall-Winter82-569
Kolb, H. and H. Lauffer, eds. Sprachliche Interferenz.*
J. Göschel, 260(IF):Band86-287
Kolb, J. - see Hallam, A.H.
Kolb, P. - see Proust, M.
Kolenda, K. Philosophy in Literature.
M.R., 185:Apr83-649
M. Rapisarda, 395(MFS):Winter82/83-725
Kolenda, K. - see Ryle, G.
Kolendo, J. L'agricoltura nell'Italia romana.
G. Barker, 313:Vol72-192
P-P. Corsetti, 555:Vol56fasc1-174
R.P. Duncan-Jones, 123:Vol132No1-72
Koliopoulos, Y. Listes.
R. Clogg, 617(TLS):12Aug83-861
Koljević, S. The Epic in the Making.*
E.C. Hawkesworth, 402(MLR):Jan82-251
Z.D. Zimmerman, 574(SEEJ):Spring82-117
Kolker, R.P. The Altering Eye.
S. Farber, 441:10Apr83-11
M. Wood, 18:Apr83-58
Kolkowicz, R. and A. Korbonski, eds. Soldiers, Peasants and Bureaucrats.
J.R. Adelman, 550(RusR):Oct82-519
Koller, E. Totentanz.
W.F. Michael, 221(GQ):Nov82-582
T. Seebass, 317:Summer82-329
Kölmel, W. Aspekte des Humanismus.
R.N. Watkins, 551(RenQ):Winter82-593
Kolschanski, G.W. Paralinguistik. (H. Zikmund, ed and trans)
B. Techtmeier, 682(ZPSK):Band34Heft3-370
Kölving, U. - see Grimm, F.M.
Komarov, B. The Destruction of Nature in the Soviet Union.*
R.A. French, 575(SEER):Jan82-146
P.P. Micklim, 104(CASS):Summer82-279
Komonen, M., ed. Tradition and Metaphor.
B. Bognar, 576:Oct82-254
Kondylis, P. Die Entstehung der Dialektik.
R.P. Horstmann, 53(AGP):Band64Heft3-335
Konhardt, K. Die Einheit der Vernunft.
U. Anacker, 687:Jan-Mar82-120

König, A.P. Denkformen in der Erkenntnis.
W. Steinbeck, 342:Band73Heft4-482
König, R. and G. Winkler. Plinius der
Ältere.
J. André, 555:Vol56fasc2-352
W. Maaz, 196:Band23Heft3/4-325
König, W. dtv-Atlas zur deutschen Sprache.
M. Philipp, 685(ZDL):3/1981-369
K-E. Sommerfeldt, 682(ZPSK):Band34
Heft2-263
Koning, H. The Kleber Flight.
639(VQR):Spring82-55
Konner, M. The Tangled Wing.
P. Engel, 441:2Jan83-11
M. Piattelli-Palmarini, 617(TLS):
18Feb83-152
Konopacki, S.A. The Descent into Words.*
P. Schäffer, 551(RenQ):Autumn82-528
Konrád, G. The Loser.*
P. Keegan, 617(TLS):14Oct83-1143
K.C. O'Brien, 362:15Sep83-23
Konrad, H.W. A Jesuit Hacienda in Colo-
nial Mexico.
N.P. Cushner, 377:Nov81-185
F.M. Spindler, 37:May-Jun82-61
Konrad, R. Reviewing German Grammar and
Building Vocabulary.
R.C. Helt, 399(MLJ):Summer82-216
Kontos, A., ed. Powers, Possessions, and
Freedom.*
D. Gauthier, 154:Jun82-353
Kontos, J.F. Red Cross — Black Eagle.
B.G. Spiridonakis, 104(CASS):Fall-
Winter82-577
"Kontrastiv Lingvistik i Danmark."
H.H. Munske, 685(ZDL):3/1981-373
Konwicki, T. A Minor Apocalypse.
I. Howe, 453(NYRB):13Oct83-19
M. Karpinski, 441:23Oct83-13
P. Kemp, 617(TLS):25Nov83-1301
Konwicki, T. The Polish Complex.*
(Polish title: Kompleks polski.)
J. Updike, 442(NY):21Feb83-130
Kooijman, K.F.M. Social and Economic
Change in a Tswana Village.
N. Mahoney, 69:Vol51No4-901
Koon, H. and R. Switzer. Eugène Scribe.*
M. Descotes, 535(RHL):May-Jun82-492
L.F. Luce, 210(FrF):Jan82-80
J.R. Williams, 207(FR):Dec82-322
Koopmann, H. Drama der Aufklärung.
S.D. Martinson, 406:Fal182-353
Koopmann, H., ed. Mythos und Mythologie
in der Literatur des 19. Jahrhunderts.*
W. Ross, 52:Band16Heft3-324
Koopmann, H. - see Heine, H.
Kooser, T. Sure Signs.*
R. Jones, 577(SHR):Summer82-280
H. Luke, 448:Vol20No1-162
Kopelev, L. Ease My Sorrows.
H. Gold, 441:18Sep83-7
L. Schapiro, 453(NYRB):13Oct83-9
Kopelev, L. Utoli moia pechali.
P. Kenez, 550(RusR):Oct82-522
Koperwas, S. Easy Money.
H. Gold, 441:9Jan83-13
Köpf, G., ed. Rezeptionspragmatik.
J.L. Sammons, 221(GQ):May82-388
Kopff, E.C. - see Otis, B.
Köpke, W. Erfolglosigkeit.*
S.L. Cocalis, 406:Spring82-103

Koppelkamm, S. Glasshouses and Wintergar-
dens of the Nineteenth Century.
J.S. Curl, 324:Dec82-62
J. Maass, 576:Dec82-348
Köppen, E. Heeresbericht.
R.C. Holub, 406:Spring82-72
Köppen, U. Die "Dialoghi d'amore" des
Leone Ebreo in ihren französischen
Übersetzungen.*
P. Chavy, 107(CRCL):Mar82-131
Kopper, J. Einführung in die Philosophie
der Aufklärung.
J-J. Wunenburger, 192(EP):Jul-Sep81-
372
Koppes, C.R. JPL and the American Space
Program.
H.S.F. Cooper, Jr., 441:9Jan83-11
J. Lighthill, 617(TLS):10Jun83-594
Koppisch, M.S. The Dissolution of Charac-
ter.
M. Moriarty, 208(FS):Oct82-471
Koppitz, H-J. Studien zur Tradierung der
weltlichen mittelhochdeutschen Epik im
15. und beginnenden 16. Jahrhundert.*
J.L. Flood, 402(MLR):Jul82-753
Kopplin, M. Das Fächerblatt von Manet bis
Kokoschka.
E.M. Landau, 471:Jul/Aug/Sep82-266
Kordecki-Widmann, A. Register zum Guten-
berg-Jahrbuch 1926-1975.
D.L. Paisey, 617(TLS):10Jun83-612
"Korean Studies." (Vol 1)
J.W. Best, 318(JAOS):Oct-Dec81-434
Korein, J., ed. Brain Death.
D.N. Walton, 154:Mar82-175
Korg, J. Language in Modern Literature.*
R.B. Hauck, 395(MFS):Winter81-388
P. Ingham, 541(RES):Feb82-65
V. Sage, 299:Spring82-148
Korhammer, M. Die monastischen Cantica
im Mittelalter und ihre altenglischen
Interlinearversionen.
G.H. Brown, 38:Band100Heft3/4-495
Korhonen, J. Studien zu Dependenz, Valenz
und Satzmodell.* (Pt 1)
G. Koller, 685(ZDL):2/1981-263
Korhonen, J. Studien zu Dependenz, Valenz
und Satzmodell. (Pt 2)
G. Koller, 685(ZDL):1/1982-123
Korhonen, J. Zu syntaktischen Ähnlich-
keiten in Luthers Evangelienübersetzung
von 1522 und in einigen früheren Überset-
zungen.
K. Gärtner, 685(ZDL):1/1982-121
Koropeckyj, I.S. and G.E. Schroeder, eds.
Economics of Soviet Regions.
H. Hunter, 550(RusR):Oct82-511
Korsten, F.J.M. Roger North (1651-1734),
Virtuoso and Essayist.
E.D. Mackerness, 179(ES):Jun82-285
Kortian, G. Metacritique.
W.V. Doniela, 63:Sep82-291
M.A.F., 543:Dec81-394
A. Rapaczynski, 185:Jul83-811
Koschorreck, W. and W. Werner. Kommentar
zum Faksimile des Codex Palatinus German-
icus 848 der Universitätsbibliothek
Heidelberg.
G.W. Radimersky, 221(GQ):May82-405
Koselleck, R. Vergangene Zukunft.
H.U. Gumbrecht, 490:Band13Heft3/4-345

Koshal, S. Ladakhi Grammar.* (B.G. Misra, ed)
G.F. Meier, 682(ZPSK):Band34Heft1-125
Kosman, M. Historia Białorusi.
M. Siekierski, 497(PolR):Vol27No1/2-176
Kosolapov, V. Mankind and the Year 2000.
G. Morgan, 154:Jun82-336
Koss, S. The Rise and Fall of the Political Press in Great Britain: The Nineteenth Century.
A. Gollin, 637(VS):Summer82-500
Kossatz-Deissmann, A. Dramen des Aischylos auf westgriechischen Vasen.
A.J.N.W. Prag, 303(JoHS):Vol 102-293
Kostash, M. Long Way From Home.
J. Baglow, 529(QQ):Spring82-185
A. Suknaski, 102(CanL):Spring82-137
Kostelanetz, R. - see Stein, G.
Koster, D.N., ed. American Literature and Language.
27(AL):Oct82-483
K.B. Harder, 424:Jun82-123
K.M. Roemer, 26(ALR):Autumn82-286
Kostiainen, A. The Forging of Finnish-American Communism, 1917-1924.
D. Kirby, 575(SEER):Jan82-126
Koszarski, R. The Man You Loved to Hate.
G. Nowell-Smith, 617(TLS):18Nov83-1277
B. Shulgasser, 441:28Aug83-13
Kosztolnyik, E.J. Five Eleventh Century Hungarian Kings.
J.J. Santa-Pinter, 104(CASS):Fall-Winter82-566
Kotošixin, G. O Rossii v carstvovanie Alekseja Mixajloviča.* (A.E. Pennington, ed)
H. Leeming, 575(SEER):Jan82-85
Kotzwinkle, W. Christmas at Fontaine's.*
A. Horowitz, 617(TLS):25Nov83-1329
Kouidis, V.M. Mina Loy.*
H.M. Dennis, 677(YES):Vol 12-341
Kouwenhoven, J.A. Half a Truth is Better Than None.
G.A. Cevasco, 324:Sep83-633
Kouznetsov, E. Lettres de Mordovie.
A. Suied, 450(NRF):Jan82-148
Kovács, E., ed. Katholische Aufklärung und Josephinismus.
W.R. Ward, 161(DUJ):Jun82-286
Kovács, K.S. "Le Rêve et la vie."
A. Green, 208(FS):Oct82-483
Kovel, J. The Age of Desire.
P. Roazen, 529(QQ):Winter82-910
Kovel, R. and T. Kovels' Know Your Antiques.
J.V. Turano, 16:Spring82-75
Kovrig, B. Communism in Hungary.
P. Pastor, 497(PolR):Vol27No1/2-178
Kovtun, G.J. Tomáš G. Masaryk, 1850-1937.
G.H. Bolsover, 575(SEER):Apr82-318
Kowalski, R. Logic for Problem Solving.
D.W. Loveland, 316:Jun82-477
Kowsky, F.R. The Architecture of Frederick Clarke Withers and the Progress of the Gothic Revival in America after 1850.
S.B. Landau, 576:Mar82-71
Kowsky, F.R. and others. Buffalo Architecture.
M.L. Peckham, 576:Oct82-245
Kozicki, H. Tennyson and Clio.*
M.L. Greenberg, 301(JEGP):Jan82-135

Kpomassie, T-M. An African in Greenland.
P. Zweig, 441:10Jul83-7
Kraft, J. - see Bynner, W.
Kraft, K-F.O. Iweins Triuwe.*
J.A. Schultz, 405(MP):May83-406
Krailsheimer, A. Pascal.*
J. Cruickshank, 402(MLR):Jan82-205
Krainz, C. Soziolinguistische, lernpsychologische und didaktische Problematik von Fehleranalysen.
F.J. Hausmann, 257(IRAL):Nov82-325
Kramer, B. and others. Kölner Papyri (P. Köln). (Vol 3)
A. Bülow-Jacobsen, 123:Vol132No1-115
Kramer, D., ed. Critical Approaches to the Fiction of Thomas Hardy.*
K. Brady, 637(VS):Spring82-390
R.P. Draper, 541(RES):Feb82-104
M. Williams, 447(N&Q):Jun81-276
Kramer, D. - see Hardy, T.
Krämer, J., ed. Pfälzisches Wörterbuch. (Vol 3, Pts 22 and 23)
D. Karch, 685(ZDL):1/1982-84
Kramer, J., ed. Studien zum Ampezzanischen.
E. Kühebacher, 685(ZDL):3/1981-397
Krämer, J. Unser Sprachschatz.
I. Guentherodt, 685(ZDL):1/1982-85
Kramer, J.E. The American College Novel.
D.G. Hale, 365:Fall82-168
Kramer, L., ed. The Oxford History of Australian Literature.*
J. Croft, 71(ALS):May82-397
B. Elliott, 71(ALS):May82-393
B. King, 569(SR):Fall82-634
P. Pierce, 381:Oct81-367
J. Tulip, 405(MP):Nov82-220
Kramer, M. Invasive Procedures.
J. McGinniss, 441:18Sep83-12
Kramer, R. In Defense of the Family.
J.K. Davison, 441:8May83-18
Kramer, S.N. From the Poetry of Sumer.
H. Limet, 318(JAOS):Oct-Dec81-439
Kramer, W. and others, eds. Gedenkschrift für Heinrich Wesche.
F. Simmler, 685(ZDL):3/1982-366
Krammer, R. Arbeitersport in Österreich.
F.L. Carsten, 575(SEER):Jan82-138
Kramrisch, S. Exploring India's Sacred Art. (B.S. Miller, ed)
D.M. Knipe, 469:Vol18No4-116
T. Maxwell, 617(TLS):23Dec83-1438
Kramsch, C.J. Discourse Analysis and Second Language Teaching.
B. Powell, 399(MLJ):Winter82-448
Krantz, J. Mistral's Daughter.
G. Glueck, 441:2Jan83-10
Kranzmayer, E. Laut- und Flexionslehre der deutschen zimbrischen Mundart.
W.J. Koelkock, 221(GQ):Nov82-582
Krapf, L. and C. Wagenknecht - see Weckherlin, G.R.
Krashen, S.D. Principles and Practice in Second Language Acquisition.
K.J. Krahnke, 608:Jun83-300
Krasnov, V. Solzhenitsyn and Dostoevsky.*
M. Futrell, 104(CASS):Spring82-145
Kratz, D.M. Mocking Epic.
A.G. Elliott, 589:Apr82-387
J. Ziolkowski, 121(CJ):Feb/Mar83-266
Kratzenstein, M. Survey of Organ Literature and Editions.
J. Dalton, 410(M&L):Apr81-217

Kratzmann, G. Anglo-Scottish Literary
Relations, 1430-1550.*
  P. Bawcutt, 677(YES):Vol 12-236
  R.D.S. Jack, 588(SSL):Vol 17-280
  J. Kerling, 179(ES):Apr82-162
  M.P. McDiarmid, 571(ScLJ):Winter82-55
  W. Scheps, 551(RenQ):Spring81-130
Kraulis, J.A., ed. The Art of Canadian
Nature Photography.*
  529(QQ):Summer82-459
Kraume, H. Die Gerson-Übersetzungen
Geilers von Kaysersberg.
  N.F. Palmer, 402(MLR):Jul82-752
Kraus, F.R. Altbabylonische Briefe in
Unschrift und Übersetzung. (Heft 7)
  S. Greengus, 318(JAOS):Apr-Jun81-257
Kraus, J. Hans E. Nossack.
  H.E. Vinica, 221(GQ):Nov82-618
Kraus, J.W. Messrs. Copeland and Day, 69
Cornhill, Boston, 1893-1899.*
  R.E. Stoddard, 517(PBSA):Vol76No3-359
Kraus, M.P. Allen Ginsberg.
  L. Bartlett, 50(ArQ):Summer82-183
Krause, D. and R.G. Lowery, eds. Sean
O'Casey Centenary Essays.*
  B.L. Smith, 329(JJQ):Winter82-201
Krauss, H., ed. Europäisches Hochmittel-
alter.
  P. Zumthor, 547(RF):Band94Heft4-478
Kreider, J.F. The Solar Heating Design
Process.
  M.M. Sizemore, 505:Oct82-126
Kreidl, J.F. Jean-Luc Godard.
  A. Sarris, 18:Apr83-59
Kreisel, H. The Almost Meeting and Other
Stories.*
  N. Besner, 102(CanL):Autumn82-125
  S. Scobie, 529(QQ):Autumn82-654
Kreiter, J.A. Le Problème du paraître
dans l'oeuvre de Mme. de Lafayette.
  N. Aronson, 475:Vol6Pt2-394
Kreitman, E. Deborah.
  H. Maccoby, 362:1Sep83-21
  S.S. Prawer, 617(TLS):29Apr83-419
Krekić, B. Dubrovnik, Italy and the Bal-
kans in the late Middle Ages.
  D. Abulafia, 575(SEER):Oct82-622
Kremer, L. Grenzmundarten und Mundartgren-
zen.
  H-J. Gernentz, 682(ZPSK):Band35Heft5-
  589
Kremnitz, G. Das Okzitanische.
  N.B. Smith, 207(FR):Oct82-203
Kren, G.M. and L. Rappoport. The Holo-
caust and the Crisis of Human Behavior.
  T. Ziolkowski, 569(SR):Fall82-592
Kresic, S., ed. Contemporary Literary Her-
meneutics and Interpretation of Classi-
cal Texts.
  M. Heath, 123:Vol32No2-281
  P.A. Johnson, 478:Oct82-220
Kress, G. and R. Hodge. Language as Ideol-
ogy.*
  B.M. Berry, 599:Winter82-90
  J. Higginbotham, 482(PhR):Jan82-131
Kretzmann, N., ed. Infinity and Continu-
ity in Ancient and Medieval Thought.*
  L. Sweeney, 319:Jul83-399
  639(VQR):Summer82-100
Kretzmann, N. - see Paul of Venice

Kreutzer, W. Stile der portugiesischen
Lyrik im 20. Jahrhundert.
  G.M. Moser, 238:Mar82-146 and
  238:Sep82-479
  J. Parker, 86(BHS):Jan82-82
Kreyling, M. Eudora Welty's Achievement
of Order.*
  T.D. Young, 569(SR):Spring82-xliii
Kriedte, P. Peasants, Landlords and
Merchant Capitalists.
  G. Parker, 617(TLS):23Sep83-1022
Krieger, E. A Marxist Study of Shake-
speare's Comedies.*
  A. Leggatt, 677(YES):Vol 12-259
  P.N. Siegel, 599:Winter82-94
Krieger, M. Arts on the Level.*
  W.B. Bache, 395(MFS):Summer82-345
  L. Shiner, 478:Oct82-221
  J. Stolnitz, 289:Winter82-99
Krieger, M. Poetic Presence and Illusion.*
  W.B. Bache, 395(MFS):Summer81-383
Krige, J. Science, Revolution and Discon-
tinuity.
  S.W. Gaukroger, 393(Mind):Jul82-473
  M. Ring, 518:Apr82-98
Krimmer, S. and A. Lawson - see "Barbara
Baynton"
Kripke, S. La logique des noms propres.
  J. Largeault, 542:Jul-Sep82-542
Kripke, S.A. Wittgenstein on Rules and
Private Language.
  P.F. Strawson, 617(TLS):11Feb83-123
Krishna, G., ed. Contributions to South
Asian Studies I.
  C. Hallisey, 318(JAOS):Oct-Dec81-503
Krishna, V., ed. The Alliterative Morte
Arthure.
  K.H. Göller, 38:Band100Heft1/2-193
Kristeller, P.O. Renaissance Thought and
its Sources. (M. Mooney, ed)
  M.J.B. Allen, 551(RenQ):Winter81-555
  K. Lloyd-Jones, 125:Winter82-215
  S. Otto, 53(AGP):Band64Heft1-85
Kristeva, J. Desire in Language.* (L.S.
Roudiez, ed)
  J. Arac, 395(MFS):Winter82/83-723
  E. Block, 659(ConL):Winter83-512
  W. Domingo, 478:Oct82-215
Kristol, A.M. Color.
  J. Bourguignon, 553(RLiR):Jan-Jun81-
  237
Kristol, I. Reflections of a Neoconserva-
tive.
  J. Fallows, 61:Oct83-110
  P. Johnson, 441:2Oct83-7
Kritzman, L.D. Destruction/Découverte.*
  H.H. Glidden, 188(ECr):Summer82-65
  V. Kahn, 546(RR):Jan82-114
  D. Maskell, 208(FS):Jul82-323
  G.P. Norton, 551(RenQ):Summer82-309
Kroeber, A.L. Yurok Myths.
  N.R. Grobman, 582(SFQ):Vol143No3/4-346
Kroetsch, R. Field Notes.
  J. Kertzer, 198:Apr82-116
  B. Whiteman, 298:Summer82-150
Kroetsch, R. The Sad Phoenician.
  D.S. West, 102(CanL):Winter81-122
Krohn, R. - see Gottfried von Strassburg
Kröhnke, F. Jungen in schlechter Gesell-
schaft.
  D. Sudhoff, 680(ZDP):Band101Heft4-619

Kuné, J.H. Die Auferstehung Christi im deutschen religiösen Drama des Mittelalters.*
E.S. Dick, 406:Spring82-96
Kunen, J.S. "How Can You Defend Those People?"
T. Ehrlich, 441:20Nov83-11
Kunene, M. Emperor Shaka the Great.
A. Barnard, 69:Vol51No1-536
Kunert, G. Stilleben.
M. Hamburger, 617(TLS):7Oct83-1075
Küng, H. Does God Exist?* (French title: Dieu existe-t-il?)
L. Dupré, 322(JHI):Jul-Sep82-517
R. Prévost, 192(EP):Oct-Dec82-502
Küng, H. and E. Schillebeeckx. Consensus in Theology? (L. Swidler, ed)
C. Davis, 529(QQ):Spring82-225
Kunnas, T. Nietzsche ou l'esprit de contradiction.*
E. Joos, 154:Mar82-150
Kunstmann, P. - see "Treize Miracles de Notre-Dame"
Kuntz, M.L. Guillaume Postel, Prophet of the Restitution of All Things.
E.F. Hirsch, 319:Jan83-99
Kunze-Götte, E. Corpus Vasorum Antiquorum. (Deutschland, Vol 37)
J.M. Hemelrijk, 394:Vol35fasc3/4-444
Künzig, J. and W. Werner-Künzig, eds. Lied- und Erzählgut der Resi Klemm aus Almáskamarás im ungarischen Banat.
E. Moser-Rath, 196:Band23Heft1/2-134
Kunzle, D. Fashion and Fetishism.*
M. Connor, 127:Summer82-165
Künzle, P. Heinrich Seuses Horologium Sapientiae.
H.J. Vermeer, 224(GRM):Band32Heft2-250
Kuoni, B. Cestería Tradicional Ibérica.
B.S. Holland, 139:Aug/Sep82-22
Kuper, L. Genocide.*
639(VQR):Summer82-89
Kupferschmid, G.S. Y tú, ¿qué dices?
F.W. Medley, Jr., 399(MLJ):Winter82-439
Kupper, H.J. Robert Burns im deutschen Sprachraum unter besonderer Berücksichtigung der schweizerdeutschen Übersetzungen von August Corrodi.*
M. Lord, 549(RLC):Oct-Dec82-515
Kuretsky, S.D. The Paintings of Jacob Ochterveldt (1634-1682).*
C. Brown, 39:Mar82-210
Kurita, V. The Second Big Book of Afghans.
M. Cowan, 614:Fall83-23
Kuriyama, C.B. Hammer or Anvil.*
C.J. Summers, 301(JEGP):Apr82-254
Kuroda, S-Y. The 'W'hole of the Doughnut.
G. Mallinson, 361:Jan82-96
A.R. Tellier, 189(EA):Jan-Mar82-72
Kurosawa, A. Something Like an Autobiography.*
J. Kirkup, 617(TLS):18Nov83-1290
Kurrik, M.J. Literature and Negation.
E. Engelberg, 125:Spring82-306
Kurt, C. Seemännische Fachausdrücke bei Homer.
J.B. Hainsworth, 123:Vol32No2-269
Kurtzman, J.G. Essays on the Monteverdi Mass and Vespers of 1610.
D. Arnold, 410(M&L):Jan81-88

Kurz, G., D. Müller and W. Nicolai, eds. Gnomosyne.
P. Chuvin, 555:Vol56fasc2-315
Kurze, W. Codex diplomaticus Amiatinus.
L.E. Boyle, 589:Oct82-908
Kurzke, H. Auf der Suche nach der verlorenen Irrationalität.
T.J. Reed, 402(MLR):Oct82-998
Kurzman, D. Ben-Gurion.
J. Feron, 441:25Dec83-4
Kurzweil, E. The Age of Structuralism.*
A. Jackson, 208(FS):Jan82-105
L.K. Penrod, 188(ECr):Spring82-92
R. Selden, 161(DUJ):Dec81-156
Kurzweil, E. and W. Phillips, eds. Writers and Politics.
D.A.N. Jones, 362:23Jun83-26
Kushner, D. The Witness and Other Stories.
W. Grady, 102(CanL):Spring82-115
Kushner, E. and R. Struc, eds. Actes du VIIe Congrès de l'Association Internationale de Littérature Comparée/Proceedings of the 7th Congress of the International Comparative Literature Association. (Vols 1 and 2)
G.M. Vajda, 52:Band16Heft2-171
Kutsche, P. and J.R. Van Ness. Cañones.
584(SWR):Summer82-v
Kux, M. Moderne Dichterdramen.
G. Brude-Firnau, 221(GQ):May82-457
H. Feldkamp, 72:Band218Heft2-413
M. Jacobs, 402(MLR):Oct82-1001
Kuzma, G. Adirondacks.
M. Sanders, 584(SWR):Summer82-350
Kuzminsky, K.K. and G.L. Kovalev, eds. The Blue Lagoon Anthology of Modern Russian Poetry.* (Vol 1)
J. Graffy, 575(SEER):Apr82-285
Kvideland, R., ed. Glunten og riddar Rev. Eventyr frå Nord-Norge.
K. Schier, 196:Band23Heft1/2-136
Kvideland, R., ed. Lita-Frid-Kirsti.*
B. af Klintberg, 64(Arv):Vol36-210
"Kvinnen i russisk litteratur."
A. Bäckström, 172(Edda):1982/3-188
Kwanten, L. Imperial Nomads.*
P.D. Buell, 293(JASt):Feb82-331
Kwock, C.H. and V. McHugh, eds and trans. Old Friends From Far Away.
V. Young, 472:Spring/Summer83-168
Kwofie, E.N. The Acquisition and Use of French as a Second Language in Africa.
W. Bal, 209(FM):Jan82-87
Kwofie, E.N. Teaching a Foreign Language to the West African Student.
W. Bal, 209(FM):Jan82-86
Kynaston, D. Bobby Abel.
T.D. Smith, 617(TLS):28Jan83-91

Labalme, P.H., ed. Beyond Their Sex.
R.C. Trexler, 551(RenQ):Winter81-565
Labandeira Fernández, A. - see Rodríguez de Lena, P.
Labaree, B.W. Colonial Massachusetts.*
F. Shuffelton, 173(ECS):Summer83-415
Labarge, M.W. Medieval Travellers.
J. Sumption, 617(TLS):18Feb83-165
Labé, L. Oeuvres complètes. (E. Giudici, ed)
Y. Bellenger, 535(RHL):Sep-Dec82-869
M-R. Logan, 551(RenQ):Winter82-649

Labhardt, R. Metapher und Geschichte.
  J. Villwock, 224(GRM):Band32Heft2-240
Laborderie, J. Le dialogue platonicien de
  la maturité.*
  Y. Lafrance, 154:Mar82-165
Labov, W. and B.S. Weinreich - see Wein-
  reich, U.
Labowsky, L. Bessarion's Library and the
  Biblioteca Marciana.*
  M.D. Feld, 517(PBSA):Vol76No3-362
  M.J.C. Lowry, 123:Vol32No1-84
  J. Monfasani, 551(RenQ):Summer82-265
Labrie, R. The Art of Thomas Merton.*
  E. Griffin, 178:Sep82-385
  M.W. Higgins, 106:Spring82-127
Labrousse, E. Bayle.
  A. Ryan, 362:17Mar83-22
Lacan, J. Le Séminaire.* (Bk 3)
  A. Calame, 450(NRF):Apr82-132
La Capra, D. "Madame Bovary" on Trial.
  R. Chambers, 400(MLN):Dec82-1251
  W. Fowlie, 569(SR):Summer82-lxiv
La Capra, D. A Preface to Sartre.*
  R. Goldthorpe, 208(FS):Jan82-98
  C. Howells, 323:Jan82-89
La Capra, D. and S.L. Kaplan, eds. Mod-
  ern European Intellectual History.
  P. Burke, 617(TLS):8Jul83-723
"Lace."
  R.L. Shep, 614:Spring83-16
Lacey, A.R. Modern Philosophy.
  483:Apr82-280
Lacey, L., ed. Lunenburg County Folklore
  and Oral History.
  J.D.A. Widdowson, 203:Vol93No1-125
Lach, D.F. Asia in the Making of Europe.
  (Vol 2, Bks 2 and 3)
  E.G. Pulleyblank, 318(JAOS):Jul-Sep81-
  388
La Charité, R.C. Recreation, Reflection
  and Re-creation.*
  R.M. Berrong, 400(MLN):May82-1010
  T. Cave, 535(RHL):May-Jun82-453
  A. Glauser, 551(RenQ):Autumn82-500
  F. Rigolot, 210(FrF):May82-189
Lachenaud, G. Mythologies, religion et
  philosophie de l'histoire de Hérodote.
  J. Laborderie, 555:Vol55fasc2-333
Lachmann, K. - see Wolfram von Eschenbach
Lachmann, R., ed. Die Makarij-Rhetorik
  (Knigi sut' ritoriki dvoi po tonku v
  voprosech spisany).
  A.R. Hippisley, 575(SEER):Jan82-89
Lachtman, H. - see London, J.
Lackey, L.M. The Pottery of Acatlán.
  584(SWR):Summer82-v
Laclavetine, J-M. Loin d'Aswerda.
  A. Clerval, 450(NRF):Jun82-124
de Laclos, P-A.C. Oeuvres complètes.* (L.
  Versini, ed)
  P-E. Levayer, 535(RHL):Jul-Aug82-661
"Laclos et le libertinage, 1782-1982."
  D. Coward, 617(TLS):16Dec83-1408
Lacocque, A. The Book of Daniel.
  S.A. Kaufman, 318(JAOS):Apr-Jun81-250
Lacombe, A. Des Compositeurs pour l'image.
  P. O'Connor, 617(TLS):6May83-470
Lacombe, O. Indianité.
  L. Sternbach, 318(JAOS):Oct-Dec81-480
Lacorne, D. Les Notables rouges.
  F. Busi, 207(FR):Feb83-496
Lacoste, J. La philosophie de l'art.
  P. Somville, 542:Jan-Mar82-97

Lacoue-Labarthe, P. Le sujet de la philoso-
  ophie.
  C. Chalier, 192(EP):Oct-Dec81-488
Lacouture, J. Léon Blum.*
  R.O. Paxton, 453(NYRB):20Jan83-16
Lacouture, J. François Mauriac.
  D. O'Connell, 207(FR):Dec82-330
Lacroix, B. Folklore de la mer et reli-
  gion.
  G. Thomas, 102(CanL):Spring82-130
Lacroix, J. Le personnalisme, sources,
  fondements, actualité.
  A. Reix, 542:Oct-Dec82-677
Lacy, N.J. The Craft of Chrétien de
  Troyes.*
  R.T. Pickens, 210(FrF):May82-186
Ladbury, A. The Dressmaker's Dictionary.
  P. Bach, 614:Winter83-16
Ladd, D.R., Jr. The Structure of Intona-
  tional Meaning.*
  R. Gunter, 355(LSoc):Aug82-297
  G. Knowles, 297(JL):Mar82-202
Ladd, J.D. SBS: The Invisible Raiders.
  C. Wain, 362:18Aug83-21
Ladero Quesada, M.A. and M. González
  Jiménez. Diezmo eclesiástico y produc-
  ción de cereales en el reino de Sevilla
  (1408-1503).
  J. Boswell, 589:Jan82-145
Ladurie, E.L. - see under Le Roy Ladurie,
  E.
Madame de Lafayette. Histoire de la Prin-
  cesse de Montpensier sous le règne de
  Charles IXème roi de France; Histoire de
  la Comtesse de Tende.* (M. Cuénin, ed)
  N. Aronson, 475:Vol9No17-756
Madame de Lafayette. La Princess de
  Clèves. (ed unknown)
  F. Taliaferro, 135:Jun82-144
Marquis de Lafayette. Lafayette in the
  Age of the American Revolution. (Vols
  2-4) (S.J. Idzerda and others, eds)
  B.A. Chernow, 656(WMQ):Oct82-719
La Feber, W. Inevitable Revolutions.
  A. Stepan, 441:6Nov83-12
Lafitau, J-F. Moeurs des sauvages améri-
  cains comparées aux moeurs des premiers
  temps. (E.H. Lemay, ed)
  A. Pagden, 617(TLS):14Oct83-1131
Lafleur, B. Dictionnaire des expressions
  idiomatiques françaises.
  G. Matoré, 209(FM):Oct82-354
Lafond, J. and A. Redondo, eds. L'image
  du monde renversé et ses représentations
  littéraires et para-littéraires de la
  fin du xvie siècle au milieu du xviie
  siècle.*
  P. Rudnytsky, 551(RenQ):Autumn81-443
Laforgue, J. Les Complaintes, l'Imitation
  de Notre Dame la Lune. (P. Reboul, ed)
  D. Arkell, 208(FS):Apr82-223
  D. Grojnowski, 535(RHL):Sep-Dec82-940
Laforgue, J. Moralités légendaires.* (D.
  Grojnowski, ed)
  C.W. Thompson, 402(MLR):Apr82-458
La France, M. Denise Pelletier, ou la
  folie du théâtre.
  L.E. Doucette, 627(UTQ):Summer82-481
Lafrance, Y. La théorie platonicienne de
  la Doxa.
  Y. Brès, 542:Apr-Jun82-462
  J.W. Dye, 319:Jul83-393
  T.M. Robinson, 627(UTQ):Summer82-503

Lagemann, E.C. A Generation of Women.
   A.C. Fellman, 106:Spring82-61
Lagerkvist, P. Mariamne.
   J-L. Gautier, 450(NRF):Jan82-150
Lagerroth, E. Litteraturvetenskapen vid
en korsväg.
   A. Linneberg, 172(Edda):1982/5-314
Lago, M. - see Burne-Jones, E.C.
Lago, M. and P.N. Furbank - see Forster,
E.M.
de Laguna, A.R-S. - see under Rodríguez-
Seda de Laguna, A.
Lahousse, A. Le vocabulaire de la cosméto-
logie en français contemporain.
   R. Arveiller, 209(FM):Apr82-171
   H.J. Wolf, 547(RF):Band94Heft1-96
Lahr, J. Coward the Playwright.*
   C. Hawtree, 364:Dec82/Jan83-139
Laine, M. Bibliography of Works on John
Stuart Mill.
   W. Thomas, 617(TLS):15Apr83-387
Lainé, P. Terre des ombres.
   V. Beauvois, 450(NRF):Jun82-116
Lainez, M.M. The Wandering Unicorn.
   P-L. Adams, 61:Jul83-108
   C. Greenland, 617(TLS):22Apr83-399
   442(NY):4Jul83-90
Laird, C. The Word.
   639(VQR):Spring82-57
Lakebrink, B. Kommentar zu Hegels Logik
in seiner "Enzyklopädie" von 1830.*
(Vol 1)
   K. Hedwig, 319:Jul82-317
Lakeman, E. Power to Elect.
   D. Butler, 617(TLS):7Jan83-4
Lakoff, G. and M. Johnson. Metaphors We
Live By.*
   W.C. Booth, 185:Apr83-619
   R.R. Butters, 579(SAQ):Winter82-128
   T.S. Champlin, 518:Apr82-111
   W.T. Gordon, 320(CJL):Spring82-81
   J.M. Lawler, 350:Mar83-201
   W.N., 102(CanL):Spring82-163
   F.H. Nuessel, Jr., 361:Feb82-185
   M.K. Smith, 35(AS):Summer82-128
   B.M.H. Strang, 402(MLR):Jan82-134
Lakoff, S., ed. Science and Ethical Re-
sponsibility.
   M.S.M., 185:Jan83-440
Lal, B.K. Contemporary Indian Philosophy.
   W. Halbfass, 318(JAOS):Oct-Dec81-474
Lam, W.M.C. Perception and Lighting as
Formgivers for Architecture.
   S. Matthews, 505:Apr82-204
Lamarque, P., ed. Philosophy and Fiction.
   C. Norris, 617(TLS):23Sep83-1024
Lamb, C. Lamb as Critic. (R. Park, ed)
   J.H. Alexander, 677(YES):Vol 12-293
   J. Haefner, 481(PQ):Summer82-365
   S. Jones, 447(N&Q):Oct81-440
   W.J.B. Owen, 541(RES):Nov82-486
Lamb, C. and M.A. Tales from Shakespeare.*
   (E. van Bergen and S. Barbour, eds)
   M. Allentuck, 570(SQ):Spring82-123
Lamb, D. The Africans.
   A. Cowell, 441:6Feb83-7
   M. Crowder, 617(TLS):16Sep83-982
Lamb, D. Hegel.
   W.V. Doniela, 63:Jun82-189
   H.S. Harris, 319:Oct82-441

Lamb, D. Language and Perception in Hegel
and Wittgenstein.
   N. Gerth, 482(PhR):Oct82-638
   H.S. Harris, 319:Oct82-441
Lamb, H.H. Climate History and the Modern
World.
   E. Le Roy Ladurie, 617(TLS):21Jan83-47
Lamb, M. "Antony and Cleopatra" on the
English Stage.*
   T.R. Griffiths, 611(TN):Vol36No1-38
Lamb, P.F. and K.J. Hohlwein. Touchstones.
   G.A. De Candido, 441:20Mar83-16
Lamb, V. and J. Holmes. Nigerian Weaving.
   P.J. Shea, 2(AfrA):May82-85
Lambdin, T.O. Introduction to Classical
Ethiopic (Ge'ez).
   J. Fellman, 318(JAOS):Oct-Dec81-459
Lambert, A.M. Storage of Textiles and
Costumes.
   R.L. Shep, 614:Fall83-23
Lambert, B., ed. Music in Colonial Mass-
achusetts: 1630-1820. (Vol 1: Music in
Public Places.)
   N. Cooke, 432(NEQ):Sep82-457
Lambert, D. The Red Dove.*
   E. Hunter, 441:25Sep83-21
Lambert, G. Running Time.*
   E. Jakab, 441:1May83-14
   442(NY):25Apr83-153
Lambert, J. - see Gide, A. and D. Bussy
Lambert, K. and G.G. Brittan, Jr. An
Introduction to the Philosophy of
Science. (2nd ed)
   P. Teller, 316:Jun82-476
Lambert, M. Dickens and the Suspended
Quotation.*
   M. Moseley, 569(SR):Winter82-83
Lambert, S. Matisse, Lithographs.
   R. Hobbs, 59:Dec82-511
Lambertino, A. Max Scheler.
   F. Volpi, 687:Apr-Jun81-316
Lambourne, L. Utopian Craftsmen.*
   W.S. Ayres, 576:Dec82-352
   P. Skipwith, 90:May82-309
Lambourne, L. and J. Hamilton, comps.
British Watercolours in the Victoria and
Albert Museum.*
   D. Robinson, 39:Sep82-200
Lambranzi, G. Neue und curieuse theatral-
ische Tantz-Schul.
   W. Dimter, 684(ZDA):Band111Heft2-78
Lambton, A. Snow and Other Stories.
   D. Montrose, 617(TLS):21Oct83-1157
de Lamennais, F. Correspondance Générale.
(Vols 8 and 9) (L. Le Guillou, ed)
   A.R. Vidler, 208(FS):Oct82-480
Lamming, R.M. The Notebook of Gismondo
Cavalletti.
   T. Sutcliffe, 617(TLS):16Dec83-1412
Lamont, C. - see Scott, W.
Lamont, C. and L. - see Masefield, J.
Lamont, W.D. Law and Moral Order.
   A.H. Lesser, 518:Jan82-55
Lamont, W.M. Richard Baxter and the Mil-
lenium.
   J.R. Jacob, 173(ECS):Summer82-457
Lamott, A. Rosie.
   442(NY):19Dec83-140
Lamotte, É. - see "The Teaching of Vimala-
kīrti"
L'Amour, L. The Lonesome Gods.
   M. Watkins, 441:24Apr83-16
   442(NY):16May83-133

Lampe, J.R. and M.R. Jackson. Balkan
Economic History, 1550-1950.
639(VQR):Autumn82-127
Lampl, H. and A.A. Hansen-Löve, eds.
Marina Cvetaeva.
S.C. Capus, 575(SEER):Oct82-618
Lamson, C. "Bloody Decks and a Bumper
Crop."
D. Kodish, 292(JAF):Apr-Jun82-237
Lamy, L. Egyptian Mysteries.
J.A. West, 469:Vol8No3-116
Lancashire, I., ed. Two Tudor Interludes.*
S. Carpenter, 541(RES):Nov82-461
J.S. Colley, 130:Summer82-193
Lancaster, C. The Japanese Influence in
America.
E. Seidensticker, 441:11Dec83-14
Lance, H.D. The Old Testament and the
Archaeologist.
A. Phillips, 617(TLS):1Jul83-702
"Lancelot, roman en prose du XIIIe
siècle."* (Vols 5 and 6) (A. Micha, ed)
F. Lecoy, 554:Vol 102No1-130
Lanchester, E. Elsa Lanchester Herself.
J. Houseman, 441:17Apr83-7
B. Weeks, 18:Jul-Aug83-55
Land, A.C. Colonial Maryland.
T.O. Hanley, 656(WMQ):Oct82-693
Land, L.K. - see Nicholson, H.B. and A.
Cordy-Collins
Landa, L.A. Essays in Eighteenth-Century
English Literature.*
P. Harth, 191(ELN):Sep82-61
S.S., 189(EA):Oct-Dec82-495
H.M. Solomon, 577(SHR):Winter82-69
566:Autumn82-60
Landeira, R. An Annotated Bibliography of
Gabriel Miró (1900-1978).
S.E. Ugalde, 552(REH):Jan82-153
Landeira, R., ed. Critical Essays on
Gabriel Miró.*
E.S. Morby, 345(KRQ):Vol29No1-107
Landerman, P. Vocabulario Quechua del
Pastaza.
G.F. Meier, 682(ZPSK):Band34Heft4-503
Landes, D.S. Revolution in Time.
E.J. Hobsbawm, 453(NYRB):8Dec83-35
T. Kidder, 441:23Oct83-3
Landi, A. Antroponimia Siceliota.
E.E. Rice, 123:Vol32No2-225
Landino, C. Disputationes Camaldulenses.
(P. Lohe, ed)
R. Deakins, 551(RenQ):Autumn81-389
Landon, H.C.R. Haydn. (Vols 1, 3 and 4)
B. Churgin, 173(ECS):Spring83-346
Landon, H.C.R. Haydn: A Documentary
Study.*
S. Sadie, 415:Mar82-187
Landow, G.P., ed. Approaches to Victorian
Autobiography.*
A.F.T. Lurcock, 541(RES):Feb82-97
W.A. Madden, 125:Fall01-101
Landow, G.P. William Holman Hunt and
Typological Symbolism.*
J. Christian, 90:Jan82-37
Landow, G.P. Victorian Types, Victorian
Shadows.*
L. Ormond, 90:Dec82-777
H. Sussman, 301(JEGP):Oct82-577
Landry, G. Sept-Iles Racontée.
G. Thomas, 102(CanL):Spring82-130
Lane, G. Chicago Churches and Synagogues.
T.M. Karlowicz, 576:May82-165

Lane, J. I Want to Tell You Lies.*
D. Barbour, 648(WCR):Summer81-83
Lane, M. Gold and Silver Needlepoint.
P. Bach, 614:Fall83-20
Lane, P. The Measure.
P. Herman, 137:Aug82-12
I. Sowton, 102(CanL):Winter81-102
Lane, P. Old Mother.
S. Gingell, 628(UWR):Spring-Summer83-
91
D. Gutteridge, 99:Mar83-34
Lane, R. Images from the Floating World.
H.A. Link, 39:Aug82-121
Lang, C.Y. and E.F. Shannon, Jr. - see
Tennyson, A.
Lang, D. The Wild Flower Finder's Calen-
dar.
R.I. Ross, 617(TLS):1Jul83-692
von Lang, J., with C. Sibyll - see Eich-
mann, A.
Langacker, R.W. - see Kalectaca, M.
Lange, O. The Land of the Long Shadow.
R. Gish, 649(WAL):Summer82-193
Lange, P., G. Ross and M. Vannicelli.
Unions, Change and Crisis.
P. Allum, 617(TLS):22Apr83-407
Lange, W. Theater in Deutschland nach
1945.
S. Gittleman, 221(GQ):Mar82-282
Lange, W-D., ed. Französische Literatur
des 19. Jahrhunderts.*
S. Himmelsbach, 535(RHL):Sep-Dec82-928
Langenbacher, J. Das "néo-français."
G. Holtus, 553(RLiR):Jul-Dec82-495
"Langenscheidts Grosswörterbuch Franzö-
sisch." (new ed) (Pt 1: Französisch-
Deutsch.) (E. Weis, ed)
F.J. Hausmann, 257(IRAL):Feb82-73
Langer, G. Das Märchen in der tschech-
ischen Literatur von 1790 bis 1860.*
W.F. Schwarz, 52:Band16Heft3-320
Langer, L.L. Versions of Survival.
T. Ziolkowski, 569(SR):Fall82-592
Langevin, G. Issue de secours.
M.G. Rose, 207(FR):May83-980
Langfeldt, G. and Ø. Ødegård. Den retts-
psykiatriske erklaering om Knut Hamsun.
Y. Mazor, 563(SS):Autumn82-313
Langguth, A.J. Saki.*
H.H. Watts, 395(MFS):Summer82-281
Langhans, E.A. Restoration Promptbooks.
R.D. Hume, 612(ThS):May82-124
Langker, R. Flash in New South Wales.
J.S. Ryan, 67:Nov82-220
Langley, L.D. The United States and the
Caribbean, 1900-1970.*
C. Pérotin, 189(EA):Jul-Sep82-358
Langner, H. Untersuchungen zur Mundart
und zur Umgangssprache im Raum um Witten-
berg.
D. Stellmacher, 685(ZDL):2/1981-252
Lanham, R.A. Literacy and the Survival of
Humanism.
T. Paulin, 617(TLS):30Dec83-1448
Lankheit, K. Die Modellsammlung der
Porzellan-Manufaktur Doccia.
C. Avery, 39:Oct82-277
Lanner, R.M. The Piñon Pine.
J. Hart, 649(WAL):Summer82-167
Lanning, G. and M. Mueller. Africa Under-
mined.
J. Doherty, 69:Vol51No1-533

Laster, A. Pleins feux sur Victor Hugo.
F. Bassan, 446(NCFS):Fall-Winter82/83-
189
Laszlo, E. and D. Keys, eds. Disarmament.
S.P., 185:Oct82-220
Latacz, J. Kampfparänese, Kampfdarstel-
lung und Kampfwirklichkeit in der
"Ilias," bei Kallinos und Tyrtaios.
F.M. Combellack, 122:Jan82-62
"Lateinisches Hexameter-Lexikon."* (Pt 1)
(O. Schumann and B. Bischoff, comps)
E.J. Kenney, 123:Vol32No2-220
J. Soubiran, 555:Vol56fasc1-149
"Lateinisches Hexameter-Lexikon." (Pts 2
and 3) (O. Schumann, ed)
J. Soubiran, 555:Vol56fasc1-151
Latham, I. Joseph Maria Olbrich.
H-W. Kruft, 576:Mar82-67
Latham, J. Unpacking Mr. Jones.
G. Szirtes, 617(TLS):15Jul83-757
Latham, R. and W. Matthews, eds. The
Diary of Samuel Pepys. (Vols 10 and 11)
C. Driver, 362:24Feb83-26
D. Nokes, 617(TLS):18Mar83-263
V.S. Pritchett, 453(NYRB):27Oct83-56
Lathem, E.C. - see Cook, S.J.
Lathrop, T.A. The Evolution of Spanish.*
J.M. Lipski, 238:May82-318
R. Penny, 86(BHS):Apr82-147
M.C. Resnick, 304(JHP):Fall82-57
Latini, B. Tesoretto. (D. Baker, ed and
trans)
M. Moog-Grünewald, 52:Band16Heft2-189
La Touche, R. John Ruskin and Rose La
Touche.* (V.A. Burd, ed)
P.F., 189(EA):Jul-Sep82-371
M. Hardman, 677(YES):Vol 12-321
Latour, B. and S. Woolgar. Laboratory
Life.
V. van Themaat, 679:Band13Heft1-166
Latrobe, B.H. The Journals of Benjamin
Henry Latrobe 1799-1820. (Vol 3) (E.C.
Carter 2d and others, eds)
639(VQR):Winter82-16
Lattimore, R. - see "Acts and Letters of
the Apostles"
de Lattre, A. La Bêtise d'Emma Bovary.
B.F. Bart, 207(FR):Dec82-324
de Lattre, A. La Doctrine de la réalité
chez Proust.*
M. Mein, 208(FS):Apr82-228
Lau, J.S.M., C.T. Hsia and L.O. Lee, eds.
Modern Chinese Stories and Novellas 1919-
1949.
J. Wills, 268(IFR):Winter83-59
639(VQR):Winter82-8
Lau, J.S.M. and T.A. Ross, eds. Chinese
Stories from Taiwan: 1960-1970.
W.L.Y. Yang, 318(JAOS):Oct-Dec81-426
Lauben, P. A Surfeit of Alibis.*
N. Callendar, 441:20Nov83-41
Laudan, H. Science and Hypothesis.
H. Lehman, 154:Dec82-780
T. Nickles, 486:Dec82-653
Laude, J. Le dict de Cassandre.
M. Collot, 98:Oct82-866
Lauer, R., ed. Europäischer Realismus.
B. Zimmermann, 133:Band15Heft4-376
Laufer, B. Kleinere Schriften von Bert-
hold Laufer. (Pt 2) (H. Walravens, ed)
J.W. de Jong, 259(IIJ):Jan82-68

Lauffer, H. Der Lehnwortschatz der alt-
hochdeutschen und altsächsischen Pruden-
tiusglossen.
T. Klein, 684(ZDA):Band111Heft1-12
Laufs, M. Walter Jens.
M. Gerber, 221(GQ):Mar82-285
Laufs, M. Politik und Recht bei Innozenz
III.
J.M. Powell, 589:Oct82-909
Laughlan, W.F. - see Hogg, J.
Laughlin, R.M. Of Cabbages and Kings.
G.H. Gossen, 292(JAF):Apr-Jun82-225
Laughlin, R.M. Of Shoes and Ships and
Sealing Wax.
G.H. Gossen, 292(JAF):Apr-Jun82-225
Launey, M. Introduction à la Langue et à
la Litterature Azteques.* (Vol 1)
[entry in prev was of Vols 1 and 2]
F. Karttunen, 269(IJAL):Jan82-101
Launitz-Schürer, L.S., Jr. Loyal Whigs
and Revolutionaries.
D.R. Gerlach, 656(WMQ):Apr82-378
Laurence, D.H. - see Shaw, G.B.
Laurence, M. Patricia Morley.
L.K. MacKendrick, 198:Jul82-96
Laurens, A-F. and O. Touchefeu. Corpus
Vasorum Antiquorum. (France, fasc 29)
B.A. Sparkes, 303(JoHS):Vol 102-285
Laurens, H. The Papers of Henry Laurens.
(Vols 6-9) (G.C. Rogers, Jr. and D.R.
Chesnutt, eds)
R.M. Weir, 656(WMQ):Oct82-716
Laurenson, D., ed. The Sociology of Lit-
erature: Applied Studies.
R. Schwartz, 125:Winter82-204
Laurent, J. Les Sous-Ensembles flous.
F. de Martinoir, 450(NRF):Jan82-110
Laurent, M. Le Terrorisme linguistique.
G. Cesbron, 356(LR):Feb82-88
Laurenti, J.L. and A. Porqueras-Mayo. The
Spanish Golden Age (1472-1700).
T.S. Beardsley, Jr., 240(HR):Spring82-
231
D.W. Cruickshank, 402(MLR):Jul82-746
Lauterer, J. Wouldn't Take Nothin' for My
Journey Now.*
R. Manley, 292(JAF):Oct-Dec82-479
Lauth, R., H. Jacob and H. Gliwitzky - see
Fichte, J.G.
Comte de Lautréamont. Maldoror and Poems.
(P. Knight, ed and trans)
D. Hillery, 161(DUJ):Dec81-153
La Valley, A.J., ed. Mildred Pierce.
J. Basinger, 18:Jul-Aug82-72
Lavater, J.C. Aphorisms on Man (1788).
J. La Belle, 88:Fall82-126
Lavater, J.C. La physiognomonie, ou
l'art de connaître les hommes d'après
les traits de leur physionomie, leurs
rapports avec les divers animaux, leurs
penchants, etc. (1775-1778).
J-C. Lebensztejn, 98:Jan82-3
Laver, J. The Phonetic Description of
Voice Quality.
M.R. Key, 567:Vol40No1/2-173
F. Nolan, 297(JL):Sep82-442
Lavin, I. Bernini and the Unity of the
Visual Arts.*
F.S. Licht, 54:Sep82-513
J. Montagu, 90:Apr82-240
L.R. Rogers, 89(BJA):Winter82-87

Lavin, I. Drawings by Gianlorenzo Bernini from the Museum der Bildenden Künste, Leipzig, German Democratic Republic.*
  J.S. Held, 551(RenQ):Winter82-630
Lavin, M.A. Piero della Francesca's Baptism of Christ.*
  R. Cocke, 59:Dec82-508
  F. Russell, 39:May82-411
de Lavinheta, B. Explanatio compendiosaque applicatio Artis Raymundi Lulli.
  A. Llinarès, 192(EP):Jul-Sep81-357
Lavis, G. and M. Stasse. Les Chansons de Thibaut de Champagne.
  A. Gier, 547(RF):Band94Heft4-452
Lavroukine, N. and L. Tchertkov, with C. Robert. D.S. Mirsky.
  H.E. Bowman, 104(CASS):Spring82-144
  E. Delavenay, 189(EA):Jul-Sep82-351
  G.S. Smith, 575(SEER):Jul82-453
Law, R. The Horse in West African History.
  R. Harris, 69:Vol52No1-81
Law, V. The Insular Latin Grammarians.
  T.M. Charles-Edwards, 617(TLS):1Apr83-337
Law-Yone, W. The Coffin Tree.
  P-L. Adams, 61:Jun83-105
  E. Milton, 441:15May83-12
Lawler, D.L. Approaches to Science Fiction.
  C.B. Hunter, 561(SFS):Jul82-225
Lawler, T. The One and the Many in the "Canterbury Tales."*
  D. Mehl, 38:Band100Heft3/4-497
  H. Suhamy, 189(EA):Oct-Dec82-454
Lawler, T.M.C., G. Marc'hadour and R.C. Marius - see More, T.
Lawlor, R. Sacred Geometry.
  P. Tabor, 46:Sep82-94
  J.A. West, 469:Vol18No3-116
Lawrence, B.B. Notes from a Distant Flute.*
  S. Vahiduddin, 485(PE&W):Jan82-118
Lawrence, D.H. Apocalypse and the Writings on Revelation. (M. Kalnins, ed)
  H.T. Moore, 402(MLR):Apr82-433
  D.R. Schwarz, 395(MFS):Winter81/82-682
Lawrence, D.H. The Complete Poems. (V. de Sola Pinto and F.W. Roberts, eds)
  J. Silkin, 493:Dec81-35
  J. Silkin, 565:Vol23No1-31
Lawrence, D.H. The Letters of D.H. Lawrence.* (Vol 1) (J.T. Boulton, ed)
  H.T. Moore, 402(MLR):Oct82-945
Lawrence, D.H. The Letters of D.H. Lawrence.* (Vol 2) (G.J. Zytaruk and J.T. Boulton, eds)
  J. Meyers, 395(MFS):Summer82-274
Lawrence, K. The Inanna Poems.
  P. Mitcham, 102(CanL):Spring82-92
  B. Whiteman, 198:Apr82-112
Lawrence, K.R. The Odyssey of Style in "Ulysses."
  M.P. Gillespie, 594:Fall82-293
  D. Hayman, 141:Fall82-400
  P. Herring, 659(ConL):Fall83-387
  M.B. Pringle, 268(IFR):Winter83-70
  M.T. Reynolds, 395(MFS):Winter82/83-629
  295(JML):Dec82-478
Lawrence, M.G. Make No Little Plans.
  S. McQuillin, 576:Oct82-246

Lawrence, P.R. and D. Dyer. Renewing American Industry.
  L. Caplan, 441:16Oct83-19
"The Laws of the Muromachi Bakufu." (K. Grossberg and K. Nobuhisa, trans)
  A. Goble, 293(JASt):Feb82-358
Lawson, B.S. Joaquin Miller.*
  S. Cohen, 577(SHR):Summer82-277
Lawson, C. The Chalumeau in Eighteenth-Century Music.
  N. Shackleton, 415:Oct82-694
Lawson, W. The Western Scar.
  J. Booth, 617(TLS):15Apr83-386
Lawton, A. Vadim Shershenevich.
  H. Stephan, 574(SEEJ):Fall82-361
Layamon. Brut. (Vol 2) (G.L. Brook and R.F. Leslie, eds)
  L. Braswell, 178:Jun82-237
Layman, R. Dashiell Hammett.
  R.E. Stoddard, 517(PBSA):Vol76No2-232
Layton, I. Europe and Other Bad News.
  P. Mitcham, 102(CanL):Autumn82-122
  M.B. Oliver, 198:Oct82-105
  B. Whiteman, 298:Summer82-150
Layton, I. The Love Poems of Irving Layton.*
  D. Watmough, 102(CanL):Winter81-146
Layton, R. The Anthropology of Art.*
  J. Picton, 59:Jun82-219
  P. Stevens, Jr., 2(AfrA):Aug82-8
Lazard, M. Le Théâtre en France au XVIe siècle.*
  J. Bailbé, 535(RHL):Sep-Dec82-868
Lazare, B. L'antisémitisme, son histoire et ses causes.
  A. Reix, 542:Oct-Dec82-660
Lea, K.M. and T.M. Gang - see Tasso, T.
Lea, S. Searching the Drowned Man.*
  C. Fogel, 152(UDQ):Summer82-152
  R. Pybus, 565:Vol23No3-61
Leach, C. Texas Station.
  N. Callendar, 441:6Nov83-53
Leach, D., ed. Generative Literature and Generative Art.
  E. Kafalenos, 268(IFR):Summer83-143
Leach, W. True Love and Perfect Union.*
  N.F. Cott, 453(NYRB):17Mar83-36
Leader, Z. Reading Blake's Songs.*
  J. Blondel, 189(EA):Jul-Sep82-333
  M.L. Johnson, 301(JEGP):Oct82-572
Leake, R.E. Concordance des "Essais" de Montaigne.
  C. Clark, 208(FS):Oct82-463
  R.C. La Charité, 210(FrF):May82-191
Leamer, L. Make-Believe.
  N. Lemann, 441:26Jun83-7
  G. Vidal, 453(NYRB):29Sep83-28
Leante, C. Capitán de Cimarrones.
  O. Rossardi, 37:Sep-Oct82-64
Leapman, M. Barefaced Cheek.
  S. Jenkins, 362:7Jul83-28
  O.R. McGregor, 617(TLS):22Jul83-771
Leapman, M. The Companion Guide to New York.
  C. Hitchens, 617(TLS):30Sep83-1066
  N. Kenyon, 362:28Jul83-22
Lear, J. Aristotle and Logical Theory.*
  J. Corcoran and M. Scanlan, 479(PhQ):Jan82-76
  P.T. Geach, 483:Oct82-557
  I. Mueller, 482(PhR):Oct82-625
  P. Thom, 518:Apr82-73

Lears, T.J.J. No Place of Grace.*
   M. Goldstein, 569(SR):Spring82-xlviii
Leary, L. Ralph Waldo Emerson.*
   E. Wagenknecht, 677(YES):Vol 12-308
Leary, T. Flashbacks.
   H. Gold, 441:3Jul83-10
   G. Strawson, 617(TLS):25Nov83-1325
Leasor, J. Who Killed Sir Harry Oakes?
   J. Symons, 617(TLS):25Nov83-1305
Least Heat Moon, W. [W. Trogden] Blue
   Highways.
   J. Crace, 617(TLS):26Aug83-902
   N. Perrin, 441:6Feb83-1
   J. Updike, 442(NY):2May83-121
Leatherbarrow, W.J. Fedor Dostoevsky.
   L. Koehler, 574(SEEJ):Summer82-243
   N. Rzhevsky, 550(RusR):Oct82-527
Leaton, A. Good Friends, Just.
   M.K. Benet, 617(TLS):19Aug83-875
Leavis, F.R. The Critic as Anti-Philoso-
   pher.* (G. Singh, ed)
   W. Scammell, 364:Nov82-78
   N. Shrimpton, 362:10Mar83-23
Leavis, F.R. "Reading Out Poetry" and
   "Eugenio Montale: A Tribute."*
   R. Wellek, 402(MLR):Jul82-710
Lebensztejn, J-C. Zigzag.
   D. Semin, 98:Oct82-883
Lebeuf, R. Cosmic Presence.
   M. Adam, 542:Oct-Dec82-678
Leblanc, B.B. Faut divorcer!
   C.F. Coates, 207(FR):Mar83-663
Le Blanc, H. Bernadette Dupuis ou La
   Mort apprivoisée.
   H.R. Runte, 102(CanL):Autumn82-144
Le Bossu, R. Traité du poème épique.
   U. Dietsche, 475:Vol9No17-781
Le Bot, M. L'oeil du peintre.
   G. Quinsat, 450(NRF):Jun82-131
   O. Kaeppelin, 98:Dec82-1061
Le Boullec, A. - see Clement of Alexandria
Le Bouthillier, C. Isabelle-sur-mer.
   R. Boudreau, 102(CanL):Winter81-169
Le Bras, H. and E. Todd. L'Invention de
   la France.
   J-F. Brière, 207(FR):Feb83-495
Le Bris, M. Journal du Romantisme.
   T. Cordellier, 450(NRF):Mar82-125
Le Brocquy, L. A la recherche de W.B.
   Yeats.
   B. Guinness, 39:Sep82-201
Le Brun, C. A Method to Learn to Design
   the Passions (1734).*
   P-G.B., 189(EA):Oct-Dec82-495
Lecaye, A. Les Pirates du Paradis.
   M.A., 561(SFS):Jul82-221
Lech, R.B. All the Drowned Sailors.
   R.J. Margolis, 441:22May83-18
Lechanteur, J. Atlas linguistique de la
   Wallonie. (Vol 4)
   L. de Cock, 553(RLiR):Jan-Jun81-262
Lecker, P. and J. David, eds. The Anno-
   tated Bibliography of Canada's Major
   Authors.* (Vol 1)
   D. Staines, 365:Fall82-166
   D. Stephens, 178:Mar82-96
Lecker, R. and J. David, eds. The Anno-
   tated Bibliography of Canada's Major
   Authors.* (Vol 2)
   M.J. Edwards, 102(CanL):Summer82-151
   D. Staines, 365:Fall82-166

Le Clair, T. and L. McCaffery, eds. Any-
   thing Can Happen.
   D. Montrose, 617(TLS):23Sep83-1025
Le Clézio, J.M.G. La Ronde et autres
   faits divers.
   M. Le Clézio, 207(FR):Mar83-667
Le Comte, E. A Dictionary of Puns in
   Milton's English Poetry.*
   A. Burnett, 391:Mar82-12
Lecomte, M. Les Minutes insolites.
   J. Laurans, 450(NRF):Jan82-108
Lecuire, P. Textes.
   P. Bady, 98:Mar82-273
Lederer, D.P. Custom Draperies.
   P. Bach, 614:Winter83-21
Leduc, J. - see McMicking, T.
Ledwidge, B. De Gaulle.
   S. Hoffmann, 441:20Mar83-3
   F. Kersaudy, 617(TLS):4Feb83-99
   442(NY):25Apr83-154
Lee, A. Russian Journal.*
   E. Kagan-Kans, 550(RusR):Jul82-339
Lee, A.R., ed. Black Fiction.*
   M. Fabre, 677(YES):Vol 12-362
   R. Willett, 447(N&Q):Oct81-469
Lee, B. The Novels of Henry James.*
   J.W. Tuttleton, 677(YES):Vol 12-328
Lee, B. Theory and Personality.*
   A.D. Moody, 402(MLR):Jan82-192
   A.D. Nuttall, 541(RES):Feb82-110
   T. Pinkney, 366:Autumn82-248
Lee, C. and G. De Vos. Koreans in Japan.
   R.H. Mitchell, 407(MN):Autumn82-408
   Ōsawa Shin'ichirō, 285(JapQ):Oct-Dec82-
   488
Lee, H. Elizabeth Bowen.*
   C.W. Barrow, 174(Éire):Fall82-152
   M.M. Rowe, 395(MFS):Summer82-280
Lee, H. - see Smith, S.
Lee, H.Y. The Politics of the Chinese
   Cultural Revolution.
   J. Unger, 318(JAOS):Oct-Dec81-431
Lee, L. Two Women.
   A. Huth, 362:8Dec83-30
Lee, L.L. and M. Lewis, eds. Women, Women
   Writers, and the West.
   M. Gilliland, 106:Spring82-75
   L. Waldeland, 395(MFS):Winter81/82-725
Lee, L.O-F. - see Průšek, J.
Lee, P.H., ed. The Silence of Love.
   V. Young, 249(HudR):Spring82-139
Lee, S.J. Aspects of European History,
   1494-1789.
   J. Black, 161(DUJ):Dec81-121
Leech, G.N. and M.H. Short. Style in Fic-
   tion.
   J. Pauchard, 189(EA):Oct-Dec82-450
   V. Raskin, 395(MFS):Winter82/83-653
Leed, R.L., A.D. Nakhimovsky and A.S. Nak-
   himovsky. Beginning Russian. (Vol 1)
   M.I. Levin, 558(RLJ):Winter-Spring82-
   277
   J.S. Levine, 574(SEEJ):Summer82-254
   C.E. Townsend, 399(MLJ):Summer82-219
Leedy, W.C., Jr. Fan Vaulting.*
   F. Bucher, 54:Sep82-508
   N. Coldstream, 90:Mar82-166
   R. Mark, 589:Jan82-146
Lees-Milne, A. and R. Verey, eds. The
   Englishman's Garden.
   R.I. Ross, 617(TLS):25Feb83-192

Lees-Milne, J. Caves of Ice.
    V. Glendinning, 617(TLS):4Mar83-207
    A. Watkins, 362:14Apr83-30
Lees-Milne, J. The Country House.
    B. Gutteridge, 364:Feb83-119
Lees-Milne, J. The Last Stuarts.
    C. Bingham, 617(TLS):30Dec83-1464
Lefebvre, C., L. Drapeau and C. Dubuison,
    eds. Le français parlé en milieu popu-
    laire. (No 1)
    B. Laks, 355(LSoc):Dec82-463
Lefèbvre, C., H. Magloire-Holly and N.
    Piou, eds. Syntaxe de l'haïtien.
    D. Bickerton, 350:Sep83-704
    C. Corne, 350:Sep83-705
Lefebvre, H. La présence et l'absence.*
    R.S., 543:Sep81-145
Lefever, E.W. and E.S. Hunt, eds. The
    Apocalyptic Premise.
    E. Grossman, 441:30Jan83-14
Lefèvre, E. Der "Phormio" des Terenz und
    der "Epidikazomenos" des Apollodor von
    Karystos.*
    E. Fantham, 122:Oct82-365
Lefèvre d'Étaples, J. Quincuplex Psalte-
    rium.*
    K.M. Hall, 208(FS):Apr82-194
Lefèvre d'Étaples, J. - see under
    Bedouelle, G.
Leffland, E. Last Courtesies and Other
    Stories.*
    B. Lyons, 573(SSF):Winter82-88
Leffler, M.P. The Elusive Quest.*
    A. Orde, 161(DUJ):Dec81-131
Lefkowitz, M.R. The Lives of the Greek
    Poets.*
    J. Fairweather, 123:Vol32No2-183
Lefler, H.T. and W.S. Powell. Colonial
    North Carolina.*
    F. Shuffelton, 173(ECS):Summer83-415
Lefort, C. L'invention démocratique. Per-
    manence du théologico-politique?
    C. Mouchard, 98:Apr82-281
Lefort, C. Sur une colonne absente.*
    J-L. Bentajou, 98:May82-462
Lefrançois, T. Nicolas Bertin, 1668-1736.
    P. Conisbee, 59:Sep82-363
Legány, D. Ferenc Liszt and His Country
    1869-1873.
    A. Walker, 617(TLS):11Nov83-1250
"The Legend of Duke Ernst."* (J.W. Thomas
    and C. Dussère, eds and trans)
    P.A. Giangrosso, 589:Apr82-437
    D.K. Watkins, 301(JEGP):Jan82-77
Legendre, P. Paroles poétiques échappées
    du texte.
    J. le Hardi, 450(NRF):Dec82-101
"Fernand Léger."
    J.B., 55:Nov82-52
Leggatt, A. Ben Jonson.*
    J. Arnold, 568(SCN):Spring-Summer82-1
    R.S. Peterson, 551(RenQ):Winter82-666
Legge, S. Affectionate Cousins.
    R. Fréchet, 189(EA):Apr-Jun82-228
    D. Middleton, 598(SoR):Winter83-219
Leggett, G. The Cheka.
    L.H. Siegelbaum, 550(RusR):Apr82-210
    P.S. Squire, 575(SEER):Jan82-132
    639(VQR):Winter82-21
Leghorn, L. and K. Parker. Woman's Worth.
    A.S., 185:Oct82-212

Le Goff, J. La naissance du Purgatoire.
    J-C. Bonne, 98:Dec82-1006
    A-C. Brès, 542:Jul-Sep82-540
    J-P. Guinle, 450(NRF):Feb82-138
Legon, R.P. Megara.
    G. Huxley, 123:Vol32No2-227
Le Guillou, L. - see de Lamennais, F.
Le Guin, U.K. The Eye of the Heron.
    P-L. Adams, 61:Feb83-105
    G. Jonas, 441:22May83-15
Le Guin, U.K. Hard Words and Other Poems.*
    J.D. McClatchy, 491:Sep82-348
Leheny, J. - see Addison, J.
Lehman, D. and C. Berger, eds. James
    Merrill.
    R.W. Flint, 441:13Mar83-6
    D.W. Hartnett, 617(TLS):9Dec83-1384
Lehman, P. and W. Luhr. Blake Edwards.*
    M. Meisel, 18:Jun82-71
Lehmann, D. and others. Lire en français
    les sciences économiques et sociales.
    C. Le Goff, 207(FR):Mar83-650
Lehmann, G. James Bond, héros mythique.
    S. Dutruch, 189(EA):Jan-Mar82-103
Lehmann, G. Kants Tugenden.
    W. Steinbeck, 342:Band73Heft2-253
Lehmann, J. The Strange Destiny of Rupert
    Brooke.*
    S. Rudikoff, 31(ASch):Autumn82-563
Lehmann, P.L. and R. Wolff. Das Stefan-
    George-Seminar 1978 in Bingen am Rhein.
    B. Sorg, 52:Band16Heft1-113
Lehmann, P.W. Cyriacus of Ancona's Egyp-
    tian Visit and Its Reflections in Gen-
    tile Bellini and Hieronymus Bosch.
    C. Dempsey, 551(RenQ):Spring81-123
Lehnert, M. Altenglisches Elementarbuch.
    (9th ed)
    P.T. Roberge, 685(ZDL):3/1982-372
Lehrman, E. A Guide to the Russian Texts
    of Tolstoi's "War and Peace."
    T.R. Beyer, Jr., 558(RLJ):Winter-
    Spring82-289
    V.O. Buyniak, 104(CASS):Spring82-133
Le Huenen, R. and P. Perron. Le Roman de
    Balzac. Balzac — Sémiotique du person-
    nage romanesque.
    M. van Schendel, 627(UTQ):Fall81-112
Leib, M. Poetics of the Holy.
    B. Berry, 141:Fall82-389
Leibbrandt, G. Little Paradise.
    C. Berger, 102(CanL):Autumn82-153
Leibniz, G.W. Discourse on the Natural
    Theology of the Chinese.* (H. Rosemont,
    Jr. and D.J. Cook, eds and trans)
    R.J. Mulvaney, 485(PE&W):Jan82-105
Leibniz, G.W. New Essays on Human Under-
    standing.* (P. Remnant and J. Bennett,
    eds and trans)
    E.J. Ashworth, 154:Sep82-593
    P.J. Fitzpatrick, 83:Spring82-154
    N. Jolley, 518:Apr82-84
Leibniz, G.W. Sämtliche Schriften und
    Briefe, Politischer und historischer
    Briefwechsel. (Vol 10, Pt 1)
    A. Robinet, 192(EP):Apr-Jun81-246
"Leibniz à Paris (1672-1676)."
    N. Jolley, 53(AGP):Band64Heft2-202
"Annie Leibovitz: Photographs."
    S.N., 441:23Oct83-31
Leifer, M. Indonesia's Foreign Policy.
    P. Carey, 617(TLS):2Dec83-1355

213

Lennon, T.M., J.M. Nicholas and J.W. Davis, eds. Problems of Cartesianism.
J. Cottingham, 617(TLS):11Nov83-1239
Le Normand, A. La Tradition classique et l'esprit romantique.
N. Penny, 59:Jun82-243
Lent, J. Rock Solid.
B. Meyer, 102(CanL):Spring82-88
Lentfoehr, T. Words and Silence.
M.W. Higgins, 106:Spring82-127
Lentricchia, F. After the New Criticism.*
C. Altieri, 478:Oct82-210
J.W. Davidson, 477(PLL):Winter82-428
D.H. Hirsch, 569(SR):Winter82-119
R. Magliola, 395(MFS):Winter81/82-759
C. Norris, 184(EIC):Jan82-89
J. Rolleston, 579(SAQ):Winter82-114
Lenz, C.R.S., G. Greene and C.T. Neely, eds. The Woman's Part.*
J.A. Roberts, 570(SQ):Winter82-533
K. Smidt, 179(ES):Feb82-74
Lenz, F.W. and C.A. Behr - see Aristides
Lenz, H. Erinnerung an Eduard.
S. Dickson, 268(IFR):Summer83-147
Lenz, H. Zeitlebens.
B. Bayen, 450(NRF):Mar82-143
Lenz, S. The Heritage.
639(VQR):Winter82-20
Lenz, S. Der Verlust.*
D. Myers, 268(IFR):Summer83-156
de León, J.L.S.P. - see under Ponce de León, J.L.S.
León, L.C. - see under Castañeda León, L.
Léon, P. and M. Rossi, eds. Problèmes de prosodie, I.
C. Pye, 350:Jun83-437
Léon, P. and J. Yashinsky, eds. Options nouvelles en didactique du français langue étrangère.
E.A. Fong, 207(FR):May83-960
Leonard, A. and J. Terrell. Patterns of Paradise.
M. Adams, 2(AfrA):Feb82-80
Leonard, E. LaBrava.
N. Johnston, 441:27Nov83-12
442(NY):19Dec83-142
Leonard, E. Split Images.*
T.J. Binyon, 617(TLS):22Apr83-400
Leonard, E. Stick.
G. Stade, 441:6Mar83-11
442(NY):7Mar83-139
Leonard, E. George Tyrrell and the Catholic Tradition.
E. Duffy, 617(TLS):9Sep83-970
Leont'ev, K. Pis'ma k Vasiliju Rozanovu. (B.A. Filippova, ed)
V. Terras, 574(SEEJ):Fall82-359
Leontiev, A.A. Psychology and the Language Learning Process. (C.V. James, ed and trans)
K.L. Black, 399(MLJ):Winter82-415
Leopardi, G. The Moral Essays.
N. Bliven, 442(NY):24Oct83-158
E. White, 441:19Jun83-10
Leopardi, G. Moral Tales.
D.J. Enright, 362:5May83-27
Leopardi, G. Pensieri.*
639(VQR):Summer82-99
Lepage, Y.G. - see Richard de Fournival
Lépine, N. Paraphrases et hommages.
F. Lurçat, 450(NRF):Nov82-118
Leppmann, W. Rilke.
P.P. Brodsky, 221(GQ):Nov82-603

Lepre, M.Z. L'interiezione vocativale nei poemi omerici.
P.V. Jones, 123:Vol32No1-88
Lepschy, G.C. Saggi di linguistica italiana.
F. Murru, 260(IF):Band86-301
Lepsius, R. Standard Alphabet for Reducing Unwritten Languages and Foreign Graphic Systems to a Uniform Orthography in European Letters.* (2nd ed) (J.A. Kemp, ed)
G.F. Meier, 682(ZPSK):Band35Heft3-346
Le Quesne, A.L. Carlyle.*
I. Campbell, 571(ScLJ):Winter82-91
Le Quesne, L. The Bodyline Controversy.
M. Davie, 617(TLS):24Jun83-657
Lequin, F. Het Personeel van de verenigde Oost-Indische Compagnie in Azie in de Achttiende eeuw, meer in het bijzonder in de vestiging Bengalen.
C.R. Boxer, 617(TLS):7Jan83-9
Lerat, P. Le Ridicule et son expression dans les comédies françaises de Scarron à Molière.
J. Émelina, 535(RHL):May-Jun82-467
de Lerma, D-R. Bibliography of Black Music.
B.L. Hampton, 187:May83-382
Lermontov, M.I. Issledovanija i materialy.
L. Koehler, 574(SEEJ):Winter82-478
Lerner, L. Love and Marriage.*
P. Boumelha, 541(RES):Aug82-345
A. Dommergues, 189(EA):Oct-Dec82-438
P.M. Spacks, 402(MLR):Jan82-157
Lerner, L., ed. Reconstructing Literature.
I. Salusinszky, 617(TLS):28Oct83-1178
Leroi-Gourhan, A. The Dawn of European Art.
P.J. Ucko, 617(TLS):7Jan83-21
Leroi-Gourhan, A. Le Fil du temps.
D.A. Roe, 617(TLS):17Jun83-621
Leroi-Gourhan, A. Les Racines du Monde.
T. Cordellier, 450(NRF):Sep82-143
Lerond, A. Dictionnaire de la prononciation.*
F. Carton, 209(FM):Oct82-344
Le Roy Ladurie, E. Carnival.
T.C. Curtis, 366:Spring82-122
Le Roy Ladurie, E. Love, Death and Money in the Pays d'Oc.* (French title: l'Argent, l'amour et la mort en pays d'oc.)
P. Johnson, 362:10Feb83-23
Le Roy Ladurie, E. The Mind and Method of the Historian.
W.H.D., 185:Oct82-203
Le Roy Ladurie, E. Paris-Montpellier, P.C.-P.S.U. 1945-63.*
H. Peyre, 207(FR):Mar83-654
Lesher, S. Media Unbound.
S. Bedell, 441:16Jan83-10
Lesky, A. Greek Tragic Poetry.
D. Bain, 617(TLS):15Jul83-756
W.E. McCulloh, 344:Fall83-125
Leslau, W. Etymological Dictionary of Gurage (Ethiopic).
J. Fellman, 318(JAOS):Oct-Dec81-457
Leslie, A. A Story Half Told.
V. Glendinning, 617(TLS):17Jun83-626
Leslie, B.R. Ronsard's Successful Epic Venture.*
I.D. McFarlane, 551(RenQ):Autumn81-441
M. Smith, 208(FS):Apr82-197

214

Leslie, J. Value and Existence.*
  M. Adam, 542:Oct-Dec82-682
Leslie, S.W. Boss Kettering.
  B.A. Weisberger, 441:19Jun83-11
Lessem, A.P. Music and Text in the Works
  of Arnold Schoenberg: the Critical Years,
  1908-1922.
  D. Puffett, 410(M&L):Jul/Oct81-404
Lessenich, R.P. Lord Byron and the Nature
  of Man.*
  T. von Bremen, 38:Band100Heft3/4-543
Lesser, R. Etruscan Things.
  R.B. Shaw, 441:4Sep83-8
Lessing, D. Documents Relating to the
  Sentimental Agents in the Volyen Empire.
  E. Rothstein, 441:3Apr83-7
Lessing, D. The Sentimental Agents in
  the Volyen Empire.
  P. Kemp, 362:30Jun83-28
  F.L. Wallis, 617(TLS):3Jun83-562
Lessing, G.E. Die Erziehung des Menschen-
  geschlechts. (L.F. Helbig, ed)
  M. Lichterfeld, 221(GQ):Jan82-116
"Lessing Yearbook." (Vols 11 and 12) (E.P.
  Harris, ed)
  A. Scott-Prelorentzos, 564:Nov82-296
"Lessing Yearbook." (Vol 13) (R.E. Schade,
  ed)
  A. Scott-Prelorentzos, 564:Nov82-296
Lester, G.A., ed. Three Late Medieval
  Morality Plays.
  J.J.A., 148:Autumn82-92
"Lettres des premiers Chartreux." (Vol 2)
  R.B. Marks, 589:Jan82-192
Letwin, S.R. The Gentleman in Trollope.*
  N. Annan, 453(NYRB):3Feb83-7
Leube, E. and A. Noyer-Weidner, eds. Apol-
  linaire.
  P. Gifford, 208(FS):Jan82-93
Leuchtenburg, W.E. In the Shadow of FDR.
  G.C. Ward, 441:25Dec83-9
Leumann, M., J.B. Hofmann and A. Szantyr.
  Lateinische Grammatik. (Vol 3)
  J. André, 555:Vol155fasc2-369
Levenson, J.C. and others - see Adams, H.
Lever, J. Architects' Designs for Furni-
  ture.
  F.J.B. Watson, 324:Aug83-569
Lever, J. Soccer Madness.
  B. Glanville, 617(TLS):30Sep83-1067
Lever, M. Le Roman français au XVIIème
  siècle.
  N. Aronson, 207(FR):Mar83-629
Levere, T.H. Poetry Realized in Nature.
  G. Durrant, 627(UTQ):Summer82-425
Leverenz, D. The Language of Puritan Feel-
  ing.*
  D. Tallack, 541(RES):Nov82-500
Leverson, A. The Little Ottleys.
  P. Craig, 617(TLS):13May83-499
  G. Mortimer, 364:Feb83-120
Levertov, D. Light Up the Cave.
  K.M. Hammond, 152(UDQ):Summer82-155
Lévesque, G. Louis Hémon, aventurier ou
  philosophe?*
  L. Rochette, 102(CanL):Spring82-94
Levet, J.P. Le vrai et le faux dans la
  pensée grecque archaïque. (Vol 1)
  W.J. Verdenius, 394:Vol135fasc1/2-156
Levey, M. The Painter Depicted.
  A. Ross, 364:Apr/May82-7
  E. Young, 39:Aug82-129

Levey, M. Painting in Eighteenth-Century
  Venice. (2nd ed)
  J. Steer, 324:Dec82-63
Levi, A. and M. La "Tabula Peutingeriana."
  B.L. Trell, 124:Mar/Apr83-250
Levi, H. Tangle Your Web and Dosey-Do.
  R. Smith, 296(JCF):No33-124
Levi, I. The Enterprise of Knowledge.
  L.J. Cohen, 393(Mind):Apr82-297
  J.H. Fetzer, 518:Jan82-35
  R.H.T., 543:Mar82-610
Levi, M.A. Pericle.
  J.D. Smart, 303(JoHS):Vol 102-268
Levi, P. Atlas of the Greek World.
  H.J.K. Usher, 123:Vol132No1-55
  P. Zweig, 441:4Dec83-71
Lévi-Strauss, C. The Way of the Masks.
  W. Suttles, 469:Vol8No2-106
  442(NY):3Jan83-72
Levin, B. Conducted Tour.*
  A. Jacobs, 415:Apr82-260
Levin, B. Enthusiasms. Speaking Up.
  J. Symons, 617(TLS):23Dec83-1440
Levin, D. - see Parkman, F.
Levin, G. Richardson the Novelist.*
  W. Füger, 38:Band100Heft1/2-216
Levin, H. Grand Delusions.
  R. Blount, Jr., 61:Nov83-142
  B. Yates, 441:25Sep83-12
Levin, H. Memories of the Moderns.*
  W.B. Bache, 395(MFS):Summer82-345
  M. Maddocks, 569(SR):Fall82-569
Levin, I.D. Ossian v russkoi literature.
  E. Kagan-Kans, 550(RusR):Jan82-99
Levin, K. Freud's Early Psychology of the
  Neuroses.
  J.B., 543:Mar82-612
Levin, M.E. Metaphysics and the Mind-Body
  Problem.*
  W.G. Lycan, 486:Mar82-142
  P.F. Snowdon, 393(Mind):Jul82-461
Levin, M.R. Ending Unemployment.
  A. Hacker, 453(NYRB):30Jun83-27
Levin, R. New Readings vs. Old Plays.*
  R.L. Heffner, 481(PQ):Winter81-125
  E.A.J. Honigmann, 677(YES):Vol 12-245
  J.L. Levenson, 539:Aug83-216
Levin, Y.D. Ossian v russkoy literature.
  S. Karlinsky, 575(SEER):Jul82-440
Levinas, E. De Dieu qui vient à l'idée.
  A. Reix, 542:Oct-Dec82-681
Levinas, E. Existence and Existents.*
  M. Adam, 542:Oct-Dec82-682
  N. Keohane-O'Connor, 323:Jan82-94
Levinas, E. L'au-delà du verset.
  A. Reix, 542:Oct-Dec82-680
Levine, A. Liberal Democracy.
  W.A. Galston, 185:Apr83-601
Levine, G. The Realistic Imagination.*
  W.K. Buckley, 594:Spring82-123
  M. Gorra, 31(ASch):Summer82-436
  J. Halperin, 579(SAQ):Summer82-354
  S. Hudson, 577(SHR):Fall82-363
  J. McMaster, 405(MP):Aug82-96
  R.M. Polhemus, 191(ELN):Sep82-74
  D.R. Schwarz, 395(MFS):Winter81/82-682
  L.J. Swingle, 661(WC):Summer82-159
Levine, G. and U.C. Knoepflmacher, eds.
  The Endurance of "Frankenstein."*
  B.F. Fisher 4th, 191(ELN):Sep81-67
  R. Jackson, 677(YES):Vol 12-301
  S. Prickett, 541(RES):May82-216

Levine, P. One For The Rose.*
  E. Grosholz, 249(HudR):Summer82-319
  L.L. Martz, 676(YR):Autumn82-63
  D. St. John, 42(AR):Spring82-232
  P. Stitt, 219(GaR):Fall82-675
  639(VQR):Summer82-92
Levine, R.T. - see Middleton, T.
Levine, S. and J. Koenig, eds. Why Men
  Rape.
  W.L. Marshall and J. Darke, 529(QQ):
  Summer82-434
Levinson, H.S. The Religious Investiga-
  tions of William James.
  S.J. Whitfield, 432(NEQ):Mar82-149
Levinson, R. and W. Link. Stay Tuned.*
  P. Brantlinger, 128(CE):Sep82-475
Levis, L. The Dollmaker's Ghost.*
  D. St. John, 42(AR):Spring82-229
  S. Sandy, 491:Aug82-293
  V. Young, 249(HudR):Spring82-139
Levit, H. Views of Rome, Then and Now.
  R. Middleton, 576:Dec82-333
Levitt, J.H. For Want of Trade.
  P.V. Bergstrom, 656(WMQ):Oct82-712
Le Vot, A. F. Scott Fitzgerald.
  W.H. Pritchard, 441:3Apr83-8
Lévy, B-H. L'Idéologie française.*
  W.N. Greenberg, 207(FR):Feb83-502
  A.Y. Kaplan, 400(MLN):May82-1021
Levy, B.J. Nine Verse Sermons by Nicholas
  Bozon.
  I. Short, 208(FS):Oct82-458
Levy, D.G. The Ideas and Careers of Simon-
  Nicolas-Henri Linguet.
  R.I. Boss, 173(ECS):Spring83-332
Levy, D.J. Realism.
  P. Gottfried, 396(ModA):Summer/Fall82-
  415
Levy, D.W. Techniques of Irony in Anatole
  France.
  D. Bresky, 446(NCFS):Fall-Winter82/83-
  178
Levy, F. "Le Mariage de Figaro."*
  J-P. de Beaumarchais, 535(RHL):Jan-
  Feb82-125
Levy, I.H. - see "The Ten Thousand Leaves"
Levy, I.J. and J. Loveluck, eds. Simposio
  Carlos Fuentes.
  C. Tatum, 238:May82-316
Levy, J.M. Beethoven's Compositional
  Choices.
  D. Matthews, 617(TLS):17Jun83-625
Levy, K.L. Tomás Carrasquilla.
  S. Menton, 240(HR):Spring82-235
  H.H. Orjuela, 238:Mar82-149
Levy, P. Moore.*
  N. Griffin, 556:Summer81-71
Lévy, S. The Play of the Text.
  S. Gavronsky, 210(FrF):Sep82-278
  M. Pierssens, 546(RR):Jan82-124
  639(VQR):Summer82-80
Lewald, H.E. and D.A. Yates. El Espíritu
  de la Juventud.
  C. Baker, 399(MLJ):Autumn82-354
  J.K. Feisthamel, 238:May82-321
Lewalski, B.K. Protestant Poetics and the
  Seventeenth-Century Religious Lyric.*
  R.C. Hassel, 570(SQ):Spring82-119
  J.N. King, 541(RES):Feb82-81
  L.L. Martz, 405(MP):Nov82-168

Lewanski, R.C., ed. Eastern Europe and
  Russia/Soviet Union: A Handbook of West
  European Archival and Library Resources.
  P.K. Grimsted, 14:Summer82-328
  P.K. Grimsted, 104(CASS):Fall-Winter82-
  513
Lewin, M.Z. Hard Line.
  T.J. Binyon, 617(TLS):19Aug83-890
  N. Callendar, 441:16Jan83-26
Lewis, A.W. Royal Succession in Capetian
  France.
  G. Duby, 617(TLS):21Jan83-62
Lewis, B. The Muslim Discovery of Europe.*
  J.D. Gurney, 617(TLS):11Mar83-241
Lewis, C. The Merton Tradition and Kine-
  matics in Late Sixteenth and Early Seven-
  teenth Century Italy.
  E.J. Allin, 539:May83-150
  E.D. Sylla, 551(RenQ):Summer82-289
Lewis, C. Saggitarious Rising.
  A.J., 617(TLS):20May83-527
Lewis, C.S. Studies in Medieval and
  Renaissance Literature. (W. Hooper, ed)
  H. Cooper, 447(N&Q):Apr81-185
Lewis, D. The Drawings of Andrea Palla-
  dio.*
  W. Cross, 43:Band12Heft1-84
Lewis, D. The Good Fight.
  G.M. Hicks, 150(DR):Summer82-340
  L. Panitch, 99:Oct82-31
Lewis, D. Inscriptiones Graecae. (Vol 1,
  fasc 1)
  M.J. Osborne, 123:Vol32No2-255
Lewis, D.L. When Harlem Was in Vogue.*
  J.R. Berry, 95(CLAJ):Sep81-117
Lewis, E.G. Bilingualism and Bilingual
  Education.
  R.V. Teschner, 399(MLJ):Summer82-198
Lewis, H.D. Jesus in the Faith of Chris-
  tians.
  H. Price, 483:Oct82-555
Lewis, H.R. Unsolvable Classes of Quanti-
  ficational Formulas.
  D. Rödding, 316:Mar82-221
Lewis, I.M. A Modern History of Somalia.
  H.S. Lewis, 69:Vol51No4-898
Lewis, J. The Birthday of the Infanta.*
  J. Finlay, 598(SoR):Winter83-181
Lewis, J. Poems Old and New, 1918-1978.*
  J.D. McClatchy, 491:Sep82-349
  T. Trusky, 649(WAL):Spring82-86
  639(VQR):Autumn82-135
Lewis, J. The Politics of Motherhood.
  N. Black, 529(QQ):Summer82-449
Lewis, J., with H. Gluck. Jerry Lewis in
  Person.
  C. Brown, 617(TLS):9Sep83-957
  L. Grossberger, 18:Dec82-72
Lewis, J.D. and R.L. Smith. American Soci-
  ology and Pragmatism.*
  J. Campbell, 619:Winter82-105
  R.R., 543:Sep81-147
  J. Walton, 319:Apr83-258
Lewis, J.R. The Victorian Bar.
  Z. Cowen, 617(TLS):1Apr83-320
Lewis, L. Guido Cantelli.
  N. Goodwin, 415:Apr82-263
Lewis, N. Cuban Passage.*
  639(VQR):Autumn82-131
Lewis, N. Naples '44.
  L.D., 617(TLS):24Jun83-683
Lewis, N. Paperchase.
  S. Sadie, 415:Apr82-260

Lindwall, B. Det tidiga 1800-talet.
  I. Sjöström, 341:Vol51No1-37
Ling, T. Buddhism, Imperialism, and War.*
  C. Hallisey, 318(JAOS):Oct-Dec81-504
Ling, X. - see under Xu Ling
Lingenfelter, R.E. The Hardrock Miners.
  F.R. Peterson, 649(WAL):Summer82-184
Lings, M. Muhammad.
  R. Irwin, 617(TLS):12Aug83-864
"Lingua e storia in puglia." (fasc 5 and
  6)
  S. Lazard, 553(RLiR):Jul-Dec81-519
"Linguistics in the Netherlands 1980."
"Linguistics in the Netherlands 1981."
  (S. Daalder and M. Gerritsen, eds of
  both)
  D.J. Napoli, 350:Mar83-225
Linguiti, G.L. Imre Lakatos e la "filoso-
  fia della scoperta."
  J. Largeault, 542:Jan-Mar82-107
Link, A.S. and others - see Wilson, W.
Link, H. Rezeptionsforschung. (2nd ed)
  W. Schmidt, 682(ZPSK):Band35Heft6-
  733
Link, J. and others. Literatursoziolo-
  gisches Propädeutikum.
  J.L. Sammons, 221(GQ):Mar82-228
Linke, K., ed. Die Fragmente des Grammati-
  kers Dionysios Thrax [together with]
  Haas, W., ed. Die Fragmente der Gram-
  matiker Tyrannion und Diokles [together
  with] Neitzel, S., ed. Apions Glōssai
  Homērikai.
  A.R. Dyck, 122:Jul82-270
Linker, R.W. A Bibliography of Old French
  Lyrics.*
  T.H. Newcombe, 402(MLR):Oct82-948
Linney, R. Jesus Tales.
  J.L. Halio, 598(SoR):Winter83-203
Lintott, A. Violence, Civil Strife and
  Revolution in the Classical City.
  P. Green, 617(TLS):11Feb83-125
Lion-Goldschmidt, D. and J-C. Moreau-
  Gobard. Chinese Art: Bronzes, Jade,
  Sculpture, Ceramics.
  M. Medley, 39:Sep82-197
Liou-Gille, B. Cultes "héroïques" romains.
  J-C. Richard, 555:Vol56fasc1-172
Lipkin, S. Dekada.
  G.A. Hosking, 617(TLS):7Oct83-1096
Lipking, L., ed. High Romantic Argument.*
  J. Arac, 661(WC):Summer82-147
  K. McSweeney, 529(QQ):Spring82-113
  D.H. Reiman, 191(ELN):Dec81-133
  M. Storey, 175:Summer82-157
Lipking, L. The Life of the Poet.*
  R. Bush, 141:Fall82-395
  D. Davie, 405(MP):Feb83-337
  J. Green, 134(CP):Fall82-96
  J. Olney, 569(SR):Summer82-456
Lipman, J. Nevelson's World.
  J. Russell, 441:4Dec83-65
Lipp, S. Leopoldo Zea.*
  A. Donoso, 258:Jun82-203
Lippard, L. Ad Reinhardt.
  R. Cohen, 55:Nov82-44
Lippard, L.R. Overlay.
  S. Gablik, 441:17Apr83-9
Lippincott, L. Selling Art in Georgian
  London.
  P. Rogers, 617(TLS):2Dec83-1337

Lippit, N.M. Reality and Fiction in Mod-
  ern Japanese Literature.*
  P.I. Lyons, 293(JASt):Nov81-139
Lipset, S.M., ed. The Third Century.
  A.L. Stinchcombe, 185:Oct82-114
Lipset, S.M. and W. Schneider. The Confi-
  dence Gap.
  T.J. Lowi, 441:10Apr83-7
Lipsius, J. and P. Cunaeus. Two Neo-Latin
  Menippean Satires.* (C. Matheeussen and
  C.L. Heesakkers, eds)
  C. Dessen, 551(RenQ):Autumn81-392
Lipsky, M. Street-Level Bureaucracy.
  C.N. Stone, 185:Apr83-588
Lipson, A., with S.J. Molinsky. A Russian
  Course. (Pt 1)
  J.J. Rinkus, 399(MLJ):Summer82-220
Lipton, D.R. Ernst Cassirer.
  J.M. Krois, 319:Apr82-209
Liria Montañés, P. - see Mandeville, J.
Lisboa, E. - see de Sena, J.
Lisci, L.G. - see under Ginori Lisci, L.
Lish, G. Dear Mr. Capote.
  G. Stade, 441:12Jun83-9
Liska, G. Russia and the Road to Appease-
  ment.
  D. Holloway, 617(TLS):21Jan83-57
Lisle, L. Portrait of an Artist.*
  A. Davis, 106:Spring82-109
  R. Murray, 648(WCR):Apr83-50
Liss, P.K. Atlantic Empires.
  J.S. Bromley, 617(TLS):9Dec83-1370
Listad, M. From Dr. Mather to Dr. Seuss.
  M. Chassagnol, 189(EA):Jul-Sep82-358
Lister, R. George Richmond.
  V. Powell, 39:Aug82-125
Lister, R.H. and F.C. Chaco Canyon.
  L. Milazzo, 584(SWR):Spring82-v
Liszt, F. The Letters of Franz Liszt to
  Olga von Meyendorff 1871-1886. (E.N.
  Waters, ed)
  A. Walker, 414(MusQ):Jan82-128
Litman, T.A. Les Comédies de Corneille.
  G.J. Mallinson, 402(MLR):Oct82-955
"La Littérature et les autres arts."
  U. Weisstein, 107(CRCL):Mar82-103
"Les Littératures de Langues Européennes
  au Tournant du Siècle." (Ser A, Vols
  1-3)
  Y. Chevrel, 107(CRCL):Dec81-558
Littlefield, D.C. Rice and Slaves.
  P.D. Morgan, 656(WMQ):Oct82-709
Littlefield, D.F., Jr. and J.W. Parins. A
  Biobibliography of Native American Writ-
  ers, 1772-1924.
  A. Krupat, 649(WAL):Nov82-267
  A.L.B. Ruoff, 50(ArQ):Autumn82-272
Litvak, L. Transformación industrial y
  literatura en España (1895-1905).
  J. Butt, 86(BHS):Apr82-157
  I.R.M. Galbis, 238:Sep82-464
Litvinoff, E. Falls the Shadow.
  M. Haltrecht, 617(TLS):21Oct83-1170
Liu Junwen. Beijing.
  D. Davin, 617(TLS):24Jun83-656
Liu, T-J. Trade on the Han River and Its
  Economic Development, 1800-1911.
  R.H. Myers, 293(JASt):Nov81-118
Lively, P. Next to Nature, Art.*
  J. Mellors, 364:Jul82-94
Lively, P. Perfect Happiness.
  J. Mellors, 362:22Sep83-25
  J. Motion, 617(TLS):30Sep83-1059

[continuing]
    T.M. Lennon, 319:Apr83-276
    J.W. Yolton, 518:Jul82-155
Loeber, R. A Biographical Dictionary of
    Architects in Ireland 1660-1720.*
    D. Fitz Gerald, 39:Feb82-137
Loeschen, J.R. The Divine Community.
    R.A. Muller, 551(RenQ):Winter82-618
Loetscher, H. Herbst in der grossen
    Orange.
    J.J. White, 617(TLS):7Oct83-1094
Loewe, M. Ways to Paradise.
    D. Bodde, 244(HJAS):Jun82-321
    Y-H. Jan, 485(PE&W):Oct82-465
    Y-S. Yü, 293(JASt):Nov81-81
Loewinsohn, R. Magnetic Field(s).
    T. Le Clair, 441:31Jul83-1
Löffler, F. Otto Dix.
    O. Conzelmann, 471:Jul/Aug/Sep82-267
    T. Hilton, 617(TLS):25Mar83-291
Lofmark, C. The Authority of the Source
    in Middle High German Narrative Poetry.
    J.A. Schultz, 222(GR):Fall82-164
Löfstedt, E. Il latino tardo.
    F. Kerlouégan, 555:Vol56fasc2-340
Löfstedt, J-I. Chinese Educational Policy.
    D.L. Layman, 293(JASt):Feb82-333
Loftis, J. - see Halkett, A. and A. Fan-
    shawe
Logan, C. Selected Poems of Christina
    Logan.
    G. Chase, 526:Autumn82-80
Logan, J. The Bridge of Change.*
    R. Phillips, 461:Spring-Summer82-98
    S. Sandy, 491:Aug82-293
Logan, J. Only the Dreamer Can Change the
    Dream.*
    R. Phillips, 461:Spring-Summer82-98
    639(VQR):Spring82-59
Logan, R.W. and M.R. Winston, eds. Dic-
    tionary of American Negro Biography.
    H.L. Gates, Jr., 441:1May83-13
Logan, W. Sad-Faced Men.
    D. Hall, 271:Winter82-169
    I. Salusinszky, 617(TLS):9Dec83-1384
Lohe, P. - see Landino, C.
Lohmeier, D. and B. Olsson, eds. Welt-
    liches und geistliches Lied des Barock.*
    H.K. Krausse, 564:Feb82-74
Lohner, E., ed. Der amerikanische Roman
    im 19. und 20. Jahrhundert.
    M. Schulze, 72:Band218Heft1-188
Lohnes, W.F.W. and F.W. Strothmann.
    German. (3rd ed)
    M.P. Alter, 399(MLJ):Spring82-103
Lohse, B. Martin Luther.
    H.G. Haile, 221(GQ):Jan82-112
Łojek, J. Przed Konstytucją Trzeciego
    Maja.
    W.H. Zawadzki, 575(SEER):Jan82-117
Lomas, H. Public Footpath.
    J. Saunders, 565:Vol23No3-73
Lomas, P. The Case for a Personal Psycho-
    therapy.
    E.K. Ledermann, 437:Spring82-196
Lomask, M. Aaron Burr: The Conspiracy and
    Years of Exile, 1805-1836.
    N. Bliven, 442(NY):10Jan83-93
    E.L. McKitrick, 441:23Jan83-6
Lombard, J. Courtilz de Sandras et la
    crise du roman à la fin du grand siècle.*
    V. Mylne, 402(MLR):Apr82-451
    R. Zuber, 535(RHL):May-Jun82-476

de Lombardi, L.B. - see under Boscán de
    Lombardi, L.
Lombardi, R.P. and A. Boero de Peters.
    Modern Spoken Spanish.
    D. Rissel, 399(MLJ):Summer82-229
Lommel, H. Kleine Schriften. (K.L.
    Janert, ed)
    J.W. de Jong, 259(IIJ):Jul80-237
    L. Sternbach, 318(JAOS):Jul-Sep81-377
Lomnäs, E., I. Bengtsson and N. Castegren,
    eds. Franz Berwald.*
    R. Layton, 410(M&L):Jul/Oct82-299
London, H.L. and A.L. Weeks. Myths that
    Rule America.
    L.W. Beilenson, 396(ModA):Summer/
    Fall82-428
London, J. Curious Fragments. Jack Lon-
    don: No Mentor But Myself. (D.L. Walker,
    ed of both)
    J. Tavernier-Courbin, 106:Winter82-363
London, J. Jack London in "The Aegis."
    (J. Sisson 3d, ed)
    E. Labor, 573(SSF):Fall82-394
London, J. Sporting Blood. (H. Lachtman,
    ed)
    R.L. Buckland, 573(SSF):Spring82-180
    D.L. Walker, 649(WAL):Nov82-270
London, J. Works. (D. Pizer, ed)
    H. Beaver, 617(TLS):3Jun83-567
London, V.C.M., ed. The Cartulary of
    Bradenstoke Priory.
    C. Ross, 325:Apr82-36
"London Politics 1713-1717."
    H.T. Dickinson, 566:Autumn82-61
The Marquess of Londonderry. The London-
    derry Album.
    A.J. Heesom, 161(DUJ):Dec81-114
Londré, F.H. Tom Stoppard.*
    M.G. Rose, 130:Winter82/83-381
Londré, F.H. Tennessee Williams.*
    I.R. Hark, 130:Spring82-84
Long, C.A. and C. Arthur-Killingley. The
    Badgers of the World.
    E. Neal, 617(TLS):16Dec83-1414
Long, D.E. The Hajj Today.
    W.R. Roff, 318(JAOS):Apr-Jun81-221
Long, L. and T. The Handbook for Latchkey
    Children and Their Parents.
    J.K. Davison, 441:25Dec83-11
Long, M. At the Piano with Fauré.
    R. Howat, 415:May82-333
Long, M.H. and others. Reading English
    for Academic Study.*
    K. Perkins, 399(MLJ):Spring82-77
Long, R-C.W. Kandinsky.*
    J.E. Bowlt, 550(RusR):Jan82-111
    M. Clarke, 575(SEER):Jan82-107
    K.C. Lindsay, 54:Dec82-678
    O.K. Werckmeister, 59:Jun82-231
Long, R.E. The Achieving of "The Great
    Gatsby."*
    J. Griffin, 106:Fall82-253
Long, R.E. The Great Succession.*
    R.A. Hocks, 183(ESQ):Vol128No4-261
Long, T.H. and others. Longman Dictionary
    of English Idioms.
    H. Appia, 189(EA):Apr-Jun82-197
    B. Cottle, 541(RES):Aug82-303
Longeon, C. Bibliographie des oeuvres
    d'Etienne Dolet, écrivain, éditeur et
    imprimeur.
    J. Bailbé, 535(RHL):Sep-Dec82-863
                                    [continued]

221

Longeon, C. Bibliographie des oeuvres
d'Etienne Dolet, écrivain, éditeur et
imprimeur. [continuing]
    J.R. Henderson, 551(RenQ):Summer81-238
    D. Maskell, 354:Mar82-84
Longeon, C. - see Dolet, É.
de Longepierre, M.B. Electre. (T. Tobari,
ed)
    P. Hourcade, 475:Vol9No17-804
Longford, E. Elizabeth R.
    A. Howard, 362:13Oct83-25
    P. Worsthorne, 617(TLS):18Nov83-1293
Longford, E. Eminent Victorian Women.
    639(VQR):Spring82-53
Longhi, R. A propos de Masolino et de
Masaccio.
    R. Micha, 98:Feb82-184
Longley, D. and M. Shain. Dictionary of
Information Technology.
    A. Hyman, 617(TLS):25Feb83-193
Longley, E. - see Durcan, P.
Longley, M. Selected Poems 1963-1980.*
    S. Fauchereau, 98:Jun-Jul82-628
Longmate, N. The Bombers.
    N. Cameron, 617(TLS):12Aug83-850
Longo, M.R., ed. Maori e Pakeha.
    S.F.D. Hughes, 395(MFS):Spring81-173
Longstreth, R. At the Edge of the World.
    P. Goldberger, 441:11Dec83-13
Lonie, I.M. The Hippocratic Treatises "On
Generation," "On the Nature of the
Child," "Diseases IV."
    A.E. Hanson, 124:Mar/Apr83-249
Lonis, R. Guerre et religion en Grèce à
l'époque classique.*
    P. Roesch, 555:Vol56fasc2-321
Lønning, P. Cet effrayant pari.*
    N. Boyle, 208(FS):Apr82-200
Lönnqvist, B. Suomenruotsalaiset, kansa-
tieteellinen tutkielma kieliryhmästä.
    M-A. Elfving, 563(SS):Spring82-171
Lonoff, S. Wilkie Collins and His Victor-
ian Readers.
    N. Page, 445(NCF):Mar83-610
Loos, A. Spoken into the Void.
    P. Engel, 441:2Jan83-11
Lope, H-J., ed. Aufsätze zum 18. Jahrhun-
dert in Frankreich.*
    F. Deloffre, 547(RF):Band94Heft2/3-332
Lope, H.J., ed. Studia Belgica.
    J. Hennig, 52:Band16Heft3-328
    M. Mat-Hasquin, 547(RF):Band93Heft3/4-
440
de Lope, P.O. - see under Ontañón de Lope,
P.
Lope Blanch, J.M. Investigaciones sobre
dialectología mexicana.
    P.M. Boyd-Bowman, 240(HR):Summer82-373
Lope Blanch, J.M. - see de Texeda, J.
Lopez, E.H. Conversations with Katherine
Anne Porter.*
    R.H. Brinkmeyer, Jr., 585(SoQ):Summer
82-109
    J.N. Gretlund, 577(SHR):Spring82-171
    J. Rickert, 584(SWR):Winter82-116
López de Abiada, J.M., ed. Actas de las
jornadas suizo-italianas de Lugano, 22-
24 de febrero de 1980.
    B.M. Damiani, 547(RF):Band94Heft2/3-
364
López de Ayala, P. Rimado de Palacio.
(G. Orduna, ed)
    E.W. Naylor, 304(JHP):Winter83-146

López de Mendoza, I. Los sonetos "al
itálico modo." (J.M. Sola-Solé, ed)
    D. Briesemeister, 547(RF):Band93
Heft3/4-482
López Estrada, F. and others. Doce comen-
tarios a la poesía de Manuel Machado.
    C. Iranzo, 241:Jan82-79
Lorant, T. Batsford Book of Hand and
Machine Knitted Laces.
    P. Bach, 614:Fall83-16
Loraux, N. L'invention d'Athènes.
    R. Seager, 303(JoHS):Vol 102-267
Lorca, F.G. Deep Song and Other Prose.*
(C. Maurer, ed and trans)
    M. Jacobson, 399(MLJ):Spring82-95
Lorca, F.G. Oeuvres complètes. (Vol 1)
(A. Belamich, ed)
    J-L. Gautier, 450(NRF):May82-138
Lord, B.B. Spring Moon.
    42(AR):Winter82-117
Lord, G. Tooth and Claw.
    B. Morton, 617(TLS):2Sep83-940
Lord, W. The Miracle of Dunkirk.
    B. Bond, 617(TLS):6May83-455
    R. Walters, 441:9Jan83-16
Lo Ré, A.G. La leyenda de doña María
Coronel.
    G.P. Andrachuk, 238:Mar82-141
    F. Pierce, 86(BHS):Jan82-69
Lorenz, C.M. Lorelei Two.
    H. Bevington, 441:22May83-11
    442(NY):6Jun83-144
Lorenz, D.C.G. Ilse Aichinger.
    J. Glenn, 221(GQ):Mar82-278
Lorenz, K. The Foundations of Ethology.
    S.R.L. Clark, 617(TLS):24Jun83-658
Lorenzatos, Z. The Lost Center and Other
Essays in Greek Poetry.*
    J.R. Clark and A.L. Motto, 436(NewL):
Fall82-104
Lorimer, D.L.R. - see Mueller-Stellrecht,
I.
Lorimer, J., ed. Canada's Oil Monopoly.
    N. Ward, 529(QQ):Winter82-900
Lorimer, W.L. - see "The New Testament in
Scots"
de Lorimier, C. At War with the Americans.
(P. Aichinger, ed and trans)
    G.W., 102(CanL):Summer82-173
Lörinczy, E.B. A magyar mássalhangzó-
kapcsolódások denszere és törvényszerü-
ségei.
    M. Katzschmann, 685(ZDL):1/1982-101
de L'Orme, P. Architecture.
    N. Miller, 576:Oct82-260
Lorrah, J. and J. Lichtenberg. Channel's
Destiny.
    G. Jonas, 441:23Jan83-24
de Lorris, G. and Jean de Meun - see under
Guillaume de Lorris and Jean de Meun
Losse, D.N. Rhetoric at Play.*
    G. Defaux, 551(RenQ):Autumn82-504
Lott, E. Vedantic Approaches to God.
    L.T. O'Neil, 485(PE&W):Apr82-218
Lottman, H.R. The Left Bank.* (French
title: La Rive gauche.)
    K. Bieber, 207(FR):Mar83-652
    J. Mellors, 364:Aug/Sep82-120
Lotze, D.P. Wilhelm Busch.
    C.P. Magill, 402(MLR):Jan82-239
Lotze, D.P. Imre Madách.
    P. Sherwood, 402(MLR):Oct82-1006

Louchheim, K., ed. The Making of the New Deal.
R.J. Margolis, 441:18Dec83-14
Loudon, J.C. On the Laying Out, Planting and Managing of Cemeteries and On the Improvement of Churchyards. (new ed)
A. Whittick, 324:Feb83-158
Loudon, J.H. James Scott and William Scott, Bookbinders.*
M.M. Foot, 78(BC):Autumn82-378
Lough, J. Seventeenth-Century French Drama: The Background.*
R.J. Melpignano, 475:No16Pt2-399
Louis XIV. Manière de montrer les jardins de Versailles. (S. Hoog, ed)
G. Walton, 576:Dec82-356
Louis, F.D. Swift's Anatomy of Misunderstanding.
R.W. Uphaus, 566:Autumn82-50
Louis-Jensen, J., J. Helgason and P. Springborg, eds. Opuscula. (Vol 7)
M. Cormack, 563(SS):Autumn82-315
Loup, J. Can the Third World Survive?
C. Marcy, 441:21Aug83-11
Louth, A. Discerning the Mystery.
J. Drury, 617(TLS):19Aug83-878
Louth, A. The Origins of the Christian Mystical Tradition.
W.E., 543:Dec81-396
R.P. Hardy, 589:Jul82-635
Love, F.R. Nietzsche's Saint Peter.
R. Hollinrake, 410(M&L):Jan/Apr82-113
R.L.J., 412:Aug-Nov81-288
Love, H. The Golden Days of Australian Opera.
J. Hibberd, 381:Sep82-381
Love, N. Generative Phonology.
J. Klausenburger, 350:Sep83-608
D.C. Walker, 361:Nov/Dec82-369
Loveland, A.C. Southern Evangelicals and the Social Order, 1800-1860.
R.M. Calhoon, 656(WMQ):Apr82-386
F. Hobson, 392:Winter81/82-73
M.R. Winchell, 585(SoQ):Fall181-88
Lovell, M. Apple to the Core.
N. Callendar, 441:6Nov83-53
Lovesey, P. The False Inspector Dew.*
639(VQR):Autumn82-130
Lovesey, P. Keystone.
T.J. Binyon, 617(TLS):23Sep83-1011
N. Callendar, 441:11Dec83-38
Lovoll, O.S., ed. Makers of an American Immigrant Legacy.
B.J. Nordstrom, 563(SS):Winter82-98
Low, D., ed. 30 Kansas Poets.
M. Lammon, 436(NewL):Winter82/83-108
Lowance, M.I., Jr. The Language of Canaan.*
E. Elliott, 301(JEGP):Jul82-461
D. Levin, 656(WMQ):Jul82-540
Lowe, B., P.J. Marshall and J.A. Woods, comps. The Correspondence of Edmund Burke. (Vol 10: Index)
C. Price, 541(RES):Nov82-474
Lowe, D. Turgenev's Fathers and Sons.
P. Waddington, 617(TLS):30Dec83-1453
Lowe, D. - see Turgenev, I.
Lowe, D.M. History of Bourgeois Perception.
K. Minogue, 617(TLS):25Feb83-195
Löwe, H-D. Antisemitismus und reaktionäre Utopie.
G. Surh, 550(RusR):Oct82-485

Lowe, J. Kennedy.
J. Maslin, 441:4Dec83-12
Lowe, S.D. Stieglitz.
H. Kenner, 441:20Feb83-5
442(NY):4Apr83-134
Löwenhardt, J. Decision Making in Soviet Politics.
D.D. Barry, 550(RusR):Oct82-501
A. Brown, 627(TLS):1Apr83-333
Löwenhardt, J. The Soviet Politburo.
A. Brown, 617(TLS):1Apr83-333
Lowenstein, J.I. Marx Against Marxism.
C. Melakopides, 529(QQ):Spring82-148
Lowenthal, R. - see Borkenau, F.
Lowerson, J.R., ed. Southern History.
R. Dunning, 325:Apr82-46
Lowery, R.G., ed. Essays on Sean O'Casey's Autobiographies.
F. McCluskey, 305(JIL):Sep82-110
Lowery, R.G. - see Atkinson, B.
Lowery, R.G. - see "O'Casey Annual No. 1"
Löwith, K. Sämtliche Schriften. (Vol 1) (K. Stichweh and M.B. de Launay, eds)
C.C., 227(GCFI):Sep-Dec82-379
Lowitt, R. and M. Beasley - see Hickok, L.
Lowndes, W. The Theatre Royal at Bath.
I. Colegate, 617(TLS):11Mar83-236
Lowry, B. and E.E. Gunter - see Michel, L.
Lowry, J.M.P. The Logical Principles of Proclus' "Stoicheiōsis Theologikē" as Systematic Ground of the Cosmos.*
J. Trouillard, 192(EP):Jul-Sep81-358
Lowry, S.P. Familiar Mysteries.
J. Peradotto, 124:Sep/Oct82-57
Lowther, P. Final Instructions. (D. Sturmanis and F. Candelaria, eds)
M. Bowering, 102(CanL):Spring82-77
Loyer, O. L'Anglicanisme de Richard Hooker.
G.R. Dunstan, 189(EA):Apr-Jun82-207
Lozza, G. Plutarco, "De Superstitione."
J. Boulogne, 555:Vol56fascl-136
B. Hillyard, 123:Vol32No2-275
Lu Hsun. A Brief History of Chinese Fiction.
D.E. Pollard, 617(TLS):24Jun83-677
Lu Xun. The Complete Stories of Lu Xun.
G. Kearns, 249(HudR):Autumn82-499
Lu Xun. Selected Poems.
D.E. Pollard, 617(TLS):24Jun83-677
Luard, N. The Last Wilderness.
639(VQR):Winter82-28
de Lubac, H. Recherches dans la foi.
G. Madec, 192(EP):Jul-Sep81-359
Lubbers, K. Typologie der Short Story.
A. Klein, 38:Band100Heft1/2-244
de Lubicz, R.A.S. - see under Schwaller de Lubicz, R.A.
Lubin, G. - see Sand, G.
Lubomirski, E. Kartki z mego życia.
N. Stone, 617(TLS):7Jan83-3
Lubrano, L.L. and S.C. Solomon, eds. The Social Context of Soviet Science.
V. Shlapentokh, 550(RusR):Apr82-222
Lucas, J. The Longest Flight.
D. Durrant, 364:Nov82-87
Lucas, J., ed. The 1930s.*
G. Reeves, 677(YES):Vol 12-354
Lucas, J. Romantic to Modern Literature.
G. Hough, 617(TLS):4Mar83-217
Lucas, J.R. On Justice.*
W.A. Galston, 185:Oct82-156

Lydall, J. and I. Strecker. The Hamar of
Southern Ethiopia.
D. Turton, 69:Vol51No1-537
Lydon, M. Perpetuum Mobile.
K. Aspley, 402(MLR):Jul82-734
G.H. Bauer, 188(ECr):Spring82-95
L. Oppenheim, 210(FrF):Jan82-89
L.S. Roudiez, 207(FR):Dec82-328
S. Sykes, 208(FS):Jan82-102
J. Waelti-Walters, 546(RR):May82-399
L. Welch, 478:Oct82-211
Lyle, G. Beyond My Expectations.
P. Bixler, 42(AR):Spring82-235
Lynch, B. Perpetual Star.
T.F. Merrill, 305(JIL):Sep82-3
Lynch, D. Yeats.*
H.J. Levine, 675(YER):Jun82-138
Lynch, J. Argentine Dictator Juan Manuel
de Rosas, 1829-1852.*
J.T. Criscenti, 263(RIB):Vol32No2-215
Lynch, K. A Theory of Good City Form.
H. Blumenfeld, 529(QQ):Autumn82-685
Lynch, K.T. and H.W. Slotkin. Processing
Manual for the Institute Archives and
Special Collections, M.I.T. Libraries.
B.D. Bishop, 14:Summer82-329
Lynch, L.W. Eighteenth-Century Novelists
and the Novel.*
A.D. Hytier, 399(MJL):Spring82-79
Lyne, R.O.A.M. The Latin Love Poets from
Catullus to Horace.*
J.A. Barsby, 67:Nov82-194
J. Chomarat, 555:Vol56fasc2-349
D. West, 313:Vol172-209
"George Platt Lynes Photographs 1931-1955."
(J. Woody, ed)
R. Philp, 151:Feb82-82
Lynn, C. Wallpaper in America.
S.J. Dornsife, 576:Mar82-69
Lyon, J.K. Bertolt Brecht in America.*
O.G. Brockett, 130:Summer82-198-
R.J. Ley, 397(MD):Dec82-571
S. Mews, 301(JEGP):Jul82-393
H.W. Seliger, 564:Nov82-302
M. Swales, 529(QQ):Spring82-200
295(JML):Dec82-415
Lyons, A. At the Hands of Another.
N. Callendar, 441:23Oct83-38
Lyons, F.S.L. Culture and Anarchy in
Ireland 1890-1939.*
P-Y. Petillon, 98:Jun-Jul82-537
B.S.G. Stewart, 447(N&Q):Oct81-454
Lyons, F.S.L. and R.A.J. Hawkins, eds.
Ireland Under the Union.
A.J. Heesom, 161(DUJ):Jun82-294
Lyons, J. Eléments de sémantique.
R. Martin, 553(RLiR):Jan-Jun81-232
Lyons, J. Language and Linguistics.*
J. Pauchard, 189(EA):Oct-Dec82-449
N. Rojas, 399(MLJ):Winter82-445
Lyons, J. Language, Meaning and Context.
G. Hammarström, 67:May82-94
D. Schiffrin, 350:Jun83-441
Lyons, L. and K. Levin. Wegman's World.
S. Schwartz, 453(NYRB):18Aug83-44
Lyons, W.E. Emotion.
G. Nerlich, 63:Mar82-90
A.R. White, 518:Jan82-51
Lyons, W.E. Gilbert Ryle.
J.B., 543:Jun82-882
A. Palmer, 483:Jul82-418
R.B.S., 185:Oct82-210

[continued]

[continuing]
E.D. Sprague, 518:Jan82-23
A.R. White, 479(PhQ):Jan82-88
Lysenko, V. A Crime Against The World.
S. Mills, 617(TLS):16Dec83-1414
Lytle, G.F., ed. Reform and Authority in
the Medieval and Reformation Church.
D. Janz, 539:Aug83-225
Lyttelton, G. and R. Hart-Davis. The
Lyttleton Hart-Davis Letters.* (Vol 4)
(R. Hart-Davis, ed)
P. Vansittart, 364:Aug/Sep82-138
Lyttelton, G. and R. Hart-Davis. The
Lyttleton Hart-Davis Letters. (Vol 5)
(R. Hart-Davis, ed)
H. Carpenter, 617(TLS):13May83-478
C. Hawtree, 364:Feb83-118
H. Wackett, 362:19May83-18
Lyttelton, H. The Best of Jazz 2.
M. Harrison, 415:Aug82-549

"MLA Directory of Periodicals."* (E.M.
Mackesy, K. Mateyak and N.B. Hoover, eds)
C.S. Bronson, 207(FR):Dec82-309
Ma, N.C., S. Ma and H.M. Yamawaki. Mrs.
Ma's Japanese Cooking.
W. and C. Cowen, 639(VQR):Spring82-68
Ma, Y.W. and J.S.M. Lau, eds. Traditional
Chinese Stories.
R.C. Hessney, 318(JAOS):Apr-Jun81-230
Maas, P. Marie.
D. Goddard, 441:3Jul83-6
Maasen, M. and J. Goossens. Limburgs Idio-
ticon.
U. Scheuermann, 685(ZDL):1/1982-94
Maass, J. Kleist.
J. Agee, 441:24Jul83-3
S. Spender, 453(NYRB):10Nov83-45
442(NY):12Sep83-157
Maass, M. Die geometrischen Dreifüsse von
Olympia.
P. Cartledge, 303(JoHS):Vol 102-289
Macadam, A. Florence.
90:Apr82-264
McAlexander, H.H. The Prodigal Daughter.*
F. Hobson, 9(AlaR):Jul82-234
W. Mixon, 392:Fall82-453
P. Skaggs, 26(ALR):Autumn82-279
27(AL):Oct82-471
McAllester, D.P., ed and trans. Hogans.
C. Heth, 292(JAF):Oct-Dec82-473
McAnany, E., J. Schnitman and N. James,
eds. Communication and Social Structure.
A.S. Tan, 583:Summer83-400
MacAndrew, E. The Gothic Tradition in Fic-
tion.*
F. Garber, 149(CLS):Fall82-394
S. Gresham, 577(SHR):Winter82-70
T. Heller, 50(ArQ):Spring82-87
I. Ousby, 637(VS):Autumn81-105
R. Paulson, 173(ECS):Summer83-427
Macandrew, H. Ashmolean Museum, Oxford,
Catalogue of the Collection of Drawings.
(Vol 3)
N. Turner, 90:Mar82-161
Macandrew, H. and H. Brigstocke, comps.
Poussin: Sacraments and Bacchanals.
A. Blunt, 208(FS):Jul82-327
McAndrew, J. Venetian Architecture of the
Early Renaissance.*
D. Hemsoll, 59:Mar82-120
W. Wolters, 43:Band12Heft2-186

MacDougall, N., ed. Church, Politics and Society.
B. Lenman, 617(TLS):30Dec83-1464
McDowell, F.P.W. E.M. Forster. (rev)
A.M. Wyatt-Brown, 395(MFS):Winter82/83-641
McDowell, G.L. Equity and the Constitution.
B.N.E., 185:Apr83-642
McDowell, J. - see Evans, G.
McDowell, J.H. Children's Riddling.
C.W. Sullivan 3d, 292(JAF):Jan-Mar82-90
B. Sutton-Smith, 355(LSoc):Apr82-150
McDowell, M.B. Carson McCullers.
M. Chew, 585(SoQ):Fall81-85
MacEachern, R. - see Thomas, A.
Maceda, J. A Manual of a Field Music Research with Special Reference to Southeast Asia.
R.A. Sutton, 187:Jan83-140
McElrath, J.R., Jr. and A.P. Robb - see Bradstreet, A.
McElvaine, R.S., ed. Down and Out in the Great Depression.
A. Schlesinger, Jr., 441:6Feb83-3
A. Sinclair, 617(TLS):3Jun83-574
442(NY):14Mar83-158
McEvedy, C. The Penguin Atlas of African History.
P. Richards, 69:Vol51No1-530
McEvoy, J. The Philosophy of Robert Grosseteste.
J. North, 617(TLS):21Oct83-1163
A.B. Wolter, 319:Jul83-400
McEwan, I. The Comfort of Strangers.*
J.R. Banks, 148:Summer82-27
P. Craig, 617(TLS):21Jan83-69
P. Lewis, 565:Vol23No2-44
McEwan, N. The Survival of the Novel.
V.R., 617(TLS):22Apr83-415
C. Sprague, 395(MFS):Summer82-275
MacEwen, G. The T.E. Lawrence Poems. Earthlight.
G. Johnson, 99:Dec82/Jan83-42
McEwen, J.S. - see Princess Alice, Duchess of Gloucester
McEwen, T. Fisher's Hornpipe.
V. Bourjaily, 441:14Aug83-13
442(NY):12Sep83-154
Macey, S.L. Clocks and the Cosmos.*
J.E. Chamberlin, 178:Sep82-368
McFadden, D. My Body Was Eaten By Dogs.
B. Whiteman, 298:Summer82-150
McFadden, D. A Trip Around Lake Huron.
S. Neuman, 102(CanL):Spring82-125
McFadden, G. Discovering the Comic.
R.B. Hauck, 395(MFS):Winter82/83-720
R.K. Simon, 141:Fall82-386
McFarland, T. Romanticism and the Forms of Ruin.*
P.M.S. Dawson, 405(MP):Feb83-321
L.R. Furst, 131(CL):Summer82-281
A.C. Goodson, 191(ELN):Sep82-70
J.A.W. Heffernan, 661(WC):Summer82-125
Macfarlane, A. The Justice and the Mare's Ale.
P.B. Munsche, 529(QQ):Autumn82-656
639(VQR):Spring82-44
McFarlane, B. Martin Boyd's Langton Novels.
J. Croft, 71(ALS):May82-400

McFarlane, B., ed. A Political Economy of S.E. Asia in the 1980's.
G. Gran, 293(JASt):Feb82-421
McFarlane, I.D. Buchanan.
M. Lee, Jr., 551(RenQ):Winter82-644
J.B. Trapp, 617(TLS):15Jul83-755
McFarlane, I.D., ed. Renaissance Latin Poetry.*
L. Forster, 447(N&Q):Dec81-530
H. Kelliher, 402(MLR):Oct82-910
McFarlane, I.D. and I. Maclean, eds. Montaigne.
D.G. Coleman, 617(TLS):13May83-496
McFarlane, J., ed. Slaves of Love and Other Norwegian Short Stories.
A. Born, 617(TLS):4Feb83-116
J. Mellors, 362:13Jan83-23
McFarlane, K.B. England in the Fifteenth Century.
C. Ross, 617(TLS):25Nov83-1302
MacFarquhar, R. The Origins of the Cultural Revolution. (Vol 2)
D.C. Wilson, 617(TLS):5Aug83-836
McFeely, W.S. Grant.*
G. Davenport, 249(HudR):Spring82-123
McGaha, M.D., ed. Approaches to the Theater of Calderón.
D.G. Lanoue, 304(JHP):Spring82-252
McGaha, M.D., ed. Cervantes and the Renaissance.
M.Z. Hafter, 551(RenQ):Summer81-268
F. Pierce, 402(MLR):Oct82-975
McGaha, M.D. The Theatre in Madrid during the Second Republic.*
D. Gagen, 86(BHS):Apr82-159
K. Pörtl, 547(RF):Band94Heft1-140
McGahern, J. The Barracks. The Dark.
P. Craig, 617(TLS):18Nov83-1294
McGahern, J. Getting Through.*
J. Kilroy, 569(SR):Winter82-89
McGann, J.J. - see Lord Byron
McGhee, R.D. Marriage, Duty, and Desire in Victorian Poetry and Drama.*
L. Poston, 637(VS):Autumn81-95
McGilligan, P., ed. Yankee Doodle Dandy.
J. Basinger, 18:Jul-Aug82-72
McGinley, P. Foggage.
M. Richler, 441:25Dec83-6
442(NY):19Dec83-140
McGinley, P. Fox Prints.
P. Craig, 617(TLS):16Sep83-1001
McGinley, P. Goosefoot.*
P. Craig, 617(TLS):11Feb83-130
McGinn, B. Visions of the End.*
G. Leff, 366:Autumn82-257
McGinn, C. The Character of Mind.
J. Lear, 617(TLS):11Mar83-246
McGinn, C. The Subjective View.
T. Nagel, 617(TLS):18Nov83-1283
McGinniss, J. Fatal Vision.
J. Barthel, 441:25Sep83-12
R. Stone, 231:Oct83-69
442(NY):30Oct83-130
McGinniss, J. Going to Extremes.
V.P. Cohen, 649(WAL):Nov82-290
McGough, R. Waving at Trains.
L. Mackinnon, 617(TLS):8Apr83-356
McGowan, R. and J. Hands. Don't Cry For Me, Sergeant-Major.
G. Wheatcroft, 617(TLS):13May83-490
McGown, J. A Perfect Match.
T.J. Binyon, 617(TLS):23Sep83-1011
McGrady, D. - see de Vega Carpio, L.

McNamara, E. Forcing the Field.
  L. Welch, 198:Oct82-99
Macnamara, J. Names for Things.
  O.J.F., 185:Apr83-630
McNaughton, H. New Zealand Drama.
  D. Carnegie, 130:Fall82-275
Macnaughton, W.R., ed. Critical Essays on
  John Updike.
  W.T.S., 395(MFS):Winter82/83-689
Macnaughton, W.R. Mark Twain's Last Years
  as a Writer.
  D.J. Dooley, 178:Dec82-513
Macneil, I.R. The New Social Contract.
  R. Hardin, 185:Oct82-168
McNeil, J. Little Brother.
  T.J. Binyon, 617(TLS):23Dec83-1437
MacNeil, R. The Right Place at the Right
  Time.*
  C. Hitchens, 617(TLS):7Oct83-1082
McNeill, W.H. The Pursuit of Power.*
  G. Best, 617(TLS):4Mar83-210
  N. Bliven, 442(NY):12Sep83-150
  J. Keegan, 453(NYRB):20Jan83-9
McNeish, J. Joy.
  J. Neville, 617(TLS):12Aug83-866
McNeley, J.K. Holy Wind in Navajo Philos-
  ophy.
  C.L. Rawlins, 649(WAL):Winter83-354
MacNicholas, J. James Joyce's "Exiles."
  V. Mahon, 402(MLR):Jan82-188
MacNiven, I.S. and H.T. Moore - see Ald-
  ington, R. and L. Durrell
McPhee, J. Basin and Range.*
  S. Brown, 569(SR):Spring82-250
  R. Holscher, 181:Spring82-161
  C. Vita-Finzi, 617(TLS):18Feb83-150
McPhee, J. In Suspect Terrain.
  M. Kakutani, 441:30Jan83-1
MacPhee, R. Maggie.* Scarecrow.
  R. Geiger, 198:Oct82-120
Macpherson, C.B. Burke.*
  J. Cannon, 83:Spring82-143
MacPherson, I., ed. The Manueline Succes-
  sion.
  D. MacKenzie, 382(MAE):1982/1-130
Macpherson, I. - see Manuel, J.
McPherson, J. Bimbashi McPherson: A Life
  in Egypt. (B. Carman and J. McPherson,
  eds)
  P.H. Newby, 362:27Oct83-28
Macpherson, J. Poems Twice Told.
  T.D. MacLulich, 628(UWR):Fall-Winter82-
  132
Macpherson, J. The Spirit of Solitude.
  D. Bromwich, 617(TLS):6May83-467
  T.D. MacLulich, 628(UWR):Fall-Winter82-
  132
McPherson, S. Patron Happiness.
  W. Logan, 617(TLS):10Jun83-614
MacPike, L. Dostoevsky's Dickens.
  A.R. Durkin, 395(MFS):Summer82-329
  D. Fanger, 445(NCF):Sep82-236
Macquarrie, J. In Search of Humanity.
  S.R. Sutherland, 617(TLS):1Apr83-332
McQueen, H. Gone Tomorrow.
  K. Tsokhas, 381:Dec82-499
McRae, R. Leibniz.
  J. Barnouw, 173(ECS):Fall81-102
  J. Tlumak, 449:Mar82-154
MacRéamoinn, S., ed. The Pleasures of
  Gaelic Poetry.
  P. Craig, 617(TLS):21Oct83-1162

McRobbie, K. Hole.*
  D. Barbour, 648(WCR):Summer81-80
Macrorie, K. Searching Writing.
  E. Lindemann, 128(CE):Apr82-358
MacShane, D. François Mitterrand.*
  442(NY):23May83-122
MacShane, F. The Life of John O'Hara.
  M. Light, 395(MFS):Winter81/82-734
  T.K. Meier, 219(GaR):Spring82-223
  B. Miller, 31(ASch):Winter81/82-120
MacShane, F. - see Chandler, R.
McSparran, F., ed. Octavian Imperator
  edited from MS BL Cotton Caligula A II.*
  G. Guddat-Figge, 38:Band100Heft1/2-179
  T. Turville-Petre, 677(YES):Vol 12-229
McSweeney, K. Tennyson and Swinburne as
  Romantic Naturalists.*
  D.G. Riede, 301(JEGP):Oct82-587
  A. Sinfield, 529(QQ):Autumn82-666
  H.F. Tucker, Jr., 591(SIR):Winter82-
  693
McSweeney, K. - see Wilson, A.
McTaggart, L. Kathleen Kennedy.
  A. Shapiro, 441:20Nov83-16
McVay, G. Isadora and Esenin.*
  A.C. Wright, 104(CASS):Spring82-141
McWhirter, G. God's Eye.
  S. Scobie, 529(QQ):Autumn82-654
McWhirter, G. The Island Man.
  D. Barbour, 648(WCR):Jun82-33
  M.T. Lane, 198:Oct82-94
  L. Lemire-Tostevin, 102(CanL):Spring82-
  141
McWilliam, C. The Buildings of Scotland,
  Lothian except Edinburgh.
  D. Watkin, 39:Aug82-128
McWilliams, R.G. - see Iberville, P.L.
Madan, T.N. and others. Doctors and
  Society.
  J. Kirkpatrick, 293(JASt):Nov81-179
de Madariaga, I. Russia in the Age of
  Catherine the Great.*
  N. Andreyev, 575(SEER):Jan82-113
  N.V. Riasanovsky, 550(RusR):Jan82-73
Madden, D. On the Big Wind.
  J.M. Davis, Jr., 152(UDQ):Spring81-117
Madden, D. A Primer of the Novel.
  E. Echevarria, 395(MFS):Summer81-398
Madden, F. Sir Frederic Madden at Cam-
  bridge.* (T.D. Rogers, ed)
  A.E.B. Owen, 325:Oct82-123
Madden, F. and D.K. Fieldhouse, eds.
  Oxford and the Idea of Commonwealth.
  H.S. Ferns, 617(TLS):7Jan83-16
Maddow, B. The Photography of Max Yavno.*
  J. Simpson, 55:Jan82-31
Maddox, B. The Marrying Kind.*
  J. Ryle, 617(TLS):18Mar83-262
Maddox, L. Nabokov's Novels in English.
  N. Tredell, 617(TLS):10Jun83-608
Madell, G.C. The Identity of the Self.
  G.N.A. Vesey, 518:Oct82-224
Madge, N., ed. Families at Risk.
  H. Rubinstein, 617(TLS):9Sep83-968
Maeder, E., ed. An Elegant Art.
  R.L. Shep, 614:Spring83-19
Maeroff, G.I. Don't Blame the Kids.
  P. Rothman, 42(AR):Spring82-240
Maes-Jelinek, H. Wilson Harris.
  J-P. Durix, 617(TLS):8Apr83-346
Maffei, D. Giuristi medievali e falsifi-
  cazioni editoriali del primo Cinquecento.
  P.O. Kristeller, 551(RenQ):Summer82-273

232

Maixner, P., ed. Robert Louis Stevenson: The Critical Heritage.*
  H-P. Breuer, 395(MFS):Summer82-263
  J. Calder, 402(MLR):Oct82-937
Majer, D. "Fremdvölkische" im Dritten Reich.
  F.L. Carsten, 575(SEER):Jan82-140
Majmin, E.A. and M.A. Černyšev - see Venevitinov, D.V.
Major, A. Inspector Therrien.
  H.R. Runte, 102(CanL):Winter81-124
Major, J.R. Representative Government in Early Modern France.
  J.M. Hayden, 551(RenQ):Spring82-102
Major, K. Far from Shore.
  J.K. Kealy, 102(CanL):Summer82-154
Majorano, M. - see Perez Pardal, V.
Makepeace, R.W. Marxist Ideology and Soviet Criminal Law.
  P.H. Juviler, 550(RussR):Apr82-220
Maki, J.M., ed and trans. Japan's Commission on the Constitution: The Final Report.*
  J.M. Ramseyer, 293(JASt):Nov81-142
Makin, B. An Essay to Revive the Antient Education of Gentlewomen.
  D. Reep, 568(SCN):Fall82-49
"Making Paper."
  R.H. Hoffman, 614:Spring83-18
Makowsky, V.A. - see Blackmur, R.P.
Makuck, P. Breaking and Entering.*
  D. Flower, 249(HudR):Summer82-274
Malachi, Z. - see "Amadís de Gaula"
Malamud, B. God's Grace.*
  A.H. Rosenfeld, 390:Nov82-55
Malamud, B. The Stories of Bernard Malamud.
  R. Alter, 441:16Oct83-1
Malaurie, J. The Last Kings of Thule.
  B. Lopez, 469:Vol8No2-118
Malcolm, J. Psychoanalysis.
  D. Kirsner, 381:Sep82-420
  P. Roazen, 639(VQR):Autumn82-710
  D.F. Sadoff, 42(AR):Spring82-242
Malcolm, N. Memory and Mind.*
  B.A., 543:Mar82-615
Maldonado, B.P. - see under Pavón Maldonado, B.
Male, R.R. Enter, Mysterious Stranger.*
  T. Martin, 395(MFS):Winter81/82-712
Male, R.R., ed. Money Talks.*
  D.B. Kesterson, 573(SSF):Spring82-184
  R.P. Weeks, 395(MFS):Summer82-295
Malebranche, N. Dialogue between a Christian Philosopher and a Chinese Philosopher on the Existence and Nature of God. (D.A. Iorio, trans)
  D.E. Mungello, 485(PE&W):Jan82-107
  D. Radner, 482(PhR):Oct82-628
Malebranche, N. Oeuvres.* (Vol 1) (G. Rodis-Lewis, with G. Malbreil, eds)
  J-L. Marion, 192(EP):Jan-Mar81-95
Malebranche, N. The Search after Truth [and] Elucidations of the Search after Truth.
  H.M.B., 543:Dec81-398
  D. Garber, 486:Mar82-146
  J.R. Milton, 84:Jun82-223
Malekin, P. Liberty and Love.
  M.J.M. Ezell, 184(EIC):Jan82-69

de Malesherbes, C-G.D. Mémoires sur la librairie et sur la liberté de la presse.* (G.E. Rodmell, ed)
  S. Diaconoff, 207(FR):Oct82-154
  J. Proust, 535(RHL):Jan-Feb82-115
Maleska, E.T. A Pleasure in Words. (H. Young, ed)
  C.R. Sleeth, 617(TLS):1Jul83-709
Malet, M. Nestor Makhno in the Russian Civil War.
  N. Stone, 617(TLS):27May83-532
Maletzke, G. Medienwirkungsforschung.
  P. Ruppert, 221(GQ):Nov82-573
Maley, A. and F. Grellet. Mind Matters.
  J.M. Hendrickson, 399(MLJ):Summer82-225
Maley, C.A. Dans le vent.*
  J.W. Cross, 399(MLJ):Spring82-84
Malhotra, P.L. Administration of Lord Elgin in India: 1894-99.
  A.P. Kaminsky, 293(JASt):Nov81-181
Malicet, M. Lecture psychanalytique de l'oeuvre de Claudel.
  J-N. Segrestaa, 535(RHL):Jan-Feb82-138
Maling, A. A Taste of Treason.
  T.J. Binyon, 617(TLS):30Dec83-1462
  N. Callendar, 441:25Sep83-34
Malingrey, A-M. - see Saint John Chrysostom
Malino, F. and P.C. Albert, eds. Essays in Modern Jewish History.
  D. Stone, 287:Aug/Sep82-25
Malinvaud, E. Réexamen de la théorie du chômage.
  C. Bismut, 98:Apr82-341
de Malkiel, M.R.L. - see under Lida de Malkiel, M.R.
Malkiel, Y. - see Lida de Malkiel, M.R.
de Mallac, G. Boris Pasternak.*
  J.D. Clayton, 104(CASS):Fall-Winter82-529
  A. Livingstone, 617(TLS):26Aug83-912
  E. Wasiolek, 405(MP):May83-434
  639(VQR):Summer82-87
Mallalieu, J.P.W. On Larkhill.
  K.O. Morgan, 617(TLS):29Jul83-800
Mallarmé, S. Correspondance.* (Vol 5) (H. Mondor and L.J. Austin, eds)
  U. Franklin, 207(FR):Oct82-158
  D. Leuwers, 535(RHL):Sep-Dec82-942
Mallarmé, S. Correspondance.* (Vol 6) (H. Mondor and L.J. Austin, eds)
  E. Souffrin-Le Breton, 208(FS):Apr82-219
Mallarmé, S. Correspondance.* (Vol 7 (H. Mondor and L.J. Austin, eds)
  E. Souffrin-Le Breton, 208(FS):Oct82-483
Mallarmé, S. Correspondance. (Vol 8) (H. Mondor and L.J. Austin, eds)
  J.M. Cocking, 617(TLS):29Apr83-422
Mallarmé, S. Correspondance. (Vol 9) (H. Mondor and L.J. Austin, eds)
  J.M. Cocking, 617(TLS):16Dec83-1408
Mallette, R. Spenser, Milton, and Renaissance Pastoral.*
  K.S. Datta, 551(RenQ):Summer82-322
  A.D. Needham, 568(SCN):Winter82-65
Mallik, B. Language of the Underworld of West Bengal.
  G.F. Meier, 682(ZPSK):Band34Heft1-137
Mallin, S.B. Merleau-Ponty's Philosophy.
  S.M. Corbett, 529(QQ):Summer82-347

Mann, R. After the Gold Rush.
   M. Abley, 617(TLS):25Mar83-285
Mann, T. Thomas Mann Diaries 1918-1939.*
  (H. Kesten, ed)
   D. Coles, 99:Feb83-31
   N. Mosley, 362:3Mar83-19
   S.S. Prawer, 617(TLS):25Feb83-171
   P. Vansittart, 364:Feb83-116
Mann, T. Reflections of a Nonpolitical
  Man.
   D.J. Enright, 617(TLS):5Aug83-825
   W. Laqueur, 441:15May83-11
Mann, T. Tagebücher 1918-1921.* (P. de
  Mendelssohn, ed)
   F. Rau, 224(GRM):Band32Heft3-366
Mann, T. The Yale "Zauberberg"-Manuscript.
  (J.F. White, ed)
   E. Schwarz and K. Thompson, 133:Band15
    Heft3-279
   O. Seidlin, 301(JEGP):Jul82-389
Manni, E. Geografia fisica e politica
  della Sicilia antica.
   E.E. Rice, 123:Vol32No2-225
Manning, E. Marble and Bronze.*
   C. Gere, 39:Dec82-431
Manning, K.R. Black Apollo of Science.
   S.J. Gould, 453(NYRB):24Nov83-3
Manning, O. The Levant Trilogy.
   P. Craig, 617(TLS):21Jan83-69
Manning, P.J. Byron and His Fictions.*
   A. Easson, 447(N&Q):Jun81-266
   J.S. Martin, 49:Jan82-91
   I. Scott-Kilvert, 677(YES):Vol 12-296
Manning, R. Open the Door.
   L. Taylor, 617(TLS):15Jul183-745
Manning, R.T. The Crisis of the Old Order
  in Russia.
   J. Keep, 617(TLS):27May83-531
Manns, P. Martin Luther.*
   J.M. Cameron, 453(NYRB):17Feb83-7
Manrique, J. Coplas de amor y de muerte.*
  (J.M. Aguirre, ed)
   N.G. Round, 86(BHS):Oct82-335
Mansbridge, J.J. Beyond Adversary Democ-
  racy.
   D. Braybrooke, 185:Oct82-153
Mansell, C. Head, Heart and Stone.
   G. Bitcon, 581:Dec82-470
Mansell, G. Let Truth Be Told.
   E. de Mauny, 617(TLS):15Apr83-382
Manser, A. Bradley's Logic.
   P. Geach, 617(TLS):1Jul183-693
Manser, M.H. A Dictionary of Contemporary
  Idioms.
   R. Boston, 617(TLS):23Dec83-1441
Mansfield, B.E. Phoenix of His Age.*
   J.K. Sowards, 551(RenQ):Spring81-98
Mansfield, H.C., Jr. Machiavelli's New
  Modes and Orders.
   J.H. Whitfield, 551(RenQ):Winter82-606
Mansfield, K. The Aloe: [with] Prelude.
  (V. O'Sullivan, ed)
   F. Adcock, 617(TLS):1Apr83-325
Mansfield, K. Félicité. (J.D. Delamain,
  trans)
   C. Jordis, 450(NRF):Jun82-134
Mantuanus, B. Die Fasti des Baptista Man-
  tuanus von 1516 als voklskundliche
  Quelle. (H. Trümpy, ed and trans)
   J.B. Dallet, 551(RenQ):Autumn81-407
"Manu-smriti with Nine Commentaries."
  (J.H. Dave, ed)
   L. Sternbach, 318(JAOS):Apr-Jun81-239

Manuel, F.E. and F.P. Utopian Thought in
  the Western World.*
   J.G.A. Pocock, 551(RenQ):Spring81-86
   L.T. Sargent, 322(JHI):Oct-Dec82-681
   R.J. Schoeck, 191(ELN):Sep82-24
Manuel, J. Juan Manuel, a Selection.*
  (I. Macpherson, ed)
   S. Baldwin, 589:Oct82-969
   R.B. Tate, 86(BHS):Oct82-333
"Manuscript Tanner 346."
   N.F. Blake, 179(ES):Feb82-71
Manuwald, B. Der Aufbau der lukrezischen
  Kulturentstehungslehre ("De rerum natura"
  5. 925-1457).
   D.P. Fowler, 123:Vol32No2-157
Mao Zedong. Mao Zedong and the Political
  Economy of the Border Region. (A.
  Watson, ed and trans)
   S.B. Thomas, 293(JASt):Nov81-125
Mao Zedong. Mao Zedong's "Talks at the
  Yan'an Conference on Literature and
  Art." (B.S. McDougall, ed and trans)
   B. Womack, 293(JASt):Aug82-825
Map, W. De Nugis Curialium. (M.R. James,
  ed and trans; rev by C.N.L. Brooke and
  R.A.B. Mynors)
   J.A. Burrow, 617(TLS):30Sep83-1040
Mapanje, J. Of Chameleons and Gods.
   P. Bland, 364:Jun82-73
Maquet, J., ed. On Linguistic Anthropol-
  ogy.
   Z. Salzmann, 350:Sep83-709
Marafioti, P.M. Caruso's Method of Voice
  Production.
   E. Forbes, 415:Nov82-764
Marazza, C. - see Ysambert de Saint-Ledger
Marbach, E. - see Husserl, E.
Marbod of Rennes. Marbode of Rennes'
  (1035-1123) De lapidus. (J.M. Riddle,
  ed)
   H. Bloch, 589:Oct82-914
March, A. Obra poètica completa.* (R.
  Ferreres, ed) Les poesies d'Ausiàs
  March. (J. Ferraté, ed)
   J.M. Sobré, 240(HR):Spring82-237
Marchais, P. Les processus psychopatho-
  logiques de l'adulte.
   A. Reix, 542:Jan-Mar82-90
Marchak, P. Ideological Perspectives on
  Canada.
   V. di Norcia, 99:Oct82-33
Marchand, L.A., ed. Byron's Letters and
  Journals.* (Vol 12: Index)
   J. Bayley, 453(NYRB):2Jun83-25
   F.W. Shilstone, 580(SCR):Fall82-129
   639(VQR):Summer82-88
Marchand, L.A. - see Lord Byron
Marchessault, J. La Saga des poules mouil-
  lées.
   P.G. Lewis, 207(FR):Apr83-788
Marckwardt, A.H. American English.* (2nd
  ed rev by J.L. Dillard)
   B.J. Koekkoek, 301(JEGP):Jul82-459
Marcos Marín, F. Reforma y modernización
  del español.
   C. Silva-C., 545(RPh):Nov81-427
Marcus, D. A Manual of Babylonian Jewish
  Aramaic.
   P. Coxon, 318(JAOS):Oct-Dec81-450

Marcus, J., ed. New Feminist Essays on Virginia Woolf.
K.C. Hill-Miller, 395(MFS):Winter82/83-636
V.S. Middleton, 594:Fall82-289
Marcus, J.R. The American Jewish Woman. The American Jewish Woman, 1654-1980.
A.S. Moore, 287:Jan82-24
Marcus, M. Diagnostic Teaching of the Language Arts.
B. Lommatzsch, 682(ZPSK):Band34Heft2-264
Marcus, P.L., W. Gould and M.J. Sidnell - see Yeats, W.B.
Mardaga, P. - see Rondal, J-A.
Marder, A.J. Old Friends, New Enemies.
C. Johnson, 293(JASt):May82-600
de la Mare, W. The Collected Poems of Walter de la Mare.
L. Bonnerot, 189(EA):Jan-Mar82-100
Marek, G. Cosima Wagner.
M. Tanner, 529(QQ):Autumn82-635
Marenbon, J. Early Medieval Philosophy (480-1150).
G.R. Evans, 617(TLS):14Oct83-1112
Marenbon, J. From the Circle of Alcuin to the School of Auxerre.
P.V. Spade, 319:Jan83-98
Marer, P. - see Pécsi, K.
Marer, P. and J.M. Montias, eds. East European Integration and East-West Trade.
A.H. Smith, 575(SEER):Apr82-306
Marer, P. and E. Tabaczynski, eds. Polish-US Industrial Cooperation in the 1980s.
S. Lamed, 104(CASS):Fall-Winter82-599
Maresca, T.E. Three English Epics.*
T.H. Cain, 125:Fall81-88
C. von Nolcken, 541(RES):May82-196
J.J. O'Connor, 551(RenQ):Spring81-149
Mareschal, A. La Cour bergère ou l'Arcadie de Messire Philippes Sidney. (L. Desvignes, ed)
P. Koch, 535(RHL):Sep-Dec82-886
J-P. Leroy, 549(RLC):Jul-Sep82-393
Marfurt, B. Textsorte Witz.*
E. Beneš, 685(ZDL):3/1981-406
Margalit, A., ed. Meaning and Use.*
S. Blackburn, 482(PhR):Jan82-128
Margenau, H. Physics and Philosophy.*
J.P.L., 543:Mar82-617
de Margerie, D. Duplicités.
B.L. Knapp, 207(FR):Dec82-338
F. de Martinoir, 450(NRF):Jun82-121
Margetson, S. Victorian High Society.
J. Lucas, 366:Spring82-132
Margitić, M.R. - see Corneille, P.
Margolies, E. Which Way Did He Go?
27(AL):Oct82-474
Margolies, J. The End of the Road.*
R.G. Wilson, 639(VQR):Summer82-533
Margolis, J. Art and Philosophy.*
R.J. Matthews, 289:Winter82-109
E.W. Prior, 63:Dec82-387
Margolis, J.D. Joseph Wood Krutch.*
S. Pickering, 569(SR):Summer82-474
Marguerite de Navarre. Oraison a Nostre Seigneur Jesus Christ. (R. Salminen, ed)
G. Roques, 553(RLiR):Jul-Dec82-507
Marguin, L. Poésie et liberté.
F.R. Smith, 208(FS):Jan82-104
Mariani, P. Crossing Cocytus.
H. Seidman, 441:20Feb83-6

Mariani, P. William Carlos Williams.*
W.S. Di Piero, 569(SR):Fall82-cii
A.M. Kolich, 405(MP):May83-438
J. Parini, 249(HudR):Winter82/83-633
W.H. Pritchard, 31(ASch):Summer82-440
Marie de France. Die Lais. (D. Rieger, trans)
B. Schmolke-Hasselmann, 224(GRM):Band 32Heft1-117
Marietti, M. and others. Présence et influence de l'Espagne dans la culture italienne de la renaissance.
A.D. Wright, 402(MLR):Apr82-468
Marín, F.M. - see under Marcos Marín, F.
Marin, L. Le portrait du roi.
C. Rosset, 98:Feb82-120
Marin, L. Le Récit est un piège.
P. Dandrey, 475:No16Pt2-423
Marino, A. Étiemble ou le comparatisme militant.*
M.F. Meurice, 450(NRF):Sep82-122
Marinoni, M.C., ed. Fierabras anonimo in prosa.
J. Monfrin, 554:Vol 102No4-558
Mark, R. Experiments in Gothic Structure.
P. Rice, 46:Nov82-80
Markandaya, K. Pleasure City.*
E. Claridge, 364:Oct82-107
Markandaya, K. Shalimar.
P-L. Adams, 61:Sep83-124
442(NY):10Oct83-166
Marker, F.J. and L-L. Edward Gordon Craig and "The Pretenders."
H. Lane, 627(UTQ):Summer82-433
L. Newman, 611(TN):Vol36No3-138
D. Rubin, 108:Winter82-115
Marker, L-L. and F.J. Ingmar Bergman.*
I. Wardle, 157:Winter82-44
Markévitch, I. Être et avoir été. Edition Encyclopedique des neuf symphonies de Beethoven. (Symphonies 1, 2, and 3)
F. Piatier, 607:Sep82-47
Markey, T.L. Frisian.
S.M. Embleton, 320(CJL):Fall82-182
Markey, T.L. - see Schuchardt, H. "Das Markgräflerland."
W. König, 685(ZDL):2/1981-254
Markham, B. West with the Night.
J.K.L.W., 617(TLS):23Sep83-1031
Markis, D. Quine und das Problem der Übersetzung.
W. Brüstle, 687:Apr-Jun81-310
Markov, G. The Truth that Killed.
J. Simpson, 362:13Oct83-29
Markov, V. Russian Imagism, 1919-1924.*
A.F. Zweers, 104(CASS):Spring82-137
Markowitz, A.L. Historic Preservation.
N. Thompson, 576:Mar82-70
Marks, C., with M. Soeharjo. The Indonesian Kitchen.
W. and C. Cowen, 639(VQR):Spring82-60
Marks, E.R. Coleridge on the Language of Verse.*
E. Kessler, 661(WC):Summer82-122
Marks, R. Burrell.
D. Walker, 617(TLS):4Nov83-1218
Marks, R. and others. The Burrell Collection.
D. Walker, 617(TLS):4Nov83-1218
Markstein, L. and L. Hirasawa. Developing Reading Skills — Intermediate.
E. Fischer-Kohn and J.J. Kohn, 399(MLJ):Winter82-450

Markús, G. Marxism and Anthropology.*
  T. Rockmore, 192(EP):Jul-Sep81-360
Markus, M. Tempus und Aspekt.
  G. Rauh, 260(IF):Band86-371
Markus, T.A., ed. Order in Space and
  Society.
  D. Walker, 617(TLS):22Apr83-410
Marlar, R. Decision Against England.
  A.L. Le Quesne, 617(TLS):16Sep83-987
Marlatt, D. What Matters.*
  D. Barbour, 648(WCR):Oct82-37
Marlyn, J. Putzi, I Love You, You Little
  Square.
  J.A. Wainwright, 150(DR):Summer82-324
Marmorek, J. Over a Barrel.
  C.K. Rush, 529(QQ):Winter82-902
Marmur, D. Beyond Survival.
  G. Vermes, 617(TLS):28Jan83-76
Marnham, P., ed. Night Thoughts.
  R. Davies, 617(TLS):23Dec83-1439
Marnham, P. The "Private Eye" Story.*
  C. Brown, 617(TLS):18Feb83-163
  C. Hawtree, 364:Nov82-83
Marot, C. Oeuvres complètes.* (Vol 6)
  (C.A. Mayer, ed)
  I.D. McFarlane, 402(MLR):Oct82-950
  J. Voisine, 549(RLC):Jul-Sep82-386
Márquez, A. Literatura e Inquisición en
  España (1478-1834).
  T. O'Reilly, 86(BHS):Oct82-336
Márquez, G.G. - see under García Márquez,
  G.
Marquez, T.F. - see under Falcon Marquez,
  T.
Márquez-Sterling, M. Fernán González.*
  P. Conerly, 589:Jul82-637
Marquis, A.G. Marchel Duchamp.
  B.L. Knapp, 188(ECr):Spring82-90
Marra, G. and others. Itinerari negati
  momenti della tradizione Inglese e Scoz-
  zese nel settecento, letterature moderne.
  M.P. McDiarmid, 571(ScLJ):Winter82-61
Marranca, B., ed. American Dreams.
  C. Bachman, 397(MD):Sep82-452
Marranca, B. and G. Dasgupta. American
  Playwrights.
  B.L. Knapp, 295(JML):Dec82-392
Marri, F. Glossario al milanese di Bon-
  vesin.
  E.F. Tuttle, 545(RPh):Nov81-425
Marriott, A. The Circular Coast.
  M.T. Lane, 198:Oct82-94
Marrone, S.P. William of Auvergne and
  Robert Grosseteste.
  J. North, 617(TLS):21Oct83-1163
Marrow, J.H. Passion Iconography in North-
  ern European Art of the Late Middle Ages
  and Early Renaissance.
  L. Campbell, 90:Jan82-35
  D. Freedberg, 589:Apr82-395
  A.H. Van Buren, 54:Sep82-510
Marrow, J.H. and A. Shestack, eds. Hans
  Baldung Grien.
  C. Harbison, 54:Mar82-150
  C.M. Kauffmann, 59:Sep82-373
Mars-Jones, A. Lantern Lecture.*
  J.R.B., 148:Spring82-95
Mars-Jones, A. Mae West is Dead.
  S. Pickles, 617(TLS):28Oct83-1185
Marsack, R. The Cave of Making.
  A. Thwaite, 617(TLS):14Jan83-28
Marsan, J-C. Montreal in Evolution.
  M.J. Edwards, 102(CanL):Summer82-161

Marsé, J. La muchacha de las bragas de
  oro.
  M.S. Vásquez, 152(UDQ):Fall82-36
Marsh, D. The Quattrocento Dialogue.*
  M.D. Lorch, 551(RenQ):Winter81-572
Marsh, E.L. Changed Into Words.
  D. Haskell, 581:Sep82-348
Marsh, N. Light Thickens.*
  M. Laski, 362:20Jan83-23
Marsh, P. Aggro.
  R.A. Day, 189(EA):Jan-Mar82-71
Marshall, G.C. The Papers of George Cat-
  lett Marshall.* (Vol 1) (L.I. Bland and
  S.R. Ritenour, eds)
  W.H. Cunliffe, 14:Fall82-485
Marshall, H.W. and R.E. Ahlborn. Bucka-
  roos in Paradise.
  A.J. Cofone, 649(WAL):Winter83-375
  584(SWR):Summer82-v
Marshall, J. Saltspring.
  D. Barbour, 648(WCR):Oct82-37
Marshall, P. Brown Girl, Brownstones.
  D. Pinckney, 453(NYRB):28Apr83-26
Marshall, P. Praisesong for the Widow.
  M.K. Benet, 617(TLS):16Sep83-1002
  D. Pinckney, 453(NYRB):28Apr83-26
  A. Tyler, 441:20Feb83-7
  442(NY):14Feb83-114
Marshall, P. and G. Williams, ed. The
  British Atlantic Empire Before the
  American Revolution.
  P.S. Haffenden, 656(WMQ):Jul82-529
Marshall, P.J. and G. Williams. The
  Great Map of Mankind.*
  566:Spring83-135
Marshall, R.K. Virgins and Viragos.
  R. Mitchison, 617(TLS):26Aug83-908
Marshall, T. The Elements.*
  D. Barbour, 648(WCR):Jun82-33
  M.B. Oliver, 198:Jan82-74
Marshall, W. Perfect End.
  N. Callendar, 441:17Apr83-21
Marshfield, A. The Elektra Poems.
  M. Imlah, 617(TLS):27May83-549
Marsilius of Padua. Oeuvres mineures. (C.
  Jeudy and J. Quillet, eds and trans)
  A.S. McGrade, 589:Oct82-916
Marston, J. Parasitaster, or the Fawn.*
  (D.A. Blostein, ed)
  J. Pearson, 161(DUJ):Jun82-305
Marteau, R. Atlante.
  D.W. Russell, 529(QQ):Spring82-217
Marteau, R. Mont-Royal.
  M. Deguy, 450(NRF):Mar82-121
Marteau, R. Salamander.
  G.D. Martin, 208(FS):Oct82-497
Marteau, R. Traite du blanc et des tein-
  tures/Treatise on White and Tincture.
  D.W. Russell, 529(QQ):Spring82-217
Martel, F. Le Jeu enthousiaste de ce
  qu'oublier peut concevoir.
  P.G. Lewis, 207(FR):Mar83-669
Martel, S. The King's Daughter.
  M.J. Evans, 102(CanL):Spring82-86
Martel, S. Menfou Carcajou.
  A. Mitcham, 102(CanL):Winter81-161
Martello, P.J. Teatro. (Vol 1) (H.S.
  Noce, ed)
  G. Costa, 173(ECS):Summer83-435
Marten, M., J. May and R. Taylor. Weird
  and Wonderful Wildlife.
  M. Levine, 441:11Dec83-35

Marty, S. Nobody Danced with Miss Rodeo.
 M.T. Lane, 198:Jan82-71
Martz, E.M., with R.K. McClure and W.T. La
 Moy - see Walpole, H.
Martz, L.L. Poet of Exile.*
 J. Blondel, 189(EA):Jan-Mar82-80
 L. Lerner, 131(CL):Winter82-74
 B.K. Lewalski, 301(JEGP):Apr82-262
 C.D. Murphy, 396(ModA):Spring82-213
 H. Richmond, 125:Spring82-302
 A. Rudrum, 191(ELN):Mar82-284
 E.W. Tayler, 551(RenQ):Summer81-292
Martz, L.L. and A. Williams, eds. The
 Author in His Work.
 J. Schlaeger, 38:Band100Heft1/2-242
Marucci, F. "I fogli della Sibilla."
 J-G. Ritz, 189(EA):Jul-Sep82-343
Marvan, J. Modern Lithuanian Declension.
 A. Carstairs, 353:Vol 19No5/6-550
Marvan, J. Prehistoric Slavic Contrac-
 tion.*
 F. Kortlandt, 361:Jan82-98
Marwick, A. Class.
 M.E. Rose, 366:Autumn82-261
Marx, J. Tiphaigne de la Roche.
 M.A., 561(SFS):Mar82-96
Marx, K. Critique of Hegel's "Philosophy
 of Right." (J. O'Malley, ed)
 A.W.J. Harper, 154:Jun82-399
Marx, K. Karl Marx in seinen Briefen.
 (S.K. Padover, ed)
 M. Silberman, 221(GQ):Mar82-286
Marx, K. and F. Engels. Irland — Insel in
 Aufruhr.
 J-P. Lefebvre, 98:Jun-Jul82-576
Marx, R. Histoire de la Grande-Bretagne.
 J. Leruez, 189(EA):Apr-Jun82-193
Marz, R. The Island-Maker.
 R. Tillinghast, 441:7Aug83-12
Marzellier, J. L'Economie de la Grande-
 Bretagne contemporaine.
 J. Weiller, 189(EA):Apr-Jun82-225
Masakazu, Y. - see under Yamazaki Masakazu
Masaryk, A.G. and others. Alice Garrigue
 Masaryk, 1879-1966. (R.C. Mitchell,
 comp)
 J.L.A. Horna, 104(CASS):Summer82-295
Masatoshi, with R. Bushell. The Art of
 Netsuke Carving.
 M. Birch, 60:May-Jun82-139
Masefield, J. Letters of John Masefield
 to Florence Lamont.* (C. and L. Lamont,
 eds)
 F. Berry, 447(N&Q):Aug81-362
 A.F.T. Lurcock, 541(RES):May82-230
Masefield, J. Letters to Reyna. (W.
 Buchan, ed)
 E.S. Turner, 362:10Nov83-28
Masefield, P. To Ride the Storm.
 P.W. Brooks, 324:Jan83-104
Masi, E. China Winter.
 442(NY):3Jan83-73
Masih, I.K. Plays of Samuel Beckett.
 E. Morot-Sir, 207(FR):Apr83-780
Maslow, J.E. The Owl Papers.
 442(NY):26Dec83-72
Mason, A. The Illusionist.
 D. May, 362:20Oct83-26
 N. Shack, 617(TLS):26Aug83-915
Mason, B. Michel Butor.*
 C.M. Senninger, 535(RHL):Jul-Aug82-677
Mason, B.A. Shiloh and Other Stories.*
 C. Rumens, 617(TLS):12Aug83-866

Mason, H., ed. Studies on Voltaire and
 the Eighteenty Century.* (Vol 182)
 J. Renwick, 402(MLR):Oct82-958
Mason, H., ed. Studies on Voltaire and
 the Eighteenth Century. (Vol 189)
 C. Bonfils, 535(RHL):May-Jun82-480
Mason, H. Voltaire.*
 A. Ages, 529(QQ):Autumn82-634
 W.H. Barber, 208(FS):Jul82-330
 B. Fink, 579(SAQ):Summer82-346
 H.G. Heymann, 77:Spring82-176
 M.F. O'Meara, 400(MLN):May82-1016
Mason, J.H. - see Rousseau, J-J.
Mason, M., ed. London Review of Books:
 Anthology Two.
 D.A.N. Jones, 362:23Jun83-26
Mason, M. and T.F. Rigelhof. A Beast With
 Two Backs.
 K. Thompson, 198:Apr82-109
Mason, P. The English Gentleman.*
 B. Gutteridge, 364:Dec82/Jan83-128
Mason, R. Chickenhawk.
 P-L. Adams, 61:Sep83-124
 C.D.B. Bryan, 441:16Oct83-9
 442(NY):7Nov83-185
Mass, E. Literatur und Zensur in der frü-
 hen Aufklärung.
 F. Deloffre, 547(RF):Band94Heft4-490
Mass, J.P., ed. Court and Bakufu in Japan.
 C. Steenstrup, 407(MN):Winter82-531
Mass, J.P. The Development of Kamakura
 Rule, 1180-1250.*
 P.J. Arnesen, 293(JASt):Nov81-143
Massicotte, M. Le parler rural de l'Île-
 aux-Grues (Québec).*
 P. Rézeau, 553(RLiR):Jul-Dec82-489
Massie, A. The Death of Men.*
 P. Lewis, 565:Vol23No2-44
Massie, R.K. Peter the Great.*
 J.A. Settanni, 396(ModA):Summer/Fall82-
 434
Massignon, L. The Passion of al-Hallāj,
 Mystic and Martyr of Islam.
 J. Baldick, 617(TLS):23Sep83-1023
Massinger, P. The Selected Plays of
 Philip Massinger.* (C. Gibson, ed)
 I. Donaldson, 617(TLS):280ct83-1183
Massingham, B. A Century of Gardeners.
 R.I. Ross, 617(TLS):25Feb83-192
Massoli, M. - see "Frey Íñigo de Mendoza,
 'Coplas de Vita Christi'"
Masson, A. The Pictorial Catalogue: Mural
 Decoration in Libraries.
 D. McKitterick, 78(BC):Autumn82-382
Masson, J.M. The Oceanic Feeling.
 W. Halbfass, 293(JASt):Feb82-387
Masson, O., with G.T. Martin and R.V.
 Nicholls. Carian Inscriptions from
 North Saqqâra and Buhen.
 C. Brixhe, 555:Vol55fasc1-150
Massuh, G. Borges.
 E.E. Behle, 547(RF):Band93Heft1/2-306
Mast, G. Howard Hawks, Storyteller.*
 D. Kehr, 18:May83-72
 M. Wood, 617(TLS):12Aug83-855
Masters, J. Man of War.
 T. Fitton, 617(TLS):23Dec83-1437
Masterton, G. Solitaire.
 S. Ellin, 441:13Feb83-14
Mastny, V. Russia's Road to the Cold War.*
 P. Marantz, 104(CASS):Summer82-269
Mastromarco, G. Il pubblico di Eronda.*
 A.H.M. Kessels, 394:Vol35fasc1/2-176

Mastronarde, D.J. Contact and Disconti-
nuity.
  D. Bain, 123:Vol32No1-4
  N.S. Rabinowitz, 122:Oct82-361
  J.R. Wilson, 487:Summer82-183
Matarasso, P. The Redemption of Chivalry.*
  E.M. O'Sharkey, 208(FS):Jul82-315
Matczak, S.A., ed. God in Contemporary
Thought.
  B.M.B., 543:Jun82-884
Matejič, M. and others. A Biobibliographi-
cal Handbook of Bulgarian Authors. (K.
Black, ed)
  M.S. Iovine, 104(CASS):Fall-Winter82-
  579
Matera, J., ed. The Quilter's Art.
  614:Summer83-21
Materer, T. Vortex.*
  R. Currie, 541(RES):May82-231
  S. Scobie, 675(YER):Jun82-144
  H.H. Watts, 395(MFS):Winter82/83-646
"Materiali per servire alla Storia del
Vaso François."
  J. Boardman, 123:Vol32No2-291
Mates, B. Skeptical Essays.*
  M. Smithurst, 518:Apr82-127
Matheeussen, C. and C.L. Heesakkers - see
Lipsius, J. and P. Cunaeus
Matheopoulos, H. Maestro.
  L. Schwarzbaum, 441:29May83-12
Mathes, E.W. From Survival to the Uni-
verse.
  T.M.R., 185:Oct82-199
Mathews, D.G. Religion in the Old South.
  R.M. Calhoon, 656(WMQ):Apr82-386
Mathiesen, T.J. - see Aristides
Mathieson, W.D. My Grandfather's War.
  L. McIntyre, 298:Winter82/83-130
Mathieu-Castellani, G. Mythes de l'éros
baroque.*
  C-G. Dubois, 549(RLC):Jul-Sep82-389
  L. Finas, 450(NRF):Jul-Aug82-174
  A. Gendre, 475:No16Pt2-401
Matisse, H. Jazz.
  J. Russell, 441:4Dec83-13
  C. Tomkins, 442(NY):19Dec83-124
"Henri Matisse: Paintings and Sculptures
in Soviet Museums."
  N. Watkins, 90:Sep82-563
de Matons, J.G. - see under Grosdidier de
Matons, J.
Matsche, F. Die Kunst im Dienst der
Staatsidee Kaiser Karls VI.
  H. Belting, 471:Jul/Aug/Sep82-268
Matsushita, H. Movimiento obrero argen-
tino 1930/1945.
  D. Rock, 617(TLS):23Dec83-1435
Matteini, O. Stendhal e la musica.
  V.D.L., 605(SC):15Oct82-90
de Matteis, M. Mehrsprachigkeit.
  B. Lommatzsch, 682(ZPSK):Band35Heft2-
  240
Matthes, M. and K. Quebec.
  529(QQ):Summer82-460
Matthew of Vendôme. The Art of Versifica-
tion. (A.E. Gaylon, trans)
  J.J. Murphy, 481(PQ):Summer81-423
  P.S. Noble, 382(MAE):1982/1-122
Matthew, D. The Atlas of Medieval Europe.
  R. Fletcher, 617(TLS):11Nov83-1252

Matthews, G. The Further Adventures of
Huckleberry Finn.
  Z. Leader, 617(TLS):30Sep83-1045
  T. Le Clair, 441:25Sep83-14
Matthews, G.B. Philosophy and the Young
Child.
  G.E.M. Anscombe, 484(PPR):Dec82-265
  J. Russell, 518:Apr82-125
  R. Young, 63:Jun82-196
Matthews, J. Dubious Persuasions.*
  R. Orodenker, 573(SSF):Spring82-178
Matthews, J. Voices.
  D. Bair, 441:22May83-11
  W. Maxwell, 442(NY):27Jun83-96
Matthews, J.T. The Play of Faulkner's
Language.
  A. Bleikasten, 395(MFS):Winter82/83-
  675
  R. Christiansen, 617(TLS):14Jan83-43
  D. Minter, 578:Fall83-123
  M.R. Winchell, 585(SoQ):Summer82-110
Matthews, N. and M.D. Wainwright, comps.
A Guide to Manuscripts and Documents in
the British Isles Relating to the Far
East. (J.D. Pearson, ed)
  D. Pong, 318(JAOS):Oct-Dec81-433
Matthews, P.H. Generative Grammar and
Linguistic Competence.*
  D.J. Allerton, 307:Apr82-57
  E.J. Hols, 660(Word):Dec82-257
Matthews, P.H. Morphology.*
  P. Swiggers, 353:Vol 19No5/6-541
Matthews, P.H. Syntax.
  P.L. Carrell, 399(MLJ):Summer82-202
  M.A. Covington, 350:Dec83-921
  G. Mallinson, 603:Vol6No2-271
Matthews, R.C.O., C.H. Feinstein and J.C.
Odling-Smee. British Economic Growth
1856-1973.
  D.N. McCloskey, 617(TLS):6May83-462
Matthews, V.H. Pastoral Nomadism in the
Mari Kingdom (ca. 1830-1760 B.C.).
  P. Talon, 318(JAOS):Oct-Dec81-454
Matthews, W. Flood.
  P. Stitt, 219(GaR):Fall82-675
Matthias, J. - see Jones, D.
Matthias, J. and G. Printz-Påhlson - see
"Contemporary Swedish Poetry"
Matthiessen, P. In the Spirit of Crazy
Horse.
  A.M. Dershowitz, 441:6Mar83-1
  D.P. McAllester, 469:Vol18No3-106
  R. Sherrill, 61:Mar83-112
  P. Stegner, 453(NYRB):14Apr83-21
  442(NY):11Apr83-136
Matthiessen, P. Sand Rivers.*
  639(VQR):Spring82-61
Matthieu, P. Tablettes de la vie et de la
mort. (C.N. Smith, ed)
  F. Lestringant, 535(RHL):Sep-Dec82-879
Mattison, H., S. Meiselas and F. Ruben
stein - see Forché, C.
Maturana, H.R. and F.J. Varela. Auto-
poiesis and Cognition.
  M.G., 543:Dec81-399
Matusow, B. The Evening Stars.
  C. Verderese, 441:27Nov83-16
Matvejevitch, P. Pour une poétique de
l'événement.
  J. Szávai, 549(RLC):Oct-Dec82-514
Matyas, A. History of Modern Non-Marxist
Economics.
  B. Ward, 104(CASS):Summer82-310

Maubon, C. Désir et écriture mélancoliques.
F. Assaf, 475:No16Pt2-443
Maugham, W.S. The Letters of William Somerset Maugham to Lady Juliet Duff.
(L.R. Rothschild, ed)
R. Craft, 453(NYRB):22Dec83-52
Mauguet, Z. La Fête à l'envers.
C. Mackey, 207(FR):Dec82-339
de Maupassant, G. Contes de la Bécasse.
(H. Juin, ed)
M. Donaldson-Evans, 207(FR):Dec82-325
de Maupassant, G. Contes du Jour et de la Nuit. (R. Bismut, ed)
P.J. Whyte, 208(FS):Jan82-86
de Maupassant, G. "Le Horla" et autres contes cruels et fantastiques. (M-C. Bancquart, ed)
P. Hamon, 535(RHL):May-Jun82-490
P.J. Whyte, 208(FS):Jan82-86
de Maupassant, G. Miss Harriet. (D. Fernandez, ed) Pierre et Jean. (L. Tancock, trans)
G. Hainsworth, 208(FS):Jan82-85
Maurer, C. - see Lorca, F.G.
Maurer, D.W. Language of the Underworld.*
(A.W. Futrell and C.R. Wordell, eds)
K.B. Harder, 35(AS):Winter82-288
Maurer, F., F. Stroh and R. Mulch. Südhessisches Wörterbuch. (Vol 3) (R. and R. Mulch, eds)
E. Wagner, 685(ZDL):1/1982-84
Mauriac, C. Le Rire des pères dans les yeux des enfants.
G.R. Besser, 207(FR):Oct82-173
Maurocordato, A. L'Ode de Paul Claudel (2).
J-N. Segrestaa, 535(RHL):Mar-Apr82-316
Maurud, Ø. Nabosprakforståelse i Skandinavia.
R.E. Wood, 660(Word):Apr81-68
Mauzi, R. and S. Menant. Le XVIIIe siècle. (Vol 2)
T. Logé, 356(LR):Feb82-80
Mawdsley, E. and M., eds. Blue Guide: Moscow and Leningrad.
G. Lewinson, 575(SEER):Jan82-151
Mawet, F. Recherches sur les oppositions fonctionnelles dans le vocabulaire homérique de la douleur (autor de pēma-algos).
C. Brixhe, 555:Vol56fasc1-122
Max, F.R. Der "Wald der Welt."
H.S. Daemmrich, 221(GQ):Nov82-597
Maxcey, C.E. Bona Opera.
S.H. Hendrix, 551(RenQ):Spring82-91
Maxfield, V.A. The Military Decorations of the Roman Army.
A.R. Birley, 123:Vol32No2-290
J.L.F. Keppie, 314:Vol72-185
Maximin, D. L'Isolé soleil.
C. Simra, 207(FR):May83-981
Maxwell, G. Lords of the Atlas.
G.S., 617(TLS):29Jul83-819
Maxwell, G. A Reed Shaken By the Wind.
G.S., 617(TLS):24Jun83-683
Maxwell, W. - see Warner, S.T.
Maxwell-Stuart, P.G. Studies in Greek Colour Terminology.* (Vols 1 and 2)
M. Davies, 123:Vol32No2-214
May, D. Proust.
V. Minogue, 617(TLS):27May83-548
A. Ryan, 362:17Mar83-22

"Erskine May's Parliamentary Practice."
(20th ed) (C. Gordon, ed)
B. Cocks, 617(TLS):12Aug83-849
May, G. L'autobiographie.*
J. Cruickshank, 208(FS):Jul82-367
N.C. Le Coat, 400(MLN):May82-993
T. Logé, 356(LR):May82-177
May, G.A. Social Engineering in the Philippines.
N.G. Owen, 293(JASt):Feb82-423
May, K.M. Characters of Women in Narrative Literature.
295(JML):Dec82-336
May, L. Screening Out the Past.*
K.R. Hey, 658:Winter82-294
Mayer, A., ed. Culture and Morality.
M. Douglas, 185:Jul83-786
Mayer, C.A. - see Marot, C.
Mayer, D., ed. Henry Irving and "The Bells."*
R. Jackson, 637(VS):Spring82-388
Mayer, H. Ein Deutscher auf Widerruf.
P. Brady, 617(TLS):1Apr83-339
Mayer, H.E. Bistümer, Klöster und Stifte im Königreich Jerusalem.
J.A. Brundage, 589:Jan82-131
Mayerthaler, W. Morphologische Natürlichkeit.
W. Mańczak, 603:Vol6No1-146
Mayes, H.R. The Magazine Maze.*
42(AR):Winter82-116
Maynard, O. Judith Jamison.
W. Como, 151:Mar82-89
Mayne, P. A Year in Marrakesh.
M.F., 617(TLS):11Feb83-143
Mayne, R. Postwar.
S. Jacobson, 362:13Oct83-27
Z. Steiner, 617(TLS):7Oct83-1081
Mayne, S. The Impossible Promised Land.*
E. Jones, 150(DR):Spring82-168
Mayne, S., ed. Irving Layton.*
J. Cowan, 178:Sep82-375
Mayo, E.L. Collected Poems.*
B. Howard, 271:Winter82-140
J. Ridland, 472:Spring/Summer83-191
Mayr, E. The Growth of Biological Thought.*
L. Wolpert, 617(TLS):4Mar83-216
639(VQR):Autumn82-136
Mayrhofer, M. Iranisches Personennamenbuch. (Vol 1, fasc 1)
M.J. Dresden, 318(JAOS):Oct-Dec81-466
Mays, J.B. The Spiral Stair.
R. Hatch, 296(JCF):No33-142
Mays, W. Whitehead's Philosophy of Science and Metaphysics.*
D.W.S., 543:Jun82-886
Mayzel, M. Generals and Revolutionaries.*
J. Bushnell, 550(RusR):Apr82-207
Mazgaj, P. The Action Française and Revolutionary Syndicalism.
D.H. Barry, 161(DUJ):Dec81-132
Mažiulis, V. Prūsų kalbos paminklai II.
W.R. Schmalstieg, 215(GL):Fal182-208
Mazu. Le Entretiens. (C. Despeux, ed and trans)
F.A. Jamme, 450(NRF):May82-137
Mazur, O. The Wild Man in the Spanish Renaissance and Golden Age Theater.
A. Parodi, 547(RF):Band94Heft4-506
K. Whinnom, 86(BHS):Oct82-338

Mazzaro, J. The Figure of Dante.
  J.F. Cotter, 249(HudR):Summer82-306
  R.G. Williams, 385(MQR):Fall83-667
Mazzaro, J. Postmodern American Poetry.*
  L. Orr, 659(ConL):Fall83-402
Mazzoleni, G. I buffoni sacri d'America e
il ridere secondo cultera.
  D. Gifford, 203:Vol93No1-122
Mazzotta, G. Dante, Poet of the Desert.*
  M. Shapiro, 276:Spring82-57
Mead, G. The Surrealist Image.
  R. Cardinal, 208(FS):Jul82-358
Mead, P. Be Faithful Go.
  G. Catalano, 381:Oct81-349
Mead, P. The Eye in the Air.
  S. Bidwell, 617(TLS):6May83-455
Meade, M. Sybille.
  M. Warner, 441:17Apr83-15
Mealing, M. Coyote's Running Here.
  B. Pirie, 102(CanL):Autumn82-139
Measeles, E.B. Lee's Ferry.
  L.C. Powell, 50(ArQ):Spring82-89
Mebane, M. Mary.
  V.A. Smith, 569(SR):Spring82-xxxvii
  639(VQR):Winter82-18
Mecham, F. "John O'Brien" and the Boree
Log.
  C. Hadgraft, 71(ALS):Oct82-547
Medawar, P. Pluto's Republic.
  442(NY):7Feb83-121
Medawar, P. and J.H. Shelley, eds. Struc-
ture in Science and Art.
  N. Bryson, 90:Sep82-569
Medawar, P.B. and J.S. Aristotle to Zoos.
  J. Bernstein, 441:2Oct83-11
Međedović, A. Ženidba Vlahinjić Alije.
  (D.E. Bynum, ed)
  J. Dittmar, 196:Band23Heft3/4-329
"Medical Treatment and Criminal Law: Work-
ing Paper 26." [Law Reform Commission of
Canada]
  B. Hoffmaster, 154:Sep82-560
de' Medici, L. Lettere, IV (1479-1480).
  (N. Rubinstein, ed)
  F. Chiappelli, 551(RenQ):Autumn82-474
Medina, A. Reflection, Time and the
Novel.*
  T. Hawkes, 447(N&Q):Aug81-378
Medina, J.T. Spanish Realism.
  R.B. Klein, 238:Mar82-144
Medish, V. The Soviet Union.
  D. Lieven, 575(SEER):Apr82-303
Medley, M. T'ang Pottery and Porcelain.*
  U. Roberts, 60:May-Jun82-143
Medley, R. Drawn from the Life.
  H. Carpenter, 617(TLS):16Dec83-1394
de Medrano, L.S. - see under Sáinz de
Medrano, L.
Medsger, B. Framed.
  R.J. Margolis, 441:20Nov83-42
  442(NY):3Sep83-114
Medvedev, R. Khrushchev.
  A. Brown, 617(TLS):1Apr83-333
  L. Schapiro, 453(NYRB):28Apr83-7
Medvedev, R.A., with P. Ostellino. Roy
Medvedev: On Soviet Dissent.* (G.
Saunders, ed)
  P. Petro, 104(CASS):Summer82-272
Medvedev, Z. Andropov.
  J.M. Burns, 441:6Nov83-13
  L. Schapiro, 617(TLS):8Jul83-719
  J. Simpson, 362:16Jun83-23

Medwall, H. The Plays of Henry Medwall.*
  (A.H. Nelson, ed)
  C. Gauvin, 189(EA):Oct-Dec82-455
  M. Stevens, 589:Oct82-918
Meek, C.E. The Commune of Lucca under
Pisan Rule, 1342-1369.
  S.R. Blanshei, 589:Jan82-151
Meeker, J. The Comedy of Survival.
  D. Wann, 152(UDQ):Spring82-115
Meeker, R.H. Newspaperman.
  E. Diamond, 441:25Sep83-13
Meeks, W.A. The First Urban Christians.
  R.M. Brown, 441:3Apr83-10
  J.L. Houlden, 617(TLS):7Oct83-1103
  E.H. Pagels, 453(NYRB):21Jul83-41
van der Meer, C.L.J. Rural Development in
Northern Thailand.
  C. Vaddhanaphuti, 293(JASt):Aug82-893
van der Meer, W. Hindustani Music in the
20th Century.
  N. Nalbandian, 293(JASt):Feb82-408
  N. Sorrell, 410(M&L):Jul/Oct81-425
Megas, G.A. To elleniko paramythi.
  M. Meraklis, 196:Band23Heft3/4-330
Megged, A. The Short Life.
  A.H. Rosenfeld, 390:Mar82-53
Meggs, P.B. A History of Graphic Design.
  S.H., 441:4Sep83-17
Mehaud, C., ed. Mouvements de populations
dans L'Océan Indien.
  M. Bloch, 69:Vol51No1-539
Mehendale, M.A. Nirukta Notes.* (Ser 2)
  R. Rocher, 318(JAOS):Oct-Dec81-469
Mehlberg, H. Time, Causality and Quantum
Theory.
  J. Butterfield, 518:Apr82-94
Mehlman, J. Cataract.*
  M.A. Rabb, 173(ECS):Winter82/83-204
Mehlman, J. A Structural Study of Auto-
biography.
  K. Gore, 208(FS):Jul82-369
Mehra, P. The North-Eastern Frontier.
  (Vol 1)
  R.J. Young, 318(JAOS):Oct-Dec81-499
Mehring, W. Les Müller, une dynastie
allemande.
  L. Arénilla, 450(NRF):Dec82-112
Mehrota, R.R. Sociology of Secret Lan-
guages.
  M.M. Bryant, 660(Word):Dec82-262
Mehrotra, S.R. Towards India's Freedom
and Partition.
  D. Arnold, 293(JASt):Aug82-871
Mehta, V. A Family Affair.*
  J. Grigg, 362:17Feb83-22
  T. Raychaudhuri, 617(TLS):11Mar83-234
Mehta, V. Vedi.*
  J. Grigg, 362:17Feb83-22
  J. Mortimer, 617(TLS):18Feb83-154
Meier, C. Die Entstehung des Politischen
bei den Griechen.
  R. Seager, 303(JoHS):Vol 102-266
Meier, C. and U. Ruberg, eds. Text und
Bild.
  M.W. Wierschin, 589:Jul82-639
Meier, G.F. and B. Handbuch der Linguis-
tik und Kommunikationswissenschaft.
  (Vol 1)
  A.F. Majewicz, 360(LP):Vol125-132
Meier, J-P. L'Esthétique de Moses Men-
delssohn (1729-1786).
  O.F. Best, 406:Summer82-201

Meiggs, R. Roman Ostia. (2nd ed)
   J. Feye, 394:Vol35fasc3/4-447
Meiggs, R. Trees and Timber in the An-
cient Mediterranean World.
   P. Green, 617(TLS):24Jun83-647
   P.H. Newby, 362:14Apr83-30
Meigret, L. Le Traité de la Grammaire
française (1550).* (F.J. Hausmann, ed)
   C. Demaizière, 535(RHL):Sep-Dec82-864
   J. Stéfanini, 209(FM):Jul82-277
Meigret, L. Traité touchant l'escriture
françoise. (K. Cameron, ed)
   A.H. Diverres, 402(MLR):Jan82-199
Meigs, M. Lily Briscoe.
   M.C. Creelman, 627(UTQ):Summer82-469
   J. Farnsworth, 526:Autumn82-78
   H. Kirkwood, 99:Jun/Jul82-41
   D. Watmough, 102(CanL):Autumn82-162
Meijering, E.P. Calvin wider die Neu-
gierde.
   D.C. Steinmetz, 551(RenQ):Winter82-622
Meilaender, G.C. Friendship.
   D.E.M., 185:Jul83-823
Meillier, C. Callimaque et son temps.*
   C. Dobias-Lalou, 555:Vol55fasc1-161
Mein, M. Thèmes proustiens.
   G. Craig, 402(MLR):Oct82-963
   R. Gibson, 208(FS):Apr82-227
Meinertzhagen, R. Kenya Diary (1902-1906).
   X.S., 617(TLS):24Jun83-683
Meinke, P. Trying to Surprise God.
   J.D. McClatchy, 491:Sep82-349
Meisel, J. Barons of the Welsh Frontier.
   C. Bullock-Davies, 382(MAE):1982/2-264
   R.B. Patterson, 589:Jan82-153
Meisel, J.M. and M.D. Pam, eds. Linear
Order and Generative Theory.*
   R.C. De Armond, 320(CJL):Spring82-73
   J. Lenerz, 603:Vol6No2-275
Meisel, P. The Absent Father.*
   K.C. Hill, 177(ELT):Vol25No2-117
   V.S. Middleton, 594:Fall82-289
   V. Shaw, 402(MLR):Oct82-941
Meiss, M. and E.H. Beatson, eds. "La Vie
de Nostre Benoit Sauveur Ihesuscrist" et
"La Saincte Vie de Nostre Dame" trans-
latee a la requeste de tres hault et
puissant prince Iehan, duc de Berry.*
   G. Hasenohr, 554:Vol 102No3-352
Meissner, F-J. Wortgeschichtliche Unter-
suchungen im Umkreis von französisch
"Enthousiasme" und "Génie."*
   R. Martin, 553(RLiR):Jan-Jun81-256
Meister, B. Nineteenth-Century French
Song.*
   R. Orledge, 410(M&L):Jul/Oct81-442
   42(AR):Summer82-369
Meizel, J.E. Spanish for Medical Person-
nel.
   H.J. Dennis, 238:Mar82-155
Mejías, H.A. and G. Garza-Swan. Nuestro
español.
   W.F. García, 238:May82-320
de Mejo, O. My America.
   B. Dobell, 441:4Dec83-64
Mejor, M. Buddyzm.
   L. Sternbach, 318(JAOS):Oct-Dec81-480
Melanchthon, P. Melanchthons Briefwechsel.
(Vols 2 and 3) (H. Scheible, ed)
   S.H. Hendrix, 551(RenQ):Spring82-91

"Mélanges de langue et de littérature fran-
çaises du Moyen Age et de la Renaissance
offerts à Charles Foulon par ses collè-
gues, ses élèves et ses amis."* (Vol 1)
   E.R. Sienaert, 356(LR):May82-161
   N.B. Smith, 589:Jan82-193
"Mélanges de littérature et d'histoire
offerts à Georges Couton."
   H. Peyre, 207(FR):Apr83-769
"Mélanges d'études anciennes offerts à
Maurice Lebel."
   É. des Places, 555:Vol55fasc2-356
Melchinger, S. Die Welt als Tragödie.*
(Vol 1)
   C. Leach, 123:Vol132No2-273
   E. Simon, 52:Band16Heft1-76
Melchinger, S. Die Welt als Tragödie.*
(Vol 2)
   E. Simon, 52:Band16Heft3-313
Melchiori, G. - see Joyce, J.
Mel'čuk, I.A. Towards a Language of Lin-
guistics. (P. Luelsdorff, ed)
   D. Zager, 350:Dec83-920
Meldau, R. Sinnverwandte Wörter der eng-
lischen Sprache.
   H. Käsmann, 38:Band100Heft3/4-474
Meléndez Ch., C. - see del Valle, J.C.
Mellard, J.M. The Exploded Form.*
   M. Courturier, 189(EA):Oct-Dec82-491
   T. Martin, 395(MFS):Winter81/82-712
   M.F. Schulz, 301(JEGP):Jan82-148
Mellen, J. Privilege.*
   M. Secrest, 364:Dec82/Jan83-119
Meller, H. London Cemeteries.
   A. Whittick, 324:Feb83-158
Mellers, W. Bach and the Dance of God.
   G. Ridout, 627(UTQ):Winter81/82-216
   U. Siegele, 410(M&L):Jul/Oct81-357
Mellers, W. Beethoven and the Voice of
God.
   G. Abraham, 617(TLS):4Mar83-206
   H. Cole, 362:23Jun83-28
Melli, E. - see Buvalelli, R.
Mellick, J.S.D. - see "Henry Kingsley"
Mellinkoff, R. The Mark of Cain.
   J.H. Bentley, 589:Jul82-686
Mellor, A.K. English Romantic Irony.*
   C. Dawson, 191(ELN):Sep81-69
   F.W. Shilstone, 577(SHR):Winter82-73
   S.M. Sperry, 637(VS):Winter82-252
   S.M. Tave, 480(P&R):Spring82-145
   P.L. Thorslev, Jr., 340(KSJ):Vol31-202
   D. Wilson, 152(UDQ):Summer81-111
Mellor, D.H. Real Time.
   T.E. Wilkerson, 483:Jul82-410
Mellor, D.H., ed. Science, Belief, and
Behaviour.*
   P. Humphreys, 482(PhR):Oct82-609
Mellor, J. The Company Store.
   R.J. Margolis, 441:4Sep83-10
Mellow, J.R. Nathaniel Hawthorne in His
Times.*
   J.L. Idol, Jr., 580(SCR):Fall82-128
   E. Wagenknecht, 591(SIR):Spring82-101
Mellown, E.W. Edwin Muir.*
   P. Dodd, 588(SSL):Vol 17-297
   R. Robertson, 447(N&Q):Aug81-366
Mel'nikov, G.P. Sistemologija i jazykovye
aspekty kibernetiki.
   B.V. Jakušin, 682(ZPSK):Band35Heft3-
348

Melnykovich, G. Reality and Expression in the Poetry of Carlos Pellicer.
P.R. Beardsell, 86(BHS):Oct82-352
Melosi, M.V. Garbage in the Cities.*
639(VQR):Autumn82-127
Meltzer, M., P.G. Holland and F. Krasno - see Child, L.M.
Melville, H. Moby-Dick; or The Whale. [The Arion Press Edition]
529(QQ):Summer82-457
Melville, J. The Ninth Netsuke.*
N. Callendar, 441:27Feb83-45
Melville, J. Sayonara, Sweet Amaryllis.
T.J. Binyon, 617(TLS):23Sep83-1011
M. Laski, 362:11Aug83-24
Melzack, R. and P.D. Wall. The Challenge of Pain.
J.F. Watkins, 617(TLS):4Mar83-208
Memon, M.U., ed. Studies in the Urdu Gazal and Prose Fiction.
D. Lelyveld, 318(JAOS):Jul-Sep81-380
M. Rahman, 293(JASt):Feb82-389
de Mena, J. Laberinto de Fortuna. (J.G. Cummins, ed)
L.V. Fainberg, 240(HR):Winter82-93
Ménager, D. Ronsard.*
I.D. McFarlane, 551(RenQ):Autumn81-441
M.C. Smith, 208(FS):Jan82-55
"Le Menagier de Paris." (G.F. Brereton and J.M. Ferrier, eds)
D. Evans, 208(FS):Apr82-187
W.W. Kibler, 207(FR):Dec82-367
F. Möhren, 553(RLiR):Jan-Jun82-218
Menaker, E. Otto Rank.
P. Grosskurth, 617(TLS):6May83-451
"Menander." (Loeb, Vol 1) (W.G. Arnott, ed and trans)
R.W., 555:Vol55fasc1-160
"Menander Rhetor." (D.A. Russell and N.G. Wilson, eds and trans)
R. Browning, 123:Vol132No2-148
G.A. Kennedy, 121(CJ):Oct/Nov82-72
Menant, S. La Chute d'Icare.
A. Gunny, 83:Autumn82-268
O. Taylor, 535(RHL):May-Jun82-477
D. Williams, 208(FS):Oct82-473
Ménard, P. Les "Lais" de Marie de France.*
R. Kroll, 224(GRM):Band32Heft1-119
Ménard, P. Syntaxe de l'ancien français. (3rd ed)
P. Swiggers, 350:Sep83-690
Mende, M. Das alte Nürnberger Rathaus. (Vol 1)
L. Silver, 551(RenQ):Winter81-587
Mendel, A.P. Michael Bakunin.*
M.A. Miller, 550(RusR):Oct82-478
L. Schapiro, 617(TLS):13May83-495
Mendelsohn, E. Zionism in Poland.
M. Malia, 453(NYRB):29Sep83-18
Mendelson, E. Early Auden.*
R. Bush, 141:Winter82-94
H. Carruth, 249(HudR):Summer82-334
W. Harmon, 577(SHR):Fall83-374
L. McDiarmid, 659(ConL):Spring83-94
J. Matthias, 598(SoR):Winter83-184
D. O'Hara, 295(JML):Dec82-402
Mendelssohn, M. Jérusalem ou Pouvoir religieux et judaïsme. (D. Bourel, ed and trans)
A. Reix, 542:Oct-Dec82-660
de Mendelssohn, P. - see Mann, T.
Méndez, J.M.R. - see under Rodríguez Méndez, J.M.

Mendizabal, J.C., ed. Basque Artistic Expression. (Vol 2)
R.M. Frank, 238:Dec82-660
de Mendoza, I.L. - see under López de Mendoza, I.
"Frey Íñigo de Mendoza, 'Coplas de Vita Christi.'"* (M. Massoli, ed)
F. Domínguez, 241:Jan82-82
Mendras, H. and others. La Sagesse et le désordre.
J-P. Ponchie, 207(FR):Feb83-499
Meneghini, G.B., with R. Allegri. My Wife Maria Callas.*
S. Pickles, 617(TLS):11Mar83-243
H. Wackett, 362:27Jan83-19
Menéndez Pidal, R. Reliquias de la poesía épica española, acompañadas de Epopeya y romancero, I. (D. Catalán, ed)
D. Hook, 86(BHS):Apr82-149
Menger, K. Selected Papers in Logic and Foundations, Didactics, Economics.*
G.P., 543:Jun82-887
Menger, L. Theodore Sturgeon.
D.M. Hassler, 561(SFS):Nov82-336
Menhennet, A. The Romantic Movement.*
A.P. Cottrell, 301(JEGP):Apr82-291
Menichelli, G.C. and G.C. Roscioni, eds. Studi e ricerche di letteratura e linguistica francese I.
F. Claudon, 535(RHL):Sep-Dec82-993
Menne, A. Einführung in die Methodologie.
K. Jacobi, 679:Band13Heft2-403
Mennell, S., ed. Lettre d'un pâtissier anglois, et autres contributions à une polémique gastronomique du XVIIIe siècle.
B. Fink, 83:Autumn82-275
Menocal, N.G. Architecture as Nature.*
L.S. Weingarden, 576:Mar82-74
Mensch, J.R. The Question of Being in Husserl's Logical Investigations.
A. Reix, 542:Jan-Mar82-68
Mentrup, W., ed. Konzepte zur Lexikographie.
E. Haggblade, 350:Dec83-921
Mentrup, W., ed. Materialen zur historischen entwicklung der gross- und kleinschreibungsregeln.*
M.H. Folsom, 133:Band15Heft3-286
Mepham, J. and D.H. Ruben, eds. Issues in Marxist Philosophy.*
R. Poole, 482(PhR):Oct82-632
Merchant, C. The Death of Nature.
M.C. Horowitz, 551(RenQ):Summer82-294
M. Jacob, 322(JHI):Apr-Jun82-331
K. Squadrito, 125:Spring82-318
Mercier, P., ed. La Facture de clavecin du XVE au XVIIIe siècle.
H. Schott, 410(M&L):Jul/Oct81-368
Mercier, V. Beckett/Beckett.*
D.L. Eder, 367(L&P):Vol30No2-83
Merin, J. and E.B. Burdick. International Directory of Theatre, Dance and Folklore Festivals.
J. Wilson, 187:Jan83-125
Merino, C.C. - see under Codoñer Merino, C.
Merino, J.A. Humanismo existencial en Merleau-Ponty.
S. Délivoyatzis, 192(EP):Jul-Sep81-361
A. Reix, 542:Jan-Mar82-69
Meriwether, J.B. and M. Millgate, eds. Lion in the Garden.*
295(JML):Dec82-441

Merk, F. History of the Westward Movement.
   M.J. Rohrbough, 658:Summer/Autumn82-
   147
Merlan, F. Mangarayi.
   B.J. Blake, 361:Nov/Dec82-383
Merle, R. Paris ma bonne ville.
   R.D. Frye, 207(FR):Dec82-340
Merquior, J.G. Rousseau and Weber.
   G. Roth, 185:Jan83-401
   S.G.S., 543:Dec81-402
Merrett, R.J. Daniel Defoe's Moral and
   Rhetorical Ideas.*
   D. Oakleaf, 49:Jul82-89
Merrill, J. The Changing Light at Sand-
   over.
   R.W. Flint, 441:13Mar83-6
   H. Kenner, 231:Sep83-69
   R. Mazzocco, 453(NYRB):16Jun83-41
Merrill, J. From the First Nine.
   R.W. Flint, 441:13Mar83-6
   R. Mazzocco, 453(NYRB):16Jun83-41
Merrill, J. Scripts for the Pageant.*
   R. Tillinghast, 569(SR):Spring82-291
Merry, B. Anatomy of the Spy Thriller.
   L.N. Landrum, 395(MFS):Summer81-401
   B. Lenz, 38:Band100Heft1/2-253
Mersenne, P.M. Correspondance du P. Marin
   Mersenne. (Vol 14) (A. Beaulieu, ed)
   A. Robinet, 192(EP):Apr-Jun81-247
Merser, C. Honorable Intentions.
   A. Shapiro, 441:20Nov83-16
Mertian, I. Allgemeine Sprachkunde. (H.E.
   Brekle, ed)
   W. Neumann, 682(ZPSK):Band35Heft3-353
Mertin, R-G. Ariano Suassuna: "Romance
   d'A Pedra do Reino."
   C. Slater, 240(HR):Winter82-113
Merwin, W.S. Opening the Hand.
   D. Bromwich, 441:9Oct83-12
Merwin, W.S. Unframed Originals.*
   G.C., 569(SR):Fall82-cviii
Merwin, W.S. - see Follain, J.
Merwin, W.S. and J.M. Masson - see "San-
   skrit Love Poetry"
Mesa-Lago, C. The Economy of Socialist
   Cuba.
   J.I. Domínguez, 263(RIB):Vol32No2-219
Meschonnic, H. Critique du rythme.
   J. Réda, 450(NRF):Sep82-136
Meschonnic, H. Jona et le signifiant
   errant.
   G. Sartoris, 450(NRF):Mar82-132
Mesh-hadi, N. Die Einschätzung der Alche-
   mie in Faust-Deutungen.
   F.L. Borchardt, 221(GQ):Jan82-120
Meslier, J. Oeuvres complètes. (Vol 3)
   (R. Desné, ed)
   J. Varloot, 535(RHL):Jan-Feb82-111
"Le curé Meslier et la vie intellectuelle,
   religieuse et sociale (fin XVIIe-début
   XVIIIe siècle)."
   J. Varloot, 535(RHL):Jan-Feb82-111
Messadi, M. Le Barrage.
   C. Zimra, 207(FR):Feb83-514
"A Message from the Falklands: The Life
   and Gallant Death of David Tinker, Lieut.
   RN."
   C. Wain, 362:3Mar83-20
Messenger, B. Picking Up the Linen
   Threads.
   R.S. McCarl, 650(WF):Apr82-153

Messenger, C.K. Sport and the Spirit of
   Play in American Fiction.
   R.B. Nye, 27(AL):May82-301
   W.J. Palmer, 395(MFS):Summer82-317
   E. Segal, 617(TLS):10Jun83-609
Messerli, D. - see Barnes, D.
Mészáros, I. The Work of Sartre.* (Vol 1)
   S.B. John, 402(MLR):Apr82-464
Metcalf, A.J. Evgenii Shvarts and His
   Fairy-Tales for Adults.
   D. Myers, 575(SEER):Jan82-104
Metcalf, J., ed. First Impressions.
   R.M. Brown, 198:Apr82-103
   A. Dawson, 102(CanL):Winter81-141
Metcalf, J., ed. Second Impressions.
   K. Thompson, 198:Apr82-109
Metcalf, J. and L. Rooke, eds. Best
   Canadian Stories.
   M.L. Drache, 99:Jun/Jul82-42
Metcalf, P. James Knowles.*
   C.L. Brooks, 541(RES):May82-226
   J.M. Crook, 447(N&Q):Dec81-565
   K.O. Garrigan, 576:Mar82-66
Metcalf, T.R. Land, Landlords, and the
   British Raj.
   B. Stein, 293(JASt):May82-620
Métellus, J. La famille Vortex.
   R. Buss, 617(TLS):6May83-464
Métellus, J. Jacmel au crépuscule.*
   L. Kovacs, 450(NRF):Mar82-124
"Méthodes chez Pascal."*
   R. Sasso, 192(EP):Oct-Dec81-489
"Met'qvelebis analizis sak'itxebi." (Vol
   5)
   G.F. Meier, 682(ZPSK):Band34Heft1-126
Mettig, V. Russische Presse und Sozialis-
   tengesetz.
   R.E. Zelnik, 550(RusR):Oct82-484
Metz, C. The Imaginary Signifier.
   S. Chatman, 18:Jul-Aug83-56
Metze, E., ed. Aufgabenbezogene Kommunika-
   tion bei älteren Vorschulkindern.
   G. Michel, 682(ZPSK):Band34Heft6-749
Metzger, R. and others. Corpus Vasorum
   Antiquorum. (Schweiz, fasc 5)
   B.A. Sparkes, 303(JoHS):Vol 102-285
Mew, C. Collected Poems and Prose. (V.
   Warner, ed)
   A. Leighton, 493:Jun82-73
Mewshaw, M. Short Circuit.
   D.E. Rosenbaum, 441:7Aug83-9
Meyendorff, J. Byzantium and the Rise of
   Russia.
   P. Bushkovitch, 550(RusR):Apr82-198
   A. Kazhdan, 589:Jan82-155
Meyendorff, J. The Orthodox Church.
   P. Bushkovitch, 550(RusR):Oct82-537
Meyer, D. Victoria Ocampo.
   A. Blasi, 238:May82-312
Meyer, M.K. and P.W. Filby, eds. Who's
   Who in Genealogy and Heraldry.
   K.B. Harder, 424:Sep82-199
Meyer, P. Québec.
   G.R. Montbertrand, 207(FR):Apr83-802
Meyer, P. and S. Rudy, eds. Gogol and
   Dostoevsky.
   R.L. Chapple, 104(CASS):Spring82-130
Meyer, S.E. A Treasury of the Great Chil-
   dren's Book Illustrators.
   J. Updike, 441:4Dec83-7
Meyer-Clason, C. Erstens die Freiheit.
   W.A. Luchting, 399(MLJ):Summer82-222

Meyer-Minnemann, K. Der spanischamerikan-
ische Roman des Fin de siècle.
 W. Theile, 72:Band218Heft1-235
Meyers, J. The Enemy.*
 M. Magalaner, 395(MFS):Winter82/83-649
 P. Widdowson, 366:Spring82-134
 639(VQR):Autumn82-122
Meyers, J., ed. Hemingway: The Critical
Heritage.
 R. Fleming, 234:Fall82-83
Meyers, J. Homosexuality and Literature.
 R. Hindmarsh, 72:Band218Heft2-398
Meyers, J., ed. Wyndham Lewis.*
 R. Currie, 541(RES):Aug82-358
 B. Murray, 395(MFS):Summer81-330
 P. Widdowson, 366:Spring82-134
Meyers, W.E. Aliens and Linguists.*
 W.A. Quinn, 599:Winter82-80
Meynell, H. Freud, Marx and Morals.
 A.P. Simonds, 185:Jul83-792
Meynell, H.A. The Intelligible Universe.
 J.C.A. Gaskin, 518:Oct82-243
Meynell, L. Silver Guilt.
 T.J. Binyon, 617(TLS):11Mar83-248
Miall, D.S., ed. Metaphor.
 M. Johnson, 290(JAAC):Summer83-463
 F. Nuessel, 350:Dec83-942
Miasnikov, V.S. Imperiia Tsin i russkoe
gosudarstva v XVII veke.
 C.M. Foust, 104(CASS):Fall-Winter82-
 543
Micha, A. Etude sur le "Merlin" de Robert
de Boron, roman du XIIIe siècle.
 J.C. Payen, 382(MAE):1982/2-257
Micha, A. - see "Lancelot, roman en prose
du XIIIe siècle"
Prince Michael of Greece. Louis XIV.
 L. Norton, 617(TLS):9Sep83-965
Michalson, D. and C. Aires. Spanish Gram-
mar.
 H. Wozniak-Brayman, 238:Mar82-155
Michaud, S. - see Tristan, F.
Michaud, S.G. and H. Aynesworth. The Only
Living Witness.
 T. Chaffin, 441:24Apr83-16
Michaud-Latremouille, A. Chansons de
Grand'mère.
 G. Thomas, 102(CanL):Spring82-130
Michaux, H. Affrontements.
 J-P. Cauvin, 207(FR):Dec82-341
Michaux, H. Poteaux d'angle.*
 M. Bishop, 207(FR):Dec82-342
Michaux, J-P., ed. George Gissing.*
 S. Monod, 189(EA):Jul-Sep82-346
Michel, A. - see Ballanche, P.S.
Michel, A. - see de Balzac, H.
Michel, A. - see Faivre, A. and F. Tristan
"Dan Michel's 'Ayenbite of Inwyt.'"*
 (Vols 1 and 2) (R. Morris, ed; rev by P.
 Gradon)
 G. Jack, 382(MAE):1982/2-239
Michel, J-B. Phonétique, phonologie et
morphosyntaxe d'un créole haïtien.
 A. Bollée, 72:Band218Heft1-209
Michel, L. The Red Virgin. (B. Lowry and
E.E. Gunter, eds and trans)
 S.P. Conner, 446(NCFS):Spring-Summer83-
 405
Michel, M., ed. Pouvoir et vérité.
 M. Adam, 542:Oct-Dec82-684

di Michele, M. Bread and Chocolate [to-
gether with] Wallace, B. Marrying into
the Family.*
 D. Barbour, 648(WCR):Jun82-33
 J.A. Wainwright, 102(CanL):Winter81-
 148
 B. Whiteman, 529(QQ):Spring82-223
 N. Zacharin, 137:Aug82-50
di Michele, M. Tree of August.
 R. Sward, 137:Winter82-109
Michelini, G. La linguistica testuale e
l'indoeuropeo: il passivo.
 W.R. Schmalstieg, 215(GL):Spring82-71
Michels, V. Materialen zu Hermann Hesses
"Der Steppenwolf."
 M. Boulby, 221(GQ):May82-452
Michels, V. Mittelhochdeutsche Grammatik.*
 (5th ed) (H. Stopp, ed)
 J. Göschel, 685(ZDL):3/1981-377
Michener, J.A. Poland.
 W. Schott, 441:4Sep83-5
Michener, J.A. Space.*
 P.K. Bell, 617(TLS):25Feb83-200
Michie, J. New and Selected Poems.
 A. Hollinghurst, 617(TLS):30Sep83-1061
Michiko, I. Story of the Sea of Camellias.
 J. Kirkup, 617(TLS):23Sep83-1029
Michon, J. Mallarmé et "Les Mots
anglais."*
 G. Chesters, 208(FS):Jan82-88
Mickel, E.J. and J.A. Nelson, eds. The
Old French Crusade Cycle. (Vol 1)
 P. Ménard, 545(RPh):Nov81-413
Micros, M. Upstairs Over the Ice Cream.*
 D. Barbour, 648(WCR):Jun82-33
 D. O'Rourke, 102(CanL):Autumn82-149
 E. Trethewey, 198:Oct82-111
Middell, E. and others, eds. Exil in den
USA.*
 A. von Bormann, 406:Fall82-345
Middlebrook, M. The Kaiser's Battle.
 N., 617(TLS):24Jun83-683
Middleton, C. - see von Goethe, J.W.
Middleton, D. Crossroads of Modern War-
fare.
 R.F. Weigley, 441:29May83-8
Middleton, R., ed. The Beaux Arts and
Nineteenth Century French Architectural
History.
 A. Betsky, 505:Dec82-96
 M.K. Meade, 46:Aug82-70
Middleton, R. and D. Horn, eds. Popular
Music I.
 J. Porter, 187:May83-364
Middleton, S. Entry into Jerusalem.
 A. Brownjohn, 617(TLS):4Feb83-104
 J. Mellors, 362:17Feb83-24
Middleton, T. The Selected Plays of
Thomas Middleton.* (D.L. Frost, ed)
 T. Donaldson, 617(TLS):200ct83-1183
Middleton, T. The Widow. (R.T. Levine,
ed)
 P.C. Kolin, 568(SCN):Spring-Summer82-
 8
Midgley, G. - see Bunyan, J.
Midgley, M. Heart and Mind.*
 M. Douglas, 185:Jul83-786
 483:Jan82-146
Midwinter, E. W.G. Grace.
 T. Mason, 637(VS):Winter82-259
Mieder, W., ed. Deutsche Sprichwörter und
Redensarten. Grimms Märchen — modern.
 D. Ward, 650(WF):Apr82-164

Miehe, G. Die Sprache der älteren Swahili-Dichtung.
K. Legère, 682(ZPSK):Band34Heft5-636
Migel, P. Great Ballet Prints of the Romantic Era.
R. Philp, 151:Feb82-82
"Leberecht Migge, 1881-1935: Gartenkultur des 20. Jahrhunderts."
C.C. Collins, 576:Dec82-358
Mignani, R., M.A. Di Cesare and G.F. Jones, eds. A Concordance to Juan Ruiz, "Libro de Buen Amor."
L.V. Fainberg, 545(RPh):Feb82-556
Mignani, R., M.A. Di Cesare and G.F. Jones, comps. Ruiziana.
L.V. Fainberg, 545(RPh):Feb82-556
Mignini, F. Ars imaginandi.
D.P. Verene, 319:Jul83-406
Mignolo, W.D. Elementos para una teoría del texto literario.
G. Costa, 545(RPh):Nov81-436
Mignot, C. - see Le Muet, P.
Mihăilescu-Bîrliba, V. La Monnaie romaine chez les Daces orientaux.
R. Reece, 575(SEER):Jul82-473
Mihályi, G. Az életkudarcok írója.
T. Gorilovics, 535(RHL):Sep-Dec82-958
Mijuskovic, B.L. Loneliness in Philosophy, Psychology, and Literature.*
G. Parloff, 107(CRCL):Jun82-247
Mikhail, E.H. An Annotated Bibliography of Modern Anglo-Irish Drama.
354:Dec82-467
Mikhail, E.H., ed. The Art of Brendan Behan.*
D. Kiberd, 541(RES):May82-237
Mikhail, E.H., ed. Brendan Behan: Interviews and Recollections.
P. Craig, 617(TLS):22Apr83-412
Mikhail, E.H. Lady Gregory, An Annotated Bibliography of Criticism.
354:Dec82-467
Mikhail, E.H. A Research Guide to Modern Irish Dramatists.
354:Dec82-468
Mikhail, E.H., ed. Oscar Wilde: Interviews and Recollections.
N. Shrimpton, 447(N&Q):Feb81-91
"Mikkyō daijiten." (rev)
J.W. de Jong, 259(IIJ):Jan82-67
Mikos, S. Wolne Miasto Gdańsk a Liga Narodów.
A-C. Carls, 497(PolR):Vol27No1/2-163
Mila, M. L'arte di Verdi.
J. Budden, 410(M&L):Jan/Apr82-94
Milbauer, B., with B.N. Obrentz. The Law Giveth.
D. Margolick, 441:27Nov83-15
Milburn, J. British Business and Ghanaian Independence.
R. Jeffries, 69:Vol51No4-887
Milbury-Steen, S.L. European and African Stereotypes in Twentieth-Century Fiction.*
H.H. Watts, 395(MFS):Winter81/82-702
Miles, B. and J.C. Trewin, eds. Curtain Calls.*
S. Morley, 157:Summer82-50
Miles, P. and H. Pitcher - see Chekhov, A.
Milgate, W. - see Donne, J.

Milhous, J. Thomas Betterton and the Management of Lincoln's Inn Fields, 1695-1708.*
R. Berry, 108:Summer82-150
B.S. Hammond, 541(RES):Aug82-333
A. Kaufman, 301(JEGP):Oct82-570
E. Rothstein, 173(ECS):Winter81/82-226
Miliband, R. Capitalist Democracy in Britain.
G. Marshall, 617(TLS):28Jan83-90
Mill, J.S. The Collected Works of John Stuart Mill.* (Vol 1: Autobiography and Literary Essays.) (J.M. Robson and J. Stillinger, eds)
I.B. Nadel, 627(UTQ):Summer82-429
C.R. Sanders, 579(SAQ):Summer82-350
529(QQ):Summer82-456
Mill, J.S. The Collected Works of John Stuart Mill.* (Vol 9: An Examination of Sir William Hamilton's Philosophy and of the Principal Philosophical Questions Discussed in his Writings.) (J.M. Robson, ed)
D.A. Rees, 303(JoHS):Vol 102-260
J. Skorupski, 479(PhQ):Apr82-171
Millar, F., with others. The Roman Empire and its Neighbors. (2nd ed)
P. MacKendrick, 121(CJ):Apr/May83-360
Millar, G.J. Tudor Mercenaries and Auxiliaries, 1485-1547.
W.T. MacCaffrey, 551(RenQ):Winter81-604
Millar, J.R. The ABCs of Soviet Socialism.
J. Thornton, 550(RusR):Apr82-221
639(VQR):Winter82-14
Millares Carlo, A. Bibliografía de Andrés Bello. (3rd ed)
D. Oberstar, 552(REH):Jan82-123
de Mille, A. Reprieve.
R. Philp, 151:Jan82-90
Miller, A.C. Sir Richard Grenville of the Civil War.
J.R. Conners, 568(SCN):Spring-Summer82-20
Miller, B.S. - see Kramrisch, S.
Miller, C. Guardians of the Singreale.
639(VQR):Autumn82-132
Miller, C.H. Auden.
J. Atlas, 61:Feb83-100
M. Bayles, 441:21Aug83-14
R. Craft, 453(NYRB):22Dec83-50
Miller, C.H., ed. Moriae Encomium id est Stultitiae Laus.
R. Kassel, 547(RF):Band93Heft1/2-228
Miller, C.H. - see Erasmus
Miller, D. Philosophy and Ideology in Hume's Political Thought.*
T.D. Campbell, 518:Oct82-206
Miller, D. and L. Siedentop, eds. The Nature of Political Theory.
J. Dunn, 617(TLS):27May83-535
Miller, D.A. Narrative and its Discontents.*
W.B. Bache, 395(MFS):Summer82-345
N. Baym, 301(JEGP):Oct82-543
W.L. Reed, 141:Winter82-78
D.H. Richter, 405(MP):Feb83-287
Miller, D.C. - see Lieberman, W.S. and L. Boltin
Miller, E.E. Season of Hunger/Cry of Rain.
B. Brown, 95(CLAJ):Jun82-478

Miller, G., ed. Letters of Edward Jenner
and other Documents concerning the Early
History of Vaccination.
  R. Porter, 617(TLS):30Dec83-1450
Miller, G. A Pennsylvania Album.
  J.R. Jeffrey, 658:Summer/Autumn82-175
Miller, H. The World of Lawrence.* (E.J.
  Hinz and J.J. Teunissen, eds)
  B. Caplan, 219(GaR):Spring82-194
  M. Magalaner, 395(MFS):Summer81-307
  C. Rossman, 659(ConL):Fall83-406
Miller, J. History and Human Existence
  from Marx to Merleau-Ponty.*
  M. Jay, 125:Winter82-191
Miller, J. Life Amongst the Modocs.
  N.J. Engberg, 649(WAL):Winter83-361
  R.C. Longtin, 26(ALR):Autumn82-284
Miller, J. States of Mind.
  R. Dinnage, 453(NYRB):18Aug83-36
  A. Ryan, 362:2Jun83-23
  S. Sutherland, 617(TLS):17Jun83-641
Miller, J. and B. Van Loon. Darwin for
  Beginners.*
  R.C. Lewontin, 453(NYRB):16Jun83-21
Miller, J.C. Building Poe Biography.
  A. Hammond, 183(ESQ):Vol28No3-197
Miller, J.C., ed. Poe's Helen Remembers.*
  T.C. Carlson, 392:Winter81/82-77
  A. Hammond, 183(ESQ):Vol28No3-197
Miller, J.C. - see Poe, E.A.
Miller, J.E., Jr. The American Quest for
  a Supreme Fiction.*
  J.M. Cox, 27(AL):Oct82-449
Miller, J.H. Fiction and Repetition.*
  D.P. Deneau, 268(IFR):Winter83-64
  M. Fischer, 290(JAAC):Summer83-452
  W.L. Reed, 594:Winter82-377
  M. Ryan, 400(MLN):Dec82-1242
  D.F. Sadoff, 42(AR):Summer82-361
Miller, K. Tiger the Lurp Dog.
  J. Charyn, 441:20Nov83-14
Miller, M. The Logic of Language Develop-
  ment in Early Childhood.*
  P. Fletcher, 320(CJL):Spring82-79
Miller, M.A. A Rainbow in Your Hands.
  R.L. Shep, 614:Spring83-22
Miller, N. Heavenly Caves.
  N. Prendergast, 127:Fall82-263
  D. Stroud, 324:Aug83-570
Miller, N.K. The Heroine's Text.*
  J. De Jean, 173(ECS):Fall82-93
  A. Morvan, 189(EA):Apr-Jun82-215
  R. Niklaus, 535(RHL):Sep-Dec82-905
  M.A. Rabb, 191(ELN):Sep82-59
  P. Rogers, 366:Autumn82-260
Miller, P.B. - see von Kleist, H.
Miller, R.A. Japan's Modern Myth.
  B.E. Wallacker, 350:Sep83-701
Miller, R.A. Origins of the Japanese Lan-
  guage.*
  S. Miyagawa, 399(MLJ):Spring82-114
  J.M. Unger, 293(JASt):Nov81-145
Miller, R.A. Studies in the Grammatical
  Tradition in Tibet.
  J.W. de Jong, 259(IIJ):Jan80-86
Miller, R.B., ed. Black American Litera-
  ture and Humanism.
  J. Benson, 392:Spring82-131
  E. Guereschi, 395(MFS):Winter82/83-682
Miller, R.F. Dostoevsky and "The Idiot."*
  A.R. Durkin, 395(MFS):Summer82-329
  V. Terras, 574(SEEJ):Summer82-242
                              [continued]

[continuing]
  W.M. Todd 3d, 550(RusR):Oct82-528
  E. Wasiolek, 131(CL):Fall82-377
Miller, R.H. - see Harington, J.
Miller, S.C. Benevolent Assimilation.*
  H. Brogan, 617(TLS):13May83-476
Miller, T. On the Border.
  D. Schmidt, 649(WAL):Spring82-74
Millgate, M. Thomas Hardy.*
  M. Engel, 676(YR):Winter83-279
  D. Kramer, 445(NCF):Mar83-604
  W. Scammell, 364:Aug/Sep82-118
  M. Shaw, 493:Jan83-64
  639(VQR):Autumn82-120
Millichap, J. Lewis Milestone.
  J. Gallagher, 200:Feb82-124
Milligan, D. Reasoning and the Explana-
  tion of Actions.*
  J.E. Tiles, 483:Jan82-142
Millman, R. Britain and the Eastern Ques-
  tion, 1875-1878.
  R.J. Crampton, 161(DUJ):Dec81-123
Millner, F.L. The Operas of Johann Adolf
  Hasse.
  D. Libby, 415:Jul82-479
Millon, H.A., ed. Studies in Italian Art
  and Architecture, 15th through 18th Cen-
  turies.
  L. Partridge, 551(RenQ):Summer82-302
Mills, A.D. The Place-Names of Dorset.*
  (Pts 1 and 2)
  G.F. Jensen, 447(N&Q):Apr81-176
Mills, D.R. Lord and Peasant in Nine-
  teenth Century Britain.
  H. Perkin, 637(VS):Spring82-382
Mills, E.L., ed. The Papers of John Pea-
  body Harrington in the Smithsonian Insti-
  tution. (Vol 1)
  W. Bright, 350:Jun83-450
Mills, H. Mailer.*
  J. Crace, 617(TLS):9Dec83-1385
Mills, J. Lizard in the Grass.
  A. Blott, 198:Jan82-87
  P. Milner, 529(QQ):Summer82-424
  G. Woodcock, 102(CanL):Winter81-125
Mills, R.J., Jr. - see Ignatow, D.
Millstein, G. God and Harvey Grosbeck.
  E. Jakab, 441:28Aug83-11
Milne, G. Stephen Crane at Brede.
  R.A. Cassell, 395(MFS):Winter81/82-717
  E. Nettels, 136:Vol 14No1-69
Milne, J. London Fields.
  L. Jones, 617(TLS):17Jun83-622
Milner, A. John Milton and the English
  Revolution.*
  R.T. Fallon, 391:Mar82-16
Milner, J-C. De la syntaxe à l'interpréta-
  tion.*
  M. Dominicy, 540(RIPh):Vol36fasc3-380
Milner, M. - see Bertrand, A.
Miloslavskij, I.G. Voprosy slovoobrazo-
  vatel'nogo sinteza.
  A. Bartoszewicz, 559:Feb82-301
Milosz, C. Emperor of the Earth.
  T. Venclova, 395(MFS):Winter82/83-717
Milosz, C. The Issa Valley.*
  B.T. Birmelin, 363(LitR):Spring83-460
Milosz, C. Native Realm.*
  D. McDuff, 565:Vol123No3-56
Milosz, C. Selected Poems.*
  J. Flavin, 396(ModA):Winter82-89

249

Milosz, C. The Witness of Poetry.
  H. Gifford, 617(TLS):9Sep83-953
  A. Kazin, 441:1May83-1
Milroy, L. Language and Social Networks.*
  C. Feagin, 35(AS):Fal182-208
  R.A. Hudson, 297(JL):Mar82-197
Milton, J. The Complete Poems. (G. Camp-
  bell, ed)
  J.B., 189(EA):Oct-Dec82-494
Milton, J. Complete Prose Works of John
  Milton.* (Vol 7) (rev) (R.W. Ayers, ed)
  R.T. Fallon, 568(SCN):Winter82-61
  C.S. Hunter, 551(RenQ):Winter81-627
  R. Lejosne, 189(EA):Oct-Dec82-464
Milton, J.R. The Novel of the American
  West.*
  M. Gilliland, 106:Spring82-75
  J.J. Wydeven, 395(MFS):Summer81-381
Milton, N.D. The China Option.
  E. Hunter, 441:9Jan83-13
Milton, S. - see Stroop, J.
"Milton Studies."* (Vol 12) (J.D. Sim-
  monds, ed)
  D. Chambers, 541(RES):May82-203
"Milton Studies."* (Vol 14) (J.D. Sim-
  monds, ed)
  J. Blondel, 189(EA):Oct-Dec82-465
Minden, M.R. Arno Schmidt.
  A. Phelan, 617(TLS):27May83-550
Mindt, D. Moderne Linguistik.
  D. Kastovsky, 38:Band100Heft3/4-442
Miner, E. and V.A. Dearing, with others -
  see Dryden, J.
Miner, E. and G.R. Guffey - see Dryden, J.
Miner, E. and H. Odagiri, eds and trans.
  The Monkey's Straw Raincoat and Other
  Poetry of the Bashō School.
  S.D. Carter, 244(HJAS):Dec82-643
  M. Ueda, 407(MN):Summer82-259
  639(VQR):Summer82-94
Ming, K. - see under Kao Ming
Ming-le, Y. - see under Yao Ming-le
Miniconi, P. and G. Devallet - see Silius
  Italicus, T.C.
"Des Minnesangs Frühling." (36th ed) (H.
  Moser and H. Tervooren, eds)
  M.G. Scholz, 224(GRM):Band32Heft4-476
Minnion, J. and P. Bolsover, eds. The CND
  Story.
  L. Freedman, 617(TLS):18Mar83-261
Minogue, V. Nathalie Sarraute and the War
  of the Words.*
  C. Britton, 402(MLR):Apr82-466
  R. Gibson, 208(FS):Apr82-230
  B. Stoltzfus, 395(MFS):Winter81/82-651
Minot, S. Surviving the Flood.
  J.L. Halio, 598(SoR):Winter83-203
  L. Jones, 617(TLS):11Mar83-249
Minta, S. Petrarch and Petrarchism.*
  W.H. Bryant, 134(CP):Fal182-94
  P. Hainsworth, 161(DUJ):Jun82-298
  F. Mouret, 549(RLC):Jul-Sep82-385
Minter, D. William Faulkner.*
  P.R. Broughton, 27(AL):Mar82-131
  J.G. Watson, 395(MFS):Summer81-365
  42(AR):Winter82-119
  529(QQ):Summer82-457
Mintz, J.R. The Anarchists of Casas
  Viejas.*
  R.L. Kagan, 441:30Jan83-12
Miquel, P. Eugène Isabey 1803-1886, La
  Marine au XIXe siècle.
  J. Ingamells, 90:Dec82-775

Miquel, P. Felix Ziem, 1821-1911.
  R. Jullian, 39:Jun82-510
Mira de Amescua. El animal profeta. (B.
  Wilds, ed)
  A.A. Heathcote, 86(BHS):Jan82-73
de Miranda, L. Solidão Provisória.
  L.D. Miller, 399(MLJ):Spring82-109
de Miranda, P.Á. - see under Álvarez de
  Miranda, P.
Mirandé, A. and E. Enríquez. La Chicana.
  M. Bornstein, 152(UDQ):Fal181-113
Miri, S., ed. Religion and Society of
  North-East India.
  R.M. Eaton, 293(JASt):May82-623
Mirié, S. Das Thronraumareal des Palastes
  von Knossos.
  R. Hägg, 121(CJ):Oct/Nov82-77
Miron, G. The Agonized Life.* (M.
  Plourde, ed and trans)
  D. Barbour, 648(WCR):Jun82-33
  D.W. Russell, 529(QQ):Spring82-217
"The Mirroure of the Worlde."
  M. Keen, 90:May82-311
"Miscellanea in onore di Eugenio Manni."
  É. des Places, 555:Vol55fasc2-359
Mischke, R. Launcelots allegorische Reise.
  H. Sauer, 72:Band218Heft1-172
von Mises, L. Epistemological Problems of
  Economics. The Theory of Money and
  Credit.
  A. Kemp, 396(ModA):Summer/Fal182-403
Mishima, Y. Une soif d'amour.
  L. Kovacs, 450(NRF):Sep82-153
Misra, B.G. - see Koshal, S.
Misra, K.P., ed. Afghanistan in Crisis.
  A.S. Ahmed, 293(JASt):Nov81-73
Mistry, F. Nietzsche and Buddhism.
  D. Thatcher, 564:Sep82-227
Mitchell, A. For Beauty Douglas.*
  E. Larrissy, 493:Sep82-61
Mitchell, A. The German Influence in
  France after 1870.
  D.H. Barry, 161(DUJ):Jun82-292
Mitchell, B. Italian Civic Pageantry in
  the High Renaissance.
  R.C. Trexler, 551(RenQ):Summer81-248
Mitchell, B. and F.C. Robinson. A Guide
  to Old English. (rev)
  M. Godden, 617(TLS):8Jul83-736
Mitchell, B.L. Edmund Ruffin.
  639(VQR):Autumn82-118
Mitchell, C. Billy Graham.
  M.R. Winchell, 585(SoQ):Fal181-88
Mitchell, D. Britten and Auden in the
  Thirties: The Year 1936.*
  J. Matthias, 598(SoR):Winter83-184
  A. Whittall, 410(M&L):Jul/Oct81-428
  A. Wilde, 295(JML):Dec82-404
Mitchell, D. and H. Keller - see "Music
  Survey"
Mitchell, G. The Greenstone Griffins.
  T.J. Binyon, 617(TLS):1Jul83-696
Mitchell, J. - see O'Casey, S.
Mitchell, J.D. Theatre.
  M. Kahan, 617(TLS):2Sep83-925
Mitchell, J.T. A Thematic Analysis of Mme
  d'Aulnoy's "Contes de Fées."*
  H.T. Barnwell, 208(FS):Jan82-65
Mitchell, K. Sinclair Ross.
  W.J. Keith, 627(UTQ):Summer82-455

250

Mitchell, L.C. Witnesses to a Vanishing
America.*
   K.E. Eble, 27(AL):Mar82-122
   L.N. Neufeldt, 301(JEGP):Oct82-591
   A.M. Woodlief, 577(SHR):Spring82-169
   D. Wyatt, 639(VQR):Spring82-340
Mitchell, R.C. - see Masaryk, A.G. and
others
Mitchell, R.L. Corbière, Mallarmé, Valéry.
   D.M. Betz, 207(FR):Apr83-777
   L.M. Porter, 210(FrF):Sep82-275
   V.L. de Vivero, 446(NCFS):Fall-Winter
   82/83-171
Mitchell, R.L., ed. Pre-Text/Text/Context.
   J.P. Houston, 210(FrF):Jan82-81
Mitchell, S. The Fallen Angel.
   E. Showalter, 637(VS):Spring82-393
Mitchell, S. - see Rilke, R.M.
Mitchell, S. and M. Rosen, eds. The Need
for Interpretation.
   D. Papineau, 617(TLS):4Nov83-1222
Mitchell, T.C., ed. Music and Civilisa-
tion.
   A. Baines, 410(M&L):Jul/Oct81-391
Mitchell, T.N. Cicero: The Ascending
Years.*
   C. Leach, 447(N&Q):Aug81-382
Mitchell, W.J.T., ed. The Language of
Images.
   J.A. Richardson, 289:Winter82-115
Mitchell, W.J.T., ed. On Narrative.
   M.B. Wiseman, 290(JAAC):Summer83-456
Mitchell, W.O. How I Spent My Summer
Holidays.
   G. Hamel, 198:Jul82-79
   W.H.N., 102(CanL):Spring82-4
   G. Woodcock, 529(QQ):Winter82-744
Mitchinson, D. - see "Henry Moore Sculp-
ture with Comments by the Artist"
Mitchison, N. The Corn King and the
Spring Queen.
   P. Craig, 617(TLS):18Nov83-1294
Mitchison, N. Not By Bread Alone.
   B. Morton, 617(TLS):17Jun83-642
Mitchison, R. Lordship to Patronage.
   G. Donaldson, 617(TLS):30Dec83-1464
Mitchner, S. Rosamund's Vision.
   D. Cole, 441:11Dec83-18
   442(NY):28Nov83-188
Mitford, T.B. The Nymphaeum of Kafizin,
the Inscribed Pottery.
   J. Pouilloux, 555:Vol56fasc1-99
Mithun, M. and H. Woodbury, eds. Northern
Iroquoian Texts.
   A.O. Wiget, 292(JAF):Oct-Dec82-477
Mittelmann, H. Die Utopie des weiblichen
Glücks in den Romanen Theodor Fontanes.
   L.S. Pickle, 221(GQ):Mar82-264
Mittelstaedt, P. Quantum Logic.
   P. Gibbins, 84:Jun82-209
Mittenzwei, W. Exil in der Schweiz.
   A. Stephan, 406:Fall82-346
Mitterand, H. Le Discours du roman.*
   J. Dubois, 535(RHL):Sep-Dec82-990
Mitterer, B. Zur Dichtung Jorge Guilléns.
   G. Güntert, 547(RF):Band93Heft1/2-304
Mixon, W. Southern Writers and the New
South Movement, 1865-1913.
   T. Bonner, Jr., 392:Fall82-457
   B. Hitchcock, 577(SHR):Summer82-275

Miyazaki Tōten. My Thirty-Three Years'
Dream. (Etō Shinkichi and M.B. Jansen,
trans)
   J.K. Fairbank, 453(NYRB):14Apr83-16
   I. Nish, 617(TLS):4Feb83-114
Moag, R.F. Fiji Hindi.
   S.K. Gambhir, 318(JAOS):Oct-Dec81-506
Moat, J. Mai's Wedding.
   J. Mellors, 362:18Aug83-23
Möbius, H. Der Positivmus in der Litera-
tur des Naturalismus.
   R.C. Cowen, 406:Spring82-108
   L.S. Pickle, 221(GQ):May82-435
Mocega-González, E.P. Alejo Carpentier.
   J. Gledson, 86(BHS):Oct82-352
"Modèles et moyens de la réflexion poli-
tique au XVIIIe siècle." (Vol 2)
   H-G. Funke, 72:Band218Heft2-477
Modell, J.S. Ruth Benedict.
   G.W. Stocking, Jr., 441:22May83-12
"Modern Public Records."
   M. Brichford, 14:Fall82-477
Modgil, S., C. Modgil and G. Brown, eds.
Jean Piaget.
   M. Richards, 617(TLS):23Sep83-1009
Modiano, P. De si braves garçons.
   C. Dis, 450(NRF):Dec82-93
Modjeska, D. Exiles at Home.
   C. Munro, 71(ALS):Oct82-533
   S. Sheridan, 381:Apr82-89
Moessner, L. Morphonologie.
   R. Ködderitzsch, 260(IF):Band86-325
Moffat, G. Hard Road West.
   J. Lloyd, 649(WAL):Winter83-357
Moffitt, I. The Retreat of Radiance.
   T.J. Binyon, 617(TLS):30Dec83-1462
Mogelon, A. Miller Brittain in Focus.
   F. Rasky, 73:May/Jun/Jul82-85
Moggach, D. Porky.
   K.C. O'Brien, 362:14Jul83-28
   G. Strawson, 617(TLS):3Jun83-562
Mohiddin, A. African Socialism in Two
Countries.
   S. Kruks, 69:Vol52No2-115
Mohn, H.R. Sten på sten.
   R. Eide, 172(Edda):1982/5-309
Mohr, W. Wolfram von Eschenbach.
   D.H. Green, 402(MLR):Jan82-227
Möhren, F. Le renforcement affectif de la
négation par l'expression d'une valeur
minimale en ancien français.
   F-J. Klein, 547(RF):Band94Heft2/3-280
   G. Straka, 553(RLiR):Jul-Dec81-492
von Mohrenschildt, D. Toward a United
States of Russia.
   E.C. Thaden, 550(RusR):Jul82-325
Moignet, G. Systématique de la langue
française. (J. Cervoni, K. Schlyter
and A. Vassant, eds)
   P. Blumenthal, 547(RF):Band94Heft2/3-
   273
   M. Wilmet, 553(RLiR):Jan-Jun82-192
Moir, A. Caravaggio.
   F. Haskell, 453(NYRB):12May83-25
Moirand, S. Situations d'écrit.
   R.H. Simon, 207(FR):May83-961
Moise, E.E. Land Reform in China and
North Vietnam.
   D.J. Duncanson, 617(TLS):19Aug83-883
Mojsisch, B. Die Theorie des Intellekts
bei Dietrich von Freiberg.
   J-F. Courtine, 192(EP):Oct-Dec81-476
Mojsisch, B. - see von Freiberg, D.

Mokyr, J. Why Ireland Starved.
  J. Lee, 617(TLS):23Sep83-1016
Molesworth, C. Donald Barthelme's Fiction.
  C. Baxter, 141:Summer82-300
  D.J. Cahill, 659(ConL):Fall83-395
  C.D. Farmer, 268(IFR):Winter83-69
  J. Klinkowitz, 580(SCR):Fall82-127
Moleta, V. Guinizzelli in Dante.
  M. Marti, 228(GSLI):Vol 159fasc508-599
de Molina, T. - see under Tirso de Molina
Moline, J. Plato's Theory of Understand-
  ing.
  D. Keyt, 319:Oct83-551
Molino, J. and J. Tamine. Introduction à
  l'analyse linguistique de la poésie.
  J.P. Houston, 207(FR):May83-934
Molitor, J.W. Architectural Photography.
  C. Robinson, 576:Mar82-79
Mollat, M. and P. Tombeur. Conciles oecu-
  méniques médiévaux.
  U-R. Blumenthal, 589:Jan82-157
Moller, M.E. Thoreau in the Human Commu-
  nity.*
  M. Granger, 189(EA):Jul-Sep82-360
  L. Lane, Jr., 106:Fall82-199
  J. Loesberg, 506(PSt):Sep82-258
Molnar, T. Theists and Atheists.*
  J.D. Collins, 396(ModA):Spring82-196
Molony, C., H. Zobl and W. Stölting, eds.
  Deutsch im Kontakt mit anderen Sprachen/
  German in Contact with Other Languages.*
  E. Weiszhar, 685(ZDL):1/1982-97
Mols, M., ed. Integración y cooperación
  en América Latina.
  A. Cohen, 263(RIB):Vol32No3/4-376
Molyneux, J. Leon Trotsky's Theory of
  Revolution.
  R.D. Rucker, 550(RusR):Oct82-499
Mommsen, H. Corpus Vasorum Antiquorum.
  (Deutschland, Vol 45)
  B.A. Sparkes, 303(JoHS):Vol 102-285
Mommsen, K. Goethe und 1001 Nacht.
  H. Eichner, 406:Fall82-327
Mommsen, W.J. and G. Hirschfeld, eds.
  Social Protest, Violence and Terror in
  Nineteenth and Twentieth Century Europe.
  J. Joll, 617(TLS):4Mar83-210
Mon, F. fallen stellen.
  J. Adler, 617(TLS):4Mar83-223
Monaghan, D. Jane Austen.*
  F.B. Pinion, 541(RES):Nov82-484
  B. Roth, 173(ECS):Spring82-350
Monaghan, D., ed. Jane Austen in a Social
  Context.*
  J.J. Gold, 405(MP):Feb83-313
Monaghan, J. The Neo-Firthian Tradition
  and its Contribution to General Lin-
  guistics.*
  V. Salmon, 260(IF):Band86-306
Monahan, M.J. - see Brontë, C.
Moncel, C. Exposé de poétique. (Vols 2
  and 3)
  P. Somville, 542:Jan-Mar82-98
Mondlane, E. The Struggle for Mozambique.
  S. Uys, 617(TLS):16Sep83-983
Mondor, H. and L.J. Austin - see Mallarmé,
  S.
Monegal, E.R. and E.M. Santí - see under
  Rodríguez Monegal, E. and E.M. Santí
Monette, M. Le Double Suspect.
  E. Dansereau, 102(CanL):Spring82-84
Monette, P. No Witnesses.
  M. Perloff, 385(MQR):Winter83-130

Money, K. Anna Pavlova.
  G. Annan, 617(TLS):18Mar83-264
  A. Kisselgoff, 441:2Jan83-4
"Money Income of Households, Families,
  and Persons in the United States: 1981."
  A. Hacker, 453(NYRB):30Jun83-27
Monférier, J., ed. François Mauriac et
  son temps.
  F. Lioure, 535(RHL):Mar-Apr82-323
Mongrédien, G. and J. Robert. Les Comé-
  diens français du XVIIe siècle, Diction-
  naire biographique suivi d'un inventaire
  des troupes (1590-1710) d'après des
  documents inédits. (3rd ed)
  A. Blanc, 535(RHL):Sep-Dec82-895
Mongrédien, J. Catalogue thématique de
  l'oeuvre complète du compositeur Jean-
  François Le Sueur (1760-1837).* Jean-
  François Le Sueur.*
  D. Charlton, 451:Fall82-166
Moñino, A.R.R. - see under Rodríguez
  Moñino, A.R.
Monk, L., ed. Canada With Love.
  F. Rasky, 73:Summer83-53
Monk, P. The Smaller Infinity.
  D.J. Dooley, 99:Oct82-30
Monk, S.H., A.E.W. Maurer and V.A. Dear-
  ing, with others - see Dryden, J.
Monkman, L. A Native Heritage.*
  A.G. Bailey, 105:Spring/Summer82-106
  J. Bell, 529(QQ):Winter82-888
  J.E. Chamberlin, 627(UTQ):Summer82-445
  C. Gerson, 102(CanL):Autumn82-136
Monod-Fontaine, I. Matisse.
  N. Watkins, 90:Sep82-563
Monro, H. The Sonneteer's History of Phi-
  losophy.
  G. Nerlich, 63:Sep82-298
Monsarrat, A. An Uneasy Victorian.*
  C. MacKay, 594:Summer82-218
  J. McMaster, 637(VS):Spring82-377
  S. Monod, 189(EA):Apr-Jun82-221
Monsen, R.J. and K.D. Walters. National-
  ized Companies.
  R.L. Heilbroner, 453(NYRB):8Dec83-23
Monsky, S. Midnight Suppers.
  A. Gottlieb, 441:13Feb83-26
Monsman, G. Walter Pater's Art of Auto-
  biography.*
  S. Bassett, 637(VS):Summer82-497
  A.F.T. Lurcock, 541(RES):Feb82-97
  J. Pilling, 301(JEGP):Jul82-453
  I. Small, 89(BJA):Summer82-284
  D.E. Van Tassel, 395(MFS):Summer81-337
  P. Zietlow, 191(ELN):Dec81-152
Monson, D.A. Les "ensenhamens" occitans.*
  É. Schulze-Busacker, 554:Vol 102No4-
  571
Monson, K. Alma Mahler.
  G. Annan, 453(NYRB):29Sep83-4
Montague, J. The Rough Field. (3rd ed)
  J. Parini, 569(SR):Fall82-623
Montague, J. Selected Poems.*
  C. Hope, 364:Dec82/Jan83-106
  E. Larrissy, 493:Sep82-61
  T. Parkinson, 219(GaR):Fall82-662
  C. Ricks, 441:22May83-15
Montague, R. Formal Philosophy. (R.H.
  Thomason, ed)
  J. Barwise and J. Moravcsik, 316:Mar82-
  210

Moors, K.F. Glaucon and Adeimantus on Justice.
J. Annas, 123:Vol32No2-283
Moorsom, S. In the Shadow of the Paradise Tree.
C. Hope, 617(TLS):3Jun83-582
Moortgat, M., H. van der Hulst and T. Hoekstra, eds. The Scope of Lexical Rules.
T. Wasow, 350:Dec83-905
Moose, M.H. Three of a Kind.
W. Grady, 102(CanL):Spring82-115
Mora, G. - see Cabanis, P-J.G.
Mora, J.F. - see under Ferrater Mora, J.
Morahan, S. A Woman's Place.
H. Marlborough, 385(MQR):Winter83-143
Morales, A.J. La Capilla Real de Sevilla.
F. Marías, 48:Apr-Jun80-215
Morales, A.J. La iglesia de San Lorenzo de Sevilla.
M. Estella, 48:Apr-Jun82-219
Morales, A.J. La obra renacentista del Ayuntamiento de Sevilla.
P. Navascués, 48:Jan-Mar82-122
Morales Carrión, A., with others. Puerto Rico.
R. Carr, 453(NYRB):18Aug83-14
Morales-Pino, A. La peste de Santos Gil.
G.E. Wade, 238:Dec82-665
Moran, E.F. Developing the Amazon.
M. Karash, 37:Jul-Aug82-63
Moran, J.C. An F. Marion Crawford Companion.
517(PBSA):Vol76No4-502
Moran, J.H. Education and Learning in the City of York, 1300-1560.
C.R. Davey, 325:Apr82-41
Moran, R. high rise sniper.
D. Haskell, 581:Sep82-348
Morani, M. La tradizione manoscritta del "De natura hominis" di Nemesio.
R. Browning, 123:Vol132No2-149
É. des Places, 555:Vol56fasc2-334
Morath, I. and A. Miller. Chinese Encounters.
L. Yang, 399(MLJ):Spring82-115
Moraud, Y. La Conquête de la liberté de Scapin à Figaro.
J. Emelina, 535(RHL):Sep-Dec82-894
Moravia, A. 1934.
S. Kauffmann, 231:Apr83-63
S. Spender, 453(NYRB):30Jun83-25
J. Whittam, 617(TLS):4Nov83-1214
M. Wood, 441:8May83-11
Morawetz, T. The Philosophy of Law.*
W.H. Wilcox, 482(PhR):Oct82-648
Morche, G. Muster und Nachahmung.
E. Higginbottom, 410(M&L):Jan81-76
Mordden, E. The American Theatre.
W.J. Meserve, 651(WHR):Winter82-370
R. Moody, 27(AL):May82-303
Mordden, E. The Hollywood Musical.*
M. Wood, 18:Dec81-77
Mordden, E. Movie Star.
R. Sklar, 441:2Oct83-12
More, C. Skill and the English Working Class, 1870-1914.
R. Price, 637(VS):Autumn81-111
More, T. The Complete Works of St. Thomas More. (Vol 6: A Dialogue Concerning Heresies) (T.M.C. Lawler, G. Marc'hadour
[continued]

[continuing]
and R.C. Marius, eds)
N. Barker, 617(TLS):25Feb83-199
R. Pineas, 551(RenQ):Winter82-617
More, T. The Complete Works of St. Thomas More.* (Vol 9: The Apology) (J.B. Trapp, ed)
N. Barker, 617(TLS):25Feb83-199
J. McConica, 551(RenQ):Summer81-262
More, T. The Tower Works: Devotional Writings. (G.E. Haupt, ed)
C. Smith, 377:Mar82-61
Moreau, J. Stoïcisme, épicurisme, tradition hellénique.*
J. Frère, 192(EP):Jan-Mar81-96
Morel, J. and A. Viala - see Racine, J.
Morella, J. and E.Z. Epstein. Rita.
M. Haskell, 441:300ct83-9
Morello, J. Jean Rotrou.*
H.C. Knutson, 210(FrF):Jan82-75
Morenas, F. Le Cinéma ambulant en Provence.
J. Paulhan, 207(FR):Mar83-661
Moreno, C.F., J. Ortega and I.A. Schulman - see under Fernández Moreno, C., J. Ortega and I.A. Schulman
Moreno-Durán, R.H. El Toque de Diana.
O. Rossardi, 37:Jan-Feb82-63
Morère, P. L'Oeuvre de James Beattie.*
L. Marcil-Lacoste, 189(EA):Apr-Jun82-217
Moretta, E.L. La poesía de Xavier Villaurrutia.
H. Wozniak-Brayman, 238:May82-315
Moretti, F. Signs Taken For Wonders.
E.W. Said, 441:4Sep83-9
M. Sprinker, 617(TLS):15Jul83-761
Moretto, G. Etica e storia in Schleiermacher.
F. Volpi, 489(PJGG):Band89Heft2-437
Morewedge, P., ed. Islamic Philosophical Theology.
C.E.B., 543:Dec81-404
Morgan, C. and D. Langford. Facts and Fallacies.
639(VQR):Summer82-99
Morgan, E., ed. Scottish Satirical Verse.
R. McQuillan, 571(ScLJ):Spring82-28
Morgan, F. The Female Wits.
A.H. Scouten, 566:Autumn82-62
Morgan, F. Northbook.*
C.B. Cox, 148:Winter82-87
E. Grosholz, 434:Summer83-634
G.E. Murray, 385(MQR):Fall83-643
Morgan, F. Refractions.
D. Schier, 569(SR):Fall82-lxxxiv
Morgan, J., C. O'Neill and R. Harré. Nicknames.
G.A. Fine, 292(JAF):Jan-Mar82-92
Morgan, K.L. Children of Strangers.
D.L. Closson, 582(SFQ):Vol43No3/4-344
Morgan, P.F. Literary Critics and Reviewers in Early Nineteenth-Century Britain.
P. O'Leary, 617(TLS):16Dec83-1396
Morgan, P.F. - see Jeffrey, F.
Morgan, R. Trunk and Thicket.*
F. Muratori, 448:Vol120No1-140
Morgan, S. In the Meantime.*
B. Roth, 173(ECS):Spring82-351
R.L. Snyder, 594:Summer82-207

Morgan, T. Churchill 1874-1915.*
 J. Grigg, 362:28Apr83-22
 J.A. Turner, 617(TLS):17Jun83-626
 P. Vansittart, 364:Mar83-100
Morgan, T. Maugham.*
 R.L. Calder, 49:Apr82-89
Morgan, W. The Almighty Wall.
 P. Goldberger, 441:11Dec83-13
Morgan, W.J., ed. Naval Documents of the
 American Revolution. (Vol 8)
 S.G. Morse, 432(NEQ):Mar82-130
Morgan, W.N. Prehistoric Architecture in
 the Eastern United States.*
 J.M. Dixon, 505:Feb82-140
Morgen, A. and B. Purdie, eds. Ireland.
 G. Eley, 385(MQR):Winter83-107
Morgenstern, S. The Silent Gondoliers.
 D. Quammen, 441:6Nov83-14
Mori, O. Frases infinitivas preposicion-
 ales en la zona significativa causal.
 O. Akhmanova and O. Aleksandrova,
 257(IRAL):Nov82-328
Morice, D. Poetry Comics.
 G. Burns, 584(SWR):Autumn82-465
Morice, D. Quicksand Through the Hour-
 glass.
 D. Lehman, 181:Winter-Spring83-166
Morin, A. Ombres fidèles. Solitude
 d'été.
 R. Bréchon, 98:Nov82-949
Morin, E. The Dust of Our City.
 M. Lammon, 436(NewL):Winter82/83-106
Morita, J.R. Kaneko Mitsuharu.*
 S. Rabson, 293(JASt):Nov81-147
Moritz, A.F. Black Orchid. Signs and
 Certainties.
 P. Miller, 526:Summer82-116
Moritz, A.F. Music and Exile.
 B. Meyer, 102(CanL):Spring82-88
Morley, F. Literary Britain.*
 D. Davie, 569(SR):Winter82-79
Morley, J.W., ed. The Fateful Choice.*
 R. Dingman, 293(JASt):Nov81-150
Morley, P. Margaret Laurence.
 W.N., 102(CanL):Summer82-163
Morley, S. Tales from the Hollywood Raj.
 J. Marsh, 617(TLS):18Nov83-1291
Morley, T.P., ed. Moral, Ethical, and
 Legal Issues in the Neurosciences.
 J.D., 185:Apr83-645
Morrell, E. A Visitor's Guide to China.
 D. Davin, 617(TLS):24Jun83-656
Morrell, J. and A. Thackray. Gentlemen of
 Science.
 G. Himmelfarb, 617(TLS):6May83-453
Morri, A., ed. É Vangëli śgönd S. Matí.
 G. Schlemmer, 547(RF):Band94Heft1-105
Morrice, P. The Schweppes Guide to Scotch.
 D. Daiches, 617(TLS):23Dec83-1442
Morrill, J., ed. Reactions to the English
 Civil War 1642-1649.
 I. Roots, 617(TLS):4Mar83-222
Morris, G.R. This Loving Darkness.
 M.R. Coke, 402(MLR):Jul82-751
 G. Edwards, 86(BHS):Apr82-158
Morris, D. Inrock.
 J. Mellors, 362:30Jun83-28
Morris, D. and others. Gestures.
 A. Kendon, 567:Vol37No1/2-129
Morris, H. Peru.
 M. Kinzie, 29:Jul/Aug83-33
 R. Tillinghast, 441:7Aug83-12

Morris, J. 100 Years of Canadian Drawings.
 A. Purdy, 102(CanL):Spring82-132
 F.K. Smith, 529(QQ):Spring82-172
Morris, J., ed. The Oxford Book of
 Oxford.*
 H. Lee, 447(N&Q):Jun81-278
Morris, J. Sultan in Oman.
 K.A.M., 617(TLS):23Sep83-1031
Morris, J. A Venetian Bestiary.*
 D. Gillard, 362:20Jan83-26
Morris, J. - see Ruskin, J.
Morris, J. and S. Winchester. Stones of
 Empire.
 J.M. Richards, 617(TLS):2Dec83-1350
Morris, J.H.C. Thank You, Wodehouse.
 H.H. Watts, 395(MFS):Winter82/83-646
Morris, M. Crossroads.
 S. Isaacs, 441:13Mar83-10
Morris, M. and P. Patton - see Foucault, M.
Morris, M.F. Le Chevalier de Jaucourt.*
 M.B. Lacy, 207(FR):Oct82-153
 J. Lough, 208(FS):Jan82-69
Morris, N. Madness and the Criminal Law.
 D.C. Anderson, 441:6Feb83-12
Morris, R. The Character of King Arthur
 in Medieval Literature.
 B. O'Donoghue, 617(TLS):18Mar83-276
Morris, R. Haig.*
 M. Beloff, 617(TLS):7Jan83-18
Morris, R. - see "Dan Michel's 'Ayenbite
 of Inwyt'"
Morris, W. The Courting of Marcus Dupree.
 P-L. Adams, 61:Dec83-116
 D. Bradley, 441:18Dec83-11
Morris, W. Friday's Footprint.*
 M. Grossman, 125:Fall81-91
Morris, W. The Ideal Book. (W.S. Peter-
 son, ed)
 D.J.R.B., 441:30Jan83-14
 S. Carter, 617(TLS):2Sep83-943
Morris, W. Solo.
 J. Atlas, 441:5Jun83-7
 442(NY):12Sep83-158
Morris, W. Will's Boy.
 M. Washington, 649(WAL):Spring82-68
 639(VQR):Winter82-16
"Wright Morris: Photographs and Words."*
 (J. Alinder, ed)
 P-L. Adams, 61:Mar83-117
Morris-Jones, W.H. and G. Fischer, eds.
 Decolonisation and After.
 A.H.M. Kirk-Greene, 69:Vol51No3-802
Morris le Bour'his, J. Robert Hugh Benson,
 homme de foi et artiste.
 F. Frost, 189(EA):Oct-Dec82-478
Morrison, A. The Hole in the Wall.
 J.K.L. Walker, 617(TLS):4Mar83-205
Morrison, B. Seamus Heaney.*
 A. Young, 493:Jan83-61
Morrison, B. and A. Motion, eds. The
 Penguin Book of Contemporary British
 Poetry.*
 H. Haughton, 617(TLS):28Jan83-78
Morrison, B.M., M.P. Moore and M.U.I.
 Lebbe, eds. The Disintegrating Village.
 J. Brow, 293(JASt):Nov81-182
Morrison, H.R. The Masque of St. Eadmunds-
 burg.
 T.A. Shippey, 617(TLS):21Jan83-69
Morrison, J.R., with W.C. Kidney. Winches-
 ter.
 D.J. Hibbard, 658:Spring82-90

Morrison, P. and others. Powers of Ten.
S.J. Gould, 441:4Dec83-15
"Stanley Morrison and D.B. Updike: Se-
lected Correspondence." (D. McKitterick,
ed)
H. Williamson, 447(N&Q):Dec81-568
Morrison, T. Tar Baby.*
C. Colter, 436(NewL):Fall82-108
Morrissey, C.T. Vermont.
T.D.S. Bassett, 432(NEQ):Jun82-297
Morrissey, L.J. Henry Fielding.*
D.L. Vander Meulen, 173(ECS):Summer83-
439
Morrow, A. The Queen.
D.A.N. Jones, 617(TLS):29Apr83-428
Morrow, B. and S. Cooney. A Bibliography
of the Black Sparrow Press, 1966-1978.
L. Bartlett, 50(ArQ):Summer82-183
Morrow, B. and B. Lafourcade. A Bibliogra-
phy of the Writings of Wyndham Lewis.*
E.M. Wallace, 677(YES):Vol 12-342
Morrow, M. Indian Rawhide.
R.M. Boyer, 292(JAF):Apr-Jun82-211
Morse, C.C. The Pattern of Judgment in
the "Queste" and "Cleanness."*
B.S. Levy, 589:Jan82-158
Morse, D. Perspectives on Romanticism.*
A. Rodway, 89(BJA):Summer82-281
Morse, R.A., ed. The Politics of Japan's
Energy Strategy.
Ikuta Toyoaki, 285(JapQ):Jul-Sep82-375
Morson, G.S. The Boundaries of Genre.
A.R. Durkin, 395(MFS):Summer82-329
W.J. Leatherbarrow, 89(BJA):Autumn82-
373
V. Terras, 104(CASS):Fall-Winter82-521
W.M. Todd 3d, 574(SEEJ):Winter82-481
D. Watson, 561(SFS):Jul82-217
Mortelier, C. - see Prévert, J.
Mortimer, E. Faith and Power.
B. Lewis, 453(NYRB):30Jun83-35
C.C. O'Brien, 362:17Mar83-20
E.R.J. Owen, 617(TLS):22Apr83-405
Mortimer, J. In Character.
C. Brown, 617(TLS):3Jun83-581
Mortimer, P. The Handyman.
A. Duchêne, 617(TLS):20May83-510
K.C. O'Brien, 362:14Jul83-28
Mortimer, R. A Portrait of the Author in
Sixteenth-Century France.
D. Shaw, 354:Jun82-196
Morton, A. Frames of Mind.*
A. Palmer, 518:Oct82-226
Morton, B.N. and D.C. Spinelli - see de
Beaumarchais, P.A.C.
Morton, F. A Nervous Splendor.
J.B. Berlin, 406:Summer82-211
Morton, J. English Grammar for Students
of French.*
R.E. Hiedemann, 399(MLJ):Spring82-83
Morton, J. - see Gide, A. and J. O'Brien
Morton, J. and J.C. Marshall, eds. Psy-
cholinguistics 2.
J.F. Kess, 567:Vol137No3/4-369
Morton, W.F. Tanaka Giichi and Japan's
China Policy.*
B.W. Kahn, 293(JASt):Feb82-364
Mosel, U. Tolai and Tok Pisin.
R.A. Hall, Jr., 350:Jun83-449
Moser, C.A. Denis Fonvizin.
G.S. Smith, 402(MLR):Jul82-762

Moser, H., H. Rupp and H. Steger, eds.
Deutsche Sprache.
F. Simmler, 685(ZDL):2/1981-244
Moser, H. and H. Tervooren - see "Des
Minnesangs Frühling"
Moser, T.C. The Life in the Fiction of
Ford Madox Ford.*
T.K. Bender, 577(SHR):Fall82-372
J.A. Bryant, Jr., 569(SR):Winter82-100
R.A. Cassell, 136:Vol 14No2-137
K. Cohen, 141:Winter82-81
M. De Koven, 395(MFS):Winter81/82-701
C. Kahane, 454:Fall82-76
J. Meyers, 191(ELN):Dec81-161
S. Weintraub, 598(SoR):Winter83-233
J. Wiesenfarth, 295(JML):Dec82-448
Moser, W. "L'Éducation sentimentale" de
1869 et la poétique de l'oeuvre autonome.
P. Berthier, 535(RHL):Sep-Dec82-932
Mosher, S.W. Broken Earth.
R. Bernstein, 441:30Oct83-3
Moskos, C.C., Jr. Greek Americans.
R. Clogg, 617(TLS):12Aug83-861
"Moskva zlatoglavaja."*
M. Winokur, 574(SEEJ):Spring82-111
Mosley, N. Beyond the Pale.
R. Skidelsky, 617(TLS):11Nov83-1242
P. Worsthorne, 362:8Dec83-28
Mosley, N. The Rules of the Game.*
P. Vansittart, 364:Mar83-100
Mosley, P. The Settler Economies.
C. Ehrlich, 617(TLS):7Oct83-1097
Moss, H. Whatever Is Moving.
D. St. John, 42(AR):Spring82-233
Moss, J., ed. The Canadian Novel. (Vol 2)
C. Gerson, 102(CanL):Winter81-166
Moss, R. and A. de Borchgrave. Monimbo.
T.J. Binyon, 617(TLS):2Dec83-1358
S. Ellin, 441:14Aug83-13
Moss, T. Hosiery Seams on a Bowlegged
Woman.
J. Ditsky, 628(UWR):Spring-Summer83-82
Mossay, J., with G. Lafontaine - see Saint
Gregory of Nazianzus
Mossberg, C.L. Scandinavian Immigrant
Literature.
A.R. Huseboe, 649(WAL):Summer82-176
Mosshammer, A.E. The "Chronicle" of Euse-
bius and Greek Chronographic Tradition.*
R. Drews, 122:Apr82-178
Mossiker, F. Madame de Sévigné.
P-L. Adams, 61:Nov83-148
Mossman, E. - see Pasternak, B.
Mossman, J., ed. Pseudonyms and Nicknames
Dictionary.*
R. Eddison, 611(TN):Vol36No2-86
Mossner, E.C. The Life of David Hume.*
(2nd ed)
R. Sasso, 192(EP):Oct-Dec81-472
Mosso, S. Fede, storia e morale.
M. Hany, 192(EP):Jul-Sep82-361
Most, G.W. and W.W. Stowe, eds. The
Poetics of Murder.
M. Bayles, 441:25Sep83-16
"Mostra di Opere di Arte Restaurate nelle
Province di Siena e Grosseto, 11."
F. Russell, 39:May82-411
Motion, A. Philip Larkin.
R. Brown, 617(TLS):1Apr83-322
Motion, A. Secret Narratives.
T. Dooley, 617(TLS):19Aug83-886

Motteux, P.A. and J. Eccles. The Rape of
  Europa by Jupiter (1694) and Acis and
  Galatea (1701).
    566:Spring83-144
Motyl, A.J. The Turn to the Right.*
    O.W. Gerus, 104(CASS):Summer82-287
Moulden, J. Songs of the People. (Pt 1)
    L.E. McCullough, 292(JAF):Apr-Jun82-
    249
Moules, J. Our Gracie.
    G. Kaufman, 362:6Oct83-23
Moulin, J-P. La France et ses populations.
    S. Smith, 207(FR):Dec82-359
Moulton, C. Aristophanic Poetry.
    A.H. Sommerstein, 123:Vol32No2-274
Mount, F. The Subversive Family.*
    N. Berry, 364:Dec82/Jan83-130
Mountjoy, R.J. Nightwind.
    S. Lukas, 649(WAL):Summer82-190
Moureau, F. Dufresny, auteur dramatique
  (1657-1724).*
    R.L. Dawson, 173(ECS):Fall82-80
de Mourgues, O. Quelques paradoxes sur le
  classicisme.
    P. France, 208(FS):Jul82-327
de Mourgues, O. Two French Moralists.*
    L.K. Horowitz, 188(ECr):Fall82-86
Moutote, D. Égotisme français moderne.
    I-M. Frandon, 535(RHL):Jan-Feb82-135
Moutsopoulos, E. Conformisme et déforma-
  tion.*
    J-J. Wunenburger, 192(EP):Jul-Sep82-
    363
Moutsopoulos, E. La critique du platon-
  isme chez Bergson.
    J-M. Gabaude, 192(EP):Jul-Sep82-370
    J-M. Gabaude, 542:Jan-Mar82-70
Moutsopoulos, E. Le problème de l'imagin-
  aire chez Plotin.*
    J-M. Gabaude, 192(EP):Jul-Sep82-370
Movellán, A.V. - see under Villar Movellán,
  A.
Mowrer, O.H., ed. Psychology of Language
  and Learning.*
    E. Bialystok, 399(MLJ):Summer82-195
Moynihan, M. God on Our Side.
    D. Hibberd, 617(TLS):15Jul83-762
Mucha, A. The Art Nouveau Style Book.
    L. Ormond, 39:Aug82-123
Mück, H-D. Untersuchungen zur Überliefer-
  ung und Rezeption spätmittelalterlicher
  Lieder und Spruchgedichte im 15. und 16.
  Jahrhundert.*
    H. Heinen, 406:Winter82-493
    F.V. Spechtler, 680(ZDP):Band101Heft1-
    153
Mück, H-D. and U. Müller - see "Jahrbuch
  der Oswald-von-Wolkenstein-Gesellschaft"
Mudford, P. The Art of Celebration.*
    M. Harris, 72:Band218Heft2-393
Mudrick, M. Nobody Here but Us Chickens.*
    G. Woodcock, 569(SR):Summer82-466
Mueller, D. Kurze Krimis.
    I.H. McCoy, 399(MLJ):Autumn82-339
Mueller, D.C., ed. The Political Economy
  of Growth.
    T.W. Hutchison, 617(TLS):2Sep83-923
Mueller, L. The Need to Hold Still.*
    R. Tillinghast, 569(SR):Spring82-291
Mueller-Stellrecht, I. Materialien zur
  Etnographie von Dardistan (Pakistan) aus
  den nachgelassenen. (Vol 1) (D.L.R.
                        [continued]

[continuing]
  Lorimer, comp)
    J.W. Anderson, 293(JASt):Feb82-390
Mugnier-Pollet, L. La philosophie poli-
  tique de Spinoza.
    A. Reix, 192(EP):Apr-Jun81-243
Muhammad, S. - see Ali, M.M. and M.S.
Mühl, K. "Verwandlung" im Werk Rilkes.
    B.L. Bradley, 221(GQ):Nov82-604
Muhlenfeld, E. Mary Boykin Chesnut.*
    F. Allen, 577(SHR):Summer82-268
    A.F. Scott, 579(SAQ):Autumn82-469
Muhlstein, A. Baron James.
    G. Annan, 453(NYRB):18Aug83-22
    J. Russell, 441:4Sep83-7
Muhr, R. Sprachwandel als soziales Phäno-
  men.
    J. Heath, 350:Jun83-455
Muir, E. Civic Ritual in Renaissance
  Venice.*
    R. Finlay, 551(RenQ):Autumn82-476
    R.C. Trexler, 589:Jul82-642
Muir, E. Scottish Journey. (T.C. Smout,
  ed)
    P. Dodd, 588(SSL):Vol 17-297
Muir, E. Uncollected Scottish Criticism.*
  (A. Noble, ed)
    W.R., 148:Summer82-92
Muir, H. Many Men and Talking Wives.
    J.L. Halio, 598(SoR):Winter83-203
Muir, J. John Muir: To Yosemite and Be-
  yond. (R. Engberg and D. Wesling, eds)
    D. Fussell, 506(PSt):Dec82-348
Muir, K. Shakespeare's Sonnets.*
    T.W. Craik, 161(DUJ):Jun82-307
    C.P. Marsh, 95(CLAJ):Jun83-478
    D.L. Peterson, 191(ELN):Dec81-141
Muir, K. Shakespeare's Tragic Sequence.*
  Shakespeare's Comic Sequence.*
    M. Charney, 402(MLR):Apr82-407
    E.A.J. Honigmann, 447(N&Q):Apr81-188
Muir, K. - see Ellis-Fermor, U.
Muir, K. - see Shakespeare, W.
Muir, K. - see "Shakespeare Survey"
Muir, K. and S. Wells, eds. Aspects of
  "Hamlet."
    E.A.J. Honigmann, 447(N&Q):Apr81-189
Muir, M. A History of Australian Chil-
  dren's Book Illustration.
    G. Cavaliero, 324:Mar83-228
Mukařovský, J. The Word and Verbal Art.*
  (J. Burbank and P. Steiner, ed and trans)
    C.E. Reeves, 567:Vol139No1/2-115
Mulcahy, G.A. Songs that Untune the Sky.
    S. Gingell, 628(UWR):Spring-Summer83-
    91
Mulch, R. Arnsburger Personennamen.
    E. Neuss, 685(ZDL):2/1981-267
Mulch, R. and R. - see Maurer, F., F.
  Stroh and R. Mulch
Mulder, R.J. and J.H. Timmerman. Freder-
  ick Manfred.
    J.M. Flora, 649(WAL):Summer82-162
Muldoon, P. Mules.
    J. Parini, 569(SR):Fall82-623
Muldoon, P. Quoof.
    N. Corcoran, 617(TLS):28Oct83-1180
Muldoon, P. Why Brownlee Left.*
    S. Fauchereau, 98:Jun-Jul82-628
    L.M. Harrod, 174(Éire):Fall82-145
    J. Parini, 569(SR):Fall82-623

Mulgan, R.G. Aristotle's Political The-
ory.*
  F.D. Harvey, 123:Vol32No1-48
Mulier, E.O.G.H. - see under Haitsma
Mulier, E.O.G.
Mullan, F. Vital Signs.
  M.W. Lear, 441:27Feb83-3
Mullan, W.N.B. Grillparzer's Aesthetic
Theory.
  I.F. Roe, 402(MLR):Apr82-496
Mullen, W. Choreia.
  R. Stoneman, 617(TLS):10Jun83-599
Müllenbrock, H-J. Der historische Roman
des 19. Jahrhunderts.
  E. Mengel, 189(EA):Apr-Jun82-220
Müller, H-P. Die schweizerische Sprachen-
frage vor 1914.
  J. Eichhoff, 685(ZDL):3/1982-393
Muller, J-C. Le Roi bouc émissaire.
  R. Fardon, 69:Vol52No1-95
  J. Pestieau, 154:Jun82-349
Muller, M. The Cheshire Cat's Eye.
  N. Callendar, 441:20Mar83-27
Muller, M. Préfiguration et Structure
Romanesque dans "A La Recherche du Temps
Perdu."*
  F. Pellan, 395(MFS):Winter81/82-655
Müller, R. Die epikureische Gesellschafts-
theorie.
  A. Laks, 192(EP):Jul-Sep81-362
Müller, R., E. Gabriel and W. Kraemer.
Laut und Schrift in Dialekt und Standard-
sprache.
  L. Zehetner, 685(ZDL):2/1982-266
Müller, U., ed. Oswald von Wolkenstein.*
  I. Glier, 221(GQ):Nov82-589
  H. Heinen, 406:Winter82-493
  S.L. Wailes, 564:Nov81-317
Müller, W., ed. Schülerduden.
  U. Schröter, 682(ZPSK):Band35Heft3-362
Müller, W.G. Die politische Rede bei
Shakespeare.*
  K. Tetzeli von Rosador, 72:Band218
  Heft2-435
  H. Zander, 38:Band100Heft3/4-518
Müller, W.G. Topik des Stilbegriffs.
  H. Seidler, 602:Vol 13No2-357
Müller-Schotte, H. Anschaulichkeit und
Eindringlichkeit als sprachgestaltende
Prinzipien im neueren Englisch.
  H. Käsmann, 38:Band100Heft3/4-478
Mullett, M. and R. Scott, eds. Byzantium
and the Classical Tradition.*
  N.G. Wilson, 123:Vol32No1-117
Mullett, M.A. Radical Religious Movements
in Early Modern Europe.
  J.D. Moss, 551(RenQ):Winter81-581
Mullins, E., ed. Great Paintings.
  T. Crombie, 39:Aug82-124
Mullins, E. Sirens.
  S. Altinel, 617(TLS):16Sep83-1001
Multhaup, U. James Joyce.
  R. Davis, 395(MFS):Winter81/82-676
Mulvaney, R.J. and P.M. Zeltner, eds.
Pragmatism.
  J.G. Grassi, 619:Summer82-265
  J.M.I., 185:Oct82-200
Mulvey, C. Anglo-American Landscapes.
  S. Koss, 362:16Jun83-26
Mumford, L. Sketches from Life: The Early
Years.*
  M. Filler, 45:Apr82-116
Mundal, E. - see "Gunnlaugs saga ormstungu"

Munday, A. The English Roman Life. (P.J.
Ayres, ed)
  J.N. King, 541(RES):Aug82-315
  J. Norton-Smith, 447(N&Q):Apr81-190
  V. Thomas, 506(PSt):May82-168
Münder, P. Harold Pinter und die Proble-
matik des Absurden Theaters.
  R. Halbritter, 38:Band100Heft1/2-228
Mundis, J., ed. The Dog Book.
  P-L. Adams, 61:Jul83-108
de Mundolo, S., comp. Index to Spanish
American Collective Biography. (Vol 1)
  M.H. Sable, 263(RIB):Vol32No1-68
Munemitsu, M. - see under Mutsu Munemitsu
Munévar, G. Radical Knowledge.
  S.W., 185:Jan83-419
Muñiz, C. El tintero. Miserere para
medio fraile. (L.L. Zeller, ed of both)
  M.A. Salgado, 238:Dec82-659
de Muñoz, M.B. - see Bertrand de Muñoz, M.
Muñoz, S. José María Arguedas y el mito
de la salvación por la cultura.
  J. Higgins, 86(BHS):Jan82-86
Munro, A. The Moons of Jupiter.
  B. De Mott, 441:20Mar83-1
  A. Hollinghurst, 617(TLS):6May83-457
  J. Mellors, 362:9Jun83-26
  S. Solecki, 99:Oct82-24
Munro, D. Alexandre Dumas père.*
  F. Bassan, 446(NCFS):Fall-Winter82/83-
  193
Munro, D.J. The Concept of Man in Contem-
porary China.
  S.B. Young, 485(PE&W):Oct82-453
Munroe, J.A. Colonial Delaware.
  F. Shuffelton, 173(ECS):Summer83-415
Munsche, P.B. Gentlemen and Poachers.*
  J. Cannon, 83:Autumn82-252
Munsey, B., ed. Moral Development, Moral
Education, and Kohlberg.
  T.M.R., 185:Oct82-207
Munslow, B. Mozambique.
  S. Uys, 617(TLS):16Sep83-983
Munzel, F. Karl Mays Erfolgsroman "Das
Waldröschen."
  R.A. Berman, 221(GQ):Nov82-601
Murakami Shigeyoshi. Japanese Religion in
the Modern Century.*
  P. Groner, 485(PE&W):Oct82-470
Muraro-Ganz, G. Frankreichs Weg zur Revol-
ution.
  M. Moog-Grünewald, 52:Band16Heft3-318
Murasaki, K. Karafuto ainugo — bumpōhen.
  A.F. Majewicz, 360(LP):Vol125-145
"Murasaki Shikibu: Her Diary and Poetic
Memoirs." (R. Bowring, trans)
  D. Mills, 617(TLS):9Dec83-1387
Murdoch, B.O. and M.G. Ward, eds. Studies
in Modern Austrian Literature.
  W.E. Yates, 402(MLR):Apr82-503
Murdoch, G.P. Theories of Illness.
  S.K. Ludwin, 529(QQ):Winter82-886
Murdoch, I. Nuns and Soldiers.*
  J. Sturrock, 648(WCR):Jun82-42
  P. Wolfe, 502(PrS):Summer82-92
Murdoch, I. The Philosopher's Pupil.
  P-L. Adams, 61:Aug83-100
  N. Mosley, 362:28Apr83-19
  J.C. Oates, 441:17Jul83-1
  G. Strawson, 617(TLS):29Apr83-421
  J. Updike, 442(NY):14Nov83-197

Murdoch, J. and others. The English Minia-
ture.*
    D. Farr, 324:Jul83-485
    G. Reynolds, 39:Jun82-507
Murillo, J.C. - see under Cañas Murillo, J.
Murnane, G. The Plains.
    J. Tittensor, 381:Dec82-523
Murphey, R.T. Hume and Husserl.
    M. Kroy, 63:Dec82-385
Murphy, D. Eight Feet in the Andes.
    J. Hemming, 617(TLS):16Dec83-1393
Murphy, D. Full Tilt.
    L.D., 617(TLS):18Mar83-279
Murphy, J.E. and S.M. Let My People Know.
    W. Bloodworth, 651(WHR):Summer82-191
    G. Hobson, 649(WAL):Summer82-170
Murphy, J.F. The United Nations and the
Control of International Violence.
    G. Best, 617(TLS):30Sep83-1062
Murphy, J.J., ed. Renaissance Rhetoric.
    L.V.R., 568(SCN):Winter82-87
Murphy, J.K. Will N. Harben.
    T. Bonner, Jr., 392:Fall82-457
Murphy, S. The Complete Knowledge of
Sally Fry.
    H. Davies, 617(TLS):16Sep83-1002
Murra, J.V. and R. Adorno - see Poma de
Ayala, F.G.
Murray, D.J. and P.R. Viotti, eds. The
Defense Policies of Nations.
    639(VQR):Summer82-91
Murray, G.K. Tales o a Gamie.
    J.D. McClure, 571(ScLJ):Spring82-24
Murray, H.A. Endeavors in Psychology.
    (E.S. Shneidman, ed)
    J.W. Crowley, 432(NEQ):Sep82-469
Murray, I.H. D. Martyn Lloyd-Jones.
    J. Whale, 617(TLS):1Apr83-331
Murray, J., ed. Cultural Atlas of Africa.*
    S.L. Kasfir, 2(AfrA):May82-21
    D. McMaster, 69:Vol152No1-90
Murray, J. The Proustian Comedy.*
    P. Newman-Gordon, 399(MLJ):Spring82-89
Murray, J. and R. Fulford. The Beginning
of Vision.
    K. Kritzwiser, 73:Dec82/Jan/Feb83-58
Murray, L.A. The Vernacular Republic.*
    C. James, 453(NYRB):14Apr83-31
    M. Kinzie, 29:Jul/Aug83-33
Murray, O. Early Greece.
    A.R. Burn, 303(JoHS):Vol 102-263
Murray, R. Journey.*
    M.T. Lane, 198:Oct82-94
Murrin, M. The Allegorical Epic.*
    J.M. Steadman, 551(RenQ):Autumn81-445
    B. Vickers, 401(MLQ):Sep82-291
    S. Woods, 301(JEGP):Oct82-557
Murry, J.M. The Letters of John Middleton
Murry. (C.A. Hankin, ed)
    S. Spender, 362:14Jul83-26
Murry, J.M. The Letters of John Middleton
Murry to Katherine Mansfield. (C.A. Han-
kin, ed)
    H. Bevington, 441:13Nov83-9
    C. Tomalin, 453(NYRB):24Nov83-38
    442(NY):14Nov83-208
Murtagh, K.O. Ariosto and the Classical
Simile.
    V. Tripodi, 345(KRQ):Vol129No4-435
Murtaugh, D.M. "Piers Plowman" and the
Image of God.*
    D.M.E. Gillam, 179(ES):Aug82-363
    H. White, 382(MAE):1982/1-119

Mus, P. L'Angle de l'Asie. (S. Thion, ed)
    D.P. Chandler, 293(JASt):Aug82-886
Muscarella, O.W. Ladders to Heaven.
    W.N., 102(CanL):Spring82-160
Muschamp, H. Man About Town.
    J.S., 231:Dec83-75
Muschg, A. The Blue Man.
    J. Mellors, 362:9Jun83-26
    M. Swales, 617(TLS):14Oct83-1143
"Museo del Prado: Inventarios Reales."
(Vol 2)
    T. Crombie, 39:Sep82-199
Musgrave, S. The Charcoal Burners.
    B. Godard, 198:Apr82-90
Musgrave, S. Tarts and Muggers.
    K. Irie, 526:Autumn82-84
    P. Monk, 150(DR):Spring82-167
Mushabac, J. Melville's Humor.
    C.L. Karcher, 395(MFS):Winter82/83-660
    R. Lehan, 445(NCF):Jun82-126
    27(AL):Oct82-469
Musheno, E.J. Sewing Big.
    P. Bach, 614:Summer83-22
"The Music Forum." (Vol 5) (F. Salzer, ed)
    J. Dunsby, 410(M&L):Jan/Apr82-107
"Music Survey." (new ser, 1949-1952) (D.
Mitchell and H. Keller, eds)
    S. Sadie, 415:Feb82-111
    A. Whittall, 410(M&L):Jul/Oct82-288
"Musica Asiatica." (Vol 2) (L.E.R. Picken,
ed)
    P. Row, 187:Sep83-560
"Musica Asiatica."* (Vol 3) (L.E.R.
Picken, ed) [shown in prev under ed]
    B.C. Wade, 293(JASt):Aug82-808
Musil, J. Urbanization in Socialist
Countries.*
    F.W. Carter, 575(SEER):Apr82-304
    L.A. Kosiñski, 104(CASS):Summer82-314
    R.A. Lewis, 550(RusR):Jan82-86
Musionus Rufus - see under Rufus
Muske, C. Skylight.
    S. Santos, 651(WHR):Spring82-45
Musmeci, A. L'Impossibile ritorno.
    B. Lawton, 395(MFS):Summer82-338
Müssener, H., ed. Nicht nur Strindberg.
    H. Uecker, 52:Band16Heft3-291
Musso, O. - see Euripides
Muthesius, S. The English Terraced House.*
    N. Annan, 453(NYRB):3Mar83-16
    J. Brandon-Jones, 324:Oct83-702
    F. Sheppard, 617(TLS):25Feb83-194
Mutsu Munemitsu. Kenkenroku.
    J.K. Fairbank, 453(NYRB):14Apr83-16
    L. Grove, 407(MN):Winter82-536
Muxin, A.M. Sintaksemnyj analiz i prob-
lema urovnej jazyka.
    M. Peckler, 660(Word):Aug81-160
Muyskens, J.A. and others. Rendez-vous.
    J.M. Goldman, 207(FR):May83-968
Muzzio, D. Watergate Games.
    N.R.M., 185:Jul83-835
Myachina, E.N. Languages of Asia and
Africa. (Vol 1)
    U. Gusa, 399(MLJ):Winter82-452
Mycue, E. The Singing Man My Father Gave
Me.
    J. Saunders, 565:Vol23No1-73
Mydans, S. The Vermilion Bridge.
    639(VQR):Winter82-20
Myerhoff, B. Number Our Days.
    E. Wachs, 292(JAF):Apr-Jun82-233

Neubauer, J. Novalis.*
  R. Immerwahr, 564:May82-147
  R. Leroy, 133:Band15Heft4-372
  E. Stopp, 402(MLR):Jan82-235
Neubauer, J. Symbolismus und symbolische
  Logik.*
  D.E. Wellbery, 406:Fall82-342
Neubuhr, E., ed. Geschichtsdrama.
  L. Sharpe, 402(MLR):Oct82-993
Neuer, G. and others. Deutsch aktiv 2.
  S.E. Lindenau, 399(MLJ):Autumn82-340
Neuman, F. Maneuvers.
  E. Hunter, 441:9Oct83-14
Neuman, S.C. Gertrude Stein.*
  M. Perloff, 677(YES):Vol 12-336
  E. Waterston, 106:Fall82-193
Neumann, A. Eine Auswahl aus seinem Werk.
  (G. Stern, ed)
  D. Sevin, 133:Band15Heft3-284
Neumann, B., ed. Johann Christian Edel-
  mann.
  W. Müller, 406:Summer82-207
Neumann, E. Creative Man.
  R. Davies, 529(QQ):Autumn82-471
Neumann, F. Ornamentation in Baroque and
  Post-Baroque Music.*
  P. Williams, 410(M&L):Jan/Apr82-96
Neumann, W. Bach-Dokumente. (Vol 4:
  Bilddokumente zur Lebensgeschichte
  Johann Sebastian Bachs.)
  S. Daw, 415:Jul82-477
  S. Daw, 415:Oct82-693
  R. Lam, 410(M&L):Jul/Oct81-412
Neumes, G. Religiosität, Agnostizismus,
  Objektivität.
  H. Emeis, 535(RHL):Sep-Dec82-956
Neuschäfer, H-J. Der Naturalismus in der
  Romania.*
  G. Hainsworth, 208(FS):Jul82-352
Neuschäfer, H-J. Populärromane im 19 Jahr-
  hundert von Dumas bis Zola.
  P.J. Whyte, 208(FS):Jan82-89
Neuse, E.K. Die deutsche Kurzgeschichte.
  A. Corkhill, 133:Band15Heft1/2-189
  J.H. Petersen, 680(ZDP):Band101Heft4-
  617
Neusner, J. Stranger at Home.
  R. Feldman, 287:Jun/Jul82-25
  T. Ziolkowski, 569(SR):Fall82-592
Neuss, P., ed. The Creacion of the World.
  T. Tiller, 617(TLS):21Oct83-1150
Neuss, P. - see Skelton, J.
Neustadt, B.C. Speaking of the USA. (2nd
  ed)
  D.N. Flemming, 399(MLJ):Spring82-78
Neustadt, R.E. and H.V. Fineberg. The
  Epidemic That Never Was.
  P. Engel, 441:27Mar83-16
Neusüss, A. Marximismus.
  W. Schmied-Kowarzik, 53(AGP):Band64
  Heft3-342
Neville, G.H. A Memoir of D.H. Lawrence.*
  (C. Baron, ed)
  J. Meyers, 395(MFS):Winter82/83-638
Neville, R.C. Reconstruction of Thinking.
  R.H., 543:Jun82-889
Nevo, R. Comic Transformations in Shakes-
  peare.
  M. Charney, 570(SQ):Winter82-542
  A. Leggatt, 301(JEGP):Oct82-562
  K. Smidt, 179(ES):Oct82-465
  L. Tennenhouse, 551(RenQ):Winter82-663

New, W.H., ed. A Political Art.*
  E.J. Hinz, 178:Jun82-227
"The New Testament in Scots." (W.L. Lori-
  mer, trans)
  G. Bruce, 617(TLS):23Dec83-1422
Newbolt, H. Selected Poems.
  J. Saunders, 565:Vol23No3-73
Newby, P.H. Feelings Have Changed.*
  P. Lewis, 565:Vol23No2-44
Newby, P.H. Saladin in His Time.
  P. Mansfield, 362:8Dec83-35
Newby, P.H. The Warrior Pharaohs.
  E.L. Bleiberg, 529(QQ):Winter82-879
Newcomb, A. The Madrigal at Ferrara, 1579-
  1597.*
  D. Arnold, 410(M&L):Jul/Oct81-440
  I. Fenlon, 317:Spring82-167
  L.L. Perkins, 551(RenQ):Spring81-93
Newcomb, H. and R.S. Alley. The Pro-
  ducer's Medium.
  B. Shulgasser, 441:9Oct83-18
Newcomb, K. and F. Schaefer. The Ghosts
  of Elkhorn.
  C.L. Rawlins, 649(WAL):Nov82-273
Newell, N.P. and R.S. The Struggle for
  Afghanistan.
  A.S. Ahmed, 293(JASt):Nov81-73
  P. Stuchen, 529(QQ):Winter82-850
Newey, V. Cowper's Poetry.
  G. Lindop, 617(TLS):2Dec83-1352
Newlin, D. Schoenberg Remembered.*
  J. Dunsby, 410(M&L):Jul/Oct81-402
Newman, F. The Hard-Boiled Virgin.
  M.F., 189(EA):Jul-Sep82-371
Newman, J. Foundations of Religious
  Tolerance.
  D.S., 185:Jul83-824
Newman, J.H. The Letters and Diaries of
  John Henry Newman.* (Vol 4) (I. Ker
  and T. Gornall, eds)
  D.J. De Laura, 402(MLR):Jan82-179
  A.G. Hill, 541(RES):Aug82-350
Newman, J.H. A Packet of Letters. (J.
  Sugg, ed)
  P. Kemp, 362:10Mar83-25
  I. Ker, 617(TLS):1Apr83-331
Newman, P. and others, eds. Modern Hausa-
  English Dictionary.* (2nd ed)
  K. Legère, 682(ZPSK):Band35Heft3-354
Newman, P.C. The Establishment Man.
  T. Traves, 99:Feb83-32
Newman, S.J. Dickens at Play.*
  G.H. Ford, 445(NCF):Sep82-214
  M. Moseley, 569(SR):Winter82-83
Newman, S.M. Arthur Dove and Duncan Phil-
  lips.
  A. Berman, 55:May82-29
Newmark, L., P. Hubbard and P. Prifti.
  Standard Albanian.
  B.D. Joseph, 350:Dec83-931
Newmeyer, F.J. Linguistic Theory in Amer-
  ica.*
  J. Fought, 355(LSoc):Aug82-317
  C. Platzack, 603:Vol6No2-285
  H.C. Wekker, 179(ES):Dec82-574
Newmyer, S.T. The "Silvae" of Statius.*
  F.M. Ahl, 487:Spring82-92
Newsome, D. On the Edge of Paradise.
  O. Chadwick, 366:Autumn82-266
  D.E. Nord, 506(PSt):Sep82-265
  295(JML):Dec82-410
Newton, R.P. Leaves of Quest.*
  A.D. Moody, 402(MLR):Jan82-192

Newton, S.H. Fashion in the Age of the Black Prince.*
J.A. Meisel, 589:Apr82-398
Newton-De Molina, D., ed. The Literary Criticism of T.S. Eliot.
T. Pinkney, 366:Autumn82-248
Newton-Smith, W.H. The Rationality of Science.*
C. Chauvire and A. Lewis-Loubignac, 98: Nov82-922
M.A.K., 185:Oct82-200
Newton-Smith, W.H. The Structure of Time.*
D.H. Mellor, 518:Apr82-65
G. Nerlich, 479(PhQ):Jul82-283
A. Smith, 63:Dec82-371
Ney, J.W. Semantic Structures for the Syntax of Complements and Auxiliaries in English.
G.T. Stump, 350:Dec83-923
Neyt, A. Gapping.
J.G. Kooij, 350:Mar83-196
Niatum, D. Songs for the Harvester of Dreams.*
L.L. Lee, 649(WAL):Spring82-69
Nichol, J.W. Sainte-Marie Among the Hurons.
M. Fraser, 102(CanL):Winter81-139
Nicholas of Lynn. The "Kalendarium" of Nicholas of Lynn.* (S. Eisner, ed; G. MacEoin and S. Eisner, trans)
J.C. Eade, 382(MAE):1982/2-251
M.A. Manzalaoui, 589:Jul82-646
Nicholas, H.G., ed. Washington Despatches 1941-1945.*
639(VQR):Winter82-23
Nicholl, C. The Chemical Theatre.
A. Demaitre, 577(SHR):Fall82-355
F.D. Hoeniger, 570(SQ):Summer82-248
Nichols, B. Ideology and the Image.*
B. Testa, 99:Jun/Jul82-28
Nichols, F.J., ed and trans. An Anthology of Neo-Latin Poetry.*
L. Forster, 447(N&Q):Dec81-530
H. Kelliher, 402(MLR):Oct82-910
Nichols, J. The Nirvana Blues.
L.Z. Bloom, 649(WAL):Winter83-372
Nichols, J.R. Art and Irony.
S.F.D. Hughes, 395(MFS):Winter82/83-738
Nicholson, H.B. and A. Cordy-Collins. Pre-Columbian Art from the Land Collection. (L.K. Land, ed)
E.P. Benson, 37:Mar-Apr82-55
Nicholson, N. Sea to the West.*
T. Eagleton, 565:Vol23No2-62
P. Gardner, 493:Dec81-46
B. Ruddick, 148:Summer82-53
Nicholson, T.R. The Birth of the British Motor Car 1769-1897.
H. Perkin, 617(TLS):28Jan83-89
Ní Chuilleanáin, E. The Second Voyage.
J. Parini, 569(SR):Fall82-623
Nickel, R. Xenophon.
R.W., 555:Vol55fasc1-159
Nickles, T., ed. Scientific Discovery: Case Studies.
M. Tamny, 393(Mind):Jul82-468
Nickles, T., ed. Scientific Discovery, Logic, and Rationality.*
A. Lugg, 486:Mar82-138
M. Tamny, 393(Mind):Jul82-468

Nicol, D.M. Church and Society in the Last Centuries of Byzantium.
M.J. Angold, 303(JoHS):Vol 102-297
Nicolaisen, J. Italian Opera in Transition, 1871-1893.
J. Budden, 410(M&L):Jul/Oct82-284
Nicolaisen, P. Ernest Hemingway.
H.G. Heymann, 573(SSF):Spring82-185
Nicolas, J. The Complete Cookbook of American Fish and Shellfish.
W. and C. Cowen, 639(VQR):Spring82-67
Nicolet, C. L'Idée républicaine en France.
N. Hampson, 617(TLS):8Apr83-362
Nicoll, A. The Garrick Stage.* (S. Rosenfeld, ed)
B.S. Hammond, 541(RES):Aug82-333
I. Mackintosh, 611(TN):Vol36No1-44
M. Perrin, 189(EA):Jan-Mar82-87
S. Wells, 157:Autumn82-45
C. Worth, 67:May82-77
Nicolson, A. Long Walks in France.
442(NY):3Oct83-131
Nicolson, N. and J. Trautmann - see Woolf, V.
Nicosia, G. Memory Babe.
M. Dickstein, 441:3Jul83-4
H. Williams, 617(TLS):2Dec83-1342
Nida, E.A. Exploring Semantic Structures.
G.F. Meier, 682(ZPSK):Band35Heft2-225
Nidditch, P.H. - see Locke, J.
Niebaum, H. Westfälisch.*
U. Scheuermann, 685(ZDL):3/1981-390
Niederauer, D.J. Pierre Louÿs.
L. Kamm, 207(FR):May83-948
Niehues-Pröbsting, H. Der Kynismus des Diogenes und der Begriff des Zynismus.
K. von Fritz, 52:Band16Heft2-182
Nielsen, H.F. Old English and the Continental Germanic Languages.
R.H. Bremmer, Jr., 179(ES):Dec82-565
Nielsen, K. and S.C. Patten, eds. Marx and Morality.
F. Cunningham, 99:Jun/Jul82-32
A.P.S., 185:Apr83-638
Nielson, C.R. Communication Games for English as a Second Language.
J.M. Hendrickson, 399(MLJ):Summer82-225
Nienhauser, W.H., Jr. P'i Jih-hsiu.
A.D. Syrokomla-Stefanowska, 293(JASt):Feb82-336
Niesz, A.J. Dramaturgy in German Drama.
B. Bennett, 221(GQ):Nov82-581
Nieto, J.C. Mystic, Rebel and Saint.* Juan de Valdés y los orígenes de la Reforma en España e Italia.
F. Márquez-Villanueva, 551(RenQ):Spring81-117
Nietzke, A. Windowlight.
V. Trueblood, 271:Spring82-132
te Nijenhuis, E. Musicological Literature.* (Vol 6, Pt 3) (J. Gonda, ed)
P. Row, 187:May83-386
Nijinska, B. Early Memoirs.* (I. Nijinska and J. Rawlinson, eds and trans)
R. Buckle, 31(ASch):Summer82-446
de Nijs, E.B. Faded Portraits.
H. van Neck-Yoder, 268(IFR):Summer83-154
Nikiforovskaya, N.A. Bibliograficheskoe opisanie v Rossi: ocherk istorii do serediny XIX v.
354:Dec82-473

Niles, B. Pragmatische Interpretationen
zu den Spruchtönen Walthers von der
Vogelweide.
  G. Objartel, 680(ZDP):Band101Heft1-138
Nilsen, H.N. Hart Crane's Divided Vision.
  J. Guiguet, 189(EA):Apr-Jun82-233
Nims, J.F. The Kiss.
  W. Harmon, 472:Spring/Summer83-129
  639(VQR):Autumn82-133
Nims, J.F. Sappho to Valéry.
  D.S. Carne-Ross, 31(ASch):Winter81/82-
  132
  A. Kerrigan, 569(SR):Spring82-318
Nin, A. Under a Glass Bell.
  P. Craig, 617(TLS):18Nov83-1294
Niobey, G., with others. Nouveau diction-
naire analogique.
  G. Gorcy, 209(FM):Oct82-350
Nisbet, R. The History of the Idea of Pro-
gress.*
  C.P., 189(EA):Oct-Dec82-494
  A.L. Stinchcombe, 185:Oct82-114
Nisbet, R. Prejudices.*
  D.J. Enright, 617(TLS):4Mar83-209
  I. Hacking, 453(NYRB):17Feb83-17
Nisbet, R.G.M. and M. Hubbard. A Commen-
tary on Horace: "Odes," Book II.*
  J.A. Richmond, 123:Vol32No2-159
Nishitani, K. Religion and Nothingness.
  J.N. Gray, 617(TLS):23Sep83-1023
Nissim, L. Storia di un tema simbolista.
  A. Pizzorusso, 535(RHL):Sep-Dec82-937
Nitta, Y. and H. Tatematsu, eds. Japa-
nese Phenomenology.
  B.J. Jones, 323:Jan82-96
Nitti, J.J. - see Fernández de Heredia, J.
Niven, A. D.H. Lawrence: The Writer and
His Work.*
  B. Caplan, 219(GaR):Spring82-194
Niven, J. Martin Van Buren.
  442(NY):29Aug83-92
Niven, R. Nigerian Kaleidoscope.
  D. Bates, 617(TLS):15Apr83-386
  G.E. Mercer, 324:Jul83-487
Niver, J. "Earth."
  B. Duchatelet, 535(RHL):Mar-Apr82-320
Nivison, D.S., P.J. Ivanhoe and M. Waters,
eds. A Concordance to Chu Hsi: "Ta
Hsüeh Chang Chü." A Concordance to Chu
Hsi: "Chung Yung Chang Chü."
  D.K. Gardner, 293(JASt):Feb82-337
Nixon, H.M. British Bookbindings pre-
sented by Kenneth H. Oldaker to the
Chapter Library of Westminster Abbey.
  M. Foot, 617(TLS):4Feb83-119
Nixon, R. Leaders.*
  K.S. Lynn, 617(TLS):25Mar83-287
Nizami, K.A. Supplement to Elliot and
Dowson's "History of India." (Vols 2
and 3)
  K.S. Lal, 273(IC):Apr82-165
Noble, A. - see Muir, E.
Noble, B. and G. Rollans. Alberta/The Bad-
lands.
  529(QQ):Autumn82-687
Noble, P. - see Nompar de Caumont
Noce, H.S. - see Martello, P.J.
Nogee, J.L. and R.H. Donaldson. Soviet
Foreign Policy since World War II.
  W.C. Clemens, Jr., 550(RusR):Apr82-229
Noggle, B. Working With History.
  T.E. Mills, 14:Summer82-334

Noguez, D., ed. Cinéma. (2nd ed)
  C.P. James, 207(FR):Feb83-517
Noguez, D. Ouverture des veines et autres
distractions.
  F. de Mèredieu, 450(NRF):Nov82-117
Noiray, J. La Romancier et la machine.
(Vol 1)
  B. Nelson, 208(FS):Oct82-487
Nöjd, T. Richard Hodges's "The English
Primrose" (1644).*
  N.E. Osselton, 179(ES):Apr82-170
  B. Sundby, 597(SN):Vol54No1-195
Nolan, W.F. Hammett.
  T.J. Binyon, 617(TLS):16Dec83-1394
  J. Symons, 441:8May83-7
Noll, G. Die Herkunft des St. Galler Klos-
terplanes.
  F. Bucher, 576:May82-156
Nolte, E. Marxism, Fascism, Cold War.
  J. Gray, 617(TLS):30Dec83-1459
Nompar de Caumont. Le Voyatge d'Oultremer
en Jherusalem de Nompar, seigneur de
Caumont. (P. Noble, ed)
  M.R. Morgan, 382(MAE):1982/1-123
Nonnus. Nonnos de Panopolis, "Les Diony-
siaques." (Vol 1 ed and trans by F.
Vian; Vol 2 ed and trans by P. Chuvin)
  A.H.M. Kessels, 394:Vol135fasc3/4-393
Nonweiler, B. That Other Realm of Freedom.
  S. Pickles, 617(TLS):28Oct83-1185
"Nonya Ware and Kitchen Ch'ing."
  B. Harrisson, 463:Summer82-180
  E.H. Moore, 60:Jul-Aug82-134
Noonan, H.W. Objects and Identity.*
  T. Baldwin, 483:Apr82-269
  L.F. Stevenson, 518:Jan82-1
Noone, J.B., Jr. Rousseau's Social
Contract.
  J.N. Shklar, 185:Jan83-405
Norberg, D. - see Paulinus of Aquileia
Norberg-Schulz, C. Meaning in Western
Architecture.
  A. Whittick, 89(BJA):Winter82-91
Nordal, S., ed. Völuspá.
  H. Beck, 196:Band23Heft1/2-141
Nordheider, H.W. Chorlieder des Euripides
in ihrer dramatischen Funktion.
  D. Bain, 123:Vol32No1-91
"Nordic Classicism 1910-1930."
  A. Saint, 617(TLS):25Mar83-306
Nordlinger, E.A. On the Autonomy of the
Democratic State.
  K.E.S., 185:Oct82-204
Norfleet, B.P. - see Steinmetz, J.
Norman, G. Midnight Water.
  442(NY):5Sep83-112
Norman, P. ... In the Way of Understanding.
  N. Roberts, 617(TLS):21Jan83-71
Norman, R. and S. Sayers. Hegel, Marx and
Dialectic.*
  W.V. Doniela, 63:Mar82-86
  M.G., 543:Jun82-892
Norrick, N.R. Semiotic Principles in
Semantic Theory.
  J.S. Duncan, 350:Sep83-686
Norrington, A.L.P. Blackwell's 1879-1979.
  A. Bell, 617(TLS):9Dec83-1379
Norris, C., ed. Shostakovich.*
  P. Griffiths, 415:Oct82-693
  S. Johnson, 607:Jun83-31
Norris, K. Autokinesis.
  D. Barbour, 648(WCR):Oct82-37
  P. Monk, 102(CanL):Winter81-171

Norris, K. The Book of Fall.*
D. Barbour, 648(WCR):Oct82-37
Norris, K. The Middle of the World.
E.C. Lynskey, 50(ArQ):Autumn82-278
639(VQR):Summer82-93
Norris, K. Report on the Second Half of
the Twentieth Century. The Perfect
Accident.
P. Monk, 102(CanL):Winter81-171
Norris, R.A., ed. Essays in Philosophy of
Art Education.
G.A. Mittler, 289:Spring82-121
Norris, R.A. History of Art Education.
G.A. Mittler, 289:Spring82-123
Norrman, R. The Insecure World of Henry
James's Fiction.
P. Kemp, 617(TLS):23Sep83-1025
Norrman, R. Techniques of Ambiguity in
the Fiction of Henry James.*
H-J. Lang, 72:Band218Heft1-183
Norstedt, J.A. Thomas MacDonagh.*
J.C. Beckett, 677(YES):Vol 12-337
North, E. Ancient Enemies.*
L. Jones, 364:Dec82/Jan83-136
North, H.F. From Myth to Icon.*
C.J. Classen, 123:Vol132No2-204
North, L. Bitter Grounds.
J.M. Kirk, 150(DR):Summer82-343
North, R. Of Building. (H. Colvin and J.
Newman, eds)
T. Connor, 90:Apr82-249
D. Thomson, 59:Mar82-129
Northcott, B., ed. The Music of Alexander
Goehr.
P.J.P., 412:May81-153
Northrup, D. Trade Without Rulers.
P. Richards, 69:Vol51No1-544
Nortier, M., ed. Recueil des actes de
Philippe Auguste, roi de France. (Vol 1)
J.W. Baldwin, 589:Apr82-400
Norton, L. The Sun King and his Loves.
B. Fothergill, 617(TLS):29Apr83-437
J. Rae, 362:3Mar83-23
Norton, M.B. Liberty's Daughters.
R.A. Gross, 656(WMQ):Jan82-231
E.I. Nybakken, 173(ECS):Summer83-445
Norton-Smith, J., ed. Bodleian Library MS.
Fairfax 16.
P. Gradon, 541(RES):Aug82-308
Norwid, C. Cyprian Norwid: Vade-mecum.
(R. Fieguth, ed and trans)
J. Łuczak-Wild, 688(ZSP):Band43Heft1-
213
Notker der Deutsche. Martianus Capella.*
(J.C. King, ed)
H.D. Schlosser, 133:Band15Heft1/2-147
M.W. Wierschin, 221(GQ):Jan82-110
Nottingham, P. The Technique of Bobbin
Lace.
P. Bach, 614:Spring83-23
Nourissier, F. L'Empire des nuages.
A. Clerval, 450(NRF):Jan82-114
"Nouveau Larousse des débutants."
J-M. Klinkenberg, 209(FM):Oct82-382
"Nouvelles recherches sur 'Bouvard et
Pécuchet' de Flaubert."
A. Compagnon, 208(FS):Jul82-345
Nova, C. The Good Son.*
J. Crace, 617(TLS):4Feb83-104
Novak, B. Nature and Culture.*
A. Davis, 106:Spring82-109

Novak, M. Confession of a Catholic.
J.M. Cameron, 453(NYRB):22Dec83-38
R. Gilman, 441:17Jul83-6
Novak, M. Moral Clarity in the Nuclear
Age.
J.M. Cameron, 453(NYRB):22Dec83-38
Novak, M. The Spirit of Democratic Capi-
talism.*
D. Martin, 617(TLS):2Dec83-1341
Novak, M.E. and G.R. Guffey - see Dryden,
J.
Novalis. Werke in einem Band.
B. Ajac, 98:Nov82-915
Novarr, D. The Disinterred Muse.*
T-L. Pebworth, 529(QQ):Winter82-899
R. Selden, 191(ELN):Sep82-38
J.M. Shami, 568(SCN):Spring-Summer82-
12
Nove, A. The Economics of Feasible Social-
ism.
G. Kennedy, 617(TLS):21Oct83-1154
Novo Villaverde, Y. Vicente Aleixandre:
Poeta surrealista.*
A. Byrum, 238:Sep82-466
Nowak, J. Courier From Warsaw.*
M. Malia, 453(NYRB):29Sep83-18
Nowak, L. The Structure of Idealisation.
A.T. Callinicos, 84:Mar82-97
Nowak, R.M. and J.L. Paradiso. Walker's
Mammals of the World. (4th ed)
M. Levine, 441:11Dec83-36
Nowakowski, M. The Canary and Other Tales
of Martial Law.
T. Garton Ash, 617(TLS):7Oct83-1096
Nowlan, A. I might not tell everybody
this.
A. Morton, 526:Autumn82-72
P. O'Flaherty, 99:Jun/Jul82-37
Nozick, R. Philosophical Explanations.*
P. Foot, 473(PR):4/1982-609
M. Lilla, 31(ASch):Summer82-426
A. Stark, 42(AR):Spring82-204
T.E. Wilkerson, 518:Oct82-222
Nsanze, A. Un domaine royal au Burundi:
Mbuye (env. 1850-1945).
A.A. Trouwborst, 69:Vol51No4-893
Nsekela, A.J., ed. Southern Africa.
B. Munslow, 69:Vol52No4-91
Nuchelmans, G. Late-Scholastic and
Humanist Theories of the Proposition.
S.L. Read, 518:Jan82-16
Nüesch, H-R., ed. Altwaldensische Bibelü-
bersetzung (Ms. 8 der Bibl. Munic. de
Carpentras). (Pts 1 and 2)
G. Roques, 553(RLiR):Jul-Dec81-507
Nuessel, F.H., Jr. Linguistic Approaches
to the Romance Lexicon.
R. de Gorog, 545(RPh):Nov81-389
Nündel, E. Kurt Schwitters in Selbstzeug-
nissen und Bilddokumenten.
I.M. Goessl, 221(GQ):Nov82-607
Nunes, R.A.D. História de educação no
Renascimento.
L. Demaitre, 589:Oct82-972
Núñez, J.P. - see under Paredes Núñez, J.
Núñez Cedeño, R.A. La fonología moderna y
el español de Santo Domingo.*
F.H. Nuessel, Jr., 353:Vol 19No11/12-
1185
Núñez Rodríguez, M. Arquitectura prerro-
mánica.
V. Jorge, 48:Jul-Sep82-320

Nunley, J. and H. Schaal. Reflections of African Artistry.
J. Cannizzo, 2(AfrA):Feb82-8
Nurse, D. Description of Sample Bantu Languages of Tanzania.
S. Brauner, 682(ZPSK):Band34Heft6-763
Nussbaum, M.C. - see Aristotle
Nute, D. Topics in Conditional Logic.
G.M. Hardegree, 316:Sep82-713
G. Hunter, 393(Mind):Jan82-136
Nuttall, A.D. Overheard by God.
L. Gent, 175:Spring82-59
V.R. Mollenkott, 301(JEGP):Jul82-418
Nwezeh, E.C. Africa in French and German Fiction, 1911-1933.*
M.E. Musgrave, 406:Summer82-223
Nyberg, D., ed. Giovanni Battista Piranesi. Piranesi Drawings and Etchings at the Avery Architectural Library Columbia University, New York.
R. Middleton, 576:Dec82-333
Nyberg, D. Power over Power.
T.M.R., 185:Apr83-647
Nye, R. The Facts of Life and Other Fictions.
D. Montrose, 617(TLS):17Jun83-622
Nye, W.S. Bad Medicine and Good.
A.O. Wiget, 292(JAF):Oct-Dec82-477
Nyíri, J.C., ed. Austrian Philosophy.
B.J. Jones, 323:May82-199

Oakes, J. The Ruling Race.*
639(VQR):Autumn82-126
Oakes, P. At the Jazz Band Ball.
D.A.N. Jones, 362:8Dec83-34
V. Scannell, 617(TLS):30Dec83-1463
Oakes, P. Selected Poems.
N. Corcoran, 617(TLS):27May83-549
Oakeshott, M. On History and Other Essays.
J.G.A. Pocock, 617(TLS):21Oct83-1155
Oakeshott, W. The Two Winchester Bibles.*
W. Gardner, 324:Dec82-61
S. Heslop, 59:Mar82-124
Oates, J.C. Angel of Light.*
J. Farnsworth, 526:Spring82-83
C. Gerson, 648(WCR):Spring82-61
J.L. Halio, 598(SoR):Winter83-203
Oates, J.C. A Bloodsmoor Romance.*
A. Mars-Jones, 617(TLS):28Jan83-79
Oates, J.C. Contraries.*
G. Woodcock, 569(SR):Summer82-466
Oates, J.C. Invisible Woman.
W. Harmon, 472:Spring/Summer83-129
G.E. Murray, 385(MQR):Fall83-643
Oates, J.C. A Sentimental Education.*
S. Pinsker, 573(SSF):Winter82-94
639(VQR):Winter82-19
Oates, S.B. Let the Trumpet Sound.*
M. Frady, 453(NYRB):27Oct83-79
Ó Baoill, C., ed. Eachann Bacach and other Maclean Poets.
S.P. Bayard, 568(SCN):Fall82-40
Ober, W.S. Boswell's Clap and Other Essays.*
S. Soupel, 189(EA):Apr-Jun82-196
Oberg, A. Anna's Song.*
J. Saunders, 565:Vol23No1-73
Oberhammer, G., ed. Offenbarung, geistige Realität des Menschen.
A. Wezler, 259(IIJ):Apr82-142

Oberhammer, G. Strukturen yogischer Meditation.*
D.S. Ruegg, 259(IIJ):Jan82-57
Oberhammer, G., ed. Transzendenzerfahrung.
J.W. de Jong, 259(IIJ):Apr80-154
Oberhuber, K. Raffaello.
J. Pope-Hennessy, 453(NYRB):22Dec83-44
Obermayer, A., ed. Festschrift for E.W. Herd.*
H. Böschenstein, 564:Nov81-312
Oberski, J. Childhood.
G.A. De Candido, 441:20Nov83-18
Obolensky, A.P. and N. Natov, eds. Transactions of the Association of Russian-American Scholars in the U.S.A. (Vol 14)
R.B. Anderson, 104(CASS):Fall-Winter82-523
O'Brien, C.J.H. Moll Among the Critics.
A.J. Hassall, 67:May82-76
O'Brien, D. Theories of Weight in the Ancient World. (Vol 1)
É. des Places, 555:Vol56fasc2-330
O'Brien, K.C. A Gift Horse.
J. Kilroy, 569(SR):Winter82-89
O'Brien, P., ed. Railways and the Economic Development of Western Europe 1830-1914.
S. Pollard, 617(TLS):5Aug83-828
O'Brien, S. The Indoor Park.
T. Dooley, 617(TLS):19Aug83-886
O'Brien, T. Going After Cacciato.*
T.C. Herzog, 145(Crit):Vol24No2-88
M.W. Raymond, 145(Crit):Vol24No2-97
O'Brien, W.V. The Conduct of Just and Limited War.
G. Best, 617(TLS):14Jan83-33
Ó Broin, L. No Man's Man.
C. Davidson, 617(TLS):9Sep83-971
O'Casey, S. The Essential O'Casey. (J. Mitchell, ed)
R.H., 305(JIL):Sep82-116
"O'Casey Annual No. 1." (R.G. Lowery, ed)
J.S. Bratton, 617(TLS):14Jan83-38
Ochotina, N.V., ed. Problemy fonetiki, morfologii i sintaksisa afrikanskich jazykov.
K. Huth, 682(ZPSK):Band34Heft6-764
Ochs, E. and B. Schieffelin, eds. Developmental Pragmatics.*
C.E. Snow, 355(LSoc):Dec82-455
Ochsner, J.K. H.H. Richardson: Complete Architectural Works.
C. Jencks, 617(TLS):16Sep83-985
Ockham, William of. Expositio super Libros elenchorum Aristotelis. (F. del Punta, ed)
T.M. Tomasic, 589:Jan82-203
Ockham, William of. Guillelmi de Ockham Quodlibeta Septem. (J.C. Wey, ed)
R.J. Long, 589:Jan82-181
A.H.W., 543:Oct01 147
O'Connell, D., ed. The Instructions of Saint Louis.
A. Foulet, 545(RPh):Feb82-569
L.D. Wolfgang, 207(FR):Apr83-762
O'Connell, D.P. The International Law of the Sea. (Vol 1) (I.A. Shearer, ed)
D.W. Bowett, 617(TLS):25Nov83-1304
O'Connor, C. The Judas Cry.
T.F. Merrill, 305(JIL):Sep82-3
O'Connor, F. Collected Stories.
R.F. Peterson, 573(SSF):Fall82-399
639(VQR):Spring82-53

"The Old Testament in Syriac According to
the Peshitta Version." (Pt 2, fasc 4)
J.C. Greenfield, 318(JAOS):Oct-Dec81-
442
Olden, M. Giri.
N. Callendar, 441:13Feb83-31
Oldenbourg, Z. Le Procès du rêve.*
J. Blot, 450(NRF):Jun82-113
Oldham, J. Selected Poems. (K. Robinson,
ed)
P.E. Hewison, 447(N&Q):Dec81-543
Oldroyd, D.R. Darwinian Impacts.
A. Olding, 84:Sep82-315
Olds, S. Satan Says.*
R. Jackson, 502(PrS):Spring82-91
W. Logan, 472:Spring/Summer83-211
Oldsey, B., ed. Ernest Hemingway.
R.P. Weeks, 395(MFS):Summer82-295
Oldsey, B. Hemingway's Hidden Craft.*
J. Griffin, 106:Fall82-253
Oldsey, B. - see "Dictionary of Literary
Biography"
O'Leary, P. Regency Editor.
J. Gross, 617(TLS):26Aug83-899
Olesch, R. - see Statorius, P.
Olin, J.C. Six Essays on Erasmus and a
Translation of Erasmus' Letter to Caron-
dolet, 1523.
J.D. Tracy, 551(RenQ):Spring82-90
de Oliva, F.P. - see under Pérez de Oliva,
F.
Oliver, A. The Property of a Lady.
N. Callendar, 441:30Oct83-31
M. Johnson, 617(TLS):1Apr83-324
Oliver, H. Flaubert and an English Gover-
ness.*
B.F. Bart, 535(RHL):Sep-Dec82-933
A. Fairlie, 208(FS):Apr82-213
Oliver, H. The International Anarchist
Movement in Late Victorian London.
J. Joll, 617(TLS):9Sep83-962
Oliver, H.J. - see Shakespeare, W.
Oliver, M. American Primitive.
B. Bennett, 441:17Jul83-10
Oliver, M.B. To a Sister Loneliness.
D. Barbour, 648(WCR):Summer81-80
Oliver, R. Entries.
R.L. Barth, 152(UDQ):Summer82-137
J. Finlay, 598(SoR):Winter83-178
Oliver, R. Bertram Grosvenor Goodhue.
P. Goldberger, 441:11Dec83-13
A.L. Huxtable, 453(NYRB):22Dec83-55
Oliver, R., ed. The Making of an Archi-
tect — 1881-1891.
C. Wilk, 505:Sep82-276
Oliver, R. To Be Plain.
J. Finlay, 598(SoR):Winter83-178
Oliver, R.W. Dreams of Passion.
P. Macnaughton, 214:Vol 10No38-119
Olivier, C. Les enfants de Jocaste.
D. Die, 542:Jan-Mar82-91
Olivier, L. Confessions of an Actor.*
442(NY):7Feb83-122
Ollé, F.G. - see under González Ollé, F.
Oller, J.W., Jr. and K. Perkins. Research
in Language Testing.
J.D. Brown, 355(LSoc):Aug82-325
Olleson, E., ed. Modern Musical Scholar-
ship.
K. von Fischer, 410(M&L):Jul/Oct81-432

Olmsted, F.L. The Papers of Frederick Law
Olmsted. (Vol 2) (C.E. Beveridge and
C.C. McLaughlin, with D. Schuyler, eds)
G. Davenport, 249(HudR):Spring82-123
W.K. Scarborough, 396(ModA):Summer/
Fall82-443
Olmsted, J.C. George Meredith.
R.F. Giles, 365:Winter83-24
Olney, J. Entertainments.
W. and C. Cowen, 639(VQR):Spring82-64
Olney, J. The Rhizome and the Flower.*
J.L. Allen, 577(SHR):Winter82-86
R. Davies, 529(QQ):Autumn82-471
Olney, J.B., ed. Autobiography.*
D. Barnouw, 221(GQ):Jan82-134
M. Gidley, 366:Spring82-115
C. Lang, 153:Winter82-2
Olney, J.B. Metaphors of Self.
C. Lang, 153:Winter82-2
O'Loughlin, M. Stalingrad: the Street
Dictionary.
T.F. Merrill, 305(JIL):Sep82-3
Olsen, D.J. Town Planning in London: The
Eighteenth and Nineteenth Centuries.
(2nd ed)
D. Bowen, 324:Jun83-416
Olsen, M. and G. Kelstrup, eds. Vaerk og
laeser.
A. Linneberg, 172(Edda):1982/2-122
Olson, A.M., ed. Myth, Symbol, and
Reality.
V. Cobb-Stevens, 258:Jun82-216
Olson, A.M. Transcendence and Hermeneu-
tics.
B.J. Jones, 323:Oct82-309
Olson, C. Maximus Poems.
H. Kenner, 231:Sep83-68
Olson, G. Literature as Recreation in the
Later Middle Ages.
J.A. Burrow, 617(TLS):27May83-537
Olson, M. The Rise and Decline of
Nations.*
A. Cairncross, 617(TLS):11Mar83-229
L.C. Thurow, 453(NYRB):3Mar83-9
Olson, T. Seaview.
R. De Feo, 441:19Jun83-13
Olsson, M. Intelligibility.*
S. Johansson, 597(SN):Vol154No2-321
Olszer, K.M., ed. For Your Freedom and
Ours. (2nd ed)
G.J. Lerski, 497(PolR):Vol27No1/2-164
Olszewski, E.J., with J. Glaubinger. The
Draftsman's Eye.
E.A. Carroll, 551(RenQ):Winter82-628
Olza Zubiri, J. and M.A. Jusayu. Gramá-
tica de la lengua Guajira.
G.F. Meier, 682(ZPSK):Band34Heft2-255
Omaggio, A.C. Helping Learners Succeed.
A. Papalia, 399(MLJ):Autumn82-320
O'Malley, J. - see Marx, K.
O'Malley, J.W. Praise and Blame in Renais-
sance Rome.*
J. Monfasani, 551(RenQ):Summer81-229
Oman, C.C. and J. Hamilton. Wallpapers.
C. Gere, 39:Nov82-352
O'Meally, R.G. The Craft of Ralph Elli-
son.*
K. Byerman, 395(MFS):Summer82-303
N. Harris, 459:Spring81-106
H. Jarrett, 27(AL):Dec82-620
O'Meara, D. Volkskapitalisme.
D. Welsh, 617(TLS):16Sep83-981

O'Meara, D.J., ed. Neoplatonism and Christian Thought.
C. Evangeliou, 319:Oct83-566
Ondaatje, M. Running in the Family.*
C. Reid, 617(TLS):29Jul83-811
O'Neal, H. Berenice Abbott.
J. Stokes, 617(TLS):22Apr83-401
O'Neil, L.T. Māyā in Śaṅkara.
W. Indich, 485(PE&W):Oct82-471
F. Staal, 293(JASt):Feb82-269
O'Neill, D. Sir Edwin Lutyens: Country Houses.
W.C. Miller, 505:Jul82-108
O'Neill, E. Eugene O'Neill at Work.*
(V. Floyd, ed)
J.H. Raleigh, 397(MD):Dec82-581
R.E. Spiller, 27(AL):Oct82-454
O'Neill, E. Eugene O'Neill: Poems, 1912-1944.* (D. Gallup, ed)
J. Saunders, 565:Vol23No1-73
O'Neill, E. The Theatre We Worked For.
(J.R. Bryer, ed)
J.Y. Miller, 27(AL):Dec82-622
O'Neill, F. The French Radical Party and European Integration.
D.T. Stephens, 207(FR):Dec82-364
O'Neill, J. Essaying Montaigne.*
C. Clark, 208(FS):Oct82-463
O'Neill, P. German Literature in English Translation.
R. Foot, 627(UTQ):Summer82-487
H.J. Schmidt, 399(MLJ):Autumn82-340
O'Neill, R., E.T. Cornelius, Jr. and G.N. Washburn. American Kernel Lessons: Advanced.
N.R. Tumposky, 608:Sep83-481
O'Neill, W.L. A Better World.
A. Brinkley, 441:9Jan83-7
442(NY):7Feb83-122
Onetti, J.C. Les Bas-Fonds du rêve.
F. Delay, 450(NRF):Mar82-147
Ong, W.J. Fighting for Life.
R.B. Miller, 377:Jul82-118
Ong, W.J. Orality and Literacy.
Z. Leader, 617(TLS):29Jul83-801
P. Lippert, 186(ETC.):Winter82-399
Ōno Susumu. Nihongo to tamirugo.
R.A. Miller, 350:Mar83-207
van Onselen, C. Studies in the Social and Economic History of the Witwatersrand 1886-1914.
R. Oliver, 617(TLS):25Feb83-191
Ontañón de Lope, P. Estudios sobre Gabriel Miró.
J. Matas, 240(HR):Spring82-233
Opie, I. and P. A Nursery Companion.
S. Pickering, 569(SR):Spring82-300
Opie, I. and P., eds. The Oxford Book of Narrative Verse.
A. Brownjohn, 617(TLS):23Dec83-1423
Opitz, M. Gesammelte Werke.* (Vol 2, Pt 2) (G. Schulz-Behrend, ed)
U. Maché, 222(GR):Spring82-84
U. Maché, 301(JEGP):Jan82-84
Opitz, P.J. and G. Sebba, eds. The Philosophy of Order.
T. Langan, 319:Jul83-424
Opland, J. Anglo-Saxon Oral Poetry.
D.G. Calder, 589:Apr82-401
J.J. Campbell, 301(JEGP):Apr82-249
D.K. Fry, 191(ELN):Sep81-53
S.B. Greenfield, 131(CL):Winter82-67
J. Turville-Petre, 382(MAE):1982/2-237

Oppel, H. Die Suche nach Irlands Vergangenheit und einer anglo-irischen Dichtersprache in Seamus Heaneys "North."
H. Kosok, 72:Band218Heft1-192
Oppenheim, F.E. Political Concepts.*
W.L.M., 543:Jun82-893
Oppenheim, L. Intentionality and Intersubjectivity.*
K. Aspley, 402(MLR):Jul82-734
A.C. Pugh, 208(FS):Jan82-101
F. Rechsteiner, 400(MLN):May82-1027
L.S. Roudiez, 546(RR):Mar82-271
Oppenheimer, R. Robert Oppenheimer: Letters and Recollections. (A.K. Smith and C. Weiner, eds)
B.W. Sargent, 529(QQ):Spring82-174
O'Prey, P. - see Graves, R.
Oquelí, R. - see del Valle, J.C.
Orasanu, J., M.K. Slater and L.L. Adler, eds. Language, Sex and Gender.
S. McConnell-Ginet, 350:Jun83-373
Orayen, R., ed. Ensayos Actuales sobre Adam Smith y David Hume.
J.P. Monteiro, 319:Apr82-205
"Ord til andet."
C. Henriksen, 563(SS):Winter82-75
Orduna, G. - see López de Ayala, P.
O'Regan, M. The Mannerist Aesthetic.*
A. Viala, 535(RHL):Sep-Dec82-893
Oreja, M.Á.C. - see under Castillo Oreja, M.Á.
Orenstein, F. Murder on Madison Avenue.
N. Callendar, 441:8May83-27
Oriano, M. Les Travailleurs de la frontière.
R.A. Day, 189(EA):Jul-Sep82-365
Oriard, M.V. Dreaming of Heroes.
W.J. Palmer, 395(MFS):Winter82/83-689
Origen. Origène, "Sur la Pâque." (O. Guéraud and P. Nautin, eds)
J. Irigoin, 555:Vol55fasc1-164
Orjuela, H.H. Los hijos de la salamandra.
M. Coddou, 238:Dec82-664
Orjuela, H.H. Imagen de los Estados Unidos en la poesía de Hispanoamérica.
R.G. Mead, Jr., 238:Dec82-661
Orjuela, H.H. Poesía de la América indígena.
C.E. Mace, 238:May82-311
Orlandello, J. O'Neill on Film.
J. Beaver, 200:Oct82-507
Orlando, F. Toward a Freudian Theory of Literature.*
C. Gordon, 208(FS):Jan82-110
K. Newman, 494:Spring82-173
R. Racevskis, 125:Spring82-309
Orledge, R. Debussy and the Theatre.
R.L. Smith, 617(TLS):28Jan83-88
Orledge, R. Gabriel Fauré.
R. Nichols, 410(M&L):Jan81-83
Orlova, A. Musorgsky's Days and Works.
(R.J. Guenther, ed and trans)
G. Abraham, 617(TLS):16Dec83-1405
Orlović-Schwarzwald, M. Zum Gastarbeiterdeutsch jugoslawischer Arbeiter im Rhein-Main-Gebiet.
R. Müller, 685(ZDL):2/1982-268
Orlovsky, D.T. The Limits of Reform.*
W.E. Mosse, 575(SEER):Apr82-291
Orme, N. The Minor Clergy of Exeter Cathedral 1300-1548.
D.E. Greenway, 325:Apr82-37

Ormond, R., with J. Rishel and R. Hamlyn. Sir Edwin Landseer.*
  G. Reynolds, 39:Aug82-122
Ormsby, F., ed. Poets from the North of Ireland.*
  S. Fauchereau, 98:Jun-Jul82-628
Orr, G. The Red House.*
  J. Schiff, 584(SWR):Winter82-105
Orr, J. Tragic Realism and Modern Society.*
  S. Delany, 599:Winter82-82
Orr, L., ed. De-Structing the Novel.
  M. Rapisarda, 395(MFS):Winter82/83-725
Orr, R.G. Religion in China.
  G. Pasti, Jr., 293(JASt):May82-584
Orrell, J. Fallen Empires.
  V. Keller, 108:Fall82-126
Orrell, J. The Quest for Shakespeare's Globe.
  S. Wells, 617(TLS):2Sep83-935
Orringer, N.R. Ortega y sus fuentes germánicas.*
  A. Donoso, 258:Jun82-203
  J. Herrero, 240(HR):Summer82-363
Orso, E.G. Modern Greek Humor.*
  E. Oring, 650(WF):Jan82-62
Ortalli, G. ... pingatur in Palatio ...
  H. Belting, 683:Band45Heft4-423
Ortega, M.H.S. - see under Sánchez Ortega, M.H.
Ortega Galindo, L. - see Inés de la Cruz, J.
Ortega y Gasset, J. Estudios sobre el amor. (rev)
  J.L. Gómez-Martínez, 552(REH):Oct82-467
Ortiz, A., ed. Handbook of North American Indians.* (Vol 9)
  B.L. Fontana, 50(ArQ):Spring82-81
Ortony, A., ed. Metaphor and Thought.*
  T.S. Champlin, 518:Apr82-111
Orwell, G. La Fille du Clergyman; Et Vive l'Aspidistra; Le Journal d'un Anglais moyen.
  J. Queval, 450(NRF):Apr82-138
Orwell, G. The Penguin Complete Longer Non-Fiction of George Orwell.
  J.C., 617(TLS):23Dec83-1443
Ory, P. Nizan.
  W.D. Redfern, 402(MLR):Apr82-462
Osborn, R. - see Wordsworth, W.
Osborne, C. The Life and Crimes of Agatha Christie.*
  R. Baxter, 364:Dec82/Jan83-143
Osborne, C. The World Theatre of Wagner.
  M. Tanner, 617(TLS):11Mar83-243
Osborne, H., ed. The Oxford Companion to 20th-Century Art.*
  G.A. Cevasco, 324:Jan83-107
  L.A. Reid, 89(BJA):Summer82-271
Osborne, M. Before Kampuchea.
  M. Ebihara, 293(JASt):Nov81-63
Osborne, M.L. Genuine Risk.
  S. Sherwin, 529(QQ):Summer82-444
Osburn, C.B. Research and Reference Guide to French Studies. (2nd ed)
  O. Klapp, 547(RF):Band94Heft2/3-261
  J.S. Patty, 207(FR):Apr83-759
Osgood, C.E. Lectures on Language Performance.*
  H.S. Cairns, 660(Word):Dec81-242

O'Shaughnessy, B. The Will.
  F. Jackson, 262:Jun82-255
  A.B. Levison, 185:Jul83-808
  H. Noonan, 483:Jan82-140
  J.W. Roxbee Cox, 518:Jul82-168
Oshinsky, D.M. A Conspiracy So Immense.
  R. Sherrill, 441:5Jun83-11
  442(NY):22Aug83-95
Osinga, J. Frankrijk, Vergennes en de Amerikaanse Onafhankelijkheid, 1776-1783.
  J.C. Riley, 656(WMQ):Apr82-385
Osley, A.S., ed and trans. Scribes and Sources.*
  N. Barker, 78(BC):Winter82-513
Ossar, M. Anarchism in the Dramas of Ernst Toller.*
  N. Ritter, 406:Fall82-369
Ossola, C. and A. Prosperi, eds. La Corte e il "Cortegiano."
  J. Tylus, 400(MLN):Jan82-208
Ost, H. Tizians Kasseler Kavalier.
  C. Hornig, 471:Oct/Nov/Dec82-359
Ostberg, K. The Old High German "Isidor" in its Relationship to the Extant Manuscripts (Eighth to Twelfth Century) of Isidorus' "De fide Catholica."*
  P.W. Tax, 133:Band15Heft1/2-149
Oster, D. Monsieur Valéry.
  A. Boyman, 546(RR):Nov82-526
Ostertag, H. Der Philosophische Gehalt der Wolff-Manteuffelschen Briefwechsel.
  J. Ecole, 192(EP):Jul-Sep81-344
Østerud, E. Det borgerlige subjekt.
  F. Paul, 172(Edda):1982/5-311
Ostiguy, J-R. Charles Huot.
  D.W. Rozniatowski, 529(QQ):Summer82-405
Östör, A. The Play of the Gods.
  L.A. Babb, 293(JASt):Nov81-183
Östör, Á., L. Fruzzetti and S. Barnett, eds. Concepts of Person.
  C.J. Fuller, 617(TLS):8Jul83-735
Ostriker, A. A Dream of Springtime.* The Mother/Child Papers.*
  V. Trueblood, 271:Spring82-132
Ostriker, A. A Woman Under the Surface.
  X.J. Kennedy, 491:Mar83-349
  I. Salusinszky, 617(TLS):9Dec83-1384
Ostyn, P. and F. Melka-Teichroew. La France vous parle.
  R.E. Heidemann, 399(MLJ):Summer82-207
O'Sullivan, J.N. A Lexicon to Achilles Tatius.
  F. Vian, 555:Vol55fasc2-348
O'Sullivan, M. Twenty Years A-Growing.
  L.D., 617(TLS):22Apr83-415
O'Sullivan, V. - see Mansfield, K.
Oszlak, O. La Formación del estado argentino.
  D. Rock, 617(TLS):23Dec83-1433
Otis, B. Cosmos and Tragedy. (E.C. Kopff, ed)
  P.G. Mason, 123:Vol132No2-270
  639(VQR):Spring82-57
O'Toole, J.M. Guide to the Archives of the Archdiocese of Boston.
  V.N. Bellamy, 14:Fall82-482
O'Toole, L.M. and A. Shukman, eds. Film Theory and General Semiotics. (Vol 8)
  R. Durgnat, 89(BJA):Summer82-270

Ott, K.A.   Der Rosenroman.
  F.J. Hassauer-Roos, 196:Band23Heft3/4-
  336
Ott, K.A. - see Guillaume de Lorris and
  Jean de Meun
Ott-Meimberg, M.   Kreuzzugsepos oder
  Staatsroman?
  D.H. Green, 382(MAE):1982/2-272
  D.P. Sudermann, 589:Jul82-648
Otten, R.M.   Joseph Addison.
  A. Furtwangler, 566:Spring83-133
Otten, T.   After Innocence.
  R.L. McCarron, 590:Jun83-47
Ottmann, H.   Individuum und Gemeinschaft
  bei Hegel. (Vol 1)
  K. Hartmann, 53(AGP):Band64Heft2-208
  D. Rodin, 489(PJGG):Band89Heft2-426
Otto, C.F.   Space into Light.
  W. Müller, 576:Mar82-63
O'Tuairisc, E.   Sidelines.
  T.F. Merrill, 305(JIL):Sep82-3
Ó Tuama, S., ed.   An Duanaire, An Irish
  Anthology, 1600-1900.*
  J. Dunn, 174(Éire):Fall82-116
Oudot, S. and R. Hunt.   French Today.
  A.S. Caprio, 207(FR):Feb83-528
Ouellet, F.   Economic and Social History
  of Québec, 1760-1850.
  G.W., 102(CanL):Autumn82-167
Ouellette, F.   En la nuit, la mer, poèmes
  1972-1980.
  C.F. Coates, 207(FR):Apr83-790
Oukada, L.   Louisiana French.*
  M.F., 189(EA):Jan-Mar82-115
"Our Nig." (H.L. Gates, Jr., ed)
  442(NY):20Jun83-101
Outhwaite, W.   Concept Formation in Social
  Science.
  Z. Bauman, 617(TLS):29Apr83-441
Ouvrard, H.   La Noyante.
  M. Cagnon, 207(FR):Feb83-515
Overholt, K.D.   Contemporary Puerto Rico
  as Seen Through Actual Interviews.
  J.A. Castañeda, 399(MLJ):Summer82-232
  B.P. Flam, 238:Mar82-153
Overy, P.   Paul Neagu.
  R. Demarco, 592:Vol 195No995-95
Ovid.   The Erotic Poems. (P. Green, trans)
  R. Wells, 617(TLS):14Oct83-1120
Ovid.   P. Ovid Nasonis: "Remedia Amoris."
  (A.A.R. Henderson, ed)
  L.M. Styler, 447(N&Q):Aug81-327
Ovid.   P. Ovidii Nasonis "Metamorphoses."
  (W.S. Anderson, ed)
  R.J. Tarrant, 122:Oct82-342
Owen, S.   Nursery Rhymes for the Dead.
  H. Silver, 598(SoR):Winter83-229
Owen, T.C.   Capitalism and Politics in
  Russia.
  A.J. Rieber, 104(CASS):Fall-Winter82-
  546
  R.A. Roosa, 550(RusR):Apr82-204
Owens, J.   St. Thomas Aquinas on the
  Existence of God. (J.R. Catan, ed)
  P.V. Spade, 154:Dec82-772
  S.L. Weber, 518:Oct82-205
Owens, J.   Aristotle.* (J.R. Catan, ed)
  R.G. Turnbull, 487:Winter82-366
Ownbey, R.W., ed.   Jack London.
  J. Tavernier-Courbin, 106:Winter82-363
Owsley, F.L., Jr.   Struggle for the Gulf
  Borderlands.
  M.J. McDaniel, 9(AlaR):Jan82-52

Oxenham, J.   Literacy.
  H.A., 189(EA):Jul-Sep82-369
"Oxford American Dictionary."* (E. Ehr-
  lich and others, eds)
  G.J. Forgue, 189(EA):Oct-Dec82-444
"The Oxford-Duden Pictorial English-Japa-
  nese Dictionary."
  J. McMullen, 617(TLS):30Dec83-1467
"Oxford Latin Dictionary." (fasc 7)
  (P.G.W. Glare, ed)
  J. André, 555:Vol55fasc2-367
"Oxford Latin Dictionary." [complete]
  (P.G.W. Glare, ed)
  D.J.R. Bruckner, 441:9Oct83-12
"Oxford Slavonic Papers." (new ser, Vol
  13) (J.L.I. Fennell, I.P. Foote and A.E.
  Pennington, eds)
  R.J. Parrott, Jr., 558(RLJ):Winter-
  Spring82-315
"Oxford Slavonic Papers." (new ser, Vol
  14) (J.L.I. Fennell, A.E. Pennington
  and I.P. Foote, eds)
  R.M. Davison, 402(MLR):Oct82-1002
Oz, A.   In the Land of Israel.
  I. Howe, 61:Dec83-106
  R. Rosenblatt, 441:6Nov83-1
Oz, A.   Where the Jackals Howl and Other
  Stories.
  D.P. Deneau, 573(SSF):Winter82-82
Ozanam, F.   Lettres de Frédéric Ozanam.
  (Vol 3) (D. Ozanam, with others, eds)
  J-R. Derré, 535(RHL):Mar-Apr82-309
Ozdoba, J.   Heuristik der Fiktion.*
  J. Proust, 547(RF):Band94Heft1-118
Ozer, J.S. - see "Film Review Annual, 1981"
Ozick, C.   Art and Ardor.
  K. Pollitt, 441:22May83-7
Ozick, C.   The Cannibal Galaxy.
  A. Alvarez, 453(NYRB):10Nov83-26
  E. White, 441:11Sep83-3
Ozick, C.   Levitation.*
  S. Pinsker, 573(SSF):Spring82-177
Ozment, S.   The Age of Reform, 1250-1550.
  G. Strauss, 551(RenQ):Summer81-215
Ozouf, M.   La fête révolutionnaire 1789-
  1799.
  F. George, 98:May82-394

Paavolainen, J.   Väinö Tanner. (Vol 2)
  M. Rintala, 563(SS):Spring82-189
Pacchiani, C.   Spinoza tra teologia e
  politica.
  F. Volpi, 489(PJGG):Band89Heft2-438
Pace, C.   Félibien's Life of Poussin.
  R. Verdi, 90:Dec82-769
Pace, D.   Claude Lévi-Strauss.
  F.C.T. Moore, 617(TLS):4Nov83-1224
Pacey, P.   David Jones and other Wonder
  Voyagers.
  G. Jones, 617(TLS):8Apr83-349
Pachai, B.   Land and Politics in Malawi,
  1875-1975.
  J.A. Hellen, 69:Vol51No4-900
Saint Pachomius.   Pachomian Koinonia.
  (Vols 1 and 2) (A. Veilleux, trans)
  M.A. Schatkin, 589:Oct82-948
Pachter, H.   Weimar Etudes.
  G.A. Craig, 617(TLS):8Apr83-347
Paci, F.G.   The Italians.*
  R. Hatch, 296(JCF):No33-142

Pack, R. Waking to My Name.
D. Gioia, 491:May82-102
P. Mariani, 418(MR):Winter82-715
J. Saunders, 565:Vol23No1-73
Packard, V. Our Endangered Children.
E. Chesler, 441:28Aug83-12
Packe, M. King Edward III. (L.C.B. Seaman, ed)
G. Holmes, 617(TLS):27May83-551
D. Luscombe, 362:17Feb83-23
Packman, D. Vladimir Nabokov.
N. Tredell, 617(TLS):10Jun83-608
Paden, J.N., ed. Values, Identities, and National Integration.
D. Barker, 69:Vol152No4-100
Padilla, H. En Mi Jardín Pastan Los Héroes.
O. Rossardi, 37:May-Jun82-64
Padilla, H. Legacies: Selected Poems.*
J.M. Cohen, 453(NYRB):30Jun83-32
Padoan, G. Momenti del Rinascimento veneto.*
D. Aguzzi-Barbagli, 276:Winter82-342
Padover, S.K. - see Marx, K.
Páez Ríos, E. Repertorio de Grabados Españoles en la Biblioteca Nacional.
A.E. Pérez Sánchez, 48:Jul-Sep82-318
Pagden, A. The Fall of Natural Man.
H. Kamen, 617(TLS):7Jan83-9
Page, B.I. Who Gets What From Government.
H.L. Wilensky, 441:21Aug83-10
Page, D.L. Further Greek Epigrams. (rev and ed by R.D. Dawe and J. Diggle)
H. Lloyd-Jones, 123:Vol32No2-139
Page, J.A. Perón.
R. Cox, 453(NYRB):8Dec83-18
J. Kandell, 441:4Sep83-6
Page, J.E. Reflections on the Symons Report.
R. Sullivan, 529(QQ):Winter82-839
Page, L.G. and E. Wigginton, eds. Aunt Arie.
R.J. Margolis, 441:24Jul83-16
Page, N., ed. Dickens: "Hard Times," "Great Expectations" and "Our Mutual Friend."*
R. Mason, 447(N&Q):Dec81-562
Page, N., ed. Thomas Hardy.
R.K. Anderson, 395(MFS):Summer81-333
K. Brady, 637(VS):Spring82-390
R.P. Draper, 447(N&Q):Oct81-449
M. Millgate, 445(NCF):Jun82-119
Page, N., ed. D.H. Lawrence.
J. Voelker, 395(MFS):Summer82-270
Page, N., ed. Tennyson: Interviews and Recollections.
J. Bayley, 617(TLS):18Mar83-255
Page, P.K. Evening Dance of the Grey Flies.
F. Adcock, 617(TLS):18Mar83-278
A. Mandel, 99:May82-32
G. Woodcock, 461:Fall-Winter82/83-99
Page, R. The Education of a Gardener.
E. Perényi, 453(NYRB):14Apr83-13
Page, T. Tim Page's Nam.
P-L. Adams, 61:Apr83-132
Pagels, H.R. The Cosmic Code.*
D.J. Bohm, 617(TLS):29Jul83-796
42(AR):Summer82-371
Pagis, D. Points of Departure.
A. Alcalay, 472:Spring/Summer83-85
L. Elkin, 287:Oct82-25
A. Williamson, 441:1May83-15

Pagnini, M. Pragmatica della letteratura.
V. Kapp, 72:Band218Heft1-148
Paige, C. The Right to Lifers.
S. Bolotin, 441:27Nov83-15
Paige, K.E. and J.M. The Politics of Reproductive Ritual.*
P.R.S., 185:Jan83-436
Painter, G.D. Marcel Proust.
G.S., 617(TLS):24Jun83-683
"The Painterly Print."
K.F. Beall, 127:Summer82-179
Pais, A. "Subtle is the Lord ... "*
R. Peierls, 453(NYRB):28Apr83-21
B. Pippard, 617(TLS):1Apr83-315
Pakerys, A. Lietuvių bendrines kalbos fonetikos pratybos.
E. Bukevičiūtė, 682(ZPSK):Band34Heft2-264
de Palacio, J. William Godwin et son monde intérieur.
P. Marshall, 189(EA):Jul-Sep82-335
Palacios, M.A. - see under Asín Palacios, M.
Palakshappa, T.C. Tibetans in India.
L.S. Leshnik, 318(JAOS):Oct-Dec81-500
Princesse Palatine. Lettres (1672-1722).
J. Aeply, 450(NRF):Apr82-121
Palau i Fabre, J. Picasso: Life and Work of the Early Years, 1881-1907.
L. Cooke, 59:Sep82-338
G. Tinterow, 90:Sep82-562
Paley, M.D. William Blake.
K. Garlick, 39:Jun82-510
Palisca, C.V. Baroque Music. (2nd ed)
I. Spink, 410(M&L):Jul/Oct81-432
Palisca, C.V., ed. Hucbald, Guido, and John on Music.*
C.M. Bower, 317:Spring82-157
Palla, R. - see Prudentius
Pallares, B. - see de Cervantes Saavedra, M.
Palliser, D.M. The Age of Elizabeth.
C. Haigh, 617(TLS):9Sep83-966
Pallot, J. and D.J.B. Shaw. Planning in the Soviet Union.
P.G. Toumanoff, 550(RusR):Oct82-503
Palma, A. Le "Curae" pubbliche.
A. Chastagnol, 555:Vol156fasc1-176
Palmenfelt, U. Gotländska Folksägner.
R. Bjersby, 64(Arv):Vol36-212
Palmer, A.S., P.J.M. Groot and G.A. Trosper, eds. The Construct Validation of Tests of Communicative Competence.
E.K. Horwitz, 399(MLJ):Winter82-414
Palmer, B. "Man over Money."*
W. Flynt, 577(SHR):Summer82-272
Palmer, B.D. The Making of E.P. Thompson.
J. Clare, 627(UTQ):Summer82-437
N. Rogers, 99:Oct82-25
Palmer, F. Semantik.
G. Van der Elst, 685(ZDL):3/1981-376
Palmer, F.R. Modality and the English Modals.*
G. Bourquin, 189(EA):Apr-Jun82-201
L. Haegeman, 179(ES):Jun82-273
N-L. Johannesson, 447(N&Q):Aug81-326
T.J. Taylor, 541(RES):May82-191
Palmer, F.R. Semantics. (2nd ed)
M.A. Covington, 350:Mar83-227
Palmer, J.J.N., ed. Froissart, Historian.
A.H. Diverres, 208(FS):Oct82-458
Palmer, K. - see Shakespeare, W.

Parias, L-H., ed. Histoire générale de l'enseignement et de l'éducation en France.
 E. Weber, 617(TLS):4Mar83-219
Parini, J. Anthracite Country.*
 J.F. Cotter, 249(HudR):Autumn82-471
 L.L. Martz, 676(YR):Autumn82-63
Parini, J. Theodore Roethke.
 L. Surette, 106:Spring82-135
Paris, B.J. Character and Conflict in Jane Austen's Novels.*
 F.B. Pinion, 541(RES):Nov82-484
Paris, J. Lisible/Visible.
 G. Cesbron, 356(LR):May82-179
Parish, R. - see Abbé de Choisy and Abbé de Dangeau, with P. Jurieu
Park, D. The Image of Eternity.
 R. Healey, 482(PhR):Oct82-607
Park, E. Treasures of the Smithsonian.
 B. Dobell, 441:4Dec83-12
Park, M. Travels into the Interior of Africa.
 A.H.M.K-G., 617(TLS):18Nov83-1295
Park, R. - see Lamb, C.
Parker, D. The Making of French Absolutism.
 R. Mettam, 617(TLS):25Nov83-1326
Parker, D.H. The Principles of Aesthetics.
 C. Korsmeyer, 290(JAAC):Summer83-443
Parker, F. and S.J. Russia on Canvas: Ilya Repin.
 J.E. Bowlt, 574(SEEJ):Spring82-110
 M. Chamot, 39:Feb82-136
 T.T. Rice, 90:May82-311
Parker, H.T. Motion Arrested. (O. Holmes, ed)
 A. Kisselgoff, 441:15May83-14
Parker, K., ed. The South African Novel in English.
 P. Quartermaine, 447(N&Q):Oct81-480
Parker, P.A. Inescapable Romance.*
 R.R. Wilson, 107(CRCL):Jun82-264
Parker, R. - see Baldini, G.
Parker, R. and G. Pollock. Old Mistresses.*
 D. Cherry, 59:Dec82-501
Parker, R.A., J. Leclant and J-C. Goyon. The Edifice of Taharqa by the Sacred Lake of Karnak.
 K.A. Kitchen, 318(JAOS):Oct-Dec81-438
Parker, R.B. The Widening Gyre.
 N. Callendar, 441:1May83-27
 442(NY):9May83-136
Parker, T. The People of Providence.
 P. Whitehead, 362:15Sep83-21
 P. Willmott, 617(TLS):15Jul83-759
Parkin, D., ed. Semantic Anthropology.
 T.O. Beidelman, 617(TLS):8Jul83-735
Parkin, F. Marxism and Class Theory.*
 F. Block, 125:Winter82-195
Parkinson, N. Fifty Years of Style and Fashion.
 J. Maslin, 441:4Dec83-12
Parkman, F. France and England in North America. (D. Levin, ed)
 W.P. Taylor, 453(NYRB):13Oct83-35
 C.V. Woodward, 441:3Jul83-3
Parmalee, P.L. Brecht's America.
 R.J. Ley, 397(MD):Dec82-571
 S. Mews, 221(GQ):May82-455
Parmet, H.S. JFK.
 R.J. Margolis, 441:17Apr83-16

Parr, N. James Hogg at Home.
 D. Gifford, 571(ScLJ):Winter82-84
Parret, H., ed. History of Linguistic Thought and Contemporary Linguistics.
 P. Swiggers, 353:Vol 19No3/4-379
Parret, H. and J. Bouveresse, eds. Meaning and Understanding.
 P.A. Lee, 350:Jun83-465
Parret, H., M. Sbisà and J. Verschueren, eds. Possibilities and Limitations of Pragmatics.
 D.J. Napoli, 350:Jun83-464
Parrinder, P., ed. Science Fiction: A Critical Guide.
 F. Jameson, 561(SFS):Nov82-322
Parrinder, P. Science Fiction, Its Criticism and Teaching.*
 F. Jameson, 561(SFS):Nov82-322
 J-P. Vernier, 189(EA):Jul-Sep82-350
Parrinder, P. and R. Philmus - see Wells, H.G.
Parrini, P. Una Filosofia senza dogmi.
 J. Largeault, 542:Jan-Mar82-126
Parris, L. The Tate Gallery Constable Collection.*
 G. Reynolds, 39:May82-415
Parrish, F. Bait on the Hook.
 T.J. Binyon, 617(TLS):18Feb83-149
 M. Laski, 362:19May83-24
Parrish, R., ed. Coisy and Dangeau: Quatre Dialogues [suivi de] "L'Apologie" de Pierre Jurieu.
 P. Hourcade, 475:No16Pt2-409
Parrot, N. Mannequins.
 C. Fox, 617(TLS):24Jun83-668
Parsegian, V.L., ed. Armenian Architecture.
 T.F. Mathews, 576:Oct82-259
Parshall, L.B. The Art of Narration in Wolfram's "Parzival" and Albrecht's "Jüngerer Titurel."
 O. Sayce, 131(CL):Fall82-363
Parslow, J. - see Fisher, J.
Parsons, J. The Art Fever.
 L. Milazzo, 584(SWR):Autumn82-vi
Parsons, J., ed. Erik Bergman.
 R. Layton, 607:Sep82-54
Parsons, L.A. Pre-Columbian Art.
 J.C. Berlo, 2(AfrA):Nov81-83
Parsons, T. Nonexistent Objects.*
 J. Bigelow, 63:Mar82-94
 D.W., 543:Sep81-151
Partee, B.H. Fundamentals of Mathematics for Linguists.*
 J. Pogonowski, 360(LP):Vol25-131
Partlow, R., Jr. and H.T. Moore, eds. D.H. Lawrence.*
 L. Hamalian, 363(LitR):Spring83-451
Partner, P. The Murdered Magicians.*
 R.C. Smail, 453(NYRB):24Nov83-24
Partouche, M = see "Jean Pierre Faye"
Partridge, F. Memories.
 J.L. Mitchell, 77:Spring82-182
Partridge, L. and R. Starn. A Renaissance Likeness.*
 R. Hatfield, 551(RenQ):Winter81-584
van Parys, P. Evolutionary Explanation in the Social Sciences.
 L. Apostel, 540(RIPh):Vol36fasc4-672
Pascal, R. Kafka's Narrators.
 K.J. Fickert, 268(IFR):Summer83-159

275

Pascale, R.T. and A.G. Athos. The Art of
Japanese Management.
  P.H., 617(TLS):23Sep83-1031
Pascall, R., ed. Brahms.
  E. Sams, 617(TLS):17Jun83-637
Pasche, W. Skandinavische Dramatik in
Deutschland.*
  V. Greene-Gantzberg, 301(JEGP):Jan82-
  99
  H. Uecker, 52:Band16Heft3-291
Pascoli, L. Vite de'pittori, scultori ed
architetti viventi. (V. Martinelli and
others, eds)
  C. and R. Enggass, 90:Dec82-771
Pascu, S. A History of Transylvania.
  D. Deletant, 617(TLS):29Jul83-818
Paskevska, A. Both Sides of the Mirror.
  M. Pierpont, 151:Apr82-88
Paskins, B. and M. Dockrill. The Ethics
of War.*
  C.A.J. Coady, 63:Sep82-309
Pasley, M. - see Kafka, F.
"Victor Pasmore, with a Catalogue Raisonné
of the Paintings, Constructions and
Graphics 1926-1929."*
  R. Alley, 592:Vol 195No991/992-98
Pasolini, P.P. Amado mio & Atti impuri.
  D. Robey, 617(TLS):7Jan83-23
Pasquali, G. Preistoria della poesia
romana.
  H.D. Jocelyn, 123:Vol32No2-151
Passage, C.E. Character Names in Dostoev-
sky's Fiction.
  G.R. Jahn, 395(MFS):Winter82/83-703
  N. Perlina, 550(RusR):Oct82-529
Passin, H. Encounter with Japan.
  R. Dore, 441:7Aug83-14
Pastan, L. PM/AM.
  S.M. Gilbert, 472:Spring/Summer83-147
  H. Seidman, 441:20Feb83-6
Pastan, L. Waiting for My Life.*
  S.M. Gilbert, 472:Spring/Summer83-147
  J.D. McClatchy, 491:Sep82-352
  639(VQR):Winter82-25
Pasternak, B. My Sister-Life [and] A Sub-
lime Malady. Selected Poems.
  D. McDuff, 617(TLS):1Jul83-703
Pasternak, B. Perepiska s Ol'goi Frieden-
berg. (E. Mossman, ed)
  O.R. Hughes, 550(RusR):Jan82-106
"Boris Pasternak, 1890-1960."*
  W.F. Kolonosky, 574(SEEJ):Winter82-485
Pasternak, L. The Memoirs of Leonid Pas-
ternak.*
  J. Bayley, 441:30Oct83-7
Pasteur, A.B. and I.L. Toldson. Roots of
Soul.*
  F. Akingbala, 529(QQ):Winter82-861
Pastor Poppe, R. Escritores bolivianos
contemporáneos.
  E. Font, 238:Mar82-148
Pastore, A. - see Flaminio, M.
Pastoureau, M. Traité d'héraldique.*
  G.J. Brault, 589:Oct82-921
Patai, R. The Messiah Texts.
  L. Orr, 390:Mar82-58
  S. Siporin, 292(JAF):Oct-Dec82-482
Pataki-Schweizer, K.J. A New Guinea Land-
scape.
  J.M. Street, 293(JASt):Aug82-887
Patañjali. The Yoga-Sūtra of Patañjali.
  (G. Feuerstein, ed and trans)
  A.T. de Nicolás, 485(PE&W):Jan82-113

"Patañjali's Vyākaraṇa-Mahābhāṣya, Anabhi-
hitāhnika (P.2.3.1-2.3.17)." (S.D.
Joshi and J.A.F. Roodbergen, eds)
  H. Scharfe, 260(IF):Band86-354
"Patañjali's Vyākaraṇa-Mahābhāṣya, Vib-
haktyāhnika (P. 2.3.18 - 2.3.45)." (S.D.
Joshi and J.A.F. Roodbergen, eds)
  J. Bronkhorst, 259(IIJ):Oct82-302
Pater, W. "The Renaissance:" the 1893
Text.* (D.L. Hill, ed)
  S. Bassett, 637(VS):Summer82-497
  J.B. Bullen, 301(JEGP):Jan82-141
  E.R. Hall, 148:Winter82-82
Patera, C. Cutwork Appliqué.
  M. Cowan, 614:Fall83-18
Paterson, A. The History of the Rose.
  C. Lloyd, 617(TLS):6May83-466
Paterson, A. The Law Lords.
  A.W.B. Simpson, 617(TLS):21Jan83-66
Patkar, M.M. History of Sanskrit Lexico-
graphy.
  M.M. Deshpande, 350:Dec83-933
Paton, A. Ah, But Your Land is Beautiful.*
  P. Lewis, 565:Vol23No2-44
  639(VQR):Summer82-98
Patrick, J. Architecture in Tennessee:
1768-1897.
  L. Knobel, 46:May82-74
Patrick, J.M. and R.H. Sundell, eds. Mil-
ton and the Art of Sacred Song.*
  I. Simon, 541(RES):Feb82-85
Patrides, C.A., ed. George Herbert: The
Critical Heritage.
  C.H. Sisson, 617(TLS):8Apr83-358
Patrides, C.A. Premises and Motifs in
Renaissance Thought and Literature.
  K. Duncan-Jones, 617(TLS):4Feb83-96
Patrides, C.A. and R.B. Waddington, eds.
The Age of Milton.*
  J.R. Mulder, 551(RenQ):Winter81-625
Patrie, J. The Genetic Relationship of
the Ainu Language.
  R.A. Miller, 350:Jun83-447
Patten, R.L. Charles Dickens and His Pub-
lishers.*
  D.A. Thomas, 594:Spring82-126
Pattenden, R. The Judge, Discretion, and
the Criminal Trial.
  A.W.B. Simpson, 617(TLS):24Jun83-659
Patterson, H. Class Conflict and Sectari-
anism.
  G. Eley, 385(MQR):Winter83-107
Patterson, M. The Revolution in German
Theatre, 1900-1933.
  M. Esslin, 157:Summer82-49
  J. Schlueter, 397(MD):Dec82-580
Patterson, M. Peter Stein.*
  I. Wardle, 157:Winter82-44
Patterson, N-L.G. Swiss-German and Dutch-
German Mennonite Traditional Art in the
Waterloo Region, Ontario.
  L. Doucette, 650(WF):Jul82-236
  S. Friesen, 292(JAF):Apr-Jun82-239
  J.D.A. Widdowson, 203:Vol193No1-125
Patterson, O. Slavery and Social Death.
  M. Banton, 617(TLS):9Sep83-947
  D.B. Davis, 453(NYRB):17Feb83-19
Pattison, R. The Child Figure in English
Literature.*
  G.A. Starr, 402(MLR):Apr82-415
Pattison, R. Tennyson and Tradition.*
  J.R. Reed, 125:Fall81-97

Patton, D.J. Industrial Development and
the Atlantic Fishery.
    R.E. Ommer, 150(DR):Summer82-330
Patwardhan, R.P. - see "Dadabhai Naoroji
Correspondance"
Paufler, H-D. Lateinamerikanisches Span-
isch.
    M. Perl, 682(ZPSK):Band34Heft4-492
Paul of Venice. Logica Magna. (Pt 1,
fasc 1 ed and trans by N. Kretzmann)
    K. Jacobi, 53(AGP):Band64Heft3-318
    P.V. Spade, 482(PhR):Apr82-275
    H. Weidemann, 489(PJGG):Band89Heft1-
    191
Paul of Venice. Logica Magna. (Pt 2,
fasc 6 ed by F. del Punta, trans by M.M.
Adams)
    K. Jacobi, 53(AGP):Band64Heft3-318
    H. Weidemann, 489(PJGG):Band89Heft1-
    191
Paul, A. Paracas Textiles.
    J. Povey, 2(AfrA):Nov81-85
Paul, C.B. Science and Immortality.*
    N.R. Gelbart, 173(ECS):Winter82/83-182
Paul, D.Y., with F. Wilson. Women in
Buddhism.*
    K.J. Lee, 485(PE&W):Apr82-222
    J.P. McDermott, 318(JAOS):Jul-Sep81-
    383
Paul, J. Modern Harpsichord Makers.
    H. Schott, 415:Apr82-261
Paul, S. The Lost America of Love.*
    G.F. Butterick, 659(ConL):Spring83-102
    F. Chappell, 579(SAQ):Autumn82-472
    J. Martin, 27(AL):Dec82-604
    295(JML):Dec82-358
Paulin, T. The Book of Juniper.*
    M. O'Neill, 493:Jun82-68
Paulin, T. Liberty Tree.
    M. O'Neill, 617(TLS):2Sep83-922
Paulin, T. The Strange Museum.*
    S. Fauchereau, 98:Jun-Jul82-628
Paulinus of Aquileia. L'oeuvre poétique
de Paulin d'Aquilée. (D. Norberg, ed)
    P. Meyvaert, 589:Apr82-404
Paulos, J.A. Mathematics and Humor.
    S.I. Bellman, 584(SWR):Spring82-233
Paulsen, W., ed. Österreichische Gegen-
wart.*
    R.E. Lorbe, 301(JEGP):Apr82-302
    W.E. Yates, 402(MLR):Apr82-503
Paulsen, W. - see Schirokauer, A.
Paulson, R. Literary Landscape.
    J. Barrell, 617(TLS):7Jan83-8
    R. Lister, 324:Aug83-571
    C.F. Stuckey, 55:Nov82-50
Paulson, R. Popular and Polite Art in the
Age of Hogarth and Fielding.*
    A.M. Duckworth, 173(ECS):Fall82-103
Paulson, R. Representations of Revolu-
tion (1789-1820).
    N. Hampson, 617(TLS):4Nov83-1225
    R. King, 344:Fall83-128
Paulston, C.B. Bilingual Education.*
    G.P. Orwen, 276:Autumn82-195
Pauly, T.H. An American Odyssey.
    S.S. Prawer, 617(TLS):12Aug83-854
Pausanias. Pausanias, "Graeciae descrip-
tio." (Vol 3, Bks 9 and 10) (M.H. Rocha-
Pereira, ed)
    R.W., 555:Vol56fasc2-333

Pausch, H.A., ed. Kommunikative Meta-
phorik.
    J. Villwock, 224(GRM):Band32Heft2-242
Pausch, O., ed. Germania Illuminata I.
    U. Müller, 680(ZDP):Band101Heft1-127
Pavlovski, R. Un autre oiseau dans un
autre temps.
    L. Kovacs, 450(NRF):Nov82-136
Pavlovsky, E. La mueca. El señor Galín-
dez. Telarañas. (G.O. Schanzer, ed)
    V.B. Levine, 238:Mar82-147
Pavón Maldonado, B. El arte hispano-
musulmán en su decoración floral.
    E. Arias Anglés, 48:Jan-Mar82-117
Pavone, M.A. Angelo Solimena.
    E. Waterhouse, 90:Jan82-44
Pawley, M. Building For Tomorrow.
    B. Bright, 441:23Jan83-13
Payen, J-C. Le Prince d'Aquitaine.*
    L.T.T., 382(MAE):1982/2-255
Payen, N.R. - see under Rousseau Payen, N.
Payne, A.J. Louisa May Alcott.*
    R. Asselineau, 189(EA):Jan-Mar82-113
Payne, D.R. The Scenographic Imagination.
    R. Stuart, 108:Winter82-116
Payne, F.A. Chaucer and Menippean Satire.*
    R.A. Shoaf, 589:Jul82-651
Payne, K., ed. Between Ourselves.
    J.H. Murray, 441:23Oct83-14
Payne, L. Black Novelists and the South-
ern Literary Tradition.
    W.L. Andrews, 27(AL):Mar82-137
    L. Budd, 579(SAQ):Summer82-358
    K. Byerman, 395(MFS):Summer82-303
    J.M. Reilly, 392:Fall82-449
Payne, S. and S. Murwin. Creative Ameri-
can Quilting Inspired by the Bible.
    M. Cowan, 614:Summer83-17
Payne, S.B., Jr. The Soviet Union and
SALT.*
    L. Goure, 550(RusR):Oct82-518
Paz, D.G. The Politics of Working-Class
Education in Britain, 1830-50.
    P. Gosden, 637(VS):Winter82-246
Paz, O. and C. Tomlinson. Airborn/Hijos
del Aire.*
    D. McDuff, 565:Vol23No1-59
Peace, A. Choice, Class and Conflict.
    J.S. Eades, 69:Vol151No3-801
Peace, R. The Enigma of Gogol.*
    G. Cox, 574(SEEJ):Winter82-477
    G.R. Jahn, 395(MFS):Winter82/83-703
Peale, G.C. - see Pérez de Oliva, F.
Pearce, G.F. The U.S. Navy in Pensacola.
    W.N. Still, Jr., 9(AlaR):Jan82-69
Pearce, J. Twelve Voices.
    W.J. Keith, 627(UTQ):Summer82-457
    L. McMullen, 102(CanL):Autumn82-151
Pearce, R., ed. Critical Essays on Thomas
Pynchon.
    R. Tölölyan, 434:Winter83-165
Pearce, T.M. - see Austin, M.
Pearson, C. and K. Pope. The Female Hero
in American and British Literature.
    J. Marcus, 395(MFS):Winter82/83-735
Pearson, J. Tragedy and Tragicomedy in
the Plays of John Webster.*
    D.L. Russell, 568(SCN):Spring-Summer82-
    5
Pearson, J.D. - see Matthews, N. and M.D.
Wainwright
Pearson, L. The Art of Demosthenes.
    W.N. Thompson, 583:Spring83-303

Peary, D. Cult Movies.
  J.P. Ward, 200:Apr82-253
Peary, G., ed. Little Caesar.
  J. Basinger, 18:Jul-Aug82-72
Pêcheux, M. Language, Semantics and
  Ideology. (French title: Les Véritiés
  de la Palice.)
  R. D'Amico, 504:No5-134
  G. Sampson, 617(TLS):30Sep83-1036
Pecheux, M.C. Milton: A Topographical
  Guide.
  R. Flannagan, 391:Mar82-20
  M.A. Mikolajczak, 568(SCN):Fall82-42
Peck, G.T. The Fool of God.*
  M. Davie, 382(MAE):1982/2-269
Peck, L.L. Northampton.
  J.A. Guy, 617(TLS):11Feb83-128
Peck, R.M. A Celebration of Birds.
  R. O'Hanlon, 617(TLS):16Sep83-998
Pécsi, K. The Future of Socialist Eco-
  nomic Integration. (P. Marer, ed)
  Z.M. Fallenbuehl, 104(CASS):Fall-
  Winter82-596
Pedicord, H.W. and F.L. Bergmann - see
  Garrick, D.
Pedley, J.G., ed. New Light on Ancient
  Carthage.
  H. Hurst, 123:Vol32No2-251
  L. Vann, 121(CJ):Dec82/Jan83-166
Pedretti, E. Stones.
  K. Crossley-Holland, 617(TLS):4Feb83-
  116
Pedrick, J. greenfellow.
  V. Trueblood, 271:Spring82-132
Peek, W. Attische Versinschriften.
  A.G. Woodhead, 303(JoHS):Vol 102-294
Peel, K.J. The Twelfth Night of Ramadan.
  T.J. Binyon, 617(TLS):23Dec83-1437
Peele, G. The Old Wives Tale. (P. Binnie,
  ed)
  T.W. Craik, 161(DUJ):Jun82-303
Peer, A.D. Studien zur Wortbildung in
  einer "klassischen" Transformationsgram-
  matik.
  P. Suchsland, 682(ZPSK):Band34Heft3-
  376
Peeters, B. La Bibliothèque de Villers.
  A. Calame, 450(NRF):Jan82-118
Pegg, B. Rites and Riots.
  J. Simpson, 203:Vol193No2-238
Péguy, C. and P. Marcel. Correspondance
  (1905-1914). (J. Sabiani, ed)
  R. Burac, 535(RHL):Sep-Dec82-952
Peinovich, M.P. Old English Noun Morphol-
  ogy.
  B.S. Phillips, 660(Word):Dec81-225
Peirce, C.S. The New Elements of Mathemat-
  ics. (Vols 3 and 4) (C. Eisele, ed)
  J. Zeman, 316:Sep82-705
Peithman, S. - see Poe, E.A.
Pekarik, A., ed. Ukifune.
  D. Mills, 617(TLS):9Dec83-1387
Pelenski, J., ed. The American and Euro-
  pean Revolutions, 1776-1848.
  M. Malia, 453(NYRB):29Sep83-18
"Pelete Bite: Kalabari Cut-Thread Cloth."
  R.L. Shep, 614:Summer83-21
Pelikan, J. The Christian Tradition.*
  (Vol 3)
  W.H. Principe, 589:Oct82-922
Pellegrino, E.D. and D.C. Thomasma. A
  Philosophical Basis of Medical Practice.
  D.T.O., 185:Oct82-219

Pelletier, A. - see Josephus
Pelletier, F.J., ed. Mass Terms.*
  E.S. Wheeler, 320(CJL):Spring82-95
Pelletier, J. and C. Adams. The Canadian
  Caper.
  P. Stuchen, 529(QQ):Summer82-417
Pelon, O. and others. Le palais de Malia.
  (Vol 5)
  S. Hood, 303(JoHS):Vol 102-277
Pelous, J-M. Amour précieux, amour galant
  (1654-1675).*
  N. Hepp, 535(RHL):Jan-Feb82-106
  I.W.F. Maclean, 402(MLR):Jan82-206
Pena, J. La derivación en español.
  C. Schmitt, 553(RLiR):Jun-Dec82-445
Peñalosa, F. Introduction to the Sociol-
  ogy of Language.
  P. Stevens, 355(LSoc):Dec82-484
Pencak, W. War, Politics, and Revolution
  in Provincial Massachusetts.
  G.A. Billias, 656(WMQ):Jul82-538
Pender, M. Max Frisch.
  P. Spycher, 221(GQ):Nov82-620
Peneff, J. Industriels algériens.
  K. Sutton, 69:Vol152No1-100
Penkert, S., ed. Emblem und Emblematik-
  rezeption.*
  W. Harms, 684(ZDA):Band11Heft1-39
  H-U. Kolb, 196:Band23Heft1/2-142
  M. Schilling, 52:Band16Heft1-86
Penn, J. An Ad for Murder.
  N. Callendar, 441:6Feb83-20
Penn, J. Deceitful Death.
  T.J. Binyon, 617(TLS):30Sep83-1037
Penn, W. The Papers of William Penn.
  (Vol 1) (M.M. and R.S. Dunn, eds)
  R.J. Plowman, 14:Winter82-60
Pennati, C. Sotteso blu 1974-1983.
  K. Bosley, 617(TLS):14Oct83-1136
Penniman, H.R., ed. Canada at the Polls,
  1979 and 1980.
  J. Stewart, 150(DR):Summer82-338
Penninger, F.E. William Caxton.
  N.F. Blake, 677(YES):Vol 12-237
Pennington, A.E. - see Kotošixin, G.
Pennington, K., ed. Johannis Teutonici
  Apparatus Glossarum in Compilationem
  Tertiam. (Vol 1)
  P.R. Hyams, 382(MAE):1982/2-266
Pennock, J.R. and J.W. Chapman, eds.
  NOMOS XXI.
  D. Braybrooke, 185:Oct82-139
Pennock, J.R. and J.W. Chapman, eds.
  NOMOS XXII.
  M.E. Hawkesworth, 185:Oct82-166
Pennock, J.R. and J.W. Chapman, eds.
  NOMOS XXIII.
  J.H.C., 185:Jul83-820
Pennock, J.R. and J.W. Chapman, eds.
  NOMOS XXIV.
  R.H., 185:Jan83-425
Penny, N. Piranesi.
  R. Middleton, 576:Dec82-333
Penrose, R. Scrap Book 1900-1981.
  R.S., 90:Sep82-568
Pensado, J.L. Contribución a la crítica
  de la lexicografia gallega. (Vol 1)
  J.M. Piel, 72:Band218Heft1-196
"Pensée hispanique et philosophie fran-
  çaise des Lumières."*
  R. Israël, 192(EP):Oct-Dec81-490

Perrie, W. By Moon and Sun.*
  R. Watson, 588(SSL):Vol 17-218
Perrin, U. Old Devotions.
  A. McCarthy, 441:6Feb83-10
Perrot, M. L'homme et la métamorphose.
  J. Brun, 192(EP):Jan-Mar81-97
Perrot, P. Les Dessus et les dessous de
la bourgeoisie.
  B.T. Cooper, 446(NCFS):Fall-Winter
    82/83-199
  T. Scanlan, 207(FR):Oct82-190
Perry, E.J. Rebels and Revolutionaries in
North China, 1845-1945.
  J. Fincher, 293(JASt):Feb82-339
Perry, G. Snow in Summer.*
  G. Catalano, 381:Oct81-349
Perry, J. Jack London.*
  R.W. Etulain, 649(WAL):Summer82-157
  E. Labor, 395(MFS):Winter82/83-665
  J.H. Maguire, 27(AL):Oct82-452
Perry, L. Childhood, Marriage, and Reform.
  M. Fellman, 529(QQ):Autumn82-637
Perry, M.E. Crime and Society in Early
Modern Seville.
  M.J. Thacker, 86(BHS):Apr82-150
Perry, R. Denizens.*
  C. Berger, 491:Apr82-35
Perry, R. Foul Up.
  N. Callendar, 441:9Jan83-41
Perry, R. Women, Letters, and the Novel.
  J.E. Aikins, 405(MP):Feb83-304
  B. Duyfhuizen, 454:Fall82-91
  K. Esser, 568(SCN):Winter82-75
  J. Harris, 173(ECS):Summer83-456
  M. Schonhorn, 566:Autumn82-63
Perry, T. Metzger's Dog.
  N. Callendar, 441:30Oct83-31
  442(NY):14Nov83-209
Perry, T.A. Erotic Spirituality.
  J.A. Devereux, 551(RenQ):Autumn81-456
Persius. The Satires. (J.R. Jenkinson,
ed and trans)
  R. Mayer, 123:Vol132No1-96
  T.G. Palaima, 124:Jan/Feb83-185
  J. Soubiran, 555:Vol55fasc2-374
Persius. The Satires of Persius.* (W.S.
Merwin, trans)
  D. McDuff, 565:Vol23No1-58
Persky, S. At the Lenin Shipyard.
  A.J. Matejko, 497(PolR):Vol27No3/4-196
Personneaux, L. Vicente Aleixandre ou une
poésie du suspens.
  D. Harris, 402(MLR):Oct82-978
Perus, F. Literatura y sociedad en
América Latina: El modernismo.
  M. Zimmerman, 504:No6-157
Pesce, D. Aristotele: La Poetica.
  B.R. Rees, 123:Vol132No1-100
Peschel, E.R. Four French Symbolist Poets.
  D.M. Betz, 446(NCFS):Fall-Winter82/83-
    166
  U. Franklin, 207(FR):Feb82-489
Peschlow, U., with P.I. Kuniholm and C.L.
Striker. Die Irenenkirche in Istanbul.
  J. Morganstern, 54:Dec82-657
Pesetsky, B. Author From a Savage People.
  T. Foote, 441:27Mar83-14
  442(NY):11Apr83-135
Pesetsky, B. Stories Up to a Point.*
  D. Grumbach, 219(GaR):Fall82-668
  J. Mellors, 362:6Jan83-24
  F. Taliaferro, 231:Apr83-72

Pesot, J. Silence, on parle.*
  G. Kleiber, 553(RLiR):Jul-Dec82-415
Petch, S. The Art of Philip Larkin.
  C. Pollnitz, 67:May82-81
Péter, M., ed. The Structure and Seman-
tics of the Literary Text.
  C. Fleckenstein, 682(ZPSK):Band34Heft2-
    267
Petermann, R. and P-V. Springborn, eds.
Theater und Aufklärung.
  W.D. Howarth, 208(FS):Jul82-336
Peters, D. Tikal.
  P-L. Adams, 61:Oct83-125
Peters, E. The Devil's Novice.
  T.J. Binyon, 617(TLS):2Dec83-1358
Peters, E., ed. Heresy and Authority in
Medieval Europe.
  E.K. Burger, 377:Nov81-180
Peters, E. The Sanctuary Sparrow.
  T.J. Binyon, 617(TLS):18Feb83-149
  M. Laski, 362:19May83-24
Peters, E. The Virgin in the Ice.
  442(NY):20Jun83-103
Peters, F.E. Children of Abraham.
  639(VQR):Autumn82-136
Peters, F.G. Robert Musil.*
  L.J. King, 406:Summer82-215
Peters, H. - see Donne, J.
Peters, J.M. Pictorial Signs and the Lan-
guage of Film.
  R. Durgnat, 89(BJA):Summer82-264
Peters, M. Untersuchungen zur Vertretung
der indogermanischen Laryngale im Greich-
ischen.
  L.D. Stephens, 350:Sep83-688
Peters, T.J. and R.H. Waterman, Jr. In
Search of Excellence.*
  F.R. Schumer, 441:6Mar83-16
Peters, U. Fürstenhof und höfische Dich-
tung.
  H. Szklenar, 196:Band23Heft1/2-146
Petersen, J.H. Max Frisch.*
  W. Schmitz, 72:Band218Heft2-408
Petersen, R.G. The Lost Cities of Cibola.
  K. McCarty, 50(ArQ):Autumn82-269
Petersen, W. Malthus.*
  W.H. Brock, 506(PSt):May82-173
Petersmann, H. Petrons urbane Prosa.
  G. Serbat, 555:Vol56fasc1-147
Peterson, C. Peter the Great's Administra-
tive and Judicial Reforms.*
  G. Yaney, 550(RusR):Jan82-71
Peterson, D. Petaluma's Architectural
Heritage. (G.M. Peterson, ed)
  D.J. Hibbard, 658:Spring82-90
Peterson, R. Leaving Taos.* (C. Kizer,
ed)
  R. Pybus, 565:Vol23No3-61
  G. Simon, 448:Vol20No1-145
  639(VQR):Winter82-26
Peterson, R.S. Imitation and Praise in
the Poems of Ben Jonson.
  J. Arnold, 568(SCN):Spring-Summer82-1
  I. Clark, 141:Spring82-180
  J.K. Gardiner, 191(ELN):Sep82-41
  P.L. Gaston, 477(PLL):Winter82-454
  G. Hammond, 148:Summer82-86
  A.F. Marotti, 551(RenQ):Autumn82-526
  G.F. Waller, 49:Jul82-84
Peterson, W.S. - see Browning, R. and F.
Furnivall
Peterson, W.S. - see Morris, W.

Pethick, D. First Approaches to the North-
west Coast.
C. Harris, 656(WMQ):Jul82-554
Petievich, G. To Die in Beverly Hills.
N. Callendar, 441:29May83-21
442(NY):4Jul83-92
Petiot, G. Le Robert des sports.
H. Cottez, 209(FM):Oct82-377
Petit, P. Comment va la France?
S. Smith, 207(FR):Dec82-359
"La Petite Musique de Verlaine."
C.T. Mitchell, 446(NCFS):Spring-Summer
83-383
Petitfils, P. Rimbaud.
M. Hutchinson, 617(TLS):16Sep83-979
Petöfi, J.S. and D. Franck, eds. Präsup-
positionen in Philosophie und Linguistik.
G.F. Meier, 682(ZPSK):Band34Heft2-241
Petrakis, H.M. Days of Vengeance.
P-L. Adams, 61:Sep83-125
J. Kaplan, 441:28Aug83-10
Petrarch. Selected Poems.* (A. Mortimer,
trans)
G. Costa, 545(RPh):Feb82-561
Petrarch, F. Songs and Sonnets from
Laura's Lifetime.* (N. Kilmer, trans)
D. McDuff, 565:Vol23No1-59
Petrey, S. History in the Text.*
D. Bellos, 402(MLR):Jan82-212
V. Brombert, 535(RHL):Sep-Dec82-925
R.T. Denommé, 400(MLN):May82-1006
M. Grimaud, 207(FR):Dec82-323
N. Schor, 210(FrF):Jan82-84
Petric, V., ed. Film and Dreams.
B. Steene, 18:May82-62
Petrie, D.W. Ultimately Fiction.*
K. Frank, 395(MFS):Summer82-300
295(JML):Dec82-373
Petrucelli, A.W. Liza! Liza!
J. Maslin, 441:4Dec83-73
Petschek, J.S. The Silver Bird.
E.S. Hillman, 283:Spring82-63
Pettigrew, J., with T.J. Collins - see
Browning, R.
Pettit, A.G. Images of the Mexican Amer-
ican in Fiction and Film.* (D.E. Show-
alter, ed)
M. Deutelbaum, 395(MFS):Summer82-367
Pettit, P. Judging Justice.*
J. Hampton, 482(PhR):Oct82-645
D.A.L. Thomas, 393(Mind):Jan82-153
Pettman, R. Biopolitics and International
Values.
C.R.B., 185:Oct82-219
Pétursson, M. Lehrbuch der isländischen
Sprache mit Übungen und Lösungen.
A. Liberman, 563(SS):Spring82-169
Petyt, K.M. The Study of Dialect.
G.M. Awbery, 297(JL):Sep82-431
M.I. Miller, 35(AS):Winter82-291
K. Shields, 215(CL):Winter82-273
Petzold, D. Das englische Kunstmärchen im
neunzehnten Jahrhundert.
W. Bies, 196:Band23Heft3/4-338
J.M. McGlathery, 301(JEGP):Jul82-451
Petzoldt, L., ed. Deutsche Sagen.
D. Ward, 650(WF):Apr82-164
Petzoldt, L., ed. Historische Sagen.
(Vol 2)
R. Grambo, 64(Arv):Vol36-210
Pevear, R. Exchanges.
J.F. Cotter, 249(HudR):Autumn82-471

Pevsner, N. The Englishness of English
Art.
A.J.G.H., 617(TLS):18Nov83-1295
Pevsner, N., ed. The Picturesque Garden
and its Influence Outside the British
Isles.
W.H. Adams, 127:Fall82-255
Peyrefitte, A. The Trouble with France.*
639(VQR):Spring82-48
Peytard, J. Voix et traces narratives
chez Stendhal.*
J-M. Gleize, 535(RHL):May-Jun82-484
Pfaff, R.W. Montague Rhodes James.
M.A. Rouse, 589:Jan82-195
Pfaffenberger, W. Blütezeit und nationale
Literaturgeschichtsschreibung.
W.A. Reichart, 221(GQ):May82-431
Pfeiffer, B.B. - see Wright, F.L.
Pfeiffer, J.E. The Creative Explosion.
J. Updike, 442(NY):31Jan83-120
P. Zweig, 441:2Jan83-6
Pfiffig, A.J. Etruskische Signaturen.
R. Adam, 555:Vol55fasc2-387
Pfister, M. Einführung in die romanische
Etymologie.*
H. Meier, 547(RF):Band94Heft2/3-264
W. Oesterreicher, 685(ZDL):3/1982-375
G. Roques, 553(RLiR):Jan-Jun81-235
Pfister, M. LEI: Lessico etimologico
italiano.* (Supplemento bibliografico;
Vol 1, fasc 1-3)
S. Lazard, 553(RLiR):Jan-Jun82-177
Pfleiderer, J.D. and M.J. Preston. A Com-
plete Concordance to The Chester Mystery
Plays.
C. Davidson, 130:Summer82-199
Pfoser, A. Literatur und Austromarxismus.
F. Kadrnoska, 602:Vol 13No2-354
Pharr, S.J. Political Women in Japan.
G.L. Bernstein, 293(JASt):Feb82-368
H.J. Jones, 407(MN):Autumn82-411
N.M. Lippit, 285(JapQ):Jul-Sep82-371
Phelan, J. Worlds from Words.*
W.E. Cain, 580(SCR):Fall82-118
P.J. Rabinowitz, 405(MP):May83-446
J.J. Sosnoski, 395(MFS):Summer82-358
295(JML):Dec82-381
Phelan, J.M. Disenchantment.
P. Brantlinger, 128(CE):Sep82-475
Phelps, L.R., with A.T. Alt, eds. Crea-
tive Encounter.*
E. Schürer, 133:Band15Heft4-360
Phelps, R. - see Colette
Philip, G. Oil and Politics in Latin
America.
E.N. Baklanoff, 263(RIB):Vol32No3/4-
378
L. Whitehead, 617(TLS):21Oct83-1156
Philipp, E. Dadaismus.
J.J. White, 402(MLR):Apr82-502
Philipp, G. Einführung ins Frühneuhoch-
deutsche.*
J. Schildt, 682(ZPSK):Band35Heft3-355
Philipp, M., A. Bothorel and G. Levieuge.
Atlas linguistique et ethnographique de
la Lorraine germanophone. (Vol 1)
P. Wiesinger, 685(ZDL):2/1982-237
Philippe de Thaon. Le Livre de Sibile.*
(H. Shields, ed)
A.J. Holden, 208(FS):Oct82-455
Philippe, R. Political Graphics.*
L. Golub, 62:Dec82-70

Philippi, D.L. Songs of Gods, Songs of
Humans.*
   D.W. Hughes, 187:Sep83-562
Phillips, C. Strange Fruit.
   D. Devlin, 157:Summer82-52
Phillips, D. The Coconut Kiss.*
   442(NY):27Jun83-99
Phillips, D. The Kiss.
   D. Barbour, 648(WCR):Oct82-37
   K. Norris, 137:Aug82-34
Phillips, D.L. Equality, Justice and
Rectification.*
   A.G.N. Flew, 518:Jan82-55
Phillips, D.Z. Through a Darkening Glass.
   N.F., 185:Apr83-628
Phillips, E. Sunday's Child.
   S. Kelman, 99:Jun/Jul82-33
Phillips, G.D. George Cukor.
   A. Sarris, 18:Apr83-59
Phillips, J.A. Electoral Behavior in Unre-
formed England.
   F. O'Gorman, 617(TLS):21Jan83-64
Phillips, J.K., ed. Action for the '80s.
   C.K. Knop, 399(MLJ):Autumn82-321
Phillips, J.K. Petits contes sympathiques.
Contes sympathiques.
   P. Silberman, 399(MLJ):Spring82-80
Phillips, L.B. Dictionary of Biographical
Reference. (3rd ed)
   K.B. Harder, 424:Sep82-199
Phillips, M. Duncan Phillips and his
Collection.
   A.P., 617(TLS):23Dec83-1443
Phillips, P. - see Pentland, H.C.
Phillips, R. Running on Empty.
   G.E. Murray, 249(HudR):Spring82-151
   G. Woodcock, 461:Fall-Winter82/83-99
Phillips, R. and O. Márquez. Visiones de
Latinoamérica. (2nd ed)
   R. Ruiz, 399(MLJ):Autumn82-354
   J.W. Zdenek, 238:Sep82-479
Phillipson, C. Capitalism and the Con-
struction of Old Age.
   N. Roberts, 617(TLS):18Mar83-270
Philo of Alexander. Philon d'alexandrie:
"De specialibus legibus," I et II. (S.
Daniel, ed and trans)
   J. Moreau, 192(EP):Apr-Jun81-237
"Les philosophies de l'existence et les
limites de l'homme."
   M. Adam, 542:Oct-Dec82-682
Phonai. Lautbibliothek der europäischen
Sprachen und Mundarten. (Vols 13 and 15)
   H. Schönfeld, 682(ZPSK):Band35Heft2-
218
"Photography as Fine Art."
   A. Grundberg, 441:4Dec83-77
Physick, J. The Victoria and Albert
Museum.*
   T. Russell-Cobb, 324:Apr83-292
"Physiologus." (M.J. Curley, trans)
   W.F. Hansen, 292(JAF):Apr-Jun82-219
Piaget, J. and others. Le possible et le
nécessaire. (Vol 1)
   A. Reix, 540(RIPh):Vol36fasc3-390
Piaget, J. and others. Recherche sur les
correspondances.
   A. Reix, 540(RIPh):Vol36fasc3-389
Piattelli-Palmarini, M., ed. Language and
Learning.* (French title: Théories du
langage, Théories de l'apprentissage.)
   E.W.F. Tomlin, 437:Winter81/82-99
   N.E. Wetherick, 323:Oct82-312

Picat-Guinoiseau, G. Une oeuvre méconnue
de Charles Nodier, "Faust" imité de
Goethe.
   R. Dumont, 549(RLC):Apr-Jun82-218
Piccirillo, M. - see Spijkerman, A.
Piccolpasso, C. I tre Libri dell'Arte del
Vasaio: The Three Books of the Potter's
Art.*
   J.V.G. Mallet, 90:Jan82-40
Pichanick, V.K. Harriet Martineau.
   C.D.C., 636(VP):Spring82-91
Pichois, C. Le Romantisme II, 1843-1869.*
   J. Body, 549(RLC):Oct-Dec82-513
le Pichon, Y. The World of Henri Rous-
seau.* (French title: Le monde du
douanier Rousseau.)
   C. Reid, 617(TLS):6May83-456
   A. Rey, 98:Mar82-243
Picht, R., ed. Das Bündnis im Bündnis.
   R. Morgan, 617(TLS):4Nov83-1230
Pickard, T. Hero Dust. O.K. Tree.
   D. Graham, 565:Vol23No2-74
Picken, L.E.R. - see "Musica Asiatica"
Picken, S.D.B. Shinto.
   H.B. Earheart, 529(QQ):Summer82-438
   W.M. Fridell, 293(JASt):May82-603
Pickens, R.T., ed. The Songs of Jaufré
Rudel.*
   J.H. Marshall, 402(MLR):Jan82-195
   E.R. Sienaert, 356(LR):Feb82-79
Pickering, F.P. Essays on Medieval German
Literature and Iconography.*
   I. Glier, 221(GQ):Mar82-242
Pickering, S.F., Jr. John Locke and the
Children's Books in Eighteenth-Century
England.*
   R.K. MacDonald, 566:Autumn82-64
   639(VQR):Spring82-56
Pickford, C.E., ed. Mélanges de littéra-
ture française moderne offerts à Garnet
Rees.*
   L.H. Bourke, 446(NCFS):Spring-Summer83-
402
   P. Caizergues, 535(RHL):Sep-Dec82-985
   A. Tooke, 208(FS):Jan82-111
Picoche, J. Précis de morphologie his-
torique du français.*
   G. Roques, 553(RLiR):Jan-Jun81-245
Picoche, J-L. Un romántico español.
   J.S. Herrero, 240(HR):Winter82-105
Picoche, J-L. - see Zorrilla, J.
Picon, G. Ingres.
   90:May82-328
Picone, M. "Vita nuova" e tradizione
romanza.
   J.M. Ferrante, 589:Apr82-408
Picton, J. and J. Mack. African Textiles.*
   R.L. Shep, 614:Fall83-15
   F. Willett, 59:Jun82-227
Pidal, R.M. - see under Menéndez Pidal, R.
Pidara, S.K. On Performing a Hindu Wed-
ding.
   L. Sternbach, 318(JAOS):Oct-Dec81-490
Piehl, M. Breaking Bread.
   A. Brinkley, 441:13Feb83-12
Piel, E. Der Schrecken der "wahren" Wirk-
lichkeit.
   A. Hillach, 406:Spring82-91
Piel, J. La Rencontre et la différence.
   J.V. Harari, 400(MLN):Dec82-1270
Piercy, M. Braided Lives.*
   L. Howe, 363(LitR):Fall82-177

Pierini, R.D. - see under Degl'Innocenti
Pierini, R.
Pierre, A.J. The Global Politics of Arms
Sales.*
  639(VQR):Summer82-89
Pierrot, J. The Decadent Imagination:
1880-1900.*
  K. Beckson, 177(ELT):Vol25No4-252
  N.R. Cirillo, 395(MFS):Winter82/83-730
  F.S. Heck, 207(FR):Mar83-640
  I.M. Kohn, 50(ArQ):Winter82-384
  M.G. Rose, 446(NCFS):Fall-Winter82/83-
  174
Pierson, J.D. Tokutomi Sohō, 1863-1957.*
  E.H. Kinmonth, 293(JASt):Nov81-152
Pierssens, M. The Power of Babel.*
  E. Finegan, 350:Jun83-461
  A. Jefferson, 447(N&Q):Dec81-572
Pietri, A.U. - see under Uslar Pietri, A.
Pieyre de Mandiargues, A. Un Saturne gai.
  C. Dis, 450(NRF):Nov82-111
Pifer, E. Nabokov and the Novel.*
  P. Balbert, 594:Spring82-95
  M. Bell, 402(MLR):Jan82-140
  P. Buitenhuis, 529(QQ):Spring82-206
  J. Grayson, 575(SEER):Jan82-103
  C.S. Ross, 395(MFS):Winter81/82-737
  E. Wasiolek, 131(CL):Winter82-91
Piggott, S. Scotland Before History.
  L. Alcock, 617(TLS):22Apr83-410
Pike, B. The Image of the City in Modern
Literature.*
  A. Axelrod, 580(SCR):Spring83-126
  B. Gelfant, 27(AL):Oct82-460
  W. Sypher, 569(SR):Fall82-575
  H. Wirth-Nesher, 395(MFS):Summer82-365
Pike, D. German Writers in Soviet Exile,
1933-1945.*
  L.W. Tusken, 395(MFS):Winter82/83-700
  639(VQR):Summer82-80
Pike, L. Beethoven, Sibelius and the "Pro-
found Logic."
  R.L.J., 412:May81-145
Pike, M.V. and J.G. Armstrong. A Time to
Mourn.
  B. Rotundo, 658:Summer/Autumn82-152
Pikhaus, D. Levensbeschouwing en milieu
in de Latijnse metrische inscripties.
  G.J.M. Bartelink, 394:Vol35fasc3/4-439
Pikoulis, J. The Art of William Faulkner.
  R. Christiansen, 617(TLS):14Jan83-43
  D. Minter, 578:Fall83-123
Pildas, A. and L. Smith. Movie Palaces.
  F.E.H. Schroeder, 658:Winter82-296
Pile, F., ed. Ah! Mischief.
  N. Berry, 364:Aug/Sep82-140
Pilinszky, J. Selected Poems.
  V. Trueblood, 271:Spring82-132
Pilkington, J. The Heart of Yoknapatawpha.
  A. Bleikasten, 395(MFS):Winter82/83-
  675
  M.R. Winchell, 585(SoQ):Summer82-110
Pilling, G. Marx's "Capital."*
  M.T.O., 543:Mar82-623
Pilling, J. Autobiography and Imagination.
  M. Sprinker, 284:Winter83-153
Pilz, K.D. Phraseologie.*
  B.J. Koekkoek, 221(GQ):May82-398
  W. Mieder, 196:Band23Heft1/2-147
Pim, L.R. The Invisible Additives.*
  G. Beakhurst, 529(QQ):Winter82-880

Pimental, D. and M. Food, Energy and
Society.
  R.A. Cline-Cole, 69:Vol52No1-86
Pimsleur, P. How to Learn a Foreign Lan-
guage.
  L.A. Briscoe, 399(MLJ):Spring82-69
  A.S. Caprio, 207(FR):Dec82-349
Pimsleur, P. and B. C'est la vie. (3rd
ed)
  R. Danner, 207(FR):Dec82-350
Pincher, C. Their Trade is Treachery.
  J.L. Granatstein, 529(QQ):Autumn82-529
Pines, B.Y. Back to Basics.*
  T.C. Holyoke, 42(AR):Fall82-484
Pines, P. The Tin Angel.
  P. Andrews, 441:30Oct83-14
Pinget, R. Between Fantoine and Agapa.
That Voice.
  R. Coover, 441:25Sep83-15
  J. Updike, 442(NY):11Jul83-96
Pinion, F.B. A D.H. Lawrence Companion.*
  B. Caplan, 219(GaR):Spring82-194
Pinkernell, G. François Villons "Lais."
  G. Roellenbleck, 547(RF):Band94Heft1-
  108
Pinney, T. - see Macaulay, T.B.
Pinsky, R. An Explanation of America.*
  J. Parini, 114(ChiR):Summer81-16
Pintacuda, M. La musica nella tragedia
greca.*
  A. Bélis, 555:Vol55fasc1-156
Pintaudi, R. I papiri vaticani greci
di Aphrodito.
  E.G. Turner, 123:Vol132No2-299
Pintner, W.M. and D.K. Rowney, eds. Rus-
sian Officialdom.*
  N.B. Theisman, 104(CASS):Summer82-248
Pinto, V.D. and F.W. Roberts - see under
de Sola Pinto, V. and F.W. Roberts
Pintore, F. Il matrimonio interdinastico
nel Vicino Oriente durante i secoli XV-
XIII.
  A.R. Schulman, 318(JAOS):Oct-Dec81-455
Piotrovskij, R.G., K.B. Bektaev and A.A.
Piotrovskaja. Matematičeskaja lingvis-
tika.
  H.T. Georgiev, 682(ZPSK):Band34Heft2-
  265
Piper, D. The Image of the Poet.
  R.B. Martin, 453(NYRB):21Jul83-25
  C. Reid, 617(TLS):8Apr83-344
Piper, W.B. Evaluating Shakespeare's Son-
nets.
  R. Jacobs, 541(RES):Feb82-79
  K. Muir, 570(SQ):Spring82-116
Pipes, R. U.S.-Soviet Relations in the
Era of Detente.
  A.E. Stent, 550(RusR):Jan82-91
Piquemal, A. Raymond Aron et l'ordre
international.
  A. Reix, 542:Jan-Mar82-62
Pircher, J. Das Lob der Frau im vorchrist-
lichen Grabepigramm der Griechen.
  P.A. Hansen, 123:Vol132No1-34
Pirie, D.B. William Wordsworth.*
  K. Sutherland, 148:Autumn82-77
Pirion, J-P. - see Green, J. and J.
Maritain
Pirrotta, N. and E. Povoledo. Music and
Theatre from Poliziano to Monteverdi.
  D. Stevens, 415:Jul82-479
de Pisan, C. - see under Christine de
Pisan

Pollin, B.R., ed. Word Index to Poe's Fiction.
D.B. Kesterson, 578:Spring83-102
R. Kopley, 495(PoeS):Jun82-24
J.V. Ridgely, 392:Fall82-447
Pollins, H. Economic History of the Jews in England.
B. Wasserstein, 617(TLS):19Aug83-876
Pollitt, K. Antarctic Traveller.*
D. Gioia, 249(HudR):Winter82/83-640
H. Kenner, 231:Sep83-70
W. Logan, 472:Spring/Summer83-211
R.B. Shaw, 491:Dec82-170
P. Stitt, 219(GaR):Summer82-438
639(VQR):Summer82-92
Pollock, D. Skywalking.
T. Shippey, 617(TLS):12Aug83-855
Pollock, L. The Freedom Principle.
R.G., 185:Jan83-427
Pollock, S. Blood Relations and Other Plays.
A. Filewood, 108:Spring82-200
Polomé, E.C. and C.P. Hill, eds. Language in Tanzania.
C. Gilman, 355(LSoc):Apr82-141
Polonsky, A. Politics in Independent Poland, 1921-1939.
M. Malia, 453(NYRB):29Sep83-18
Pölöskei, F. Hungary after Two Revolutions (1919-1927).
L. Congdon, 104(CASS):Summer82-299
Pols, E. The Arts of Our Being.
T.M.R., 185:Jul83-818
Polyviou, P.G. Search and Seizure.
Lord Scarman, 617(TLS):11Feb83-124
Poma de Ayala, F.G. El primer nueva corónica y buen gobierno. (J.V. Murra and R. Adorno, eds)
J. Higgins, 86(BHS):Jan82-84
Pomeau, R. - see de Voltaire, F.M.A.
Pomfret, J.E. Colonial New Jersey.
F. Shuffelton, 173(ECS):Summer83-415
Pomper, P. Sergei Nechaev.*
R. Leiter, 31(ASch):Winter81/82-136
Pompili, B. - see Borel, P.
Ponce de León, J.L.S. El arte de la conversación, el arte de la composición. (3rd ed)
M.S. Arrington, Jr., 399(MLJ):Autumn82-355
Poneman, D. Nuclear Power in the Developing World.
R.J. Barnet, 441:16Jan83-19
Ponge, F. Nioque de l'avant-printemps.
G.D. Martin, 617(TLS):5Aug83-840
Pons, A. - see Vico, G.
Pont. The British Character.
442(NY):19Dec83-140
Ponting, K. Beginner's Guide to Weaving.
R. Hoffman, 614:Fall83-17
Pontus de Tyard. Solitaire second.* (C.M. Yandell, ed)
H.H. Glidden, 207(FR):Apr83-765
Pooley, R. - see Gascoigne, G.
Poortvliet, R. Dogs.
M. Levine, 441:11Dec83-35
Pope-Hennessy, J. Luca della Robbia.*
A.M. Schulz, 551(RenQ):Autumn81-419
Pope-Hennessy, J. The Study and Criticism of Italian Sculpture.*
V. Herzner, 471:Apr/May/Jun82-167
Popelar, I. - see Baldinger, K.

Popham, M.R. and others, eds. Lefkandi I.
A.M. Snodgrass, 303(JoHS):Vol 102-279
Popkin, J.D. The Right-Wing Press in France, 1792-1800.
J.A. Leith, 173(ECS):Spring83-359
Popkin, R.H. The High Road to Pyrrhonism.* (R.A. Watson and J.E. Force, eds)
R.J. Butler, 518:Jan82-18
Popkin, R.H. The History of Skepticism from Erasmus to Spinoza.
A. Cohen, 319:Jan83-102
G. Gawlick, 53(AGP):Band64Heft1-90
D.R.L., 543:Sep81-155
C.B. Schmitt, 551(RenQ):Spring81-97
Popkin, S.L. The Rational Peasant.*
E.J. Perry, 293(JASt):Aug82-889
Popov, S. Am Ende aller Illusionen.
D. Johnson, 617(TLS):2Sep83-942
Poppe, R.P. - see under Pastor Poppe, R.
Popper, K. La quête inachevée.
J. Largeault, 542:Jan-Mar82-128
Popper, K.R. and J.C. Eccles. The Self and Its Brain.*
M.S., 543:Jun82-894
Poppi, A., ed. Storia e cultura al Santo.
F. Purnell, Jr., 551(RenQ):Spring81-89
Porch, D. The Conquest of Morocco.
P-L. Adams, 61:Apr83-133
J. Keegan, 453(NYRB):18Aug83-50
F.R. Schumer, 441:6Mar83-16
Porcher, M-C. Figures de style en Sanskrit.
L. Sternbach, 318(JAOS):Oct-Dec81-488
Porges, H. Wagner Rehearsing the "Ring."
P. Carnegy, 617(TLS):9Sep83-954
J. Kerman, 453(NYRB):22Dec83-27
Pörnbacher, K., ed. Thomas Mann, Mario und der Zauberer.
E. Schwarz and K. Thompson, 133:Band15 Heft3-279
"Isaac Porphyrogenitus: 'Praefatio in Homerum.'" (J.F. Kindstrand, ed)
F.M. Combellack, 122:Apr82-183
F. Vian, 555:Vol55fasc2-289
Porphyry. Porphyre, "De l'abstinence." (Vol 2, Bks 2 and 3) (J. Bouffartigue and M. Patillon, eds and trans)
É. des Places, 555:Vol55fasc2-352
Porte, J. - see Emerson, R.W.
Portelli, A. Saggi sulla cultura afro-americana.
C.P., 189(EA):Apr-Jun82-239
Porter, A. Music of Three More Seasons, 1977-1980.
H. Keller, 415:May82-336
Porter, C. The Complete Lyrics of Cole Porter. (R. Kimball, ed)
W. Balliett, 442(NY):26Dec83-70
E. Sirkin, 61:Dec83-113
Porter, C. Seeing and Being.*
C. Baxter, 141:Fall82-403
F. Lentricchia, 27(AL):Oct82-444
J. Michael, 400(MLN):Dec82-1254
A. Tintner, 26(ALR):Autumn82-269
Porter, D. Dickinson.*
J.L. Capps, 27(AL):May82-298
A. Gibson, 175:Spring82-68
D. O'Hara, 141:Winter82-87
295(JML):Dec82-432
Porter, D. Emerson and Literary Change.*
M. Gonnaud, 189(EA):Oct-Dec82-485

Porter, D. The Pursuit of Crime.*
B. Landon, 481(PQ):Summer82-360
J. Michael, 400(MLN):Dec82-1277
639(VQR):Summer82-80
Porter, E., W. Stegner and P. Stegner.
American Places.
F.G. Robinson, 649(WAL):Summer82-161
42(AR):Fall82-487
Porter, E.G. Schubert's Piano Works.
H. Ferguson, 410(M&L):Jul/Oct81-378
Porter, H. The Clairvoyant Goat.
R.G. Geering, 581:Mar82-109
Porter, J.A. The Drama of Speech Acts.*
J. Rees, 677(YES):Vol 12-254
Porter, L.M. The Literary Dream in French
Romanticism.*
B. Juden, 402(MLR):Jan82-213
S. Noakes, 591(SIR):Spring82-114
Porter, M. Home, Work and Class Conscious-
ness.
P. Willmott, 617(TLS):29Apr83-441
Porter, P. Collected Poems.
D. Davis, 362:18Aug83-20
B. Morrison, 617(TLS):1Apr83-321
Porter, P. English Subtitles.*
T. Eagleton, 565:Vol23No2-62
M. O'Neill, 493:Apr82-59
Porter, P. - see Roberts, M.
Porter, R. and M. Teich, eds. The Enlight-
enment in National Context.
R. Waller, 83:Spring82-145
Porter, W.E. The Italian Journalist.
L. Barzini, 617(TLS):7Oct83-1082
Porterfield, B. Texas Rhapsody.
J. Bouterse, 649(WAL):Summer82-188
L. Milazzo, 584(SWR):Spring82-v
Pörtl, K. Das lyrische Werk des Damián
Cornejo (1629-1707). (Pt 1)
M. Lentzen, 547(RF):Band93Heft1/2-300
Portmann, P.R. "Kommunikation" als Prob-
lem der Sprachdidaktik.
B.J. Koekkoek, 221(GQ):Mar82-235
W. Nemitz, 133:Band15Heft3-254
Portuondo, A.A. Diez comedias atribuidas
a Lope de Vega.*
J.A. Castañeda, 238:May82-307
Portuondo, J.A. La emancipación literaria
de Hispanoamérica.
R.A. Young, 107(CRCL):Dec81-565
Posner, R. and J.N. Green, eds. Trends in
Romance Linguistics and Philology.
(Vols 1 and 2)
D.C. Walker, 320(CJL):Fall82-193
Posse, A. La Guerre au roi.
R. André, 450(NRF):Apr82-145
Possehl, G.L., ed. Ancient Cities of the
Indus.
R. Inden, 318(JAOS):Oct-Dec81-494
Post, J.F.S. Henry Vaughan.
A. Rudrum, 617(TLS):24Jun83-681
van der Post, L. Yet Being Someone Other.*
P-L. Adams, 61:May83-105
R. Fuller, 364:Oct82-92
D. McWhorter, 441:1May83-17
W.P. Marsh, 469:Vol8No3-120
Postel, J. Genèse de la psychiatrie.
A. Reis, 542:Jan-Mar82-90
Postman, N. The Disappearance of Child-
hood.*
E. Havelock, 186(ETC.):Fall82-291
A. Wooldridge, 617(TLS):13May83-492

Potestà, G.L. Storia ed escatologia in
Ubertino da Casale.
E.R. Daniel, 589:Apr82-411
Potholm, C.P. The Theory and Practice of
African Politics.
C. Clapham, 69:Vol51No1-529
Potichnyj, P.J., ed. Poland and Ukraine.
P.J. Best, 497(PolR):Vol127No3/4-241
G.P. Kulchycky, 104(CASS):Summer82-284
Potok, C. The Book of Lights.*
639(VQR):Summer82-98
Potter, E.F., J.F. Parnell and R.P. Teul-
ings. Birds of the Carolinas.
L. Patton, 579(SAQ):Winter82-125
Potter, J. Good King Richard?
G. Holmes, 617(TLS):23Sep83-1026
Potter, J.L. Robert Frost Handbook.*
W. Tefs, 106:Fall82-223
295(JML):Dec82-452
Pottle, F.A. Pride and Negligence.*
R.D. Altick, 401(MLQ):Mar82-87
Potts, L.W. Arthur Lee.
R.R. Rea, 577(SHR):Spring82-165
Potts, T.C. Conscience in Medieval Philos-
ophy.*
E.L.F., 543:Sep81-158
Potulicki, E.B. La Modernité de la pensée
de Diderot dans les oeuvres philoso-
phiques.*
J. Chouillet, 535(RHL):Sep-Dec82-913
A. Strugnell, 208(FS):Jan82-72
Pou, S. Études sur le Rāmakerti (XVIe-
XVIIe siècles).
L. Sternbach, 318(JAOS):Oct-Dec81-484
Pou, S., ed and trans. Rāmakerti (XVIe-
XVIIe siècles).
L. Sternbach, 318(JAOS):Oct-Dec81-484
Poulenc, F. Emmanuel Chabrier.*
R. Orledge, 410(M&L):Jul/Oct82-328
Poulet, G. La Poésie éclatée.
M. Evans, 208(FS):Jan82-83
Poulton, A., comp. The Recorded Works of
Sir William Walton.*
P.J.P., 412:May81-153
Pouncey, P.R. The Necessities of War.
H.D. Westlake, 123:Vol132No1-20
Pound, E. Ezra Pound: Lettere 1907-1958.
(A. Tagliaferri, ed)
D. Anderson, 468:Spring82-171
Pound, E. and F.M. Ford. Pound/Ford.*
(B. Lindberg-Seyersted, ed)
A. Jenkins, 617(TLS):30Sep83-1057
442(NY):18Apr83-151
Pound, O.S. and P. Grover. Wyndham Lewis.*
E.M. Wallace, 677(YES):Vol 12-342
Pourrat, H. Le Trésor des contes IV.
G. Sartoris, 450(NRF):Feb82-123
Pouthier, P. Ops et la conception divine
de l'abondance dans la religion romaine
jusqu'à la mort d'Auguste.
J-C. Richard, 555:Vol56fasc2-371
Povejšil, J. Das Prager Deutsch des 17.
und 18. Jahrhunderts.
F.J. Hannig, 680(ZDP):Band101Heft3-474
B.J. Koekkoek, 221(GQ):Nov82-582
Poverman, C.E. Solomon's Daughter.
V. Nelson, 219(GaR):Summer82-463
Powell, A. Faces in My Time.*
C. Eichelberger, 295(JML):Dec82-517
J. Russell, 396(ModA):Summer/Fall82-
418
Powell, A. Messengers of Day.*
C. Eichelberger, 295(JML):Dec82-517

Powell, A. O, How The Wheel Becomes It!
D. May, 362:16Jun83-27
J.K.L. Walker, 617(TLS):24Jun83-660
Powell, A. The Strangers All Are Gone.*
M. Kakutani, 441:26Jun83-9
A. Ross, 364:Jul82-5
442(NY):22Aug83-94
Powell, A. To Keep the Ball Rolling.
A.J., 617(TLS):23Dec83-1443
Powell, A.S., comp. Istorik-Marksist,
1926-1941.
W. Zalewski, 550(RusR):Oct82-535
Powell, G. Language as Being in the Po-
etry of Yvor Winters.
R. Labrie, 106:Winter82-397
Powell, N. A Season of Calm Weather.*
T. Dooley, 617(TLS):7Jan83-17
M. O'Neill, 493:Jan83-48
Powell, R. Shakespeare and the Critics'
Debate.*
G.K. Hunter, 569(SR):Spring82-273
Powell, T.G. Mexico and the Spanish Civil
War.
R. Carr, 617(TLS):29Apr83-435
Powell, V. The Constant Novelist.
V. Glendinning, 617(TLS):29Jul83-799
Power, M.S. Hunt for the Autumn Clowns.
J. Melmoth, 617(TLS):17Jun83-622
"The Power of Design."
R.L. Shep, 614:Summer83-21
Powers, L.H. Faulkner's Yoknapatawpha
Comedy.*
T. Heller, 50(ArQ):Summer82-179
J.G. Watson, 395(MFS):Summer81-365
295(JML):Dec82-442
Powers, T. Thinking About the Next War.
M. Howard, 231:Feb83-67
J.S. Nye, Jr., 441:30Jan83-13
Powys, J.C. The Letters of John Cowper
Powys to Sven-Erik Tåckmark. (C. Hent-
schel, ed) The Letters of John Cowper
Powys to G.R. Wilson Knight. (R. Black-
more, ed)
G. Cavaliero, 617(TLS):18Nov83-1268
Powys, L. Black Laughter.
P. Redgrove, 617(TLS):27May83-536
Prada, R.R. - see under Rivadeneira Prada,
R.
Prado, C.G. Illusions of Faith.
T. Penelhum, 154:Jun82-346
P. Slater, 529(QQ):Summer82-436
Prager, E. A Visit from the Footbinder
and Other Stories.
S. Altinel, 617(TLS):11Mar83-248
J. Mellors, 362:9Jun83-26
J.W., 231:Feb83-75
Prance, C.A. Companion to Charles Lamb.
N. Berry, 617(TLS):27May83-555
J. Gross, 453(NYRB):16Jun83-11
Prandi, A. - see Bertaux, É.
Prandy, K., A. Stewart and R.M. Blackburn.
White-Collar Work.
C. Crouch, 617(TLS):25Nov83-1328
Prange, G.W., with D.M. Goldstein and K.V.
Dillon. Miracle at Midway.
N. Bliven, 442(NY):12Sep83-148
Praschek, H., ed. Gerhart Hauptmanns
"Weber."
S. Hoefert, 564:Sep82-229
Praschniker, C. and others. Forschungen
in Ephesos veröffentlicht vom Österreich-
[continued]

[continuing]
ischen Archäologischen Institut in Wien.
(Vol 6)
A. Stewart, 303(JoHS):Vol 102-282
Prater, D. and V. Michels - see Zweig, S.
Prater, D.A. Stefan Zweig.
H. Zohn, 680(ZDP):Band101Heft4-583
"La pratique des ordinateurs dans la cri-
tique des textes."
P-P. Corsetti, 555:Vol56fasc1-181
Prato, C. and D. Micalella - see Julian
Pratt, A. Archetypal Patterns in Women's
Fiction.
C.N. Davidson, 594:Fall82-297
Pratt, B. L'Évangile selon Albert Camus.
A. Bates, 67:Nov82-206
J. Sarocchi, 535(RHL):Mar-Apr82-325
Pratt, C. El anglicismo en el español
peninsular contemporáneo.
T.C. Bookless, 402(MLR):Jul82-743
L. Williams, 86(BHS):Jan82-68
Pratt, D. Alternatives to Pain in Experi-
ments on Animals.
M.A.F., 185:Jan83-439
Pratt, J.C. and V.A. Neufeldt - see Eliot,
G.
Prauss, G. Einführung in die Erkenntnis-
theorie.*
K. Ameriks, 262:Mar82-125
H-L. Ollig, 687:Jan-Mar81-160
Prawer, J. Crusader Institutions.
J. Folda, 318(JAOS):Oct-Dec81-458
Prawer, S.S. Heine's Jewish Comedy.
S.L. Gilman, 617(TLS):2Dec83-1343
Praz, M. An Illustrated History of Inte-
rior Decoration. Il mondo che ho visto.
H. Honour, 453(NYRB):3Mar83-4
Praz, M. Giovan Battista Piranesi, Le
carceri.
R. Middleton, 576:Dec82-333
"Precolumbian Art of Costa Rica."
J. Brzostoski, 139:Aug/Sep82-23
Pred, A. Urban Growth and City Systems in
the United States, 1840-1860.
J.C. Weaver, 529(QQ):Autumn82-682
Predmore, R.L. Lorca's New York Poetry.*
C. Maurer, 240(HR):Summer82-365
Preisner, R. Aspekte einer provokativen
tschechischen Germanistik. (Vol 2)
J.P. Strelka, 680(ZDP):Band101Heft4-
625
Prendergast, C. Balzac: Fiction and Melo-
drama.
A.L. Lacy, 546(RR):Mar82-262
Prenshaw, P.W., ed. Eudora Welty.
W.J. Stuckey, 395(MFS):Autumn82-507
Prescott, A.L. French Poets and the Eng-
lish Renaissance.*
M. Hughes, 549(RLC):Jan-Mar82-105
Presley, N. Never in Doubt.
L. Milazzo, 584(SWR):Spring82-v
Pressly, W.L. The Life and Art of James
Barry.*
R. Wark, 90:Mar82-159
Prest, J. The Garden of Eden.*
J.D. Hunt, 576:Dec82-360
Preston, A. Sea Combat off the Falklands.
G. Wheatcroft, 617(TLS):13May83-490
Preston, D. and S. Crazy Fox Remembers.
F.L. Lee, 649(WAL):Nov82-285
Preston, D.J. Young Frederick Douglass:
The Maryland Years.
R. Felgar, 392:Fall82-427

Preston, M.J. and J. Pfleiderer. A KWIC
Concordance to the Plays of the Wake-
field Master.
  C. Davidson, 130:Summer82-199
Preti, L. Mussolini giovane.
  T. Abse, 617(TLS):3Jun83-580
Prévert, J. Anthologie Prévert. (C. Mor-
telier, ed)
  P. Low, 67:May82-85
Prévot, J. Cyrano de Bergerac poète et
dramaturge.
  J. Morel, 535(RHL):Sep-Dec82-890
Prévot, J. - see Furetière, A.
Prewo, R. Max Webers Wissenschaftspro-
gramm.
  R. Twenhöfel, 687:Jul-Sep82-467
Preziosi, D. Architecture, Language and
Meaning.* The Semiotics of the Built
Environment.
  M. Krampen, 567:Vol37No3/4-339
Price, A. The Old Vengeful.*
  M. Laski, 362:20Jan83-23
Price, C.A. Music in the Restoration The-
atre.
  M. Laurie, 410(M&L):Apr81-197
Price, D.B. and N.J. Twombly. The Phantom
Limb Phenomenon.
  J. Forrest, 582(SFQ):Vol43No3/4-335
Price, D.C. Patrons and Musicians of the
English Renaissance.*
  N. Orme, 410(M&L):Jul/Oct82-335
Price, E. Savannah.
  E. Jakab, 441:1May83-14
Price, G. and D.A. Wells - see "The Year's
Work in Modern Language Studies"
Price, J.M. Capital and Credit in British
Overseas Trade.
  P.G.M. Dickson, 656(WMQ):Jul82-527
Price, K., ed. On Criticizing Music.
  G. Iseminger, 290(JAAC):Winter82-219
Price, M. Forms of Life.
  V. Cunningham, 617(TLS):22Jul83-790
Price, R. The Breaks.
  B. De Mott, 441:13Feb83-14
  J. Rubins, 453(NYRB):31Mar83-28
  J. Wolcott, 231:Feb83-59
  442(NY):14Feb83-114
Price, R. The Source of Light.
  J.L. Halio, 598(SoR):Winter83-203
  D. Noble, 577(SHR):Summer82-276
Price, S. and R. Afro-American Arts of
the Suriname Rain Forest.*
  D.J. Crowley, 2(AfrA):Nov81-27
Prickett, S. Romanticism and Religion.
  E.S. Shaffer, 402(MLR):Apr82-419
Prickett, S., ed. The Romantics.
  P.M.S.D., 148:Summer82-91
  A. Rodway, 89(BJA):Summer82-281
Prickett, S. Victorian Fantasy.*
  R. McGillis, 49:Apr82-85
  D. Petzold, 38:Band100Heft1/2-222
Prideaux, G.D., ed. Perspectives in Exper-
imental Linguistics.*
  P.G. Patel, 320(CJL):Fall82-189
Prideaux, G.D., B.L. Derwing and W.J.
Baker, eds. Experimental Linguistics.*
  A.R. Tellier, 189(EA):Jul-Sep82-323
Priest, R. Sadness of Spacemen.
  L. Welch, 198:Oct82-99
Priestley, B. Mingus.
  C. Fox, 617(TLS):1Apr83-319
Priestman, M. Cowper's "Task."
  G. Lindop, 617(TLS):2Dec83-1352

Prigent, C. Viallat la main perdue.
  C. Limousin, 98:May82-459
Prigogine, I. From Being to Becoming.
  K.G. Denbigh, 84:Sep82-325
Prigogine, I. Physique, temps et devenir.
  A. Reix, 542:Jan-Mar82-131
Primeau, R. Beyond "Spoon River."*
  J.E. Hallwas, 301(JEGP):Oct82-605
"John Prince, 1796-1870." (R.A. Douglas,
ed)
  M. Power, 628(UWR):Fall-Winter82-129
Prince, P. The Good Father.
  L. Jones, 617(TLS):4Nov83-1227
  J. Mellors, 362:22Sep83-25
Prindle, D.F. Petroleum Politics and the
Texas Railroad Commission.
  L. Milazzo, 584(SWR):Spring82-v
Pringle, M.B. and A. Stericker, eds. Sex
Roles in Literature.
  E.P.M. Senter, 268(IFR):Winter83-71
Pringle, P. and J. Spigelman. The Nuclear
Barons.*
  639(VQR):Spring82-46
Pringle, T. This is the Child.
  J.K. Davison, 441:24Jul83-17
Prinz, F. Gründungsmythen und Sagenchron-
ologie.*
  J.T. Hooker, 303(JoHS):Vol 102-276
  F. Vian, 555:Vol55fasc1-148
Prior, A. A Cast of Stars.
  P-L. Adams, 61:Apr83-132
Pritchard, J.B. Recovering Sarepta.
  K.N. Schoville, 318(JAOS):Oct-Dec81-
440
Pritchett, V.S. Collected Stories.*
  G. Core, 569(SR):Summer82-1xxii
Pritchett, V.S. More Collected Stories.
  M. Kakutani, 441:18Sep83-11
  H. Lee, 617(TLS):4Nov83-1214
Pritchett, V.S. The Myth Makers.*
  M. Lebowitz, 598(SoR):Winter83-247
Pritchett, V.S., ed. The Oxford Book of
Short Stories.
  D.A. Hughes, 573(SSF):Winter82-89
  529(QQ):Summer82-454
Privat, E. and R. Rolland. Bon Voisinage.
  (P. Hirsch, ed)
  B. Duchatelet, 535(RHL):Mar-Apr82-318
Probert, B. Beyond Orange and Green.
  G. Eley, 385(MQR):Winter83-107
Probyn, C.T., ed. The Art of Jonathan
Swift.
  W. Kinsley, 173(ECS):Summer82-442
Probyn, C.T., ed. Jonathan Swift.*
  J. Bull, 161(DUJ):Jun82-310
  W. Kinsley, 173(ECS):Summer82-442
Prochaska, F.K. Women and Philanthropy in
Nineteenth-Century England.
  K. Heasman, 637(VS):Winter82-251
Procter, E.S. Curia and Cortes in León
and Castile 1072-1295.*
  T.N. Bisson, 589:Jan82-165
Proctor, D. The Experience of Thucydides.
  J.D. Smart, 123:Vol32No1-19
Proctor, G.A. Canadian Music of the
Twentieth Century.*
  D. Roberts, 410(M&L):Jul/Oct81-377
Profeti, M.G. - see under Grazia Profeti,
M.
Proffer, C. and E., eds. Contemporary
Russian Prose.
  C. Avins, 574(SEEJ):Winter82-493
  A. McMillin, 617(TLS):17Jun83-639

Proffer, E., ed. Tsvetaeva.*
  J.A. Taubman, 104(CASS):Spring82-142
Proffitt, N. Gardens of Stone.
  E. Jakab, 441:13Nov83-16
"Sergei Prokofieff."
  A.F.L.T., 412:Feb82-61
Prokofiev, A. Selected Poems. (V. Bakh-
  tin, ed)
  M.K. Frank, 399(MLJ):Winter82-434
Prokosch, F. The Asiatics.
  P.K. Bell, 617(TLS):23Dec83-1420
Prokosch, F. Voices.
  J. Atlas, 61:Feb83-100
  P.K. Bell, 617(TLS):23Dec83-1420
  W.H. Pritchard, 441:29May83-6
  G. Vidal, 453(NYRB):12May83-14
Prokudin-Gorskii, S.M. Photographs for
  the Tsar. (R.H. Allshouse, ed)
  I. Vinogradoff, 31(ASch):Spring82-264
Pronko, L.C. Eugène Labiche and Georges
  Feydeau.*
  A.P. Hinchliffe, 148:Autumn82-83
Pronzini, B. Bindlestiff.
  N. Callendar, 441:18Dec83-29
Pronzini, B. Dragonfire.
  N. Callendar, 441:16Jan83-26
Propertius – see under Fedeli, P.
Prophète, J. Les Para-personnages dans
  les tragédies de Racine.
  M.B. Nelson, 207(FR):Apr83-767
"La Prosa Francese del primo seicento."
  G. Hainsworth, 208(FS):Jan82-66
von Proschwitz, G. Alexis Piron épisto-
  lier.
  J. Bourguignon, 553(RLiR):Jul-Dec82-
  507
Prose, F. Hungry Hearts.
  J. Charyn, 441:6Mar83-10
  442(NY):7Mar83-135
Pross, W. Arno Schmidt.
  R. Voris, 221(GQ):Mar82-280
Prosser, E. Shakespeare's Anonymous Edi-
  tors.
  L.A. Beaurline, 639(VQR):Autumn82-715
  P. Bertram, 551(RenQ):Summer82-332
  L.C. Keyes, 191(ELN):Sep82-32
  S. Urkowitz, 570(SQ):Spring82-117
Prottas, J.M. People-Processing.
  C.N. Stone, 185:Apr83-588
Proulx, M. Le Cri durable.
  P.G. Lewis, 207(FR):Oct82-176
Proust, J. L'Objet et le texte.
  V. Mylne, 535(RHL):Jul-Aug82-664
Proust, J., ed. Recherches nouvelles sur
  quelques écrivains des Lumières.* (Vol
  2)
  M.H. Waddicor, 208(FS):Apr82-207
Proust, M. Correspondance. (Vol 7) (P.
  Kolb, ed)
  W.C. Carter, 207(FR):Apr83-778
Proust, M. Correspondance. (Vol 9) (P.
  Kolb, ed)
  J.M. Cocking, 617(TLS):18Feb83-155
Proust, M. Matinée chez la Princesse de
  Guermantes. (H. Bonnet and B. Brun, eds)
  Poèmes. (C. Francis and F. Gontier, eds)
  J.M. Cocking, 617(TLS):18Feb83-155
Proust, M. Marcel Proust: Selected Let-
  ters (1880-1903). (P. Kolb, ed)
  D. May, 362:18Aug83-19
  V.S. Pritchett, 453(NYRB):21Jul83-3
  J. Weightman, 441:29May83-5
  442(NY):15Aug83-90

Proust, M. Remembrance of Things Past.*
  (C.K. Scott Moncrieff, T. Kilmartin and
  A. Mayor, trans)
  A. Corn, 249(HudR):Summer82-298
Proust, M. A Search for Lost Time:
  Swann's Way. (J. Grieve, trans)
  D. May, 362:18Aug83-19
Prudent, L-F. Des baragouins à la langue
  antillaise.
  A. Hull, 207(FR):Oct82-201
Prudentius. Prudenzio, "Hamartigenia."
  (R. Palla, ed and trans)
  A-M. Palmer, 123:Vol32No2-175
de Prunes, M.I.S. – see under Santa Cruz
  de Prunes, M.I.
Prunty, W. The Times Between.
  W.B. Clark, 598(SoR):Winter83-242
  J.F. Cotter, 249(HudR):Autumn82-471
  639(VQR):Summer82-92
Průšek, J. The Lyrical and the Epic.
  (L.O-F. Lee, ed)
  E. Gunn, 293(JASt):May82-585
Pruslin, S., ed. Peter Maxwell Davies.*
  A. Whittall, 410(M&L):Jan81-64
Pruuden, S., comp. Catalogue of Books and
  Periodicals on Estonia in the British
  Library Reference Division. (D.B.
  Chrastek and C.G. Thomas, eds)
  D. Kirby, 575(SEER):Jul82-477
Pryce-Jones, D. Paris in the Third Reich.*
  639(VQR):Winter82-23
Pryce-Jones, D. – see "Cyril Connolly:
  Journal and Memoir"
Prynne, J.H. Poems.
  N. Wheale, 617(TLS):24Jun83-661
Pryse, M. – see Freeman, M.E.W.
Psaar, W. and M. Klein. Sage und Sachbuch.
  G. Petschel, 196:Band23Heft3/4-339
Psyhogeos, M. Greek Anthology/Elleniko
  Anthologio.
  J.E. Rexine, 399(MLJ):Winter82-452
Puccini, D. La palabra poética de Vicente
  Aleixandre.*
  G. Connell, 86(BHS):Oct82-346
  H. Galilea, 240(HR):Winter82-109
Puccioni, G. Il problema della monografia
  storica latina.
  E. Rawson, 123:Vol32No2-283
Pucelle, J. – see Locke, J.
Pugliesi, M. – see Kant, I.
Puhvel, M. "Beowulf" and Celtic Tradi-
  tion.*
  G. Clark, 529(QQ):Autumn82-633
  N. Jacobs, 382(MAE):1982/1-112
  T.A. Shippey, 541(RES):Aug82-306
Puig, M. Eternal Curse on the Reader of
  These Pages.* (Spanish title: Maldición
  Eterna a Quien Lea Esta Páginas.)
  C. Delacre Capestany, 37:Jan-Feb82-62
  639(VQR):Autumn82-131
Puig, M. Sangre de Amor Correspondido.
  O. Rossardi, 37:Sep-Oct82-63
Puk, F.S. – see Hardy, T.
Pulaski, M.A.S. Understanding Piaget.
  E.M. Regan, 529(QQ):Autumn82-646
Pulgram, E. Italic, Latin, Italian.
  P. Flobert, 555:Vol155fasc2-367
Pullega, P. – see Lukács, G.
Pullin, F., ed. New Perspectives on Mel-
  ville.*
  S.J. Allen, 161(DUJ):Dec81-151

Quennell, P. Customs and Characters.*
  C. de Beaurepaire, 364:Dec82/Jan83-138
  E. Grossman, 441:30Jan83-14
Quesada, M.A.L. and M. González Jiménez -
  see Ladero Quesada, M.A. and M. González
  Jiménez
Questal, V. Near Mourning Ground.
  S. Brown, 493:Dec81-65
Queval, J. - see "Beowulf, l'épopée fonda-
  mentale de la littérature anglaise"
de Quevedo, F. L'heure de tous; la hora
  de todos. (J. Bourg, P. Dupont and P.
  Geneste, eds and trans)
  R.M. Price, 86(BHS):Jan82-72
Quigly, I. The Heirs of Tom Brown.*
  B. Gutteridge, 364:Oct82-101
Quill, J. Spitfire.
  J. Joss, 617(TLS):14Oct83-1109
Quilligan, M. The Language of Allegory.*
  J.D. Burnley, 541(RES):May82-238
  M.J. Murrin, 301(JEGP):Apr82-247
Quinault, P. Astrate.* (E.J. Campion, ed)
  A. Viala, 535(RHL):Jul-Aug82-655
Quine, W.V. From a Logical Point of View.
  (2nd ed, rev)
  F.B. Fitch, 316:Mar82-230
Quine, W.V. Theories and Things.*
  R.B.S., 185:Jan83-416
Quinlivan, P. and P. Rose. The Fenians in
  England 1865-1872.
  R. Foster, 617(TLS):21Jan83-48
Quinn, A.H. Edgar Allan Poe.
  A. Hammond, 183(ESQ):Vol28No3-197
Quinn, E.C. The Penitence of Adam.*
  L.R. Muir, 382(MAE):1982/2-250
Quinn, J. American Tongue and Cheek.*
  W.W. Douglas, 128(CE):Jan82-72
  J.R. Gaskin, 569(SR):Winter82-143
Quinn, J. The Wolf Last Seen.
  D. Gioia, 249(HudR):Autumn82-483
Quinn, K. - see Horace
Quinnell, A.J. Snap Shot.*
  M. Laski, 362:20Jan83-23
Quinnett, P.G. The Troubled People Book.
  B. Bright, 441:23Jan83-14
Quinones, R.J. Dante Alighieri.
  J.M. Ferrante, 589:Apr82-452
Quinsat, G. Le Sang et la mémoire.
  F. Wybrands, 450(NRF):May82-109
Quintilian. Quintilien, "Institution ora-
  toire." (Vol 6, Bks 10 and 11) (J.
  Cousin, ed and trans)
  J-M. André, 555:Vol56fasc2-344
Quinton, A. The Politics of Imperfection.
  D.D. Todd, 154:Mar82-173
Quirk, R. Style and Communication in the
  English Language.
  M. Laski, 617(TLS):22Apr83-408
Quirk, T. Melville's Confidence Man.
  L. Mackinnon, 617(TLS):15Jul83-750

Rabassa, C.C. Demetrio Aguilera-Malta and
  Social Justice.*
  P.R. Beardsell, 86(BHS):Apr82-164
Rabbitt, T. The Booth Interstate.*
  R. Tillinghast, 569(SR):Spring82-291
Rabe, S.G. The Road to OPEC.
  W.J. Burggraaff, 263(RIB):Vol32No3/4-
  380
  639(VQR):Autumn82-126

Rabinowicz, W. Universalizability.*
  D.B., 543:Mar82-625
  D. Butcher, 482(PhR):Apr82-284
Rabinowitz, S.J. Sologub's Literary Chil-
  dren.
  L. Vogel, 104(CASS):Spring82-136
  J. West, 574(SEEJ):Winter82-482
Rabkin, E.S., ed. Science Fiction.
  C. Greenland, 617(TLS):18Nov83-1294
Rabkin, N. Shakespeare and the Problem of
  Meaning.*
  J.P. Hammersmith, 577(SHR):Fall82-356
  G.K. Hunter, 569(SR):Spring82-274
  M.E. Mooney, 130:Fall82-290
  B.A. Mowat, 301(JEGP):Jul82-414
  D.J. Palmer, 551(RenQ):Autumn82-519
  K. Smidt, 179(ES):Dec82-571
Raby, J. Venice, Dürer and the Oriental
  Mode.
  R. Irwin, 617(TLS):26Aug83-897
Race, W.H. The Classical Priamel from
  Homer to Boethius.
  D.E. Gerber, 121(CJ):Apr/May83-360
Racelle-Latin, D., ed. Inventaire des
  particularités lexicales du français en
  Afrique Noire. (fasc 1 and 2)
  J-C. Corbeil, 209(FM):Jan82-74
Rachlin, H. The Encyclopedia of the Music
  Business.
  J. Bridges, 498:Vol8No3/4-138
Rachlin, N. Married to a Stranger.
  B. Thompson, 441:2Oct83-14
Rachline, M. Le dernier océan.
  L. Séjor, 98:May82-435
Racinaro, R. La crisi del marxismo nella
  revisione di fine secolo.
  M.A. Finocchiaro, 319:Jan82-100
Racine, B. Le Gouverneur de Morée.
  R. Buss, 617(TLS):7Oct83-1076
Racine, J. Théâtre complet.* (J. Morel
  and A. Viala, eds)
  J. Dubu, 535(RHL):Jul-Aug82-653
  W. Leiner, 475:Vol9No17-787
  R.P. Sussman, 207(FR):Dec82-317
Racine, P. Plaisance du Xème à la fin du
  XIIIème siècle.
  C.E. Meek, 589:Apr82-413
Rackham, O. Ancient Woodland.
  W.H. Te Brake, 589:Apr82-418
Raczymow, H. Rivières d'exil.
  V. Beauvois, 450(NRF):Jul-Aug82-171
Radcliff-Umstead, D., ed. Human Sexuality
  in the Middle Ages and Renaissance.
  P.A. Knapp, 539:Feb83-70
Rademaker, C.S.M. Life and Work of Gerar-
  dus Joannes Vossius (1577-1649).
  H.H. Rowen, 551(RenQ):Summer82-292
Rader, M. Marx's Interpretation of His-
  tory.*
  E. Kamenka, 63:Mar82-81
Radford, C. and S. Minogue. The Nature of
  Criticism.
  W. Charlton, 479(PhQ):Oct82-389
  P.S. Guptara, 366:Autumn82-254
  A. Rodway, 89(JBA):Winter82-79
  D. Wheeler, 577(SHR):Fall82-375
Radicchi, P. Giovanni Lorenzo Cattani.
  J.W. Hill, 410(M&L):Jul/Oct82-303
Radice, L. Prelude to Appeasement.
  L.A. Gebhard, 104(CASS):Fall-Winter82-
  565
  P.S. Wandycz, 550(RusR):Jul82-360

Ranawake, S. Höfische Strophenkunst.*
  U. Müller, 224(GRM):Band32Heft2-248
  P.H. Stäblein, 545(RPh):Feb82-464
Rancière, J. La nuit des prolétaires.
  J. Borreil, 98:Oct82-807
  H.L. Butler, 207(FR):Feb83-500
Rand, H. Arshile Gorky.*
  C. Donnell-Kotrozo, 290(JAAC):Summer83-461
  R. Reiff, 127:Spring82-75
  M.S. Young, 39:Nov82-348
Randal, J. The Tragedy of Lebanon.
  M. Yapp, 617(TLS):26Aug83-911
Randal, J.C. Going All the Way.
  C. Glass, 453(NYRB):29Sep83-43
  E. Mortimer, 441:10Jul83-3
Randall, J. The Farewells.
  T. Diggory, 560:Summer82-159
  W.S. Di Piero, 598(SoR):Spring83-456
  E. Grosholz, 249(HudR):Summer82-319
  C. Inez, 502(PrS):Winter82/83-89
Randall, M. The Mansions of Long Island's
  Gold Coast.
  D.J. Hibbard, 658:Spring82-90
Randall, M. Doris Tijerino. Sandino's
  Daughters.
  C. De Bresson, 99:Aug82-33
Randolph, F.L. Studies for a Byron Bibli-
  ography.
  J.D. Bone, 677(YES):Vol 12-298
  T. Hofmann, 78(BC):Summer82-257
Randsborg, K. The Viking Age in Denmark.
  H. Chickering, 589:Jul82-652
  J.J. Kudlik, 563(SS):Spring82-160
Rang, B. - see Husserl, E.
Rangel-Guerrero, D. - see Vicente, G.
Rangel-Ribeiro, V. Baroque Music.
  R. Donington, 410(M&L):Jul/Oct82-313
Ranke, K. and others, eds. Enzyklopädie
  des Märchens.* (Vol 1)
  J. Dorst, 582(SFQ):Vol43No3/4-341
Ranke, K. and others, eds. Enzyklopädie
  des Märchens.* (Vol 2)
  A. Gier, 72:Band218Heft1-142
  H. Rölleke, 52:Band16Heft1-62
Ranke, K. and others, eds. Enzyklopädie
  des Märchens. (Vol 3, Pt 1)
  A. Gier, 72:Band218Heft1-142
Rankin, M. and J. The Getaway Guide II.
  529(QQ):Autumn82-687
Rankka, E., ed. Li ver del juïse.
  G. Roques, 553(RLiR):Jul-Dec82-498
Ranney, A. Channels of Power.
  R.J. Margolis, 441:27Nov83-16
Ransford, O. Bid the Sickness Cease.
  B. Hepburn, 617(TLS):30Dec83-1450
Ranum, O. Artisans of Glory.
  J-M. Apostolidès, 153:Winter82-58
  W.J. Bouwsma, 125:Spring82-300
Ranwez, A.D. Jean-Paul Sartre's "Les
  Temps Modernes."
  H. Davies, 208(FS):Oct82-495
  A. Rizzuto, 207(FR):Oct82-163
Rao, C.H.H. and P.C. Joshi, eds. Reflec-
  tions on Economic Development and Social
  Change.
  A. Heston, 293(JASt):May82-624
Rao, K.L.S. Mahatma Gandhi and Compara-
  tive Religion.
  A.B. Creel, 293(JASt):May82-625
Rao, M.S.A. Social Movements and Social
  Transformation.
  M. Juergensmeyer, 293(JASt):Feb82-398

Rao, P.G.R. Ernest Hemingway.
  R.S. Nelson, 395(MFS):Summer81-362
Raoul, V. The French Fictional Journal.*
  A. Chevalier, 535(RHL):Sep-Dec82-989
  L.K. Penrod, 207(FR):Feb83-471
Raper, J.R. From the Sunken Garden.*
  W.J. Stuckey, 395(MFS):Autumn82-507
Raphael, C. The Springs of Jewish Life.
  G. Vermes, 617(TLS):13May83-497
Raphael, D.D. Justice and Liberty.*
  J.P. Day, 483:Apr82-278
  A.G.N. Flew, 518:Jan82-55
Raphael, D.D. Moral Philosophy.*
  N.F., 185:Jul83-818
  A.G.N. Flew, 518:Jan82-55
  E. Griffin-Collart, 540(RIPh):Vol136
  fasc3-391
Raphael, F. Byron.*
  J. Bayley, 453(NYRB):2Jun83-25
Rapoport, D.C. and Y. Alexander, eds. The
  Morality of Terrorism.
  M.A.K., 185:Jul83-840
Rapoport, L. The Lost Jews.
  Y. Shapiro, 390:Oct82-61
Rapp, G., Jr. and J.A. Gifford, eds. Troy:
  The Archaeological Geology. (Supplemen-
  tary Monograph 4)
  J.M. Cook, 617(TLS):25Feb83-198
Rappard, H.V. Psychology as Self-Knowl-
  edge.*
  F.E.E., 543:Jun82-896
Raschke, M.G. New Studies in Roman Com-
  merce with the East.
  A.F.P. Hulsewé, 293(JASt):Feb82-342
Rasmussen, S.E. London, The Unique City.
  (rev ed)
  A.J.G.H., 617(TLS):20May83-527
Rasputin, V.G. Povesti.
  D. Milivojević, 558(RLJ):Winter-
  Spring82-307
Rassam, J. Le silence comme introduction
  à la métaphysique.
  A. Reix, 542:Oct-Dec82-685
Rassias, J.A., with J. de la Chapelle-
  Skubly. Le Français.*
  J.C. Evans, 399(MLJ):Summer82-214
Rastall, R. The Notation of Western Music.
  I. Fenlon, 617(TLS):17Jun83-636
Rataboul, L.J. Le Pasteur anglican dans
  le roman victorien.*
  T.J. Winnifrith, 677(YES):Vol 12-305
Ratcliff, C. John Singer Sargent.*
  J.D., 231:Jan83-75
  S. Olson, 617(TLS):3Jun83-561
Ratcliffe, S. Campion: On Song.
  E.B. Jorgens, 551(RenQ):Winter82-655
Rathbun, W.J. and M. Knight. Yo No Bi.
  R.L. Shep, 614:Fall83-24
Ratliff, W.M. Creaciones y creadores.
  A. Dias, 399(MLJ):Summer82-227
  I.E. Stanislawczyk, 238:Sep82-475
Ratner, L.G. Classic Music.
  B. Churgin, 317:Summer82-351
Rau, W. - see "Bhartṛharis Vākyapadīya"
Rauch, I. and G.F. Carr, eds. Linguistic
  Method.*
  G.F. Meier, 682(ZPSK):Band34Heft4-493
Raugei, A.M. - see "Gautier de Dargies
  Poesie"
Raulet, G. - see Bloch, E.
Raval, S. Metacriticism.
  M. Rapisarda, 395(MFS):Winter82/83-725

Raven, S. September Castle.
　　V. Cunningham, 617(TLS):24Jun83-682
Raven, S. Shadows on the Grass.*
　　M. Meyer, 364:Aug/Sep82-131
Ravitch, D. The Troubled Crusade.
　　R. Berman, 441:18Sep83-3
　　442(NY):14Nov83-206
Raw, B.C. The Art and Background of Old
　English Poetry.*
　　M. Lehnert, 682(ZPSK):Band34Heft2-243
Rawling, T. Ghosts at my Back.
　　A. Stevenson, 617(TLS):18Feb83-160
Rawlings, H.R. 3d. The Structure of Thucy-
　dides' History.*
　　P.J. Rhodes, 161(DUJ):Jun82-276
　　H.D. Westlake, 123:Vol132No2-232
Raworth, T. Writing.
　　C. MacCabe, 617(TLS):30Dec83-1455
Rawski, T.G. Economic Growth and Employ-
　ment in China. China's Transition to
　Industrialism.
　　V.D. Lippit, 293(JASt):Aug82-817
Rawson, D.C. - see Gruzenburg, O.O.
Ray, D., ed. From A to Z.
　　639(VQR):Winter82-25
Ray, D. - see Mayo, E.L.
Ray, D.J. Aleut and Eskimo Art.
　　C.L. Rawlins, 649(WAL):Winter83-380
"Man Ray: Photographs."
　　B.L., 55:Nov82-58
　　A. Ross, 364:Oct82-3
Ray, S. The Blyton Phenomenon.*
　　B. Gutteridge, 364:Oct82-101
Ray, S.K., R.W. Cummings, Jr. and R.W.
　Herdt. Policy Planning for Agricultural
　Development.
　　T.N. Srinivasin, 293(JASt):Feb82-399
Raymond, E. We, the Accused.
　　639(VQR):Summer82-97
Raymond, F., ed. Jules Verne, Machines et
　Imaginaire.
　　S. Vierne, 535(RHL):Sep-Dec82-944
Raymond, G. Un Moulin, un village, un
　pays.
　　A. Nabarra, 207(FR):Mar83-671
de Raymond, J-F. L'improvisation.
　　M. Adam, 542:Oct-Dec82-685
Raymond, M. Romantisme et rêverie.*
　　H. Jechova, 549(RLC):Apr-Jun82-219
Raymond, M. and G. Poulet. Marcel Raymond
　— Georges Poulet, Correspondance: 1950-
　1977. (P. Grotzer, ed)
　　R. Macksey, 400(MLN):Dec82-1304
　　J. Onimus, 535(RHL):Sep-Dec82-984
Raymond, M.B. and M.R. Sullivan - see
　Browning, E.B.
"G. Raynauds Bibliographie des altfranzö-
　sischen Liedes." (Vol 1) (rev by H.
　Spanke)
　　N.B. Smith, 589:Jan82-198
　　J. Stevens, 382(MAE):1982/2-254
Raynor, H. Music in England.
　　J. Caldwell, 410(M&L):Jul/Oct81-395
Raz, J. The Authority of Law.*
　　D. Lyons, 482(PhR):Jul82-461
"Razrušennye i oskvernennye xramy."*
　　M. Winokur, 574(SEEJ):Spring82-111
Read, B. Victorian Sculpture.*
　　S. Beattie, 90:Dec82-777
　　C. Gere, 39:Dec82-431

Read, F. '76: One World and "The Cantos"
　of Ezra Pound.*
　　S.J. Adams, 106:Fall82-245
　　W. Harmon, 569(SR):Spring82-279
Read, G. Style and Orchestration.
　　D. Charlton, 410(M&L):Jan81-74
Read, M. The Story of the Shadows.
　　M. Halasa, 617(TLS):2Dec83-1356
Reader, J. Missing Links.
　　J. Jordan, 42(AR):Winter82-113
"Reader's Digest Household Medical Encyclo-
　pedia."
　　529(QQ):Summer82-458
Reading, P. Diplopic.
　　G. Ewart, 617(TLS):30Sep83-1061
Ready, R. Hazlitt at Table.
　　R.M. Wardle, 340(KSJ):Vol131-223
Reale, G. The Concept of First Philosophy
　and the Unity of the Metaphysics of
　Aristotle.* (J.R. Catan, ed and trans)
　　J. Driscoll, 482(PhR):Oct82-623
　　J.D.G. Evans, 518:Oct82-203
　　G. Seel, 53(AGP):Band64Heft3-349
Reale, G. Storia della filosofia antica.*
　　B.M.B., 543:Jun82-897
　　A.A. Long, 123:Vol132No1-38
Reale, M. Experiência e cultura.
　　Z. Kouřim, 542:Oct-Dec82-687
"Reallexikon der Assyriologie und vorder-
　asiatischen Archäologie." (Vol 5, Pts
　7/8; Vol 6, Pts 1/2)
　　P. Swiggers, 350:Mar83-226
"Reallexikon für Antike und Christentum."
　(Pts 81-83) (T. Klauser and others, eds)
　　J. André, 555:Vol55fasc1-190
Reamer, F.G. Ethical Dilemmas in Social
　Service.
　　J.D., 185:Jul83-840
Reardon-Anderson, J. Yenan and the Great
　Powers.
　　S.M. Goldstein, 293(JASt):Nov81-120
"Reason, Action and Experience."
　　J-L. Dumas, 192(EP):Apr-Jun81-230
Reavey, G. - see Yevtushenko, Y.
Reavy, J.M. The Music of Corktown.
　　L.E. McCullough, 292(JAF):Apr-Jun82-
　　249
Rebel, H. Peasant Classes.
　　J. Whaley, 617(TLS):19Aug83-885
Reboredo, V.G. - see under González
　Reboredo, V.
Reboul, P. - see Laforgue, J.
Récanati, F. Les énoncés performatifs.
　　J. Bellemin-Noel, 98:May82-406
Rechy, J. Bodies and Souls.
　　A. Cheuse, 441:10Jul83-15
"Records of The Most Ancient and Puissant
　Order of the Beggar's Benison and Merry-
　land, Anstruther."
　　A. Smith, 617(TLS):18Mar83-271
Reator, M., ed. Cowboy Life on the Texas
　Plains.
　　L. Milazzo, 584(SWR):Autumn82-vi
Réda, J., ed. Anthologie des musiciens de
　jazz.
　　J. Laurans, 450(NRF):Feb82-166
Rédei, K. Zyrian Folklore Texts.*
　　H-J. Uther, 196:Band23Heft1/2-149
Redfern, R. The Making of a Continent.
　　S.J. Gould, 441:4Dec83-75
Redgrave, M. In My Mind's Eye.
　　H. Spurling, 617(TLS):21Oct83-1149

Redgrove, P. The Apple-Broadcast and Other New Poems.*
  J. Bristow, 175:Autumn82-267
  M. O'Neill, 493:Apr82-59
Redmond, J. - see "Themes in Drama"
Redondo, A., ed. XIXe Colloque International d'Études Humanistes, Tours, 5-17 juillet 1976: L'Humanisme dans les lettres espagnoles.*
  H. Nader, 551(RenQ):Summer81-266
Redpath, P.A. A Simplified Introduction to the Wisdom of St. Thomas.
  H. Veatch, 258:Jun82-218
Redwood, C., ed. An Elgar Companion.
  M. Trend, 617(TLS):15Jul83-751
Rée, P. De l'Origine des sentiments moraux.
  T. Cordellier, 450(NRF):Jul-Aug82-182
Reece, R.H.W. The Name of Brooke.
  J.S. Bastin, 617(TLS):18Mar83-274
Reed, J. The Missionary Mind and American East Asia Policy, 1911-1915.
  J.K. Fairbank, 617(TLS):24Jun83-652
Reed, J. Sir Walter Scott.*
  K. Kroeber, 571(ScLJ):Spring82-13
Reed, J.R. The Natural History of H.G. Wells.*
  C.R. La Bossière, 268(IFR):Summer83-155
Reed, K.T. Truman Capote.
  P.T. Nolan, 573(SSF):Winter82-96
Reed, M. The Georgian Triumph 1700-1830.
  P.J. Corfield, 617(TLS):12Aug83-848
Reed, T.J. The Classical Centre.*
  A.J. Camigliano, 406:Fall82-355
Reed, W. Great American Illustrators.
  M.S. Young, 39:Mar82-212
Reed, W.L. An Exemplary History of the Novel.*
  R. Bjornson, 141:Spring82-186
  M. Spilka, 594:Spring82-128
  P. Stevick, 395(MFS):Winter81/82-748
Reeder, D.A., ed. Educating Our Masters.
  D.G. Paz, 637(VS):Autumn81-86
Reedy, G. Lyndon B. Johnson.
  M. Kempton, 453(NYRB):17Feb83-25
Rees, G. Early Railway Prints.
  J. Ranlett, 637(VS):Winter82-254
Rees, N. Slogans.
  C. Sharpe, 362:13Jan83-22
Reese, M.M. Shakespeare, His World and His Work. (rev)
  M. Eccles, 570(SQ):Winter82-537
  G.K. Hunter, 569(SR):Spring82-274
Reese, W.L. Dictionary of Philosophy and Religion.*
  G.K. Plochmann, 319:Jul82-324
Reeves, H. Patience dans l'azur.
  A. Suied, 450(NRF):Feb82-147
Reeves, J. and R. Gittings - see Hardy, T.
Reff, T. Manet and Modern Paris.
  D.H. Wright, 453(NYRB):2Jun83-6
"Reflections upon a Century of Architecture, Evansville, Indiana."
  D.J. Hibbard, 658:Spring82-90
Regan, D.H. Utilitarianism and Co-operation.*
  P. Dubois, 542:Oct-Dec82-689
Regan, T. The Case for Animal Rights.
  R. Nozick, 441:27Nov83-11
Regan, T., ed. Matters of Life and Death.*
  R. Young, 518:Jan82-60

Reger, E. Union der festen Hand.
  R.C. Holub, 406:Spring82-72
Reggiani, R. I proemi degli Annales di Ennio.*
  P. Flobert, 555:Vol56fasc2-341
Regina, V. Alcamo.
  W. Krönig, 683:Band45Heft2-211
Regn, G. Konflikt der Interpretationen.
  S. Bogumil, 547(RF):Band93Heft1/2-273
Reh, A.M. Die Rettung der Menschlichkeit.
  W. Paulsen, 222(GR):Fall82-167
Rehder, R. Wordsworth and the Beginnings of Modern Poetry.
  D. McCracken, 405(MP):May83-430
  42(AR):Summer82-367
Rehg, K.L. and D.G. Sohl. Ponapean-English Dictionary.
  G.F. Meier, 682(ZPSK):Band34Heft4-503
Reich, C. Financier.
  R. Lekachman, 441:16Oct83-14
Reich, M. Racial Inequality.
  J.L.H., 185:Jan83-437
Reich, R.B. The Next American Frontier.
  L. Caplan, 442(NY):20Jun83-97
  R. Lekachman, 441:24Apr83-1
  R.J. Samuelson, 231:Jun83-60
Reichart, W.A. and L. Schlissel - see Irving, W.
Reichelt, K. Barockdrama und Absolutismus.
  J. Hardin, 221(GQ):May82-411
Reichert, J. Making Sense of Literature.
  P.H. Fry, 107(CRCL):Mar82-87
  E. Wikborg, 179(ES):Jun82-268
Reichler, C. La diabolie, la séduction, la renardie, l'écriture.
  P. Dandrey, 475:No16Pt2-423
  H. Godin, 208(FS):Jul82-370
Reichmann, F. The Sources of Western Literacy.
  F.H. Bäuml, 589:Jul82-654
  G. Benecke, 354:Sep82-340
Reid, A. and D. Marr, eds. Perceptions of the Past in Southeast Asia.
  W.R. Roff, 293(JASt):May82-635
Reid, C. Pea Soup.*
  H. Lomas, 364:Dec82/Jan83-100
  M. O'Neill, 493:Jan83-48
Reid, D. Bertram Brooker. (2nd ed)
  N.E. Dillow, 529(QQ):Autumn82-631
Reid, I. Fiction and the Great Depression.*
  A. Pollard, 366:Autumn82-269
  E. Webby, 541(RES):Nov82-498
Reid, J.C. Acadia, Maine, and New Scotland.*
  G.T. Stewart, 656(WMQ):Oct82-694
Reid, J.P. The Briefs of the American Revolution.
  R. Middlekauf, 165(EAL):Spring83-102
Reid, J.P. In a Defiant Stance.
  639(VQR):Spring82-44
Reid, J.P. In Defiance of the Law.
  R. Middlekauf, 165(EAL):Spring83-102
  J.E. Semonche, 432(NEQ):Jun82-293
Reid, M. The Life of Ryley.
  D. Barbour, 648(WCR):Oct82-37
Reid, R. The Book of Buildings.
  529(QQ):Summer82-458
Reiersen, J.R. Pathfinder for Norwegian Emigrants.
  J.L. Sammons, 563(SS):Autumn82-307

Reiffenstein, I., ed. Österreichische Märchen.
E. Ettlinger, 203:Vol93No2-237
H-J. Uther, 196:Band23Heft3/4-332
Reiger, G. Wanderer on My Native Shore.
P-L. Adams, 61:Jun83-104
Reiher, R. Zur sprachlichen Kommunikation im sozialistischen Industriebetrieb.
J. Donath, 682(ZPSK):Band35Heft2-230
Reilly, C.W., ed. Scars Upon My Heart.*
M. Shaw, 493:Apr82-65
Reilly, E.R. - see Mahler, G. and G. Adler
Reilly, J.H. Jean Giraudoux.*
A.G. Raymond, 399(MLJ):Spring82-87
Reilly, L.C. Slaves in Ancient Greece.
O. Masson, 555:Vol55fasc2-326
Reiman, D.H., ed. English Romantic Poetry, 1800-1835.*
E.D. Mackerness, 447(N&Q):Oct81-438
E.B. Murray, 541(RES):Nov82-479
Reiman, D.H., ed. The Romantic Context: Poetry 1789-1830.
M. Butler, 541(RES):Feb82-94
Reiman, D.H., ed. The Romantic Context: Poetry; Significant Minor Poetry 1789-1830.
K. Williamson, 541(RES):Nov82-480
Rein, K. Religiöse Minderheiten als Sprachgemeinschaftsmodelle.
H. Wolf, 685(ZDL):2/1981-248
Rein, K. and R. Hildebrandt, eds. Siebenbürgisch-Deutscher Wortatlas.
E. Seidelmann, 685(ZDL):2/1982-222
Reindorf, J. Scandinavians in Africa.
M. Johnson, 69:Vol51No4-885
Reiner, E. Les doublets étymologiques.
G. Roques, 553(RLiR):Jul-Dec82-464
Reiner, E. Die etymologischen Dubletten des Französischen.
G. Schlemmer, 547(RF):Band94Heft2/3-277
Reinhartz, D. Milovan Djilas.
A.N. Dragnich, 104(CASS):Fall-Winter82-578
Reinhold, H. Der englische Roman im 18. Jahrhundert.
H. Foltinek, 224(GRM):Band32Heft1-122
Reinitz, R. Irony and Conscience.
D.W. Noble, 106:Winter82-321
R.A. Skotheim, 579(SAQ):Spring82-230
Reis, M. Lauttheorie und Lautgeschichte.
R. Hinderling, 684(ZDA):Band111Heft1-5
Reisinger, P. Idealismus als Bildtheorie.*
G. Schönrich, 687:Jan-Mar82-126
Reiss, E. William Dunbar.*
P. Bawcutt, 677(YES):Vol 12-238
L. Ebin, 588(SSL):Vol 17-288
F.H. Ridley, 551(RenQ):Spring81-132
Reiss, J. Express.
M. Kinzie, 29:Nov/Dec03 40
Reiss, T.J. Tragedy and Truth.*
T. Cave, 131(CL):Summer82-276
U. Chaudhuri, 546(RR):Nov82-516
O.B. Hardison, Jr., 551(RenQ):Spring82-126
G. Hemphill, 569(SR):Winter82-x
E. Rothstein, 301(JEGP):Jul82-421
R.M. Torrance, 191(ELN):Sep82-47
Reitz, D. Commando.
G. Wheatcroft, 617(TLS):16Sep83-983
Reitz, J.G. The Survival of Ethnic Groups.
R.T. Bowles, 298:Spring82-131

"Relire 'Les Destinées' d'Alfred de Vigny."*
J-P. Picot, 535(RHL):Mar-Apr82-305
Remacle, L. Notaires de Malmedy, Spa et Verviers.
L. de Cock, 553(RLiR):Jan-Jun81-264
Remak, H.H.H. Der Weg zur Weltliteratur.
R.L. Ackerman, 221(GQ):May82-429
H.S. Daemmrich, 678(YCGL):No30-84
Remigio dei Girolami. Contra falsos ecclesie professores. (F. Tamburini, ed)
D.R. Lesnick, 589:Oct82-929
Remini, R.V. Andrew Jackson and the Course of American Freedom, 1822-1832.*
639(VQR):Spring82-51
Remnant, M. Musical Instruments of the West.
M. Rasmussen, 410(M&L):Jan81-70
Remnant, P. and J. Bennett - see Leibniz, G.W.
Rémond, R. Les Droites en France.
D. Johnson, 617(TLS):28Jan83-90
Renard, J-C. Selected Poems.* (G.D. Martin, ed)
R. Cardinal, 402(MLR):Apr82-467
Renaud, J. Clandestine(s) ou La tradition du couchant.
P. Merivale, 102(CanL):Winter81-157
"Rencontres des peuples francophones 1979."
M. Lebel, 102(CanL):Winter81-159
Rendell, R. The Speaker of Mandarin.
T.J. Binyon, 617(TLS):13May83-498
Render, S.L. Charles W. Chesnutt.*
B. Hitchcock, 577(SHR):Summer82-274
C. Werner, 392:Winter81/82-85
de Renéville, J.R. Le philosophe retrouvé, précédé de Criton.
J-J. Wunenburger, 192(EP):Apr-Jun81-247
Rennison, J.R. Bidialektale Phonologie.
B.J. Koekkoek, 221(GQ):Nov82-583
Renouvier, C. Manuel républicain de l'homme et du citoyen (1848).* (M. Agulhon, ed)
E. Schulkind, 208(FS):Jan82-84
Renwick, R.D. English Folk Poetry.*
E.R. Long, 650(WF):Apr82-158
Renz, H. Geschichtsgedanke und Christusfrage.
N. Fischer, 342:Band73Heft1-88
Renzi, L. Einführung in die romanische Sprachwissenschaft.* (G. Ineichen, ed)
J. Albrecht, 260(IF):Band86-355
H.W. Haller, 660(Word):Dec82-268
"Répertoire des spécialistes français du XVIe siècle." "Répertoire des chercheurs étrangers spécialistes du XVIe siècle."
H. Sonneville, 356(LR):Feb82 79
"Répertoire international des Médiévistes/International Directory of Medievalists."
H. Sonneville, 356(LR):Nov82-359
"Report of the Commission of Inquiry into Incomes, Prices and Conditions of Service." [Government of Zimbabwe]
G. Williams, 69:Vol52No3-114
"Report of the President's Commission on Strategic Forces."
M. Bundy, 453(NYRB):16Jun83-3
Requardt, W. and M. Machatzke. Gerhart Hauptmann und Erkner.
R.C. Cowen, 680(ZDP):Band101Heft2-307

Rescher, N. Cognitive Systematization.*
  G. Priest, 63:Jun82-185
Rescher, N. Idéalisme contre Pragmatisme,
  Cohérence contre Succès.
  L. Apostel, 540(RIPh):Vol36fasc4-653
Rescher, N. Leibniz's Metaphysics of
  Nature.
  F. Duchesneau, 154:Jun82-391
Rescher, N. Scepticism.*
  O.A. Johnson, 484(PPR):Jun83-551
  R. McLaughlin, 63:Jun82-177
  A. O'Hear, 393(Mind):Jan82-132
Rescher, N. Unpopular Essays on Technolog-
  ical Progress.
  E.G.B., 543:Dec81-407
  D. Wells, 63:Sep82-302
Rescher, N. and R. Brandom. The Logic of
  Inconsistency.*
  D. Makinson, 316:Mar82-233
  R.G.W., 543:Mar82-627
Resnick, M.C. Introducción a la historia
  de la lengua española.
  T.A. Lathrop, 304(JHP):Spring82-239
Resnicow, H. The Gold Solution.
  N. Callendar, 441:27Nov83-28
Resnik, M.D. Frege and the Philosophy of
  Mathematics.
  J.B., 543:Sep81-160
  G. Currie, 84:Dec82-435
  C. McIntosh, 316:Jun82-475
  J.M.B. Moss, 311(JP):Sep82-497
  J.E. Tiles, 518:Jul82-164
Restany, P. Yves Klein.
  C. Nadelman, 55:Nov82-52
Resweber, J-P. La méthode interdisciplin-
  aire.
  A. Reix, 542:Oct-Dec82-689
Retamar, R.F. - see under Fernández Reta-
  mar, R.
Rétat, P., ed. L'Attentat de Damiens.
  A.D. Hytier, 173(ECS):Spring82-344
  J. Lough, 208(FS):Jul82-337
Reuber, G.L. Canada's Political Economy.
  T.L. Powrie, 529(QQ):Spring82-196
Reudenbach, B. G.B. Piranesi.
  R. Middleton, 576:Dec82-333
Reumaux, P. Jeanne aux chiens.
  N.Q. Maurer, 450(NRF):Apr82-127
Reumaux, P. Largeur des tempes.
  D. Leuwers, 450(NRF):Sep82-117
Reumaux, P. - see Guadalupi, G. and A.
  Manguel
Revard, S.P. The War in Heaven.*
  M.K. Starkman, 551(RenQ):Summer81-290
Revel, J-F. La Grâce de l'état.
  H.B. Sutton, 207(FR):Feb83-497
Reveley, E. In Good Faith.
  J. O'Faolain, 617(TLS):1Jul83-696
Revell, D. From the Abandoned Cities.
  A. Williamson, 441:13Nov83-26
Revell, P. Quest in Modern American
  Poetry.*
  R. Crowder, 27(AL):Oct82-457
Reverdy, P. Ferraille; Plein verre; Le
  Chant des morts; Bois vert [suivi de]
  Pierres blanches.
  D. Leuwers, 450(NRF):Jan82-107
Reverdy, P. Roof Slates and Other Poems
  of Pierre Reverdy.
  M. Guiney, 188(ECr):Winter82-101

"Revista Nueva, 1899." (L. Ruiz Contreras,
  ed)
  J.B. Jelinski, 238:Mar82-145
  M. Lentzen, 547(RF):Band94Heft4-509
Rewald, J. - see Pissarro, C.
Rex, J. Race Relations in Sociological
  Theory.
  R.T.B., 617(TLS):11Feb83-143
Rey, A. Le Lexique.
  J. Pleciński, 360(LP):Vol24-139
  J. Sypnicki, 360(LP):Vol24-137
Rey, A. and S. Chantreau. Dictionnaire
  des expressions et locutions.
  G. Matoré, 209(FM):Oct82-352
Rey, F. La Compagnie des Dames.
  P.A. Mankin, 207(FR):Mar83-672
Rey, P-L. L'Univers romanesque de Gobin-
  eau.
  M.D. Biddiss, 208(FS):Jul82-341
Rey-Debove, J. Le Métalangage.
  I. Tamba-Mecz, 209(FM):Apr82-152
Rey-Debove, J. and G. Gagnon. Diction-
  naire des anglicismes.*
  B. de Bessé, 209(FM):Oct82-363
  G. Price, 208(FS):Jan82-116
Rey-Flaud, H. Pour une dramaturgie du
  Moyen Age.*
  G.A. Runnalls, 208(FS):Jan82-51
Reynaert, J. De Beeldspraak van Hadewijch.
  E. Colledge, 589:Apr82-420
Reynard, J-M. Maint corps des chambres.
  P. Denis, 98:May82-457
Reynaud, J-D. and Y. Grafmeyer. Français,
  qui êtes-vous?
  E. Knox, 207(FR):Feb83-494
Reynolds, C.H.B. Sinhalese.
  L. Jayawardena and K. Matzel, 259(IIJ):
  Jan82-69
Reynolds, D.S. Faith in Fiction.*
  L. Buell, 183(ESQ):Vol128No1-63
  B.H. McClary, 27(AL):Mar82-142
Reynolds, G. Wallace Collection: Cata-
  logue of Miniatures.*
  J. Murdoch, 90:Jul82-450
Reynolds, G. - see Constable, J.
Reynolds, M.S. Hemingway's Reading, 1910-
  1940.*
  G. Monteiro, 517(PBSA):Vol76No1-95
  S. Wertheim, 234:Fall82-81
  G. Wickes, 395(MFS):Summer82-292
Reynolds, M.T. Joyce and Dante.*
  W. Harmon, 301(JEGP):Oct82-589
  D. Hayman, 594:Winter82-386
  H. Levin, 131(CL):Fall82-364
  K.E. Marre, 395(MFS):Summer82-266
  J. Voelker, 573(SSF):Spring82-187
  295(JML):Dec82-479
Reynolds, R. Who's Who in the Royal Fam-
  ily.
  D.A.N. Jones, 617(TLS):29Apr83-428
Reynolds, T.S. Stronger Than a Hundred
  Men.
  N. Smith, 617(TLS):25Nov83-1331
Reynolds, W.A. Hernán Cortés en la litera-
  tura del Siglo de Oro.
  A.E. Wiltrout, 552(REH):Jan82-116
Reznikova, N.V. Ognennaia pamiat'.
  E. Bristol, 550(RusR):Apr82-239
  A. Pyman, 575(SEER):Jul82-452
Rezvani. La Loi humaine.
  D. Boreham, 617(TLS):14Oct83-1142

Richmond, C. - see Alas, L.
Richmond, H.M. Puritans and Libertines.*
  E.E. Kuzirian, 539:May83-153
  A.L. Prescott, 551(RenQ):Autumn82-511
Richter, D. Art, Economics and Change.*
  J. Picton, 69:Vol51No4-889
Richter, M. The Politics of Conscience.
  K.A.M., 617(TLS):21Oct83-1171
Richter, M. Sprache und Gesellschaft im
  Mittelalter.*
  H. Käsmann, 38:Band100Heft3/4-455
Richter, P. and I. Ricardo. Voltaire.*
  M.L. Perkins, 210(FrF):Jan82-78
Rickard, P. and T.G.S. Combe - see Harmer,
  L.C.
Rickett, A.A. - see "Wang Kuo-Wei's Jen-
  chien Tz'u-hua"
Rickford, J.R., ed. A Festival of Guy-
  anese Words.
  R.D. Abrahams, 292(JAF):Jan-Mar82-99
Ricklefs, U. Arnims lyrisches Werk.
  R. Burwick, 406:Fall82-359
  R. Hoermann, 221(GQ):May82-423
Rickman, G. The Corn Supply of Ancient
  Rome.*
  J-C. Richard, 555:Vol56fasc2-369
Rickman, H.P. William Dilthey.*
  W. Mays, 518:Oct82-217
  T. Plantinga, 482(PhR):Jul82-448
Rickman, H.P. - see Dilthey, W.
Rico, F. Signos e indicios en la portada
  de Ripoll.
  C. Stern, 545(RPh):Aug81-302
Ricoeur, P. Hermeneutics and the Human
  Sciences.* (J.B. Thompson, ed and trans)
  P.B.F., 185:Jan83-422
Ricord, C.G.G. - see under Guez Ricord,
  C.G.
Riddle, J.M. - see Marbod of Rennes
Ridenour, R.C. Nationalism, Modernism,
  and Personal Rivalry in Nineteenth-
  Century Russian Music.*
  E. Garden, 410(M&L):Jul/Oct82-307
Rider, R.W., with D. Paulsen. Sixshooters
  and Sagebrush.*
  B.J. Stoeltje, 292(JAF):Jul-Sep82-365
Ridge, M., ed. The New Bilingualism.
  J.A. Fishman, 350:Sep83-676
Ridgely, J.V. Nineteenth-Century Southern
  Literature.
  J.C. Guilds, 27(AL):Dec82-615
Ridgeway, W.H. Community Leadership in
  Maryland, 1790-1840.
  P.F. Lachance, 106:Spring82-53
Ridgway, B.S. The Archaic Style in Greek
  Sculpture.*
  E.D. Francis and M. Vickers, 90:Jan82-
  41
Ridgway, B.S. Fifth Century Styles in
  Greek Sculpture.*
  R. Higgins, 39:May82-413
  I. Scheibler, 471:Jul/Aug/Sep82-268
Ridho, A. Oriental Ceramics. (Vol 3)
  "Skipjack," 463:Summer82-179
Ridley, J. Statesman and Saint.
  N. Bliven, 442(NY):18Apr83-142
Rieber, A.J. Merchants and Entrepreneurs
  in Imperial Russia.
  639(VQR):Summer82-84
Riede, D.G. Swinburne.*
  P. Clements, 677(YES):Vol 12-323

Riedel, N. Uwe Johnson: Bibliographie
  1959-1980. (Vol 1) (2nd ed)
  R. Pichl, 602:Vol 13No2-355
  354:Dec82-470
Riedel, N. Uwe Johnson: Bibliographie
  1959-1977.* (Vol 2)
  R. Pichl, 602:Vol 13No2-357
Riedel, W.E. Das literarische Kanadabild.
  F.H. Bastein, 564:Sep82-231
  K.P. Stich, 102(CanL):Spring82-98
Riedy, J.L. Chicago Sculpture.
  J. Zimmer, 324:Aug83-573
Riegel, L. Guerre et littérature.*
  F. Mielke, 549(RLC):Apr-Jun82-226
Rieger, G.E. Henrik Ibsen in Selbstzeug-
  nissen und Bilddokumenten.
  D.J. Parent, 221(GQ):Nov82-601
Riegl, A. Problemas de estilos.
  D. Angulo Íñiguez, 48:Apr-Jun80-212
Riehle, W. The Middle English Mystics.
  V.M. Lagorio, 589:Oct82-930
Riel, L.D. Poésies religieuses et poli-
  tiques.
  S.P. Knutson, 102(CanL):Winter81-151
"Louis Riel — Justice Must be Done."
  S.P. Knutson, 102(CanL):Winter81-151
Riessauw, A-M. Catalogue des oeuvres
  vocales écrites par des compositeurs
  européens sur des poèmes de Verlaine.
  A.F.L.T., 412:Feb81-61
Riffaterre, M. Semiotics of Poetry.*
  P. Hamilton, 541(RES):Nov82-504
Rifkin, J. Entropy.
  D. Wann, 152(UDQ):Spring82-115
Rigaud, N.J. George Etherege.
  E. Burns, 541(RES):Nov82-472
  J. Conaghan, 189(EA):Oct-Dec82-465
Rigby, T.H., A. Brown and P. Reddaway, eds.
  Authority, Power and Policy in the USSR.*
  J. Keep, 575(SEER):Apr82-297
Rigelhof, T.F. The Education of J.J. Pass.
  M. Harry, 150(DR):Winter82/83-704
Rigg, A.G., ed. Editing Medieval Texts.
  J. Gerritsen, 179(ES):Oct82-463
Riggan, W. Pícaros, Madmen, Naïfs, and
  Clowns.*
  R.B. Hauck, 395(MFS):Winter82/83-720
  A. Otten, 42(AR):Summer82-361
Riggio, T.P., J.L.W. West 3d and N.M.
  Westlake - see Dreiser, T.
Rigolot, F. Poétique et onomastique.
  P.M. Smith, 208(FS):Jan82-61
Rigolot, F. Le Texte de la Renaissance.
  T. Cave, 617(TLS):14Oct83-1123
Riiho, T. "Por" y "para."*
  G. Fält, 597(SN):Vol54No2-342
Riikonen, H. Die Antike im historischen
  Roman des 19. Jahrhunderts.*
  M. Landfester, 394:Vol35fasc3/4-448
Rile, K. Winter Music.
  F. Taliaferro, 441:31Jul83-12
Riley, B., ed. Material History Bulletin
  8.
  C. Camp, 292(JAF):Apr-Jun82-235
Riley, H.M.K. Idee und Gestaltung.*
  E. Schürer, 133:Band15Heft4-375
Riley, J.C. International Government Fi-
  nance and the Amsterdam Capital Market
  1740-1815.
  T.P. Enger, 173(ECS):Winter81/82-209
Riley, P. Kant's Political Philosophy.
  W.H. Walsh, 617(TLS):3Jun83-566

Riley, P. Will and Political Legitimacy.
  B. Goodwin, 617(TLS):25Mar83-300
Rilke, R.M. Selected Poems. (R. Bly, ed
  and trans)
  D. McDuff, 565:Vol23No1-58
Rilke, R.M. The Selected Poetry of Rainer
  Maria Rilke. (S. Mitchell, ed and trans)
  D. Donoghue, 441:30Jan83-9
  S. Spender, 453(NYRB):17Mar83-33
Rilke, R.M. An Unofficial Rilke.* (M.
  Hamburger, trans)
  M. Hofmann, 493:Jun82-79
Rimbaud, A. Oeuvres. (S. Bernard and A.
  Guyaux, eds)
  N. Osmond, 208(FS):Oct82-485
Rinaldi, N. We Have Lost Our Fathers.
  J.F. Cotter, 249(HudR):Autumn82-471
"Il Rinascimento: Interpretazioni e prob-
  lemi."*
  J.W. O'Malley, 551(RenQ):Spring81-80
Ringe, D. American Gothic.
  H. Smith, 590:Jun83-48
Ringger, K. L'Ame et la page.
  P. Berthier, 605(SC):15Apr83-433
  V. Brombert, 617(TLS):27May83-547
Ringler, S. Viten- und Offenbarungslitera-
  tur in Frauenklöstern des Mittelalters.
  P. Dinzelbacher, 684(ZDA):Band111Heft2-
  63
Rinhart, F. and M. The American Daguerreo-
  type.
  P. Haas and L. Gross, 14:Summer82-333
  J.V. Turano, 16:Winter82-80
Rink, E. Technical Americana.
  J. Bidwell, 517(PBSA):Vol76No4-500
Riordan, J. Sport in Soviet Society.
  L. Pugh, 104(CASS):Summer82-281
Ríos, A. Sleeping on Fists.
  V. Trueblood, 271:Spring82-132
Ríos, A. Whispering to Fool the Wind.
  J.D. Saldívar, 152(UDQ):Summer82-141
Ríos, E.P. - see under Páez Ríos, E.
Rioux, M. Les Québécois.
  G.R. Montbertrand, 207(FR):Apr83-802
Ripley, A. Charleston.
  639(VQR):Summer82-96
Ripley, J. "Julius Caesar" On Stage in
  England and America, 1599-1973.*
  A.W. Bellringer, 447(N&Q):Aug81-334
  R. Berry, 108:Summer82-150
  M. Mullin, 301(JEGP):Jul82-424
  S.P. Zitner, 178:Dec82-504
Ripoll, A.M. - see under Martínez Ripoll,
  A.
Ripoll, R. Réalité et mythe chez Zola.
  L. Kamm, 207(FR):Mar83-639
Ripp, V. Turgenev's Russia.*
  T.G.S. Cain, 529(QQ):Autumn82-670
  R. Freeborn, 575(SEER):Jan82-100
  J.D. Grossman, 574(SEEJ):Spring82-98
  K.A. Lantz, 104(CASS):Spring82-129
  D.E. Peterson, 395(MFS):Winter81/82-
  665
Risi, N. I Fabbricanti del "bello."
  K. Bosley, 617(TLS):140ct83-1136
Risse, W. Bibliographia logica.
  J. Ecole, 192(EP):Jul-Sep81-345
Rist, J.M., ed. The Stoics.*
  D. Sedley, 487:Summer82-198
Ritchey, D., ed. A Guide to the Baltimore
  Stage in the Eighteenth Century.
  W.J. Meserve, 612(ThS):Nov82-249

Ritchie, J.M. German Literature under
  National Socialism.
  M. Butler, 617(TLS):4Nov83-1230
Ritsos, Y. Subterranean Horses.*
  D. McDuff, 565:Vol23No1-59
Ritz, J-G. - see Hopkins, G.M.
Rivadeneira Prada, R. Rulfo en llamas.
  I.A. Luraschi, 238:Sep82-473
Rivera, E. Family Installments.*
  C.R. Hortas, 676(YR):Summer83-622
Rivera Blanco, J.J. El Palacio Real de
  Valladolid.
  P. Navascués, 48:Oct-Dec82-397
Rivera Rodríguez, T. Arquitectura del
  siglo XVIII en la provincia de Orense:
  Los Pazos Orensanos.
  I. Mateo Gómez, 48:Jul-Sep82-323
Rivers, I., ed. Books and their Readers
  in Eighteenth-Century England.*
  P.R. Backscheider, 566:Spring83-141
Rivers, J.E. Proust and the Art of Love.*
  R. Alter, 560:Fall82/Winter83-347
  N. Bailey, 208(FS):Oct82-490
  R. Gibson, 402(MLR):Jul82-729
  W. Greenberg, 188(ECr):Summer82-68
  W.L. McLendon, 579(SAQ):Spring82-234
  R. Sarkonak, 400(MLN):May82-1031
  W.A. Strauss, 131(CL):Spring82-189
  S. Willey, 400(MLN):Dec82-1265
  295(JML):Dec82-518
Rivers, W.M. Teaching Foreign Language
  Skills.* (2nd ed)
  A.C. Omaggio, 399(MLJ):Winter82-412
  D. Orrantia, 238:Dec82-670
Rivet, A. and C. Sarrau. Correspondance
  intégrale. (Vol 2) (H. Bots and P.
  Leroy, eds)
  R. Zuber, 535(RHL):Jan-Feb82-101
Rivière, J. and J. Schlumberger. Corres-
  pondance 1909-1925. (J-P. Cap, ed)
  H.T. Naughton, 188(ECr):Spring82-89
Rivington, R.T. Punting.
  B. Hepburn, 617(TLS):15Jul83-759
Rix, A. Japan's Economic Aid.
  J.C. Campbell, 293(JASt):Nov81-154
Rix, W.T., ed. Hermann Sudermann.
  R. Alter, 67:Nov82-216
  R.C. Cowen, 680(ZDP):Band101Heft2-310
Rizzi, L. Issues in Italian Syntax.
  D.J. Napoli, 350:Sep83-663
Rizzo, G. - see Donno, F.
Rizzuto, A. Camus' Imperial Vision.
  C.F. Gerrard, 207(FR):Mar83-644
  L.M. Porter, 395(MFS):Summer82-332
van Rjndt, P. Samaritan.
  S. Ellin, 441:13Feb83-14
Roach, J.G. C.L. Sonnichsen.
  G.F. Day, 649(WAL):Summer82-173
Robb, J.D. Hispanic Folk Music of New
  Mexico and the Southwest.*
  D. Clifford, 06(DHO):Apr82-162
Robbe-Grillet, A. and Y. Lenard. Le
  rendez-vous.*
  T. Carr, Jr., 399(MLJ):Summer82-205
Robbin, E. Woody Guthrie and Me.
  R.A. Reuss, 292(JAF):Jul-Sep82-365
Robbins, J.A. - see "American Literary
  Scholarship"
Robbins, K. The Eclipse of a Great Power.
  J. Harris, 617(TLS):15Apr83-382
Robbins, R.H., ed. Chaucer at Albany.
  H. Gillmeister, 72:Band218Heft1-166

Robbins, W. The Arnoldian Principle of
Flexibility.*
    S. Monod, 402(MLR):Oct82-936
Robe, S.L., ed. Hispanic Legends from New
Mexico.
    J.O. West, 650(WF):Jul82-235
Robert de Baron. Merlin le prophète, ou
le livre du graal. (E. Baumgartner,
trans)
    D.A. Fein, 207(FR):Oct82-144
Robert, M. Origins of the Novel.
    P. Stevick, 395(MFS):Winter81/82-748
    G.L. Stonum, 594:Fall82-286
Roberts, C.G.D. The Lure of the Wild.
(J.C. Adams, ed)
    R. Lecker, 102(CanL):Autumn82-141
Roberts, D. Paternalism in Early Victor-
ian England.*
    A. Heesom, 161(DUJ):Jun82-291
Roberts, G. Metropolitan Myths.
    442(NY):4Apr83-133
Roberts, J. Walter Benjamin.
    S.S. Prawer, 617(TLS):1Apr83-339
Roberts, J., ed. The Guthlac Poems of the
Exeter Book.*
    J. Rosier, 301(JEGP):Oct82-548
Roberts, J.A. Shakespeare's English
Comedy.*
    W. Green, 551(RenQ):Spring81-143
    A. Leggatt, 677(YES):Vol 12-259
    D. Lindley, 447(N&Q):Dec81-537
Roberts, J.K. Ernest Rhys.
    N. Cross, 617(TLS):18Nov83-1268
Roberts, J.R. John Donne.
    E.W. Sullivan 2d, 365:Spring83-83
Roberts, K. Heritage.
    E. Trethewey, 198:Oct82-111
Roberts, K. S'ney'mos.
    L. Ricou, 102(CanL):Spring82-90
Roberts, M., ed. The Faber Book of Modern
Verse. (4th ed rev by P. Porter)
    E. Larrissy, 493:Sep82-61
    J. Symons, 364:Oct82-65
Roberts, P. Tender Prey.
    T.J. Binyon, 617(TLS):25Nov83-1301
    S. Ellin, 441:31Jul83-13
Roberts, R. Papa Jack.
    D. McWhorter, 441:25Sep83-19
Roberts, W. Jane Austen and the French
Revolution.*
    F.W. Bradbrook, 447(N&Q):Jun81-268
    C. Kent, 125:Winter82-200
    H. Kozicki, 149(CLS):Spring82-86
    F.B. Pinion, 541(RES):Feb82-90
    B. Roth, 173(ECS):Spring82-351
    A. Wright, 677(YES):Vol 12-294
Robertson, A.S. Roman Imperial Coins in
the Hunter Coin Cabinet, University of
Glasgow. (Vol 5)
    M. Crawford, 617(TLS):1Apr83-338
Robertson, C.J.A. The Origins of the Scot-
tish Railway System 1722-1844.
    B. Lenman, 617(TLS):28Oct83-1198
Robertson, D.A. Sir Charles Eastlake and
the Victorian Art World.*
    W.L. Pressly, 54:Sep82-519
Robertson, G. People Against the Press.
    S. Jacobson, 362:30Jun83-27
    A.W.B. Simpson, 617(TLS):7Oct83-1082
Robertson, H. The Flying Bandit.
    L. Rogers, 102(CanL):Summer82-156
Robertson, M. A History of Greek Art.
    C.C. Vermeule, 39:Apr82-293

Robertson, M.E. Speak, Angel.
    S. Ellin, 441:31Jul83-13
Robertson, P. An Experience of Women.
    K.J. Crecelius, 446(NCFS):Fall-Winter
    82/83-200
    A. Goreau, 617(TLS):7Jan83-20
Robertson, P.J.M. The Leavises on Fic-
tion.*
    W.E. Cain, 594:Fall82-299
    H.H. Watts, 395(MFS):Winter82/83-646
Robertson, R. Meaning and Change.
    F.A. Hanson, 488:Mar82-98
Robertson-Mellor, G., ed. The Franco-
Italian Roland (V4).
    M. Offord, 208(FS):Jul82-315
Robichez, J. Verlaine entre Rimbaud et
Dieu.
    E. Zimmermann, 208(FS):Oct82-484
Robinet, A. Le Langage à l'âge classique.
    R.A. Watson, 319:Apr82-203
Robins, R.H. A Short History of Linguis-
tics. (2nd ed)
    P. Swiggers, 353:Vol 19No9/10-1036
Robinson, A. Selected Papers of Abraham
Robinson. (Vol 1) (H.J. Keisler, ed)
    J.T. Baldwin, 316:Mar82-197
Robinson, A. Selected Papers of Abraham
Robinson. (Vol 2) (W.A.J. Luxemburg and
S. Körner, eds)
    M. Davis, 316:Mar82-203
Robinson, B.W. The Baur Collection,
Geneva: Japanese Sword-Fittings and
Associated Metalwork.
    J. Earle, 463:Winter82/83-382
Robinson, B.W. Persian Paintings in the
John Rylands Library.*
    A. Topsfield, 90:Mar82-161
Robinson, C. French Literature in the
Twentieth Century.
    B. Stoltzfus, 395(MFS):Winter81/82-651
Robinson, C. Lucian and His Influence in
Europe.*
    B. Baldwin, 487:Autumn82-286
    C. Dessen, 551(RenQ):Autumn81-392
    C.P. Jones, 122:Jul82-268
Robinson, C.E. Shelley and Byron.
    J.D. Bone, 339(KSMB):No31-76
Robinson, D. John Barth's "Giles Goat-
Boy."
    J.Z. Guzlowski, 395(MFS):Summer82-310
Robinson, D. Chaplin.
    A. Burgess, 617(TLS):18Nov83-1263
Robinson, D. William Morris, Edward Burne-
Jones and the Kelmscott Chaucer.
    B. Crutchley, 324:Jun83-414
    K. Flint, 617(TLS):25Feb83-194
Robinson, D. Psychology and Law.
    D.N. Husak, 185:Jan83-394
Robinson, E. - see Clare, J.
Robinson, E. and R. Fitter - see Clare, J.
Robinson, F. Atlas of the Islamic World
since 1500.
    R. Irwin, 617(TLS):11Mar83-241
Robinson, F.J.G. and others. Eighteenth-
Century British Books.* (Vol 1)
    E. Rainey, 83:Spring82-131
    D.J. Shaw, 354:Dec82-453
    H.L. Snyder, 173(ECS):Spring83-342
Robinson, F.J.G. and others. Eighteenth-
Century British Books.* (Vols 2 and 3)
    E. Rainey, 83:Spring82-131
    H.L. Snyder, 173(ECS):Spring83-342

302

Rodney, R.M., comp. Mark Twain International.
  T. Wortham, 445(NCF):Mar83-619
Rodríguez, J.C. - see under Costas Rodríguez, J.
Rodríguez, J.L. El Cancionero de Joan Airas de Santiago.
  A. Gier, 553(RLiR):Jan-Jun82-176
Rodríguez, M.N. - see under Núñez Rodríguez, M.
Rodríguez, P.S. - see under Sainz Rodríguez, P.
Rodriguez, R. Hunger of Memory.*
  J.M. Davis, 152(UDQ):Fall82-91
  639(VQR):Summer82-99
Rodríguez, T.R. - see under Rivera Rodríguez, T.
Rodriguez Almeida, E. Forma Urbis Marmorea.
  D.E.E. and F.S. Kleiner, 576:Dec82-345
Rodríguez Campos, M. Venezuela, 1902.
  J. Ewell, 263(RIB):Vol32No3/4-356
Rodríguez de Lena, P. El Passo Honroso de Suero de Quiñones.* (A. Labandeira Fernández, ed)
  A. Hurtado Torres, 552(REH):Jan82-115
Rodríguez Méndez, J.M. Los inocentes de la Moncloa. (M.T. Halsey, ed)
  M.C. Dillingham, 238:Mar82-146
Rodríguez Monegal, E. and E.M. Santí. Pablo Neruda.
  C.B. Schlak, 238:May82-312
Rodríguez Moñino, A.R. Los poetas extremeños del siglo XVI.* (P. Cañada Castillo and others, eds)
  G.A. Davies, 86(BHS):Jan82-72
  G.A. Davies, 402(MLR):Jul82-748
Rodríguez-Seda de Laguna, A. Shaw en el mundo hispánico.
  E.B. Adams, 572:Vol3-246
"Rods, Bundles and Stitches."
  B.S. Holland, 139:Aug/Sep82-22
Roe, J., ed. Twentieth Century Sydney.
  B. Andrews, 71(ALS):May82-405
Roe, K. Teaching with Historical Records.
  M. Childress, 14:Summer82-332
Roehr, M. Speed Tailoring.
  P. Bach, 614:Spring83-23
Roemer, K.M., ed. America as Utopia.
  C. Elkins, 561(SFS):Nov82-325
  D. Ketterer, 27(AL):Oct82-465
Roethel, H.K. and J.K. Benjamin. Kandinsky: Catalogue Raisonné of the Oil-Paintings. (Vol 1)
  J. Gage, 617(TLS):25Nov83-1300
Roethke, T. Words for the Wind.
  K.R. Stafford, 649(WAL):Summer82-160
Roethlisberger, M. Bartholomeus Breenbergh: The Paintings.*
  M. Kitson, 39:Mar82-210
Roff, W.R., with M.L. Koch. Malaysia, Singapore, Brunei.
  C.R. Bryant, 293(JASt):May82-636
Rogers, E.R. The Perilous Hunt.*
  J.R. Burt, 238:Mar82-138
  D.L. Garrison, 400(MLN):Mar82-429
  A.G. Hauf, 86(BHS):Oct82-326
  W.E. Richmond, 650(WF):Jul82-233
Rogers, G.C., Jr. and D.R. Chesnutt - see Laurens, H.
Rogers, J. Alternate Endings.*
  D. Barbour, 648(WCR):Summer81-80
  C. Wiseman, 102(CanL):Summer82-140

Rogers, J. Separate Tracks.
  J. Melmoth, 617(TLS):11Feb83-130
Rogers, K.M. Feminism in Eighteenth-Century England.
  A. Goreau, 617(TLS):7Jan83-20
  R. Runte, 150(DR):Autumn82-516
Rogers, P. The Expectations of Light.
  D. Hopes, 236:Spring-Summer82-47
  L.L. Martz, 676(YR):Autumn82-63
  P. Stitt, 219(GaR):Summer82-438
Rogers, P. Henry Fielding.*
  J.A. Downie, 566:Autumn82-51
  T. Lockwood, 173(ECS):Summer83-436
Rogers, P. Hacks and Dunces.
  J.M. Aden, 569(SR):Spring82-xxxii
  D.J.F., 83:Spring82-164
Rogers, P. "Robinson Crusoe."
  J. Devoize, 189(EA):Apr-Jun82-214
  M.E. Novak, 402(MLR):Jan82-168
Rogers, P. - see Swift, J.
Rogers, P.T. Saul's Book.
  A. Cheuse, 441:10Jul83-15
Rogers, R. Metaphor.*
  C.L. Clark, 107(CRCL):Mar82-113
  E. Slater, 447(N&Q):Jun81-288
Rogers, R.M. and A.R. Watkins. German Through Conversational Patterns. (3rd ed)
  M.P. Alter, 399(MLJ):Spring82-104
Rogers, T.D. - see Madden, F.
Rogerson, J., ed. Beginning Old Testament Study.
  A. Phillips, 617(TLS):1Jul83-702
"Roget's II: The New Thesaurus."
  529(QQ):Summer82-458
Rogin, M.P. Subversive Genealogy.
  P. Shaw, 617(TLS):16Sep83-984
Rogosin, D. Invisible Men.
  R. Lipsyte, 441:7Aug83-9
Rohlfs, G. Calabria e Salento.
  H. Lausberg, 547(RF):Band93Heft3/4-430
Rohlfs, G. Dizionario dei cognomi e soprannomi in Calabria.
  F. Mosino, 553(RLiR):Jul-Dec81-507
Rohlfs, G. Le Gascon — Études de philologie pyrénéenne.* (3rd ed)
  G.F. Meier, 682(ZPSK):Band34Heft6-776
Rohlfs, G. Die rumänische Sprache in ihrer sprachgeographischen Beziehung zu den anderen romanischen Sprachen.
  H. Lausberg, 547(RF):Band93Heft3/4-432
Rohner, L. - see Hebel, J.P.
Rohrer, C. Die Wortzusammensetzung im modernen Französisch.
  R. Martin, 553(RLiR):Jan-Jun81-257
Rohrer, C. and N. Ruwet, eds. Actes du Colloque Franco-Allemand de Grammaire Transformationelle.
  G.F. Meier, 682(ZPSK):Band34Heft4-495
Ro'i, Y., ed. The Limits to Power.
  T.W. Cobb, 550(RusR):Jul82-345
Rojas, A. Historia de las relaciones diplomáticas entre Venezuela y los Estados Unidos, 1810-1899. (Vol 1)
  J. Ewell, 263(RIB):Vol32No3/4-356
Rojas, C. El ingenioso hidalgo y poeta Federico García Lorca asciende a los infiernos.
  K. Schwartz, 400(MLN):Mar82-443
de Rojas, F. La Celestina. (C. Alvaro, trans)
  D.S. Severin, 545(RPh):Feb82-557

304

de Rola, S.K. Balthus.
R.S. Short, 617(TLS):30Sep83-1063
Roland, A., ed. Psychoanalysis, Creativity, and Literature.*
W.T. MacCary, 367(L&P):Vol30No2-90
Rolfe, B., ed. Mimes on Miming.
M. Stephens, 609:Spring83-82
Rolin, D. Le Gâteau des Morts.
F. de Martinoir, 450(NRF):May82-114
Rolland, R. and L. Tolstoy. Monsieur le Comte.
B. Duchatelet, 535(RHL):Mar-Apr82-319
Rölleke, H. Westfälische Sagen.
G. Petschel, 196:Band23Heft3/4-340
Rolleston, S.E. Heritage Houses.
D.J. Hibbard, 658:Spring82-90
Rollins, P.C. Benjamin Lee Whorf.
D.K.H. Alford, 355(LSoc):Apr82-120
Rollins, R.M. The Long Journey of Noah Webster.*
C. Miller, 77:Spring82-179
Rollinson, P., with P. Matsen. Classical Theories of Allegory and Christian Culture.*
O.B. Hardison, Jr., 551(RenQ):Autumn82-457
M. Murrin, 405(MP):Feb83-293
Romain, A. Wörterbuch der Rechts- und Handelssprache/Dictionary of Legal and Commercial Terms.
M. Burkhard, 301(JEGP):Oct82-531
Roman, J. Exit House.
F.J. Jarrett, 529(QQ):Spring82-229
"The Romance of Tristan and Isolt." (N.B. Spector, trans)
J.L. Grigsby, 545(RPh):Feb82-532
Romano, F. Porfirio di Tiro.*
A. Meredith, 123:Vol32No1-52
"Romanos le Mélode, 'Hymnes.'" (Vol 5) (J. Grosdidier de Matons, ed and trans)
É. des Places, 555:Vol56fasc2-335
"The Romanov Family Album."
A. Kelly, 453(NYRB):16Jun83-38
Romanyshyn, R.D. Psychological Life.
D.M. Levin, 469:Vol18No2-114
Romanyuk, M. Byelorussian National Dress.
R.L. Shep, 614:Winter83-14
Rombandeeva, E.I. Sintaksis mansijskogo vogul'skogo jazyka.
L. Hartung, 682(ZPSK):Band34Heft3-378
Romeo, L. Ecce Homo!
A.S. Kaye, 320(CJL):Spring82-82
Romera Castillo, J. Estudios sobre "El Conde Lucanor."
J. England, 86(BHS):Oct82-335
Romeralo, A.S., D. Catalán and S.G. Armistead - see under Sánchez Romeralo, A., D. Catalán and S.G. Armistead
Romero, J.L. La experiencia argentina y otros ensayos.
F. Luna, 263(RIB):Vol32No1-69
Romero, L. Agua Negra.
D. Lee, 649(WAL):Nov82-291
de Romilly, J. Précis de littérature grecque.
J. Laborderie, 555:Vol56fasc1-108
M. Lebel, 487:Autumn82-284
Ronan, C.A. The Cambridge Illustrated History of the World's Science.
J.M. Ziman, 617(TLS):21Oct83-1165

Ronan, C.A. and J. Needham. The Shorter Science and Civilisation in China. (Vol 1)
F. Dagenais, 293(JASt):May82-587
Ronconi, A. and B. Scardigli, eds. Storie. (Bks 36-40)
P. Jal, 555:Vol56fasc2-342
Rondal, J-A. Langage et éducation. (P. Mardaga, ed)
L. Millet, 192(EP):Oct-Dec81-494
Rondeau, G. and others, eds. Vingt-cinq ans de linguistique au Canada, Hommage à Jean-Paul Vinay.*
P.R. Léon, 320(CJL):Fall82-184
Ronsley, J., ed. Denis Johnston, A Retrospective.
F. McCluskey, 305(JIL):Sep82-110
Rooke, L. The Birth Control King of the Upper Volta.
V. Sharman, 628(UWR):Spring-Summer83-95
Rooke, L. Cry Evil.
J. Wasserman, 102(CanL):Winter81-106
Rooke, L. Death Suite.
C. Fagan, 526:Spring82-79
Rooke, L. Shakespeare's Dog.
J. Charyn, 441:29May83-11
J.S., 231:May83-92
442(NY):13Jun83-131
Rooks, G. The Non-Stop Discussion Workbook.
S.J. Gaies, 399(MLJ):Autumn82-358
Room, A. Room's Classical Dictionary.
J.H.C. Leach, 617(TLS):20May83-520
Rooney, A. A Few Minutes with Andy Rooney.
639(VQR):Spring82-62
Roos, J. Etudes de littérature générale et comparée.
F. Jost, 149(CLS):Fall82-389
Root, W. Food.*
W. and C. Cowen, 639(VQR):Spring82-64
Root, W. Herbs and Spice.
W. and C. Cowen, 639(VQR):Spring82-64
Rooth, A.B. The Alaska Seminar.
P. Pénigault-Duhet, 189(EA):Oct-Dec82-481
Ropars-Wuilleumier, M-C. Le Texte divisé.
T. Conley, 400(MLN):Dec82-1284
Roper, A. and V.A. Dearing - see Dryden, J.
Roper, D. Reviewing before the "Edinburgh," 1788-1802.*
J.T. Boulton, 161(DUJ):Dec81-142
de Roquette-Buisson, O. The Canal du Midi.
442(NY):6Jun83-145
Rorem, N. Setting the Tone.
B. Shulgasser, 441:17Jul83-17
Rorty, R. Consequences of Pragmatism.
S. Blackburn, 617(TLS):15Jul83-746
B. Williams, 453(NYRB):28Apr83-33
Rorty, R. Philosophy and the Mirror of Nature.* (German title: Der Spiegel der Natur.)
V. Choy, 606:Sep82-515
K. Hartmann, 489(PJGG):Band89Heft1-168
R. Hollinger, 321:Vol 16No2-161
J. Poulain, 98:Feb82-130
Rosa, A.A. - see under Asor Rosa, A.
Rosa, J.G. The West of Wild Bill Hickok.
L. Milazzo, 584(SWR):Autumn82-vi
Rosaldo, M.Z. Knowledge and Passion.
J.L. Ecklund, 293(JASt):Feb82-425
Rosaldo, R. Ilongot Headhunting 1883-1974.
A.S. Bacdayan, 293(JASt):Feb82-427

Rosenfeld, S. Temples of Thespis.
　　C. Price, 447(N&Q):Feb81-86
Rosenfeld, S. - see Nicoll, A.
Rosenfield, J.M., ed. Song of the Brush.
　　"Skipjack," 463:Autumn82-285
Rosengarten, H. and M. Smith - see Brontë,
　　C.
Rosengren, I., ed. Sprache und Pragmatik.*
　　K. Nyholm, 439(NM):1982/2-219
　　A. Porsch, 682(ZPSK):Band34Heft6-771
　　P. Suchsland, 682(ZPSK):Band35Heft6-
　　734
Rosenkranz, B. Vergleichende Untersuchun-
gen der altanatolischen Sprachen.
　　E. Neu, 260(IF):Band86-339
Rosenmeyer, T.G. The Art of Aeschylus.
　　T. Gantz, 121(CJ):Feb/Mar83-264
Rosenn, K.S. Law and Inflation.
　　J.K., 185:Apr83-648
Rosenstiel, L. Nadia Boulanger.*
　　A. Fitz Lyon, 617(TLS):1Jul83-697
　　N. Rorem, 364:Dec82/Jan83-112
Rosenthal, B. City of Nature.*
　　L. Ziff, 541(RES):Aug82-371
Rosenthal, B., ed. Critical Essays on
Charles Brockden Brown.*
　　E.J. Sundquist, 580(SCR):Spring83-132
Rosenthal, G., ed. Italian Paintings XIV-
XVIIIth Centuries from the Collection of
the Baltimore Museum of Art.
　　E.W. Rowlands, 39:Dec82-432
　　E. Waterhouse, 90:May82-302
Rosenthal, H. My Mad World of Opera.*
　　C. Osborne, 364:Dec82/Jan83-141
Rosenthal, M. Constable.
　　J. Hayes, 617(TLS):25Nov83-1299
Rosenthal, M. Virginia Woolf.*
　　A. McLaurin, 447(N&Q):Aug81-363
Rosenthal, M.L. Poems 1964-1980.
　　W. Harmon, 472:Spring/Summer83-129
Rosenthal, M.L. Poetry and the Common
Life.
　　L. Mackinnon, 617(TLS):30Dec83-1455
Rosenthal, M.L. and S.M. Gall. The Modern
Poetic Sequence.
　　S. Heaney, 441:20Nov83-3
　　L. Mackinnon, 617(TLS):30Dec83-1455
Rosenthal, R. and R. Sivan. Ancient Lamps
in the Schloessinger Collection.
　　H.N. Richardson, 318(JAOS):Oct-Dec81-
　　453
Rosenthal-Schneider, I. Reality and Scien-
tific Truth. (T. Braun, ed)
　　J. Hendry, 84:Sep82-329
　　A.B. Stewart, 42(AR):Summer82-362
Rositzke, H. The KGB.
　　J.S. Zacek, 550(RusR):Oct82-505
Roskina, N. Četyre glavy.*
　　T.W. Clyman, 574(SEEJ):Summer82-249
Röslav, W. Polis und Tragödie
　　J.M. Alonso-Núñez, 123:Vol32No1-91
Rosner, D. A Once Charitable Enterprise.
　　M. Neve, 617(TLS):4Mar83-208
de Rosny, É. Les Yeux de ma chévre.
　　H. Cronel, 450(NRF):Mar82-136
Ross, A. Colours of War.
　　D.J. Enright, 362:23Jun83-26
　　F. Spalding, 617(TLS):8Jul83-731
Ross, A., ed. New Stories 7.
　　L. Jones, 364:Nov82-85
　　J. Mellors, 362:6Jan83-24

Ross, A. Ranji.
　　S. Gardiner, 362:25Aug83-24
　　P.H. Sutcliffe, 617(TLS):30Sep83-1067
Ross, A. - see Addison, J. and R. Steele
Ross, C.L. The Composition of "The Rain-
bow" and "Women in Love."*
　　K.M. Hewitt, 541(RES):Aug82-360
　　J.C.F. Littlewood, 184(EIC):Apr82-186
Ross, D. Acts of Faith.
　　M. Skakun, 287:Nov82-23
Ross, H.L. Deterring the Drinking Driver.
　　J.B. Jacobs, 453(NYRB):14Apr83-36
Ross, I.S. William Dunbar.*
　　A.B. Friedman, 589:Oct82-932
Ross, M. The Creative Arts.*
　　A. Simpson, 289:Summer82-122
Ross, M. Milena.
　　D. Durrant, 364:Mar83-109
　　L.T. Lyham, 617(TLS):6May83-457
Ross, M.H. and B.K. Walker. "On another
day ... "*
　　J. Knappert, 69:Vol51No1-534
Ross, M.J. Ross in the Antarctic.
　　P. Beck, 617(TLS):18Mar83-260
Ross, S. Lorraine McMullen.
　　L.K. MacKendrick, 198:Jul82-96
Ross, S.D. Philosophical Mysteries.
　　M. Adam, 542:Oct-Dec82-676
Ross, S.D. A Theory of Art.
　　H. Osborne, 89(BJA):Summer82-272
Ross, S.D. Transition to an Ordinal Meta-
physics.
　　M.C.M., 543:Jun82-900
　　K. Wallace, 311(JP):Apr82-222
Ross, V. Goodbye Summer.
　　V. Howard, 102(CanL):Spring82-117
Rossant, C. After-Five Gourmet.
　　W. and C. Cowen, 639(VQR):Spring82-64
Rossi, A. Serafino Aquilano e la poesia
cortigiana.
　　U. Schulz-Buschhaus, 547(RF):Band93
　　Heft3/4-478
Rossi, A. The Architecture of the City.
　　H. Blumenfeld, 529(QQ):Winter82-868
Rossi, G.C. Scritti da "Annali — Sezione
Romanza."
　　D. Briesemeister, 72:Band218Heft1-239
　　D-H. Pageaux, 549(RLC):Jan-Mar82-101
Rossi, I., ed. Structural Sociology.
　　K.S., 185:Jul83-828
Rossi, M. and others. L'intonation.
　　F. Carton, 209(FM):Jul82-271
Rossi, N., ed. Catalogue of Works by
Mario Castelnuovo-Tedesco.
　　A.F.L.T., 412:Feb81-61
Rossi, P. - see Grosseteste, R.
Rossing, N. and B. Rønne. Apocryphal —
Not Apocryphal?*
　　N. Andreyev, 575(SEER):Apr82-289
　　E.L. Keenan, 104(CASS):Spring82-95
Rossiter, M.W. Women Scientists in Amer-
ica.
　　A.K. Smith, 441:6Feb83-12
Rössler, G. Konnotationen.
　　I. Freudenschuss-Reichl, 685(ZDL):
　　1/1982-125
Rossner, J. August.
　　W. Kendrick, 441:24Jul83-1
　　A. Mars-Jones, 617(TLS):4Nov83-1227
　　J.S., 231:Sep83-75

Rousseau, J-J. Correspondance complète de Jean-Jacques Rousseau.* (Vols 28-32) (R.A. Leigh, ed)
P. Lefebvre, 535(RHL):Sep-Dec82-915
Rousseau, J-J. Correspondance complète de Jean-Jacques Rousseau. (Vol 37) (R.A. Leigh, ed)
R. Wokler, 617(TLS):2Sep83-919
Rousseau, J-J. Correspondance complète de Jean-Jacques Rousseau. (Vol 38) (R.A. Leigh, ed)
L. Gasbarrone, 207(FR):Apr83-772
R. Wokler, 617(TLS):2Sep83-919
Rousseau, J-J. Correspondance complète de Jean-Jacques Rousseau. (Vols 39 and 40) (R.A. Leigh, ed)
R. Wokler, 617(TLS):2Sep83-919
Rousseau, J-J. The Indispensable Rousseau. (J.H. Mason, ed)
R. Grimsley, 208(FS):Jan82-70
Rousseau, J-J. The Reveries of the Solitary Walker.* (C.E. Butterworth, ed and trans)
A.J. Bingham, 173(ECS):Summer83-450
A.J. Bingham, 402(MLR):Jul82-726
Rousseau, J-J. Reveries of the Solitary Walker. (P. France, trans)
R. Grimsley, 208(FS):Jul82-331
"Jean-Jacques Rousseau et la crise contemporaine de la conscience."
J-M. Ansart, 192(EP):Jul-Sep81-364
Rousseau, N. Le Déluge blanc.*
L. Rochette, 102(CanL):Autumn82-158
"Rousseau selon Jean-Jacques."*
A.J. Bingham, 173(ECS):Summer83-450
N. Suckling, 208(FS):Apr82-204
Rousseau Payen, N. La situation linguistique de Hilbesheim.
A-M. Houdebine, 209(FM):Jan82-78
Roussel, H. and F. Suard, eds. Alain de Lille, Guatier de Châtillon, Jakemart Giélée et leur temps.*
W.D. Paden, Jr., 589:Jan82-171
Rousset, J. Leurs yeux se rencontrèrent.
D. Coste, 207(FR):Apr83-760
J-Y. Tadié, 208(FS):Jul82-366
Rousset, J. Le Mythe de Don Juan.*
E. Balmas, 535(RHL):May-Jun82-501
Roustang, F. Dire Mastery.
F. Randall, 441:27Feb83-12
Roustang, F. Un Destin si funeste.
... Elle ne le lâche plus.
T.M. Kavanagh, 400(MLN):May82-981
Routh, J. and J. Wolff, eds. The Sociology of Literature: Theoretical Approaches.
R. Schwartz, 125:Winter82-204
Routley, R. Exploring Meinong's Jungle and Beyond.
N. Griffin, 154:Dec02 764
N. Griffin, 556:Winter82/83-53
Rouy, F. L'esthétique du traité moral d'après les oeuvres d'Alain Chartier.
P. Bourgain, 554:Vol 102No4-554
Roux, L. - see de Sorbière, S.
Rowe, F.W. A History of Newfoundland and Labrador.
K.S. Samuelson, 529(QQ):Spring82-208
Rowe, G.E., Jr. Thomas Middleton and the New Comedy Tradition.*
L. Salingar, 551(RenQ):Spring81-153
A. Wertheim, 301(JEGP):Jan82-112

Rowe, W. Mito e ideología en la obra de José María Arguedas.
B. Torres Caballero, 240(HR):Autumn82-505
Rowe, W.W. Nabokov's Spectral Dimension.*
J.D. Clayton, 104(CASS):Fall-Winter82-531
D.B. Johnson, 574(SEEJ):Spring82-104
C.S. Ross, 395(MFS):Winter82/83-687
Rowell, G. Mountains of the Middle Kingdom.
P. Zweig, 441:4Dec83-70
Rowell, G. The Victorian Theatre 1792-1914. (2nd ed)
C. Woodring, 130:Spring82-90
Rowland, B. Birds with Human Souls.*
W.F. Hansen, 292(JAF):Apr-Jun82-219
Rowland, B., ed. Medieval Woman's Guide to Health.
J. Stannard and L.E. Voigts, 589:Apr82-422
Rowland, C. The Open Heaven.
M. Knibb, 617(TLS):7Jan83-22
Rowley, N., comp. Law and Order in Essex.*
R.A. Lewis, 325:Oct82-120
Rowley, T. The Norman Heritage 1066-1200.
H.R. Loyn, 617(TLS):22Jul83-789
Rowse, A.L. Eminent Elizabethans.
P. Collinson, 617(TLS):13May83-484
Rowse, A.L. Shakespeare's Globe.
F. Lagarde, 189(EA):Oct-Dec82-459
Roy, A. Les Envois de l'etat au Musée de Dijon (1803-1815).
B. Scott, 39:Apr82-294
Roy, D.T. and T-H. Tsien, eds. Ancient China.
J.K. Riegel, 244(HJAS):Dec82-684
Roy, L. and L. Saia, with M. Rivard. Bachelor.
E.R. Hopkins, 207(FR):Dec82-343
Roy, P.E. Vancouver.
C. Berger, 102(CanL):Autumn82-153
Royce, J. The Spirit of Modern Philosophy.
M.G.M., 617(TLS):23Dec83-1443
Royce, K. Channel Assault.
442(NY):23May83-124
Royer, R.G. and L.W. McKim. PR Prototypes.
L.A. Strasheim, 399(MLJ):Winter82-411
Royet-Journoud, C. Travail de poésie.
F. de Laroque, 98:Feb82-165
Royle, E. and J. Walvin. English Radicals and Reformers 1760-1848.
I.J. Prothero, 617(TLS):21Jan83-65
Royle, T. The Macmillan Companion to Scottish Literature.
I. Campbell, 617(TLS):26Aug83-909
Royot, D. L'Humour américain.
H. Levin, 189(EA):Oct-Dec82-482
Royster, C. A Revolutionary People at War.*
J. Béranger, 189(EA):Jan-Mar82-106
J.K. Nelson, 9(AlaR):Jan82-54
Royster, V. My Own, My Country's Time.
W. Carroll, 441:25Dec83-8
Rozas, J.M. Sobre Marino y España.
E.L. Rivers, 552(REH):Jan82-143
Rózsa, M. Double Life.
G. Kaufman, 362:6Oct83-23
P. O'Connor, 617(TLS):6May83-470
Ruano, J.M. and J.E. Varey - see de Vega Carpio, L.

Ruben, D-H. Marxism and Materialism.*
(2nd ed)
    J. Daly, 518:Jan82-20
Rubens, B. Brothers.
    K.C. O'Brien, 362:15Sep83-23
    C. Rumens, 617(TLS):16Sep83-1001
Rubenstein, D. Marx and Wittgenstein.
    R.S. Nelsen, 185:Apr83-622
Rubenstein, R.L. The Age of Triage.
    J.S., 231:Jan83-75
Rubin, B., R. Carlton and A. Rubin. L.A.
in Installments: Forest Lawn.*
    E. Oring, 292(JAF):Jul-Sep82-366
Rubin, D., ed. Canada on Stage 1980-81.
    K. Garebian, 298:Summer82-137
Rubin, D. and A. Cranmer-Byng, eds.
Canada's Playwrights.
    L.W. Conolly, 612(ThS):May82-134
Rubin, D. and A. Wagner, eds. Directory
of Canadian Theatre Schools 1981-82.
    K. Garebian, 298:Summer82-137
Rubin, D.L. The Knot of Artifice.*
    D. Judovitz, 475:No16Pt2-428
    J.D. Lyons, 207(FR):Oct82-150
    B. Nicholas, 208(FS):Jan82-64
    B. Norman, 546(RR):May82-388
    A.J. Steele, 402(MLR):Oct82-952
Rubin, J.H. Realism and Social Vision in
Courbet and Proudhon.
    C. Frayling, 90:Aug82-515
    A. Sheon, 127:Spring82-69
Rubin, J.S. Constance Rourke and American
Culture.*
    S.I. Bellman, 50(ArQ):Spring82-91
    J. Hoopes, 658:Spring82-88
    H.D. Shapiro, 529(QQ):Spring82-19
    V. Strong-Boag, 106:Spring82-97
Rubin, L. The Nicholas Nickleby Story.
    D. Parker, 155:Summer82-111
Rubin, L.D., Jr. A Gallery of Southerners.
    G.C., 569(SR):Fall82-cx
Rubin, L.D., Jr. Surfaces of a Diamond.*
    E. Fuller, 569(SR):Summer82-1x
    639(VQR):Summer82-95
Rubin, W., ed. Pablo Picasso: A Retro-
spective.*
    N. Wadley, 592:Vol 195No993/994-103
Rubin, Z. Civil-War Propaganda and Histo-
riography.
    P. Jal, 555:Vol56fasc2-367
Rubinstein, A.Z. Soviet Foreign Policy
since World War II.
    H. Hanak, 575(SEER):Apr82-302
    R.M. Slusser, 550(RusR):Oct82-512
Rubinstein, N. - see de' Medici, L.
Rubio Cremades, E. Costumbrismo y folle-
tín.
    B.J. Dendle, 552(REH):Jan82-122
Ruble, B.A. Soviet Trade Unions.
    R.J. Osborn, 550(RusR):Jul82-342
Ruch, E.A. and K.C. Anyanwu, eds. African
Philosophy.
    S. Kruks, 69:Vol52No4-103
Rudenstine, A.Z., ed. Russian Avant-Garde
Art.*
    M. Chamot, 39:May82-414
    G.H. Roman, 127:Winter82-361
Ruderman, D.B. The World of a Renaissance
Jew.
    P.C. Ioly-Zorattini, 551(RenQ):Winter
    82-612
    A.M. Lesley, 539:Aug83-221

Rudigoz, C. Systématique génétique de la
métaphore sexuelle.
    J. De Caluwé-Dor, 189(EA):Oct-Dec82-
    434
Rudkin, D. Sons of Light. The Triumph of
Death.
    D. Devlin, 157:Summer82-52
Rudnick, H.H. - see Kant, I.
Rudnicki, A. Têtes polonaises.
    L. Kovacs, 450(NRF):May82-149
Rudolf, A. After the Dream.
    T. Eagleton, 565:Vol123No2-62
Rudolph, V.C. - see Johnson, S.
Rudy, S. and M. Taylor - see Jakobson, R.
Rueckert, W.H. Kenneth Burke and the
Drama of Human Relations.
    R.M. Adams, 617(TLS):8Jul83-715
Ruef, H. Augustin über Semiotik und
Sprache.
    S. Ebbesen, 319:Oct83-563
Ruegg, D.S. The Life of Bu Ston Rin Po
Che, with the Tibetan Text of the Bu
ston rNam thar.
    G.W. Houston, 259(IIJ):Jul80-252
Rueschemeyer, M. Professional Work and
Marriage.*
    M. Meissner, 104(CASS):Fall-Winter82-
    602
Ruether, R. and E. McLaughlin. Women of
Spirit.
    N.O. Keohane, 185:Oct82-102
Ruether, R.R. Sexism and God-Talk.
    P. Trible, 441:1May83-28
Ruffinatto, A. Struttura e significazione
del "Lazarillo de Tormes."
    M. Tietz, 72:Band218Heft1-210
Musionus Rufus. Entretiens et fragments.
(A. Jagu, ed and trans)
    J. Ecole, 192(EP):Apr-Jun81-234
Rügemer, W. Philosophische Anthropologie
und Epochenkrise.
    J-M. Gabaude and E. Harmat, 542:
    Jan-Mar82-67
Ruggerini, M.E. Le invettive di Loki.
    J. Martínez-Pizarro, 301(JEGP):Oct82-
    526
Ruggiero, G. Violence in Early Renais-
sance Venice.
    B. Pullan, 551(RenQ):Autumn81-384
Ruggiers, P.G. - see Chaucer, G.
Rugoff, M. The Beechers.
    42(AR):Winter82-122
Ruh, K. Höfische Epik des deutschen
Mittelalters. (Pt 2)
    W.H. Jackson, 402(MLR):Oct82-989
    J.F. Poag, 301(JEGP):Jul82-379
Rühmkorf, P. Walther von der Vogelweide,
Klopstock und ich.
    T. Ehlert, 680(ZDP):Band101Heft3-460
Ruiz Contreras, L. - see "Revista Nueva,
1899"
Rūķe-Draviņa, V. The Standardization
Process in Latvian.
    S.F. Kolbuszewski, 360(LP):Vol124-150
Rule, J. Outlander.
    W.N., 102(CanL):Summer82-174
Rull, E. - see Calderón de la Barca, P.
Rumens, C. Scenes from the Gingerbread
House. Star Whisper.
    F. Adcock, 617(TLS):28Oct83-1180
Rumens, C. Unplayed Music.*
    J. Saunders, 565:Vol123No3-73

Runciman, W.G. A Treatise on Social
Theory. (Vol 1)
S. Lukes, 617(TLS):5Aug83-823
Rundell, W.F., Jr. Oil in West Texas and
New Mexico.
584(SWR):Summer82-v
Rundle, B. Grammar in Philosophy.*
D.E. Cooper, 393(Mind):Jan82-134
Runnalls, G.A. - see "Le Mystère de Sainte
Venice"
Runte, R. - see "Studies in Eighteenth-
Century Culture"
Runyon, R. Fowles/Irving/Barthes.
W. Bache, 395(MFS):Winter82/83-732
Rupert of Deutz. De gloria et honore
Filii hominis super Matthaeum. (R.
Haacke, ed)
J. Van Engen, 589:Apr82-426
Ruppelt, G. Schiller im nationalsozialis-
tischen Deutschland.*
J.L. Sammons, 221(GQ):Jan82-127
Ruprecht, E. and D. Bänsch, eds. Mani-
feste und Dokumente zur deutschen Lit-
eratur — Jahrhundertwende.
H. Steinecke, 680(ZDP):Band101Heft4-
603
Ruschenbusch, E. Athenische Innenpolitik
im 5. Jahrhundert v. Chr.*
H.W. Pleket, 394:Vol35fasc3/4-424
Ruschenbusch, E. Untersuchungen zu Staat
und Politik in Griechenland vom 7.-4. Jh.
v. Chr.
H.W. Pleket, 394:Vol35fasc3/4-428
Ruscoe, J. The Italian Communist Party
1976-81.
M. Clark, 617(TLS):3Jun83-580
Rusconi, R. L'attesa della fine.
B. McGinn, 589:Apr82-428
Ruse, M. Darwinism Defended.
A.J., 185:Apr83-634
R.C. Lewontin, 453(NYRB):16Jun83-21
Ruse, M.E. Sociobiology.*
V. Pratt, 518:Jan82-61
Rushdie, S. Midnight's Children.*
U. Parameswaran, 314:Summer-Fall82-249
Rushdie, S. Shame.
D.J. Enright, 453(NYRB):8Dec83-26
D.A.N. Jones, 362:8Sep83-22
A. Mars-Jones, 617(TLS):9Sep83-949
R. Towers, 441:13Nov83-3
Rushforth, P. Kindergarten.
W. Sullivan, 569(SR):Summer82-484
Ruskin, J. Letters from the Continent
1858.* (J. Hayman, ed)
D. Johnson, 453(NYRB):31Mar83-13
P. Kemp, 362:10Mar83-25
Ruskin, J. Reflections of a Friendship.
(V. Surtees, ed)
J.L. Bradley, 161(DUJ):Dec81-150
Ruskin, J. The Stones of Venice.* (J.
Morris, ed)
K.O. Garrigan, 576:Mar82-65
Russ, C.V.J., ed. Contrastive Aspects of
English and German.
J.L. Cox, 399(MLJ):Autumn82-327
Russ, C.V.J. Historical German Phonology
and Morphology.*
N.C. Keul, 221(GQ):Jan82-107
Russ, J. How to Suppress Women's Writing.
P-J. Adams, 61:Nov83-148
Russell, C., ed. The Avant-Garde Today.
S. Mews, 221(GQ):Nov82-621
639(VQR):Winter82-8

Russell, D. The Religion of the Machine
Age. The Dora Russell Reader.
M. Warnock, 617(TLS):9Dec83-1365
Russell, D.A. Criticism in Antiquity.*
T. Cole, 569(SR):Fall82-605
H.P. Foley, 24:Winter82-466
S. Usher, 123:Vol132No2-185
Russell, D.A. Period Style for the Thea-
tre.
S. Kerwin, 108:Winter82-111
Russell, D.A. and N.G. Wilson - see "Men-
ander Rhetor"
Russell, F., ed. Art Nouveau Architecture.
D.A. Hanser, 576:Oct82-250
Russell, J. The Meanings of Modern Art.*
R. Alley, 39:Oct82-279
D. Hall, 90:Sep82-559
42(AR):Spring82-246
529(QQ):Autumn82-689
Russell, M. Backlash.
N. Callendar, 441:25Sep83-34
Russell, M. Melvin B. Tolson's "Harlem
Gallery."
R.M. Farnsworth, 436(NewL):Winter82/83-
114
Russell, N. - see "The Lives of the Desert
Fathers"
Russell, R. Valentin Kataev.
D.G.B. Piper, 402(MLR):Jul82-766
Rust, H. Jugendprobleme im Fernsehen.
P. Ruppert, 221(GQ):Nov82-573
Rustin, J. Le Vice à la mode.*
P.V. Conroy, Jr., 546(RR):Jan82-117
"Ruth."* (J.M. Sasson, trans)
M.H. Pope, 318(JAOS):Jul-Sep81-405
Rutherford, D. Stop at Nothing.
N. Callendar, 441:27Nov83-28
Ruthrof, H. The Reader's Construction of
Narrative.
R.A. Champagne, 399(MLJ):Spring82-76
W.H. Clark, Jr., 289:Summer82-113
A. Schwarz, 196:Band23Heft1/2-150
J.J. Sosnoski, 395(MFS):Summer82-358
"Rutland Record No. 1." (B. Waites, ed)
R.J. Olney, 325:Oct82-120
Rutledge, A.W. Artists in the Life of
Charleston.
C.M. Saunders, 585(SoQ):Summer82-115
M.S. Young, 39:Jan82-67
Rutsala, V. Walking Home from the Ice-
house.*
S. Sandy, 491:Aug82-293
van Rutten, P-M. Le Langage poétique de
Saint-John Perse.
R.A. Laden, 546(RR):Jan82-125
Ruttkowski, W.V., ed. Nomenclator littera-
rius.
H. Eichner, 564:May82-143
M. Schmeling, 547(RF):Band94Heft4-476
G. von Wilpert, 133:Band15Heft4-346
Rutz, P. Zweiwertige und mehrwertige
Logik.
J-L. Gardies, 542:Jan-Mar82-131
Ruud, C.A. Fighting Words.
K. Fitz Lyon, 617(TLS):7Oct83-1082
Ruwet, N. Grammaire des insultes et
autres études.
M. Dominicy, 540(RIPh):Vol36fasc3-380
M.W. Epro, 350:Sep83-685
Ruwet, N. Problems in French Syntax.
J. Klare, 682(ZPSK):Band34Heft2-245
Ryan, D. Deadlines.
442(NY):7Mar83-139

Ryan, F.L.   The Immediate Critical Recep-
tion of Ernest Hemingway.
     D.A. Daiker, 234:Spring83-62
     G. Wickes, 395(MFS):Summer82-292
Ryan, G.   The Division of Anger.
     G. Catalano, 381:Oct81-349
Ryan, M.   In Winter.*
     R. Phillips, 461:Spring-Summer82-98
     H. Raz, 502(PrS):Summer82-87
Ryan, M.   Marxism and Deconstruction.
     C. Norris, 617(TLS):7Jan83-6
     A. Parker, 400(MLN):Dec82-1217
Ryan, M.   The Politics of Penal Reform.
     A.W.B. Simpson, 617(TLS):25Nov83-1304
Ryan, M-L.   Rituel et Poésie.*
     G. Cesbron, 356(LR):May82-173
Ryan, N.   A Hitch or Two in Afghanistan.
     P. Levi, 617(TLS):4Nov83-1212
     E. Mortimer, 453(NYRB):22Dec83-3
Ryan, R.W.   Une Analyse phonologique d'un
parler acadien de la Nouvelle-Ecosse
(Canada): Région de la Baie Sainte-Marie.
     C.A. Fox, 207(FR):Dec82-353
Ryan, T.G.   Stage Left.
     K. Garebian, 298:Summer82-137
Rybakov, A.   Heavy Sand.
     P. Lewis, 565:Vol23No2-44
Rybczynski, W.   Taming the Tiger.
     L.S. Robinson, 441:6Nov83-16
Rybicki, M., ed.   Sejm Ustawodawczy
Rzeczypospolitej Polskiej 1947-1952.*
     P.J. Best, 497(PolR):Vol27No3/4-240
Ryden, H.   Bobcat Year.
     P.T. Bryant, 649(WAL):Winter83-358
Ryder, F.G. - see Keller, G.
du Ryer, P.   Clitophon.*   (L. Zilli, ed)
     P.E. Chaplin, 208(FS):Jan82-63
du Ryer, P.   Les Vendanges de Suresnes.
(L. Zilli, ed)
     A. Blanc, 535(RHL):Jan-Feb82-109
Rykwert, J.   The First Moderns.*
     A. von Buttlar, 90:Jan82-39
     J. Sweetman, 83:Autumn82-285
Ryle, G.   La notion d'esprit, pour une
critique des concepts mentaux.
     A. Reix, 192(EP):Oct-Dec81-495
Ryle, G.   On Thinking.*   (K. Kolenda, ed)
     T.A. Goudge, 154:Mar82-125
Ryōkan.   The Zen Poems of Ryōkan.   (N.
Yuasa, trans)
     K. Oderman, 584(SWR):Summer82-337
     B. Watson, 407(MN):Spring82-124

Saada, J.F. and J. Contreras - see under
Favret Saada, J. and J. Contreras
von Saalfeld, L.   Die ideologische Funk-
tion des Nibelungenliedes in der preus-
sisch-deutschen Geschichte von seiner
Wiederentdeckung bis zum Nationalsozial-
ismus.
     O. Ehrismann, 224(GRM):Band32Heft2-246
Saalman, H.   Filippo Brunelleschi: The
Cupola of Santa Maria del Fiore.*
     C. Elam, 59:Dec82-489
Saarinen, E. and others, eds.   Essays in
Honour of Jaakko Hintikka.
     J. Dancy, 393(Mind):Oct82-618
Saavedra, M.D. - see under de Cervantes
Saavedra, M.
Saba, G. - see Théophile de Viau

Sabatier, R.   Histoire de la poésie fran-
çaise: La poésie du vingtième siècle.
     G. Gouérou, 450(NRF):Jun82-94
Sabato, L.J.   The Rise of Political Consul-
tants.
     J. Latimer, 639(VQR):Summer82-519
Sabiani, J. - see Péguy, C. and P. Marcel
Sabini, J. and M. Silver.   Moralities of
Everyday Life.
     V.H., 185:Jul83-821
Sabor, P. - see Richardson, S.
Sabot, R.H.   Economic Development and
Urban Migration: Tanzania 1900-71.
     D. Wellbelove, 69:Vol51No1-541
Sacca, E.J. - see "Canadian Review of Art
Education Research"
Sachs, H.   Virtuoso.
     S. Pickles, 617(TLS):15Jul83-751
Sachs, K-J.   Mensura fistularum.   (Vol 2)
     P. Williams, 410(M&L):Jan/Apr82-127
Sack, A. and J. Yourman.   The Sack-Yourman
Study Skills Program.
     L. Hamp-Lyons, 608:Mar83-109
Sack, F.L.   Grammatik der englischen
Sprache.
     H. Bennemann, 682(ZPSK):Band34Heft3-
379
     H. Ulherr, 38:Band100Heft3/4-473
Sack, J.   Fingerprint.
     P-L. Adams, 61:Feb83-105
Sackett, R.E.   Popular Entertainment,
Class, and Politics in Munich, 1900-1923.
     J. Willett, 617(TLS):17Jun83-640
Sacks, E.   Shakespeare's Images of Preg-
nancy.*
     G.K. Hunter, 569(SR):Spring82-274
Sacks, S., ed.   On Metaphor.*
     R.A. Shiner, 478:Oct82-196
Sackville-West, V.   The Edwardians.   All
Passion Spent.
     P. Craig, 617(TLS):29Jul83-820
de Sacy, S.S. - see de Balzac, H.
Saddlemyer, A. - see Synge, J.M.
Sadie, S., ed.   The New Grove Dictionary
of Music and Musicians.*   (Vols 1-20)
     J. Boulton, 412:Aug-Nov81-268
     L.W. Brunner, 414(MusQ):Apr82-189
     B. Churgin, 414(MusQ):Apr82-228
     R. Cogan, 414(MusQ):Apr82-182
     R. Crawford, 414(MusQ):Apr82-254
     J.W. Finson, 414(MusQ):Apr82-245
     A. Forte, 414(MusQ):Apr82-161
     A.S. Garlington, Jr., 414(MusQ):Apr82-
238
     R.P. Morgan, 414(MusQ):Apr82-262
     B. Nettl, 414(MusQ):Apr82-153
     J. Peyser, 414(MusQ):Apr82-283
     J. Rifkin, 317:Spring82-182
     D. Stevens, 414(MusQ):Apr82-217
     A.F.L.T., 412:Aug-Nov81-278
     B. Taylor, 414(MusQ):Apr82-271
     F. Tirro, 414(MusQ):Apr82-207
     P. Wittke, 414(MusQ):Apr82-274
Sadie, S.   The New Grove Mozart.
     A. Blackwood, 617(TLS):9Sep83-954
Sadler, I.   The New York School.
     M.S. Young, 39:Dec82-432
Sadler, L.   Thomas Carew.*
     F.W. Fry, 447(N&Q):Feb81-73
Sadler, L.V.   John Bunyan.*
     R. Sharrock, 447(N&Q):Feb81-76

Sadler, L.V. Consolation in "Samson Agonistes."
  M.A. Radzinowicz, 677(YES):Vol 12-268
Sadoff, D.F. Monsters of Affection.
  A. Sanders, 617(TLS):25Mar83-288
Sa'edi, G-H. Dandil.
  42(AR):Spring82-247
Sáez-Godoy, L. - see de Vivar, G.
Safir, N. Moving Into Seasons.
  B.F. Lefcowitz, 363(LitR):Fall82-161
Sagan, F. musiques de scènes.
  H. Le Mansec, 207(FR):Mar83-672
Sagan, F. The Painted Lady.
  N. Johnson, 441:6Feb83-10
  F. Taliaferro, 231:Feb83-74
  442(NY):24Jan83-107
Sagar, K., ed. The Achievement of Ted Hughes.
  P. Redgrove, 617(TLS):11Nov83-1238
Sagar, K. The Art of Ted Hughes. (2nd ed)
  M. Sweeting, 161(DUJ):Jun82-320
Sagar, K. D.H. Lawrence: A Calendar of His Works.*
  B. Caplan, 219(GaR):Spring82-194
  M. Magalaner, 395(MFS):Summer81-307
Sagar, K., ed. A D.H. Lawrence Handbook.
  P.T. Whelan, 344:Summer83-130
Sagar, K. The Life of D.H. Lawrence.*
  B. Caplan, 219(GaR):Spring82-194
  D. Gutierrez, 649(WAL):Spring82-65
  C. Holmes, 366:Autumn82-264
Sagar, M.V., ed and trans. Kalpasūtra.
  E. Bender, 318(JAOS):Oct-Dec81-508
Sager, J.C., D. Dungworth and P.F. McDonald. English Special Languages.
  D.C. Andrews, 355(LSoc):Apr82-147
Sagstetter, K. Ceremony.
  V. Trueblood, 271:Spring82-132
Saher, P.J. The Conquest of Suffering.
  C. Hallisey, 318(JAOS):Oct-Dec81-506
Sahi, J. The Child and the Serpent.
  H.R.E. Davidson, 203:Vol193No2-243
  J.S. Hawley, 293(JASt):Aug82-872
Sahlin, E. "Some" and "Any" in Spoken and Written English.
  R. Hudson, 297(JL):Mar82-211
Sahlins, M. Historical Metaphors and Mythical Realities.
  K.E.S., 185:Oct82-197
Said, E.W. Covering Islam.* The Question of Palestine.
  D.C. Gordon, 42(AR):Winter82-104
Said, E.W., ed. Literature and Society.
  M. Jardine, 366:Spring82-113
Said, E.W. Orientalism.*
  D.C. Gordon, 42(AR):Winter82-104
  B.D.H. Miller, 463:Autumn82-284
Said, E.W. The World, the Text, and the Critic.
  J. Bayley, 441:27Feb83-11
  G. Weales, 344:Fall83-122
Saikaku Ihara. Some Final Words of Advice. (P. Nosco, trans)
  J.T. Araki, 407(MN):Spring82-129
Sainsbury, R.M. Russell.*
  P. Hylton, 482(PhR):Jan82-121
Saint, A. The Image of the Architect.
  L. Schwarzbaum, 441:29May83-12
  R. Scruton, 617(TLS):27May83-539
Saint, A. Lives.
  G. Catalano, 381:Oct81-349
Saint-Arnaud, Y. La Psychologie.
  F.F. Wilson, 627(UTQ):Summer82-504

de Saint-Aubin, C.G. Art of the Embroiderer.
  P. Bach, 614:Fall83-16
St. Aubyn, G. The Year of Three Kings: 1483.
  G. Wilson, 617(TLS):23Sep83-1026
de Saint-Exupéry, A. Écrits de Guerre 1939-1944.
  D. Johnson, 617(TLS):1Apr83-316
St. George, R.B. The Wrought Covenant.
  D.R. Friary, 658:Winter82-271
Saint-Gérand, J-P. Les Destinées d'un style.
  A. Jarry, 535(RHL):Mar-Apr82-303
St. John, D. Hush.
  S. Pinsker, 363(LitR):Fall82-153
St. John, D. The Shore.*
  R. Jackson, 502(PrS):Spring82-91
  R. Tillinghast, 569(SR):Spring82-291
St. John-Jones, L.W. The Population of Cyprus.
  P. Loizos, 617(TLS):23Sep83-1027
de Saint-Ledger, Y. - see under Ysambert de Saint-Ledger
Saint-Martin, F. Les Fondements topologiques de la peinture.
  F. Sparshott, 627(UTQ):Summer82-491
St. Martin, G.L. and J.K. Voorhies, eds. Écrits louisianais du dix-neuvième siècle.*
  J.J. Perret, 207(FR):Oct82-198
  L.R. Schub, 207(FR):Dec82-348
  G. Thomas, 292(JAF):Apr-Jun82-224
Abbé de Saint-Pierre. Projet pour rendre la paix perpétuelle en Europe. (S. Goyard-Fabre, ed)
  D. Leduc-Fayette, 192(EP):Oct-Dec82-473
de Ste. Croix, G.E.M. The Class Struggle in the Ancient Greek World.*
  T.D. Barnes, 487:Winter82-363
  K.R. Bradley, 24:Fall82-347
  P.A. Brunt, 313:Vol72-158
  P. Green, 617(TLS):11Feb83-125
  D.A.N. Jones, 362:27Jan83-23
Sainz, G., ed. Jaula de palabras.
  S. Menton, 238:Sep82-472
Sáinz de Medrano, L. - see Fernández de Lizardi, J.J.
Sáinz Rodríguez, P., ed. Antología de la literatura espiritual española. (Vol 1)
  A. Labandeira Fernández, 552(REH):Oct82-468
Sainz Rodríguez, P. Biblioteca Bibliografía Hispánica.
  D.S. Zubatsky, 552(REH):Jan82-124
Saisselin, R.G. The Literary Enterprise in Eighteenth-Century France.*
  J. Lough, 208(FS):Jul82-335
Saito, S., with B. Solyom. Southeast Asia Research Tools. (Vol 1)
  C.R. Bryant, 293(JASt):May82-636
Sakalis, D.T. Iōniko Lektiko ston Platōna, Meros B, Phōnētikē.
  P. Louis, 555:Vol55fasc2-341
Sakamoto, Y. Mongo goishū.
  A.J. Majewicz, 360(LP):Vol24-169
Sakellariou, M.B. Peuples préhelléniques d'origine indo-européenne.
  J. Raison, 555:Vol55fasc1-145
Sakellariou, M.B. Les Proto-grecs.
  G. Huxley, 303(JoHS):Vol 102-275
  J. Raison, 555:Vol156fasc2-305

313

Sakthivel, S. Phonology of Toda with
Vocabulary. A Grammar of the Toda
Language.
  D.W. McAlpin, 318(JAOS):Oct-Dec81-491
Sala, M. and others. El Léxico Indígena
del Español Americano.
  M. Perl, 682(ZPSK):Band34Heft2-266
Salaman, N. Dangerous Pursuits.
  J. Mellors, 362:30Jun83-28
  J.K.L. Walker, 617(TLS):1Jul83-696
Salaquarda, J., ed. Nietzsche.
  W.J.D., 543:Jun82-901
  R. Margreiter, 489(PJGG):Band89Heft2-
  428
Salbstein, M.C.N. The Emancipation of the
Jews in Britain.
  B. Wasserstein, 617(TLS):19Aug83-876
Salé, C. Les Scénaristes au travail.
  R. Hammond, 207(FR):May83-971
Salgádo, G. English Drama.*
  L. Lieblein, 568(SCN):Spring-Summer82-
  6
Salinger, W. Folly River.*
  C. Berger, 491:Apr82-35
  S. Santos, 651(WHR):Spring82-45
Salisbury, H.E. A Journey For Our Times.
  R. MacNeil, 441:15May83-11
Salkey, A. In the Hills Where Her Dreams
Live.
  J. Saunders, 565:Vol23No3-73
Sallis, J. The Gathering of Reason.
  R. Schürmann, 319:Apr83-239
Salminen, R. - see Marguerite de Navarre
Salmon, C. and D. Lombard. Les Chinois de
Jakarta.
  K. Kane, 293(JASt):May82-639
Salmon, E. Granville Barker.
  M. Holroyd, 617(TLS):13May83-485
Salmon, V. The Study of Language in 17th-
Century England.*
  B.M.H. Strang, 402(MLR):Apr82-408
Salmon, W.C., ed. Hans Reichenbach, Logi-
cal Empiricist.*
  P. Humphreys, 486:Mar82-140
Salomaa, A.K. Formale Sprachen.
  J. Kunze, 682(ZPSK):Band35Heft2-241
Salomon, B. Critical Analyses in English
Renaissance Drama.
  D. Mehl, 72:Band218Heft1-176
Salomon-Bayet, C. - see Cournot, A-A.
Salrach, J.M. El procés de formació nac-
ional de Catalunya (segles viii-ix).
  J.C. Shideler, 589:Jan82-196
Salter, C.H. Good Little Thomas Hardy.
  M. Millgate, 445(NCF):Jun82-119
  D.E. Van Tassel, 395(MFS):Summer82-255
  H.L. Weatherby, 569(SR):Spring82-313
Saltonstall, C.D. and H. A New Catalog of
Music for Small Orchestra.
  A.F.L.T., 412:Feb81-61
Salu, M., ed. Essays on "Troilus and
Criseyde."*
  D. Mehl, 38:Band100Heft1/2-189
  D. Pearsall, 161(DUJ):Jun82-299
Salvadori, M. Why Buildings Stand Up.
  R. Mark, 576:Dec82-354
Salvatore, F. Suns of Darkness.
  D. O'Rourke, 102(CanL):Autumn82-149
Salvatore, N. Eugene V. Debs.
  J. Beatty, 231:Feb83-71
  I. Howe, 453(NYRB):10Nov83-18
  D. Montgomery, 441:22May83-12

Salverson, L. Confessions of an Immi-
grant's Daughter. (K.P. Stich, ed)
  T.L. Craig, 627(UTQ):Summer82-450
Salway, P. Roman Britain.
  639(VQR):Spring82-43
Salzer, F. - see "The Music Forum"
Samatar, S.S. Oral Poetry and Somali
Nationalism.
  A. Al-Shahi, 617(TLS):25Mar83-302
Sambrook, J. - see Thomson, J.
Sammons, J.L. Heinrich Heine.*
  D.J. Constantine, 161(DUJ):Jun82-315
  J.M. Ellis, 221(GQ):Mar82-255
  L. Netter, 549(RLC):Oct-Dec82-521
  J. Winkelman, 222(GR):Spring82-85
Sammons, J.L. Literary Sociology and Prac-
tical Criticism.*
  P.A. Robberecht, 107(CRCL):Mar82-107
Sammut, A. Unfredo duca di Gloucester e
gli umanisti italiani.*
  B.C. Barker-Benfield, 354:Jun82-191
  P. Boitani, 382(MAE):1982/2-268
  V. Zaccaria, 228(GSLI):Vol 159fasc505-
  130
Samozvancev, A.M. Teoriya sobstvennosti v
drevnej Indii.
  L. Sternbach, 318(JAOS):Oct-Dec81-487
Sampson, A. The Changing Anatomy of Brit-
ain.*
  R.W. Apple, Jr., 441:15May83-1
  P. Jenkins, 453(NYRB):21Jul83-22
  442(NY):25Apr83-156
Sampson, A. Drum.
  M. Crowder, 617(TLS):16Sep83-982
Sampson, G. Schools of Linguistics.*
  G. Bourcier, 189(EA):Jul-Sep82-320
Sampson, G.R. Making Sense.*
  C. Good, 307:Apr82-56
  R.B. Lees, 84:Jun82-194
  D. Lightfoot, 297(JL):Sep82-426
  B.B. Rundle, 518:Jan82-42
Sampson, R., ed. Early Romance Texts.*
  J.T. Snow, 86(BHS):Apr82-146
  G. Straka, 553(RLiR):Jul-Dec81-487
Samson, J. The Music of Szymanowski.*
  H. Macdonald, 415:Jun82-416
Samuels, E. Bernard Berenson.*
  B. Elevitch, 418(MR):Summer82-245
Samuels, P. and H. Frederic Remington.*
  L. Milazzo, 584(SWR):Autumn82-vi
Samuelson, P. Economics from the Heart.
  R. Lekachman, 61:Jul83-96
Samway, P.H. Faulkner's "Intruder in the
Dust."
  J.G. Watson, 395(MFS):Summer81-365
Sanborn, M. Yosemite.
  S. Sargent, 649(WAL):Summer82-179
Sánchez, V. and C.S. Fuertes, eds. España
en Extremo Oriente, Filipinas, China,
Japón.*
  F.G. Ilárraz, 552(REH):Jan82-118
Sánchez-Albornoz, C. La España cristiana
de los siglos VIII al XI. (Vol 1)
  J.F. Powers, 589:Oct82-934
Sánchez Ortega, M.H. Documentación
selecta sobre la situación de los
gitanos españoles en el siglo XVIII.
  H.R. Morell, 552(REH):Jan82-119
Sánchez Romeralo, A., ed. Romancero tra-
dicional de las lenguas hispánicas.
(Vol 9)
  K. Kish, 545(RPh):May82-681

Sánchez Romeralo, A., D. Catalán and S.G. Armistead, eds. Romancero y poesía oral. (Vols 2-4)
R. Wright, 86(BHS):Oct82-324
Sancho, I. Ignatius Sancho (1729-1780); an Early African Composer in England. (J. Wright, ed)
R. Fiske, 415:Oct82-693
Sand, G. Correspondance. (Vol 15) (G. Lubin, ed)
L.J. Austin, 208(FS):Jan82-80
"The George Sand Papers."*
L.J. Austin, 208(FS):Jan82-80
Sanday, P.R. Female Power and Male Dominance.
M. Douglas, 185:Jul83-786
Sandberg, B. Die neutrale -(e)n-Ableitung der deutschen Gegenwartssprache.*
A. Lötscher, 685(ZDL):3/1981-403
Sandberg, B. Zur Repräsentation, Besetzung und Funktion einiger zentraler Leerstellen bei Substantiven.
V.M. Coombs, 301(JEGP):Jul82-377
P. Suchsland, 682(ZPSK):Band35Heft3-357
Sandeen, E.R. St. Paul's Historic Summit Avenue.
D.J. Hibbard, 658:Spring82-90
Sandel, M.J. Liberalism and the Limits of Justice.
R. Scruton, 617(TLS):13May83-482
Sandercock, L. and I. Turner. Up Where, Cazaly?
S. Alomes, 381:Dec81-534
Sanders, A. Charles Dickens Resurrectionist.
J. Lucas, 617(TLS):29Apr83-440
Sanders, C.R., J. Butt and K.J. Fielding - see Carlyle, T. and J.W.
Sanders, C.R. and K.J. Fielding - see Carlyle, T. and J.W.
Sanders, J.L. Roger Zelazny.
R.C. Schlobin, 561(SFS):Mar82-99
Sanders, L. The Seduction of Peter S.
J. Coleman, 441:24Jul83-11
Sanders, M.L. and P.M. Taylor. British Propaganda during the First World War, 1914-18.
P. Smith, 617(TLS):10Jun83-590
Sanders, N. and others. The Revels History of Drama in English.* (Vol 2)
C. Hill, 366:Autumn82-258
Sanders, W. Linguistische Stilistik.*
J. Scharnhorst, 682(ZPSK):Band34Heft5-649
Sanderson, L.P. Against the Mutilation of Women.
J. Murray, 69:Vol51No4-879
Sandford, J. Landscape and Landscape Imagery in R.M. Rilke.
M. Jacobs, 402(MLR):Oct82-997
Sandford, J. The New German Cinema.
J. Hoberman, 18:Jan-Feb83-62
Sandison, B. The Trout Lochs of Scotland.
A. Atha, 617(TLS):16Sep83-998
Sandler, L.F. The Peterborough Psalter in Brussels and Other Fenland Manuscripts.*
A. Bennett, 54:Sep82-502
Sandler, L.F. The Psalter of Robert De Lisle.
C.R. Dodwell, 617(TLS):25Nov83-1330

Sandmann, M. Subject and Predicate. (2nd ed)
K.H. Schmidt, 685(ZDL):1/1982-74
Sandmel, S. Judaism and Christian Beginnings.
R. Kimelman, 318(JAOS):Oct-Dec81-460
Sandner, D. Navaho Symbols of Healing.
D.P. McAllester, 292(JAF):Apr-Jun82-214
Sandoz, E. The Voegelinian Revolution.
J.H. Hallowell, 396(ModA):Summer/Fal182-397
Sandoz, M. Slogum House.
S. Cormier, 436(NewL):Winter82/83-118
Sandqvist, S., ed. Trois Contes Français du 14e s. tirés du Recueil Le Tombel de Chartrose.
G. Roques, 553(RLiR):Jul-Dec82-502
Sands, M. Robson of the Olympic.*
J.S. Bratton, 155:Autumn82-173
Sandy, G.N. Heliodorus.
G. Schmeling, 121(CJ):Apr/May83-365
Sandy, S. Riding to Greylock.
B. Bennett, 441:17Jul83-10
Saner, R. So This Is the Map.*
D. Asper, 152(UDQ):Summer82-157
J.D. McClatchy, 491:Sep82-351
L.L. Martz, 676(YR):Autumn82-63
B. Tremblay, 649(WAL):Summer82-182
Sanford, A.J. and S.C. Garrod. Understanding Written Language.
E. Finegan, 350:Jun83-461
Sanjdorj, M. Manchu Chinese Colonial Rule in Northern Mongolia.
P.D. Buell, 293(JASt):Feb82-343
Sankoff, G. The Social Life of Language.
D. Cram, 571(ScLJ):Winter82-54
R. Darnell, 474(PIL):Vol 14No2-297
J.A. Fishman, 399(MLJ):Spring82-74
P. Stoller, 355(LSoc):Apr82-105
Sankovitch, T. Jodelle et la Création du Masque.*
K.M. Hall, 208(FS):Oct82-462
M. Simonin, 535(RHL):Mar-Apr82-288
M-C. Wrage, 399(MLJ):Spring82-88
Sanneh, L.O. The Jakhanke.
Y. Person, 69:Vol51No3-794
de San Pedro, D. Prison of Love (1492), together with the Continuation by Nicolás Núñez (1496).* (K. Whinnom, ed and trans)
J.F. Chorpenning, 400(MLN):Mar82-428
"Sanskrit Love Poetry."* (W.S. Merwin and J.M. Masson, trans)
J.W. de Jong, 259(IIJ):Jan80-66
Santa Cruz de Prunes, M.I. La Genèse du Monde Sensible dans la Philosophie de Plotin.*
G.J.P. O'Daly, 123:Vol32No2-285
Santana, J.A. Spanish for the Professions.
J. Burckett-Evans, 399(MLJ):Winter82-441
Santareno, B. The Promise.
C.L. De Oliveira, 399(MLJ):Winter82-430
Santas, G.X. Socrates.*
J. Beatty, 319:Jul82-303
R. Kraut, 449:Sep82-479
Santerre, R., ed. Anthologie de la littérature franco-américaine de la Nouvelle-Angleterre. (Vols 5-9) [entry in prev was of Vols 1-4]
A.B. Chartier, 207(FR):Apr83-791

Santi, V.A. La "Gloria" nel pensiero di
Machiavelli.
   R. Price, 551(RenQ):Spring82-84
Santiago, D. Famous All Over Town.
   D. Quammen, 441:24Apr83-12
   442(NY):2May83-126
Marqués de Santillana. Poesías completas.*
(Vols 1 and 2) (M. Durán, ed)
   C.I. Nepaulsingh, 240(HR):Autumn82-483
   J. Piccus, 238:Mar82-139
Santinello, G., ed. Storia delle storie
generali della filosofia. (Vol 1)
   C.B. Schmitt, 617(TLS):6May83-463
Santinello, G., ed. Storia delle storie
generali della filosofia. (Vol 2)
   D. Leduc-Fayette, 542:Oct-Dec82-691
   C.B. Schmitt, 617(TLS):6May83-463
Santini, C. - see Eutropius
Santoli, A. Everything We Had.
   P. Beidler, 577(SHR):Spring82-181
Santoni, G., ed. Société et culture de la
France contemporaine.
   N. Aronson, 399(MLJ):Autumn82-333
   L.J. Haenlin, 207(FR):Oct82-185
dos Santos, A.S. Guia prático de tradução
inglesa. (2nd ed)
   F.G. Williams, 238:Dec82-671
Santos, N.E. Español Comercial.
   D.A. Klein, 238:Dec82-673
   D.E. Rivas, 399(MLJ):Autumn82-351
Santos, S. Accidental Weather.
   M. Kinzie, 29:Jan/Feb83-28
Sapergia, B. Dirt Hills Mirage.*
   P. Nightingale, 102(CanL):Autumn82-155
Saperstein, M. Decoding the Rabbis.
   M. Kellner, 589:Apr82-430
Sapir, R.B. The Body.
   D. Flower, 441:10Apr83-30
Saporoshez, A.W. and M.I. Lissina, eds.
Kommunikation mit Kindern.
   E. Metze, 682(ZPSK):Band34Heft3-372
Sapper. Bulldog Drummond.
   P. Craig, 617(TLS):19Aug83-890
Sarafis, M., ed. Greece.
   S. Wichert, 575(SEER):Apr82-300
Sarafis, S. ELAS: Greek Resistance Army.
   S. Wichert, 575(SEER):Apr82-300
Saraydar, A. Proust disciple de Stendhal.*
   H. Bonnet, 535(RHL):Sep-Dec82-955
Sareil, J. and A. Bergens. Les Joies de
la lecture.*
   G. Crouse, 399(MLJ):Summer82-210
Sargeant, W. - see "The Bhagavad Gītā"
Sargent, S. Galen Clark.
   V.P. Cohen, 649(WAL):Nov82-277
Sarkar, S. Epistemology and Ethics of
G.E. Moore.
   T.M.R., 185:Jan83-415
Sarma, M.V.R. - see under Rama Sarma, M.V.
Sarno, I.P. - see under Pepe Sarno, I.
Sárosi, B. Gypsy Music.
   S. Erdely, 187:Sep83-550
Saroyan, A. Last Rites.*
   M. Secrest, 364:Nov82-61
Saroyan, W. Births.
   J. Oppenheimer, 441:21Aug83-3
Saroyan, W. My Name is Saroyan. (J.H.
Tashjian, ed)
   J. Oppenheimer, 441:21Aug83-3
   442(NY):22Aug83-93
Sarraute, N. Enfance.
   J. Sturrock, 617(TLS):10Jun83-596

Sarraute, N. Pour un oui ou pour un non.*
   G.R. Besser, 207(FR):Apr83-791
Sarraute, N. The Use of Speech.
   442(NY):11Apr83-137
Sartin, S. A Dictionary of British Narra-
tive Painters.
   T. Crombie, 39:Jul82-66
Sartre, J-P. No Exit and Three Other
Plays.
   S. Keane, 399(MLJ):Summer82-206
Sartre, J-P. Oeuvres romanesques. (M.
Contat and M. Rybalka, with others, eds)
   G. Prince, 188(ECr):Summer82-71
Sashegyi, O. Ungarns politische Verwal-
tung in der Ära Bach, 1849-1860.
   L. Péter, 575(SEER):Jan82-124
Sasse, W. Das Glossar Koryŏ-pangŏn im
Kyerim-yusa.
   S.R. Ramsey, 318(JAOS):Oct-Dec81-425
Sasso, G. Niccolò Machiavelli.
   G. Silvano, 276:Winter82-349
Sasson, J.M. - see "Ruth"
Sassoon, S. Siegfried Sassoon Diaries,
1915-1918. The War Poems of Siegfried
Sassoon. (R. Hart-Davis, ed of both)
   D.J. Enright, 362:14Apr83-27
   D. Hibberd, 617(TLS):22Apr83-395
Sassoon, S. Siegfried Sassoon Diaries,
1920-1922.* (R. Hart-Davis, ed)
   T. Warr, 493:Apr82-67
Sassoon, S. Sassoon's Long Journey. (P.
Fussell, ed)
   D. Hibberd, 617(TLS):23Dec83-1423
Sassoon, S. Sherston's Progress.
   D.J. Enright, 362:14Apr83-27
   D. Hibberd, 617(TLS):22Apr83-395
Sastri, H.C., ed. The Philosophy of Nāgār-
juna as contained in the Ratnāvalī. (Pt
1)
   L. Hurvitz, 318(JAOS):Jul-Sep81-391
Sastri, P.A.M., ed. The Vaiṣṇava Upan-
iṣads.
   S. Elkman, 318(JAOS):Oct-Dec81-499
Sastry, R.A. Viṣṇusahasranāma.
   J.W. de Jong, 259(IIJ):Jul82-218
Satie, E. Écrits. (O. Volta, ed)
   R. Shattuck, 208(FS):Jul82-355
Satie, E. The Writings of Erik Satie. (N.
Wilkins, ed and trans)
   P. Dickinson, 410(M&L):Jul/Oct82-293
   R. Nichols, 415:Feb82-112
   R. Shattuck, 208(FS):Jul82-355
Sato, H. and B. Watson, eds and trans.
From the Country of Eight Islands.*
   639(VQR):Summer82-94
Sato, T. Currents in Japanese Cinema.
   D. Desser, 500:Winter83-59
   R. McCormick, 18:Mar83-72
   200:Nov82-572
Satow, M. and R. Desmond. Railways of the
Raj.*
   A. Heston, 318(JAOS):Oct-Dec81-500
Sattler, H.R. Dinosaurs of North America.
   529(QQ):Summer82-455
Sauder, G. Empfindsamkeit. (Vol 3)
   C.P. Magill, 402(MLR):Apr82-493
Sauer, G. - see Steinitz, W.
Sauer, G., with L. Hartung and B. Schulze -
see Steinitz, W.
Sauer, G. and B. Schulze - see Steinitz, W.
Sauer, H., ed. Theodulfi Capitula in
England.*
   G.H. Brown, 589:Apr82-432

Ščerba, L.V. Vostočnoluzickoe narečie.
   K. Gutschmidt, 682(ZPSK):Band34Heft4-
   500
Schabert, T. Gewalt und Humanität.
   R. Brague, 192(EP):Oct-Dec81-496
Schach, P., ed. Languages in Conflict.*
   H.L. Kufner, 221(GQ):Mar82-237
Schacht, R. Nietzsche.
   R. Rorty, 617(TLS):17Jun83-619
Schachter, A. Cults of Boiotia.
   E. Kearns, 123:Vol132No2-205
   L.C. Reilly, 24:Winter82-457
Schade, R.E. - see "Lessing Yearbook"
Schadendorf, W., ed. Lübecker Museumskata-
   loge. (Vol 1)
   E.M. Vetter, 471:Oct/Nov/Dec82-359
Schaeder, B. Lexikographie als Praxis und
   Theorie.
   U. Reichenbach, 221(GQ):May82-398
Schaefer, D.L. Justice or Tyranny?
   L. Fujimagari, 154:Jun82-356
Schaefer, E., ed. Medien und Deutschunter-
   richt.
   P. Ruppert, 221(GQ):Nov82-574
Schaeffer, N. The Art of Laughter.*
   R.K. Simon, 141:Fall82-386
Schaeffer, S.F. The Madness of a Seduced
   Woman.
   R. Brown, 441:22May83-14
Schaeffler, R. Frömmigkeit des Denkens?
   192(EP):Jul-Sep81-356
Schaeper, T.J. The French Council of Com-
   merce 1700-1715.
   J.M.J. Rogister, 617(TLS):5Aug83-842
Schäfer, J. Documentation in the O.E.D.*
   G. Bourcier, 189(EA):Jul-Sep82-317
   G. Bourquin, 189(EA):Apr-Jun82-203
   D.J. Lake, 447(N&Q):Apr81-189
   G.R. Proudfoot, 191(ELN):Sep81-59
   M. Stokes, 541(RES):Nov82-447
Schafer, R. The Analytic Attitude.
   B. Farrell, 617(TLS):9Sep83-968
Schäfer, W.E. Anekdote — Antianekdote.
   D. Dollenmayer, 221(GQ):Nov82-580
   K. Haberkamm, 224(GRM):Band32Heft4-463
Schakel, P.J. The Poetry of Jonathan
   Swift.*
   W. Kinsley, 173(ECS):Summer82-442
Schakel, P.J. Reading with the Heart.*
   B. Reynolds, 677(YES):Vol 12-356
Schank, G. and G. Schoenthal. Gesprochene
   Sprache.
   D. Stellmacher, 685(ZDL):3/1981-400
Schanzer, G.O. - see Pavlovsky, E.
Schaper, E. Studies in Kant's Aesthetics.*
   M. Kraft, 687:Jan-Mar81-154
Schapiro, L. and J. Godson, eds. The
   Soviet Worker.*
   H. Hunter, 550(RusR):Apr82-226
   M. Matthews, 575(SEER):Jul82-468
Schaps, D.M. Economic Rights of Women in
   Ancient Greece.*
   É. Will, 555:Vol55fasc1-152
Scharer, K. Pour une poétique des "Chi-
   mères" de Nerval.
   S. Dunn, 446(NCFS):Spring-Summer83-370
Scharf, G. Alt-Reichenau.
   W. Jungandreas, 684(ZDA):Band111Heft2-
   90
Scharfstein, B-A. The Philosophers.*
   M. Adam, 542:Oct-Dec82-676
Schatz, S.P. Nigerian Capitalism.
   P.A. Beckett, 69:Vol51No1-545

Schatz, T. Hollywood Genres.
   G. Fuller, 214:Vol 10No38-125
   L. Giannetti, 651(WHR):Summer82-178
Schaub, T.H. Pynchon: The Voice of Ambigu-
   ity.*
   S. Brivic, 295(JML):Dec82-520
   B.L. Clark, 587(SAF):Spring82-120
   D. Cowart, 301(JEGP):Apr82-285
   J.Z. Guzlowski, 395(MFS):Summer82-310
   G.O. Taylor, 27(AL):Mar82-148
   K. Tölölyan, 454:Winter83-165
Schauer, F. Free Speech.
   J.N. Gray, 617(TLS):11Mar83-247
   A. Ryan, 362:13Jan83-21
Schäufele, E. Normabweichendes Rollenver-
   halten.
   D.H. Green, 402(MLR):Jan82-227
Schavelzon, I. A contre-jour.
   L.K. Penrod, 207(FR):Apr83-793
Scheben, H. Die Krise des Modernismus in
   Peru.
   K. Meyer-Minnemann, 547(RF):Band93
   Heft3/4-495
Scheckel, R. Bildgeleitete Sprachspiele.
   P. Ruppert, 221(GQ):Nov82-573
Schecker, M., ed. Methodologie der Sprach-
   wissenschaft.
   D. Stellmacher, 685(ZDL):3/1981-371
Scheer, R., with N. Zacchino and C. Matt-
   hiessen. With Enough Shovels.*
   L. Freedman, 617(TLS):18Mar83-261
Scheerer, T.M. Ferdinand de Saussure.
   K.H. Schmidt, 547(RF):Band93Heft1/2-
   173
Scheffel, D. Kants Theorie der Substan-
   tialität.
   H. Graubner, 342:Band73Heft2-241
Scheffel, W. Aspekte der platonischen
   Kosmologie.
   J. Mansfield, 394:Vol35fasc1/2-168
   D.O., 543:Mar82-631
Scheffers, H. Höfische Konvention und die
   Aufklärung.
   J. Hardin, 564:May82-149
Scheffler, I. Beyond the Letter.*
   T.S. Champlin, 518:Apr82-111
   H-J. Eikmeyer and H. Rieser, 449:Nov82-
   626
   G. Iseminger, 289:Spring82-112
Scheible, H. Arthur Schnitzler und die
   Aufklärung.
   D.G. Daviau, 221(GQ):Mar82-265
Scheible, H. - see Melanchthon, P.
Scheick, W.J., ed. Critical Essays on
   Jonathan Edwards.
   C. Gerbaud, 189(EA):Jul-Sep82-359
Scheidegger, J. Arbitraire et motivation
   en français et en allemand.
   F-J. Klein, 547(RF):Band94Heft4-453
Schein, S.L. The Iambic Trimeter in
   Aeschylus and Sophocles.*
   J. Irigoin, 555:Vol56fasc1-125
Scheler, L. - see Tchemerzine, A.
Schell, J. The Fate of the Earth.*
   J. Elder, 434:Summer83-647
   M. Fox, 529(QQ):Winter82-923
   T.C. Holyoke, 42(AR):Fall82-483
   D.P.L., 185:Jul83-838
Schell, T. and others. The Northwest
   Adventure Guide.
   529(QQ):Autumn82-687

318

Schelle, H., ed. Christoph Martin Wieland.
  G. Müller, 684(ZDA):Band111Heft4-174
  W. Paulsen, 222(GR):Spring82-87
Schellekens, O., ed. Stendhal, le saint-
  simonisme et les industriels.*
  F.W. Saunders, 208(FS):Oct82-481
Schellenberg, J.A. The Science of Con-
  flict.
  D.S., 185:Apr83-633
Schelling, F.W.J. Le système de l'idéal-
  isme transcendantal. (C. Dubois, ed and
  trans)
  J-F. Courtine, 192(EP):Jan-Mar81-115
Schelling, F.W.J. The Unconditional in
  Human Knowledge.* (F. Marti, ed and
  trans)
  D. Loubet, 319:Jan83-109
  T.F.O., 543:Jun82-905
Schemann, H. and L. Schemann-Dias. Dic-
  ionário idiomático português-alemão.
  H. Müller, 72:Band218Heft1-201
Schemm, R. Mapping My Father.
  S. Hamill, 649(WAL):Summer82-194
  V. Trueblood, 271:Spring82-132
Schenda, R. - see Burke, P.
Schenker, A.M. and E. Stankiewicz, eds.
  The Slavic Literary Languages.
  T. Alt and W. Browne, 574(SEEJ):
    Spring82-120
  M.Z. Brooks, 497(PolR):Vol27No3/4-232
  O. Frink, 399(MLJ):Winter82-432
  C.A. Moser, 104(CASS):Spring82-115
  G. Stone, 575(SEER):Jan82-90
Schenker, W. Die Sprache Huldrych Zwing-
  lis im Kontrast zur Sprache Luthers.
  H. Moser, 685(ZDL):3/1982-397
Schepens, G. L'"autopsie" dans la méthode
  des historiens grecs du Ve siècle avant
  J-C.
  H.D. Westlake, 123:Vol132No2-230
Scherer, J.L. - see "USSR Facts and Fig-
  ures Annual"
Schesaeus, C. Opera quae supersunt omnia.*
  (F. Csonka, ed)
  G.F. Cushing, 575(SEER):Jul82-445
Schevill, J. The American Fantasies.
  R. Elman, 441:18Sep83-36
Schiavo, L. Historia y novela en Valle-
  Inclán.
  B.B. Aponte, 240(HR):Summer82-359
  R. Johnson, 238:May82-308
Schiavone, G. The Institutions of Comecon.
  A.H. Smith, 575(SEER):Apr82-306
Schicho, W. Kiswahili von Lubumbashi.
  I. Herms, 682(ZPSK):Band35Heft2-220
Schickel, R. Cary Grant.
  J. Maslin, 441:4Dec83-73
Schiebe, M.W. Das ideale Dasein bei
  Tibull und die Goldzeitkonzeption
  Vergils
  R. Maltby, 123:Vol132No2-163
Schiefer, L. Phonematik und Phonotaktik
  des Vach-Ostjakischen.
  A.F. Majewicz, 360(LP):Vol124-158
Schier, P. and M. Oum-Schier, with W.
  Jarke. Prince Sihanouk on Cambodia.
  M. Ebihara, 293(JASt):Nov81-63
Schiff, D. The Music of Elliott Carter.
  P. Griffiths, 617(TLS):17Jun83-637
Schiff, N.R. A Celebration of the 80's.
  J. Maslin, 441:4Dec83-72
Schiffer, M. Ballpark.
  639(VQR):Summer82-96

Schiffhorst, G.J., ed. The Triumph of
  Patience.*
  D. Mehl, 72:Band218Heft1-175
Schiffrin, H.Z. Sun Yat-sen.
  A.J. Gregor, 293(JASt):Aug82-820
Schillebeeckx, E. God Among Us.
  P. Hebblethwaite, 617(TLS):7Oct83-1103
Schillebeeckx, E. Jesus. Christ.
  L. Dupré, 322(JHI):Jul-Sep82-512
Schillebeeckx, E., with H. Oosterhuis and
  P. Hoogeveen. God is New Each Moment.
  P. Hebblethwaite, 617(TLS):7Oct83-1103
Schillemeit, J. - see Kafka, F.
Schiller, D. Objectivity and the News.
  S. Craig, 583:Winter83-200
Schiller, F. On the Aesthetic Education
  of Man. (E.M. Wilkinson and L.A.
  Willoughby, eds and trans)
  A.P., 617(TLS):23Sep83-1031
Schiller, F. On the Naive and Sentimental
  in Literature. (H. Watanabe-O'Kelly, ed
  and trans)
  P. Robinson, 83:Autumn82-276
Schiller, J. Physiologie et classifica-
  tion.
  G. Brykman, 542:Jan-Mar82-138
Schilling, M. Imagines Mundi.*
  D. Peil, 52:Band16Heft2-200
  P. Skrine, 402(MLR):Jul82-758
Schilpp, P.A., ed. The Philosophy of Karl
  Jaspers.
  W. Earle, 396(ModA):Spring82-197
Schimmel, A., ed and trans. Märchen aus
  Pakistan.
  H-J. Uther, 196:Band23Heft3/4-332
Schine, C. Alice in Bed.
  C. Seebohm, 441:5Jun83-14
  J. Updike, 442(NY):1Aug83-87
Schings, H-J. Der mitleidigste Mensch ist
  der beste Mensch.*
  B. Bennett, 301(JEGP):Oct82-537
  B. Duncan, 133:Band15Heft1/2-169
Schirn, M., ed. Studien zu Frege. (Vol 1)
  R.H. Stoothoff, 316:Mar82-226
Schirokauer, A. Frühe Hörspiele. (W.
  Paulsen, ed)
  R.C. Holub, 406:Spring82-72
Schirokauer, C. A Brief History of Chi-
  nese and Japanese Civilizations.
  J.M. Gentzler, 318(JAOS):Jul-Sep81-391
Schjeldahl, P. The Brute.
  D. Lehman, 181:Spring-Summer83-277
Schlaffer, H. Faust Zweiter Teil.
  H.G. Haile, 301(JEGP):Jul82-385
Schlaffer, H. Wilhelm Meister.
  C. Grawe, 67:Nov82-213
Schlee, A. The Proprietor.
  L. Marcus, 617(TLS):16Sep83-1001
  K.C. O'Brien, 362:10Nov83-30
Schlee, A. Rhine Journey.
  C. Hawtree, 364:Apr/May82-138
Schlegel, F. Die Epoche der Zeitschrift
  Concordia (6. November 1818-Mai 1823).
  (E. Susini, ed)
  M. Vetö, 192(EP):Oct-Dec81-499
Schlegel, I. Samuel Hofmann (1595-1649).
  C. Brown, 39:Mar82-210
Schlegel, R. Superposition and Inter-
  action.
  J. Largeault, 542:Jan-Mar82-140
Schleifer, R., ed. The Genres of the
  Irish Literary Revival.*
  R.M. Kain, 395(MFS):Winter81/82-671

Schlerath, B. Sanskrit Vocabulary.
  J.W. de Jong, 259(IIJ):Apr82-135
Schlereth, T.J. Artifacts and the Ameri-
  can Past.
  E.M. Fleming, 658:Winter82-269
  I.M.G. Quimby, 576:Mar82-70
Schlesinger, G.N. Aspects of Time.
  K.G. Denbigh, 393(Mind):Jan82-141
  D.P. Lackey, 449:May82-324
Schlesinger, G.N. Metaphysics.
  P. Mackie, 617(TLS):4Nov83-1222
Schlissel, L. Women's Diaries of the West-
  ward Journey.
  R.E. Carp, 649(WAL):Winter83-351
Schlobin, R.C., ed. The Aesthetics of
  Fantasy Literature and Art.
  T.A. Shippey, 617(TLS):13May83-479
Schloss, C. Flannery O'Connor's Dark
  Comedies.
  M. Chew, 585(SoQ):Fall81-85
Schlott, W. Zur Funktion antiker Gotter-
  mythen in der Lyrik Osip Mandel'stams.
  J.T. Baer, 574(SEEJ):Winter82-487
Schlotzhauer, J.M. The Curved Two-Patch
  System.
  M. Cowan, 614:Spring83-17
Schluchter, W. The Rise of Western Ratio-
  nalism.
  J.G. Morgan, 150(DR):Summer82-331
Schlueter, J. The Plays and Novels of
  Peter Handke.
  C. Bedwell, 395(MFS):Winter82/83-698
Schlütter, H-J., R. Borgmeier and H.W.
  Wittschier. Sonett.*
  B. Bjorklund, 406:Fall82-337
Schlyter, A. and T. George.
  J.C. Stone, 69:Vol51No4-899
Schmandt-Besserat, D., ed. Immortal Egypt.
  M.E. Lane, 318(JAOS):Oct-Dec81-436
Schmeling, G.L. Xenophon of Ephesus.*
  J.R. Morgan, 123:Vol32No1-95
Schmeling, M. Der Spiel im Spiel.
  V. Tasca, 549(RLC):Apr-Jun82-222
Schmeling, M., ed. Vergleichende Litera-
  turwissenschaft.
  D.J. Parent, 221(GQ):Mar82-225
  J. Voisine, 549(RLC):Apr-Jun82-205
Schmid, C. Die Mittelalterrezeption des
  18. Jahrhunderts zwischen Aufklärung
  und Romantik.
  O. Ehrismann, 224(GRM):Band32Heft4-479
Schmid, G. - see Büchner, G.
Schmidgall, G. Shakespeare and the Court-
  ly Aesthetic.*
  B.A. Mowat, 551(RenQ):Summer82-329
  D. Norbrook, 175:Autumn82-247
  J.W. Velz, 301(JEGP):Oct82-560
Schmidt, A. The Egghead Republic.
  P. Parrinder, 299:Spring82-151
Schmidt, A. History and Structure.
  42(AR):Spring82-247
Schmidt, A. Scenes from the Life of a
  Faun.
  E. Pawel, 441:8May83-11
  S.S. Prawer, 617(TLS):8Apr83-346
Schmidt, A.V.C. and N. Jacobs, eds. Medie-
  val English Romances.*
  H. Cooper, 541(RES):Nov82-454
  A. Crépin, 189(EA):Jul-Sep82-325
  A.S.G. Edwards, 589:Jul82-660

Schmidt, E-J. Stellenkommentar zum IX.
  Buch des "Willehalm" Wolframs von Eschen-
  bach.
  F.H. Bäuml, 589:Jan82-197
  M.E. Gibbs, 406:Winter82-485
Schmidt, G. "Far-Sourced Canticles."
  R. Asselineau, 549(RLC):Apr-Jun82-230
Schmidt, H. The Roots of Lo Mexicano.
  A. Donoso, 258:Jun82-203
Schmidt, J. Hegels Wissenschaft der Logik
  und ihre Kritik durch Adolf Trendelen-
  burg.
  K. Hartmann, 53(AGP):Band64Heft1-106
Schmidt, J.N. Satire: Swift und Pope.
  P. Rogers, 67(YES):Vol 1-277
Schmidt, K. Kosmologische Aspekte im
  Geschichtswerk des Poseidonios.
  I.G. Kidd, 303(JoHS):Vol 102-253
Schmidt, M. A Reader's Guide to Fifty
  British Poets 1300-1900.*
  M.A. Mikolajczak, 568(SCN):Fall82-45
Schmidt, P., ed. Meyerhold at Work.*
  M. Coiner, 42(AR):Spring82-240
Schmidt, S., ed. Märchen aus Namibia.
  E. Dammann, 196:Band23Heft1/2-123
Schmidt, W. Untersuchungen zu Aufbaufor-
  men und Erzählstil im "Daniel von dem
  blühenden Tal" des Stricker.
  P. Wiehl, 680(ZDP):Band101Heft1-143
Schmidt, W. and E. Stock, eds. Rede-
  Gespräch-Diskussion.
  E. Kurka, 682(ZPSK):Band35Heft1-109
Schmidt, W.H. The Faith of the Old Testa-
  ment.
  A. Phillips, 617(TLS):27May83-554
Schmidt-Dengler, W. Genius.*
  P.F. Veit, 406:Spring82-99
Schmidt-Künsemüller, F.A. Corpus der
  Gotischen Lederschnitteinbände aus dem
  deutschen Sprachgebiet.
  M.M. Foot, 78(BC):Spring82-113
Schmieding, W. Aufstand der Töchter.
  A. Gleason, 550(RusR):Oct82-483
Schmier, L. - see Wessolowsky, C.
Schmithausen, L. - see Hacker, P.
Schmitt, J-C. Le Saint Lévrier.
  D. Fabre, 98:Apr82-295
Schmitt, R. Einführung in die griech-
  ischen Dialekte.
  P. Swiggers, 353:Vol 19No3/4-377
Schmitt, R. Iranica Graeca Vetustiora.
  (Vol 1)
  L. Isebaert, 259(IIJ):Apr82-127
Schmitt, R. - see Simon, R.
Schmitz, D. String.
  R. Tillinghast, 569(SR):Spring82-291
Schmitz, H. Neue Phänomenologie.
  R. Schottlaender, 489(PJGG):Band89
  Heft1-162
Schmitz, U. Gesellschaftliche Bedeutung
  und sprachliches Lernen.
  R. Pape, 682(ZPSK):Band35Heft3-359
Schmitz, V.A. and F. Martini - see Gundolf,
  F.
Schmölders, C. - see "Das Ramayana des
  Valmiki"
Schmucker, J. Die Ontotheologie des vor-
  kritischen Kant.
  D.D., 543:Sep81-163
  H. Wagner, 53(AGP):Band64Heft1-96
Schnackenberg, G. Portraits and Elegies.
  E. Grosholz, 249(HudR):Summer82-319
  W. Logan, 617(TLS):10Jun83-614

Schnackenburg, B. Adriaen van Ostade, Isack van Ostade.
S. Reiss, 39:Aug82-127
K. Renger, 471:Apr/May/Jun82-168
Schnädelbach, H. Reflexion und Diskurs.
W. Hogrebe, 687:Apr-Jun82-289
Schnapper, D. Jewish Identities in France.
M.R. Marrus, 617(TLS):14Oct83-1108
Schneewind, J.B. Sidgwick's Ethics and Victorian Moral Philosophy.*
M.G. Singer, 449:May82-339
Schneider, H. Livestock and Equality in East Africa.
G. Dahl and A. Hjort, 69:Vol52No1-89
Schneider, K. Die deutschen Handschriften der Bayerischen Staatsbibliothek München. Dasselbe.
B. Schnell, 684(ZDA):Band111Heft2-92
Schneider, L.A. A Madman of Ch'u.
D. Johnson, 293(JASt):Feb82-344
M. Loewe, 203:Vol93No1-127
J.W. Schiffeler, 292(JAF):Jul-Sep82-360
Schneider, M. Die kranke schöne Seele der Revolution.
G. Kaiser, 224(GRM):Band32Heft2-234
Schneider, M. La Lumière du Nord.
P. Mahillon, 450(NRF):Nov82-114
Schneiderman, S. Jacques Lacan.
J. Malcolm, 441:3Apr83-1
Schneiders, H-W. Der französische Wortschatz zur Bezeichnung von "Schall."
R. Martin, 553(RLiR):Jan-Jun81-255
Schneidmüller, B. Karolingische Tradition und frühes französisches Königtum.
F. Behrends, 589:Jan82-173
Schneiper, Z. and D. Stock. Saint Francis of Assisi.
F. Russell, 39:Feb82-135
Schneir, W. and M. Invitation to an Inquest.
R. Radosh and J. Milton, 453(NYRB):21Jul83-17
Schnitzler, A. The Letters of Arthur Schnitzler to Hermann Bahr.* (D.G. Daviau, ed)
F.J. Beharriell, 406:Summer82-212
Schnitzler, A. La Ronde. (F. and J. Marcus, trans) Anatol. (F. Marcus, trans)
P.F. Dvorak, 399(MLJ):Winter82-423
Schnitzler, A. Arthur Schnitzler: Plays and Stories. (E. Schwarz, ed)
G. Annan, 453(NYRB):21Jul83-14
Schnitzler, A. Tagebuch 1909-1912.* (W. Welzig and others, eds)
M. Swales, 220(GL&L):Jul83-368
Schnitzler, G., ed. Dichtung und Musik.
U. Weisstein, 52:Band16Heft1-67
Schnyder, A., ed. Biterolf und Dietleib.*
T.P. Thornton, 301(JEGP):Jan82-76
Schober, O., ed. Text und Leser.
W. Schmidt, 682(ZPSK):Band35Heft5-596
Schodt, F.L. Manga! Manga!
J. Kirkup, 617(TLS):1Jul83-695
442(NY):8Aug83-93
Schoenbaum, S. William Shakespeare: Records and Images.*
A.J. Cook, 570(SQ):Winter82-530
R.A. Foakes, 354:Dec82-440
G.K. Hunter, 569(SR):Spring82-274
J.L. Murphy, 191(ELN):Sep82-30

Schoenbaum, S. Shakespeare: The Globe and the World.*
A.W. Bellringer, 447(N&Q):Dec81-536
D.S. Rodes, 570(SQ):Summer82-239
Schoffel, A. Arts primitif de l'Asie du sud-est.
L.T. Wells, Jr., 2(AfrA):May82-87
Schofield, C. Jagger.
J. Stokes, 617(TLS):22Jul83-771
Schofield, M. An Essay on Anaxagoras.*
G.B. Kerferd, 303(JoHS):Vol 102-246
A.R. Lacey, 518:Apr82-71
J. Mansfeld, 394:Vol35fasc3/4-360
D. Pralon, 555:Vol56fasc1-131
R.A. Shiner, 487:Summer82-171
Schofield, M., M. Burnyeat and J. Barnes, eds. Doubt and Dogmatism.*
S. Gaukroger, 63:Mar82-97
G.B. Kerferd, 123:Vol132No1-50
R.W. Sharples, 393(Mind):Jul82-452
S.U., 543:Sep81-165
Scholberg, K.R. and D.E. Aquí mismo.*
A. Sánchez-Rojas, 238:Mar82-155
Scholem, G. Walter Benjamin.*
J. Boyarin, 287:May82-27
A. Thorlby, 617(TLS):4Feb83-110
Scholem, G. From Berlin to Jerusalem.
S. Cain, 390:May82-59
L. Greenspan, 529(QQ):Summer82-408
Scholes, R. Fabulation and Metafiction.*
J.R. Clark, 436(NewL):Fall82-102
Scholes, R. Semiotics and Interpretation.*
N. Armstrong, 141:Fall82-382
M. Green, 363(LitR):Fall82-139
R. Pearce, 454:Fall82-83
M. Ryan, 400(MLN):Dec82-1242
J.J. Sosnoski, 329(JJQ):Summer83-466
27(AL):Oct82-476
Schölz, M.G. Hören und Lesen.
F.H. Bäuml, 589:Oct82-936
J. Bumke, 684(ZDA):Band111Heft3-116
K. Düwel, 196:Band23Heft3/4-341
D.H. Green, 402(MLR):Apr82-479
E. Haymes, 133:Band15Heft4-353
Schomann, H. Lombardei.
H-W. Kruft, 471:Oct/Nov/Dec82-360
Schönberger, O. - see Cato, M.P.
Schönfeld, H. and J. Donath. Sprache im sozialistischen Industriebetrieb.
H. Löffler, 685(ZDL):2/1981-258
Schönfeldt, A. Studien zur Morphologie des Verbs in den ost- und westpreussischen Mundarten.
K. Hameyer, 685(ZDL):3/1981-386
Schoolman, M. The Imaginary Witness.
J. Schmidt, 185:Jan83-397
Schopenhauer, A. Gesammelte Briefe.* (A. Hübscher, ed)
J. Lefranc, 192(EP):Apr-Jun81-235
Schor, N. Zola's Crowds.*
L. Frappier-Mazur, 207(FR):Dec82-325
R. Lethbridge, 208(FS):Jul82-348
Schorr, M. Red Diamond: Private Eye.
N. Callendar, 441:5Jun83-37
Schorske, C.E. Fin-de-Siècle Vienna.*
D. Barnouw, 221(GQ):May82-463
K. Rossbacher, 602:Vol 13No1-190
Schottelius, J.G. Ethica. (J.J. Berns, ed)
R.E. Schade, 133:Band15Heft1/2-163
Schouls, P.A. The Imposition of Method.*
W.S., 543:Dec81-408

Schoultz, L. The Populist Challenge.
R. Cox, 453(NYRB):8Dec83-18
Schöwerling, R. Chapbooks.
R. Wehse, 196:Band23Heft1/2-151
Schrader, M. Epische Kurzformen.
H. Bausinger, 196:Band23Heft1/2-154
Schreiber, E.G. and T.E. Maresca - see
Bernardus Silvestris
Schreiber, F.R. The Shoemaker.
A. Storr, 617(TLS):2Dec83-1351
Schreuders, P. The Book of Paperbacks.
D.J. Hall, 354:Sep82-353
Schreyer, R. Stratifikationsgrammatik.
H. Janssen, 260(IF):Band86-310
Schröder, H., ed and trans. Die Frau ist
frei geboren.
M. Lichterfeld, 221(GQ):Nov82-625
Schröder, I. Des westfränkischen Synoden
von 888 bis 987 und ihre Überlieferung.
U-R. Blumenthal, 589:Oct82-973
Schroeder, J. Pierre Reverdy.
M. Guiney, 188(ECr):Winter82-101
M. Guiney, 210(FrF):Sep82-277
Schroyer, T. Critique de la domination.
A. Reix, 542:Jan-Mar82-72
Schubert, D. Works and Days.
P. Schjeldahl, 441:25Dec83-7
Schubert, H. Das Verbotene Zimmer.
C. Russ, 617(TLS):22Jul83-788
Schuchardt, H. Pidgin and Creole Lan-
guages.* (G.G. Gilbert, ed and trans)
The Ethnography of Variation.* (T.L.
Markey, ed and trans)
J.E. Reinecke, 297(JL):Mar82-188
Schuh, W. Richard Strauss: A Chronicle of
the Early Years 1864-1898.*
M. Kennedy, 410(M&L):Jul/Oct82-329
W. Mann, 617(TLS):15Apr83-373
Schulberg, B. Moving Pictures.*
V.S. Navasky, 18:Mar82-72
Schulberg, B. Writers in America.
D. Hall, 441:17Jul83-9
Schulman, A.K. On the Stroll.
W.H. Pritchard, 249(HudR):Spring82-159
Schultheis, H. The Hidden West.*
G.C., 569(SR):Fall82-cix
Schulthess, E. Swiss Panorama.
P. Zweig, 441:4Dec83-70
Schultze, B. Studien zum politischen
Verständnis moderner englischer Unter-
haltungsliteratur.
B. Lenz, 38:Band100Heft1/2-248
Schultze, S. The Structure of Anna
Karenina.
V.E. Alexandrov, 550(RusR):Jul82-350
Schulz, G-M. Die Überwindung der Barbarei.
E. Dvoretzky, 221(GQ):Mar82-248
D.G. John, 564:May82-142
Schulz, W. Le Dieu de la Métaphysique mod-
erne. (J. Colette, ed and trans)
C. Roels, 192(EP):Jul-Sep81-366
Schulz, W. Ich und Welt.
K. Konhardt, 687:Jul-Sep82-459
Schulz-Behrend, G. - see Opitz, M.
Schumann, O. - see "Lateinisches Hexameter-
Lexikon"
Schumann, O. and B. Bischoff - see "Latein-
isches Hexameter-Lexikon"
Schunck, F. Joseph Conrad.*
W. Senn, 136:Vol 14No2-154

Schupp, V. Studien zu Williram von Ebers-
berg.*
T.L. Markey, 406:Winter82-484
P.W. Tax, 133:Band15Heft1/2-151
Schürer, E. The History of the Jewish
People in the Age of Jesus Christ
(175 B.C. - A.D. 135). (Vol 2) (G.
Vermes, F. Millar and M. Black, eds)
T. Rajak, 313:Vol72-170
Schürmann, K.E., ed. Ludwig van Beethoven:
Alle vertonten und musikalisch bearbeite-
ten Texte.
E. Forbes, 410(M&L):Jul/Oct81-355
Schuster, I., ed. Zu Alfred Döblin.
A.W. Riley, 564:Nov81-329
Schuster, P-K. Theodor Fontane.
R.L. Jamison, 406:Summer82-210
Schütrumpf, E. Die Analyse der Polis
durch Aristoteles.
M.H. Chambers, 123:Vol32No2-284
É. des Places, 555:Vol56fasc2-329
Schutte, G.J. - see Coolhaas, W.P.
Schütte, K. Proof Theory.
W.A. Howard, 316:Mar82-218
Schutte, W.M. Index of Recurrent Elements
in James Joyce's "Ulysses."
M.P. Gillespie, 395(MFS):Winter82/83-
625
Schütz-Güth, G. and H. Schütz. Typen des
britischen Arbeiterromans.*
B. Greiner, 490:Band13Heft1/2-172
Schützeichel, R., ed. Althochdeutsches
Wörterbuch. (3rd ed)
H. Penzl, 350:Mar83-229
Schützeichel, R. Die Grundlagen des west-
lichen Mitteldeutschen. (2nd ed)
W. Kleiber, 260(IF):Band86-376
Schützeichel, R., with U. Fellmann, eds.
Studien zur deutschen Literatur des Mit-
telalters.*
D.H. Green, 402(MLR):Jan82-223
Schuurman, E. Technology and the Future.*
G. Hottois, 540(RIPh):Vol36fasc1/2-195
Schuyler, J. The Morning of the Poem.*
R. Tillinghast, 569(SR):Spring82-291
Schwaller de Lubicz, R.A. Nature Word.
J.A. West, 469:Vol8No3-116
Schwamm, E. How He Saved Her.
F. Taliaferro, 441:26Jun83-12
J. Wolcott, 231:Aug83-62
Schware, R. Quantification in the History
of Political Thought.
D.A. Graber, 480(P&R):Summer82-217
Schwartz, B. Super Chief.
G. Marshall, 617(TLS):28Oct83-1175
Schwartz, B., with S. Lesher. Inside the
Warren Court.
R.J. Margolis, 441:20Nov83-42
Schwartz, H. and A. Rudolf, eds. Voices
Within the Ark.
R. Scherer, 287:Feb82-25
Schwartz, L. Diderot and the Jews.
H. Cohen, 207(FR):Feb83-484
Schwartz, L. These People.
D. Lehman, 181:Winter-Spring83-166
Schwartz, L. and S.P. Estess, eds. Eliza-
beth Bishop and Her Art.
D. Bromwich, 441:27Feb83-7
Schwartz, L.S. Disturbances in the Field.
C. See, 441:6Nov83-14
442(NY):28Nov83-188

Schwartz, M.M. and C. Kahn. Representing Shakespeare.
  A. Kirsch, 570(SQ):Summer82-252
  K. Newman, 494:Spring82-173
Schwartz, N.L., with S. Schwartz. The Hollywood Writers' Wars.*
  V.S. Navasky, 18:Mar82-72
Schwartz, R. - see Weimann, R.
Schwartz, S. The Art Presence.*
  G.A. De Candido, 441:13Feb83-16
  F. Spalding, 617(TLS):24Jun83-668
Schwartz, S.P., ed. Naming, Necessity, and Natural Kinds.
  T. Burge, 316:Dec82-911
Schwartzberg, J.E. with others, eds. A Historical Atlas of South Asia.*
  J.W. de Jong, 259(IIJ):Jan82-62
Schwarz, A. From Büchner to Beckett.*
  E. Kern, 299:Spring82-147
  J. Lyons, 214:Vol 10No38-127
Schwarz, B. Der "Pfennigstreit" in Hildesheim, 1343.
  S. Jenks, 589:Jan82-176
Schwarz, C. Der Nicht-nominale MENT-Ausdruck im Französischen.*
  G. Kleiber, 553(RLiR):Jan-Jun82-196
Schwarz, D.R. Conrad: "Almayer's Folly" to "Under Western Eyes."*
  R.K. Anderson, 395(MFS):Summer81-333
  T.K. Bender, 191(ELN):Dec81-154
Schwarz, D.R. Disraeli's Fiction.*
  T. Braun, 447(N&Q):Dec81-563
  S. Monod, 677(YES):Vol 12-312
Schwarz, E., ed. Hermann Hesses "Steppenwolf."
  G. Finney, 221(GQ):Jan82-125
Schwarz, E. - see Schnitzler, A.
Schwarz, G.S. and R.L. Wertis. Index locorum zu Kühner-Stegmann "Satzlehre."
  G. Serbat, 555:Vol56fasc2-340
Schwarzbach, F.S. Dickens and the City.*
  M. Hollington, 161(DUJ):Dec81-149
  K. Tetzeli von Rosador, 72:Band218 Heft2-445
Schwarzbaum, H. The Mishlé Shu'alim (Fox Fables) of Rabbi Berechiah Ha-Nakdan.
  D. Ben-Amos, 292(JAF):Apr-Jun82-222
  E.H. Rehermann, 196:Band23Heft3/4-343
Schwarze, C., ed. Analyse des prépositions.
  B.W. Hawkins, 350:Jun83-439
Schweeger-Hefel, A. Steinskulpturen der Nyonyosi aus Ober-Volta.
  C.M. Geary, 2(AfrA):Aug82-86
Schweickart, D. Capitalism or Worker Control?
  E. Sankowski, 185:Apr83-624
Schwengel, H. Jenseits der Ideologie des Zentrums.
  D. Kamper, 489(PJGG):Band89Heft1-211
Schwertheim, E., ed. Die Inschriften von Kyzikos und Umgebung.* (Pt 1)
  P.M. Fraser, 123:Vol132No2-301
  A.G. Woodhead, 303(JoHS):Vol 102-294
Schwitalla, J. Dialogsteuerung in Interviews.
  R. Kanth, 685(ZDL):1/1982-118
Schwob, M. Chroniques.* (J.A. Green, ed)
  J.P. Gilroy, 446(NCFS):Fall-Winter 82/83-177
  L. Kamm, 207(FR):May83-949

Schyfter, S.E. The Jew in the Novels of Benito Pérez Galdós.*
  H. Hinterhäuser, 547(RF):Band93Heft1/2-302
  J. Schraibman, 345(KRQ):Vol129No2-218
Sciascia, L. Candido.*
  P. Lewis, 565:Vol23No3-68
"Science Fiction Book Review Index, 1974-1979." (H.W. Hall, ed)
  C.E., 561(SFS):Mar82-100
Scobie, S. Leonard Cohen.*
  J. Cowan, 178:Sep82-375
Scobie, S. A Grand Memory for Forgetting.
  R. Attridge, 137:Aug82-32
  J. Bell, 526:Summer82-106
  R. Billings, 99:Jun/Jul82-35
Scobie, S. McAlmon's Chinese Opera.
  M.T. Lane, 198:Jan82-71
  G. Woodcock, 102(CanL):Winter81-97
Scodel, R. The Trojan Trilogy of Euripides.*
  R.W., 555:Vol55fasc2-337
Scofield, M. The Ghosts of "Hamlet."*
  A. Lorant, 549(RLC):Jul-Sep82-391
Sconocchia, S. Per una nuova edizione di Scribonio Largo.
  M.D. Reeve, 123:Vol132No2-277
Scott, A., ed. Scotch Passion.
  G. Ewart, 617(TLS):22Apr83-397
Scott, C. French Verse-Art.*
  J. Crow, 447(N&Q):Dec81-571
Scott, D., ed. Bread and Roses.
  T. Warr, 617(TLS):6May83-469
Scott, F.R. The Collected Poems of F.R. Scott.*
  D.M.R. Bentley, 150(DR):Spring82-153
  B. Whiteman, 298:Summer82-150
Scott, G.G. Cult and Countercult.
  J. Santino, 292(JAF):Oct-Dec82-487
Scott, H. Operation 10.*
  N. Callendar, 441:2Jan83-26
Scott, J. Corporal Smithers, Deceased.
  T.J. Binyon, 617(TLS):13May83-498
  T.J. Binyon, 617(TLS):27May83-553
Scott, J. Piranesi.
  R. Middleton, 576:Dec82-333
Scott, J.S. The Local Lads.
  N. Callendar, 441:17Apr83-21
Scott, M. Late Gothic Europe, 1400-1500.*
  C.R., 90:Mar82-200
Scott, M. Mauriac.
  J. Flower, 402(MLR):Apr82-461
  D. O'Connell, 207(FR):Dec82-330
Scott, P. Staying On.
  F. Weinbaum, 314:Winter-Spring82-225
Scott, P.H. Walter Scott and Scotland.*
  P. Garside, 571(ScLJ):Winter82-73
Scott, P.J.M. Jane Austen: A Reassessment.
  A. Leighton, 617(TLS):15Apr83-384
Scott, P.J.M. Anne Brontë.
  A. Leighton, 617(TLS):4Nov83-1217
Scott, R.I. - see Jeffers, R.
Scott, W. Scott on Himself. (D. Hewitt, ed)
  R.C. Gordon, 571(ScLJ):Spring82-11
Scott, W. Sir Walter Scott, "The Letters of Malachi Malagrowther."
  P. Garside, 571(ScLJ):Winter82-73
Scott, W. Waverley; or, 'Tis Sixty Years Since.* (C. Lamont, ed)
  J.H. Alexander, 571(ScLJ):Winter82-76

Scott, W. Waverley; Rob-Roy; La Fiancée de Lammermoor. (M. Crouzet, ed; A. Defauconpret, trans)
R. Ripoll, 535(RHL):Sep-Dec82-927
Scott Fox, D. Saint George.
B. Fothergill, 617(TLS):15Jul83-762
Scott-James, A. Sissinghurst.
L.D., 617(TLS):22Apr83-415
"Scottish Short Stories: 1983."
S. Altinel, 617(TLS):26Aug83-898
Scoufos, A-L. Shakespeare's Typological Satire.
R.P. Adams, 551(RenQ):Winter81-623
Scovell, E.J. The Space Between.*
C. Hope, 364:Dec82/Jan83-106
Scoville, H., Jr. MX.
G. Ignatieff, 529(QQ):Summer82-352
Screech, M.A. Ecstasy and "The Praise of Folly."
J.C. Olin, 551(RenQ):Spring82-88
Screech, M.A. Rabelais.*
M.B. McKinley, 639(VQR):Winter82-181
L. Schrader, 547(RF):Band93Heft1/2-255
Scribner, R.W. For the Sake of Simple Folk.
I. Gaskell, 59:Sep82-366
Scribner, S. and M. Cole. The Psychology of Literacy.
J.V. Singler, 350:Dec83-893
Scrivener, M. Radical Shelley.
S. French, 617(TLS):26Aug83-913
Scriver, S. All Star Poet.
D. Barbour, 648(WCR):Jun82-33
Scruton, R. The Aesthetics of Architecture.*
F.N. Sibley, 393(Mind):Jan82-143
W. Widdowson, 658:Summer/Autumn82-173
Scruton, R. A Dictionary of Political Thought.
D.A.N. Jones, 362:12May83-25
J. Waldron, 617(TLS):11Mar83-244
Scruton, R. From Descartes to Wittgenstein.
G. Graham, 483:Jul82-419
J. Rée, 518:Apr82-76
Scruton, R. Kant.*
483:Jul82-423
Scullard, H.H. Festivals and Ceremonies of the Roman Republic.
D.P. Harmon, 121(CJ):Dec82/Jan83-171
Scullard, H.H. Roman Britain.
G.M. Woloch, 487:Summer82-191
Scully, J. May Day.*
J. Saunders, 565:Vol23No1-73
Scully, M. Love Poems and Others.
T.F. Merrill, 305(JIL):Sep82-3
Seaborg, G.T., with B.S. Loeb. Kennedy, Khrushchev, and the Test Ban.*
639(VQR):Summer82-89
Seager, R. Pompey.*
J. Briscoe, 313:Vol72-184
B.L. Twyman, 122:Jan82-83
Seal, A. - see Gallagher, J.
Seale, W. Recreating the Historic House Interior.
S. Karr, 576:Mar82-71
Seaman, L.C.B. - see Packe, M.
Sear, F. Roman Architecture.
M. Lyttelton, 617(TLS):25Feb83-198
Searing, H. New American Art Museums.
R. Banham, 617(TLS):18Nov83-1265

Searle, E., ed and trans. The Chronicle of Battle Abbey.*
E.Z. Tabuteau, 589:Apr82-433
Searle, J.R. Expression and Meaning.*
D. Holdcroft, 518:Jan82-46
P. Lamarque, 479(PhQ):Apr82-177
B. Loar, 482(PhR):Jul82-488
Searle, J.R., F. Kiefer and M. Bierwisch, eds. Speech Act Theory and Pragmatics.
D.E.B. Pollard, 307:Apr82-60
Searles, H. Le Contre-Transfert.
H. Cronel, 450(NRF):May82-131
Sears, S.W. Landscape Turned Red.
T. Keneally, 441:7Aug83-3
Seay, A. - see Guillermus de Podio
Seay, A. - see Martinez de Biscargui
Seay, A. - see Vanneo, S.
Sebastián, S. Arte y humanismo.
D. Angulo Íñiguez, 48:Jan-Mar80-130
Sebastián, S. Contrarreforma y barroco.
F. Marías, 48:Jan-Mar82-118
Sebeok, T.A., ed. Current Trends in Linguistics. (Vol 10)
G.F. Meier, 682(ZPSK):Band34Heft4-484
Sebeok, T.A. The Play of Musement.
H. Gardner, 567:Vol138No3/4-347
P.H. Salus, 350:Mar83-237
Sebeok, T.A. and R. Rosenthal, eds. The Clever Hans Phenomenon.
M. Gardner, 567:Vol138No3/4-357
Sebeok, T.A. and J. Umiker-Sebeok. "You Know My Method."
R. Fellows, 518:Jul82-163
"IIe Colloque de linguistique russe."
V.M. Du Feu, 575(SEER):Apr82-276
Secord, P.F., ed. Explaining Human Behavior.
I.S., 185:Jul83-826
Secrest, M. Being Bernard Berenson.*
B. Elevitch, 418(MR):Summer82-245
Secret, F. Postelliana.
M.L. Kuntz, 551(RenQ):Autumn82-481
Secrétan, P. - see Bocheński, J.M.
Secundus, J. Juan Segundo: "Besos y otros poemas." (O. Gete Carpio, ed and trans)
J.B. Dallet, 551(RenQ):Autumn81-407
Sedgwick, F. From Another Part of the Island.
I. McMillan, 493:Jun82-71
Sedwick, F. Spanish for Careers.
J. Burckett-Evans, 399(MLJ):Winter82-442
Sędzik, W. Prasłowiańska terminologia rolnicza (Rośliny uprawne, Użytki rolne).
T. Lewaszkiewicz, 360(LP):Vol125-167
See, C. Rhine Maidens.*
J. Helbert, 649(WAL):Nov82-274
von See, K. Skaldendichtung.*
T.M. Andersson, 221(GQ):May82-400
F.W. Blaisdell, 406:Winter82-478
R. Frank, 301(JEGP):Jul82-396
H. Kratz, 133:Band15Heft1/2-146
J. Lindow, 589:Jan82-200
Seeber, G.C. The Abduction.
N. Callendar, 441:10Apr83-32
Seebold, E. Etymologie.
B.J. Koekkoek, 301(JEGP):Jul82-376
Seeger, A. Nature and Society in Central Brazil.
D.J. Crowley, 187:Sep83-539
Seeger, C. Studies in Musicology, 1935-1975.
S. Blum, 187:May83-360

Seelig, S.C. The Shadow of Eternity.*
J.J. Balakier, 391:Dec82-104
J. Stephens, 568(SCN):Winter82-70
639(VQR):Summer82-80
Segal, C. Dionysiac Poetics and Euripides'
"Bacchae."
O. Taplin, 617(TLS):11Mar83-242
Segal, C. - see Whitman, C.H.
Segal, G. and others. Nuclear War and
Nuclear Peace.
W. Rodgers, 362:10Mar83-23
P. Towle, 617(TLS):3Jun83-565
Segal, H. Melaine Klein.
W.C.M. Scott, 529(QQ):Summer82-431
Segre, C. Structures and Time.*
M.E. Blanchard, 567:Vol40No1/2-139
Segura, C. Marshland Brace.
442(NY):3Jan83-71
Seibert, J. Die politischen Flüchtlinge
und Verbannten in der griechischen
Geschichte.*
É. Will, 555:Vol55fasc2-332
Seid, P. Zum Thema der Langeweile bei Eça
de Queirós.
D. Woll, 547(RF):Band93Heft3/4-489
Seidel, F. Sunrise.*
R. Tillinghast, 569(SR):Spring82-291
Seidel, L. Songs of Glory.*
J.A. Franklin, 59:Sep82-375
Seidel, M. Satiric Inheritance.*
P.M. Briggs, 594:Spring82-132
D. Fairer, 402(MLR):Oct82-921
J. Lamb, 131(CL):Fall82-374
A. Varney, 447(N&Q):Dec81-553
Seidenfeld, T. Philosophical Problems of
Statistical Inference.*
C.B., 543:Jun82-907
Seidensticker, E. Low City, High City.
W.G. Beasley, 617(TLS):25Nov83-1324
R.C. Christopher, 441:11Sep83-12
Seidensticker, P. and others. Didaktik
der Grundsprache.*
H. Eilers, 685(ZDL):3/1981-407
Seidl, H. - see Aristotle
Seidler, G.L., J. Malarczyk and M. Smolka.
Some Remarks on the Polish Political
System in the Past.
M. Konick, 173(ECS):Fall81-108
Seidler, H. Österreichischer Vormärz und
Goethezeit.*
E. Beutner, 602:Vol 13No2-347
Seidman, H. Throne/Falcon/Eye.
R. Tillinghast, 441:1May83-15
Seifert, H.W., with A. Schneider and P-V.
Springborn - see Wieland, C.M.
Seiffert, H. Stil heute.
A. Porsch, 682(ZPSK):Band34Heft3-381
G. Vitt-Maucher, 406:Summer82-191
Seigfried, C.H. Chaos and Context.
E.L., 543:Jun82-909
Seiler, H., ed. Linguistic Workshop II.
G.F. Meier, 682(ZPSK):Band34Heft2-247
Seiler-Dietrich, A., ed. Märchen der
Bantu.
E. Dammann, 196:Band23Heft1/2-123
Seitel, P. See So That We May See.
E. Dammann, 196:Band23Heft1/2-157
P.M. Peek, 650(WF):Oct82-309
Sekler, E.F. Josef Hoffmann.
A.E. Sarnitz, 576:Oct82-252
Selbourne, D. The Making of "A Midsummer
Night's Dream."
M. Kahan, 617(TLS):29Jul83-817

Selcher, W.A. Brazil in the International
System.
R. Wesson, 263(RIB):Vol32No1-70
Selement, G. and B. Woolley - see Shepard,
T.
Seligman, D. Doris Lessing.
B. Draine, 365:Winter83-27
Seligman, J. The Transformation of Wall
Street.
I. Friend, 441:20Feb83-8
Seling, H. Die Kunst der Augsburger Gold-
schmiede 1529-1868.*
Y. Hackenbroch, 54:Dec82-664
J. Hayward, 39:Mar82-211
Sellars, W. Naturalism and Ontology.*
P. Kitcher, 482(PhR):Jul82-473
D.A. Kolb, 518:Apr82-108
Sellers, C.C. Mr. Peale's Museum.
S. Hart, 658:Summer/Autumn82-145
Sellin, E. Crépuscule prolongé à El Biar.
A-M. Faisandier, 207(FR):Apr83-793
Sellner, T.F. - see von Hippel, T.G.
Selma, J.V. - see under Vila Selma, J.
Selz, P. Art in Our Times.
M. Sawin, 127:Winter82-351
Selznick, I.M. A Private View.
P-L. Adams, 61:Jul83-109
M. Haskell, 441:22May83-3
A. Mars-Jones, 617(TLS):18Nov83-1291
R. Wetzsteon, 18:Sep83-79
Semaan, K.I., ed. Islam and the Medieval
West.
M.S. Khan, 273(IC):Jan82-71
Semino, I. Il problema della conoscenza
empirica nel pensiero di Alfred J. Ayer.
J. Largeault, 542:Jan-Mar82-143
Semprun, J. What a Beautiful Sunday!
R. Boyers, 617(TLS):11Nov83-1253
de Sena, J. The Poetry of Jorge de Sena.*
(F.G. Williams, ed)
E. de Lima, 238:Dec82-661
H. Macedo, 86(BHS):Oct82-347
de Sena, J. Versos e alguma prosa de
Jorge de Sena. (E. Lisboa, ed)
M. Guterres, 86(BHS):Jan82-88
Sendall, B. Independent Television in
Britain. (Vol 1)
P. Whitehead, 362:6Jan83-20
Sendall, B. Independent Television in
Britain. (Vol 2)
P. Whitehead, 362:21Jul83-26
Seneca. L. Annaei Senecae "Naturales
Quaestiones." (C. Codoñer Merino, ed
and trans)
H.M. Hine, 123:Vol32No1-30
Senelick, L., ed and trans. Russian Dra-
matic Theory from Pushkin to the Sym-
bolists.
S.M. Carnicke, 574(SEEJ):Fall82-351
F.H. Londré, 130:Winter82/83-386
Senelick, L., D.F. Cheshire and U. Sch-
neider. British Music-Hall 1840-1923.
P. Davison, 611(TN):Vol36No3-137
D.B. Wilmeth, 612(ThS):May82-131
Seneviratne, H.L. Rituals of the Kandyan
State.*
C. Hallisey, 318(JAOS):Oct-Dec81-502
Sengle, F. Biedermeierzeit.* (Vol 3)
C.P. Magill, 402(MLR):Jan82-237
Seniff, D.P. - see Alfonso XI
Senior, N. The Mushroom Jar.
J.A. Wainwright, 102(CanL):Winter81-
148

Senn, A.E. Assassination in Switzerland.
  R.K. Debo, 550(RusR):Oct82-492
Senn, W. Conrad's Narrative Voice.
  T.G. Willy, 136:Vol 14No1-71
Sennett, R. The Frog Who Dared to Croak.*
  639(VQR):Autumn82-131
Sennett, T. Great Hollywood Movies.
  J. Maslin, 441:4Dec83-72
Sennett, T. Hollywood Musicals.*
  M. Wood, 18:Dec81-77
Sentner, C. Everywhere I've Been.
  A.T. Seaman, 198:Apr82-97
Senzel, H.T. Cases.
  D. Margolick, 441:23Jan83-11
Serbat, G. Cas et fonctions.
  A. Reix, 540(RIPh):Vol36fasc3-393
Serfontein, J.H.P. Brotherhood of Power.
  B. Munslow, 69:Vol52No4-91
Serge, V. Midnight in the Century.
  B. Marshall, 617(TLS):4Feb83-116
Sergooris, G. Peter Handke und die
  Sprache.*
  W. Blomster, 406:Summer82-228
Serjeant, R.B. and R. Lewcock, eds. Sana.
  H. Kennedy, 617(TLS):8Jul83-734
Serle, J. A Plan of Mr. Pope's Garden.
  A.J. Sambrook, 566:Spring83-135
Serlio, S. The Five Books of Architecture.
  A.J.G.H., 617(TLS):18Mar83-279
Serres, M. Genèse.
  T. Cordellier, 450(NRF):Jun82-127
  W. Paulson, 446(NCFS):Spring-Summer83-
  363
Serres, M. Hermès V.
  S. Lévy, 400(MLN):May82-989
Serres, M. The Parasite.*
  639(VQR):Autumn82-115
Serroy, J. Roman et réalité.
  R.G. Hodgson, 475:Vol9No17-797
  K. Hoffmann, 400(MLN):May82-1012
Serroy, J. - see Tristan L'Hermite
Sérullaz, M. Delacroix.
  J. Whiteley, 90:Dec82-773
Servadio, G. Luchino Visconti.*
  R. Armes, 364:Aug/Sep82-112
  D. Spoto, 441:13Nov83-10
  M. Wood, 617(TLS):23Sep83-1015
Servatius, C. Paschalis II (1099-1118).
  U-R. Blumenthal, 589:Oct82-940
Server, A.W. and J.E. Keller - see Fernán-
  dez de Avellaneda, A.
Servet, M. Restitución del Cristianismo.
  (A. Alcalá, ed)
  R.H. Bainton, 551(RenQ):Winter81-583
Service, A. Edwardian Interiors.*
  A. Saint, 617(TLS):8Apr83-344
Sesé, B. Antonio Machado (1875-1939).
  B. Ciplijauskaité, 240(HR):Summer82-
  361
Seston, W. Scripta Varia.
  P. Flobert, 555:Vol55fasc2-383
Setbon, R. Libertés d'un écriture cri-
  tique, Charles Nodier.
  A. Kies, 356(LR):May82-168
Seth-Smith, M. A Classic Connection.
  R. Longrigg, 617(TLS):30Sep83-1067
Sethna, N.R. Shāl.
  R.L. Shep, 614:Spring83-23
Seton, C.P. A Private Life.*
  W.H. Pritchard, 249(HudR):Spring82-159
Seton-Watson, H. and C. The Making of a
  New Europe.*
  H. Hanak, 575(SEER):Jan82-129

Settar, S. Archaeological Survey of My-
  sore, Annual Reports, 1906-1909, 1910-
  1911, and 1912.
  J. Lowry, 463:Spring82-88
Settle, M.L. All the Brave Promises.
  S.D. Blackford, 569(SR):Spring82-305
Seung, T.K. Semiotics and Thematics in
  Hermeneutics.
  C. Norris, 617(TLS):25Mar83-304
Seung, T.K. Structuralism and Herme-
  neutics.*
  B. Lang, 290(JAAC):Spring83-348
  S.H. Watson, 478:Oct82-222
Ševčenko, I. and F.E. Sysyn, with U.M.
  Pasicznyk, eds. Eucharisterion.
  S. Akiner, 575(SEER):Apr82-273
  H. Birnbaum, 574(SEEJ):Fall82-365
"Seven Poets."
  D. Dunn, 493:Dec81-55
Severin, T. The Sindbad Voyage.
  P-L. Adams, 61:Mar83-116
  J. Carter, 362:20Jan83-24
Madame de Sévigné. Correspondance III.
  (R. Duchêne, ed)
  H.R. Allentuch, 207(FR):Dec82-318
Seward, D. Richard III.
  R.L. Storey, 617(TLS):13May83-484
Sewart, A. Drink! For Once Dead.
  T.J. Binyon, 617(TLS):18Feb83-149
Sewell, B. In the Dorian Mode.
  T.D. Smith, 617(TLS):30Sep83-1038
Sewell, B., ed. Henry Williamson.
  J.W. Blench, 161(DUJ):Jun82-257
Sexton, A. The Complete Poems.
  S.P. Edelman, 584(SWR):Winter82-98
  R.T. Smith, 577(SHR):Summer82-283
Seyfert, G. Zur Theorie der Verbgrammatik.
  G. Van der Elst, 685(ZDL):1/1982-76
Seymour, M.C. - see Hoccleve, T.
Seymour-Smith, M. Robert Graves.*
  D. Hall, 441:20Mar83-14
  I. Hamilton, 453(NYRB):18Aug83-38
  M. Imlah, 493:Sep82-67
Seymour-Ure, C. The American President.
  A. Howard, 617(TLS):4Feb83-99
de Seyssel, C. The Monarchy of France.
  (D.R. Kelley, ed)
  R.E. Giesey, 551(RenQ):Autumn82-490
  M. Prestwich, 617(TLS):14Jan83-42
Sezgin, F. Geschichte des arabischen
  Schrifttums. (Vol 6)
  G. Saliba, 318(JAOS):Apr-Jun81-219
Seznec, J. La Survivance des dieux
  antiques.
  J.M. Cocking, 208(FS):Oct82-468
Sgall, P., E. Hajičova and E. Buráňová.
  Aktuální členěni věty v čeština.
  B. Bílý, 559:Jun82-381
Shack, W.A. and P.S. Cohen, eds. Politics
  in Leadership.
  A. Kuper, 69:Vol51No1-529
Shackle, C., comp. Catalogue of the
  Panjabi and Sindhi Manuscripts in the
  India Office Library.
  I.D. Serebryakov, 259(IIJ):Apr80-167
Shackle, C., comp. A Gurū Nānak Glossary.
  R.K. Barz, 259(IIJ):Oct82-327
Shackleton, E. South.
  A.J., 617(TLS):29Jul83-819
Shackleton Bailey, D.R. Profile of
  Horace.*
  S. Commager, 453(NYRB):3Feb83-40

Shackleton Bailey, D.R. Towards a Text of "Anthologia Latina."
  J. André, 555:Vol55fasc1-185
  J.M. Hunt, 122:Jul82-253
Shackleton Bailey, D.R. - see Cicero
Shaffer, D.L. Justice or Tyranny?
  W.P. Baumgarth, 258:Jun82-213
Shaffer, E. - see "Comparative Criticism"
Lord Shaftesbury - see under Cooper, A.A.
Shahar, D. Le Jour de la Comtesse.
  J. Blot, 450(NRF):Feb82-152
Shaheen, M. George Meredith.
  W.F. Wright, 637(VS):Winter82-248
Shahrani, M.N.M. The Kirghiz and Wakhi of Afghanistan.*
  A.S. Ahmed, 293(JASt):Nov81-73
Shakespeare, W. The Arden Shakespeare: Hamlet.* (H. Jenkins, ed)
  G.F. Parker, 97(CQ):Vol 11No3-411
Shakespeare, W. As You Like It.* (R. Knowles, ed)
  H.W. Gabler, 72:Band218Heft2-424
Shakespeare, W. Coriolan (The Tragedy of Coriolanus). (H. Fluchère, ed and trans)
  G. Bullough, 189(EA):Oct-Dec82-458
Shakespeare, W. Measure for Measure.* (M. Eccles, ed)
  K. Smidt, 179(ES):Oct82-467
Shakespeare, W. A Midsummer Night's Dream.* (H.F. Brooks, ed)
  G. Taylor, 447(N&Q):Aug81-332
Shakespeare, W. Poems (1640). (H.M. Klein, ed)
  T.G.S. Cain, 447(N&Q):Aug81-384
Shakespeare, W. Richard III. (J. Hankey, ed)
  P.C. McGuire, 570(SQ):Summer82-241
Shakespeare, W. Rikardo Tria.
  M. Boulton, 447(N&Q):Jun81-286
Shakespeare, W. Shakespeare Stories. (G. Gordon, ed)
  J. Mellors, 362:13Jan83-23
  442(NY):22Aug83-93
Shakespeare, W. Shakespeare's Plays in Quarto. (M.J.P. Allen and K. Muir, eds)
  F. Bowers, 250(HLQ):Spring82-174
Shakespeare, W. Shakespeare's Sonnets.* (S.C. Campbell, ed) Shakespeare's Sonnets. (W.G. Ingram and T. Redpath, eds)
  K. Muir, 570(SQ):Spring82-116
Shakespeare, W. The Taming of the Shrew. (H.J. Oliver, ed) Henry V. (G. Taylor, ed) Troilus and Cressida. (K. Muir, ed)
  N. Alexander, 617(TLS):29Jul83-815
  F. Kermode, 453(NYRB):28Apr83-30
Shakespeare, W. Trollus and Cressida. (K. Palmer, ed)
  F. Kermode, 453(NYRB):28Apr83-30
"Shakespeare Jahrbuch, 116."
  D. Aubawlen, 189(FA):Oct-Dec82-460
"Shakespeare Survey."* (Vol 31) (K. Muir, ed)
  R.S. White, 447(N&Q):Apr81-185
"Shakespeare Survey."* (Vol 32) (K. Muir, ed)
  T. Hawkes, 541(RES):Aug82-316
  R.S. White, 447(N&Q):Apr81-185
"Shakespeare Survey." (Vol 35) (S. Wells, ed)
  J. Hankey, 617(TLS):8Apr83-359
Shalamov, V. Kolyma Tales.*
  E. Levin, 473(PR):1/1982-154

Shales, T. On the Air!*
  H. Rosenberg, 18:Jan-Feb83-63
Shallis, M. On Time.
  D. Finkelstein, 469:Vol8No3-102
Shalvey, T. Claude Lévi-Strauss.
  M.S., 543:Mar82-631
Shannon, E. Up in the Park.
  D. McWhorter, 441:7Aug83-18
Shannon, M.O., ed. Modern Ireland.
  G. Eley, 385(MQR):Winter83-108
Shanquan. Henan.
  R.V. Des Forges, 293(JASt):May82-588
Shapiro, A. After the Digging.*
  T. Diggory, 560:Summer82-159
  E. Grosholz, 249(HudR):Summer82-319
Shapiro, A.M., J.R. Bryer and K. Field. Carson McCullers.
  W.J. Stuckey, 395(MFS):Autumn82-507
Shapiro, B.J. Probability and Certainty in Seventeenth-Century England.
  R. Porter, 617(TLS):20May83-518
Shapiro, K. Collected Poems.
  D.H. Sullivan, 648(WCR):Spring82-56
Shapiro, M. Hieroglyph of Time.
  P. Bondanella, 131(CL):Spring82-183
Shapiro, M.H. and R.G. Spence, Jr. Bioethics and Law.
  D.T.O., 185:Oct82-216
Shapiro, M.J. Language and Political Understanding.
  R.B.S., 185:Jan83-426
Sharaf, M. Fury on Earth.
  R. Dinnage, 617(TLS):1Jul83-691
  W. Kendrick, 441:3Apr83-1
  A. Ryan, 362:2Jun83-23
  442(NY):7Mar83-138
Sharma, B.R., ed. Kṣudrakalpasūtra of Maśaka Gārgya with the Commentary of Śrī Śrīnivāsa.
  L. Sternbach, 318(JAOS):Oct-Dec81-482
Sharma, M. The Politics of Inequality.
  J.M. Mahar, 293(JASt):Nov81-189
Sharma, R.S. "The Rainbow."
  J. Meyers, 395(MFS):Winter82/83-638
Sharma, S. Kāṅgaṛī.
  L. Sternbach, 318(JAOS):Oct-Dec81-482
Sharma, T.R.S. Robert Frost's Poetic Style.
  27(AL):Oct82-474
Sharp, F.M. The Poet's Madness.*
  K. Oderman, 584(SWR):Autumn82-458
  G.M. Sakrawa, 222(GR):Spring82-88
  R. Schier, 301(JEGP):Jul82-391
Sharp, R. Knowledge, Ideology and the Politics of Schooling.
  D. Hogan, 185:Jan83-410
Sharp, R.A. Keats, Skepticism, and the Religion of Beauty.
  J. Donovan, 339(KSMB):No31-71
  A. Elliott, 541(RES):Aug82-370
Sharpe, J.A. Crime in Seventeenth Century England.
  P. Slack, 617(TLS):28Oct83-1182
Sharpe, J.A. Defamation and Sexual Slander in Early Modern England.
  C. Cross, 325:Apr82-43
Sharpe, K. Sir Robert Cotton, 1586-1631.*
  D. Underdown, 551(RenQ):Summer81-264
  D. Vaisey, 541(RES):May82-201
Sharpe, T. Vintage Stuff.*
  L. Jones, 364:Dec82/Jan83-136

Sharrer, H.L., ed. The Legendary History of Britain in Lope García de Salazar's "Libro de las bienandanzas e fortunas."*
J.R. Burt, 552(REH):Jan82-132

Sharrock, R. and J.F. Forrest - see Bunyan, J.

Shastri, K.C. Bengal's Contribution to Sanskrit Grammar in the Paninian and Candra Systems. (Pt 1)
G.F. Meier, 682(ZPSK):Band34Heft1-133

Shatz, M.S. Soviet Dissent in Historical Perspective.
S. Monas, 104(CASS):Summer82-271
P. Pomper, 550(RusR):Apr82-228

Shaumyan, S.K. Applicational Grammar as a Semantic Theory of Natural Language.
G. Van der Elst, 685(ZDL):1/1982-73

Shaw, B.D. and R.P. Saller - see Finley, M.I.

Shaw, D.L. Nueva narrativa hispanoamericana.
I.M. Zuleta, 263(RIB):Vol32No2-220

Shaw, G. The Cost of Authority.
J.L. Houlden, 617(TLS):13May83-494

Shaw, G.B. Arms and the Man: A Facsimile of the Holograph Manuscript. Candida and How He Lied to Her Husband: Facsimiles of the Holograph Manuscripts. You Can Never Tell: A Facsimile of the Holograph Manuscript.
E.B. Adams, 572:Vol3-222

Shaw, G.B. The Collected Screenplays of Bernard Shaw.* (B.F. Dukore, ed)
G. Weales, 219(GaR):Winter82-923

Shaw, G.B. The Devil's Disciple: A Facsimile of the Holograph Manuscript. The Man of Destiny and Caesar and Cleopatra: Facsimiles of the Holograph Manuscripts. Captain Brassbound's Conversion: A Facsimile of the Holograph Manuscript.
G. Larson, 572:Vol3-224

Shaw, G.B. The Doctor's Dilemma: A Facsimile of the Holograph Manuscript.
A. Zucker, 572:Vol3-232

Shaw, G.B. Major Barbara: A Facsimile of the Holograph Manuscript.
F.P.W. McDowell, 572:Vol3-227

Shaw, G.B. Shaw and Ibsen.* (J.L. Wisenthal, ed)
A.M. Gibbs, 541(RES):Nov82-497
S. Williams, 107(CRCL):Jun82-297
J. Woodfield, 178:Dec82-517

Shaw, G.B. Shaw's Music.* (D.H. Laurence, ed)
C. Barker, 97(CQ):Vol 11No1-265
D. Harris, 135:May82-144
S. Weintraub, 572:Vol3-235

Shaw, G.B. Widowers' Houses: Facsimiles of the Shorthand and Holograph Manuscripts and the 1893 Published Text. The Philanderer: A Facsimile of the Holograph Manuscript. Mrs. Warren's Profession: A Facsimile of the Holograph Manuscript.
B.B. Watson, 572:Vol3-219

Shaw, G.B. and A. Douglas. Bernard Shaw and Alfred Douglas: a Correspondence.* (M. Hyde, ed)
A. Phillips, 364:Mar83-115
442(NY):7Mar83-137

Shaw, G.B. and F. Harris. The Playwright and the Pirate. (S. Weintraub, ed)
N. Grene, 617(TLS):8Apr83-359
442(NY):7Mar83-136

Shaw, I. Paris/Magnum.
L. Zelevansky, 55:Nov82-62

Shaw, J.H. Motivierte Komposita in der deutschen und englischen Gegenwartssprache.
G. Deimer, 38:Band100Heft1/2-153
K. Faiss, 257(IRAL):May82-163

Shaw, J.S. The Management of Scottish Society 1707-1764.
B. Lenman, 617(TLS):11Nov83-1258

Shaw, P. American Patriots and the Rituals of Revolution.*
J. Conforti, 432(NEQ):Mar82-125
C. Royster, 656(WMQ):Jul82-548

Shaw, R.B. The Call of God.
D. Benet, 391:Dec82-105
R. Selden, 617(TLS):24Jun83-681

Shawcross, J.T. With Mortal Voice.*
R. Flannagan, 391:May82-49

She, L. - see under Lao She

Sheard, W.S. Antiquity in the Renaissance.*
C. Dempsey, 551(RenQ):Spring81-123

Shearer, I.A. - see O'Connell, D.P.

Shearson, W.A. The Notion of Encounter.
J.B. Hoy, 154:Sep82-549

Sheck, L. Amaranth.
P. Stitt, 219(GaR):Spring82-184

Sheckley, R. Dramocles.
G. Jonas, 441:6Nov83-38

Shedden, L. Mining Photographs and other Pictures. (R. Wilkie and B. Buchloh, eds)
A. Grundberg, 441:4Dec83-77

Sheed, W. Clare Boothe Luce.*
639(VQR):Summer82-88

Sheffield, C. Man on Earth.
S.J. Gould, 441:4Dec83-74

Shehaby, N. The Propositional Logic of Avicenna.
G.F. Meier, 682(ZPSK):Band34Heft1-134

Shehan, L. A Blessing of Years.
P. Hebblethwaite, 617(TLS):12Aug83-864

Sheidley, W.E. Barnabe Googe.
L.V.R., 568(SCN):Fall82-58

Shelah, S. Classification Theory and the Number of Nonisomorphic Models.
V. Harnik, 316:Sep82-694

Sheldon, G.W., ed. Artistic Country-Seats.
R.G. Wilson, 658:Winter82-281

Sheldon, S. Master of the Game.*
P.K. Bell, 617(TLS):25Feb83-200

Shell, S.M. The Rights of Reason.*
V. Gerhardt, 342:Band73Heft2-247
J. Iwanicki, 529(QQ):Spring82-213
A.L., 185:Oct82-209
R.C.S. Walker, 393(Mind):Apr82-291

Shelley, M. Frankenstein.
B. Johnson, 153:Summer82-2

Shelley, M.W. The Letters of Mary Wollstonecraft Shelley.* (Vol 1) (B.T. Bennett, ed)
D.D. Fischer, 591(SIR):Fall82-523
W. Keach, 184(EIC):Jan82-82

Shelley, M.W. The Letters of Mary Wollstonecraft Shelley. (Vol 2) (B.T. Bennett, ed)
L.A. Marchand, 441:16Oct83-12

Shelley, P.B. Shelley on Love. (R.
Holmes, ed)
506(PSt):Dec82-357
Shellim, M. Oil Paintings of India and
the East by Thomas Daniell R.A. 1749-
1840 and William Daniell R.A. 1769-1837.
J.E. van Lohuizen-de Leeuw, 57:Vol43
No3-247
Shelnutt, E. The Formal Voice.
J. Baskin, 676(YR):Autumn82-xvii
Shelp, E.E., ed. Justice and Health Care.
T.M.R., 185:Oct82-217
Shelton, K.J. The Esquiline Treasure.
M.A.R. Colledge, 123:Vol32No2-295
Shennan, J.H. Philippe, Duke of Orléans,
Regent of France 1715-1723.*
J. Lough, 208(FS):Jan82-68
Shenton, G. The Fictions of the Self.*
M. Davanture, 535(RHL):Sep-Dec82-949
Shepard, J. Flights.
F. Busch, 441:9Oct83-15
Shepard, S. True West.
D. Devlin, 157:Summer82-52
Shepard, T. Thomas Shepard's Confessions.
(G. Selement and B. Woolley, eds)
N. Pettit, 432(NEQ):Dec82-596
Shepelev, L.E. Tsarizm i burzhuaziia vo
vtoroi polovine XIX veka.
T.C. Owen, 550(RusR):Jul82-327
Shepherd, S. Amazons and Warrior Women.*
J.C.B., 148:Summer82-91
S. Clark, 539:Aug83-230
Sheppard, A.D.R. Studies on the Fifth and
Sixth Essays of Proclus' Commentary on
the "Republic."*
H.J. Blumenthal, 319:Jan83-96
Sheppard, F.H.W., ed. Survey of London.
(Vol 41)
M. Girouard, 617(TLS):2Dec83-1350
Sheridan, A. Michel Foucault.*
J. Bernauer, 258:Mar82-87
Sheridan, E.R. Lewis Morris, 1671-1746.
R.R. Rea, 577(SHR):Spring82-165
Sheridan, J.J. - see Alan of Lille
Sherlock, K., comp. A Bibliography of
Timor.
E. Traube, 293(JASt):Aug82-891
Sherman, C.R., with A.M. Holcomb, eds.
Women as Interpreters of the Visual
Arts, 1820-1979.
H.E. Roberts, 637(VS):Summer82-512
Sherman, L.B. Fires on the Mountain.
F.A.K. Yasamee, 575(SEER):Jan82-127
Sherman, P. Expeditions to Nowhere.
B. Patton, 649(WAL):Summer82-164
G.W., 102(CanL):Winter81-173
Sherrill, R. The Oil Follies of 1970-1980.
J. Fallows, 441:27Nov83-7
Sherrill, R.A. The Prophetic Melville.*
H. Beaver, 677(YES):Vol 12-320
J-J. Mayoux, 189(EA):Jan-Mar82-111
Sherrin, N. A Small Thing — Like an Earth-
quake.
J. Stokes, 617(TLS):11Mar83-237
Sherry, C. Wordsworth's Poetry of the
Imagination.*
J.H. Averill, 301(JEGP):Jan82-119
J.W. Page, 405(MP):Nov82-205
Sherwin, B.L. Mystical Theology and
Social Dissent.
C. Abramsky, 617(TLS):18Nov83-1286
Sherwood, J. Death at the BBC.
N. Callendar, 441:11Dec83-38

Shevelov, G.Y. A Historical Phonology of
the Ukrainian Language.*
J. Göschel, 685(ZDL):3/1982-379
H. Leeming, 575(SEER):Jul82-441
Shibles, W. Good and Bad are Funny Things.
Ethics for Children. Emotion. Humor.
Time.
J.V. Brown, 154:Mar82-160
Shields, C. Happenstance.*
J. Parks, 526:Spring82-77
Shields, H. - see Philippe de Thaon
Shields, K., Jr. Indo-European Noun In-
flection.
A.R. Bomhard, 215(GL):Winter82-269
S.G. Thomason, 350:Sep83-687
Shier, L.A. Terracotta Lamps from Karanis,
Egypt.
R. Reece, 123:Vol32No2-296
Shigematsu, S., ed and trans. A Zen For-
est.
R. Epp, 407(MN):Summer82-261
Shigeyoshi, M. - see under Murakami Shi-
geyoshi
Shih T'ao. Philosophy of Painting by Shih
T'ao. (E.J. Coleman, ed and trans)
S. Addiss, 318(JAOS):Apr-Jun81-236
"Shikinaisha chōsa hōkoku." (fasc 24)
F.G. Bock, 318(JAOS):Oct-Dec81-432
Shillony, B-A. Politics and Culture in
Wartime Japan.
M.R. Peattie, 407(MN):Winter82-545
Shils, E. The Calling of Sociology and
Other Essays on the Pursuit of Learning.
R.R., 543:Sep81-167
Shils, E. The Constitution of Society.
S.D.J., 185:Jul83-829
Shimomiya, T. Zur Typologie des Georg-
ischen.
G.F. Meier, 682(ZPSK):Band34Heft6-769
Shimura, M. and C-W. Schümann. Textile
Designs of Art Nouveau.
R.L. Shep, 614:Spring83-24
Shipler, D.K. Russia.
M.D. Shulman, 441:20Nov83-1
Shipp, G.P. Modern Greek Evidence for the
Ancient Greek Vocabulary.*
S. Levin, 215(GL):Spring82-44
B. Newton, 320(CJL):Fall82-188
J-L. Perpillou, 555:Vol56fasc1-118
Shirley, G. Belle Starr and Her Times.
L. Milazzo, 584(SWR):Autumn82-vi
Shivers, A.S. The Life of Maxwell Ander-
son.
J. Logan, 441:11Sep83-11
Shivers, L. Here to Get My Baby Out of
Jail.
D. Quammen, 441:24Apr83-12
L. Taylor, 617(TLS):11Nov83-1256
442(NY):18Apr83-148
Shkurinov, P.S. Pozitivizm v Rossii XIX
veka.
J.P. Scanlan, 550(RusR):Apr82-203
Shloss, C. Flannery O'Connor's Dark Come-
dies.*
L.Y. Gossett, 579(SAQ):Spring82-243
D. McGifford, 106:Winter82-389
W.J. Stuckey, 395(MFS):Autumn82-508
Shneidman, E.S. - see Murray, H.A.
Shneidman, N.N. Soviet Literature in the
1970's.*
D. Milivojević, 558(RLJ):Winter-
Spring82-299
M. Raskin, 395(MFS):Summer81-412

Shochat, Y. Recruitment and the Programme of Tiberius Gracchus.*
  J-C. Richard, 555:Vol55fasc1-185
Shoemaker, W.H. The Novelistic Art of Galdós.*
  M. Gordon, 86(BHS):Jan82-75
Shōkō, K. - see under Kabutogi Shōkō
Shope, R.K. The Analysis of Knowing.
  J. Hornsby, 617(TLS):2Sep83-941
Shopen, T., ed. Languages and their Status. Languages and their Speakers.
  A.F. Majewicz, 360(LP):Vol25-140
Shore, B. Sala'ilua.
  J. Clifford, 617(TLS):13May83-475
Short, E. I Knew My Place.
  N. Nicholson, 617(TLS):27May83-540
  J. Vaizey, 362:5May83-25
Short, J.F., Jr., ed. The State of Sociology.
  K.S., 185:Jul83-829
Short, K.R.M., ed. Feature Films as History.
  M.H. Bernstein, 400(MLN):Dec82-1289
  J. Rosenbaum, 18:Apr82-71
Short, K.R.M., ed. Film and Radio Propaganda in World War II.
  I. Kershaw, 617(TLS):30Sep83-1064
Short, P. The Dragon and the Bear.*
  R. Bernstein, 441:6Feb83-7
Shorter, E. A History of Women's Bodies.*
  M. Drabble, 362:24Feb83-23
  L.J. Jordanova, 617(TLS):29Apr83-436
  L. Stone, 441:2Jan83-6
Shortt, S.E.D., ed. Medicine in Canadian Society.*
  W.N., 102(CanL):Spring82-160
  W.P. Ward, 529(QQ):Autumn82-676
Shouldice, L., ed and trans. Contemporary Quebec Criticism.*
  K. Mezei, 107(CRCL):Mar82-133
  J. Warwick, 178:Mar82-117
Shoup, P.S. The East European and Soviet Data Handbook.*
  A. Korbonski, 550(RusR):Jan82-88
  J. Thornton, 104(CASS):Fall-Winter82-585
Showalter, D.E. Little Man, What Now?
  J.D. Noakes, 617(TLS):17Jun83-640
Showalter, D.E. - see Pettit, A.G.
Shrader-Frechette, K.S. Nuclear Power and Public Policy.*
  C.E.S. Franks, 529(QQ):Summer82-426
Shrimpton, G.S. and D.J. McCargar, eds. Classical Contributions.
  W.G. Forrest, 487:Autumn82-288
Shrubb, P. A List of All People and Other Stories.
  S. Moore, 581:Jun82-238
Shtromas, A. Political Change and Social Development.
  A. Katsenelinboigen, 550(RusR):Jul82-340
Shudakov, G., with O. Suslova and L. Ukhtomskaya. Pioneers of Soviet Photography.
  A. Grundberg, 441:4Dec83-14
Shue, V. Peasant China in Transition.
  T. Tang, 293(JASt):Aug82-822
Shukla, N.S., ed and trans. Le Karṇānanda de Kṛṣṇadāsa.
  C.S.J. White, 318(JAOS):Oct-Dec81-492
Shulman, A.K. On the Stroll.
  M.K. Benet, 617(TLS):1Jul83-696

Shulman, D.D. Tamil Temple Myths.*
  D. Hudson, 293(JASt):Feb83-400
Shulman, J. The Photography of Architecture and Design.
  C. Robinson, 576:Mar82-79
Shumway, M. Practicing Vivaldi.
  J.L. Asper, 152(UDQ):Summer82-150
Shurr, W.H. Rappaccini's Children.
  W.B. Dillingham, 569(SR):Summer82-1xx
  J.R. Moore, 573(SSF):Summer82-289
  L.P.S., 27(AL):May82-311
Shuter-Dyson, R. and C. Gabriel. The Psychology of Musical Ability.
  A. Hickman, 410(M&L):Jul/Oct82-336
Shuttle, P. The Child-Stealer.
  F. Adcock, 617(TLS):28Oct83-1180
Shuttle, P. Éclats de pluie sur le jardin du zodiaque.
  R. Blin, 450(NRF):May82-143
Shuy, R.W. and A. Shnukal, eds. Language Use and the Uses of Language.
  C.M. Scotton, 350:Jun83-453
Sibum, N. Loyal and Unholy Hours.
  D. Barbour, 648(WCR):Summer81-82
Sicard, M. La Critique littéraire de Jean-Paul Sartre.
  R. Goldthorpe, 208(FS):Jan82-98
Sicart, Á. Pintura medieval: La Miniatura.
  C. Muñoz Delgado, 48:Oct-Dec82-395
Siciliano, E. Pasolini.* (Italian title: Vita di Pasolini.)
  M. Silverman, 18:Sep82-76
Siciliano, E. La Voce di Otello.
  G. Sertoli, 617(TLS):1Apr83-336
Sicker, P. Love and the Quest for Identity in the Fiction of Henry James.*
  A.W. Bellringer, 402(MLR):Apr82-429
  J.C. Rowe, 445(NCF):Jun82-113
Sickman, L. and others. Eight Dynasties of Chinese Painting.
  J. Hay, 55:Mar82-29
Siclier, J. La France de Pétain et son cinéma.
  J. Paulhan, 207(FR):Apr83-784
Sider, D. - see Anaxagoras
Sidhwa, B. The Bride.
  J. Mellors, 364:Mar83-106
Sidlauskas, S. Intimate Architecture.
  R.L. Shep, 614:Summer83-19
Siebenmann, G., ed. Die lateinamerikanische Hacienda.
  A. Blasi, 240(HR):Autumn82-501
Siebenschuh, W.R. Fictional Techniques and Factual Works.
  J. Sturrock, 617(TLS):5Aug83-841
Sieber, H. Language and Society in "La vida de Lazarillo de Tormes."*
  G. Sobejano, 240(HR):Autumn82-488
Sieber, R. African Furniture and Household Objects.*
  F. Willett, 59:Jun82-227
Siebert, E. Kleist.
  K. Kanzog, 72:Band218Heft2-403
Siebert, R.J. Hegel's Philosophy of History.
  W.C. Gay, 125:Summer82-441
Siefken, H. Thomas Mann, Goethe: "Ideal der Deutschheit."*
  K. Bullivant, 220(GL&L):Oct82/Jan83-148
  M. Hoppe, 405(MP):May83-441
Siegel, L. Fires of Love: Waters of Peace.
  D. Murphy, 617(TLS):1Jul83-708

Siegel, L. Sacred and Profane Dimensions
of Love in Indian Traditions as Exempli-
fied in the "Gītagovinda" of Jayadeva.*
  J.W. de Jong, 259(IIJ):Jan80-62
Siegel, P.J. Alfred de Musset.
  P. Berthier, 446(NCFS):Fall-Winter
  82/83-190
Siegel, R. In a Pig's Eye.
  D. Gioia, 491:May82-102
Siegert, R. Aufklärung und Volkslekture.*
  D.C.G. Lorenz, 221(GQ):May82-417
Sieghart, P. The International Law of
Human Rights.
  C. Gray, 617(TLS):20May83-521
  D. Pannick, 362:10Feb83-25
Siegman, A.W. and S. Feldstein, eds. Of
Speech and Time.*
  P. Alkon, 113:Spring82-80
Siegmund, G. Buddhism and Christianity.
  P. Novak, 485(PE&W):Jul82-346
von Siegroth-Nellessen, G. Versuch einer
exakten Stiluntersuchung für Meister
Eckhart, Johannes Tauler und Heinrich
Seuse.
  F. Tobin, 406:Winter82-495
Siemek, M.J. Idea transcendentalizmu u
Fichtego i Kanta.
  B. Andrzejewski, 342:Band73Heft4-483
Sigrid, J. L'Ange couteau.
  I.H. Coleman, 207(FR):Mar83-673
Sikes, H.M., with W.H. Bonner and G. Lahey
- see Hazlitt, W.
Silcox, D.P. and M. Weiler. Christopher
Pratt.
  K. Kritzwiser, 73:Dec82/Jan/Feb83-58
Silenstam, M. Les Phrases qui contiennent
une complétive.*
  K.E.M. George, 208(FS):Jul82-374
Silgardo, M., R.D. Rose and S. Rodrigues.
3 Poets.
  S. Brown, 493:Dec81-65
Silius Italicus, T.C. Silius Italicus,
"La guerre punique." (Vol 1) (P. Mini-
coni and G. Devallet, eds and trans)
  C. Moussy, 555:Vol55fasc1-174
Silk, M.S. and J.P. Stern. Nietzsche on
Tragedy.
  J.E. Atwell, 290(JAAC):Summer83-465
  R. Nicholls, 131(CL):Spring82-187
  E.J.M. West, 478:Oct82-219
Sillitoe, A. The Lost Flying Boat.
  B. Hardy, 617(TLS):11Nov83-1256
  J. Mellors, 362:15Dec83-30
Sills, D. - see "Biographical Supplement
to The International Encyclopedia of the
Social Sciences"
de Silva, P. An Introduction to Buddhist
Psychology.
  C. Hallisey, 318(JAOS):Oct-Dec81-504
Silver, A. Bernard Shaw.ᴬ
  C.A. Berst, 401(MLQ):Jun82-190
  639(VQR):Summer82-88
Silver, A. Thimblerig.
  R. Runnells, 108:Fall82-126
Silver, I. Ronsard and the Hellenic
Renaissance in France.* (Vol 2)
  T. Cave, 551(RenQ):Autumn82-509
  F. Rigolot, 405(MP):Aug82-83
  P.M. Smith, 208(FS):Oct82-462
Silverberg, R. Sunrise on Mercury.
  C. Greenland, 617(TLS):11Mar83-249

Silverman, D. and B. Torode. The Material
Word.*
  R. Arnaud, 189(EA):Apr-Jun82-200
  L. Brodkey and M. Boyd, 355(LSoc):
  Aug82-308
  S. Kappeler, 208(FS):Jan82-115
Silverman, D.P. Reconstructing Europe
after the Great War.*
  639(VQR):Summer82-82
Silverman, H.J., ed. Piaget, Philosophy
and the Human Sciences.
  F.E.E., 543:Jun82-910
Silverman, R.A. Law and Urban Growth.
  P. Finkelman, 432(NEQ):Mar82-152
Silverstein, J. Burmese Politics.
  J.A. Wiant, 293(JASt):Feb82-428
Silvestris, B. - see under Bernardus
Silvestris
Simenon, G. Aunt Jeanne.
  442(NY):29Aug83-92
Simenon, G. The Lodger.
  J. Symons, 441:30Oct83-12
Simenon, G. The Long Exile.
  P. Keegan, 617(TLS):29Jul83-804
  442(NY):14Mar83-157
Simenon, G. Maigret Afraid.
  442(NY):5Sep83-116
Simenon, G. Maigret and the Nahour Case.
  442(NY):17Jan83-114
Siṃhabhūpāla II. The Rasārṇavasudhākara
of Siṃhabhūpāla. (T. Venkatacharya, ed)
  L. Sternbach, 318(JAOS):Apr-Jun81-240
Simic, C. Austerities.
  A. Williamson, 441:1May83-15
Simis, K. USSR: Secrets of a Corrupt
Society.
  L. Schapiro, 453(NYRB):20Jan83-3
  C. Wheeler, 362:6Jan83-23
Simison, G. Disturbances.
  C. Wiseman, 102(CanL):Summer81-140
  N. Zacharin, 526:Winter82-84
Simkin, T., R.S. Fiske and S.F. Melcher.
Krakatau.
  P-L. Adams, 61:Nov83-149
Simmel, G. The Problems of the Philosophy
of History.*
  T.E. Huff, 488:Mar82-81
  T.E. Huff, 488:Jun82-205
Simmler, F. Graphematisch-phonematische
Studien zum althochdeutschen Konsonantis-
mus.
  H. Penzl, 350:Mar83-229
Simmler, F. Die westgermanische Konsonant-
engemination im Deutschen unter beson-
derer Berücksichtigung des Althochdeut-
schen.
  R. Hinderling, 684(ZDA):Band111Heft1-1
Simmonds, J.D. - see "Milton Studies"
Simmons, A.J. Moral Principles and Politi-
cal Obligation.*
  P. Carrive, 192(EP):Jul-Sep81-368
  D.L.N., 543:Jun82-911
Simmons, D.D. Personal Valuing.
  T.M.R., 185:Jul83-825
Simmons, G. Peckinpah.
  M. Haskell, 441:27Mar83-12
Simmons, J. and W. Mares. Working To-
gether.
  S. Lohr, 441:6Mar83-12
Simões, M. García Lorca e Manuel da Fon-
seca.
  J. Parker, 86(BHS):Oct82-346

Simon, C. Les Géorgiques.*
D. Sherzer, 207(FR):Apr83-794
Simon, J. Paradigms Lost.*
W.W. Douglas, 128(CE):Jan82-72
I.B. Holley, Jr., 579(SAQ):Winter82-119
Simon, J. Something to Declare.
S. Farber, 441:10Apr83-11
Simon, J. Wahrheit als Freiheit.*
H. Holzhey, 687:Jan-Mar82-117
Simon, J.L. The Ultimate Resource.*
639(VQR):Winter82-12
Simon, K. Bronx Primitive.*
G.C., 569(SR):Fall82-cviii
Simon, L. Of Virtue Rare.*
639(VQR):Summer82-87
Simon, M.A. Understanding Human Action.
J.D., 185:Apr83-631
Simon, P. The Tongue-Tied American.
F.M. Grittner, 399(MLJ):Summer82-191
Simon, R. Gramsci's Political Thought.
M. Clark, 617(TLS):3Jun83-580
Simon, R. Kleine Schriften. (R. Schmitt, ed)
J.W. de Jong, 259(IIJ):Jan82-64
L. Sternbach, 318(JAOS):Jul-Sep81-377
Simon, R. and A. Smart. The Art of Cricket.
A. Ross, 617(TLS):16Sep83-987
Simon-Vandenbergen, A.M. The Grammar of Headlines in "The Times" 1870-1970.
J. Pauchard, 189(EA):Oct-Dec82-450
Simons, G. Are Computers Alive?
H.C. Longuet-Higgins, 617(TLS):28Oct83-1177
Simons, M.A. Sémiotisme de Stendhal.*
P. Berthier, 535(RHL):May-Jun82-482
Simonsuuri, K. Homer's Original Genius.*
J. Richetti, 107(CRCL):Jun82-279
Simpson, C. Emma.
B. Fothergill, 617(TLS):25Nov83-1303
Simpson, D. Fetishism and Imagination.
E. Hollahan, 454:Spring83-259
D. Trotter, 617(TLS):1Jul83-707
Simpson, D. Irony and Authority in Romantic Poetry.*
S.M. Tave, 402(MLR):Jan82-174
P.L. Thorslev, Jr., 340(KSJ):Vol31-202
Simpson, D. The Political Economy of Growth.
T.W. Hutchison, 617(TLS):2Sep83-923
Simpson, D. Puppet for a Corpse.
T.J. Binyon, 617(TLS):15Apr83-374
M. Laski, 362:19May83-24
Simpson, D. C.F.A. Voysey.
W.C. Miller, 505:Jul82-108
Simpson, D. Winning Elections.
L.L. Kaid, 583:Spring83-302
Simpson, E. Poets in Their Youth.*
J.B. Gilbert, 385(MQR):Winter83-151
W. Harmon, 344:Summer83-112
N. Miller, 42(AR):Fall82-485
M. Mudrick, 249(HudR):Autumn82-460
M. Perloff, 29:May/Jun83-32
R. Tillinghast, 434:Spring83-428
Simpson, G.G. Splendid Isolation.*
R.O., 617(TLS):23Dec83-1443
Simpson, H. D.H. Lawrence and Feminism.
P. Boumelha, 617(TLS):25Feb83-176
P.T. Whelan, 344:Summer83-130
Simpson, J. Matthew Arnold and Goethe.*
J. Boening, 52:Band16Heft2-214
C. Dawson, 541(RES):Feb82-102

Simpson, J. British Dragons.
B. White, 203:Vol93No2-235
Simpson, J. A Fine and Private Place.
M. Laski, 362:11Aug83-24
Simpson, J. - see Adam, W.
Simpson, J.A., ed. The Concise Oxford Dictionary of Proverbs.
A. Brownjohn, 617(TLS):25Feb83-193
H. Kenner, 231:May83-84
Simpson, L. Caviare at the Funeral.*
R. Pybus, 565:Vol23No3-60
639(VQR):Winter82-25
Simpson, L.P. The Brazen Face of History.*
W. French, 395(MFS):Winter82/83-656
E.N. Harbert, 587(SAF):Spring82-119
W.C. Havard, 569(SR):Winter82-114
W. Prunty, 639(VQR):Winter82-152
Simpson, M. Making Arrangements.
H. Lomas, 364:Feb83-73
W. Scammell, 617(TLS):7Jan83-17
Simpson, M.S. The Officer in Nineteenth-Century Russian Literature.
J. Bushnell, 550(RusR):Oct82-524
Simpson, R.A. Selected Poems.
D. Haskell, 581:Sep82-348
Sims, J. and P.W. Peterson. Better Listening Skills.
L. Hamp-Lyons, 608:Mar83-109
Sinclair, A. Jack.
J. Tavernier-Courbin, 106:Winter82-363
Sinclair, A., R.J. Jarvella and W.J.M. Levelt, eds. The Child's Concept of Language.
E. Mayr, 685(ZDL):1/1982-105
R. Thiele, 682(ZPSK):Band34Heft2-249
Sinclair, C. Bedbugs.*
L. Jones, 364:Nov82-85
Sinclair, C. The Brothers Singer.
H. Maccoby, 362:1Sep83-21
S.S. Prawer, 617(TLS):29Apr83-419
Sinclair, G. and M. Wolfe, eds. The Spice Box.
E.S. Fisher, 627(UTQ):Summer82-447
L. Shohet, 102(CanL):Autumn82-161
Sinclair, K.V. French Devotional Texts of the Middle Ages.
P.B. Grout, 402(MLR):Jan82-194
P. Rézeau, 554:Vol 102No2-137
Sinden, D. A Touch of the Memoirs.*
D. Hughes, 157:Autumn82-45
Sinfield, A. Literature in Protestant England 1560-1660.
H.R. Woudhuysen, 617(TLS):13May83-484
Singal, D.J. The War Within.*
J.H. Justus, 344:Summer83-128
R.H. King, 578:Spring83-122
C.V. Woodward, 453(NYRB):3Mar83-31
Singer, D. The Road to Gdansk.
A. Korbonski, 550(RusR):Jan82-93
Singer, I.B. The Collected Stories of Isaac Bashevis Singer.*
S. Pinsker, 573(SSF):Summer82-294
F. Tuohy, 364:Dec82/Jan83-124
Singer, I.B. Lost in America.
M. Bernheim, 390:Aug/Sep82-62
Singer, I.B. The Penitent.
H. Bloom, 441:25Sep83-3
Singer, I.B. Reaches of Heaven.
J. Goldin, 31(ASch):Winter81/82-128
Singer, I.J. The Brothers Ashkenazi.
H. Maccoby, 362:1Sep83-21
S.S. Prawer, 617(TLS):29Apr83-419

Singer, P. The Expanding Circle.*
  A.L. Caplan, 185:Apr83-603
  R. Trigg, 518:Jul82-190
Singer, P. Hegel.
  R. Plant, 617(TLS):15Apr83-385
  A. Ryan, 362:17Mar83-22
Singer, P. Marx.
  C. Melakopides, 529(QQ):Spring82-148
Singer, P. Practical Ethics.*
  R.G. Frey, 393(Mind):Apr82-304
Singh, C. Textiles and Costumes from the
  Maharaja Sawai Man Singh II Museum.*
  M.W. Meister, 318(JAOS):Oct-Dec81-476
Singh, G. - see Leavis, F.R.
Singleton, F.B. Regional Economic Inequal-
  ities.
  D.A. Dyker, 575(SEER):Apr82-317
Sinha, J.P. The Mahābhārata.
  L. Sternbach, 318(JAOS):Oct-Dec81-481
Sini, C. Semiotica e filosofia.
  R.P.H., 543:Sep81-168
Sinisgalli, L. The Ellipse.
  K. Bosley, 617(TLS):25Mar83-286
Sipriot, P. Montherlant sans masque.
  (Vol 1)
  P. McCarthy, 617(TLS):17Jun83-627
Siraisi, N.G. Taddeo Alderotti and His
  Pupils.
  R.C. Dales, 377:Nov82-186
  C.B. Schmitt, 551(RenQ):Summer82-269
Siris, P. The Peking Mandate.
  P. van Rjndt, 441:30Oct83-32
Siska, H.S. People of the Ice.
  M. Whitaker, 102(CanL):Spring82-95
Sisler, R. Passionate Spirits.
  W.N., 102(CanL):Spring82-161
Sisson, J., 3d - see London, J.
Sito Alba, M. Montherlant et l'Espagne.*
  R.J. Golsan, 207(FR):Oct82-160
Sitta, H., ed. Ansätze zu einer pragmat-
  ischen Sprachgeschichte.*
  F. Simmler, 685(ZDL):3/1982-384
"Six Poètes 1." "Six Poètes 2."
  D.E. Rivas, 207(FR):Oct82-177
Sjölin, J-G. Den surrealistiska erfaren-
  heten.
  G. Sörbom, 341:Vol51No1-41
Skagestad, P. The Road of Inquiry.*
  S. Haack, 619:Spring82-197
Skal, D.J., ed. Graphic Communications for
  the Performing Arts.
  S. Elchen, 108:Winter82-113
Skapski, J. Green Water Blues.
  D. Barbour, 648(WCR):Summer81-82
Skard, S. Classical Tradition in Norway.
  D. Buttry, 301(JEGP):Jan82-101
  S. Lyngstad, 563(SS):Winter82-91
Skarda, P.L. and N.C. Jaffe, eds. The
  Evil Image.
  566:Autumn82-58
Skei, H.H. William Faulkner.
  27(AL):Oct82-475
Skelton, G. Richard and Cosima Wagner.
  R. Anderson, 415:Jun82-416
  M. Kennedy, 410(M&L):Jul/Oct82-331
Skelton, J. Magnificence.* (P. Neuss, ed)
  S. Carpenter, 541(RES):Nov82-461
  J.S. Colley, 130:Summer82-193
  N. Davis, 447(N&Q):Oct81-437
"John Skelton: The Complete English Poems."
  (J. Scattergood, ed)
  J.A. Burrow, 617(TLS):15Apr83-372

Skelton, R. The Collected Shorter Poems,
  1947-1977.
  R. Billings, 526:Winter82-72
  S. Hamill, 649(WAL):Spring82-85
  J.D. McClatchy, 491:Jun82-170
  F. Sparshott, 102(CanL):Spring82-134
  P. Stevens, 628(UWR):Fall-Winter82-122
Skelton, R. Landmarks.*
  M.B. Oliver, 198:Jan82-74
Skelton, R. - see Synge, J.M.
Skendi, S. Balkan Cultural Studies.*
  G. Schöpflin, 575(SEER):Oct82-627
  S.D. Spector, 104(CASS):Summer82-305
Skiadas, A.D., ed. Archaikos Lyrismos I.
  D.E. Gerber, 121(CJ):Apr/May83-366
Skidelsky, R. John Maynard Keynes. (Vol
  1)
  A. Cairncross, 617(TLS):4Nov83-1209
  N. Mosley, 362:10Nov83-25
Skiles, D. Miss America.*
  J. Mellors, 362:6Jan83-24
Skinner, D. Thomas George Lawson.
  G.M. Fyle, 69:Vol51No4-882
Skinner, Q. Machiavelli.
  H.K. Moss, 402(MLR):Apr82-472
Sklar, L. Space, Time, and Spacetime.
  J. Largeault, 542:Jul-Sep82-545
Sklar, M. and J. Mulac, eds. Editor's
  Choice.
  J. Griffith, 436(NewL):Fall82-114
Skolling, H.G. Charter 77 and Human
  Rights in Czechoslovakia.
  D.W. Paul, 104(CASS):Fall-Winter82-593
Skoyles, J. A Little Faith.
  F. Muratori, 448:Vol20No1-166
  J. Schiff, 584(SWR):Spring82-237
Skrine, P.N. The Baroque.*
  M. Hollington, 161(DUJ):Dec81-141
Skrynnikov, R.G. Ivan the Terrible. (H.F.
  Graham, ed)
  D. Atkinson, 550(RusR):Apr82-199
Skulsky, H. Metamorphosis.
  H. Levin, 131(CL):Spring82-171
Skura, M.A. The Literary Use of the Psy-
  choanalytic Process.*
  L.K. Bundtzen, 405(MP):Aug82-110
  A. Kirsch, 570(SQ):Summer82-252
  C. Snider, 395(MFS):Winter81/82-765
  M. Steig, 648(WCR):Oct82-46
  R.P. Wheeler, 301(JEGP):Oct82-540
Skurnowicz, J. Romantic Nationalism and
  Liberalism.
  D. Stone, 104(CASS):Fall-Winter82-561
Skvorecky, J. The Bass Saxophone.
  P. Stevens, 102(CanL):Summer82-131
Skvorecky, J. The Swell Season.
  G. Josipovici, 617(TLS):12Aug83-866
  J. Mills, 648(WCR):Apr83-49
  M. Thorpe, 99:Dec82/Jan83-40
Skydsgaard, O. La combinatoria sintáctica
  del infinitivo español, I-II.
  K. Karlson, 545(RPh):Nov81-356
Skynner, R. and J. Cleese. Families.
  A. Clare, 617(TLS):11Nov83-1236
Skyrms, B. Causal Necessity.*
  M.B., 543:Jun82-913
Skyttä, K. Tuntematon Kekkonen.
  M. Rintala, 563(SS):Spring82-191
Slade, C., ed. Approaches to Teaching
  Dante's "Divine Comedy."
  A.K. Cassell, 276:Autumn82-187
  I.A. Portner, 276:Autumn82-189

Slater, A.P. Shakespeare the Director.
F. Kermode, 453(NYRB):28Apr83-30
Slater, C. Defeatists and their Enemies.*
J.N. Green, 208(FS):Jul82-372
D.R. Watson, 402(MLR):Oct82-966
Slater, C. Stories on a String.
M. Silverman, 263(RIB):Vol32No3/4-381
Slater, M. Dickens and Women.
N. Auerbach, 344:Fall83-131
H. Lee, 617(TLS):11Mar83-232
E.S. Turner, 362:10Feb83-24
Slater, M. Humour in the Works of Marcel
Proust.*
G. Craig, 402(MLR):Oct82-963
M. Thomas, 447(N&Q):Dec81-570
Slaughter, C. The Banquet.
M.K. Benet, 617(TLS):27May83-553
Slaughter, M.M. Universal Languages and
Scientific Taxonomy in the Seventeenth
Century.
M.A. Covington, 350:Dec83-920
V. Salmon, 617(TLS):14Jan83-37
Slights, C.W. The Casuistical Tradition
in Shakespeare, Donne, Herbert, and
Milton.*
W.H. Chelline, 130:Winter82/83-382
G. Hemphill, 569(SR):Winter82-x
H. MacCallum, 627(UTQ):Summer82-415
Sligo, J. The Concert Master.
M. Laski, 362:11Aug83-24
Sloane, D.E.E. Mark Twain as a Literary
Comedian.
R. Lehan, 445(NCF):Jun82-128
J.S. Whitley, 447(N&Q):Aug81-354
Sloate, D. A Taste of Earth, A Taste of
Flame.
R. Geiger, 198:Oct82-120
Slobin, M. Tenement Songs.
E. Koskoff, 187:May83-377
Sløk, J. Da Kierkegaard tav.
M. Plekon, 563(SS):Summer82-264
Sloman, A. The Computer Revolution in Phi-
losophy.*
M. Ringle, 449:Mar82-170
Słomczyński, K. and T. Krauze, eds. Class
Structure and Social Mobility.
S. Andreski, 575(SEER):Jan82-150
Šlosar, D. Slovotvorný vývoj českého slo-
vesa.
Z. Salzmann, 350:Sep83-696
Sloterdijk, P. Kritik der zynischen Ver-
nunft.
M. Rosen, 617(TLS):7Oct83-1092
Sluga, H.D. Gottlob Frege.*
P. Long, 479(PhQ):Apr82-173
J.M. Vickers, 319:Jan83-123
I.P. Wilson, 518:Jul82-166
Słupski, Z. - see "Dictionary of Oriental
Literature"
Slusser, G.E., G.R. Guffey and M. Rose,
eds. Bridges to Science Fiction.
D.N. Samuelson, 561(SFS):Nov82-333
Slusser, M.S. Nepal Mandala.
S. Digby, 617(TLS):19Aug83-889
Small, I., ed. The Aesthetes.
C. Donnell-Kotrozo, 289:Fall82-119
N. Shrimpton, 447(N&Q):Feb81-91
Smallwood, R.L. and S. Wells - see Dekker,
T.
Smart, B. Foucault, Marxism and Critique.
J. Gray, 617(TLS):30Dec83-1459

Smetana, J. and M-R. Myron. Mélange lit-
téraire. (2nd ed)
J.M. Goldman, 207(FR):Apr83-815
Smethurst, W. Jennifer's Friends.
J.K.L. Walker, 617(TLS):22Apr83-400
Smidt, K. Unconformities in Shakespeare's
History Plays.
I. Salusinszky, 617(TLS):14Jan83-43
Smith, A., ed. George Eliot.*
K. McSweeney, 637(VS):Autumn81-109
Smith, A. Lectures on Rhetoric and Belles
Lettres. (J.C. Bryce, ed)
B. Vickers, 617(TLS):23Sep83-1024
Smith, A. Adam Smith: Essays on Philosoph-
ical Subjects. (W.P.D. Wightman, J.C.
Bryce and I.S. Ross, eds)
J.L. Mackie, 541(RES):Aug82-338
Smith, A., with C. Sanger. Stitches in
Time.
P. Stuchen, 529(QQ):Autumn82-648
Smith, A.H. The Planned Economies of
Eastern Europe.
G. Kennedy, 617(TLS):21Oct83-1154
Smith, A.H., G.M. Baker and R.W. Kenny -
see Bacon, N.
Smith, A.J. Literary Love.
J. Briggs, 617(TLS):2Dec83-1352
Smith, A.K. and C. Weiner - see Oppen-
heimer, R.
Smith, B.F. The Shadow Warriors.
E. Barker, 617(TLS):2Dec83-1339
T. Powers, 453(NYRB):12May83-29
P. Taubman, 441:21Aug83-10
Smith, B.H. On the Margins of Discourse.*
M. Finlay-Pelinski, 107(CRCL):Mar82-56
C. Norris, 402(MLR):Jan82-136
S. Raval, 50(ArQ):Spring82-85
Smith, B.S. Russian Orthodoxy in Alaska.
R. Polchaninoff, 550(RusR):Jan82-70
Smith, C. The Making of the "Poema de mio
Cid."
B. Tate, 617(TLS):5Aug83-838
Smith, C.B. - see under Babington Smith, C.
Smith, C.D. The Early Career of Lord
North the Prime Minister.
J.J. Hecht, 173(ECS):Summer83-432
R.R. Rea, 577(SHR):Winter82-71
Smith, C.M. A Monograph: The Physical
Browning.
J.W. Herring, 85(SBHC):Fall82-64
Smith, C.M. Reverend Randollph and the
Unholy Bible.
N. Callendar, 441:1May83-27
Smith, C.N. - see Matthieu, P.
Smith, D. Above Timberline. (A. Anderson,
Jr., ed)
P.T. Bryant, 649(WAL):Spring82-80
Smith, D. Dream Flights.*
S. Sandy, 491:Aug82-293
P. Stitt, 219(GaR):Fall82-675
639(VQR):Spring82-60
Smith, D. Goshawk, Antelope.*
S. Sandy, 491:Aug82-293
Smith, D. Homage to Edgar Allan Poe.*
639(VQR):Spring82-60
Smith, D. In the House of the Judge.
R.W. Flint, 441:13Feb83-15
Smith, D. Lewis Jones.
K.O. Morgan, 617(TLS):8Apr83-349
Smith, D. The Light of Our Bones.
D. Barbour, 648(WCR):Summer81-84

Smith, D., ed. The Pure Clear Word.*
  K. Callaway, 472:Spring/Summer83-58
  W. Harmon, 569(SR):Fall82-612
Smith, D. Scarecrow.*
  D. Barbour, 648(WCR):Summer81-83
Smith, D. Socialist Propaganda in the
  Twentieth-Century British Novel.*
  J. Lucas, 677(YES):Vol 12-348
Smith, D.B. Inside the Great House.*
  R. Isaac, 656(WMQ):Jan82-226
  N.R. Johnson, 569(SR):Spring82-xxxv
Smith, D.E. The Regional Decline of a
  National Party.
  G.R. Davy, 150(DR):Summer82-333
  W.P. Irvine, 529(QQ):Summer82-340
Smith, D.F. and M.L. Lawhon. Plays about
  the Theatre in England, 1737-1800.
  B.S. Hammond, 541(RES):Aug82-333
  R.D. Hume, 130:Spring82-88
Smith, D.G. The Music Stops and the Waltz
  Continues.
  J. Melmoth, 617(TLS):18Nov83-1269
Smith, D.H. and others. Participation in
  Social and Political Activities.
  J. Smith, 185:Jan83-411
Smith, D.M. Guide to Bishops' Registers
  of England and Wales: A Survey from the
  Middle Ages to the Abolition of Episco-
  pacy in 1646.
  R.H. Helmholz, 589:Jul82-687
Smith, D.M. A Supplementary Guide to the
  Archive Collections in the Borthwick
  Institute of Historical Research.
  D.M. Barratt, 325:Oct82-129
Smith, D.M. - see under Mack Smith, D.
Smith, E. The Compleat Housewife: or
  Accomplished Gentlewoman's Companion.
  C. Driver, 617(TLS):23Dec83-1442
Smith, E. The Irish Journals of Elizabeth
  Smith, 1840-1850. (D. Thomson, with M.
  McGusty, eds)
  P. Diskin, 447(N&Q):Oct81-441
Smith, E.C. and L.F. Luce, eds. Toward
  Internationalism.
  H. Tonkin, 355(LSoc):Dec82-462
Smith, E.M.G. Mrs. Humphry Ward.
  F.R., 189(EA):Oct-Dec82-496
Smith, F.K. André Biéler.
  A. Davis, 529(QQ):Spring82-170
  F. Rasky, 73:Summer83-52
Smith, F.N. Language and Reality in
  Swift's "A Tale of a Tub."*
  W. Kinsley, 173(ECS):Summer82-442
  C.J. Rawson, 541(RES):Aug82-327
Smith, G.B., ed. Public Policy and Admin-
  istration in the Soviet Union.
  R. Cornell, 104(CASS):Fall-Winter82-
  586
Smith, G.E.K. - see under Kidder Smith,
  G.E.
Smith, G.H. The Explorations of the La
  Vérendryes in the Northern Plains, 1738-
  43. (W.R. Smith, ed)
  R.R. Johnson, 173(ECS):Fall82-75
Smith, G.K. - see under Kinross Smith, G.
Smith, H. Peter De Wint 1784-1849.
  J. Gage, 617(TLS):29Apr83-438
Smith, H., ed. Learning from Shōgun.*
  C.C. Hurst 3d, 293(JASt):Nov81-158
Smith, H. The Tension of the Lyre.*
  S. Woods, 551(RenQ):Winter82-657

Smith, H.D. A Descriptive Bibliography of
  the Printed Texts of the Pāñcarātrāgama.
  F. Wilson, 293(JASt):Feb82-402
Smith, H.F. The Popular American Novel,
  1865-1920.*
  G. Wickes, 395(MFS):Summer81-358
Smith, H.L., Jr. and others. 25 Years of
  Record Houses.
  J.M. Davern, 45:Nov81-59
Smith, I.C. - see under Crichton Smith, I.
Smith, J. An Apology for Loving the Old
  Hymns.
  H. Vendler, 472:Spring/Summer83-116
Smith, J. Death Turns a Trick.
  N. Callendar, 441:27Feb83-45
Smith, J. A Landscape of My Own.
  E. Larrissy, 493:Sep82-61
Smith, J.C. The Day the Music Died.
  G. Lewis, 498:Vol8No1-63
Smith, J.H., ed. The Literary Freud.*
  B. Jean, 148:Summer82-88
  E. Slater, 447(N&Q):Aug81-371
  M. Steig, 648(WCR):Oct82-46
Smith, J.I. and Y.Y. Haddad. The Islamic
  Understanding of Death and Resurrection.
  S. Vahiduddin, 273(IC):Apr82-166
Smith, J.L., comp. An Annotated Biblio-
  graphy of and about Ernesto Cardenal.*
  H.C. Woodbridge, 552(REH):Jan82-126
Smith, J.M., ed. Evolution Now.
  R.C. Lewontin, 453(NYRB):16Jun83-21
Smith, K. Fox Running.
  R. Garfitt, 617(TLS):24Jun83-661
  D. Graham, 565:Vol23No2-74
Smith, K. The Poet Reclining. Abel Baker
  Charlie Delta Epic Sonnets. Burned
  Books.
  R. Garfitt, 617(TLS):24Jun83-661
Smith, L. The Japanese Print since 1900.
  E. Seidensticker, 441:11Dec83-33
Smith, L. Oral History.
  F. Busch, 441:10Jul83-15
  F. Taliaferro, 231:Jul83-74
Smith, L.R., ed. The New Italian Poetry.
  J. Saunders, 565:Vol23No3-73
Smith, M. Doctor Blues.
  J. McConkey, 441:17Jul83-11
Smith, M. Montaigne and the Roman Censors.
  C. Clark, 208(FS):Oct82-463
Smith, M.E. Too Soon the Curtain Fell.
  D. Gardner, 627(UTQ):Summer82-442
  L. Lawrence, 108:Spring82-206
Smith, M.M. Playing Side Two.
  M. Lammon, 436(NewL):Winter82/83-106
Smith, N., ed. A Collection of Ranter
  Writings from the 17th Century.
  S. Wintle, 617(TLS):16Sep83-992
Smith, N. and D. Wilson. Modern Linguis-
  tics.*
  P. Collins, 320(CJL):Spring82-68
Smith, N.B. and J.T. Snow, eds. The Expan-
  sion and Transformation of Courtly Liter-
  ature.*
  E. Rozgonyi-Szilágyi, 549(RLC):Jan-
  Mar82-97
Smith, N.C. James Hogg.
  D. Gifford, 571(ScLJ):Winter82-84
Smith, N.J.H. Man, Fishes, and the Ama-
  zon.
  S.H. Weitzman, 37:Jul-Aug82-61
Smith, P. The Nation Comes of Age.
  639(VQR):Spring82-43

Smith, P. Realism and the Progress of Science.*
  A. Morton, 479(PhQ):Jul82-288
Smith, P.C. - see Gadamer, H-G.
Smith, P.F. Architecture and the Human Dimension.
  W.C. Watt, 290(JAAC):Summer83-450
Smith, P.L. The Problem of Values in Educational Thought.
  T.M.R., 185:Jul83-837
Smith, P.M. On the Hymn to Zeus in Aeschylus' "Agamemnon."
  P.G. Mason, 123:Vol32No2-271
Smith, P-M. - see Estienne, H.
Smith, R. Trial by Medicine.
  T.M.R., 185:Oct82-217
Smith, R.B. and W. Watson, eds. Early Southeast Asia.
  K.L. Hutterer, 293(JASt):May82-559
Smith, R.H. Patches of Godlight.
  H.H. Watts, 395(MFS):Winter81/82-702
Smith, R.J. The "Ecole Normale" and the Third Republic.
  H.C. Staples, 207(FR):Mar83-655
Smith, R.T. Rural Route.
  D. Secreast, 577(SHR):Summer82-278
Smith, S. Inviolable Voice.
  S. Ellis, 617(TLS):18Feb83-167
Smith, S. Lowestoft Porcelain in Norwich Castle Museum.
  G. Wills, 39:Apr82-297
Smith, S. Stevie Smith: A Selection. (H. Lee, ed)
  V. Feaver, 617(TLS):5Aug83-840
Smith, S.B. Sensualities. Scurrilities.
  T.F. Merrill, 305(JIL):Sep82-3
Smith, S.M. The Other Nation.*
  L. James, 637(VS):Winter82-260
  S. Monod, 189(EA):Jan-Mar82-90
Smith, T. De Republica Anglorum. (M. Dewar, ed)
  C.S.L. Davies, 617(TLS):11Feb83-128
Smith, T.L. Revivalism and Social Reform.
  M.R. Winchell, 585(SoQ):Fall81-88
Smith, V., ed. Young St. Poets Anthology.
  D. Haskell, 581:Sep82-348
Smith, W.D. The Hippocratic Tradition.
  J. Scarborough, 24:Fall82-340
Smith, W.F. Noticiario.
  D.M. Franzblau, 238:Sep82-478
Smith, W.H., with others, comps. The Yale Edition of Horace Walpole's Correspondence. (Vols 44-48)
  R. Halsband, 617(TLS):4Nov83-1228
Smith, W.H.C. Napoleon III.
  T. Judt, 617(TLS):22Apr83-409
Smitherman, G., ed. Black English and the Education of Black Children and Youth.
  J.L. Zorn, 128(CE):Mar82-314
Smithers, A.J. Dornford Yates.*
  B. Andrews, 364:Jul82-85
Smithers, J. Combined Forces.
  M. Trend, 617(TLS):19Aug83-890
Smitten, J.R. and A. Daghistany, eds. Spatial Form in Narrative.
  N. Baym, 301(JEGP):Oct82-543
  R.K. Cross, 445(NCF):Sep82-243
  R. Gullón, 405(MP):Feb83-340
  S.G. Kellman, 395(MFS):Summer82-349
  W. Sypher, 569(SR):Fall82-575
  M. Torgovnick, 579(SAQ):Autumn82-475
  639(VQR):Winter82-7

Smoldon, W.L. The Music of the Medieval Church Dramas. (C. Bourgeault, ed)
  A. Hughes, 589:Jul82-663
Smollett, T. Travels through France and Italy.* (F. Felsenstein, ed)
  J.A. Downie, 506(PSt):May82-171
  J.V. Price, 447(N&Q):Dec81-556
  G.S. Rousseau, 402(MLR):Apr83-413
Smout, T.C. - see Muir, E.
Smuda, M. Der Gegenstand in der bildenden Kunst und Literatur.*
  K.L. Pfeiffer, 52:Band16Heft1-63
Smullyan, R. Alice in Puzzleland. 5000 B.C. and Other Philosophical Fantasies.
  H. Kenner, 231:Mar83-64
Smullyan, R. The Chess Mysteries of the Arabian Knights.
  P.F.S., 617(TLS):18Nov83-1295
Smullyan, R. The Lady or the Tiger?
  H. Kenner, 231:Mar83-64
  P.F.S., 617(TLS):24Jun83-683
Smuszkiewicz, A. Stereotyp fabularny fantastyki naukowej.
  E. Stachniak, 561(SFS):Jul82-221
Snell, B., ed. Frühgriechische Lyriker.
  D. Arnould, 555:Vol56fasc2-320
Snell, B. Der Weg zum Denken und zur Wahrheit.
  S.R. Slings, 394:Vol135fasc3/4-356
Snellgrove, D.L., ed and trans. The Nine Ways of Bon.
  G.W. Houston, 293(JASt):Aug82-824
Snellgrove, D.L. and T. Skorupski. The Cultural Heritage of Ladakh. (Vol 2)
  J. Lowry, 463:Winter82/83-383
Snodgrass, A. Archaic Greece.
  A.R. Burn, 303(JoHS):Vol 102-263
Snodgrass, W.D. If Birds Build With Your Hair.
  D. Gioia, 249(HudR):Autumn82-483
Snow, E.A. A Study of Vermeer.*
  M.M. Kahr, 54:Jun82-338
  P.C. Sutton, 551(RenQ):Spring81-126
Snow, J. The Poetry of Alfonso X, El Sabio.
  P.O. Gericke, 545(RPh):Feb82-554
Snow, K. Wonders.*
  C. Berger, 491:Apr82-35
Snow, P. Stranger and Brother.*
  P-L. Adams, 61:Apr83-133
  D.A.N. Jones, 617(TLS):7Jan83-4
Snowden, F.M. Before Color Prejudice.
  K. Hopkins, 617(TLS):21Oct83-1152
Snyder, F.G. Capitalism and Legal Change.
  R.H.B., 185:Oct82-197
Snyder, G. Axe Handles.
  M. Kinzie, 29:Nov/Dec83-40
Snyder, G. The Real Work.* (S. McLean, ed)
  R. Jones, 584(SWR):Spring82-246
Snyder, J.M. Puns and Poetry in Lucretius' "De Rerum Natura."
  D. Clay, 24:Summer82-220
  R. Minadeo, 121(CJ):Apr/May83-361
  D.A. West, 123:Vol32No1-25
Snyder, S. The Comic Matrix of Shakespeare's Tragedies.*
  B. McElroy, 405(MP):Aug82-86
  J. Rees, 677(YES):Vol 12-257
  G. Taylor, 541(RES):Feb82-76
Soames, S. and D.M. Perlmutter. Syntactic Argumentation and the Structure of Eng-
[continued]

[continuing]
lish.*
    T.J. Taylor, 541(RES):Feb82-63
Sobchack, V.C. The Limits of Infinity.
    A. Gordon, 561(SFS):Mar82-93
Sobel, R. Gogol's Forgotten Book.
    D. Rancour-Laferriere, 104(CASS):Fall-
    Winter82-519
    N. Rzhevsky, 550(RusR):Jul82-349
Sobin, A. The Sunday Naturalist.
    I. Salusinszky, 617(TLS):9Dec83-1384
Sochen, J. Consecrate Every Day.
    A.S. Moore, 287:Jan82-24
Södergård, Ö., ed. La Chirurgie de l'Abbé
    Poutrel.
    R. Roques, 553(RLiR):Jul-Dec82-501
Södergran, E. Love and Solitude.
    A. Swanson, 563(SS):Autumn82-323
Soichi Iijima, Seiji Imahori and Kanesa-
    buro Gushima, eds. Hiroshima and Naga-
    saki.
    Toyoda Toshiyuki, 285(JapQ):Apr-Jun82-
    244
Sokel, W.H., A.A. Kipa and H. Ternes, eds.
    Probleme der Komparatistik und Interpre-
    tation.
    R. Immerwahr, 107(CRCL):Dec81-580
Sökeland, W. Indirektheit von Sprechhand-
    lungen.
    P. Suchsland, 682(ZPSK):Band35Heft3-
    366
Sokolowski, R. Presence and Absence.
    E.S. Casey, 543:Mar82-557
Solá, M.M. Poesía política en Pablo Ner-
    uda.
    L.F. González-Cruz, 238:Dec82-663
de Sola Pinto, V. and F.W. Roberts - see
    Lawrence, D.H.
Sola-Solé, J.M. El alfabeto monetario de
    las cecas "libio fenices."
    T.V. Higgs, 238:May82-319
    K-H. Schmidt, 547(RF):Band93Heft3/4-
    417
Sola-Solé, J.M. Los sonetos "al itálico
    modo" del Marqués de Santillana.*
    J.F. Burke, 238:Sep82-462
Sola-Solé, J.M. - see López de Mendoza, I.
de Solare, B.E.E. - see under Entenza de
    Solare, B.E.
Soldevila Durante, I. La novela desde
    1936.
    R.C. Spires, 240(HR):Summer82-371
Solé-Leris, A. The Spanish Pastoral
    Novel.*
    F. Pierce, 402(MLR):Apr82-477
Solensten, J. Good Thunder.
    F. Busch, 441:24Jul83-10
Söll, L. Gesprochenes und geschriebenes
    Französisch.* (2nd ed) (F.J. Hausmann,
    ed)
    A. Greive, 547(RF):Band93Heft1/2-193
    K. Hunnius, 72:Band218Heft2-450
Sollenberger, E., comp. Organ Composi-
    tions of the Twentieth Century (se-
    lected).
    A.F.L.T., 412:Feb81-61
Sollers, P. Femmes.
    S. Romer, 617(TLS):8Apr83-346
Sollertinsky, D. and L. Pages from the
    Life of Dmitri Shostakovich.*
    M. Barry, 410(M&L):Jul/Oct81-430

Söllner, A. Einführung in die römische
    Rechtsgeschichte. (2nd ed)
    W.M. Gordon, 123:Vol132No1-103
Solman, P. and T. Friedman. Life and
    Death on the Corporate Battlefield.
    R. Lekachman, 441:13Feb83-13
Solmsen, F. Isis among the Greeks and
    Romans.
    J.G. Griffiths, 123:Vol132No1-53
    Tran Tam Tinh, 487:Summer82-195
Solo, R.A. and C.W. Anderson, eds. Value
    Judgement and Income Distribution.
    C.N.S., 185:Jan83-436
Solomon, B.P. Short Flights.
    C. See, 441:17Jul83-8
    442(NY):5Sep83-113
Solomon, C. and R. The Complete Curry
    Cookbook.
    W. and C. Cowen, 639(VQR):Spring82-68
Solomon, H.M. Sir Richard Blackmore.*
    A. Pailler, 189(EA):Oct-Dec82-469
Solomon, J. and O., comps. Zickary Zan.
    J. Cech, 582(SFQ):Vol43No3/4-353
Solomon, R.H., ed. Asian Security in the
    1980s.
    M. Yahuda, 293(JASt):Nov81-89
Solovieff, G. - see Madame de Staël
Solovyov, V. and E. Klepikova. Yuri Andro-
    pov.
    J.M. Burns, 441:6Nov83-13
Solta, G.R. Einführung in die Balkanlin-
    guistik mit besonderer Berücksichtigung
    des Substrats und des Balkanlatein-
    ischen.
    D. Deletant, 575(SEER):Apr82-274
    C. Schmitt, 553(RLiR):Jul-Dec82-429
Solway, D. Mephistopheles and the Astro-
    naut.*
    K. Norris, 137:Aug82-34
Solway, D. Selected Poems.
    J. Peirce, 99:Oct82-27
Solzhenitsyn, A. Prisoners.
    M. Nicholson, 617(TLS):17Jun83-639
Solzhenitsyn, A. Victory Celebrations.
    M. Nicholson, 617(TLS):17Jun83-639
de Somaize, A.B. Le Procès des Précieuses,
    en vers burlesques. (E. Biancardi, ed)
    N. Aronson, 475:Vol9No17-800
Somers, J. The Diary of a Good Neighbour.
    P-L. Adams, 61:May83-103
Somerset Fry, P. and F. The History of
    Scotland.*
    442(NY):14Feb83-119
Somerville, E.A.Œ. and M. Ross. The Irish
    R.M.
    P. Craig, 617(TLS):13May83-499
Sommant, M. Dictionnaire des mots
    abstraits.
    M. Cranston, 207(FR):Mar83-625
Sommer, F. Schriften aus dem Nachlass.
    (B. Forssman, ed)
    O. Masson, 555:Vol55fasc1-154
Sommer, S. Lifetime.
    639(VQR):Spring82-55
Sommers, F. The Logic of Natural Lan-
    guage.*
    P.F. Strawson, 311(JP):Dec82-786
Sommers, R.J. Richmond Redeemed.
    A.P. McDonald, 9(AlaR):Jan82-66
Song, B-S. Source Readings in Korean
    Music.*
    K.L. Pratt, 293(JASt):Aug82-851

337

Song, Y-Y. Bertolt Brecht und die chinesische Philosophie.*
A. Hsia, 133:Band15Heft1/2-180
Sonne, B. The Happy Family.
A. Fienup-Riordan, 292(JAF):Oct-Dec82-475
von Sonnenburg, H. Raphael in der Alten Pinakothek.
J. Pope-Hennessy, 453(NYRB):22Dec83-44
Sonnichsen, C.L. The Ambidextrous Historian.
L. Milazzo, 584(SWR):Winter82-v
C.S. Peterson, 649(WAL):Summer82-172
Sontag, S. A Susan Sontag Reader.*
M. Mudrick, 231:Feb83-62
H.P., 617(TLS):21Oct83-1171
Sontag, S. - see Barthes, R.
Soong, S.C., ed. Song Without Music.
E. Kaplan, 134(CP):Spring82-79
Sopena, F. - see de Falla, M.
Soper, K. On Human Needs.*
S.K., 185:Apr83-633
Sopher, D.E., ed. An Exploration of India.*
M.N. Pearson, 318(JAOS):Jul-Sep81-382
Sophocles. Oedipus the King. (R. Bagg, trans)
P. Roche, 385(MQR):Fall83-655
Sophocles. Tragicorum Graecorum Fragmenta.* (Vol 4) (S. Radt, ed)
W.J. Verdenius, 394:Vol35fasc1/2-163
Sophocles. Tragoediae.* (Vol 2) (R.D. Dawe, ed)
J. Irigoin, 555:Vol55fasc2-336
Soproni, S. Der spätrömische Limes zwischen Esztergom und Szentendre.
R.S.O. Tomlin, 123:Vol32No2-253
Sorabji, R. Necessity, Cause and Blame.*
S. Gaukroger, 63:Dec82-363
A. Gotthelf, 319:Oct83-561
H. Weidemann, 53(AGP):Band64Heft3-301
de Sorbière, S. Relation d'un voyage en Angleterre.* (L. Roux, ed)
J. Lough, 189(EA):Jul-Sep82-327
J. Trethewey, 535(RHL):Sep-Dec82-897
D.A. Watts, 475:No16Pt2-436
Sorel, C. Histoire comique de Francion (livres I à VII). (Y. Giraud, ed)
G. Berger, 475:Vol19No17-776
Sorell, W. Dance in its Time.*
M.J. Warner, 529(QQ):Winter82-874
Sørensen, P.M. Norrønt nid.*
C.J. Clover, 301(JEGP):Jul82-398
Soriano, O. Carteles de Invierno.
O. Rossardi, 37:Sep-Oct82-63
Sorkin, M. Hardy Holzman Pfeiffer.
L. Knobel, 46:Apr82-81
Sorlin, P. The Film in History.
J. Rosenbaum, 18:Apr82-71
Sorokin, B. Tolstoy in Prerevolutionary Russian Criticism.*
V. Terras, 149(CLS):Spring82-79
Sorrel, N. and R. Narayan. Indian Music in Performance.
R. Widdess, 415:May82-336
Sorrels, C.A. US Cruise Missile Programs.
L. Freedman, 617(TLS):26Aug83-900
Sorrentino, G. Abberation of Starlight.*
G.W. Jarecke, 577(SHR):Spring82-159
Sorrentino, G. Blue Pastoral.
P-L. Adams, 61:Jun83-105
J. Conarroe, 441:19Jun83-13

Sorrentino, G. Crystal Vision.
W.H. Pritchard, 249(HudR):Spring82-159
639(VQR):Spring82-53
Sorrentino, G. Mulligan Stew.*
P. Lewis, 565:Vol23No1-51
Sosa, E., ed. Essays on the Philosophy of Roderick M. Chisholm.
F. Feldman, 482(PhR):Jul82-476
Sosa, E., ed. The Philosophy of Nicholas Rescher.
L. Antony, 482(PhR):Jul82-481
Sosa, M. and B. Harvey - see Tynianov, Y.
Sōseki, N. I Am a Cat. Mon.
J. Updike, 442(NY):3Jan83-66
Sosin, J.M. English America and the Restoration Monarchy of Charles II.
A. Olson, 656(WMQ):Jul82-525
Sosin, J.M. English America and the Revolution of 1688.
P. Marshall, 617(TLS):8Jul83-730
Sőtér, I. and I. Neupokoyeva, eds. European Romanticism.*
P.N. Gilbertson, 107(CRCL):Jun82-282
R. von Tiedemann, 52:Band16Heft1-90
Soto, G. Where Sparrows Work Hard.
V. Armour-Hileman, 152(UDQ):Summer82-154
Souchal, F. French Sculptors of the 17th and 18th Centuries: The Reign of Louis XIV.* (Vol 1)
N. Penny, 59:Jun82-243
Souchal, F. French Sculptors of the 17th and 18th Centuries: The Reign of Louis XIV.* (Vol 2)
T. Hodgkinson, 39:Feb82-129
N. Penny, 59:Jun82-243
Souchal, F., with F. de la Moureyre. Les Frères Coustou et l'évolution de la sculpture française du Dôme des Invalides aux Chevaux de Marly.
G. Weber, 471:Jan/Feb/Mar82-80
Souche-Dagues, D. - see Hegel, G.W.F.
Součková, M. Baroque in Bohemia.*
J.D. Naughton, 575(SEER):Apr82-290
R. Weltsch, 104(CASS):Spring82-148
Soueif, A. Aisha.
J. Mellors, 362:21Jul83-27
G. Strawson, 617(TLS):8Jul83-725
"Les Sources en musicologie."
D. Leech-Wilkinson, 410(M&L):Jul/Oct82-338
Sousa, R.W. The Rediscoverers.
M.L. Daniel, 238:Dec82-660
Souster, R. Collected Poems of Raymond Souster.* (Vol 1)
D. Barbour, 648(WCR):Jun82-33
Souster, R. Collected Poems of Raymond Souster. (Vol 2)
D. Barbour, 648(WCR):Jun82-33
A. Brooks, 526:Summer82-108
B. Whiteman, 198:Jul82-101
Soutet, O. La Littérature française de la Renaissance.*
T. Thomson, 208(FS):Jan82-62
"South Africa: Time Running Out."
B. Munslow, 69:Vol152No4-91
Southerland, E. Let the Lion Eat Straw.
E. Stetson, 459:Summer/Winter81-224
Southern, E. Biographical Dictionary of Afro-American and African Musicians.
D-R. de Lerma, 187:Sep83-543

Spencer, B.T. Patterns of Nationality.
  J. Cohn, 395(MFS):Winter83/83-658
  W.B. Rideout, 27(AL):Dec82-602
Spencer, E. The Stories of Elizabeth
  Spencer.*
  R. Buffington, 569(SR):Spring82-264
  D.J. Enright, 617(TLS):15Jul83-745
  639(VQR):Winter82-18
Spencer, M.C. Michel Butor.
  A. Waite, 546(RR):Jan82-126
Spencer, M.C. Charles Fourier.
  C. Crossley, 208(FS):Oct82-478
  L. Kamm, 207(FR):Apr83-775
Spencer, R. The Spencers on Spas.
  M. Neve, 617(TLS):21Oct83-1149
Spencer, S. Collage of Dreams. (rev)
  E.J. Hinz, 106:Winter82-373
Spencer, T.J.B. - see Ford, J.
Spender, D. Man Made Language.*
  R.M. Hogg, 148:Spring82-91
Spender, S. The Thirties and After.
  G. Reeves, 677(YES):Vol 12-354
Spender, S. and D. Hockney. China Diary.*
  J.R. Banks, 148:Winter82-81
  A. Ross, 364:Dec82/Jan83-132
  A. Sutherland, 362:3Feb83-26
  442(NY):14Mar83-160
Spengemann, W.C. The Adventurous Muse.
  L. Buell, 183(ESQ):Vol28No1-63
Spengemann, W.C. The Forms of Autobiog-
  raphy.*
  M. Gidley, 366:Spring82-115
  C. Lang, 153:Winter82-2
  K.E. Welch, 481(PQ):Spring82-227
Spenser, E. The Faerie Queene.* (A.C.
  Hamilton, ed)
  S. Dorangeon, 189(EA):Apr-Jun82-211
"Spenser Studies." (Vol 1) (P. Cullen and
  T.P. Roche, Jr., eds)
  S. Dorangeon, 189(EA):Apr-Jun82-208
  B. Sherry, 67:May82-74
"Spenser Studies." (Vol 3) (P. Cullen and
  T.P. Roche, Jr., eds)
  H.R. Woudhuysen, 617(TLS):12Aug83-867
Sperber, D. Le Savoir des anthropologues.
  M. Bloch, 617(TLS):11Feb83-136
Sperlich, N. and E.K. Guatemalan Back-
  strap Weaving.*
  R.M. Boyer, 292(JAF):Apr-Jun82-211
Sperling, D. and G. Mingay. Mrs. Hurst
  Dancing and Other Scenes from Regency
  Life 1812-1823.*
  P-L. Adams, 61:Feb83-105
  M.D. Kierstead, 442(NY):11Apr83-131
Sperlinger, D., ed. Animals in Research.
  M.A.F., 185:Jan83-439
Speroni, C. and C.L. Golino. Basic Ital-
  ian. (5th ed)
  J.B. Funigiello, 399(MLJ):Spring82-110
Sperry, R. Science and Moral Priority.
  P. Engel, 441:27Mar83-18
  K. Lennon, 617(TLS):22Jul83-784
Spevack, M. A Complete and Systematic
  Concordance to the Works of Shakespeare.
  (Vol 9)
  R. Harrier, 551(RenQ):Spring82-117
Sphrantzes, G. The Fall of the Byzantine
  Empire.* (M. Philippides, trans)
  V. Christides, 551(RenQ):Autumn82-458
Spicker, S.F., J.M. Healey, Jr. and H.T.
  Engelhardt, Jr., eds. The Law-Medicine
  Relation.
  J.C.M., 185:Oct82-218

Spieckermann, M-L. William Wotton's "Re-
  flections upon Ancient and Modern Learn-
  ing" im Kontext der englischen "Querelle
  des anciens et des modernes."
  H.J. Real, 566:Autumn82-6
Spiegelberg, H. The Context of the Phenom-
  enological Movement.
  W.R. McKenna, 319:Apr83-266
Spieler, S. Autonomie oder Reglementier-
  ung.
  S.D. Kassow, 550(RusR):Oct82-486
  J.J. Tomiak, 575(SEER):Oct82-628
Spielrein, S. Entre Freud et Jung.
  J. le Hardi, 450(NRF):Apr82-134
Spies, W., ed. Pablo Picasso: Sammlung
  Marina Picasso.
  L. Cooke, 59:Sep82-338
Spijkerman, A. The Coins of the Decapolis
  and Provincia Arabia. (M. Piccirillo,
  ed)
  G.W. Bowersock, 313:Vol72-197
Spilka, M. Virginia Woolf's Quarrel with
  Grieving.*
  M. Di Battista, 659(ConL):Spring83-90
  D. Doner, 395(MFS):Winter81/82-686
  D.L. Eder, 152(UDQ):Winter82-104
  J. Gindin, 301(JEGP):Jul82-455
  J. Naremore, 141:Winter82-83
  R.D. Newman, 577(SHR):Winter82-81
  S.L. Proudfit, 191(ELN):Sep82-90
Spiller, R.E. Late Harvest.*
  K. Lincoln, 651(WHR):Winter82-364
Spinelli, D.C. A Concordance to Mari-
  vaux's Comedies in Prose.*
  J. Whatley, 207(FR):Dec82-321
de Spinoza, B. Sämtliche Werke.* (Vols 1-
  7) (C. Gebhardt, ed)
  O. Pfersmann, 489(PJGG):Band89Heft1-
  202
de Spinoza, B. Tractatus politicus/Traité
  politique.* (P-F. Moreau, trans)
  R. Sasso, 192(EP):Apr-Jun82-249
Spinrad, N. The Void Captain's Tale.
  G. Jonas, 441:22May83-15
Spires, E. Globe.*
  D. Gioia, 249(HudR):Winter82/83-640
  D. St. John, 42(AR):Spring82-229
  P. Stitt, 219(GaR):Spring82-184
  639(VQR):Winter82-27
Spitz, L.W., ed. Humanismus und Reforma-
  tion als kulturelle Kräfte in der deut-
  schen Geschichte.
  E. Bernstein, 221(GQ):Nov82-592
Spitzer, L. Essays on Seventeenth-Century
  French Literature. (D. Bellos, ed and
  trans)
  A.J. Krailsheimer, 617(TLS):13May83-
  496
Spitzer, L. and J. Brody. Approches tex-
  tuelles des "Mémoires" de Saint-Simon.*
  B. Cap, 207(FR):Feb83-480
  M. Guggenheim, 210(FrF):Jan82-70
  P. Hourcade, 535(RHL):Mar-Apr82-293
Spivack, K. Swimmer in the Spreading Dawn.
  B.F. Lefcowitz, 363(LitR):Fall82-161
  J.D. McClatchy, 491:Sep82-351
Spivey, T.R. The Journey Beyond Tragedy.*
  P. Stevick, 395(MFS):Winter81/82-748
  295(JML):Dec82-339
Sponsler, L.A. Women in the Medieval
  Spanish Epic and Lyric Traditions.
  K. Kish, 241:May82-89

Stampfle, F. Giovanni Battista Piranesi, Drawings in the Pierpont Morgan Library.*
R. Middleton, 576:Dec82-333
Stampp, K.M. The Imperiled Union.
L.H. Johnson 3d, 579(SAQ):Winter82-105
C.P., 189(EA):Oct-Dec82-497
Stanford, W.B. Enemies of Poetry.*
R.A., 189(EA):Jul-Sep82-369
H. Adams, 191(ELN):Dec81-166
S. Trombley, 541(RES):Nov82-502
G.J. de Vries, 394:Vol35fasc3/4-447
Stang, S.J., ed. The Presence of Ford Madox Ford.
R. Brebach, 395(MFS):Winter81/82-698
J.A. Bryant, Jr., 569(SR):Winter82-100
S. Weintraub, 598(SoR):Winter83-233
Stange, K. Nocturnal Rhythms.*
R. Sward, 137:Winter82-103
Stankiewicz, W.J. Approaches to Democracy.*
R.J. Burkhardt, 518:Oct82-248
Stankiewicz, W.J., ed. The Tradition of Polish Ideals.
M.B. Biskupski, 104(CASS):Fall-Winter 82-559
Stanković, S. The End of the Tito Era.
D. Wilson, 575(SEER):Apr82-305
Stanley, J.L. The Sociology of Virtue.*
S.K., 185:Apr83-638
Stanley, L.C. The Foreign Critical Reputation of F. Scott Fitzgerald.*
R.S. Nelson, 395(MFS):Summer81-362
Stanley, T.A. Ōsugi Sakae, Anarchist in Taishō Japan.
S.S. Large, 407(MN):Winter82-541
Stanton, D.C. The Aristocrat as Art.*
P.R. Berk, 568(SCN):Fall82-37
É. Carassus, 535(RHL):Sep-Dec82-936
Stanton, R.J. Truman Capote.*
R. Asselineau, 189(EA):Jan-Mar82-113
Stanwood, P.G. - see Hooker, R.
Stanzel, F.K. Theorie des Erzählens.*
J.H. Petersen, 490:Band13Heft1/2-155
Stapleton, M. The Cambridge Guide to English Literature.
C. Rawson, 617(TLS):20May83-508
Starbuck, G. The Argot Merchant Disaster.
R.W. Flint, 441:13Feb83-15
Stark, F. Letters. (Vols 7 and 8) (C. Moorehead, ed) Rivers of Time.
P.L. Fermor, 617(TLS):29Apr83-434
Stark, F. The Valley of the Assassins and Other Persian Travels. The Southern Gates of Arabia.
G.J.S., 617(TLS):11Feb83-143
Stark, J.O. Pynchon's Fictions.*
B.L. Clark, 395(MFS):Summer81-379
D. Seed, 447(N&Q):Oct81-468
K. Tölölyan, 454:Winter83-165
42(AR):Winter82-120
Starn, R. Contrary Commonwealth.
J.K. Hyde, 617(TLS):30Dec83-1465
Starobinski, J. Montaigne en mouvement.
T. Cave, 617(TLS):3Jun83-579
Starobinski, J. Words upon Words.
P. Hamilton, 541(RES):Nov82-504
R. Kilpatrick, 402(MLR):Jan82-138
Starr, C.G. The Roman Empire: 27 B.C.-A.D. 476.*
442(NY):24Jan83-107
Starr, J.B. Continuing the Revolution.
B. Womack, 293(JASt):Aug82-825

Starr, P. The Social Transformation of American Medicine.
H.J. Geiger, 441:9Jan83-1
Starr, S.F. Red and Hot.
T. Bethell, 231:Apr83-74
E. Hobsbawm, 617(TLS):12Aug83-852
A. Lee, 441:17Apr83-1
"Statistical Abstract of the United States: 1982-83." (103d ed)
J. Jencks, 441:10Apr83-7
Statorius, P. Polonicae grammatices institutio. (R. Olesch, ed)
H. Leeming, 575(SEER):Oct82-613
Stauffer, G.B. The Organ Preludes of Johann Sebastian Bach.
R. Stinson, 414(MusQ):Jul82-419
Staum, M.S. Cabanis.
L.S. Greenbaum, 173(ECS):Spring83-336
Staves, S. Players' Sceptres.*
E. Mackenzie, 541(RES):Aug82-323
M.H. Wikander, 125:Spring82-304
Stavola, T.J. Scott Fitzgerald.*
J. Newman, 161(DUJ):Jun82-318
M. Hoffman, 367(L&P):Vol30No1-44
Stead, C. Divine Substance.*
S.M. Cohen, 449:May82-334
Stead, C.K. Geographies.
P. Bland, 364:Feb83-79
Stead, C.K. In the Glass Case.
P. Bland, 364:Jul82-95
Stearns, A. Batsford Book of Crochet.
C.J. Mouton, 614:Winter83-13
Stearns, M., Jr. Crimean Gothic.
E. Seebold, 260(IF):Band86-364
Stearns, M.L. Haida Culture in Custody.
G.W., 102(CanL):Summer82-173
Stebbins, S. Maxima in minimis.
C. Daxelmüller, 196:Band23Heft1/2-158
T.P. Saine, 133:Band15Heft3-267
Steedman, C. The Tidy House.
R. Dinnage, 617(TLS):29Apr83-425
Steegmuller, F. - see Flaubert, G.
Steel, D. Changes.
J. Bass, 441:11Sep83-20
Steel, G.H. Chronology and Time in "A la Recherche du temps perdu."*
M. Mein, 402(MLR):Jan82-216
Steel, R. Walter Lippmann and the American Century.*
G.S. Smith, 529(QQ):Spring82-2
Steele, E. Carlo Goldoni.
P. Rink, 97(CQ):Vol 11No2-339
Steele, J. Soviet Power.
M. Beissinger, 441:25Dec83-10
Steele, P. Jonathan Swift, Preacher and Jester.
W. Kinsley, 173(ECS):Summer82-442
van Steenberghen, F. Maître Siger de Brabant. Thomas Aquinas and Radical Aristotelianism.
E.P. Mahoney, 319:Oct82-429
Steensma, R.C. Dr. John Arbuthnot.*
S.S., 189(EA):Jul-Sep82-370
Steer, J. Alvise Vivarini.*
T. Puttfarken, 59:Dec82-497
A. Thomas, 324:Feb83-157
Steermann-Imre, G. Untersuchung des Königswahlmotivs in der indischen Märchenliteratur: Pañcadivyādhivāsa.
J.W. de Jong, 259(IIJ):Jan80-64
Stefanile, F., ed and trans. The Blue Moustache.
D. McDuff, 565:Vol23No1-59

Steltzer, U. Inuit.
  P-L. Adams, 61:Apr83-133
Stendhal. Chroniques 1825-1829. (H. Mar-
  tineau, ed)
  R. Denier, 605(SC):15Apr83-427
Stendhal. De l'Amour. (V. del Litto, ed)
  V. Brombert, 617(TLS):27May83-547
Stendhal. Oeuvres intimes. (Vol 1) (V.
  Del Litto, ed)
  K. Ringger, 605(SC):15Apr83-424
  E.J. Talbot, 446(NCFS):Fall-Winter
  82/83-154
Stendhal. Oeuvres intimes. (Vol 2) (V.
  Del Litto, ed)
  V. Brombert, 617(TLS):27May83-547
  K. Ringger, 605(SC):15Apr83-424
Stendhal. Le Rose et le Vert, Mina de
  Vanghel et autres nouvelles. (V. Del
  Litto, ed)
  G. Moinet, 605(SC):15Apr83-429
Stendhal. Vie de Henry Brulard.
  G. Strickland, 402(MLR):Apr82-454
"Stendhal e Milano."
  V. Brombert, 617(TLS):27May83-547
Stent, A. From Embargo to Ostpolitik.*
  R.P. Morgan, 617(TLS):1Apr83-334
Stenzel, H. Der historische Ort Baude-
  laires.
  R.A. York, 402(MLR):Apr82-455
Štěpán, J. Složite souvětí s řetězcovou
  závislostí.
  B. Lommatzsch, 682(ZPSK):Band34Heft5-
  650
Stephan, A. Die deutsche Exilliteratur
  1933-1945.*
  A. von Bormann, 406:Fall82-344
Stephan, H. "Lef" and the Left Front of
  the Arts.
  V.D. Barooshian, 550(RusR):Apr82-241
  J.L. Laychuk, 104(CASS):Fall-Winter82-
  556
Stephanopoulos, T.K. Umgestaltung des
  Mythos durch Euripides.
  D. Bain, 123:Vol32No2-136
  G. Ronnet, 555:Vol56fasc1-128
Stephen, A. The "Dreadnought" Hoax.
  M.F., 617(TLS):21Oct83-1171
Stephen, D. Bodach the Badger.
  D. Profumo, 617(TLS):2Sep83-940
Stephen, S. Waiting for the Stones.
  D. Barbour, 648(WCR):Jun82-33
  R.J. Merrett, 529(QQ):Winter82-893
  E. Trethewey, 198:Oct82-111
Stephens, A. In Plain Air.
  M. Kinzie, 29:Jul/Aug83-33
Stephens, A. Nacht, Mensch und Engel.
  B. Maché, 406:Summer82-217
Stephens, F.C. The Hartley Coleridge Let-
  ters.
  R. Woof, 402(MLR):Jan82-178
Stephens, J.C., ed. The Guardian.
  P. Rogers, 617(TLS):14Oct83-1115
Stephens, J.N. The Fall of the Florentine
  Republic 1512-1530.
  P. Partner, 617(TLS):11Nov83-1252
Stephens, J.R. The Censorship of English
  Drama, 1824-1901.*
  R. Jackson, 611(TN):Vol36No2-92
Stephenson, H. Claret and Chips.*
  S.H. Beer, 617(TLS):3Jun83-563
Stepto, R.B. From Behind the Veil.*
  K.E. Byerman, 594:Summer82-214
[continued]

[continuing]
  M. Fabre, 402(MLR):Apr82-414
  G. Moore, 447(N&Q):Oct81-470
Sterba, J.P. The Demands of Justice.*
  T.A. Shipka, 518:Jul82-181
Sterling, C. The Terror Network.*
  C.C. Joyner, 639(VQR):Winter82-176
Stern, F.C. F.O. Matthiessen.
  E. Current-Garcia, 577(SHR):Winter82-
  78
  B. Duffey, 27(AL):Oct82-461
  295(JML):Dec82-497
  639(VQR):Autumn82-117
Stern, G. The Red Coal.*
  L.M. Rosenberg, 584(SWR):Spring82-244
  D. St. John, 42(AR):Spring82-226
  S. Sandy, 491:Aug82-293
Stern, G. - see Neumann, A.
Stern, J. Lewis Carroll's Library.
  P. Heath, 191(ELN):Dec82-126
  W.J. Smith, 283:Spring82-60
  354:Dec82-468
Stern, J.P. A Study of Nietzsche.*
  E.L. Jurist, 222(GR):Winter82-43
Stern, M., ed. Expressionismus in der
  Schweiz.
  M. Adams, 67:Nov82-215
  W. Paulsen, 133:Band15Heft4-380
Stern, M., ed. Greek and Latin Authors on
  Jews and Judaism.
  M.D. Goodman, 123:Vol32No2-262
Stern, S. Women Composers.
  A.F.L.T., 412:Feb81-61
Sternbach, L. Bibliography on "dharma"
  and "artha" in Ancient and Mediaeval
  India.
  J.W. de Jong, 259(IIJ):Jan80-84
Sternbach, L. A Descriptive Catalogue of
  Poets Quoted in Sanskrit Anthologies and
  Inscriptions. (Vol 1)
  P.L. Bhargava, 318(JAOS):Oct-Dec81-477
Sternbach, L. Poésie sanskrite conservée
  dans les anthologies et les inscriptions.
  (Vol 1)
  F. Staal, 293(JASt):Feb82-269
Sternhell, Z. Ni Droite ni gauche.
  R.O. Paxton, 617(TLS):7Oct83-1078
Stettler, B. - see Tschudi, A.
Steube, A. Temporale Bedeutung im Deuts-
  chen.
  B. Comrie, 350:Sep83-696
Steuernagel, G.A. Political Philosophy as
  Therapy.
  H. Jansohn, 687:Jan-Mar81-157
Steven, R. Classes in Contemporary Japan.
  J.A.A. Stockwin, 617(TLS):25Nov83-1324
Stevens, D. - see Monteverdi, C.
Stevens, P. Coming Back.
  L. Welch, 198:Oct82-99
Stevens, R.P. Kant on Moral Practice.
  T. Auxter, 319:Oct83-573
Stevenson, A. Minute by Glass Minute.*
  C. Rumens, 617(TLS):6May83-469
Stevenson, J.V. Through the Kaleidoscope.
  J. Mellors, 362:30Jun83-28
Stevenson, R., ed. Time Remembered — Alan
  Bush.
  C. Rice, 607:Sep82-57
Stevenson, R.L. Doktoro Jekyll Kaj Sin-
  joro Hyde.
  M. Boulton, 447(N&Q):Aug81-382

Stevenson, R.L. An Old Song and Edifying
  Letters of the Rutherford Family.* (R.G.
  Swearingen, ed)
    J. Campbell, 617(TLS):11Feb83-140
Stevick, P. Alternative Pleasures.*
    C. Caramello, 395(MFS):Summer82-355
    R. Wasson, 141:Spring82-197
Stewart, A.M. - see Wedderburn, R.
Stewart, B. and M. Cutten. The Shayer
  Family of Painters.*
    T. Crombie, 39:Nov82-353
Stewart, F.M. Ellis Island.
    D. Cole, 441:6Mar83-28
Stewart, G. A New Mythos.*
    C.N. Davidson, 594:Summer82-213
Stewart, G. The Tenth Virgin.
    E. Jakab, 441:13Nov83-18
Stewart, G.M. The Literary Contributions
  of Christoph Daniel Ebeling.*
    G. Bersier, 406:Summer82-200
Stewart, J.B. The Partners.
    N. Johnston, 441:6Mar83-13
Stewart, J.I.M. A Villa in France.*
    442(NY):7Mar83-136
Stewart, M. Monkey-Shines.
    J.B., 231:Sep83-76
    N. Shack, 617(TLS):6May83-465
Stewart, M.A. - see Boyle, R.
Stewart, P. Cascades.
    F. Muratori, 448:Vol20No1-131
Stewart, S. Nonsense.*
    J.H. McDowell, 567:Vol39No1/2-167
Stewart, S. Yellow Stars and Ice.*
    J.D. McClatchy, 491:Sep82-352
    639(VQR):Winter82-25
Stewart, V.L., ed. Justice and Troubled
  Children around the World. (Vol 2)
    T.M.R., 185:Oct82-216
Stewart, W.K. Time Structure in Drama.*
    E. Waniek, 406:Summer82-202
Stich, K.P. - see Salverson, L.
Stichweh, K. and M.B. de Launay - see
  Löwith, K.
Stierlin, H. Art of the Aztecs.
    P-L. Adams, 61:Mar83-116
Stilgoe, J.R. Common Landscape of America,
  1580-1845.*
    N. Prendergast, 127:Fall82-265
Stilgoe, J.R. Metropolitan Corridor.
    D. Greenberg, 441:18Dec83-12
Stiller, J., ed. Schrifttum über Polen
  (ohne Posener Land), 1966-70.
    N. Davies, 575(SEER):Jul82-477
Stillinger, J. - see Keats, J.
Stillman, L.K. La Théâtralité dans
  l'oeuvre d'Alfred Jarry.*
    M. Kesting, 547(RF):Band94Heft1-131
Stillman, Y.K. Palestinian Costume and
  Jewelry.
    E. Whelan, 318(JAOS):Apr-Jun81-225
Stimm, H., ed. Zur Geschichte des gespro
  chenen Französisch und zur Sprachlenkung
  im Gegenwartsfranzösischen.
    M. Wandruszka, 547(RF):Band93Heft1/2-
    198
Stinchcombe, W. The XYZ Affair.
    G.L. Lint, 656(WMQ):Apr82-394
Stirling, J. and others. James Stirling:
  An Architectural Design Profile.
    A.L. Huxtable, 453(NYRB):8Dec83-29
Stirnimann, H. Die Pangwa von S.W.-
  Tansania.
    T.O. Beidelman, 69:Vol51No1-536

Stites, F.N. John Marshall.
    P. Finkelman, 432(NEQ):Jun82-301
    K. Newmyer, 656(WMQ):Apr82-392
Stivers, R. Evil in Modern Myth and
  Ritual.
    T.M.R., 185:Jul83-824
Stock, B. The Implications of Literacy.
    M. Chibnall, 617(TLS):22Jul83-789
Stock, I. Fiction as Wisdom.
    J.M. Mellard, 395(MFS):Summer81-391
Stock, R.D. The Holy and the Demonic from
  Sir Thomas Browne to William Blake.*
    G.S. Rousseau, 566:Spring83-140
Stockanes, A.E. Ladies Who Knit for a
  Living.*
    S. Disbrow, 502(PrS):Fall82-88
    639(VQR):Spring82-55
Stockenström, W. The Expedition to the
  Baobab Tree.
    D. Sweetman, 617(TLS):16Dec83-1413
Stockwell, A.J. British Policy and Malay
  Politics during the Malayan Union Experi-
  ment, 1942-1948.
    J. Butcher, 293(JASt):Feb82-432
Stockwood, M. Chanctonbury Ring.*
    G. Irvine, 617(TLS):14Jan83-32
Stoddard, P.H., D.C. Cuthell and M.W.
  Sullivan, eds. Change and the Muslim
  World.
    639(VQR):Summer82-90
Stoddart, D.R., ed. Geography, Ideology
  and Social Concern.
    J.L.G., 185:Jan83-434
Stoessl, F. C. Valerius Catullus.
    R.T. van der Paardt, 394:Vol35fasc3/4-
    404
Stojan, P.E. Bibliografio de Internacia
  Lingvo.
    G.F. Meier, 682(ZPSK):Band35Heft5-595
Stökl, G. Der russische Staat in Mittel-
  alter und früher Neuzeit. (M. Alexander,
  H. Hecker and M. Lammich, eds)
    M. Szeftel, 575(SEER):Jul82-457
Stoler, J.A. and R.D. Fulton. Henry Field-
  ing.*
    D.L. Vander Meulen, 173(ECS):Summer83-
    439
Stoljar, S. Moral and Legal Reasoning.*
    L.J. Cohen, 482(PhR):Jan82-141
Stolpe, B. Adjö till Änglar.
    S. Mitchell, 563(SS):Spring82-184
Stommel, H. and E. Volcano Weather.
    T. Ferris, 441:31Jul83-8
Stone, A. Now for the Turbulence.
    E. Jakab, 441:28Aug83-11
    442(NY):3Oct83-128
Stone, D.D. The Romantic Impulse in Vic-
  torian Fiction.*
    S. Hudson, 577(SHR):Winter82-74
    K. Kroeber, 191(ELN):Dec81-156
    S. Monod, 189(EA):Jul-Sep82-339
    S.M. Sperry, 637(VS):Winter82-252
Stone, G. and D. Lowenstein, eds. Lowen-
  stein.
    R.J. Margolis, 441:17Jul83-16
Stone, G.W., Jr., ed. The Stage and the
  Page.
    M.S. Auburn, 566:Spring83-138
    J. Gray, 405(MP):May83-426
Stone, G.W., Jr. and G.M. Kahrl. David
  Garrick.*
    M.E. Novak, 570(SQ):Summer82-251

345

Stone, H. Dickens and the Invisible
World.*
  R. Bennett, 541(RES):Aug82-357
  E.M. Eigner, 677(YES):Vol 12-317
  L. Haring, 292(JAF):Oct-Dec82-468
Stone, J. In All This Rain.
  J. Saunders, 565:Vol23No1-73
Stone, J.C. A Guide to the Administrative
Boundaries of Northern Rhodesia.
  A.H.M. Kirk-Greene, 69:Vol51No3-802
Stone, M.E. Scriptures, Sects and Visions.
  A. Phillips, 617(TLS):1Jul83-702
Stone, N. Europe Transformed 1878-1919.
  D. Johnson, 617(TLS):22Apr83-406
Stone, P.W.K. The Textual History of
"King Lear."*
  P. Edwards, 402(MLR):Jul82-694
Stone, R. Dog Soldiers.
  F.W. Shelton, 145(Crit):Vol24No2-74
Stone, R. A Flag for Sunrise.*
  B. Allen, 569(SR):Summer82-493
  W.H. Pritchard, 249(HudR):Spring82-159
  42(AR):Summer82-374
Stone, R.M. Let the Inside be Sweet.
  J.C. Dje Dje, 187:Sep83-544
Stone, S.H. French Hand Sewing.
  P. Bach, 614:Winter83-17
Stoneman, R., ed. Daphne into Laurel.
  R. Wells, 617(TLS):15Apr83-380
Stopp, H. Schreibsprachwandel.*
  D. Nerius, 682(ZPSK):Band34Heft2-251
Stopp, H. - see Michels, V.
Storey, D. A Prodigal Child.*
  V. Glendinning, 441:10Apr83-15
  J. Mellors, 364:Jul82-87
Storey, G. and K.J. Fielding - see Dickens,
C.
Storey, R.F. Pierrot.*
  W.D. Howarth, 208(FS):Jan82-114
Storing, H.J., with M. Dry. What the Anti-
Federalists Were For.*
  E.S., 185:Apr83-643
Storm, T. and E. Esmarch. Theodor Storm —
Ernst Esmarch, Briefwechsel.* (A.T.
Alt, ed)
  C.A. Bernd, 301(JEGP):Jan82-93
  H. Slessarev, 221(GQ):May82-430
Storm, T. and T. Fontane. Theodor Storm —
Theodor Fontane: Briefwechsel. (J.
Steiner, ed)
  H. Wetzel, 564:Nov82-299
Stössel, A. Nupe Kakanda Basa-Nge.
  A. Rubin, 2(AfrA):Nov81-22
Stouck, D. Willa Cather's Imagination.
  A. Collins, 178:Mar82-108
Stout, J. The Flight from Authority.
  J.D., 185:Apr83-629
Stout, W., with W. Service. The Dinosaurs.
  529(QQ):Autumn82-690
Stove, D. Popper and After.
  D. Papineau, 617(TLS):1Jul83-693
Stow, R. To the Islands. (rev)
  S. Thomas, 581:Sep82-288
Stowe, W.W. Balzac, James, and the Realis-
tic Novel.
  P. Kemp, 617(TLS):23Sep83-1025
Stowell, H.P. Literary Impressionism,
James and Chekhov.*
  A.W. Bellringer, 402(MLR):Apr82-429
  M.E. Grenander, 651(WHR):Spring82-83
  R.A. Hocks, 183(ESQ):Vol28No4-261
  V. Kalina-Levine, 149(CLS):Spring82-77

van Straaten, Z., ed. The Basic Concepts
of Philosophy.
  483:Jan82-147
van Straaten, Z., ed. Philosophical Sub-
jects.*
  C.J.F. Williams, 518:Jan82-33
Strachan, H. European Armies and the Con-
duct of War.
  G. Best, 617(TLS):11Nov83-1240
Strachey, B. Remarkable Relations.*
  P-L. Adams, 61:Jan83-103
  M. Moran, 556:Winter81/82-151
  442(NY):10Jan83-98
Strachey, B. and J. Samuels - see Beren-
son, M.
Strachey, J. and F. Partridge. Julia.
  L. Bennetts, 441:16Oct83-12
  R. Dinnage, 617(TLS):13May83-478
  V. Glendinning, 362:28Apr83-27
  442(NY):12Sep83-155
Strachey, L. The Shorter Strachey.* (M.
Holroyd and P. Levy, eds)
  G. Merle, 189(EA):Jan-Mar82-96
Straight, M. After Long Silence.
  P-L. Adams, 61:Apr83-132
  N. Annan, 617(TLS):11Mar83-227
  M. Jay, 362:10Mar83-22
  L.H. Lapham, 441:20Feb83-1
  H.R. Trevor-Roper, 453(NYRB):31Mar83-3
Straka, G. Les Sons et les mots.*
  W.A. Bennett, 208(FS):Jul82-373
Strand, B. Kvinnor och män i Gesta Dan-
orum.
  J.M. Jochens, 589:Jul82-667
Strand, M., ed. Art of the Real.
  J. Russell, 441:4Dec83-65
Strand, M. Selected Poems.*
  L. Bartlett, 50(ArQ):Autumn82-275
  D. Reiter, 152(UDQ):Spring81-123
Strandberg, V. A Faulkner Overview.
  A. Bleikasten, 395(MFS):Winter82/83-
675
  L.P. Simpson, 27(AL):Dec82-617
Strange, H. Rural Malay Women in Tradi-
tion and Transition.
  R. Provencher, 293(JASt):Aug82-892
Strange, K.H. Climbing Boys.
  N. Roberts, 617(TLS):28Jan83-77
Strässner, M. Analytisches Drama.
  E.M. Chick, 221(GQ):May82-395
Stratos, A.N. Byzantium in the Seventh
Century. (Vol 5)
  P. Charanis, 589:Oct82-913
Stratton, C. and M.M. Scott. The Art of
Sukhothai.
  60:Jul-Aug82-136
Stratton, J.L. Pioneer Women.*
  C.A. Martin, 651(WHR):Summer82-188
Straub, P. Floating Dragon.
  A. Bold, 617(TLS):11Mar83-249
  R. Freedman, 441:6Mar83-10
Straughan, R. I Ought to But.
  V.H., 185:Jul83-819
Straus, B. The Maladies of Marcel Proust.
  G. Brée, 651(WHR):Winter82-361
Strauss, D. Die erotische Dichtung von
Robert Burns.
  M.P. McDiarmid, 588(SSL):Vol 17-291
Strauss, J. Winter Driving.
  G. Catalano, 381:Oct81-349
  D. Haskell, 581:Sep82-348

Strauss, R. and H. von Hofmannsthal. The
Correspondence between Richard Strauss
and Hugo von Hofmannsthal. (H. Hammel-
mann and E. Osers, trans)
    J.B., 412:Feb81-60
Strauss, W.L. Albrecht Dürer: Woodcuts
and Woodblocks.
    J.C. Hutchison, 54:Jun82-332
    P. Strieder, 90:Oct82-638
Strauss, W.L. and M. van der Meulen, with
others. The Rembrandt Documents.
    B.P.J. Broos, 600:Vol 12No4-245
Strawson, P.F. The Bounds of Sense.
    K. Davies, 484(PPR):Mar83-401
Streeback, N. The Films of Burt Reynolds.
    M. Buckley, 200:Apr82-253
Streefland, P. The Sweepers of Slaughter-
house.
    R. Kurin, 293(JASt):Feb82-403
Street, D., G.T. Martin, Jr. and L.K.
Gordon. The Welfare Industry.
    C.N. Stone, 185:Apr83-588
Street, J.S. French Sacred Drama from
Bèze to Corneille.
    A. Levi, 617(TLS):14Oct83-1123
Strelcyn, S. Catalogue of Ethiopian Manu-
scripts in the British Library Acquired
since the Year 1877.
    E. Isaac, 318(JAOS):Jul-Sep81-414
Strelka, J. Esoterik bei Goethe.
    G. Brude-Firnau, 222(GR):Spring82-83
    K. Weissenberger, 133:Band15Heft4-371
Strelka, J. Methodologie der Literatur-
wissenschaft.*
    A.T. Alt, 406:Summer82-188
Strelka, J. Werk, Werkverständnis, Wer-
tung.
    D.E. Wellbery, 406:Summer82-190
Strelka, J. Stefan Zweig.
    H. Zohn, 680(ZDP):Band101Heft4-583
Strelsky, K. and C. Wolkonsky - see
Tolstoy, A.
"The Stretchford Chronicles."
    J. O'Sullivan, 31(ASch):Spring82-295
Strevens, P. Teaching English as an Inter-
national Language.
    P. Westney, 257(IRAL):Nov82-323
Strickland, G. Structuralism or Criti-
cism?*
    D. Boak, 67:May82-70
    A. Jefferson, 208(FS):Apr82-238
    G.C. Lepschy, 97(CQ):Vol 11No2-353
    R. Wellek, 402(MLR):Oct82-906
Strindberg, A. Apologia and Two Folk
Plays.
    M. Mattsson, 563(SS):Summer82-270
Stringer, D. Custom Tailoring.
    P. Bach, 614:Summer83-17
Strobach, H., ed. Deutsche Volksdichtung.
    R. Schenda, 196:Band23Heft1/2-161
Strobel, G. and W. Wolf - see Wagner, R.
Strobos, P. Treading Water.
    J.L. Halio, 598(SoR):Winter83-203
Strømberg, U. and J. Wiingaard, eds. Den
levende Ibsen.
    B.D. Knuttgen, 563(SS):Autumn82-310
Strong, R. Britannia Triumphans.
    G. Martin, 39:Nov82-347
Strong, R. The English Renaissance Minia-
ture.
    M. Jordan, 617(TLS):5Aug83-832

Strong, R. The Renaissance Garden in
England.
    T. Comito, 551(RenQ):Winter81-615
Stroop, J. The Stroop Report. (S. Milton,
ed and trans)
    G.J. Lerski, 497(PolR):Vol27No1/2-168
Stroop, J., ed. Toelichting bij de Taal-
atlas van Noord- en Zuid-Nederland II.
    U. Scheuermann, 685(ZDL):2/1982-241
Strosetzki, C. Konversation.*
    J-P. Chauveau, 535(RHL):Jan-Feb82-103
    J. Thomas, 547(RF):Band93Heft1/2-262
Stroud, B. Hume.
    D.C. Long, 449:Sep82-474
Stroud, M.D. - see Calderón de la Barca, P.
Stroud, R. The Axones and Kyrbeis of
Drakon and Solon.
    É. Will, 555:Vol55fasc2-333
Strouse, J. Alice James.*
    N. Baym, 301(JEGP):Jan82-144
    M. Bell, 473(PR):2/1982-309
    J. Lidoff, 184(EIC):Jul82-286
    J. Rivkin, 114(ChiR):Summer81-49
    M.C. Rodgers, 436(NewL):Fall82-98
Strout, C. The Veracious Imagination.
    L.B. Goodheart, 639(VQR):Winter82-165
    D.W. Noble, 106:Winter82-321
Strowski, F., F. Geblin and P. Villey -
see de Montaigne, M.
Strozzi, T. Die "Borsias" des Tito
Strozzi. (W. Ludwig, ed)
    G. Roellenbleck, 547(RF):Band93Heft1/2-
    222
Struss, L. Epische Idealität und histor-
ische Realität.
    L.S. Crist, 207(FR):Oct82-143
Struthers, J.R., ed. Before the Flood ...
    B. Cameron, 198:Jul82-89
Stubbings, F., ed. The Statutes of Sir
Walter Mildmay for Emmanuel College.
    J. Catto, 617(TLS):8Jul83-720
Stubblebine, J.H. Duccio di Buoninsegna
and His School.*
    F. Ames-Lewis, 161(DUJ):Dec81-111
    M. Boskovits, 54:Sep82-496
Stubbs, J.C. - see Fellini, F.
Stubbs, P. Women and Fiction.*
    P. Boumelha, 541(RES):Aug82-345
    J. Marcus, 395(MFS):Winter82/83-735
Stuckenschmidt, H.H. Ravel.
    A. Suied, 450(NRF):Jun82-144
Stuckey, W.J. The Pulitzer Prize Novels.
(2nd ed)
    G. Woodcock, 569(SR):Spring82-240
    295(JML):Dec82-327
Stucky, S. Lutoslawski and his Music.*
    H.R.N. Macdonald, 607:Dec82-37
"Studi di Filologia Romanza e Italiana
offerti a Gianfranco Folena dagli
allievi padovani."
    P. Baldan, 220(CCLI):Vol 159fasc508-
    604
"Studi Filosofici, I: Studi su Jean-
Jacques Rousseau."
    N. Suckling, 208(FS):Apr82-204
"Studien zur allgemeinen und vergleichen-
den Sprachwissenschaft."
    G.F. Meier, 682(ZPSK):Band34Heft5-643
"Studies in Attic Epigraphy, History, and
Topography presented to Eugene Vander-
pool."
    S. Van de Maele, 487:Winter82-373

"Studies in Eighteenth-Century Culture."*
(Vol 9) (R. Runte, ed)
  E. Caramaschi, 549(RLC):Oct-Dec82-506
  J.C. O'Neal, 546(RR):May82-389
"Studies in Slavic and General Linguis-
tics." (Vol 1) (A.A. Barentsen, B.M.
Groen and R. Sprenger, eds)
  J. Miller, 402(MLR):Jan82-254
Stueck, W.W., Jr. The Road to Confronta-
tion.
  J. Merrill, 293(JASt):Aug82-853
Sturluson, S. Snorre Sturlassons Edda.
(A. Grape, G. Kallstenius and O. Thorell,
eds)
  H. Fix, 684(ZDA):Band111Heft1-20
Sturmanis, D. and F. Candelaria - see
Lowther, P.
Stürmer, M. Handwerk und höfische Kultur.
  P. Thornton, 39:Aug82-128
Sturrock, J., ed. Structuralism and
Since.*
  J.M. Cocking, 208(FS):Oct82-502
St'urua, N. Sit'q'va rogorc enobrisi
erteuli.
  G.F. Meier, 682(ZPSK):Band35Heft6-739
Stutley, M. Ancient Indian Magic and Folk-
lore.
  H.R.E. Davidson, 203:Vol93No2-243
  H.B. Reynolds, 293(JASt):May82-626
Stutman, S. - see Wolfe, T. and A. Bern-
stein
Styan, J.L. Modern Drama in Theory and
Practice.
  295(JML):Dec82-394
Styron, W. Sophie's Choice.* (French
title: Le Choix de Sophie.)
  R. Asselineau, 189(EA):Oct-Dec82-492
Styron, W. This Quiet Dust and Other Writ-
ings.*
  P. Kemp, 617(TLS):10Jun83-592
Suard, F. Guillaume d'Orange.*
  B. Guidot, 547(RF):Band93Heft1/2-250
Suarès, J-C. The Indispensable Cat.
  P-L. Adams, 61:Aug83-101
  M. Levine, 441:11Dec83-35
Suares, J.C. Manhattan.
  G. Baker, 135:Jan82-12
Suárez, M.M., ed. La Lengua Sáliva.
  H.E. Manelis Klein, 269(IJAL):Oct82-
  484
Suárez-Torres, J.D. Contrastes culturales.
  D.A. Klein, 399(MLJ):Summer82-228
  H.D. Oberhelman, 238:Sep82-476
Subtelny, O. The Mazepists.
  N.V. Riasanovsky, 550(RusR):Jul82-324
Sucksmith, H.P. - see Dickens, C.
Suda, Z. Zealots and Rebels.
  V.V. Kusin, 575(SEER):Jan82-143
Sudnow, D. Pilgrim in the Microworld.
  H. Gardner, 441:27Mar83-12
Sugarman, R.I. Rancor against Time.
  R.A., 543:Sep81-170
  J.E. Llewelyn, 323:May82-203
Sugarman, S. Children's Early Thought.
  P.E. Bryant, 617(TLS):16Dec83-1407
Sugden, R. The Political Economy of Pub-
lic Choice.
  J.K., 185:Apr83-632
Sugg, J. - see Newman, J.H.
Sugg, R.S., Jr., ed. Walter Anderson's
Illustrations of Epic and Voyage.*
  P.E. Parnell, 568(SCN):Winter82-79
  G. Snyder, 585(SoQ):Fall81-92

Suhamy, H. Les Figures de style.
  P.R., 189(EA):Jul-Sep82-369
Suhrawardī, S.Y. The Mystical and Vision-
ary Treatises.
  J. Baldick, 617(TLS):4Mar83-221
Sukale, M., ed. Moderne Sprachphilosophie.
  G. Van der Elst, 685(ZDL):3/1981-372
Suknaski, A. In the Name of Narid. (D.
Cooley, ed)
  A.L. Amprimoz, 526:Winter82-81
  R. Attridge, 137:Aug82-32
  M.T. Lane, 198:Jan82-71
Suleiman, S.R. and I. Crosman, eds. The
Reader in the Text.*
  W.E. Cain, 580(SCR):Fall82-118
  T.M. Lentz, 480(P&R):Spring82-142
  D. Lodge, 494:Winter82-185
  R. Selden, 161(DUJ):Jun82-269
  J.J. Sosnoski, 395(MFS):Winter81/82-
  753
  M. Steig, 128(CE):Feb82-182
Sulivan, J. L'Écart et l'Alliance.
  P.J.T. Gormally, 207(FR):Apr83-795
  J. Grosjean, 450(NRF):May82-123
Sullerot, E. L'Amant.
  M. Maione, 207(FR):Feb83-516
Sullivan, A.T. Thomas-Robert Bugeaud.
  F.V. Parsons, 617(TLS):5Aug83-842
Sullivan, C., ed. Nude.
  A. Ross, 364:Jun82-99
Sullivan, F. Spy Wednesday's Kind.*
  D. Asper, 152(UDQ):Spring81-120
Sullivan, M. Symbols of Eternity.*
  W. Watson, 89(BJA):Spring82-178
Sullivan, M.C. A Middle High German Bene-
dictine Rule.
  C.V.J. Russ, 685(ZDL):3/1981-409
Sullivan, R., ed. Fine Lines.
  D. Grumbach, 219(GaR):Fall82-668
Sultana, D., ed. New Approaches to
Coleridge.
  R. Ashton, 661(WC):Summer82-120
Sumarah Adhyatman. Antique Ceramics Found
in Indonesia.
  J.W. Lydman, 60:Sep-Oct82-134
Sumarah Adhyatman, ed. The Adam Malik
Ceramic Collection.
  J.W. Lydman, 60:Sep-Oct82-134
Sumarokov, A.P. and N.M. Karamzin. Se-
lected Aesthetic Works of Sumarokov and
Karamzin. (H.M. Nebel, Jr., ed and
trans)
  L. O'Bell, 399(MLJ):Winter82-436
Summers, A. Throb.
  J. Maslin, 441:4Dec83-73
Summers, C.J. Christopher Isherwood.
  H.H. Watts, 395(MFS):Winter81/82-702
Summers, C.J. and T-L. Pebworth. Ben Jon-
son.*
  S. Pearl, 447(N&Q):Dec81-538
Summers, C.J. and T-L. Pebworth, eds.
"Too Rich to Clothe the Sunne."
  C.D. Lein, 405(MP):May83-413
  M.E. Rickey, 551(RenQ):Spring82-130
  J.R. Roberts, 568(SCN):Winter82-66
Summers, D. Michelangelo and the Language
of Art.*
  C. Hope, 59:Jun82-247
  D. Rosand, 551(RenQ):Autumn82-465
Summers, J.L. and R. Chartrand. Military
Uniforms in Canada 1665-1970.
  W.N., 102(CanL):Winter81-183

Swales, M. A Student's Guide to Thomas
   Mann.
     H. Siefken, 402(MLR):Jan82-244
Swan, C.T. The Old French Prose Legend of
   Saint Julian the Hospitaller.*
     A. Fontana, 547(RF):Band93Heft1/2-244
Swan, O.E. First Year Polish.
     C.Y. Bethin, 574(SEEJ):Fall82-377
     M.G. Levine, 399(MLJ):Winter82-438
Swanson, G. Swanson on Swanson.*
     W.D. Blackmon, 152(UDQ):Spring81-116
Swanton, M. - see "Beowulf"
Swantz, M-L. and H. Jerman, eds. Jipemoyo.
   (Vol 1)
     M. Etherton, 69:Vol51No4-863
Swarp, F.M. The Poet's Madness.
     U.H. Peters, 221(GQ):May82-446
Swearingen, R.G. The Prose Writings of
   Robert Louis Stevenson.*
     R. Kiely, 637(VS):Autumn81-87
Swearingen, R.G. - see Stevenson, R.L.
Swedenberg, H.T., Jr. and V.A. Dearing -
   see Dryden, J.
Swedenborg, E. "Jean Barois" de Roger
   Martin Du Gard.*
     F. Pellan, 395(MFS):Winter81/82-655
Sweeney, M. A Dream of Maps.*
     T.F. Merrill, 305(JIL):Sep82-3
Swellengrebel, J.L. In Leijdeckers voet-
   spoor. (Vols 1 and 2)
     J.M. Echols, 318(JAOS):Jul-Sep81-377
Swenson, A. and P-C. Chang. Architectural
   Education at IIT: 1938-1978.
     J. Winter, 46:Mar82-60
Swiatecka, M.J. The Idea of the Symbol.
     J.R. Barth, 591(SIR):Winter82-703
     J.L. Mahoney, 661(WC):Summer82-124
     D. Wesling, 506(PSt):Sep82-256
Swick, E., ed. Trio. Quartet.
     J. Schillinger, 399(MLJ):Summer82-221
Swidler, L. - see Küng, H. and E. Schille-
   beeckx
Swift, E. Principia Martindale.
     M. Harris, 441:13Mar83-11
     442(NY):6Jun83-142
Swift, G. Learning to Swim and Other
   Stories.*
     L. Jones, 364:Nov82-85
     J. Mellors, 362:6Jan83-24
Swift, G. Waterland.
     A. Hollinghurst, 617(TLS):7Oct83-1073
     D. May, 362:20Oct83-26
Swift, J. Jonathan Swift: The Complete
   Poems. (P. Rogers, ed)
     R. Wendorf, 617(TLS):22Jul83-787
Swinburne, R. The Existence of God.*
     S.R. Sutherland, 393(Mind):Apr82-310
Swinburne, R. Space and Time.
     T.E. Wilkerson, 483:Jul82-410
Swindell, L. Charles Boyer.
     G. Kaufman, 362:6Oct83-23
Swinden, P. Paul Scott — Images of India.*
     H.H. Watts, 395(MFS):Winter81/82-702
Syberberg, H-J. Hitler, a Film from Ger-
   many.
     J. Hoberman, 18:Nov82-76
Sykes, C.S. Black Sheep.*
     M. Bayles, 441:13Mar83-12
Sykes, S. Les Romans de Claude Simon.
     A.B. Duncan, 402(MLR):Jan82-219
Sylvere, A. Toinou.
     G.J. Barberet, 207(FR):Apr83-803

Syme, R. History in Ovid.
     L. de Blois, 394:Vol35fasc3/4-412
     J-M. Frécaut, 555:Vol56fasc2-350
Syme, R. Roman Papers I-II.* (E. Badian,
   ed)
     J. Beaujeau, 555:Vol56fasc1-171
Syme, R. Some Arval Brethren.
     C.P. Jones, 123:Vol32No1-70
Symons, J. Critical Observations.*
     G. Woodcock, 569(SR):Summer82-466
Symons, J. The Detling Murders.*
     R. Baxter, 364:Aug/Sep82-142
Symons, J. The Detling Secret.
     M. Cantwell, 441:20Mar83-12
     442(NY):7Feb83-123
Symons, J. The Great Detectives.*
     C. Osborn, 364:Apr/May82-140
Symons, J. The Name of Annabel Lee.
     T.J. Binyon, 617(TLS):18Nov83-1269
Symons, J. The Tell-Tale Heart.
     A. Hammond, 183(ESQ):Vol28No3-197
Symons, J. The Tigers of Subtopia.
     R. Baxter, 364:Aug/Sep82-142
     M. Cantwell, 441:20Mar83-12
     442(NY):14Feb83-120
Synes, E. Deutschunterricht und Ideologie.
     E. Schwarz, 133:Band15Heft3-253
Synge, J.M. The Collected Letters of John
   Millington Synge. (Vol 1) (A. Saddle-
   myer, ed)
     P. Craig, 617(TLS):2Sep83-937
Synge, J.M. Collected Works. (Vols 1-4)
   (R. Skelton, ed)
     J. Elsom, 617(TLS):25Mar83-295
Synge, J.M. Deirdre des douleurs [suivi
   de] Les Noces du ferblantier.
     J. Guérin, 450(NRF):Sep82-154
Synodinou, K. On the Concept of Slavery
   in Euripides.
     J. Hangard, 394:Vol35fasc1/2-164
"Synthesis." (Vol 7)
     M. Schmeling, 547(RF):Band94Heft2/3-
   290
Szabo, M.E. Algebra of Proofs.
     G.E. Minc, 316:Dec82-904
Szabolcsi, M. Attila József.
     P. Sherwood, 402(MLR):Jul82-767
Szanto, G. Not Working.
     N. Callendar, 441:6Feb83-20
Szarkowski, J. The Idea of Louis Sullivan.
     W. McQuade, 135:Mar82-152
Szarkowski, J. and M.M. Hambourg. The
   Work of Atget. (Vol 1)
     J. Guimond, 219(GaR):Winter82-894
     J. Stokes, 617(TLS):22Apr83-401
Szarkowski, J. and M.M. Hambourg. The
   Work of Atget.* (Vol 2)
     J. Stokes, 617(TLS):22Apr83-401
Szarkowski, J. and M.M. Hambourg. The
   Work of Atget. (Vol 3)
     A. Grundberg, 441:4Dec83-14
Szarota, E.M. Das Jesuitendrama im deut-
   schen Sprachgebiet.* (Vol 2, Pts 1 and
   2)
     R. Aulich, 133:Band15Heft4-356
Szechter, S. A Stolen Biography.
     G. Mikes, 617(TLS):27May83-538
Szilard, L. Leo Szilard: His Version of
   the Facts. (S.R. Weart and G.W. Szilard,
   eds)
     B.W. Sargent, 529(QQ):Spring82-174
Szirtes, G. Homage to Cheval.
     I. McMillan, 493:Jun82-71

Tarica, R. Imagery in the Novels of Andrě Malraux.
C. Moatti, 535(RHL):Sep-Dec82-969
Tarnawsky, G. and P. Kilina - see "Ukrainian Dumy"
Tarrant, N. Collecting Costume.
R. Shep, 614:Fall83-18
Tartakowsky, D. Les Premiers Communistes français.
E. Busi, 207(FR):Feb83-496
Tarvainen, K. Einführung in die Dependenzgrammatik.
M.A. Covington, 350:Mar83-227
Tashjian, J.H. - see Saroyan, W.
Tashjian, N. Armenian Lace. (J. and K. Kliot, eds)
R.L. Shep, 614:Summer83-15
Tasker, J. Savage Arena.
442(NY):13Jun83-132
Tasolambros, F.L. In Defence of Thucydides.*
D. Lateiner, 122:Jul82-264
Tassi, R. Sutherland: The Wartime Drawings.*
F. Spalding, 90:Jan82-46
Tasso, T. Creation of the World (Il Mondo Creato). (J. Tusiani, trans)
R. Flannagan, 391:Dec82-101
Tasso, T. Godfrey of Bulloigne. (K.M. Lea and T.M. Gang, eds)
H.D. Brumble 3d, 568(SCN):Fall82-40
D. Moore, 481(PQ):Fall82-494
Tatar, M.M. Spellbound.*
A.J. Niesz, 406:Spring82-83
Tatarkiewicz, W. A History of Six Ideas.*
N. Wolterstorff, 484(PPR):Mar83-407
Tate, A. The Poetry Reviews of Allen Tate 1924-1944. (A. Brown and F.N. Cheney, eds)
L. Mackinnon, 617(TLS):6May83-448
Tate, C., ed. Black Women Writers at Work.
A. Tyler, 441:29May83-6
Tate, J. Constant Defender.
A. Corn, 441:4Sep83-8
Tate, T.W. and D.L. Ammerman, eds. The Chesapeake in the Seventeenth Century.*
R.R. Beeman, 658:Spring82-86
Tatlow, A. The Mask of Evil.*
I. Solbrig, 406:Summer82-224
Tatum, J. Apuleius and The Golden Ass.*
C. Moussy, 555:Vol56fasc1-166
Tatum, S. Inventing Billy the Kid.
L. Milazzo, 584(SWR):Autumn82-vi
Taube, M. Tibetische Handschriften und Blockdrucke.
J.W. de Jong, 259(IIJ):Jul80-263
Taubert, G. Rechtschaffener Tantzmeister oder gründliche Erklärung der Frantzösischen Tantz-Kunst.
W. Dimter, 684(ZDA):Band111Heft2-78
Tausky, T.E. Sara Jeannette Duncan.
C. Gerson, 102(CanL):Spring82-113
C. Thomas, 178:Mar82-103
F. Zichy, 298:Summer82-143
Tausky, T.E. - see Duncan, S.J.
Tavris, C. Anger.
E. First, 441:30Jan83-7
Tawa, N. A Sound of Strangers.
E.J.P. O'Connor, 187:May83-380
Tayler, E.W. Milton's Poetry.*
M. Evans, 541(RES):Aug82-318

Taylor, A. Caroline Minuscule.*
N. Callendar, 441:23Oct83-38
Taylor, A. Magic and English Romanticism.*
D. Degrois, 189(EA):Apr-Jun82-219
S.M. Tave, 402(MLR):Jan82-174
Taylor, A. Notes and Tones.
J. Stokes, 617(TLS):12Aug83-852
Taylor, A.B. - see Lindsay, A.
Taylor, A.J.P. A Personal History.
J. Gross, 441:25Sep83-7
P. Johnson, 362:26May83-18
J. Keegan, 453(NYRB):13Oct83-5
R. Skidelsky, 617(TLS):27May83-540
Taylor, B. Eve and the New Jerusalem.
J.A. Banks, 617(TLS):25Mar83-311
Taylor, B. The Green Avenue.*
J.C. Beckett, 677(YES):Vol 12-337
P. McIvor, 174(Éire):Summer82-134
R.C. Petersen, 177(ELT):Vol25No1-50
Taylor, B. and E. Brewer. The Return of King Arthur.
T.A. Shippey, 617(TLS):4Nov83-1208
Taylor, C. Hegel.
B. Dinkel, 489(PJGG):Band89Heft1-173
Taylor, C. Village and Farmstead.
M.W. Beresford, 617(TLS):21Oct83-1166
Taylor, D. Hardy's Poetry, 1860-1928.*
M. Bird, 175:Autumn82-262
K. Brady, 637(VS):Spring82-390
W.E. Buckler, 191(ELN):Sep82-87
H.L. Weatherby, 569(SR):Spring82-313
Taylor, D. Mother Love.
G. Clifford, 617(TLS):24Jun83-660
E. Jakab, 441:13Nov83-16
Taylor, D.S. Thomas Chatterton's Art.*
D.W. Lindsay, 677(YES):Vol 12-287
Taylor, E. In a Summer Season. The Soul of Kindness.
J. Grant, 617(TLS):1Jul83-711
Taylor, E. The Unpublished Writings of Edward Taylor. (T.M. and V.L. Davis, eds)
J. Gatta, 568(SCN):Fall82-51
F. Murphy, 432(NEQ):Mar82-120
R. Pooley, 402(MLR):Oct82-923
Taylor, E.R. Marcel Proust and His Contexts.*
J. Murray, 207(FR):May83-953
Taylor, F. - see Goebbels, J.
Taylor, F. - see James, M.R.
Taylor, G. - see Shakespeare, W.
Taylor, G. - see under Wells, S.
Taylor, G.R. The Great Evolution Mystery.
M. Bayles, 441:15May83-18
J. Durant, 617(TLS):6May83-466
Taylor, H.A. The Arrangement and Description of Archival Materials.
M. Cook, 325:Oct82-126
Taylor, I.C. Das Bild der Witwe in der deutschen Literatur.
H. Wilfert, 221(GQ):May82-396
Taylor, J. and J. Andrews. John Andrews.
R. Giurgola, 505:Jun82-119
Taylor, J.C., J. Dillenberger and R. Murray. Perceptions and Evocations.
B. Groseclose, 658:Spring82-87
Taylor, J.G. From Modernization to Modes of Production.
A.L. Stinchcombe, 185:Oct82-114
Taylor, J.R. Strangers in Paradise.
S. Kauffmann, 441:10Jul83-12
S.S. Prawer, 617(TLS):11Mar83-233

Taylor, L. and I. Maar. The American Cowboy.
　　N. Lemann, 441:11Dec83-34
Taylor, L.A. Only Half a Hoax.
　　N. Callendar, 441:18Dec83-29
Taylor, M. Community, Anarchy and Liberty.
　　J. Waldron, 617(TLS):4Mar83-218
Taylor, M. Shakespeare's Darker Purpose.
　　S. Wells, 617(TLS):2Sep83-935
Taylor, M.C. Journeys to Selfhood.*
　　J.W. Elrod, 319:Jan83-113
Taylor, R. Art, an Enemy of the People.
　　C. Keil, 187:May83-366
Taylor, R. Beyond Art.*
　　A.J. Skillen, 89(BJA):Spring82-174
Taylor, R. The Court and Kitchen of Mrs. Elizabeth commonly called Joan Cromwell. (D. Clinton and M. Liquorice, eds)
　　C. Driver, 617(TLS):23Dec83-1442
Taylor, R. Literature and Society in Germany 1918-1945.
　　H.J. Hoffmann and B.A. Beckett-Hoffman, 593:Fall82-276
　　G.B. Pickar, 395(MFS):Summer82-326
Taylor, R. Robert Schumann.*
　　J. Chernaik, 364:Mar83-116
Taylor, R. Workers and the New Depression.
　　C. Crouch, 617(TLS):25Nov83-1328
Taylor, R.H. The Neglected Hardy.
　　M. Casserley, 617(TLS):4Feb83-112
Taylor, R.J. Colonial Connecticut.*
　　F. Shuffelton, 173(ECS):Summer83-415
Taylor, S. Germany 1918-1933.
　　J.D. Noakes, 617(TLS):17Jun83-640
Taylor, W. Equational Logic.
　　H. Werner, 316:Jun82-450
Taylor, W. Faulkner's Search for a South.
　　L. Mackinnon, 617(TLS):3Jun83-568
Taylor-Martin, P. John Betjeman.
　　C. Raine, 617(TLS):11Mar83-235
Tchaikovsky, P.I. Piotr Ilich Tchaikovsky: Letters to his Family. (P.M. Young, ed)
　　D. Brown, 415:Jan82-32
　　J. Warrack, 410(M&L):Jan/Apr82-138
Tchemerzine, A. Bibliographie d'éditions originales et rares d'auteurs français des XVe, XVIe, XVIIe et XVIIIe siècles. (with annotations by L. Scheler)
　　G. Barber, 617(TLS):15Jul83-763
"The Teaching of Vimalakīrti." (É. Lamotte, trans)
　　J.W. de Jong, 259(IIJ):Jul80-254
Teague, E.H. Henry Moore.
　　90:Sep82-591
Teahan, T., with J. Dunson. The Road to Glountane.
　　L.E. McCullough, 292(JAF):Apr-Jun82-249
"Techniques of the World's Great Painters."
　　J. Burr, 39:Aug82-128
Tedeschi, R. - see Gide, A. and D. Bussy
Tegethoff, W. Mies van der Rohe.
　　W. Pehnt, 471:Oct/Nov/Dec82-361
Teichmann, H. Fonda: My Life.
　　P. Anderson, 200:Jan82-60
Teichner, W. Kants Transzendentalphilosophie.
　　H. Jansohn, 342:Band73Heft2-238
Tekinay, A. Materialen zum vergleichenden Studium von Erzählmotiven in der deutschen Dichtung des Mittelalters und den
[continued]

[continuing]
Literaturen des Orients.
　　E.A. Metzger, 221(GQ):Mar82-230
Telfer, E. Happiness.*
　　J. Annas, 393(Mind):Apr82-287
　　M.B. Green, 185:Jan83-395
di Tella, G. Argentina Under Perón, 1973-76.
　　H.S. Ferns, 617(TLS):21Oct83-1156
Telle, É-V. - see Le Chevalier de Berquin
Teloh, H. The Development of Plato's Metaphysics.
　　K. Dorter, 154:Dec82-775
　　K.M. Sayre, 319:Jul83-391
Temperley, N., ed. The Athlone History of Music in Britain.* (Vol 5)
　　A. Jacobs, 415:Aug82-547
Tempesti, F. - see Collodi, C.
Temple, N. John Nash and the Village Picturesque.*
　　K. Woodbridge, 39:Feb82-135
Temporini, H. Die Frauen am Hofe Trajans.
　　A. Chastagnol, 555:Vol55fasc2-386
Ten, C.L. Mill on Liberty.
　　R.J. Arneson, 185:Jan83-399
　　E. Rapaport, 518:Jul82-161
"The Ten Thousand Leaves."* (Vol 1) (I.H. Levy, trans)
　　T.B. Hare, 293(JASt):May82-597
　　Saeki Shōichi, 285(JapQ):Jan-Mar82-122
Tengström, E. A Study of Juvenal's Tenth Satire.*
　　J. Hellegouarc'h, 555:Vol56fasc2-352
Tennant, E. Hotel De Dream.
　　P. Craig, 617(TLS):1Jul83-711
Tennant, E. Woman Beware Woman.
　　J. Motion, 617(TLS):2Dec83-1345
Tennant, R. Joseph Conrad.*
　　T.K. Bender, 577(SHR):Fall82-370
　　J. Halperin, 395(MFS):Summer82-260
　　295(JML):Dec82-426
Tennenbaum, S. Yesterday's Streets.*
　　639(VQR):Spring82-54
Tennyson, A. The Letters of Alfred, Lord Tennyson.* (Vol 1) (C.Y. Lang and E.F. Shannon, Jr., eds)
　　R.D. Altick, 639(VQR):Summer82-507
　　L.K. Hughes, 636(VP):Summer82-199
Tennyson, B.D. Canadian Relations with South Africa.
　　D. Middlemiss, 150(DR):Winter82/83-717
Tennyson, G.B. Victorian Devotional Poetry.*
　　R. Beum, 569(SR):Winter82-i
　　C. Dawson, 301(JEGP):Apr82-278
　　J.R. Griffin, 134(CP):Fall82-114
　　S.I. Gurney, 396(ModA):Summer/Fall82-445
　　W.S. Johnson, 405(MP):Aug82-101
　　G.P. Landow, 191(ELN):Sep82-84
　　W.D. Shaw, 637(VS):Autumn81-84
　　R.H. Tener, 49:Jul82-86
"Lady Tennyson's Journal."* (J.O. Hoge, ed)
　　R.D. Altick, 639(VQR):Summer82-507
　　H. Bryant, 580(SCR):Fall82-132
Tenorio, H.A. - see under Alvarado Tenorio, H.
Teodorsson, S-T. The Phonology of Attic in the Hellenistic Period.
　　J. Irigoin, 555:Vol55fasc1-159
　　W.F. Wyatt, Jr., 122:Jan82-73

Theroux, P. The Kingdom by the Sea.
  J. Campbell, 617(TLS):28Oct83-1192
  W. Sheed, 61:Oct83-104
  K. Waterhouse, 362:6Oct83-24
  A. Waugh, 441:23Oct83-9
Theroux, P. The London Embassy.*
  J. Moynahan, 441:20Mar83-1
  R. Towers, 453(NYRB):2Jun83-42
Theroux, P. The Mosquito Coast.*
  W.H. Pritchard, 249(HudR):Spring82-159
Thesen, S. Artemis Hates Romance.*
  D. Barbour, 648(WCR):Oct82-37
Thesiger, W. The Marsh Arabs.
  G.S., 617(TLS):24Jun83-683
Thesing, W.B. The London Muse.
  H.B. Bryant, 580(SCR):Spring83-128
  F. Schwarzbach, 617(TLS):14Jan83-29
Thévenin, A. Enseigner les différences.
  J-P. Berwald, 399(MLJ):Summer82-204
Thew, H. The Public Enemy. (H. Cohen, ed)
  J. Gallagher, 200:Mar82-189
Thibault, P., ed. Le français parlé.*
  B. Laks, 355(LSoc):Dec82-463
Thieberger, R., ed. Hermann Broch und
  seine Zeit.
  E. Schlant, 221(GQ):May82-447
Thiele, D. Bertolt Brecht.
  D. Wöhrle, 602:Vol 13No1-198
Thiele, R. Satanismus als Zeitkritik bei
  Joris-Karl Huysmans.
  R. Lloyd, 208(FS):Apr82-220
Thieme, U. Studien zum Jugendwerk Arnold
  Schönbergs.
  A. Clayton, 410(M&L):Jul/Oct82-320
Thies, W.J. When Governments Collide.
  G.M. Kahin, 293(JASt):May82-640
Thill, A. "Alter ab illo."
  C. Moussy, 555:Vol56fasc1-162
Thion, S. - see Mus, P.
Thireau, J-L. Charles Dumoulin (1500-
  1566).
  D.R. Kelley, 551(RenQ):Summer81-236
"Thirty Minor Upanishads, including the
  Yoga Upanishads." (K.N. Aiyar, trans)
  A. Wayman, 485(PE&W):Jul82-360
This, B. La Requête des Enfants à Naître.
  R. Porter, 617(TLS):29Apr83-436
Thiselton, A.C. The Two Horizons.
  R.E.P., 543:Sep81-172
Thom, P. The Syllogism.
  P.M. Simons, 479(PhQ):Apr82-175
Thom, R. Modèles mathématiques de la mor-
  phogenèse.
  J. Largeault, 542:Jul-Sep82-556
Thomaj, J., X. Lloshi and M. Samara, eds.
  Fjalor i gjuhës së sotme shqipe.
  O. Buchholz and W. Fiedler, 682(ZPSK):
  Band34Heft6-756
Thomas, A. Latakia.
  D. Cooper-Clark, 102(CanL).Winter81-
  104
Thomas, A. Real Mothers.
  R. Lecker, 102(CanL):Autumn82-141
  A. Todkill, 526:Autumn82-87
Thomas, A. Songs and Stories from Deep
  Cove, Cape Breton. (R. MacEachern, ed)
  D. Kodish, 292(JAF):Apr-Jun82-237
Thomas, A.R. Areal Analysis of Dialect
  Data by Computer, a Welsh Example.
  R.A. Fowkes, 660(Word):Aug81-173
  C.L. Houck, 35(AS):Summer82-143
Thomas, B. Golden Boy.
  J. Marsh, 617(TLS):18Nov83-1291

Thomas, C. Christianity in Roman Britain
  to AD 500.
  J.F. Kelly, 589:Oct82-942
Thomas, C. L'Ashram de l'Amour.
  P. Gaeffke, 293(JASt):May82-626
Thomas, C. Quilting Teachers Handbook.
  M. Cowan, 614:Fall83-23
Thomas, C. and J. Lennox. William Arthur
  Deacon.
  M.A. Peterman, 298:Fall82-146
Thomas, D. Robert Browning.
  P-L. Adams, 61:Mar83-116
  D.J.R. Bruckner, 441:13Mar83-9
  I. Ehrenpreis, 453(NYRB):29Sep83-41
  W. Scammell, 364:Feb83-98
Thomas, D. Naturalism and Social Science.*
  T. Airaksinen, 486:Mar82-144
Thomas, D.M. Ararat.
  R.M. Adams, 453(NYRB):16Jun83-34
  M. Amis, 61:Apr83-124
  D. Johnson, 441:27Mar83-7
  A. Ryan, 362:3Mar83-23
  G. Strawson, 617(TLS):25Feb83-175
Thomas, D.M. Birthstone.
  P. Craig, 617(TLS):21Jan83-69
Thomas, D.M. Dreaming in Bronze.*
  H. Lomas, 364:Jul82-66
  P. Swinden, 148:Winter82-74
Thomas, D.M. Selected Poems.
  N. Corcoran, 617(TLS):29Jul83-813
Thomas, D.M. The White Hotel.*
  F. Conroy, 473(PR):1/1982-142
  M. Hollington, 381:Sep82-363
  P. Lewis, 565:Vol23No1-51
  W.H. Pritchard, 249(HudR):Spring82-159
  W. Sullivan, 569(SR):Summer82-484
  P. Swinden, 148:Winter82-74
Thomas, E. The Letters of Edward Thomas
  to Jesse Berridge. (A. Berridge, ed)
  D. Hibberd, 617(TLS):4Nov83-1204
Thomas, E. Louise Michel.
  G.W., 102(CanL):Winter81-184
Thomas, F. and O. Johnston. Disney Anima-
  tion.
  N. Roddick, 617(TLS):25Feb83-178
  M. Vaughan, 18:Jan/Feb82-68
Thomas, G. and M. Morgan-Witts. Pontiff.
  I. Vinogradoff, 617(TLS):16Dec83-1406
Thomas, G.S. Trees in the Landscape.
  S. Leathart, 617(TLS):16Sep83-998
Thomas, G.S. - see Jekyll, G. and E. Maw-
  ley
Thomas, H. Joueur surpris.
  F.C. St. Aubyn, 207(FR):May83-985
Thomas, J.B. Shop Boy.
  P. Willmott, 617(TLS):27May83-540
Thomas, J.D. The epistrategos in Ptole-
  maic and Roman Egypt. (Pt 1)
  R.P. Salomons, 394:Vol135fasc3/4-438
Thomas, J.E. Musings on the "Meno."
  C.J. McKnight, 518:Jan82-12
Thomas, J.L. Alternative America.
  A. Kazin, 441:24Apr83-9
  442(NY):25Apr83-155
Thomas, J.M.C., L. Bouquiaux and F.
  Cloarec-Heiss. Initiation à la phoné-
  tique.
  G.F. Meier, 682(ZPSK):Band35Heft5-593
Thomas, J.W. and C. Dussère - see "The
  Legend of Duke Ernst"

Thomas, K. Man and the Natural World.
　H. Erskine-Hill, 617(TLS):20May83-511
　S. Hampshire, 453(NYRB):2Jun83-17
　N. Perrin, 441:24Apr83-8
　A. Ryan, 362:14Apr83-29
　442(NY):23May83-121
Thomas, L. Late Night Thoughts on Listen-
　ing to Mahler's Ninth Symphony.
　442(NY):26Dec83-73
Thomas, L. The Youngest Science.
　J. Bernstein, 442(NY):14Feb83-109
　W. Gaylin, 441:27Feb83-3
　S.J. Gould, 453(NYRB):21Jul83-12
Thomas, L.L. Ordnung und Wert der Unord-
　nung bei Bertolt Brecht.
　J.K. Lyon, 221(GQ):Mar82-282
Thomas, M., ed. The BBC Guide to Parlia-
　ment, 1983.
　G. Kaufman, 362:27Oct83-31
Thomas, M.C. The Making of a Feminist.
　(M.H. Dobkin, ed)
　M. Moran, 556:Winter81/82-155
Thomas, P. Robert Kroetsch.*
　R. Brown, 627(UTQ):Summer82-462
　J. Kertzer, 198:Apr82-116
Thomas, P. Karl Marx and the Anarchists.*
　W.J.D., 543:Dec81-415
Thomas, R.S. Later Poems, 1972-1982.
　D. Davis, 362:28Jul83-23
　G. Lindop, 617(TLS):16Dec83-1411
Thomas, W. The Philosophical Radicals.*
　D. Roberts, 637(VS):Autumn81-91
Thomas, W.K. The Fizz Inside.*
　R. Hatch, 102(CanL):Summer82-157
Thomason, R.H. - see Montague, R.
Thomke, H. - see Wetter, J.
Thompson, C.P. The Poet and the Mystic.
　D.H. Darst, 546(RR):Nov82-528
Thompson, C.R. - see Erasmus
Thompson, D., ed. Change and Tradition in
　Rural England.*
　A.B. Ferguson, 579(SAQ):Winter82-120
Thompson, D. Raphael.
　D. Rosand, 617(TLS):21Oct83-1147
Thompson, E.P. Beyond the Cold War.*
　M. Howard, 231:Feb83-69
Thompson, F.M.L., ed. Horses in European
　Economic History.
　J. Clutton-Brock, 617(TLS):16Dec83-
　1410
Thompson, G. Nobody Cared for Kate.
　N. Callendar, 441:4Sep83-20
　442(NY):12Sep83-159
Thompson, G.R. and V.L. Lokke, eds.
　Ruined Eden of the Present.
　R. Lehan, 445(NCF):Jun82-125
　C.N. Watson, Jr., 495(PoeS):Jun82-22
Thompson, H.W. Body, Boots and Britches.
　S.J. Bronner, 292(JAF):Jan-Mar82-98
Thompson, J.B. - see Ricoeur, P.
Thompson, J.C., P.W. Stanley and J.C.
　Perry. Sentimental Imperialists.
　O. Schell, 293(JASt):Feb82-307
Thompson, J.G. A Reader's Guide to Fifty
　British Plays: 1660-1900.
　566:Spring83-144
Thompson, J.K. Policies and Programmes
　for Disabled People in the Commonwealth.
　B. Windeyer, 324:Nov83-777
Thompson, J.M. Revolutionary Russia, 1917.
　R.G. Suny, 550(RusR):Jul82-331
　639(VQR):Spring82-43

Thompson, J.O. Echo and Montana.
　P. Mitcham, 102(CanL):Spring82-92
Thompson, K. Shacking Up.*
　J. Mills, 198:Apr82-95
Thompson, K.W. Winston Churchill's World
　View.
　N. Stone, 453(NYRB):10Nov83-43
Thompson, K.W. Cold War Theories.* (Vol
　1)
　639(VQR):Spring82-46
Thompson, R. Unfit for Modest Ears.*
　D.C. Kay, 447(N&Q):Jun81-265
Thompson, S.O. American Book Design and
　William Morris.
　J. Roberts, 354:Dec82-459
Thompson, V. and R. Adloff. Conflict in
　Chad.*
　D.B.C. O'Brien, 69:Vol52No4-97
Thomsen, C.W. Das Groteske und die
　Englische Literatur.
　A. Clayborough, 179(ES):Aug82-367
Thomsen, R. King Servius Tullius.*
　P.G. Walsh, 313:Vol72-175
Thomson, D. Dandiprat's Days.
　J. Mellors, 362:13Oct83-31
　J.K.L. Walker, 617(TLS):21Oct83-1157
Thomson, D. A Descriptive Catalogue of
　Middle English Grammatical Texts.
　O.S. Pickering, 72:Band218Heft2-418
Thomson, D. In Camden Town.
　S. Jenkins, 362:20Oct83-29
　J.K.L. Walker, 617(TLS):21Oct83-1157
Thomson, D., with M. McGusty - see Smith,
　E.
Thomson, D.F.S. - see "Catullus"
Thomson, G., ed. Identities.
　D. Dunn, 493:Dec81-55
　C. Lamont, 571(ScLJ):Spring82-25
Thomson, G. The Museum Environment.
　H. Lank, 90:May82-313
Thomson, G., ed. National Gallery Techni-
　cal Bulletin. (Vol 4)
　H. Lank, 90:Jan82-36
Thomson, G. A Spurious Grace.
　C. Milton, 571(ScLJ):Spring82-19
Thomson, G.L. Scribe.
　N. Barker, 78(BC):Winter82-513
Thomson, J., ed. New Zealand Literature
　to 1977.*
　S.F.D. Hughes, 395(MFS):Spring81-173
Thomson, J. The Seasons. (J. Sambrook,
　ed)
　B.B. Redford, 405(MP):Nov82-193
Thomson, J. To Make a Killing.*
　M. Laski, 362:20Jan83-23
Thomson, J.A.F. Popes and Princes, 1417-
　1517.
　D.S. Chambers, 551(RenQ):Autumn82-450
　D. Williman, 589:Jan82-178
Thomson, J.A.F. The Transformation of
　Medieval England 1370-1529.
　J.R. Maddicott, 617(TLS):12Aug83-865
Thomson, J.C., Jr., P.W. Stanley and J.C.
　Perry. Sentimental Imperialists.
　639(VQR):Winter82-20
Thomson, J.J. Acts and Other Events.*
　M. Bratman, 449:Sep82-467
Thomson, J.K.J. Clermont-de-Lodève 1633-
　1789.
　D. Parker, 617(TLS):14Jan83-42
Thomson, P. Shakespeare's Theatre.
　S. Wells, 617(TLS):2Sep83-935

Thomson, R.M. Manuscripts from St. Albans
Abbey, 1066-1235.
R. McKitterick, 617(TLS):15Jul83-763
Thorburn, D. and H. Eiland, eds. John
Updike.*
W.T.S., 395(MFS):Summer81-374
Thoreau, H.D. Journal. (Vol 1) (J.C.
Broderick, general ed)
P.F. Gura, 432(NEQ):Sep82-448
G. Hendrick, 301(JEGP):Oct82-594
529(QQ):Summer82-454
Thoreau, H.D. Journal 1837-1861. (K.
White, ed; R. Michaud and S. David,
trans)
C. Jordis, 450(NRF):Sep82-150
Thoreau, H.D. Ktaadn.
L. Lane, Jr., 506(PSt):May82-174
Thornberry, R.S. André Malraux et
l'Espagne.
H-G. Funke, 72:Band218Heft1-227
Thornburg, N. Dreamland.
P. Van Rjndt, 441:25Sep83-20
Thorndike, J.J., Jr., ed. Three Centuries
of Notable American Architects.
J.F. O'Gorman, 576:Mar82-68
Thornton, E.M. Freud and Cocaine.
A. Storr, 617(TLS):18Nov83-1266
Thornton, R. Temple of Flora.* (R. King,
ed)
H. Brooke, 39:Feb82-133
Thornton, R.D. William Maxwell to Robert
Burns.
A. Noble, 571(ScLJ):Winter82-68
Thornton, R.K.R. - see Gurney, I.
Thornton, R.K.R. and T.G.S. Cain - see
Hilliard, N.
"The Thornton Manuscript (Lincoln Cathe-
dral MS 91)."
M. Seymour, 354:Dec82-428
Thorp, J. Free Will.*
M. Levin, 529(QQ):Winter82-904
P. Simpson, 63:Dec82-374
Thorpe, J. Frontiersmen of the Spirit.
M.P. Gillespie, 395(MFS):Winter82/83-
625
Thorpe, J. John Milton.
D.J. Enright, 617(TLS):25Nov83-1306
Thrane, T. Referential-Semantic Analysis.
G. Bourcier, 189(EA):Apr-Jun82-202
Threatte, L. The Grammar of Attic Inscrip-
tions.* (Vol 1)
J. Irigoin, 555:Vol56fasc1-110
A.H. Sommerstein, 303(JoHS):Vol 102-
256
Threlfall, R. and G. Norris. A Catalogue
of the Compositions of S. Rachmaninoff.
G. Abraham, 415:Jun82-416
P.W. Jones, 410(M&L):Jul/Oct82-346
Thubron, C. and others. The Ancient Mar-
iners.
42(AR):Winter82-118
Thuente, M.H. W.B. Yeats and Irish Folk-
lore.*
B. Tippett, 366:Autumn82-265
Thuillier, G. Bureaucratie et Bureau-
crates en France au XIXe siècle.
A-M. Buaoui-Baron, 535(RHL):Sep-Dec82-
934
Thulstrup, N. and M.M. - see von Kloeden,
W. and others

Thum, B. Aufbruch und Verweigerung.
P. Giloy-Hirtz, 680(ZDP):Band101Heft3-
448
D.H. Green, 402(MLR):Oct82-984
Thun, H. Probleme der Phraseologie.
H. Kröll, 547(RF):Band93Heft1/2-174
Thunecke, J., with E. Sagarra, eds. For-
men realistischer Erzählkunst.*
F. Martini, 680(ZDP):Band101Heft2-262
Thurber, J. Selected Letters of James
Thurber.* (H. Thurber and E. Weeks, eds)
27(AL):Oct82-474
Thurin, E.I. Emerson as Priest of Pan.
H. Aspiz, 27(AL):Oct82-447
Thurley, G. Counter-Modernism in Current
Critical Theory.
B. Bergonzi, 617(TLS):28Oct83-1178
Thurmair, G. Einfalt und einfaches Leben.
B. Bjorklund, 406:Spring82-102
Thurman, J. Isak Dinesen.*
R. Fuller, 364:Feb83-100
W. Maxwell, 442(NY):28Mar83-113
J. Rascoe, 231:Mar83-67
H. Spurling, 617(TLS):21Jan83-49
Thurman, R.A.F. - see "The Holy Teaching
of Vimalakīrti"
Thurow, L.C. Dangerous Currents.
J.K. Galbraith, 61:Jun83-102
J. Tobin, 231:Nov83-64
D.H. Wrong, 441:5Jun83-12
Thwaite, A., ed. Larkin at Sixty.*
M. Imlah, 493:Jun82-9
J. Wolcott, 231:Nov83-57
Thweatt, V. La Rochefoucauld and the
Seventeenth-Century Concept of the Self.*
J-P. Dens, 210(FrF):Jan82-73
E. Jellinek, 475:Vol9No17-806
A.H.T. Levi, 402(MLR):Jan82-207
C. Strosetzki, 547(RF):Band94Heft4-487
Thwin, M.A. Burma.
C.R. Bryant, 293(JASt):May82-636
Tibbetts, A.M. and C. What's Happening to
American English?
M. Hinden, 289:Spring82-108
Tibble, A. - see Clare, J.
Tibble, A. and R.K.R. Thornton - see Clare,
J.
Tichy, S. The Hands in Exile.
A. Williamson, 441:13Nov83-26
Tidholm, H. The Dialect of Egton in North
Yorkshire.
B.K. Dumas, 350:Jun83-441
Tidrick, K. Heart-Beguiling Araby.
R.W. Bulliet, 579(SAQ):Summer82-351
Tiedemann, R. - see Benjamin, W.
Tiefenbrun, S.W. Signs of the Hidden.*
M. Grimaud, 567:Vol38No1/2-177
S. Romanowski, 475:No16Pt2-441
R.W. Tobin, 207(FR):Dec82-316
Tiefenthaler, S.L. Jerzy Kosinski.
W. Hölbling, 602:Vol13No1-204
Tierney, B. and P. Linehan, eds. Author-
ity and Power.*
N.G. Round, 86(BHS):Oct82-329
Tierney, M. Eoin MacNeill. (F.X. Martin,
ed)
G. Eley, 385(MQR):Winter83-107
Tiffin, C. and H., eds. South Pacific
Stories.
E. Webby, 381:Jul81-200
Tihanya, E. - see under Joyce, D.
Tiles, J.E. Things that Happen.
N. Unwin, 518:Apr82-106

Toland, J. Infamy.*
  L.G. Gerber, 50(ArQ):Autumn82-283
Tolchin, S.J. and M. Dismantling America.
  R.E. Litan, 441:16Oct83-15
Toliver, H. The Past that Poets Make.
  M. Megaw, 175:Summer82-172
  J. Wittreich, 301(JEGP):Jul82-429
Tolkien, J.R.R. The Monsters and the
  Critics and Other Essays. (C. Tolkien,
  ed) Finn and Hengest. (A. Bliss, ed)
  The Old English Exodus. (J. Turville-
  Petre, ed)
  M. Godden, 617(TLS):8Jul83-736
Tolksdorf, U. Eine ostpreussische Volk-
  serzählerin.
  E. Moser-Rath, 196:Band23Heft1/2-164
Toloudis, C. Jacques Audiberti.*
  J-J. Roubine, 535(RHL):Sep-Dec82-979
"Tolstoi aujourd'hui."
  P. Carden, 104(CASS):Spring82-131
Tolstoy, A. Out of the Past.* (K.
  Strelsky and C. Wolkonsky, eds)
  X. Gasiorowska, 550(RusR):Oct82-520
  D. Senese, 104(CASS):Fall-Winter82-558
Tolstoy, N. Stalin's Secret War.*
  L. Schapiro, 453(NYRB):20Jan83-3
  639(VQR):Autumn82-127
Tolstoy, N. The Tolstoys.
  J. Bayley, 362:20Oct83-22
  A.G. Cross, 617(TLS):2Dec83-1338
  H. Robinson, 441:6Nov83-3
Tomalin, R. W.H. Hudson.*
  R. Blythe, 441:13Mar83-8
Tomasetti, G. Man of Letters.
  P. Pierce, 381:Dec81-522
  N. Shack, 617(TLS):16Dec83-1412
Tomback, R.S. A Comparative Semitic Lexi-
  con of the Phoenician and Punic Lan-
  guages.
  P.T. Daniels, 318(JAOS):Jul-Sep81-411
Tombs, R. The War against Paris 1871.*
  N. Hampson, 208(FS):Jul82-354
Tomerlin, J.B. - see Austin, S.F. and D.G.
  Burnet
Tomita, J. and N. Japanese Ikat Weaving.
  P. Bach, 614:Summer83-19
Tomlinson, B.R. The Political Economy of
  the Raj, 1914-1947.
  M.D. Morris, 293(JASt):Feb82-405
Tomlinson, C. The Flood.*
  T. Eagleton, 565:Vol23No2-62
  M. O'Neill, 493:Apr82-59
  A. Young, 148:Winter82-67
Tomlinson, C., ed. The Oxford Book of
  Verse in English Translation.*
  P. Danchin, 189(EA):Oct-Dec82-430
  A. Kerrigan, 569(SR):Spring82-318
  R. Lattimore, 249(HudR):Spring82-154
Tomlinson, C. Poetry and Metamorphosis.
  A. Elliot, 617(TLS):14Oct83-1120
Tomlinson, C. Some Americans.*
  A. Young, 148:Winter82-67
Tomlinson, R. La Fête galante.
  J.F. Jones, Jr., 546(RR):Nov82-523
  S. Jones, 208(FS):Jul82-329
  G.E. Rodmell, 83:Spring82-161
Tomory, W.M. Frank O'Connor.*
  J.L. Schneider, 395(MFS):Winter81/82-
  679
Tomosugi, T. A Structural Analysis of
  Thai Economic History.
  H.L. Lefferts, Jr., 293(JASt):Feb82-
  434

Tompkins, J.P., ed. Reader-Response Criti-
  cism.*
  W.E. Cain, 580(SCR):Fall82-118
  M. Grimaud, 290(JAAC):Fall82-108
  D.H. Hirsch, 569(SR):Winter82-119
  J.J. Sosnoski, 395(MFS):Winter81/82-
  753
  M. Steig, 128(CE):Feb82-182
Tompkins, S.R. The Secret War, 1914-1918.
  D.R. Jones, 150(DR):Summer82-335
Tong, X. - see under Xiao Tong
Toole, J.K. A Confederacy of Dunces.*
  J.L. Halio, 598(SoR):Winter83-203
  L.G. Harvey, 436(NewL):Fall82-120
Tooley, M. Abortion and Infanticide.
  M. Warnock, 617(TLS):23Dec83-1424
van den Toorn, P.C. The Music of Igor
  Stravinsky.
  G. Abraham, 617(TLS):17Jun83-635
Topol, E. and F. Neznansky. Red Square.
  E. de Mauny, 617(TLS):18Feb83-149
  P. van Rjndt, 441:30Oct83-32
Toporišič, J. and V. Gjurin, eds. Sloven-
  ska zvrstna besedila.
  J. Paternost, 215(GL):Fall82-196
Toporov, V.N. Axmatova i Blok.
  S. Ketchian, 574(SEEJ):Winter82-483
Topping, D.M., P.M. Ogo and B.C. Dungca.
  Chamorro-English Dictionary.
  G.F. Meier, 682(ZPSK):Band34Heft1-139
Topsfield, L.T. Chrétien de Troyes.*
  E.M. Ghil, 188(ECr):Summer82-63
  P.S. Noble, 208(FS):Apr82-183
  L.M. Paterson, 382(MAE):1982/1-126
  D.J. Shirt, 402(MLR):Jul82-716
Torberg, F. Süsskind von Trimberg.
  T. Ehlert, 680(ZDP):Band101Heft3-460
Torgovnick, M. Closure in the Novel.*
  W.B. Bache, 395(MFS):Summer82-345
  N. Baym, 301(JEGP):Oct82-543
  A. Jefferson, 208(FS):Oct82-498
  K. Lawrence, 454:Winter83-177
  W.L. Reed, 141:Winter82-78
  D.H. Richter, 405(MP):Feb83-287
  C. Torsney, 284:Winter83-149
Tornay, S., ed. Voir et nommer les cou-
  leurs.*
  D. Vallier, 98:Jan82-61
Toro Jiménez, F. La política de Venezuela
  en la Conferencia Interamericana de Con-
  solidación de la Paz.
  J. Ewell, 263(RIB):Vol32No3/4-356
della Torre, P.F. Thatcher.
  M. Clark, 617(TLS):2Dec83-1340
Torrens, R.A. - see under Arrillaga
  Torrens, R.
Torres, R. Perfil de la creación musical
  en la nueva canción chilena desde sus
  orígenes hasta 1973.
  M. Agosin, 263(RIB):Vol32No3/4-382
de Torres Villarroel, D. Los desahuciados
  del mundo y de la gloria. (M.M. Pérez,
  ed)
  C. Chaves McClendon, 552(REH):Jan82-
  127
de Torres Villarroel, D. Vida. (D.
  Chicharro, ed)
  I.L. McClelland, 86(BHS):Oct82-344
Torretti, R. Manuel Kant.
  M.P.M. Caimi, 342:Band73Heft3-360

359

Torretti, R. Philosophy of Geometry from Riemann to Poincaré.*
  R.B. Angel, 154:Jun82-384
  J. Largeault, 542:Jul-Sep82-565
  L.S., 543:Mar82-633
Torrey, E.F. The Roots of Treason.
  R. Coles, 441:23Oct83-11
  442(NY):26Dec83-73
Tortel, J. Le discours des yeux.
  G. Arseguel, 98:Nov82-977
Tosh, J. Clan Leaders and Colonial Chiefs in Lango.
  J.C. Miller, 69:Vol51No3-804
Tossell, W.E. Partnership in Development.
  J.W. Grove, 529(QQ):Autumn82-641
Tōten, M. - see under Miyazaki Tōten
Toth, S.A. Blooming.
  E. Twining, 152(UDQ):Summer82-129
Totman, C. Japan before Perry.
  M.B. Jansen, 407(MN):Winter82-535
Tou-hui, F. - see under Fok Tou-hui
Touhill, B.M. William Smith O'Brien and His Irish Revolutionary Companions in Penal Exile.*
  G.B. Beadle, 174(Éire):Fall82-137
  S. Cronin, 174(Éire):Summer82-156
Touloudis, C. Jacques Audiberti.
  J.G. Miller, 210(FrF):Sep82-282
Touraine, A. and others. Solidarity: Poland 1980-81.
  T. Garton Ash, 617(TLS):9Sep83-969
  M. Malia, 453(NYRB):29Sep83-18
  J. Simpson, 362:4Aug83-21
Touratier, C. La Relative.
  G. Kleiber, 553(RLiR):Jul-Dec81-482
  A. Lorian, 209(FM):Apr82-159
  P. Monteil, 555:Vol55fasc2-370
Tourneur, C. The Plays of Cyril Tourneur.* (G. Parfitt, ed)
  I. Donaldson, 617(TLS):28Oct83-1183
Tourney, L.D. Joseph Hall.*
  G.K. Hunter, 677(YES):Vol 12-263
  B. Vickers, 551(RenQ):Summer81-285
Tournier, M. The Four Wise Men.* Friday. The Ogre. Gemini. Le Vent du Paraclet.
  R. Shattuck, 453(NYRB):28Apr83-8
Tournier, M. Gilles et Jeanne.
  M. Warner, 617(TLS):19Aug83-879
Tournier, M. and É. Boubat. Vues de dos.
  F. de Mèredieu, 450(NRF):Mar82-161
Toury, G. In Search of a Theory of Translation.*
  K. Reiss, 72:Band218Heft2-380
Toussaint, B. Qu'est-ce que la sémiologie?
  P. Swiggers, 567:Vol138No3/4-369
Tovar, A. Mitología e ideología sobre la lengua vasca.
  L. Bloom, 238:Sep82-467
Tovey, D.F. Essays in Musical Analysis.
  C. Barker, 97(CQ):Vol 11No3-429
  C. MacDonald, 607:Sep82-56
Tower, B.S. Klee and Kandinsky in Munich and at the Bauhaus.
  P.V., 90:Sep82-592
Towers, R. The Summoning.
  W. Kendrick, 441:16Oct83-11
Townsend, C.E. Czech through Russian.
  E. McKee, 399(MLJ):Autumn82-348
Townsend, J.R. Written For Children.
  L.D., 617(TLS):21Oct83-1171
Townsend, J.R. and R.C. Bush, comps. The People's Republic of China. (2nd ed)
  J.T. Miller, 293(JASt):May82-590

Townshend, A. The Poems and Masques of Aurelian Townshend. (C.C. Brown, ed)
  K. Duncan-Jones, 617(TLS):11Nov83-1257
Toynbee, A. and D. Ikeda. Choisir la vie.
  M. Adam, 542:Oct-Dec82-661
Trabant, J. Elemente der Semiotik.
  L. Pap, 567:Vol37No3/4-333
Tracey, M. A Variety of Lives.
  P. Fox, 362:22Sep83-21
Trachsler, E. Der Weg im mittelhochdeutschen Artusroman.*
  I. Glier, 221(GQ):Mar82-241
Trachtenberg, A. The Incorporation of America.
  G. Gunn, 676(YR):Winter83-296
Trachtenberg, S., ed. American Humorists, 1800-1950.
  T. Wortham, 445(NCF):Mar83-620
Tracy, J., ed. Masterworks of Crime and Mystery.
  N. Callendar, 441:9Jan83-41
"Tradicionnyj fol'klor Novgorodskoj oblasti."
  J.L. Conrad, 292(JAF):Jan-Mar82-95
"La Traduzione."
  G.F. Meier, 682(ZPSK):Band34Heft2-236
Traeger, J. Mittelalterliche Architekturfiktion.*
  E.C. Fernie, 90:Jan82-43
Trager, F.N. and W.J. Koenig, with Y. Yi. Burmese Sit-Tāns 1764-1826.
  J.C. Scott, 293(JASt):Feb82-436
Train, J. Remarkable Words with Astonishing Origins.
  J.A., 35(AS):Fall82-224
Trajtenbrot, B.A. Los algoritmos y la resolución automática de problemas.
  G.W. Jones, 316:Sep82-702
Tran, Q-P. William Faulkner and the French New Novelists.*
  J.G. Watson, 395(MFS):Summer81-365
Tranel, B. Concreteness in Generative Phonology.
  J. Casagrande, 207(FR):Dec82-352
  P. Hagiwara, 399(MLJ):Autumn82-335
  J. Klausenburger, 350:Sep83-608
"Transactions of the Fifth International Congress on the Enlightenment." (Vol 1)
  J. Balcou, 535(RHL):Jul-Aug82-659
"Transactions of the Fifth International Congress on the Enlightenment." (Vol 4)
  J. Biard-Millérioux, 535(RHL):Sep-Dec82-911
Transtrŏmer, T. Selected Poems.
  J. Lutz, 563(SS):Autumn82-324
  D. McDuff, 565:Vol23No1-58
Trapido, B. Brother of the More Famous Jack.*
  D. Durrant, 364:Nov82-87
  D. Wells, 441:16Jan83-23
Trapnell, W.H. Voltaire and the Eucharist.
  B.E. Schwarzbach, 83:Autumn82-272
Trapp, J.B. - see More, T.
Trapp, K.R. Ode to Nature.
  R.I. Weidner, 658:Summer/Autumn82-162
Traubel, H. With Walt Whitman in Camden.* (Vol 6) (G. Traubel and W. White, eds)
  M. Hindus, 646(WWR):Jun-Sep-Dec82-99
Traugott, E.C., R. La Brum and S. Shepherd, eds. Papers from the Fourth International Conference on Historical Linguis-
                    [continued]

[continuing]
tics, Stanford, March 26-30, 1979.
    P. Baldi, 399(MLJ):Spring82-71
    P. Beade, 361:Mar/Apr82-357
Traugott, E.C. and M.L. Pratt. Linguistics for Students of Literature.*
    P.C. Collins, 215(GL):Spring82-65
    J.L. Subbiondo, 179(ES):Apr82-180
"Travaux de linguistique québécoise."
    (Vols 2 and 3) (L. Boisvert, M. Juneau
    and C. Poirier, eds)
    P.T. Ricketts, 208(FS):Jan82-119
"Travaux de l'institut de Phonétique
    d'Aix." (Vol 5)
    G.F. Meier, 682(ZPSK):Band35Heft5-596
Traven, B. The Night Visitor and Other
    Stories.
    L. Jones, 617(TLS):26Aug83-898
Traver, R. Laughing Whitefish.
    E. Hunter, 441:30Oct83-14
Traversa, V. Parola e Pensiero.* (3rd ed)
    M. Fanelli, 276:Autumn82-192
Travis, P.W. Dramatic Design in the
    Chester Cycle.
    C. Davidson, 405(MP):May83-408
Travitsky, B., ed. The Paradise of Women.
    639(VQR):Winter82-8
Treadgold, W.I. The Nature of the "Bibliotheca" of Photius.
    N.G. Wilson, 589:Oct82-943
Treasure, G.R.R. Seventeenth-Century
    France.
    R. Mettam, 208(FS):Jul82-329
Trebach, A.S. The Heroin Solution.
    F. Zimring, 617(TLS):10Jun83-610
Treece, P. A Man for Others.
    J. Gross, 453(NYRB):17Feb83-3
Trefil, J.S. From Atoms to Quarks.
    B. Castel, 529(QQ):Winter82-918
Trefil, J.S. The Moment of Creation.
    A.P. Lightman, 441:25Sep83-9
Trefil, J.S. The Unexpected Vista.
    H.R. Pagels, 441:24Apr83-7
Trefusis, V. Hunt the Slipper.
    P. Craig, 617(TLS):18Nov83-1294
Tregear, M. Catalogue of Chinese Greenware in the Ashmolean Museum, Oxford.
    L. Craighill, 318(JAOS):Jul-Sep81-394
Tregear, M. Song Ceramics.
    M.A. Cort, 139:Oct/Nov82-32
    M. Medley, 39:Nov82-349
Tregear, M., O. Impey and J. Allen. Eastern Ceramics and Other Works of Art from
    the Collection of Gerald Reitlinger.
    "Skipjack," 463:Spring82-90
Treglown, J., ed. Spirit of Wit.
    D. Nokes, 617(TLS):8Apr83-358
Treglown, J. - see Lord Rochester
Treherne, J. The Galapagos Affair.
    J. Stokes, 617(TLS):13May83-476
    E.S. Turner, 362:26May83-22
Trein, F. Die Autonomie der Theorie bei L.
    Althusser in ihrer rationalistischen
    Begründung.
    H. Faes, 542:Jan-Mar82-73
"Treize Miracles de Notre-Dame." (P.
    Kunstmann, ed)
    J-C. Aubailly, 547(RF):Band94Heft4-483
    F. Collins, 627(UTQ):Summer82-407
    G. Roques, 553(RLiR):Jan-Jun82-215
Trelford, D., ed. Sunday Best 3.
    R. Davies, 617(TLS):23Dec83-1439

de Trémaudan, A-H. Histoire de la nation
    métisse dans l'Ouest-canadien.
    S.P. Knutson, 102(CanL):Winter81-151
Tremblay, M. Les Anciennes Odeurs.
    E.R. Hopkins, 207(FR):Apr83-796
Tremblay, M. Damnée Manon. Sacrée Sandra.
    Sainte-Carmen of the Main. The Impromptu of Outremont.
    T. McNamara, 526:Summer82-111
    D. Rubin, 108:Fall82-124
Trenn, T.J. and R.K. Merton - see Fleck, L.
Trenschel, W. Das Phänomen der Nasalität.
    G. Meinhold, 682(ZPSK):Band34Heft2-254
"Trésor de la langue française." (Vol 5)
    (P. Imbs, ed)
    H.J. Wolf, 547(RF):Band93Heft1/2-179
"Trésor de la langue française du XIXe et
    du XXe siècle (1789-1960)." (Vol 8)
    (B. Quemada, ed)
    V. Väänänen, 439(NM):1982/2-216
Trethewey, E. In the Traces.
    L. Welch, 198:Oct82-99
Trevanian. The Summer of Katya.
    E. Hunter, 441:3Jul83-9
    442(NY):22Aug83-93
Trevelyan, H. Goethe and the Greeks.
    R.B. Harrison, 123:Vol32No2-265
Trevino, L. and S. Blair. Supermex.
    P-L. Adams, 61:Feb83-105
Trevor, W. Beyond the Pale and Other
    Stories.*
    639(VQR):Summer82-95
Trevor, W. Fools of Fortune.
    P. Craig, 617(TLS):29Apr83-421
    D.J. Enright, 362:9Jun83-24
    M. Gordon, 453(NYRB):22Dec83-53
    F. Taliaferro, 231:Oct83-74
    R. Towers, 441:2Oct83-1
Trevor, W. Lovers of Their Own Time and
    Other Stories.
    J. Kilroy, 569(SR):Winter82-89
Trevor, W. The Stories of William Trevor.
    M. Gordon, 453(NYRB):22Dec83-53
    F. Taliaferro, 231:Oct83-74
    R. Towers, 441:2Oct83-1
Trexler, R.C. Public Life in Renaissance
    Florence.*
    H. Butters, 551(RenQ):Autumn82-468
    R. Starn, 589:Oct82-944
Tribble, E. - see Wilson, W. and E.B. Galt
Tributsch, H. How Life Learned to Live.
    H.R. Pagels, 441:24Apr83-7
Tributsch, H. When the Snakes Awake.
    P-L. Adams, 61:Jan83-107
    B. Bright, 441:23Jan83-13
Trifonov, I. Mise à mort d'un pigeon.
    J. Blot, 450(NRF):Jul-Aug82-200
Trigg, R. Reality at Risk.*
    M.B.C., 543:Mar82-634
    C.W. Gowans, 258:Mar82-98
    G.A.J. Rogers, 318:Apr02-102
    J.E. Tiles, 393(Mind):Oct82-622
Trigg, R. The Shaping of Man.
    O. O'Neill, 617(TLS):11Mar83-245
Trillin, C. Third Helpings.
    C. Claiborne, 441:17Apr83-13
Trinder, B. The Making of the Industrial
    Landscape.
    J. Butt, 617(TLS):25Mar83-285
Trinder, B. Victorian Banbury.
    P. Horn, 617(TLS):4Mar83-222

Trinkaus, C. The Poet as Philosopher.*
  P. Hainsworth, 447(N&Q):Jun81-261
  R. Witt, 551(RenQ):Summer81-228
Tripathy, A.K. The Art of Aldous Huxley.
  H.H. Watts, 395(MFS):Summer82-281
Tripet, A. La Rêverie littéraire.*
  R. Grimsley, 208(FS):Jul82-331
Triska, J.F. and C. Gati, eds. Blue-
  Collar Workers in Eastern Europe.*
  A. Braun, 104(CASS):Fall-Winter82-600
Tristan L'Hermite. Le Page disgracié. (J.
  Serroy, ed)
  F. Assaf, 475:No16Pt2-443
  J-P. Chauveau, 535(RHL):Sep-Dec82-877
Tristan, F. Lettres. (S. Michaud, ed)
  J. Gaulmier, 535(RHL):Mar-Apr82-307
Tristan, F. Le Tour de France, Journal
  1843-1844.
  L. Czyba, 535(RHL):Mar-Apr82-307
"Trivialliteratur?"
  E. Caramaschi, 549(RLC):Oct-Dec82-511
  T.M. Scheerer, 72:Band218Heft2-394
Trocmé, H. Les Américains et leur archi-
  tecture.
  R.A. Day, 189(EA):Jul-Sep82-357
Trogdon, W. - see under Least Heat Moon, W.
Trollope, A. Marion Fay. (R.H. Super, ed)
  J. Keates, 617(TLS):20May83-513
Trombley, S. "All That Summer She Was
  Mad."*
  R.S., 148:Summer82-92
Trotter, D. The Poetry of Abraham Cowley.
  D. Hopkins, 677(YES):Vol 12-269
  A. Rudrum, 447(N&Q):Aug81-337
Trousson, R., ed. Thèmes et Figures du
  Siècle des Lumières.*
  H-G. Funke, 547(RF):Band93Heft3/4-450
Trousson, R. Thèmes et mythes.
  G. Cesbron, 356(LR):Aug82-273
Troy, T.F. Donovan and the CIA.
  T. Powers, 453(NYRB):12May83-29
Troyat, H. Alexander of Russia.
  J.H. Billington, 441:20Feb83-8
  N. Bliven, 442(NY):18Apr83-146
Troyat, H. The Children.
  J. Pilling, 617(TLS):14Oct83-1143
Troyen, C. The Boston Tradition.
  N. Harris, 432(NEQ):Sep82-455
de Troyes, C. - see under Chrétien de
  Troyes
Truchet, J., ed. Recherches de thématique
  théâtrale.
  E. Henein, 475:No16Pt2-454
  A. Niderst, 535(RHL):Sep-Dec82-891
Trudgill, P. On Dialect.
  R.B. Le Page, 617(TLS):20May83-524
Trudgill, P. Sociolinguistics.
  K. Reichl, 38:Band100Heft3/4-485
Trueba, H.T., G.P. Guthrie and K.H. Au,
  eds. Culture and the Bilingual Class-
  room.
  J. Edwards, 399(MLJ):Summer82-197
Trueblood, P.G., ed. Byron's Political
  and Cultural Influence in Nineteenth-
  Century Europe.
  H. de Almeida, 340(KSJ):Vol31-210
  D.H. Reiman, 579(SAQ):Autumn82-478
Truitt, A. Daybook.
  C.N., 55:Nov82-52
Truman, H.S. Dear Bess. (R.H. Ferrell,
  ed)
  G.C. Ward, 441:7Aug83-1
  442(NY):12Sep83-157

Trümpy, H. - see Mantuanus, B.
Trusted, J. The Logic of Scientific Infer-
  ence.
  J.E. Adler, 479(PhQ):Jul82-291
Trypanis, C.A. Greek Poetry.*
  M. Grant, 441:9Jan83-33
"Tsá' Ászi'."
  L.J. Sass, 292(JAF):Jan-Mar82-96
Tsakirides, E. Spoken Greek. (Step 1)
  J.E. Rexine, 399(MLJ):Spring82-113
Tsangadas, B.C.P. The Fortifications and
  Defense of Constantinople.
  J.H. Rosser, 589:Jan82-179
  S. Runciman, 31(ASch):Winter81/82-126
Tschauder, G. Existenzsätze.
  M. Katzschmann, 260(IF):Band86-332
Tschudi, A. Chronicon Helveticum. (Vol 3)
  (B. Stettler, ed)
  S. Rowan, 589:Jul82-687
Tsigakou, F-M. The Rediscovery of Greece.*
  P. Conner, 90:Jan82-39
  R. Higgins, 39:May82-413
Tsong-ka-pa. Tantra in Tibet. (J.
  Hopkins, ed and trans)
  J.W. de Jong, 259(IIJ):Jul80-261
Tsongas, P. The Road from Here.
  W.S. Burke, 396(ModA):Spring82-211
Tsuji, S. Japanese Cooking.*
  W. and C. Cowen, 639(VQR):Spring82-68
no Tsurayuki, K. The Tosa Diary. (W.N.
  Porter, trans)
  Takeda Katsuhiko, 285(JapQ):Jan-Mar82-
  120
Tsuzuki, C. Edward Carpenter 1844-1929.
  K. Willis, 556:Winter82/83-61
Tsvetaeva, M. A Captive Spirit.* (J.M.
  King, ed and trans)
  J.A. Taubman, 104(CASS):Spring82-142
Tsvetaeva, M. The Dêmesne of the Swans/
  Lebedinyi stan.* (R. Kemball, ed and
  trans)
  J.A. Taubman, 104(CASS):Spring82-142
Tsvetayeva, M. Selected Poems of Marina
  Tsvetayeva.* (E. Feinstein, trans)
  639(VQR):Summer82-93
Tubiana, M.J. and J. The Zaghawa from an
  Ecological Perspective.
  E. Conte, 69:Vol51No3-799
Tucci, G. The Religions of Tibet.*
  G.R. Elder, 485(PE&W):Jan82-117
Tuck, R. Natural Rights Theories.*
  T.L. Thorson, 319:Jan83-101
Tucker, D.F.B. Marxism and Individualism.*
  B. Warren, 63:Mar82-84
Tucker, H.F., Jr. Browning's Beginnings.*
  C.T. Christ, 401(MLQ):Jun82-185
  T.J. Collins, 301(JEGP):Jul82-444
  J.A. Dupras, 85(SBHC):Fall82-57
  J.F. Hulcoop, 150(DR):Spring82-162
  J. Maynard, 85(SBHC):Fall82-62
  D. Mermin, 591(SIR):Winter82-689
  L. Poston, 579(SAQ):Spring82-239
Tucker, P.H. Monet at Argenteuil.*
  R. Jay, 446(NCFS):Spring-Summer83-389
Tucker, P.L. Time and History in Valle-
  Inclán's Historical Novels and "Tirano
  Banderas."*
  M. Bieder, 593:Fall82-274
Tucker, R.W. and D.C. Hendrickson. The
  Fall of the First British Empire.
  R. Middlekauff, 617(TLS):14Oct83-1121
  G.S. Wood, 453(NYRB):3Feb83-16

Turnock, D. The Historical Geography of
 Scotland Since 1707.
   B.P. Lenman, 617(TLS):18Mar83-272
Turow, J. Entertainment, Education, and
 the Hard Sell.
   A. Alexander, 583:Winter83-199
Turville-Petre, J. - see Tolkien, J.R.R.
Tusa, A. and J. The Nuremberg Trial.
   K. Kyle, 362:15Dec83-27
Tushnet, M. The American Law of Slavery,
 1810-1860.
   W.L. Barney, 9(AlaR):Apr82-150
Tuska, J. The Vanishing Legion.
   R. Bann, 200:Aug-Sep82-442
Tutorow, N.E. The Mexican-American War.
   B.J. Robinson, 263(RIB):Vol32No2-222
Tveten, J.L. Coastal Texas.
   L. Milazzo, 584(SWR):Autumn82-vi
Twain, M. The Adventures of Tom Sawyer by
 Mark Twain: A Facsimile of the Author's
 Holograph Manuscript. (P. Baender, ed)
   Z. Leader, 617(TLS):30Sep83-1045
Twain, M. A Connecticut Yankee in King
 Arthur's Court.* (B.L. Stein, ed)
   H.G. Baetzhold, 405(MP):Nov82-217
   H. Parker, 301(JEGP):Oct82-596
Twain, M. Early Tales and Sketches.*
 (Vol 1) (E.M. Branch and R.H. Hirst,
 with H.E. Smith, eds) The Adventures of
 Tom Sawyer; Tom Sawyer Abroad; Tom
 Sawyer, Detective. (J.C. Gerber, P.
 Baender and T. Firkins, eds) The Prince
 and the Pauper. (V. Fischer and L.
 Salamo, with M.J. Jones, eds)
   H. Parker, 301(JEGP):Oct82-596
Twain, M. Early Tales and Sketches. (Vol
 2) (E.M. Branch and R.H. Hirst, with H.E.
 Smith, eds)
   H. Parker, 301(JEGP):Oct82-596
   H. Springer, 445(NCF):Mar83-608
Twain, M. Mississippi Writings. (G.
 Cardwell, ed)
   H. Beaver, 617(TLS):3Jun83-567
   Z. Leader, 617(TLS):30Sep83-1045
Twain, M. The Selected Letters of Mark
 Twain.* (C. Neider, ed)
   J.W. Gargano, 573(SSF):Fall82-393
   27(AL):Oct82-487
Twain, M. A Tramp Abroad.
   J.K.L.W., 617(TLS):22Apr83-415
Twain, M. Mark Twain's Notebooks and
 Journals.* (Vol 3) (F. Anderson and
 others, eds)
   M.J. Fertig, 26(ALR):Spring82-131
   H. Parker, 301(JEGP):Oct82-596
Twersky, I. Introduction to the Code of
 Maimonides (Mishneh Torah).
   W.Z. Harvey, 319:Apr82-200
Twichell, C. Northern Spy.*
   J.D. McClatchy, 491:Sep82-350
Twigg, A. For Openers.
   T. Goldie, 102(CanL):Spring82-146
"Twin Figures from West Africa."
   J. Povey, 2(AfrA):Nov81-85
Twitchell, J.B. The Living Dead.*
   C.D.C., 636(VP):Spring82-91
   S. Gresham, 577(SHR):Winter82-70
   I. Ousby, 637(VS):Autumn81-105
   J. Wilt, 591(SIR):Spring82-107
Twiti, W. The Art of Hunting (1327).* (B.
 Danielsson, ed)
   M. Thiébaux, 301(JEGP):Jul82-407

Twohig, D. and W. Abbot - see Washington,
 G.
Tyacke, S. English Map-Making 1500-1650.
   E.M.J. Campbell, 617(TLS):30Dec83-1468
de Tyard, P. - see under Pontus de Tyard
Tygiel, J. Baseball's Great Experiment.
   P-L. Adams, 61:Aug83-100
   R. Lipsyte, 441:7Aug83-9
   442(NY):30ct83-132
Tyler, A. Dinner at the Homesick Restau-
 rant.*
   G. Kearns, 249(HudR):Autumn82-499
Tyler, R.W. and S.D. Elizondo. The Charac-
 ters, Plots and Settings of Calderon's
 Comedias.
   W.R. Blue, 238:Dec82-657
   R. Minian de Alfie, 547(RF):Band94
    Heft2/3-371
Tyler, S.A. The Said and the Unsaid.
   R. Chatterjee, 350:Jun83-423
Tynianov, Y. The Problem of Verse Lan-
 guage. (M. Sosa and B. Harvey, eds and
 trans)
   B.P. Scherr, 574(SEEJ):Spring82-107
   E. Stankiewicz, 104(CASS):Fall-Winter
    82-526
Tynn, M.B., ed. The Science Fiction Refer-
 ence Book.
   R.M.P., 561(SFS):Jul82-224
Tyrrell, I. The Survival Option.
   W. Rodgers, 362:10Mar83-23
   J. Warnock, 617(TLS):29Apr83-426
Tyrrell, J. and R. Wise. A Guide to Inter-
 national Congress Reports in Musicology
 1900-1975.
   P.W. Jones, 410(M&L):Jan/Apr82-126
Tyson, C.N. The Red River in Southwestern
 History.
   L. Milazzo, 584(SWR):Spring82-v
Tyson, G.P. Joseph Johnson.*
   O.M. Brack, Jr., 173(ECS):Summer82-484
   F.H. Ellis, 541(RES):Feb82-88
   R.J. Roberts, 447(N&Q):Feb81-84
Tyssens, M., ed and trans. Le Voyage de
 Charlemagne à Jérusalem et à Constantin-
 ople.*
   A. Iker-Gittleman, 545(RPh):Nov81-442
Tytler, G. Physiognomy in the European
 Novel.*
   J. Mileham, 210(FrF):Sep82-285
Tzonev, S. Le Financier dans la comédie
 française sous l'ancien régime.
   M.R. Margitić, 475:No16Pt2-458

"USSR Facts and Figures Annual." (Vol 5)
 (J.L. Scherer, ed)
   B.M. Barr, 104(CASS):Fall-Winter82-583
   M. McCauley, 575(SEER):Apr82-317
Ubersfeld, A. Claudel, Autobiographie et
 Histore.
   J.P. Gilroy, 207(FR):Apr83-779
Učida, N. Hindi Phonology.
   E. Bender, 318(JAOS):Oct-Dec81-510
   L.A. Schwarzschild, 259(IIJ):Apr80-169
Ude, W. Becoming Coyote.
   J.L. Davis, 649(WAL):Winter83-380
Udolph, J. Studien zu slavischen Gewässer-
 namen und Gewässerbezeichnungen.*
   H. Leeming, 575(SEER):Jan82-87
Uecker, H., ed. Der Wiener Psalter.
   M.E. Kalinke, 563(SS):Autumn82-316

Ueding, G., with B. Steinbrink. Hoffmann und Campe.
J.L. Sammons, 221(GQ):May82-472
von Uexküll, T., ed. Lehrbuch der Psychosomatischen Medizin.
E. Baer, 567:Vol37No1/2-165
Ugenti, V. - see "Luciferi Calaritani, 'De regibus apostaticis [et] Moriendum esse pro Dei Filio'"
Uglow, J.S. The Macmillan Dictionary of Women's Biography.
L. Sage, 617(TLS):28Jan83-77
Ugrinsky, A. and others, eds. Heinrich von Kleist Studies.
G. Brude-Firnau, 221(GQ):Jan82-122
J.M. Grandin, 301(JEGP):Jul82-388
Uher, L. Humans and Other Beasts.
P. Monk, 529(QQ):Summer82-419
B. Pell, 102(CanL):Spring82-128
N. Zacharin, 137:Aug82-9
Uhlenbeck, E.M. Studies in Javanese Morphology.
J.M. Echols, 318(JAOS):Oct-Dec81-496
Uhlig, C. Hofkritik im England des Mittelalters und die Renaissance.
E. Danninger, 72:Band218Heft2-415
Ukaji, M. Imperative Sentences in Early Modern English.*
J. Monaghan, 38:Band100Heft1/2-156
"Ukrainian Dumy."* (G. Tarnawsky and P. Kilina, trans)
R.B. Klymasz, 292(JAF):Apr-Jun82-245
Ulam, A.B. Dangerous Relations.
A. Dallin, 441:27Mar83-9
Ulam, A.B. Russia's Failed Revolutions.*
M.N. Hagopian, 396(ModA):Summer/Fall82-457
C. Johanson, 529(QQ):Summer82-442
D.W. Treadgold, 550(RusR):Apr82-201
Ullman, L. Natural Histories.
C. Berger, 491:Apr82-35
Ulloa, J., ed. José Lezama Lima.
A.A. Fernández-Vázquez, 345(KRQ):Vol29No1-108
Ulreich, J.C., Jr. - see Barfield, O.
Ulrich, E.C., Jr. The Qumran Text of Samuel and Josephus.
W.S. Lasor, 318(JAOS):Oct-Dec81-451
Umpierre, G. Songs in the Plays of Lope de Vega.
D. Rogers, 86(BHS):Apr82-153
Ünal, A. Ein Orakeltext über die Intrigen am hethitischen Hof.
G. Beckman, 318(JAOS):Jul-Sep81-410
Unbescheid, G. Kānphaṭā.
A. Bharati, 293(JASt):Aug82-873
"The Undercover Story."
R.L. Shep, 614:Summer83-23
Underhill, R. The Truman Persuasions.
C.A. Smith, 583:Winter83-196
Underwood, T.L. - see Bunyan, J.
Ungar, F. - see von Goethe, J.W.
Unger, A.L. Constitutional Development in the USSR.
W.E. Butler, 575(SEER):Oct82-635
Unger, J., ed. Barnboken som livsorientering.
A-M. Rasmussen, 563(SS):Spring82-188
Unger, L. Eliot's Compound Ghost.
P. Gray, 617(TLS):11Feb83-142
Unger, R.W. The Ship in the Medieval Economy, 600-1600.
T.J. Runyan, 589:Jul82-671

Unger-Hamilton, C. Keyboard Instruments.
C. Ehrlich, 415:Jun82-417
Unruh, J.D., Jr. The Plains Across.
M.J. Rohrbough, 658:Summer/Autumn82-147
Unschuld, P.U. Medizin und Ethik — Sozialkonflikte im China der Kaiserzeit.
M. Porkert, 318(JAOS):Oct-Dec81-430
Unseld, S. The Author and His Publisher.*
G. Woodcock, 569(SR):Spring82-240
Unsworth, B. The Rage of the Vulture.
T.R. Edwards, 441:13Mar83-7
442(NY):14Mar83-156
Unverfehrt, G. Hieronymus Bosch.
W.S. Gibson, 90:Jan82-35
Unwin, T.A. - see Flaubert, G.
Uo, D.K. [D.C. Waugh]. Slavyanskiye rukopisi sobraniya F.A. Tolstogo.
W.F. Ryan, 575(SEER):Oct82-637
Updike, J. Bech is Back.*
W. Boyd, 364:Feb83-111
D. Montrose, 617(TLS):14Jan83-30
P. Whitehead, 362:13Jan83-19
Updike, J. Hugging the Shore.
D. Donoghue, 441:18Sep83-1
S. Schwartz, 453(NYRB):24Nov83-26
J. Wolcott, 231:Sep83-63
Updike, J. Rabbit Is Rich.*
B. Allen, 569(SR):Summer82-493
J.L. Halio, 598(SoR):Winter83-203
B. and L. Quart, 390:Nov82-60
P. Wolfe, 502(PrS):Fall82-86
Uphaus, R.W. The Impossible Observer.*
R.L. Brett, 541(RES):May82-206
C. Rawson, 83:Spring82-159
S. Soupel, 189(EA):Jan-Mar82-88
Uphaus, S.H. John Updike.
S. Fogel, 106:Fall82-267
W.T.S., 395(MFS):Summer81-374
Upitis, L. Latvian Mittens/Latviesu Cimdi.
R.L. Shep, 614:Winter83-18
Upton, L.F.S. Micmacs and Colonists.*
G.A. Rawlyk, 529(QQ):Spring82-210
Urban, G.R., ed. Stalinism.
R. Hingley, 617(TLS):18Mar83-269
Urbanski, M.M.O. Margaret Fuller's "Woman in The Nineteenth Century."*
V. Strong-Boag, 106:Spring82-97
Urdang, C. The Lone Woman and Others.*
R. Jackson, 502(PrS):Spring82-91
Urdang, L., A. Humez and H.G. Zettler, eds. Suffixes and Other Word-Final Elements of English.
K.B. Harder, 424:Sep82-199
Ure, J. The Quest for Captain Morgan.
J. Morgan, 617(TLS):9Dec83-1370
Ureland, P.S., ed. Sprachkontakte im Nordseegebiet.
P.T. Roberge, 685(ZDL):2/1982-243
Ureña, E.M. La Crítica Kantiana de la Sociedad y de la Religión.
M. Caimi, 342:Band/3Heft1-90
Urkowitz, S. Shakespeare's Revision of "King Lear."*
P. Edwards, 402(MLR):Jul82-694
J.W. Velz, 130:Spring82-79
Urmson, J.O. Berkeley.*
483:Jul82-423
Urofsky, M.I. A Voice That Spoke for Justice.
M. Zoltan, 287:Aug/Sep82-27
Urquhart, F. Seven Ghosts in Search.
A. Bold, 617(TLS):30Dec83-1462

Urquhart, J. Animals on the Farm.
  J. Clutton-Brock, 617(TLS):23Sep83-
  1013
Usborne, R. Clubland Heroes.
  D.J., 617(TLS):21Oct83-1171
Usher, D. The Economic Prerequisite to
  Democracy.
  B.R.G., 185:Jan83-424
Usherwood, S. and E. The Counter-Armada,
  1596.
  K.R. Andrews, 617(TLS):30Dec83-1466
Uslar Pietri, A. La Isla de Robinson.
  O. Rossardi, 37:Jan-Feb82-63
Usmiani, R. Michel Tremblay.
  S. Ross, 150(DR):Autumn82-509
  D. Rubin, 108:Fall82-124
Ustinov, P. My Russia.
  N. Tolstoy, 617(TLS):1Jul83-703
  442(NY):2May83-130
Uther, H-J. Behinderte in populären Erzäh-
  lungen.
  H. Trümpy, 196:Band23Heft1/2-166
Uturgaidze, T. Kartuli enis ponemat'uri
  st'rukt'ura.
  G.F. Meier, 682(ZPSK):Band35Heft5-599

Väänänen, V. Introduction au latin vul-
  gaire. (3rd ed)
  J.N. Adams, 123:Vol132No2-287
  P. Flobert, 555:Vol56fasc1-95
  C.D. Lanham, 439(NM):1982/4-475
  H. Lausberg, 547(RF):Band94Heft4-451
Vadim, R. The Hungry Angel.
  M. Simpson, 441:11Dec83-16
Vagianos, S.C. - see under Caides Vagianos,
  S.
Vaidyanathan, S., ed. Studies in Dravid-
  ian Linguistics, No. 1.
  S.B. Steever, 350:Dec83-933
Vaillancourt, S. Perspectives françaises
  2.
  B.G. Marckel, 399(MLJ):Winter82-419
  P. Siegel, 207(FR):Feb83-529
Vaillant, G.E. The Natural History of
  Alcoholism.
  S. Peele, 441:26Jun83-10
Vainshtein, S. Nomads of South Siberia.*
  (C. Humphrey, ed) [shown in prev under
  Vainstein]
  T.J. Barfield, 293(JASt):Aug82-828
Vaizey, J. Breach of Promise.
  N. Annan, 362:6Oct83-22
  K.O. Morgan, 617(TLS):11Nov83-1243
Vaizey, J. The Squandered Peace.
  N. Annan, 453(NYRB):27Oct83-89
  W. Rodgers, 362:21Apr83-22
  Z. Steiner, 617(TLS):7Oct83-1081
Vaizey, M. The Artist as Photographer.
  J. Naughton, 362:6Jan83-22
Vakalopoulos, A.E. Istoria tou Neou
  Ellinismou. (Vols 5 and 6)
  R. Clogg, 617(TLS):12Aug83-861
Vala, V. Une Perle blanche à Terre-de-
  Haut.
  M.G. Paulson, 207(FR):Mar83-675
Valbuena-Briones, Á. Calderón y la
  comedia nueva.
  A.E. Foley, 240(HR):Autumn82-491
Valcárcel, E.D. - see under Díaz Valcár-
  cel, E.

Valdés, G., A.G. Lozano and R. García-
  Moya, eds. Teaching Spanish to the
  Hispanic Bilingual.
  N.J. Dyer, 238:Sep82-474
  J.R. Gutiérrez, 399(MLJ):Summer82-234
Valdés, J. Lecturas básicas: A Civiliza-
  tion Reader. (2nd ed)
  M.S. Arrington, 399(MLJ):Spring82-97
  R. Romeu, 238:Sep82-477
Valdes, M.J. and O.J. Miller, eds. Inter-
  pretation of Narrative.*
  T. Rajan, 627(UTQ):Fall81-93
Valdivieso, E. Pintura sevillana del
  siglo XIX.
  E. Arias Anglés, 48:Apr-Jun82-218
Valdivieso, L.T. Bibliografía de un tea-
  tro "silenciado."
  R.C. Manteiga, 552(REH):Jan82-136
Valdman, A. and A. Highfield, eds. Theo-
  retical Orientations in Creole Studies.*
  C. Corne, 350:Mar83-176
  A. Hull, 35(AS):Summer82-139
  S.G. Thomason, 355(LSoc):Dec82-478
Valdovinos, J.M.C. and J.M. García López -
  see under Cruz Valdovinos, J.M. and J.M.
  García López
Vale, J. Edward III and Chivalry.
  S. Anglo, 617(TLS):23Sep83-1026
Vale, M. The Gentleman's Recreations.
  R. Ralph, 447(N&Q):Feb81-72
Vale, N. Knitting 1920's and 1930's
  Originals.
  R.L. Shep, 614:Winter83-18
Valencia, P. and F. Merlonghi. En con-
  tacto.*
  D.R. McKay, 238:Dec82-673
Valenta, J. Soviet Intervention in Czecho-
  slovakia, 1968.
  A.R. De Luca, 104(CASS):Summer82-269
Valentin, J-M., ed. Gegenreformation und
  Literatur.
  P. Skrine, 402(MLR):Jul82-757
  B.L. Spahr, 133:Band15Heft1/2-159
Valenziani, E. and P. Veneziani, with G.
  Sciascia Villani, comps. Indice Gene-
  rale degli Incunaboli delle Biblioteche
  d'Italia. (Vol 6)
  D.E. Rhodes, 354:Mar82-87
Valenzuela, L. The Lizard's Tail.
  A. Josephs, 441:20Oct83-15
"Paul Valéry, 3."
  P. Jourdan, 535(RHL):Jul-Aug82-677
Valesio, P. Novantiqua.
  S. Deetz, 480(P&R):Summer82-207
Valette, J-P., G.S. Kupferschmid and R.
  Valette. Con mucho gusto.*
  R.T. Douglass, 399(MLJ):Spring82-99
Valette, R.M. Nouvelles lectures libres.
  J.A. Reiter, 207(FR):Oct82-196
  L. Vines, 399(MLJ):Winter82-420
Valin, J. Day of Wrath.
  T.J. Binyon, 617(TLS):19Aug83-890
Valin, J. Natural Causes.
  N. Callendar, 441:4Sep83-20
Valis, N.M. The Decadent Vision in Leo-
  poldo Alas.
  F. García Sarriá, 86(BHS):Apr82-155
  J.W. Kronik, 238:Sep82-463
  E. Sánchez, 395(MFS):Summer82-335
Valiuddin, M. The Quranic Ṣūfism. (2nd
  ed)
  S. Vahiduddin, 485(PE&Q):Apr82-219
Valk, G.M. - see Kaiser, G.

van der Valk, M. - see Eustathius
Valla, L. On Pleasure: De Voluptate.*
  (A.K. Hieatt and M. Lorch, eds and trans)
    L.V. Ryan, 551(RenQ):Spring81-91
del Valle, J.C. Escritos de José Cecilio
  del Valle. (C. Meléndez Ch., ed)
    J.M. García Laguardia, 263(RIB):Vol32
      No2-218
del Valle, J.C. José del Valle, Antolo-
  gía.* (R. Oquelí, ed)
    M. Rodríguez, 37:May-Jun82-60
Vanbrugh, J. L'épouse outragée. (M-L.
  Fluchère, trans)
    M.S. Plaisant, 566:Autumn82-5
Van Buren, P. Discerning the Way.
    A.J. Wolf, 287:Mar82-27
Vance, C. Hard Choices.
    M. Frankel, 441:29May83-3
    S. Hoffmann, 453(NYRB):29Sep83-48
    442(NY):4Jul83-91
Van Cleve, S. 40 Years' Gatherin's.
    C. Beyers, 649(WAL):Spring82-76
Van Daalen, L.A. Vālmīki's Sanskrit.
    R.P. Goldman, 293(JASt):Aug82-874
Vandegans, A. Aux origines de "Barabbas,"
  "Actus tragicus" de Michel de Ghelderode.
    R. Frickx, 535(RHL):Mar-Apr82-327
Van D'Elden, K.H. West German Poets on
  Society and Politics.
    K. Menges, 149(CLS):Spring82-82
Vanden Bemden, Y. Corpus Vitrearum
  Belgique. (Vol 4)
    W. Cole, 90:Aug82-508
Van den Broeck, J., ed and trans. La
  Saveur de l'Immortel (A-p'i-t'an Kan
  Lu Wei Lun).
    J. May, 259(IIJ):Jul80-251
Van der Cruysse, D. La Mort dans les
  "Memoires" de Saint-Simon.
    R.A. Picken, 207(FR):Apr83-767
Vanderhaeghe, G. Man Descending.
    C. Fagan, 99:Sep82-34
Vander Motten, J.P. Sir William Killigrew
  (1606-1695).
    J.S. Johnston, Jr., 405(MP):May83-416
    I. Simon, 179(ES):Oct82-475
Vander Veer, G.L. Philosophical Skepti-
  cism and Ordinary-Language Analysis.*
    R.P.M., 543:Jun82-914
Van Deth, J-P. and J. Puyo, eds. Actes du
  colloque international "Langues et coop-
  eration européenne."
    J. Pauchard, 189(EA):Apr-Jun82-199
Van Devanter, L., with C. Morgan. Home
  Before Morning.
    P-L. Adams, 61:May83-103
    H.R., 231:May83-91
Van de Vate, D., Jr. Romantic Love.*
    J.T. Wood, 480(P&R):Fall82-277
Vandromme, P. Robert Le Vigan, compagnon
  et personnage de L-F. Céline.
    S.L. Luce, 207(FR):Feb83-491
Van Duyn, M. Letters from a Father and
  Other Poems.*
    M.L. Rosenthal, 441:13Mar83-6
Van Dyk, J. In Afghanistan.
    E. Mortimer, 453(NYRB):22Dec83-3
Van Fossen, R.W. - see Chapman, G., B.
  Jonson and J. Marston
Van Houton, G. Canada's Party of Social-
  ism.
    I. Abella, 99:Aug82-35

Van Inwagen, P., ed. Time and Cause.*
    R. Swinburne, 393(Mind):Jan82-139
Vankóné, D.J. Falum Galgamácsa.
    G.F. Cushing, 575(SEER):Jul82-470
Van Louhuizen-de Leeuw, J.E., ed. South
  Asian Archaeology 1975.
    L.S. Leshnik, 318(JAOS):Apr-Jun81-247
Van Lustbader, E. Black Heart.
    J. Sullivan, 441:10Apr83-29
Vanneo, S. Recanetum — Liber II, XX-
  XXXVII (On Proportions). (A. Seay, ed
  and trans)
    A.E. Walters, 308:Fall82-349
Vannier, B. L'inscription du corps.
    G. Jacques, 356(LR):Nov82-362
Van Noten, F., with others. The Archaeol-
  ogy of Central Africa.
    C.T. Shaw, 617(TLS):4Feb83-118
Vannoy, R. Sex Without Love.*
    R.C. Solomon, 482(PhR):Oct82-653
Van Parijs, P. Evolutionary Explanation
  in the Social Sciences.*
    J. Elster, 262:Sep82-378
Van Peursen, C.A. Le corps — l'âme —
  l'esprit.
    C. Chalier, 192(EP):Jul-Sep81-363
Van Rillaer, J. Les illusions de la psy-
  chanalyse.
    J-M. Gabaude, 542:Jan-Mar82-94
Vansittart, P. Three Six Seven.
    D. Durrant, 364:Mar83-109
    J. Mellors, 362:10Mar83-27
    O. Murray, 617(TLS):4Mar83-205
Vansittart, P., ed. Voices from the Great
  War.*
    S.S., 148:Spring82-94
Van Wart, A. Positionings.
    M. Bowering, 102(CanL):Spring82-77
Van Windekens, A.J. Le tokharien con-
  fronté avec les autres langues indo-
  européennes.* (Vols 1-3)
    W. Stefański, 360(LP):Vol24-143
Van Young, E. Hacienda and Market in
  Eighteenth-Century Mexico.*
    A.F. Chaves, 37:May-Jun82-62
Van Zanten, D. - see Egbert, D.D.
Varanini, G., L. Banfi and A. Ceruti Bur-
  gio, eds. Laude cortonesi dal secolo
  XIII al XV.
    C. Del Popolo, 228(GSLI):Vol 159
      fasc506-293
Vareille, J-C. Alain Robbe-Grillet
  l'étrange.
    B. Stoltzfus, 207(FR):May83-957
Varela, B. Lo chino en el habla cubana.*
    M. Torreblanca, 238:May82-318
Varey, S. - see "Lord Bolingbroke: Contri-
  butions to the 'Craftsman'"
Varga, A.K. - see under Kibedi Varga, A.
Vargas Llosa, M. Aunt Julia and the
  Scriptwriter.* (Spanish title: La tia
  Julia y el escribidor.)
    N. Shakespeare, 617(TLS):20May83-510
Vargas Llosa, M. La Guerra del Fin del
  Mundo.
    O. Rossardi, 37:Jul-Aug82-64
Varley, C. Frederick H. Varley.
    N.E. Dillow, 529(QQ):Winter82-857
Varley, H., ed. Color.
    529(QQ):Summer82-455
Varley, J. Millennium.
    G. Jonas, 441:31Jul83-13

Varloot, J. and P. Jansen, eds. L'année
1768 à travers la presse traitée par
ordinateur.
   P. Rétat, 535(RHL):Sep-Dec82-906
Varma, D.P., ed. Gothic Novels. (Ser 3)
   R. Paulson, 173(ECS):Summer83-427
Varma, S. G.A. Grierson's Linguistic
Survey of India.
   L. Sternbach, 318(JAOS):Oct-Dec81-489
Varro. Varron, "Satires Ménippées.* (Vol
5) (J-P. Cèbe, ed and trans)
   P. Flobert, 555:Vol56fasc2-341
Varró, R. Dialektik in der lebenden Natur.
   J-M. Gabuade and E. Harmat, 542:
      Jan-Mar82-67
Vas, Z. Viszontagságos életem. Akkori
önmagunkról.
   G. Mikes, 617(TLS):11Mar83-250
Vasari, G. Artists of the Renaissance.
(G. Bull, ed and trans)
   M. Larsen, 324:Sep83-630
Vasi, S. and J. Tomasino. Exercises in
Spanish.
   M.J. Schneider, 399(MLJ):Summer82-231
   A.J. Vetrano, 238:May82-322
Vasta, E. and Z.P. Thundy, eds. Chau-
cerian Problems and Perspectives.
   D.C. Baker, 191(ELN):Sep81-56
   J.D. Burnley, 541(RES):Nov82-455
van der Vat, D. The Last Corsair.
   P. Dickens, 617(TLS):30Dec83-1466
"The Vatican Collections: The Papacy and
Art."
   D.H. Wright, 453(NYRB):2Jun83-6
Vattimo, G. Le avventure della differenza.
   T.H., 543:Sep81-174
Vaughan, A. Signalman's Twilight.
   V. Powell, 617(TLS):9Sep83-971
Vaughan, A.T. and E.W. Clark, eds. Puri-
tans Among the Indians.
   J. Axtell, 432(NEQ):Mar82-123
Vaughan, D. Portrait of an Invisible Man.
   E. Rhodes, 617(TLS):18Nov83-1276
Vaughan, E.C. Some Desperate Glory.*
   T. Warr, 493:Apr82-67
Vaughan, J.L. and O.A. Gianniny, Jr.
Thomas Jefferson's Rotunda Restored 1973-
76.
   J.M. Dickey, 576:May82-167
Vaughan, S.L. Holding Fast the Inner
Lines.
   A.G. Marquis, 161(DUJ):Dec81-128
Vaughan, W. German Romantic Painting.*
   K. Andrews, 39:Sep82-196
   J. Gage, 90:Aug82-514
   M. Morton, 127:Summer82-163
Vaughn, K.I. John Locke.*
   P. Murray, 319:Jan83-103
Vaughn, S.N. The Abbey of Bec and the
Anglo-Norman State 1034-1136.
   V. Chandler, 589:Oct82-947
Vázquez-Ayora, G. Introducción a la tra-
ductología.
   L.V. Fainberg, 545(RPh):Nov81-423
de la Vega, J.S.L. - see under Lasso de la
Vega, J.S.
de la Vega, O.F. and J.E. Hernández-Miy-
ares - see under Fernández de la Vega, O.
and J.E. Hernández-Miyares
de Vega Carpio, L. La francesilla. (D.
McGrady, ed)
   R.W. Tyler, 238:Dec82-656

de Vega Carpio, L. Peribáñez y el Comenda-
dor de Ocaña. (J.M. Ruano and J.E.
Varey, eds)
   M.D. Stroud, 238:Mar82-142
de Vega Carpio, L. El perro del horte-
lano.* (V. Dixon, ed)
   J.B. Rotta, 238:Dec82-656
Veidle, V. - see under Weidlé, V.
Veit, W., ed. Captain James Cook. (Vol 2)
   J.A. Hay, 402(MLR):Oct82-927
Vejdle, V. - see under Weidlé, V.
van der Vekene, E., with P. Hamanová and
H.M. Nixon. Les reliures aux armoiries
de Pierre Ernest de Mansfeld.*
   A. Hobson, 90:Oct82-636
"The Willem van de Velde Drawings in the
Boymans-van Beuningen Museum Rotterdam."
   P. Eikemeier, 471:Jan/Feb/Mar82-75
Veldman, H. La Tentation de l'inacces-
sible.
   R.A. Champagne, 210(FrF):Sep82-281
Velie, A.R. Four American Indian Literary
Masters.
   27(AL):Oct82-472
Véliz, C. The Centralist Tradition of
Latin America.*
   J. Fisher, 86(BHS):Jan82-83
Vellacott, J. Bertrand Russell and the
Pacifists in the First World War.
   T.C. Kennedy, 556:Summer81-83
Vellev, J., ed. Romanske Stenarbejder 1.
   E.B. Hohler, 341:Vol15No2-83
Vel'tman, A.F. Povesti i rasskazy. (J.M.
Akutin, ed)
   J.J. Gebhard, 574(SEEJ):Spring82-93
Vendler, H. The Odes of John Keats.
   F. Kermode, 441:27Nov83-9
Vendler, H. Part of Nature, Part of Us.*
   L. Surette, 106:Spring82-135
Vendrovskaya, L. and G. Kaptereva. Evgeny
Vakhtangov.
   R. Cottrell, 617(TLS):2Sep83-928
Vendryes, J. Lexique étymologique de
l'irlandais ancien: Lettres T-U.
   W. Meid, 260(IF):Band86-362
Venevitinov, D.V. Stixotvorenija, Proza.
(E.A. Majmin and M.A. Černyšev, eds)
   I.K. Lilly, 574(SEEJ):Spring82-95
Venezky, R.L. and A.D. Healey. A Micro-
fiche Concordance to Old English.
   D.K. Fry, 191(ELN):Sep82-11
Venkata Ramanan, K. Nāgārjuna's Philoso-
phy as Presented in the Mahā-Prajñāpāra-
mitā-Śāstra.
   W. Halbfass, 318(JAOS):Oct-Dec81-474
Venkatacharya, T. The Rasārṇavasudhākara
of Siṃhabhūpāla.
   J.W. de Jong, 259(IIJ):Apr82-138
Venkatacharya, T. - see Siṃhabhūpāla II
Ventriglia, L. Conversations of Miguel
and Maria.
   B. Murphy, 608:Mar83-123
Venturi, F. Roots of Revolution.
   E.W., 617(TLS):29Jul83-819
Venturi, F. Settecento riformatore.
   M.S. Miller, 173(ECS):Winter82/83-230
Venturi, F. Studies in Free Russia.
   R. Pipes, 617(TLS):14Oct83-1114
Venturi, L. Historia de la crítica de
Arte.
   D. Angulo Íñiguez, 48:Apr-Jun80-212
Veny, J. Els parlars.
   T.D. Cravens, 350:Sep83-692

Vera, E.G. - see under Gascón Vera, E.

Vera, P.J. Tiempo de Muñecos.
J.D. Suárez-Torres, 37:Jan-Feb82-61

Vercors. Cent Ans d'Histoire de France. (Vol 1)
K. Bieber, 207(FR):Dec82-344

Verdi, G. Don Carlos. (U. Günther and L. Petazzoni, eds)
A. Porter, 317:Summer82-360

Verdi, G. Rigoletto. (M. Chusid, ed)
C. Rosen, 453(NYRB):27Oct83-33

Verdier, P. Le couronnement de la Vierge.
J.D. Breckenridge, 589:Jul82-673
P. Williamson, 90:Jan82-44

Verdon, J. Les Loisirs en France au Moyen Age.
H.H. Kalwies, 207(FR):Oct82-189

Verdonk, R.A. La lengua española en Flandes en el siglo XVII.
R.J. Penny, 86(BHS):Jan82-69

Ver Eecke, J., ed and trans. Le Dasavat-thuppakarana.
C. Hallisey, 318(JAOS):Oct-Dec81-503

Veremis, T. and O. Dimitrakopoulos, eds. Meletimata gyro apo ton Venizelo kai tin epokhi tou.
R. Clogg, 617(TLS):12Aug83-861

Verene, D.P. Vico's Science of Imagination.*
R.D., 543:Jun82-916
E.W. Strong, 319:Apr83-273
W.H. Walsh, 89(BJA):Autumn82-378

Verene, D.P. - see Cassirer, E.

Vergara, L. Rubens and the Poetics of Landscape.
A.M. Wagner, 617(TLS):25Mar83-284

Vergés, P. Sólo Cenizas Hallarás.
O. Rossardi, 37:Jan-Feb82-63

Vergil. The Aeneid. (R. Fitzgerald, trans)
P-L. Adams, 61:Dec83-117
D.S. Carne-Ross, 453(NYRB):27Oct83-3
C.H. Sisson, 441:16Oct83-13

Vergil. Virgil: The "Eclogues" and "Georgics." (R.D. Williams, ed)
P. Flobert, 555:Vol55fasc2-373
K.W. Gransden, 313:Vol72-207

Vergil. Virgil: "The Georgics."* (R. Wells, trans)
J. Griffin, 493:Sep82-75

Vergo, P. Art in Vienna 1898-1918.
D. Barnouw, 221(GQ):May82-463

Vergote, A. Dette et désir.
C. Chalier, 192(EP):Apr-Jun82-245
L. Dupré, 322(JHI):Jul-Sep82-505

Verhesen, F. L'Archée.
D.L., 450(NRF):Jan82-155

Verheyen, E. The Palazzo del Te at Mantua.
C.H. Clough, 39:Sep82-194

Verkest, S. Crocheting Storybook Hand Puppets.
M. Cowan, 614:Spring83-17

Verlaine, P. Poésies (1866-1880). (M. Décaudin, ed)
A. Guyaux, 535(RHL):Sep-Dec82-938

Verlet, P. Les meubles français du XVIIIe siècle.
P. Hughes, 39:Nov82-351
F.J.B. Watson, 324:May83-353

Verleun, J.A. The Stone Horse.*
C.R. La Bossière, 136:Vol 14No2-135

Vermaseren, M.J., ed. Die orientalischen Religionen im Römerreich.
R.M. Ogilvie, 123:Vol132No2-286

Vermes, G., F. Millar and M. Black - see Schürer, E.

Vermes, P. Buber on God and the Perfect Man.
D.W. Hardy, 617(TLS):18Feb83-166

Vermeule, E. Aspects of Death in Early Greek Art and Poetry.*
R. Higgins, 39:Sep82-199

Vernay, H. Syntaxe et sémantique.
O. Gsell, 547(RF):Band94Heft1-92

Vernay, P., ed. Maugis d'Aigremont.
M. Bambeck, 547(RF):Band94Heft2/3-316
P.E. Bennett, 402(MLR):Apr82-444
L.S. Crist, 589:Apr82-438
W.G. Van Emden, 208(FS):Jan82-46

Vernes, P-M. La ville, la fête, la démo-cratie.
S. Goyard-Fabre, 192(EP):Apr-Jun82-246

Vernier, F. L'écriture et les Textes.
B. Langen, 504:No5-122

Vernière, P. - see Locke, J.

Vernois, P. La Dramaturgie poétique de Jean Tardieu.
J. Guérin, 450(NRF):May82-151
E. Jacquart, 207(FR):Mar83-645

Verpoorten, J-M. L'ordre des mots dans l'Aitareya-brāhmaṇa.
J.W. de Jong, 259(IIJ):Apr82-136

Verrier, A. Through the Looking Glass.
K. Jeffery, 617(TLS):20May83-519

Verriere, J. La population de l'Irlande.
P-Y. Petillon, 98:Jun-Jul82-537

Verschuren, H. Jean Pauls "Hesperus" und das zeitgenössische Lesepublikum.
J. Campe, 72:Band218Heft2-405

Versini, L. Le Roman épistolaire.*
F. Jost, 173(ECS):Winter82/83-188
V. Mylne, 208(FS):Jul82-333

Versini, L. - see de Laclos, P-A.C.

Vértes, E. Morphonematische Untersuchung der ostjakischen Vokalharmonie.
G. Sauer, 682(ZPSK):Band35Heft2-234

Vescovini, G.F. - see under Federici Vescovini, G.

Vessillier-Ressi, M. Le Métier d'auteur.
R. Findlater, 617(TLS):8Jul83-722

Vet, C. Temps, aspects et adverbes de temps en français contemporain.*
R. Martin, 553(RLiR):Jul-Dec81-503
F. Nef, 361:May82-93

Vetö, M. Eléments d'une doctrine chré-tienne du mal.
R. Kühn, 489(PJGG):Band89Heft2-434

Vetta, M. - see Theognis

Vetter, T. Maṇḍanamiśra's Brahmasiddhiḥ.
A.W. Thrasher, 259(IIJ):Apr80-155

Vetter, T. Studien zur Lehre und Entwick-lung Śaṅkaras. (N° 6)
J.A. Taber, 485(PE&W):Apr82-213

Vetterling-Braggin, M., ed. Sexist Lan-guage.*
S. McConnell-Ginet, 350:Jun83-373
T.M.R., 185:Oct82-212

Vetterling-Braggin, M., F.A. Elliston and J. English, eds. Feminism and Philoso-phy.*
M. Fox, 154:Mar82-141

Veyne, P. Les Grecs ont-ils cru à leurs mythes?
J. Griffin, 617(TLS):22Apr83-398

Virtanen, K. Settlement or Return.
  D. Kirby, 575(SEER):Jan82-126
Visca, A.S. and J.C. Da Rosa - see de
  Ibarbourou, J.
Vishniac, R. A Vanished World.
  A. Grundberg, 441:4Dec83-77
de Visser, J., B. Simpkins and R. Taylor.
  The Yellowhead Route.
  529(QQ):Summer82-459
Visson, L. Sergei Esenin.*
  J.A. Taubman, 550(RusR):Jul82-354
Viswanathan, S. The Shakespeare Play as
  Poem.*
  J.A. Bryant, Jr., 130:Summer82-188
  R. Fraser, 405(MP):Nov82-181
  G.K. Hunter, 569(SR):Spring82-274
Vital, D. Zionism: The Formative Years.
  Z. Frazer, 287:Nov82-21
Vitéz de Zredna, I. Opera quae supersunt.
  (I. Boronkai, ed)
  M.D. Birnbaum, 551(RenQ):Summer82-271
Vitsaxis, V.G. Hindu Epics.
  A.T. Embree, 318(JAOS):Oct-Dec81-494
Vitukhin, I., ed. Soviet Generals Recall
  World War II.
  T.J. Uldricks, 550(RusR):Jul82-336
Vitzthum, R.C. Land and Sea.
  J.D. Eberwein, 173(ECS):Winter81/82-
  218
de Vivar, G. Crónica y relación copiosa y
  verdadera de los Reinos de Chile (1558).
  (L. Sáez-Godoy, ed)
  D. Briesemeister, 72:Band218Heft2-468
Vivas Gallardo, F. Venezuela en la
  Sociedad de las Naciones: 1920-1939.
  J. Ewell, 263(RIB):Vol132No3/4-356
Vives, J.L. Against the Psuedodialecti-
  cians.* (R. Guerlac, ed and trans)
  N.W. Gilbert, 589:Apr82-440
Vives, J.L. Epistolario. (J. Jiménez
  Delgado, ed)
  E.J. Neugaard, 552(REH):May82-316
Vizinczey, S. An Innocent Millionaire.
  T.J. Binyon, 617(TLS):15Apr83-375
  J. Mellors, 362:14Apr83-32
Vladimov, G. Vernyj Ruslan.
  D. Milivojević, 558(RLJ):Winter-
  Spring82-301
Vleeskens, C. Full Moon Over Lumpini Park.
  G. Bitcon, 581:Dec82-470
Vleeskens, C. Orange Blizzard.
  D. Haskell, 581:Sep82-348
Vliegenthaart, A.W. Bildersammlung der
  Fürsten zu Salm.
  A. Laing, 90:Dec82-763
  E. Young, 39:Apr82-293
van der Vliet, E.C.L. Strabo over landen,
  volken en steden.
  A. Dirkzwager, 394:Vol35fasc3/4-381
Voelkle, W. The Stavelot Triptych.
  D. Buckton, 90:Jan82-42
Voelkle, W.M., ed. Masterpieces of Medie-
  val Painting: The Art of Illumination.
  L.M.C. Randall, 377:Nov81-181
Voetz, L. Komposita auf "-man" im Althoch-
  deutschen, Altsächsischen und Altnieder-
  fränkischen.
  N.R. Wolf, 685(ZDL):1/1982-77
Vogel, C. Indian Lexicography.*
  L. Sternbach, 318(JAOS):Jul-Sep81-379
Vogel, J., ed. Die sowjetische Interven-
  tion in Afghanistan.
  H. Hanak, 575(SEER):Apr82-310

Vogel, J. Leos Janáček.
  M.J. Anderson, 607:Dec82-43
Vogel, S., ed. For Spirits and Kings.*
  D.H. Ross, 2(AfrA):May82-12
von der Vogelweide, W. - see under Walther
  von der Vogelweide
Vogt, G.L. and J.B. Jones, eds. Literary
  and Historical Editing.
  P. Davison, 354:Jun82-207
Vogt, J. Portuguese Rule on the Gold
  Coast, 1469-1882.
  P.E.H. Hair, 69:Vol52No1-94
Voigt, E.B. The Forces of Plenty.
  B. Bennett, 441:17Jul83-10
Vojnovič, V.N. Pretendent na Prestol.*
  S. Kryzytski, 558(RLJ):Winter-Spring82-
  323
Volk, P. Rokokoplastik in Altbayern, Bay-
  risch-Schwaben und im Allgäu.
  E. Zimmermann, 471:Apr/May/Jun82-169
Volokh, A., with M. Manus. The Art of
  Russian Cusine.
  M. Burros, 441:11Dec83-36
Volpe, C. and M. Lucco. L'opera completa
  di Sebastiano del Piombo.
  C. Hope, 90:Oct82-637
Vol'pert, L.I. Puškin i Psixologičeskaja
  Tradicija vo Francuzskoj Literature.*
  J.D. Clayton, 558(RLJ):Winter-Spring82-
  287
Volta, O. - see Satie, E.
de Voltaire, F.M.A. Candide ou l'optim-
  isme. (R. Pomeau, ed)
  V.W. Topazio, 207(FR):Dec82-321
de Voltaire, F.M.A. Correspondance.
  (Vols 1-3) (T. Besterman, ed; adapted
  by F. Deloffre)
  A. Magnan, 535(RHL):Jul-Aug82-656
de Voltaire, F.M.A. Erzählungen, Dialoge,
  Streitschriften. [no ed shown]
  J. von Stackelberg, 547(RF):Band94
  Heft4-494
de Voltaire, F.M.A. Romans et Contes. (F.
  Deloffre and J. van den Heuvel, eds)
  J. Bourguignon, 553(RLiR):Jan-Jun81-
  266
"Voltaire and the English."*
  J.H. Brumfitt, 208(FS):Apr82-203
Von Baich, P. The Old Kingston Road.
  529(QQ):Summer82-460
Vones, I. Die "Historia Compostellana"
  und die Kirchenpolitik des nordwest-
  spanischen Raumes, 1070-1130.
  L.H. Nelson, 589:Jul82-676
Von Leyden, R., D. Duda and M. Roschan-
  zamir. Spielkarten-Bilder in persischen
  Lackmalereien.
  N.M. Titley, 463:Summer82-179
Vonnegut, K. Deadeye Dick.*
  W. Boyd, 364:Feb83-111
  A. Mars-Jones, 617(TLS):25Feb83-175
  J. Mellors, 362:17Feb83-24
Voorwinden, N. and M. de Haan. Oral
  Poetry.
  A.J. Holden, 554:Vol 102No2-268
Vorbichler, A. Die Oralliteratur der
  Balese-Efe im Ituri-Wald (Nordost-
  Zaïre).
  R. Vossen, 69:Vol51No1-534
Voss, R. Der Tanz und seine Geschichte.
  W. Dimter, 684(ZDA):Band111Heft2-78

Vosters, S.A. Los Países Bajos en la
literatura española. (Pt 1)
   J. Lechner, 549(RLC):Jan-Mar82-108
   N.G. Round, 86(BHS):Oct82-331
Vovelle, M. Idéologies et mentalités.
   P. Higonnet, 617(TLS):14Oct83-1141
Voyles, J.B. Gothic, Germanic, and North-
west Germanic.
   E.A. Ebbinghaus, 215(GL):Fall82-194
"Voz'mi na radost'."
   J. Graffy, 575(SEER):Jul82-448
Vrana, S.A. Interviews and Conversations
with 20th-Century Authors Writing in
English.
   R.F. Kiernan, 365:Fall82-165
de Vries, A.B., M. Toth-Ubbens and W.
Froentjes. Rembrandt in the Maurits-
huis.*
   C. Brown, 39:Mar82-210
de Vries, J. Grundbegriffe der Scholastik.
   J-F. Courtine, 192(EP):Oct-Dec81-500
   J.O., 543:Dec81-380
"Výslovnost spisovné češtiny."
   E. Eichler, 682(ZPSK):Band34Heft3-385

de Waal, F. Chimpanzee Politics.*
   A. Manning, 362:1Sep83-20
Wacher, J. The Coming of Rome.
   R. Goodburn, 123:Vol132No2-296
Wachtel, C. Joe the Engineer.
   J. Moynahan, 441:10Apr83-14
Wackernagel, J. Kleine Schriften. (Vols
1-3) (B. Forssman, ed)
   J.W. de Jong, 259(IIJ):Oct82-308
Wacziarg, F. and A. Nath. Rajasthan.
   S. Digby, 617(TLS):1Apr83-335
Waddington, P. Turgenev and England.*
   W.B. Edgerton, 678(YCGL):No30-85
   E. Kagan-Kans, 550(RusR):Jan82-103
   H. Orel, 131(CL):Summer82-283
   C.J.G. Turner, 104(CASS):Fall-Winter82-
524
   R. Whittaker, 574(SEEJ):Fall82-355
   J. Woodward, 402(MLR):Jan82-250
   N.G. Zekulin, 395(MFS):Winter82/83-707
Waddington, P. Turgenev and George Sand.
   E. Kagan-Kans, 550(RusR):Jan82-103
   L. Schapiro, 402(MLR):Apr82-505
   N.G. Zekulin, 395(MFS):Winter82/83-707
Wade, B.C. Music in India.
   R.B. Qureshi, 187:Sep83-555
Wade, M. Nadine Gordimer.
   R. Mane, 189(EA):Apr-Jun82-228
Wade, T.L.B. The Russian Preposition "do"
and the Concept of Extent.
   S. Marder, 575(SEER):Jan82-154
Wadley, S.S., ed. The Powers of Tamil
Women.
   P.G. Price, 293(JASt):May82-628
Wadlington, M.J. The Custom Touch.
   P. Bach, 614:Winter83-15
de Waelhens, A. Le Duc de Saint-Simon,
Immuable comme Dieu et d'une suite
enragée.
   M.S. Koppisch, 475:Vol9No17-810
Wagar, W.W. Terminal Visions.
   A. Burgess, 617(TLS):18Mar83-256
Wagaw, T.G. Education in Ethiopia.
   R. Pankhurst, 69:Vol51No1-538
Wagenknecht, C. Deutsche Metrik.
   B. Bjorklund, 133:Band15Heft4-349

Wagenknecht, E. The Novels of Henry James.
   P. Kemp, 617(TLS):23Sep83-1025
Wagenknecht, E. Henry David Thoreau.
   R. Asselineau, 189(EA):Oct-Dec82-486
   J.A. Christie, 27(AL):Mar82-126
   L. Lane, Jr., 106:Fall82-199
Wagenknecht, E. Utopia Americana.
   L. Mendelsohn, 561(SFS):Mar82-96
Wager, W. Designated Hitter.
   N. Callendar, 441:10Apr83-32
Waggoner, H.H. American Visionary Poetry.
   I. Salusinszky, 617(TLS):13May83-493
Wagner, A., ed. Canada's Lost Plays.
(Vol 3)
   R. Plant, 102(CanL):Spring82-103
Wagner, C. Cosima Wagner's Diaries.*
(Vol 1) (M. Gregor-Dellin and D. Mack,
eds)
   E. Salzman, 414(MusQ):Jul82-337
Wagner, C. Cosima Wagner's Diaries.*
(Vol 2) (M. Gregor-Dellin and D. Mack,
eds)
   R.L.J., 412:Feb81-59
   E. Salzman, 414(MusQ):Jul82-337
Wagner, F.J. J.H. Shorthouse.
   H.D. Spear, 447(N&Q):Oct81-447
Wagner, K. Herr und Knecht.
   M. Brändle, 67:May82-91
Wagner, L., ed. Critical Essays on Joyce
Carol Oates.
   Z. Mistri, 395(MFS):Summer81-377
Wagner, L.W. Dos Passos.*
   J. Griffin, 106:Fall82-253
Wagner, L.W. Ellen Glasgow.
   L. Auchincloss, 578:Spring83-100
Wagner, R. Dichtungen und Schriften. (D.
Borchmeyer, ed)
   J. Kerman, 453(NYRB):22Dec83-27
Wagner, R. My Life. (M. Whittall, ed)
   J. Kerman, 453(NYRB):22Dec83-27
Wagner, R. Three Wagner Essays.* (R.L.
Jacobs, trans)
   J. Kerman, 453(NYRB):22Dec83-27
Wagner, R. Richard Wagner: Sämtliche
Briefe.* (Vol 4) (G. Strobel and W.
Wolf, eds)
   R. Strohm, 410(M&L):Jul/Oct81-434
Wagner, R-L. Essais de linguistique fran-
çaise.*
   M. Wilmet, 553(RLiR):Jan-Jun82-191
Wagner, S. A Piece of My Mind.
   J. Riemer, 390:Feb82-60
Wagner, W., ed. Theodor Fontane, Schach
von Wuthenow.
   H-G. Richert, 133:Band15Heft1/2-172
Waguet, J-P. Poing Soleil.
   J. Paulhan, 207(FR):Apr83-797
Wahl, A., ed. Die altprovenzalische Über-
setzung des Liber Scintilarum.
   G. Roques, 553(RLiR):Jul-Dec82-504
Wahrig, G., ed. dtv-Wörterbuch der deut-
schen Sprache.
   K-E. Sommerfeldt, 682(ZPSK):Band34
Heft3-390
Wahrig, G., H. Krämer and H. Zimmermann –
see "Brockhaus Wahrig Deutsches Wörter-
buch"
Waibl, E. Gesellschaft und Kultur bei
Hobbes und Freud.
   R. Thurnher, 53(AGP):Band64Heft1-92
Wain, J. Poems 1949-1979.
   M. Imlah, 493:Apr82-55
   J. Saunders, 565:Vol23No3-73

Wainwright, D. Broadwood by Appointment.*
  B. Shulgasser, 441:30Oct83-18
Wainwright, H. and D. Elliott. The Lucas
Plan.
  C. Crouch, 617(TLS):25Nov83-1328
Waites, B. - see "Rutland Record No. 1"
Wajsbrot, C. Une vie à soi.
  P.L. Bowles, 617(TLS):15Jul83-760
Wakefield, G.S., ed. A Dictionary of
Christian Spirituality.
  R. Morgan, 617(TLS):2Dec83-1353
Walach, D. Der aufrechte Bürger, seine
Welt und sein Theater.
  S.D. Martinson, 221(GQ):May82-419
Walbank, M.B. Athenian Proxenies of the
Fifth Century B.C.*
  A.G. Woodhead, 303(JoHS):Vol 102-294
Walcott, D. The Fortunate Traveller.*
  P. Bland, 364:Jun82-73
  X.J. Kennedy, 491:Mar83-349
  M. O'Neill, 493:Jun82-68
  639(VQR):Autumn82-133
Wald, A.M. The Revolutionary Imagination.
  P. Schjeldahl, 441:10Jul83-14
Wald, K.D. Crosses on the Ballot.
  J. Cornford, 617(TLS):22Jul83-770
Waldeck, P.B. The Split Self from Goethe
to Broch.*
  G. Brude-Firnau, 564:Feb81-91
  J.J. White, 402(MLR):Apr82-493
Waldeland, L. John Cheever.
  S.I. Bellman, 573(SSF):Spring82-182
Walden, H.T. 2d. The Last Pool.
  W. Zander, 135:Apr82-134
Walder, D. Dickens and Religion.*
  G.H. Ford, 445(NCF):Sep82-214
  A. Wilson, 155:Summer82-110
Waldman, D. Anthony Caro.*
  J. McEwen, 90:Sep82-567
Walens, S. Feasting With Cannibals.*
  J.J. Cove, 529(QQ):Winter82-887
Waley, A. A Half of Two Lives.*
  H. Carpenter, 441:24Apr83-10
  H.R., 231:Apr83-76
  A. Ross, 364:Nov82-96
Waley, D. George Eliot's Blotter.
  W. Baker, 354:Mar82-80
Waley, P. - see "Curial and Guelfa"
Walicki, A. A History of Russian Thought
From the Enlightenment to Marxism.*
  D.W. Treadgold, 396(ModA):Winter82-86
Walicki, A. Philosophy and Romantic
Nationalism.
  M. Malia, 453(NYRB):29Sep83-18
Walker, A. Joan Crawford.
  M. Haskell, 441:30Oct83-9
  A. Mars-Jones, 617(TLS):18Nov83-1291
Walker, A. In Search of Our Mothers' Gar-
dens.
  442(NY):7Nov83-184
Walker, A. Franz Liszt. (Vol 1)
  L. Beckett, 617(TLS):17Jun83-623
  H. Cole, 362:8Sep83-20
  E. Hoffman, 441:3Apr83-8
  G. Steiner, 442(NY):13Jun83-126
Walker, A.G.H. Die nordfriesische Mundart
der Bökin`gharde.
  B.J. Koekkoek, 221(GQ):Nov82-583
Walker, C.B.F. Cuneiform Texts from Baby-
lonian Tablets in the British Museum.
(Pt 52)
  S. Greengus, 318(JAOS):Apr-Jun81-257

Walker, C.D. Dictionnaire inverse de
l'ancien français.
  W.J. Ashby, 350:Jun83-443
  G. Roques, 553(RLiR):Jun-Dec82-453
Walker, D.C. An Introduction to Old
French Morphophonology.
  J. Klausenburger, 207(FR):Apr83-809
  J. Klausenburger, 350:Sep83-608
Walker, D.D. Clio's Cowboys.
  H.P. Hinton, 651(WHR):Summer82-183
Walker, D.L. - see London, J.
Walker, D.M. The Oxford Companion to Law.*
  P-G. Boucé, 189(EA):Apr-Jun82-198
Walker, D.P. Unclean Spirits.*
  R.H. Robbins, 551(RenQ):Summer82-297
Walker, G.F. Gossip.
  A. Messenger, 102(CanL):Spring82-101
Walker, G.J. Spanish Politics and Impe-
rial Trade, 1700-1789.
  W.J. Callahan, 173(ECS):Fall82-82
Walker, J. Portraits: 5,000 Years.
  C. Tomkins, 442(NY):19Dec83-126
Walker, J. Portraiture.
  J. Russell, 441:4Dec83-65
Walker, J. The Reverend Dr. John Walker's
Report on the Hebrides of 1764 and 1771.
(M.M. McKay, ed)
  R.A. Rauschenberg, 173(ECS):Summer83-
443
Walker, J. Walker's Rhyming Dictionary of
the English Language. (rev by L.H. Daw-
son; supp comp by M. Freeman)
  T. Disch, 617(TLS):20May83-509
Walker, J. - see Cunninghame Graham, R.B.
Walker, J.A. The Japanese Novel of the
Meiji Period and the Ideal of Individual-
ism.*
  M.G. Ryan, 244(HJAS):Dec82-702
Walker, J.A. Van Gogh Studies.
  R. Pickvance, 39:Sep82-201
Walker, M. Robert Penn Warren.*
  T.A. Westendorp, 125:Spring82-310
Walker, N. Punishment, Danger and Stigma.*
  R.S. Gerstein, 185:Jan83-408
  J. Kleinig, 63:Jun82-193
Walker, S. Animal Thought.
  A. Manning, 362:1Sep83-20
  S. Stich, 617(TLS):29Apr83-424
Walker, S. The Poetry of Judith Wright.
  M. Duwell, 71(ALS):May82-410
Walker, S. and A. Burnett. The Image of
Augustus.
  J. Mitchell, 59:Jun82-256
Walker, S.F. Theocritus.*
  M. Campbell, 123:Vol32No1-94
  D.M. Halperin, 121(CJ):Dec82/Jan83-159
Walker, T. The High Path.
  E. Blishen, 617(TLS):14Jan83-32
  P. Dickinson, 364:Mar83-105
Walker, W. A Dime to Dance By.
  442(NY):15Aug83-90
Wall, C.C. George Washington.
  E.L. Shepard, 77:Summer82-273
Wall, I.M. French Communism in the Era of
Stalin.
  R.W. Johnson, 617(TLS):30Dec83-1461
Wall, K. L'inversion dans la subordonnée
en français contemporain.*
  K.J. Danell, 597(SN):Vol154No2-339
  K. Klingebiel, 545(RPh):Nov81-400
Wall, M.B. and R.J. Dack, with J.R. Warnke.
Balustrades and Gingerbread.
  D.J. Hibbard, 658:Spring82-90

Wallace, B. - see under di Michele, M.
Wallace, C.M. The Design of "Biographia Literaria."
   P. Hamilton, 617(TLS):16Sep83-1000
Wallace, D.R. The Klamath Knot.
   P-L. Adams, 61:Feb83-105
   C.D. May, 441:20May83-15
   P. Zaleski, 469:Vol8No2-97
Wallace, E. The Mind of Mr. J.G. Reeder.
   P. Craig, 617(TLS):19Aug83-890
Wallace, J. Joe Wallace Poems.
   M. Acorn, 102(CanL):Summer82-126
Wallace, J.D. Virtues and Vices.*
   S.B. Cunningham, 154:Mar82-133
   C.D. MacNiven, 488:Jun82-221
   R. de Sousa, 449:Mar82-161
Wallace, R. Plums, Stones, Kisses and Hooks.*
   S.C. Behrendt, 502(PrS):Summer82-91
Wallace, R. and C. Zimmerman, eds. The Work.
   K. Garebian, 99:Feb83-28
   M. Page, 648(WCR):Apr83-51
Wallace, S.E. and A. Eser, eds. Suicide and Euthanasia.
   T.M.R., 185:Apr83-645
Wallach, L. Diplomatic Studies in Latin and Greek Documents from the Carolingian Age.
   R.J. Schoeck, 121(CJ):Dec82/Jan83-162
Wallach-Faller, M. Ein alemannischer Psalter aus dem 14. Jahrhundert.
   K. Kirchert, 684(ZDA):Band111Heft3-130
Wallbank, F.W. The Hellenistic World.
   S.M. Burstein, 121(CJ):Feb/Mar83-262
Wallenstein, K. Corpus Vasorum Antiquorum. (Deutschland, Vol 44)
   B.A. Sparkes, 303(JoHS):Vol 102-285
Waller, M. Democratic Centralism.*
   S.S. Vosper, 575(SEER):Jul82-465
Waller, M.R. Petrarch's Poetics and Literary History.*
   S.L. Bermann, 546(RR):May82-385
   A.S. Bernardo, 551(RenQ):Winter81-560
   A.F. Nagel, 131(CL):Fall82-367
Waller, P.J. Town, City and Nation: England 1850-1914.
   R. Floud, 617(TLS):16Dec83-1410
Wallerstein, N. Language and Culture in Conflict.
   L.M. Crawford-Lange, 608:Dec83-673
Walliczek, W. - see Kuhn, H.
Wallis, H., ed. The Maps and Text of the Boke of Idrography presented by Jean Rotz to Henry VIII now in the British Library.
   N. Barker, 617(TLS):6May83-471
Wallis, P.J. The Book Trade in Northumberland and Durham to 1860. The North-East Book Trade to 1860.
   D. Pearson, 83:Autumn82-265
   E.A. Swaim, 517(PBSA):Vol176No3-358
Walliser, S. That Nature is a Heraclitean Fire and of the Comfort of the Resurrection.*
   L. Moessner, 38:Band100Heft1/2-225
Wallner, B., ed. The Middle English Translation of Guy de Chauliac's Treatise on Wounds.* (Pt 2)
   L.E. Voigts, 589:Jan82-201
Wallot, H. L'Accès au monde littéraire ou Éléments pour une critique littéraire
                                          [continued]

[continuing]
   chez Maurice Merleau-Ponty.
   G. Cesbron, 356(LR):Feb82-87
Walls, J. and Y. - see "West Lake"
Walpole, H. Horace Walpole's Miscellaneous Correspondence. (W.S. Lewis and J. Riely, with others, eds)
   T.J. McCormick, 39:Aug82-127
Walpole, H. The Yale Edition of Horace Walpole's Correspondence. (Vol 43) (E.M. Martz, with R.K. McClure and W.T. La Moy, comps)
   R. Halsband, 617(TLS):4Nov83-1228
Walpole, H. and others - see under Sayers, D.L. and others
Walravens, H. - see Laufer, B.
Walrod, M.R. Discourse Grammar in Ga'dang.
   P.S. Frank, 355(LSoc):Apr82-145
Walser, M. The Swan Villa.*
   J. Neves, 617(TLS):6May83-464
Walser, R. North Carolina Legends.
   R. Manley, 292(JAF):Oct-Dec82-479
Walser, R. Selected Stories.*
   J. Mellors, 362:13Jan83-23
Walsh, J. American War Literature: 1914 to Vietnam.
   S. Fender, 617(TLS):22Apr83-395
Walsh, J.E. The Bones of St. Peter.
   P. Hebblethwaite, 617(TLS):9Sep83-970
Walsh, J.E. Growing Up In British India.
   H. Toye, 617(TLS):9Sep83-971
Walsh, M.J. Vatican City State.
   P. Hebblethwaite, 617(TLS):13May83-494
Walsh, P.G. - see "Andreas Capellanus on Love"
Walsh, S. Bartók Chamber Music.
   P. Griffiths, 415:Nov82-764
Walsh, T.J. Second Empire Opera.*
   S. Huebner, 414(MusQ):Jul82-416
Walsh, W. F.R. Leavis.*
   R. Wellek, 402(MLR):Jul82-710
Walsh, W. R.K. Narayan.
   R. Davies, 617(TLS):4Mar83-205
   M. Hulse, 364:Mar83-119
Walsh, W. Patrick White: "Voss."
   J.F. Burrows, 677(YES):Vol 12-360
Walshe, P. Church versus State in South Africa.
   P. Hinchliff, 617(TLS):7Oct83-1103
Walter, H. La Dynamique des phonèmes dans le lexique français contemporain.
   F. Abel, 72:Band218Heft2-456
Walther von der Vogelweide. Die gesamte Überlieferung der Texte und Melodien. (H. Brunner, U. Müller and F.V. Spechtler, eds)
   E. Nellmann, 680(ZDP):Band101Heft3-453
Walton, D. Evening Out.
   R. Banks, 441:20Feb83-6
Walton, D.N. Brain Death.
   L.C. Becker, 482(PhR):Oct82-656
Walton, I. The Compleat Angler 1653-1676. (J. Bevan, ed)
   D. Profumo, 617(TLS):29Jul83-798
Walton, T. Louie and Women.
   V. Bourjaily, 441:14Aug83-13
   442(NY):16May83-133
Walzer, M. Spheres of Justice.
   R. Dworkin, 453(NYRB):14Apr83-4
   M.J. Sandel, 441:24Apr83-1
   J. Waldron, 617(TLS):23Dec83-1424

Warren, B. Semantic Patterns of Noun-Noun Compounds.*
    H. Sauer, 38:Band100Heft1/2-148
Warren, D. and J. Cagney. James Cagney.
    J. Marsh, 617(TLS):18Nov83-1291
Warren, G.H. Fountain of Discontent.
    D.F. Long, 432(NEQ):Jun82-309
Warren, M.A. The Nature of Women.*
    N.O. Keohane, 185:Oct82-102
Warren, M.E. and M. Baltimore.
    B. Dobell, 441:4Dec83-64
Warren, P. Elstree: The British Hollywood.
    G. Kaufman, 362:6Oct83-23
    617(TLS):18Nov83-1264
Warren, P. Irish Glass.*
    G. Wills, 39:Nov82-349
Warren, R.P. Being Here.*
    C. Molesworth, 473(PR):4/1982-620
    D.H. Sullivan, 648(WCR):Spring82-56
Warren, R.P. Rumor Verified.*
    L.L. Martz, 676(YR):Autumn82-63
    P. Stitt, 219(GaR):Spring82-184
    V. Young, 249(HudR):Spring82-139
    639(VQR):Spring82-58
Warrier, A.G.K. God in Advaita.
    S. Mayeda, 318(JAOS):Oct-Dec81-475
Warshawsky, A.G. The Memories of an American Impressionist. (B.L. Bassham, ed)
    H.W. Morgan, 658:Summer/Autumn82-166
von Wartburg, W. Französisches Etymologisches Wörterbuch. (fasc 142 ed by C.T. Gossen)
    G. Roques, 553(RLiR):Jan-Jun82-185
Wartelle, A. Bibliographie d'Eschyle 1518-1974.
    L.K., 450(NRF):Jan82-155
Wartofsky, M.W. Models.
    J.R. Wettersten, 679:Band13Heft1-170
Warwick, C. Princess Margaret.
    A. Huth, 362:21Apr83-21
    D.A.N. Jones, 617(TLS):29Apr83-428
Washington, G. The Papers of George Washington: The Journal of the Proceedings of the President, 1793-1797. (D. Twohig and W. Abbot, eds)
    639(VQR):Summer82-87
Wasow, T. Anaphora in Generative Grammar.*
    A.R. Tellier, 189(EA):Jan-Mar82-72
Wasson, B. Count No 'Count.
    442(NY):4Jul83-92
Watanabe-O'Kelly, H. - see Schiller, F.
Waterer, J.W. Leather and the Warrior.
    E. Marx, 324:Jan83-108
Waterhouse, E. The Dictionary of British Eighteenth-Century Painters.*
    J. Egerton, 90:Mar82-164
Waterhouse, K. In the Mood.
    J. Mellors, 362:30Jun83-28
    J.K.L. Walker, 617(TLS):13May83-481
Waterhouse, R. A Heidegger Critique.
    A.G. Pleydell-Pearce, 323:May82-206
Waterman, A. Out for the Elements.*
    P. Bland, 364:Jun82-73
    C.B. Cox, 148:Winter82-3
    M. O'Neill, 493:Apr82-59
Waters, E.N. - see Liszt, F.
Waters, F. Mountain Dialogues.
    C.L. Adams, 649(WAL):Spring82-61
Waterson, N. Uzbek-English Dictionary.*
    G.L. Lewis, 402(MLR):Jan82-255
Waterton, B. Pettranella.
    M. Whitaker, 102(CanL):Summer82-142

Watkin, D. The English Vision.*
    J.M. Crook, 617(TLS):7Jan83-19
Watkin, D. Athenian Stuart.
    J.M. Richards, 617(TLS):7Jan83-19
Watkins, A. Brief Lives.*
    442(NY):21Feb83-134
Watkins, F.C. Then and Now.
    W. Harmon, 578:Spring83-119
Watkins, G. Portrait of a Friend.
    D. Abse, 617(TLS):5Aug83-839
Watson, A. - see Mao Zedong
Watson, C.N. The Novels of Jack London.
    H. Beaver, 617(TLS):3Jun83-567
Watson, G. The Shorter New Cambridge Bibliography of English Literature.*
    P. Davison, 354:Jun82-188
Watson, G.J. Drama.
    K. Mrosovsky, 617(TLS):2Sep83-927
Watson, G.J. Irish Identity and the Literary Revival.*
    P. Faulkner, 161(DUJ):Jun82-316
    P-Y. Petillon, 98:Jun-Jul82-537
Watson, H.L. Jacksonian Politics and Community Conflict.
    639(VQR):Summer82-82
Watson, I. Song and Democratic Culture in Britain.
    S. Frith, 617(TLS):2Dec83-1356
Watson, J.R., ed. Everyman's Book of Victorian Verse.
    A. Shelston, 148:Autumn82-81
Watson, P. Double-Dealer.
    W. Mostyn-Owen, 617(TLS):30Sep83-1063
Watson, R. Night Blooming Cactus.*
    K. Cherry, 134(CP):Spring82-100
Watson, R. Rumours of Fulfilment.*
    442(NY):21Feb83-133
Watson, R.A. and J.E. Force - see Popkin, R.H.
Watson, W. Art of Dynastic China.
    "Skipjack," 463:Autumn82-285
Watson, W., ed. The Great Japan Exhibition Catalogue.
    D. Newman, 463:Spring82-88
Watson, W. The Knight on the Bridge.*
    D. Durrant, 364:Nov82-87
    D. Quammen, 441:6Nov83-14
Watson-Williams, H. The Novels of Nathalie Sarraute.
    C.A. Hingley, 67:Nov82-208
Watt, C. The Christian Watt Papers. (D. Fraser, ed)
    J. Hunter, 617(TLS):26Aug83-910
Watt, I. Conrad in the Nineteenth Century.*
    K. Carabine, 191(ELN):Sep81-75
    C. Eichelberger, 295(JML):Dec82-426
    I. Ousby, 97(CQ):Vol 11No1-275
Watten, B. Complete Thought.
    D. Hall, 271:Winter82-175
Wattenmaker, B.S. and V. Wilson. A Guidebook for Teaching Foreign Language.*
    R.W. Newman, 207(FR):Oct82-197
    W. Woodhouse, 238:Dec82-670
Watters, D. "With Bodilie Eyes."
    A.I. Ludwig, 165(EAL):Winter82/83-251
Watts, C. R.B. Cunninghame Graham.
    D. Campbell, 617(TLS):30Sep83-1039
Watts, C. - see Cunninghame Graham, R.B.
Watts, D.A. Cardinal de Retz.*
    H. De Ley, 475:No16Pt2-460

Watts, E.S. The Businessman in American Literature.
  G. Ewart, 617(TLS):11Mar83-229
Watzlawick, P. and J.H. Weakland. Sur l'interaction.
  F. Flahault, 98:May82-442
Waugh, D.C. - see under Uo, D.K.
Waugh, E. Grandeur et décadence; Scoop; Le Cher Disparu; Retour à Brideshead.
  C. Jordis, 450(NRF):Jan82-145
Waugh, E. The Letters of Evelyn Waugh.*
  (M. Amory, ed)
  J. Meyers, 395(MFS):Summer81-352
  G.S. Rousseau, 579(SAQ):Summer82-338
Waugh, H. Kate's House.
  T. Mars, 617(TLS):14Oct83-1110
  K.C. O'Brien, 362:10Nov83-30
Way, B. Audience Participation.
  J. Doolittle, 108:Spring82-198
Way, B. F. Scott Fitzgerald and the Art of Social Fiction.*
  R. Bromley, 366:Autumn82-271
  S. Egan, 447(N&Q):Oct81-465
  R.S. Powell, 148:Spring82-85
  D. Seed, 677(YES):Vol 12-352
  G. Wickes, 395(MFS):Summer82-292
Wayman, A. Yoga of the Guhyasamājatantra.
  P. Kvaerne, 259(IIJ):Jul80-242
  L. Sternbach, 318(JAOS):Oct-Dec81-481
Wayman, T., ed. Going for Coffee.*
  D. Barbour, 648(WCR):Summer81-82
  T. Goldie, 102(CanL):Summer82-149
  J. Lent, 137:Aug82-30
Wayman, T. A Planet Mostly Sea.* Living on the Ground.*
  D. Barbour, 648(WCR):Summer81-84
Wearing, J. The L-Shaped Party.
  W.P. Irvine, 529(QQ):Summer82-340
Wearing, J.P. American and British Theatrical Biography.
  C. Price, 447(N&Q):Dec81-569
Wearing, J.P. The London Stage 1900-1909.
  J. Ellis, 570(SQ):Summer82-245
Wearing, J.P. The London Stage 1910-1919.
  V. Ellis, 617(TLS):2Sep83-938
Weart, S.R. and G.W. Szilard - see Szilard, L.
Weaver, D.H. and others. Media Agenda-Setting in a Presidential Election.
  R.A. Weaver, 583:Spring83-305
Weaver, R.L. and N.W. A Chronology of Music in the Florentine Theater 1590-1750.
  W. Dean, 410(M&L):Jan81-84
Webb, B. The Diary of Beatrice Webb. (Vol 2) (N. and J. MacKenzie, eds)
  S.R. Letwin, 362:20Oct83-23
Webb, B. My Apprenticeship.
  I.B. Nadel, 506(PSt):Sep82-269
Webb, B.L. Poetry on the Stage.
  T. Griffiths, 402(MLR):Oct82-938
Webb, I. From Custom to Capital.*
  P. Christmas, 405(MP):Nov82-214
  M. Cotsell, 155:Summer82-116
  J. Halperin, 395(MFS):Summer82-259
Webb, J. A Country Such As This.
  D. Evanier, 441:13Nov83-14
Webb, J. Fields of Fire.
  E.F. Palm, 145(Crit):Vol24No2-105
Webb, J.C. Mechanism, Mentalism and Metamathematics.*
  J.B., 543:Sep81-176   [continued]

[continuing]
  J.R. Lucas, 84:Dec82-441
  C. Mortensen, 63:Dec82-379
Webb, P. Wilson's Bowl.
  D. Barbour, 648(WCR):Oct82-37
  W.J. Keith, 102(CanL):Winter81-99
  A. Mandel, 198:Jan82-63
  B. Whiteman, 137:Aug82-16
Webb, S.S. The Governors-General.
  J. Béranger, 189(EA):Jan-Mar82-81
Webb, T., ed. English Romantic Hellenism: 1700-1824.
  R. Bentman, 566:Spring83-136
Webb, V. Archaic Greek Faience.
  E.J. Peltenburg, 303(JoHS):Vol 102-290
Webb, W.L., ed. The Bedside "Guardian" 32.
  R. Davies, 617(TLS):23Dec83-1439
Webber, J.M. Milton and his Epic Tradition.*
  A. Burnett, 402(MLR):Jan82-161
  M. Evans, 541(RES):Aug82-318
Webber, L.R. Japanese Woodblock Prints.
  U. Roberts, 60:Mar-Apr82-134
Weber, A. Die Entwicklung der Rahmenerzählungen Nathaniel Hawthornes.
  E.O. Fink, 72:Band218Heft1-193
Weber, B.N. and H. Heinen, eds. Bertolt Brecht.
  M. Hays, 397(MD):Sep82-443
von Weber, C.M. Writings on Music. (J. Warrack, ed)
  W. Dean, 415:Dec82-842
  M.C. Tusa, 451:Spring83-272
Weber, E., ed. Texte zur Romantheorie II (1732-1780).
  G. Hoffmeister, 221(GQ):May82-397
  F. Wahrenburg, 680(ZDP):Band101Heft2-289
Weber, E. - see Guillaumin, E.
Weber, H., ed. Die Generallinie.
  F.L. Carsten, 575(SEER):Oct82-631
Weber, M. Rescher and Knies.* Critique of Stammler.*
  T.E. Huff, 488:Mar82-81
  T.E. Huff, 488:Jun82-205
Weber, R. The Literature of Fact.*
  M. Cross, 599:Fall82-462
  S. Fogel, 106:Fall82-267
  J. Hollowell, 395(MFS):Summer82-312
Weber, R., ed. The Reporter as Artist.
  M. Cross, 599:Fall82-462
Weber, S. Unwrapping Balzac.*
  P. Imbert, 107(CRCL):Dec81-547
  L.A. Russell, 446(NCFS):Spring-Summer 83-367
Weber, S. and H. Sussman - see "Glyph"
Webster, E. The Venetian Spy-Glass.
  T.J. Binyon, 617(TLS):13May83-498
  T.J. Binyon, 617(TLS):8Jul83-732
Webster, G. The Republic of Letters.*
  R.H. Pearce, 27(AL):Oct82-464
  R.D. Stock, 396(ModA):Winter82-102
Wechsler, J., ed. On Aesthetics in Science.
  R. Payne, 152(UDQ):Winter82-119
Wechsler, S. Low-Fire Ceramics.
  D. Rhodes, 139:Feb/Mar82-43
Weckermann, H-J. Verständigungsprobleme in Shakespeares Dramen.*
  D. Mehl, 72:Band218Heft1-177

Weckherlin, G.R. Stuttgarter Hoffeste.*
Essais van Hulsen/Matthäus Merian,
"Repraesentatio Der fürstlichen Aufzug
und Ritterspil."* (L. Krapf and C.
Wagenknecht, eds of both)
   B. Becker-Cantarino, 221(GQ):May82-414
Wedberg, A. Antiquity and the Middle Ages.
483:Oct82-567
Wedderburn, R. The Complaynt of Scotland
(c. 1550) by Mr. Robert Wedderburn.*
(A.M. Stewart, ed)
   A.H. MacLaine, 541(RES):Feb82-73
Weeks, J. Capital and Exploitation.
A.L., 185:Jan83-432
Wegelin, E.A. Urban Low-Income Housing
and Development.
   T. McGee, 293(JASt):Feb82-412
Wegman, W. Man's Best Friend.
   S. Schwartz, 453(NYRB):18Aug83-44
Wehle, W., ed. Nouveau Roman.
   L. Hill, 208(FS):Jan82-103
   B. Wichmann, 395(MFS):Summer81-408
Wehle, W. Novellenerzählen.
   G. Demerson, 549(RLC):Jul-Sep82-381
Wehner, W.L. Humanism and the Aesthetic
Experience in Music.
   G.L. Knieter, 289:Fall82-121
Wehrli, M. Geschichte der deutschen Lit-
eratur von den Anfängen bis zur Gegen-
wart. (Vol 1)
   H. Emmel, 221(GQ):May82-408
   D.H. Green, 402(MLR):Oct82-984
Wehrli, R. G.C. Lichtenbergs ausführliche
Erklärung der Hogarthischen Kupferstiche.
   H-G. Schwarz, 564:May82-146
Wehse, R. Schwanklied und Flugblatt in
Grossbritannien.*
   N. Würzbach, 38:Band100Heft1/2-196
Wei Chuang. The Song-Poetry of Wei Chuang
(836-910 A.D.). (J.T. Wixted, trans)
   D.J. Levy, 293(JASt):Feb82-346
Wei, W. - see under Wang Wei
Wei, W. and others - see under Wang Wei
and others
Weidlé, V. Èmbriologiia poèzii.
   V.E. Alexandrov, 550(RusR):Apr82-234
   T. Eekman, 104(CASS):Spring82-122
   A. McMillin, 575(SEER):Jan82-155
   B.P. Scherr, 574(SEEJ):Fall82-353
Weigel, S. Flugschriftenliteratur 1848 in
Berlin.*
   J. Schildt, 682(ZPSK):Band34Heft3-386
Weiger, J.G. The Individuated Self.*
   F.G. Salinero, 552(REH):Jan82-134
Weigle, M. and K. Fiore. Santa Fe and
Taos.
   L. Milazzo, 584(SWR):Autumn82-vi
Weijnen, A. and others - see "Atlas Lingu-
arum Europae"
Weil, S. and L. Rameau. Trésors des
expressions françaises.
   P-L. Rey, 450(NRF):Mar82-123
Weimann, J.M. The Fair Women.
   J.V. Turano, 16:Spring82-76
Weimann, R. Shakespeare and the Popular
Tradition in the Theater.* (R. Schwartz,
ed and trans)
   P. Davison, 677(YES):Vol 12-250
Weimar, K. Enzyklopädie der Literaturwis-
senschaft.*
   D.H. Miles, 221(GQ):May82-391
   J. Schmidt, 564:May82-144

Weinberg, J.R. Ockham, Descartes, and
Hume.
   R.H. Popkin, 319:Jan82-97
de Weinberg, M.B.F. - see under Fontanella
de Weinberg, M.B.
Weinberger, C.W. Department of Defense
Annual Report to the Congress, Fiscal
Year 1984.
   E. Rothschild, 453(NYRB):14Apr83-40
Weinbrot, H.D. Augustus Caesar in "Augus-
tan" England.*
   B. Nugel, 38:Band100Heft3/4-535
   I. Simon, 179(ES):Feb82-78
Weinbrot, H.D. Alexander Pope and the Tra-
ditions of Formal Verse Satire.
   I. Salusinszky, 617(TLS):15Apr83-380
   H. Weber, 566:Spring83-129
Weiner, R.R. Cultural Marxism and Politi-
cal Sociology.
   A.P.S., 185:Apr83-634
Weingartner, F. - see Friess, H.L.
Weinraub, B. Bylines.
   C. Schine, 441:19Jun83-12
Weinreich, U. On Semantics.* (W. Labov
and B.S. Weinreich, eds)
   R.I. Binnick, 320(CJL):Spring82-64
Weinstein, A. Fictions of the Self: 1550-
1800.*
   R. Goldberg, 208(FS):Jan82-109
   S.G. Kellman, 454:Fall82-81
   B. McCrea, 301(JEGP):Jul82-431
   A.M. Moore, 131(CL):Summer82-279
   D. Wheeler, 577(SHR):Fall82-359
Weinstein, E.A. Woodrow Wilson.
   T.L. McDorman, 150(DR):Autumn82-514
Weinstein, N. Whaddaya Say?
   R.F. Van Trieste, 608:Mar83-129
Weintraub, S., ed. Modern British Drama-
tists, 1900-1945.
   P. Davison, 354:Dec82-463
Weintraub, S. The Unexpected Shaw.
   N. Grene, 617(TLS):8Apr83-359
Weintraub, S. - see "Dictionary of Lit-
erary Biography"
Weintraub, S. - see Shaw, G.B. and F.
Harris
Weir, J.E. - see Baxter, J.K.
Weir, R.F., ed. Death in Literature.*
   D. Schier, 569(SR):Winter82-viii
Weis, E. - see "Langenscheidts Grosswörter-
buch Französisch"
Weisberg, G. The Drawings and Water
Colors of Léon Bonvin.
   R. Jay, 446(NCFS):Fall-Winter82/83-188
Weisberg, G.P. The Realist Tradition.*
   M.S. Kinsey, 446(NCFS):Fall-Winter
82/83-186
Weiskel, T.C. French Colonial Rule and
the Baule Peoples.
   E. Terray, 69:Vol52No1-92
Weisman, J. Watchdogs.
   E. Jakab, 441:22May83-43
Weiss, B. and L.C. Pérez - see de la
Cueva, J.
Weiss, N.J. Farewell to the Party of
Lincoln.
   C.V. Woodward, 453(NYRB):8Dec83-14
Weiss, P. You, I, and the Others.*
   R.J. Bernstein, 543:Dec81-349
   A.B.W., 543:Mar82-638
Weiss, R. The Aramaic Targum of Job.
   F.S. Greenspahn, 318(JAOS):Oct-Dec81-
452

Weiss, T. The Man from Porlock.*
    C. Wilmer, 617(TLS):6May83-469
Weiss, T. Recoveries.*
    X.J. Kennedy, 491:Mar83-349
    C. Wilmer, 617(TLS):6May83-469
Weiss, T. Views and Spectacles.
    D. Gioia, 491:May82-102
Weiss, T. and R. - see "Quarterly Review
    of Literature Poetry Series"
Weiss, U. Das philosophische System von
    Thomas Hobbes.
    W. Bartuschat, 489(PJGG):Band89Heft1-
    213
Weiss, W. Das Drama der Shakespeare-Zeit.
    K.P. Steiger, 72:Band218Heft2-422
Weissman, F.S. Du Monologue intérieur à
    la Sous-conversation.*
    V. Minogue, 208(FS):Jan82-100
Weissman, J. - see Carruth, H.
Weissman, N.B. Reform in Tsarist Russia.
    D.T. Orlovsky, 104(CASS):Fall-Winter82-
    553
    M.M. Szeftel, 550(RusR):Jul82-328
Weisz, G. The Emergence of Modern Univer-
    sities in France, 1863-1914.
    M. Larkin, 617(TLS):29Jul83-818
Weisz, J. Das Epigramm in der deutschen
    Literatur des 17. Jahrhunderts.
    K.F. Otto, Jr., 406:Winter82-498
    J.A. Parente, Jr., 221(GQ):Mar82-233
Weitzmann, K. and others. The Icon.
    C. Mango, 617(TLS):20May83-523
Weitzmann-Fiedler, J. Romanische gravi-
    erte Bronzeschalen.
    H.L. Kessler, 589:Oct82-954
    C. Nordenfalk, 341:Vol51No1-34
Weizsäcker, E. Die Weizsäcker-Papiere
    1900-1932. (L.E. Hill, ed)
    P. Kennedy, 617(TLS):10Jun83-604
Welch, D. Propaganda and the German
    Cinema 1933-1945.
    I. Kershaw, 617(TLS):6May83-454
Welch, D. In Youth is Pleasure.
    A.J.G.H., 617(TLS):28Jan83-79
Welch, L. Orage with Gurdjieff in America.
    M. Heyneman, 469:Vol8No1-110
Welch, R. Irish Poetry from Moore to
    Yeats.*
    T. Eldemann, 305(JIL):Sep82-116
    R. Tracy, 174(Éire):Fall82-141
Welcome, J. Irish Horse-Racing.
    A. Ross, 364:Feb83-5
Welcome, J. The Sporting World of R.S.
    Surtees.*
    N. Woodin, 364:Aug/Sep82-125
Welish, M. Handwritten.* Two Poems.
    D. Lehman, 181:Winter-Spring83-166
Wellek, R. Four Critics.
    M. Buccó, 651(WHR):Winter82-374
    F.W. Conner, 290(JAAC):Winter82-229
Wellek, R. and A. Ribeiro, eds. Evidence
    in Literary Scholarship.*
    P.R. Backscheider, 173(ECS):Winter81/
    82-221
    H.K. Miller, 402(MLR):Jan82-147
Wellings, E.M. Vintage Cricketers.
    P.H. Sutcliffe, 617(TLS):16Sep83-987
Wellington, M.A. and M. O'Nan, eds. Ro-
    mance Literary Studies.*
    R.B. Klein, 552(REH):May82-315
Wells, D.F. and H. Cole, eds. Mississippi
    Heroes.
    M.C. Brown, 585(SoQ):Spring82-92

Wells, G. and others. Learning Through
    Interaction.
    S. Foster, 350:Mar83-238
Wells, G.A. The Historical Evidence for
    Jesus.
    J.D.M. Derrett, 617(TLS):18Feb83-166
Wells, H.G. H.G. Wells's Literary Criti-
    cism. (P. Parrinder and R. Philmus, eds)
    J. Huntington, 395(MFS):Summer81-327
Wells, J. Anyone for Denis?
    D. Devlin, 157:Summer82-52
Wells, R. Insurrection.
    R. Foster, 617(TLS):23Sep83-1016
Wells, R.H. Spenser's "Faerie Queene" and
    the Cult of Elizabeth.
    J. Wilson, 617(TLS):29Apr83-442
Wells, S. Modernizing Shakespeare's Spel-
    ling [together with] Taylor, G. Three
    Studies in the Text of "Henry V."*
    A. Hammond, 570(SQ):Autumn82-412
    R.K. Turner, Jr., 551(RenQ):Autumn81-
    450
Wells, S. Shakespeare, the Writer and His
    Work. Shakespeare: An Illustrated Dic-
    tionary.
    E. Quinn, 570(SQ):Spring82-127
Wells, S. - see "Shakespeare Survey"
Wells, T. The Technique of Electronic
    Music.
    R.D. Morris, 308:Fall82-331
Welsch, R.L., ed. Mister, You Got Your-
    self a Horse.
    C.L. Rawlins, 649(WAL):Nov82-290
Welsh, A. Reflections on the Hero as
    Quixote.*
    R. Björnson, 141:Spring82-186
    J.R. Holstun, 49:Jan82-88
    S.G. Kellman, 395(MFS):Summer82-349
    S.M. Tave, 445(NCF):Jun82-110
    566:Spring83-137
Welsh-Ovcharov, B. Vincent van Gogh and
    the Birth of Cloisonism.
    F. Orton and G. Pollock, 59:Sep82-341
Welty, E. The Collected Stories of Eudora
    Welty.*
    R. Buffington, 569(SR):Spring82-264
Welty, E. The Ponder Heart.
    P. Craig, 617(TLS):18Nov83-1294
Welzig, W. and others - see Schnitzler, A.
Wemple, S.F. Women in Frankish Society.
    V.M. Lagorio, 377:Jul82-115
Wendel, H. Danton.
    R.C. Holub, 406:Spring82-72
Wendland, H. Deutsche Holzschnitte bis
    zum Ende des 17. Jahrhunderts.
    N. Powell, 39:Aug82-128
Wendler, J., ed. 75 Jahre Phoniatrie.
    H. Ulbrich, 682(ZPSK):Band34Heft6-776
Wendorf, P. Peacefully. In Berlin.
    S. Altinel, 617(TLS):11Feb83-130
Wendorf, R. William Collins and Eigh-
    teenth-Century English Poetry.*
    M.R. Pownall, 566:Spring83-136
    P.M. Spacks, 401(MLQ):Jun82-179
Wendorf, R. and C. Ryskamp - see Collins,
    W.
Wendt, H.F., ed. Langenscheidts Kurzgram-
    matik Deutsch.
    H. Meier, 682(ZPSK):Band34Heft6-762
Weng, W-G. and Y. Boda, eds. The Palace
    Museum, Peking.*
    M. Medley, 617(TLS):1Apr83-335

Wenisch, F. Spezifisch anglisches Wortgut
in den nordhumbrischen Interlinearglos-
sierungen des Lukasevangeliums.*
  A. Cameron, 589:Oct82-956
Wennberg, B. French and Scandinavian
Sculpture in the Nineteenth Century.
  P. Cannon-Brookes, 39:Aug82-125
Wenzel, S. Verses in Sermons.*
  C. von Nolcken, 447(N&Q):Feb81-65
  O.S. Pickering, 72:Band218Heft1-170
Werewere-Liking. Une Nouvelle Terre suivi
de Du Sommeil d'injuste, Théâtre-Rituel.
  H.A. Waters, 207(FR):Mar83-676
Werkmeister, W.H., ed. Facets of Plato's
Philosophy.*
  D.J.Z., 543:Dec81-417
Werlen, I. Lautstrukturen des Dialekts
von Brig im schweizerischen Kanton Wal-
lis.
  W. Haas, 685(ZDL):2/1982-262
Werlich, D.P. Research Tools for Latin
American Historians.
  J. Fisher, 86(BHS):Jan82-89
Werlich, E. Typologie der Texte. A Text
Grammar of English.
  R. Zimmermann, 257(IRAL):Feb82-77
Werner, C.H. Paradoxical Resolutions.
  T. Schaub, 659(ConL):Winter83-524
Werner, E. Die Verbalperiphrase im Mittel-
französischen.
  W. Dietrich, 547(RF):Band93Heft3/4-420
  M. Wilmet, 554:Vol 102No3-410
Werner, G. Herr Arnes pengar.
  M. Setterwall, 563(SS):Winter82-93
Werner, H-G., ed. Lessings-Konferenz
Halle 1979.
  A. Scott-Prelorentzos, 221(GQ):Mar82-
  249
Werner, J. Gesellschaft in literarischer
Form.
  H.J. Schmidt, 221(GQ):Nov82-595
Wertime, T.A. and J.D. Muhly. The Coming
of the Age of Iron.
  J.F. Healy, 123:Vol32No1-82
Wertmüller, L. The Head of Alvise.*
  V. Rothschild, 617(TLS):11Mar83-248
Wesche, U. Byron und Grabbe.
  G. Hoffmeister, 301(JEGP):Apr82-293
Weschler, L. Seeing Is Forgetting the
Name of the Thing One Sees.*
  G. Marzorati, 55:Sep82-27
Wescott, R.W. Sound and Sense.
  D. Hymes, 350:Mar83-226
Wesley, M. Jumping the Queue.
  M. Johnson, 617(TLS):17Jun83-642
  M. Laski, 362:11Aug83-24
Wesley-Smith, P. Unequal Treaty 1898-1997.
  W.K.K. Chan, 293(JASt):Nov81-127
Wessell, L.P., Jr. Karl Marx, Romantic
Irony, and the Proletariat.*
  H. White, 591(SIR):Spring82-105
Wessolowsky, C. Reflections of Southern
Jewry. (L. Schmier, ed)
  H.S. Marks, 9(AlaR):Oct82-282
Wesson, R. The United States and Brazil.
  R.M. Schneider, 263(RIB):Vol32No1-72
West, D. and T. Woodman, eds. Creative
Imitation and Latin Literature.
  K. Galinsky, 122:Jan82-76
West, J.F. Faroese Folktales and Legends.
  J. Simpson, 203:Vol93No2-238
West, J.L.W. 3d and others - see Dreiser,
T.

West, M. The World is Made of Glass.
  P. van Rjndt, 441:3Jul83-9
West, M.L. Delectus ex Iambis et Elegis
Graecis.
  A.M. Bowie, 123:Vol32No2-269
  J. Péron, 555:Vol56fasc1-125
West, N. A Matter of Trust.
  N. Annan, 617(TLS):11Mar83-227
West, P. The Very Rich Hours of Count von
Stauffenberg.*
  R. Christ, 473(PR):3/1982-469
West, S.H. Vaudeville and Narrative.
  R.E. Strassberg, 318(JAOS):Oct-Dec81-
  427
West, T.G. Plato's "Apology of Socrates."*
  G.J. de Vries, 394:Vol35fasc1/2-167
  M.D. Yaffe, 154:Jun82-364
"West Lake." (J. and Y. Walls, trans)
  F.H. Mayer, 292(JAF):Jul-Sep82-359
Westbrook, W.W. Wall Street in the Ameri-
can Novel.*
  M. Chénetier, 189(EA):Apr-Jun82-231
  W. French, 395(MFS):Winter82/83-656
Westfall, R.S. Never at Rest.*
  A.R. Hall, 84:Sep82-305
  M. Jacob, 173(ECS):Spring83-317
  R. Penrose, 617(TLS):16Sep83-980
  P. Rogers, 83:Spring82-148
  G.S. Rousseau, 566:Autumn82-65
Westin, A. Newswatch.
  S. Bedell, 441:16Jan83-10
Westlake, D.E. Why Me.
  H. Gold, 441:9Jan83-13
Westphal, M., ed. Method and Speculation
in Hegel's Phenomenology.
  M.A.G., 185:Apr83-640
Westphal-Schmidt, C. Studien zum "Renne-
wart" Ulrichs von Türheim.*
  E.C. Lutz, 406:Winter82-489
Westrup, J.A. Purcell. (rev by N. For-
tune)
  J.M., 189(EA):Jul-Sep82-370
"Westward for Smelts." (H.M. Klein, ed)
  T.G.S. Cain, 447(N&Q):Aug81-384
Wetherell, W.D. Souvenirs.
  W.H. Pritchard, 249(HudR):Spring82-159
  639(VQR):Winter82-18
Wetsel, D. L'Ecriture et le reste.
  H.M. Davidson, 546(RR):Nov82-519
Wetter, J. Karl von Burgund.* (H. Thomke,
ed)
  G.C. Schoolfield, 301(JEGP):Jan82-80
  P. Skrine, 402(MLR):Apr82-488
Wettstein, R.H. Eine Gegenstandstheorie
der Warheit.
  W. Hogrebe, 342:Band73Heft1-87
Wexler, D.B. Mental Health Law.
  D.T.O., 185:Oct82-218
Wexler, J.P. Laura Riding's Pursuit of
Truth.*
  P. Hobsbaum, 677(YES):Vol 12-346
  T.D. Young, 569(SR):Summer82-1xvi
Wexler, P. Critical Social Psychology.
  D. Ingleby, 617(TLS):16Dec83-1407
Wey, J.C. - see Ockham, William of
Weydt, H., ed. Die Partikeln in der deut-
schen Sprache.
  B. Hilgendorf, 353:Vol 19No9/10-1031
Whalen, P. Enough Said.
  J.D. McClatchy, 491:Sep82-353
Whaley, J., ed. Mirrors of Mortality.
  C. Howells, 83:Autumn82-284
Whalley, G. - see Christian, E.

Whalley, G. - see Coleridge, S.T.
Whalley, J.I. The Pen's Excellencie.
  N. Barker, 78(BC):Winter82-513
Whalley, P. The Mortician's Birthday
Party.
  T.J. Binyon, 617(TLS):23Dec83-1437
Wharton, E. The House of Mirth.
  L.D., 617(TLS):8Apr83-360
Wharton, E. Roman Fever.
  P. Craig, 617(TLS):29Jul83-820
Wharton, W. Dad.*
  M. Maddocks, 569(SR):Winter82-107
Whatley, C.A., ed. John Galt 1779-1979.*
  E. Frykman, 588(SSL):Vol 17-275
Wheat, C. Dead Man's Thoughts.
  N. Callendar, 441:23Oct83-38
Wheatcroft, A. The World Atlas of Revolu-
tions.
  G. Best, 617(TLS):14Oct83-1130
Wheaton, B.K. Savoring the Past.
  J. Grigson, 617(TLS):23Dec83-1442
  G. Levitas, 441:24Jul83-7
Whedon, J. Two and Two Together.
  442(NY):24Oct83-163
Wheeler, D.L. Republican Portugal.
  N.J. Lamb, 86(BHS):Jan82-80
Wheeler, K.M. The Creative Mind in Cole-
ridge's Poetry.
  P.M.S. Dawson, 148:Summer82-87
  A.J. Harding, 401(MLQ):Jun82-181
  T. McFarland, 676(YR):Autumn82-95
  A. Reed, 661(WC):Summer82-116
Wheeler, K.M. Sources, Processes and
Methods in Coleridge's "Biographia
Literaria."
  J. Colmer, 67:May82-79
  R. Gravil, 72:Band218Heft2-441
  J.W. Wright, 661(WC):Summer82-114
Wheeler, M. The Art of Allusion in Victor-
ian Fiction.*
  J. Dusinberre, 447(N&Q):Aug81-350
Wheeler, M.C. Britain and the War for
Yugoslavia, 1940-1943.*
  D. Stafford, 104(CASS):Summer82-267
Wheeler, P. Bodyline.
  A. Hislop, 617(TLS):16Sep83-1002
Wheeler, R.P. Shakespeare's Development
and the Problem Comedies.
  D. Bevington, 301(JEGP):Jul82-411
  M. Burns, 539:Aug83-226
  C.W. Cary, 130:Fall82-272
Wheelwright, J. Collected Poems of John
Wheelwright. (A.H. Rosenfeld, ed)
  P. Schjeldahl, 441:10Jul83-14
Whelan, R. Double Take.
  J. Simpson, 55:Nov82-59
Wheldon, D. The Viaduct.
  J. Mellors, 362:14Apr84-32
  L. Taylor, 617(TLS):1Apr83-324
Whelpton, J. Jang Bahadur in Europe.
  E. Gellner, 617(TLS):23Dec83-1438
Whiffen, M. and F. Koeper. American Archi-
tecture 1607-1976.
  M.G. Broderick, 46:Nov82-81
  R.G. Wilson, 639(VQR):Summer82-533
Whinnom, K. La poesía amatoria de la
época de los Reyes Católicos.
  E.M. Gerli, 304(JHP):Fall82-60
Whinnom, K. - see de San Pedro, D.
Whitcombe, R.T. The New Italian Cinema.
  R. Armes, 364:Aug/Sep82-113

White, A. As Once in May. (S. Chitty, ed)
  A. Calder-Marshall, 617(TLS):30Dec83-
  1463
White, A. Names and Nomenclature in
Goethe's "Faust."*
  M.C. Crichton, 406:Fall82-355
  D.W.J. Vincent, 564:May81-177
White, A. The Uses of Obscurity.
  R.A. Hocks, 183(ESQ):Vol128No4-261
  E. Hollahan, 594:Fall82-294
  H. Wirth-Nesher, 395(MFS):Summer82-365
  R.B. Yeazell, 445(NCF):Mar83-611
White, D.A. Heidegger and the Language of
Poetry.*
  G.L. Bruns, 107(CRCL):Mar82-90
White, D.S. Black Africa and de Gaulle.
  A.H.M. Kirk-Greene, 69:Vol51No3-802
White, E. A Boy's Own Story.*
  A. Hollinghurst, 617(TLS):19Aug83-875
  J. Mellors, 362:18Aug83-23
White, E.W. A History of English Opera.
  H. Cole, 362:8Sep83-20
  J. Glover, 617(TLS):21Oct83-1151
White, H. The Men Were There Then.
  D. Zieroth, 648(WCR):Apr83-47
White, H. Studies in Theocritus and other
Hellenistic Poets.*
  F. Cairns, 123:Vol32No1-93
White, J. Central Administration in Nige-
ria, 1914-1918.*
  A.E. Afigbo, 69:Vol52No4-95
White, J. Duccio.*
  M. Boskovits, 54:Sep82-496
White, J. Rothschild Buildings.
  R.V. Steffel, 637(VS):Autumn81-101
White, J.D. Guidelines for College Teach-
ing of Music Theory.
  B.B. Campbell, 308:Fall82-356
White, J.F. - see Mann, T.
White, J.L. The Salt Ecstacies.
  D. Wojahn, 271:Spring82-158
White, K. - see Thoreau, H.D.
White, M. What Is and What Ought to Be
Done.
  A. Duff, 483:Oct82-562
  S. Nathanson, 258:Sep82-211
  E.R., 185:Jan83-413
White, N.P. Plato on Knowledge and Real-
ity.
  M.A. Stewart, 449:May82-317
White, P. Flaws in the Glass.*
  S.F.D. Hughes, 395(MFS):Winter82/83-
  738
  B. Kiernan, 581:Jun82-165
  L.T. Lemon, 502(PrS):Fall82-92
  S. Tatum, 649(WAL):Winter83-382
White, R.B., Jr., ed. The Dress of Words.
  P. Rogers, 541(RES):Feb82-83
White, R.L. Pär Lagerkvist in America.
  S.F.D. Hughes, 395(MFS):Summer81-403
White, S.D. Sir Edward Coke and "The
Grievances of the Commonwealth," 1621-
1628.
  L.A. Knafla, 551(RenQ):Autumn82-496
White, T. Catch a Fire.
  J. Wiener, 441:14Aug83-11
White, T.D. Johnnie Cross.
  B. Hardy, 617(TLS):7Oct83-1095
  J. Mellors, 362:15Dec83-30
White, T.H. America in Search of Itself.*
  K.S. Lynn, 617(TLS):10Jun83-595
  P. Whitehead, 362:16Jun83-24

White, V. Pa Ndau.
  R.L. Shep, 614:Winter83-20
Whitehouse, R. A London Album.
  B. Jay, 637(VS):Summer82-515
Whitelaw, M. - see Lord Dalhousie
Whitelock, D., ed. English Historical
  Documents, c. 500-1042. (2nd ed)
  C. Sisam, 541(RES):Nov82-452
Whiteman, B. Inventions.*
  D. Barbour, 648(WCR):Jun82-33
Whiteside, T. The Blockbuster Complex.*
  G. Woodcock, 569(SR):Spring82-240
Whiteson, L. White Snake.
  M. Thorpe, 99:Aug82-34
Whitfield, J.H. A Short History of Ital-
  ian Literature.
  G. Faustini, 399(MLJ):Spring82-111
Whitford, F. Egon Schiele.*
  N. Powell, 39:Apr82-294
Whiting, A.S. Siberian Development and
  East Asia.
  H. Hunter, 550(RusR):Jul82-343
Whiting, C. Death of a Division.
  639(VQR):Winter82-22
Whitman, C.H. The Heroic Paradox. (C.
  Segal, ed)
  H. Lloyd-Jones, 617(TLS):17Jun83-628
Whitman, W. American Bard. (W. Everson,
  ed)
  L.L. Martz, 676(YR):Autumn82-63
  W. White, 646(WWR):Mar82-36
  639(VQR):Spring82-60
Whitman, W. City of Orgies and Other
  Poems. (J.L. Lembo, ed)
  M.J. Killingsworth, 646(WWR):Jun-Sep-
  Dec82-103
Whitman, W. Leaves of Grass.* (S. Brad-
  ley and others, eds)
  R. Asselineau, 189(EA):Oct-Dec82-487
  R. Nelson, 639(VQR):Winter82-157
Whitmarsh, A. Simone de Beauvoir and the
  Limits of Commitment.
  A. Cismaru, 395(MFS):Winter82/83-711
  J. Forbes, 208(FS):Apr82-232
  S. Reynolds, 402(MLR):Oct82-967
Whittaker, R. The Faith and Fiction of
  Muriel Spark.
  P. Raine, 617(TLS):1Jul83-710
Whittall, A. The Music of Britten and
  Tippett.*
  S. Johnson, 607:Dec82-35
Whittall, M. - see Wagner, R.
Whitten, L. A Killing Pace.
  N. Callendar, 441:18Sep83-45
Whitton, K.S. Dietrich Fischer-Dieskau
  Mastersinger.*
  E. Forbes, 415:Aug82-549
Whitton, K.S. The Theatre of Friedrich
  Dürrenmatt.*
  C.N. Genno, 564:Sep81-254
Whitworth, J. Poor Butterflies.
  N. Corcoran, 617(TLS):27May83-549
"Who Owns Appalachia?"
  R.J. Margolis, 441:23Oct83-16
"Who's Who in the Theatre."* (17th ed)
  (I. Herbert, with C. Baxter and R.E.
  Finley, eds)
  R. Findlater, 157:Winter82-45
"Who's Who 1983."
  G. Wheatcroft, 617(TLS):20May83-520
Whynes, D.K. and R.A. Bowles. The Eco-
  nomic Theory of the State.
  M.W., 185:Jan83-424

Whyte, I.B. - see under Boyd Whyte, I.
Whyte, J. Gallimaufry.
  R. Geiger, 198:Oct82-120
Wich, R. Sino-Soviet Crisis Politics.*
  J. Radvanyi, 550(RusR):Apr82-232
Wichmann, S. Japonisme.*
  D. Sutton, 39:Jan82-8
Wicht, W. Virginia Woolf, James Joyce,
  T.S. Eliot.
  M.T. Reynolds, 395(MFS):Winter82/83-
  629
Wick, W.C. George Washington.
  J.V. Turano, 16:Autumn82-89
Wickens, H.M. Beginner's Guide to Spin-
  ning.
  R. Hoffman, 614:Fall83-17
Wickens, P.L. The Industrial and Commer-
  cial Workers' Union of Africa.
  R.D. Grillo, 69:Vol51No1-531
Wickert, E. The Middle Kingdom.
  D. Davin, 617(TLS):30Sep83-1060
Wickham, C.J. Early Medieval Italy.*
  D. Herlihy, 589:Oct82-957
Wickham, G. Early English Stages, 1300 to
  1660.* (Vol 3)
  D. Bevington, 589:Apr82-441
  C. Davidson, 130:Spring82-86
  A. Gurr, 570(SQ):Summer82-247
Wicks, C.B. The Parisian Stage.* (Pts 1-
  5)
  O. Krakovitch, 535(RHL):Jul-Aug82-673
Wickwire, F.B. and M. Cornwallis: The
  Imperial Years.
  S.R. Frey, 173(ECS):Winter82/83-224
  R.E. Johnson, 9(AlaR):Jan82-55
Widdess, D.R. and R.F. Wolpert, eds.
  Music and Tradition.*
  J.B. Katz, 410(M&L):Jan/Apr82-104
Widdowson, P., ed. Re-Reading English.*
  F. Whitehead, 437:Autumn82-388
Wideman, J.E. Sent for You Yesterday.
  A. Cheuse, 441:15May83-13
Widmer, K. Edges of Extremity.*
  R.B. Hauck, 395(MFS):Summer81-388
  P. Stevick, 473(PR):2/1982-315
Widmer, K. Paul Goodman.
  B. Vincent, 189(EA):Jul-Sep82-364
Widmer, U. Liebesnacht.
  A. Phelan, 617(TLS):7Oct83-1094
Wiecker, R., ed. Text & Kontext.
  M. Gerber, 406:Fall82-349
Wieczynski, J.L., ed. The Modern Encyclo-
  paedia of Russian and Soviet History.
  (Vol 17)
  D.W. Spring, 575(SEER):Jan82-108
Wied, A. Bruegel.*
  H. Langdon, 90:Jan82-36
Wiedemann, C., ed. Literatur und Gesell-
  schaft im deutschen Barock.
  J. Hardin, 406:Fall82-352
Wiedemann, K. Arbeit und Bürgertum.*
  J. Rosellini, 406:Spring82-81
Wiedemann, T. Greek and Roman Slavery.
  M. Golden, 487:Autumn82-280
  C.G. Starr, 24:Winter82-459
Wiedmann, A. Romantic Roots in Modern Art.
  M. Peckham, 591(SIR):Summer82-259
Wieland, C.M. Wielands Briefwechsel.
  (Vol 4) (H.W. Seifert, with A. Schneider
  and P-V. Springborn, eds)
  W. Paulsen, 222(GR):Winter82-41

Wiener, M. English Culture and the Decline of the Industrial Spirit, 1850-1980.*
  P. Stansky, 637(VS):Winter82-240
"Wiener Studien." (Vol 12)
  S. Saïd, 555:Vol55fasc1-169
Wier, D. The 8-Step Grapevine.*
  R. Jackson, 502(PrS):Spring82-91
Wierlacher, A., ed. Fremdsprache Deutsch.
  G. Träbing, 67:May82-98
Wierlacher, A. - see "Jahrbuch Deutsch als Fremdsprache 7"
Wierzbicka, A. The Case for Surface Case.*
  J.S. Levine, 574(SEEJ):Fall82-373
Wierzbicka, A. Lingua Mentalis.*
  R. Darnell, 474(PIL):Vol 14No4-540
  J.D. McCawley, 350:Sep83-654
Wiesel, E. The Testament.* (French title: Le Testament d'un poète juif assassiné.)
  P. Lewis, 565:Vol23No1-51
  A.H. Rosenfeld, 390:Jan82-51
Wieseltier, L. Nuclear War, Nuclear Peace.
  M. Bundy, 441:9Oct83-1
Wiesenfarth, J. - see Eliot, G.
Wiethase, I. Sprachwerke — Sprechhandlungen.
  H. Ulbrich, 682(ZPSK):Band34Heft5-650
Wiethölter, W. Witzige Illumination.*
  S.L. Cocalis, 406:Spring82-103
  M.R. Higonnet, 301(JEGP):Jan82-87
Wigforss, E. Skrifter i urval, I-IX.
  T. Tilton, 563(SS):Spring82-186
Wiggins, D. Sameness and Substance.*
  T. Baldwin, 483:Apr82-269
  H.M. Cartwright, 482(PhR):Oct82-597
  L.F. Stevenson, 518:Jan82-1
Wightman, W.P.D., J.C. Bryce and I.S. Ross - see Smith, A.
Wigley, J. The Rise and Fall of the Victorian Sunday.
  G.W. Olsen, 637(VS):Autumn81-97
Wigmore, J.H., ed. Law and Justice in Tokugawa Japan. (Pt 6-G)
  Y. Kawashima, 293(JASt):Aug82-845
Wijnands, P. and J.M. Ost. Mots d'aujourd'hui néerlandais-français, français-néerlandais.
  J-C. Boulanger, 209(FM):Oct82-358
Wijsenbeek-Wijler, H. Aristotle's Concept of Soul, Sleep and Dreams.
  P.H. Schrijvers, 394:Vol35fasc1/2-172
von Wilamowitz-Moellendorff, U. History of Classical Scholarship.* (H. Lloyd-Jones, ed)
  D.A.N. Jones, 362:27Jan83-23
Wilber, D.N. Iran. (9th ed)
  A.H.H. Abidi, 273(IC):Oct82-319
Wilberforce, W. Journey to the Lake District from Cambridge. (C.E. Wrangham, ed)
  D.A.N. Jones, 362:11Aug83-22
Wilbers, S. The Iowa Writers' Workshop.
  42(AR):Winter82-121
Wilbur, J.B. and H.J. Allen. The Worlds of Plato and Aristotle. The Worlds of the Early Greek Philosophers.
  L.E. Rose, 484(PPR):Jun83-556
Wilcox, J. Modern Baptists.
  A. Tyler, 441:31Jul83-1
  442(NY):18Jul83-96
Wild, D. Nicolas Poussin.*
  O. Bätschmann, 683:Band45Heft1-82
  R. Verdi, 90:Apr82-247

Wild, I. Zur Überlieferung und Rezeption des "Kudrun"—Epos.
  T. Nolte, 406:Winter82-486
Wild, P. Clarence King.
  A.R. Huseboe, 649(WAL):Summer82-176
Wild, P. Enos Mills.
  G.F. Day, 649(WAL):Summer82-173
Wild, P. Rainbow.
  E.C. Lynskey, 50(ArQ):Summer82-185
  E.C. Lynskey, 649(WAL):Winter83-368
Wild, R., ed. Johann Georg Hamann.
  M.L. Baeumer, 406:Spring82-97
Wild, R., ed. How to Manage.
  P. Gorb, 324:Oct83-700
Wilde, A. Horizons of Assent.*
  C. Caramello, 395(MFS):Summer82-355
  A.N. Jeffares, 651(WHR):Spring82-77
  K. Lawrence, 454:Winter83-177
  D.H. Miles, 221(GQ):Nov82-569
  W. Sypher, 569(SR):Fall82-575
  R. Wasson, 141:Spring82-197
  295(JML):Dec82-375
Wilde, W.H. and T.I. Moore - see Gilmore, M.
Wilder, A.N. Thornton Wilder and His Public.*
  F. Baldanza, 395(MFS):Summer81-370
Wilding, M. Political Fictions.*
  L. Hergenhan, 71(ALS):May82-413
  L.L. Lee, 599:Winter82-72
  V.S. Middleton, 594:Summer82-204
  M. Sperber, 395(MFS):Summer81-396
  S. Trombley, 541(RES):Nov82-502
Wildman, A.K. The End of the Russian Imperial Army.
  R. Stites, 104(CASS):Summer82-263
  N. Stone, 575(SEER):Jul82-474
  M. Szeftel, 161(DUJ):Dec81-129
Wildman, S. David Cox 1783-1859.
  A. Wilton, 324:Nov83-780
Wilds, B. - see Mira de Amescua
Wiles, P., ed. The New Communist Third World.
  C. Clapham, 69:Vol52No4-99
Wiles, T.J. The Theater Event.*
  M. Breslow, 529(QQ):Spring82-191
  B.M. Hobgood, 289:Winter82-113
  N.C. Schmitt, 397(MD):Dec82-588
Wilhelm, J.J. - see Arnaut Daniel
Wilhelmsen, F.D. Citizen of Rome.
  P.F. Lawler, 396(ModA):Summer/Fall82-408
Wilk, C. Marcel Breuer, Furniture and Interiors.
  A.W., 90:Sep82-592
Wilkes, G.A. The Stockyard and the Croquet Lawn.*
  J. Croft, 71(ALS):May82-397
  B. Elliott, 71(ALS):May82-393
Wilkie, R. and B. Buchloh - see Shedden, L.
Wilkin, K. Pierre Gauvreau.
  C.A. Phillips, 529(QQ):Winter82-854
Wilkins, B.T. Has History Any Meaning?
  W.H. Dray, 488:Sep82-336
  H. Putnam, 125:Spring82-291
Wilkins, E.H. Studies on Petrarch and Boccaccio.
  T. Barolini, 551(RenQ):Summer81-226
Wilkins, N. Music in the Age of Chaucer.*
  D. Fallows, 447(N&Q):Jun81-255
  J. Michon, 189(EA):Jan-Mar82-76
  K. Reichl, 38:Band100Heft3/4-501
Wilkins, N. - see Satie, E.

Wilkinson, E. Japan versus Europe.
R.T.B., 617(TLS):18Mar83-279
Wilkinson, E.M. and L.A. Willoughby - see
Schiller, F.
Wilkinson, G. Turner on Landscape.
G. Reynolds, 617(TLS):29Apr83-438
Wilkinson, J. Seasonings Cookbook for
Quantity Cuisine.
W. and C. Cowen, 639(VQR):Spring82-67
Wilkinson, J.D. The Intellectual Resist-
ance in Europe.*
A.L., 185:Oct82-199
J. Miller, 560:Summer82-139
A. Wald, 385(MQR):Winter83-157
Will, G.F. The Pursuit of Virtue and
Other Tory Notions.*
W. McGurn, 396(ModA):Summer/Fall82-405
639(VQR):Summer82-92
Will, G.F. Statecraft as Soulcraft.
J. Fallows, 61:May83-98
M.J. Sandel, 441:17Jul83-6
Willan, A. French Regional Cooking.
W. and C. Cowen, 639(VQR):Autumn82-140
Willard, N. Household Tales of Moon and
Water.
D. Walker, 199:Spring83-77
Willems, D. Syntaxe, lexique et séman-
tique.
M.W. Epro, 350:Dec83-929
Willett, J. and R. Manheim - see Brecht, B.
Willett, J. and R. Manheim, with E. Fried -
see Brecht, B.
Willetts, W. Chinese Calligraphy.
Liu Liang-yu, 60:May-Jun82-142
Willey, M. "Théâtres populaires" d'au-
jourd'hui en France et en Angleterre
(1960-1975).
C. Campos, 189(EA):Jan-Mar82-104
Willey, T.E. Back to Kant.*
R. Malter, 342:Band73Heft1-92
William of Conches. Glosae in Iuvenalem.
(B. Wilson, ed)
J. Newell, 589:Oct82-959
Williams, A.L. An Approach to Congreve.*
M. Cordner, 179(ES):Apr82-175
J.H. O'Neill, 161(DUJ):Dec81-139
Williams, B. Descartes.*
G.A.J. Rogers, 483:Apr82-263
Williams, B., ed. Obscenity and Film Cen-
sorship.
B.B., 185:Oct82-211
Williams, B., ed. The Subscription Book
of Bishops Tounson and Davenant, 1620-
40.
D. Robinson, 325:Apr82-38
Williams, C. The Arthurian Poems.
S. Medcalf, 617(TLS):21Oct83-1150
Williams, C.G.S. Madame de Sévigné.
H.R. Allentuch, 207(FR):Feb83-482
Williams, C.K. Tar.
L. Simpson, 441:27Nov83-13
Williams, D. Mr. George Eliot.
R. Ashton, 617(TLS):24Jun83-650
Williams, D., ed. The Horseman's Compan-
ion.
639(VQR):Spring82-62
Williams, D. Incidents in My Own Life
Which Have Been Thought of Some Impor-
tance. (P. France, ed)
D.O. Thomas, 83:Spring82-153
Williams, D. The River Horsemen.
R.C. Davis, 102(CanL):Autumn82-134
D. Duffy, 529(QQ):Winter82-761

Williams, D. Treasure Preserved.
N. Callendar, 441:25Sep83-34
Williams, D. A World of his Own.*
G. Mortimer, 364:Nov82-97
Williams, D. and S. Mead. Tennessee Wil-
liams.
P-L. Adams, 61:Jun83-104
P. Engel, 441:7Aug83-15
Williams, D.A., ed. The Monster in the
Mirror.*
E. Caramaschi, 549(RLC):Apr-Jun82-223
Williams, D.R. Trapline Outlaw.
G.W., 102(CanL):Summer82-175
Williams, F. Callimachus, "Hymn to
Apollo."*
W.H. Mineur, 394:Vol35fasc3/4-377
Williams, F.G. - see de Sena, J.
Williams, G. Change and Decline.
J.C. Bramble, 313:Vol72-210
Williams, G. Figures of Thought in Roman
Poetry.*
L. Duret, 555:Vol56fasc2-346
K. Quinn, 487:Spring82-89
A. Sheppard, 161(DUJ):Jun82-277
Williams, G. Pomeroy.*
S. Altinel, 617(TLS):12Aug83-867
Williams, G. Technique and Ideas in the
"Aeneid."
N.M. Horsfall, 617(TLS):15Apr83-380
Williams, G.H. The Mind of John Paul II.
M. Malia, 453(NYRB):29Sep83-18
Williams, H.A. Some Day I'll Find You.
A. Webster, 617(TLS):18Feb83-154
Williams, J. Lettering in Embroidery.
P. Bach, 614:Winter83-19
Williams, J. Pariah.
E. Milton, 441:18Sep83-14
442(NY):10Oct83-167
Williams, J. White River.
E. Webby, 381:Jul81-200
Williams, J.C., ed. Preservation of Paper
and Textiles of Historical and Artistic
Value.
A.D. Baynes-Cope, 325:Oct82-124
Williams, J.H. Hidden Identities.*
S. Regan, 493:Sep82-64
Williams, J.M. From That Terrible Field.
(J.K. Folmar, ed)
H. Hattaway, 9(AlaR):Oct82-277
Williams, M. Distractions.*
S. Sandy, 491:Aug82-293
Williams, M. Groundless Belief.
P. Horwich, 449:May82-312
Williams, M.D. Source: Music of the Avant
Garde.
D.C., 412:May81-154
Williams, O.F. and J.W. Houck, eds. The
Judeo-Christian Vision and the Modern
Corporation.
D.S., 185:Jul83-842
Williams, P. A New History of the Organ.*
J. Dalton, 410(M&L):Jul/Oct81-370
Williams, P. The Organ Music of J.S. Bach.
J. Dalton, 410(M&L):Jul/Oct82-347
Williams, P.M. - see Gaitskell, H.
Williams, P.V.A., ed. The Fool and the
Trickster.*
D.M.E. Gillam, 179(ES):Apr82-159
D. Norbrook, 447(N&Q):Feb81-71
G.S. Rousseau, 402(MLR):Jan82-145
Williams, P.W. Popular Religion in Amer-
ica.
D.E. Byrne, Jr., 292(JAF):Oct-Dec82-484

Williams, R. Cobbett.
  A. Ryan, 362:17Mar83-22
  J. Stevenson, 617(TLS):9Dec83-1380
Williams, R. Towards 2000.
  J. Morgan, 617(TLS):4Nov83-1223
  W. Rodgers, 362:15Dec83-22
Williams, R.C. Russian Art and American
  Money, 1900-1940.
  G. Lewinson, 575(SEER):Jan82-133
Williams, R.D. - see Vergil
Williams, R.H. Dream Worlds.*
  B.T. Cooper, 446(NCFS):Spring-Summer83-
  403
  A.J., 185:Apr83-636
  M. Larkin, 617(TLS):4Mar83-220
Williams, R.L. The Horror of Life.*
  L.R. Furst, 131(CL):Winter82-83
  B. Stoltzfus, 395(MFS):Winter81/82-651
Williams, S. and R. Burgos-Sasscer. Ex-
  ploraciones Chicano-Riqueñas.
  D.N. Flemming, 399(MLJ):Summer82-233
  O.U. Somoza, 238:Dec82-668
Williams, S.A. Some One Sweet Angel Chile.
  B. Brown, 95(CLAJ):Mar82-365
Williams, S.H. and F.W. Madan. The Lewis
  Carroll Handbook.* (rev by R.L. Green
  and D. Crutch)
  P. Heath, 191(ELN):Dec82-126
Williams, T.H. The History of American
  Wars: From Colonial Times to World War I.
  639(VQR):Winter82-24
Williams, U. and W. Williams-Krapp, eds.
  Die "Elsässische Legenda Aurea." (Vol 1)
  N.F. Palmer, 402(MLR):Apr82-486
  H-G. Richert, 133:Band15Heft1/2-155
Williams, W. The Tragic Art of Ernest
  Hemingway.*
  J.M. Flora, 573(SSF):Summer82-285
  S. Pinsker, 395(MFS):Winter82/83-673
  M. Reynolds, 27(AL):Oct82-454
Williams, W.P., ed. Index to the Statio-
  ners' Register, 1640-1708.*
  M.S. Friedman, 365:Winter83-34
Williams-Ellis, A. All Stracheys are
  Cousins.
  H. Spurling, 617(TLS):11Mar83-237
  E.S. Turner, 362:24Feb83-24
Williams-Knapp, W. Überlieferung und Gat-
  tung.
  R. Bergmann, 684(ZDA):Band111Heft4-164
  T. Nolte, 406:Winter82-491
Williams-Mitchell, C. Dressed for the Job.
  R.L. Shep, 614:Fall83-19
Williamsen, V.G., ed. An Annotated, Ana-
  lytical Bibliography of Tirso de Molina
  Studies, 1627-1977.* (W. Poesse, comp)
  J.H. Parker, 552(REH):May82-319
Williamsen, V.G. The Minor Dramatists of
  Seventeenth-Century Spain.
  T.A. O'Connor, 304(JHP):Fall82-76
Williamson, A. Presence.
  R.W. Flint, 441:13Feb83-15
Williamson, D. Don's Party. The Club.
  Travelling North.
  W. Fairhead, 108:Fall82-130
Williamson, D.S. Shandy.*
  C. Kerr, 102(CanL):Spring82-149
Williamson, H.G.M. Israel in the Books of
  Chronicles.
  J.H. Hayes, 318(JAOS):Oct-Dec81-445
Williamson, J., ed. Teaching Science Fic-
  tion.
  C.B. Hunter, 561(SFS):Nov82-337

Williamson, J.W. The Myth of the Con-
  queror.*
  P.V. Marinelli, 539:Feb83-68
Willing, J.Z. The Lively Mind.
  S. Reznitsky, 186(ETC.):Fall82-296
Willis, B., with A. Lee. The Captain's
  Diary.
  A.L. Le Quesne, 617(TLS):16Sep83-987
Willis, J. Screen World (1982 Film
  Annual).
  M. Buckley, 200:Nov82-570
Willmott, P. A Green Girl.
  M. Forster, 617(TLS):21Oct83-1149
Wills, G. Confessions of a Conservative.*
  G. Feaver, 529(QQ):Spring82-29
Wills, G. Explaining America.*
  G. Feaver, 529(QQ):Spring82-29
  J.R. Pole, 656(WMQ):Apr82-370
  A.J. Reck, 619:Winter82-91
Wills, G. The Kennedy Imprisonment.*
  L. Goldstein, 385(MQR):Winter83-156
Wills, G. Lead Time.
  R. Sherrill, 441:3Jul83-2
Wilmer, C. Devotions.
  T. Dooley, 617(TLS):7Jan83-17
Wilmerding, J. American Light.*
  D.A. Kilgo, 658:Winter82-277
Wilmeth, D.B. George Frederick Cooke.*
  A. Hare, 611(TN):Vol36No3-140
  A. Woods, 612(ThS):Nov82-245
Wilmeth, D.B. The Language of American
  Popular Entertainment.
  W. Green, 612(ThS):Nov82-256
Wilmeth, D.B. Variety Entertainment and
  Outdoor Amusements.
  M. Matlaw, 612(ThS):Nov82-258
Wilmot, J. - see under Lord Rochester
Wilmut, R. Tony Hancock "Artiste."
  A.J.H., 617(TLS):18Mar83-279
von Wilpert, G., ed. Lexikon der Weltlit-
  eratur. (Vol 2) (2nd ed)
  G. Müller, 597(SN):Vol54No1-186
Wilson, A. Diversity and Depth in Fiction.
  (K. McSweeney, ed)
  J. Bayley, 617(TLS):16Sep83-978
Wilson, A. Setting the World on Fire.*
  J.L. Halio, 598(SoR):Winter83-203
Wilson, A.N. The Laird of Abbotsford.*
  P. Garside, 571(ScLJ):Spring82-8
Wilson, A.N. The Life of John Milton.
  D.J. Enright, 617(TLS):4Feb83-100
  M. Meyer, 364:Feb83-95
  A. Watkins, 362:27Jan83-21
Wilson, A.N. Scandal.
  D.A.N. Jones, 362:8Sep83-22
  J.K.L. Walker, 617(TLS):9Sep83-949
Wilson, A.N. Wise Virgin.*
  M. Gorra, 441:27Nov83-12
  L. Jones, 364:Dec82/Jan83-136
Wilson, B. Fundamental Car.
  V. Trueblood, 271:Spring82-132
Wilson, B. - see William of Conches
Wilson, C. Bernard Shaw.
  R.J. Steen, 214:Vol 10No38-123
Wilson, C.N., ed. Why the South Will Sur-
  vive.
  W.W. Braden, 583:Fall82-89
  L.W. Dunbar, 639(VQR):Autumn82-702
Wilson, C.N. - see Calhoun, J.C.
Wilson, C.R. Baptized in Blood.
  F. Hobson, 392:Winter81/82-73

Wilson, D., ed. Sight and Sound — A Fifti-
eth Anniversary Selection.
R. Armes, 364:Mar83-119
Wilson, D.J. Arthur O. Lovejoy and the
Quest for Intelligibility.
J. Guttmann, 529(QQ):Spring82-215
D.W. Noble, 106:Winter82-321
S. Pickering, 569(SR):Summer82-474
G.A. Press, 319:Apr83-254
Wilson, D.M. and O. Klindt-Jensen. Viking
Art. (2nd ed)
H. Chickering, 589:Jul82-689
Wilson, D.R. Air Photo Interpretation for
Archaeologists.
P.G. Dorrell, 617(TLS):23Sep83-1028
Wilson, E. The Forties. (L. Edel, ed)
D. Donoghue, 617(TLS):5Aug83-827
J. Gross, 453(NYRB):10Nov83-22
D.A.N. Jones, 362:29Sep83-23
A. Kazin, 61:Apr83-126
R.W.B. Lewis, 441:22May83-1
442(NY):23May83-121
Wilson, E. The Lost Treasure of Casa Loma.
J.K. Kealy, 102(CanL):Summer82-154
Wilson, E. The Mental as Physical.*
J. Levin, 482(PhR):Apr82-295
Wilson, E. Mirror Writing.
H. Harris, 364:Apr/May82-137
Wilson, E. The Portable Edmund Wilson.
(L.M. Dabney, ed)
J. Gross, 453(NYRB):10Nov83-22
R.W.B. Lewis, 441:22May83-1
L. Ziff, 617(TLS):15Jul83-749
Wilson, E. The Thirties.* (L. Edel, ed)
B. Gallagher, 152(UDQ):Winter82-90
J.V. Hagopian, 395(MFS):Winter81/82-
732
Wilson, E. Erica Wilson's Smocking.
R.L. Shep, 614:Fall83-19
Wilson, E.G. John Clarkson and the Afri-
can Adventure.
P.E.H. Hair, 83:Autumn82-259
Wilson, E.M. Spanish and English Litera-
ture of the 16th and 17th Centuries.*
G. Edwards, 402(MLR):Jul82-747
J.H. Parker, 238:Mar82-141
Wilson, E.M. and D.W. Cruickshank. Samuel
Pepys's Spanish Plays.
J.E. Varey, 402(MLR):Oct82-977
Wilson, F. The Joy of Building.
D. Upton, 658:Summer/Autumn82-171
Wilson, H. The Skedule.
E. Webby, 381:Jul81-200
Wilson, J. Entertainments for Elizabeth
I.*
S. Fulton, 611(TN):Vol36No3-134
P. Walls, 410(M&L):Jul/Oct81-378
Wilson, J.Q. The Politics of Regulation.
D.J. Senese, 396(ModA):Spring82-209
Wilson, M.D. Descartes.*
G.A.J. Rogers, 483:Apr82-263
Wilson, M.I. Organ Cases of Western
Europe.*
A. Laing, 90:Feb82-106
Wilson, N.G. Scholars of Byzantium.
R. Browning, 617(TLS):29Jul83-802
D. Hunt, 362:16Jun83-26
Wilson, R.B.J. Henry James's Ultimate
Narrative: "The Golden Bowl."*
J. Rambeau, 395(MFS):Winter82/83-662
R.B. Yeazell, 445(NCF):Mar83-611

Wilson, R.G. and S.K. Robinson. The Prai-
rie School in Iowa.
D.J. Hibbard, 658:Spring82-90
Wilson, S. Creative Knitting.
C.J. Mouton, 614:Spring83-17
Wilson, W. The Papers of Woodrow Wilson.
(Vols 25 and 27-31) (A.S. Link and
others, eds)
R.A. Hohner, 106:Fall82-213
Wilson, W. and E.B. Galt. A President in
Love.* (E. Tribble, ed)
F.C. Rosenberger, 639(VQR):Spring82-
366
Wilson, W.D. The Narrative Strategy of
Wieland's "Don Sylvio von Rosalva."
M. Boulby, 221:Nov82-298
Wilt, J. Ghosts of the Gothic.*
M. Baumgarten, 191(ELN):Sep82-103
S. Gresham, 577(SHR):Winter82-70
J. Halperin, 395(MFS):Summer81-341
I. Ousby, 637(VS):Autumn81-105
R.L. Snyder, 594:Summer82-207
Wilton, A. J.M.W. Turner: France, Italy,
Germany, Switzerland.
C.F. Stuckey, 55:Nov82-50
Wilton-Ely, J. The Mind and Art of Gio-
vanni Battista Piranesi. Piranesi.
R. Middleton, 576:Dec82-333
Wiltse, D. The Serpent.
J. Coleman, 441:24Jul83-11
Winans, R.B. A Descriptive Checklist of
Book Catalogues Separately Printed in
America 1693-1800.*
S. Botein, 517(PBSA):Vol76No2-223
P. Drummey, 432(NEQ):Jun82-311
Winchell, M.R. Joan Didion.
A. Arthur, 649(WAL):Spring82-93
"Windows at Tiffany's."
J. Simpson, 55:Jan82-31
Windsor, A. Peter Behrens.*
P. Davey, 46:May82-74
M. Richardson, 90:Oct82-639
Wing, D., comp. Short Title Catalogue of
Books Printed in England, Scotland, Ire-
land, Wales and British America and of
English Books Printed in Other Countries,
1641-1700.* (Vol 2, 2nd ed) (T.J. Crist,
ed)
J.M. Perlette, 365:Spring83-79
Winge, M. Den Kunst at blive en god Pige,
Hustru, Moder og Husmoder- om pigelaes-
ning og pigeopdragelse i Danmark til ca.
1900.
T. Steinfeld, 172(Edda):1982/1-55
Winiger, J. Feuerbachs Weg zum Humanis-
mus.
J-P. Osier, 192(EP):Jul-Sep81-370
Winklehner, B. Die Tugenden der antiken
Philosophenschulen bei Michel de Mon-
taigne.
R. Bernoulli, 535(RHL):Sep-Dec82-874
Winkler, P., ed. Methoden der Analyse von
Face-to-Face-Situationen.
P.R. Portmann, 196:Band23Heft3/4-347
Winks, R.W., ed. Detective Fiction.
B. Benstock, 149(CLS):Spring82-88
Winn, J.A. Unsuspected Eloquence.
C.S. Brown, 219(GaR):Summer82-449
J.T. Dzieglewicz, 405(MP):May83-449
A.J. Sabol, 141:Fall82-379
Winn, M. Children Without Childhood.
M. Scarf, 441:24Jul83-8
442(NY):18Jul83-99

Wolff, U. Hermann Hesse: "Demain."
J. Mileck, 221(GQ):Mar82-274
Wolfram von Eschenbach. Parzival. (A.T.
Hatto, trans)
E.J. Morrall, 161(DUJ):Dec81-134
Wolfram von Eschenbach. Parzival. (K.
Lachmann, ed; W. Spiewok, trans)
J.W. Thomas, 133:Band15Heft4-352
Wolfram, H. Geschichte der Goten.* (2nd
ed)
W. Goffart, 589:Apr82-444
Wolfram, W. and D. Christian. Appalachian
Speech.
M. Montgomery, 35(AS):Summer82-134
Wolfson, N. CHP: The Conversational His-
torical Present in American English Nar-
rative.
R.K.S. Macaulay, 350:Sep83-694
Wolgast, E.H. Equality and the Rights of
Women.*
N.O. Keohane, 185:Oct82-102
S. Sherwin, 529(QQ):Summer82-444
Wolgemuth, C. Gramática náhuatl del muni-
cipio de Mecayapana, Veracruz.
R.W. Langacker, 350:Jun83-451
Wolin, R. Walter Benjamin.
M. Rosen, 617(TLS):4Feb83-109
Wolitzer, H. In the Palomar Arms.
J.C. Oates, 441:5Jun83-14
Wolitzer, M. Sleepwalking.*
V. Rothschild, 617(TLS):1Apr83-325
42(AR):Summer82-374
Wolkstein, D. and S.N. Kramer. Inanna.
H. Bloom, 453(NYRB):13Oct83-7
P. Michalowski, 441:25Sep83-31
M. Weigle, 469:Vol8No4-95
Wollen, P. Readings and Writings.
S. Chatman, 18:Jul-Aug83-56
Wollheim, R. Art and its Objects.* (2nd
ed)
W. Charlton, 89(BJA):Winter82-78
M. Podro, 90:Feb82-100
Wollheim, R. and J. Hopkins, eds. Philo-
sophical Essays on Freud.
K. Wilkes, 617(TLS):11Mar83-245
Wollin, L. Svensk Latinöversättning I.
I. Haskå, 596(SL):Vol36No2-174
Woloch, I. The French Veteran from the
Revolution to the Restoration.
J.C. White, 173(ECS):Winter81/82-228
Wolski, W. Schlechtbestimmtheit und Vag-
heit.
B.J. Koekkoek, 221(GQ):Mar82-235
Wolterstorff, N. Art in Action.
N. Klinghoffer, 396(ModA):Winter82-99
F.D. Martin, 289:Spring82-114
Wolterstorff, N. Works and Worlds of Art.*
A. Harrison, 518:Apr82-116
P. Lewis, 479(PhQ):Apr82-185
J.O, Urmson, 410(M&L):Jul/Oct81-400
Wolz, H.G. Plato and Heidegger.
K. Seeskin, 319:Oct83-556
"The Women's Annual: 1980." (B. Haber, ed)
I. Thompson, 365:Winter83-37
"Women's Day: Prize Winning Quilts, Cover-
lets and Afghans."
M. Cowan, 614:Winter83-22
Wong, M.G. Nun.
E. Kennedy, 441:10Apr83-12
Wongar, B. Babaru.
R. Banks, 441:20Feb83-6

Wood, A., ed. Times Guide to the House of
Commons.
G. Kaufman, 362:27Oct83-31
Wood, A.W. Karl Marx.
R. Bhaskar, 518:Oct82-214
G. Duncan, 479(PhQ):Oct82-385
R. Schacht, 319:Jul83-403
A.P. Simonds, 185:Jul83-792
P. Singer, 63:Jun82-191
Wood, B.S. Children and Communication.
(2nd ed)
W. Haynes, 583:Fall82-93
Wood, C. The Pre-Raphaelites.*
G. Reynolds, 39:Aug82-122
Wood, H. Third Class Ticket.
J. Drew, 99:Jun/Jul82-41
Wood, J. and J.S. Gilchrist. The Campus
Survival Cookbook No. 2.
W. and C. Cowen, 639(VQR):Spring82-66
Wood, J.B. The Nobility of the "Election"
of Bayeux, 1463-1666.
J.H.M. Salmon, 551(RenQ):Spring81-111
Wood, J.C. British Economists and the
Empire.
S.G. Checkland, 617(TLS):4Nov83-1210
Wood, R. Howard Hawks.
D. Kehr, 18:May83-72
Wood, S. Bazaar.*
R. Phillips, 461:Spring-Summer82-98
D. St. John, 42(AR):Spring82-228
S. Santos, 651(WHR):Spring82-45
Wood, T. Dead in the Water.
N. Callendar, 441:18Dec83-29
Woodard, K. The International Energy Rela-
tions of China.
B.J. Esposito, 293(JASt):Feb82-348
Woodbridge, A. and H.C. - see Johnston, M.
Woodcock, G. The Canadians.*
P. Pénigault-Duhet, 189(EA):Jan-Mar82-
105
Woodcock, G. Ivan Eyre.
W.N., 102(CanL):Autumn82-185
Woodcock, G. Letter to the Past.
M. Abley, 617(TLS):20May83-517
Woodcock, G. Thomas Merton, Monk and Poet.
M.W. Higgins, 106:Spring82-127
Woodcock, G. The Mountain Road.*
D. Barbour, 648(WCR):Summer81-80
R.J. Merrett, 529(QQ):Summer82-422
Woodcock, G. A Picture History of British
Columbia.
C. Berger, 102(CanL):Autumn82-153
Woodcock, G. Taking It to the Letter.
J. Heath, 627(UTQ):Summer82-460
Woodcock, G. The World of Canadian Writ-
ing.*
F. Zichy, 298:Summer82-143
Woodhead, A.G. The Study of Greek Inscrip-
tions. (2nd ed)
L.H. Jeffrey, 123:Vol132No2-299
Woodhouse, A. and D. Bush. A Variorum Com-
mentary on the Poems of John Milton.
(Vol 2)
C. Schaar, 179(ES):Feb82-75
Woodhouse, C.M. Karamanlis.
R. Clogg, 617(TLS):12Aug83-861
Woodress, J. - see "American Literary
Scholarship"
Woodruff, P. - see Plato
Woods, D. Asking for Trouble.
639(VQR):Spring82-52

Woods, O. and J. Bishop. The Story of The
Times.
  O.R. McGregor, 617(TLS):16Dec83-1395
Woods, P.D. French-Indian Relations on
the Southern Frontier, 1699-1762.
  J.L. Wright, Jr., 656(WMQ):Oct82-698
Woods, R.D. Reference Materials on Latin
America in English: The Humanities.*
  J. Gledson, 86(BHS):Jan82-89
Woods, S. Run Before the Wind.
  N. Callendar, 441:29May83-21
Woods, S.E. Ottawa.
  C. Berger, 102(CanL):Autumn82-153
Woodward, A. Ezra Pound and "The Pisan
Cantos."*
  S.J. Adams, 106:Fall82-245
  W. Harmon, 577(SHR):Winter82-83
  P. Makin, 402(MLR):Apr82-431
Woodward, C.V. - see Chesnut, M.
Woodward, J.B. Ivan Bunin.*
  B.H. Monter, 104(CASS):Spring82-140
Woodward, J.B. Gogol's "Dead Souls."*
  M. Beresford, 161(DUJ):Dec81-148
  A.H. Karriker, 558(RLJ):Winter-
    Spring82-291
Woodward, K. At Last, the Real Distin-
guished Thing.*
  B. Duffey, 579(SAQ):Spring82-237
  W. Harmon, 577(SHR):Spring82-175
  R. Labrie, 106:Winter82-397
  S. Paul, 301(JEGP):Apr82-282
  H.F. Smith, 675(YER):Jun82-141
  295(JML):Dec82-359
Woodward, K. Jipping Street.
  L.D., 617(TLS):20May83-527
Woodward, P. Condominium and Sudanese
Nationalism.
  P.M. Holt, 69:Vol51No3-793
Woody, J. - see "George Platt Lynes Photo-
graphs 1931-1955"
Woolf, H., ed. The Analytic Spirit.
  W.C. Anderson, 98:Dec82-1023
Woolf, L. An Autobiography. (Vol 1)
  I.B. Nadel, 506(PSt):Sep82-269
Woolf, S. A History of Italy 1700-1860.
  B. Moloney, 83:Spring82-146
Woolf, V. The Diary of Virginia Woolf.*
  (Vols 1 and 2) (A.O. Bell, with A.
  McNeillie, eds)
  B. Ruddick, 148:Spring82-86
Woolf, V. The Diary of Virginia Woolf.*
  (Vol 3) (A.O. Bell, with A. McNeillie,
  eds)
  A.L. McLaughlin, 395(MFS):Summer81-320
Woolf, V. The Letters of Virginia Woolf.
  (Vol 6) (N. Nicolson and J. Trautmann,
  eds)
  D. Doner, 395(MFS):Winter81/82-686
  K.C. Hill, 177(ELT):Vol25No2-117
Woolf, V. The London Scene.*
  442(NY):17Jan83-113
Woolfe, R., Jr. Steeplechasing.
  P-L. Adams, 61:Jun83-105
Woolhouse, R.S. Locke.
  D. Smith, 617(TLS):11Nov83-1239
Woozley, A.D. Law and Obedience.*
  M.D. Yaffe, 154:Jun82-364
  C.M. Young, 482(PhR):Jan82-109
Worakawinto, P.M.T. A Village Ordination.
  D.K. Swearer, 318(JAOS):Oct-Dec81-497
Wordie, J.R. Estate Management in Eigh-
teenth-Century England.
  L. Colley, 617(TLS):22Jul83-785

Wordsworth, J. William Wordsworth.
  D. Bromwich, 617(TLS):9Sep83-963
Wordsworth, W. Benjamin the Waggoner.*
  (P.F. Betz, ed)
  P. Magnuson, 661(WC):Summer82-130
  D.H. Reiman, 591(SIR):Fall82-502
Wordsworth, W. The Borderers. (R. Osborn,
  ed)
  D. Bromwich, 617(TLS):9Sep83-963
  J. Robinson, 661(WC):Summer82-128
Wordsworth, W. The Poems. (J.O. Hayden,
  ed)
  529(QQ):Autumn82-690
Wordsworth, W. The Prelude 1799, 1805,
  1850. (J. Wordsworth, M.H. Abrams and
  S. Gill, eds)
  D.H. Reiman, 591(SIR):Fall82-502
Wordsworth, W. and D. The Letters of Wil-
liam and Dorothy Wordsworth.* (2nd ed)
  (Vol 5) (A.G. Hill, ed)
  J.H. Averill, 591(SIR):Fall82-496
  S. Logan, 447(N&Q):Aug81-344
Wordsworth, W. and M. The Love Letters of
William and Mary Wordsworth.* (B. Dar-
lington, ed)
  P.M. Spacks, 591(SIR):Winter82-661
  639(VQR):Summer82-88
Wormald, F. and P.M. Giles. A Descriptive
Catalogue of the Additional Illuminated
Manuscripts in the Fitzwilliam Museum.
  N. Barker, 78(BC):Winter82-523
Wormell, D. Sir John Seeley and the Uses
of History.*
  C. Parker, 366:Spring82-121
Wormser, B. The White Words.
  M. Kinzie, 29:Jul/Aug83-33
  H. Vendler, 472:Spring/Summer83-116
Worrall, A.J. Quakers in the Colonial
Northeast.
  M.B. Endy, Jr., 656(WMQ):Jul82-545
Worth, G.J. Dickensian Melodrama.*
  C.P. Havely, 447(N&Q):Oct81-443
Worth, K. The Irish Drama of Europe from
Yeats to Beckett.*
  P. Faulkner, 161(DUJ):Jun82-316
Worth, S. Studying Visual Communication.
  (L. Gross, ed)
  J.M. Carroll, 567:Vol40No3/4-371
Worth, W. The Chapel of Our Lady of Talpa.
  J.S. Griffith, 292(JAF):Jul-Sep82-367
Wortham, T., with C.K. Lohmann and D.
Nordloh - see Howells, W.D.
Worthen, J. D.H. Lawrence and the Idea of
the Novel.*
  H.T. Moore, 402(MLR):Oct82-945
Wouters, A. The Grammatical Papyri from
Graeco-Roman Egypt.
  M.D. MacLeod, 303(JoHS):Vol 102-258
  N.G. Wilson, 123:Vol32No1-116
Wrangham, C.E. - see Wilberforce, W.
Wratislaw, T. Oscar Wilde. (K. Beckson,
  ed)
  D.E. Van Tassel, 395(MFS):Summer81-337
Wrede, C. Leonhard von München, der
Meister der Prunkurkunden Kaiser Ludwigs
des Bayern.
  B. Ross, 589:Jul82-689
Wretö, T. J.L. Runeberg.*
  V. Zuck, 222(GR):Winter82-44
Wright, A.W. G.D.H. Cole and Socialist
Democracy.
  M. Bentley, 161(DUJ):Jun82-296

Wright, C. Paintings in Dutch Museums.
T. Crombie, 39:Sep82-199
Wright, C. The Southern Cross.*
X.J. Kennedy, 491:Mar83-349
V.L. Nielsen, 649(WAL):Nov82-268
D. St. John, 42(AR):Spring82-230
P. Stitt, 219(GaR):Spring82-184
Wright, C. Wittgenstein on the Founda-
tions of Mathematics.*
J.R. Cameron, 518:Apr82-86
D.A. Gillies, 84:Dec82-422
P. Roeper, 63:Dec82-376
H.D. Sluga, 262:Mar82-115
Wright, C.D. Translations of the Gospel
Back into Tongues.
R.B. Shaw, 441:4Sep83-8
D. Walker, 199:Spring83-77
Wright, E. The Night The Gods Smiled.
T.J. Binyon, 617(TLS):13May83-498
T.J. Binyon, 617(TLS):27May83-553
N. Callendar, 441:18Dec83-29
Wright, E.L. The Jester Hennets.
J. Saunders, 565:Vol23No3-73
Wright, F.L. Letters to Apprentices.
(B.B. Pfeiffer, ed)
A. Saint, 617(TLS):16Sep83-985
Wright, G. Building the Dream.
639(VQR):Spring82-62
Wright, G. France in Modern Times. (3rd
ed)
H. Peyre, 207(FR):Oct82-188
Wright, G. Insiders and Outliers.
J. Paulhan, 207(FR):Feb83-501
Wright, G. Moralism and the Model Home.*
D. Schuyler, 658:Summer/Autumn82-157
von Wright, G.H. and H. Nyman - see Witt-
genstein, L.
von Wright, G.H., with H. Nyman - see
Wittgenstein, L.
Wright, J. This Journey.*
K. Callaway, 472:Spring/Summer83-58
S. Friebert, 199:Spring83-87
W. Harmon, 569(SR):Fall82-612
P. Stitt, 219(GaR):Winter82-911
Wright, J. - see Sancho, I.
Wright, K. Bump-Starting the Hearse.
G. Ewart, 617(TLS):30Sep83-1061
Wright, M.R. - see Empedocles
Wright, O. The Modal System of Arab and
Persian Music A.D. 1250-1300.
D. Wulstan, 410(M&L):Jan81-77
Wright, R. Late Latin and Early Romance
in Spain and Carolingian France.
M. Torreblanca, 304(JHP):Winter83-141
Wright, R.B. Final Things.
J. Kertzer, 198:Jan82-81
Wright, R.B. The Teacher's Daughter.
M. Yearsley, 99:Dec82/Jan83-40
Wright, R.T. and B. Herger. The Canadian
Rockies.
529(QQ):Autumn82-687
Wright, S. Meditations in Green.
W. Kendrick, 441:6Nov83-7
Wright, S.L. Quilts from Happy Hands.
M. Cowan, 614:Winter83-21
Wright, W. The Von Bülow Affair.
D. Clendinen, 441:3Jul83-10
Wringe, C.A. Children's Rights.*
J.M.G., 185:Apr83-647
Wrong, D.H. Power.
Q. Gibson, 488:Dec82-452

Wu, W.F. The Yellow Peril.*
J. Cohn, 395(MFS):Winter82/83-658
B. Raffel, 152(UDQ):Summer82-151
Wucherpfennig, W. Kindheitskult und Irra-
tionalismus in der Literatur um 1900.
D. Dethlefsen, 564:Nov81-324
J. Michaels, 406:Fall82-366
Wüest, J. La Dialectalisation de la Gallo-
Romania.
M. Offord, 208(FS):Apr82-191
Wuilleumier, P. - see Tacitus
Wuketits, F.M. Wissenschaftstheoretische
Probleme der modernen Biologie.
G. Vollmer, 687:Jan-Mar82-125
Wunderlich, D. Arbeitsbuch Semantik.
K-E. Sommerfeldt, 682(ZPSK):Band35
Heft6-740
Wunderlich, W. Die Spur des Bundschuhs.
T.F. Sellner, 221(GQ):Nov82-622
Wurm, S.A., ed. New Guinea and Neighbour-
ing Areas.*
J. Haiman, 320(CJL):Spring82-59
Würtz, D. Das Verhältnis von Beobachtungs-
und theoretischer Sprache in der Erkennt-
nistheorie Bertrand Russells.
H-J. Dahms, 167:May82-405
Würzbach, N. Anfänge und gattungstypische
Ausformung der englischen Strassenbal-
lade 1550-1650.
V.E. Neuburg, 196:Band23Heft1/2-167
Wüscher, H.J. Liberty, Equality and
Fraternity in Wordsworth: 1791-1800.
M. Friedman, 661(WC):Summer82-133
M. Moorman, 161(DUJ):Jun82-312
Wuttke, D., with K.G. Heise - see Warburg,
A.M.
Wyatt, D. Prodigal Sons.*
W.B. Bache, 395(MFS):Summer81-383
G.O. Carey, 573(SSF):Winter82-85
Wyatt, R. Foreign Bodies.
M. Penman, 99:Sep82-33
Wyatt-Brown, B. Southern Honor.*
D.H. Donald, 441:24Apr83-8
W.S. McFeely, 617(TLS):18Feb83-153
L.H. MacKethan, 578:Fall83-113
Wycherley, W. The Plays of William Wycher-
ley.* (A. Friedman, ed)
H. Love, 402(MLR):Jan82-164
J.P. Vander Motten, 179(ES):Apr82-173
Wycherley, W. The Plays of William Wycher-
ley. (P. Holland, ed)
I. Donaldson, 617(TLS):28Oct83-1183
Wyeth, B.J. Christina's World.
P-L. Adams, 61:Jan83-103
Wylder, D.E. Emerson Hough.
R.L. Gale, 649(WAL):Nov82-271
Wylie, R.F. The Emergence of Maoism
B. Womack, 293(JAST):Aug82-825
Wyman, W.D. Wisconsin Folklore.
J.P. Leary, 292(JAF):Apr-Jun82-227
Wymer, T.L. and others. Intersections.
C.B. Hunter, 561(SFS):Jul82-225
Wynand, D. One Cook, Once Dreaming.*
M. Abley, 102(CanL):Spring82-76
Wynand, D. Pointwise.
D. Barbour, 648(WCR):Summer81-80
Wynar, L.R. and P. Kleeberger. Slavic
Ethnic Libraries, Museums and Archives
in the United States.*
J.E.O. Screen, 575(SEER):Jan82-157

Yin, J. The Soviet View on the Use of
Force in International Law.
W.E. Butler, 575(SEER):Apr82-316
York, A. The Combination.
N. Callendar, 441:29May83-21
York, A. In This House There Are No
Lizards.*
D. Barbour, 648(WCR):Summer81-80
York, T. Trapper.
R.C. Davis, 102(CanL):Autumn82-134
Yorke, M. Find Me A Villain.
T.J. Binyon, 617(TLS):22Apr83-400
Yorke, M. Eric Gill.*
A. Causey, 90:Sep82-566
J. Glancey, 46:Apr82-80
Yorks, S.A. The Evolution of Bernard Shaw.
W.S. Smith, 572:Vol3-245
Young, A. Ask Me Now.
G. Hobson, 649(WAL):Spring82-87
Young, A. The Blues Don't Change.
W. Harmon, 472:Spring/Summer83-129
Young, A. Dada and After.*
D.A. Callard, 364:Apr/May82-136
B. Martin, 148:Winter82-59
Young, A. Danta Gradha.
T. Eagleton, 565:Vol23No2-62
Young, A.M. and others. The Paintings of
James McNeill Whistler.*
P. Conrad, 637(VS):Spring82-378
Young, A.R. Henry Peacham.
G. Parfitt, 447(N&Q):Feb81-72
Young, D. - see Wang Wei and others
Young, D.J. The Structure of English
Clauses.
G. Bourcier, 189(EA):Jul-Sep82-318
T. Thrane, 603:Vol6No1-157
Young, E.B. Lincoln Center.
M. Morgan, 576:Mar82-78
Young, H. - see Maleska, E.T.
Young, H.T. The Line in the Margin.*
J. Wilcox, 88:Spring83-235
Young, K., W.C.F. Bussink and P. Hasan.
Malaysia.
L.T. Ghee, 293(JASt):Feb82-438
Young, P. Power of Speech.
R.J. Overy, 617(TLS):5Aug83-828
Young, P.M. George Grove 1820-1900.
S. Banfield, 410(M&L):Jul/Oct81-437
Young, P.M. - see Tchaikovsky, P.I.
Young, P.T. The Look of Music.
R. Leppert, 658:Winter82-274
Young, R., ed. Untying the Text.
D.H. Miles, 221(GQ):Nov82-569
C. Rubino, 400(MLN):Dec82-1213
Young, R.V. Richard Crashaw and the
Spanish Golden Age.
A. Rudrum, 617(TLS):24Jun83-681
Young, T.D. The Past in the Present.*
C. Bohner, 395(MFS):Winter82/83-680
J.E. Brown, 577(SHR):Summer82-270
M. Kreyling, 27(AL):Mar82-138
Young, T.D. and J.J. Hindle - see Bishop,
J.P. and A. Tate
Young Bear, R. Winter of the Salamander.*
J. Saunders, 565:Vol23No1-73
Young-Bruehl, E. Hannah Arendt.*
J.H.S., 185:Apr83-637
Young-Bruehl, E. Freedom and Karl Jas-
pers's Philosophy.
L.G., 185:Jul83-833
Youngkin, S.D., J. Bigwood and R. Cabana,
Jr. The Films of Peter Lorre.
J. Beaver, 200:Oct82-508

Youngs, F.A., ed. Guide to the Local Ad-
ministrative Units of England. (Vol 1)
R.B. Pugh, 325:Apr82-45
Yourcenar, M. A Coin in Nine Hands.
J. Mellors, 362:14Apr83-32
M. Tilby, 617(TLS):1Apr83-325
J. Weightman, 441:30Jan83-10
Yourcenar, M. Comme l'eau qui coule.*
C. Dis, 450(NRF):Sep82-125
Yourcenar, M. Fires.*
E. Crim, 31(ASch):Summer82-444
W.G. Regier, 502(PrS):Summer82-96
Yourcenar, M. Oeuvres romanesques.
J. Weightman, 617(TLS):22Jul83-767
Youssef, Z. La Poésie de l'eau dans les
"Fables" de La Fontaine.
J-H. Périvier, 207(FR):May83-945
Yovel, Y. Kant and the Philosophy of His-
tory.*
E. Schaper, 518:Oct82-210
Yovel, Y., ed. Philosophy of History and
Action.*
L. Holborow, 393(Mind):Oct82-629
Ysambert de Saint-Ledger. Le Miroir des
Dames. (C. Marazza, ed)
W. Rothwell, 208(FS):Jan82-50
Yu, A.C. - see "The Journey to the West"
Yü, C-F. The Renewal of Buddhism in China.
M. Levering, 293(JASt):Aug82-833
Yu, P. - see Wang Wei
Yü-hsin, W. - see under Wang Yü-hsin
Yu-Ning, L. - see under Li Yu-Ning
Yuan Hung-Tao. Pilgrim of the Clouds.
W. Schultz, 318(JAOS):Apr-Jun81-235

Zaborska, M. Seeing Stone.
D. Barbour, 648(WCR):Summer81-81
Zac, S. Philosophie, théologie et poli-
tique dans l'oeuvre de Spinoza.*
R. Sasso, 192(EP):Jan-Mar81-102
Zach, N. The Static Element.
E. Hirsch, 441:6Feb83-11
Zacharasiewicz, W. Die Klimatheorie in
der englischen Literatur und Literatur-
kritik von der Mitte des 16. bis zum
frühen 18. Jahrhundert.*
J. Schäfer, 38:Band100Heft3/4-510
Zacharias, L. Lessons.*
639(VQR):Summer82-96
Zagagi, N. Tradition and Originality in
Plautus.*
E. Segal, 24:Summer82-217
Zagari, L. and P. Chiarini, eds. Zu Hein-
rich Heine.
J.L. Sammons, 221(GQ):Mar82-260
Zagorin, P. Rebels and Rulers, 1500-1660.
H.G. Koenigsberger, 617(TLS):21Jan83-
63
Zahn, P. Ein konstruktiver Weg zur Mass-
theorie und Funktionanalysis.
F. Richman, 316:Sep82-703
Zainaty, C. La morale d'Avempace.
J. Jolivet, 192(EP):Jan-Mar81-108
Zajadacz, F. Motivgeschichtliche Unter-
suchungen zur Artusepik.
D.H. Green, 402(MLR):Jan82-227
Zajda, J.I. Education in the USSR.
G.Z.F. Bereday, 550(RusR):Jan82-84
Zaliznjak, A.A. Glagol'naja akcentuacija
v južnovelikorusskoj rukopisi XVI v.
W. Lehfeldt, 559:Jun82-377

Wright, C. Paintings in Dutch Museums.
   T. Crombie, 39:Sep82-199
Wright, C. The Southern Cross.*
   X.J. Kennedy, 491:Mar83-349
   V.L. Nielsen, 649(WAL):Nov82-268
   D. St. John, 42(AR):Spring82-230
   P. Stitt, 219(GaR):Spring82-184
Wright, C. Wittgenstein on the Founda-
   tions of Mathematics.*
   J.R. Cameron, 518:Apr82-86
   D.A. Gillies, 84:Dec82-422
   P. Roeper, 63:Dec82-376
   H.D. Sluga, 262:Mar82-115
Wright, C.D. Translations of the Gospel
   Back into Tongues.
   R.B. Shaw, 441:4Sep83-8
   D. Walker, 199:Spring83-77
Wright, E. The Night The Gods Smiled.
   T.J. Binyon, 617(TLS):13May83-498
   T.J. Binyon, 617(TLS):27May83-553
   N. Callendar, 441:18Dec83-29
Wright, E.L. The Jester Hennets.
   J. Saunders, 565:Vol23No3-73
Wright, F.L. Letters to Apprentices.
   (B.B. Pfeiffer, ed)
   A. Saint, 617(TLS):16Sep83-985
Wright, G. Building the Dream.
   639(VQR):Spring82-62
Wright, G. France in Modern Times. (3rd
   ed)
   H. Peyre, 207(FR):Oct82-188
Wright, G. Insiders and Outliers.
   J. Paulhan, 207(FR):Feb83-501
Wright, G. Moralism and the Model Home.*
   D. Schuyler, 658:Summer/Autumn82-157
von Wright, G.H. and H. Nyman - see Witt-
   genstein, L.
von Wright, G.H., with H. Nyman - see
   Wittgenstein, L.
Wright, J. This Journey.*
   K. Callaway, 472:Spring/Summer83-58
   S. Friebert, 199:Spring83-87
   W. Harmon, 569(SR):Fall82-612
   P. Stitt, 219(GaR):Winter82-911
Wright, J. - see Sancho, I.
Wright, K. Bump-Starting the Hearse.
   G. Ewart, 617(TLS):30Sep83-1061
Wright, M.R. - see Empedocles
Wright, O. The Modal System of Arab and
   Persian Music A.D. 1250-1300.
   D. Wulstan, 410(M&L):Jan81-77
Wright, R. Late Latin and Early Romance
   in Spain and Carolingian France.
   M. Torreblanca, 304(JHP):Winter83-141
Wright, R.B. Final Things.
   J. Kertzer, 198:Jan82-81
Wright, R.B. The Teacher's Daughter.
   M. Yearsley, 99:Dec82/Jan83-40
Wright, R.T. and B. Herger. The Canadian
   Rockies.
   529(QQ):Autumn82-687
Wright, S. Meditations In Green.
   W. Kendrick, 441:6Nov83-7
Wright, S.L. Quilts from Happy Hands.
   M. Cowan, 614:Winter83-21
Wright, W. The Von Bülow Affair.
   D. Clendinen, 441:3Jul83-10
Wringe, C.A. Children's Rights.*
   J.M.G., 185:Apr83-647
Wrong, D.H. Power.
   Q. Gibson, 488:Dec82-452

Wu, W.F. The Yellow Peril.*
   J. Cohn, 395(MFS):Winter82/83-658
   B. Raffel, 152(UDQ):Summer82-151
Wucherpfennig, W. Kindheitskult und Irra-
   tionalismus in der Literatur um 1900.
   D. Dethlefsen, 564:Nov81-324
   J. Michaels, 406:Fall82-366
Wüest, J. La Dialectalisation de la Gallo-
   Romania.
   M. Offord, 208(FS):Apr82-191
Wuilleumier, P. - see Tacitus
Wuketits, F.M. Wissenschaftstheoretische
   Probleme der modernen Biologie.
   G. Vollmer, 687:Jan-Mar82-125
Wunderlich, D. Arbeitsbuch Semantik.
   K-E. Sommerfeldt, 682(ZPSK):Band35
   Heft6-740
Wunderlich, W. Die Spur des Bundschuhs.
   T.F. Sellner, 221(GQ):Nov82-622
Wurm, S.A., ed. New Guinea and Neighbour-
   ing Areas.*
   J. Haiman, 320(CJL):Spring82-59
Würtz, D. Das Verhältnis von Beobachtungs-
   und theoretischer Sprache in der Erkennt-
   nistheorie Bertrand Russells.
   H-J. Dahms, 167:May82-405
Würzbach, N. Anfänge und gattungstypische
   Ausformung der englischen Strassenbal-
   lade 1550-1650.
   V.E. Neuburg, 196:Band23Heft1/2-167
Wüscher, H.J. Liberty, Equality and
   Fraternity in Wordsworth: 1791-1800.
   M. Friedman, 661(WC):Summer82-133
   M. Moorman, 161(DUJ):Jun82-312
Wuttke, D., with K.G. Heise - see Warburg,
   A.M.
Wyatt, D. Prodigal Sons.*
   W.B. Bache, 395(MFS):Summer81-383
   G.O. Carey, 573(SSF):Winter82-85
Wyatt, R. Foreign Bodies.
   M. Penman, 99:Sep82-33
Wyatt-Brown, B. Southern Honor.*
   D.H. Donald, 441:24Apr83-8
   W.S. McFeely, 617(TLS):18Feb83-153
   L.H. MacKethan, 578:Fall83-113
Wycherley, W. The Plays of William Wycher-
   ley.* (A. Friedman, ed)
   H. Love, 402(MLR):Jan82-164
   J.P. Vander Motten, 179(ES):Apr82-173
Wycherley, W. The Plays of William Wycher-
   ley. (P. Holland, ed)
   I. Donaldson, 617(TLS):28Oct83-1183
Wyeth, B.J. Christina's World.
   P-L. Adams, 61:Jan83-103
Wylder, D.E. Emerson Hough.
   R.L. Gale, 649(WAL):Nov82-271
Wylie, R.F. The Emergence of Maoism.
   B. Womack, 293(JASt):Aug82-825
Wyman, W.D. Wisconsin Folklore.
   J.P. Leary, 292(JAF):Apr-Jun82-227
Wymer, T.L. and others. Intersections.
   C.B. Hunter, 561(SFS):Jul82-225
Wynand, D. One Cook, Once Dreaming.*
   M. Abley, 102(CanL):Spring82-76
Wynand, D. Pointwise.
   D. Barbour, 648(WCR):Summer81-80
Wynar, L.R. and P. Kleeberger. Slavic
   Ethnic Libraries, Museums and Archives
   in the United States.*
   J.E.O. Screen, 575(SEER):Jan82-157

Wyrwa, T. La pensée politique polonaise à l'époque de l'humanisme et de la Renaissance.
W. Weintraub, 551(RenQ):Spring81-105
Wyss, U. Die wilde Philologie.*
L. Denecke, 684(ZDA):Band111Heft4-176
P.W. Tax, 133:Band15Heft4-350

Xaburgaeva, G. Ètnonimy Povesti vremennyx let v svjazi s zadačami rekonstrukcii vostočnoslavjanskogo glottogeneza. Stanovlenie russkogo jazyka.
G.Y. Shevelov, 559:Jun82-353
Xanthakis-Karamanos, G. Studies in Fourth-Century Tragedy.
W.G. Arnott, 303(JoHS):Vol 102-255
Xianzu, T. - see under Tang Xianzu
Xiao Tong. Wen xuan or Selections of Refined Literature. (Vol 1) (D.R. Knechtges, trans)
D. Hawkes, 617(TLS):24Jun83-655
Xu Ling. New Songs From a Jade Terrace. (A. Birrell, trans)
D. Hawkes, 617(TLS):24Jun83-655
Xuequin, C. - see under Cao Xuequin
Xun, L. - see under Lu Xun

Yahuda, J. Hebrew is Greek.
J. Barr, 617(TLS):22Apr83-408
Yahya, D. Morocco in the Sixteenth Century.
A.C. Hess, 69:Vol52No4-98
Yalouris, N. and others. The Search for Alexander.
A.F. Stewart, 54:Jun82-321
Yamanaka, N. The Kimono Book.
P. Bach, 614:Winter83-17
Yamazaki Masakazu. Mask and Sword.
J.K. Gillespie, 293(JASt):May82-607
Yandell, C.M. - see Pontus de Tyard
Yaney, G. The Urge to Mobilize.
N. Stone, 617(TLS):27May83-532
Yang Jiang. A Cadre School Life.
W.J.F. Jenner, 617(TLS):24Jun83-676
Yannella, D. and J.H. Roch, eds. American Prose to 1820.
A. Hook, 402(MLR):Oct82-922
Yanov, A. The Origins of Autocracy.*
D.H. Kaiser, 104(CASS):Fall-Winter82-537
A. Kelly, 453(NYRB):17Feb83-34
M. Raeff, 550(RusR):Oct82-474
Yansané, A.Y., ed. Decolonization and Dependency.
J. Doherty, 69:Vol52No1-98
Yao Ming-le. The Conspiracy and Death of Lin Biao. (British title: The Conspiracy and Murder of Mao's Heir.)
Liang Heng, 453(NYRB):21Jul83-35
O. Schell, 441:15May83-3
D. Wilson, 617(TLS):24Jun83-656
Yarbrough, T.E. Judge Frank Johnson and Human Rights in Alabama.
D.E. Alsobrook, 9(AlaR):Apr82-149
Yarwood, E. Vsevolod Garshin.
P. Henry, 402(MLR):Apr82-507
N. Rzhevsky, 550(RusR):Oct82-530
Yates, B. The Decline and Fall of the American Automobile Industry.
W. Serrin, 441:3Jul83-10

Yates, D. Blind Corner.
P. Craig, 617(TLS):19Aug83-890
Yates, P.L. Mexico's Agricultural Dilemma.
R.T. Edminster, 263(RIB):Vol32No1-73
Yates, R. Liars in Love.
K. Cushman, 573(SSF):Summer82-292
Yates, V. Listening and Notetaking. (2nd ed)
L. Hamp-Lyons, 608:Mar83-109
Yau, J. Corpse and Mirror.
R. Elman, 441:18Sep83-36
Yavetz, Z. Julius Caesar and his Public Image.
T.P. Wiseman, 617(TLS):24Jun83-648
Yazdani, Z. Hyderabad during the Residency of Henry Russell 1811-1820.
R. Rocher, 318(JAOS):Oct-Dec81-470
Yeager, G.M. Barros Arana's "Historia general de Chile."
S. Collier, 263(RIB):Vol32No2-223
"The Yearbook of English Studies."* (Vol 8) (G.K. Hunter and C.J. Rawson, eds)
J. Bull, 366:Spring82-110
D. Tallack, 541(RES):Aug82-363
"The Yearbook of English Studies."* (Vols 9 and 10) (G.K. Hunter and C.J. Rawson, eds)
J. Bull, 366:Spring82-110
"The Year's Work in Modern Language Studies." (Vol 41) (G. Price and D.A. Wells, eds)
A.H. Diverres, 208(FS):Jan82-115
Yeats, J.B. Letters to his son W.B. Yeats and others 1869-1922. (J. Hone, ed)
R. Foster, 617(TLS):1Jul83-691
Yeats, W.B. A Critical Edition of Yeats's "A Vision." (G.M. Harper and W.K. Hood, eds)
B. Dolan, 305(JIL):Sep82-114
W. Gould, 447(N&Q):Oct81-458
Yeats, W.B. Per Amica Silentia Lunae.
R. Fréchet, 189(EA):Jan-Mar82-99
Yeats, W.B. The Secret Rose. (P.L. Marcus, W. Gould and M.J. Sidnell, eds)
S.B., 675(YER):Jun82-145
R. Bonaccorso, 174(Éire):Summer82-155
Yeazell, R.B. - see James, A.
Yehoshua, A.B. Between Right and Right.*
J. Riemer, 390:Apr82-62
Yelaja, S.A., ed. Ethical Issues in Social Work.
J.D., 185:Apr83-648
Yeni-Komshian, G.H., J.F. Kavanagh and C.A. Ferguson, eds. Child Phonology.* (Vol 2) [entry in prev was of Vols 1 and 2]
J.E. Hoard, 215(GL):Summer82-128
Yerkes, D. The Two Versions of Waerferth's Translation of Gregory's "Dialogues."*
R.I. Page, 382(MAE):1982/1-115
J. Roberts, 447(N&Q):Apr81-179
Yerushalmi, Y.H. Zakhor.
H. Bloom, 453(NYRB):17Feb83-23
Yeshurun, A. The Syrian-African Rift and Other Poems.
N. Stiller, 287:Mar82-28
Yevtushenko, Y. The Poetry of Yevgeny Yevtushenko. (G. Reavey, ed and trans)
D. McDuff, 565:Vol23No1-59
Yin, J. Soviet Military Doctrine.
J.N. Westwood, 575(SEER):Apr82-316

WITHDRAWAL